Professional Oracle Weblogic Server

D1573019

Professional
Oracle® WebLogic Server

Robert Patrick
Gregory Nyberg
Philip Aston
with Josh Bregman and Paul Done

WILEY

Wiley Publishing, Inc.

Professional Oracle® WebLogic Server

Published by
Wiley Publishing, Inc.
10475 Crosspoint Boulevard
Indianapolis, IN 46256
www.wiley.com

To Chintana and Tony–
For their patience, love, and support.
— Robert

For my Father–
A good man I should have known better.
— Greg

To all who have worked to make WebLogic Server what it is today,
and to those dreaming about its future.
— Philip

About the Authors

Robert Patrick is a VP in Oracle's Fusion Middleware Development organization, responsible for a team of Solution Architects (known as the A-Team) covering EMEA, APAC, and Latin America engagements. Robert has over 16 years experience in the design and development of distributed systems, and he specializes in designing and troubleshooting large, high performance, mission-critical systems built with various middleware technologies. Prior to joining Oracle, Robert spent $7\frac{1}{2}$ years working for BEA Systems (most recently as their Deputy CTO) where he spent most of his time advising Fortune 1000 companies how to best apply middleware technology to solve their business problems. He has written papers, magazine articles, and was one of the co-authors of the previous edition of *Mastering BEA WebLogic Server* (Wiley, 2003) as well as speaking at various industry conferences.

Greg Nyberg has over 20 years of experience in the design and development of object-oriented systems and specializes in large mission-critical systems using WebLogic Server. Mr. Nyberg is one of the co-authors of the previous edition of *Mastering BEA WebLogic Server* (Wiley, 2003) and is the author of the book *WebLogic Server 6.1 Workbook for Enterprise JavaBeans, 3rd Edition* (O'Reilly & Associates, 2002). Mr. Nyberg has spoken to local and national users' groups on a variety of topics over the last decade, focusing on pragmatic approaches to Enterprise Java architecture and team development. Mr. Nyberg is currently Senior Development Engineer, the Senior Director, IT, at Carlson Hotels Worldwide, and is responsible for application development and technical architecture.

Philip Aston has specialized in WebLogic Server since joining BEA Professional Services in 2000. He currently works for Oracle's SOA Consulting team in the UK. Philip is hands-on with customers most days, helping them to extract the best value from their investment in WebLogic Server. Philip is the developer of The Grinder, a popular Java load-testing tool, is co-author of *J2EE Performance Testing with BEA WebLogic Server* (Expert Press 2002, APress 2003), and has also written for the *WebLogic Developers Journal* and *BEA dev2dev* (now part of the Oracle Technology Network).

Contributing Authors

Josh Bregman has nearly 15 years experience architecting Java and Java EE-based security and identity management solutions. Josh is a Consulting Solutions Architect at Oracle where he advises Oracle and its key customers on technology, architecture, and implementation best practices. Prior to joining Oracle, Josh worked at BEA Systems for 3 years as the Enterprise Security Specialist for the Americas. In this role, Josh worked with customers to develop security solutions for WebLogic Server and related BEA technologies. Before joining BEA, Josh worked at Netegrity/CA for 5 years where he designed and developed a number of Java based security products, including IdentityMinder and SiteMinder Application Server Agents for BEA WebLogic Server and IBM WebSphere. Josh has also held engineering positions at GTE/Verizon Labs and IBM Global Services. Josh holds a B.A. in Mathematics from the University of Rochester and had spoken at a number of industry conferences including the RSA Conference and Oracle Open World. Josh is the also the author of the Oracle Fusion Security blog at http://fusionsecurity.blogspot.com.

Paul Done joined BEA Professional Services in early 2005, having worked for the previous 6 years for other J2EE Application Server vendors (SilverStream, Novell eXtend). He is now an Oracle Middleware consultant based in the UK, following Oracle's acquisition of BEA. This is Paul's second spell at Oracle, having worked in Oracle Product Development in the '90s, developing the Oracle's Designer 2000 product. Paul specializes in Oracle's WebLogic Server, Service Bus and JRockit JVM technologies. He also is the developer of an open source monitoring tool for WebLogic, called 'DomainHealth,' and a is a contributor to articles on Dev2Dev and Oracle Technology Network (OTN).

Credits

Executive Editor
Robert Elliott

Project Editor
Christopher J. Rivera

Technical Editors
Prasanth Pallamreddy
Matthew Shinn
Ryan Eberhard
Tom Barnes
Will Hopkins
Naresh Revanuru
Derek Sharpe

Production Editor
Eric Charbonneau

Copy Editor
Kim Cofer

Editorial Director
Robyn B. Siesky

Editorial Manager
Mary Beth Wakefield

Production Manager
Tim Tate

Vice President and Executive Group Publisher
Richard Swadley

Vice President and Executive Publisher
Barry Pruett

Associate Publisher
Jim Minatel

Project Coordinator, Cover
Lynsey Stanford

Proofreader
Jen Larsen, Word One

Indexer
Jack Lewis

Cover Photo
© Ryan McVay / Digital Vision / Getty Images

Contents

Contents

Contents

Contents

Contents

Contents

Introduction

Professional Oracle WebLogic Server is different from other books about WebLogic Server and Java EE technologies.

First, it is an advanced-level book designed to complement the Oracle online documentation and other introductory books on Java EE and WebLogic Server technologies, providing intermediate- to advanced-level developers, architects, and administrators with in-depth coverage of key Java EE development and deployment topics. We skip the basic material, avoid duplicating basic references or information easily obtained elsewhere, and focus on information and techniques not available anywhere else. Written by a team of Oracle insiders and experts in the development of enterprise-class Java EE applications, this book starts where other books and references stop.

Second, this is a book with an *opinion*. Rather than simply articulating the options available to solve a given problem and leaving it up to you to decide, we share our thought process and give you concrete recommendations and best practices for use in your own application-development and administration efforts. Different design solutions, architectures, construction techniques, deployment options, and management techniques are presented and explained — but we do not stop there. We go on and explain the benefits of a given alternative and when to use it. We want you to understand not just how things *can* be done, but also how they *should* be done.

Finally, the primary example application built and described in these pages is a realistic, complex application that highlights many of the features of Java EE technologies in general and Oracle WebLogic Server 11g in particular. The example application leverages key technologies such as JSP, Spring MVC, EJB 3.0, JPA, JMS, and Web Services to demonstrate their use, and the text walks you through each decision made during the design, development, and deployment of the application to assist you in making similar decisions in your own efforts.

Who This Book Is For

Professional Oracle WebLogic Server is not intended to be a primer or introductory book on Java EE technologies or the WebLogic Server environment. Written as an advanced-level book with minimal coverage of basic concepts, this book is for experienced developers and WebLogic Server administrators looking to take their knowledge of these technologies to the next level.

What This Book Covers

This book is focused on Java EE development, deployment, and administration using the latest release of Oracle WebLogic Server, 11g. Many of the technologies, frameworks, deployment techniques, and management tools described in the book require this version of WebLogic Server and the latest versions of the Java EE environment and various libraries and frameworks. The primary example application built in the book, bigrez.com, also requires WebLogic Server 11g.

That said, the authors do not subscribe to the newer-is-always-better school of technology. Where it makes sense, tried-and-true versions of Java EE frameworks and libraries are used in the examples if these choices meet our requirements and get the job done.

The following is a partial list of the technologies and frameworks described, compared, and used (or not used) in this book and its examples:

- ❑ EJB 3.0, JPA, OpenJPA, Kodo, TopLink
- ❑ Java 6, Spring 2.5 MVC, Jakarta Struts 1.2, JSP 2.0, Tiles 2.0
- ❑ JMS 1.1, SOAP 1.1, JAX-WS 2.1
- ❑ JAAS, SAML 1.1 and 2.0, XACML, SSL, TLS 1.0, JSSE
- ❑ JMX, SNMP, WLST, WLDF

How This Book Is Structured

Professional Oracle WebLogic Server is organized around three key themes:

- ❑ Walking you through the design, construction, and deployment of a realistic example application.
- ❑ Discussing advanced topics and best practices in areas such as security, administration, performance tuning, and configuration of WebLogic Server environments.
- ❑ Providing you with best practices for developing, deploying, and managing your own WebLogic Server applications.

The first 10 chapters focus on the first theme, and the next 5 target the second theme; best practices are a focus throughout the entire book. Here is a brief description of each chapter to help you understand the scope and organization of the book:

Chapter 1 reviews key web application concepts and technologies and then discusses advanced topics such as JSTL, the expression language, custom tags, and servlet filtering.

Chapter 2 examines the presentation-tier requirements that drive web application architectures, compares three different candidate architectures, and makes specific recommendations to help you choose an appropriate architecture for your WebLogic Server application.

Chapter 3 details the design of the presentation tier of a fairly large and complex Java EE application. Topics include alternative page assembly techniques, business-tier interfaces, and the requirements of the example application that led to the chosen design.

Chapter 4 walks through the construction of the Spring MVC– and JSP-based example web application. Construction techniques unique to WebLogic Server are emphasized along with the components and techniques resulting from the choice of presentation approach, web application architecture, and business-tier interaction techniques.

Chapter 5 discusses the steps required to package and deploy a WebLogic Server web application with an emphasis on WebLogic Server–specific techniques and best practices.

Chapter 6 examines options and best practices for implementing Enterprise JavaBeans (EJB) and related persistence technologies in WebLogic Server 11g. After a brief review of EJB technology, the focus turns to the JPA persistence specification and the OpenJPA and Kodo implementations. The final half of the chapter then discusses key EJB-related features in WebLogic Server 11g and explains how best to leverage them in your development efforts.

Chapter 7 walks through the design and construction of the business tier of the example application started in Chapters 1–4, highlighting key concepts and best practices. Candidate business-tier architectures are first identified and examined in light of a representative set of business-tier requirements. Next, the techniques required to implement the chosen EJB architecture are covered in detail to highlight implementation details and best practices. Finally, the chosen JPA implementation (Kodo) is swapped out in favor of an alternative implementation (TopLink) to show the ease with which this can be done.

Chapter 8 discusses the steps required to package and deploy WebLogic Server enterprise applications. The basic structures of EJB modules and enterprise applications are reviewed, techniques for packaging JPA persistent units are discussed, Ant-based build processes are presented, options for packaging enterprise applications are compared, and deployment techniques for WebLogic Server development environments are examined.

Chapter 9 reviews web services technology, describes WebLogic Server 11g support for web services, and presents key best practices related to web services. Example web services are created using WebLogic Server utilities, advanced web services features in WebLogic Server are discussed, and a web service is built to interface with the primary example program in the book.

Chapter 10 presents information and best practices related to the WebLogic Server JMS implementation. Topics include JMS clustering and high availability, the various JMS client options, WebLogic JMS provider configuration, JMS application design considerations, building applications that leverage WebLogic JMS, and integrating with external JMS providers.

Chapter 11 covers important topics related to WebLogic Server security, including the WebLogic Server Security Service, the WebLogic Security Framework and its built-in providers, integrating with external authentication providers, setting up secure client-server and server-to-server communication, managing application security, and configuring WebLogic Server for single sign-on.

Chapter 12 focuses on WebLogic Server administration and the architecture of the WebLogic Server product. This is not a users' guide to the administration console, but rather an in-depth look at the internal architecture of WebLogic Server, a discussion of important administrative concepts such as server health states and network channels, and a thorough treatment of the configuration, monitoring, and management of WebLogic Server and WebLogic Server–based applications.

Chapter 13 presents best practices for delivering and troubleshooting scalable high-performance systems. It includes a discussion of core principles and strategies for scalable Java EE systems, a collection of important design patterns and best practices that affect performance and scalability, and steps and techniques you can use to improve performance and solve scalability issues in your systems.

Chapter 14 rounds out the discussion of development-related best practices with recommendations in key areas related to the development environment. Topics include development environment hardware and software, proper installation of WebLogic Server in the development environment, organizing your project directory structure, establishing a build process, choosing appropriate development tools, and creating a unit testing infrastructure for your project.

Chapter 15 discusses strategies and best practices for deploying WebLogic Server applications in a production environment, focusing on production deployment strategies, global traffic management solutions, and production security best practices.

What You Need to Use This Book

The examples and best practices in this book are based on Oracle's WebLogic Server 11g application server, available from the Oracle download site at http://otn.oracle.com/. Download and install this product if you plan to build and deploy any of the example applications.

The WebLogic Server 11g installer includes a version of Eclipse suitable for viewing and editing the example code. Alternatively, you may prefer to use Oracle JDeveloper 11g, or another Java development tool. Chapter 14 contains full details about how to install and configure Eclipse and JDeveloper.

Finally, the main example program in this book assumes that you have a copy of the Oracle RDBMS available in your environment. We used the full Oracle Database 10g. Oracle Database 11g, or the 10g Express Edition (also known as Oracle XE) should also work fine. See the Oracle download site at http://otn.oracle.com/database for a trial copy of the database software.

Source Code

As you work through the examples in this book, you may choose either to type in all the code manually or to use the source code files that accompany the book. All of the source code used in this book is available for download at www.wrox.com. Once at the site, simply locate the book's title (either by using the Search box or by using one of the title lists) and click the Download Code link on the book's detail page to obtain all the source code for the book.

Because many books have similar titles, you may find it easiest to search by ISBN; this book's ISBN is 978-0-470-48430-2.

Once you download the code, just decompress it with your favorite compression tool. Alternately, you can go to the main Wrox code download page at www.wrox.com/dynamic/books/download.aspx to see the code available for this book and all other Wrox books.

Errata

We make every effort to ensure that there are no errors in the text or in the code. However, no one is perfect, and mistakes do occur. If you find an error in one of our books, like a spelling mistake or faulty piece of code, we would be very grateful for your feedback. By sending in errata you may save another reader hours of frustration and at the same time you will be helping us provide even higher quality information.

To find the errata page for this book, go to www.wrox.com and locate the title using the Search box or one of the title lists. Then, on the book details page, click the Book Errata link. On this page you can view all errata that has been submitted for this book and posted by Wrox editors. A complete book list including links to each book's errata is also available at www.wrox.com/misc-pages/booklist.shtml.

If you don't spot "your" error on the Book Errata page, go to www.wrox.com/contact/techsupport. shtml and complete the form there to send us the error you have found. We'll check the information and, if appropriate, post a message to the book's errata page and fix the problem in subsequent editions of the book.

Online Appendix

Within the text of this book, the authors occasionally refer you to online information available at sites like http://otn.oracle.com/ and http://java.sun.com/ to supplement the discussions within this book. The authors found that in many cases the desired reference URLs were both long — making them nearly impossible to type accurately — and had a tendency to change over time as documentation was modified and expanded. For this reason, actual addresses for additional reference material are not included in this text. Instead, an online Appendix available at www.wrox.com/ compiles and organizes all referenced URLs by chapter. The text itself refers to these links by number, e.g., Link 3-1. If you are interested in locating and reading online reference information mentioned in the text, download the online Appendix from www.wrox.com/ and use the addresses found therein.

p2p.wrox.com

For author and peer discussion, join the P2P forums at p2p.wrox.com. The forums are a web-based system for you to post messages relating to Wrox books and related technologies and interact with other readers and technology users. The forums offer a subscription feature to e-mail you topics of interest of your choosing when new posts are made to the forums. Wrox authors, editors, other industry experts, and your fellow readers are present on these forums.

At http://p2p.wrox.com you will find a number of different forums that will help you not only as you read this book, but also as you develop your own applications. To join the forums, just follow these steps:

1. Go to p2p.wrox.com and click the Register link.
2. Read the terms of use and click Agree.
3. Complete the required information to join as well as any optional information you wish to provide and click Submit.
4. You will receive an e-mail with information describing how to verify your account and complete the joining process.

You can read messages in the forums without joining P2P but in order to post your own messages, you must join.

Once you join, you can post new messages and respond to messages other users post. You can read messages at any time on the Web. If you would like to have new messages from a particular forum e-mailed to you, click the Subscribe to this Forum icon by the forum name in the forum listing.

For more information about how to use the Wrox P2P, be sure to read the P2P FAQs for answers to questions about how the forum software works as well as many common questions specific to P2P and Wrox books. To read the FAQs, click the FAQ link on any P2P page.

Building Web Applications in WebLogic

Web applications are an important part of the Java Enterprise Edition (Java EE) platform because the Web components are responsible for key client-facing presentation and business logic. A poorly designed web application will ruin the best business-tier components and services. In this chapter, we review key web application concepts and technologies and their use in WebLogic Server, and we provide a number of recommendations and best practices related to web application design and construction in WebLogic Server.

This chapter also provides the foundation for the discussion of recommended web application architectures in Chapter 2 and the construction and deployment of a complex, realistic web application in Chapters 3, 4, and 5.

Java Servlets and JSP Key Concepts

In this section we review some key concepts related to Java servlets and JavaServer Pages. If you are unfamiliar with these technologies, or if you need additional background material, you should read one of the many fine books available on the subject. Suggestions include *Head First Servlets and JSP: Passing the Sun Certified Web Component Developer Exam* by Bryan Basham et. al. (O'Reilly & Associates, 2008), *Java Servlet Programming Bible* by Suresh Rajagopalan et. al. (John Wiley & Sons, 2002), and *Java Servlet Programming* by Jason Hunter (O'Reilly & Associates, 2001).

Characteristics of Servlets

Java servlets are fundamental Java EE platform components that provide a request/response interface for both Web requests and other requests such as XML messages or file transfer functions. In this section, we review the characteristics of Java servlets as background for a comparison of servlets with JavaServer Pages (JSP) technology and the presentation of best practices later in the chapter.

Servlets Use the Request/Response Model

Java servlets are a request/response mechanism: a programming construct designed to respond to a particular request with a dynamic response generated by the servlet's specific Java implementation. Servlets may be used for many types of request/response scenarios, but they are most often employed in the creation of HyperText Transfer Protocol (HTTP) responses in a web application. In this role, servlets replace other HTTP request/response mechanisms such as Common Gateway Interface (CGI) scripts.

The simple request/response model becomes a little more complex once you add chaining and filtering capabilities to the servlet specification. Servlets may now participate in the overall request/response scenario in additional ways, either by preprocessing the request and passing it on to another servlet to create the response or by postprocessing the response before returning it to the client. Later in this chapter, we discuss servlet filtering as a mechanism for adding auditing, logging, and debugging logic to your web application.

Servlets Are Pure Java Classes

Simply stated, a Java servlet is a pure Java class that implements the `javax.servlet.Servlet` interface. The application server creates an instance of the servlet class and uses it to handle incoming requests. The `Servlet` interface defines the set of methods that should be implemented to allow the application server to manage the servlet life cycle (discussed later in this chapter) and pass requests to the servlet instance for processing. Servlets intended for use as HTTP request/response mechanisms normally extend the `javax.servlet.http.HttpServlet` class, although they may implement and use the `Servlet` interface methods if desired. The `HttpServlet` class implements the `Servlet` interface and implements the `init()`, `destroy()`, and `service()` methods in a default manner. For example, the `service()` method in `HttpServlet` interrogates the incoming `HttpServletRequest` object and forwards the request to a series of individual methods defined in the `HttpServlet` class based on the type of request. These methods include the following:

- ❑ `doGet()` for handling GET, conditional GET, and HEAD requests

- ❑ `doPost()` for POST requests

- ❑ `doPut()` for PUT requests

- ❑ `doDelete()` for DELETE requests

- ❑ `doOptions()` for OPTIONS requests

- ❑ `doTrace()` for TRACE requests

The `doGet()`, `doPost()`, `doPut()`, and `doDelete()` methods in `HttpServlet` return a BAD_REQUEST (400) error as their default response. Servlets that extend `HttpServlet` typically override and implement one or more of these methods to generate the desired response. The `doOptions()` and `doTrace()` methods are typically not overridden in the servlet. Their implementations in the `HttpServlet` class are designed to generate the proper response, and they are usually sufficient.

A minimal HTTP servlet capable of responding to a GET request requires nothing more than extending the `HttpServlet` class and implementing the `doGet()` method.

WebLogic Server provides a number of useful sample servlets showing the basic approach for creating HTTP servlets. These sample servlets are located in the `samples/server/examples/src/examples/webapp/servlets` subdirectory beneath the WebLogic Server home directory, a directory we refer to as `$WL_HOME` throughout the rest of the book.

Creating the HTML output within the servlet's `service()` or `doXXX()` method is very tedious. This deficiency was addressed in the Java EE specification by introducing a scripting technology, JavaServer Pages (JSP), discussed later in this chapter.

Servlets Must Be Registered in the Application

Servlets will only be invoked by the application server if they have been registered in the application and associated with a specific URL or URL pattern. The standard mechanism for registering a servlet involves `<servlet>` and `<servlet-mapping>` elements within the application's `web.xml` file as shown here:

```
<servlet>
  <servlet-name>SimpleServlet</servlet-name>
  <servlet-class>
    professional.weblogic.ch01.example1.SimpleServlet
  </servlet-class>
</servlet>

<servlet-mapping>
  <servlet-name>SimpleServlet</servlet-name>
  <url-pattern>/simple</url-pattern>
</servlet-mapping>
```

When a user accesses the specified URL, `/simple`, the application server will invoke the `doGet()`, `doPost()`, or other `doXXX()` method on the servlet class.

WebLogic Server provides an alternate annotation-based technique for registering servlets and specifying the mapped URL pattern: The `@WLServlet` annotation. The following annotation, placed at the top of the `SimpleServlet` source file, eliminates the need for `web.xml` entries for this servlet:

```
@WLServlet (
    name = "SimpleServlet",
    mapping = {"/simple"}
)
public class SimpleServlet extends HttpServlet
{
...
}
```

The `@WLServlet` annotation syntax includes all of attributes available in the `web.xml` technique, including `loadOnStartup`, `initParams`, and `runAs` values. This annotation technique represents a viable, if non-standard, approach for registering and configuring servlets in your application.

Servlets Have a Life Cycle

A servlet is an instance of the `Servlet` class and has a life cycle similar to that of any other Java object. When the servlet is first required to process a request, the application server loads the servlet class, creates an instance of the class, initializes the instance, calls the servlet's `init()` method, and calls the `service()` method to process the request. In normal servlet operation, this same instance of the `Servlet` class will be used for all subsequent requests.

Servlets may be preloaded during WebLogic Server startup by including the `<load-on-startup>` element in the `web.xml` file for the web application or by including the `loadOnStartup` attribute in the `@WLServlet` annotation block in the servlet's class definition. You can also provide initialization parameters in the `web.xml` file using `<init-param>` elements or by including them in the `@WLServlet` annotation block. WebLogic Server will preload and call `init()` on the servlet during startup, passing the specified initialization parameters to the `init()` method in the `ServletConfig` object.

An existing servlet instance is destroyed when the application server shuts down or intends to reload the servlet class and create a new instance. The server calls the `destroy()` method on the servlet prior to removing the servlet instance and unloading the class. This allows the servlet to clean up any resources it may have opened during initialization or operation.

Servlets Allow Multiple Parallel Requests

Servlets are normally configured to allow multiple requests to be processed simultaneously by a single servlet instance. In other words, the servlet's methods must be thread-safe. You must take care to avoid using class- or instance-level variables unless access is made thread-safe through synchronization logic. Typically, all variables and objects required to process the request are created within the `service()` or `doXXX()` method itself, making them local to the specific thread and request being processed.

Best Practice

Servlets that allow multiple parallel requests must be thread-safe. Do not share class- or instance-level variables unless synchronization logic provides thread safety.

Servlets may be configured to disallow multiple parallel requests by defining the servlet class as implementing the `SingleThreadModel` interface:

```
...
public class TrivialSingleThreadServlet
    extends HttpServlet implements SingleThreadModel
{
    public void init(ServletConfig config) throws ServletException
    {
        super.init(config);
        System.out.println("Here!");
    }
...
```

This simple change informs the application server that it may not process multiple requests through the same servlet instance simultaneously. Although WebLogic Server continues to implement this mechanism for enforcing single-threaded servlets, the Servlet 2.4 specification has deprecated its use. The specification encourages developers to protect critical sections of servlet code using synchronization logic. Of course, using synchronization logic around non-thread-safe code comes with a price — it invariably creates bottlenecks and latency in high volume systems as threads wait for their turn to execute the protected code. If the code within the critical section takes too long to execute, overall performance and scalability of your system will suffer. Avoid using the SingleThreadModel interface in your applications. Design your servlets be thread-safe and minimize their use of synchronization blocks.

Best Practice

Avoid using single-threaded servlets. Design your servlets be thread-safe and minimize their use of synchronization blocks to avoid potential performance issues.

Servlets May Access Request Data

The HttpServletRequest parameter passed in to the service() or doXXX() method contains a wealth of information available to the servlet during the processing of the request. Useful data in the HttpServletRequest is summarized in Table 1-1.

This is not an exhaustive list of the methods available on the HttpServletRequest class or its superclass, ServletRequest. Refer to the servlet documentation at Link 1-1 in the book's online Appendix at http://www.wrox.com or a good reference book on servlets for a complete list including parameter types, return types, and other details.

Servlets Use Session Tracking

A servlet is a request/response mechanism that treats each incoming request as an independent processing event with no relationship to past or future requests. In other words, the processing is stateless. The HTTP protocol is also a stateless protocol: Each request from the web browser is independent of previous or subsequent requests. Linking current requests to previous requests from the same client requires a mechanism for preserving context or state information from request to request. A number of HTML-based techniques exist for preserving context or state information:

❑ *Cookies* may be set in responses and passed back to the server on subsequent requests.

❑ *URL-rewriting* may be used to encode small amounts of context information on every hyperlink on the generated page.

❑ *Hidden form fields* containing context information may be included in forms.

These techniques all have limitations, and none provides the robust data types and flexibility needed to implement true state management. Fortunately, the session tracking capability defined in the Java EE servlet model provides an excellent solution.

Session tracking provides a flexible hashtable-like structure called an HttpSession that can be used to store any serializable Java object and make it available in subsequent requests. To identify the specific client making the request and look up its session information, session tracking uses a cookie or URL-encoded session ID passed to the server on subsequent requests. In WebLogic Server, this session ID has the name JSESSIONID by default and consists of a long hash identifying the client plus creation-time and cluster information. The format of the session ID is

```
JSESSIONID=SESSION_ID!PRIMARY_JVMID_HASH!SECONDARY_JVM_HASH!CREATION_TIME
```

Table 1-1: Information Available in the HttpServletRequest

Type of Information	Access Methods
Parameters passed in the query string or through form input fields	getParameterNames(), getParameter(), getParameterValues(), getQueryString()
Server information	getServerName(), getServerPort()
Client characteristics	getRemoteAddr(), getRemoteHost(), getAuthType(), getRemoteUser()
Request information	getContentType(), getContentLength(), getProtocol(), getScheme(), getRequestURI()
HTTP headers	getHeaderNames(), getHeader(), getIntHeader(), getDateHeader()
Cookies sent by browser	getCookies()
Session information	getSession(), getRequestedSessionId(), isRequestedSessionIdValid(), ...

WebLogic Server uses exclamation marks to separate portions of the session ID. The first portion is used by the session tracking implementation in WebLogic Server to look up the client's HttpSession object in the web application context. Subsequent portions of the session ID are used to identify primary and secondary servers for this client in a WebLogic Server cluster and to track the creation time for this session. Chapter 12 discusses WebLogic Server clustering in detail as part of the discussion of administration best practices.

Using session tracking in a servlet is as simple as calling the getSession() method on the passed-in HttpServletRequest object to retrieve or create the HttpSession object for this client and then utilizing the HttpSession interface to get and set attributes in the session.

WebLogic Server supports several forms of session persistence, a mechanism for providing session failover. The two most commonly used forms are in-memory replication and JDBC persistence. When using these types of session persistence, be careful not to place very large objects in the `HttpSession`. WebLogic Server tracks changes to the session object through calls to the `setAttribute()` method. At the end of each request, the server will serialize each new or modified attribute, as determined by the arguments to any `setAttribute()` calls, and persist them accordingly.

Recognize that persisting a session attribute will result in WebLogic Server serializing the entire object graph, starting at the root object placed in the `HttpSession`. This can be a significant amount of data if the application stores large, coarse-grained objects in the session. Multiple fine-grained objects can provide superior performance, provided that your application code updates only a subset of the fine-grained objects (using `setAttribute`) in most cases. We talk more about in-memory session replication and clustering in Chapter 12.

Best Practice

Use session tracking to maintain state and contextual information between servlet requests. When using session persistence, avoid placing large objects in the session if your application tends to update only a small portion of these objects for any particular request. Instead, use multiple fine-grained objects to reduce the cost of session persistence.

To summarize, servlets are a reliable pure Java mechanism for processing HTTP requests. It can be tedious to generate the HTML response through the simple `println()` methods available on the response `Writer` object, however. As we discuss in Chapter 2, servlets are better suited for processing incoming requests and interacting with business objects and services than for the generation of HTML responses.

If servlets are a tedious way to create HTML, what is available in the Java EE specification for efficiently creating HTML responses? JavaServer Pages technology, the subject of the next section of this chapter, is specifically design to be a powerful tool for creating HTML.

Characteristics of JavaServer Pages

JavaServer Pages (JSP) technology was introduced in the Java EE platform to provide an alternative to servlets for the generation of server-side HTML content. Although a detailed discussion of JSP technology is beyond the scope of this book, some key concepts and characteristics are worth a brief review.

JSP Is a Scripting Technology

Recall that one of the important characteristics of servlets is their pure Java nature. Servlets are Java classes that are written, compiled, and debugged much like any Java class. JavaServer Pages, on the other hand, are a script-based technology similar to Microsoft's Active Server Pages (ASP) technology or Adobe's Cold Fusion scripting language. Like these scripting languages, special tags and script elements are added to a file containing HTML to produce a combination of static and dynamic content. In the case of JSP, these added elements are Java code or special JSP tags that interact with JavaBeans and other Java EE components in the application.

JSP Pages Are Converted to Servlets

The key to understanding JSP pages is to recognize that the JSP file itself is simply the input for a multistep process yielding a servlet. In the key processing step, the JSP page is parsed by the application server and converted to the equivalent pure Java servlet code. All text that is not part of JSP tags and scripting elements is assumed to be part of the HTTP response. This text is placed in output writing calls within the generated servlet method that processes requests. All Java scripting elements and tags become additional Java code in the servlet. The generated servlet is then compiled, loaded, and used to process the HTTP request in a manner identical to a normal servlet.

Figure 1-1 depicts this process for a trivial JSP page with a small amount of scripted Java code embedded on the page. The sample.jsp page is converted to the equivalent pure Java servlet code, compiled into a servlet class, and used to respond to the original and subsequent HTTP requests.

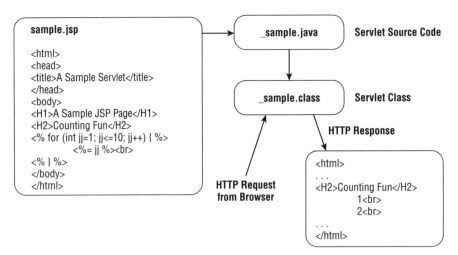

Figure 1-1: JSP page is converted to a servlet.

The parsing, conversion, compiling, and classloading steps required to accomplish this transformation are handled by the application server. You don't have to perform any of these steps ahead of time or register the resulting servlet — all of this is done automatically by the server. Note that the processing and compiling can be done prior to deployment using utilities provided by WebLogic Server, a technique known as precompiling the JSP pages.

In WebLogic Server, the resulting servlet is a subclass of weblogic.servlet.jsp.JspBase by default. JspBase is a WebLogic-provided class that extends HttpServlet and forwards service() calls to a method called _jspService(). You may also create a custom base class for JSP-generated servlets to replace the default JspBase class.

Many Tags and Scripting Elements Are Available

JSP technology provides a rich set of scripting elements and tags for creating dynamic content. Table 1-2 lists some of the important elements available.

Table 1-2: JSP Syntax Elements

Element	Syntax	Description
Scriptlet	<% *scriptlet code* %>	Java code placed directly in _jspservice() method at this location.
Declaration	<%! *declaration* %>	Java code placed within the generated servlet class above the _jspservice() method definition. This usually defines class-level methods and variables.
Expression	<%= *expression* %>	Java expression evaluated at run time and placed in the HTML output.
page	<%@ page *attribute="value"* ... %>	Controls many page-level directive attributes and behaviors. Important attributes include import, buffer, errorPage, and extends.
include	<%@ include file="*filename*" %>	Inserts the contents of the specific file in the JSP page and parses/compiles it.
taglib	<%@ taglib uri="*...*" prefix="*...*" %>	Defines a tag library and sets the prefix for subsequent tags.
jsp:include	<jsp:include page="*...*" />	Includes the response from a separate page in the output of this page.
jsp:forward	<jsp:forward page="*...*" />	Abandons the current response and passes the request to a new page for processing.
jsp:useBean	<jsp:useBean id="*...*" class="*...*" scope="*...*" />	Declares the existence of a bean with the given class, scope, and instance name.

Many more elements and tags are available. A detailed discussion of these elements is beyond the scope of this book. Consult one of the books listed at the beginning of this chapter for a complete list of JSP elements and tags, or browse Sun's JSP area at Link 1-2 for more information.

All Servlet Capabilities Are Available

Because JSP pages are converted to servlets, all of the capabilities and techniques available in servlets are also available in JSP pages. The HttpServletRequest and HttpServletResponse parameters are available, along with a number of predefined variables available in the JSP page, as listed in Table 1-3.

JSP scriptlet code may access these implicit objects directly because all scriptlet code is placed in the generated _jspService() method code below the definition of these objects. Nevertheless, the direct use of implicit objects in JSP scriptlet code is considered poor form. The JavaServer Pages Standard Tag Library (JSTL), discussed later in this chapter, provides access to data stored within these implicit objects — and many others — in a much safer and more standard way.

Table 1-3: JSP Implicit Objects

Object	Type	Description
request	javax.servlet.http.HttpServletRequest	Provides access to request information and attributes set at the request scope.
response	javax.servlet.http.HttpServletResponse	Reference to the response object being prepared for return to the client.
pageContext	javax.servlet.jsp.PageContext	Provides access to attributes set at the page scope.
session	javax.servlet.http.HttpSession	Session object for this client; provides access to attributes set at the session scope.
application	javax.servlet.ServletContext	Application context; provides access to attributes set at the application scope.
out	javax.servlet.jsp.JspWriter	PrintWriter object used to place text output in the HTTP response.
config	javax.servlet.ServletConfig	Reference to the servlet configuration object set during initialization; provides access to initialization parameters.

Session tracking is available by default in JSP pages. If your application is not using session tracking, you should disable it to avoid unnecessary session persistence. Although there is no explicit way to disable session tracking for the entire web application, servlets will not create sessions unless the servlet code calls the getSession() method. JSP pages may disable sessions using the page directive:

```
<%@ page session="false" %>
```

Even if your JSP does nothing with the session information, WebLogic Server must persist the last access time for the session at the end of the request processing. It is best to disable session tracking explicitly in JSP pages that do not use it.

> **Best Practice**
>
> Disable session tracking in JSP pages that do not require this feature to avoid unnecessary session persistence.

Like servlets, JSP pages are normally multithreaded and may process multiple requests simultaneously. The same thread-safety restrictions that apply to servlets also apply to JSP pages unless the JSP is configured to be single threaded. In a JSP page a special `page` directive is used to configure this attribute:

```
<%@ page isThreadSafe="false" %>
```

If the `isThreadSafe` attribute is set to `false`, the resulting servlet will implement the `SingleThreadModel` interface. This technique, like the related servlet technique, is deprecated in the Servlet 2.4 specification and should be avoided.

> **Best Practice**
>
> Avoid declaring JSP pages to be single threaded. Code that is not thread-safe should be encapsulated in some other Java class and controlled using synchronization blocks.

JSP Response Is Buffered

As we said, servlets and JSP pages are request/response mechanisms: An HTTP request is made by the browser, and an HTML response is generated by the servlet or JSP page. In both cases, this response is normally *buffered*, or held in memory on the server temporarily, and sent back to the calling browser at the end of the processing.

By default, output created in the generated servlet code is buffered, along with HTTP headers, cookies, and status codes set by the page. Buffering provides you with these important benefits:

❑ Buffered content may be discarded completely and replaced with new content. The `jsp:forward` element relies on this capability to discard the current response and forward the HTTP request to a new page for processing. Note that the `errorPage` directive uses `jsp:forward` to send the processing to the error page if an error is caught in the JSP page, so buffering is also required for proper error page handling.

❑ Buffering allows the page to add or change HTTP headers, cookies, and status codes after the page has begun placing HTML content in the response. Without buffering, it would be impossible to add a cookie in the body of the JSP page or change the response to be a redirect (302) to a different page once output is written because the headers and cookies have already been sent.

When the buffer fills, the response is committed, and the first chunk of information is sent to the browser. Once this commit occurs, the server will no longer honor jsp:forward, HTTP header changes (such as redirects), or additional cookies. The server will generate an IllegalStateException if any of these operations is attempted after the buffer fills and the response is committed.

The default size of the JSP output buffer is 8KB in WebLogic Server, which you can control using the page directive in each JSP page:

```
<%@ page buffer="32kb" %>
```

Output buffering may also be turned off using this directive by specifying none for a size, but this practice is not recommended.

Output buffers should be set to at least 32KB in most applications to avoid filling the buffer and committing the response before the page is complete. The minor additional memory requirement (32KB times the number of threads) is a small price to pay for correct error page handling and the ability to add cookies and response headers at any point in large pages.

Best Practice

Always use output buffering in JSP pages. Increase the size of the buffer to at least 32KB to avoid redirect, cookie, jsp:forward, and error page problems.

JSP Pages Have Unique Capabilities

Unique capabilities are available in JSP pages that are not present in servlets. The most important of these is the ability to embed custom XML tags within the JSP page.

Custom tags provide a mechanism to interact with a custom developed Java class that encapsulates business logic, presentation logic, or both. Custom tag elements are placed in the JSP page by the developer and then parsed and preprocessed by the application server during the conversion from JSP to servlet. The tag elements are converted by the server to the Java code required to interact with the tag class and perform the desired function. Later in this chapter we discuss custom tags and commonly used tag libraries in more detail and present best practices for their use in WebLogic Server.

To summarize, JavaServer Pages technology is a scripting language used to create HTML responses. JSP pages are converted to pure Java servlets by the application server during processing, and they can perform nearly any task a pure Java servlet can perform. JSP pages also have unique directives, features, and customization capabilities unavailable to servlets.

Why not use JSP for everything and forget servlets completely? Although it is possible to do so, servlets often provide a better mechanism for implementing presentation-tier business logic. Chapter 2 addresses this issue in detail and provides guidance for the proper use of each technology.

Web Application Best Practices

Now that you have reviewed some of the key concepts related to web applications in WebLogic Server, it's time to dig in and discuss best practices. So many options are available to designers and developers of Java EE web applications that it would require an entire book to list and explain all of the web application best practices we could conceivably discuss. In this section, we've attempted to discuss the best practices we feel are applicable to the widest variety of development efforts or are most likely to improve the quality or performance of your WebLogic Server web applications.

The best practices contained in this chapter cover everything from recommended techniques for using custom tags to proper packaging of your web application to caching page content for performance. They are presented in no particular order of importance, because the importance of a given best practice depends greatly on the particular application you are building.

Ensure Proper Error Handling

Unhandled exceptions that occur during the execution of a servlet or JSP-generated servlet cause the processing of that page to stop. Assuming the response has not been committed, the JSP output buffer will be cleared and a new response generated and returned to the client. By default, this error response contains very little useful information apart from the numeric error code.

What you need is a friendly, informative error page containing as much information as possible to help during debugging. Fortunately, there is a built-in mechanism for specifying a custom error page for use in handling server errors during processing.

First, you construct an error page to present the error information to the user in a friendly fashion. At a minimum, it should display the exception information and a stack trace. To be more useful during debugging, it can display all request and HTTP header information present using the methods available on the `HttpServletRequest` object. Portions of an example error page are shown in Listing 1-1. The entire page is available on the companion web site located at `http://www.wrox.com/`.

Listing 1-1: ErrorPage.jsp.

```
<%@ page isErrorPage="true" %>
<html>
<head><title>Error During Processing</title></head>
<body>
<h2>An error has occurred during the processing of your request.</h2>
<hr>
<h3><%= exception %></h3>
<pre>
<%
    ByteArrayOutputStream ostr = new ByteArrayOutputStream();
    exception.printStackTrace(new PrintStream(ostr));
    out.print(ostr);
%>
</pre>
```

Continued

Listing 1-1: ErrorPage.jsp. *(continued)*

```
<hr>
<h3>Requested URL</h3>
<pre>
<%= HttpUtils.getRequestURL(request) %>
</pre>

<h3>Request Parameters</h3>
<pre>
<%
Enumeration params = request.getParameterNames();
while(params.hasMoreElements()){
    String key = (String)params.nextElement();
    String[] paramValues = request.getParameterValues(key);
    for(int i = 0; i < paramValues.length; i++) {
        out.println(key + " : "  + paramValues[i]);
    }
}
%>
</pre>

<h3>Request Attributes</h3>
<pre>
...
</pre>

<h3>Request Information</h3>
<pre>
...
</pre>

<h3>Request Headers</h3>
<pre>
...
</pre>
```

Second, place a `<%@ page errorPage=" ... " %>` directive on all JSP pages in the application specifying the location of this error JSP page. Listing 1-2 presents a simple example JSP page that declares the error page explicitly. Normally, you would do this through a common include file shared by all pages rather than including the directive on every page.

Listing 1-2: ErrorCreator.jsp.

```
<%@ page errorPage="ErrorPage.jsp" %>
<html>
<head></head>
<body>
<!-- Do something sure to cause problems -->
<% String s = null; %>
The string length is: <%= s.length() %><p>
</body>
</html>
```

Accessing the `ErrorCreator.jsp` page from a browser now causes a useful error message to be displayed to the user. The page could conform to the look and feel of the site itself and could easily include links to retry the failed operation, send an email to someone, or go back to the previous page.

As an alternative to specifying the `errorPage` on each individual JSP page, a default error-handling page may be specified for the entire web application using the `<error-page>` element in `web.xml`:

```
<error-page>
    <error-code>500</error-code>
    <location>/ErrorPage.jsp</location>
</error-page>
```

These two mechanisms for specifying the error page may look very similar but are, in fact, implemented quite differently by WebLogic Server. The `<%@ page errorPage="..." %>` directive modifies the generated servlet code by placing all JSP scriptlet code, output statements, and other servlet code in a large try/catch block. Specifying the error page in `web.xml` does not affect the generated servlet code in any way. Instead, uncaught exceptions that escape the `_jspService()` method in the original page are caught by the web container and forwarded to the specified error page automatically.

Which technique is best? Unless the target error page must differ based on the page encountering the error, we recommend the `<error-page>` element in `web.xml` for the following reasons:

❑   A declarative and global technique has implicit benefits over per-page techniques. Individual pages that require different error pages can easily override the value in `web.xml` by including the `page` directive.

❑   The information describing the original page request is more complete if the `<error-page>` element is used rather than the `page` directive. Specifically, calling `request.getRequestURL()` in the error page returns the URL of the original page rather than the URL of the error page, and additional attributes are placed on the request that are not present if the `page` directive is employed.

Best Practice

Create a friendly and useful error page, and make it the default error page for all server errors using the `<error-page>` element in `web.xml`. Override this default error page using the `page` directive in specific pages, if necessary.

Use JSTL Tags to Reduce Scriptlet Code

The JavaServer Pages Standard Tag Library (JSTL) is a custom tag library that encapsulates many core functions required within JSP pages and virtually eliminates the need for JSP scriptlet code. Common constructs, such as conditionals, loops, accessing request or session data, placing data in the response HTML output, formatting output, displaying language-sensitive strings, and many other functions, are implemented in the JSTL library in a standard way. JSTL represents a huge improvement over the old `jsp:useBean` and `jsp:getProperty` techniques.

Custom tags can be difficult to create, but no knowledge of their construction is required to use them successfully. All you need is a good reference on the tag library you are trying to use and a basic understanding of the syntax for calling custom tags within your JSP pages.

Calling Custom Tags in JSP Pages

Custom tags are invoked within JSP pages by embedding the appropriate XML tags in your page using the syntax

```
<prefix:tagname attribute1="value1" ...  attributeN="valueN" />
```

or

```
<prefix:tagname attribute1="value1" ...  attributeN="valueN" >
  ...
</prefix:tagname>
```

The prefix represents the short name you gave a particular library when it was declared in your page, the tagname is the specific tag or function identifier within the library, and the attribute/value pairs are the data or settings needed by the tag for proper operation.

For example, if you've declared the JSTL core library using a prefix c with a taglib directive like this:

```
<%@ taglib prefix="c" uri="http://java.sun.com/jstl/core" %>
```

you would invoke the out tag within the JSTL core library to display the contents of the request parameter employeeNum using the following syntax:

```
<c:out value="${requestScope.employeeNum}"/>
```

The equivalent scriptlet code, for comparison purposes, might look like this:

```
<%= request.getParameter("employeeNum") %>
```

Although this JSTL example does not appear to be significantly shorter or simpler than using scriptlet code in this trivial example, the difference becomes much larger with more complex operations.

Using Expression Language in JSTL Calls

The JSTL libraries support the use of Expression Language (EL) within many of the attribute/value pairs supplied to the custom tags. To understand the difference between an invocation with and without EL support, consider the following two calls to the out tag in the core JSTL library:

```
<c:out value="requestScope.employeeNum" />
```

```
<c:out value="${requestScope.employeeNum}" />
```

The first call passes a simple string to the tag implementation via the value attribute. This string is simply placed in the output response being generated by the JSP, and the users would see the string requestScope.employeeNum on their web page.

The second call informs the custom tag implementation that it is using the EL syntax by including ${ ... } characters within the value attribute passed to the tag. The tag sees this syntax and treats the string within the braces as an expression that should be parsed and treated as a request for data from some source available to the page.

By specifying `requestScope` in the expression, we are indicating that the tag should look only in the `HttpServletRequest` object, and by specifying `employeeNum` we are telling the tag which parameter or attribute we want from the request object. The tag will find the object located in the request under this key, invoke `toString()` on it, and place the result in the output. The users will, hopefully, see a valid employee number on their web page.

As a second example, consider the following tag invocation:

```
<c:out value="${employee.myAddress.line1}" />
```

This example does not specify a source scope (`requestScope`, `sessionScope`, and so on), and has three parts. The tag implementation will perform the following steps as it parses and processes this expression:

- ❏ It will first search within all of the scopes available to it (starting with `pageScope` and ending with `applicationScope`) for some attribute stored using `employee` as the key. Let's assume it finds an object of the class `CompanyEmployee` located in the `HttpSession` stored with this key.

- ❏ The tag will then examine the retrieved `CompanyEmployee` object and attempt to invoke a `get` method based on the next identifier in the expression. In this case the method attempted would be `getMyAddress()`. Assuming such a method exists, the underlying `Address` object is extracted and the processing continues.

- ❏ The tag will next attempt to invoke `getLine1()` on the `Address` object and extract the resulting object, most likely a simple `String` object in our example.

- ❏ Finally, the tag will invoke `toString()` on the object returned by `getLine1()` to obtain the text that should be placed in the HTML response output.

This *chaining* of identifiers using the dot operator is very common in JSTL attribute values. It allows access to specific nested properties within objects stored on the request or session with a simple, compact syntax.

Entries in a `List` or `Map` object can be accessed with the same dot operator or through the use of an alternate bracket syntax as shown in these two equivalent tag invocations:

```
<c:out value="${sessionScope.stateNames.NY}" />

<c:out value="${sessionScope.stateNames["NY"]}" />
```

Hard-coding the map's key into the JSP page is clearly of limited value, and it too can be replaced by an expression that returns the key to be used in the `Map` lookup. The following example replaces the fixed value of `NY` with the value passed in through a request parameter called `stateCode`:

```
<c:out value="${sessionScope.stateNames[param.stateCode]}" />
```

In this example we look in the session for the `Map`, and look in the passed-in request parameters for the key. These are two examples of implicit objects that are available within the Expression Language. Table 1-4 presents a complete set of these implicit objects.

Table 1-4: JSP Implicit Objects

Identifier	Description
pageScope	Map containing page-scoped attributes
requestScope	Map containing request-scoped attributes
sessionScope	Map containing session-scoped attributes
applicationScope	Map containing application-scoped attributes
param	Map containing the primary values of the request parameters
paramValues	Map containing all values of the request parameters as String arrays
header	Map containing the primary values of the request headers
headerValues	Map containing all values of the request headers as String arrays
cookie	Map containing all cookies accompanying the request
initParam	Map containing the context initialization parameters of the web application
pageContext	The PageContext instance for the page, providing access to all JSP implicit objects

Although the Expression Language syntax is very powerful, it can be a bit confusing at times. Find a good reference on JSTL, including the EL, and refer to it often until you get the hang of it. You'll find that 95% or more of your custom tag invocations will use the EL syntax for one or more of the attributes in the tag, because it is the only recommended way to pass dynamic data into the tags.

Above all, resist the temptation to use the old-style scriptlet code in your JSP pages. With a little experimentation, you'll find there is very little you can do in scriptlet code that you cannot accomplish with JSTL and the Expression Language syntax.

Best Practice

Master the Expression Language (EL) syntax and use it extensively in the JSTL tags within your JSP pages. Use expressions in a clear and consistent manner to improve readability, choosing appropriate operators and constructs. Avoid JSP scriptlet code if at all possible.

JSTL Contains Five Tag Libraries

The JavaServer Pages Standard Tag Library (JSTL) contains the following tag libraries:

❑ The JSTL `core` library contains tags for common operations such as flow control (conditionals, looping), generating output, setting variables, and creating standard HTML links. Nearly every application makes use of the core library.

❑ The JSTL `fmt` library contains tags that perform formatting operations such as looking up and displaying localized messages, generating formatted output using templates, parsing text, and so on. Many applications use this library.

❑ The JSTL `sql` library provides a tag-based approach for executing SQL statements from within JSP pages. Because this is rarely a good idea, this library is rarely used.

❑ The JSTL `XML` library provides tags that query and display elements and attributes within XML documents using the XPath syntax. It can be a viable alternative to using complex XSLT transformations when trying to display XML data as HTML output.

❑ The JSTL `functions` library contains tags that reproduce the `String` functions available in Java code. The use of this library should be avoided in favor of performing text-related searches, substrings, or other functions in Java code prior to invoking the JSP page.

A detailed look at the tags, attributes, and correct usage of each of these JSTL libraries is beyond the scope of this book. The example web application built in subsequent chapters will make extensive use of the `core` and `fmt` libraries within its JSP pages, and there will be ample opportunity at that time to highlight the important tags and their correct usage.

Best Practice

Plan to use the JSTL `core` and JSTL `fmt` libraries in all of your web applications. These two libraries provide the most generally useful tags and will be required for all but the simplest JSP pages.

Use Custom Tags for Selected Behaviors

Custom tags are a powerful mechanism for extending the basic JSP tag syntax to include custom developed tags for interacting with Java components, modifying response content, and encapsulating page logic. The JSTL tag libraries discussed previously are good examples of custom tags that can reduce or eliminate the need for scriptlet code in the JSP page and improve maintainability.

The power of custom tags comes with a cost, of course: complexity. Custom tags add an entirely new layer to the architectural picture and require a strictly defined set of classes and descriptor files to operate. Although a detailed description of the steps required to create custom tags is beyond the scope of this text, it is instructive to review the key concepts to frame the recommendations we will be making.

Custom Tag Key Concepts

Custom tags require a minimum of three components:

❏ The *Tag Handler Class* is a Java class implementing either the `javax.servlet.jsp.tagext.Tag` or `BodyTag` interfaces. The tag handler class defines the behavior of the tag when invoked in the JSP page by providing set methods for attributes and implementations for key methods such as `doStartTag()` and `doEndTag()`.

❏ The *Tag Library Descriptor* (TLD) file contains XML elements that map the tag name to the tag handler class and provide additional information about the tag. This file defines whether the tag contains and manipulates JSP body content, whether it uses a tag extra information class, and the name of the library containing this tag.

❏ *JSP Pages* contain `<%@ taglib ... %>` declarations for the tag library and individual tag elements in the page itself to invoke the methods contained in the tag handler class.

Custom tags may also define a *Tag Extra Information* (TEI) class, extending `javax.servlet.jsp.tagext.TagExtraInfo`, that defines the tag interface in detail and provides the names and types of scriptlet variables introduced by the tag. During page generation, the JSP engine uses the TEI class to validate the tags embedded on the page and include the correct Java code in the generated servlet to introduce variables defined by the custom tag.

Custom Tags are Different from Tag Files

Don't confuse custom tags with the new *tag files* functionality added in the JSP 2.0 specification: They are quite different in both intent and implementation.

As stated above, custom tags provide a powerful mechanism for extending the basic JSP tag syntax to include custom developed tags for interacting with Java components. They efficiently and safely replace the use of scriptlet code required to call methods on these Java components.

Tag files, on the other hand, provide a new way to include shared pieces of JSP-generated output within a main page. They are essentially an alternative to the use of `<jsp:include>` actions or `<%@ include file="..." %>` directives, and provide no direct access to utility Java classes or other Java components. Shared JSP pages and page fragments previously located with other JSP content are renamed to end with a `.tag` suffix and moved to a special `tags` directory below `WEB-INF`. These shared pages and fragments are then included in the main page content using new custom tags.

Apart from simplifying the passing of parameters to a shared JSP page, and providing the ability for the called tag file to control when the body of the calling tag is evaluated and inserted in the output, it is difficult to find any advantage that would pay for the complexity tag files add to an application. If you find the older, simpler methods for sharing JSP pages and fragments unable to accommodate your needs, consider using the new tag files mechanism, but don't convert simple JSP pages and fragments to tag files without a good reason.

We will not be covering the creation or use of tag files in this book, nor will we be using them in the example programs.

> **Best Practice**
>
> The JSP 2.0 tag files mechanism provides a new approach for sharing and including JSP pages and page fragments that might make sense if the older `<jsp:include>` action and `<%@include file="..." %>` directive do not meet your needs. Be sure there is sufficient value in changing to the new approach since it represents additional complexity.

Custom Tag Use Is Easy — Development Is Complex

It is important to keep the appropriate goal firmly in mind when evaluating a new technology or feature for potential use on your project. In the case of technologies such as custom tags, the goal is to improve the readability and maintainability of the JSP pages. The assumption is that by reducing or eliminating scriptlet code the page will be easier to understand and maintain, which is true enough, but the JSP pages are only one part of the total system being developed. The beans and custom tags are part of the system as well, and any improvement in maintainability of the JSP pages must be weighed against the complexity and maintenance requirements of the beans and tags themselves.

Custom tag development, in particular, is complex. The complexity is not evident until the tasks being performed become more realistic, perhaps requiring TEI classes, body content manipulation, handling of nested tags, or other more advanced behaviors. Examine the source code for some tag libraries available in the open source community to get a sense of the requirements for a realistic, production-ready tag library. Is your development team ready to tackle this level of development? Are the people being earmarked for maintenance of the application capable of maintaining, extending, or debugging problems in the tag library? These are valid questions you should consider when making your decision to build a custom tag library.

Using custom tags, on the other hand, is relatively easy. As you saw in the discussion of the JSTL libraries, it requires a simple declaration at the top of the JSP page and a few straightforward XML elements in the page to invoke a custom tag and produce the desired behavior.

In the end, the decision comes down to the benefits of using custom tags versus the effort to develop and maintain the custom tags. Clearly a tag that is developed once and used on many pages may pay for itself through the incremental benefits accrued across multiple uses. Taken to the limit, the most benefit will come from a tag used in many pages that is acquired rather than internally developed, eliminating all development and maintenance effort on the tag itself. This should be your goal: Use custom tags, but don't develop them.

> **Best Practice**
>
> Custom tags are easy to use but difficult to develop and maintain, so make every effort to locate and use existing tag libraries from reputable sources rather than developing your own custom tags.

Table 1-5: Custom Tag Sources

Location	Description
http://jakarta.apache.org/taglibs	This source has a number of open source tag libraries, providing everything from string manipulation to regular expression handling to database access. It also hosts an implementation of the JSTL specification.
http://jakarta.apache.org/struts	Struts is a model-view-controller framework that includes a number of useful tag libraries.
http://www.servletsuite.com/jsp.htm	This commercial vendor, with more than 350 different tag libraries, offers free binary download and evaluation.

In additional to the standard JSTL tag libraries packaged in WebLogic Server, useful tag libraries are available from various vendors and open source communities. Table 1-5 provides a short list to get you started in your search.

We will be using selected custom tags from the Spring MVC framework in the example application in Chapters 3 and 4 to create HTML form elements with automatic handling of posted data during processing.

Use Servlet Filtering for Common Behaviors

Servlet filtering, a feature of servlets introduced in the Servlet 2.3 specification, provides a declarative technique for intercepting HTTP requests and performing any desired preprocessing or conditional logic before the request is passed on to the final target JSP page or servlet. Filters are very useful for implementing common behaviors such as caching page output, logging page requests, providing debugging information during testing, and checking security information and forwarding to login pages. Figure 1-2 illustrates the basic components of the filtering approach and shows the incoming HTTP request passing through one or more `Filter` classes in the `FilterChain` collection defined for this page request.

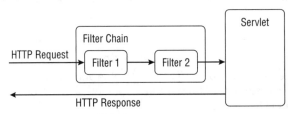

Figure 1-2: Servlet filtering.

Placing a filter in the path of a particular servlet or JSP request is a simple two-step process: Build a class that implements the `javax.servlet.Filter` interface, and register that class as a filter for the desired pages and servlets using either entries in the web.xml descriptor file or annotations in the filter class. To illustrate this process, we will build and deploy a simple but useful filter that intercepts servlet and JSP requests and logs HttpServletRequest information before passing the request on to the intended JSP page or servlet.

Building a Simple SnoopFilter Filter Class

The first step is the construction of a filter class called SnoopFilter that implements the javax.servlet.Filter interface and performs the desired logging of request information. Simply put, the doFilter() method writes information from the HttpServletRequest object to System.out before forwarding to any additional filters in the filter chain or to the final destination page itself. The source for SnoopFilter is available from the companion web site (http://www.wrox.com/).

Registering SnoopFilter in the Application

Registering a filter normally requires a set of elements in the web application descriptor file, web.xml. These elements declare the filter class and define the pages or servlets to which the filter should be applied. In this simple example, you want all pages and servlets in the application to be filtered through SnoopFilter, and the web.xml file includes the following elements:

```
<filter>
  <filter-name>SnoopFilter</filter-name>
  <display-name>SnoopFilter</display-name>
  <description></description>
  <filter-class>
    professional.weblogic.ch01.example1.SnoopFilter
  </filter-class>
</filter>

<filter-mapping>
  <filter-name>SnoopFilter</filter-name>
  <url-pattern>/*</url-pattern>
</filter-mapping>
```

The <url-pattern>/*</url-pattern> element declares that all pages and servlets in the application should be filtered using SnoopFilter, so every page request will go through the filter before normal processing begins. The server's stdout stream will therefore contain detailed request information for every page request, which is potentially very useful during development and debugging.

Clearly the same general logging capability could have been placed in a helper class, custom tag, or simple scriptlet included in each JSP page or servlet, but the ability to control the specific pages or groups of pages using the SnoopFilter in a declarative manner (via <url-pattern> elements) has significant advantages.

WebLogic Server also supports an annotation-based approach for registering a filter and specifying the URL pattern. The following @WLFilter syntax is equivalent to the web.xml entries shown above:

```
@WLFilter (
    name = "SnoopFilter",
    mapping = {"/*"}
```

```
)
public class SnoopFilter implements Filter
{
    ...
}
```

Although this is obviously a simple example, SnoopFilter illustrates the value of filters for preprocessing activities such as logging, auditing, or debugging in Java EE web applications. Filters are not
limited to writing output to stdout; they can easily write information to separate log files, insert rows
in database tables, call EJB components, add or modify request attributes, forward the page request
to a different web application component, or perform any other desired behavior unconditionally
or based on specific request information. They are a very powerful tool in the Java EE servlet
specification.

Best Practice

Use filters to implement common behaviors such as logging, auditing, and security
verification for servlets and JSP pages in your web applications.

Response Caching Using the CacheFilter

WebLogic Server includes a filter called CacheFilter that provides page-level response caching for web
applications. This filter operates at the complete page level rather than surrounding and caching only
a section of JSP content in a page. The CacheFilter may also be used with servlets and static content,
unlike the related wl:cache custom tag, which works only in JSP pages.

The CacheFilter is registered like any other servlet filter. Define the filter in the web.xml file, and
specify the <url-pattern> of the page or pages to cache. Use initialization parameters in the filter
registration to define timeout criteria and other cache control values. For example, to cache the
response from a specific JSP page for 60 seconds, register the CacheFilter using elements similar to
the following:

```
<filter>
  <filter-name>CacheFilter1</filter-name>
  <filter-class>weblogic.cache.filter.CacheFilter</filter-class>
  <init-param>
    <param-name>timeout</param-name>
    <param-value>60</param-value>
  </init-param>
</filter>
...
<filter-mapping>
  <filter-name>CacheFilter1</filter-name>
  <url-pattern>CacheFilterTest1.jsp</url-pattern>
</filter-mapping>
```

The CacheFilterTest1.jsp page will execute the first time the URL is accessed by any client, and the
content of the HTTP response will be cached by the filter and used for all subsequent access requests for
60 seconds.

Additional initialization parameters for the `CacheFilter` include the following:

Name   The name of the cache. It defaults to the request URI.

Timeout   Timeout period for the cached content. It defaults to seconds, but it may be specified in units of `ms` (milliseconds), `s` (seconds), `m` (minutes), `h` (hours), or `d` (days).

Scope   The scope of the cached content. Valid values are request, session, application, and cluster. Note that `CacheFilter` does not support page scope. It defaults to application scope.

Key   The names of request parameters, session attributes, and other variables used to differentiate cached content. The key is supplied using a `scope.name` syntax, with possible scope values of parameter, request, application, and session. Multiple keys can be supplied, separated by commas.

Vars   The names of variables used or calculated by the page that should be cached alongside the HTTP output. When the cached version of the page is retrieved and used, these cached variables will be placed in their respective scopes as if the page had executed again. It uses the same syntax as the key parameter.

Size   The maximum number of unique cache entries based on `key` values. It defaults to unlimited.

Max-cache-size   The maximum size of a single cache entry. It defaults to 64k.

Very simple JSP pages or servlets may be cacheable using only a `timeout` setting as long as the output does not depend on any request or session variables. Most pages, however, will require the use of the `key` initialization parameter to create multiple cached versions of the page, one for each value of the key specified in this setting.

The `CacheTest2.jsp` example program in Listing 1-3 is an example of a page that depends on a single request parameter, `howmany`, and will require a different cached version of the output for each value of that parameter.

Listing 1-3: CacheTest2.jsp.

```
<HTML>
<BODY>
<%
int jj = Integer.parseInt(request.getParameter("howmany"));
System.out.println("Inside JSP page with howmany of " + jj);
%>
<H2>We're going to count from 1 to <%= jj %><H2>
<%
for (int ii = 1; ii <= jj; ii++) {
    out.print(ii + "<br>");
}
%>
</BODY>
</HTML>
```

The `CacheFilter` would be registered to cache this page content with a dependency on the `howmany` request parameter as follows:

```
<filter>
  <filter-name>CacheFilter2</filter-name>
```

```
      <filter-class>weblogic.cache.filter.CacheFilter</filter-class>
      <init-param>
        <param-name>timeout</param-name>
        <param-value>60</param-value>
      </init-param>
      <init-param>
        <param-name>key</param-name>
        <param-value>parameter.howmany</param-value>
      </init-param>
   </filter>
   ...
   <filter-mapping>
      <filter-name>CacheFilter2</filter-name>
      <url-pattern>CacheFilterTest2.jsp</url-pattern>
   </filter-mapping>
```

Accessing this page with a specific value of howmany in the query string causes the entire page to be executed one time. Subsequent page hits with the same howmany parameter value will return the same content without executing the page. Supplying a different value for howmany will cause the page to be executed for that value and the contents cached using that key value. In other words, if you hit the page five times with different howmany values, you've created five different cached versions of the HTTP response using the howmany value as the key. This technique is very slick and very powerful for improving site performance.

WebLogic Server also includes a wl:cache custom tag that provides a very similar caching capability for any JSP content placed in the body of the custom tag. It has the ability to cache based on key values, like CacheFilter, and can cache small portions of a JSP page rather than an entire page. However, the CacheFilter approach has an obvious advantage over the wl:cache technique: Caching is performed using a declarative technique rather than embedding custom tags in the page itself. This defers the definition of caching behavior to deployment time and allows easier control of the caching parameters and scope using the web.xml descriptor elements.

Best Practice

Use the CacheFilter instead of wl:cache tags for page-level response caching whenever possible to provide better flexibility during deployment.

Note that a JSP page included using the <jsp:include> action is considered a separate page for the purposes of caching. It can therefore be configured to cache independently from the parent page, which may be helpful. Recognize, however, that this included page will not be invoked if the parent page execution is skipped due to caching. Plan accordingly!

Creating Excel Files Using Servlets and JSP Pages

Creating spreadsheets using servlets and JSP pages is a useful way to provide users with results they can sort, manipulate, and print using Microsoft Excel or other spreadsheet applications. Servlets are the preferred mechanism, but JSP pages can also be used if you take steps to avoid unintended newline characters in the output stream.

To create a spreadsheet using a servlet, build the servlet in the normal manner but set the content type to application/vnd.ms-excel in the response header to indicate that the response should be interpreted as a spreadsheet. Data written to the response Writer object will be interpreted as spreadsheet data, with tabs indicating column divisions and newline characters indicating row divisions. For example, the SimpleExcelServlet servlet in Listing 1-4 creates a multiplication table using simple tabs and newlines to control the rows and columns in the result.

Listing 1-4: SimpleExcelServlet.java.

```java
package professional.weblogic.ch01.example2;

import java.io.*;
import javax.servlet.*;
import javax.servlet.http.*;

public class SimpleExcelServlet extends HttpServlet
{
    public static final String CONTENT_TYPE_EXCEL =
        "application/vnd.ms-excel";

    public void doGet(HttpServletRequest request,
                      HttpServletResponse response)
        throws IOException
    {
        PrintWriter out = response.getWriter();
        response.setContentType(CONTENT_TYPE_EXCEL);

        out.print("\t"); // empty cell in upper corner
        for (int jj = 1; jj <= 10; jj++) {
            out.print("" + jj + "\t");
        }
        out.print("\n");

        for (int ii = 1; ii <= 10; ii++) {
            out.print("" + ii + "\t");
            for (int jj = 1; jj <= 10; jj++) {
                out.print("" + (ii * jj) + "\t");
            }
            out.print("\n");
        }
    }
}
```

Normal registration of this servlet in web.xml is all that is required in most cases.

```xml
<servlet>
  <servlet-name>SimpleExcelServlet</servlet-name>
  <servlet-class>
    professional.weblogic.ch01.example2.SimpleExcelServlet
  </servlet-class>
</servlet>

<servlet-mapping>
```

```
    <servlet-name>SimpleExcelServlet</servlet-name>
    <url-pattern>/simpleexcel</url-pattern>
</servlet-mapping>
```

As noted earlier, WebLogic Server supports a @WLServet annotation for registering servlets and specifying URL patterns. In this case, the SimpleExcelServlet source file could include the following @WLServlet annotation to eliminate the need for web.xml entries:

```
@WLServlet (
    name = "SimpleExcelServlet",
    mapping = {"/simpleexcel"}
)
public class SimpleExcelServlet extends HttpServlet
{
    ...
}
```

In both registration approaches, users accessing the /simpleexcel location will be presented with a spreadsheet embedded in their browser window. The servlet may also be registered for a <url-pattern> that includes an .xls file extension to assist the users by providing a suitable default file name and type if they choose to use Save As... from within the browser:

```
<servlet-mapping>
  <servlet-name>SimpleExcelServlet</servlet-name>
  <url-pattern>/multitable.xls</url-pattern>
</servlet-mapping>
```

Simple tab- and newline-based formatting may be sufficient in many cases, but you can achieve additional control by building HTML tables and using HTML formatting options such as <b> and <i> in the generated output. Because the content type was specified as ms-excel, these HTML tags are interpreted by the browser and spreadsheet application as equivalent spreadsheet formatting options.

The FancyExcelServlet example servlet in Listing 1-5 builds the same multiplication table as SimpleExcelServlet but uses HTML to control formats and cell sizes.

Listing 1-5: FancyExcelServlet.java.

```
package professional.weblogic.ch01.example3;

import java.io.*;
import javax.servlet.*;
import javax.servlet.http.*;

public class FancyExcelServlet extends HttpServlet
{
    public static final String CONTENT_TYPE_EXCEL =
        "application/vnd.ms-excel";

    public void doGet(HttpServletRequest request,
                      HttpServletResponse response)
        throws IOException
```

```
    {
        PrintWriter out = response.getWriter();
        response.setContentType(CONTENT_TYPE_EXCEL);

        out.print("<table border=1>");
        out.print("<tr>");
        out.print("<td> </td>"); // empty cell in upper corner
        for (int jj = 1; jj <= 10; jj++) {
            out.print("<td><b>" + jj + "</b></td>");
        }
        out.print("</tr>");

        for (int ii = 1; ii <= 10; ii++) {
            out.print("<tr>");
            out.print("<td><b>" + ii + "</b></td>");
            for (int jj = 1; jj <= 10; jj++) {
                out.print("<td>" + (ii * jj) + "</td>");
            }
            out.print("</tr>");
        }
        out.print("</table>");
    }
}
```

You can also use JSP pages to create spreadsheets with one complication: The output of a JSP page often contains many unintended newline characters caused by extra whitespace around directives and scriptlet tags, making it difficult to control the spreadsheet formatting when using simple tab and newline techniques. HTML formatting similar to the FancyExcelServlet works better in JSP pages used to create spreadsheets. Listing 1-6 presents the JSP equivalent to the FancyExcelServlet.

Listing 1-6: FancyExcelPage.jsp.

```
<% response.setContentType("application/vnd.ms-excel"); %>
<html>
<body>
<table border=1>
<tr>
  <td> </td>
  <% for (int jj = 1; jj <= 10; jj++) { %>
    <td><b><%= jj %></b></td>
  <% } %>
</tr>
<% for (int ii = 1; ii <= 10; ii++) { %>
  <tr>
    <td><b><%= ii %></b></td>
    <% for (int jj = 1; jj <= 10; jj++) { %>
      <td><%= (ii * jj) %></td>
    <% } %>
  </tr>
<% } %>
</table>
</body>
</html>
```

Viewing Generated Servlet Code

Viewing the servlet code generated for a particular JSP page can be instructive while learning JSP technology and useful during the testing and debugging process. Often the error report received during the execution of the JSP page indicates the line in the generated servlet code, but finding the JSP scriptlet code or tag that caused the error requires inspection of the Java code.

Generated Java servlet code will be kept alongside the generated servlet class files if the `keepgenerated` parameter is set to `true` in the `<jsp-descriptor>` section of the `weblogic.xml` descriptor file. The equivalent option for keeping the generated Java code for JSP pages compiled using the `weblogic.appc` utility or `wlappc` Ant task is `keepgenerated` placed on the command line or within the Ant task invocation.

By default, the generated servlet classes and Java code will be placed in a temporary directory structure located under the domain root directory. The name of this temporary directory depends on the names of the server, enterprise application, and web application, and it typically looks something like `servers/myserver/tmp/_WL_user/_appsdir_myapp_dir/wx8qxk/jsp_servlet`. This default location may be overridden using the `<working-dir>` option in the `weblogic.xml` descriptor file.

Chapter Review

In this chapter we reviewed the key concepts related to web applications in WebLogic Server and presented a number of important best practices designed to improve the quality and performance of your web applications.

Most of this chapter has been at the detailed design and implementation level, the *trees*, in a sense. In the next two chapters we step back and look at the *forest* for a few minutes by examining the importance of the overall web application architecture, the selection of a suitable presentation template technique, and the application of a model-view-controller pattern and framework for form and navigation handling.

2

Choosing a Web Application Architecture

The Java EE specification defines many different technologies in great detail, but it does not actually define the architecture of a Java EE application. For example, the EJB specification describes the behaviors and characteristics of Enterprise JavaBean components and the rules that dictate how they are to be managed by the application server, but the specification does not define the proper choice for a given application. It is up to the system architect on the project to define rules governing the use of session beans, message-driven beans, and other EJB components.

Similarly, the Java EE specification defines the three key technologies for web applications, Java servlets, JavaServer Faces, and JavaServer Pages, but it does not specify how they should be used in an application. As a result, the Java EE community has adopted a wide variety of de facto standards and design patterns for designing web applications based on lessons learned by early adopters.

This chapter examines the presentation requirements that drive web application architectures and makes specific recommendations to help you choose an appropriate architecture for your WebLogic Server application.

Architecture Key Concepts

Before embarking on a discussion of presentation requirements and architecture drivers, we need to step back and review some key concepts related to Java EE architecture.

Java EE Application Tiers

The Java EE specification and related documentation from Sun describe the Java EE platform as a distributed application environment organized in three tiers: client, business, and enterprise information systems (EIS) or data. Although this is a useful organization, it lumps all of the application server–hosted components in the business tier. It is more common to break up this middle tier into two separate tiers, presentation and business, containing presentation-related components and business-related components, respectively. This organization is depicted in Figure 2-1.

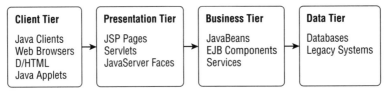

Figure 2-1: Java EE application tiers.

A related rule of thumb states that a component in a given tier may communicate directly only with components in adjacent tiers. JSP pages may not access the database directly, for example. Presentation-tier components must request information from components in the business tier, which then request data from the database or other data-tier systems as required. The advantages of this approach include the flexibility to leverage the same business components across multiple presentation-tier components and the reduction in coupling between nonadjacent layers.

There is nothing particularly new or revolutionary about organizing components in tiers. Three-tier and *n*-tier client/server technologies have followed this model for years, and even so-called two-tier systems often had stored procedures and other middle-tier business services. The benefits of organizing components in tiers or layers are well known and accepted in the industry, but this layered organization hardly defines an application architecture.

Model-View-Controller Architecture

One design pattern often cited as a web application architecture is the model-view-controller (MVC) pattern. This pattern has its roots in the Smalltalk world, where applications often used sophisticated techniques for viewing business information (the model) using interfaces (views) that were updated and managed automatically by controller objects whenever business objects changed state.

When architects discuss the model-view-controller pattern today, they usually mean a watered-down version of the original. Essentially, the MVC pattern has become another layered architecture, where view components must interact with a controller component to gain access to model data. As shown in Figure 2-2, the Java EE technologies have shuffled around a bit, but the left-to-right interactions implicit in a tiered architecture are still present.

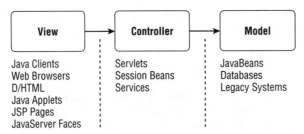

Figure 2-2: Java EE components mapped to MVC pattern.

There is more to the model-view-controller pattern than simply layering components and mandating left-to-right communication paths, of course. The MVC design pattern also commonly defines an approach for important presentation-tier behaviors such as defining navigational flow through the site and processing HTML form submissions.

Common Java EE Design Patterns

The Java EE architectural community has rallied around a number of important design patterns based on the seminal work, *Design Patterns*, by Erich Gamma, Richard Helm, Ralph Johnson, and John Vlissides (Addison-Wesley, 1995) and more recent books such as *Core J2EE Patterns: Best Practices and Design Strategies 2nd Edition* by Deepak Alur, John Crupi, and Dan Malks (Prentice Hall PTR, 2003) and *Expert One-on-One J2EE Design and Development* by Rod Johnson (Wrox, 2002). Patterns such as the *session façade* and *value object* are so prevalent now in application design that they have become, in a sense, part of the Java EE platform. Every architect should read these works and be well versed in the advantages and disadvantages of each design pattern before sitting down to build a system.

These common Java EE design patterns still have some rough edges, however. Often they tackle problems individually, leaving the proper combination of many different (and possibly conflicting) patterns as an exercise for the architect. Some of the patterns introduce additional layers in the architecture, ostensibly to reduce coupling between the layers already defined. We wonder how much decoupling is truly advantageous to the development and maintenance effort taken as a whole. By the time you implement the *business delegate*, *service locater*, *session façade*, *value object assembler*, and *composite entity* patterns in the business tier, for example, the resulting system may not be an improvement over the starting point.

The Java EE community has not yet reached the point where complete, end-to-end architectures incorporating a select set of well-understood design patterns are documented and available for new architectural efforts. We hope to address this deficiency in some small way in this chapter and subsequent chapters on EJB architecture by presenting complete, realistic example applications employing a consistent set of Java EE design patterns. The success or failure of your WebLogic Server project may depend more on the proper selection of architecture than on any other decision you make during development, so take the time to understand the issues involved before you start designing or coding.

Now that we have discussed some basic concepts related to web application architecture, it is time to dig in and discuss the issues that drive presentation-tier architecture design decisions.

Presentation-Tier Architecture Selection

The high-level depiction of Java EE application tiers in Figure 2-1 defined the presentation tier as containing Java servlets, JavaServer Faces, and JSP pages. When we talk about presentation-tier architecture, we are essentially defining the manner in which these three types of components will be combined to create a user interface that meets the explicit and implicit requirements for the presentation tier of the application.

Understanding these explicit and implicit requirements is the goal of the next section.

Presentation-Tier Requirements

Defining the presentation-tier architecture is much like designing the application itself: It must depend on the requirements. You don't build a customer management system if the users want an accounting system, and you shouldn't design the presentation tier without understanding presentation-tier requirements.

We're not talking about understanding the user-interface requirements of the system, but rather the general requirements of any well-behaved web application. Examples include good form validation and error handling, robust handling of bookmarks and browser *Back* buttons, ability to change graphics or page arrangements quickly, and helpful pop-ups and dialogs. Users are becoming more familiar and comfortable with the Web and are demanding robust behavior from their custom-built web applications. Meanwhile, the large commercial sites keep raising the bar with respect to usability. Users see constant improvements in areas such as page layout customization, form validation, pick lists and pop-ups, and many other areas, and they wonder why you can't implement something similar for their project.

A detailed discussion of state-of-the-art AJAX-powered technologies and site design is beyond the scope of this book. If you are interested in user-controlled page layout and content customization, you should investigate Oracle's WebLogic Portal product. Our focus is presentation-tier architecture rather than detailed site design and human factors engineering.

Achieving many of the basic usability and flexibility requirements of a site can be helped or hindered a great deal by the choice of presentation-tier architecture. These are some of the presentation-tier requirements:

❑   Display requirements

❑   Form/update requirements

❑   Navigation requirements

The following sections document these requirements and the ways they affect the required architecture.

Display Requirements

Display requirements include all of the user-interface requirements related to the presentation of data on web pages. As discussed in Chapter 1, JSP pages are considered the best mechanism for creating HTML responses containing dynamic content. We assume you're using JSP pages for display behavior unless otherwise noted.

In this section, we discuss some of the key display-related requirements that affect presentation-tier architecture decisions. At a minimum, the architecture must support the following:

❑   *Displaying model data* in various modes and forms

❑   *Displaying lists* of objects with flexible sorting, paging, and form input capabilities

❑   *Controlling page availability and model data presentation* based on user authorization

❑   *Internationalization* of all appropriate content on pages

❑   *Producing flexible and maintainable pages* allowing for multiple deployments and efficient future modifications

Displaying Model Data

Applications must be able to display model data on view-only web pages for inspection by the user. The architecture must provide a straightforward mechanism to retrieve the model object and place properly formatted attribute values in the HTML response. JSP pages offer expression scriptlets and custom tags in the JSTL core library for the purpose of embedding the model data in the response, and they require only some mechanism for retrieving the proper model object and making it available in the proper context for display.

Displaying Model Data in a Form

You will often want to allow the creation and modification of model objects through an HTML form with input elements corresponding to the model object attributes. The presentation-tier architecture must provide a mechanism to retrieve the proper model object (or create an empty object) and populate the form elements with the properly formatted attribute values.

Techniques for populating form elements with model data are simple enough for text input fields, requiring a snippet in the JSP page something like this:

```
<tr>
  <td nowrap>Middle name:</td>
  <td><INPUT TYPE='text' NAME='middleName'
      value='<c:out value="${person.middleName}"/>' size='50'></td>
</tr>
```

Techniques become more challenging when the form elements are formatted dates, select lists, checkboxes, radio buttons, and other fields requiring some form of mapping from the attribute value in the model object to the proper display format or selected value on the page. Your presentation-tier architecture must recognize the need for these complex form elements and provide convenient and reliable mechanisms for producing them.

Displaying a List of Model Objects

No web application is complete without a search page for choosing criteria and a results page showing a list of model objects meeting the search criteria. Search criteria pages are typically straightforward HTML forms with no new requirements for the presentation-tier architecture. Search result pages, on the other hand, can often present a host of interesting challenges for the presentation tier:

❏   You should be able to sort results by different columns, perhaps by clicking the desired column title.

❏   You may need to buffer and page results, presenting only a subset of the results on the page at one time and allowing the user to scroll through the results via Previous and Next buttons.

❏   Although most search result pages are simple views of the model data with perhaps a link to drill in and edit the corresponding object, some list pages may require form elements such as checkboxes or input fields associated with each row. The architecture should therefore support the creation of HTML forms containing multiple model objects in a list.

Creating search result pages containing lists of model objects can be accomplished with JSP pages using straightforward scriptlet looping code or iterator custom tags without much trouble. You can also accommodate sorting, results pagination, and multi-object forms through relatively simple techniques. The presentation-tier architecture should define the standard approach for accomplishing these tasks in a manner consistent with the solutions for other display-related requirements.

Presenting Role-Based Views of Data

Most web applications require user authentication in some form or another, and many applications limit or modify the data presented to the user depending on their authorization. It may be as simple as identifying pages in the site available to particular users and using the declarative security provided through the web.xml descriptor file for the web application. If that's the case for you, consider yourself fortunate. Web applications commonly require much more sophisticated role- or user-based control of the pages and data presented. Some typical requirements include the following:

❑ Selected pages or whole areas of the site are available or off limits based on user or role.

❑ Navigation devices such as menus, navigation bars, and hyperlinks must reflect the user or role by eliminating or disabling links leading to off-limit pages.

❑ Pages may be available to certain users or roles but exhibit display differences or limited functionality depending on the user. Forms may treat some fields as read-only for certain users, for example, or omit certain information completely.

❑ Page display and functionality may differ depending on both user information and attribute information in the model object itself. For example, modifying customer information might require that the user be a salesperson in that customer's region.

Are you beginning to get the picture? Many application development efforts have abandoned the simplistic declarative security model offered by Java EE in favor of a custom-built authorization framework providing some or all of these features. The presentation-tier architecture you select should provide a mechanism for integrating with your chosen security system and meeting your role- and user-based display requirements.

Of course, writing your own authorization framework comes at a price. You are depending on your developers not only to understand all of the facets of writing a security framework but also to use it properly to protect your application's resources. Chapter 11 describes the WebLogic Server security model in detail, including the WebLogic Server extensions that allow you to address some of these authorization flexibility issues without writing your own security framework.

Internationalization

Your web application may need to support internationalized content and display formats as part of a comprehensive globalization, localization, and internationalization (GLI) strategy.

Internationalization, often abbreviated as i18n, requires the removal of all language- and culture-specific items from the application source code and display pages. All displayed text, images with embedded text, informational and error messages, button labels, and other language-specific resources should be packaged independently from the application and presented using language-specific mechanisms in the display pages. Date formats, monetary and numeric formats, and other display formats may also require internationalization.

Localization, abbreviated l10n, takes this process one step further by tailoring the application look and feel, site content, currency conversions, business processes, and design considerations based on language and cultural considerations. More than just translating content, localization ensures that users feel the site has been designed specifically for them. Applications cannot be localized unless they are first internationalized.

Globalization seeks to ensure that all customers receive a similar quality of experience regardless of language, culture, and location. It builds on internationalization and localization and ensures the proper language- and location-specific handling of customer interactions at all levels in the system. This might include global site hosting, global content management, multilingual customer support facilities, global invoicing and fulfillment, and many other issues not directly related to the web application itself.

A complete discussion of internationalization is beyond the scope of this book. We will consider internationalization requirements when choosing a web application architecture, but we will not include internationalized content or behavior in our example applications.

Display Flexibility and Maintainability

The final display-related requirement emphasizes planning for the future in the design of the web application.

First, unless the application is a short-lived throwaway, it will undergo maintenance and enhancement at some time in the future. Plan for this eventuality by designing in the right level of flexibility and modularity from the start.

Next, don't assume that the layout, look and feel, style sheets, images, logos, or any other visual elements will remain constant over time. Customer-facing web sites are part of the brand image of the company, and companies are continually updating their sites to adopt the latest marketing and branding directions. Even internal sites can undergo significant modification in display characteristics when functionality is added or removed or usability issues necessitate major changes to the site.

Finally, your site may need to be flexible enough to use in an application service provider (ASP) environment. The site appearance, colors, behaviors, and even layout may need to be easily customizable for multiple clients. You cannot copy the site and tweak it for the new client; you'll end up with multiple copies of the site to maintain, enhance, and update with desired functionality and look-and-feel changes. That's not where you want to be.

How might these relatively fuzzy requirements for flexibility and maintainability affect the presentation-tier architecture?

- ❑ Style sheets are critical for defining fonts, sizes, colors, and other display attributes. Every single table cell, input field, and piece of text on the site should use a `class` attribute.

- ❑ Define page layout details such as the overall HTML table structure in a way that allows modification in the future. For example, if the header, body, footer, and gutter contents and sizes are specified on every page in the site (a technique often referred to as the *composite view pattern*), how easy will it be to shuffle the table structure around and move advertisements from the left to the right gutter? Not easy at all if you must edit every page to change the location of the `<jsp:include>` actions.

- ❑ Modularity of display content is important. Any common element, whether it is a copyright message or a navigation bar, should be separated from surrounding content and placed in its own JSP page for inclusion via `<jsp:include>` actions or `<%@ include file="..." %>` directives.

We discuss various template and page assembly options in Chapter 3 to provide some best practices related to display flexibility and maintainability, and in Chapter 4 we build an example web application that demonstrates many of the topics outlined here.

Form/Update Requirements

The requirements in the previous section dealt primarily with the flow of data from the model to the view and with the proper formatting and display of that data. This next set of presentation-tier requirements deals with data flow in the opposite direction, from the view back to model components, normally through the posting of HTML forms. Figure 2-3 illustrates the basic flow of this data and the role of the presentation tier in the transfer process. Remember that we're talking about only presentation-tier requirements in this section, so this discussion does not cover business-tier requirements, such as transactional behavior or object-relational mapping.

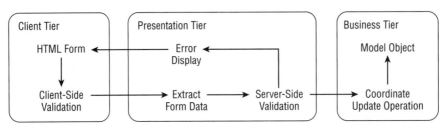

Figure 2-3: Steps required during form processing.

In this section we walk through the process from the HTML form to the model object, highlighting the presentation-tier requirements. At a minimum, the architecture must support the following:

❑   *Client-side validation* to provide immediate feedback to users when input does not meet constraints

❑   *Extraction of HTML form data* to facilitate subsequent validation and transfer steps

❑   *Server-side validation* to catch input errors before transferring data to model objects

❑   *Display of errors and original data* in the HTML form to allow user correction and resubmission

❑   *Efficient interaction with the business tier* to coordinate transactions properly and meet the interface requirements imposed by the business-tier architecture without undue complexity

Client-Side Validation

Although client-side validation is not strictly part of the presentation-tier architecture, it's commonly used, and it's important in the overall design of the view-to-model transfer process. Users expect form pages to warn them if required fields are left blank or inconsistent selections are made, without requiring a round trip to the server. You can apply client-side validation techniques in a light manner, perhaps checking only for required fields, or your design can include heavier levels of validation, such as checking fields for valid formats and content consistent with other fields.

Client-side validation is almost universally performed with JavaScript code that is executed just before submitting the form contents to the target. Errors are often displayed in a JavaScript alert window, and the cursor is placed in the offending field. A detailed examination of the mechanisms for providing client-side validation is beyond the scope of this book.

You should recognize that including client-side validation of fields in your application does not eliminate the need for server-side validation of the same required fields and formatting rules. Users may turn off JavaScript in their browsers or bypass the validation in other ways, causing invalid data to be passed to the server for processing.

> **Best Practice**
>
> Use client-side validation to enhance the usability of the application, but do not rely solely on it for field validation. Perform the same validation in the server-side processing.

Remember that all fields appearing on the HTML form are visible to the user if he or she looks at the HTML source, so creating spurious form submissions with bad input data or even different hidden field values is a trivial matter for someone who wants to bypass your validation and security requirements. Design accordingly.

Extracting Form Data

The HTML form data is presented to the server-side processing component, normally a servlet or controller class, as a series of parameters in the HttpServletRequest object. The first step in server-side processing is normally extracting the form data and placing it in an intermediate Java object appropriate for server-side validation and subsequent transfer operations. The type of Java object is determined by the presentation-tier architecture, but it is often a simple JavaBean, value object, or other straightforward data structure.

Note that you can perform most server-side validation by examining the HttpServletRequest parameters themselves without first extracting the data to an intermediate object, but this direct inspection technique has at least two negative effects:

❑ Directly examining request parameters places the validation logic in the presentation-tier component itself rather than encapsulating the validation rules in an object used exclusively for this purpose. Many server-side validation rules involve multiple form fields and their interrelationships, and this logic is best encapsulated in the object containing all the attributes.

❑ If errors are encountered during server-side validation, the intermediate object plays a valuable role in preserving the original form input data for redisplaying it to the user. Without this object, it can be difficult to redisplay the HTML form properly to the user. We discuss this requirement in more detail in a moment.

> **Best Practice**
>
> Extract HTML form data to a special purpose intermediate object before performing server-side validation to improve encapsulation and assist in redisplaying the form data in case of validation errors.

You can extract HTML form data with an ugly and error-prone process of retrieving the parameter values field by field from the `HttpServletRequest` and placing them in the corresponding attributes of the intermediate object using code like this:

```
person.setLastName(request.getParameter("lastName"));
```

Instead, the presentation tier should provide helper methods or standard techniques for extracting form data and placing it in the intermediate object.

Server-Side Validation

Once the HTML form data has been placed in an intermediate object, the presentation-tier components should perform server-side validation to identify problems with the incoming data, collect all of the resulting error messages, and display them to the user. Server-side validation should include simple required field checks as well as all formatting validation, interrelated field rules, and foreign key constraints.

Do not use the database constraints to perform input validations. The database may very well have the same validation rules embedded in constraints, but you should not use these constraints as the primary line of defense against such data errors. Catching the problems during server-side validation will avoid starting and rolling back transactions in the business tier of your application. This will improve system performance and reduce database-related exceptions, which might mask or be confused with true errors needing attention during testing or production operation.

> ### Best Practice
> Perform all server-side validation in application code rather than by relying on database constraints. This improves performance and reduces confusion during testing.

Don't stop performing server-side validation upon encountering the first error. The validation process should collect all errors encountered and make them available for display to the user for input correction and resubmission, as discussed next.

> ### Best Practice
> Server-side validation should collect and return all errors encountered in the submitted data rather than stopping with the first error. This provides a clearer picture of the validation requirements and reduces user frustration.

Displaying Errors

Errors discovered in server-side processing must be sent back to the client for display. This is easier said than done because users expect to see the original form and input data along with the error messages. The presentation-tier architecture must therefore include a mechanism for displaying the errors on the original HTML form and allowing resubmission through the same validation process.

Note that normally the input data is not contained in a model object yet, so the redisplayed form cannot simply be an instance of the typical HTML form display of a model object (a requirement outlined earlier in this chapter). Instead, you need to display the input data submitted during the previous iteration without having created a model object. This represents a new display requirement not previously identified because previously you always displayed the contents of a model object in the HTML form. How the presentation tier preserves the submitted input data and makes it available for the redisplay of the HTML form depends on the architecture.

The error messages themselves may be presented in a separate section of the redisplayed form, as shown in Figure 2-4, or may cause individual error messages to appear near the offending fields. Other designs may present the errors as a pop-up alert window and highlight offending fields with appropriate colors or formats. The type of error display is an application-specific requirement negotiated with the users, but the presentation-tier architecture may need to support general or field-specific errors and should be selected with this flexibility in mind.

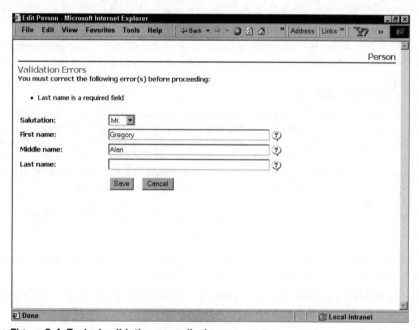

Figure 2-4: Typical validation error display.

Interacting with the Business Tier to Update Model Objects

Once the form data has been extracted and validated, the presentation tier must interact with the business-tier components to perform the desired object creation, update, or deletion. The details of this interaction will depend greatly on the business-tier architecture and the type of intermediate object created during HTML form extraction.

In most cases the business-tier architecture utilizes a different set of model objects than the intermediate objects used in the presentation tier. The data in the intermediate objects must therefore be transferred to the model objects before invoking the business-tier services. This is very common in real-world applications, because the presentation-tier objects are typically designed to support individual web pages in the application whereas model objects are mapped more closely to the database entities or backend services.

You must consider business-tier and presentation-tier architecture together to produce a good, efficient design. A key goal is to provide the right level of separation and encapsulation of the work required to perform the overall HTML form-to-model object transfer process without requiring numerous extra bean objects and hundreds of lines of related get/set transfer code. Don't lose sight of this goal in your zeal to minimize coupling between the tiers or create reusable services.

> **Best Practice**
>
> Presentation-tier architecture requirements depend on the business-tier architecture and interfaces. Design the overall architecture with the requirements of both tiers in mind to avoid unnecessary complexity.

Obviously, the presentation-tier architecture is a little more complicated than just some JSP pages and a servlet for handling forms. The next few sections round out the presentation-tier requirements.

Navigation Requirements

The previous sections outlined the requirements for the presentation of model data and the processing of form submissions as an isolated event, but in a large web application, the individual search pages, results pages, model display pages, HTML forms, and other pages are all connected to form the overall web site. Users navigate through the web site performing the desired activities and receiving the proper display pages by clicking appropriate hyperlinks or navigation control elements in the site. These navigation activities impose significant requirements on the presentation-tier architecture.

Defining the related presentation-tier requirements depends less on how navigation is accomplished visually than on the answers to questions such as these:

❑ How are these navigational controls and links established? Does each page have hard-coded links representing all of the paths available to the user?

❑ Will individual pages or sections of pages be reused in multiple areas of the current application or in other applications?

❑ Does the presence or absence of navigation links depend on some state in the system, such as an attribute of a model object or the identity of the user? Where are these rules implemented?

❑ On which page does the user end up after submitting a form and performing a processing step? Is this target page hard-coded in the processing component? How is branching logic that depends on the outcome of the processing implemented?

❑ Does the site guard against multiple form submissions and improper use of the back/forward capability of browsers? Can the user safely bookmark pages deep within the site?

These are significant and involved questions. The answers applicable in your application may drive your presentation-tier architecture in many different ways and require significant infrastructure development. We'll boil these questions and issues down to three main requirements: basic navigation definition, outcome-based navigation, and submission/bookmark controls.

Basic Navigation Definition

Web applications are complex, interconnected sets of pages tied together with hyperlinks and other navigational controls. The specific target page for each link or control must obviously be specified somewhere in the architecture, but not necessarily in the JSP pages themselves. It may be more consistent with good maintainability and flexibility to defer the target page definition to some other component in the presentation-tier architecture.

Consider the following example snippet from a display JSP page that establishes a simple link to edit a particular person.

```
...
Display person elements
...
<a href="EditPerson.jsp?id=...">[Edit]</a>
```

The target page, `EditPerson.jsp`, is hard-coded in the JSP page, making it painful to change the name of the target page without affecting every page that links to this target page. Reusing this display page elsewhere in this application or subsequent applications is also made more difficult. The coupling between pages is strong and implemented in the pages themselves.

Contrast that snippet with a different JSP snippet using a general servlet as a controller to accept requests and pass the user to the proper page.

```
...
Display person elements
...
<a href="ActionServlet?action=editperson&id=...">[Edit]</a>
```

The `ActionServlet` would receive the `action` parameter in the `HttpServletRequest` and perform a lookup or conditional branching of some sort to determine the name of the target page, forwarding or redirecting the user to that page, as appropriate. The specific technique used to perform this activity is determined by the presentation-tier architecture.

We recommend that you use some form of controller servlet or other similar mechanism outside of the JSP pages themselves to define basic site navigation. Therefore, the presentation-tier architecture must enable and support this capability.

Best Practice

Avoid hard-coding navigational links and controls in JSP pages. Use controller servlets or other presentation-tier components to define basic navigational logic.

Outcome-Based Navigation

Defining outcome-based navigation is, in some ways, the flip side of the previous section. In the previous section, the navigational information was removed from the JSP pages and placed in a controller layer of some sort. In this section, the outcome of a processing step defines the next page displayed for the user, and this navigational information too must be removed from an inappropriate place and delegated to the controller layer.

For example, a processing step that creates new users on the site may want to send a user to the `CreationComplete.jsp` page if the creation was successful and to the `CreationProblem.jsp` page if not. Where are these specific page names defined in the application? The name could be embedded in the processing component itself, as indicated by the following code snippet.

```
public void service(HttpServletRequest request,
                    HttpServletResponse response)
    throws ServletException, IOException
{
    ...
    boolean result = service.createUser(userinfo);
    String nextpage =
        (result ? "CreationComplete.jsp" : "CreationProblem.jsp");
    RequestDispatcher disp = request.getRequestDispatcher(nextpage);
    disp.forward(request, response);
}
```

In this crude example, the processing servlet will forward control depending on the outcome of the call to the service. Clearly, the hard-coding of the target pages in the servlet affects the maintainability and reusability of this component, making the coupling with the JSP page names and locations very strong. Although the controller or processing servlet is the right layer to determine the target page, hard-coding the names in the controller is not appropriate.

We recommend that navigation information that depends on outcomes of processing steps, model object states, or other branching conditions should be defined in the controller layer using an external definition mechanism, such as a properties file or XML descriptor, to define the target page names. This minimizes coupling between controller-layer components and the display pages and allows for efficient maintenance and reuse of both controller and display components.

Best Practice

Avoid hard-coding page names in controller servlets and other components. Use an external file or descriptor to define page names based on outcomes or branch conditions.

Submission/Bookmark Controls

It's a common lament for web application designers: site development would be easy if it weren't for the users! Users will explore every corner of the site, set and use bookmarks deep in the site, and make use of the Back and Forward functions of their browsers with wild abandon. Be prepared for the worst!

Although a complete discussion of this topic is beyond the scope of this book, there is at least one concrete requirement that you should impose on the presentation-tier architecture: the site must guard against multiple submissions or out-of-order submissions of HTML forms. Users may, by accident or intent, submit a form one time and perhaps continue to navigate through the site, then back up to the HTML form page again, and resubmit the form with the same or modified data. How will your site react if the form was used to place an order or create a new record?

Solutions to this problem vary from architecture to architecture, but they normally employ some form of token or timestamp in the form that is good for only a single submission. Preventing multiple form submissions and handling them properly when they occur represent important requirements for the presentation-tier architecture.

> **Best Practice**
>
> Include safeguards in your presentation-tier components to prevent erroneous form submissions and handle user bookmarking and back/forward navigation properly.

We've barely scratched the surface of issues related to navigation definition and the handling of special situations and conditions caused by user activity. Clearly, additional requirements might affect the presentation-tier architecture, such as support for navigation bars or menus, security-based navigation behavior, customizing navigation on a per-user basis, and many others. The important thing to note is that achieving good maintainability and reusability of presentation-tier components imposes significant requirements on the presentation-tier architecture, which must be taken into consideration during architecture selection and design.

Building a Presentation-Tier Architecture

The preceding sections identified a number of important requirements imposed on the presentation-tier architecture based on typical user interface requirements and good design principles. These requirements represent a tall order for any architecture and may seem somewhat daunting at this point.

Fortunately, you don't have to build a presentation-tier architecture from scratch unless you feel compelled to do so. A number of good presentation-tier frameworks are available in the open source community, including Spring MVC and Struts.

We need to finish up our general discussion of the presentation-tier architecture selection process with a few additional items, and then we will present a brief comparison of a typical hand-made presentation-tier architecture, the Spring MVC framework, and the Struts 1.2 framework using the requirements discussed so far as the basis for comparison.

Other Architecture Considerations

Requirements imposed on the presentation-tier architecture are important but are not the only considerations that affect the selection or design of an architecture. Essentially, the requirements specify a minimum set of behaviors for the presentation tier but do not actually define the solution. The solution itself should take into account other factors, such as the following:

❑   What is the experience level of the Java EE development team? What about the team expected to perform ongoing maintenance and enhancements after the application rolls out? There is almost always a trade-off between flexibility and maintainability of the design and the apparent complexity of the original development. Find the right balance.

❑   Does it make sense to impose requirements such as the elimination of hard-coded navigation links based on the site size, need for reuse, and other factors? Can a compromise set of rules be established that mandates the use of controller navigation control in some areas but not others?

❑   Will performance be adversely affected by presentation-tier design decisions? Creating additional layers in the architecture and steps in processes such as form submission have a performance cost associated with them. Weigh this cost against the benefits of the additional design elements to justify the design.

❑ Is the design consistent with WebLogic Server clustering and other production environment deployment practices and options? Don't preclude the use of clustering through some design feature or assumption, for example, or assume that the web application will always be collocated with the EJB components if this is not true.

In the end, the presentation-tier architecture design or selection process comes down to a judgment call based on all of the available information and requirements. There is no single correct answer or even a set of hard-and-fast rules to go by. What makes sense for one application or development team may not make sense for a different development effort.

One fact remains: The presentation tier defines the behaviors closest to the user, and because of this it is subject to the highest variability of inputs, must react to the need for constant change, and can make or break your development effort. Don't rush the design decisions or jump on any given framework bandwagon unless you understand the details and have a clear picture of the costs and benefits for your application.

Candidate Presentation-Tier Architectures

In this section, we briefly compare three candidate presentation-tier architectures, summarizing their individual solutions to the presentation-tier requirements outlined in the previous section. The first architecture, a *JSP-centric architecture*, uses JSP pages alone to meet the presentation-tier requirements in a fairly *low-tech* approach to the problem. The second architecture, Struts 1.2, is a *servlet-centric architecture* that uses JSP pages and servlets in a more complex and flexible model-view-controller design and represents an established, well-understood option. The third architecture, Spring MVC, is newer alternative, very similar to Struts, that represents a more state-of-the-art presentation-tier architecture.

The comparison will be performed by examining the components and techniques necessary to build a simple *Person Tracker* web application using each architecture. The Person Tracker application maintains a list of people and allows users to view the list and edit individuals. It employs a simple stateless service Java object, `PersonService`, as the business-tier component responsible for managing model objects. `PersonService` is a simple Java class that maintains a list of `Person` objects in memory and provides a straightforward interface for retrieving, creating, and updating people.

The complete source code for all three solutions is available on the companion web site (`http://www.wrox.com/`).

JSP-Centric Architecture

The JSP-centric architecture we chose for this comparison uses only a single presentation-tier technology, JSP pages, to produce a web application meeting the presentation-tier requirements. The emphasis is on reducing complexity by eliminating all layers, technologies, and components not absolutely necessary to the design.

Figure 2-5 presents a high-level picture of the JSP components and their interactions in the architecture. Note that although everything in the presentation tier is implemented as JSP pages, there is still a controller component (called an *action page* in this architecture). This approach is basically an all-JSP implementation of the model-view-controller architecture.

The following list summarizes the JSP-centric solution according to the major presentation-tier requirements outlined in the previous section. Examine the downloadable example programs to understand better how these requirements were satisfied in the JSP-centric architecture.

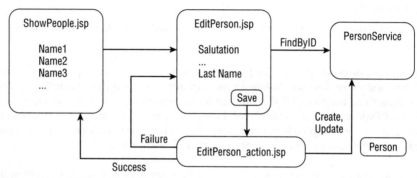

Figure 2-5: JSP-centric architecture components.

JSP pages perform display tasks JSP pages are responsible for all of the display-related requirements outlined in the previous section. JSP pages fetch data from the service using scriptlet code or custom tags, create list displays by looping through collections of model objects, and create HTML forms containing model data for display and modification.

Action JSP pages process form submissions Specialized JSP pages, called *action pages*, are used to process HTML form submissions. Action pages extract form data using scriptlet code, custom tags, or similar techniques, validate the data, and interact with the business-tier components. Errors are handled by forwarding back to the form page after creating a list of errors in the `HttpServletRequest`. Form data is redisplayed on the form for correction by special code that looks for it in the request. Significant scriptlet code is required on form pages and action pages to implement all of the form submission and error redisplay rules outlined previously.

Navigation controlled by view and action pages Basic navigation definition and outcome-based navigation are implemented in the JSP display pages and action pages using straightforward links and URLs. Navigation information could be stored in external files to reduce coupling at the expense of complexity. Submission controls are implemented using a custom token–based approach involving a hidden HTML form field and matching session attribute. HTTP redirects are used after form submissions, where possible, to alleviate bookmark and browser-navigation issues.

The benefits of the JSP-centric approach include the following:

- ❏ The number of components required to build a given application is small.
- ❏ The number of technologies used is small, reducing the learning curve for inexperienced developers.
- ❏ JSP pages can be modified and redeployed to a running instance of WebLogic Server very quickly, speeding turnaround time in a prototyping or UI brainstorming effort.

The drawbacks include the following:

❏ Architecture tends to produce a tightly coupled application with hard-coded page names.

❏ Action JSP pages are primarily Java code but cannot be developed, compiled, and debugged as easily as pure Java code.

❏ Large amount of scriptlet code is required in JSP pages to implement all presentation-tier requirements.

❏ Reuse of processing and validation logic is hampered by its placement in form-specific action JSP pages.

Given the existence of good open source frameworks such as Struts and Spring MVC, the wealth of documentation and examples available using these frameworks, and the availability of developers with experience using these frameworks, it is difficult to recommend a JSP-centric architecture under any circumstances. Whatever time you might save during construction by keeping the number of components and technologies minimal will be lost, eventually, as you maintain and tweak your custom-built JSP components to handle changing business or navigational requirements.

JSP-centric architectures might be appropriate in throwaway prototyping efforts, given the quick turnaround JSP pages enjoy when it comes to redeployment, but otherwise this architecture and others like it should be avoided.

Best Practice

Consider a simple JSP-centric approach for throwaway prototyping efforts to speed redeployment, but avoid it for all other applications.

Servlet-Centric Architecture: Struts

The first servlet-centric architecture chosen for this comparison leverages an open source framework called Struts to avoid building the required support components and logic from scratch. We're going to use a small subset of the components and features in the Struts 1.2 framework, concentrating primarily on the features related to form handling and navigation.

Figure 2-6 presents a high-level view of the JSP, servlet, form, and model components and their interactions in the Struts architecture chosen for this application.

There are still two main JSP pages, ShowPeople.jsp and EditPerson.jsp, but the components responsible for processing forms and controlling navigation have changed considerably in the new architecture. A new PersonForm object has been introduced for use by the EditPerson.jsp page and related processing, and new *action* components are present for processing user actions. More components are required in the Struts servlet-centric approach, overall, than in the JSP-centric architecture depicted in Figure 2-5.

Let's list the presentation-tier requirements in the same manner as before and examine how the Struts architecture meets them in our example application. We again refer you to the downloadable source code for a detailed examination of this solution.

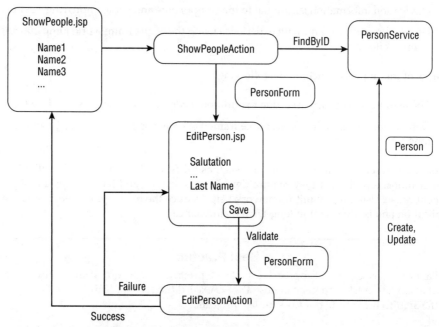

Figure 2-6: Struts servlet-centric architecture components.

JSP pages perform display tasks   JSP pages are again responsible for all of the display-related requirements. JSP pages use special Struts custom tags to create HTML forms, favor retrieving model data from JavaBeans located in the HttpServletRequest rather than fetching it directly, and avoid hard-coding links to other pages by referencing controllers rather than display pages. Struts also provides tags for internationalization and simple role-based conditional logic.

Controller components process form submissions   A centralized controller servlet invokes *action* classes to process HTML form submissions and interact with business-tier components. Specialized Java objects, called *form beans*, are used to extract and validate the HTML form data. Errors are handled by forwarding back to the form page after creating a list of errors in the HttpServletRequest for display by Struts tags on the form. Form data is automatically redisplayed on the form for correction. No scriptlet code is required to satisfy form submission requirements.

Navigation controlled by configuration files   Basic and outcome-based navigation information is stored in an external configuration file, struts-config.xml. This file is also used by the controller servlet to relate JSP display pages, form beans, and action classes across the application. Submission controls are implemented using a built-in, token-based approach involving a hidden HTML form field and matching session attribute. HTTP redirects are used after form submissions, where possible, to alleviate bookmark and browser navigation issues.

The benefits of the Struts-based servlet-centric approach include the following:

❑   Display logic, processing logic, and form validation are encapsulated in different components, improving application flexibility and reuse.

❑   Pure Java code in controller components is easier to develop with IDE tools than scriptlet code within JSP action pages.

❑   Navigation information is external to the components and code, improving flexibility and reuse.

❑   Developers can be found with experience using the Struts framework, jump-starting your development effort.

Drawbacks of this approach include the following:

❑   The learning curve increases, due to additional components and files required for operation.

❑   Dependence on an older open source framework such as Struts 1.2 may become an issue in the long term.

We recommend a servlet-centric architecture such as the Struts 1.2 framework for all but the smallest web applications, especially if they require flexible organization and have a substantial potential for component reuse. Using a prebuilt framework helps reduce the development effort and complexity of the application and is important in long-term maintenance.

Best Practice

Favor the servlet-centric approach for all web projects. The flexibility and reuse benefits of a servlet-centric approach almost always exceed the costs of learning and adopting the architecture for all but the simplest projects.

Servlet-Centric Architecture: Spring MVC

The second servlet-centric architecture chosen for this comparison leverages the Spring 2.5 MVC framework as an alternative to the Struts framework. Spring MVC is part of a larger Spring open source framework that defines a comprehensive approach for building Java EE applications that are modular, easy to test, and easily reusable. Spring uses a technique known as Dependency Injection to connect objects and services via declarative mechanisms rather than runtime lookups or hard-coded connections. Spring MVC uses this same technique to wire together the model, view, and controller components in the presentation tier to achieve the desired navigational and form submission logic in your web application.

The newer Spring 2.5 MVC framework, though much more configurable and extensible than Struts, actually shares many key concepts with its older brother.

❑   Both have Java classes, acting as controllers in the MVC parlance, whose job it is to prepare data for display on view components and process data coming in via HTML form submissions. Struts calls these *action* classes; Spring MVC calls these *controllers*.

❑   Both make use of standard view components such as JSP pages for rendering HTML output, and both provide custom tag libraries for accessing functions and data on JSP pages in a standard way.

❑   Both also have intermediate objects used by the controllers to pass data to and receive data from the view components. Struts uses *form beans* for this function; Spring MVC has *command* classes.

❑   Both of these frameworks make use of a dispatcher servlet for accepting and forwarding HTTP requests to the proper controller class depending on configuration information.

❑   Finally, both use an external configuration file to specify all of the mappings, relationships, navigational rules, and other connections between components in the web tier.

A dyed-in-the-wool Spring MVC fan might take issue with this simplistic comparison by pointing out some of the significant differences between the frameworks. For example, Spring MVC provides a wide variety of *controller* types tailored for different types of activity, whereas Struts 1.2 basically supports a single *action* interface. Spring MVC also has a richer set of interception points available in the flow that handles form submittal and other complex tasks, making it easier to override default behaviors. These and other differences notwithstanding, there is value in recognizing the similarities — especially if you are migrating from Struts to Spring MVC and need to get a handle on all the new terminology and classes!

Figure 2-7 presents a high-level view of the JSP, controller, command, and model components and their interactions in the Spring MVC architecture chosen for this example application.

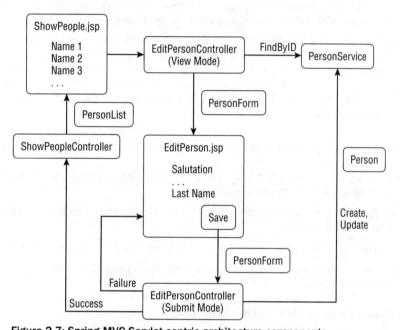

Figure 2-7: Spring MVC Servlet-centric architecture components.

As in the Struts version, two main JSP pages are responsible for view-related functions: ShowPeople.jsp displays a list of people and EditPerson.jsp allows the viewing and editing of a single person. The *action* classes in the Struts version were replaced with *controller* classes in the Spring MVC version with some rearrangement to make proper use of the built-in SimpleFormController form-handling functionality in the EditPersonController class.

The Spring MVC version utilizes two *command* classes as intermediate objects between the controllers and the JSP pages: the PersonList object is created by the SimpleFormController and displayed by the ShowPeople.jsp page, and PersonForm is created by EditPersonController and displayed by the EditPerson.jsp page. HTML form submissions from the edit page come back into the EditPersonController and are validated and processed in a manner very similar to the Struts version of this same process.

The number of components and complexity of the Spring MVC application is comparable to the Struts version. Let's examine the presentation-tier requirements again and see how the Spring MVC architecture meets them in our example application.

JSP pages perform display tasks   JSP pages continue to be responsible for all of the display-related requirements. Spring-provided custom tags retrieve data from the command classes and create HTML forms. Links point at controllers via mappings in the Spring MVC configuration file.

Controller components prepare data for views and process form submissions   A centralized dispatcher servlet invokes *controller* classes to prepare data for viewing, process HTML form submissions, and interact with business-tier components. Specialized Java objects, called *commands*, are used to pass data to view pages and to extract and validate the HTML form data. Errors are handled by forwarding back to the form page after creating a list of errors in the HttpServletRequest for display by Spring tags on the form. Form data is automatically redisplayed on the form for correction. No scriptlet code is required to satisfy form submission requirements.

Navigation controlled by configuration files   Basic and outcome-based navigation information is stored in an external configuration file, in this case exampleapp-servlet.xml. This file connects components together via dependency injection and allows the Spring MVC infrastructure to relate JSP display pages, controller classes, and command classes across the application. Although there is no built-in submission control technique, a session-token approach is easily added to the form processing controllers.

The benefits of the Spring MVC–based approach are, essentially, the same as the Struts-based approach.

❏   Display logic, processing logic, and form validation are encapsulated in different components, improving application flexibility and reuse.

❏   Pure Java code in controller components is easier to develop with IDE tools than scriptlet code within JSP action pages.

❏   Navigation information is external to the components and code, improving flexibility and reuse.

❏   Developers can be found with experience using the Spring MVC framework, jump-starting your development effort.

Benefits unique to the Spring MVC approach include:

❏   Rich flow of control within the form submission process provides a very good mechanism for intercepting and overriding selected default behaviors.

❏   Dependency injection provides a mechanism to *mock up* or simulate business-tier components within the controller components, easing unit testing of presentation-tier logic.

Drawbacks of this approach include:

❏   The learning curve increases, due to additional components and files required for operation. Spring MVC is worse than Struts in this respect due simply to the breadth and depth of the framework and its component classes and flows.

❏   Dependence on an open source framework such as Spring MVC may become an issue in the long term.

Given Spring MVC's similarity to Struts, and our earlier recommendation that you consider Struts for almost all web projects, it should come as no surprise that we feel the same, in general, about Spring MVC. It is a very powerful and flexible servlet-based MVC framework that meets nearly all of the presentation-tier requirements out of the box and will undoubtedly replace Struts as the framework of choice very soon, if it hasn't already.

Our only reservation in recommending Spring MVC is simply that many web applications do not require the power and flexibility it provides. Is your development team ready and able to decide how best to use the flexibility of Spring MVC without false starts and rework? It's not as easy as you might think — there are many ways to achieve the same ends, each with its own set of pros and cons.

The bottom line is this: If you are comfortable with Struts, and find that it does the job for you, it may be hard to justify the expense of converting all of your existing applications to Spring MVC. If you are fortunate enough to have no applications requiring migration, and feel confident in your team's ability to tackle Spring MVC, then go for it.

Best Practice

Spring MVC is a step above Struts in flexibility and power, and is fast becoming the de facto standard for Java EE web development. If you have the technical prowess to handle the complexity, it definitely makes sense to use Spring MVC, but don't chase new technology for technology's sake — make it earn its way into your environment!

Chapter Review

We've covered a lot of information in this chapter. We began by defining some key architecture concepts and design patterns related to web applications, including the model-view-controller pattern.

We then defined the requirements of a robust presentation-tier architecture in terms of display capabilities, form submission and processing requirements, and navigation controls. We discussed how meeting these requirements represents a significant design challenge for a home-grown, custom developed architecture, thereby leading us to search for a prebuilt presentation-tier framework to speed development and improve maintenance.

Three candidate architectures were then compared in the context of the presentation-tier requirements defined earlier, and recommendations were provided to guide your selection of presentation-tier architecture based on project and team attributes.

It's time to apply what you learned in Chapters 1 and 2. In the next two chapters, we design and build the presentation-tier components of a larger example application. This example program, a hotel reservation web site, will provide a realistic platform for our examination of deployment issues, JMS best practices, security, application management, Web Services, and business-tier architecture selection in succeeding chapters.

3

Designing an Example Java EE Application

In this chapter and the next, we explore the design and construction of a realistic example application. By realistic, we mean an example of sufficient size and complexity that key technology elements are useful and demonstrated in the example. The example also helps you explore decisions you must make during application development in WebLogic Server and provides a context for sidebars and notes on best practices.

This chapter details the design of the presentation tier of a fairly large and complex Java EE application. We cover different topics related to the example program throughout the book. For example, Chapter 4 walks through many of the presentation-tier components and discusses the techniques used in their construction. Chapter 7 details the design and development of the business-tier components and their interaction with the database.

We discuss issues and decisions in roughly the same order they were encountered during the actual design and development of the example application. We begin by examining the system requirements for the example application, a web-based hotel reservation system.

Application Requirements

The example application is a web-based reservation system for hotels, bed-and-breakfasts, and resorts.

Specific requirements include the following:

- ❑ The system must provide a user site with a basic property search, pricing, room availability, and reservation capability.

- ❑ Property information must be created and maintained through an administration site providing pages for maintenance of property data including basic property information, room types, rate, inventory, and targeted marketing offers. Properties must be able to view and maintain their own information through the administration site.

□ Users must be able to create profiles containing guest information to speed subsequent reservations.

□ Marketing offers should be targeted to users based on the last property search performed or hotel selected.

□ The application must employ a relational database to store all property, guest, and reservation information.

Sound challenging enough? Don't forget the ever-present requirements for high performance and good scalability, maintainability, and reliability. Sounds like a job for Java EE and WebLogic Server!

We're going to call our web-based reservation application `bigrez.com`.

Business Domain Models

The `bigrez.com` system employs a relational database to store all business domain objects. Although Chapter 7 provides object models and discusses the business domain and business-tier components in more detail, we present the database model at this point to illustrate the scope of the business domain and provide a framework for discussing presentation-tier design. Figure 3-1 shows the logical database design of `bigrez.com`.

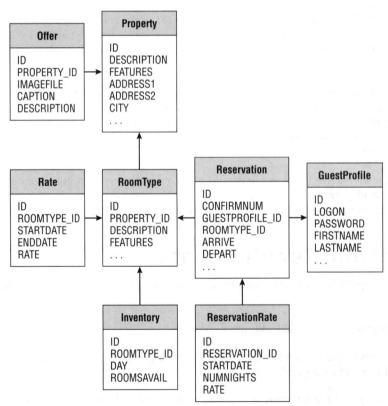

Figure 3-1: `bigrez.com` logical database design.

The data model in Figure 3-1 illustrates the key objects and relationships present in the business domain of this system. For example, each property has a set of room types, with related inventory and rate records defining the availability and price for that type of room for a particular date.

Our task in the user-facing web application portion of `bigrez.com` is to hide this complex set of business objects and related processes and give the user an easy-to-use, step-by-step process for finding and booking the right room on the right dates. The administration site will present a view of this data more directly related to the database design.

Presentation Requirements

The `bigrez.com` user-facing site must walk the user through the reservation process by presenting forms and pages in a logical order and building the reservation visually on one side of the screen. The basic layout illustrated in Figure 3-2 shows the key elements of the display.

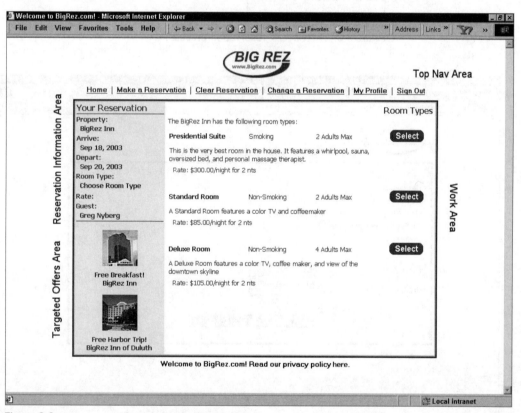

Figure 3-2: `bigrez.com` **basic presentation layout.**

The user will interact primarily with HTML forms and content presented in the work area, while the progress of the reservation is displayed in the reservation information area. The reservation information area can also be used as a navigation device to revisit a previous page in the process (for example, to change dates) by clicking links in the area.

The basic reservation process is illustrated by Figure 3-3. This diagram represents the basic course through the reservation process. The actual process is subject to many detours and alternate courses not depicted in this figure, based on user navigation decisions. We cover some of these alternate courses during the discussion of the reservation information area later in the chapter.

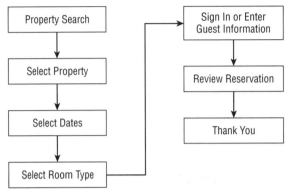

Figure 3-3: `bigrez.com` **reservation process.**

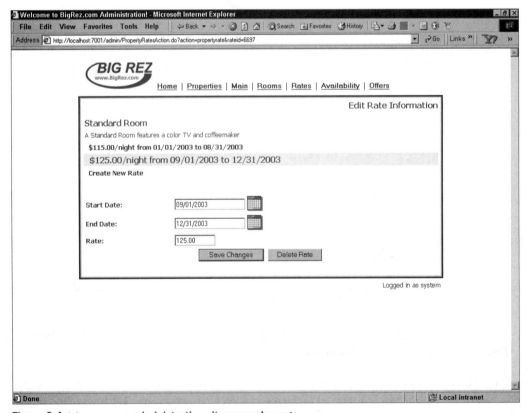

Figure 3-4: `bigrez.com` **administration site example page.**

We must implement many business rules related to site navigation and the reservation process in the presentation tier of the application. For example, the user may not skip ahead and choose a room type before selecting a property and arrival/departure dates because the available room types are dependent on these choices. The user may, however, skip ahead and sign in or provide guest information at any point in the process. Note that the web application architecture defines, among other things, where business rules such as these are implemented in the presentation tier.

The `bigrez.com` application also requires an administration site allowing authorized users to create and maintain the properties and related information used by the reservation process. Figure 3-4 presents an example page in the administration site, showing the basic structure of a page.

Both the user site and the administration site must meet all of the presentation-tier requirements discussed in Chapter 2, including display-related requirements, form/update requirements, and navigation requirements.

The `bigrez.com` site is not a small application. There are more than 20 JSP pages in the user site and another 15 pages in the administration site. We believe an example application of this size provides a more realistic platform for the construction, deployment, and management discussions to follow.

Web Application Architecture

Chapter 2 discussed the selection of a web application architecture and presented a brief comparison of three specific architectures: a JSP-centric approach and two servlet-centric frameworks (Struts and Spring MVC). We need to choose an architecture for `bigrez.com` that will meet the requirements and provide good maintainability and flexibility.

As discussed in Chapter 2, there are advantages and disadvantages to all three architectures. Although the JSP-centric approach is simpler, and might make our job easier in this chapter and the next as we design and construct the example application, the resulting architecture would not be suitable for many medium to large applications. We're focusing on best practices in this book, and we feel a servlet-centric approach should be considered a best practice for most production applications.

We've chosen to use the Spring MVC framework, rather than Struts, simply as an acknowledgment that examples using newer technologies and frameworks are of more interest to the developer community. Either framework would have met the requirements.

The web application architecture for `bigrez.com` will therefore adopt the Spring MVC architecture described in Chapter 2 and implemented in the Person Tracker example program. Display JSP pages will present beans, forms, and business data to the user, and user actions and submitted HTML forms will be processed by the page-specific `Controller` classes. The difference is that `bigrez.com` requires much more sophistication both in terms of navigation and interaction with the business layer. We discuss both of these areas in detail in a later section.

One key aspect of the chosen architecture is that controller components are responsible for loading required data into the proper context for display in the JSP pages. `Controller` classes should interact with the business-tier components to retrieve the desired data and place it in the `HttpServletRequest` before forwarding to the next display JSP page. If the JSP page includes an HTML form, the `Controller` class will populate the form bean and place it in the request for use by the page.

Presentation Approach

The Spring MVC architecture selected for bigrez.com uses JSP pages for all display-related components. JSP pages will therefore be used to display business data, forms, search results, and all visual elements that define the overall design of the site. As shown in Figure 3-2, the site includes navigation bars, headers and footers, and a left-side gutter containing the current reservation information and targeted offers. We must now decide how this overall table structure will be defined and who will be responsible for assembling the generated HTML into a single response to the user.

A very common design pattern, the *composite view pattern*, is often used for this purpose. This pattern recognizes the importance of placing individual pieces of content in separate view components, in our case either standalone JSP pages or snippets of JSP code. As discussed in the literature, the overall page is then assembled by some manager or controller in the architecture that knows the proper placement of each view component on the final page and is responsible for creating the top-level HTML tags and structure for the page. The specific technique used to include the separate view components is not defined by the pattern and can include translation-time <%@ include file="..." %> directives, dynamic <jsp:include> actions, or more sophisticated techniques using helper objects or custom tags.

We'll employ the composite view pattern in the construction of our example application by breaking the overall page into six different view components, as illustrated by Figure 3-5. Each of these view components will be a separate, standalone JSP page included in the overall HTML response using some type of dynamic include capability. The information generated by the primary display page will be located in the framed area to the right of the reservation information and offers areas in the left gutter.

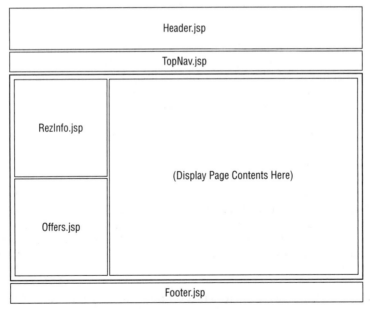

Figure 3-5: bigrez.com **primary view components and layout.**

So far, so good, but we're not done yet. Which component or page, exactly, is going to define the overall page structure, generate the top-level HTML tags such as <body> and <table>, and use <jsp:include>

actions or other techniques to assemble the page? Will each display page in the site include the proper view components to assemble the overall response, a commonly used technique we've labeled *self-assembly*? Will some master page or template be responsible for creating the overall HTML response and including the specific display page in the response, a technique we've called *master page assembly*? Or, should a separate view assembler combine layout or template information with individual page contents to create the overall response, a technique we've labeled *external view assembly*? We examine these options in more detail and make a design decision for the bigrez.com example application.

Self-Assembly

In the self-assembly technique, the display page assembles all of the supporting pieces of the overall response. The display page basically includes the view components or code snippets required to create the proper HTML table structure and embed all of the headers, footers, and other visual elements in their proper locations. The SimpleHome_SA.jsp page, presented in Listing 3-1, illustrates how the bigrez.com home page might be constructed using the self-assembly technique.

Listing 3-1: SimpleHome_SA.jsp showing self-assembly.

```
<!DOCTYPE HTML PUBLIC "-//W3C//DTD HTML 4.0 Transitional//EN">

<html>
<head>

  <title>Welcome to BigRez.com!</title>

  <link rel=stylesheet type="text/css" href="css/StyleMaster.css">
  <script src="/js/DatePicker.js"></script>

</head>

<body bgcolor="#FFFFFF">

<table align="center" width="725" cellpadding="0" cellspacing="0" border="0">
  <tr>
    <td>
      <table align="center" cellpadding="0" cellspacing="10">
        <tr>
          <td align="center">
            <jsp:include page="/Header.jsp"></jsp:include>
          </td>
        </tr>
        <tr>
          <td>
            <jsp:include page="/TopNav.jsp"></jsp:include>
          </td>
        </tr>
      </table>
    </td>
  </tr>
</table>
```

Continued

Listing 3-1: SimpleHome_SA.jsp showing self-assembly. *(continued)*

```
<table align="center" width="725" cellpadding="0" cellspacing="0"
      border="0">
  <tr>
    <td width="175" valign="top" bgcolor="#EEEEEE">
      <table width="175" border="0" cellpadding="0" cellspacing="0">
      <tr>
        <td><jsp:include page="/RezInfo.jsp"/></td>
      </tr>
      <tr>
        <td><jsp:include page="/Offers.jsp"/></td>
      </tr>
      </table>
    </td>
    <td width="1" >
      <img src="images/space.gif" width="1" height="1">
    </td>
    <td width="550" valign="top">
      Home Page Contents Here..
    </td>
  </tr>
</table>

<table align="center" width="725" cellpadding="0" cellspacing="0"
      border="0">
  <tr>
    <jsp:include page="/Footer.jsp"/>
  </tr>
</table>

</body>
</html>
```

The five common components (`Header.jsp`, `TopNav.jsp`, `RezInfo.jsp`, `Offers.jsp`, and `Footer.jsp`) are included in the HTML response at the proper location in the overall page structure and table layout. In this simple technique, a large amount of the structure and layout would have to be copied to all display pages in the site, making maintenance and customization for different installations difficult. This simple type of self-assembly is suitable for only the smallest web applications.

The basic self-assembly approach can be improved by combining the sections above and below the display page content itself in additional intermediate view components, as illustrated in the `BetterHome_SA.jsp` example in Listing 3-2.

Listing 3-2: BetterHome_SA.jsp showing improved self-assembly.

```
<jsp:include page="/Top_SA.jsp">
  <jsp:param name="title" value="Welcome to BigRez.com!"/>
</jsp:include>
```

```
<table align="center" width="725"
       cellpadding="0" cellspacing="0" border="0">
  <tr>
    <jsp:include page="/LeftSide_SA.jsp"/>
    <td width="1" >
      <img src="images/space.gif" width="1" height="1">
    </td>
    <td width="550" valign="top">
      Home Page Contents Here..
    </td>
  </tr>
</table>

<jsp:include page="/Bottom_SA.jsp"/>
```

These new intermediate view components, Top_SA.jsp, LeftSide_SA.jsp, and Bottom_SA.jsp, basically contain the HTML and lower-level <jsp:include> tags previously contained in the display page itself, thereby reducing the amount of content copied on each display page. This technique represents a significant improvement over the simple technique, although it too has limitations as the complexity of the page structure surrounding the display content increases.

Because the title of the HTML page is now defined in the common Top_SA.jsp, each display page must provide the title to the included JSP using a request parameter:

```
<jsp:include page="/Top_SA.jsp">
  <jsp:param name="title" value="Welcome to BigRez.com!"/>
</jsp:include>
```

The Top_SA.jsp page must define the title using the passed-in request parameter:

```
<head>
  <title><%= request.getParameter("title") %></title>
  ...
</head>
```

Note that these self-assembly examples did not include all of the visual elements desired for the bigrez.com site (see Figure 3-2) in order to keep the examples simple. For example, the table containing the LeftSide_SA.jsp component and the actual display page content should have been surrounded by a two-color border. This would complicate the table structure copied in each display page.

One thing to keep in mind before including scriptlet code such as request.getParameter("title") in your JSP pages is the danger this creates in the form of cross-site scripting (XSS) vulnerabilities. As written, the contents of the title request parameter will be copied directly into the output HTML response without any filtering or checking. A malicious user could create a URL with the title parameter set to inject JavaScript in the response, cause an unsuspecting user to invoke that URL via a redirect from another site or other mechanism, and thereby gain access to protected data or services. XSS vulnerabilities can be avoided by filtering request parameters through a utility such as the built-in WebLogic Server utility method weblogic.servlet.security.Utils.encodeXSS() to replace dangerous characters with their safe "escaped" HTML equivalents before displaying them on your pages. For more information on XSS vulnerabilities and their mitigation, see Link 3-1 in the book's online Appendix at http://www.wrox.com.

Some form of self-assembly would probably work for the `bigrez.com` site, but we're looking for a technique that provides more flexibility and is easier to maintain. Imagine, for example, that we want to move the reservation information and targeted offers from the left gutter to the right gutter or that we need to add a completely new view component, perhaps something like a bread-crumb navigator, in the table containing the display page. Both of these changes would require touching all of the display pages to modify the table structure and `<jsp:include>` actions to reflect the new layout and components.

We'd also like to be able to deploy the same application for multiple hotel chains or customers. What if a potential new customer demands a different layout? The display pages or intermediate view components would have to be copied and edited to create a new layout, hurting maintainability, or would require conditional code to assemble the page differently based on the client, adding complexity. Neither solution provides a clean, easy mechanism to reuse the application in the face of significant layout changes.

No matter how sophisticated the include process becomes through the use of custom tags, view helpers, or even framework components meant for this purpose, the basic concept of self-assembly is inherently flawed. The individual display pages should know little or nothing about the way in which they are assembled to form the overall page, and self-assembly in all its forms breaks this rule.

What we need is an implementation of the *composite view* pattern that completely separates the overall structure and layout of the page from the contents of the display area. In the next section, we discuss one useful solution: *master page assembly*.

Master Page Assembly

The self-assembly approach, discussed in the previous section, separated the complete page contents into individual view components and made it the responsibility of the display page itself to include these components in the correct manner to build the full HTML response. The display page was in charge of the assembly process. In the master page assembly approach, on the other hand, the display page is simply another piece of content included in the overall response by a *master* page. As shown in Figure 3-6, the master page is now in charge of the assembly process and defines the overall page structure and layout.

This seems simple enough as a concept, but how can the same master page be used for all the different display pages in the site? How does the master page know which display page to include?

The trick to making this technique work is the runtime evaluation of a `<jsp:include>` action placed in the master page to include the proper content page. Recall that the `<jsp:include>` action had two basic forms. The first is a version using a statically defined page name:

```
<jsp:include page="/Home.jsp" />
```

The second is a version with the page name defined using a runtime expression:

```
<jsp:include page="<%= variablename %>" />
```

The version using a runtime expression as the page name provides one straightforward way to share the same master page across many display pages. In its simplest form, the `Master.jsp` page looks for a particular request parameter, `page`, and uses it in a `<jsp:include>` action to include the proper page in the display area in the overall template defined in the master page.

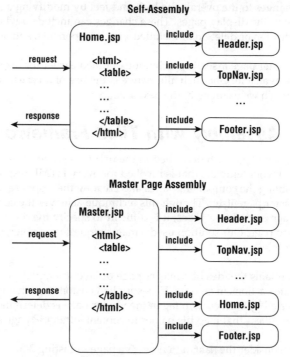

Figure 3-6: Comparison of self-assembly and master
page assembly.

```
...
<% String pagename = request.getParameter("page"); %>
...
<body>
<table>
...
    <% try { %>
    <jsp:include page="<%= pagename %>"/>
    <% }
        catch (IOException e) {
    %>
      <jsp:include page="Blank.jsp"/>
    <% } %>
...
</table>
</body>
```

All of the display pages are then accessed using URLs with the master page name and a query string
parameter defining the display page. For example, http://servername:port/Master.jsp?page=
Home.jsp would invoke the Master.jsp master page and provide the name of the display page to
include, in this case Home.jsp. Hyperlinks within the pages would likewise specify URLs containing this
syntax:

```
<A HREF="Master.jsp?page=ViewProperty.jsp">...</A>
```

We can now make changes to the overall site look and feel by modifying a single page, Master.jsp, without touching any of the display pages. These changes can include a wholesale rearranging of the page structure, the addition or deletion of included view components, and any other desired changes.

We could select the master page assembly technique outlined earlier for bigrez.com and be content, but better alternatives are available. One such alternative is the use of an *external view assembly* framework such as Tiles, an approach we examine in the next section.

External View Assembly with Tiles Framework

The master page assembly approach described in the previous section has, at its heart, the idea of a single master page or layout template that is invoked for every HTML response. That master page was responsible for assembling the component pieces and creating the response using simple <jsp:include> actions within the master page itself. Though this technique achieves the core requirement for reusing shared JSP elements across multiple pages, it is difficult to specify the dynamic content and elements that differ from page to page. Our solution used a magic request parameter, page, to specify the included content page, for example.

The Tiles framework retains the idea of a master page or layout template, but eliminates the awkward dynamic <jsp:include> actions in favor of Tiles-supplied custom tags that perform the same basic function. The content inserted by each custom tag in the master page is determined by an XML configuration file containing tiles *definitions* that map tile names to content, often JSP page snippets.

As a simple example, consider the Master_Tiles.jsp page in Listing 3-3.

Listing 3-3: Master_Tiles.jsp showing simple Tiles master page.

```
<tiles:insertAttribute name="top"/>

<table align="center" width="725"
       cellpadding="0" cellspacing="0" border="0">
  <tr>
    <tiles:insertAttribute name="leftside"/>
    <td width="1" >
      <img src="images/space.gif" width="1" height="1">
    </td>
    <td width="550" valign="top">
      <tiles:insertAttribute name="body"/>
    </td>
  </tr>
</table>

<tiles:insertAttribute name="bottom"/>
```

A simple tiles definition using this master page might look as follows:

```
<definition name="homepage" page="Master_Tiles.jsp">
    <put name="top" value="Top.jsp" />
    <put name="leftside" value="LeftSide.jsp" />
    <put name="body" value="Home.jsp" />
    <put name="bottom" value="Bottom.jsp" />
</definition>
```

Struts actions or Spring MVC controllers now specify the homepage tiles definition as their destination, rather than a specific JSP page or servlet. The Tiles framework prepares the request context with the attributes specified in the definition and invokes the master page to create the HTML response by assembling the output from the specified pages.

Tiles definitions can inherit from each other, making it very easy to create multiple definitions that use a single master page without having to re-specify the static attributes in each definition, as shown here.

```
<definition name="defaultlayout" page="Master_Tiles.jsp">
    <put name="top" value="Top.jsp" />
    <put name="leftside" value="LeftSide.jsp" />
    <put name="body" value="Empty.jsp" />
    <put name="bottom" value="Bottom.jsp" />
</definition>

<definition name="homepage" extends="defaultlayout">
    <put name="body" value="Home.jsp" />
</definition>

<definition name="profilepage" extends="defaultlayout">
    <put name="body" value="Profile.jsp" />
</definition>
```

The Tiles framework provides a very powerful mechanism for assembling JSP pages from reusable content components. We make use of Tiles in the bigrez.com example program in the next chapter and show you more details on the proper configuration and setup of this framework.

Business-Tier Interfaces

Now that we've identified the mechanisms for displaying data and handling navigation and form submission, it is time to discuss the heart of any presentation-tier architecture: interfacing with business-tier components.

First, we need to look ahead a bit to Chapter 7, where we discuss the design and development of the EJB components for this application. Clearly the business-tier interfaces available to the web application depend on the architecture of the business tier. Although we thoroughly discuss the choice of business-tier architecture in Chapter 7, what you need to know here is that we decided to use EJB 3.0 stateless session beans (SLSB) for services, use JPA for persistence management, and pass the JPA-managed domain objects freely between the web layer and the business services. The implications of these decisions on business-tier interfaces include:

❑ Presentation-tier components will call the SLSB business services, passing in whatever parameters or domain objects are required by the services. Services will, in most cases, return data to the presentation components in the form of domain objects or lists of domain objects, which the presentation layer can then freely use in rendering pages.

❑ Controller components will normally place domain objects in forms, thereby giving the view JSP pages direct access to domain object data for view or edit operations.

❑ Relationships between domain objects may or may not be populated within results returned to the presentation tier by the business services. The presentation components need to be aware of the rules for automatic population of children within various domain objects, for example, and not simply assume that all children are available within any domain object returned by the services.

❑　Changes made to domain objects must be explicitly sent back to the services for update in the database. The presentation tier is responsible for knowing which domain objects need to be sent.

❑　Optimistic locking techniques in JPA mandate certain presentation-tier behavior to store version information in the HTTP session and provide it again during update requests.

❑　By default, transactions will always start and end at the session bean boundary. If multiple service calls must be in a single coordinated transaction, a separate service request should be defined that manages the transaction and calls other back-end services from within this single transaction.

All in all, the decision to pass the JPA-managed domain objects between tiers saves considerable work creating and populating separate data transfer objects. This represents one of the huge benefits of EJB 3.0 with JPA persistence over EJB 2.0 container-managed persistence (CMP) entity beans. The use of CMP entity beans created a whole host of problems when we tried to use them directly in the presentation tier (a technique we called *direct interaction* and covered in the previous edition of this book), and mandated the creation of a full set of data transfer objects for inter-tier communication purposes if we did not.

The following sections provide more detail on the key implications of our decision to use EJB 3.0, SLSB services, and JPA-managed domain objects.

Controllers Call Business Services

Consistent with basic tenets of the model-view-controller architecture, only the controller components will request business services from the stateless session bean (SLSB) components. The JSP view components will never call business services, either directly or indirectly, to acquire model data required for presentation on the page.

Controllers that require business services will define attributes for the desired SLSB components, with associated get/set methods, and have references to these EJB components injected via the Spring MVC configuration file.

```
<beans>
    <bean id="propertyServicesReference"
          class="org.springframework.jndi.JndiObjectFactoryBean">
        <property name="jndiName"
                  value="java:/comp/env/ejb/PropertyServices"/>
    </bean>

    . . .

    <bean id="propertySearchController"
          class="com.bigrez.web.PropertySearchController">
        <property name="formView" value="chooseproperty"/>
        <property name="successView" value="propertylist"/>
        <property name="bindOnNewForm" value="true"/>
        <property name="commandName" value="propertySearchForm"/>
        <property name="commandClass"
```

```
                    value="com.bigrez.web.PropertySearchForm"/>
        <property name="propertySearchForm">
            <bean class="com.bigrez.web.PropertySearchForm"/>
        </property>
        <property name="propertyServices"
                ref="propertyServicesReference"/>
    </bean>

    ...

</beans>
```

Note that we are using a special Spring utility class, JndiObjectFactoryBean, to find the EJB component in the web application's local JNDI tree and inject a reference into our Spring MVC controller object. In order for the factory to find it in the JNDI tree, we must also create a reference in the web application's web.xml file.

```
<ejb-local-ref>
    <ejb-ref-name>ejb/PropertyServices</ejb-ref-name>
    <local>com.bigrez.service.PropertyServices</local>
    <ejb-link>PropertyServicesImpl</ejb-link>
</ejb-local-ref>
```

With this wiring process complete, the controller can simply invoke business services through the injected reference without performing any JNDI lookup or other steps.

```
List<Property> propertyList =
    propertyServices.findByCityAndState(form.getCity(), form.getStateCode());
form.setPropertyList(propertyList);
```

The ability to inject EJB 3.0 SLSB components into the Spring MVC controllers is very powerful. It simplifies the controller code dramatically, stays true to inversion-of-control principles, and makes it easy to inject mock versions of the services for unit testing. All in all, a simple and elegant solution.

> **Best Practice**
>
> Use the JndiObjectFactoryBean to inject references to EJB 3.0 components into your Spring MVC controllers and avoid explicit JNDI lookups.

Controllers Populate Forms for JSPs

The JSP view components assume that all model data required for the rendering of the page is located on a single *form* object placed in the request or session context by the controller class preceding the JSP page. The required data might be made available to the JSP page in two ways:

❑   We could define attributes on the form object for all required data and have the controller class copy values from domain object attributes into corresponding form attributes.

❑   We could simply attach domain objects to the form and allow the JSP to access the nested model data directly.

69

We've chosen the second approach for most controllers and pages. Although there are cases where additional attributes are required on the form object to support specific presentation logic or formatting, generally it is fine to have the JSP components access the model data through the form-to-object reference without duplicating fields in the form itself.

When this approach is used, the JSP page will have JSTL and Spring form-related tags that use the dot operator to access the nested data within the domain object held by the form.

In the previous section we showed how the controller class fetches a list of properties from the business service and attaches the list to the form object. The following code snippet shows how a JSP page can loop over the list and display information about each property using the nested notation.

```
<c:forEach var="property"
           items="${propertySearchForm.propertyList}">
  <tr>
    <td width="80" align="center">
      <img src="<c:url value='/images/${property.imageFile}'/>"
           alt="" width="70" height="70">
    </td>
    <td width="100%" align="left">
      <table cellspacing="0" cellpadding="0" border="0">
        <tr>
          <td align="left">
            <c:url var="viewproperty" value="/viewproperty.do">
              <c:param name="id"
                       value="${property.externalIdentity}"/>
            </c:url>
            <a class="table-link"
               href="<c:out value='${viewproperty}'/>">
              <c:out value='${property.description}'/>
            </a>
          </td>
        </tr>
        <tr>
          <td align="left">
            <span class="table-data">
              <c:out value='${property.address.address1}'/>
            </span>
          </td>
        </tr>
        <c:if test='${not empty property.address.address2}'>
        <tr>
          <td align="left">
            <span class="table-data">
              <c:out value='${property.address.address2}'/>
            </span>
          </td>
        </tr>
        </c:if>
        ...
      </table>
    </td>
  </tr>
</c:forEach>
```

Updates Require Explicit Service Calls

The chosen approach to business layer interaction allows the presentation layer to acquire, hold, store in the session, modify, and otherwise manipulate domain objects and their relationships. These domain objects are *disconnected* from the entity manager in the service layer and become the responsibility of the presentation layer components.

This approach has a great many advantages, and at least one distinct disadvantage: The presentation tier needs to make explicit update calls to the services whenever domain objects contain modified data or relationships.

This may not sound like a big deal, but as objects get more complex and the process of making changes to the objects extends to, for example, multiple pages in the application, it can become quite difficult to know what exactly needs to be sent to the services for update. Many developers code their submit processing controllers always to send the object to the service without evaluating whether the user actually modified any of the fields, simply because the alternative can be daunting. Our controllers in bigrez.com will do this as well to keep things simple.

Relationships in Presentation Components

Business domain objects are rarely simple, disconnected objects containing only attribute data. They invariably have relationships with children, sibling, and parent objects. Presentation-tier components will often need to traverse these relationships while displaying information or performing validation or other logic. Because our domain objects are disconnected from the entity manager, relationships are not automatically populated as they are requested, but must be instantiated ahead of time by the initial service request or by subsequent calls to the service.

Note that one of the significant benefits of the direct interaction EJB 2.0 CMP approach used in the previous edition of this book was the ability of presentation-tier components such as JSP pages and Controller classes to work directly with the object lattice and relationships implemented in the entity beans themselves. There was no need to write session bean methods that fetch and return lattices of value objects simulating the entity bean relationships or implement some form of lazy instantiation of relationship collections in parent value objects. When the entity beans were used directly, all retrieving of relationships and related beans was managed automatically by the CMP code in the container, as was all updating of modified attributes and relationships in any entity beans touched in the transaction.

Our solution in this version of the example application will be to examine the presentation-tier components that use the domain objects, identify the children objects needed when displaying or manipulating the domain objects, and create services that automatically fetch the required children objects when retrieving parent domain objects. For example, whenever a Property object is fetched, the service will automatically fetch and attach the appropriate list of RoomType and Offer children objects before returning the Property. It would be straightforward to make the code that populates these children objects within the service conditional based on a passed-in Boolean parameter — feel free to adopt this technique if you see value in doing so within your own applications.

The presentation tier is also responsible for updating relationships between disconnected domain objects in a manner that allows an update-related service request to make all of the necessary changes in the database to reflect the new or modified relationships. The EJB 2.0 CMP approach allowed presentation-tier components simply to add or remove relationships between the entity beans in a natural manner and the container sorted out and implemented the required changes in the database. In a service-based approach with disconnected domain objects we need to know a little more about how relationships are being modeled and then determine which service methods to use to add or remove objects from those relationships.

The bigrez.com administration web site code listings in Chapter 4 will show examples of adding and removing objects from relationships using the available service methods.

Chapter Review

The following list summarizes the design decisions we've made for the bigrez.com application:

❏   The bigrez.com application includes a separate user site and administration site, with different processes and visual designs.

❏   The application meets the presentation-tier requirements for basic display, navigation, and form validation and submission outlined in Chapter 2.

❏   We'll use the Tiles framework to assemble our pages with a master layout page that defines the overall structure of pages in the site.

❏   We'll use a servlet-centric architecture with the Spring MVC framework to implement a model-view-controller approach in the presentation tier.

❏   Presentation-tier components will access business-tier components using EJB 3.0 stateless session bean services and disconnected domain objects.

Are you ready to look at the code and see how it all comes together? Turn to the next chapter, and get to it!

Building an Example Web Application

In this chapter, we walk through the construction of a realistic example web application, `bigrez.com`. Because this book is intended for intermediate- to advanced-level developers and architects, we assume that you understand the basic steps required to construct a Java EE web application. Our emphasis is on any construction techniques unique to WebLogic Server as well as the components and techniques required for the `bigrez.com` application resulting from the choice of presentation approach, web application architecture, and the use of EJB 3.0 stateless session bean services and disconnected domain objects.

The construction of the web application portion of `bigrez.com` involves the following steps:

1. Constructing the application skeleton, including master layout pages, descriptor files, build files, and all required directory structures and configuration files

2. Identifying and constructing the specific JSP display pages, form beans, and controller components required to implement the user and administration site behaviors

Additional steps are required to construct the necessary business-tier components and related persistence logic. These steps are covered in Chapter 7.

Overview of Application Components

The `bigrez.com` example is large enough that we will start our discussion of its contents by presenting a list of the major groups of components in the application and a high-level picture of the project directory structure. These will help you understand the role of the components listed in this chapter in the overall application design. Note that complete source listings of all components would require a prohibitive amount of space, so we are including only listings of key components that emphasize steps and techniques covered in the text. You are encouraged to download the complete example program and installation instructions from the companion web site (`http://www.wrox.com/`).

The application components have been split into eight separate groups:

❑ **User site display components** including display JSP pages, JSP include files, style sheets, and key configuration and descriptor files, located in the `web-user/WebContent` subdirectory

❑ **Administration site display components** including the same types of components for the administration web application, located in the `web-admin/WebContent` subdirectory

❑ **User site source components** including Spring MVC controllers, forms, and other Java components for the user web application, located in the `web-user/src` subdirectory

❑ **Administration site source components** including the same types of components for the administration web application, located in the `web-admin/src` subdirectory

❑ **Common web source components** including base classes and utility classes for use by both user and administration web applications, located in the `web-common/src` subdirectory

❑ **EJB service components** used by both sites to encapsulate persistence services and complex business logic, located in the `services` subdirectory

❑ **Domain objects** representing the primary business domain entities stored in the database and modeled in the persistence layer, located in the `domain` subdirectory

❑ **Web services components**, located in the `webservices` subdirectory

These groups are reflected in the overall structure of the project directory depicted in Figure 4-1. This structure incorporates the development environment best practices discussed in Chapter 14.

Many of the directories shown in Figure 4-1 contain components required during the build and packaging process, topics we cover in Chapters 5 and 8. This chapter emphasizes the presentation-tier components in the `web-user`, `web-admin`, and `web-common` directories.

All source code, web components, images, and key configuration files are located in the project directory structure. The build process, driven by `build.xml` files located in the project root directory and most project subdirectories, assembles the components appropriately and creates a single enterprise application archive (EAR) file for deployment to WebLogic Server. Chapter 5 discusses deployment and management of WebLogic Server web applications. Chapter 8 covers the steps required to package and deploy the complete `bigrez.com` application.

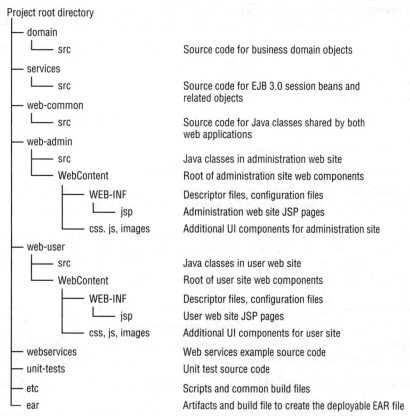

Project root directory	
└─ domain	
└─ src	Source code for business domain objects
└─ services	
└─ src	Source code for EJB 3.0 session beans and related objects
└─ web-common	
└─ src	Source code for Java classes shared by both web applications
└─ web-admin	
├─ src	Java classes in administration web site
└─ WebContent	Root of administration site web components
├─ WEB-INF	Descriptor files, configuration files
│ └─ jsp	Administration web site JSP pages
└─ css. js, images	Additional UI components for administration site
└─ web-user	
├─ src	Java classes in user web site
└─ WebContent	Root of user site web components
├─ WEB-INF	Descriptor files, configuration files
│ └─ jsp	User web site JSP pages
└─ css, js, images	Additional UI components for user site
└─ webservices	Web services example source code
└─ unit-tests	Unit test source code
└─ etc	Scripts and common build files
└─ ear	Artifacts and build file to create the deployable EAR file

Figure 4-1: Project directory structure for the bigrez.com application.

Constructing the Application Skeleton

The first step when creating a new web application is the construction of the application skeleton. In the bigrez.com web application, this skeleton consists of the minimum components required to configure and boot the user and administration web sites and display their respective home pages. This is not simply a Home.jsp page for each site, remember. We are using a Spring MVC architecture and a Tiles-based view assembly approach, so the skeleton must include the basic configuration files and components required to implement our chosen approach.

The skeleton web applications for both sites consist of similar components, with examples listed here for the user web application:

❑ The DefaultLayout.jsp template page for the site, defining the overall page layout and included components

❑ Supporting view components such as `Header.jsp`, `TopNav.jsp`, `Footer.jsp`, and placeholder versions of view components such as `RezInfo.jsp` and `Offers.jsp`

❑ The `web.xml` and `weblogic.xml` descriptor files, including JSP configuration elements and the servlet mappings from `*.do` to the Spring MVC `DispatcherServlet`

❑ A placeholder `HomeController` component in the `src` subdirectory that simply returns the success view result

❑ A placeholder Spring MVC `userapp-servlet.xml` file with sufficient configuration information to map the `/home.do` URL to the `HomeController` component and configure Tiles as the view resolver for presentation assembly

❑ A placeholder `Home.jsp` page, to use as a test page to validate the skeleton configuration

❑ A placeholder `tiles-config.xml` file to configure Tiles to use the `DefaultLayout.jsp` page and inject the `Home.jsp` body page for the initial *home* Tiles definition

These skeleton components, once deployed to the user web application in the domain, are sufficient to present the `Home.jsp` page in the display area of the layout when the `home.do` URL is accessed from a browser. On a typical development project, the skeleton components are then placed in source code control to form the starting point for the web application construction tasks to follow.

Best Practice

Begin construction by building an application skeleton containing the minimum number of components necessary to configure and start the web application.

Constructing the User Site Components

Once the application skeleton is in place, additional view components are added in a piecewise fashion to flesh out the application. The construction of the user site in `bigrez.com` was broken down into three primary sections:

❑ *Reservation information components* responsible for the display of the reservation information area on the left side of the page

❑ *Core reservation process components* providing the main site functionality of finding properties, selecting dates, room types, and rates and making reservations

❑ *Targeted offers components* generating the targeted marketing offers in the left gutter depending on the user's recent search results and selections

In the following sections, we examine each of these sections of the user site in some detail, highlighting key components and techniques in each section.

Reservation Information Components

Creating a reservation requires a multiple-step process. Intermediate results must be stored in the `HttpSession` on behalf of the user, a technique much like a shopping cart in an e-commerce site. The bigrez.com application uses a serializable value object called `ReservationInfo` to store this information in the `HttpSession` using the session attribute key `rezinfo`. As the user selects a property, selects dates, selects a room type, and signs in to the site, the related information is saved or updated in the `ReservationInfo` object in the session. The `ReservationInfo` class is a simple value object with private attributes and appropriate get and set methods, so a complete listing is not required. For reference, the `ReservationInfo` class has the following attributes:

```
private String lastSearchCity;
private String lastSearchState;
private String propertyId;
private Property property;
private String roomTypeId;
private RoomType roomType;
private String guestProfileId;
private GuestProfile guestProfile;
private Date arriveDate;
private Date departDate;
private List<ReservationServices.RateDetails> rezRates;
```

The current reservation information is displayed on the left side of the screen on every page in the user site in a small reservation information area generated by the `RezInfo.jsp` display JSP page. Figure 3-2 in the previous chapter showed this reservation information area in the context of the overall display. As the user selects a property, selects dates, or completes additional steps in the process, the reservation information area changes to reflect these selections.

Note that we have used the domain objects `Property`, `RoomType`, and `GuestProfile` as child objects of our `ReservationInfo` main object to hold data such as the property name, room description, and guest names required for display, rather than creating individual `String` fields for this purpose. These domain objects are serializable Java objects and can therefore be placed in the `HttpSession` legally and safely. Using child domain objects instead of individual `String` fields in an `HttpSession` storage object is a design decision that often makes sense.

The `RezInfo.jsp` page generates the reservation information area using straightforward JSTL `out` and `formatDate` tags to retrieve information from the `ReservationInfo` object and its children:

```
<c:out value="${rezinfo.property.description}"/>
...
<f:formatDate value="${rezinfo.arriveDate}" pattern="MMM dd, yyyy"/>
...
<c:out value="${rezinfo.roomType.description}"/>
```

Collections contained in the `ReservationInfo` object may be examined using JSTL `forEach` tags.

```
<c:set var="rezrates" value="${rezinfo.rezRates}"/>
...
  <tr>
    <td>
      <span class="sidebar-title">Rate:</span>
      <c:forEach var="rezrate" items="${rezrates}">
        <br> 
        <span class="sidebar-data"><c:out value="${rezrate.numberOfNights}"/>
        nts @ $<c:out value="${rezrate.price.amount}"/>/nt</span>
```

```
     </c:forEach>
   </td>
 </tr>
```

The `ReservationInfo` object may also be used in JSTL `if` tags to display information conditionally. For example, we want to display the string `Choose Property` for the property description if the user has not yet selected a property for this reservation. Rather than performing this logic in the `ReservationInfo` value object or creating a separate helper class, we've made use of these `if` tags to control the display:

```
<a class="sidebar-link" href="<c:url value='/chooseproperty.do'/>">
  <c:if test="${empty rezinfo.propertyId}">
    Choose Property
  </c:if>
  <c:if test="${not empty rezinfo.propertyId}">
    <c:out value="${rezinfo.property.description}"/>
  </c:if>
</a>
```

Best Practice

Do not place conditional display logic, such as replacing empty values with default messages, in value objects. Use custom tags or other view components to create conditional displays.

The displayed values in the reservation information area are also used as navigation links, allowing the users to select their desired property, dates, or room type, jump back to a previous decision, or log in before creating a reservation. As the code snippet shows, the target URL for the property description — whether or not the user has already selected a property — is `chooseproperty.do`. All hyperlinks in this JSP page and every other JSP page in the site use this `<desiredaction>.do` approach rather than hard-coding page or controller names in the display JSP pages. These `*.do` locations are mapped in the `web.xml` file to the default `DispatcherServlet` in Spring MVC, which then instantiates and uses a page-specific controller class to handle the request.

If you examine the code for the `RezInfo.jsp` page, you may notice that the user can click on the `Choose Room Type` link and invoke the `selectroomtype.do` action without regard for the status of the property or dates selection. In the main reservation flow, depicted in Figure 3-3 in the previous chapter, the choice of property and dates precedes the choice of room type. In fact it is impossible to select a room type prior to knowing these other two items. We had two choices on the `RezInfo.jsp` page in terms of handling this dependency:

❑ Implement the checks for property and dates on the page itself using additional JSTL `if` tags to check for the presence of a `Property` object and arrival and departure dates in the `ReservationInfo` object. If these dependencies are not met, the `Choose Room Type` link could be disabled, or it could invoke the `chooseproperty.do` or `selectdates.do` actions rather than `selectroomtype.do`. In this option the page itself is responsible for dependency checks.

❑ Allow the page to invoke the `selectroomtype.do` action regardless of dependencies and then implement checks in the invoked controller to force the user to make property or dates selections first. In this option the controller is responsible for checking dependencies.

We chose the second approach to keep the page simple and ensure that complex business and dependency rules are kept in Java code where they are easier to create and maintain. We examine the code in the SelectRoomTypeController that implements this logic in the next section as we walk through the reservation process and examine each component in turn.

In summary, the reservation information area of the bigrez.com user site is designed to display the current status of the reservation process and allow the user to jump directly to certain steps in the process, subject to business rules enforced in the SelectRoomTypeController component. The display area is created by the RezInfo.jsp display JSP page using data stored in the HttpSession in the ReservationInfo value object.

The reservation information area design and the chosen implementation techniques provide a good model for a shopping cart or other multi-step process in your Java EE web applications.

Core Reservation Process Components

The core reservation process, illustrated in Figure 3-3, walks the user step-by-step through the selection of required elements of a reservation. In this section, we examine a few of the presentation-tier components in detail to illustrate the solutions employed for common requirements in Java EE web applications.

Defining Navigation Paths

The reservation process involves a fair number of separate display JSP pages, controller classes, and related form objects and value objects. Table 4-1 provides a list of the primary components in the reservation process, and Table 4-2 completes the picture with non-core pages and related components. Note that most pages have a single controller class that prepares form information for display and handles user form submission for that page, a relationship described in Chapter 2 when we discussed the SimpleFormController class. Some relationships are not quite as clean and are explained in the text to follow.

> **Best Practice**
>
> Use a standard naming convention for display pages, controller classes, and form objects to make relationships between components clear without inspecting the configuration files.

As discussed in Chapter 2, the servlet-centric web application architecture dictates certain rules and principles related to presentation-tier components and their relationships. One key principle is the separation of roles between display components, controller components, and navigational control facilities. The bigrez.com application meets the requirements by adopting the following rules:

❑ Display JSP pages must use <desiredaction>.do controller invocations for all hyperlinks and form-posting targets. The controller is always responsible for determining the next page in the process based on the user's action, the current state, and navigation control information.

❑ Controller components do not refer directly to display JSP page names when specifying the next page for display. Tiles definition names are used in the controller configurations and injected into controllers.

Table 4-1: Core Reservation Process Primary Components

Display Component	Related Controller Components	Form Object
PropertySearch.jsp PropertyList.jsp	PropertySearchController.java	PropertySearchForm.java
ViewProperty.jsp	ViewPropertyController.java	ViewPropertyForm.java
SelectDates.jsp	SelectDatesController.java	SelectDatesForm.java
SelectRoomType.jsp	SelectRoomTypeController.java	SelectRoomTypeForm.java
GuestInformation.jsp	GuestInformationController.java	GuestInformationForm.java
ReviewReservation.jsp	ReviewReservationController.java	ReviewReservationForm.java
ReservationThankYou.jsp		

Table 4-2: Additional Web Application Components

Display Component	Related Controller Components	Form Object
Home.jsp	HomeController.java	
Login.jsp	LoginController.java	LoginForm.java
ViewProfile.jsp	ViewProfileController.java	ViewProfileForm.java
Offers.jsp	OffersPreparer.java	

Two critical aspects of this design are the Spring MVC configuration file, userapp-servlet.xml, and the Tiles configuration file, tiles-config.xml. The userapp-servlet.xml file defines the mapping of action links such as chooseproperty.do to their related controller components as well as many other relationships between forms, controllers, and other Spring MVC elements. The tiles-config.xml file defines the mapping between tiles definitions and the actual JSP page names inserted in the body of the layout, among other things. Please download the source code for bigrez.com from the companion web site (http://www.wrox.com/) and review these files before proceeding.

The userapp-servlet.xml file also defines the basic course, or *happy path*, through the reservation process by defining successView mappings in each core reservation controller. For example, the next page after SelectDates is SelectRoomType, but rather than hard-coding this relationship in any JSP or controller component, the mapping is placed in the definition of the SelectDatesController component in this file and is injected into the `successView` attribute of the `SimpleFormController` base class for this controller:

```
<bean id="selectDatesController"
      class="com.bigrez.web.SelectDatesController">
   <property name="formView" value="selectdates"/>
   <property name="successView" value="redirect:selectroomtype.do"/>
   <property name="bindOnNewForm" value="true"/>
   <property name="commandName" value="selectDatesForm"/>
   <property name="commandClass" value="com.bigrez.web.SelectDatesForm"/>
   <property name="selectDatesForm">
       <bean class="com.bigrez.web.SelectDatesForm"/>
   </property>
   <property name="validator">
       <bean class="com.bigrez.web.SelectDatesForm"/>
   </property>
</bean>
```

By default, a `SimpleFormController` subclass will place the `successView` in the `ModelAndView` object it returns when it exits the `onSubmit()` method successfully.

In theory, you can change the order of the reservation process by simply modifying the entries in `userapp-servlet.xml` to indicate the new `successView` mappings for each page in the process. Modifying the page flow may require some changes in related controller classes to implement the modified flow properly, but these changes should be minimal.

Controller components that do not follow this simple `successView` chain or that need to indicate a different target page also use logical page mappings defined in the configuration file. This turns out to be a bit tricky in Spring MVC if the controller needs to redirect the user based on rules implemented in the controller code itself, a topic we discuss in the next section.

Choosing Spring MVC Components

Before explaining the choices made in the `bigrez.com` example program, a caveat: This book is not intended to be a primer on the Spring MVC framework, nor can it spend a large amount of time considering the pros and cons of using different design patterns and Spring-provided components. The topic is simply too large and is well-covered by existing books and resources on the web in any case. We instead present the choices made — and the design principles and requirements that led to those choices — in the hope that our thought process, if not our specific choices, can be of use to you.

Spring MVC is a very deep and robust framework containing a wide variety of controller types, handler mapping components, view resolvers, locale resolvers, theme resolvers, validation utilities, and other components. There is no right way to create a Spring MVC application, although there are likely many wrong ways. Meeting the presentation-tier design requirements while avoiding an overly complex, inflexible, and hard to understand and maintain application will be our goal. Piece of cake!

First, we need to decide on the type of controller components to use. We'll focus on two different requirements: basic controller logic, resulting in either success or failure and returning the target view and model objects, and form submission processing with the full set of logic described in Chapter 2.

Choosing Basic Controller Components

Spring provides a number of abstract controller classes designed to handle controller logic, the most basic being `AbstractController`. Any subclass of this class need only define the behavior of one method, `handleRequestInternal()`, and return a `ModelAndView` object representing the desired target view and any model objects required by that view.

```
public class SampleController extends AbstractController
{
    public ModelAndView handleRequestInternal(HttpServletRequest request,
                                              HttpServletResponse response)
        throws Exception
    {
        ModelAndView result = new ModelAndView("showtime");
        result.addObject("now", new Date());
        return result;
    }
}
```

This simple controller returns a `ModelAndView` object specifying `showtime` as the desired view and places the current time in the result under the key `now`. We could adopt this design for our simple controllers as well, except for one issue: The target view name is defined in the controller code, rather than in the `userapp-servlet.xml` configuration file. Because one of our design principles is to avoid hard-coding such navigation definitions in the components themselves, we need a mechanism to move this to the configuration file.

The Spring-provided class `ParameterizableViewController` is an improvement over `AbstractController`. It contains a single attribute, `viewName`, used by a built-in `handleRequestInternal()` method to construct a `ModelAndView` object and return it. The `viewName` value can be injected using the configuration file, thereby eliminating the hard-coding of navigation information in controller code. This class does not, however, give the controller the ability to handle a failure case and return a different failure-view value, a feature we need for our application. Only a single view name is configurable and returnable by the class.

To meet our needs, we've created a simple concrete subclass of the Spring MVC `AbstractController` class, called `SimpleSuccessFailureController`, that adds two view-name attributes, `successView` and `failureView`, and provides a default implementation of `handleRequestInternal()` that returns a `ModelAndView` object based on the success view:

```
package com.bigrez.web;

public class SimpleSuccessFailureController extends AbstractController
{
    private String successView;
    private String failureView;

    protected ModelAndView handleRequestInternal(HttpServletRequest request,
                                                 HttpServletResponse response)
        throws Exception
    {
        return new ModelAndView(getSuccessView());
    }
}
```

```
        // get/set methods
        ...
    }
```

Controllers that have no business logic, and always return the success view, can use this class directly, as shown here:

```
<bean id="dumbController" class="com.bigrez.web.SimpleSuccessFailureController">
    <property name="successView" value="dumbpage"/>
</bean>
```

Controllers that have business logic, or need to decide whether to return the success or failure view, can subclass from the SimpleSuccessFailureController class and return ModelAndView objects based on these attributes:

```
package com.bigrez.web;

public class LogoutController extends SimpleSuccessFailureController
{
    protected ModelAndView handleRequestInternal(HttpServletRequest pRequest,
                                                 HttpServletResponse pResponse)
        throws Exception
    {
        ReservationInfo rezinfo = (ReservationInfo)
            pRequest.getSession().getAttribute("rezinfo");
        if (rezinfo != null && rezinfo.getGuestProfile() != null) {
            rezinfo.setGuestProfile(null);
            rezinfo.setGuestProfileId("");
            return new ModelAndView(getSuccessView());
        }
        else {
            return new ModelAndView(getFailureView());
        }
    }
}
```

In this example the controller knows whether or not the operation was successful, but does not have the target view pages hard-coded within it. The configuration file defines the two views by injecting them into the successView and failureView attributes:

```
<bean id="logoutController" class="com.bigrez.web.LogoutController">
    <property name="successView" value="home"/>
    <property name="failureView" value="home"/>
</bean>
```

We've elected to send both success and failure cases to the same target view page, home, but we can easily change our minds at a later date.

A number of controllers in the user and administration web applications in bigrez.com use the SimpleSuccessFailureController to perform basic business logic and return a success or failure view. Examine the ClearReservationController, LogoutController, and HomeController for examples.

83

> **Best Practice**
>
> Avoid hard-coding target view names in controller components. Use the
> `ParameterizableViewController` provided by Spring if you only require a
> success view, and use a class like `SimpleSuccessFailureController` if you need both
> success and failure views.

Choosing Form-Processing Controller Components

The second type of controller we must select focuses on the displaying and processing of user-submitted HTML forms. Spring MVC again provides a variety of controller classes designed to help manage the form submission process, including `AbstractCommandController`, `AbstractFormController`, `SimpleFormController`, and `AbstractWizardFormController`. We might start with a basic abstract controller and build up to a custom-built form-processing controller class, or use the `SimpleFormController` without customization to keep things simple. We could try the wizard-based controller for our reservation process, or we might implement the step-by-step process as a series of simple controllers. Choosing the right approach, and the right controller class, will make a big difference in our success.

First, we'll eliminate the idea of building something ourselves. As discussed in Chapter 2, the complexity of form display, submission, validation, error redisplay, and other related behaviors will overwhelm us if we attempt to handle everything ourselves. For this reason alone it makes sense to start with a framework-supplied controller class such as `SimpleFormController` and see how far that takes us.

> **Best Practice**
>
> Don't build your own form-handling controller classes based on `AbstractForm
> Controller` — it's way too much work! Find a way to leverage an existing class such
> as `SimpleFormController` and override its behavior if necessary.

Second, do we really need to introduce the `AbstractWizardFormController` into the mix to implement our multi-step reservation process? Does it provide enough value over the alternative, a JSP page, `SimpleFormController`-based controller, and form object for each step? It helps to phrase the question in this manner to remind ourselves that each major framework component we select introduces a learning curve and additional complexity.

We've elected to stick with the `SimpleFormController` alone for the `bigrez.com` example program. It is possible that a wizard-based approach, in the hands of a master, might yield a more elegant and compact set of components — but our goals are clarity, ease of maintenance, and flexibility, rather than elegance. We'll therefore adopt an approach that leverages a single form-handling controller type and separates the components related to each page in a clear and straightforward manner, as indicated by Table 4-1 earlier in this chapter. After all, clarity has a quality — and elegance — all its own.

A detailed discussion of `SimpleFormController` is beyond the scope of this book. Fortunately it works well out of the box and hides most of the complexity associated with form binding, submission, and other related tasks, and needs little discussion. We'll use it for handling form display and submission processing in a fairly straightforward manner, adopting the following guidelines and usage rules:

❑ Business object retrieval and form preparation will take place in the overridden method `onBindOnNewForm()` within our `SimpleFormController` subclass. This method will be called when an HTTP GET request is made to the URL mapped to our controller instance.

❑ Form validation will be accomplished by implementing the `Validator` interface in the form class itself. We've elected to place validation logic in the form, rather than creating additional validation classes, in an attempt to keep the overall class count down and keep logic that depends on form attributes close to those attributes.

❑ Form submission processing will take place in the overridden method `onSubmit()` within our subclass. This method will be called when an HTTP POST request is made to the URL mapped to our controller instance.

❑ The `formView` and `successView` target values will be injected using the configuration file, but can be overridden in select cases should errors in processing occur within the controller code.

By adopting `SimpleFormController`, we've simplified the Java code required to implement the form submission logic described in Chapter 2 by limiting it to a small set of well-defined methods within two classes we create. You can't ask for much more than that!

Choosing Handler and Resolver Components

We've chosen a basic controller, `SimpleSuccessFailureController`, for straightforward controller logic, and the `SimpleFormController` approach for form-based logic. These controllers constitute the core presentation-tier components in our system, but they are not sufficient to complete our design. We also need to choose an approach for mapping URL values to specific controllers, known as a *handler mapping*, as well as our desired mechanism for resolving view names into specific display pages or other view components.

Spring provides two primary handler mapping components: `BeanNameUrlHandlerMapping` and `SimpleUrlHandlerMapping`. Both are designed to examine an incoming URL and return the correct `HandlerExecutionChain`, normally consisting of zero or more `HandlerInterceptor` classes and a specific controller to be invoked for that URL.

`BeanNameUrlHandlerMapping` relies on an exact match between the name given to the controller in the configuration file and the URL itself. That level of coupling between URL values and controller names is undesirable, in our opinion.

`SimpleUrlHandlerMapping` uses specific mappings defined in the configuration file to associate a URL with a controller. For example, the following partial listing from the user web application's `userapp-servlet.xml` configuration file shows the basic use of this handler mapping:

```xml
<bean id="handlerMapping"
    class="org.springframework.web.servlet.handler.SimpleUrlHandlerMapping">
  <property name="interceptors">
    <list>
      <ref bean="loggingViewInterceptor"/>
    </list>
  </property>
  <property name="mappings">
    <value>
      /home.do=homeController
      /login.do=loginController
```

```
                /logout.do=logoutController
                /viewprofile.do=viewProfileController
                /clearreservation.do=clearReservationController
                /chooseproperty.do=propertySearchController
                /viewproperty.do=viewPropertyController
                /selectdates.do=selectDatesController
                /selectroomtype.do=selectRoomTypeController
                /guestinformation.do=guestInformationController
                /reservationreview.do=reservationReviewController
                /thankyou.do=thankYouController
            </value>
        </property>
    </bean>
```

Note that each URL is of the form <desiredaction>.do, as discussed previously, and that each URL maps to a single controller bean. Though not perfect, this approach meets our goal of flexibility and clarity.

The handler mapping configuration includes a single interceptor, loggingViewInterceptor, which will be included on every HandlerExecutionChain returned by the handler mapping. We've defined this interceptor in the configuration file as shown here:

```
<bean id="loggingViewInterceptor"
      class="com.bigrez.web.LoggingViewInterceptor">
</bean>
```

This class implements the HandlerInterceptorAdapter interface and defines preHandle() and postHandle() methods to be invoked before and after the controller handleRequest() method is called, respectively.

Simply put, interceptors give us a way to perform actions, before and after the controller is invoked, for whatever purposes we see fit. In our case we've included a simple logging interceptor to output request and response information to the log for each invocation.

Our last decision, the choice of a *view resolver*, is easy: We're using the Tiles framework for assembly of our display JSP pages, so we will be using the Spring-supplied UrlBasedViewResolver configured to resolve view names as Tiles definitions:

```
<bean id="viewResolver"
      class="org.springframework.web.servlet.view.UrlBasedViewResolver">
    <property name="viewClass"
              value="org.springframework.web.servlet.view.tiles2.TilesView"/>
</bean>
```

If a controller returns a ModelAndView object containing the view name propertylist, for example, the view resolver will invoke the Tiles framework and cause it to render the Tiles definition propertylist, combining its master layout page and all other common and overridden tiles within the definition. The following partial listing of the tiles-config.xml file shows the propertylist definition for reference:

```
<definition name="defaultLayout" template="/WEB-INF/jsp/common/DefaultLayout.jsp">
    <put-attribute name="header" value="/WEB-INF/jsp/common/Header.jsp" />
    <put-attribute name="topnav" value="/WEB-INF/jsp/common/TopNav.jsp" />
```

```
        <put-attribute name="rezinfo" value="/WEB-INF/jsp/common/RezInfo.jsp" />
        <put-attribute name="offers" value="offers" />
        <put-attribute name="footer" value="/WEB-INF/jsp/common/Footer.jsp"/>
    </definition>
    ...
    <definition name="propertylist" extends="defaultLayout">
        <put-attribute name="body" value="/WEB-INF/jsp/PropertyList.jsp"/>
    </definition>
```

You may have noticed one unusual element in this listing: the `offers` tile in the `defaultLayout` definition does not refer to a specific JSP page, as do all the others, but instead refers to yet another Tiles definition, `offers`. This second level of indirection is required to add a `preparer` to the `offers` definition, as shown in this snippet from that same file:

```
<definition name="offers" template="/WEB-INF/jsp/common/Offers.jsp"
            preparer="com.bigrez.web.OffersPreparer"/>
```

By configuring the `offers` tile in this manner, the `execute()` method on the `OffersPreparer` class is invoked just before the tile is rendered, providing us with a convenient mechanism to prepare or load something in the `HttpServletRequest` context required by the `Offers.jsp` page. We explain this in more detail later in the chapter when we talk about the targeted offers portion of the page.

One final note on view resolving: The view name returned by the controller may refer to a Tiles definition, as described earlier, or may be an HTTP redirect to a different controller, as highlighted here:

```
<bean id="selectDatesController"
      class="com.bigrez.web.SelectDatesController">
    <property name="formView" value="selectdates"/>
    <property name="successView" value="redirect:selectroomtype.do"/>
    ...
</bean>
```

The `formView` value, `selectdates`, will resolve to a Tiles definition called `selectdates` and will be treated as a `RequestDispatcher.forward()` transfer to the components involved, meaning that `HttpServletRequest` and `HttpServletResponse` data will be carried along to the view components. In particular, the controller's form object, normally stored in the request scope, will be available to the target view components and underlying JSP pages.

The `successView` value, `redirect:selectroomtype.do`, instructs the `UrlBasedViewResolver` that it should bypass all normal resolving logic and simply return a `RedirectView` object to the calling `DispatcherServlet`, which will then return an HTTP redirect to the user's browser with the URL specified after the `redirect:` prefix. In addition, any objects in the `ModelAndView` returned by the controller will be placed in the URL as query string parameters, a behavior that can be handy as well as dangerous.

By specifying this `redirect:` prefix in the `successView` value in the `userapp-servlet.xml` file, rather than having the controller create and return a `RedirectView` object itself, we've successfully kept navigation details in the configuration file where they belong. Note that the controller is unaware that returning the `successView` will result in a redirect, and may therefore attach objects to the `ModelAndView` it creates and returns without regard for their appropriateness in a redirect scenario.

Best Practice

Use the `redirect:` prefix in view names to perform HTTP redirects upon successful completion of controller processing and avoid hard-coding this navigation information in the controllers themselves. Keep in mind that objects in the returned `ModelAndView` are placed in the query string during redirects.

Now that we have discussed the Spring MVC components we're going to use and have walked through some of the common design approaches we've adopted, let's examine selected pages and controller components in the site to learn more about its construction.

Property Search/Selection Pages

As indicated in Table 4-1, the first three pages in the reservation process consist of `PropertySearch.jsp`, a simple search page allowing users to pick the desired city or state to use in finding a property, the `PropertyList.jsp` page for displaying the results of a property search, and the `ViewProperty.jsp` page for displaying a single property and asking the users to select it for their reservation.

For reference purposes, the URL for the search page is `chooseproperty.do`, the mapped controller is `PropertySearchController`, and the form object associated with the controller is `PropertySearchForm`. The pertinent portion of the `userapp-servlet.xml` file is shown here:

```
<bean id="propertySearchController"
      class="com.bigrez.web.PropertySearchController">
  <property name="formView" value="chooseproperty"/>
  <property name="successView" value="propertylist"/>
  <property name="bindOnNewForm" value="true"/>
  <property name="commandName" value="propertySearchForm"/>
  <property name="commandClass" value="com.bigrez.web.PropertySearchForm"/>
  <property name="propertySearchForm">
      <bean class="com.bigrez.web.PropertySearchForm"/>
  </property>
  <property name="propertyServices" ref="propertyServicesReference"/>
</bean>
```

`PropertySearchController` is a `SimpleFormController`-based component, meaning that the initial HTTP GET request will invoke the `onBindOnNewForm()` method where we prepare the form for display, and the subsequent HTTP POST submission of form information will invoke `onSubmit()` where we perform the search and move to the next page in the process.

The display page itself, `PropertySearch.jsp`, is rather unremarkable, containing simple `<form:select>` tags for creating a droplist of state codes and city names, as shown in this code snippet:

```
<form:select path="stateCode">
  <form:option value="">Choose...</form:option>
  <form:options items="${stateCodeList}" itemValue="value" itemLabel="label"/>
</form:select>
```

More interesting is the `onSubmit()` method in the controller that processes the submitted selections and performs a search for matching properties using a service defined in the business tier of the application.

```
protected ModelAndView onSubmit(HttpServletRequest request,
                                HttpServletResponse response, Object command,
                                BindException errors)
    throws Exception
{
    PropertySearchForm form = (PropertySearchForm) command;
    List<Property> propertyList =
        propertyServices.findByCityAndState(form.getCity(), form.getStateCode());
    form.setPropertyList(propertyList);
    // update the ReservationInfo in the session to reflect this location info
    ReservationInfo rezinfo =
        (ReservationInfo) request.getSession().getAttribute("rezinfo");
    rezinfo.setLastSearchCity(form.getCity());
    rezinfo.setLastSearchState(form.getStateCode());
    return super.onSubmit(request, response, command, errors);
}
```

The first half of the method is pretty straightforward. The controller makes a call to `findByCityAndState()` in the property service, which returns a list of `Property` domain objects that match the passed-in city and state values. We attach this list to the form using `setPropertyList()`, making it available to the `successView` component downstream of us.

The second half of the method updates the `HttpSession`-based `ReservationInfo` object with the city and state values selected by the user. These stored values are used by the `OffersPreparer` to generate a list of targeted offers based on the user's last city and state, a topic we cover later in this chapter.

As shown in the `userapp-servlet.xml` snippet, this particular controller's `successView` is a forward to a Tiles definition named `propertylist`. There is no `redirect:` prefix in this view definition, so the list of `Property` objects placed in the request-scope form object will be available in the downstream page for display.

The `propertylist` Tiles definition renders the downstream `PropertyList.jsp` page within the body of the master layout, giving the user a list of properties that met the city and state chosen in the form, as shown in Figure 4-2.

The `PropertyList.jsp` page is fairly straightforward, so rather than including a listing of the entire page, we'll examine a few key elements.

First, the main loop iterating through the list of properties uses a standard JSTL `forEach` tag as shown here:

```
<c:forEach var="property" items="${propertySearchForm.propertyList}">
  <tr>
    ...
  </tr>
</c:forEach>
```

Note that the JSTL tag accesses the list by specifying the form name, as defined in the configuration elements for the controller, and the name of the list. The tag will return each underlying `Property` object in turn, referring to it by the name `property` in the body of the `forEach` tag.

Figure 4-2: Property list page.

The property name, description, image, and other elements are rendered to the HTML output using straightforward JSTL `out` tags within the body of the `forEach` tag, as shown in this example snippet:

```
<tr>
  <td align="left">
    <span class="table-data">
      <c:out value='${property.address.address1}'/>
    </span>
  </td>
</tr>
```

There are two different action links on this page: the property description itself, and the *Select* button on the right side of the page. The property description link invokes the `viewproperty.do` action in an HTTP GET mode, with the intent of displaying more information about a single property using the `ViewProperty.jsp` page and giving the users the chance to select that property for their reservation using that page. The following code snippet shows the creation of this HTTP GET link to the `viewproperty.do` action using the JSTL `url` and `out` tags:

```
<td align="left">
  <c:url var="viewproperty" value="/viewproperty.do">
    <c:param name="id" value="${property.externalIdentity}"/>
  </c:url>
  <a class="table-link" href="<c:out value='${viewproperty}'/>">
```

```
        <c:out value='${property.description}'/>
      </a>
    </td>
```

The *Select* link on the right side of `PropertyList.jsp` is special — we want to bypass the `ViewProperty.jsp` display page and pretend that the user has actually selected the property on that page for his reservation. This will be an HTTP POST request to the `viewproperty.do` action, so we need to create a POST request on our page and supply the needed object identifier, as shown in this snippet of code from the `PropertyList.jsp` page:

```
<td>
  <form method="post" action="<c:url value='/viewproperty.do'/>">
    <input type="hidden" name="id"
      value="<c:out value='${property.externalIdentity}'/>"/>
    <input type="image" src="<c:url value='/images/selectbutton.gif'/>" border="0"/>
  </form>
</td>
```

For reference, the `viewproperty.do` action maps to the `ViewPropertyController`, a form called `ViewPropertyForm`, a Tiles definition called `viewproperty`, and ultimately to the `ViewProperty.jsp` display page. If invoked in HTTP GET mode, users are simply presented with information on a single property and a button for indicating that they wish to select that property for their reservation. The selection process causes an HTTP POST to the `viewproperty.do` action, the `onSubmit()` method on the `ViewPropertyController` is invoked, the selected property is attached to the `ReservationInfo` object in the `HttpSession`, and the `successView` for the controller is followed to the next page in the process.

Whether the user went through the `viewproperty.do` action sequence the normal way, or bypassed the GET mode and display page entirely by selecting the property directly from the list page, the end result is the same: A `Property` domain object is attached to the `ReservationInfo` object, and the user is redirected to the next page in the process: `SelectDates.jsp`.

Date Selection Page

The `SelectDates.jsp` page allows users to choose the arrival and departure date for their stay at the property they selected in the preceding step.

The URL for the date-selection page is `selectdates.do`, the mapped controller is `SelectDatesController`, the form object associated with the controller is `SelectDatesForm`, the Tiles definition is `selectdates`, and the display page is `SelectDates.jsp`. The pertinent portion of the `userapp-servlet.xml` file is shown here:

```
<bean id="selectDatesController"
    class="com.bigrez.web.SelectDatesController">
  <property name="formView" value="selectdates"/>
  <property name="successView" value="redirect:selectroomtype.do"/>
  <property name="bindOnNewForm" value="true"/>
  <property name="commandName" value="selectDatesForm"/>
  <property name="commandClass" value="com.bigrez.web.SelectDatesForm"/>
  <property name="selectDatesForm">
      <bean class="com.bigrez.web.SelectDatesForm"/>
  </property>
  <property name="validator">
```

```
            <bean class="com.bigrez.web.SelectDatesForm"/>
        </property>
    </bean>
```

Like many of the controllers in the reservation process, `SelectDatesController` is a `SimpleFormController`-based component. The `onBindOnNewForm()` method is used to prepare the form data for display, and `onSubmit()` is used to process form submission and move to the next page in the process.

The `SelectDates.jsp` page presents the user with a simple form requesting an arrival and departure date (see Figure 4-3). Calendar icons next to each field use JavaScript to pop up a calendar window allowing the user to pick dates. We're not going to cover this feature in the book, but feel free to look at the downloadable code if you're interested in how these buttons work.

Figure 4-3: Select dates page.

The user chooses the desired dates and submits the form back to the `SelectDatesController` for processing. As shown in the configuration file snippet, this particular controller has defined a *validator* that should be called after submitted data has been bound to the form but before the `onSubmit()` method is invoked. As discussed earlier in this chapter, we've elected to have the form class itself implement the

Validator interface, thus requiring the implementation of two methods shown in the following snippet from the SelectDatesForm.java file:

```java
public void validate(Object form, Errors errors)
{
    SelectDatesForm datesform = (SelectDatesForm) form;
    if (FormUtils.assertNonEmpty(errors, datesform.getArriveDate(),
                            "error.selectdates.arriveempty")) {
        FormUtils.assertValidDate(errors, datesform.getArriveDate(),
                            "error.selectdates.arriveinvalid");
    }
    if (FormUtils.assertNonEmpty(errors, datesform.getDepartDate(),
                            "error.selectdates.departempty")) {
        FormUtils.assertValidDate(errors, datesform.getDepartDate(),
                            "error.selectdates.departinvalid");
    }
    if (errors.getErrorCount() == 0) {
        try {
            Date arrive = DateHelper.parse1(datesform.getArriveDate());
            Date depart = DateHelper.parse1(datesform.getDepartDate());
            if (arrive.equals(depart) || arrive.after(depart)) {
                errors.reject("error.selectdates.arriveafterdepart");
            }
        }
        catch (ParseException e) {
            errors.reject("error.validationproblem");
        }
    }
}

public boolean supports(Class pClass)
{
    return pClass.equals(SelectDatesForm.class);
}
```

The validate() method examines the data in the incoming form and flags problems using the reject() method in the Errors object passed in to the validate() method. We've implemented some simple validation rules in a helper class called FormUtils just for convenience, as you can see from the listing.

Should the validate() method reject the form data, the onSubmit() method in the controller class will not be invoked. Instead the display page will be redisplayed with the form data representing the last set of input from the user along with any binding errors present in the request. The SelectDates.jsp page displays any bind-related errors using the following Spring custom tags:

```html
<spring:hasBindErrors name="selectDatesForm">
  <tr>
    <td>
      <span class="error-header1">Errors<br></span>
      <span class="error-header2">You must correct the following error(s)
          before proceeding:</span>
```

```
      <ul>
        <form:errors path="*" htmlEscape="false" cssClass="error-text"/>
      </ul>
    </td>
  </tr>
</spring:hasBindErrors>
```

As shown in the `validate()` method, errors are generated using key values such as `error.selectdates`
`.arriveafterdepart`. The error messages themselves are stored in an `errors.properties` file
located in the `WEB-INF/classes` directory and are loaded by configuring a resource bundle in the
`userapp-servlet.xml` file as shown here:

```
<bean id="messageSource"
    class="org.springframework.context.support.ResourceBundleMessageSource">
    <property name="basenames">
        <list>
            <value>errors</value>
        </list>
    </property>
</bean>
```

Should the submitted form data pass the tests in the `validate()` method, the `onSubmit()` method in the
controller is invoked to process the form submission. As shown here, the method is very straightforward,
simply storing the chosen dates in the `ReservationInfo` object in the `HttpSession` and returning the
success view:

```
protected ModelAndView onSubmit(HttpServletRequest request,
                                HttpServletResponse response,
                                Object command, BindException errors)
    throws Exception
{
    SelectDatesForm form = (SelectDatesForm) command;
    // update the ReservationInfo in the session to reflect this date info
    ReservationInfo rezinfo =
        (ReservationInfo) request.getSession().getAttribute("rezinfo");
    rezinfo.setArriveDate(DateHelper.parse1(form.getArriveDate()));
    rezinfo.setDepartDate(DateHelper.parse1(form.getDepartDate()));
    return super.onSubmit(request, response, command, errors);
}
```

The success view for this controller is a redirect to the next page in the process, `selectroomtype.do`,
where rates, room types, and availability information for the selected property and arrival/departure
dates are calculated and displayed for user selection.

Availability Display and Room Type Selection Page

The next step in the reservation process is the selection of a specific room type for the chosen property,
subject to availability, and the viewing of rate information for the dates of the stay.

As shown in Figure 4-4, the `SelectRoomType.jsp` page presents the users with a list of room types, rates,
and availability information to assist them in choosing the desired room for their stay. Rooms that are not

available for the entire duration of the stay are not available for selection and indicate the specific nights they are unavailable. We talk more about rates and availability when we walk through some pages in the administration site, so for now let's concentrate on how this content is retrieved by the controller and rendered by the JSP page.

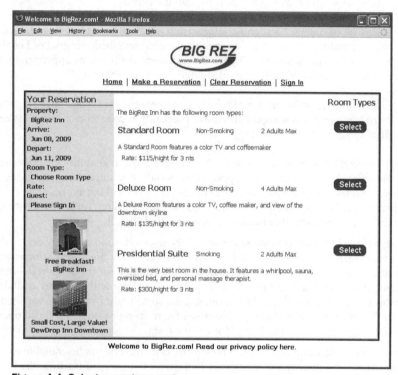

Figure 4-4: Select room type page.

The URL for the availability display and room type selection page is selectroomtype.do, the mapped controller is SelectRoomTypeController, the form object associated with the controller is SelectRoomTypeForm, the Tiles definition is selectroomtype, and the display page is SelectRoomType.jsp. The pertinent portion of the userapp-servlet.xml file is shown here:

```
<bean id="selectRoomTypeController"
     class="com.bigrez.web.SelectRoomTypeController">
   <property name="formView" value="selectroomtype"/>
   <property name="successView" value="redirect:guestinformation.do"/>
   <property name="overrideChoosePropertyView" value="redirect:chooseproperty.do"/>
   <property name="overrideSelectDatesView" value="redirect:selectdates.do"/>
   <property name="bindOnNewForm" value="true"/>
   <property name="commandName" value="selectRoomTypeForm"/>
   <property name="commandClass" value="com.bigrez.web.SelectRoomTypeForm"/>
   <property name="selectRoomTypeForm">
       <bean class="com.bigrez.web.SelectRoomTypeForm"/>
   </property>
   <property name="reservationServices" ref="reservationServicesReference"/>
```

```
                <property name="propertyServices" ref="propertyServicesReference"/>
        </bean>
```

The `SelectRoomTypeController` is a `SimpleFormController` subclass, like the previous controllers. The `onBindOnNewForm()` method is used to prepare the form data for display, and `onSubmit()` is used to process form submission and move to the next page in the process.

By the way, if this set of names, files, and configuration information seems repetitive and obvious to you by now, that's great news! That would mean we've accomplished our goal of keeping things clear, consistent, easy-to-understand, and simple! We'll continue to list them, as appropriate, to help connect the text discussion with the code in the downloadable example program.

Unlike previous controllers with very simple `onBindOnNewForm()` methods, the `SelectRoomTypeController` needs to perform some important logic in the form preparation code in `onBindOnNewForm()` before the page can be displayed:

❏ First, we need to verify that we are ready to perform the availability and rates search. The users should have already selected a property, arrival date, and departure date earlier in the process. If not, we must redirect them to `chooseproperty.do` or `selectdates.do` to complete those steps. Our earlier decision deferred this logic to the controller, rather than trying to code it in the `RezInfo.jsp` page, and that means we now must address it.

❏ Next, we need to take what we know about the user's desired property and arrival/departure dates and search the inventory and rates database for all of the information required to populate the display page. This includes all room type information for the property — whether or not all room types are available for the dates in question — along with rate and availability information for those dates. If a room type is unavailable for some night in the stay, we need to know which night. Prices may change during the course of a multi-night stay, and those price changes must also be reflected in the rates data placed in the form.

❏ Finally, the availability and room type information must be made available to the display JSP page in a manner that facilitates display to the user without undue difficulty.

The good news, from our perspective as a presentation-tier developer, is that the business-tier developer is on the hook for performing all of the complex logic to satisfy the second requirement in the preceding list. Poor guy! Examine the `ReservationServicesImpl` class and focus on the `calculateRatesAndAvailability()` method if you want to see how the service performs the required room type, rate, and availability checking logic.

The bad news is that we need to figure out how to satisfy the first item — checking to make sure the users are ready for this step and redirecting them elsewhere if not — and that simple requirement turns out to be trickier than you might think given some limitations in the `SimpleFormController` class and the mechanism we've adopted for handling HTTP GET requests.

The problem is simple: HTTP GET processing in `SimpleFormController` assumes the `formView` is always the target page and provides no easy way to override this behavior. In particular, methods like `onBindOnNewForm()` and `formBackingObject()` occur early in the overall flow in `SimpleFormController`'s implementation of `handleRequest()` and have no *hooks* for changing the returned `ModelAndView` object to reflect a different view. Instead, `SimpleFormController` waits until the very end of the final step in the overall flow, in a method called `showForm()`, to call `getFormView()` and place that view name in newly created `ModelAndView` object and return it.

We can jury-rig something to give us the behavior we want in a variety of ways, of course, but we're looking for something that feels clean and is easy to understand and configure. One option might be an additional `HandlerInterceptorAdapter` class configured with a `preHandle()` method that checks for the necessary prerequisites. Unfortunately, this step is so early in the call stack that it is impossible to make use of view names, so any HTTP redirection must be done manually through `HttpServletResponse` methods. A different interceptor approach might be to check for the prerequisites in the `onBindOnNewForm()` method and note their absence in the `HttpServletRequest` in some agreed-upon attribute, and then check for that attribute in the interceptor's `postHandle()` method, modifying the `ModelAndView` object passed in to `postHandle()` as appropriate. Both of these techniques seem overly complex and kludgy.

One rule of thumb in the override-to-fix-it game is to start by focusing on the method with which you are dissatisfied. In this case we dislike the default behavior of the `showForm()` method that unconditionally calls the `getFormView()` method to create the final `ModelAndView` object. That's where we will turn our attention.

Two options spring to mind: We can either override the `getFormView()` method in our subclass to return values conditionally, or we can override the `showForm()` method to be aware of our prerequisites and return something other than `getFormView()` if they are not met. We've chosen the second approach, overriding `showForm()`, because it has all of the necessary objects available for evaluating the prerequisites and returning the correct view, whereas `getFormView()` would have to rely on instance variables in the controller, or some other equally ugly solution, to acquire references to the `HttpSession` and other required objects.

The `SelectRoomTypeController` overridden version of `showForm()` is shown in this partial listing:

```
protected ModelAndView showForm(HttpServletRequest request,
                                HttpServletResponse response,
                                BindException errors, Map controlModel)
    throws Exception
{
    ReservationInfo rezinfo =
        (ReservationInfo) request.getSession().getAttribute("rezinfo");
    if (rezinfo.getProperty() == null) {
        return new ModelAndView(getOverrideChoosePropertyView());
    }
    else if (rezinfo.getArriveDate() == null || rezinfo.getDepartDate() == null) {
        return new ModelAndView(getOverrideSelectDatesView());
    }
    return super.showForm(request, response, errors, controlModel);
}
```

If the `Property` reference in the `ReservationInfo` object is not defined, the method returns the view name stored in the `overrideChoosePropertyView` attribute. In the same way, the `overrideSelectDatesView` value is returned if the arrival and departure dates are not present. These override view values are injected by the configuration information for the controller to avoid hard-coding them in the `showForm()` method as shown here:

```
<bean id="selectRoomTypeController"
      class="com.bigrez.web.SelectRoomTypeController">
    ...
    <property name="overrideChoosePropertyView" value="redirect:chooseproperty.do"/>
    <property name="overrideSelectDatesView" value="redirect:selectdates.do"/>
    ...
</bean>
```

The onBindOnNewForm() method in our controller needs to check for these same prerequisites to avoid null pointer exceptions, but does not have to throw an error or otherwise handle their absence. The showForm() method will catch this at the end of the overall flow and deal with it properly.

Creating a custom showForm() method is not a perfect solution to our problem, but it does give us a clean way to override the default formView value with injected values.

> **Best Practice**
>
> Consider overriding the showForm() method in your SimpleFormController-based controllers to check for important prerequisites and return a view name other than the default formView value if they are not met.

As shown in the following listing, the controller code to invoke the business service and retrieve the availability and room type information is deceptively simple:

```
protected void onBindOnNewForm(HttpServletRequest request,
                               Object command, BindException pErrors)
    throws Exception
{
    SelectRoomTypeForm form = (SelectRoomTypeForm) command;
    ReservationInfo rezinfo =
        (ReservationInfo) request.getSession().getAttribute("rezinfo");
    if (rezinfo.getProperty() != null
        && rezinfo.getArriveDate() != null && rezinfo.getDepartDate() != null) {
        // everything is fine, do the rate/availability search using the given info
        List<AvailabilityAndRates> availrates =
            reservationServices.calculateRatesAndAvailabilty(rezinfo.getProperty(),
                rezinfo.getArriveDate(), rezinfo.getDepartDate());
        form.setProperty(rezinfo.getProperty());
        form.setAvailRates(availrates);
    }
}
```

Each AvailabilityAndRates object returned by the services contains a RoomType domain object, a List of RateDetails objects, and a List of Date objects representing blocking — or unavailable — days during the stay for this particular room type. A RateDetails object represents one chunk of dates within the overall stay that came from a single Rate row in the database, and therefore contains a starting date, a price, and a number of nights.

The returned list of AvailabilityAndRates objects is placed in the form object and control is passed to the SelectRoomType.jsp page via the selectroomtype Tiles definition. By encapsulating the complex business logic associated with room type and availability searching within a service, the presentation-tier code remains straightforward and focused on appropriate logic.

> **Best Practice**
>
> Favor encapsulating complex business logic in session beans to improve efficiency and maintainability.

The `SelectRoomType.jsp` page is presented in Listing 4-1 in its entirety because it contains some interesting features and highlights the power of JSTL tags when dealing with nested data structures such as `AvailabilityAndRates`.

Listing 4-1: SelectRoomType.jsp.

```
<%@ include file="/WEB-INF/jsp/common/Include.jspf" %>

<table width="100%" cellspacing="5" cellpadding="0">
  <tr>
    <td class="page-header" align="right">Room Types</td>
  </tr>
  <tr>
    <td class="page-text">
The <c:out value="${selectRoomTypeForm.property.description}"/> has
the following room types:</td>
  </tr>
  <tr>
  <td>
  <table width="100%" cellspacing="0" cellpadding="3" border="0">
  <c:forEach var="availrate" items="${selectRoomTypeForm.availRates}">
    <c:set var="roomtype" value="${availrate.roomType}"/>
    <tr>
      <td width="30%" align="left" class="table-header">
        <c:out value="${roomtype.description}"/>
      </td>
      <td width="25%" class="table-data">
        <c:if test="${roomtype.smokingFlag}">Smoking</c:if>
        <c:if test="${not roomtype.smokingFlag}">Non-Smoking</c:if>
      </td>
      <td width="25%" class="table-data">
        <c:out value="${roomtype.maximumAdults}"/> Adults Max
      </td>
      <c:if test="${empty availrate.blockingDates}">
        <td width="20%" align="center">
          <form method="post"
              action="<c:url value='/selectroomtype.do'/>">
            <input type="hidden" name="id"
            value="<c:out value='${roomtype.externalIdentity}'/>"/>
            <input type="image"
                src="<c:url value='/images/selectbutton.gif'/>" border="0"/>
          </form>
        </td>
      </c:if>
      <c:if test="${not empty availrate.blockingDates}">
        <td class="table-header" width="20%" align="center">
          Unavailable
        </td>
      </c:if>
    </tr>
    <tr>
      <td colspan="3" class="table-data">
        <c:out value="${roomtype.features}" escapeXml="false"/>
```

Continued

Listing 4-1: SelectRoomType.jsp. *(continued)*

```
            </td>
        </tr>
        <c:forEach var="ratedetail" items="${availrate.rates}">
          <tr>
              <td colspan="3" class="table-data">
                  Rate: $
                <c:out value="${ratedetail.price.amount}"/>/night for 
                <c:out value="${ratedetail.numberOfNights}"/> nts
              </td>
          </tr>
        </c:forEach>
        <c:forEach var="blocker" items="${availrate.blockingDates}">
          <tr>
            <td colspan="3" class="table-data">
                Not Available on
              <f:formatDate value="${blocker}" pattern="MM/dd/yyyy"/>
            </td>
          </tr>
        </c:forEach>
        <tr><td> </td></tr>
      </c:forEach>
      </table>
      </td>
      </tr>
    </table>
```

Some key things to note in the listing of SelectRoomType.jsp include:

❑   The use of nested forEach loops to iterate over the set of AvailabilityAndRates objects in the form and then within the list of RateDetails child objects nested below that object.

❑   The conditional logic checking for an empty list of blocking dates to determine if the room type is available for booking.

❑   The implementation of the Select button on the right side of the page for room types available for booking. Because this is a SimpleFormController-based process, we need to invoke the controller using HTTP POST when the user is making a selection.

The SelectRoomTypeController.onSubmit() method is invoked when the user chooses one of the displayed room types using the Select button. This method is responsible for recording the user's selection in the ReservationInfo object in the HttpSession, as shown here:

```
protected ModelAndView onSubmit(HttpServletRequest request,
                                HttpServletResponse response,
                                Object command, BindException errors)
     throws Exception
{
    SelectRoomTypeForm form = (SelectRoomTypeForm) command;
    ReservationInfo rezinfo =
        (ReservationInfo) request.getSession().getAttribute("rezinfo");
```

```
RoomType roomType =
    propertyServices.findRoomTypeByExternalIdentity(form.getId());
List<ReservationServices.RateDetails> rateDetails =
    reservationServices.calculateRates(roomType, rezinfo.getArriveDate(),
                                       rezinfo.getDepartDate());
rezinfo.setRoomTypeId(form.getId());
rezinfo.setRoomType(roomType);
rezinfo.setRezRates(rateDetails);
return super.onSubmit(request, response, command, errors);
}
```

Note that we are re-fetching the chosen `RoomType` object based on the selected `id` value submitted by the form page, and we are calling a slightly different reservation service to re-fetch the rate details for a single room type and set of arrival/departure dates. We cannot make use of the previous list of `AvailabilityAndRates` objects fetched in the `onBindOnNewForm()` method prior to displaying the page because they were only available in the `HttpServletRequest` during the previous controller and view invocation, and were not placed in the `HttpSession`, so they are not present in this instance of the form.

The next page in the reservation process, `GuestInformation.jsp`, is a fairly straightforward HTML form used to collect guest information and credit card information for the reservation. It is a typical set of components consisting of controller, form, Tiles view, and display page along the lines of previous examples. You can examine these components in the downloaded example code if desired, but we do not discuss the page or related components in this text.

Reservation Creation Process

The final step in the reservation process begins with the confirmation page shown in Figure 4-5. The `ReviewReservation.jsp` display page displays information from a newly created `Reservation` business domain object created by the controller but not yet saved to the database. The user examines the contents and clicks the confirmation button to make the reservation official.

The URL for the review reservation page is `reviewreservation.do`, the mapped controller is `ReviewReservationController`, the form object is `ReviewReservationForm`, the Tiles definition is `reviewreservation`, and the display page is `ReviewReservation.jsp`. The pertinent portion of the `userapp-servlet.xml` file is shown here:

```xml
<bean id="reservationReviewController"
    class="com.bigrez.web.ReservationReviewController">
  <property name="formView" value="reviewreservation"/>
  <property name="successView" value="redirect:thankyou.do"/>
  <property name="bindOnNewForm" value="true"/>
  <property name="commandName" value="reviewReservationForm"/>
  <property name="commandClass" value="com.bigrez.web.ReviewReservationForm"/>
  <property name="reviewReservationForm">
      <bean class="com.bigrez.web.ReviewReservationForm"/>
  </property>
  <property name="sessionForm" value="true"/>
  <property name="reservationServices" ref="reservationServicesReference"/>
  <property name="profileServices" ref="profileServicesReference"/>
</bean>
```

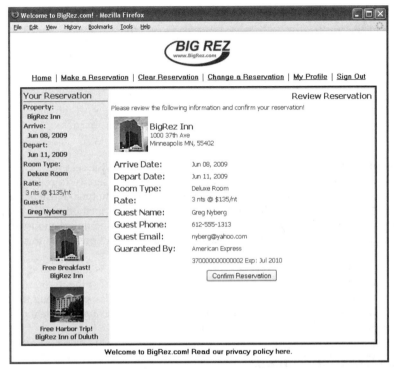

Figure 4-5: Review reservation page.

Note that this controller is configured to use a session form, meaning that the form object will be placed in the HttpSession at the end of the HTTP GET processing and will be retrieved from the session before the binding of submitted data into the form during HTTP POST processing. In practical terms, the objects we attach to the form in the onBindOnNewForm() method will be there when we receive the form again in onSubmit(), simplifying the logic for creating the final, saved reservation in the database.

The onBindOnNewForm() method creates a Reservation object using data from the ReservationInfo object as shown in this partial listing:

```
protected void onBindOnNewForm(HttpServletRequest request,
                        Object command, BindException errors)
   throws Exception
{
   ReviewReservationForm form = (ReviewReservationForm) command;
   ReservationInfo rezinfo =
      (ReservationInfo) request.getSession().getAttribute("rezinfo");
   Reservation reservation = new Reservation();
   reservation.setArrivalDate(rezinfo.getArriveDate());
   reservation.setDepartureDate(rezinfo.getDepartDate());
   reservation.setCard(rezinfo.getGuestProfile().getCard());
   reservation.setGuestProfile(rezinfo.getGuestProfile());
   reservation.setRoomType(rezinfo.getRoomType());
   form.setReservation(reservation); // ready for review
```

Chapter 4: Building an Example Web Application

```
        form.setProperty(rezinfo.getProperty());
        form.setReservationRates(rezinfo.getRezRates());
    }
```

The `onSubmit()` method sends the `Reservation` object to the `createReservation()` service in the business layer, as shown in this listing:

```
    protected ModelAndView onSubmit(HttpServletRequest request,
                                    HttpServletResponse response,
                                    Object command, BindException errors)
    throws Exception
{
    ReviewReservationForm form = (ReviewReservationForm) command;
    Reservation finalreservation =
        reservationServices.createReservation(form.getReservation(),
                                              form.getReservationRates());
    ReservationInfo rezinfo =
        (ReservationInfo) request.getSession().getAttribute("rezinfo");
    rezinfo.clearAllButProfile();
    // re-fetch the latest profile to make sure our version number matches..
    GuestProfile profile = rezinfo.getGuestProfile();
    GuestProfile newprofile =
        profileServices.findByLogonAndPassword(profile.getLogon(),
                                               profile.getPassword());
    rezinfo.setGuestProfileId(newprofile.getExternalIdentity());
    rezinfo.setGuestProfile(newprofile);
    // Need to stash the completed reservation somewhere for the "thank you" page
    request.getSession().setAttribute("finalreservation", finalreservation);
    return super.onSubmit(request, response, command, errors);
    }
```

The `createReservation()` service performs a variety of functions: It saves the new `Reservation` object in the database, including its child `ReservationRate` objects, assigns a confirmation number, decrements any inventory values for room type and day combinations with limited availability, and sends a confirmation email to the guest. Once the reservation is complete the `onSubmit()` method clears information from the `ReservationInfo` object in the session, re-fetches the `GuestProfile` object to ensure our copy matches the latest version in the database, and places the completed reservation in the `HttpSession` in an agreed-upon location for use by the next page in the process, the `ReservationThankYou.jsp` page.

The user is presented with the thank-you page, and the process is complete!

Targeted Offers Components

To round out our discussion of the user site in `bigrez.com`, in this section we briefly examine the targeted offers area on the left side of the page. As shown in Figure 3-2 in the previous chapter, this area presents a small number of offers containing a graphic, caption, and related property name. Clicking an offer simply displays the normal property information page for the given hotel, a simplification we chose for this example application. In a real site, clicking an offer might display a special page with detailed information about the offer and provide a shortcut for selecting a specific rate or room type in the hotel, for example.

Like the reservation information area on the left side of the page, the offers area is part of the master layout and will be displayed every time a display page is shown. Unlike the reservation information area, the data to be displayed in the offers area must be calculated every time based on the latest selections of city, state, and property by the user of the site. For example, if the user has indicated a preference to stay in Minneapolis by selecting that city in the PropertySearch.jsp page, any offers for properties located in Minneapolis should have precedence over offers in other cities.

We've elected to perform the complex business logic required to determine the offers to be displayed in a service method on a session bean, consistent with our philosophy of encapsulating such logic in services rather than performing it in presentation-tier components. The only question remaining is who will invoke this service each time the page is displayed and place the offers information in the request for rendering into the HTML output?

The Tiles framework provides a very slick mechanism for preparing data just prior to invoking the JSP underlying a given Tiles component. As mentioned earlier in this chapter, we've defined the defaultLayout in the tiles-config.xml file to include an OffersPreparer class as part of the definition of the offers tile. The pertinent sections of the configuration file are shown here:

```
<definition name="offers" template="/WEB-INF/jsp/common/Offers.jsp"
    preparer="com.bigrez.web.OffersPreparer"/>

<definition name="defaultLayout" template="/WEB-INF/jsp/common/DefaultLayout.jsp">
    <put-attribute name="header" value="/WEB-INF/jsp/common/Header.jsp" />
    <put-attribute name="topnav" value="/WEB-INF/jsp/common/TopNav.jsp" />
    <put-attribute name="rezinfo" value="/WEB-INF/jsp/common/RezInfo.jsp" />
    <put-attribute name="offers" value="offers" />
    <put-attribute name="footer" value="/WEB-INF/jsp/common/Footer.jsp"/>
</definition>
```

The OffersPreparer class defines an execute() method as follows:

```
public void execute(TilesRequestContext tilesContext,
                    AttributeContext attributeContext)
    throws PreparerException
{
    Map<String,Object> lSessionMap = tilesContext.getSessionScope();
    Map<String,Object> lRequestMap = tilesContext.getRequestScope();
    ReservationInfo rezinfo = (ReservationInfo) lSessionMap.get("rezinfo");
    try {
        List<Offer> offers =
            propertyServices.getOffersForDisplay(rezinfo.getProperty(),
                                        rezinfo.getLastSearchCity(),
                                        rezinfo.getLastSearchState(),
                                        getMaximumOffers());
        lRequestMap.put("offers", offers);
    }
    catch (EntityNotFoundException e) {
        lRequestMap.put("offers", new ArrayList<Offer>());
    }
    super.execute(tilesContext, attributeContext);
}
```

The Offers.jsp page finds the List of fetched Offer objects in the request scope under the key offers, loops through them, and displays the targeted offers to the user using standard JSTL forEach and out tags.

That's it! We are now ready to proceed to the construction of the administration site components including pages for entering, updating, and deleting all of the information used by the bigrez.com user site.

Construction of Administration Site Components

The construction of the administration site in bigrez.com is broken down into two primary sections:

❑ *Authentication/authorization components* controlling access to site components

❑ *Property maintenance components* providing pages for creating, modifying, and deleting all of the property information required to drive the user site

Note that the administration site is designed to be a completely separate web application deployed to WebLogic Server alongside the user site. The administration site has its own web.xml file, adminapp-servlet.xml Spring MVC configuration file, tiles-config.xml file, and a completely independent set of display and controller components. Certain Java code components in the web-common area are shared between the two applications, as are all of the EJB services and domain objects.

We next examine the two sections of the administration site, highlighting key components and techniques in each section as appropriate.

Authentication/Authorization Components

The administration site in bigrez.com is not available to the general user community. To gain access to the administration site you must have a login and password defined as a bigrez.com system administrator in the WebLogic Server security realm.

We've employed the standard Java EE web application security mechanisms provided by WebLogic Server as a starting point for this application. More advanced WebLogic Server–specific security mechanisms are discussed in Chapter 11. Standard web application security relies on three primary components:

❑ The definition of users and groups in the application server environment using administration tools provided by WebLogic Server

❑ Declaring web application security in the web.xml file for the application and specifying the roles having access to specific web components

❑ Defining the mapping between the roles defined in the web.xml file and the principals, either users or groups, defined in the environment

Using the WebLogic Server administration console, create a BigRezAdministrators group in the realm and then create a bigrez.com administrator user and make it a member of that group. Chapter 5 walks through this process in detail.

Next, declare and configure web application security in the `web.xml` descriptor file for the administration site using the standard descriptor elements. Define a `security-constraint` element to secure all of the controller invocation URL values in the administration site using a `*.do` URL pattern with the `<auth-constraint>` tag specifying that only the `bigrezadmin` role may access these resources:

```
<security-constraint>
  <web-resource-collection>
    <web-resource-name>Dispatcher Servlet</web-resource-name>
    <url-pattern>*.do</url-pattern>
    <http-method>GET</http-method>
    <http-method>POST</http-method>
  </web-resource-collection>
  <auth-constraint>
    <role-name>bigrezadmin</role-name>
  </auth-constraint>
</security-constraint>
```

Next, configure the web application to use form-based authentication. This requires a `<login-config>` element defining the authentication method and the pages to use for requesting login information from the user and for reporting login problems:

```
<login-config>
  <auth-method>FORM</auth-method>
  <form-login-config>
    <form-login-page>/login.do</form-login-page>
    <form-error-page>/login.do?error=true</form-error-page>
  </form-login-config>
</login-config>
```

The web container is responsible for displaying the specified login page whenever a user requests a resource in the site for which they are not authorized. In our case, because all `*.do` mappings are considered secure, and all JSP pages are hidden under the `WEB-INF/jsp` subdirectory, there is nothing available to a user without logging in.

Note that the `login.do` URL specified for this form-based login page is not a simple JSP display page. When the Web container requests the `login.do` URL it will cause the Spring MVC `DispatcherServlet` to be invoked, which will then call the controller mapped to the `/login.do` URL and invoke a view resolver to render the `successView` returned by that controller. The success view, `login`, represents a Tiles definition, so Tiles will be invoked to assemble and render the entire page, one piece of which is the `Login.jsp` page with the fields for username and password in the center of the display. Whew! Fortunately the web container allows all of that forwarding and invoking to occur before we are actually logged in because it is aware that the login page itself may require such functionality.

We examine `Login.jsp` in a moment, but first let's finish the required descriptor entries in `web.xml`:

```
<security-role>
  <role-name>bigrezadmin</role-name>
</security-role>
```

These elements simply declare the existence of the security roles used in the `<auth-constraint>` elements earlier in the descriptor. Note that this security role is not the same as the `BigRezAdministrators` group defined in the WebLogic Server realm. Although WebLogic Server will automatically map roles to groups in the realm if the names are identical, this is not a best practice. A separate set of elements in `weblogic.xml` should be used to map roles to principals, either groups or users, in the realm. For `bigrez.com`, the mapping element in `weblogic.xml` looks like this:

```
<security-role-assignment>
  <role-name>bigrezadmin</role-name>
  <principal-name>BigRezAdministrators</principal-name>
</security-role-assignment>
```

> ### Best Practice
>
> Always map the roles defined in `web.xml` to principals (groups or users) defined in the realm using explicit `<security-role-constraint>` entries in `weblogic.xml` rather than relying on automatic matching of role names to principal names.

As shown in Listing 4-2, the `Login.jsp` page follows the basic rules of form-based authentication. It defines an HTML form with the action `j_security_check` containing input fields `j_username` and `j_password`. This page will be displayed automatically by the web container whenever a user attempts to access any controlled resource in the application.

Listing 4-2: Login.jsp.

```
<%@ include file="/WEB-INF/jsp/common/Include.jspf" %>

<table width="100%" cellspacing="5" cellpadding="0">
  <tr>
    <td class="page-header" align="right">Login</td>
  </tr>
  <tr>
    <td class="page-text">Please log in to Administration Site:</td>
  </tr>
  <c:if test="${not empty param.error}">
    <tr><td> </td></tr>
    <tr><td class="error-header2">Invalid Administrator ID
          or Password. Please try again.</td></tr>
  </c:if>
  <tr><td> </td></tr>
  <tr>
    <td>
      <form method="POST" action="j_security_check">
        <table width="50%" border="0" cellspacing="0" cellpadding="0">
          <tr>
            <td width="50%" class="page-label">Administrator ID:</td>
            <td width="50">
            <input type="text" name="j_username" size="15" maxlength="15" value=""/>
            </td>
          </tr>
          <tr>
            <td class="page-label">Password:</td>
```

Continued

Listing 4-2: Login.jsp. *(continued)*

```
        <td>
          <input type="password" name="j_password" size="15"
                 maxlength="15" value=""/>
        </td>
      </tr>
      <tr><td colspan="2"> </td></tr>
      <tr>
        <td align="center" colspan="2">
          <input type="submit" value="Submit"/>
        </td>
      </tr>
    </table>
  </form>
 </td>
 </tr>
</table>
```

When the user submits the form, the container intercepts the request and attempts to authenticate using the default security realm and the supplied username and password. If the supplied data is not correct, the container forwards the user to the page defined in the web.xml file in the <form-error-page> element, normally an error page of some sort. We've added a twist here by defining the error page to be the login page again with an error parameter set as shown here:

```
<form-error-page>/login.do?error=true</form-error-page>
```

In the Login.jsp page, we can now sense the presence of this error request parameter, using standard JSTL tags or any normal scriptlet-based mechanism, and conditionally display an error message at the top of the page:

```
<c:if test="${not empty param.error}">
  <tr><td> </td></tr>
  <tr><td class="error-header2">Invalid Administrator ID or Password.
          Please try again.</td></tr>
</c:if>
```

The login form will therefore be redisplayed to the user in the case of login errors with this additional error message at the top.

Now let's move on to discuss a few of the property maintenance components in the administration site to complete our examination of the bigrez.com web application.

Property Maintenance Components

Table 4-3 lists the primary presentation-tier components responsible for maintenance of property information in the administration site. Once a property is chosen using the PropertyList page, the user can update five different types of information: main property information, room types in the property, rates for a given room type, availability of a given room type, and the targeted offers for the property.

Table 4-3: Property Maintenance Primary Components

Display Component	Related Controller Component	Form Object
PropertyList.jsp	PropertyListController.java	PropertyListForm.java
PropertyMain.jsp	PropertyMainController.java	PropertyMainForm.java
PropertyRooms.jsp	PropertyRoomsController.java	PropertyRoomsForm.java
PropertyRoom.jsp	PropertyRoomController.java	PropertyRoomForm.java
PropertyRates.jsp	PropertyRatesController.java	PropertyRatesForm.java
PropertyRate.jsp	PropertyRateController.java	PropertyRateForm.java
PropertyAvails.jsp	PropertyAvailsController.java	PropertyAvailsForm.java
PropertyAvail.jsp	PropertyAvailController.java	PropertyAvailForm.java
PropertyOffers.jsp	PropertyOffersController.java	PropertyOffersForm.java
PropertyOffer.jsp	PropertyOfferController.java	PropertyOfferForm.java

These maintenance components are intended to demonstrate proper use of the Spring MVC framework across a variety of different form types and update requirements. As shown in the table, all of the display JSP pages use a similarly named `Controller` class, and all pages use form objects to store data for display and update. Consistent with the user web application, all relationships between these components are defined in the administration site `adminapp-servlet.xml` Spring MVC configuration file. Tiles definitions are placed in the `tiles-config.xml` file, as before.

The following sections examine selected pages in the administration site to highlight additional techniques and best practices.

Property Main Form

The main property maintenance page, `PropertyMain.jsp`, is a standard HTML form page using a form object and `Controller` class to process updates. As shown in Figure 4-6, the page presents all of the basic property information for update by the user.

The `PropertyMain.jsp` display page uses the Spring MVC `form` tags and JSTL tags to create the HTML form. No JavaScript field validation was employed in these pages, to keep them simple.

Form validation is performed by the `validate()` method in the form object in a manner similar to previous examples. The controller class, `PropertyMainController`, accepts the submitted form once it has been validated and processes the changes in the `onSubmit()` method, as shown in Listing 4-3.

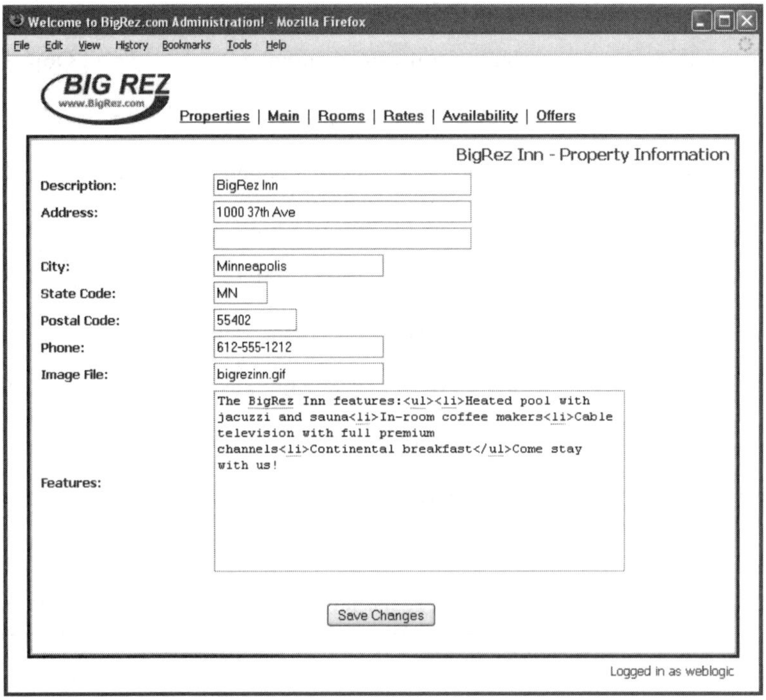

Figure 4-6: Property main page.

Listing 4-3: PropertyMainController.java.

```java
package com.bigrez.admin.web;

import java.util.logging.Level;
import java.util.logging.Logger;

import javax.servlet.http.HttpServletRequest;
import javax.servlet.http.HttpServletResponse;

import org.apache.commons.lang.StringUtils;
import org.springframework.beans.BeanUtils;
import org.springframework.validation.BindException;
import org.springframework.web.servlet.ModelAndView;
import org.springframework.web.servlet.mvc.SimpleFormController;

import weblogic.logging.LoggingHelper;

import com.bigrez.domain.Property;
import com.bigrez.service.PropertyServices;

public class PropertyMainController extends SimpleFormController
{
    private PropertyServices propertyServices;
```

```java
private PropertyMainForm propertyMainForm;
final Logger logger = LoggingHelper.getServerLogger();

@Override
protected void onBindOnNewForm(HttpServletRequest request,
                               Object command,
                               BindException errors)
    throws Exception
{
    logger.log(Level.INFO,
               "PropertyMainController::onBindOnNewForm()");
    PropertyMainForm form = (PropertyMainForm)command;
    String id = form.getId();
    Property prop = null;
    if (StringUtils.isNotEmpty(id)) {
        // specific property was chosen and passed to
        // us, honor that choice
        prop = propertyServices.
            findPropertyByExternalIdentity(id);
        request.getSession().setAttribute("currentProperty",
                                          prop);
    }
    else {
        // no property choice specified, use
        // Property object in session
        prop = (Property)request.getSession().
            getAttribute("currentProperty");
    }
    // The form has copies of the property and address
    // fields to avoid binding into the actual session
    // version of the property object
    BeanUtils.copyProperties(prop, form,
        new String[]{"roomTypes","offers","address"});
    BeanUtils.copyProperties(prop.getAddress(), form);
    logger.log(Level.INFO,
        "PropertyMainController::onBindOnNewForm() complete");
}


@Override
protected ModelAndView onSubmit(HttpServletRequest request,
                                HttpServletResponse response,
                                Object command,
                                BindException errors)
    throws Exception
{
    logger.log(Level.INFO,
        "PropertyMainController::onSubmit(" + command + ")");
    PropertyMainForm form = (PropertyMainForm) command;
    // Copy the field values back into the session
    // version of the property
    Property prop = (Property)
        request.getSession().getAttribute("currentProperty");
    BeanUtils.copyProperties(form, prop, new String[]{"id"});
```

Continued

111

Listing 4-3: PropertyMainController.java. *(continued)*

```
            BeanUtils.copyProperties(form, prop.getAddress());

            // update the property in the database
            propertyServices.createOrUpdate(prop);

            // re-fetch the entire Property lattice to
            // update the session copy
            Property updatedprop =
                propertyServices.findPropertyByExternalIdentity(
                    prop.getExternalIdentity());
            request.getSession().setAttribute("currentProperty",
                                              updatedprop);

            logger.log(Level.INFO,
                "PropertyMainController::onSubmit(" + command +
                                              ") complete");
            ModelAndView result =
                super.onSubmit(request, response, command, errors);
            result.addObject("success","true");
            return result;
        }


    public PropertyServices getPropertyServices()
    {
        return propertyServices;
    }

    public void setPropertyServices(PropertyServices
                                    pPropertyServices)
    {
        propertyServices = pPropertyServices;
    }

    public PropertyMainForm getPropertyMainForm()
    {
        return propertyMainForm;
    }

    public void setPropertyMainForm(PropertyMainForm
                                    pPropertyMainForm)
    {
        propertyMainForm = pPropertyMainForm;
    }
}
```

The pertinent portion of the `adminapp-servlet.xml` file is shown here:

```
<bean id="propertyMainController"
      class="com.bigrez.admin.web.PropertyMainController">
    <property name="formView" value="propertymain"/>
    <property name="successView" value="redirect:propertymain.do"/>
```

```
<property name="overridePropertyListView" value="redirect:propertylist.do"/>
<property name="bindOnNewForm" value="true"/>
<property name="commandName" value="propertyMainForm"/>
<property name="commandClass" value="com.bigrez.admin.web.PropertyMainForm"/>
<property name="propertyMainForm">
    <bean class="com.bigrez.admin.web.PropertyMainForm"/>
</property>
<property name="sessionForm" value="true"/>
<property name="validator">
    <bean class="com.bigrez.admin.web.PropertyMainForm"/>
</property>
<property name="propertyServices" ref="propertyServicesReference"/>
</bean>
```

Although the `PropertyMainController` is basically a straightforward implementation of the `SimpleFormController` design pattern, with `onBindOnNewForm()` and `onSubmit()` methods performing the key logic, there is one design decision worth examining in more detail. We've chosen to duplicate property-related attributes in the `PropertyMainForm` object for use in the HTML form, copying data between the `Property` domain object and the form as necessary, rather than placing a reference to the current `Property` domain object in the form object and mapping form fields directly to nested attributes in the domain object. The reason is fairly simple: We need to avoid corrupting the official session-based copy of the `Property` object under certain error conditions.

Consider the following sequence of events:

1. The current `Property` domain object in the session is attached to the form object.
2. The user makes changes to the data on the HTML form, including a blanking out of the property description.
3. Form data is posted back to the controller, bound into the form object and nested `Property` object by the `SimpleFormController` infrastructure, but fails validation.
4. The user is presented with an error page, but chooses not to correct the error and instead moves to a different page in the administration site.

We're left with corrupt information in the `Property` domain object attached to the form, which happens to be the same object we have stored in the `HttpSession` as our official *current* property in the administration site.

We could modify the `Property` domain class, and its nested `Address` class, to implement the `Cloneable` interface and properly clone itself and its children using the `clone()` method. The `onBindOnNewForm()` method could then clone the official `Property` domain object in the session and attach a clone to the form object. A perfectly viable solution, perhaps, but a modification of this complexity in a domain object just to satisfy a UI requirement seems awkward and counter-intuitive.

We chose to replicate the needed fields in the form object and avoid attaching the `Property` object to the form, thereby avoiding all possibility of binding bad data into the official `Property` object. The `PropertyMainForm` therefore contains a series of primitive attributes, as shown here:

```
private String id;
private String description;
```

```
private String address1;
private String address2;
private String city;
private String stateCode;
private String postalCode;
private String phone;
private String imageFile;
private String features;
```

The `PropertyMainController` carefully copies data from the `Property` domain object to the form attributes, and from the form attributes back to the `Property` object, using a Spring-provided utility class called `BeanUtils` as shown in Listing 4-3.

Rate Maintenance Pages

The `PropertyRates.jsp` page displays a complete set of room types and rates available for the current property, as shown in Figure 4-7. Users click on any one of the existing rate entries for a given room type or on the link to create a new rate. The associated controller class, `PropertyRatesController`, placed the needed room type and rate information in the `PropertyRatesForm` during `onBindOnNewForm()` processing, and the page simply iterates and displays the list of room types and rates using JSTL `forEach` and `out` tags.

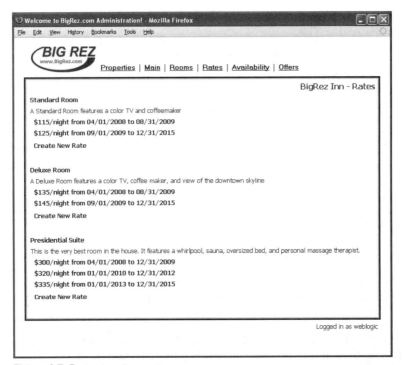

Figure 4-7: Property rates page.

The only tricky aspect worth examining here is the mechanism used to pass rate information for each room type to the page. The `RoomType` domain object does not have a bidirectional relationship to its child `Rate` domain objects. In other words, although `Rate` has a reference to its parent `RoomType`, the `RoomType` class does not have a list of associated child `Rate` objects. The choices that led to this design are discussed in Chapter 7. We cannot, therefore, simply attach a list of `RoomType` objects with their children `Rate` objects to the `PropertyRatesForm` and be done. We decided to store the `Rate` objects in a separate construct — we chose to use a `Map` keyed by room type identity — and find the rates for a given room type in that construct during the display page processing.

The `PropertyRatesForm` therefore contains a `Map` for storing this information, and a helper method for adding a list of `Rate` objects to the map, as shown in this partial listing:

```
public class PropertyRatesForm
{
    private List<RoomType> roomTypes;
    private Map<String,List<Rate>> ratesByRoomType;

    ...

    public Map<String, List<Rate>> getRatesByRoomType()
    {
        return ratesByRoomType;
    }

    public void addRateListToMap(RoomType roomType, List<Rate> rates)
    {
        if (ratesByRoomType == null) {
            ratesByRoomType = new HashMap<String,List<Rate>>();
        }
        ratesByRoomType.put(roomType.getExternalIdentity(), rates);
    }
}
```

The `onBindOnNewForm()` method loops over the `RoomType` objects for the current `Property` and fetches the current list of `Rate` objects for that room type, placing each `List` in the form's `Map` using the helper method, as shown here:

```
List<RoomType> roomTypes = prop.getRoomTypes();
for (RoomType room : roomTypes) {
    List<Rate> rates = propertyServices.findRatesByRoomType(room);
    form.addRateListToMap(room, rates);
}
```

Finally, the `PropertyRates.jsp` page loops over the list of `RoomType` objects and finds the associated list of rates in the `Map` using a special syntax in the `items` attribute of the inner `forEach` loop tag.

Listing 4-4 presents the complete contents of the `PropertyRates.jsp` page for your examination.

Listing 4-4: PropertyRates.jsp.

```
<%@ include file="/WEB-INF/jsp/common/Include.jspf" %>

<c:set var="property" value="${sessionScope.currentProperty}"/>

<table width="100%" cellspacing="5" cellpadding="0">
  <tr>
    <td class="page-header" align="right"><c:out
value="${property.description}"/> - Rates</td>
  </tr>
  <tr>
    <td>
      <table width="100%" cellspacing="0" cellpadding="3" border="0">
        <c:forEach var="roomtype" items="${propertyRatesForm.roomTypes}">
          <tr>
            <c:url var="propertyroomurl" value="/propertyroom.do">
              <c:param name="id"
                        value="${roomtype.externalIdentity}"/>
            </c:url>
            <td align="left">
              <a class="table-link"
                 href="<c:out value='${propertyroomurl}'/>">
                <c:out value="${roomtype.description}"/>
              </a>
            </td>
          </tr>
          <tr>
            <td class="table-data">
              <c:out value="${roomtype.features}"/>
            </td>
          </tr>
          <c:set var="id" value="${roomtype.externalIdentity}"/>
          <c:forEach var="rate"
            items="${propertyRatesForm.ratesByRoomType[id]}">
            <tr>
              <c:url var="propertyrateurl" value="/propertyrate.do">
                <c:param name="roomId" value="${roomtype.externalIdentity}"/>
                <c:param name="id" value="${rate.externalIdentity}"/>
              </c:url>
              <td><a class="table-link" href="<c:out value='${propertyrateurl}'/>">
                    $<c:out value='${rate.price.amount}'/>/night from
                   <f:formatDate value="${rate.startDate}" pattern="MM/dd/yyyy"/> to
                    <f:formatDate value="${rate.endDate}" pattern="MM/dd/yyyy"/></A>
              </td>
            </tr>
          </c:forEach>
          <c:url var="newpropertyrateurl" value="/propertyrate.do">
            <c:param name="roomId" value="${roomtype.externalIdentity}"/>
            <c:param name="id" value=""/>
          </c:url>
          <tr>
            <td>  <a class="table-link" href="<c:out
```

```
            value='${newpropertyrateurl}'/>">Create New Rate</a></td>
          </tr>
          <tr><td> </td></tr>
        </c:forEach>
      </table>
    </td>
  </tr>
</table>
```

Links on the `PropertyRates.jsp` page invoke the `propertyrate.do` action, mapped in the `adminapp-servlet.xml` file to the `PropertyRateController` and associated form and page. The resulting page, depicted in Figure 4-8, is used to create or modify a single `Rate` object for a given room type. The controller is a standard `SimpleFormController` subclass, with code in the `onBindOnNewForm()` and `onSubmit()` methods to handle HTTP `GET` and `POST` invocations, respectively. Examine the downloadable source code if you are interested in the implementation details.

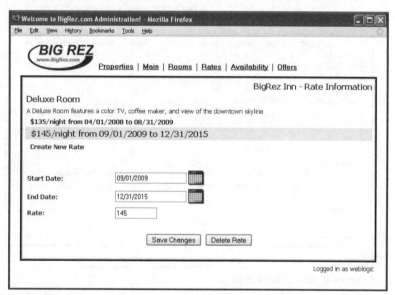

Figure 4-8: Property rate page.

Availability Maintenance Pages

We're down to one final set of maintenance pages to examine: the `PropertyAvails.jsp` list page and the `PropertyAvail.jsp` availability update page. These pages are designed to present the user with a high-level view of room availability at the current property and provide a mechanism for modifying that availability. Availability may be modified by closing out rooms on certain dates or by limiting the number of rooms available on certain dates.

Availability in the `bigrez.com` system is stored in the `Inventory` table as a sparse series of rows linked to room types. For example, if the `Deluxe` room type is not available for the date 11/15/2009, there will be a row in the `Inventory` table linked to that room type having a date stamp of 11/15/2009 with a

ROOMSAVAIL value of zero. A non-zero value for inventory indicates that the room is currently available, but only a limited number of rooms remain. The term *sparse* in the previous sentence indicates that the absence of a row in the database for a particular room type and date means no limit or problem with that date instead of implying that there is no inventory available on that date.

Let's look at the list page for availability, PropertyAvails.jsp. As shown in Figure 4-9, the availability list page presents the user with a high-level view of availability over a nine-month period, providing counts of closed days (days with zero inventory) and days with some control (either closed or limited remaining inventory).

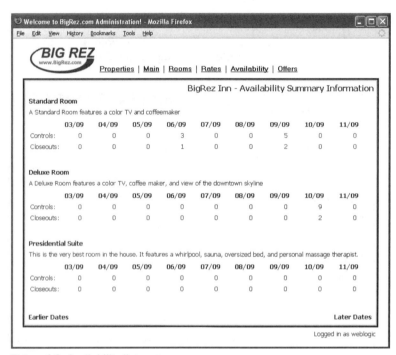

Figure 4-9: Availability list page.

This display represents a great deal of information and a fair number of calculations, so we've chosen to implement the business logic required to collect all of these counts as a session bean façade that returns a set of value objects. Consistent with other pages in the site requiring complex value objects for display, the controller class responsible for preparing the form object, in this case PropertyAvailsController, invokes the proper calculation method on the session bean and places the list of AvailabilitySummary objects in the PropertyAvailsForm object for display by the page, as shown here:

```
protected void onBindOnNewForm(HttpServletRequest request,
                               Object command, BindException errors)
    throws Exception
{
    PropertyAvailsForm form = (PropertyAvailsForm) command;
    Property prop = (Property) request.getSession().getAttribute("currentProperty");
    if (prop != null) {
```

```
        String startDateAsString = form.getStartDate();
        Date startDate = new Date();
        if (StringUtils.isNotEmpty(startDateAsString)) {
            try {
                startDate = DateHelper.parse3(startDateAsString);
            }
            catch (Exception ignore) {}
        }
        int numberOfMonths = 9;
        List<AvailabilitySummary> availsummaries =
            reservationServices.calculateAvailabilitySummary(prop, startDate,
                                                       numberOfMonths);
        form.setAvailabilitySummaries(availsummaries);
        form.setStartDate(DateHelper.format3(startDate));
        form.setNumMonths(numberOfMonths);
    }
    return;
}
```

Straightforward JSTL forEach and out tags are used to render this availability information to the page as shown in Figure 4-9.

This page also contains hyperlinks designed to drill in on a given month to view the details for the month and edit the availability as well as links to scroll forward and backward in time. Examine the source code for PropertyAvails.jsp in the downloadable example code to see how these links are created in the page.

For this discussion, we'll simply state that the user clicks a hyperlink on the summary page, which provides the target controller class, PropertyAvailController, with the parameters necessary to prepare the proper information in the form to forward to the maintenance page, PropertyAvail.jsp, depicted in Figure 4-10. This page uses the form object PropertyAvailForm, which contains date attributes used for navigation and a List of String values representing the inventory values for each day in the month:

```
private String roomId;
private RoomType roomType;
private List<String> availability;
private String startDate;
private String editDate;
```

The PropertyAvailController.onBindOnNewForm() method prepares the PropertyAvailForm object by calling a service method provided by the business layer to fetch a list of Integer values. These values represent the availability information for the specific room type and date range, and are placed in the form as shown here:

```
protected void onBindOnNewForm(HttpServletRequest request,
                               Object command, BindException errors)
    throws Exception
{
    PropertyAvailForm form = (PropertyAvailForm) command;
    Property prop = (Property) request.getSession().getAttribute("currentProperty");
    if (prop != null) {
        RoomType roomType =
            propertyServices.findRoomTypeByExternalIdentity(form.getRoomId());
```

```
    form.setRoomType(roomType);
    String editDateAsString = form.getEditDate();
    Date editDate = DateHelper.parse3(editDateAsString);
    Date endDate = DateHelper.addMonths(editDate, 1);
    List<Integer> availabilityValues =
        reservationServices.calculateAvailability(roomType, editDate, endDate);
    List<String> availability = new ArrayList<String>();
    for (Integer value : availabilityValues) {
        if (value == ReservationServices.UNCONTROLLED) {
            // service returns -1 values for missing days, we show as blank
            availability.add("");
        }
        else {
            availability.add(value.toString());
        }
    }
    form.setAvailability(availability);
}
return;
}
```

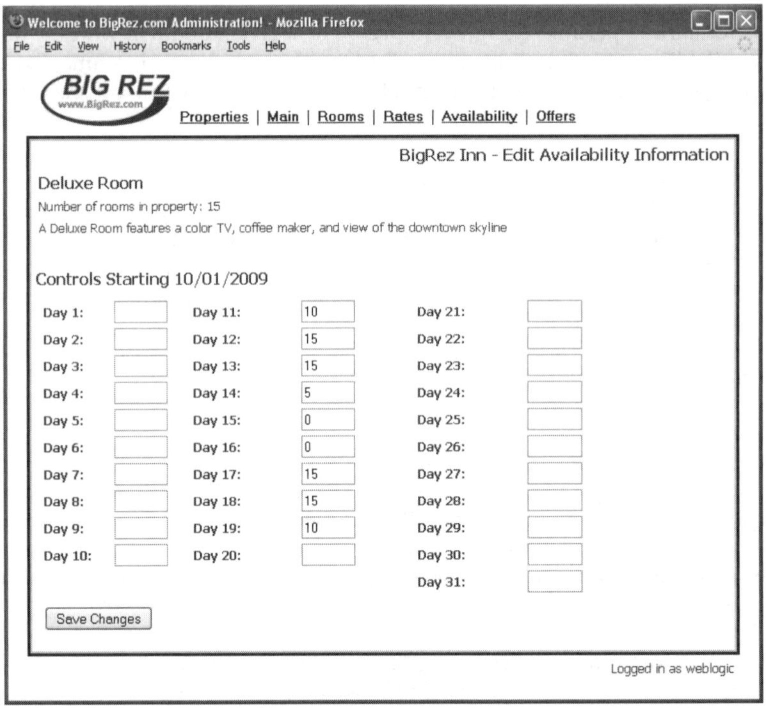

Figure 4-10: Availability maintenance page.

The returned list will contain an entry for every day in the date range, with special UNCONTROLLED values present for days that do not have any Inventory row in the database. We use a list of String objects in the form and convert these UNCONTROLLED value rows into empty strings in the form's list of values.

The `PropertyAvail.jsp` page presents the list of availability counts and allows the user to add, delete, or modify the existing values. Mapping HTML input fields to each of the values in the form's `availability` list requires a JSTL `forEach` iterator with the `varStatus` attribute included to keep track of the index for the current row. As shown here, the `status.count` value can then be used both for displaying the day number in front of the input field and for indexing within the form's availability list:

```
<c:forEach var="av" items="${propertyAvailForm.availability}" varStatus="status">
  <tr>
    <td width="50%" class="page-label">
      Day <c:out value="${status.count}"/>:</td>
    <td>
      <form:input path="availability[${status.count-1}]" size="5"></form:input>
    </td>
  </tr>
  ...
</c:forEach>
```

Examine the full source listing in the downloadable example program to see how this `status.count` value is also used to create multiple columns on the display page.

The user makes changes to the values on the page and submits the form back to the `PropertyAvailController` using an HTTP `POST` request. The `SimpleFormController` infrastructure calls `validate()` in the `PropertyAvailForm` where we check to make sure the entered values are either empty, indicating an uncontrolled day, or numeric. Once validation succeeds the `onSubmit()` method in our controller is invoked to process the form submission using the code shown here:

```
protected ModelAndView onSubmit(HttpServletRequest request,
                                HttpServletResponse response, Object command,
                                BindException errors)
    throws Exception
{
    PropertyAvailForm form = (PropertyAvailForm) command;
    RoomType roomtype = form.getRoomType();
    Date startDate = DateHelper.parse3(form.getEditDate());
    List<String> enteredStrings = form.getAvailability();
    List<Integer> availableRoomsByDay = new ArrayList<Integer>();
    for (String enteredString : enteredStrings) {
        if (StringUtils.isEmpty(enteredString)) {
            availableRoomsByDay.add(new Integer(ReservationServices.UNCONTROLLED));
        }
        else {
            availableRoomsByDay.add(new Integer(enteredString));
        }
    }
    reservationServices.updateInventory(roomtype, startDate, availableRoomsByDay);
    ModelAndView result = super.onSubmit(request, response, command, errors);
    // help list page stay where it was before coming here
    result.addObject("startDate", form.getStartDate());
    return result;
}
```

We simply convert our list of `String` objects back into a list of `Integer` objects, including `UNCONTROLLED` values for days with no control, and send the resulting list to the service for processing. What could be easier? It is up to the business service to decide how to implement this updateinventory() mechanism. It may delete all existing Inventory rows for the date range in question and re-insert the appropriate rows for any controlled days we pass to it, or it may compare the existing Inventory rows to our list and *patch* the database by making only the necessary changes. As presentation-tier developers we are not overly concerned about the implementation as long as it works.

Note that before returning the ModelAndView result our onSubmit() method adds the start date from the incoming form to the result using the key startDate:

```
ModelAndView result = super.onSubmit(request, response, command, errors);
// help list page stay where it was before coming here
result.addObject("startDate", form.getStartDate());
return result;
```

We are doing this because the successView value for this controller uses a redirect: prefix to send the user back to the PropertyAvails.jsp page, depicted in Figure 4-9, and we want to pass the start date value back to that page. That way the PropertyAvails.jsp page will display the same date range as it did before the user clicked on a particular month to come to the maintenance page. Recall that objects placed on the ModelAndView object will be included in the query string returned on the HTTP redirect, so the target controller and page will have the start date value available. We talked about this redirect: plus ModelAndView result object trick earlier in this chapter and promoted it as a best practice. Fortunately we also found a use for it in bigrez.com so you can see how it works!

Administration Controller Form View Overrides

One final topic and we're done with our discussion of the administration web site components.

Like the SelectRoomTypeController in the user web application, all of our property maintenance controllers need to be careful that a user doesn't navigate to a controller dependent on a Property object in the HttpSession without first selecting a Property from the property list page. We're careful to disable the links in the navigation bar in the header using conditional code that checks for a selected property in the HttpSession, but the user might save a bookmark to one of our detail pages and thereby invoke a controller without a Property object in the session.

Our administration controllers are SimpleFormController subclasses, as in the user site, so we have the same problem: the onBindOnNewForm() method gives us no mechanism to override the formView value defined in the configuration file in order to send the user somewhere else if no Property is available in the session. Identical to the solution we adopted for the SelectRoomTypeController in the user site, we'll override the default behavior of the showForm() method in all of our administration controllers to check for the presence of a Property object in the session and return a special ModelAndView object if it is not present. An example from the PropertyAvailsController is shown here:

```
protected ModelAndView showForm(HttpServletRequest request,
                                HttpServletResponse response,
                                BindException errors, Map controlModel)
    throws Exception
{
    Property prop = (Property) request.getSession().getAttribute("currentProperty");
    if (prop == null) {
        return new ModelAndView(getOverridePropertyListView());
    }
```

```
            return super.showForm(request, response, errors, controlModel);
        }
```

The `overridePropertyListView` view name is injected by the configuration file, to avoid hard-coding it in the controller, and is set for all controllers to redirect to the `propertylist.do` action. That's all there is to it!

Chapter Review

This chapter examined the construction process for the `bigrez.com` example application and presented a detailed discussion of selected presentation-tier components. Key concepts such as navigation control, presenting the progress through the reservation process, form validation techniques, handling errors, and securing the administration site were included in the discussion.

In the next chapter, we talk about packaging and deploying web applications in WebLogic Server and begin walking through the packaging and deployment of the `bigrez.com` web application components.

5

Packaging and Deploying WebLogic Web Applications

This chapter discusses the steps required to package and deploy a WebLogic Server web application. Consistent with the intermediate to advanced nature of this book, we assume that you have some knowledge of the Java EE specification and the required elements in a well-structured web application. Our emphasis will be on the techniques applicable to a WebLogic Server deployment rather than a generic Java EE environment. We also assume a basic level of experience with the Ant build tool provided by the Apache Software Foundation. See the Ant home page at http://jakarta.apache.org/ant for online documentation.

Figure 5-1 presents the basic process for packaging and deploying a web application using WebLogic Server. The basic steps in the process are as follows:

1. Create web.xml and weblogic.xml descriptor files.
2. Organize the web application components in the proper directory structure.
3. Precompile JSP pages and place the generated class files in the web application structure.
4. Deploy the application to WebLogic Server as an exploded or archived web application.

The rest of this chapter discusses each of the steps in this process and the tools available in WebLogic Server to perform each activity.

Packaging Web Applications

You package web applications for deployment in WebLogic Server by creating the correct web application directory structure and placing in that structure the view components, images, class libraries, and descriptor files required for the application. In this section, we briefly review the structure of a standard Java EE web application, examine key elements in the web.xml and weblogic.xml descriptor files, and present a build process for creating web applications using the Ant utility.

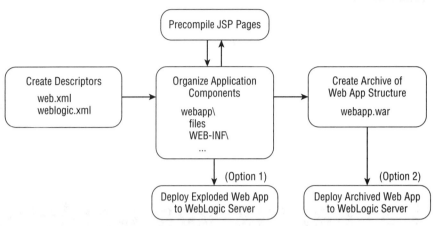

Figure 5-1: Basic packaging and deployment process.

Web Application Directory Structure

The standard web application directory structure, depicted in Figure 5-2, defines the proper location for all of the components required for the application. Viewable components, such as JSP pages, static HTML pages, images, and other content intended for viewing by client browsers, are normally placed directly below the root directory in the structure. Internal files, such as Java classes, libraries, and descriptors, are placed in the WEB-INF directory. If access to JSP pages always utilizes controllers or other view-rendering components, the JSP pages themselves may be placed in a subdirectory of the WEB-INF directory, as shown in Figure 5-3, to enhance security. Browsers cannot access JSP pages or any other files placed within the WEB-INF directory structure, so don't place images, style sheets, or any other files referred to on your pages beneath WEB-INF if the browser will need to access them directly.

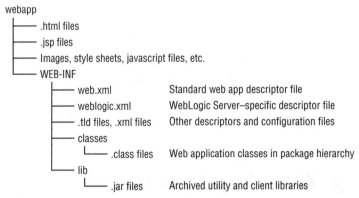

Figure 5-2: Standard web application directory structure.

Hyperlinks, include directives, and c:url custom tags in the view pages must reflect any directory structure present in the web application, so it is important to make these organizational decisions early in the development process. Recognize that a good hierarchical organization allows the use of directories in the `url-pattern` descriptor elements to better configure security, servlet mapping, filter mapping, and other features.

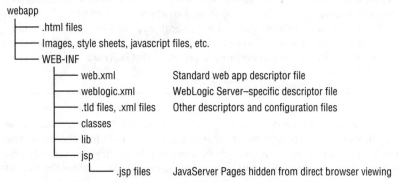

Figure 5-3: Alternate web application directory structure.

When organizing your web applications, be aware of the important difference between separate directories in a single web application and separate web applications:

❑ *Separate directories* in the same web application represent a purely organizational structure. Components in all directories of a web application share the same `HttpSession` data, classloader, `WEB-INF/lib` libraries, application-scoped variables, authentication information, servlet and JSP configuration, and all parameters defined at the web application level in the `web.xml` or `weblogic.xml` descriptors.

❑ *Separate web applications* may look similar to separate directories from the point of view of the user, differing only by the context path in the URL (for example, `/user/main.jsp` versus `/admin/main.jsp`). In the application server, however, separate web applications are treated much differently than separate directories in the same web application. Each web application will use a different classloader, need its own copies of `WEB-INF/lib` libraries, have its own set of descriptor files and application-scoped variables, and store separate `HttpSession` data for the user. The only information shared by both web applications, essentially, is authentication information. Even this can be scoped to each web application separately, if desired, creating completely independent applications.

Generally speaking, you should use separate directories in a single web application when the directories represent different areas of the same site, the directories share the same `WEB-INF/lib` libraries and descriptors, and you need a single `HttpSession` preserved across the directories. Use separate web applications when there is a strong need to isolate the sections of the overall application from each other.

One caveat worth mentioning here: WebLogic Server includes a *session sharing* feature that allows you to configure two or more web applications located in the same enterprise application to share `HttpSession` data for a user. Enable session sharing by including the `<wls:sharing-enabled>` element in the `weblogic-application.xml` file, enabling this feature for the enterprise application, and then enabling it in each participating web application in its individual `weblogic.xml` file using the `<wls:sharing-enabled>` element. This session-sharing feature gives you the isolation benefits of using multiple web applications while sharing `HttpSession` data between the applications, a potent combination worth considering for large applications.

> **Best Practice**
>
> Use separate directories in a single web application to share all context and session information automatically. Choose separate web applications to provide the maximum isolation between the sections of the overall application. Consider using the WebLogic Server session-sharing feature to share HttpSession data between web applications in the same enterprise application if this choice simplifies your architecture.

The bigrez.com application uses two separate web applications, user and admin, rather than a single web application with separate directory structures. We made this choice because the two sites are intended for completely different sets of users and have different security and auditing rules, and because there is no requirement to share HttpSession data across the two sites.

Internal Components

The WEB-INF directory contains all of the internal components, including configuration and supporting files for the application. Files located in WEB-INF are not accessible directly by the client browser.

As described in Chapter 1, any Java class files or resource files located in the WEB-INF/classes directory are loaded automatically by the web application classloader and made available to all components in the web application. In a similar manner, all Java archive (.jar) files placed in WEB-INF/lib are loaded automatically and made available to the web application. Note that class files located in /classes are loaded before archives in /lib, an important distinction if individual classes are defined in both locations.

> *Class files located in* WEB-INF/classes *are loaded before archives in* WEB-INF/lib. *If the same class is located in both places, the version in* WEB-INF/classes *will be used in the application.*

The remaining files in WEB-INF are descriptor files used by the container to deploy and configure the web application properly at runtime. These files are discussed in the following section.

Web Application Descriptor Files

WebLogic Server uses two primary descriptor files to deploy the web application properly: web.xml and weblogic.xml. See the WebLogic Server documentation at Link 5-1 and Link 5-2 for a complete listing of the elements and structure of web.xml and weblogic.xml, respectively. These link references can be found in the book's online Appendix at http://www.wrox.com/.

In this section we examine the descriptor files in bigrez.com to help you understand key elements and best practices related to these files.

Standard web.xml Descriptor File

The web.xml descriptor file is defined by the Java EE specification and is used by WebLogic Server to control basic configuration and deployment of the application. Table 5-1 outlines the high-level sections of the web.xml file and lists the key elements used in each section.

Table 5-1: Sections of the web.xml Descriptor File

web.xml Section	Purpose and Key Top-Level XML Elements
Deployment attributes	Defines graphics and descriptions used by deployment and management tools. `<icon>`, `<display-name>`, `<description>`, `<distributable>`
Context parameters	Defines parameters and values placed in a web application context, making them available in application components. `<context-param>`
Filter information and mapping	Provides deployment information, name, class, initialization parameters, and URL mappings for filters in the application. `<filter>`, `<filter-mapping>`
Application listeners	Defines listener classes used to intercept application events. `<listener>`
Servlet information and mapping	Provides deployment information, name, class, initialization parameters, security roles, and URL mappings for servlets in the application. `<servlet>`, `<servlet-mapping>`
Session configuration	Defines the timeout value for `HttpSession` information. `<session-config>`
MIME mapping	Defines MIME types for file extensions. `<mime-mapping>`
Welcome pages	Provides a list of default pages for unspecified page requests. `<welcome-file-list>`
Error pages	Defines the error page to be displayed in case of specific HTTP error code or Java exception. `<error-page>`
JSP tag libraries	Identifies and maps tag library definition (`.tld`) file to a specific URI name. `<taglib>`
Resource references	Defines an external resource available in the web application. `<resource-env-ref>`, `<resource-ref>`
Security information	Defines the security authorizations required to access sets of web pages, the technique used to authenticate a user, and security roles valid in the application. `<security-constraint>`, `<login-config>`, `<security-role>`
Environment entries	Defines a data value available in the environment. `<env-entry>`
EJB references	Defines EJB components available to web application components using environment lookups. `<ejb-ref>`, `<ejb-local-ref>`

The `bigrez.com` application consists of two separate web applications, `user` and `admin`. Each application has a `web.xml` descriptor file containing the elements required for proper operation of the web components in the application. Please download these files from `http://www.wrox.com/` and examine them before proceeding.

We'll now walk through the `web.xml` file for the administration site and highlight some sections worth noting in that file. We won't examine the `web.xml` file for the user site because it contains a subset of the elements in the administration version.

The first section in `web.xml` defines a filter used to log all activity on the administration site:

```xml
<!-- define auditing filter to log all admin activity -->
<filter>
  <filter-name>AuditFilter</filter-name>
  <filter-class>com.bigrez.web.AuditFilter</filter-class>
</filter>

<filter-mapping>
  <filter-name>AuditFilter</filter-name>
  <url-pattern>*.do</url-pattern>
</filter-mapping>
```

The `AuditFilter` is invoked for all requests matching the URL pattern `*.do`. The `doFilter()` method in the `AuditFilter` class simply logs the request and its parameters to the standard logging facility and invokes the next filter, if any, in the chain:

```java
public void doFilter(ServletRequest request,
                     ServletResponse response, FilterChain chain)
    throws IOException, ServletException
{
    HttpServletRequest req = (HttpServletRequest) request;
    StringBuffer auditentry = new StringBuffer();
    auditentry.append(req.getRemoteAddr() + " " + req.getRemoteUser() +
                      " " + req.getRequestURI());

    Enumeration<String> e = req.getParameterNames();
    if (e.hasMoreElements()) {
        while (e.hasMoreElements()) {
            String name = e.nextElement();
            auditentry.append(" " + name + "=" + req.getParameter(name));
        }
    }

    logger.log(Level.INFO, auditentry.toString());

    // continue processing any other filters
    chain.doFilter(request, response);
}
```

The next section of the administration `web.xml` file configures the Spring MVC `DispatcherServlet` used by the application and provides the required startup and mapping information:

```
<servlet>
  <servlet-name>adminapp</servlet-name>
  <servlet-class>
      org.springframework.web.servlet.DispatcherServlet
  </servlet-class>
  <load-on-startup>1</load-on-startup>
</servlet>

<servlet-mapping>
  <servlet-name>adminapp</servlet-name>
  <url-pattern>*.do</url-pattern>
</servlet-mapping>
```

Based on this snippet from the `web.xml` file, the `DispatcherServlet` will be loaded when the application starts up, will intercept and process all URLs matching the `*.do` pattern, and will locate and read the Spring MVC configuration file that defines all controllers, handlers, view resolvers, and other presentation-layer components in the web application. In our case, because the `DispatcherServlet` is being registered using a `<servlet-name>` of `adminapp`, the configuration file will be named `adminapp-servlet.xml`. We discussed the contents of this Spring MVC configuration file in detail in Chapter 4 and will not cover it here.

The `bigrez.com` user web application adds an additional component in its version of the `web.xml` file, `InitializationListener`, a servlet context event listener class used to preload selected information in to the web application context for use in drop-down lists in the display pages.

We've used a listener class as an initialization component rather than defining a server-level `StartupClass` object for a number of reasons:

❑ A server-level startup class must be defined in the system classpath for the class to be available during server startup. Application classes should generally not be loaded in the system classpath because this practice inhibits redeployment of the application and is the root cause of many `NoClassDefFoundError` exceptions.

❑ A class located in the system classpath can use only classes that are available in that classloader. This restriction often necessitates moving additional classes to the system classpath, which in turn uses other classes that must also be promoted to the system classpath, a vicious cycle that is difficult to break.

❑ Classes present in the system classpath cannot be deployed automatically by WebLogic Server to managed servers in the domain. The classes must be manually copied to each server in the domain and made available in the system classpath during server startup.

Servlet context event listener classes are a much better alternative for initialization components because they avoid the system classpath issues completely, have visibility to all classes defined or available in the web application, and are reinitialized whenever their hosting web application is redeployed. The web application containing the initialization listener class may also be configured to always deploy after any EJB components in the same overall application, thereby allowing the initialization servlet to access the EJB components reliably.

Best Practice

Use servlet context event listener classes as initialization components rather than defining server-level `StartupClass` classes. Listener-based initialization classes reload when the web application is redeployed and avoid the problems associated with classes located in the system classpath.

In the next section of `web.xml` we define the default welcome page, `propertylist.do`, and the error page to display when an HTTP 404 or 500 error code falls out of a controller or JSP invocation:

```
<welcome-file-list>
  <welcome-file>/propertylist.do</welcome-file>
</welcome-file-list>

<error-page>
  <error-code>404</error-code>
  <location>/WEB-INF/jsp/NotFoundPage.jsp</location>
</error-page>

<error-page>
  <error-code>500</error-code>
  <location>/WEB-INF/jsp/ErrorPage.jsp</location>
</error-page>
```

Note that although the welcome page definition can use the `*.do` syntax, the error pages must invoke the corresponding display JSP pages directly to avoid losing the error information in the HTTP request.

The administration site employs standard Java EE security to control access to pages in the application, and the next few sections of `web.xml` contain the elements necessary to enable and configure this security. These elements, `<security-constraint>`, `<login-config>`, and `<security-role>`, are explained in detail in Chapter 4 and are not discussed here. The login page, `Login.jsp`, is also listed and described in Chapter 4.

The final section of the administration site `web.xml` file contains `<ejb-local-ref>` elements required to map EJB reference names to actual session beans in the application, as shown here.

```
<ejb-local-ref>
  <ejb-ref-name>ejb/PropertyServices</ejb-ref-name>
  <local>com.bigrez.service.PropertyServices</local>
  <ejb-link>PropertyServicesImpl</ejb-link>
</ejb-local-ref>
```

```
<ejb-local-ref>
  <ejb-ref-name>ejb/ReservationServices</ejb-ref-name>
  <local>com.bigrez.service.ReservationServices</local>
  <ejb-link>ReservationServicesImpl</ejb-link>
</ejb-local-ref>

<ejb-local-ref>
  <ejb-ref-name>ejb/ProfileServices</ejb-ref-name>
  <local>com.bigrez.service.ProfileServices</local>
  <ejb-link>ProfileServicesImpl</ejb-link>
</ejb-local-ref>
```

With these mappings in place, the EJB session beans required by the Spring MVC controllers can be injected using simple pairs of elements in the `adminapp-servlet.xml` file as shown in this example.

```
<bean id="propertyServicesReference"
      class="org.springframework.jndi.JndiObjectFactoryBean">
    <property name="jndiName" value="java:/comp/env/ejb/PropertyServices"/>
</bean>

<bean id="propertyListController"
      class="com.bigrez.admin.web.PropertyListController">
    ...
    <property name="propertyServices" ref="propertyServicesReference"/>
</bean>
```

The `JndiObjectFactoryBean` utility class performs a lookup in the JNDI tree for the specified name and will find an instance of the correct `PropertyServicesImpl` session bean using that name due to the `<ejb-local-ref>` mapping element in the `web.xml` file. The `propertyServicesReference` bean will then be available for injection into controllers.

This multi-step configuration process can be a little confusing at first, but once you have the references in place, it is very easy to make services available to controllers using simple injection. This technique also avoids resorting to JNDI lookups or *locator* patterns within the controller code.

That's all there is to the administration site `web.xml` file.

weblogic.xml Descriptor File

The `weblogic.xml` descriptor file is a WebLogic Server–specific file used to control WebLogic Server–specific features and provide extensions to the basic configuration and deployment features in `web.xml`. Table 5-2 outlines the high-level sections of the `weblogic.xml` file and lists the key elements used in each section. See the online documentation at Link 5-2 for a complete listing.

The `weblogic.xml` descriptors for both sites in `bigrez.com` require only a handful of elements to configure their respective web applications properly. Listing 5-1 presents the administration site version of this file.

Table 5-2: Sections of the weblogic.xml Descriptor File

weblogic.xml Section	Purpose and Key Top-level XML Elements
Deployment attributes	Defines information used by deployment and management tools. `<description>`, `<weblogic-version>`
Security role/principal mapping	Assigns specific principals in the security realm to a role defined in the `web.xml` descriptor, supplementing any realm assignments. `<security-role-assignment>`, `<run-as-role-assignment>`
Resource references	Provides the physical location (JNDI name) of resources and EJB components declared in the `web.xml` file using `<resource-ref>`, `<ejb-ref>`, and `<ejb-local-ref>` elements. `<reference-descriptor>`
Message destination references	Provides the physical location (JNDI name) and initial context factory for message destinations declared in the web.xml file. `<message-destination-descriptor>`
Session configuration	Defines detailed `HttpSession` configuration parameters such as persistence technique, cookie name, and so on. `<session-descriptor>`
JSP configuration	Defines parameters for JSP compilation. `<jsp-descriptor>`
Container configuration	Defines miscellaneous parameters controlling container behavior for forwards and HTTP redirects. Also defines how frequently servlets and resources are checked and reloaded, if necessary. `<container-descriptor>`
Character set parameters	Defines character set mappings for incoming request data. `<charset-params>`
Directory mapping information	Defines alternate locations for files matching specific URL patterns. `<virtual-directory-mapping>`
URL matching class	Defines the custom class used to perform URL pattern matching. `<url-match-map>`
Security permission	Specifies a single security permission associated with the Java SE sandbox. `<security-permission>`
Context root information	Defines the context root for the web application. Used when the web application is not deployed in an enterprise application (`.ear`) file with an `application.xml` file defining this value. `<context-root>`

weblogic.xml Section	Purpose and Key Top-level XML Elements
Work manager configuration	Specifies a custom work manager for the entire web application. `<wl-dispatch-policy>`
Servlet configuration	Defines principals to be used during servlet initialization, execution, and destruction. May also specify execute queue used for a servlet. `<servlet-descriptor>`
Work manager definition	Defines a web application–scoped work manager along with its request class and any constraints. `<work-manager>`
Logging configuration	Defines logging settings for this web application independent of server settings. `<logging>`
Library reference configuration	Defines library modules required by the web application. `<library-ref>`
FastSwap configuration	Defines settings for the FastSwap class-reloading feature and enables it for this web application. `<fast-swap>`

Listing 5-1: Administration site weblogic.xml descriptor file.

```
<?xml version="1.0" encoding="UTF-8"?>
<wls:weblogic-web-app
  xmlns:wls="http://xmlns.oracle.com/weblogic/weblogic-web-app"
  xmlns:xsi="http://www.w3.org/2001/XMLSchema-instance"
  xsi:schemaLocation="http://xmlns.oracle.com/weblogic/weblogic-web-app
    http://www.oracle.com/technology/weblogic/weblogic-web-
  app/1.0/weblogic-web-app.xsd">

<wls:weblogic-version>10.3</wls:weblogic-version>

<wls:session-descriptor>
  <wls:persistent-store-type>
    REPLICATED_IF_CLUSTERED</wls:persistent-store-type>
</wls:session-descriptor>

<wls:jsp-descriptor>
  <wls:keepgenerated>true</wls:keepgenerated>
  <wls:page-check-seconds>1</wls:page-check-seconds>
  <wls:precompile>false</wls:precompile>
  <wls:precompile-continue>false</wls:precompile-continue>
  <wls:debug>true</wls:debug>
```

Continued

Listing 5-1: Administration site weblogic.xml descriptor file. *(continued)*

```
    </wls:jsp-descriptor>

    <wls:security-role-assignment>
      <wls:role-name>bigrezadmin</wls:role-name>
      <wls:principal-name>BigRezAdministrators</wls:principal-name>
    </wls:security-role-assignment>

</wls:weblogic-web-app>
```

We've defined only four sections in this file, and within these sections only a small number of elements.

The <weblogic-version> section simply identifies the target version of WebLogic Server for informational purposes only.

The <session-descriptor> section contains a single element defining the store type to be REPLICATED_IF_CLUSTERED. If this application is deployed in a single-server environment, the store type will default to MEMORY. If the application is deployed in a clustered environment, the user HttpSession data will be replicated across the servers in the cluster using the standard in-memory-based replication.

The <jsp-descriptor> section contains some parameters defining both non-default values and values we must revisit and modify when making a production release. The <page-check-seconds> parameter, for example, should be set to — or allowed to default to — the value –1 in production to disable all page checking and recompilation.

The <security-role-assignment> section maps the roles defined in the web.xml file to principals, either groups or users, in the WebLogic Server security realm defined in the domain. This topic is discussed in more detail in Chapters 4 and 11.

The following list identifies a number of the sections we did not require in the weblogic.xml file and explains our rationale for excluding them to give you an idea about when they might be required in your development efforts:

Context Root Information   We will be deploying the user and admin web applications in an enterprise application (.ear) file. The context root will be defined in the application.xml file.

Resource References   EJB components can be injected into our web application components based solely on the ejb-local-ref entries in the web.xml file. No matching ejb-reference-description elements are required here.

Directory Mapping Information   Images are placed in the user and admin web applications rather than mapped to a separate directory using this section.

Dispatch Policy and Work Manager Information   Our web application will use the default work manager in the environment rather than targeting a special version.

Logging Configuration   We have no need to supplement logging performed across the entire WebLogic Server runtime instance with special logging for our web application.

FastSwap Information   We are not making use of the new FastSwap capability in our example application. This topic is discussed in Chapter 14 when we describe development environment best practices.

Most web applications require very little configuration information in the weblogic.xml file because the default values for weblogic.xml are often sufficient.

Precompiling JSP Components

At some point in the packaging process you have a decision to make: Should JSP pages in the application be processed and compiled by the server when the page is first accessed by a user, or should all pages be precompiled before deploying the application? Precompiling improves site performance and ensures that all JSP pages in the site compile before deployment takes place. Without precompiling the JSP pages, syntax errors in scriptlet code and custom-tag elements will not be caught until a user accesses the page.

Best Practice

All production and test deployments should include precompiled JSP pages. Development deployments intended for use on the developer's workstation may use precompiled pages or on-the-fly compilation.

Precompiling of JSP pages is one of the many tasks accomplished by the WebLogic Server application compiler, weblogic.appc. This utility is capable of compiling application components and building enterprise application (.ear) files, EJB archive (.jar) files, web application (.war) files, and exploded versions of these files, in addition to performing JSP precompilation.

Because weblogic.appc is such a key part of the overall build process, including the incorporation of EJB components, we discuss the use of weblogic.appc in the bigrez.com build process in Chapter 8, after we've covered the rest of the application components.

You can use weblogic.appc to validate the descriptors and precompile the JSP files in a web application by invoking the utility and passing it the root directory for the application:

```
java -classpath ... weblogic.appc src/web-user
```

Integrating weblogic.appc in your build.xml file is accomplished using an Ant task, wlappc. The build.xml file for the Chapter 2 example application includes a jspc-webapps target for precompiling the JSP files in the three web applications contained in that example using the wlappc task:

```
<taskdef name="wlappc" classname="weblogic.ant.taskdefs.j2ee.Appc"
  classpathref="dev.classpath"/>

<target name="jspc-webapps">
  <!-- Pre-compile webapp1 JSP pages to src/web1/WEB-INF/classes -->
```

```
    <wlappc source="${srcweb1}"
            classpathref="dev.classpath" verbose="true">
    </wlappc>
    <!-- Pre-compile webapp2 JSP pages to src/web2/WEB-INF/classes -->
    <wlappc source="${srcweb2}"
            classpathref="dev.classpath" verbose="true">
    </wlappc>
    <!-- Pre-compile webapp3 JSP pages to src/web3/WEB-INF/classes -->
    <wlappc source="${srcweb3}"
            classpathref="dev.classpath" verbose="true">
    </wlappc>
</target>
```

This target will scan the web application directories for all files ending in .jsp and perform the same servlet generation and compilation steps performed by the application server at runtime. The resulting Java source files and classes are placed in the /WEB-INF/classes directory and can be deployed to this same location in the exploded or archived web application. The weblogic.appc compiler requires the same descriptor files, library archive files, and Java class files as the runtime container requires. The WEB-INF directory must therefore contain the appropriate descriptors, and the classpath for weblogic.appc or wlappc must include all required directories and archive files.

Note that the generated code in the precompiled class is very picky about the timestamp of the associated JSP file. If the JSP file in the deployed web application is older or newer than the file used to create the precompiled class, the precompiled class will be ignored at runtime, and the normal on-the-fly JSP compilation will occur. To avoid this problem, be careful to preserve the file timestamp when copying JSP files from the area used to create the precompiled classes to an exploded application structure or staging area.

If you want to avoid all possibility of recompiling JSP pages within the running server, consider replacing the default servlet that handles JSP pages, JSPServlet, with the JSPClassServlet handler servlet. JSPClassServlet will find and execute precompiled JSP classes located in the WEB-INF/classes directory of your web application, but will not check the underlying JSP pages for changes or timestamp differences, nor will it ever compile or recompile a page. In fact, you can eliminate the JSP pages completely in the deployed application — all you need are the precompiled class files!

To replace the normal JSPServlet handler with the JSPClassServlet, register the new servlet in your web.xml file and map it to all JSP pages using entries similar to the following code snippet:

```
<servlet>
  <servlet-name>JSPClassServlet</servlet-name>
  <servlet-class>weblogic.servlet.JSPClassServlet</servlet-class>
</servlet>

<servlet-mapping>
  <servlet-name>JSPClassServlet</servlet-name>
  <url-pattern>*.jsp</url-pattern>
</servlet-mapping>
```

This registration and mapping of `JSPClassServlet` will override the default mapping of JSP pages to `JSPServlet` and eliminate the compiling of JSP pages in your running server.

Best Practice

Replace the normal `JSPServlet` with the `JSPClassServlet` when deploying to test and production environments. `JSPClassServlet` eliminates the potential for page recompilation and removes the need for a Java compiler in the running environment.

There is one additional best practice to discuss related to precompiling JSP pages. It is a rather mundane recommendation, but it can be costly if you do not follow it. Any partial pages or snippets of scriplet code included in the actual JSP pages using `<%@ include file="..." %>` should have a file extension other than `.jsp`. The `.jspf` file extension is recommended in the JSP specification, but any extension will work.

Why is using a different extension important? The `weblogic.appc` compiler typically scans the web application directory and compiles all files that match the desired file name (`*.jsp`) and will probably not be able to compile any partial pages it encounters. They were never intended to be standalone pages yielding their own servlet classes — they are simply snippets of HTML or JSP code included in a master JSP page. Many developers wait to begin precompiling their JSP pages until late in the development cycle and learn this lesson the hard way.

Note that this practice applies only to the static `<%@ include file="snippet.jspf" %>` directive and not to the dynamic `<jsp:include file="header.jsp"/>` action. The dynamic action assumes the target page is a standalone JSP page capable of being converted to a Java servlet, so the target page should be included in the precompilation process and should retain the `.jsp` file extension.

Best Practice

Use the `.jspf` file extension for all partial pages and JSP snippets included in JSP pages using the static `<%@ include file="..." %>` directive to avoid precompilation problems.

Creating an Exploded Web Application

As discussed earlier in this chapter, WebLogic Server web applications contain components, descriptor files, classes, libraries, and other files organized in a directory structure defined by the Java EE specification with the addition of the WebLogic Server–specific `weblogic.xml` file. To create an exploded web application you must simply assemble your source files and compiled class files into a valid directory structure similar to Figure 5-2 or 5-3.

In `bigrez.com`, we are deploying the `user` and `admin` web applications in archived (`.war`) format in an archived enterprise application (`.ear`) file as part of the development build process. We'll defer the discussion of the `bigrez.com .ear` format and build process to Chapter 8 and instead examine the construction and deployment of the Chapter 2 example web application as an exploded web application at this time.

Recall that the Chapter 2 example application consisted of three separate web applications demonstrating the implementation of a simple application for editing and viewing information about people. The three versions of the application demonstrated the use of a JSP-centric architecture, a Struts-based servlet-centric architecture, and a Spring MVC–based servlet-centric architecture. All three versions had simple domain objects and simulated services to avoid complicating the example with EJB components or database access code.

The working directory for the Chapter 2 example application consisted of the source components and directories shown in Figure 5-4. Source code files for the domain and simulated service classes were located in a set of individual source directories under the `src/java` root directory, and the three web applications themselves were located under the `src` directory.

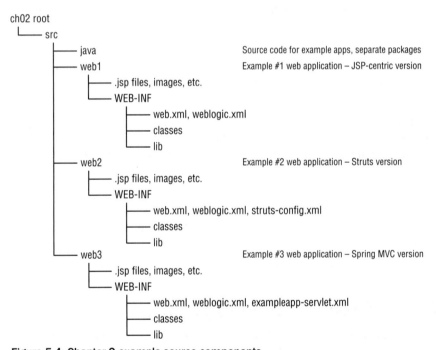

Figure 5-4: Chapter 2 example source components.

To construct and deploy these as exploded web applications, we need to compile the three sets of domain and service classes, place them in the `WEB-INF/classes` directory structures below the corresponding web root directories, and deploy the web applications to the WebLogic Server instance running on our machine. We'll now examine the `build.xml` tasks required for each of these steps. For reference, a complete listing of the Chapter 2 example `build.xml` file is provided in Listing 5-2.

140

Listing 5-2: Chapter 2 example program build.xml file.

```xml
<?xml version="1.0" encoding="UTF-8"?>
<project basedir="." default="deploy" name="Chapter 2 Example">
  <property file="${basedir}/build.properties"/>

  <!-- set global properties for this build -->
  <property name="src" value="${basedir}/src"/>
  <property name="lib" value="${basedir}/lib"/>
  <property name="srcjava1" value="${src}/java/webapp1"/>
  <property name="srcjava2" value="${src}/java/webapp2"/>
  <property name="srcjava3" value="${src}/java/webapp3"/>
  <property name="srcweb1" value="${src}/web1"/>
  <property name="srcweb2" value="${src}/web2"/>
  <property name="srcweb3" value="${src}/web3"/>
  <property name="domain.dir" value="${DOMAIN_HOME}/${DOMAIN}"/>
  <property name="autodeploy" value="${domain.dir}/autodeploy"/>
  <property name="deploy.dir" value="${autodeploy}"/>
  <property name="webapp1.dir" value="${deploy.dir}/webapp1"/>
  <property name="webapp2.dir" value="${deploy.dir}/webapp2"/>
  <property name="webapp3.dir" value="${deploy.dir}/webapp3"/>

  <!-- Set up the development classpath -->
  <path id="dev.classpath">
    <pathelement location="${JAVA_HOME}/lib/tools.jar"/>
    <pathelement location="${WEBLOGIC_HOME}/server/lib/weblogic.jar"/>
    <pathelement location="${WEBLOGIC_HOME}/server/lib/api.jar"/>
    <pathelement location="${lib}/spring.jar"/>
    <pathelement location="${lib}/spring-webmvc.jar"/>
    <pathelement location="${lib}/struts.jar"/>
    <pathelement location="${lib}/log4j.jar"/>
  </path>

  <target name="clean">
    <delete includeEmptyDirs="true">
      <fileset dir="${srcweb1}/WEB-INF/classes"/>
      <fileset dir="${srcweb2}/WEB-INF/classes"/>
      <fileset dir="${srcweb3}/WEB-INF/classes"/>
    </delete>
  </target>

  <target name="makeapp">
    <!-- Make classes directories -->
    <mkdir dir="${srcweb1}/WEB-INF/classes"/>
    <mkdir dir="${srcweb2}/WEB-INF/classes"/>
    <mkdir dir="${srcweb3}/WEB-INF/classes"/>
  </target>

  <target name="compile">
    <javac deprecation="true" classpathref="dev.classpath"
      destdir="${srcweb1}/WEB-INF/classes"
      srcdir="${srcjava1}">
      <include name="**/*.java"/>
```

Continued

Listing 5-2: Chapter 2 example program build.xml file. *(continued)*

```xml
      </javac>
      <javac deprecation="true" classpathref="dev.classpath"
        destdir="${srcweb2}/WEB-INF/classes"
        srcdir="${srcjava2}">
        <include name="**/*.java"/>
      </javac>
      <javac deprecation="true" classpathref="dev.classpath"
        destdir="${srcweb3}/WEB-INF/classes"
        srcdir="${srcjava3}">
        <include name="**/*.java"/>
      </javac>
    </target>

    <taskdef name="wlappc"
             classname="weblogic.ant.taskdefs.j2ee.Appc"
             classpathref="dev.classpath"/>

    <target name="jspc-webapps">
      <!-- Pre-compile webapp1 JSP pages -->
      <wlappc source="${srcweb1}"
              classpathref="dev.classpath" verbose="true">
      </wlappc>
      <!-- Pre-compile webapp2 JSP pages -->
      <wlappc source="${srcweb2}"
              classpathref="dev.classpath" verbose="true">
      </wlappc>
      <!-- Pre-compile webapp3 JSP pages -->
      <wlappc source="${srcweb3}"
              classpathref="dev.classpath" verbose="true">
      </wlappc>
    </target>

    <target name="deploy" depends="makeapp, compile, jspc-webapps">
      <!-- Copy all of the web application files to the webapp# -->
      <copy todir="${webapp1.dir}">
        <fileset dir="${srcweb1}" includes="**/*.*"/>
      </copy>
      <copy todir="${webapp2.dir}">
        <fileset dir="${srcweb2}" includes="**/*.*" excludes="**/*.properties"/>
      </copy>
      <copy todir="${webapp3.dir}">
        <fileset dir="${srcweb3}" includes="**/*.*" excludes="**/*.properties"/>
      </copy>
      <!-- Copy the web application classes to the webapp#/WEB-INF/classes -->
      <copy todir="${webapp1.dir}/WEB-INF/classes">
        <fileset dir="${srcweb1}/WEB-INF/classes" includes="*.class" />
      </copy>
      <copy todir="${webapp2.dir}/WEB-INF/classes">
        <fileset dir="${srcweb2}/WEB-INF/classes" includes="*.class" />
        <fileset dir="${srcweb2}/WEB-INF" includes="*.properties" />
      </copy>
```

```
    <copy todir="${webapp3.dir}/WEB-INF/classes">
      <fileset dir="${srcweb3}/WEB-INF/classes" includes="*.class" />
      <fileset dir="${srcweb3}/WEB-INF" includes="*.properties" />
    </copy>
  </target>

  <target name="redeploy">
    <touch file="${deploy.dir}/webapp1/WEB-INF/REDEPLOY"/>
    <touch file="${deploy.dir}/webapp2/WEB-INF/REDEPLOY"/>
    <touch file="${deploy.dir}/webapp3/WEB-INF/REDEPLOY"/>
  </target>

</project>
```

As indicated in the listing, the default task for the build script is `deploy`, a task that invokes `makeapp`, `compile`, and `jspc-webapps` before performing the actual deployment to WebLogic Server.

The `makeapp` task simply ensures that the necessary `WEB-INF/classes` directories exist in each of the web applications.

Compilation of the domain and service classes is accomplished by a `compile` task that invokes the `javac` built-in task and directs the output to the corresponding web application `classes` directory as shown in this snippet from the `build.xml` listing.

```
  <target name="compile">
    <javac deprecation="true" classpathref="dev.classpath"
      destdir="${srcweb1}/WEB-INF/classes" srcdir="${srcjava1}">
      <include name="**/*.java"/>
    </javac>
    ...
  </target>
```

The three `srcweb` and `srcjava` properties are defined earlier in the `build.xml` file, as is `dev.classpath`. Note that libraries required for compilation are stored in the root-level `lib` directory, whereas libraries required for deployment with the web applications are placed in each `WEB-INF/lib` directory.

After compiling the source files, the `deploy` task invokes the `jspc-webapps` task to precompile the JSP pages and place the resulting class files in the `WEB-INF/classes` directory within each web application.

Once everything is compiled and ready, the exploded web applications are complete. The final step is the deployment of all three applications to the WebLogic Server domain running on the local workstation. For simplicity this final deployment task was accomplished using the `autodeploy` directory in the domain root directory, one of three deployment techniques discussed later in this chapter. The deploy task basically copies the contents of the three web applications, with all JSP files, libraries, and class files contained therein, to the `autodeploy` directory. The resulting `webapp1`, `webapp2`, and `webapp3` subdirectories in the `autodeploy` directory are automatically read, validated, and deployed by WebLogic Server to the administration server on the local machine. That's all there is to it!

Once deployed, the exploded versions of the web applications located in autodeploy can be updated with source code changes using the same deploy task with a few caveats and notes:

❑   Changes to class files will be copied to a running application by the deploy task but may not be sensed by the server and reflected in the application unless the web application is redeployed. A separate redeploy task is provided in the build.xml file to *touch* the WEB-INF/REDEPLOY file in each application and signal WebLogic Server to reload all classes and redeploy the application. We talk about this more later in this chapter along with techniques to reload modified classes automatically without redeploying the entire application.

❑   Changes to JSP pages will be copied by the deploy task to the running version of the application in the autodeploy directory and will be reflected in the application on the next request for the associated page. This is a very efficient way to perform quick, iterative development of JSP pages, and is one advantage of using exploded applications for local deployments.

One final note: Be careful not to confuse the deployment of an exploded application via copying to the autodeploy directory, as was done here, with the deployment of the same application using the wldeploy Ant task or weblogic.Deployer utility. In the first case a copy of the application is promoted into the running environment; in the second, the environment is running the application directly from the source location. Later in this chapter, we talk more about these two techniques and discuss the pros and cons of each.

Now that we've shown you how to create an exploded web application, along with one way to deploy it, we will briefly cover the creation of a web application archive file before diving in to the deployment options in more depth.

Creating a Web Application Archive File

A web application archive file, or .war file, contains all of the web application components, descriptors, and supporting classes in a single file. The internal structure of the .war file is identical to the equivalent exploded web application deployment directory.

Creating a .war file is easy enough in theory; you simply execute the appropriate jar command to include all of the desired web application components and supporting files in the archive. In practice, you need a mechanism to assemble the proper components and files in a staging area in preparation for the standard jar utility, or you need a better jar technique that allows you to piece together components and supporting classes from various locations in a single archive. Either solution works, but we prefer the latter.

The recommended archive technique uses the war task in Ant to build the archive from a variety of files. The war task, like the basic jar Ant task, allows the definition of multiple fileset embedded elements, each with flexible and powerful controls for including and excluding files from the archive. The war task adds a number of special elements that automatically place the specified files in their proper locations in the web application directory structure.

Creating a .war file for each of the web applications in the Chapter 2 example program would require simple build.xml tasks similar to the following.

```
<target name="war3" depends="makeapp, compile, jspc-webapps">
  <war webxml="${srcweb3}/WEB-INF/web.xml"
       warfile="${src}/webapp3.war">
    <zipfileset dir="${srcweb3}" excludes="**/*.properties"/>
    <zipfileset dir="${srcweb3}/WEB-INF"
       includes="*.properties" prefix="WEB-INF/classes"/>
  </war>
</target>
```

In the `bigrez.com` build process, the `.war` file for each web application is created using tasks such as this in the `build.xml` file.

```
<target name="do.package" depends="common.do.package">
  <war webxml="webContent/WEB-INF/web.xml"
       warfile="${output.dir}/bigrez-web-admin.war"
       manifest="webContent/META-INF/MANIFEST.MF">
    <zipfileset dir="webContent"/>
    <zipfileset dir="${output.dir}" includes="**/*.jar" prefix="WEB-INF/lib"/>
  </war>
</target>
```

That's all you need to create the web application archive from the web components in the `WebContent` area of each application and the supporting libraries in the `WEB-INF/lib` area. The simplicity of this step is a direct result of the directory structure and practices we've adopted in the development environment.

Deploying Web Applications

Now that we've reviewed the structure of a web application, the contents of its descriptor files, and the techniques available for creating an exploded web application and archive file, it is time to examine the options for deploying web applications to WebLogic Server. This part of the chapter concentrates on the techniques from the developer's point of view — how to deploy the application in a single server or workstation environment for the purposes of development and unit testing. Chapter 12 describes techniques and best practices in a multi-server, managed, clustered environment.

There are three basic ways to deploy a web application, or any other Java EE application, in a WebLogic Server environment:

❑   Automatic deployment

❑   WebLogic deployer utility or Ant task

❑   WebLogic Console deployment

We examine each option in the following sections, followed by a brief discussion of the steps required to configure security information for proper `admin` site operation.

Automatic Deployment

Automatic deployment is the simplest technique available for deploying an application to an administration server or a combined administration/managed server. If automatic deployment is enabled during the startup process, the administration server will constantly scan the autodeploy directory for new applications as well as modifications to existing applications. When a new application is placed in the autodeploy directory, the administration server immediately attempts to load and deploy the application. When an existing, deployed application is modified, the server immediately attempts to undeploy the old version and deploy the new version of the application.

This is exactly the sort of behavior a developer prefers during development and unit testing. Changes can be made to the application and redeployed rapidly to a running server without requiring a complete restart of the server, a big advantage in an iterative development and testing process.

Two steps are required to deploy an application using automatic deployment.

First, automatic deployment must be enabled for the administration server. In the startWebLogic command or shell script used to start the server, make sure that the PRODUCTION_MODE variable is either set to false or not set, which is the default. This variable is used by the script to control the value of the weblogic.ProductionModeEnabled property in the java command line used to start the server. A value of true means production mode, and false means development mode, which will enable auto-deployment, among other things.

Next, copy the web application archive file or exploded web application directory structure to the autodeploy directory in the domain. Although applications can be located almost anywhere in the directory structure in general, automatic deployment works only for applications placed in the autodeploy directory. As indicated in Figure 5-5, an archive file should be located directly in the autodeploy root directory, not in a subdirectory, and an exploded application should include a top-level directory.

The archive root name, webapp1, and top-level directory name, webapp2, will be used by the server as the initial name and root context for the deployed applications. You can specify a different root context using the <context-root> element in the weblogic.xml descriptor file in the web application. When the new file or directory structure appears in the autodeploy directory the administration server will immediately sense the new application and attempt to deploy it. Assuming the archive or directory is well structured and contains the required descriptor files, the new application will be deployed and ready for use. Mission accomplished!

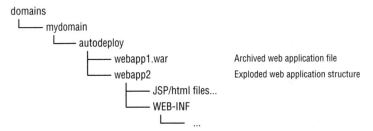

Figure 5-5: Web applications deployed in the autodeploy directory.

The Chapter 2 example application uses this automatic deployment technique, as described in the previous section of this chapter. The deploy task in the build.xml file places the exploded application files in the autodeploy directory in preparation for automatic deployment. No additional steps or tasks are required to deploy the application or modify the contents of the deployed application, although for reasons we describe in a moment, you may need to signal the server when a modification is made to the exploded application to force a full redeployment.

Applications deployed using archive files can be redeployed automatically by simply overwriting the existing version of the archive file in the autodeploy directory. This rule holds for all archive types, including web application .war files, EJB .jar files, and enterprise application .ear files. The server senses the timestamp change for the file and automatically undeploys the old application and deploys the new version of the application.

Applications deployed using exploded formats present a problem for the server: Which file timestamp should be monitored to sense a change in the application and force a full redeployment? There could be hundreds or thousands of files in the exploded directory structure, making it impossible to monitor all of them for changes. WebLogic Server chose to introduce a special file, REDEPLOY, for this very purpose. The contents of this file do not matter; only the timestamp matters. If you touch the file or otherwise modify its timestamp, the server redeploys the application. The REDEPLOY file is located in the META-INF directory in enterprise applications and in the WEB-INF directory in web applications.

The Chapter 2 example is a set of three web applications, so there are REDEPLOY files located in the WEB-INF directories used for this purpose. A redeploy task in the build.xml file touches all three of the REDEPLOY files to cause a redeployment of the exploded applications:

```
<target name="redeploy">
  <touch file="${deploy.dir}/webapp1/WEB-INF/REDEPLOY"/>
  <touch file="${deploy.dir}/webapp2/WEB-INF/REDEPLOY"/>
  <touch file="${deploy.dir}/webapp3/WEB-INF/REDEPLOY"/>
</target>
```

Recognize that the new versions of the application files in the exploded directory structure must already be present before requesting the redeployment, or a race condition could occur.

Given the added complexity described here, why would you choose to deploy to a workstation or single server environment using an exploded web application? Simply put, the ability to modify JSP pages and web application classes without redeploying the entire web application, or the enclosing enterprise application, provides a big benefit in an iterative development process. There can be a significant overhead associated with redeployment of archived applications due to the all-or-nothing redeployment this technique mandates. For example, if the web application is part of an archived enterprise application, all of the EJB components in the application will be undeployed and redeployed, initialization classes will be invoked again, and you may even have to re-login and start your testing process from scratch if HttpSession information is lost. This is clearly a lot of effort to make and view a simple JSP change.

With an exploded deployment, you simply edit the JSP pages in the working area and invoke a copying function, like the deploy task in the Chapter 2 example's build script, to copy the modified pages to the exploded web application. As you continue browsing the site, new pages will be recompiled by the server when they are accessed by the browser because the timestamp on the JSP file no longer matches the timestamp in the generated class file. WebLogic Server keeps track of files included using the <%@ include file="..." %> directive as well, so changes to .jspf files will also cause the correct JSP pages to be recompiled as they are accessed. Remember that this timestamp checking is controlled by the <page-check-seconds> parameter set in weblogic.xml. The default value is one second when running in development mode, so the behavior described here will apply unless you disable it using that parameter or switch to production mode, where the default value is disabled.

In a similar fashion, classes in the WEB-INF/classes directory of your exploded web application can be overwritten with new versions and WebLogic Server will reload the new classes on the fly. This functionality is controlled by the <servlet-reload-check-secs> element in the weblogic.xml file, an element whose name is somewhat misleading since all web application classes are candidates for reloading — not just servlets, as the name (and online documentation) suggests. In development mode the default value of `<servlet-reload-check-secs>` is 1, meaning that classes in `WEB-INF/classes` will be checked every second for changes and possible reloading. Production environments have a value of –1 by default, meaning that classes will never be checked or reloaded by this mechanism. `HttpSession` data for users is retained when web application classes are reloaded as long as the modified classes do not invalidate previously stored data in the session.

The bottom line is that exploded application deployment allows changes to JSP pages and web application classes without requiring a full redeployment of the entire application. This all adds up to a clear advantage to using an exploded application structure during development.

Best Practice

Use exploded application structures for deployment on developer workstations to allow fine-grained updates to JSP pages and web application classes without requiring a complete redeployment of the enclosing application. Automatic deployment is sufficient for these installations if you have a good technique for touching the REDEPLOY file to cause full redeployments on demand.

WebLogic Deployer Utility and Ant Task

The default WebLogic Server installation includes a utility, `weblogic.Deployer`, providing a command-line technique for deploying and managing applications. The `weblogic.Deployer` utility mirrors the deployment functions available through the WebLogic Console, including the deployment of new applications, redeployment of modified applications, undeploying existing applications, and modifying the targeted servers for an application. The `weblogic.Deployer` utility also provides an upload capability to move applications from a staging directory to the proper directory in the administration server in preparation for deployment.

The `weblogic.Deployer` utility is invoked using the following basic syntax:

```
java weblogic.Deployer [options] [action] [files]
```

As before, we'll concentrate here on the actions and options necessary to deploy and redeploy an application to a standalone server instance in a simple development environment. Chapter 12 discusses deployment of applications in production environments including the mechanisms available in WebLogic Server for redeploying applications without impacting active user sessions.

The following steps are required to deploy a web application manually using the `weblogic.Deployer` utility:

1. Start the WebLogic Server instance using the `startWebLogic` script or other mechanism.

2. Build the web application as either an exploded directory structure or archive (`.war`) file using the normal Ant build process. Normally this build script will place the application in some `build` or `output` directory within your source code directory structure.

3. If desired, copy the application files or archive file from this build directory to a staging directory on your machine. Copying the application before deploying it will insulate the running version of the application from any builds you make in your source area until you are ready to deploy them.

4. Deploy the application using the deploy action in the weblogic.Deployer utility.

The first two steps are self-explanatory. The Deployer utility only works if there is a running WebLogic Server administration server with which to communicate, and the build itself must be complete before deployment can occur. As the optional third step notes, it is often useful to separate the running version of the application from the version in the build directory of your source code structure by performing a distinct *copy* step to create another copy of the application in a staging directory. This step is not required for deployment, because the Deployer utility can easily deploy the application directly from the build directory or other directory within the source area, but it may prove helpful to you. If you decide to copy the application to a staging directory, we suggest a directory such as myapps in the domain directory structure to avoid confusion.

The webapp1 application may now be deployed from the web archive file webapp1.war using the command:

```
java weblogic.Deployer -adminurl t3://localhost:7001 -name webapp1
   -source /domains/mydomain/myapps/webapp1.war -targets myserver -deploy
```

You can deploy exploded applications such as webapp2 in this manner by referring to the root directory of the exploded web application in the source option:

```
java weblogic.Deployer -adminurl t3://localhost:7001 -name webapp2
   -source /domains/mydomain/myapps/webapp2 -targets myserver -deploy
```

Redeploying a modified application is accomplished using the redeploy action and specifying the name of the application, as shown here:

```
java weblogic.Deployer -adminurl t3://localhost:7001 -name webapp2 -redeploy
```

The example command lines shown so far require you to enter the administrator's username and password to complete the operation. You can specify these values on the command line with the user and password options:

```
java weblogic.Deployer -user weblogic -password weblogic1 ...
```

Other useful options include debug and verbose, providing details during the deployment operations to assist in troubleshooting problems.

Using the weblogic.Deployer utility to deploy web applications replaces the automatic deployment performed by WebLogic Server when running in development mode and changes how the server reacts to updated versions of the application files. In general, you must use the redeploy action before a running copy of the application will reflect application updates. WebLogic Server will not automatically redeploy the application based on a timestamp change in the REDEPLOY file or archive file itself as it does when deployment is accomplished using the autodeploy directory. Changes to JSP pages in exploded web applications will still cause automatic recompilation of the page when a user accesses it.

Because the automatic deployment feature affects only applications placed in the `autodeploy` directory, you may combine automatic and manual deployment in the same domain. Leave `PRODUCTION_MODE` set to `false` in the start script, place applications using automatic deployment in the `autodeploy` directory, and place applications using manual deployment in an alternate directory such as `myapps`. Use the `weblogic.Deployer` utility to deploy the applications in `myapps` manually, and allow WebLogic Server to deploy the applications in `autodeploy` automatically.

WebLogic Server includes an Ant task, `wldeploy`, providing the same basic functions as the `weblogic.Deployer` utility. Deploying the exploded `webapp2` web application from the `/myapps` directory requires an Ant target similar to the following:

```
<target name="deploy2">
  <wldeploy verbose="true" user="weblogic" password="weblogic1"
            adminurl="t3://localhost:7001" action="deploy"
            source="${domain.dir}/myapps/webapp2" />
</target>
```

Best Practice

Favor the new `wldeploy` Ant task over the command-line `weblogic.Deployer` utility when manually deploying or redeploying applications. It provides the same functionality and is much easier to integrate in the overall build and deployment process.

See the Oracle online documentation for more information on both the `weblogic.Deployer` utility (at Link 5-3) and the related `wldeploy` Ant task (at Link 5-4).

WebLogic Console Deployment

You can use the WebLogic Console to deploy and manage web applications in a combined administration/managed server instance or across complex clusters of managed servers. In this chapter, we're interested in the simple case of a combined or standalone server instance suitable for development and unit testing on a workstation. Deploying a web application to a standalone server instance involves the following steps:

1. Start the WebLogic Server instance in either production mode or development mode.
2. Optionally, copy the exploded archive file or web application directory structure to a suitable staging directory such as `<domainroot>/myapps`.
3. Deploy the application using the WebLogic Console.

Once the server is running and the applications to be deployed are in place, open the WebLogic Console and click the `Deployments` link in the left-hand navigation pane. Click the `Install` button and navigate to the location of your exploded or archived application. Your application archive files or exploded directory structures should be listed, as shown in Figure 5-6.

Select one of the displayed web applications using the radio buttons. The WebLogic Console displays a set of forms allowing you to choose the type of deployment, the name to use for the deployment, and the security and staging models, and gives you the option to perform additional configuration steps before deployment. The application will automatically be targeted to the combined administration and managed server, if applicable, requiring little or no manual configuration.

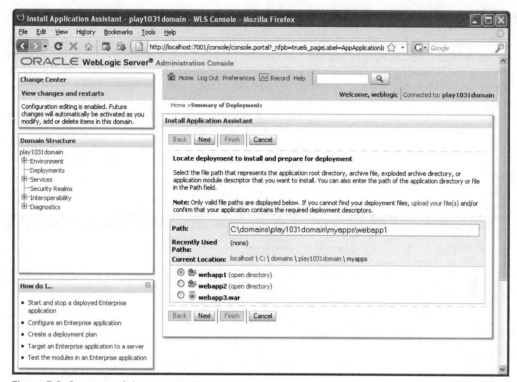

Figure 5-6: Contents of the myapps directory.

Once you click `Finish` on the final form in the process, your application will be loaded and deployed to the server, and you'll end up on the `Overview` tab for the deployment. The new application has now been deployed to the server and is ready for use. Note that in production mode you'll need to start the application before using it.

Once the application is deployed using the WebLogic Console, redeployment and modification behavior follow the same rules outlined in the previous section. Modified JSP pages in an exploded application may be recompiled by the server as the pages are encountered, depending on the value of `<page-check-seconds>`, but all other application changes will require a redeployment using either the WebLogic Console or a utility such as `weblogic.Deployer` or `wldeploy`.

Redeploying an application using the WebLogic Console does not require that you delete and reinstall the application. Simply open the list of deployed applications by clicking the Deployments link in the left-hand navigation pane, check the box next to the application, and click the Update button below the list. This has the same effect as the `redeploy` action in the `Deployer` utility.

Best Practice

Manual application deployment using the WebLogic Console requires a number of steps to perform and is not required for developer workstation deployments. Use automatic deployment or one of the deployment utilities outlined in the previous section in these environments.

Creating Required Users and Groups for `BigRez.com`

The `bigrez.com` application includes two separate web applications, `user` and `admin`. As we discussed in Chapter 4, the `admin` web application uses standard Java EE security features to control access to the property maintenance pages. The required users and groups must be created in the default security realm in WebLogic Server to complete the deployment of the `bigrez.com` web applications.

After starting the domain, open the WebLogic Console and click the `Security Realms` link in the navigation pane on the left. The right side will display a list of realms, including a default realm called `myrealm`. Click the `myrealm` link and navigate to the `Users and Groups` tab, and then open the `Groups` tab within this folder. You should see a list on the right side containing the default groups in the security realm, as shown in Figure 5-7.

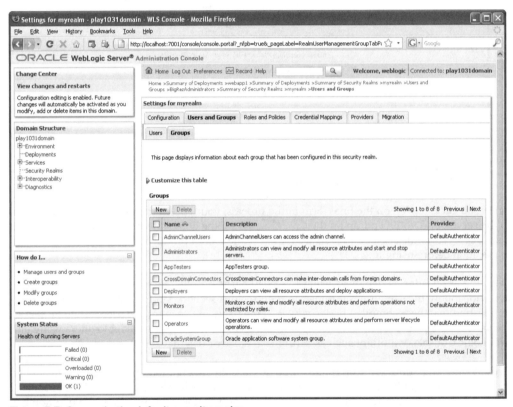

Figure 5-7: Groups in the default security realm.

Click the `New` button and fill out the form, as shown in Figure 5-8, to create the new `BigRezAdministrators` group required by the `admin` web application. Click `OK` to create the group.

Next, click the `Users` tab within the `Users and Groups` folder on the right side of the screen. The list on the right will most likely show only the `weblogic` user and any other users you may have created for

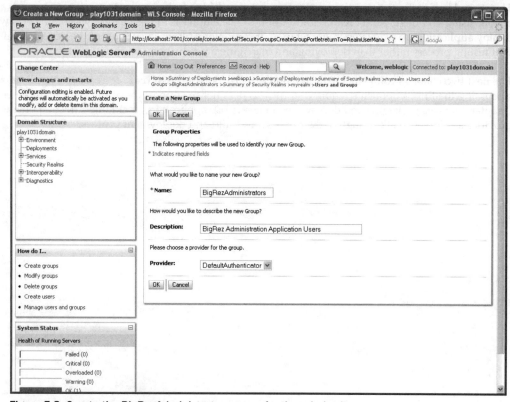

Figure 5-8: Create the BigRezAdministrators group for the admin site.

testing purposes. Click the New button and create a BIGREZADMIN user, assigning it a valid password and clicking the OK button. Once the user is created, click the newly created user in the list of users, navigate to the Groups tab in the resulting folder, and make the user a member of the BigRezAdministrators group.

The required user and group are now available in the security realm. Property administrators may log in to the admin site using the BIGREZADMIN username and password and maintain property information for all properties.

Chapter Review

This chapter discussed the steps required to package and deploy a web application to the WebLogic Server environment.

The first half of the chapter reviewed the structure of a web application and the contents of the web application descriptor files web.xml and weblogic.xml. Ant-based techniques for assembling web applications, precompiling JSP components, and creating exploded and archived web applications were then presented. Some portions of the bigrez.com build process were also presented to illustrate best practices in these areas.

The second half of the chapter discussed techniques available for deploying and redeploying web applications using WebLogic Server features and utilities. The emphasis in this chapter was on the best way to deploy applications to a developer workstation or standalone server in support of the development and unit testing process rather than deploying and managing a production server environment.

The next two chapters complete the design and construction of the bigrez.com example application by discussing the EJB components required in the business tier to support the application requirements. Chapter 8 revisits packaging and deployment of enterprise applications, including EJB components, and provides a complete walkthrough of the bigrez.com build and deployment process.

6

Building Enterprise JavaBeans in WebLogic Server

This chapter examines best practices related to the implementation of Enterprise JavaBeans (EJB) technology in the WebLogic Server product. Chapters 7 and 8 walk through the development and deployment of an example EJB application to highlight related best practices.

This chapter is not intended as a primer, introduction, or reference for EJB technology. Our primary emphasis is the EJB container in WebLogic Server and its unique features and capabilities. If you're unfamiliar with the basics of EJB, we suggest you study *Mastering Enterprise JavaBeans 3.0*, by Rima Patel Sriganesh, Gerald Brose, and Micah Silverman (Wiley, 2006), a complete treatment of EJB technology.

We begin by briefly reviewing some EJB terms and key concepts to support the discussions that follow. The second half of the chapter discusses EJB features that are specific to WebLogic Server.

EJB Technology Overview

The Enterprise JavaBeans (EJB) specification defines a server-side component technology designed to support the construction of distributed enterprise-class applications. We'll break apart the definition of EJB and examine key concepts.

EJB is a specification It is not a set of classes, code, or reference implementation components. Vendors such as Oracle are expected to build application servers that implement EJB technology according to the specification.

EJB is a component technology Component technologies emphasize the encapsulation of business logic in *components* deployed in and managed by a *container*. The EJB specification carefully defines the interactions between components and their containers to ensure portability and consistency between EJB container vendors.

EJB supports distributed applications   EJB components may be distributed across multiple servers or processes with a limited impact on component developers, a concept known as *location transparency*.

EJB is designed for enterprise-class applications   The EJB specification is very concerned with transactions, security, concurrency, and memory management because these areas are important for large, mission-critical applications.

To remain consistent with the target audience for this book, intermediate- to advanced-level developers and architects, we will not discuss every detail of developing EJB components. We assume that you have already built some simple EJB components and are familiar with the key steps and concepts involved, and that you would rather learn about more advanced topics and best practices for developing EJB applications.

This book and its associated example code use EJB 3.0 throughout. WebLogic Server has supported EJB 3.0 since version 10.0 and continues to support the old EJB 2.x APIs as required by the EJB 3.0 specification. If you are only familiar with applications built using earlier versions of the specification, we hope this book will persuade you of EJB 3.0's many advantages and guide you in building your own EJB 3.0 applications.

The next chapter discusses the development and packaging of the `bigrez.com` example EJB application and covers some of the tools and best practices related to the development process. Chapter 14 is dedicated to development best practices, so there is no lack of information on this topic in this book.

EJB 3.0

The EJB 3.0 specification made major changes to the EJB specification to address the most significant and much criticized shortcomings of the programming API of previous versions. These changes have a large impact on the way Java EE applications are developed.

Although the core concepts and runtime behavior for session beans and message-driven beans remain largely unchanged, EJB 3.0 introduces significant changes to their programming model.

Annotation-based Programming   Java 5 annotations are used to declare that a Java class is an EJB, and to control how the container applies its services to manage the EJB (in particular, declarative security and transaction management), largely doing away with the need for deployment descriptors. Deployment descriptors may still be used, but they have been relegated to a deployment time override mechanism, rather than a mandatory part of EJB development.

Prior to EJB 3.0, it was common to use technologies such as XDoclet or WebLogic Server's EJBGen to generate EJB 2.x deployment descriptors and reduce the development effort required to manage multiple Java files and deployment descriptors for each EJB. EJB 3.0 annotation-based programming is a direct evolution of these approaches and supersedes them.

EJBs are Plain Old Java Objects (POJOs)   EJBs no longer need to implement specific lifecycle callbacks. Instead, they use Java annotations to declare only the events in which they are interested. EJB business interfaces are not required to extend `javax.ejb.EJBObject` or `javax.ejb.EJBLocalObject`, and remote business methods need not throw `java.rmi.RemoteException`. Home interfaces are no longer required.

Dependency Injection   References to other EJBs and resources such as data sources can be automatically resolved and set by the container, freeing your EJB code from explicitly having to look up such resources from JNDI. Not only does this simplify your code, it also allows the EJB container to perform more deployment time validation. References to external components are declared with annotations, and the EJB container is responsible for resolving these references at deployment time. An EJB can be used as a plain Java class outside of the container, allowing it easily to be unit tested.

In contrast to the evolutionary changes made to session beans and message-driven beans, the support for persistent, database-backed beans has been radically overhauled. EJB 2.x entity beans are supported for backward compatibility only. In EJB 3.0, entities are lightweight components managed by the Java Persistence API (JPA) rather than full Enterprise Java Beans.

The Spring Framework

The need for the radical overhaul of the EJB specification was largely driven by competition from a single alternative product — *The Spring Framework* (`http://www.springsource.org/`). The Spring Framework provides an alternative to EJB, but embraces other Java EE technologies including the Java Persistence API. Spring championed dependency injection and the benefits of using POJOs for enterprise Java applications, and revolutionized the way Java EE applications are developed.

The Spring Framework can be used with Java EE 5, and in conjunction with, or as an alternative to, EJB 3.0. WebLogic Server's EJB 3.0 container is itself implemented using Spring, based on the Pitchfork project, which was co-developed by SpringSource and WebLogic Server engineers. WebLogic Server has specific support for Spring applications, including a console extension, integration of WebLogic Server transaction features, and support for the Spring Acegi security model.

We like the Spring Framework. However, EJB 3.0 is sufficient to develop full enterprise applications in a clean, understandable style and we will not use the Spring Framework in this book.

EJB Component Types

The EJB 3.0 specification defines the following types of EJB components:

❑   Stateless session bean (SLSB)

❑   Stateful session bean (SFSB)

❑   Message-driven bean (MDB)

Each of these component types fulfills a different design requirement for enterprise-class distributed systems. The following sections review each of these types and look at a few simple examples to complete our discussion of EJB key concepts.

The EJB 3.0 specification requires the container to support EJB 2.x entity beans for backward compatibility. We are focusing exclusively on the new programming model provided by EJB 3.0, so will not consider EJB 2.x entity beans. We cover JPA entities later in this chapter.

Stateless Session Beans

Stateless session bean (SLSB) components are designed to service requests using a classic stateless request/response style. Setting aside complexities related to bean lifecycle and pooling, an SLSB is not unlike a shared static class used as a service (like the `PersonService` class in Chapter 2). The SLSB has a set of methods, exposed through local or remote business interfaces, which can be called by clients to request particular services. Data is passed to the SLSB methods using method parameters, and results are returned, typically, through the return type of the method. This is classic request/response design.

Generally speaking, SLSB components are suitable for encapsulating business processes rather than business data. SLSB components often have names like `AccountingService` or `ContractManager`, signifying their role as controller code or services related to certain business domains. Method names normally make clear the particular service exposed by the interface.

```
@EJB
AccountingService aService;  // Container will inject an SLSB instance.
...
float tax = aService.calculateTax(income, expenses);
System.out.printf("The IRS is only taking $%f this year!", tax);
```

Clients are given a particular instance of the SLSB for use during the single request/response cycle, and there is no guarantee that subsequent requests from the same client will be handled by the same instance of the SLSB. In general, SLSB components should not have client-associated instance variables, although it is possible to use instance variables to cache connections to shared resources or shared read-only data if desired. Just recognize that each invocation of the SLSB is independent from past and future invocations from the same client, and you can't make assumptions about the contents of the instance variables.

Here's an implementation of the `AccountingService` SLSB.

```
// AccountingService.java
public interface AccountingService
{
    float calculateTax(float income, float expenses);
}

// AccountingServiceImpl.java
import javax.ejb.Stateless;

@Stateless
public class AccountingServiceImpl implements AccountingService
{
    public float calculateTax(float income, float expenses)
    {
        return (income - expenses) * 0.25;
    }
}
```

This is radically simpler than an EJB 2.x session bean. No `ejb.xml` or `weblogic-ejb.xml` deployment descriptors are required — deployment information such as the JNDI name to use can be specified using annotations. Home interfaces are not required. The bean does not have to implement `javax.ejb.SessionBean`, nor does its business interface have to extend `javax.ejb.EJBObject`. If we chose to ignore the annotation, the bean is a plain old Java object (POJO) that is easy to use and test outside of the Java EE container.

SLSB components have distinct advantages over simple static classes:

❑   EJB developers do not have to write thread-safe code. The EJB container prevents more than one thread at a time from using a given bean instance.

❑   EJBs can declare references to resources they require, including other EJBs. The EJB container is responsible for resolving these references when the EJB is deployed. This is an important feature when developing a set of interdependent components that otherwise have their own independent development lifecycles. Before such dependency injection became popular, EJB applications would manage dependencies using the Service Locator pattern, which results in verbose configuration files, and brittle, environment-specific lookup code directly within the EJBs.

❑   EJBs optionally can provide remote services over Java RMI. This support is declared for an EJB 3.0 session bean business interface using a simple annotation, without it having to implement `java.rmi.Remote`, or its remote methods needing to declare that they throw `RemoteException`. Client applications benefit from location transparency. So long as clients do not rely on side effects resulting from running within the same JVM as a locally deployed EJB, they can access local and remote EJBs in the same way.

❑   Transaction control and security constraints are implemented by the EJB container and declared using standard annotations or deployment descriptor elements. Transaction and security contexts are automatically propagated to SLSB methods without requiring extra method parameters, a common approach in a static class.

❑   Annotations have sensible defaults that reflect common usage. Although our `AccountingServiceImpl` example specifies neither the `@TransactionManagement` nor the `@TransactionAttribute` annotations, the container will ensure that a transaction is active before calling the `calculateTax()` implementation, and if it had to start a transaction, that transaction is committed before control is returned to the client.

SLSB components are often used to implement the session façade design pattern. The business process encapsulated by an SLSB may include complex calculations and interactions with additional EJB components, including both SLSB and JPA entities. The SLSB façade provides a simpler interface to this complex process. The SLSB also provides a convenient mechanism for ensuring transactional integrity. The container is often configured to require or start a transaction whenever an SLSB method is invoked, thereby ensuring that all operations in the method are part of the same transaction.

We'll make use of SLSBs and the session façade pattern in the example application in Chapter 7. A set of SLSBs provides a simplified set of services to the web application layer and the web services interface. The SLSBs contain business logic that transforms the more complex entity model into results that are more directly of use to the web application views. All interaction with the database is performed through this session façade, with the SLSBs managing the transaction boundaries.

Stateful Session Beans

Stateful session bean (SFSB) components combine the request/response mechanism of stateless session beans with the storage of state information between method invocations. Clients are given a dedicated instance of the SFSB to use for multiple method invocations, and subsequent requests from the same client are guaranteed to be handled by the same instance of the SFSB bean. Thus, the client has a conversation with a particular SFSB instance. These beans should have instance variables that store the intermediate state of the process being modeled by the SFSB. If there are no instance variables, there's no reason to use a stateful session bean.

SFSB components are normally used to implement multi-step business processes that require retention of state information from step to step. They fall somewhere between SLSB and JPA entities in terms of function and naming, and they often have names like `Reservation` or `ReservationProcess`. Method names on SFSB components also tend to fall somewhere between SLSB and entities, and they may have set methods for updating the state information in the bean as well as methods that perform business processing.

```
// EJB is bound into local environment using a class level annotation
@EJB(name="ejb/sfsb", beanInterface=Reservation.class)
...
Reservation reservation =
    (Reservation) initialContext.lookup("java:comp/env/ejb/sfsb");
...
reservation.setProperty(...);
reservation.setDates(...);
reservation.setGuestInformation(...);
...
String confirmnum = reservation.performBooking();
System.out.println("Your confirmation number is: " + confirmnum);
```

In this example code, we've used an SFSB to maintain information about the customer's selections during the reservation process before invoking the final `performBooking()` method to make the reservation. The set method invocations are shown as if they occurred in the same block of code, but this is not required. As long as the client holds on to and uses the same SFSB reference, the invocations will be processed by the same instance of the SFSB.

The preceding example binds the EJB to the client's local environment, and then performs a JNDI lookup in the `java:comp/env` namespace to obtain a reference to an SFSB instance. The EJB container creates a new instance of the SFSB for every JNDI lookup. Suppose instead we had injected the EJB reference directly into a field of the client class.

```
@EJB
Reservation reservation;
```

Now the client container will create and inject a `Reservation` instance into the annotated field for each new instance of the client class. If the client is itself an SFSB, this may well be what you want. On the other hand, if the client is a stateless component such as a servlet, you will want to create and manage different `Reservation` instances for different user sessions. The `bigrez.com` example application, introduced in Chapters 3 and 4, uses a value object placed in the `HttpSession` to store intermediate results and passes this value object to a method on a stateless session bean to perform the final booking. Essentially, we store the intermediate data in the HTTP session rather than just storing a reference to a client-specific SFSB. Both techniques are viable ways to manage conversational state on behalf of a user. When creating a web application, we favor the `HttpSession` approach for the simple reason that SFSB components increase the complexity of the overall system and may introduce unnecessary transaction and security processing mandated by the EJB specification. SFSBs are more appropriate for maintaining a client's server-side state for remote clients — that is, clients not in the same JVM.

WebLogic Server provides replication of SFSB data across a cluster, a topic discussed later, so both techniques have similar failover capabilities. When you try to use an SFSB from a web application client where both the `HttpSession` and the SFSB are using in-memory replication, the failover scenarios can get a little bit complex. We recommend using `HttpSession` objects to hold client session state for web applications, and an SFSB only for applications where the client is not a web application.

Best Practice

Avoid using stateful session beans for web application client data more readily stored in the `HttpSession`. Although both SFSB and `HttpSession` data can be configured to be replicated for failover in WebLogic Server, complexity considerations favor the use of `HttpSession` storage when possible. Use an SFSB for situations where the client is not a web application.

If you decide to use stateful session beans, you should consider the following additional points:

❏ SFSB components normally disallow concurrent access, although WebLogic Server does include a flag to cause concurrent invocations to block rather than throw an exception. In a web application multiple requests from the same user may be processed simultaneously, a condition that might require simultaneous access to the client-associated SFSB.

❏ If an SFSB throws a `RuntimeException` the container destroys the instance of the bean and all associated state information is lost, as required by the EJB specification.

❏ SFSB components are not appropriate for long-term storage of state. Replication of SFSB data can allow the state to survive the failure or restart of a single server instance, but provides no strong transactional guarantees. Use JPA entities to store data that must survive the client restarting the browser session or returning to the application after an extended period of time.

❏ If an SFSB uses bean-managed transaction demarcation, it is possible that a business method that started a transaction does not commit or rollback the transaction. In this case, the container is required to retain the association between the SFSB instance and the transaction across multiple method calls. This may be appropriate for some unusual scenarios, but in general it will lead to an application that does not scale well and is difficult to manage.

Although there may be specific applications for which the SFSB component is well suited, it is generally best to use `HttpSession` objects for short-lived, client-specific data and JPA entities or other database-backed storage for long-lived data.

Message-Driven Beans

Message-driven bean (MDB) components were added in the EJB 2.0 specification to address a significant hole in the integration of EJB and Java Message Service (JMS) technology. EJB components are capable of acting as JMS producers, creating and sending messages to JMS destinations, but prior to EJB 2.0 there was no way for an EJB component to act as an asynchronous JMS consumer. There was nothing preventing a stateless session bean from invoking `receive()` and waiting for a message, of course, but this synchronous operation has the potential to block the thread indefinitely.

MDBs behave like SLSBs but with a system-defined, asynchronous interface. The EJB 2.1 specification expanded the role of MDBs beyond JMS, to supporting other messaging systems. MDBs can now receive messages from JCA resource adapters; however, they are most commonly used to receive and process JMS messages.

Because their interfaces are fixed, MDBs are very simple to write. Here's an example JMS MDB.

```
@MessageDriven( ...)
public class MyMDB implements javax.jms.MessageListener
{
    public void onMessage(Message msg)
    {
        System.out.println("Received a message");
    }
}
```

Despite the simplicity of implementation, the container provides many useful services to an MDB. JMS sessions are automatically pooled and managed. Transactions can be container-managed, in which case, a JTA transaction is automatically started when a message is passed to the MDB; if the transaction rolls back, the message is not removed from the JMS destination.

WebLogic Server provides additional MDB features including transaction batching; automatic enlistment of foreign JMS servers in transactions; temporary suspension on repetitive exceptions; and automatic re-establishment of JMS connections.

We talk more about JMS and MDBs in Chapter 10.

Interceptors

EJB 3.0 allows a session or message-driven bean to be associated with one or more interceptor classes. Interceptor classes provide a simple way of introducing *cross-cutting* functionality to every EJB method, and to deploy it against a number of EJBs. For example, an interceptor class could be used to audit all business method calls to an EJB. An interceptor class can also be configured to receive the PostConstruct, PreDestroy, PostActivate, or PrePassivate lifecycle callbacks.

Let's look at a simple interceptor that logs the entry and exit of all business method calls.

```
import java.util.logging.Level;
import java.util.logging.Logger;
import javax.interceptor.AroundInvoke;
import javax.interceptor.InvocationContext;
import weblogic.logging.LoggingHelper;

public class LoggingInterceptor
{
    private Logger logger = LoggingHelper.getServerLogger();

    @AroundInvoke
    public Object audit(InvocationContext ic) throws Exception
    {
        String context = ic.getMethod().toGenericString();
        try {
            logger.log(Level.INFO, "entering " + context);
            Object result = ic.proceed();
```

```
            logger.log(Level.INFO, "exiting " + context);
            return result;
        }
        catch (Exception e) {
            logger.log(Level.INFO, "exception in " + context, e);
            throw e;
        }
    }
}
```

The `@AroundInvoke` annotation identifies the `audit()` method as an interceptor method. The container will call this interceptor method when a client invokes any business method. The interceptor method has control over whether to pass the invocation onto the bean instance. It can do such things as modifying the parameters using the `InvocationContext.setParameters()` method, handle exceptions thrown from bean instance, or modify the return value. Our interceptor simply logs the entry and exit events to the WebLogic Server log, invoking the business method with the `ic.proceed()` call in between.

The interceptor class is associated with an EJB as using the `@javax.interceptor.Interceptors` annotation on methods to which it should be applied, or on the EJB class if the interceptor should be applied to all methods. Multiple interceptors can be applied to the same method. Alternatively, interceptors can be specified in the `ejb-jar.xml` deployment descriptor.

Interceptors are occasionally useful, but are not a full aspect-oriented programming (AOP) mechanism. Their primary drawbacks are that they can only be applied to EJB methods; that they cannot be configured separately outside of the EJB deployment; and the specification of the methods to which they should apply is simplistic compared to the power of the Spring Framework or AspectJ pointcut expressions.

Best Practice

If you find yourself regularly using interceptors, consider whether you should be using a more sophisticated AOP tool such as AspectJ or the Spring Framework.

The Java Persistence API

The Java Persistence API is a standard interface that provides Object Relational Mapping (ORM) services to Java applications. These services allow an application to interact with a relational database by making changes to instances of application-specific Java classes. The JPA engine performs the appropriate mapping between the Java classes and the relational database tables.

JPA History

Many different ORM technologies influenced the evolution of the JPA standard. Perhaps the least influential was the entity beans facility of the EJB 2.x specification. EJB 2.x provides container-managed persistence (CMP) services, which allow a straightforward mapping between relational tables and managed beans. Entity beans were the most criticized feature of EJB 2.x. Complaints included:

❏   The simplicity of the mapping. The specification allowed for mapping a single table to a single entity bean, and did not support inheritance between entity bean classes. While some implementations provided for more sophisticated mapping strategies, they were not portable and still did not support inheritance.

❏ The weight of the API. Each entity bean required home and business interfaces, plus deployment descriptors. The mapping between the bean and the database tables had to be specified fully in the deployment descriptor. Tools such as EJBGen were created to reduce the development overhead, but they were a band-aid rather than a satisfactory solution.

❏ The runtime cost. Because entity beans were full EJBs, they had to support declarative security and transaction management and remote invocation. Many argued that these services were not appropriate in an ORM tool.

❏ Ease of testing. Entity beans could only be tested within an EJB container.

Despite these limitations, EJB 2.x entity beans have been applied successfully in large Java EE deployments. Nevertheless, Java EE architects increasingly turned to sophisticated and mature ORM products from more focused providers. These included Oracle's TopLink, JBoss's Hibernate, and Solarmetric's Kodo. Solarmetric was purchased by BEA, and Kodo is now included in Oracle WebLogic Server.

The persistence layer is a significant part of most enterprise applications, and there was a pressing need for a common standard. Some products implemented the Java Data Objects (JDO) standard, Kodo being the most well-known commercial implementation.

JPA has successfully combined the best features of EJB CMP, JDO, and proprietary products, and today TopLink, Hibernate, Kodo, and others all implement JPA.

With the acquisition of BEA, Oracle found itself with two market-leading JPA implementations — Kodo and TopLink. Kodo has been the JPA provider in WebLogic Server since version 10.0, but TopLink is Oracle's strategic product, and will replace Kodo in a future version of WebLogic Server. We show in Chapter 7 how using JPA allows us to easily change `bigrez.com` from Kodo to TopLink.

Best Practice

Favor JPA over proprietary persistence APIs. This allows flexibility in porting your application between different ORM providers.

When BEA bought Solarmetric in 2005, it donated the bulk of the Kodo source code to the Apache Software Foundation to create the open source OpenJPA project. Kodo is now based upon an OpenJPA foundation, but provides additional features and performance enhancements.

Similarly, TopLink has spawned the open source Eclipse Persistence Platform (EclipseLink) project, an Eclipse Foundation project led by Oracle. EclipseLink is the reference implementation for the JPA 2.0 specification. In contrast to Kodo and OpenJPA, functionality and performance of EclipseLink has not been restricted with respect to the commercial TopLink product. The additional features in TopLink are limited to those necessary for integration with WebLogic Server and Oracle SOA Suite.

OpenJPA and Kodo

OpenJPA has many features over and above those required by the JPA specification. These include:

❑ Custom fetch groups, for grouping associated fields to improve performance.

❑ A detachment API, which allows more control over when entity instances are *detached* from being managed by the container.

❑ Large result sets and large collection fields, backed by database cursors.

❑ Unidirectional OneToMany relationships with a foreign key rather than a join table.

❑ Fewer restrictions on entity classes. For example, they can be final.

WebLogic Server 10.3 includes the Enterprise Edition of Kodo. Kodo Enterprise Edition is built on OpenJPA, but adds many features not found in the open source version, including:

❑ Batching of JDBC statements for performance.

❑ Optimization of eager loading of related entities.

❑ Lock groups.

❑ Data and query caching.

❑ Profiler and management console tools.

❑ SQL queries.

❑ Managed transactions, and XA support.

❑ Custom class mappings.

❑ Remote entity managers.

We consider only the most commonly used features in this book; please refer to the Kodo documentation for more details.

Most of the additional Kodo features enhance runtime performance. It is important to realize that all ORM tools are not created equal. The lengthy histories of Kodo and TopLink have provided the experience that sets them apart as market leaders.

JPA Concepts

JPA entities are simple Java classes with Java 5 annotations to indicate how they should be mapped to the database.

Client applications manage entity instances using an EntityManager. The facilities that the EntityManager provides correspond to those provided by the home interface of an EJB 2.x CMP entity bean; namely the ability to create, find, and destroy entity instances, reflecting the changes in the underlying relational database.

Each `EntityManager` manages an independent set of entities known as a *persistence context*. When used in a container such as that provided by WebLogic Server, the `EntityManager` can be injected directly into an EJB or servlet using the `@PersistenceContext` annotation. A separate persistence context is managed for each JTA transaction, and injection allows the container automatically to provide the application with an appropriate `EntityManager`. The changes made to the set of entities are persisted back to the database when the JTA transaction commits.

EJB 2.x CMP entity beans also associate a set of changes with the current transaction, and use the transaction scope to minimize the number of required reads and writes to the database. This optimization is particularly important when dealing with complex transactions that affect many entities, and may well read and write the same entity many times. In JPA, the notion of a persistence context makes this management explicit.

`EntityManager`s can also be used outside of a container, for example, in a standalone Java application. This is an important difference to EJB 2.x entity beans. We have used this facility in the `bigrez.com` unit tests to test the entity classes from JUnit test classes. When used outside a container, an `EntityManagerFactory` is used to create an `EntityManager`, and transactions can be managed through the `EntityTransaction` interface.

A JPA Sample

A complete discussion of JPA is beyond the scope of this book. In this section, we develop a simple example that illustrates the features of JPA and provides a basis for many of the complex topics and WebLogic Server–specific discussion that follows. The `bigrez.com` example program uses JPA entities for all business objects and relationships and provides a more realistic example.

Here is an example of a JPA entity representing a Person.

```
import javax.persistence.Entity;
import javax.persistence.Id;

@Entity
public class Person
{
    @Id
    private long id;
    private String salutation;
    private String firstName;
    private String lastName;

    public Person() { }

    public Person(long id, String salutation, String firstName, String lastName)
    {
        this.id = id;
        setSalutation(salutation);
        setFirstName(firstName);
        setLastName(lastName);
    }

    public long getId() { return id; }
```

```
    public String getSalutation() { return salutation; }
    public void setSalutation(String salutation) { this.salutation = salutation; }

    public String getFirstName() { return firstName; }
    public void setFirstName(String firstName) { this.firstName = firstName; }

    public String getLastName() { return lastName; }
    public void setLastName(String lastName) { this.lastName = lastName; }
}
```

Person is a simple Java class with a number of fields that follows the JavaBeans conventions for get and set methods. You have to look hard to spot the annotations — there are only two. The first is the @javax.persistence.Entity class annotation; the second is the @javax.persistence.Id annotation on the id field. Despite this, there is a wealth of mapping metadata derived from JPA defaults and the conventions followed by the class.

❑ The class is mapped to a table named PERSON.

❑ The fields salutation, firstName, and lastName are mapped to the columns SALUTATION, FIRSTNAME, and LASTNAME. These columns can contain NULL, do not have a UNIQUE constraint, and are 255-character VARCHAR fields.

❑ The id field is the primary key for the class, and is mapped to the number column ID.

These conventions go a long way to make programming JPA entities very similar to programming plain Java classes. By default, all primitive and String fields of a JPA entity are expected to map to a database column. If you don't want a particular field to be persisted, you should indicate this by making it transient, or with the @javax.persistence.Transient annotation. If you want to map a field to a column with a different name, or to control other aspects of the column mapping such as the column type, uniqueness, or null constraints, you can use the @javax.persistence.Basic and @javax.persistence.Column annotations to provide the supporting metadata.

Annotations can also be used on a property method pair, such as getLastName() and setLastName(), rather than the field that they use. This can be useful when migrating EJB 2.x entity beans to JPA. It also allows the JPA container to benefit from validation and conversion logic in the methods. On the other hand, because the specification does not define how often, when, or in what order the container will call the property methods, adding code to the property methods can have unexpected side effects. Also, the application code must always use the property methods, and not access the field directly. The JPA specification does not support mixing field and property annotations — you should use one of these access methods within an entity class hierarchy. We find field level annotations simpler, and rarely use property method annotations.

Despite all of this cleverness, a small deployment descriptor is required. This is called persistence.xml and is usually packaged in the META-INF directory of the jar file containing the persistent classes. Here's an example of a persistence.xml file for an application to be deployed in a Java EE environment.

```
<?xml version="1.0" encoding="UTF-8"?>
<persistence version="1.0" ... namespace declarations ...>
  <persistence-unit name="ExamplePU">
    <jta-data-source>datasource.jta.example</jta-data-source>
    <non-jta-data-source>datasource.nonjta.example</non-jta-data-source>
  </persistence-unit>
</persistence>
```

The descriptor defines a *persistence unit*, which is the set of classes and mapping metadata used by a particular set of entity managers. The terminology can be a little confusing at first. An *entity manager factory* creates *entity managers* (the runtime Java instance) for a particular *persistence unit* (the configuration). Each entity manager manages a *persistence context* (a set of entity instances).

It is important to understand the lifecycle of JPA entities with respect to the persistence context. A newly created instance of an entity is not associated with any persistence context. If it is used in a call to the entity manager `persist()` method, it obtains a persistent identity and becomes *managed* by the persistence context. Each persistence context has at most one instance of an entity with a given identity. Entity instances found by calling a query method are also managed. The fields of managed entities are populated automatically from the database, and changes to the fields are sent to the database when the persistence context is flushed, such as when the JTA transaction commits. When the transaction commits, an entity becomes *detached* from the persistence context, and changes to the entity are no longer synchronized to the database. The entity manager `remove()` method is used to schedule a managed entity for deletion from the database when the transaction commits.

Each persistence unit has a name. Our example is called `ExamplePU`. This allows application code to work with multiple persistence units, which may be necessary if the application uses more than one database. The persistence unit to use can be specified using the `unitName` element of the `@PersistenceContext` annotation. Applications that have a single persistence unit don't need to set `unitName`.

Our example persistence unit declares that it uses two JDBC data sources by supplying their JNDI names. The first data source should support global JTA transactions. This is the primary data source used to persist changes made by the application. The second data source is not transactionally aware, and is used by the JPA container whenever it needs to access the database independently of the current JTA transaction.

We've written a simple stateless session bean that provides a method to create a `Person`.

```
import javax.ejb.Stateless;
import javax.persistence.EntityManager;
import javax.persistence.PersistenceContext;

@Stateless
public class PersonSLSBImpl implements PersonSLSB
{
    @PersistenceContext
    private EntityManager entityManager;

    public Person createPerson(int id, String salutation,
                                String firstName, String lastName)
    {
        Person person = new Person(id, salutation, firstName, lastName);
        entityManager.persist(person);
        return person;
    }
}
```

The implementation is straightforward, and shows how easy it is to use JPA entities from a session bean. When called, this will execute the following prepared statement to create a new row in the `Person` database table.

```
INSERT INTO Person (id, firstName, lastName, salutation) VALUES (?, ?, ?, ?)
```

The `EntityManager` is injected into the SLSB using the `@PersistenceContext` annotation. To ensure the correct persistence context is obtained, JPA code deployed to a container should use the `@PersistenceContext` annotation or look up the `EntityManager` in JNDI. Both of these methods result in a container-managed persistence context. There is no need to pass `EntityManager` instances to other EJBs; simply inject the `EntityManager` into each EJB and the container will ensure the persistence context is propagated with the JTA transaction. The alternative is to use application-managed persistence contexts that are created from an `EntityManagerFactory`. Application-managed persistence contexts are more troublesome to manage: they must be created and closed at the right points, and associated with the JTA transaction if necessary.

> ### Best Practice
> Use container-managed persistence contexts whenever possible. It is rarely necessary to use application-managed persistence contexts in code deployed to a Java EE server.

Persistent units deployed to a Java EE 5 application server will use JTA transactions, unless overridden using the `transaction-type` element. If the `EntityManager` for a JTA persistence unit is called without a current JTA transaction, a `TransactionRequiredException` will be thrown. The SLSB conveniently takes care of this for us. It will run the `createPerson()` method in a container-managed transaction (due the defaults for the `@TransactionManagement` and `@TransactionAttribute` annotations).

Special care is required when using JPA directly in web applications. Many threads can call the same servlet at once, so if you must use an `EntityManager` directly from servlet code, use a JNDI lookup in your service method. Using annotations will cause the container to inject a single `EntityManager` into the servlet when it is created, and this will not be thread-safe. It is usually better to wrap the JPA code in an SLSB, and rely on the SLSB for transaction management and thread safety.

When using JPA with a stateful session bean, you will probably want to add `type=PersistenceContextType.EXTENDED` to the `@PersistenceContext` annotation. This special extended persistence context is only supported for SFSBs, and causes a single persistence context to be used for every call to a particular instance of the SFSB. If the SFSB uses container-managed transactions, the persistence context will be used for multiple transactions and will not have to be refreshed from the database on every request. The application can control synchronization with the database by calling the entity manager's `refresh()` or `flush()` methods.

> ### Best Practice
> Use container-managed data sources and JTA transaction management when using JPA with a Java EE application server. The EJB API makes this natural. It ensures transactional integration with other global transaction–aware resources managed by the container, such as JMS destinations.
>
> Favor container-managed transactions using session beans over bean-managed transactions. This avoids repetitive, boilerplate code.

`Person` has an `id` field of type `long` that is the primary key for the entity, and is used as the foreign key to maintain relationships to other entities. There are two schools of thought on primary key columns for object mappings. One holds that the primary key should be some real-world attribute of the entity — sometimes known as a *business key*; this is the more purist, database-centric approach. The other school holds that primary keys should be opaque and system-allocated. One advantage of the second approach is that it is does not require a complex transaction should the business key representing an entity ever change. Suppose, for example, we chose to use a person's name as the primary key. If a person changes his or her name, all other tables that refer to the row in the PERSON table will need to be updated. Another is that it does not place artificial constraints on the data — two individuals can have the same name. A third advantage is that we can use a common type for the primary key for all entity classes, and abstract out common functionality for allocating a primary key and finding an entity by a primary key to a common base class.

Generated Values

Having decided that the system should allocate primary keys, let's modify Person so that the id field is generated, and remove the need to pass it to the constructor.

```
@Id
@GeneratedValue
private long id;
...
public Person(String salutation, String firstName, String lastName)
{
    setSalutation(salutation);
    setFirstName(firstName);
    setLastName(lastName);
}
...
```

The @javax.persistence.GeneratedValue annotation specifies that the JPA provider should pick an appropriate generation strategy for the database being used. When used with an Oracle database, OpenJPA uses a table called OPENJPA_SEQUENCE_TABLE. The strategy can be changed with the strategy annotation element. We use element this in the bigrez.com implementation to specify that a database sequence should be used. With the table and database sequence strategies (GenerationType.TABLE and GenerationType.SEQUENCE), you can use the generator element to refer to a separately-defined generator. These generators are defined with the SequenceGenerator or TableGenerator annotations. The annotations can override the name of the table and columns or sequence from the defaults chosen by the provider; and can set the initial value and number of values to allocate for each request.

The third generated value strategy is GenerationType.IDENTITY, which indicates that a database auto-increment or identity column should be used. It might seem a good idea to use the database's native support for generating unique identity values, but this strategy has a number of downsides. Not all databases have such support for native identity columns, so the persistence provider may have to use another database mechanism. For example, when used with the Oracle database, OpenJPA uses a combination of triggers and sequences. If your database does support identity columns, it may also restrict them to be primary key columns, or require at most one identity column per table. Finally, after persisting a new entity using the identity strategy, the JPA provider must immediately retrieve the generated value from the database because it may be required by the application code, or to associate the entity with another entity. This prevents the provider from optimizing performance by batching inserts into the entity's table.

> The `GenerationType.IDENTITY` strategy for generating identities prevents the persistence provider from batching inserts, and is likely to perform slower than the `GenerationType.TABLE` or `GenerationType.SEQUENCE` strategies.

The JPA specification only requires support for the `@GeneratedValue` annotation on identity fields. Open-JPA supports the use of the annotation on non-identity fields, but this is not portable.

Using JPA Entities in a Java SE Environment

Let's now look at how we can use our entity outside of a container. This is particularly valuable for unit testing. We developed the persistence layer of `bigrez.com` iteratively using a test-driven development approach. A set of JUnit 4 unit tests allowed us to test the persistence layer fully before we deployed it to WebLogic Server. Here's a `persistence.xml` for using `Person` outside of a container.

```xml
<?xml version="1.0" encoding="UTF-8"?>
<persistence version="1.0" ... namespace declarations ...>
  <persistence-unit name="ExampleTestPU">
    <class>example.Person</class>
    <properties>
      <property name="openjpa.ConnectionDriverName"
                value="oracle.jdbc.OracleDriver"/>
      <property name="openjpa.ConnectionURL"
                value="jdbc:oracle:thin:@localhost:1521:orcl"/>
      <property name="openjpa.ConnectionUserName" value="sampleuser"/>
      <property name="openjpa.ConnectionPassword" value="password"/>
      <property name="openjpa.Log" value="DefaultLevel=TRACE"/>
      <property name="openjpa.jdbc.SynchronizeMappings" value="buildSchema"/>
    </properties>
  </persistence-unit>
</persistence>
```

This is a little longer than the descriptor we used to deploy to the server. We have added the following items:

❑ Provider-specific properties containing the database connection information. These properties should not be used when deploying to WebLogic Server because it is better to use WebLogic Server managed data sources.

❑ The `openjpa.Log` property is set to TRACE so we can monitor Kodo's activity and examine the generated SQL. This property is ignored when deploying to WebLogic Server — use the WebLogic Server debug facility instead.

❑ The `openjpa.jdbc.SynchronizeMappings` property is set to `buildSchema`. This is a very useful feature for rapid development of new entities. When set, Kodo will examine the database schema, and issue the appropriate SQL statements to create tables that don't already exist.

❑ A `<class/>` element that explicitly lists our entity class.

We didn't need to list our entity classes for Java EE deployment; the container is required by the specification to scan the classes in the jar file at deployment time looking for annotated classes. For portable Java SE deployment outside of a container, the classes must be explicitly listed. Kodo has a special runtime enhancer agent (see the next section, "Persistent Class Enhancement"), which can discover entities if they are not listed, but this process involves scanning every class for metadata and significantly increases classloading times.

Optionally, the classes can be explicitly listed in a separate orm.xml mapping file. This file can also be used to provide mapping metadata as an alternative to using annotations. We discuss best practice for using orm.xml later in this chapter.

Java SE code must use an EntityManagerFactory to obtain an EntityManager. Additionally, the persistent unit's transaction-type defaults to RESOURCE_LOCAL (that is, local database transactions) because JTA transactions are not available. Application code should manage transactions through the EntityTransaction interface. For example:

```
EntityManagerFactory emf = Persistence.createEntityManagerFactory("ExampleTestPU");
EntityManager em = emf.createEntityManager();
em.getTransaction().begin();
// JPA application code goes here.
em.getTransaction().commit();
em.close();
```

If you wish to deploy JPA code written for Java SE to a Java EE container, it often needs modification to remove hard-coded dependencies on an EntityManagerFactory or EntityManager transaction management. The reverse is not true, and is one benefit of EJB 3.0's use of dependency injection. It is easy to write a J2SE wrapper around an SLSB that creates an appropriate EntityManager and manually injects it into the annotated field in the SLSB class. This does require that the wrapper code can access the field. When writing SLSBs, we often add methods to provide access to unit test code in the same package. For example:

```
@PersistenceContext
private EntityManager entityManager;
/** For unit tests. */
void setEntityManager(EntityManager entityManager)
{
    this.entityManager = entityManager;
}
```

Best Practice

Add access methods to your EJBs and other Java EE components, so that unit tests can simulate the container dependency injection and populate annotated fields.

The access methods can be package scope, and need not corrupt a component's public interface.

When running in a Java SE environment, be sure that you are using the correct classpath. It should contain the com.bea.core.kodo jar files from the modules subdirectory of the Oracle Middleware Home directory. Otherwise you might end up using plain OpenJPA and not benefiting from Kodo's enterprise features. We ran into this when developing the `bigrez.com` unit tests, and experienced problems related to database constraints until we added Kodo to the classpath. OpenJPA inserts records into the database in the order that you persist the corresponding objects. Kodo is aware of the database constraints and reorders SQL statements to avoid these problems.

Because Kodo is a commercial tool, you should also check with your Oracle representative that using Kodo outside of WebLogic Server is covered by your license agreement.

Persistent Class Enhancement

To optimize performance and implement lazy loading, OpenJPA and Kodo require that the byte code of persistent classes be modified with an *enhancer* tool. The enhancer is run automatically on deployment to a Java EE 5 environment.

For Java SE deployments, the enhancer can either be run manually over the compiled classes as part of a build, or through a Java 5 agent. If neither of these are done, Kodo will generate subclasses of the persistent classes, and issue a warning that the application will run less efficiently, and that references between entities will always be resolved eagerly. We have also witnessed differences in behavior between JPA code run through the enhancer and JPA code relying on generated subclasses. Consequently we recommend always running the enhancer.

The runtime agent is useful when developing Java SE code in an IDE, as it doesn't require a separate compile stage. Simply add the argument `-javaagent:/oracle/middleware/modules/org.apache.openjpa_1.0.0.0_1-1-1-SNAPSHOT.jar` (where `/oracle/middleware` is the Oracle Middleware Home directory) to the Java command line.

When using the runtime enhancer, it is a good idea to list the entities in the persistence unit. As noted previously, this is required if you want your persistence context to be portable between JPA providers. Additionally, if the classes are not listed, the enhancer checks every class that is classloaded, which can be slow and can even cause deadlocks.

Build-time enhancement is useful as part of the formal build process for your code. There are advantages to build-time enhancement when deploying to a Java EE environment as well, including catching errors before deployment time, and speeding up deployment. To enhance your classes at build time, either use the `org.apache.openjpa.enhance.PCEnhancer` utility directly from the command line or use the `kodoc` Ant task, as shown here.

```
<taskdef name="kodoc"
         classname="kodo.ant.PCEnhancerTask"
         classpathref="wls.classpath"/>
<kodoc>
  <classpath refid="build.classpath"/>
  <config propertiesFile="${classes.dir}/META-INF/persistence.xml"/>
  <fileset dir="${src.dir}">
    <include name="**/entities/*.java" />
  </fileset>
</kodoc>
```

Starting in WebLogic Server 10.3, the WebLogic Server `appc` compiler also performs build-time enhancement for Kodo-managed persistence units that it finds in the application.

Best Practice

When working with OpenJPA or Kodo, always ensure persistent classes to be deployed in a Java SE environment are enhanced at build time or by using the runtime agent.

Relationships

The efficient mapping and management of relationships between entities is a key feature of an ORM system. Let's create a new entity class that has a relationship to `Person`. Our new entity represents a team of individuals.

```
@Entity
public class Team
{
    @Id
    @GeneratedValue
    private long id;
    private String name;
    @OneToMany
    private Set<Person> teamMembers = new HashSet<Person>();

    public Team() { }
    public Team(String name) { setName(name); }

    public long getId() { return id; }

    public void setName(String name) { this.name = name; }
    public String getName() { return name; }

    public void addTeamMember(Person person) { this.teamMembers.add(person); }

    public Set<Person> getTeamMembers()
    {
        return Collections.unmodifiableSet(teamMembers);
    }
}
```

The `Team` entity is linked to the `Person` entity through its `teamMembers` field. Unlike basic attributes, relationship fields must be explicitly annotated. We have used the `@OneToMany` annotation to specify that each `Team` is associated with many `Person` instances. JPA also supports `OneToOne` and `ManyToMany` relationships.

The *many* end of a relationship can be mapped to a `java.util.Collection`, `java.util.List`, `java.util.Set`, or `java.util.Map`. The field should be initialized to an appropriate implementation, but this may be replaced by a provider-specific implementation when an entity is refreshed from the database. Applications should not depend on the order of the elements in a collection unless the relationship is also annotated with `javax.persistence.OrderBy` and the application takes care not to alter the order.

Because we only set an annotation on the Team class, our relationship is unidirectional. You can navigate from a Team instance to a related Person, but not from a Person to its Team.

The natural database schema mapping for a one-to-many relationship would be a foreign key column in the PERSON table that refers to the TEAM table. JPA does not support this mapping for unidirectional one-to-many relationships, because it would require the mapping for the entity that owns the relationship (Team) to influence the mapping for the entity that is otherwise ignorant of the relationship (Person). Instead, JPA requires the introduction of a separate join table for unidirectional one-to-many mappings. OpenJPA supports unidirectional one-to-many mappings using a foreign key, but this is not portable.

Let's make our relationship bidirectional. To do this, we add a Team field to Person, and annotate it with ManyToOne, and add a mappedBy element to the @OneToMany annotation.

```
@Entity
public class Person
{
    @ManyToOne
    Team team;
    ...
}

@Entity
public class Team
{
    ...
    @OneToMany(mappedBy="team")
    private Set<Person> teamMembers = new HashSet<Person>();
    ...
    public void addTeamMember(Person person)
    {
        this.teamMembers.add(person);
        person.team = this;
    }
    ...
}
```

Now that the relationship is bidirectional, the JPA mapping uses a foreign key column on the PERSON table. The default name of the column is TEAM_ID, the ID part being derived from the name of the TEAM primary key column.

Best Practice

When creating bidirectional relationships, use the mappedBy element on one entity, rather than annotating both entities with mapping data. This follows the *Don't Repeat Yourself* principle, and avoids the opportunity for the mappings to be inconsistent.

JPA requires that the application maintain both ends of bidirectional relationships. If you modify the field at one end, you must make the corresponding changes to the field at the other end. We've made this a little easier to manage by updating the Person.team field in addTeamMember().

Best Practice

JPA requires you to maintain both sides of a bidirectional relationship manually. Don't provide direct access to modify the association fields through the entities' public interfaces. Instead, write helper methods in one or both entities to encapsulate the work to correctly maintain the relationship.

Cascading Operations

All of the association annotations have a `cascade` element. This accepts an array of `CascadeType` values that control which entity manager operations carried out on the owning entity are automatically cascaded to the related entities. Four entity manager operations can be cascaded: `persist()`, `remove()`, `refresh()`, and `merge()`. By default, no operations are cascaded. The operation may recursively be applied through the association fields of the related entities, again according to the `cascade` element setting.

Cascading can be seen as a convenience feature that frees programmers from having to apply the same entity manager operation to related entities, and to their related entities, potentially several levels deep. It also affects whether related entities are managed as a group, which can have positive and negative effects on performance. Finally, it can reflect whether the association types represent *composition* (where an entity cannot exist without its parent) or *aggregation.*

Cascading `persist()` operations usually makes sense. If the related entities are already persisted, no action is taken. When the container attempts to flush a newly persisted entity that has a `cascade=CascadeType.PERSIST` association, but some of the related entities have not been persisted, it may throw an exception due to database foreign key constraints. If you experience problems when cascading `persist()` due to foreign key constraints, don't be tempted not to cascade `persist()`. Instead, you should ensure you have flushed the parent entities before you create the child entities.

`CascadeType.REMOVE` should be used only where there is a composition relationship between the entity and its related entities. That is, the entity *owns* the related entities, and the related entities cannot exist independently of the owner.

In our simple model, it would probably not be right to cascade `remove()` through the `Team.teamMembers` association, because a `Person` may validly belong to no `Team`. It certainly would not be right to cascade `remove()` through `Person.team` to the `Team` without also cascading through `Team.teamMembers`, because removing a `Person` would delete the `Team` and leave any other members of the team with a dangling foreign key reference. If the database schema has foreign key constraints, the transaction will fail when committed. If there are no foreign key constraints, the database will be left in an inconsistent state.

What about `CascadeType.MERGE` and `CascadeType.REFRESH` cascade types? Clearly, you should not apply them to every association, or `merge()` and `refresh()` operations will walk every reachable entity. Think twice before applying them to `@ManyToOne` associations — will the target entity propagate the operation through the inverse link and affect more entities than you intended? Our preference is to use these cascade types only for closely related entities.

Best Practice

Set `cascade=CascadeType.PERSIST` on your associations by default; there's little reason not to.

Only set `cascade=CascadeType.REMOVE` for associations that represent composition relationships. Never set `CascadeType.REMOVE` on `@ManyToOne` or `@ManyToMany` associations without also setting it on the inverse association field of the target entity.

Think carefully before applying `cascade=CascadeType.MERGE` or `cascade=CascadeType.REFRESH` to a `@ManyToOne` association.

Here are the changes to `Person` and `Team` to cascade persist operations.

```
@Entity
public class Person
{
    ...
    @ManyToOne(cascade=CascadeType.PERSIST)
    Team team;
    ...
}

@Entity
public class Team
{
    ...
    @OneToMany(mappedBy="team", cascade=CascadeType.PERSIST)
    private Set<Person> teamMembers = new HashSet<Person>();
    ...
}
```

JPQL Queries

Entities that already exist in the database can be loaded into a persistence context using the `EntityManager.find()` method, or by using a query.

An entity can be looked up by primary key using the `EntityManager.find()` method. This method is equivalent to the EJB 2.x `findByPrimaryKey()` method. It should always be used if the primary key is known, because it will not contact the database if the entity is already in the persistence context.

Queries provide more general access to entities. Queries are written in the Java Persistence Query Language (JPQL), which is largely derived from the EJB 2.x Enterprise JavaBeans Query Language (EJB QL). We do not have the space here to discuss the details of the JPQL language, but it is easy to pick up if you are familiar with SQL or EJB QL.

Queries can either be *named queries* or *dynamic queries*. Named queries are static queries that are predefined in metadata — either in a class level annotation or in `orm.xml`. They are accessed using the `EntityManager.createNamedQuery()` method. Dynamic queries are created using `EntityManager.createQuery()`. They are appropriate when the form of the query expression is not fully known until run time.

Named queries have several advantages over dynamic queries. There is more opportunity for the container to cache the result of query parsing and compilation, so they are more efficient. They can easily be overridden. Dynamic query expressions are strings constructed by the application, and are often derived from user input. Unless care is taken, these expressions may be vulnerable to SQL injection attacks. Named queries don't suffer from this risk because variable information is supplied as named query parameters that are mapped directly to prepared statement bind variables. API extensions to allow safe dynamic queries to be constructed are a feature of the JPA 2.0 specification, and so will be supported in a Java EE 6 and a future version of WebLogic Server.

A downside to named queries is that their names must be globally unique, and are not checked at compile time. We recommend qualifying each query with the name of the owning entity, and referring to the query using a constant field.

Here's an example of a named query that finds all members of a team with a given name.

```
@NamedQuery(name = Person.QUERY_BY_TEAM_NAME,
            query = "select p from Person p where p.team.name = :teamName")
@Entity
public class Person
{
    public static final String QUERY_BY_TEAM_NAME = "Person.queryByTeamName";
    ...
}
```

The query parameter `teamName` will be mapped to a prepared statement bind variable. This allows for efficient execution and protects against SQL injection. The query is used as follows.

```
Query query = em.createNamedQuery(Person.QUERY_BY_TEAM_NAME);
query.setParameter("teamName", "Blue");
List<Person> blueTeamMembers = query.getResultList();
```

Queries need not return entities. Here's a query that returns an ordered list of team names.

```
@NamedQuery(name = Team.QUERY_NAMES,
            query = "select distinct t.name from Team t order by o.name")
```

JPA also supports native SQL queries, created using the `EntityManager.createNativeQuery()` method. Native SQL queries are not portable across databases, and are only appropriate where JPQL cannot be used.

Best Practice

Where possible, use named queries in preference to dynamic queries or native queries.

The JPA container will populate the persistence context with the results of a JPQL query. Only information retrieved by the query will be used, so related entities will not be loaded if the query doesn't join across the relationships and they are not eagerly fetched. (We discuss eager fetching shortly). If you detach the entities returned by a query, for example, and you return a list of the entities to a client, their association fields will be null. The client might reasonably expect the associations to be populated. You can force a JPQL query to load related entities, even if it doesn't refer to the entities in a WHERE clause, by using a *fetch join*. Usually you will want to use a left outer join. Here's a query that ensures that the teamMembers fields of the returned Teams are populated.

```
@NamedQuery(name = Team.QUERY_BY_TEAM_NAME,
            query = "select distinct t from Team t left join fetch t.teamMembers
                     where t.team.name = :teamName")
```

Fetch joins behave like normal joins, and the result will include a reference to the Team for each of its team members. When using fetch joins, you can add the distinct keyword to remove the duplicate results.

> **Best Practice**
>
> When writing a JPQL query, ask yourself whether the result should include associated entities that are not otherwise referenced in the query and are not eagerly fetched. If so, use fetch joins to populate the association fields.

JPQL Bulk Updates

JPQL may also be used to perform a bulk update against the database. Bulk updates are executed in the database, without the need to pull the data into application server memory. The update expression is written using JPQL in terms of the application object model, and is portable across different data stores.

```
Query bulkUpdate =
  em.createQuery(
    "update Person p set p.team = " +
    "(select t from Team t where t.name = 'The Boys' ) " +
    "where p.salutation = 'Mr'");
bulkUpdate.executeUpdate();
```

Kodo generates the following SQL for this example.

```
UPDATE Person t0 SET t0.TEAM_ID = (SELECT t1.id FROM Team t1 WHERE (t1.name =
?)) WHERE (t0.salutation = ?)
```

Bulk updates are an effective way to make mass changes to the database. This is not often required by an online transaction processing application, but may be useful for batch updates and schema migration applications.

You should be aware of the following before using bulk updates.

❑ The results of bulk updates are not synchronized with the persistence context. Consequently, it is best not to mix bulk updates in the same transaction as normal JPA code.

❑ Bulk updates do not automatically update optimistic locking version columns, nor check whether optimistic locking assertions have been violated. If you wish the bulk operations to interact correctly with other application transactions, the update expression should explicitly update the value of the version column, if desired, and explicitly verify that the version column has the correct value. We discuss optimistic locking at length later in this chapter.

Best Practice

Use bulk updates where you can for wholesale changes to the database, such as might be required by batch processing or for schema version migration applications.

Be careful when mixing bulk updates with other JPA operations. The results are not automatically synchronized with the persistence context, and you should ensure the update expressions perform any necessary version updates and checks.

Embedded Entity Classes

JPA provides the notion of embedded entity classes to allow entities to be composed of smaller, fine-grained classes. Instances of embedded entity classes are value objects that have no persistent identity of their own. They are wholly owned by a single entity. An instance of an embeddable class cannot be shared between two entities.

Embeddable classes are marked with the `@javax.persistence.Embeddable` annotation. The owning entity can have one or more fields of an embeddable class, each indicated with a `@javax.persistence.Embedded` annotation. The attributes of an embeddable class are mapped with metadata (as annotations, or in `orm.xml`) as if they were expanded in line in the owning entity.

Embedded entity classes allow the identification and grouping of attributes to create a more appropriate Java class model. This can be independent of the underlying schema; that is, the schema has no notion of a distinct object. Embeddable class can also be used to map the Java class model to a denormalized database schema; in this case the schema has multiple tables, each of which contains the columns corresponding to the embeddable class's attributes.

You can find examples of embedded entity classes in the `bigrez.com` application. For example, both the `GuestProfile` and the `Reservation` entities use the `CardDetails` embedded class.

Eager and Lazy Fetching

If you have an entity with a large field that is infrequently accessed, you might not want the field to be brought back into memory every time the entity is refreshed from the database. If so, you can add an explicit `@javax.persistence.Basic` annotation to those fields with a `fetch=FetchType.LAZY` element. The field will then be fetched on demand.

The `fetch=FetchType.LAZY` element can also be added to `@OneToOne` and `@ManyToOne` associations to change their default, eager loading behavior.

`@OneToMany` and `@ManyToMany` associations are lazy by default; they can be made eager using `fetch=FetchType.EAGER`. This is appropriate if you know the collections are small and likely to be accessed.

Configuring fields for lazy loading can be very useful when tuning an application. However, be aware that the JPA specification defines `FetchType.LAZY` as a hint that the container is free to ignore. Also, lazily fetched fields and associations are ignored when entities are detached from the persistence context, or reattached with an `EntityManager.merge()` operation. Consequently, lazy loading is vendor-specific behavior.

Later in this chapter we describe our preference for setting vendor-specific behavior in deployment descriptors, rather than annotations. It is also a good idea to keep tuning information in descriptors, because it can change with different environments, particularly between databases of different sizes.

Best Practice

Tune large and infrequently accessed fields and associations to be fetched lazily from the database. Tune small, or very frequently accessed fields and associations to be eagerly fetched.

Fetch behavior is vendor-specific, and may need to be tuned per environment, so it is generally best set in the `orm.xml` descriptor and not in annotations.

Optimistic Locking and Version Fields

Java EE applications typically support simultaneous access by many thousands of users. A key consideration for a persistent Java EE application is how to manage concurrency. In particular, how do you ensure that changes made by a user affect other users in a well-defined manner?

Three common approaches exist: *database locking*, *pessimistic locking*, and *optimistic locking*.

Database Locking The database locking strategy uses a database lock to ensure that only one user can update the database row for a particular entity for the duration of a transaction.

Database locking provides a basis for the application to interact safely with other applications that access the database. The database will prevent the other applications from updating the locked data, and the transaction isolation level will determine the consistency of each application's view of the data. The other applications can use the same, well-defined database locking so their changes are not overwritten.

A second advantage of using database locks is that the database will guarantee that the locks are released when the transaction commits or rolls back.

Database locking has several negative consequences.

Unless applications take care to acquire and release locks in a well-defined order, there is the possibility of encountering a deadlock between two application transactions. The database will detect the deadlock and cause one of the application transactions to rollback.

Database locks can negatively affect scalability and performance. The database must do more work to implement the locking. Application transactions may have to wait to obtain a lock. Applications that use database locking may require a more strict database isolation level than those that use optimistic locking. This too negatively affects performance. There is no application tier caching so the container is forced to read all of the data used by a transaction from the database. There is no way to share data read by one transaction with subsequent transactions.

181

The final and most important deficiency with database locking concerns correct application behavior. The transaction controls the granularity of database access. Every time an application starts a new transaction and reads data from the database, that data may have changed. This creates problems for conversational applications that use one transaction to present a view of the database to the user (perhaps as an HTML form), and another transaction to write updates back to the database (perhaps the result of the user submitting the form). What happens if some other user updates the same data after the view has been obtained but before the update is written back? The second transaction will blindly overwrite the changes made by the other user, resulting in lost updates.

Pessimistic Locking   With pessimistic locking, the application takes out locks on an area of the database that can survive multiple transactions. The locks might be implemented in the application (in which case, no other application will understand and respect them), or with database features.

Pessimistic locking might be suitable for departmental applications serving a small user base, but is impractical for the typical Java EE application.

Optimistic Locking   With optimistic locking, when a user starts to use an entity, data is read from a row in the database. The user modifies the entity and when the data is written back to the database, the container checks that no other thread or process has updated the row in the interim. This is how optimistic concurrency gets its name. Instead of taking out a pessimistic lock on an area of the database between the read and the write, the code executing on behalf of the user *optimistically* assumes that no other code has updated the data and attempts to do the write.

How does the container check whether an entity the application is trying to write back to the database is out of date — that is, whether someone else has changed the database since the entity was read? Several common strategies exist, ranging from checking all attributes of the entity, through to managing a separate version attribute. An important point is that this version information is managed with the entity itself. This allows optimistic locking to be used as a basis for safely caching entities across many separate transactions.

What are the attributes of an application that is suited to the optimistic concurrency strategy?

First of all, there should be low probability of write contention. It should be unlikely that two users will be attempting to write to the same entity at the same time. Optimistic concurrency is not a good fit for a single entity instance that must frequently be read and later updated by many users. This does not rule out many readers. Optimistic concurrency is a great fit for applications that have many readers and few writers for each entity.

Secondly, the application must be designed to handle write failures in a reasonable manner. This usually involves presenting the user with a message such as "Another user has altered this account, please refresh your view and try again." Such a message might be annoying for the user but is unlikely to occur due to the low write contention. Contrast this with pessimistic locking where it is possible to inform the user "Another user is altering this account, please open it read-only." What if this other user has gone for a two-hour lunch? This is the reason pessimistic locking can only scale to a small population of users that work in the same office where they all know about the activities of their peers. Systems that use pessimistic locking may have to incorporate complex lock override mechanisms to resolve such problems.

Fortunately the typical Java EE application (a multi-user e-commerce system with a web interface and a database partitioned into user accounts) can be designed to satisfy both of these requirements.

There is a third requirement that is important if the application system is not the only system that writes to the database, namely that all systems that update the database must use the same convention to mark a row as updated. We will see that JPA provides support for optimistic locking based upon an application defined *version* attribute. OpenJPA supports other conventions, including one based purely on changes made to the business data, which may make interoperability with other systems easier to arrange.

EJB 2.x neither defines nor mandates a locking strategy. For EJB 2.x WebLogic Server supports database locking (the *database concurrency strategy*), optimistic locking, plus two other locking strategies. The *exclusive concurrency strategy* uses Java locking, but only works in a single JVM so is impractical for real-world applications. The *read-only concurrency strategy* does not support update and allows stale reads; it can be considered overly optimistic. The *optimistic concurrency strategy* is a full optimistic locking implementation that was introduced in WebLogic Server 7.0. Despite clear benefits to optimistic locking, most EJB 2.x WebLogic Server implementations use the database concurrency strategy. Perhaps one reason for this is WebLogic Server–specific configuration (the version field information is specified in `weblogic-ejb-jar.xml`) and APIs (`weblogic.ejb.OptimisticConcurrencyException`) were required.

JPA assumes optimistic locking, and provides good support for implementing it. Importantly, the API has been standardized, so applications that rely on optimistic locking should be portable between JPA providers. In particular, a standard exception (`javax.persistence.OptimisticLockException`) is thrown to the application for optimistic lock failures. Applications must add a version field to each entity they wish to protect with optimistic locking, indicated by a `@javax.persistence.Version` annotation. OpenJPA provides other options for change detection; we look at those later in this chapter.

The optimistic concurrency strategy ensures that the row in the database has not changed during the lifecycle of the bean. This is accomplished in WebLogic Server by saving, in the entity bean instance, the values of specific fields as they existed during the database read invocation. These saved values are then used in database update operations to verify that the database row has not changed by including them in the WHERE clause of the SQL UPDATE statement.

Table 6-1 presents a simple example for two clients accessing and attempting to modify the same entity.

Here are the changes to the Person entity to add support for optimistic locking.

```
@Entity
public class Person
{

    @Version
    private long version;
    ...
```

An attribute marked with `@Version` and the corresponding column in the database table is all that is required to enable optimistic locking support. The application should not attempt to update the version field itself; it is managed entirely by the JPA container.

The following driver code creates a scenario in which `OptimisticLockException` is thrown. Two `EntityManagers` are used to simulate the actions of two distinct users.

```
// User 1 creates a Person.
EntityManager em = emf.createEntityManager();
em.getTransaction().begin();
Person person = new Person("Mr", "Phil", "Aston");
em.persist(person);
em.getTransaction().commit();
```

```
// User 2 changes our Person.
EntityManager em2 = emf.createEntityManager();
em2.getTransaction().begin();
Person person2 = em2.find(Person.class, person.getId());
person2.setFirstName("Bob");
em2.getTransaction().commit();

// Time passes... Imagine that person is stored in User 1's HTTPSession.

// User 1 changes our person.
person.setLastName("Smith");
em.getTransaction().begin();
em.merge(person);
try {
  em.flush(); // Will throw an OptimisticLockException.
}
catch (OptimisticLockException e) {
}
```

In the preceding example, flush() was called explicitly to push changes out to the database. The JPA provider is required to throw OptimisticLockException if any entity with a version field has been modified concurrently. Explicitly calling flush() allows the application to detect early that an optimistic exception will occur and perhaps take some corrective action. The options for this corrective action are limited because the current transaction will have been marked for rollback.

Furthermore, because a third party can update the database at any time, the application must always be prepared to handle an optimistic locking failure at commit time. This typically involves an exception handler in the presentation layer that catches the exception and presents a page to the users explaining that their attempted update failed. Alternatively, the application may retry its operations in a new transaction a number of times. This is common for applications driven by JMS messages. It is up to the caller performing the business method that caused the exception to determine whether it is safe to retry the operation by starting the transaction again, reacquiring the bean instance with updated data from the database, and reapplying the desired changes. Normally, it is not safe simply to reapply the changes without asking for user permission. It may also be necessary to check whether the row still exists in the database to determine the proper course of action. The safest technique is to report the concurrency exception to the user and ask him or her to determine the correct action.

It is also reasonable for a session façade EJB not to try to handle the OptimisticLockException, and to rely on its caller to do so. Often the end user will have called the session EJB based on a view obtained a minute or two earlier. Key entities from the view will have been resupplied to the session EJB, and an optimistic lock failure might arise because the entity version fields are out of step with the database. The end user will almost certainly want to know that another user is altering the same part of the database.

Best Practice

Include exception handling code in client applications to trap and handle OptimisticLockExceptions thrown by the container at the end of a bean lifecycle. In some cases, particularly for message-driven bean implementations, the operation can simply be retried, but often the user must be informed of the error and given the opportunity to select a course of action.

Table 6-1: Optimistic Concurrency Example

Client #1 Thread Activity	Client #2 Thread Activity
The client starts a transaction and finds a reference to entity 101.	
The JPA container loads entity 101 from the database into the client's persistent context. The value of the entity's version field is read as 3.	The client starts a transaction and finds a reference to entity 101.
The client changes the values of some of the entity's attributes.	The JPA container loads entity 101 from the database into the client's persistent context. The value of the entity's version field is read as 3.
The client attempts to commit its transaction, causing the persistent context to be flushed to the database.	
The JPA container performs the database update. The SQL expression is of the form elements UPDATE ... set version=4 ... WHERE version=3	The client changes the values of some of the entity's attributes.
The database transaction branch is committed and the results of the transaction become visible to others.	The client attempts to commit its transaction, causing the persistent context to be flushed to the database.
The container returns control back to the client, indicating the commit completed successfully.	The JPA container performs the database update. The SQL expression is of the form elements UPDATE ... set version=4 ... WHERE version=3. This update fails because the database VERSION column now has the value 4. The JPA container marks the transaction for rollback and throws an OptimisticLockException to the client.

When catching exceptions from a commit or a rollback, beware that the OptimisticLockException may be wrapped in another exception. For applications using the JPA transaction management, this might be a javax.persistence.RollbackException. For Java EE applications using JTA transaction management, the OptimisticLockException will probably be wrapped in a javax.transaction.RollbackException. Clients who wish to handle optimistic concurrency failures must unwrap the exception they catch and look for an OptimisticLockException. This can be done by calling the isOptimisticLockingException() method shown here.

```
public static final boolean isOptimisticLockingException(Throwable t)
{
    while (t != null && t.getCause() != t) {
        if (t instanceof OptimisticLockException) {
            return true;
```

```
        }
        t = t.getCause();
    }
    return false;
}
```

Explicit Locking

Optimistic locking only protects against concurrent modifications to the same entities. It does not stop an application from using stale data from an entity it has loaded, but not changed.

For example, consider an application transaction that queries the `Person` entities for a particular `Team`, uses this to create a string describing the members of team, then writes this description to a field of the `Team` entity. Because the transaction has not modified any of the `Person` entities, the optimistic locking assertion on the SQL update will only check the version column for the `Team` entity. If a separate transaction concurrently updates a `Person`'s name, there is a danger that the team description will be out of date.

To protect against this non-repeatable read scenario, the application can use the `EntityManager.lock()` method to take out read locks on each `Person` it reads from.

```
StringBuilder sb = new StringBuilder();
for (Person p : team.getTeamMembers()) {
    if (sb.length() > 0) {
        sb.append(", ");
    }
    em.lock(p, LockModeType.READ);
    sb.append(p.getFirstName());
}
team.setDescription(sb.toString());
```

The `lock()` method name is a little misleading because it doesn't necessarily need to lock anything. The implementation may take out a database lock on the entity row, or simply add the supplied entity to the list of entities to be checked for version changes when the persistence context is flushed or committed.

Calling `lock()` with a lock mode of `LockModeType.WRITE` behaves in the same way, but also causes the version column to be updated when the persistence context is next flushed or committed. Because the transaction will then hold a write lock on the row, this will prevent other transactions from updating the entity until the transaction commit completes.

Best Practice

If your application reads data from an entity it does not update, and then uses that data to update another entity, you should strongly consider taking out a read lock on the entity to ensure your transaction leaves the database in a consistent state.

If you wish to prevent other concurrent transactions from updating an entity, take out a write lock instead and `flush()` the persistence context. This will likely acquire a database lock on the row, so be wary of using write locks in lengthy transactions because they will constrain performance and increase the probability of database deadlocks.

Writing a Web Layer Suited to Optimistic Locking

One final nuance related to optimistic concurrency and web applications is worth discussing: there is a difference between enforcing concurrency in the context of a container transaction and ensuring that multiple users do not perform conflicting updates. Consider a typical web application having an HTML form used to edit entity data. The form might be populated with entity data during one *read* transaction, and sent to the user's browser for update. Later, the updated fields may be posted to a controller or action JSP page, and used to modify entity data during a second *write* transaction. Optimistic concurrency ensures integrity during each of the two transactions, but it does not inherently prevent two users from viewing the same entity data simultaneously and submitting conflicting changes one at a time. To understand why, note that the write transaction will re-read all the entity data from the database, including the version column. Each write transaction will succeed for both users, one after another, because value of the version column does not change between the start and end of the transaction.

To avoid this, the web layer should hold on to the version information associated with the entities used to render a particular view, and resubmit the version information with the write transaction. Two straightforward implementation strategies exist: store the original entities in the HTTP session, or extract the version information and place it in hidden form fields.

> **Store view entities in the HTTP session**   With this strategy, the web layer stores the detached entities used to render the view in the HTTP session. It returns those same entities (with the fields updated to reflect user edits) as parameters to the write transaction. Instead of re-reading the entities from the database, the write transaction uses the `EntityManager.merge()` method to merge the supplied entities into its persistence context. The original version field will then be used by optimistic locking assertion to ensure that no other user has modified the data in the meantime.

> **Store version information in hidden fields**   The web layer can store the value of the identity and version fields in hidden fields on the HTML form. When the form is submitted, the web layer creates new detached entity instances, including the user edits, sets the value of identity and version fields from the hidden form fields, then submits the new entities as parameters to the write transaction. The write transaction uses `EntityManager.merge()` to merge the supplied entities into its persistence context with optimistic locking checks.

> It is valid for the application to set the version field of a newly created instance that also has the identity field set. All other attempts to modify the version field are invalid, and will be detected as such by OpenJPA.

The first approach is simple in JPA terms, but requires the web layer to keep a set of entities in the session for each page flow the user begins. This uses more memory, and if the user leaves the page and never returns, the HTTP session may fill up with unused information.

The second approach involves copying additional information out of the entities into the HTML form, and the application must handle the otherwise opaque identity and version fields. This copying can almost certainly reuse whatever existing approach the application uses for populating a form with entity data. It has the distinct advantage of not requiring any session state; however, it is not compatible with the Kodo surrogate version column and lock group features — we discuss this later in this chapter.

The combination of this type of application-level check and the server-based optimistic concurrency logic provides a strong level of concurrency control for your application.

Best Practice

To take full advantage of optimistic locking, allowing it to work across multiple transactions and to synchronize a view of application data with an associated user edit, the web layer and other user interfaces need to manage version information associated with each view.

Inheritance

Support for mapping inheritance hierarchies is one of the touted advantages of JPA over EJB 2.x entity beans. In practice, inheritance is an advanced feature that is rarely appropriate.

JPA supports three mapping strategies. Each has advantages and disadvantages. There is no general-purpose, efficient mapping of inheritance hierarchies to the relational model.

The *single table* strategy maps all the classes in the inheritance hierarchy to the same table. A special discriminator column in the table is used to store the entity class for a row. This is a simple, fast strategy. The table will contain columns that are only used by some of the derived classes, and will be NULL in rows for entities belonging to other classes. The presence of many optional columns is undesirable from a relational design perspective, and prevents the use of database constraints to maintain structural integrity.

In the *joined tables* strategy, each class in the hierarchy maps to its own table. The table for the most abstract class contains a discriminator column. This approach produces a normalized database schema, but leads to more complex, slower SQL statements. When entities are loaded from the database, the query has to join tables for subclasses to the superclass tables. Similarly, updates to a single entity affect multiple rows.

The *table per class* strategy maps each concrete (non-abstract) class to its own table. Each table contains all of the information for a particular entity type. A discriminator column is not required, so it conceivably could be retrofitted to an existing schema. This strategy does not require unnormalized tables with empty columns, and the SQL statements for basic operations operate on a single table so are straightforward and efficient. Nevertheless, it has a number of significant limitations if you wish to treat the entities in a polymorphic manner. You cannot map to a non-leaf entity class (that is, an entity class from which another entity is derived) using an inverse foreign key — to what table would the key refer? Also, identity lookups and queries require multiple SELECT statements or a complex UNION.

It is common wisdom that inheritance is often overused in object-oriented design. Often, aggregation and composition are more appropriate and lead to simpler, flexible, and less brittle implementations. This principle becomes even more important with the added complexity of mapping between the object and relational models. Only use inheritance where you truly need polymorphic behavior from your entity object model.

JPA also provides for *mapped superclasses*. Mapped superclasses are similar to embedded classes, and allow the abstraction of the behavior of fields that are common to many entities. This is not a strategy for entity inheritance mapping. The superclass is not an entity itself; its fields are mapped to columns that are present in each of the entity's tables.

We often create a utility mapped superclass that deals with identity and versioning concerns. This superclass can provide standard implementations of hashCode() and equals(), as well as utility methods common to each entity class. See bigrez.com for an example.

Applying JPA

Although JPA is a relatively new specification, it builds on experience derived from mature products such as Kodo, TopLink, and Hibernate. The breadth and detail of the specification can be a little daunting to the first-time user. In practice, it is straightforward to apply.

The following list is our recommended approach for applying JPA effectively.

❑ Don't start off by attempting to learn the entire specification — look for additional features as you need them.

❑ Create a utility mapped superclass that deals with identity and versioning concerns.

❑ Apply the *Don't Repeat Yourself* principle. If your schema tables repeatedly use the same group of columns, use embedded entities to map these to a single Java class.

❑ Use inheritance between entities with caution. It is rarely appropriate, and has significant performance costs due to the mismatch between inheritance and the relational model.

❑ Your schema will most likely outlive your application, and will be used by other applications. Allowing the JPA provider to generate the schema can be useful for rapid prototyping, but the database schema, rather than your object model, should be considered authoritative.

❑ Use SLSBs to manage transactions, and use container-managed persistence contexts.

❑ Estimate the scope of each transaction. How many entities will it affect? Apply lazy loading to avoid unnecessarily loading large collections into memory.

❑ Use optimistic locking. Design optimistic locking exception handling mechanisms into the layers that call JPA.

❑ Don't be afraid to use advanced features of your JPA provider, but minimize the points in your application that rely on them. For example, avoid proprietary annotations and make the corresponding changes in a deployment descriptor instead.

And our most important piece of advice:

❑ Write full unit tests for your entity classes. Set `openjpa.Log` property to `TRACE`, and check that the generated SQL is as you would expect. This will give you confidence that the JPA provider is performing correctly, and provide early warning of potential performance problems. The `openjpa.Log` property is ignored when deploying to WebLogic Server — use the WebLogic Server debug facility instead.

Now that we've completed our review of EJB key concepts and looked at a few generic EJB examples, it is time to dive in to the unique features and capabilities of the WebLogic Server EJB container.

WebLogic Server EJB Container

Our discussion of WebLogic Server EJB features concentrates on features useful in the creation of classic Java EE applications using EJB components for the business layer of the application. We start with a brief review of the EJB container and the lifecycle of EJB components in the WebLogic Server container implementation. The next section documents WebLogic Server EJB features common to many of the EJB component types. The remainder of the chapter is then spent discussing features applicable to specific types of EJB components.

WebLogic Server has so many EJB-related features and configuration parameters that we had to make some choices in the interest of space. The theme for this book is best practices, after all, and some advanced features and capabilities represent more useful and important concepts for typical Java EE applications than others. The next chapter applies the best practices discussed here to a realistic Java EE application.

EJB Container Basics

The EJB container is a fundamental part of the EJB architecture. In a nutshell, the EJB container provides the environment used to host and manage the EJB components deployed in the container. The container is responsible for providing a standard set of services, including caching, concurrency, persistence, security, transaction management, and locking services. The container also provides distributed access and lookup functions for hosted components, and it intercepts all method invocations on hosted components to enforce declarative security and transaction contexts.

The EJB container is not a single Java class, nor is it a single API or service accessible to the contained components or external client code. It is more of an abstract concept implemented by each server vendor in a unique fashion. Note that most of the unique features of WebLogic Server described in the remaining sections of this chapter are actually features of the EJB container itself.

EJB Lifecycle in WebLogic Server

One of the key responsibilities of the EJB container is the management of EJB component lifecycles. Bean instances are pooled and reused by the container to reduce the number of object instantiations. Rather than spend time reviewing the complex and confusing processes involved in pooling, passivation, activation, and other memory-management issues, we'll take a more pragmatic approach by concentrating on the key lifecycle events of an EJB component from the point of view of a client of the component.

Given that approach, the lifecycle of a stateless session bean, for example, becomes fairly simple:

1. The client obtains a reference to the SLSB. There are three options here. First, the reference can be injected into the client via an @EJB annotation. Second, the reference can be bound into the client's local java:comp/env environment, using the @EJB annotation at class-level or a deployment descriptor entry, and the client can retrieve the reference with a JNDI lookup. Third, the client can look up the SLSB in the server's global JNDI tree. The client can also use the EJB 2.1 client view to look up the SLSB Home interface, using any of the three methods, and call create(). (The EJB 2.1 client view allows EJB 2.x clients to call EJB 3.0 beans, providing backward compatibility, as required by the specification).

2. The client invokes a business method on the bean reference.

3. The container can reuse an existing instance of the SLSB from a pool, if available, or can instantiate a new bean instance. If a bean instance is newly created, the container will first perform dependency injection. If the SLSB implements the optional javax.ejb.SessionBean interface, the container will call setSessionContext(). The session context will also be injected to any SessionContext field marked with the @Resource annotation. After completing injection of the session context and other dependencies, the container will call any methods marked with the @PostConstruct annotation.

4. The container starts a transaction, if appropriate. This is controlled by the `@javax.ejb.TransactionManagement` and `@javax.ejb.TransactionAttribute` annotations.

5. The container invokes the called business method on the bean instance, and the bean performs the desired operation.

6. The container commits the transaction, if appropriate.

7. The results of the business method call are returned to the client.

8. The client may invoke additional business methods on the bean reference, each of which may end up invoking methods on a different bean instance.

9. At some point, if the container decides to reduce the size of the bean instance pool, the container invokes any `@PreDestroy` methods on the bean instance, or `ejbRemove()` if the bean implements the `SessionBean` interface. It is important to understand that this decision is not related to any client action.

`@PostConstruct` methods are equivalent to EJB 2.x `ejbCreate()` methods, and are good places to load cached data in an SLSB instance, or perform other initialization steps such as JNDI lookups, or obtain an expensive connection to a backend resource. Although SLSBs are stateless from the point of view of the client, the bean instances are reused and may cache data in internal member variables.

The application should not assume that `@PreDestroy` methods will always be called. For example, bean instances can be destroyed without the `@PreDestroy` methods being called if a method throws a system exception. Similarly, the server might crash without calling these methods.

There is a stronger link between the lifecycle of a stateful session bean and the client's use of its reference.

1. The client obtains a reference to the SFSB through one of the previously described methods.

2. The container instantiates a new bean instance. The container will perform dependency injection. If the SLSB implements the optional `javax.ejb.SessionBean` interface, the container will call `setSessionContext()`. The session context will also be injected to any `SessionContext` field marked with the `@Resource` annotation. Any methods marked with the `@PostConstruct` will then be called.

3. The client invokes a business method on the bean reference.

4. The container starts a transaction, if appropriate.

5. The container invokes a business method on the bean instance, and the bean performs the desired operation.

6. The container commits the transaction, if appropriate.

7. The results of the business method call are returned to the client.

8. The client may invoke additional business methods on the bean reference and is assured that these additional calls will go to the same instance of the bean.

9. The client calls a method annotated with `@javax.ejb.Remove` when it is done with the SFSB.

10. The container invokes any `@PreDestroy` methods on the bean instance, or `ejbRemove()` if the bean implements the `SessionBean` interface.

Like SLSB components, `@PostConstruct` methods are called once when an SFSB instance is created and are appropriate places for creating internal caches or performing other initialization steps. Of course, the cache is specific to the particular client's session so you could just as easily use lazy initialization because, either way, the client will be waiting on the initialization work.

This very brief introduction to the lifecycle of session EJB components represents a simplified view of the process. Additional complexities are introduced by limitations in the pool and cache sizes that you need to understand to configure your application properly. We cover some of these complexities in a subsequent section on setting pool sizes and configuring passivation.

General WebLogic Server EJB Features

This section discusses some of the important general features of the WebLogic Server EJB container related to all types of EJB components. Subsequent sections detail WebLogic Server features related to specific EJB types.

EJB Deployment/Redeployment

One important feature of the WebLogic Server EJB container is the ability to deploy and redeploy EJB components easily. Chapter 8 discusses the basic EJB packaging and deployment process, and it compares various options for deploying EJB components in WebLogic Server.

Dynamic EJB Compilation

The normal packaging and deployment technique for EJB components involves the execution of the WebLogic Server application compiler appc to create a complete EJB archive file containing all of the runtime container classes required for the EJB components. The complete EJB archive file is then deployed to WebLogic Server using one of the techniques discussed in Chapter 8.

Here's a terminal session showing the effect of compiling an EJB jar with appc. Initially, the EJB jar just contains the implementation class MyEJBImpl, the business interface MyEJB, and a jar manifest. After appc has been run on the jar file, it contains several other generated classes.

```
% jar tf myejb.jar
META-INF/MANIFEST.MF
example/MyEJBImpl.class
META-INF/
example/
example/MyEJB.class
% java weblogic.appc myejb.jar
% jar tf myejb.jar
META-INF/MANIFEST.MF
META-INF/
_WL_GENERATED
example/
example/MyEJBImpl.class
example/MyEJBImpl_ehtkps_Impl.class
example/MyEJB.class
example/MyEJBImpl_ehtkps_Intf.class
example/MyEJBImpl_ehtkps_MyEJBImpl.class
```

It is possible to deploy the raw EJB archive file to WebLogic Server, without first running it through appc. When this is done, the actual compilation step is deferred until the EJB container processes the archive file during the deployment of the application. WebLogic Server will also recompile on deployment if it detects that any of the files in the jar archive have changed or if the jar was created using a different version of the compiler, even if the difference is only a service pack. This information is stored in the _WL_GENERATED file. Automatic compilation on deployment is a good development time convenience, but will increase the length of time it takes your EJB to deploy.

A further advantage of running appc is that it will enhance persistent classes.

Best Practice

To minimize deployment time, your formal build scripts should include an appc stage. For this to be effective, the version of appc must be taken from a WebLogic Server installation with the same version and service pack as the expected production environment.

EJB Remote Business Interfaces and JNDI

Session beans can define remote business interfaces by annotating them with javax.ejb.Remote.

```
// MyEJB.java
package example;

public interface MyEJB
{
    String helloWorld();
}

// MyEJBImpl.java
package example;

import javax.ejb.Remote;
import javax.ejb.Stateless;

@Stateless
@Remote
public class MyEJBImpl implements MyEJB
{
    @Override
    public String helloWorld()
    {
        return "Hello world";
    }
}
```

Remote clients can look up the session bean in JNDI and invoke it over RMI. The Java EE 5 specification does not define a portable way to map the EJB to a well-known name in JNDI. Standardized mappings will be included in Java EE 6, and a future version of WebLogic Server. In the meantime, the mapping to JNDI is vendor-specific behavior.

WebLogic Server provides two options for mapping a session bean's remote business interface into the global JNDI tree. The mapping can be specified in the `weblogic-ejb-jar.xml` deployment descriptor, or the `mappedName` element of the `@Stateless` or `@Stateful` annotations can be used.

Here's an example `weblogic-ejb-jar.xml` descriptor that maps the `MyEJB` remote business interface to the global JNDI name `ejbs.MyEJB`.

```
<weblogic-ejb-jar xmlns="http://xmlns.oracle.com/weblogic/weblogic-ejb-jar"
                  xmlns:j2ee="http://java.sun.com/xml/ns/javaee"
                  xmlns:xsi="http://www.w3.org/2001/XMLSchema-instance"
                  xsi:schemaLocation="http://xmlns.oracle.com/weblogic/weblogic-ejb-
jar http://www.oracle.com/technology/weblogic/weblogic-ejb-jar/1.0/weblogic-ejb-
jar.xsd">
  <weblogic-enterprise-bean>
    <ejb-name>MyEJBImpl</ejb-name>
    <stateless-session-descriptor>
      <business-interface-jndi-name-map>
        <business-remote>example.MyEJB</business-remote>
        <jndi-name>ejbs.MyEJB</jndi-name>
      </business-interface-jndi-name-map>
    </stateless-session-descriptor>
  </weblogic-enterprise-bean>
</weblogic-ejb-jar>
```

The value set in the `<ejb-name>` element must match the name of the EJB. There is no direct relation between the name of the EJB and its JNDI names. The name can be set using the `name` element of the `@Stateless` or `@Stateful` annotations, and defaults to the unqualified name of the bean class. The `<business-interface-jndi-name-map>` element has at most one mapping for each remote business interface of the EJB. Take care when specifying the `<ejb-name>` and `<business-remote>` values. If you misspell these, WebLogic Server will not complain when the EJB is deployed; the EJB will simply not be bound to the JNDI name.

The other way to bind a session bean into the global JNDI tree is to use the `mappedName` element of the `@Stateless` or `@Stateful` annotations.

```
@Stateless(mappedName="myEjb")
@Remote
public class MyEJBImpl implements MyEJB
{
    ...
```

A bean can have multiple remote interfaces. The JNDI name used by WebLogic Server is the supplied `mappedName` further qualified with the remote interface class name. In our example, the global JNDI name will be `myEJB#example.MyEJB`. The way the JNDI name is constructed is specific to WebLogic Server. The EJB specification explicitly warns that using `mappedName` is non-portable.

There are two minor disadvantages to using `mappedName` to bind an EJB into the global JNDI tree. First, it does not allow an arbitrary JNDI name to be specified — the interface name will always be appended. Second, it is specified within the source code, but is non-portable. We generally prefer to keep vendor-specific behavior in deployment descriptors, but the simplicity of placing all the binding information in a single annotation is a compelling counter-argument. We will use the `mappedName` element for this unless there is a strong requirement to write portable code.

One reason to implement a remote business interface is to allow a session EJB to be called from RMI clients or code running in other servers. WebLogic Server 11g can interoperate with clients running on WebLogic Server 8.1 or later. However, the EJB 3.0 client view is only supported with clients running against WebLogic Server 10.0 or later. Unlike EJB 2.1 remote interfaces, an EJB 3.0 remote business interface is not required to be a valid RMI interface. Earlier versions of WebLogic Server do not have the client side classes necessary to call the non-RMI interfaces. If you need to call a session EJB from WebLogic Server 9.2 or earlier, and other clients that are not EJB 3.0 aware, you should either add an EJB 2.1 client view to the EJB, or ensure that the remote business interface is also a valid RMI interface — that is, it extends `java.rmi.Remote` and each method declares that it throws `RemoteException`. You will also need to ensure the client is using a version of the remote business interface compiled with a compatible version of `javac`.

> For an EJB to be called remotely by a client running on WebLogic Server 9.2 or earlier, it must either implement an EJB 2.1 client view or ensure that its remote business interface is a valid RMI interface.

References between EJBs

EJBs rarely exist in isolation. Their implementations often need to call other EJBs, and require a way to look up these EJBs. The EJB specification allows an EJB to declare references to other EJBs, either in its deployment descriptor, or by using the `@EJB` annotation. This avoids the need to hard code the global JNDI names or locations of the referenced beans in the EJB implementation code. The references can be customized by modifying the deployment descriptor or using a deployment plan. This makes the EJB a more reusable component.

The `<ejb-ref>` and `<ejb-local-ref>` elements in the `ejb-jar.xml` descriptor are used to map references to other EJBs into the local `java:comp/env` environment. The application code then uses logical JNDI names in the `java:comp/env` namespace, and the deployment descriptor specifies how the container should resolve these names.

Setting up an EJB reference in deployment descriptors requires coordinated changes to the code, the `ejb-jar.xml` descriptor, and sometimes the `weblogic-ejb-jar.xml` descriptor as well. The annotation and dependency injection features introduced in EJB 3.0 are much more convenient. The `@EJB` annotation keeps the declaration of an EJB reference within the code, but the mapping can still be overridden if necessary in a deployment descriptor.

In this section, we discuss the details of setting up references to EJBs in the same application, and to EJBs in other applications. We end this section with a discussion of the WebLogic Server pass-by-reference optimization

Referring to EJB Components in the Same Application

It is very common for EJB components to refer to other EJB components contained in the same Java EE application. All EJB components in the same EJB archive file are in the same application, as are all EJB components in different archive files packaged in a single enterprise application (`.ear`).

EJBs can, of course, look up each other directly using known global JNDI names.

```
Context ctx = new InitialContext();
MyOtherEJB myOtherEJB = (MyOtherEJB)ctx.lookup("myejbs.MyOtherEJB");
```

This technique increases the coupling between EJB components because the global JNDI name of the referenced EJB is hard coded in multiple places. When a global JNDI lookup is used directly, the container knows nothing of the reference.

Alternatively, an EJB reference can be declared to the container. The container resolves the target EJB during deployment, and makes it available in the local `java:comp/env` environment.

```
MyOtherEJB myOtherEJB = (MyOtherEJB)ctx.lookup("java:comp/env/ejb/MyEJB");
```

EJB 3.0 has added a `lookup()` convenience method to `EJBContext` that provides direct access to an EJB's environment without the need to use JNDI APIs, so the following will also work.

```
@Resource
SessionContext sessionContext;
...
MyOtherEJB myOtherEJB = (MyOtherEJB)context.lookup("ejb/MyEJB");
```

There are three ways to map an environment entry to the target EJB.

In the first approach, the referring component declares the reference by including an `<ejb-ref>` element (for remote business interfaces) or an `<ejb-local-ref>` element (for local business interfaces) in the `ejb-jar.xml` descriptor.

```
<session>
  <ejb-name>MyEJBImpl</ejb-name>
  <ejb-local-ref>
    <ejb-ref-name>ejb/MyOtherEJB</ejb-ref-name>
    <local>example.MyOtherEJB</local>
  </ejb-local-ref>
</session>
```

The `<ejb-local-reference-description>` element in the `weblogic-ejb-jar.xml` descriptor is then used to map this reference to a particular global JNDI name.

```
<ejb-local-reference-description>
  <ejb-ref-name>ejb/MyOtherEJB</ejb-ref-name>    <!-- Matches name in ejb-jar.xml -->
  <jndi-name>myejbs.MyOtherEJB</jndi-name>
</ejb-local-reference-description>
```

In the second approach, the referring component includes an `<ejb-link>` element in the `<ejb-local-ref>` element in `ejb-jar.xml`, specifying the name of the other EJB component.

```
<ejb-local-ref>
  <ejb-ref-name>ejb/MyOtherEJB</ejb-ref-name>
  <local>example.MyOtherEJB</local>
  <ejb-link>MyOtherEJBImpl</ejb-link>
</ejb-local-ref>
```

With this approach there is no need to bind the referenced EJB into the global JNDI tree. No elements are required in the `weblogic-ejb-jar.xml` descriptor, which means the code is portable between containers. The container automatically maps the `ejb/MyOtherEJB` reference to the `example.MyOtherEJB` business interface and binds it to the referring EJB's environment at `java:comp/env/ejb/MyOtherEJB`. The name `MyOtherEJBImpl` is the logical name of the EJB set using the `name` element of the `@Stateless` or `@Stateful` annotations or, by default, the unqualified name of the bean class. The `<ejb-link>` element may also provide the name of the EJB archive file hosting the desired component.

```
<ejb-link>another.jar#MyOtherEJB</ejb-link>
```

This is necessary only if two EJBs are in two different archive files and use the same logical name.

The third approach uses the `@EJB` annotation on the referring EJB class.

```
@EJB(name="ejb/MyOtherEJB", beanInterface=example.MyOtherEJB.class)
@Stateless
@Remote
public class MyEJBImpl implements MyEJB
{
    ...
}
```

This approach is similar to using an `<ejb-local-ref>`, but has the benefit of requiring no deployment descriptor entries. A JNDI lookup of `java:comp/env/ejb/MyOtherEJB` is still required.

The `@EJB` annotation also supports a `beanName` element, which is interpreted in the same way as the value of an `<ejb-link>` element. In this case we've left it out, so the container will attempt to resolve the reference based on the type of the business interface. This will work, so long as a single EJB implements that business interface. The container will perform similar *auto-wiring* if we declare an `<ejb-ref>` or an `<ejb-local-ref>` without an `<ejb-link>` or a binding in `weblogic-ejb-jar.xml`.

Finally, EJB 3.0 dependency injection can be used to remove the need for an explicit lookup. The `@EJB` annotation is used again, but applied to a field of the referring EJB, rather than at class level.

```
@Stateless
@Remote
public class MyEJBImpl implements MyEJB
{
    @EJB
    private MyOtherEJB myOtherEJB;
    ...
}
```

It doesn't get much simpler than this. When `MyEJBImpl` is deployed, the container will inject a reference to an EJB with the appropriate business interface. This is portable and requires no deployment descriptor entries. The EJB will be bound to `java:comp/env/example.MyEJBImpl/myOtherEJB`, but because the container has set the reference, there is no need for a JNDI lookup. The `beanInterface` and `beanName` elements can be used for disambiguation if the reference type is a superclass of the business interface, or if it is implemented by multiple EJBs in the application.

A further benefit of using dependency injection is that the implementation class can be constructed easily in a unit test context, where the value of the `@EJB` field is set directly by the unit test code. As we

197

noted earlier in this chapter, it is a best practice to add access methods to your EJBs so that unit tests can simulate the container dependency injection and populate annotated fields.

> **Best Practice**
>
> Use `@EJB` annotations, or `<ejb-ref>`/`<ejb-local-ref>` deployment descriptor elements, rather than direct lookup using global JNDI names, to reduce coupling between components.
>
> In most applications, using dependency injection with the `@EJB` annotation will be the simplest approach and will allow your EJB code to be unit tested easily.

Referring to External EJB Components

EJB components located in different enterprise application archive (`.ear`) files or other EJB jar files not part of the current application, are considered external components whether or not they run in the same WebLogic Server instance. These components are not part of the same deployment, so the `<ejb-link>` mechanism for referring to other components is not available. Components must use either global JNDI names or include appropriate `<ejb-ref>` elements in `ejb-jar.xml` and `<ejb-reference-description>` elements in the `weblogic-ejb-jar.xml` descriptor to look up external components. Note that local business interfaces can only be used within an application, so external components must be looked up and invoked through their remote business interfaces.

Because the components are external to the current application and more likely to change their global JNDI names, we suggest you use `<ejb-ref>` and `<ejb-reference-description>` elements instead of directly using global JNDI names.

The `<ejb-reference-description>` allows lookup of components in the host WebLogic Server's global JNDI tree. If the location of the referenced EJB is truly remote, use WebLogic Server's Foreign JNDI Provider feature to create a binding in the global JNDI tree, and place the configuration of its physical location under the administrator's control.

> **Best Practice**
>
> Use `<ejb-ref>` and `<ejb-reference-description>` elements to access EJB components in other applications.
>
> If the referenced EJB is truly remote, use WebLogic Server's Foreign JNDI Provider feature to map its location into the local server's global JNDI tree.

Calling Components by Reference

The Java EE specification requires that EJB components invoked through their remote interfaces must use pass-by-value semantics, meaning that method parameters are copied during the invocation. Changes made to a parameter in the bean method are not reflected in the caller's version of the object. Copying method parameters is required in the case of a true remote invocation, of course, because the parameters are serialized by the underlying RMI infrastructure before being provided to the bean method. Pass-by-value semantics are also required between components located in different enterprise applications in the same Java virtual machine due to classloader constraints.

EJB components located in the same enterprise application archive (.ear) file are loaded by the same classloader and have the option of using pass-by-reference semantics for all invocations, eliminating the unnecessary copying of parameters passed during the invocation and improving performance. Set the <enable-call-by-reference> parameter to true in the weblogic-ejb-jar.xml descriptor file to enable this feature for each bean in your application. Local references always use pass-by-reference semantics and are unaffected by the <enable-call-by-reference> setting.

When you deploy an EJB with a remote interface and do not enable call by reference, WebLogic Server will issue a warning of the performance cost. You can disable this warning by adding <disable-warning>BEA-010202</disable-warning> to the weblogic-ejb-jar.xml descriptor, or by using the @weblogic.javaee.DisableWarnings annotation.

> The default value of **<enable-call-by-reference>** was **true** in WebLogic Server 7.0 but is **false** in WebLogic Server 8.1 and later to comply with Sun's Java EE licensing policy changes that require all Java EE compatible servers to support the specification with their out-of-the-box configuration. Be sure to set **<enable-call-by-reference>** to true for all beans in your application that have remote business interfaces to avoid parameter copying unless your application requires copying for functional correctness.

Transaction Isolation

A purist would expect the effects of an uncommitted transaction not to be visible to other transactions. The transactions are said to be *isolated* from one another. Achieving this level of isolation is costly from a performance perspective, and in the real world it is common to relax the isolation requirements.

The JDBC API has four increasing levels of transaction isolation; they can be set on a per-transaction basis. These are described in Table 6-2.

Table 6-2: JDBC Isolation Levels

Isolation Level	Description
READ_UNCOMMITTED	Transactions can view uncommitted changes made by other transactions.
READ_COMMITTED	Protects against *dirty reads*. Transactions can view only committed changes made by other transactions.
REPEATABLE_READ	Protects against *non-repeatable reads*. Once a transaction has read a row, it will not see changes made to that row by other transactions.
SERIALIZABLE	Protects against *phantom reads*. A transaction will receive consistent answers if it queries the same table twice. It will not see new rows committed by other transactions between the two queries.

Your database may not support all four levels. The Oracle database only supports READ_COMMITTED and SERIALIZABLE.

JPA maintains a consistent persistence context in memory, and can use optimistic locking to ensure the consistency of the persistence context. Optimistic locking requires that the JDBC isolation level is at least `READ_COMMITTED`. It's usually not necessary to set the JDBC isolation level higher than this — the caching of data in each transaction's persistence context will protect against non-repeatable and phantom reads, and optimistic locking will ensure that the database is consistent after flushing the persistence context.

You may need to consider setting a stricter isolation level than `READ_COMMITTED` for transactions that use JPQL queries because they are partially evaluated against the database, and then augmented by information in the persistence context. This is a phantom read problem. The results of a query may contain changes that others have committed since the transaction began, and so not match the existing persistence context. This can be protected against using a `SERIALIZABLE` isolation level, but this is rarely required, because few transactions query the same information twice with JPQL, and if the application accesses the data again, it usually does so from the persistence context.

Here's another example that can be solved by using the `SERIALIZABLE` transaction isolation level. Consider two transactions working on two `Account` entities, each containing $100. The first transaction finds the `Account` entity for account 1, and then later finds the `Account` entity for account 2. In between the two finds, the second transaction transfers $50 from account 1 to account 2. If the isolation level is `REPEATABLE_READ` or less, when the first transaction looks at the balance of each `Account`, it will find the first has $100 and the second has $150 — an extra $50 has been created. Let's consider some options to prevent this problem and provide the first transaction with the correct total of $200.

❑   Use the `SERIALIZABLE` isolation level. This will solve the problem, but can be expensive in performance terms, particularly if applied to every transaction.

❑   Take out `LockModeType.READ` locks on the accounts using the `EntityManager.lock()`. This works if `Account` is a versioned entity (it has a `@Version` column). Rather than give the first transaction the correct answer, it will ensure that the first transaction fails with an `OptimisticLockException`. This is an appropriate solution if the chance of concurrent modification is small, or if there is a requirement to notify the user of concurrent attempts to modify the account.

❑   Take out `LockModeType.WRITE` locks on the accounts, and flush the persistent context so no others transactions can write to it. Again, `Account` needs to be a versioned entity. If the flush succeeds, the second transaction will receive an `OptimisticLockException` and the first will be able to commit. For `LockModeType.WRITE`, most implementations, including OpenJPA, will hold a database lock on the account rows. Like the `SERIALIZABLE` option, this has negative performance consequences, but at least the application can apply write locks selectively.

The first transaction could use a single JPQL query to find both accounts using one SQL statement. This solution is simple, and efficient. It does not extend to more complex scenarios; for example, reading a consistent view of two entities of unrelated types. However, it should be favored as a good way to enforce read consistency.

The transaction level can be set using the `<transaction-isolation>` element of the `weblogic-ejb-jar.xml` descriptor, or with the WebLogic Server–specific annotation `@weblogic.javaee.TransactionIsolation`. If the `<transaction-isolation>` element isn't used, the database's default transaction isolation level will apply. The default transaction isolation for the Oracle database is `READ_COMMITTED`.

Here's a `weblogic-ejb-jar.xml` descriptor that configures all EJB methods for the `PropertyServicesImpl` EJB to use the `READ_COMMITTED` isolation level.

```xml
<weblogic-ejb-jar xmlns="http://xmlns.oracle.com/weblogic/weblogic-ejb-jar"
                  xmlns:j2ee="http://java.sun.com/xml/ns/javaee"
                  xmlns:xsi="http://www.w3.org/2001/XMLSchema-instance"
                  xsi:schemaLocation="http://xmlns.oracle.com/weblogic/weblogic-ejb-
jar http://www.oracle.com/technology/weblogic/weblogic-ejb-jar/1.0/weblogic-ejb-
jar.xsd">
  <transaction-isolation>
    <isolation-level>TransactionReadCommitted</isolation-level>
    <method>
      <ejb-name>PropertyServicesImpl</ejb-name>
      <method-name>*</method-name>
    </method>
  </transaction-isolation>
</weblogic-ejb-jar>
```

Best Practice

The `READ_COMMITTED` transaction isolation level is appropriate for most transactions that use JPA and optimistic locking.

A more strict isolation level may be required for transactions that perform several JPQL queries, or use features that bypass the JPA persistence context, such as Kodo's large result set proxies (described later). This can limit performance and scalability.

Before you increase the isolation level, consider whether you can achieve your consistency goals by using JPQL to read related entities using a single SQL operation, or by using Entity Manager locks.

Session Bean Features

We'll now consider WebLogic Server–specific features related to session bean components and their management by the container.

Stateless Session EJB Pooling

WebLogic Server maintains a pool of stateless session EJB instances for each SLSB deployment. This pool improves performance, because a client request can be handled immediately by any free initialized EJB instance. By default, the pool starts empty, and grows on demand. This can be controlled with the `<initial-beans-in-free-pool>` and `<max-beans-in-free-pool>` deployment descriptor parameters.

The SLSB pool can also shrink in size. A bean instance will be removed if it has been idle for more than the value of `<idle-timeout-seconds>` (by default, 600 seconds), and there are more than `<initial-beans-in-free-pool>` beans in the pool.

The default value of 0 for <initial-beans-in-free-pool> is fine for most SLSB deployments. You may wish to set <initial-beans-in-free-pool> if your SLSB is particularly expensive to initialize so that you force the initialization of a number of bean instances at deployment time, and you ensure that pool shrinking does not discard these beans.

The default value of 1000 for <max-beans-in-free-pool> is also appropriate for most SLSB deployments. Unless an SLSB recursively calls itself (the only way that a single execute thread might require more than one active instance of the SLSB), this default limit will not practically be reached. If you set <max-beans-in-free-pool>, you are choosing deliberately to throttle your application. If there are no idle bean instances, an execute thread making a new request will block until a bean becomes available or the transaction times out. If remote clients call the SLSB, it is a good idea to use the <dispatch-policy> deployment descriptor element to assign the EJB instance to a custom work manager with a <max-threads-constraint> set to the same value as <max-beans-in-free-pool>. The <max-threads-constraint> will mean that surplus requests are left in the self-tuning thread pool's execute queue, rather than requiring an execute thread. The <max-beans-in-free-pool> setting is still required to ensure that non-remote calls to the SLSB (which will not use the work manager specified by the <dispatch-policy>) do not cause the pool size to increase beyond the desired limit.

Best Practice

The default pool settings for stateless session beans are usually appropriate. Set <initial-beans-in-free-pool> if an SLSB is expensive to initialize. Set <max-beans-in-free-pool> if you wish to constrain the number of concurrent requests to the SLSB.

If you set <max-beans-in-free-pool> and your SLSB is called by remote clients, consider associating the bean with a custom work manager that has a <max-threads-constraint> of the same size as <max-beans-in-free-pool>.

Stateless session beans provide a simple way to implement a managed resource pool. Suppose you use an SLSB to control access to a backend resource with which you communicate over a TCP socket. Each SLSB instance manages its own TCP connection, which is initialized in a @PostConstruct method. The <initial-beans-in-free-pool> parameter controls the initial number of connections in the pool, and the <max-beans-in-free-pool> parameter controls the maximum number of connections.

Best Practice

Stateless session beans are an effective way to implement a managed resource pool.

Stateful Session EJB Cache Management

WebLogic Server creates stateful session bean instances as they are needed to service client requests. Between requests these instances reside in a bean-specific cache in the *active* state, ready for the next request. The size of the cache is limited by the <max-beans-in-cache> element in the weblogic-ejb-jar.xml deployment descriptor file. The default value is 1000. So long as your application never requires more than `<max-beans-in-cache>` instances of the SFSB at any given time to service all concurrent clients, there is no contention for the cache and performance is optimal. If you limit the number of beans in the cache, WebLogic Server may be forced to manage the cache in a fairly active manner using the following rules.

❏ If the cache is full, bean instances that are not being used at that moment for client requests are subject to passivation. Setting the `<idle-timeout-seconds>` parameter has no effect on this rule because the server must make room for additional instances.

❏ If bean-managed transaction demarcation is used, a transaction may not be committed or rolled back at the end of a business method call. This leaves the bean instance associated with the transaction, pinned in the cache, and not eligible for passivation. Earlier in this chapter, we noted applications that keep transactions open between SFSB calls do not scale well and are difficult to manage.

❏ If the cache is full and all instances are currently pinned in the cache fulfilling client requests, WebLogic Server throws a `CacheFullException`. It will not block and wait for an instance to become available for passivation. If container-managed transaction demarcation is used, this condition cannot occur if the `<max-beans-in-cache>` setting is higher than the maximum number of execute threads and the processing of each client request uses a single SFSB.

❏ Passivation logic is controlled by the `<cache-type>` and `<idle-timeout-seconds>` elements in the descriptor. The default setting for `<cache-type>`, not recently used (NRU), passivates beans only when the number of active beans approaches the `<max-beans-in-cache>` setting. An alternative `<cache-type>` value, least recently used (LRU), passivates based on both the maximum cache size and when the bean hasn't been used for longer than the value of the `<idle-timeout-seconds>` setting. The NRU strategy is lazy; the LRU strategy is eager. Although the LRU setting can be a convenient way of enforcing idle timeouts on the resources the objects encapsulate, it requires the container to keep track of the bean's access time and maintain an ordered list that gets updated after each bean access. Unless you have a good reason to need idle timeouts strictly enforced, most applications should retain the default NRU algorithm.

❏ In addition to its role with the LRU cache type, the `<idle-timeout-seconds>` property has another purpose. It is the default timeout value for passivated instances, unless the separate `<session-timeout-seconds>` property has been set. Passivated instances that have been unused for longer than this timeout are subject to removal from disk storage during cache maintenance. If the container removes an SFSB in this way, it does not invoke `@PreDestroy` or `ejbRemove()` methods.

❏ If the `<idle-timeout-seconds>` property is set to zero, beans are simply removed when chosen for passivation and are never passivated to disk storage. This can be a useful option to avoid passivating old instances representing lost clients or transactions that were completed long before. Of course, this can also cause long-running clients to lose their sessions if the `<max-beans-in-cache>` is not properly tuned.

Recall that passivation of beans refers to the serialization of non-transient data in the bean to disk storage to release the memory used by the bean. The next request for the passivated bean will require activation, the reverse process, where bean elements are read from the disk store and the active bean instance is recreated in memory. Needless to say, passivation and activation cycles can be extremely expensive. You should monitor the amount of passivation activity occurring in your system using the WebLogic Console and tune the `<max-beans-in-cache>` setting to reduce or eliminate this activity to achieve high performance.

> **Best Practice**
>
> Avoid excessive passivation of stateful session beans by setting `<max-beans-in-cache>` high enough to meet the instance requirements for the expected maximum concurrent user count.

Your application should always call a `@Remove` method to delete the active bean instance from the cache when a client is through using the instance. Failure to call a `@Remove` method leaves the bean instance in the active state and consumes one slot in the cache, requiring eventual passivation by WebLogic Server during cache management to make room for additional client beans.

> **Best Practice**
>
> Always call a `@Remove` method on a stateful session bean after you are done using it to delete it from the bean cache to free up memory and prevent unnecessary passivation.

The `<idle-timeout-seconds>` setting clearly is very important in cache management. The bean is subject to passivation once the timeout expires, assuming the LRU algorithm is being used, and may be removed from storage completely after the timeout period passes again. The default timeout value, 600 seconds, may be too short if users are likely to pause between requests for a longer period of time. If you are using SFSBs with a web application, it might make sense to set this timeout value equal to the `HttpSession` timeout value for your web application, for example, to be more consistent. Otherwise, review your business requirements and set the `<idle-timeout-seconds>` to the lowest value possible that still meets your application's requirements.

> **Best Practice**
>
> Set the `<idle-timeout-seconds>` to the lowest value possible while still meeting your business requirements for the application.

In-Memory Replication for Stateful Session EJBs

Stateful session bean components are used to encapsulate client-specific data and processes that must maintain state across multiple method invocations. These invocations may be separated by periods as short as milliseconds or as long as hours, subject to timeout settings. State that is maintained across multiple invocations would be lost if the SFSB was deployed to a single server instance that failed or became unavailable to the client. Fortunately, WebLogic Server provides failover for stateful session beans deployed in a cluster, just as it does for `HttpSession` data through the use of in-memory replication.

Figure 6-1 illustrates the basic in-memory replication scenario and shows communication paths before and after the failure of Server2. In this example, Client155 was using the SFSB155 component hosted on

Server2 as the primary copy of the bean. When that server failed, Client155 was automatically redirected to the backup copy of the SFSB155 component hosted on the other server. This failover logic is provided by the replica-aware stub object used by the client for all communication with the bean. The stub acts as a proxy for the bean in much the same way the web server plug-in acts as a proxy for web applications and provides failover in the presentation tier.

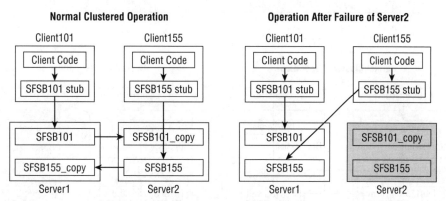

Figure 6-1: The replica-aware stub provides SFSB failover.

Changes made to the primary copy of an SFSB component are copied to the replicated version on the backup server at the end of a committed transaction involving the SFSB component. Note that modified SFSB data may be lost if either server fails during the post-commit transfer of data to the backup server because the replication is done outside the scope of the transaction.

Although we generally recommend storing session data in the HttpSession and using HttpSession replication alone when possible, you might consider using SFSB replication to store business data or the intermediate results of a multi-step process under some conditions. Figure 6-2 illustrates the web application replication scenario using an HttpSession to store the replica-aware stub object and a replicated SFSB component to store the business data.

Note that both the web application and EJB components are located on the same machine. Failure of that machine will cause the web server plug-in to fail over to servlets and JSPs to a WebLogic Server instance running on another machine. How can you be sure that the backup copy of the SFSB data will be located on the same machine as the backup copy of the HttpSession data, as illustrated in Figure 6-2? Just as WebLogic Server always prefers to communicate with EJB components located in the same application as the web application components, it normally configures the failover copies of both the HttpSession data and the replicated SFSB data on the same backup server.

Unfortunately, the collocation of both kinds of backup data is not guaranteed to occur in all conditions. If the HttpSession secondary and the SFSB secondary are located on different machines, you can easily get into a situation where a single client request involves calling from one WebLogic Server cluster member to another to process the request. Performance will suffer if this scenario occurs, and the large number of cross-server messages and the threads consumed by these messages also expose your application to a potential deadlock condition discussed in Chapter 13.

> Be careful when storing SFSB references in the `HttpSession` because in-memory replication doesn't guarantee collocation of secondary objects and may lead to excessive server-to-server calls in the same cluster after a primary server failure. Not only will this kill your performance, but it also will expose your application to potential deadlock situations.

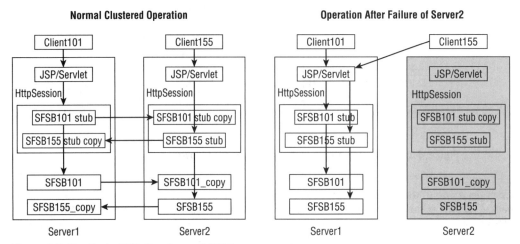

Figure 6-2: Replicated HttpSession and SFSB component.

Recognize that SFSB replication is more costly in terms of memory and performance than `HttpSession` replication because there is no simple way for the container to determine which portions of the bean have changed. Whereas `HttpSession` replication relies on `setAttribute()` calls to determine the data that must be sent to the backup server, SFSB replication requires before and after images of the SFSB to determine changes requiring replication at the end of the transaction. For efficiency, the server keeps the after image from the last transaction to use as the before image for the next; this means that you have two copies of the bean in memory in the primary server and one in the secondary server.

Why would you use replicated SFSB components when `HttpSession` replication fills essentially the same role? Web applications should probably stick with `HttpSession` replication to maximize performance and avoid introducing additional complexity, but not all applications are web applications. Replicated SFSB components allow non-web applications to maintain state between method invocations in a fully clustered fashion as well.

Configuring SFSB components for in-memory replication requires a `<replication-type>` element in the descriptor for the stateless session bean in `weblogic-ejb-jar.xml`.

```
<stateful-session-clustering>
  ...
  <replication-type>InMemory</replication-type>
</stateful-session-clustering>
```

Handles to Session Beans

EJB 2.x defines the concept of a *handle* to an EJB. A handle is an object that represents a remote EJB instance. It can be serialized to a persistent store, or perhaps sent to a different client process. When deserialized, it can be used to access the EJB so long as the EJB still exists on the server.

Although the simplified EJB 3.0 API does not include support for handles, WebLogic Server provides an extension API to generate handles for EJB 3.0 session beans with remote business interfaces. The RMI stub to a remote business interface can be cast to the `weblogic.ejb.spi.BusinessObject` interface. `BusinessObject` has a `_WL_getBusinessObjectHandle()` method that returns a handle. The handle implements `weblogic.ejb.spi.BusinessHandle`. The handle's `getBusinessObject()` method can be used to restore a reference to the session EJB's business interface.

> **Best Practice**
>
> The `weblogic.ejb.spi.BusinessHandle` API is convenient, but is proprietary and will tie your code to WebLogic Server. If you need to create a handle to a session bean, consider modifying your bean to support the EJB 2.1 client view, and then using the standard `javax.ejb.Handle` API.

Idempotent Methods

Session beans can declare to the container that some of their methods are *idempotent*; that is, they have the same result if called once as if they are called multiple times. For example, a `setAddress()` method may well be idempotent, because setting the same information again won't change anything and concurrency can be handled by standard transaction and optimistic locking features. On the other hand, `creditAccount(Money amount)` certainly isn't idempotent.

Idempotent methods are declared using the `<idempotent-methods>` element of the `weblogic-ejb-jar.xml` descriptor, or the `@weblogic.javaee.Idempotent` annotation.

WebLogic Server takes advantage of knowing a method is idempotent when making remote calls to a cluster. If a remote call fails, and the EJB client stub knows it didn't manage to establish the connection to the server, it can always retry the operation on another server in the cluster. If a remote call fails in flight, *and the method is idempotent*, the EJB stub can always retry the operation on another server.

With modern, reliable networks this automatic retry may not seem a huge advantage. It can be of benefit if you wish to restart a server with minimal disruption to its clients.

> **Best Practice**
>
> When deploying remotely accessed EJBs to a cluster, consider declaring the idempotent methods in `weblogic-ejb-jar.xml`. This will reduce disruption to clients that are accessing a server when it fails or is shutdown.

Message-Driven Bean Features

Message-driven bean (MDB) components provide a bridge between JMS and EJB components by listening on JMS destinations and invoking EJB components. A number of WebLogic Server–specific features are available to improve the reliability and performance of MDB components.

MDBs are pooled in a manner very similar to SLSBs. The initial and maximum number of MDB instances can be controlled using the `<initial-beans-in-free-pool>` and `<max-beans-in-free-pool>` parameters in `weblogic-ejb-jar.xml`. Unless a custom work manager with a `<max-threads-constraint>` is specified using the `<dispatch-policy>`, an upper limit of 16 MDB instances is enforced. This upper limit is a significant difference compared to the behavior of WebLogic Server 8.1. In 8.1, the upper limit of an untuned MDB was a function of the size of the default execute thread pool.

Limiting the number of instances provides a simple mechanism to throttle the processing of incoming JMS messages. You may wish to do this to match the availability of resources used by an MDB, for example, the number of JDBC connections in a connection pool, or to set the priority of JMS requests versus other synchronous requests. A custom work manager should be used if more precise control is required.

WebLogic Server supports the clustering of JMS destinations and the migration of MDB components from failed servers to operational servers using administrative functions. MDB components may also be deployed across all servers in a cluster to provide high levels of performance and availability.

WebLogic Server permits MDB components to be deployed against third-party JMS providers while retaining proper container-managed transactional behaviors. WebLogic Server achieves this by starting a new transaction, enlisting the remote JMS destination within the transaction, polling for a message, and rolling back the transaction if none is found.

WebLogic Server can batch multiple calls to `onMessage()` for the receipt of messages in a single container-managed transaction. This can improve performance by spreading the cost of the transaction management across multiple `onMessage()` calls. Transaction batching does not require any change to user code; it is enabled by setting the `<max-messages-in-transaction>` deployment descriptor element. Because more work is done in a transaction, you may also need to increase the transaction timeout using `<trans-timeout-seconds>`.

Should the transaction batch fail due to a transaction timeout, WebLogic Server will temporarily reduce the batch size and resubmit the messages in smaller batches. Should the batch fail due to an `onMessage()` call throwing an exception or marking the transaction for rollback, WebLogic Server will reprocess each of the messages in an individual transaction.

Transaction batching is not suited for all applications. It may cause unexpected problems if the `onMessage()` relies on the transaction to isolate the effects of its work from other calls to `onMessage()`.

Additionally, if the `onMessage()` method is likely to call `setRollbackOnly()`, WebLogic Server will often have to reprocess messages in individual transactions, making transaction batching ineffective.

MDBs can be used with WebLogic Server's advanced JMS features, such as Store-And-Forward and Unit-Of-Order.

Chapter 10 discusses WebLogic Server JMS and MDB features and best practices in more depth.

OpenJPA and Kodo Features

In this section, we consider OpenJPA and Kodo-specific features. In what follows, when we refer to "Kodo" we are discussing a Kodo-only feature; when using "OpenJPA," we are discussing a feature available in both products.

Many of the OpenJPA and Kodo features we discuss here are set using product-specific annotations, and there is no option to use a vendor descriptor instead.

> **Many OpenJPA and Kodo features require the use of product-specific annotations. Using these annotations will make your application code less portable, and you should consider this when weighing the benefits of using the feature.**

The Kodo Deployment Descriptor

Kodo-specific configuration can be provided in a `persistence-configuration.xml` file, placed alongside the `persistence.xml` file. Unlike the JPA `persistence.xml` descriptor, this file is optional. When the `persistence-configuration.xml` is present, it must contain the entire Kodo-specific configuration, and the `persistence.xml` file should not contain any OpenJPA or Kodo properties.

The `persistence-configuration.xml` file allows you to keep the standard descriptor clean and portable. The XML format provides validation, and traps errors in the spelling of configuration item names. A further advantage of providing a `persistence-configuration.xml` file is that the WebLogic Console deployment tabs will provide advanced configuration support.

Kodo also allows the configuration using the standard `<properties>` element of the standard `persistence.xml` file. This is generally better for Java SE deployments. WebLogic Server 10.3 introduced support for using `persistence-configuration.xml` in a Java SE environment. However, doing this requires `weblogic.jar` to be on the `CLASSPATH`, a `SerializedSystemIni.dat` security salt file must be present in the working directory, and you will need to overwrite the default values of several properties, including `openjpa.TransactionMode` and `openjpa.NonTransactionalWrite` to make them suited for the Java SE environment.

> ### Best Practice
>
> Use the `persistence-configuration.xml` descriptor to set Kodo configuration for Java EE deployments.
>
> Use the standard JPA `<properties>` element to set Kodo configuration for Java SE deployments.

Although you have to choose one or the other of `persistence-configuration.xml` or `<properties>`, both support the full range of Kodo configuration. The naming convention for the descriptor elements differs from that of the property names. In the sections that follow, we refer to the OpenJPA and Kodo configuration settings using their full property names. They can be converted to the corresponding `persistence-configuration.xml` element by taking the last part of the name, placing hyphens between the words, and converting it to lowercase. For example, `openjpa.TransactionMode` becomes `<transaction-mode>`.

Fetch Groups

OpenJPA allows a set of fields to be grouped together into a *fetch group*. The fields in a fetch groups are loaded together, and fetch groups can be used to tune eager loading behavior. If you are familiar with WebLogic Server's EJB 2.x CMP implementation, you will recognize fetch groups as being similar to the field group feature.

A field can belong to several fetch groups. All fields that use JPA eager fetching belong to the predefined *default* fetch group, but custom fetch groups may also be defined.

Suppose you are developing an application to provide access to a defect-tracking database. A typical user might submit a query for known defects that affect a planned release of a product. The application will return a list of summary details for each product, perhaps containing a defect ID, a description field, the defect's severity, the date the defect was recorded, and one or two other fields. The user may then select one of the defects from the returned list, and be presented with full details covering perhaps 50 fields, some of them large. There are two types of queries that we wish to support — let's call them `getDefectSummaries()` and `getDefectDetail()`. This sort of user interaction is very common in online applications.

With standard JPA features, you might consider one of the following approaches.

❑ Model the database using a single `Defect` entity, and configure all of the fields to be eagerly loaded (the JPA default for basic fields). This approach will unnecessarily affect the performance of `getDefectSummaries()`, because the fields of every `Defect` returned by the query will be fully populated from the database, even though the information is unlikely to be used. A further problem is that the result will take up a large amount of memory, and perhaps may not even fit into the available memory.

❑ Model the database using a single `Defect` entity, configure the summary fields to be eagerly loaded, and the detail fields to be lazily loaded using `fetch=FetchType.LAZY`. This approach works well for `getDefectSummaries()`, because only the information that is required to populate the summary list will be loaded from the database. It is disastrous for the performance of `getDefectDetail()`; every field in the defect detail page will cause a separate query to the database.

❑ Model the database using `DefectSummary` and `DefectDetail` entities. Configure the one-to-one association between `DefectSummary` and `DefectDetails` to be lazily loaded, and all other fields to be eagerly loaded. This approach works well for both `getDefectSummaries()` and `getDefectDetail()`. However, you have been forced to introduce a boundary into your object model based solely on expected usage patterns. If the usage pattern changes, for example, if a field is moved from the details page to the summary page, you will have to refactor your code.

OpenJPA fetch groups provide a straightforward, configuration-based answer to this problem, and allow you to control the field loading separately from your object model. One simple answer, assuming the model uses a single `Defect` entity, would be to configure the summary fields to be eagerly loaded, the detail fields to be lazily loaded, and further configure the detail fields to belong to a *detail* custom fetch group. This means that when one of the detail fields is loaded, all of the detail fields will be loaded.

Fetch groups are configured using OpenJPA-specific annotations. Here's what our `Defect` entity might look like.

```
@Entity
@FetchGroups({
    @FetchGroup(name="detail", attributes={
        @FetchAttribute(name="additionalDetails"),
        @FetchAttribute(name="workLog"),
    })
})
public class Defect
{
    ...
    @Basic(fetch=FetchType.LAZY)
    private String additionalDetails;
    @Basic(fetch=FetchType.LAZY)
    private String workLog;
    ...
}
```

Custom fetch groups are particularly powerful when you wish to tune the loading behavior of groups of associated entities. You can control the group of entities and the subsets of their fields to be loaded, and also limit the depth to which recursive relationships will be traversed.

Best Practice

Configure OpenJPA fetch groups according to expected usage patterns to ensure you are loading the data you need and no more in the fewest number of SQL statements.

Examine the generated SQL during pre-production testing to confirm that your expectations were correct, and refine the fetch groups if necessary.

Also recognize one danger inherent in the use of fetch groups: Because the entity data might be fetched in multiple queries it is possible to have an entity in memory that represents data from different points in time, potentially representing inconsistent states. With typical transaction isolation settings, if another transaction made changes to the database between the first and second fetches you make, your copy of the bean might contain some data that reflects the update and some that does not. Optimistic concurrency will avoid corruption of the database itself, but your display or business logic might show inconsistent data.

> Using fetch groups to support partial loading of a bean's data can cause the bean to have inconsistent data loaded, with each group loaded at different points in time. Use caution when defining fetch groups to make sure that all interdependent fields are in the same group.

OpenJPA also provides a `FetchPlan` API for dynamic control of eagerly loaded fields. This might be useful in our defect tracking application if the fields that appear on the summary page are not fixed, but are selected according to user preference. The field groups or individual fields to load eagerly can be dynamically set based on the user preferences for each transaction. Similar to the `@FetchGroup` annotation, this is a valuable feature, so you may be willing to use it at the cost of tying your application to a vendor-specific API.

Eager Fetching

Eager fetching optimizes the number of SQL queries required when performing eager loading. Eager fetching is a Kodo feature, so is available in WebLogic Server but is not part of OpenJPA.

Eager fetching is on by default, and it is unlikely that you will have to tune it. It is useful to understand what it does so you can interpret the SQL statements that Kodo generates.

Loading an entity often requires querying across multiple tables, either because of associations to related entities or embedded classes or because of inheritance mappings. With eager fetching, Kodo produces a combined query that uses appropriate joins (often left outer joins) to retrieve all of the required data in a single database query. By default, eager fetching uses the *parallel* mode. In this mode, a further refinement causes several selects to be issued to load multiple entities that have eager relationships. Using a separate select for each entity avoids transferring more data than necessary from the database. In contrast, an outer join across multiple tables can return the same information in multiple rows. As the name suggests, these selects are issued in parallel, further improving performance.

Optimistic Locking Version Strategies

To apply optimistic locking in standard JPA code, you use the `@Version` annotation. JPA allows each entity to have at most a single `@Version` column, which must be mapped to the primary table for the entity and have one of the types `int`, `Integer`, `short`, `Short`, `long`, `Long`, `Timestamp`.

OpenJPA and Kodo provide more flexibility, but taking advantage of this requires the use of custom annotations and restricts portability. The JPA specification hints that additional mechanisms may be standardized by a future version of specification.

Support for other Version Field Types

In addition to the types supported by the JPA standard, OpenJPA allows version fields of type `byte` and `Byte`.

Kodo (but not OpenJPA) also allows you to specify a surrogate version column; that is, one that doesn't map to a field of the entity class, using the `@kodo.persistence.jdbc.LockGroupVersionColumn` annotation. If you use this feature, Kodo manages the version information for detached entities in hidden fields of the enhanced entity classes, and your application can neither read nor write it. Similarly, the version fields are not available to bulk update statements that use pure JPQL, so they can't be updated or verified.

> If you use Kodo's surrogate version column feature, you cannot externalize an entity's version information, and so cannot use the *Store version information in hidden fields* strategy we previously discussed.
>
> Additionally, you cannot extend JPQL bulk update statements to update and verify version information.

State Comparison Version Strategy

OpenJPA allows for versioning without any version column. Instead, an entity instance keeps a record of the original database state of the fields that are read during the transaction, and uses this to form the optimistic locking assertion in the WHERE clause of the SQL statements it uses to write to the database.

This *state comparison* strategy can be applied using the @org.apache.openjpa.persistence.jdbc. VersionStrategy annotation.

```
import org.apache.openjpa.jdbc.meta.strats.StateComparisonVersionStrategy;
import org.apache.openjpa.persistence.jdbc.VersionStrategy;
@VersionStrategy(StateComparisonVersionStrategy.ALIAS)
@Entity
public class Person
{
    ...
}
```

With versioning based on a version column, the UPDATE statement for modifying the firstName attribute of our Person entity will look something like this.

```
UPDATE Person SET firstName = ?, version = ? WHERE id = ? AND version = ?
```

The following shows how the statement changes when the state comparison versioning strategy is used.

```
UPDATE Person SET firstName = ? WHERE id = ? AND firstName = ? AND lastName = ? AND salutation = ?
```

The major advantage of the state comparison strategy is that it doesn't require a version column. This allows it to be used with an existing database schema, without requiring modifications.

The state comparison version strategy has a number of disadvantages.

❑　Each entity must keep a copy of the original value of every field that is read, and must send this back to the database with every update operation. This will impact performance for entities that have many columns.

❑　The strategy only checks the fields that are read during the transaction, and so lazily loaded fields will be ignored if they are not otherwise used. This may allow two transactions to update different parts of an entity independently without causing a locking exception. Depending on your application, this may be allowable, or even desirable because it increases concurrency. With lazily loaded fields, the state comparison strategy is more subtle and less predictable than the version column strategy.

❑ Only fields with simple, exact types are considered. For example, columns with a `float`, `BLOB`, or `Collection` value will not be taken into account. If a transaction only changes such a field, other concurrent transactions will not detect its update.

Best Practice

If you cannot modify the database schema to add a version column, consider using the OpenJPA state comparison versioning strategy.

Be aware of the performance cost of using this strategy with entities that have a large number of fields; that its behavior can be less predictable when used with lazily loaded fields; and that the strategy only detects changes in fields with simple, exact types.

Lock Groups

Optimistic locking in JPA works at entity granularity. Sometimes you may want to lock at a finer-grained level (allowing separate application threads to concurrently update different fields of the same entity), or not at all (that is, a commit will always overwrite the contents of the database). This can be achieved using Kodo's *lock groups* feature.

Lock groups are applied using the `@kodo.persistence.LockGroup` annotation. The following example shows our `Person` entity with added lock groups.

```
@Entity
public class Person
{
    @Id
    private long id;
    private String salutation;
    private String firstName;
    private String lastName;
    @LockGroup("location")
    private Location location;
    @LockGroup("location")
    private Date trackingDate;
    ...
}
```

Here we're assuming that the `location` and `trackingDate` fields are updated regularly by a separate tracking system. We don't want optimistic locking exceptions to be generated when committing a transaction that has modified the user's name if the tracking system has concurrently updated the location.

If the latest position set by the tracking system is acceptable, we might go further and disable optimistic locking entirely for these fields. To achieve this, we would simply annotate the fields with `@LockGroup(LockGroup.NONE)`.

> **Best Practice**
>
> Consider applying Kodo lock groups if you find contention between two types of transaction that update separate parts of an entity.
>
> You should also ask yourself whether you could split the entity into two separate entities and so remove the need to use a Kodo-specific feature. This will most likely require that the database schema is refactored but may lead to a more normalized schema that is a better fit for your application.

The implementation of lock groups requires a separate version column for each lock group. You must remove any existing @Version annotations from your code and add a @LockGroupVersionColumn annotation for each lock group.

```
@LockGroupVersionColumns({
  @LockGroupVersionColumn(), // Default lock group.
  @LockGroupVersionColumn(lockGroup="location"),
  })
@Entity public class Person {.. }
```

The column mappings for the version columns can be overridden using elements of the @LockGroupVersionColumn annotation.

Lock groups require the use of the surrogate version columns. You can't map these version columns to fields of your entity classes. The restrictions we mentioned earlier regarding surrogate version columns also apply to the lock groups feature.

Large Result Sets

Some database queries can return large amounts of data, perhaps more than will fit into the available memory. This data can take a significant amount of time to transfer between the database server and the application server. An application may find the information it needs in the early rows returned by a query, and not have to retrieve the later rows. OpenJPA provides features to allow an application to handle such large result sets efficiently.

Queries with Large Result Sets

When executing a database query, OpenJPA's default behavior is to load the entire result into memory. OpenJPA handles large result sets by loading the query results bit by bit as you iterate over the query result, and so allows you to deal with large tables containing millions of rows that might not fit into available memory.

To enable support for large result sets, you must set the openjpa.FetchBatchSize parameter. FetchBatchSize should be set to a positive number corresponding to the number of rows to retrieve at a time, or to 0 to use the JDBC driver's default batch size.

If your JDBC driver supports it, you can also set openjpa.jdbc.ResultSetType to one of forward-only, scroll-sensitive, or scroll-insensitive and FetchDirection to one of forward, reverse, or `unknown` to control the type of cursor used. Refer to the Javadoc for `java.sql.ResultSet` for details.

Finally, you can set the `openjpa.jdbc.LRSSize` parameter to control the strategy that OpenJPA uses to determine the size of a collection backed by a large result set whenever the application requests it. Under the default value of `query`, OpenJPA will issue a `SELECT COUNT(*)` query when the application first requests the size. If set to `last`, and you have set `ResultSetType` to `scroll-sensitive` or `scroll-insensitive`, this setting will use the JDBC driver's support for scrollable result sets to find the index of the last element. Otherwise, or if `LRSSize` is set to `unknown`, the size will always be reported as `Integer.MAX_VALUE`.

> Depending on the use of transactions and the transaction isolation level, the observed size of a collection may change during the course of iterating over a large result set. Further, if `openjpa.jdbc.LRSSize` is set to `last`, some JDBC drivers will load the entire result set into memory, negating the value of the large result set feature.
>
> Your application will be more robust if you avoid calling `size()` on large collections, and simply rely on iterating over collections.

Here's a `persistence-configuration.xml` that sets the `FetchBatchSize` parameter to 10.

```xml
<?xml version="1.0" encoding="UTF-8"?>
<persistence-configuration xmlns="http://www.bea.com/ns/weblogic/persistence-configuration"
                           xmlns:xsi="http://www.w3.org/2001/XMLSchema-instance"
                           xsi:schemaLocation="http://www.w3.org/2001/XMLSchema-instance http://www.bea.com/ns/weblogic/persistence-configuration">
  <persistence-unit-configuration name="BigRezDomain">
    <fetch-batch-size>10</fetch-batch-size>
  </persistence-unit-configuration>
</persistence-configuration>
```

Large Result Set Proxies

In addition to the large result set support for query operations, OpenJPA allows `Collection` and `Map` fields to be marked as a *large result set* field, using the `@org.apache.openjpa.persistence.LRS` annotation. OpenJPA handles such fields by delegating the collection operations to a database cursor, using a *large result set proxy*.

> ### Best Practice
> Large collections don't map well to an in-memory object model. If you are considering using the support for large result set proxies, question carefully whether the association belongs in your entity model. An entity with large collections is not well suited to detachment. Further, an OpenJPA-specific annotation is required. You may be better off using a JPQL query instead, and tuning `openjpa.FetchBatchSize` to prevent the whole result set from being loaded at once.

Second-level Caching

The JPA standard defines how entity instances should be cached in the persistence context. It does not specify any support for caching shared data between persistence contexts, typically called a *second-level* or *L2* cache; however, because JPA uses plain Java objects and has an optimistic locking model, it is straightforward for vendors to provide such a cache.

Kodo supports second-level caches, which it refers to as *data caches*. Configuring a data cache can dramatically increase performance with no changes to application code.

Data cache comes in several flavors. Of these, two are implemented entirely by Kodo: the *concurrent* data cache and the *least recently used* data cache. The least recently used data cache uses a smarter eviction scheme, but this requires more synchronization so the concurrent data cache generally gives better performance.

The other types of data cache rely on third-party distributed cache products, namely Gemstone's *GemFire* and Oracle's *Coherence*. Coherence Enterprise Edition is part of the WebLogic Suite and is included in many WebLogic Server licenses. We discuss how to use Coherence as a data cache a little later.

Tuning Data Caches

The concurrent and least recently used data caches have `CacheSize` and `SoftReferenceSize` parameters. The `CacheSize` parameter controls the basic size of the cache, and defaults to 1000. When the cache overflows, surplus entities are maintained with soft references so are at the mercy of the garbage collector. By default, the number of softly referenced entries is unlimited, but this can be constrained with the `SoftReferenceSize` parameter.

You can configure an eviction schedule for all types of data cache. The eviction schedule specifies the times and dates at which all the entries in the data cache will be cleared.

Multiple caches can be created. By default, entity instances are stored in the default cache. You can use the `@org.apache.openjpa.persistence.DataCache` annotation to specify that a different cache should be used for an entity class.

Cache entries are subject to a global `DataCacheTimeout` property. If a value retrieved from the cache is older than this value, it is discarded. The property defaults to no timeout. You can override the timeout on a per entity class basis using the `@DataCache` annotation.

Here's a sample `persistence-configuration.xml` using these features.

```
<?xml version="1.0" encoding="UTF-8"?>
<persistence-configuration xmlns=...>
  <persistence-unit-configuration name="BigRezDomain">
    <data-caches>
      <kodo-concurrent-data-cache>
        <name>default</name>
        <cache-size>100</cache-size>
        <soft-reference-size>1000</soft-reference-size>
        <!-- 2am every Sunday. -->
        <eviction-schedule>00,00 02 * * 1</eviction-schedule>
      </kodo-concurrent-data-cache>
```

```
      </data-caches>
      <data-cache-timeout>1000</data-cache-timeout>
      <single-jvm-remote-commit-provider/>
   </persistence-unit-configuration>
</persistence-configuration>
```

> Data caches work best when your system has exclusive access to the database tables.
> Data caches may not be appropriate if the information in your database is updated
> frequently by other systems or applications. Because the data cache has no way of
> learning about these updates, your application will often encounter optimistic lock
> failures. It is also at risk of presenting stale data to the user.
>
> By tuning the DataCacheTimeout, or choosing not to cache certain entity types, you
> may be able to reduce these problems to an acceptable level.

Configuring a Data Cache for Multiple JVMs

You may have noticed the `<single-jvm-remote-commit-provider>` element in the preceding sample
`persistence-configuration.xml`. This configures a trivial *remote commit provider*, telling Kodo not to
synchronize the cache information with other JVMs.

This is rarely appropriate in a production WebLogic Server deployment. The application will typically be
deployed over one or more clusters, each containing multiple managed servers. In these situations, you
will want to configure a different remote commit provider so that the managed servers' data caches can
be synchronized. Otherwise your application will suffer from optimistic locking and stale data problems,
similar to those that occur when a separate system is updating the database.

Kodo provides two built-in remote commit providers that can be used, one based on TCP sockets and
one on JMS topics. The JMS provider is preferred over the TCP provider in a Java EE environment like
WebLogic Server because it is integrated with the server's threading, monitoring, and configuration
features.

Better still, an alternative, more powerful approach is to use a third-party distributed cache. A dedicated
distributed caching product will provide sophisticated tuning and monitoring features, and will allow
you fine-grained control over where your objects are cached. You may even choose to store the objects
outside of WebLogic Server, in a separate tier of standalone Java virtual machines. We show you how to
use Oracle Coherence with Kodo next.

Using Oracle Coherence as a Second-Level Cache

Oracle Coherence is installed as a separate product from WebLogic Server. You should modify your
WebLogic Server `setDomainEnv.sh` or `setDomainEnv.cmd` script to add the `coherence.jar` file in the
Coherence `lib` directory to the `CLASSPATH`.

Coherence can be sensitive to the correct network configuration. Before you use it with Kodo, test that you
can run Coherence in a standalone manner by using the standard `cache-server.sh` and `coherence.sh`
command-line tools. You may need to add Coherence-specific properties to the Java command line. For
example, on an Ubuntu Linux machine, we find we need to add `-Djava.net.preferIPv4Stack=true`.

Having made these changes and restarted your server, you can modify your application to use the Coherence data cache implementation and redeploy. The Coherence implementation is controlled with the `TangosolDataCache` and `TangosolQueryCache` properties. (Tangosol was the company that developed Coherence, and was bought by Oracle in 2007). The query cache property determines whether query results (essentially the object identities) should be cached in the data store and returned for subsequent queries using the same parameters.

Here's a suitable `persistence-configuration.xml` to enable Coherence as a second-level cache.

```xml
<?xml version="1.0" encoding="UTF-8"?>
<persistence-configuration ...>
  <persistence-unit-configuration name="BigRezDomain">
    <data-caches>
      <tangosol-data-cache>
        <name>default</name>
      </tangosol-data-cache>
    </data-caches>
    <data-cache-timeout>1000</data-cache-timeout>
    <query-caches>
      <tangosol-query-cache/>
    </query-caches>
  </persistence-unit-configuration>
</persistence-configuration>
```

The type of the Coherence cache can be set using the `<tangosol-cache-type>` child element of `<data-cache>`. The allowed different cache types are *named*, *distributed*, and *replicated*. These control the cache topologies — that is, how the cached objects are shared between JVMs. We recommend that you omit the cache type from `persistence-configuration.xml`, in which case it will default to *named*, and instead control the cache topology and other Coherence settings by adding a `tangosol-coherence-override.xml` file to the server classpath. Refer to the Coherence user guide for more details.

Controlling Flush Behavior

When preparing to evaluate a JPQL query, OpenJPA will consider whether it might be affected by changes made to the current transaction's persistence context that have not yet been flushed to the database. If so, it will either evaluate the query in memory against the persistence context, or first flush the changes before making a database query.

If you set the `openjpa.IgnoreChanges` property to `true`, OpenJPA will instead ignore any changes that have not been flushed, and execute the query directly against the database. This is faster, but the application will then have to call `flush()` whenever it wants to be sure the results of the query are consistent with other changes made in the transaction.

Managed Inverses

We mentioned earlier in this chapter that JPA requires an application to keep bidirectional relationships consistent by making changes to both fields.

219

OpenJPA can automatically manage inverse relationships. This is enabled by setting the openjpa.InverseManager property to true. With this setting, OpenJPA detects changes to either side of an association, and automatically corrects the other side on flush(). This is a convenience for the programmer, but at the expense of non-portable code. It also opens the possibility of subtle bugs in application code due to the inconsistency of the Java references before the persistence context has been flushed.

OpenJPA can also be configured to log a warning or throw an exception when it detects an inconsistent bidirectional association. This is more useful because it can be used as an assertion mechanism to detect programming errors. To log inconsistencies, the openjpa.InverseManager property should be set to true(Action=warn). To throw an exception, use true(Action=exception) instead.

Whether inconsistencies in the bidirectional associations are corrected, or just detected, the checks have a performance overhead. The cost depends on the number of objects in the association. Because of this, OpenJPA does not check large result set fields by default. You can enable checking by setting the openjpa.ManageLRS to true.

Best Practice

Don't rely on OpenJPA's managed inverse feature because it has a performance cost and makes your application non-portable. Fix your code instead.

Set openjpa.InverseManager to true(Action=exception) in development and functional test environments. This will assert that your application is correctly maintaining bidirectional relationships. Do not use this setting in performance test and production environments because it will negatively impact performance.

Mixed Inheritance Strategies

The JPA standard only supports a single strategy for a given inheritance hierarchy. Kodo allows you to use a mix of inheritance mapping strategies for a single inheritance hierarchy. This can be configured solely in the deployment descriptors, so it need not affect the portability of your code. As we pointed out early in this chapter, you should use inheritance with caution.

Prepared Statement Caching

OpenJPA uses JDBC prepared statements for every SQL statement it executes. Prepared statements make life easier for the database, and significantly improve performance. Each JDBC connection has a cache of prepared statements. If an application regularly uses more distinct statements than the cache can hold, OpenJPA will often have to re-initialize prepared statements, losing their performance benefit.

When using OpenJPA in a standalone manner, the size of this cache is controlled by the ConnectionFactoryProperties /MaxCachedStatements property, and defaults to 50 statements.

When deploying OpenJPA in WebLogic Server using container-managed data sources, WebLogic Server manages prepared statement caching for each data source. The default size of the WebLogic Server prepared statement cache is a rather miserly 10. The data source pages in the WebLogic Console provide monitoring of the prepared statement cache statistics (you have to select the Customize this table link and choose the prepared statement attributes). The statistics are also available via the `DataSourceMBean`. You should monitor these statistics and increase the cache size, as needed.

Deployment Descriptors or Annotations?

EJB 3.0 introduces annotation-based programming. This provides the developer with a choice as to whether to include metadata as annotations, or to use the traditional Java EE method — deployment descriptors.

Annotations are simple to apply, and can result in much cleaner, more comprehensible code.

Deployment descriptors exist to capture environmental or product-specific differences. Extracting these specific configuration details out of code can make it portable across environments, application servers, database schemas, and database servers. Deployment descriptor elements always override their annotation counterparts. They can also be further customized with deployment plans.

Two classes of descriptor exist — standards-defined descriptors such as `ejb-jar.xml` and `persistence.xml`, and vendor-specific descriptors, such as `weblogic-ejb-jar.xml` and `persistence-configuration.xml`.

When assessing where to set a particular item of metadata, we think of the hierarchy shown in Figure 6-3: code (annotations) ⇨ standard descriptors ⇨ vendor descriptors ⇨ deployment plans. We aim to specify each item of metadata at the highest level that doesn't constrain portability. For example, the `<ejb-link>` mechanism allows us to describe the relationships between our application EJBs. These relationships are the same whether the application is deployed to WebLogic Server, or to another Java EE 5 application server. Because `<ejb-link>` is set in the standard `ejb-jar.xml` descriptor, we have not constrained portability, so we prefer it to the alternative of using the WebLogic Server–specific `<ejb-reference-description>` setting in `weblogic-ejb-jar.xml`. We can go further. We can use the `@EJB` annotation directly in the code without sacrificing any portability but gaining much simplicity. In this case, annotations are to be preferred.

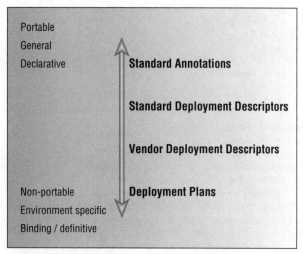

Figure 6-3: The various ways to provide deployment metadata

Be wary of product-specific annotations. Using these annotations makes your code directly dependent on a vendor's container and therefore harder to port should the need arise. Sometimes, a product annotation is required to access a product feature of significant value. You should first look for an option to configure this feature externally in a deployment descriptor. For example, use the `<enable-call-by-reference>` element in the `weblogic-ejb-jar.xml` deployment descriptor in preference to the `@weblogic.javaee.CallByReference` annotation. Similarly, if portability is a concern, you should avoid standard annotations that have vendor-specific behavior, such as the `mappedName` element of the `@Stateless` and `@Stateful` annotations.

Aim to make your JPA code portable across both databases and containers. Isolate database- or container-specific features in deployment descriptors, and use annotations to describe only logical aspects of your schema. As we have noted, some useful features of OpenJPA and Kodo, for example fetch groups, can only be controlled using a product annotation.

Don't hard code environmental information in annotations, for example IP addresses, host names, or URLs. These will almost certainly vary between the various environments to which your application will be deployed. Put them in a descriptor (a standard descriptor if possible), and customize them per environment with deployment plans.

Deployment Plans

Deployment plans are a good way to customize settings for a particular environment. They can even add missing information to a descriptor — the only requirement is that the descriptor file exists. For example, a deployment plan can be used to set the global JNDI name for the remote business interface `example.MyEJB` of the `MyEJBImpl` session bean.

```xml
<?xml version='1.0' encoding='UTF-8'?>
<deployment-plan xmlns="http://xmlns.oracle.com/weblogic/deployment-plan"
                 xmlns:xsi="http://www.w3.org/2001/XMLSchema-instance"
                 xsi:schemaLocation="http://xmlns.oracle.com/weblogic/deployment-
plan http://xmlns.oracle.com/weblogic/deployment-plan/1.0/deployment-plan.xsd"
                 global-variables="false">
  <application-name>wls1031domain</application-name>
  <variable-definition>
    <variable>
      <name>WeblogicEnterpriseBean_MyEJBImpl_jndiName_12326136237900</name>
      <value>my.jndi.name</value>
    </variable>
  </variable-definition>
  <module-override>
    <module-name>Test</module-name>
    <module-type>ejb</module-type>
    <module-descriptor external="false">
      <root-element>weblogic-ejb-jar</root-element>
      <uri>META-INF/weblogic-ejb-jar.xml</uri>
      <variable-assignment>
        <name>WeblogicEnterpriseBean_MyEJBImpl_jndiName_12326136237900</name>
        <xpath>/weblogic-ejb-jar/weblogic-enterprise-bean/[ejb-
name="MyEJBImpl"]/stateless-session-descriptor/business-interface-jndi-name-
map/[business-remote="example.MyEJB"]/jndi-name</xpath>
      </variable-assignment>
    </module-descriptor>
```

```
      </module-override>
   </deployment-plan>
```

This plan will work with an application that contains the following basic `weblogic-ejb-xml.jar` file.

```
<weblogic-ejb-jar xmlns="http://xmlns.oracle.com/weblogic/weblogic-ejb-jar"
    xmlns:xsi="http://www.w3.org/2001/XMLSchema-instance"
    xsi:schemaLocation="http://xmlns.oracle.com/weblogic/weblogic-ejb-jar
                        http://xmlns.oracle.com/weblogic/weblogic-ejb-jar/1.0/
weblogic-ejb-jar.xsd ">
</weblogic-ejb-jar>
```

We cover deployment plans in more depth in Chapter 12.

Annotations, Descriptors, Plans, and Dependency Injection

Consider how dependency injection works with annotations, deployment descriptors, and deployment plans.

We've already spent some time looking at injection of `@EJB` and `@PersistenceContext` resources, so for a change our next examples inject more general settings, using the `@javax.annotation.Resource` annotations. Many different types of resources can be injected to fields annotated with `@Resource`, including data sources, JMS queues and topics, and EJB context variables. We'll illustrate how to inject a simple integer that is a parameter for our application logic.

You can mix annotations, deployment descriptors, and deployment plans. A field in an EJB class can have a reasonable default value that can be overridden if necessary. Here's a session bean that declares a searchDepth parameter.

```
package example;
...
@Stateless
@Remote
public class MyEJBImpl implements MyEJB
{
    @Resource
    int searchDepth = 7;

    ...
}
```

This parameter has been given a default value of 7. Because it has been annotated with `@javax.annotation.Resource`, it can be overridden if necessary in a deployment descriptor or plan. Here's what to add to the `ejb-jar.xml` deployment descriptor to change the value to 10.

```
...
  <session>
    <ejb-name>MyEJBImpl</ejb-name>
    <env-entry>
      <env-entry-name>example.MyEJBImpl/searchDepth</env-entry-name>
```

```
        <env-entry-type>java.lang.Integer</env-entry-type>
        <env-entry-value>10</env-entry-value>
      </env-entry>
    </session>
  ...
```

By default, the `<env-entry-name>` is derived from the fully qualified class name of the EJB implementation, and the field name, but it can be overridden with the `name` element of the `@Resource` parameter. As well as allowing the descriptor to refer to the annotated field, this name is used to bind the value into the local JNDI namespace. In our case, the JNDI name will be `java:comp/env/example.MyEJBImpl/searchDepth`.

The resource setting can be further overridden in a deployment plan. Deployment plans can only set atomic values and not add arbitrary XML content, so the `ejb-jar.xml` must already have an `<env-entry>` element for `searchDepth`. You might wonder how our previous sample deployment plan set the JNDI name, despite the lack of the `<weblogic-enterprise-bean>`, `<stateless-session-descriptor>`, and `<business-interface-jndi-name-map>` elements in the deployment descriptor. The plan works only because during deployment, WebLogic Server builds an implicit descriptor that contains these elements. This isn't the case for `<env-entry>` elements.

Here's a plan that sets `searchDepth` to 11.

```
<?xml version='1.0' encoding='UTF-8'?>
<deployment-plan xmlns="http://xmlns.oracle.com/weblogic/deployment-plan"
                 xmlns:xsi="http://www.w3.org/2001/XMLSchema-instance"
                 xsi:schemaLocation="http://xmlns.oracle.com/weblogic/deployment-
plan http://xmlns.oracle.com/weblogic/deployment-plan/1.0/deployment-plan.xsd"
                 global-variables="false">
  <application-name>wls1031domain</application-name>
  <variable-definition>
    <variable>
      <name>EnterpriseBean_MyEJBImpl_searchDepth</name>
      <value>11</value>
    </variable>
  </variable-definition>
  <module-override>
    <module-name>ResourceInjection</module-name>
    <module-type>ejb</module-type>
    <module-descriptor external="false">
      <root-element>ejb-jar</root-element>
      <uri>META-INF/ejb-jar.xml</uri>
      <variable-assignment>
        <name>EnterpriseBean_MyEJBImpl_searchDepth</name>
        <xpath>/ejb-jar/enterprise-beans/session/[ejb-name="MyEJBImpl"]/env-
entry/[env-entry-name="example.MyEJBImpl/searchDepth"]/env-entry-value</xpath>
      </variable-assignment>
    </module-descriptor>
  </module-override>
</deployment-plan>
```

It is possible to inject a value or resource into a field of an EJB without it even being marked with an annotation using the `<injection-target>` descriptor element. Here's an example.

```
...
  <session>
    <ejb-name>MyEJBImpl</ejb-name>
    <env-entry>
      <env-entry-name>searchDepth</env-entry-name>
      <env-entry-type>java.lang.Integer</env-entry-type>
      <env-entry-value>3</env-entry-value>
      <injection-target>
        <injection-target-class>example.MyEJBImpl</injection-target-class>
        <injection-target-name>searchDepth</injection-target-name>
      </injection-target>
    </env-entry>
  </session>
...
```

Injecting dependencies to fields without annotations may seem convenient, but can be confusing to someone just reading the source code. Apply with caution.

Best Practice

EJB developers should declare all fields they expect to be injected with an annotation such as `@Resource`, `@EJB`, or `@PersistenceContext`.

Be wary of using the `<injection-target>` element in `ejb-jar.xml` to inject values and resources into unannotated fields. Relying on this feature makes the EJB source code harder to understand and maintain.

Chapter Review

This chapter began with a review of key EJB concepts and terminology and a discussion of the EJB lifecycle in the WebLogic Server EJB container. Each of the EJB component types was identified, and a few simple examples were presented in preparation for the subsequent discussions.

The bulk of the chapter was dedicated to presenting WebLogic Server–specific features and capabilities related to EJB components. Many of these features are relatively new in the WebLogic Server product and require careful configuration to achieve the desired performance or reliability benefits. The discussion of each feature was accompanied by a best practice indicating its usefulness for typical EJB applications and highlighting any limitations or configuration recommendations.

How should you design your EJB application? Which WebLogic Server configuration options should you employ to improve performance? In the vernacular of the Java EE architect, it depends. It depends on your specific requirements for performance, concurrency control, remote interface availability, and many other issues. It is impossible to provide a single, overriding recommendation for EJB design or configuration. It's up to you to decide.

To help you make these important decisions for your project, the next chapter includes a discussion of the key application drivers, the selection of a business layer architecture, and the appropriate configuration options for the example EJB application, `bigrez.com`.

7

Building an Example EJB Application

In this chapter, we walk through the design and implementation of the business layer of the `bigrez.com` example application, highlighting key concepts and best practices. Though this chapter is not a full tutorial for constructing EJB components or the business layer of Java EE applications, it provides insight into the construction of the example application, along with useful techniques that you can apply in your projects.

This chapter is organized like Chapters 2 through 4, with the discussion proceeding from requirements to architecture and then to implementation.

❑ We identify a set of business layer requirements to guide the architecture selection process.

❑ We identify and examine candidate architectures in light of the requirements to gauge their relative value for our application.

❑ We examine selected business layer components required for the `bigrez.com` application to highlight implementation details and best practices.

Finally, we look at the necessary changes should we want to switch the JPA provider from WebLogic Server's Kodo implementation to Oracle's TopLink implementation, which will replace Kodo in a future version of WebLogic Server.

We start with the requirements.

Business Layer Requirements

As we stated in Chapter 2, you should identify and consider as many requirements as you can before choosing a design. We spent a fair amount of time identifying the many presentation layer requirements that a web application must address, before selecting the Spring MVC–based presentation layer architecture. Requirements such as error handling and form redisplay led us to choose a robust servlet-centric presentation layer framework rather than a simpler JSP-centric approach. We'll now follow the same strategy and identify the key business layer requirements that drive our choice of architecture to ensure that we make the right decision.

As in Chapter 2, when we talk about requirements in this section we mean the general requirements of a business layer architecture, rather than the specific requirements of a given application. Application requirements matter in the architecture selection, but many common business layer requirements apply to all applications.

We walk through the business layer, from the business logic requirements through to the database access requirements, and identify key requirements that will be useful in evaluating candidate business layer architectures.

Business Logic Requirements

The first set of business layer requirements is derived from the business logic requirements for the application. Most applications have specific business logic requirements based on the required application behaviors and functions. Unlike the requirements for data access or object-relational mapping, it is difficult to generalize and identify business logic requirements that are common to applications. We focus on the common requirements shared by all Java EE business layers.

Encapsulation and the Business Layer Interface

The first common requirement is the need to give the presentation layer a simple, straightforward interface. The business layer implementation may be complex and involve many steps, but this should not concern the author of the presentation layer. The implementation is said to be *encapsulated*. A good principle is to expose the minimum you can get away with — sometimes referred to as the *principle of least exposure*. By following this principle, you reduce the dependencies between the presentation layer and the business layer, decreasing the likelihood that a change to the business layer will necessitate corresponding changes to the presentation layer. The two layers are then said to be *more loosely coupled*.

The business layer interface is usually more coarse-grained than the implementation. For example, the interface may expose a getAccountProfile() service that returns a single AccountProfile object. The implementation of this operation can do whatever is necessary to calculate the result; this may involve calling several other services, merging many small objects, and using complex object-oriented patterns. As well as simplifying the client, a coarse-grained interface may provide performance benefits in a distributed, transactional environment by eliminating multiple transactions and the need for multiple distributed requests from the client to the service. This is commonly known as the *session façade* pattern.

The standard way to implement a session façade with Java EE is to use session EJBs, and most often these are stateless session EJBs. As illustrated in Figure 7-1, the session façade pattern provides client components with a simple service interface. Each session bean encapsulates the service's business logic. The manipulation of the domain object model (usually database-backed), the use of container services such as JPA entity managers, and use of other application services, are all hidden from the client. Without the façade, the client component would be required to initiate and manage transactions, make multiple calls to session beans and other business layer components, directly use JPA to interact with the database, and trap and handle all business exceptions.

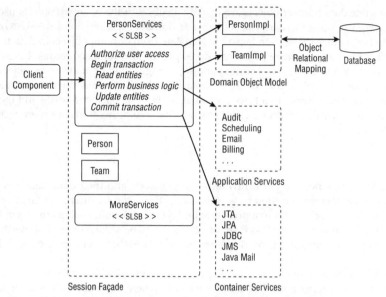

Figure 7-1: Session façade encapsulates complex business logic.

To sum up, the chosen business layer architecture must provide a mechanism for encapsulating complex business logic and provide a straightforward interface for client components.

Transaction Management and Security

The business layer should be responsible for managing transaction boundaries, ensuring that the effects of a service call are atomic and only persisted and made visible to other transactions if the call completes successfully.

The session façade is the ideal place to manage transaction boundaries. EJB provides good, declarative mechanisms to apply transactions.

The session façade is also a good point at which to apply security policy checks to make sure the user is authorized to use the service. This is often implemented using Java EE declarative security, which we cover in depth later in Chapter 11.

The Domain Model and Data Transfer Objects

To make best use of the Java language, you will want to implement your business logic using a *domain model* of Java objects. Here, domain refers to the application domain, and classes in the domain model represent things that are meaningful in the application's business context. Many domain objects are long lived, and in the next section, we consider the best way to map the persistent parts of the domain model to a database.

The session façade interface needs to transfer objects back and forth to the client. These objects typically contain only state and no behavior (in line with the session façade's role of simplifying the client interface), and are referred to as *data transfer objects* or DTOs.

The session façade data transfer objects are usually a subset of the business objects used in the domain object model. For example, there may be a `Customer` domain class and a `CustomerDTO` data transfer class. Some approaches require the session façade to translate from domain objects to data transfer objects, and vice versa. This has the advantage that it can decouple the two representations. Classes in the domain model can change without requiring corresponding changes to the data transfer object classes; instead, the translation code is simply changed. Disadvantages include the need to write and maintain two similar sets of classes, the need to write repetitive code that copies data back and forth, and the performance cost of the copying. In general, architectural approaches that avoid this translation are more efficient and easier to maintain.

Validation

The business layer may need to perform validation of objects and their data elements. As discussed in Chapter 2, the data values submitted by a web application user are often validated both on the page itself, perhaps via JavaScript, and in a presentation layer component such as the form bean or controller class. Many applications consider this level of validation to be sufficient, and allow the business layer components to perform operations on client-provided data without repeating the validation checks.

Other applications have more rigorous requirements and must include validation checks on all data sent to the business layer components. This may be the case where the presentation layer and business layer are deployed to separate physical tiers (so the business layer is directly accessible over the network and is more exposed to a malicious user), or where the business layer has several distinct presentation clients. The need for validation in the business layer may not be present in the original application, but it can occur once the component is reused in a subsequent application. For example, a component intended for use with a web application having validation checks in the presentation layer might eventually be reused by a different application that does not include presentation layer validation.

The business layer architecture should provide a mechanism for validating objects and data and returning validation errors in much the same way the controller components provided this functionality in the presentation layer.

Object-Relational Mapping Requirements

Moving further into the business layer toward the database, the next set of requirements concerns the mechanisms for mapping domain objects to the relational database technology. These object-relational mapping (ORM) requirements define the functions necessary to translate between object technology and relational database representations of the data.

Mapping Simple Classes

The simplest form of object-relational mapping is the simple one-to-one mapping of a business object to a database table. The characteristics of this type of mapping include the following:

❑   Each instance of the business object is represented by a row in the database table.

❑   The attributes in the business object are all scalars, strings, or other simple data types.

❑   Each attribute maps to a single column in the database table.

The object-relational mapping technology must allow for a straightforward mapping of business objects to tables, including support for basic create, read, update, and delete (CRUD) operations.

It is possible to design a database schema where a single business object is spread across multiple tables. Inserting the business object creates a row in each table, removing the object deletes the corresponding row in each table, and modifying the object updates all of the rows. The ORM technology must allow for objects that span tables in a database, and maybe even across multiple databases.

You often want to use objects that contain arbitrary subsets of data from one or more tables. One good example of such a *projection* object is a query result object that contains a subset of data from a table needed for the presentation of search results.

For example, suppose we are querying for a list of `Person` objects. The `PERSON` table might have 20 or more columns, so a result list containing many full `Person` business objects may need a large amount of memory, network bandwidth, and so on. If the user interface needs to display only the first and last name, a specialized projection object could be defined that contains only those two attributes from the `Person` table plus the table primary key. The mapping technology must allow fetching a list of these projection objects from the table using SQL statements that fetch only the required fields.

It is also valuable to create projection objects that span multiple tables, again containing only the necessary attributes for the specific requirement being satisfied. A highly normalized database will require multi-table projection objects for best query performance. The query that fetches the multi-table projection object should perform the join using the database rather than trying to fetch objects for each table in to memory and joining them by hand. The ORM technology should allow for projection objects that define a subset of columns from one or more tables.

Mapping Associations

Associations are relationships between objects. Associations can be one-to-one, one-to-many, many-to-one, or many-to-many. Associations are normally between objects of different classes, but some may be *reflexive*, that is, they can be from an object of one class to an object of the same class.

In a relational database, relationships between rows are implemented using foreign key relationships between tables. They can be easily navigated starting from either end of the association — this is *bidirectional* navigation. In Java, an association is implemented using a reference field of the object corresponding to one end of the association, and because the reference can only be traversed in one direction it is *unidirectional*. Where necessary, a complementary reference may be added to allow traversal in the other direction.

For example, an `Employee` class may have a many-to-one relationship to itself through the field `manager`. This is reflexive and unidirectional. If we want to navigate in the other direction, we can add a `reports` field, representing a one-to-many relationship to the employee's direct reports. This bidirectional navigation does not come for free. When we change an employee's manager, we must also take care to update the list of reports for the old and the new managers.

The difference between the natural bidirectional navigation of associations possible in a relational database and the frequent need to manage a pair of unidirectional references in an object model is one example of the mismatch between object and relational technologies. We would like our ORM technology to manage all the gritty details of translating between these two worlds.

Here's another example. A common form of association is the many-to-many relationship between two entities that have independent lifetimes. For example, in Figure 7-2, the relationship between students at a school and the courses offered at the school is contained in a separate relationship table, `ENROLLMENT`.

The ENROLLMENT relationship table exists to indicate that a particular student is taking a particular course, and can also include additional information related directly to this relationship. In this example, the student's grade in the specific course would be stored in the ENROLLMENT table, not in the STUDENT or COURSE table.

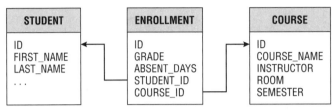

Figure 7-2: The ENROLLMENT table implements a many-to-many association.

Due to differences between the object and relational models, a relationship looks different in memory than it does in a database. In memory, objects are linked by Java references in an *object graph*. The object-relational mapping technology must provide mechanisms for both creating the interconnected series of objects in memory when reading tables, and writing out the interconnected objects to the proper database tables when making changes.

Ideally, the ORM technology should be capable of the following:

❑　Automatically creating the object graph during a fetch operation, linking business objects appropriately, and pre-fetching some or all of the graph during the initial database operation.

❑　Automatically walking through all of the relationships in the object graph and performing the necessary and appropriate CRUD operations on the objects to save any changes.

❑　Where required in the object model, managing bidirectional references.

You often want to defer the fetching of related objects until the time they are actually required. In many cases, the source object may be all that is required to perform a calculation or present some business data to the user, and it is a waste of resources to populate fully the object graph with all related objects. This technique of waiting to fetch children is referred to as *lazy instantiation*.

The ORM technology should therefore allow the following:

❑　Fetching an object plus all of its related objects, and their related objects, recursively. This is called a *deep* or full fetch of the entire object graph starting with the parent object.

❑　Fetching only the object without fetching any related objects, often called a *shallow* fetch.

The term *composition* refers to ownership, or parent-child, associations, in which the child cannot exist without the parent. For example, the associations between students, enrollments, and courses are not composition relationships, because students can exist without courses, and courses can exist without students, but the association between a SCHOOL and a DEPARTMENT can be considered composition, because the departments cannot exist without the school.

With composition, there is typically a one-to-many relationship between the parent and the child table. Where there is a one-to-one relationship, you may be able simply to fold the child data back into the parent table.

Some basic rules apply in composition:

❏ Deleting the parent is dependent on having no remaining children in the database. This is normally enforced by the referential integrity constraints in the database. Automatic deletion of children during a parent delete is possible, but it must occur before the parent is deleted.

❏ Inserting child rows also depends on the existence of the parent row for the referential integrity constraints to allow the insert.

Updating the parent primary key becomes a pain, requiring a multi-step process of copying the parent row, changing the children to refer to the new parent row, and then deleting the original parent row. This operation is costly and should be avoided by using immutable keys for primary key identifiers if at all possible.

To sum up, the chosen business layer architecture must support flexible, efficient, and safe techniques for modeling and managing complex relationships.

Mapping Inheritance

Java is an object-oriented language, and one of the strengths of object-oriented technology is the concept of inheritance. Inheritance can be difficult to implement in an object-relational mapping environment, however, because normal database systems do not provide a native technique for inheriting and extending tables.

Three primary techniques are available for mapping inheritance to a set of database tables: horizontal partitioning, typed partitioning, and vertical partitioning. Figure 7-3 depicts these three techniques for a simple example containing a single base class, `Person`, and two subclasses, `Employee` and `Customer`.

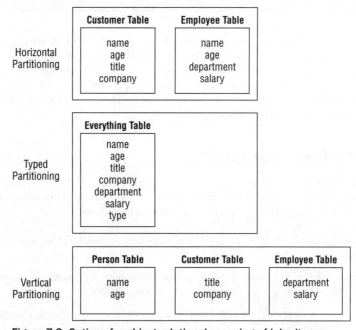

Figure 7-3: Options for object-relational mapping of inheritance.

In horizontal partitioning, only concrete subclass objects are mapped to tables. These tables include all of the base class and subclass attributes. This approach may improve performance because only one table needs to be accessed for instances of a given concrete class.

In typed partitioning, all classes in an inheritance tree are mapped to a single table containing all attributes required for all subclass objects. A type column is used to distinguish which type of object is stored in each row of the table, and many type-specific columns in the table will be empty for a given object.

Finally, in vertical partitioning, every class in the inheritance tree maps to a table in the database. Fetching data for a concrete subclass involves a join operation between the base table and the concrete subclass table.

All three techniques for mapping inheritance in the database are viable, but clear advantages and disadvantages are present in some of them. Designing the database to match the object inheritance tree exactly, represented in the vertical partitioning technique, can dramatically affect performance and complicate the data access services by requiring joins during all CRUD operations. On the other hand, the placement of all attributes for all object types in a single table, the typed partitioning technique, sacrifices a great deal of flexibility and maintainability to achieve fast and simple queries and CRUD operations. The horizontal partitioning scheme often represents the best compromise between flexibility and performance, and it can also be implemented easily with a variety of ORM technologies including JPA.

Best Practice

Horizontal partitioning provides the simplest and most efficient method for modeling inheritance in a relational database.

All of the object-relational mapping requirements discussed in this section are important in real-world applications containing large, complex object models. Simple architectures may have no problem implementing the business logic and simple object-relational mapping requirements discussed in this section, but they often break down when they encounter more complex requirements in the object model such as nested composition or multiple sets of associated objects. Don't adopt an architecture that will not support the long-term needs in these areas.

Data Access Requirements

The business layer must provide basic data access services to support the object-relational mapping and business logic requirements outlined previously. Although this is not a complete list, most applications require at least the following set of data access services and functions:

- ❑ Basic create, read, update, and delete operations at an object level to meet basic object persistence requirements.
- ❑ Creation of custom SQL statements to perform complex logic without resorting to fetching objects and performing logic in business layer components.
- ❑ Standardized mechanisms for handling large result sets and limiting returned results.
- ❑ Standardized mechanisms for handling and reporting data-related errors.

❑ Efficient bulk insert, update, and delete mechanisms to avoid reading and updating multiple objects one at a time.

❑ Concurrency control (optimistic or pessimistic locking) to eliminate the loss of data in the event of multiple simultaneous update transactions.

Other Business Layer Requirements

Finally, many applications have additional business layer requirements in the following areas:

❑ Creation of detailed audit trails of business layer service requests, data access, data manipulation, and other activities. The audit tracks who, what, when, and even why these activities were performed.

❑ Robust logging and instrumentation capability. It is used to troubleshoot system problems during system development and to provide usage profiling information during production operation.

❑ High levels of performance and scalability. These are normally expressed as overall system requirements, of course, but the business layer architecture plays a large role in ensuring good performance. The architecture must represent sound design principles and leverage all of the appropriate clustering, caching, and performance-related features of the application server hosting the components.

Review of Business Layer Requirements

Table 7-1 summarizes all of the requirements outlined in this section and provides the set of criteria we'll use to evaluate candidate business layer architectures for the bigrez.com application.

Business Layer Architecture Options

Chapter 3 introduced the bigrez.com example application and described the web application architecture chosen for the presentation layer. The next step in the construction is the selection of a business layer architecture based on the general business layer requirements outlined in the previous sections and our particular application requirements for bigrez.com.

In contrast to the presentation layer, fewer architectures are worth considering for the business layer. We examine three candidate business layer architectures in this chapter:

❑ Stateless session EJBs using JDBC to perform SQL operations.

❑ Stateless session EJBs using EJB 2.1 Container-Managed Persistence (CMP) entity beans for persistence operations.

❑ Stateless session EJBs using JPA for persistence operations.

All three of the candidate architectures use stateless session EJBs to provide the required session façade. We discuss the advantages of using SLSBs in the following section. Occasionally, you will find a need for a stateful session façade, and so may consider using stateful session EJBs as well, but this is rarely appropriate for applications such as bigrez.com that have a stateful presentation layer.

Table 7-1: Summary of Business Layer Requirements

Requirement	Description
Session façade	Straightforward technique available to encapsulate complex or multi-step business processes behind a simplified interface of services.
Transaction and security management	Declarative specification of transaction management and security policies.
Audit, logging, and instrumentation	Techniques available to log, audit, and instrument business layer activity at the method level.
Translation between the domain model and DTOs	Easy translation to and from the DTOs used in the business layer interface.
Validation	Ability to perform business layer validation.
Simple object-relational mapping	Basic create, read, update, and delete operations on simple objects that map to one or more tables.
Associations	Ability to map relationships and perform all required CRUD operations on complex object graphs. Support for lazy fetching.
Inheritance and polymorphism	Ability to map inheritance in the object model to the database.
Advanced data access operations	Limiting result sets, performing dynamic queries, bulk operations, and concurrency controls.
Performance and scalability	Good performance and scalability. The ability to use caches to share effort across many requests.

The candidates differ then in what they use for object-relational mapping. Here JPA has significant benefits, and you can treat the following discussion as a justification for our choice to use JPA over previously popular implementation technologies.

Moving outside the constraints of plain Java EE, you also might consider more proprietary frameworks such as the Spring Framework or Oracle's Application Development Framework (ADF) Business Components. A complete survey of all possible architectures is beyond the scope of this book. Use the discussion in this chapter to aid you in choosing the right architecture for your application by applying a similar selection process that considers your particular business layer requirements and limitations.

SLSBs and the Session Façade Requirements

Stateless session EJBs easily meet the first three of our requirements; namely the need for a way to implement a session façade, support for declarative security and transaction management, and audit, logging, and administration.

We'll briefly contrast some of the advantages of using SLSBs over the alternative implementation of a *pure Java* session façade.

First, SLSBs support both dependency injection and JNDI binding, and allow the links from clients to the façade beans to be overridden in deployment descriptors. As you saw in Chapter 6, the @EJB annotation is often all that client code requires to refer to an EJB. Such declarative coupling of components is important for code that must work in many different environments, and that needs to be easy to unit test. In contrast, a pure Java session façade implementation has to choose between hard coding the links (making unit testing hard, and the code very brittle), using the *Service Locator* pattern (which often means a dependency on custom framework code and verbose, application-specific property files), or using a third-party dependency injection tool such as the Spring Framework.

Second, the SLSB threading model means that a service author rarely has to consider concurrency. In contrast, a pure Java session façade would require the author to code each service implementation carefully to be thread-safe.

Third, SLSBs support declarative security and transaction policies that link directly into the services provided by the application server, and can be specified using annotations or deployment descriptors. A pure Java session façade would either have to code support for transactions and security into every service implementation, or use complicated aspect-oriented programming techniques to support transactions and security in a generic manner.

Fourth, SLSBs can be called remotely. It is easy to modify interfaces defined at the service level to support remote method invocation. The main change is that the data transfer objects must be *serializable* to enable passing by value via remote (RMI) invocations. As well as allowing access to clients in different physical tiers, remote invocation supports clients deployed in different classloaders such as those packaged in a separate enterprise application. Remote invocation is not required for bigrez.com, but may be for other applications.

Fifth, application servers provide deployment and monitoring facilities for managing SLSBs. Additional audit, logging, and instrumentation facilities can be added using custom interceptors.

Finally, SLSBs are defined by a standard. They are portable between Java EE application servers. There is a large talent pool of Java developers who understand SLSBs.

We'll use EJB 3.0 SLSBs for bigrez.com, and compare the remaining requirements against our candidate architectures.

Stateless Session EJBs with JDBC

The first candidate business layer architecture uses SLSBs to encapsulate all business logic, a pass-by-value technique to accept and return business objects, and simple JDBC functionality to implement persistence. Figure 7-4 illustrates this architecture for a simple application containing a single service and business object.

As shown in the figure, each business layer request is implemented as a separate method on the service. Process encapsulation is achieved by creating coarse-grained methods on the service that encapsulate multi-step processes. All of the object-relational mapping requirements and data access requirements are implemented with custom Java code and SQL statements. You can develop methods to find business objects by any number of criteria, and a general find method accepting the actual WHERE clause for the SQL statement is also possible.

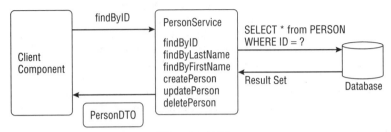

Figure 7-4: Stateless Session EJBs with JDBC

All the business layer requirements can be met with this architecture, although some require a large amount of custom coding. JDBC is a foundational layer used by the other technologies we consider, and anything achievable with EJB 2.1 CMP or JPA is achievable with JDBC plus custom code. You can essentially do anything in this architecture because you control, and are responsible for writing, everything in the service. Recognize, however, that with this control and flexibility comes additional complexity: You must code everything yourself, including all object-relational mapping and advanced data access operations. The effort to implement advanced features quickly makes the off-the-shelf alternatives more attractive. In assessing the capabilities of JDBC, we'll assume that the custom coding is limited to implementing CRUD operations as SQL statements in stateless *data access objects* (DAOs), and mapping to and from DTOs.

Table 7-2 presents a list of the business layer requirements and describes the capabilities and limitations of this SLSB and JDBC-based architecture in each area.

The stateless session EJBs with JDBC architecture doesn't line up well with our requirements.

Historically, straight JDBC would be used occasionally to complement EJB 2.1 CMP entity beans. For example, JDBC might be required to make a call to a database stored procedure. JPA provides support for native SQL queries, allowing arbitrary SQL to be used, so there is no longer a good use case for using JDBC directly.

We don't want the effort of hand coding the database access for our bigrez.com application and it needs to perform well. Let's move on to the next candidate and see if it represents an improvement.

Stateless Session EJBs with EJB 2.1 CMP Entity Beans

The second candidate architecture resembles the first choice in some respects. It also uses stateless session EJBs, but it replaces the JDBC-based data access logic with an entity bean layer modeling the business objects. As shown in Figure 7-5, the stateless service acts as a session façade encapsulating both business logic and the basic persistence operations for business objects.

Table 7-2: JDBC Architecture Requirements Analysis

Requirement	Support provided by the architecture	
Translation between the domain model and DTOs	Poor	Repetitive, error-prone custom code is required. The application must maintain a separate set of DTO classes, translate from JDBC result sets to these DTO objects, and in the other direction, map from the DTO objects to parameters of JDBC statements. The alternative approach of using JDBC RowSets is even less desirable because it does not provide the client with an object-oriented view and fails to encapsulate the implementation.
Validation	Acceptable	Validation can be performed in the SLSB or the DTO classes.
Simple object-relational mapping	Acceptable	Custom code required. The SQL statements required for basic CRUD operations are coded in data access objects (DAOs) in the business layer. The SQL statements can be arbitrarily complex, and can easily support projection or mapping to multiple tables. The DAO implementations must be careful to close JDBC resources after use.
Associations	Poor	Support for each association must be hand coded into DAOs using SQL. Support for lazy fetching is not achievable without making the DAOs stateful.
Inheritance and polymorphism	Poor	Inheritance mapping must be hard coded into each DAO.
Advanced data access operations	Poor	There is no way to batch JDBC operations between different DAOs that may be used in a single transaction. Concurrency control must be coded consistently into every DAO. A mistake in a single DAO can open up the application to concurrency issues.
Performance and scalability	Poor	Stateless DAOs cannot cache by definition. Not only does this prevent us caching between requests, it prevents us caching within a single transaction. A DAO cannot use results from other DAOs, or even previous calls to itself within a transaction. Even if we relax the restriction that the DAO be stateless, it is hard to see how a generic cache might be easily applied. Caching requires a standard CRUD interface, a consistent object model with well-defined keys, and consistently implemented locking features. You should have reached for one of the more advanced architectures well before this point.

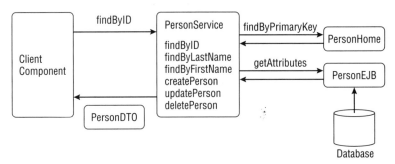

Figure 7-5: Stateless Session EJBs with EJB 2.1 CMP entity beans

Each business layer request is implemented as a separate method on the service, meeting the process encapsulation, validation, and other business layer requirements in the same manner as the first architecture. We've just swapped out the JDBC-based persistence layer and replaced it with EJB 2.1 container-managed persistence (CMP) entity beans. The entity beans are responsible for all data access services and for meeting some, if not all, of the object-relational mapping requirements. Using CMP beans eliminates the hand coding of persistence logic and provides access to all of the persistence optimization capabilities of the WebLogic Server EJB container.

We don't propose to describe the details of EJB 2.1 entity beans here. We briefly covered some drawbacks of EJB 2.1 entity beans in Chapter 6. If you are unfamiliar with EJB 2.1, it will help to know that an entity EJB is a full EJB component, like a session bean, and so can be invoked remotely, and have declarative security and transaction management policies.

The client component requesting the business service is not allowed to communicate directly with the entity bean in this architecture, nor can entity beans be passed to services or be returned by them. A separate set of data transfer objects is used to communicate with the service. These DTOs almost invariably contain a mirror image of the attributes in the entity bean. The SLSB is responsible for copying data back and forth between value objects and the related entity beans in addition to performing any business logic contained in the service itself.

Table 7-3 presents our list of business layer requirements and describes the capabilities and limitations of this SLSB and EJB 2.1 CMP entity bean architecture in each area.

As you might expect, the EJB 2.1 CMP entity bean architecture scores significantly higher against our requirements than direct JDBC.

We identify two significant disadvantages with the EJB 2.1 CMP entity bean architecture for `bigrez.com`:

❑   The requirement for the data transfer object classes, and the need to map back and forward between entity beans and their external representation.

❑   The mappings to the database are defined by the container vendor, and so are non-portable. The mapping features depend upon the maturity of the particular container.

Table 7-3: EJB 2.1 CMP Entity Bean Architecture Requirements Analysis

Requirement	Support provided by the architecture	
Translation between the domain model and DTOs	Poor	Repetitive, error-prone custom code is required. The application must maintain a separate set of DTO classes, translate from entity beans to these DTO objects, and in the other direction, map from the DTO objects to the entity beans. CMP entity beans are a better solution than the direct use of JDBC, because the container manages the mapping from the raw result set to Java and can deal with database-specific details for mapping special types such as large object columns.
Validation	Acceptable	Validation can be performed in the SLSB, the DTO classes, or the entity beans.
Simple object-relational mapping	Good in WebLogic Server, but non-portable.	This is core CMP entity bean functionality. However, the EJB specification does not define how an entity bean is mapped to a database. This is left entirely to the container vendor. Consequently, the specification of the mapping to the database is not portable between application servers. Vendors may differ on support for advanced features such as mapping to multiple tables.
Associations	Good in WebLogic Server, but non-portable.	As for the ORM mapping, the details and level of support for features such as lazy loading is vendor specific.
Inheritance and polymorphism	None	EJB 2.1 does not support inheritance relationships between entities.
Advanced data access operations	Good in WebLogic Server, but non-portable.	Again, the EJB specification leaves the details to the product vendor. WebLogic Server uses JDBC batching, supports field groups (for projection), and provides support for pessimistic and optimistic locking schemes.
Performance and scalability	Acceptable	EJB 2.1 entity beans are often criticized for the container overhead. So long as entity beans are not invoked remotely (considered to be extremely poor practice), the container overhead need not be overly large. One significant advantage over plain JDBC is the transaction level caching. An entity bean's state is read from the database only once per transaction. WebLogic Server provides support for second level caching of entity bean state, with cluster-wide invalidation.

To dwell on the first of these disadvantages, some subtle, but significant, drawbacks are inherent in the conversion from DTOs to entity beans in the services. The handling of associations can be significantly more complex when all relationships must be represented in the object graph for the purposes of communication with the services. As a simple example of this problem, consider the case of a parent-child relationship between two objects and the logic required in the services to maintain these objects and their relationships. You would need SLSB operations to perform at least the following services:

❑   Fetching one or more parent objects using supplied criteria, and returning the parent objects plus child objects for each parent if desired by the client. The service would fetch the parent entity beans, walk through the list creating the parent value objects, optionally iterate on the child relationship fields to fetch each child entity bean, create a value object for each child, and place it in the object graph.

❑   Fetching one or more child objects using supplied criteria, including the parent object for each child if desired by the client. The service would fetch the child entity beans, walk through the list creating each child value object, optionally traverse the relationship to the parent entity bean, create a value object for the parent, and place it in the graph.

❑   Updating a parent object, including the update of any attached child objects. The service must determine the proper insert, update, or delete operation to perform for each child value object in the graph. Child value objects would require a status flag set by the client, or separate lists of child objects would have to be supplied by the client representing each desired type of operation. The service would fetch and update the parent entity bean using the data in the parent value object, then fetch and process each child object according to the required operation.

The difficulty in using value objects only intensifies when many-to-many relationships and other complex associations are modeled in the entity beans. The simple copying of DTOs to entity beans quickly becomes a nightmare if the object graph becomes large and complex. Remember that making multiple calls to the service to process portions of the object graph may not be a viable solution if you have strict requirements for transactional consistency. To ensure consistency, the service must begin and end the transaction in a single method call, so all of the required value objects, relationships, and required CRUD operations must be represented by the parameters and data structures passed to the service in that single method invocation.

EJB 2.1 CMP is a step forward over direct use of JDBC, but still has its drawbacks. We'll move on to consider stateless session EJBs with JPA.

Stateless Session EJBs with JPA

The final candidate architecture has two significant differences to the EJB 2.1 CMP architecture. Obviously, JPA replaces EJB 2.1 CMP. The other difference, which is enabled by JPA, is that the JPA entity object is used as the data transfer object, eliminating the need to maintain a separate set of classes and for additional translation and copying in the stateless session bean. Figure 7-6 depicts this architecture.

The session bean interacts with the JPA entity manager to perform CRUD operations on entity instances. The set of entities for a particular request is managed in a persistence context specific to the request. The diagram shows an entity being passed directly back to the client; it is automatically *detached* (disassociated from the persistence context) when the request transaction completes. The client receives a plain Java object that is no longer associated with the database, with its attributes reflecting the state of the entity when the transaction committed.

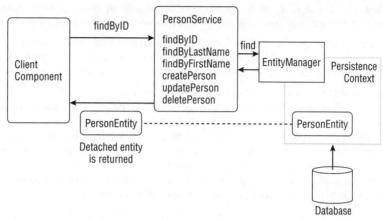

Figure 7-6: Stateless session EJBs with JPA

More complex interactions with the session bean might return an entity that has references to other entities. If the other entities were also loaded in the persistence context (which will depend on whether the associations are set to be lazy or eager, or whether the session bean traversed the relationships), they too will be detached and the result will be an object graph.

Up until this point, we've assumed that each request will use a single transaction that is managed by the session façade. This is not the only approach, so, for completeness, we will take a little time to consider the pros and cons of this approach, together with some alternatives:

Session Façade with Disconnected Entities: This is our preferred approach. The session façade defines the transaction boundary and produces disconnected object graphs. Transactions and the JPA persistence context have the same life cycle.

This is simple, and understandable. Nevertheless, the object graph the façade returns to the client must be populated with all the information needed by the client, or the client must make further calls to the session façade to retrieve information. This may require the client to provide additional parameters that control the scope of the results, or to make additional transactional calls to retrieve information (sacrificing read consistency).

Transaction Around Page Rendering: This approach moves the responsibility for transaction management to the client.

Doing this allows the client to work with managed entities in the persistence context, and lazily load attributes and associations as needed. Otherwise, this is not an attractive approach. Encapsulation is broken, because the client can directly update the database. Database locks will be held for longer, because the page must be rendered before the transaction commits. It is unsuitable for update operations because the transaction demarcation is outside the page rendering, making it hard for the web layer to deal with transactional failure.

Open Session in View: This is a pattern popularized by Hibernate, and implemented by several web frameworks.

The pattern involves committing the service layer transaction at the end of the service call, but keeping the JPA persistence context open. New read-only transactions are started as necessary for rendering the view, and re-use the persistence context. If the view requires information that is not already part of the persistence context, further queries are made to the database to retrieve it.

Some frameworks explicitly define a service transaction and a view transaction as part of the request processing life cycle, still using a single persistence context bridge for both. This has the advantage that all of the view rendering is wrapped up in a single view transaction.

This approach also allows the client to work with managed entities in the persistence context, and lazily load attributes and associations as needed. Nevertheless, it has many disadvantages. It can be harder to understand and debug. It is inherently non-atomic; for example, the view transactions might include the results of someone else's update. It may be more inefficient, as there are multiple queries across two or more transactions, where one might have sufficed. Container-managed entity managers can't be used, because they associate the persistence context with the transaction. It is more work to implement, and requires a custom servlet filter or request listener to ensure the entity manager is correctly closed when the servlet request processing finishes.

The client can modify the detached objects it receives, and pass them back to the session façade as parameters to update operations. The session bean can then *merge* these objects into the persistence context for the new request. This works well in conjunction with JPA's support for optimistic locking, because the detached objects will maintain version information, and the merge operation will fail if some other transaction has concurrently modified the entity's database row. We described how a presentation layer might manage these detached objects in its HTTP session in "Writing a Web Layer Suited to Optimistic Locking" in Chapter 6.

If the entities are to be used across a remote interface, they should implement `java.io.Serializable`.

Using entities as DTOs couples the presentation layer more tightly to the business layer, because they both share a single entity object model. Changes to the business layer's entity model will directly affect clients. In practice, this is unlikely to be a problem. There is usually no advantage to be gained by maintaining two similar object models, and translating backward and forward. If you find a client does need a different view of an entity, consider whether that view could be an interface that the entity implements, allowing you to pass the entity instance directly back to the client without additional translation.

Table 7-4 presents our list of the business layer requirements and describes the capabilities and limitations of the SLSB and JPA architecture.

The SLSB and JPA architecture meets our requirements very well.

The bigrez.com Implementation

Unsurprisingly, we've chosen to implement the bigrez.com application using the stateless session EJB with JPA architecture, and to use our entities as data transfer objects across the session façade.

In this section, we walk through the implementation of various parts of the bigrez.com business layer. We start with the database schema, look at the domain object model, and then at the implementation of the business services and session façade. We also consider how to write effective unit tests for a business layer, and the changes required to support optimistic locking.

Table 7-4: JPA Architecture Requirements Analysis

Requirement	Support provided by the architecture	
Translation between the domain model and DTOs	Good	Using the JPA entities as DTOs means no translation is required.
Validation	Acceptable	Validation can be performed in the SLSB, the DTO classes, or the entity classes. If the entities are used as DTOs, the JPA annotations on entity fields that define constraints such as the column length can also be used by presentation layer frameworks to provide additional validation in the user interface.
Simple object-relational mapping	Good	JPA provides strong support for object-relational mapping, and standardizes the mapping to relational databases.
Associations	Good	JPA provides good support for associations, including defining advanced features such as lazy loading. (The vendor may choose not to implement lazy loading, but the interface remains the same.)
Inheritance and polymorphism	Good	JPA defines various ways to map a class hierarchy of entities to database tables.
Advanced data access operations	Good	JPA defines advanced features such as optimistic locking. Other features, such as the JDBC batching feature of Kodo, depend on the quality of provider implementation. Usually, these features can be applied without making an application non-portable.
Performance and scalability	Good	The persistence context provides transaction level caching. An entity's state is read from the database only once per transaction. The default optimistic locking approach is appropriate for most applications and scales well. The clean POJO-based model allows an implementation easily to introduce second level caching.

Database Schema

The first version of the bigrez.com application was developed for the book *Mastering BEA WebLogic Server: Best Practices for Building and Deploying J2EE Applications* by Gregory Nyberg and Robert Patrick with Paul Bauerschmidt, Jeff McDaniel, and Raja Mukherjee (Wiley, 2003). The business layer was based on EJB 2.0 stateless session beans and CMP entity beans, which was the most appropriate technology available when the book was written.

We've completely rewritten `bigrez.com` for this book, using EJB 3.0 stateless session beans and JPA for the business layer. It is common to have to fit a JPA application to an existing schema or one defined by another group, so we've decided to keep the database schema as close to the original as possible.

The `bigrez.com` schema is presented in Figure 7-7.

The top left-hand side of Figure 7-7 shows the tables containing information that changes rarely. A row in the PROPERTY table represents a particular hotel. Each hotel has a number of ROOMTYPES such as `standard double`, `executive`, or `penthouse`. Hotels vary widely, so there is no standard room type model that applies to all hotels. The marketing department can associate OFFERS with each property — this is important for `bigrez.com` because we will present the offers on our web pages. The corporation can control the rates charged for each room type.

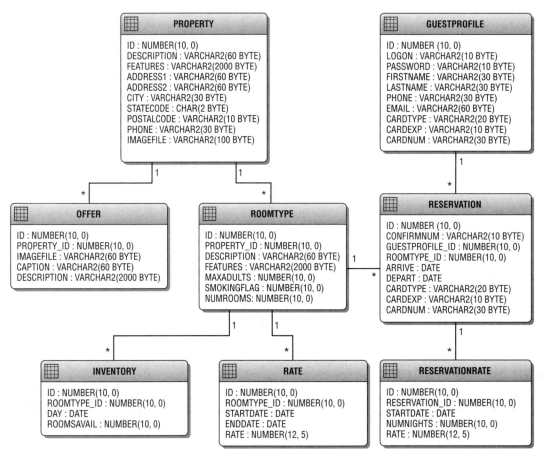

Figure 7-7: `bigrez.com` database schema.

The INVENTORY table holds the number of rooms of a particular type available on a particular day. You might think that this could be calculated from reservation information, but that would neglect bookings made directly with the hotel that bypass the reservation system. Additionally, last-minute cancellations and no-shows are a fact of life for hotels, so the hotel managers need enough flexibility to overbook rooms and control the level of overbooking. Also, notice there is no model of specific rooms; the front desk is given free reign to assign guests to rooms on arrival.

The right-hand side of Figure 7-7 shows the three tables that support the reservation system. The GUESTPROFILE holds information about guests making reservations. The RESERVATION table holds information about specific reservations, including the guest information used when booking. A real-world system would likely separate out the credit card information to a separate table, or a separate database, so more rigorous security can be applied to the data. The RESERVATIONRATE table stores information about the quoted room rates at the time a reservation was made.

Domain Model

Now, consider the JPA model corresponding to the database schema, which also serves as our domain model. This is shown in Figure 7-8. These classes exist in the com.bigrez.domain package.

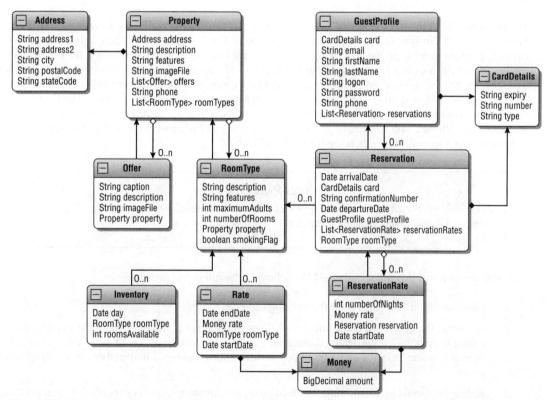

Figure 7-8: bigrez.com **domain model.**

The correspondence with the database schema is strong. There are two interesting points of difference to note.

First, some classes don't have a one-to-one correspondence with a table, namely `Address`, `CardDetails`, and `Money`. We've separated these in the domain model using JPA embedded classes, allowing us to have a better object model without normalizing the database schema. The `CardDetails` and `Money` classes are also embedded in multiple entities, so we have less code to maintain.

> **Best Practice**
>
> Use embedded entity classes to create a more appropriate, fine-grained Java object model without requiring a change to the database schema.

Second, not all associations are mapped in a bidirectional manner. For example, there is a Java reference from `Inventory` to `RoomType`, but `RoomType` does not have a collection of references to `Inventory`. This is because we found no need for the bidirectional navigation when writing the business logic associated with the entities. None of our code needs to find all the `Reservation` entities or all of the `Inventory` entities or all of the `Rate` entities for a `RoomType`. There is code that needs to find *some* of the `Inventory` or `Rate` entities, but these are always queries constrained by a date range so are implemented using JPQL queries.

The benefits of not creating references in both directions are that we do not need to worry about keeping the two references in sync (a JPA requirement we discussed in Chapter 6), and there is less code to write. Further, because there is no need to navigate the missing references, there is no need for the related entities to be part of a disconnected object graph that would require more memory. For example, suppose a transaction returns a detached `Property` reference to a client, and that the transaction fully loads all of its `RoomType` entities, and all of the related `Inventory`, `Rate`, and `Reservation` entities. The `Property` has no references to these classes, so the client will just receive the `Property`, and its related `Address`, `Offer`, and `RoomType` entities. The `Inventory`, `Rate`, and `Reservation` instances used by the transaction will be eligible for garbage collection when the transaction finishes.

> **Best Practice**
>
> Create bidirectional references for associations between entities only when you find you need them. Often, a unidirectional reference is sufficient and simpler.

How did we arrive at this domain model? We followed the following process:

❏   Generate the JPA entities from the existing schema.

❏   Reformat the generated code, and tweak some of the class or member names as needed. For example, rename the generated `Guestprofile` class to `GuestProfile`, or expand the `numnights` field to `numberOfNights` and add a `@Column` annotation to keep it mapped to the `NUMNIGHTS` column.

❏   Refine the model by identifying coherent groups of attributes, and encapsulating them in their own embedded classes.

❑ For each association, make a guess at how we might need to traverse it, and add either a unidirectional reference or a bidirectional pair of references.

❑ Following the best practice identified in Chapter 6, write helper methods to maintain the integrity of bidirectional reference pairs.

❑ Following the best practice identified in Chapter 6, add `cascade=CascadeType.PERSIST` to all of the associations. Add `CascadeType.REMOVE` to those composition associations.

❑ Extract superclasses for the entities and the embedded classes, and use these to implement common functionality such as identity and versioning.

❑ Write unit tests for the domain classes.

After you've been through this process once, it becomes quite natural, and you can quickly develop a rough cut of the domain model that lets you get started with the service implementations. As you implement the first few services, you'll find ways in which the domain model needs to be refined. Typical changes include adding an inverse reference to an association to make it bidirectional; changing whether an association is loaded lazily or eagerly; finding other opportunities to extract embedded classes; adding `Cascade.MERGE` or `CascadeType.REFRESH` to associations; and adding named JPQL queries.

Best Practice

Don't try to perfect your JPA object model in isolation. Iteratively develop the entity classes in conjunction with the service code that uses it.

We've already discussed the embedded classes, and whether associations should be implemented in a unidirectional or bidirectional manner. We now consider the other steps in the process, starting with how to generate JPA classes from a schema.

Generating the JPA Classes from the Schema

Many tools will generate JPA code from a database schema. When we developed `bigrez.com`, we used the Eclipse IDE's Dali Java Persistence API tools. Dali is part of the Eclipse Web Tools Platform Project, and can be installed via the Eclipse update manager.

To generate JPA classes from a schema with Dali, follow these steps:

1. Open the Data Source Explorer view, and create a database connection to the database schema you wish to map.

2. Create a new JPA project, choosing `None` as the target runtime, and the database connection you created in step 1.

3. Right-click the project, and chose `Generate Entities from Tables`. A dialog will appear. Select your database connection, and then on the next page in the dialog, select all the tables you want to map to entities and type in the Java package name you want to use. Select `Finish` and the entities will be created.

OpenJPA also has good support for generating JPA classes through its reverse mapping tool. To use this tool, first create a `persistence.xml` containing database connection properties. (See "Using JPA

Entities in a Java SE Environment'' in Chapter 6 for an example.) Then, set your environment for running WebLogic Server and run the tool using the `org.apache.openjpa.jdbc.meta.ReverseMappingTool` class.

```
%  . /oracle/middleware/wlserver_10.3/server/bin/setWLSEnv.sh
%  java org.apache.openjpa.jdbc.meta.ReverseMappingTool -properties persistence.xml
-pkg com.bigrez.domain -schema bigrez -annotations true -inverseRelations false
```

Refer to the OpenJPA documentation for details of the many options you can specify. Here we have used `-annotations true`, so the tool will add metadata annotations to the generated entities, and `-inverseRelations false`, which fits our preference of selectively adding bidirectional reference pairs.

As we pointed out in Chapter 6, the database schema is likely to outlive your application and be used by other applications. Normally, you will want to design this schema carefully, and so it makes sense to generate the JPA model from the schema. On occasion, you may wish instead to generate the schema from your domain model. If so, you can set the `openjpa.jdbc.SynchronizeMappings` property to `buildSchema`. This modifies the database schema to match your mappings, and is particularly useful for rapid prototyping.

Generic JPA Functionality

There is common functionality that we want all of our JPA entities to share. For example, the `equals()` method should compare entity instances using the primary key. We've extracted a `DomainEntity` super-class for the entity classes, and a `ValueObject` superclass for the embedded classes. This is shown in Figure 7-9. These classes exist in the `com.bigrez.jpa` package.

`ValueObject` is simple. Because we will use our domain classes as data transfer objects, it implements `Serializable`. It contains two utility methods, `nullSafeEquals()` and `nullSafeHashCode()`, which subclasses can use to avoid repetitive checks for `null` values in their value-based `equals()` and `hashCode()` method implementations. `ValueObject` also provides a `toString()` method that returns a standard format string, including the implementation class name, the hash code, and a description that subclasses have to provide by implementing the abstract `toStringDescription()` method. The implementation class is calculated by looking for the most derived class that has a package name starting `com.bigrez`. This will filter out any subclasses that have been added by the JPA provider as part of its enhancement process.

`DomainEntity` is a little more complicated. The class's primary responsibility is to handle all of the common functionality related to identity. The primary key columns of all of the `bigrez.com` entities are of type `NUMBER(10)`, which is mapped to a `long` field in the domain model. By declaring `DomainEntity` as a mapped superclass, it can manage the primary key in the `id` field that all of the subclasses inherit. `DomainEntity` uses the `@GeneratedValue` and `@SequenceGenerator` annotations to generate primary keys from a database sequence, so a public `setID()` method is not required.

Clients require a string representation of an entity's identity. Web applications often use such identity strings to add context information to URLs. We have declared the `DomainEntity.getID()` method to be `protected`, so it can't be called directly by clients. This is deliberate, and for two reasons. First, we decided not to expose our primary keys outside of the domain model implementation, retaining the freedom to change the primary key representation if we need to at a later date. Second, the primary key only makes sense in conjunction with the class with which it is associated, so providing a client with just a `long` value is not particularly helpful. The client would be required to keep track of the entity class for which the `long` was a primary key and supply the entity class when it wanted to use the primary key for look up. Instead, a client should call `getExternalIdentity()`, which provides a string encoding both the entity class and the primary key. At a later date, the client can call the static method `findByExternalIdentity()` to convert the encoded string to an entity. All of this functionality is implemented in the `DomainEntity` class, so can be inherited easily by the concrete entity classes.

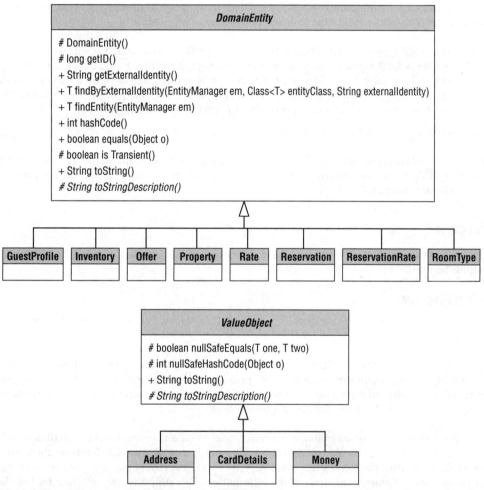

Figure 7-9: `bigrez.com` **domain model superclasses.**

Unlike `ValueObject` subclasses, which need to do a field-by-field value-based equality calculation, the equality of an entity class is based purely on its primary key. `DomainEntity` implements `equals()` and `hashCode()` based on the entity class and the primary key, and all subclasses inherit this behavior. `DomainEntity` implements `toString()` in a similar manner to `ValueObject`; subclasses simply need to override `toStringDescription()` to provide additional information from their significant fields.

Best Practice

`DomainEntity` and `ValueObject` contain generic functionality that should be useful to any JPA implementation. Feel free to use these classes in your projects.

Changes to the *bigrez.com* Schema

We aimed to make the minimum number of changes to the original database schema. By and large, we achieved this. The following is a list of differences from the original:

❑ The COMMON_SEQUENCE database table has been replaced by a database sequence. Although JPA defines a database table–backed generator strategy, it requires that the table has both a primary key and a value column. The original `bigrez.com` implementation used a table with a single column holding the sequence value, so is not compatible with the JPA table generator. We felt a database sequence was more appropriate for the Oracle database anyway.

❑ We removed a redundant foreign key between RESERVATION and PROPERTY.

These are minor changes, and arguably we would have made these improvements whether or not we were using JPA. A more significant change is the version column we added to support optimistic locking. We describe this later in this chapter.

Services

Now we have a robust domain model, let's consider the implementation of the session façade and the business services.

Session Façade

Figure 7-10 shows the `bigrez.com` service interface. These classes exist in the `com.bigrez.service` package.

Following the session façade pattern, the service methods are tuned to the needs of the presentation layer. We've split the services into three groups. The profile services deal with guest profiles. The property services deal with the administration of properties, marketing offers, and rates. The reservation services deal with availability checking and making reservations.

We've used a subset of classes from the domain model as data transfer objects. Not all domain model classes are exposed. In particular, `Inventory` and `ReservationRate` are hidden from the client, and instead the client uses the `AvailabilitySummary`, `AvailabilityAndRates`, and `RateDetails` interfaces that provide more appropriate views of the information. This simplifies the interface for the client. It also helps performance because each `RoomType` can have many `Inventory` entities, but the client is only interested in availability for a limited time period and not all of the `Inventory` entities.

The package contains a number of application exceptions. We've used checked application exceptions for problems that the client can reasonably be expected to handle. For example, a `DuplicateKeyException` will be thrown if the client tries to create a guest with the same logon name as an existing guest. The implementation may throw unchecked exceptions for other conditions, such as not being able to connect to the database; for these problems, the client can do little more than present a *technical error* page to the user.

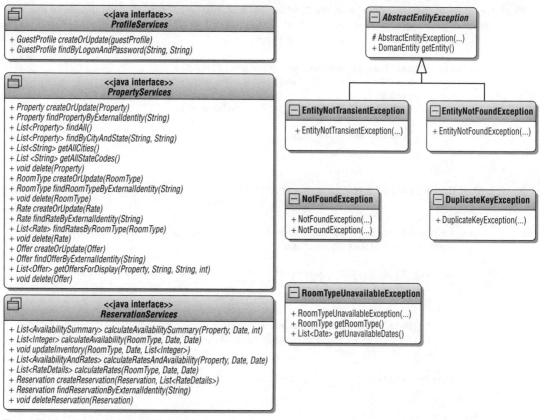

Figure 7-10: `bigrez.com` **service interface.**

The interfaces and classes in the `com.bigrez.service` package are pure Java, and so are easy to mock up for unit testing.

Service Implementation

The services are implemented using three stateless session EJBs in the `com.bigrez.service.impl` package. Let's look at the simplest implementation, the `ProfileServicesImpl` EJB.

Because the presentation layer is packaged in the same enterprise application, we use `ProfileServices` as a local interface. The EJB also declares an `entityManager` field, which the container will set up when it deploys the application.

```
@Stateless
@Local
public class ProfileServicesImpl implements ProfileServices
{
    @PersistenceContext
    private EntityManager entityManager;
```

Next, we come to the creation of a utility `JPABaseDAO` instance. We'll consider the details of this data access object class in a bit; for now just note that `ProfileServicesImpl` implements `getEntityManager()` to allow the utility class access to the entity manager.

```
private JPABaseDAO<GuestProfile> guestProfileDAO =
    new JPABaseDAO<GuestProfile>() {
        @Override
        protected EntityManager getEntityManager()
        {
            return entityManager;
        }
    };
```

Now, look at the two method implementations:

```
@Override
public GuestProfile createOrUpdate(GuestProfile guestProfile)
    throws DuplicateKeyException
{
    GuestProfile result = guestProfileDAO.createOrUpdate(guestProfile);
    try {
        entityManager.flush();
    }
    catch (PersistenceException e) {
        throw new DuplicateKeyException("GuestProfile exists with logon name '"
                            + guestProfile.getLogon() + "'");
    }
    return result;
}

@Override
public GuestProfile findByLogonAndPassword(String logon, String password)
    throws NotFoundException
{
    return guestProfileDAO.findOne(GuestProfile.QUERY_BY_LOGON_AND_PASSWORD,
                            logon, password);
}
```

That's the full `ProfileServicesImpl` EJB. The other EJBs are a little more complex, but all three follow the same pattern.

The EJB method implementations are simple because they delegate the interaction with the entity manager to the data access object. Let's have a quick look at this class. You can see its methods in Figure 7-11.

The `JPABaseDAO` is a generic abstract base class that encapsulates CRUD operations with the JPA entity manager. To use the class, a subclass is created for a particular JPA entity class, and `getEntityManager()` is overridden to supply the entity manager. The class provides various methods that map frequently used JPA operations to a form more suited to the EJB implementations, and avoids much repetitive code.

Here's one of the methods, `findOne()`, which wraps up the invocation of a named JPQL query when a single result is expected. The `ProfileServicesImpl` EJB used this method to implement `findByLogonAndPassword()`.

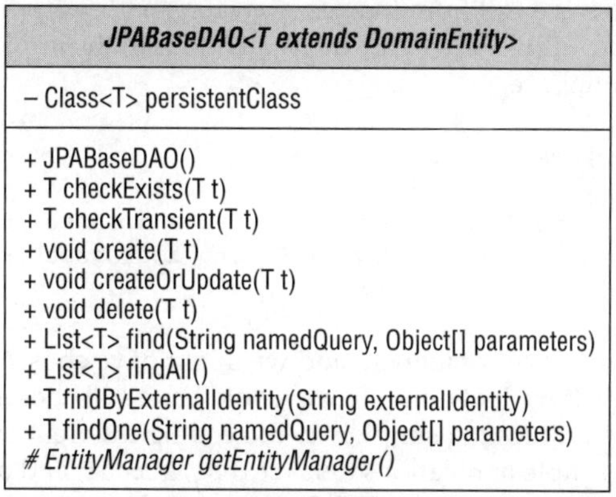

```
JPABaseDAO<T extends DomainEntity>

– Class<T> persistentClass

+ JPABaseDAO()
+ T checkExists(T t)
+ T checkTransient(T t)
+ void create(T t)
+ void createOrUpdate(T t)
+ void delete(T t)
+ List<T> find(String namedQuery, Object[] parameters)
+ List<T> findAll()
+ T findByExternalIdentity(String externalIdentity)
+ T findOne(String namedQuery, Object[] parameters)
# EntityManager getEntityManager()
```

Figure 7-11: The JPABaseDAO class.

```java
public T findOne(String namedQuery, Object... parameters)
    throws NotFoundException
{
    try {
        Query query = getEntityManager().createNamedQuery(namedQuery);
        int i = 0;
        for (Object p : parameters) {
            query.setParameter(++i, p);
        }
        return (T)query.getSingleResult();
    }
    catch (NoResultException e) {
        throw new NotFoundException(e);
    }
}
```

The findOne() method deals with the translation of the JPA NoResultException to the more neutral NotFoundException session façade exception; it returns an instance of the correct entity type, so the client doesn't need to concern itself with casting. It also simplifies the Query interface: the client calls one method, passing all of the query parameters, rather than having to make repeated calls to setParameter() itself.

Best Practice

Follow the *Don't Repeat Yourself* principle and encapsulate repetitive CRUD operations in a generic data access object class. You can use the JPABaseDAO class in your own projects if it fits your needs.

Email Integration

The bigrez.com application sends an email notification to the guest when a reservation is made or canceled.

The first step in this process is a call from the ReservationServicesImpl EJB to an EmailServicesImpl EJB. The EmailServicesImpl EJB is used only internally, so is in the implementation package. It supports a simple EmailServices interface.

```
interface EmailServices
{
    void sendReservationConfirmedEmail(String addressee, Reservation reservation);
    void sendReservationCancelledEmail(String addressee, Reservation reservation);
}
```

EmailServicesImpl is an internal component and we might have chosen to implement it as a plain Java class, rather than as an EJB. If we had done so, we would have still chosen to separate an EmailServices interface because it makes unit testing simpler, so the coding difference between plain Java and EJB amounts to adding a few simple annotations (@Stateless, @Local, and a couple for dependency injection). We get many advantages of using an EJB. First, the client can use dependency injection to obtain a reference to the EJB and we can let the container worry about managing the life cycle of EJB instances. Had we used plain Java we would have needed to create a factory or register the component with a service locator class. Second, we can use dependency injection within the EJB to obtain references to other services; we do so for EmailServicesImpl to look up a JMS connection factory and destination. Third, the container ensures our code will only be invoked by one thread at a time, pooling and creating additional EJB instances as necessary. Fourth, we can monitor our EJB through the WebLogic Console or using JMX.

EmailServicesImpl's primary responsibility is the creation of a formatted email from a Reservation, together with an appropriate subject line depending on whether the reservation was confirmed or canceled. Having done so, it places the information on a JMS queue, for later processing by a separate EmailMDBImpl EJB. We have used a JMS queue to separate the sending of an email message into its own, repeatable transaction. This means that the original transaction (the reservation booking or cancellation) will not be delayed or aborted if the remote mail server is unavailable. Further, our data sources and JMS connection factories are configured to participate in the same global transaction using XA. We use this to ensure that emails are sent only if the original transaction succeeded. If the reservation transaction calls sendReservationConfirmedEmail() and then fails to commit, perhaps because of an optimistic locking exception, the transaction will also rollback the sending of the JMS message and no email will be sent out.

The JMS queue also provides a simple, configuration-based mechanism for retrying failed attempts to send the email. This is important, because the email server is remote and may be down for maintenance or not contactable due to a network issue. We cover how to configure message redelivery in Chapter 10.

Best Practice

Introduce a JMS queue where you need to split an operation into two separate transactions, and ensure the second transaction is started if and only if the first one commits successfully.

You can configure WebLogic Server's JMS redelivery capabilities to retry the second transaction a number of times, or to move it to an error queue for an administrator's attention.

As promised, the dependency injection of JMS resources into `EmailServicesImpl` is simple:

```
@Resource(mappedName="bigrez.jms.connectionfactory")
private ConnectionFactory jmsConnectionFactory;
@Resource(mappedName="bigrez.jms.emailQueue")
private Destination emailQueue;
```

The `mappedName` elements refer to the JNDI names of the connection factory and queue that are set in the domains configuration. WebLogic Server will inject wrapped versions of the JMS resources that have built-in pooling and error recovery. See Chapter 10 for more details on JMS wrappers.

Let's look at the other end of the queue, and the `EmailMDBImpl` EJB. This is a message-driven bean that will remove messages from the queue, and send out email messages.

```
@MessageDriven(mappedName = "bigrez.jms.emailQueue",
              activationConfig = {
                  @ActivationConfigProperty(propertyName = "destinationType",
                                            propertyValue = "javax.jms.Queue")
              }
)
public class EmailMDBImpl implements MessageListener
{
    public static final String EMAIL_SUBJECT = "EMAIL_SUBJECT";
    public static final String EMAIL_ADDRESSEE = "EMAIL_ADDRESSEE";
    @Resource
    private MessageDrivenContext context;
    @Resource(mappedName="bigrez.mail.session")
    private Session mailSession;
    @Resource
    private String sender = "reservations@bigrez.com";

    @Override
    public void onMessage(Message message)
    {
        // Send email message.
    }
}
```

The `activationConfig` element indicates that the MDB should be deployed to receive messages from a JMS queue, and the `mappedName` element supplies the JNDI name of the queue.

The MDB has the default transaction configuration, so will use container-managed JTA transactions. When a message arrives, the container will start a new transaction and call the `onMessage()` method. Our implementation makes use of the injected JavaMail `Session` to convert the received JMS message into an email, and send it using the WebLogic Server mail session that is bound to the JNDI name `bigrez.mail.session`.

The `bigrez.com` EJB module doesn't use deployment descriptors. We've chosen to use annotations to inject the required resources. This is a good development time convenience, but a disadvantage of this approach is that the application's dependencies are not readily apparent to or easily changeable by an administrator. To determine the dependencies without attempting to deploy the application, the administrator would have to read all of the application code. We addressed this by supplying a WLST script that creates the required resources. We also include a sample deployment plan in the downloadable examples that would allow our administrator to override these injected dependency JNDI names, should the need arise.

When writing error-handling logic in message-driven beans, you should decide whether an exception should rollback the current transaction. If you rollback the transaction, the message will be eligible for redelivery. If you don't rollback, you effectively have consumed the message. Rolling back the transaction is appropriate for transient errors, where redelivery in a new transaction might succeed. We do this in `EmailMDBImpl` if we received a `MessagingError` from the email system. You shouldn't rollback if you know the message can never be processed; instead you should log the problem or perhaps place the message directly on an error queue for the attention of an administrator. For example, when `EmailMDBImpl` fails to parse the recipient's email address, it logs a warning but does not rollback the transaction. Such messages are sometimes referred to as *poison messages*, and we further discuss how to handle them in Chapter 10.

The container will automatically rollback the transaction if the MDB throws a `RuntimeException`. It is poor practice to rely on this, because the container will also discard the MDB instance; a high error rate would negate the value of MDB pooling. Instead, you should use the JTA or EJB APIs to mark the transaction for rollback and return from the `onMessage()` method. `EmailMDBImpl` does this by calling `setRollbackOnly()` on the injected `MessageDrivenContext`.

Alternatively, you can throw `weblogic.ejb.NonDestructiveRuntimeException` or an exception that derives from that class. In this case, the container will not destroy the MDB instance. Further, if the exception is thrown repeatedly, the MDB will be automatically suspended according to the `<init-suspend-seconds>` and `<max-suspend-seconds>` settings. We cover these settings in Chapter 8.

Best Practice

Only mark an MDB transaction for rollback if there is a chance that reprocessing the message will succeed. Otherwise, raise an administrative alert, perhaps by placing the message directly on an error queue.

To force the rollback of an MDB transaction, use the JTA or EJB API or throw a `weblogic.ejb.NonDestructiveRuntimeException`, rather than throwing any other type of `RuntimeException`.

Logging Interceptor

We configured all of the `bigrez.com` EJBs to use a simple interceptor that logs the entry and exit points of EJB methods to the WebLogic Server log. Using such an interceptor provides traceability for debugging without having to clutter the implementation with repetitive logging code. It could easily be converted to provide an audit trail.

Unit Tests

In Chapter 6, we mentioned that unit tests allow JPA code to be developed in an iterative fashion, and recommended it as a best practice. For the `bigrez.com` service layer, our unit tests provide full coverage for both the JPA domain model and the service implementation.

Thanks to the sea change in Java API design that has occurred over the past few years, and in particular to dependency injection, JPA and EJB 3.0 classes are particularly easy to test. Our unit tests are based on JUnit 4, and we used the Mockito library, which allows interfaces and classes to be easily mocked up. All of our tests run outside of WebLogic Server, and are integrated into the standard Ant build files. Although an application server is not required, the unit tests are written to rely upon access to a running database. It would not be simple to simulate a database with mock objects, and doing so would reduce the value of the unit tests, because their behavior may change subtly with different database implementations. We want to be sure that our tests run correctly with the version of the database we plan to use in the production environment.

A test utility class of note is `AbstractEntityManager`. All of our JPA unit test classes that require an entity manager extend from this base class. Its main purpose is to provide access to an entity manager, begin an entity manager transaction before each test method is called, and rollback the transaction after the test method. By rolling back after each method, we leave the database in a known state for the next test. Some unit tests require that there are no rows in a database table, so they delete all the rows with a JPQL query in a separate setup method. Again, because we rollback the transaction after the test, deleting the rows does not affect other transactions.

We will cover unit testing in greater depth in Chapter 14. Having a solid set of unit tests allows us to remain confident that the code still works as designed after making a significant change. One such change is to add support for optimistic locking. Let's look at what was entailed.

Adding Optimistic Locking

The main changes required to add optimistic locking support to `bigrez.com` were to the database schema. Columns must be added to each table to store the version information. We could have avoided the need to change the schema by using OpenJPA's state comparison versioning strategy, but a number of drawbacks to this strategy were covered in Chapter 6. Instead, we went ahead and added a version column to each entity table:

```
create table PROPERTY (ID NUMBER(10) NOT NULL,
                       VERSION NUMBER(4) NOT NULL,
                       DESCRIPTION VARCHAR2(60) NOT NULL,
                       ...
```

Thanks to JPA's strong support for optimistic locking, the code changes to the domain model turned out to be very simple. As all of our entities inherit from the `DomainEntity` mapped superclass, we just added a version field to that class.

```
@SuppressWarnings("unused")
@Version
private int version;
```

The `@SuppressWarnings` annotation is to placate the Java compiler, which would otherwise warn that the version field is never used.

With these changes applied, all of our existing unit tests still passed. We added a couple more tests to check that concurrent modifications result in the appropriate optimistic locking exceptions.

The business layer propagates optimistic locking exceptions directly to the presentation layer as runtime exceptions. In Chapter 6, we mentioned that JPA could nest an `OptimisticLockException` inside other exceptions. The presentation layer shouldn't need to know the back end is implemented using JPA, but unfortunately there is no easy way for the business layer to unwrap `OptimisticLockExceptions` and translate them to an implementation-neutral exception. Optimistic lock exceptions are most likely to occur when a transaction commits, and the container handles the commit outside the scope of any business layer application code. We could `flush()` the entity manager at the end of each session bean method and translate any optimistic lock exceptions at that point; however, this would still not catch optimistic locking failures that occur between the `flush()` and the commit point, and would reduce efficiency by increasing the length of time we hold database locks.

To allow the presentation layer to determine whether a given exception is caused by an optimistic locking failure, we added the `isOptimisticLockingException()` method presented in Chapter 6 as a static utility method in the domain model package. This at least removes the need for the presentation layer to depend directly on JPA.

In summary, JPA made it very easy to add optimistic locking to the `bigrez.com` business layer.

Using TopLink instead of Kodo

We close this chapter by looking at how to switch the JPA provider used by `bigrez.com` from Kodo to Oracle TopLink.

Why Would You Want to Use TopLink?

In Chapter 6, we covered the history of Kodo, TopLink, and their open source offspring, OpenJPA and the Eclipse Persistence Platform (EclipseLink).

Let's briefly review pros and cons of switching the JPA provider to TopLink. Kodo is the default JPA provider for WebLogic Server 10.3.1 and earlier. It has integration into the WebLogic Console and logging subsystems. TopLink is Oracle's strategic JPA provider, and will replace Kodo as the default JPA provider in a future version of WebLogic Server.

Both Kodo and TopLink are mature, sophisticated products that are fully supported by Oracle, and both are delivered in the WebLogic Server 11g installation. At the time of writing there is no compelling technical reason to advocate one over the other. You might consider using TopLink for one of the following reasons:

- ❏ You prefer TopLink to Kodo, or want to take advantage of a particular TopLink feature.
- ❏ You are already using TopLink for other applications.
- ❏ You wish to check that your application will be easy to port to TopLink, perhaps to prepare for the day it becomes the default provider in WebLogic Server.
- ❏ You wish to use JPA 2.0 features. EclipseLink is the reference implementation for JPA 2.0. There are no plans to make Kodo JPA 2.0 compliant.

Changes to `bigrez.com` to use TopLink

This section discusses the necessary changes to convert the `bigrez.com` application to use TopLink.

Change the Persistence Provider

Our standard `bigrez.com persistence.xml` doesn't specify a JPA provider, so WebLogic Server will use the default provider, Kodo. To change the provider to TopLink, we alter the `persistence.xml` file to specify the EclipseLink JPA provider.

```
<?xml version="1.0" encoding="UTF-8"?>
<persistence version="1.0" ... namespace declarations ...>
  <persistence-unit name="BigRezDomain" transaction-type="JTA">
    <provider>org.eclipse.persistence.jpa.PersistenceProvider</provider>
    <jta-data-source>bigrez.datasource.jta</jta-data-source>
    <non-jta-data-source>bigrez.datasource.nonjta</non-jta-data-source>
  </persistence-unit>
</persistence>
```

TopLink is included in the WebLogic Server 11g installation, and no further changes are needed to the WebLogic Server domain before our application can be deployed.

TopLink Enhancement

The business layer build file runs the Kodo enhancer over the entities. This must be disabled, because it will not work with the TopLink provider in the `persistence.xml` file. Doing so also avoids incompatibilities between the Kodo and TopLink enhancement.

TopLink can dynamically enhance the entity classes at runtime, but following the advice in Chapter 6 you may wish to enhance the classes statically at build time. This can be achieved using the `org.eclipse.persistence.tools.weaving.jpa.StaticWeaveAntTask` Ant task.

```
<taskdef name="weave"
         classname="org.eclipse.persistence.tools.weaving.jpa.StaticWeaveAntTask"
         classpathref="wls.classpath"/>
<weave source="${classes.dir}"
       target="${classes.dir}"
       persistenceinfo="${common.basedir}/../unit-tests/src">
  <classpath refid="build.classpath"/>
</weave>
```

There's a minor difference in style between the Kodo enhancer that we covered in Chapter 6 and the TopLink enhancer. The Kodo enhancer Ant task allows the classes to enhance to be passed in a nested file set. The TopLink enhancer expects the classes to be listed in the referenced `persistence.xml`. The `persistence.xml` we package in the application doesn't list the entities, so we've pointed the enhancer at the `persistence.xml` used by our unit tests, which does.

Running the Unit Tests

Because the TopLink classes are referred to by `weblogic.jar`, no changes are required to the classpath in the unit test build file.

If you are launching the unit tests from an IDE that doesn't understand manifest classpath entries, you will need to add the EclipseLink jar file to the classpath. You can find this jar file in the `modules` subdirectory of the WebLogic Server installation. It is named `org.eclipse.persistence_1.0.0.0_1-1-0.jar` in WebLogic Server 10.3.1.

The unit tests have their own `persistence.xml`, configured for a Java SE environment. The EclipseLink provider must also be set in this file.

Fix Incompatibilities

We ran the unit tests against the `bigrez.com` business layer, and found the following three differences of implementation between Kodo and TopLink:

- ❑ There were differences in the result sets produced by JPQL fetch joins.

- ❑ A bug in the application exposed a difference in the behavior of cascaded persist operations that repersist a removed entity.

- ❑ The application was using a Kodo extension that allows generators to be used on non-identity fields.

Recall that a fetch join is used to retrieve associations as a side effect of the execution of a query, even if the associations are not otherwise referred to in the query. Here's an example from the JPA specification:

```
SELECT d FROM Department d LEFT JOIN FETCH d.employees WHERE d.deptno = 1
```

The left join ensures that the `employees` field of the returned `Department` is populated; otherwise it would be `null`. The JPA specification goes on to say the following:

> A fetch join has the same join semantics as the corresponding inner or outer join, except that the related objects specified on the right-hand side of the join operation are not returned in the query result or otherwise referenced in the query. Hence, for example, **if department 1 has five employees, the above query returns five references to the department 1 entity**.
>
> Source — *JSR 220: Enterprise JavaBeansTM, Version 3.0 Java Persistence API.*

Kodo returns a single reference to the `Department` in this case, whereas TopLink returns five. The Kodo behavior is perhaps more intuitive, and provides the result we want, but TopLink is compliant with the specification. Fortunately it is simple to modify the query so that both products return a single result by using the `DISTINCT` keyword:

```
SELECT DISTINCT d FROM Department d LEFT JOIN FETCH d.employees WHERE d.deptno = 1
```

The second difference is quite subtle. One of our unit tests deletes a `Reservation` that was associated with a `GuestProfile`, detaches the `GuestProfile`, and then later merges the `GuestProfile` back into the persistence context. Due to a bug in `bigrez.com`, the `GuestProfile` maintained a link to the deleted `Reservation`. Kodo ignored this reservation when the `GuestProfile` was merged, but TopLink cascaded a persist operation to the reservation and recreated it, causing a unit test assertion to fail. By the letter of the JPA specification, the TopLink behavior is correct: persisting a removed entity should cause it to become managed again. The fundamental problem was the application bug in `ReservationServicesImpl.deleteReservation()` that left a bidirectional association in an inconsistent state. We fixed this method to set the GuestProfile reference to null when deleting the reservation.

The third problem found by our unit tests was due to the use of a Kodo extension feature. The JPA specification only allows the @GeneratedValue annotation to be used for identity columns, yet the application had applied it to the Reservation.confirmationNumber field.

```
@Column(name="CONFIRMNUM")
@GeneratedValue(strategy=GenerationType.SEQUENCE, generator="CommonSequence")
private String confirmationNumber;
```

This is a useful feature, but not portable. We provided an alternative implementation that calculates a confirmation number in memory.

```
@Column(name="CONFIRMNUM")
/* @GeneratedValue(strategy=GenerationType.SEQUENCE,
generator="CommonSequence") */
private String confirmationNumber;
...
@PrePersist
public void calculateConfirmationNumber()
{
    if (confirmationNumber == null) {
        confirmationNumber =  String.valueOf(Math.abs((int)System.nanoTime()));
    }
}
```

The @javax.persistence.PrePersist annotation registers the calculateConfirmationNumber() to be called whenever the entity is persisted by the entity manager. The confirmation number is simply derived from the result of System.nanoTime(). It is a good enough way to generate a confirmation number because there is no need for the number to be globally unique.

With two minor changes to the code, and one bug fix, all of our unit tests now pass under both Kodo and TopLink.

Test the Integrated Application

With the unit tests all passing, we now have a lot of confidence that the integrated application will work with TopLink. We built the application EAR file and deployed it to WebLogic Server — bigrez.com is now running on TopLink!

Summary

With very little change to the code, we now have an implementation that we can deploy using either Kodo or TopLink, just by changing the provider in persistence.xml. We didn't set out to write the bigrez.com business layer in a particularly portable fashion, we simply found standard JPA features to be sufficient and didn't need to exploit advanced Kodo features. If we were happy to rely on dynamic enhancement, we might even do this with a deployment plan.

The unit tests were a very useful tool for identifying how the application may behave differently, or just not work, when running under TopLink.

Best Practice

If you are writing JPA code that must be portable between JPA providers, you should write full unit tests and regularly run them against at least two JPA implementations.

Chapter Review

This chapter examined the process for selecting a business layer architecture and constructing the business layer components for the `bigrez.com` example application. Important business layer requirements were identified, candidate architectures were outlined and mapped against the requirements, and a specific architecture was chosen for the example application. The chosen stateless session EJB with JPA architecture has clear advantages over the other candidates.

We considered various aspects of the `bigrez.com` implementation, including the database schema, domain object model, and the implementation of the business services and session façade. We saw that JPA made it very simple to add support for optimistic locking.

Finally, we investigated what would be required to deploy `bigrez.com` using TopLink instead of Kodo as the JPA provider. JPA allows us to switch between TopLink and Kodo by changing a single line in a deployment descriptor.

In the next chapter, we discuss packaging and deploying this application using WebLogic Server–specific tools and techniques.

8

Packaging and Deploying WebLogic Applications

This chapter covers the steps required to package and deploy WebLogic Server applications. Chapter 5 looked at the basic packaging of web applications. This chapter covers how to create enterprise applications from web application and EJB modules; how classloading works in a WebLogic Server application; how to provide common functionality as Java EE optional packages or WebLogic Server shared libraries; and how to include JDBC, JMS, and WLDF resources in the application.

Individual web applications and EJB packages are generically referred to as *modules*. A Java EE enterprise application is composed of one or more modules, and has an optional deployment descriptor called application.xml. It is packaged in an .ear (*Enterprise Archive*) file, which can be deployed as a unit to an application server. Web applications and EJBs are by far the most commonly used module types. Java EE defines two other module types: client applications and resource adapters, but we don't cover either of these in any depth. Later in the chapter you see that WebLogic Server allows for other types of modules that contain JDBC, JMS, and WLDF resources, and that enterprise applications can also contain bundled libraries. At the end of this chapter, we show how the bigrez.com application is packaged and deployed.

Creating an EJB Archive File

Just like web applications, EJBs are packaged into archive files to be deployed either standalone to a server or included in an enterprise application.

An EJB module contains one or many EJBs, and like a web application, can have associated deployment descriptors. We briefly touched upon the EJB deployment descriptors in Chapter 6, mainly to note that they are not mandatory for an EJB 3.0 module because many standard Java EE settings can be specified using annotations.

The EJB module we created for `bigrez.com` does not use deployment descriptors. Such a module is very easy to package — you just compile your classes and use the familiar `jar` tool to create an archive file. We walked through the process in Chapter 6. The resulting `.jar` file can be deployed directly to a WebLogic Server instance. Two things enable this simple packaging.

Annotations   We covered the benefits of annotations at length in Chapter 6. Before EJB 3.0, an EJB developer had to spend a lot of time keeping deployment descriptors in line with the EJB code. Annotations make deployment descriptors optional for most EJBs, and no deployment descriptors means there's less to package.

Dynamic Compilation   WebLogic Server automatically compiles applications if necessary when they are deployed. It is unnecessary to precompile an EJB module with the `appc` compiler before it can be deployed, but as we noted in Chapter 6, you might wish to do so to discover any errors when the application is built, and to minimize deployment time.

EJB Deployment Descriptors

Some EJB features can only be specified using deployment descriptors, so here we consider them in a little more depth. You may also want to use deployment descriptors to override the values set by annotations in the application code for a specific environment.

An EJB module may contain three descriptor files; all three are optional. If they exist, the descriptors are packaged in a top-level `META-INF` directory in the EJB jar file. The first descriptor is defined by Java EE and is named `ejb-jar.xml`. The second descriptor contains WebLogic Server settings, and is named `weblogic-ejb-jar.xml`. It is common for `ejb-jar.xml` to declare logical items required by the EJB code that must be bound into the WebLogic Server environment in `weblogic-ejb-jar.xml`. For example, a security role defined in `ejb-jar.xml` must be mapped to externally configured security principals in `weblogic-ejb-jar.xml`. Here, you'll recognize a similar pattern to the web application descriptor `web.xml`, which is defined by Java EE, and `weblogic.xml`, which contains WebLogic Server–specific settings.

EJB 2.x entity beans using container-managed persistence require a third descriptor called `weblogic-cmp-rdbms-jar.xml` if they are to be deployed to WebLogic Server. This file contains object relational mapping information. We don't cover EJB 2.x entity beans in this book, so won't consider this file further, nor the many `<entity-descriptor>` settings that can be configured in `weblogic-ejb-jar.xml` to tune EJB 2.x entities.

Tip to Remember

Don't be confused by the fact the WebLogic Server reference documentation for `weblogic-ejb-jar.xml` refers to the `2.1` version of the descriptors. This is to distinguish the documentation from that of the EJB 1.1 descriptor.

The `2.1` descriptor applies equally to EJB 2.x and EJB 3.0 deployments.

A complete discussion of the contents of the `ejb-jar.xml` and `weblogic-ejb-jar.xml` files is beyond the scope of this book. The WebLogic Server online documentation is your best reference source for this information: See Link 8-1 in the book's online Appendix at http://www.wrox.com/. We'll satisfy ourselves by summarizing the WebLogic Server settings that are commonly used for EJB 3.0 beans, many of which we mentioned in passing in Chapter 6.

JNDI Bindings and References to EJBs and Other Resources

In Chapter 6, we showed how to bind an EJB remote business interface to a JNDI name using the `<business-interface-jndi-name-map>` element in `weblogic-ejb-jar.xml`. We called this out as a best practice compared to the alternative of using the non-portable `mappedName` element of the `@Stateless` or `@Stateful` annotations. We didn't need to use the `<business-interface-jndi-name-map>` element for `bigrez.com` because it doesn't contain any EJBs that have remote business interfaces.

We also looked at how to use deployment descriptors to define references to other EJBs, both within the same enterprise application using `<ejb-link>`, and in other applications using `<ejb-ref>` and `<ejb-reference-description>`. Please refer back to Chapter 6 for details.

An EJB can declare other types of resources in `ejb-jar.xml` that it expects the container to bind into its `java:comp/env` JNDI environment namespace. The EJB specification provides the `<resource-env-ref>` element that can be used to bind elements from the global JNDI tree into the EJB's environment. Each `<resource-env-ref>` must be mapped using the `<resource-env-description>` element in `weblogic-ejb-jar.xml` to a specific resource by specifying its global JNDI name or its location in another application module.

There is also a `<resource-ref>` element that can be used to bind JDBC data sources, JMS connection factories, JavaMail sessions, and `java.net.URL` resources into an EJB's environment. The common link between these types of resources, and the reason that they are declared with a different element, is that they are container-managed factories that the application uses to create other resources. Each `<resource-ref>` must be mapped using the `<resource-description>` element in `weblogic-ejb-jar.xml` to a specific resource by specifying its global JNDI name or its location in another application module.

The `@javax.ejb.Resource` annotation may be used instead of `<resource-ref>` or `<resource-env-ref>` elements. This annotation is a jack-of-all-trades. We used it in Chapter 6 as an alternative to the `<env-ref>` descriptor element, and to inject EJB context variables. Whatever the resource type, `@Resource` can be used to inject resources directly into application code, or be applied at the class level to bind resources to the `java:comp/env` environment namespace. You can still use `<resource-env-description>` and `<resource-description>` elements in `weblogic-ejb-jar.xml` to bind the `@Resource` declarations to real resources.

We used `@Resource` in the `bigrez.com EmailServicesImpl` session EJB to inject a JMS connection factory and a JMS destination, using the `mappedName` annotation element to provide the global JNDI names of these resources directly.

```
@Resource(mappedName="bigrez.jms.connectionfactory")
private ConnectionFactory jmsConnectionFactory;
@Resource(mappedName="bigrez.jms.emailQueue")
private Destination emailQueue;
```

You can think of the `mappedName` value as providing an optional default value, which can be overridden in the deployment descriptors and further customized using a deployment plan, just as you saw in Chapter 6 for `<env-entry>`. You must specify the binding somewhere though. If we choose to leave out the mapped names, or simply want to override the values, we can do so in `weblogic-ejb-jar.xml` as follows.

```
<weblogic-ejb-jar xmlns="http://xmlns.oracle.com/weblogic/weblogic-ejb-jar"
                  xmlns:j2ee="http://java.sun.com/xml/ns/javaee"
                  xmlns:xsi="http://www.w3.org/2001/XMLSchema-instance"
                  xsi:schemaLocation="http://xmlns.oracle.com/weblogic/weblogic-ejb-
jar http://www.oracle.com/technology/weblogic/weblogic-ejb-jar/1.0/weblogic-ejb-
jar.xsd">
  <weblogic-enterprise-bean>
    <ejb-name>EmailServicesImpl</ejb-name>
    <resource-description>
      <res-ref-name>
        com.bigrez.service.impl.EmailServicesImpl/jmsConnectionFactory
      </res-ref-name>
      <jndi-name>bigrez.jms.connectionfactory</jndi-name>
    </resource-description>
    <resource-env-description>
      <resource-env-ref-name>
        com.bigrez.service.impl.EmailServicesImpl/emailQueue
      </resource-env-ref-name>
      <jndi-name>bigrez.jms.emailQueue</jndi-name>
    </resource-env-description>
  </weblogic-enterprise-bean>
</weblogic-ejb-jar>
```

Here, we've used a `<resource-description>` element to bind the JMS connection factory, and a `<resource-env-description>` for the JMS destination. The default reference name is formed from the fully qualified class name and the annotated field name. If you want to use a different name, you can use the `name` element of the `@Resource` annotation, but there is little reason to do so.

Bindings to Logical JMS Message Destinations

The preceding resource mappings are scoped to individual EJBs. For example, if desired, two different EJBs can use the same `java:comp/env` binding to point to two different resources.

It is common for multiple components in an enterprise application to need to access a JMS queue or topic. To remove the need for repetitive configuration, Java EE provides a way for *logical* JMS destinations to be declared once, and shared between multiple EJBs in an application. The `<message-destination>` element is used to declare a logical destination in `ejb-jar.xml`, and it is bound to a physical topic or queue using the `<message-destination-descriptor>` element in `weblogic-ejb-jar.xml`. Individual EJBs then declare references to the `<message-destination>` using the `<message-destination-ref>` element in `ejb-jar.xml` or the `@Resource` annotation. As you might expect, a message-driven bean can also refer to the logical destination as its source, using the `<message-destination-link>` element. There is no corresponding element to `<message-driven-destination-ref>` in `weblogic-ejb-jar.xml`, because it is simply a pointer to the `<message-driven-destination>` and there is nothing specific to WebLogic Server to customize.

Let's modify our `bigrez.com` example to use a logical message destination. We'll still inject the destination into the code, but we need to modify our code slightly. When injecting logical message destinations, the type of the field must be `Queue` or `Topic`, so we've changed the type of the field to be `Queue`, rather than `Destination`.

```
@Resource
private javax.jms.Queue emailQueue;
```

Here's the `ejb-jar.xml` descriptor that declares the `<message-destination>` and injects a reference into the `emailQueue` field.

```xml
<?xml version="1.0"?>
<ejb-jar xmlns:xsi="http://www.w3.org/2001/XMLSchema-instance"
         xmlns="http://java.sun.com/xml/ns/javaee"
         xmlns:ejb="http://java.sun.com/xml/ns/javaee/ejb-jar_3_0.xsd"
         xsi:schemaLocation="http://java.sun.com/xml/ns/javaee
http://java.sun.com/xml/ns/javaee/ejb-jar_3_0.xsd"
         version="3.0">
  <enterprise-beans>
    <session>
      <ejb-name>EmailServicesImpl</ejb-name>
      <message-destination-ref>
        <message-destination-ref-name>
          com.bigrez.service.impl.EmailServicesImpl/emailQueue
        </message-destination-ref-name>
        <message-destination-usage>Produces</message-destination-usage>
        <message-destination-link>myDestination</message-destination-link>
      </message-destination-ref>
    </session>
  </enterprise-beans>
  <assembly-descriptor>
    <message-destination>
      <message-destination-name>myDestination</message-destination-name>
    </message-destination>
  </assembly-descriptor>
</ejb-jar>
```

We didn't specify the `name` element in the `@Resource` annotation, so it is linked to the `<messsage-destination-ref>` element using the default name derived from the EJB class and the field name. The `<message-destination-ref>` element then further refers to the `<message-destination>` element by name. We could have left out the `<message-destination-ref>` element entirely by adding `name="myDestination"` to the `@Resource` annotation. The `<message-destination>` can be defined in a different EJB jar file in the same application. If there is a chance that there are multiple destinations with the same name in different EJB jar files, the `<message-destination-link>` text can be qualified using the form `otherejb.jar#myDestination`.

The `<message-destination>` is bound to a physical queue in `weblogic-ejb-jar.xml` as follows.

```xml
<weblogic-ejb-jar xmlns=...>
  <message-destination-descriptor>
    <message-destination-name>myDestination</message-destination-name>
    <destination-jndi-name>bigrez.jms.emailQueue</destination-jndi-name>
  </message-destination-descriptor>
</weblogic-ejb-jar>
```

> **Best Practice**
>
> Use the Java EE `<message-destination>` element to set logical JMS destinations only when the message destination is used by multiple components in your application. If this doesn't apply to your application, logical destinations add unwanted complexity.

Security Settings

We look at how to configure declarative security policies for session EJBs and web application modules in Chapter 11, and also show how to use the `<run-as>` element in `ejb-jar.xml` and `<run-as-role-assignment>` in `weblogic-ejb-jar.xml` to override the caller's identity with a fixed identity.

WebLogic Server allows fine-grained control over the identity used to perform particular EJB life cycle operations, using the `<create-as-principal-name>`, `<passivate-as-principal-name>`, and `<remove-as-principal-name>` settings. These are occasionally required to escalate the privileges of a session or message-driven bean, or to refine the identity set with `<run-as-role-assignment>`, otherwise these life cycle operations will be performed as the anonymous user.

For example, suppose a session bean declares a reference to a JMS queue using the `@Resource` annotation, and that the JMS queue is bound into the JNDI tree with a security policy that only allows it to be looked up by members of the `jmsusers` group. To allow the EJB to be initialized, the `<create-as-principal-name>` element could be used to specify a user belonging to the `jmsusers` group.

Transaction Settings

We looked at the `<transaction-isolation>` settings in Chapter 6, and covered the Java EE `@TransactionManagement` and `@TransactionAttribute` annotations, which generally are to be preferred to the equivalent `<transaction-type>` and `<container-transaction>` elements in `ejb-jar.xml`.

The `<transaction-descriptor>` element of `weblogic-ejb-jar.xml` allows the transaction timeout to be customized for an EJB's container-managed transactions.

```
<weblogic-enterprise-bean>
  <ejb-name>MyEJBImpl</ejb-name>
  <transaction-descriptor>
    <trans-timeout-seconds>100</trans-timeout-seconds>
  </transaction-descriptor>
</weblogic-enterpise-bean>
```

This setting applies only to new transactions started by container when the EJB is called. It has no effect for calls to the EJB that use an existing transaction, so the EJB's `@TransactionAttribute` must either be `REQUIRES_NEW` or `REQUIRED` (the default value), and in the latter case the there must not be an existing transaction when the call to the EJB is made. You may need to use the `<transaction-descriptor>` element to increase the transaction timeout for an EJB that performs a lengthy database operation, or for a message-driven bean that uses transaction batching. It is better to relax the transaction timeout for specific EJBs than to increase the global default for the whole WebLogic domain.

WebLogic Server 9.0 introduced automatic retries for container-managed transactions. This is configured using the `<retry-methods-on-rollback>` element.

```
<retry-methods-on-rollback>
  <retry-count>2</retry-count>
  <method>
    <ejb-name>MyEJBImpl</ejb-name>
    <method-name>*</method-name>
  </method>
</retry-methods-on-rollback>
```

This setting also applies only to container-managed transactions started by the EJB. You must be careful that methods you configure for retry do not have nontransactional side effects that would cause a retried transaction to produce an invalid result.

In practice, automatic retries of EJB container-managed transactions are of limited use. This in contrast with the JMS retry feature we describe in Chapter 10. Retries are most useful where a transaction may fail due to a temporary condition, such as a database being restarted. JMS retries are performed asynchronously, and allow a retry delay to be configured to make it more likely that the transaction is retried after the temporary condition has been cleared. In contrast, EJB retries are performed immediately, and so any retried transaction is likely to fail for the same reason as the original transaction.

Free Pool Settings

In Chapter 6, we covered the `<initial-beans-in-free-pool>`, `<max-beans-in-free-pool>`, and `<idle-timeout-seconds>` elements that are used to tune the pooling behavior of stateless session beans and message-driven beans. There is rarely any need to tune the default settings for stateless session beans. Here's an example that configures a message-driven bean pool to contain three instances that are pre-initialized on deployment.

```
<message-driven-descriptor>
  <pool>
    <max-beans-in-free-pool>3</max-beans-in-free-pool>
    <initial-beans-in-free-pool>3</initial-beans-in-free-pool>
  </pool>
</message-driven-descriptor>
```

Stateful Session Bean Cache Settings

We also covered the SFSB `<max-beans-in-cache>`, `<cache-type>`, `<idle-timeout-seconds>`, `<session-timeout-seconds>`, and `<replication-type>` settings. Here's an example that configures a cache that can hold up to 5000 instances of a bean in memory, eagerly passivates instances that haven't been used for ten minutes from memory to disk, and if they still haven't been used for a further hour then discards the copies on disk when convenient.

```
<stateful-session-cache>
  <max-beans-in-cache>5000</max-beans-in-cache>
  <idle-timeout-seconds>600</idle-timeout-seconds>
  <session-timeout-seconds>3600</session-timeout-seconds>
  <cache-type>LRU</cache-type>
</stateful-session-cache>
```

Message-Driven Bean Settings

In addition to the `<pool>` element, many other WebLogic Server–specific settings can be configured for message-driven beans in `weblogic-ejb-jar.xml`.

The basic connection information can be set using `<provider-url>`, `<initial-context-factory>`, `<connection-factory-jndi-name>`, and `<destination-jndi-name>`. Of these, `<destination-jndi-name>` is most commonly used, although the destination JNDI name can also be set with the `mappedName` element of the `@MessageDriven` annotation, or with a `<message-destination-link>`. The default message-driven bean connection factory usually suffices when connecting to a collocated destination, but a custom JMS connection factory can be configured using `<connection-factory-jndi-name>`. The other two elements, `<provider-url>` and `<initial-context-factory>`, are necessary only when connecting to remote or foreign JMS providers without using WebLogic JMS's Foreign Server feature. We look integration with remote and foreign JMS providers in Chapter 10. These three elements can also be set in code using the WebLogic Server `@weblogic.javaee.MessageDestinationConfiguration` annotation.

The `<max-messages-in-transaction>` element enables the MDB transaction-batching feature we covered in Chapter 6, and controls the maximum number of messages per transaction.

The `<jms-client-id>`, `<generate-unique-jms-client-id>`, and `<durable-subscription-deletion>` elements are used to set the client ID used for durable subscriptions to JMS topics. See Chapter 10 for more details.

The `<init-suspend-seconds>` and `<max-suspend-seconds>` elements control what happens when a message-driven bean repeatedly throws an exception with the same message. After ten such exceptions have been thrown in succession, WebLogic Server will write a message to the server log file, and suspend the JMS connection associated with the MDB for the period set by `<init-suspend-seconds>`. After this period has expired, the connection will be resumed and the message will be redelivered to the MDB. If the MDB still repeatedly throws exceptions, the JMS connection will be suspended again, but this time for double the period. This process will continue, with the suspension period doubled every time, until the MDB no longer throws exceptions. The `<max-suspend-seconds>` element can be used to specify a maximum time a connection will be suspended. Automatic MDB suspension allows WebLogic Server applications to cope more gracefully with temporary resource outages without entering a tight loop, repeatedly failing to process messages. It focuses on problems that affect the processing of many messages, and so complements the JMS redelivery features, which deal with the processing of individual messages. The default value of `<init-suspend-seconds>` is 5 seconds, and the default value of `<max-suspend-seconds>` is 60 seconds, so an MDB that throws exceptions will be initially paused for 5 seconds, then for periods of 10, 20, 40, 60, 60, 60 . . . . seconds. The default values are fine for most applications. If you want to disable the feature, set `<max-suspend-seconds>` to 0.

The `<jms-polling-interval-seconds>` element controls the frequency at which an MDB will attempt to reconnect to a destination that is unavailable. The default value is 10 seconds. While an MDB is unable to connect to its destination, a message will be printed to the server log every 10 minutes.

Tuning and Optimization Settings

Several miscellaneous settings in `weblogic-ejb-jar.xml` can be used to tune the performance of an EJB.

The most important of these is `<dispatch-policy>`. This allows a custom work manager to be specified for a message-driven bean or for remote requests to a session bean. It is common to use a custom work manager to tune the number of threads an MDB will use for processing messages. We cover work managers in more detail in Chapters 12 and 13, and how to tune MDB concurrency in Chapter 10.

The `<enable-call-by-reference>` setting enables a performance optimization that applies if you make calls to an EJB's remote business interface within the same enterprise application. By default, WebLogic Server fully serializes all parameters and returned objects for all calls to a remote business interface method to comply with the Java EE specification. The receiving EJB deserializes the parameters and so receives a copy of each parameter *by value*. Serialization is required when communicating remotely using RMI, or when making a call between unrelated classloaders — for example, a call between two separate enterprise applications. Setting `<enable-call-by-reference>` to `True` causes WebLogic Server to skip serialization and deserialization for calls made between components within the same enterprise application, and instead passes the parameters and return value *by reference*. Essentially, WebLogic Server behaves as if the remote business interface is actually a local business interface. This can result in a significant performance boost, but the caller must guard against side effects arising from any changes the EJB makes to the parameters. The origin of this setting dates back to much earlier versions of WebLogic Server, before the introduction of local interfaces in EJB 2.0. If you have control over the application, it is better to add a local interface; this is both explicit and portable.

> **Best Practice**
>
> Instead of using the `<enable-call-by-reference>` setting, add a local business interface to your EJBs for calls within the same enterprise application.

The `<idempotent-method>` setting is used to mark methods that can safely be retried. We covered this in Chapter 6.

The `<network-access-point>` setting is used to configure a custom network channel for remote calls to EJBs. RMI calls that arrive via other network channels will be rejected, so this can be used to enforce a security restriction on how an EJB is accessed. We cover the configuration of network channels in Chapter 12.

The `<remote-client-timeout>` element is another RMI setting. If set, WebLogic Server clients will abort remote EJB method calls that fail to return within the configured timeout period, and throw a `weblogic.rmi.extensions.RequestTimeOutException` to the client application. If the method call is transactional and the value is greater than the transaction timeout, the transaction timeout will be used instead. The EJB method will not be not interrupted if its client times out.

Packaging JPA Persistence Units

In Chapters 6 and 7 we examined the content of the `persistence.xml` deployment descriptor that defines a JPA persistence unit. All that remains is to provide the details of how the descriptor should be packaged in an application.

The packaging of a persistence unit for a Java EE application is straightforward. Persistence units can be defined in a module, such as an EJB or web application, or at application level. Persistence units defined in a module are scoped to the module, and are not visible from other modules in the application. Application-scoped persistence units are visible to all modules in the application. There can be only one persistence unit with a given name within a scope.

The `persistence.xml` file can be included in the following locations.

❑ In a web application, below `WEB-INF/classes`, or in a `.jar` file in `WEB-INF/lib` (module-scoped).

❑ In an EJB (module-scoped).

❑ In an application, either in a bundled library belonging to the application, or in the application's `APP-INF/classes` directory (application-scoped). We look at bundled libraries and `APP-INF/classes` later in this chapter.

In each case, the `persistence.xml` file should be located below a `META-INF` directory. This rule is applied consistently, so its correct path in a web application's `classes` directory is the unusual looking `WEB-INF/classes/META-INF/persistence.xml`.

Any associated `orm.xml` mapping file or Kodo-specific `persistence-configuration.xml` should be placed alongside the `persistence.xml` descriptor.

In practice, many JPA applications deal with a single logical schema, and use a single persistence unit. Multiple persistence units are only required when an application must deal with more than one database, or when it has several distinct types of transaction, each of which deals exclusively with a disjoint part of a large schema.

Enterprise Applications

You have a number of ways to package and deploy an application consisting of EJB and web application modules.

1. **Standalone modules.** Deploy the EJB archives and web applications directly to the server as standalone applications. The web application components can access the EJB components using remote business interfaces.

2. **Enterprise application archive.** Package the EJB and web applications into an enterprise application archive (`.ear`) file, which is deployed as a unit to the server.

3. **Exploded enterprise application.** Package the EJB and web applications into an enterprise application directory structure, which is deployed as a unit to the server. Support for this unarchived deployment format is a WebLogic Server extension to Java EE. In WebLogic Server parlance, it is called an *exploded* deployment.

The first option, standalone deployment of EJB archives and web applications, is depicted in Figure 8-1. Each EJB archive and web application is deployed as an independent Java EE application in WebLogic Server using one of the standard deployment techniques (discussed later in this chapter).

ejbarchive1.jar	*EJB archive file*
ejbarchive2.jar	*EJB archive file*
webapp1.war	*Archived web application file*
webapp2	*Exploded web application structure*

```
      ├── JSP/html files
      └── WEB-INF
```

Figure 8-1: EJBs and web applications deployed as separate applications.

This technique is not recommended for the following reasons.

❏ Each application is loaded with a separate, independent application classloader (see Figure 8-2). Because each classloader is independent, classes loaded by one application classloader are not visible to classes loaded by other application classloaders. For a web application to invoke EJBs, it must include a copy of the client-related EJB classes necessary to communicate with the EJB components (typically remote business interfaces, and any classes used as arguments, return types, or exceptions by the methods of the business interfaces). As the number of web applications and EJBs increases, the management of these client classes becomes tedious and error prone.

❏ Because the application classes are loaded in separate unrelated classloaders, and each module classloader has its own versions of the classes, communication between the modules must use remote interfaces and RMI serialization to avoid ClassCastException errors. The overhead of this serialization is acceptably small when making a remote network call, but is overly costly for more frequent, local communication between an application's modules.

❏ Applications are difficult to manage as a single unit because they are not, in fact, a single application in the view of the server. For example, controlling the order of deployment during server startup becomes an issue with this technique, and the WebLogic Server staging and deployment features are unable to process multiple applications as a single deployment unit.

❏ There is no way to share a JPA persistence context across modules, or configure application-wide resources.

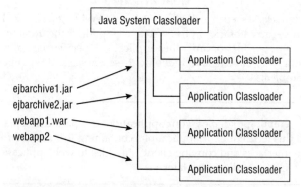

Figure 8-2: Separate classloader used for each application.

All classloaders used for the separate applications are children of the Java system classloader. The classes in the system classloader (configured by the CLASSPATH environment variable) are used for the server process itself during startup. Components in a child classloader may refer to classes present in parent classloaders, meaning that your EJB and web applications can use classes loaded by the system classloader. An acceptable alternative to placing client .jar files for each EJB archive in each web application might appear to be to put such files in the system classpath, making the client classes available to all child classloaders and therefore to all of your application components. Don't fall into this trap! There are two very good reasons to avoid using the system classloader for application classes.

❑   Placing application-related classes in the system classpath prevents a complete redeployment of your application because classes loaded by the system classloader cannot be removed and reloaded. If you need to change any classes loaded through the system classloader, you will have to restart the whole server for the changes to be picked up. Similarly, you cannot use the WebLogic Server FastSwap feature with classes on the system classpath.

❑   Classes in the parent classloader cannot refer directly to classes in children classloaders. If any class in the system classloader attempts to use a class found only in the EJB archive or web application lib or classes directory, you will get a ClassNotFoundException or a NoClassDefFoundError exception. If you address this problem by moving more and more classes to the system classpath, pretty soon you'll find that every class in your application winds up in the system classloader and all hope for hot redeployment is gone.

We recommend that only classes required for system-wide components be present in the system classpath and therefore loaded by the Java system classloader, for example, JDBC driver classes. Even classes such as logging utilities and frameworks used by your application do not belong in the system classpath. There are better locations for such libraries in an enterprise application. We cover this topic in detail later in this chapter when we consider bundled libraries, optional packages, and shared Java EE libraries.

WebLogic Server uses a separate classloader to load classes from the domain lib directory. This classloader is a child of the system classloader, and a parent of the application classloaders. The classes and resources in any .jar file placed in the directory is automatically available to all applications. However, the domain lib classloader does not support redeployment, dynamic reloading, or FastSwap, and cannot refer directly to code in the application classloaders. You should consider the domain lib directory to be roughly equivalent to the system classpath, and using it for application classes.

Best Practice

Place only system classes, such as JDBC drivers and WebLogic Server classes, or particularly large third-party libraries in the system classpath or the domain lib directory. Don't place client .jar files or any other application-specific classes in the system classpath or you will not be able to redeploy these classes and will likely encounter classloading problems.

Although it might be tempting to deploy your application as separate independent archives, we recommend that you avoid this technique for applications containing EJB archive files. Once you get in the habit of using remote interfaces and copying client .jar files to web applications, it may be difficult to migrate to the better techniques discussed later.

Best Practice

Avoid deploying EJB archives and related web applications as separate, independent applications in WebLogic Server.

Enterprise Application Directory Structure

The other two options for EJB deployment involve creating an enterprise application containing all of the EJB archives and web application components. The options differ only in the final packaging step: should the enterprise application be deployed as an exploded directory or as a single enterprise archive (.ear) file? We address that question later in this chapter. Here we review the contents of an enterprise application and examine the enterprise application descriptor files that allow us to configure the application components.

Figure 8-3 presents the standard directory structure and contents of an enterprise application. The key difference from the previous EJB deployment option is the bigapp enterprise application root directory. This directory contains all of the individual application components. The server treats everything in the bigapp directory as a single Java EE application, eliminating many of the problems associated with standalone modules.

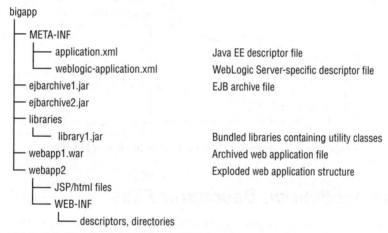

Figure 8-3: Standard enterprise application directory structure.

The EJB archives and web application components are placed at the root level of the enterprise application directory structure along with a META-INF directory containing optional descriptors and any other directories required by your application.

Bundled libraries can be included in an enterprise application in several ways. In Figure 8-3, we have shown them in a libraries directory to be loaded using the manifest Class-Path technique. We discuss the use of manifest Class-Path entries and the other ways to package bundled libraries later in this chapter.

Compared to deploying the modules in a standalone fashion, an important difference in this deployment option is the structure of the classloaders used to load application classes. When deployed standalone, each EJB archive and web application is loaded in a separate classloader descended directly from the Java system classloader (see Figure 8-2). When EJB modules and web applications are placed in an enterprise application structure, however, WebLogic Server uses the classloader structure depicted in Figure 8-4.

All EJB modules, along with bundled libraries, are loaded by a single top-level application classloader, thereby permitting local interfaces and direct Java method calls between components in these EJB modules. More importantly, the web application classloaders are children of the application classloader rather than siblings of it. Recall that a child classloader is able to refer to all classes loaded by its parent classloader, so the web application components also have full access to the classes in the EJB modules. This *child-sees-parent* visibility has two important ramifications.

❏ Web applications may use local EJB interfaces and make Java method calls to EJB components located in the same enterprise application. There is no need to use remote interfaces or Serializable parameters and return types, although their use is not precluded in this option.

❏ There is no need for the web applications to include client EJB classes, because they have full visibility to these classes by virtue of the parent application classloader.

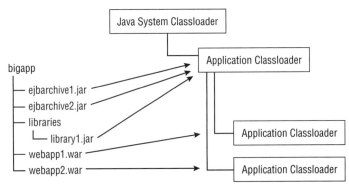

Figure 8-4: Classloader hierarchy in an enterprise application.

Enterprise Application Descriptor Files

The META-INF directory in the enterprise application directory structure may contain two optional descriptor files used to control the deployment of the components and resources in the enterprise application. The first descriptor file is application.xml, a standard file defined by the Java EE specification. The second file, weblogic-application.xml, is a WebLogic Server–specific descriptor file used to configure shared caches and resources common to all components in the enterprise application.

Standard application.xml Descriptor File

The application.xml descriptor file is defined by the Java EE specification and defines the basic configuration and deployment of the application. Table 8-1 outlines the high-level sections of the application.xml file and lists the key elements used in each section.

The module definitions are the most significant information in the application.xml descriptor. The bigrez.com application takes advantage of the application.xml descriptor being optional in Java EE 5, and does not define one, which brings up the interesting question of how the container knows what the application's modules are without a descriptor. This is done by convention, following the rules listed in Table 8-2. These rules apply only if there is no application.xml descriptor; if a descriptor is provided, its <module> elements fully specify the application's modules.

Listing 8-1 presents an example of an application.xml descriptor that we could have used had we chosen to define one for bigrez.com.

Table 8-1: Sections of the application.xml Descriptor

application.xml Section	Purpose and Key Top-Level XML Elements
Deployment attributes	Defines optional descriptions and graphical icons used by deployment and management tools. The standard WebLogic Sever tools do not use this information. `<icon>`, `<display-name>`, `<description>`
Module definitions	Defines the location of each module contained in the enterprise application. The `connector` and `java` module types are for resource adapters and client modules respectively. `<module>`, `<connector>`, `<ejb>`, `<java>`, `<web>`
Security information	Defines application-wide security roles available for all modules. `<security-role>`
Library directory	Optional specification of a directory that contains bundled libraries. `<library-directory>`

Table 8-2: Conventions Used to Identify an Application's Modules when no application.xml Descriptor is Provided

File Characteristics	Interpretation
Name ends in `.war`.	Web application module. The context root is derived from the file name by removing `.war`.
Name ends in `.rar`.	Resource adapter module.
Directory named `lib`.	Directory containing bundled libraries.
Name ends in `.jar`, and contains a jar file manifest with a `Main-Class` attribute, or a `META-INF/application-client.xml` descriptor.	Application client module.
Name ends in `.jar`, and contains a `META-INF/ejb-jar.xml` descriptor or any class with an EJB component annotation.	EJB module.
Other files.	Not treated as modules.

Listing 8-1: Sample bigrez.com application.xml descriptor file.

```
<?xml version="1.0">
<application xmlns:xsi="http://www.w3.org/2001/XMLSchema-instance"
             xmlns="http://java.sun.com/xml/ns/javaee"
             xmlns:application=
```

Continued

Listing 8-1: Sample bigrez.com application.xml descriptor file. *(continued)*

```
"http://java.sun.com/xml/ns/javaee/application_5.xsd"
   xsi:schemaLocation="http://java.sun.com/xml/ns/javaee
http://java.sun.com/xml/ns/javaee/application_5.xsd" version="5">
  <display-name>BigRezServicesEAR</display-name>
  <module>
    <ejb>BigRezServices.jar</ejb>
  </module>
  <module>
    <web>
      <web-uri>BigRezWebUser.war</web-uri>
      <context-root>user</context-root>
    </web>
  </module>
  <module>
    <web>
      <web-uri>BigRezWebAdmin.war</web-uri>
      <context-root>admin</context-root>
    </web>
  </module>
  <module>
    <web>
      <web-uri>BigRezWebServices.war</web-uri>
      <context-root>webservices</context-root>
    </web>
  </module>
</application>
```

Web application modules must specify a URI context root with the `<context-root>` element. This over-rides any value set in the web application itself. An empty `<context-root>` will make the web application the default for the application server.

If there is no `application.xml` descriptor, the context root for a web module is derived from the relative file name of the web module file by removing its `.war` extension.

Best Practice

Use an empty `<context-root>` element in the `application.xml` descriptor to specify the server's default web application.

---

weblogic-application.xml Descriptor File

The `weblogic-application.xml` descriptor is a WebLogic Server–specific file used to configure resources and control WebLogic Server features at the enterprise application level. This descriptor file is optional.

Table 8-3 outlines the high-level sections of the `weblogic-application.xml` file and lists the key elements in each section. Refer to the WebLogic Server online documentation for complete information about this descriptor file and its elements (see Link 8-2).

Table 8-3: Sections of the weblogic-application.xml Descriptor

weblogic-application.xml Section	Purpose and Key Top-Level XML Elements
EJB configuration	Defines application-wide EJB 2.x CMP entity bean caches and MDB startup policies. `<ejb>`, `<entity-cache>`, `<start-mdbs-with-application>`
XML configuration	Defines XML parsing, document building, and transformation factories for use in this application. Also defines XML entity mapping information. `<xml>`, `<parser-factory>`, `<entity-mapping>`
JDBC connection pool configuration	Deprecated method of packaging a JDBC data source in an application. Use the `<module>` element to deploy a JDBC module instead. `<jdbc-connection-pool>`
Security information	Provides security role mappings for the application. `<security-role-assignment>`
Container behavior	Various minor parameters affecting container behavior, including the character encoding used by web applications. `<application-param>`
Classloader hierarchy	Allows a custom classloader structure for the application. Rarely required. `<classloader-structure>`, `<module-ref>`
Listener, startup, and shutdown	Registers custom listeners, startup classes, and shutdown classes. `<listener>`, `<startup>`, `<shutdown>`
WebLogic Server module configuration	Defines WebLogic Server JDBC, JMS, and WLST application-scoped modules in a similar way to the use of `<module>` in `application.xml` for standard Java EE modules. `<module>`
Library references	Declares shared Java EE libraries used by the application. `<library-ref>`
Work Manager settings	Allows the application's work manager to be tuned. Used to override the priority the server gives to requests for this application. `<work-manager>`
Administration mode stuck threads trigger	Declares that the server should transition the application to administration mode if more than the configured number of threads have been *stuck* working on application requests for a period of time. This behavior can also be defined by customizing the work manager. `<application-admin-mode-trigger>`

Continued

Table 8-3: Sections of the weblogic-application.xml Descriptor *(continued)*

weblogic-application.xml Section	Purpose and Key Top-Level XML Elements
HTTP session configuration	Allows control over the HTTP sessions for web applications belonging to the application. If this is provided, it takes precedence over the descriptor in the individual web applications. Setting session parameters at the application level is mostly of use when you also set the `<sharing-enabled>` to enable sharing of a single HTTP session between all of the web applications. `<session-descriptor>`
FastSwap enablement	Used to enable WebLogic Server FastSwap. FastSwap is an extension to Java 6 class redefinition, which allows newly compiled code to be immediately used without having to redeploy the application, thus speeding up development cycles. `<fast-swap>`

The most important of the settings are those for configuring application-scoped modules and library references. We cover the details of these later in this chapter. The other settings are things to be reached for as and when you need them.

The `bigrez.com` `weblogic-application.xml` file, presented in Listing 8-2, is brief and simply enables the FastSwap feature. You see how the FastSwap feature speeds up development cycles in Chapter 14.

Listing 8-2: bigrez.com weblogic-application.xml descriptor file.

```
<?xml version="1.0"?>
<weblogic-application
    xmlns="http://xmlns.oracle.com/weblogic/weblogic-application"
    xmlns:xsi="http://www.w3.org/2001/XMLSchema-instance"
    xsi:schemaLocation="http://xmlns.oracle.com/weblogic/weblogic-
application http://www.oracle.com/technology/weblogic/weblogic-
application/1.0/weblogic-application.xsd">
  <fast-swap><enabled>true</enabled></fast-swap>
</weblogic-application>
```

We've discussed the structure and contents of an enterprise application. We can now consider exploded enterprise applications, which are most suitable for development and unit test environments, and archived enterprise applications, which are better for applications to be promoted to test and production environments.

Exploded Deployments

The Java EE specification requires that an enterprise application is packaged in an `.ear` file archive, and also that all modules and bundled libraries contained in the application are packaged in `.war`, `.rar`, or `.jar` archive files.

As an extension to the Java EE–defined behavior, WebLogic Server allows standalone modules and enterprise applications to be deployed in an unarchived form known as an *exploded* directory structure. This exploded directory structure matches that of its archived equivalent. You can create an exploded application from an `.ear` file by using the `jar` command to extract the `.ear` file's contents to a directory. You can then use the exploded directory structure as an argument to any of the WebLogic Server deployment tools, just as you would an archived module or application. We cover the deployment options in depth at the end of this chapter.

You can mix exploded and archived modules within an enterprise application, whether or not the application itself is exploded. For example, in Figure 8-3 `webapp1` is archived and `webapp2` is exploded.

The conventions described in Table 8-2 also apply to exploded web applications. This means that any directory that has a name ending `.war` is a web application that can be deployed to WebLogic Server. Things are nearly as simple for enterprise applications, except that an enterprise application must have at least one module. For example, a directory called `myapp.ear` containing a subdirectory called `webapp.war` is a valid enterprise application.

What are the advantages of using an exploded directory structure? The main benefit is a much faster development cycle.

❑ Application files can be changed and the application redeployed without a separate repackaging build stage.

❑ JSPs and static web application resources such as HTML, image, CSS, and JavaScript files can be changed in place without redeploying the application. WebLogic Server regularly checks whether such files have changed according to the `<page-check-secs>` and `<resource-reload-check-secs>` settings in the `weblogic.xml` descriptor. The settings determine how regularly the container checks for changes, and default to 1 second when the server is started in development mode and −1 (no change detection) in production mode. JSP files that have changed are compiled on the fly. To allow the JSPs to be reloaded individually without the need for the web application to be redeployed, WebLogic Server creates a separate classloader for each JSP as a child of the web application classloader.

❑ WebLogic Server also supports change detection for servlets and other web application classes according to the `<servlet-reload-check-secs>` setting in `weblogic.xml`. The default for this setting is 1 second in development mode, and −1 (no change detection) in production mode. If checking is enabled and a change to any class loaded by the web application classloader is detected, the container will create a new classloader for the servlet's web application and reload the classes. The container will also strive to maintain the old session state, servlet listeners, and so on. In terms of cost, this is similar to a redeployment of the web application.

❑ The classes and resources in a classloader are units of redeployment. WebLogic Server allows the *partial redeployment* of a module, such as a web application, that belongs to an exploded enterprise application, without the need to redeploy the entire enterprise application. This feature is used by WebLogic Server–aware Integrated Development Environments (IDEs) such as the Oracle Enterprise Pack for Eclipse (OEPE) to speed up deployment when a developer changes only part of an application.

❑ If the WebLogic Server FastSwap feature is enabled, application classes that are recompiled can immediately be reloaded in the running application without redeploying the application. This on-the-fly class replacement is very quick, and works for classes loaded in any of the application's modules. FastSwap works only with exploded applications, where the class has its own file on disk. We cover FastSwap in Chapter 14.

In short, you should use exploded applications for fast, interactive development. In Chapter 14, we look at how to configure popular IDEs to compile classes automatically into an exploded application structure. We also cover WebLogic Server's split development directory feature that allows static resources, deployment descriptors, and JSP files to be picked up directly from the project source directory, removing the need to copy these to the same location to which classes are compiled, and for the different modules of an application to be located in separate project directories.

We prefer to use archived applications for production deployment, because the configuration management is easier with a single file, but exploded applications have clear advantages in development environments.

> **Best Practice**
> Use exploded applications in your development environment for faster turnaround.

Bundled Libraries

A *bundled library* is simply a .jar file, containing code and resources, that is included in the application. A bundled library might contain a component of the application — for example, JPA entity model code, a company's standard foundation classes, common resources used by all of the web application modules, client jar files for accessing remote EJBs, or third-party product library code. In fact, any code that an application relies on or wishes to manage as a unit can be packaged in a bundled library.

In the early days of Java EE, before support for bundled libraries or even enterprise applications was available, it was common to package such library code on the system classpath. Bundled libraries provide three advantages over packaging classes on the system classpath. First, an application using bundled libraries is more self-contained and has fewer dependencies on a particular server configuration. This makes the application easier to manage and deploy. Second, as described earlier in this chapter, bundled libraries are loaded in the application's classloader. This allows changes to the bundled libraries to be made effective by redeploying the application, without needing to restart the server. Third, applications that rely on slightly different versions of the same bundled library can each have their own copies and be deployed to the same server. This can be important where two teams are producing applications to be deployed to a common server. For example, if one team needs to use a later version of a third-party product, such as Spring MVC, they can do so without requiring the other team to upgrade at the same time.

The drawbacks of bundled libraries over packaging classes on the system classpath are that they increase the size of applications, and that if many applications include the same bundled library their combined memory footprint can be much larger. There's a clear trade-off here between the benefit of self-contained, independent applications, and the inefficiency of managing multiple copies of the bundled libraries. Most often, bundled libraries will win.

You have four different ways to include bundled libraries in an application.

Manifest Class-Path Header A module in the application (including EJB, web application, resource adapter modules) can include a Class-Path header in its META-INF/MANIFEST.MF file that refers to a list of .jar files. These .jar files will be loaded as bundled libraries, and can be placed anywhere in the application directory structure. Each Class-Path list entry is treated as a path relative to the referring module. The process is transitive: Any `Class-Path` manifest headers in the `.jar` files will be used recursively to load other bundled libraries.

Web Application WEB-INF/lib   In Chapter 5, you saw that web applications provide a built-in mechanism to load utility archives in the same classloader as the web application itself: the `WEB-INF/lib` directory. Any `.jar` file placed in that directory will be loaded automatically by the web application classloader, and its classes will be available to the web application components. These `.jar` files can have manifest `Class-Path` headers that reference further bundled libraries. There is also a `WEB-INF/classes` directory for unarchived class and resource files.

Classes and resources loaded from `WEB-INF/classes`, `WEB-INF/lib`, or bundled libraries referred by libraries in `WEB-INF/lib`, are loaded in the web application classloader, and are not visible to the application's other modules. Refer back to Figure 8-4 and the associated discussion for detail.

WebLogic APP-INF/lib   Since version 8.1, WebLogic Server has allowed `.jar` files to be included as bundled libraries in an `APP-INF/lib` directory. These `.jar` files can have manifest `Class-Path` headers that refer to further bundled libraries. WebLogic Server also supports an `APP-INF/classes` directory for unarchived class and resource files. These `APP-INF` directories provide the same type of behavior as the `WEB-INF` directories do for web applications, but load classes into the application classloader.

Java EE 5 Application Library Directory   Java EE 5 introduced a similar feature to the WebLogic Server `APP-INF/lib` directory. Any `.jar` files in a Java EE application's library directory will be treated as a bundled library and loaded in the application classloader. These `.jar` files can have manifest `Class-Path` headers that refer to further bundled libraries.

The default library directory is called `lib`, but this can be changed using the `<library-directory>` element of the `application.xml` descriptor. An empty `<library-directory>` element means there is no library directory.

There is no Java EE equivalent to the WebLogic Server `APP-INF/classes` directory.

Best Practice

Prefer the Java EE library directory to the similar WebLogic Sever `APP-INF/lib` feature, because the former is portable between Java EE containers. If you are upgrading an older WebLogic Server application, you can simply set `<library-directory>` to `APP-INF/lib`.

Let's consider an example of packaging bundled libraries. Recall the scheme depicted in Figure 8-4. The two EJB modules and the two web application modules will be loaded automatically according to the conventions listed in Table 8-2. Nevertheless, the `library1.jar` file will not be automatically loaded and must be specially handled. The two most obvious options for doing so are defining a Java EE library directory or adding a manifest `Class-Path` entry.

The library directory option requires adding an `application.xml` descriptor to a `META-INF` directory and using the `<library-directory>` element to set the Java EE library directory to `libraries`. Because a descriptor has been provided, the default identification of modules by convention no longer applies, so the descriptor must fully specify each of the application's modules. Alternatively, the `libraries` directory could be renamed to `lib`, allowing the application to continue to rely on Java EE defaults and conventions.

The manifest `Class-Path` entry option requires adding a `META-INF/MANIFEST.MF` file to one or more of the EJB and web application modules.

```
Manifest-Version: 1.0
Class-Path: libraries/library1.jar
```

Modern Java EE development environments will automatically create and maintain these `Class-Path` headers in manifest files. If you edit the files by hand, be aware that lines in manifest files are limited to 72 characters. Long `Class-Path` headers may be continued onto subsequent lines by starting each such line with a single space.

It is generally poor practice to include two versions of the same class or resource in an application. The manifest `Class-Path` header is the only packaging method to allow control over the precedence of classes in bundled libraries. The order is not defined for the three other methods. We have seen subtle problems arise from assuming that the order is defined, such as where an application had been running reliably for years until the environment's file system was changed and the loading order of `WEB-INF/lib` libraries suddenly changed, causing the application to malfunction.

With the `Class-Path` header, the bundled libraries that appear earlier in the `Class-Path` header have the higher priority. This can be useful if two bundled libraries contain the same classes and you need to ensure that one is given priority. One use case is to *patch* a particular class or file of a third-party bundled library without altering the library itself.

Best Practice

Endeavor not to package more than one version of a class or resource in an application. Remove duplicates from bundled libraries.

If an application must contain multiple versions of a class or resource in two different bundled libraries, use the `Class-Path` header to define a fixed order of precedence.

Shared Java EE Libraries and Optional Packages

WebLogic Server provides two ways to package and manage libraries to be shared between applications: optional packages and shared Java EE libraries. There's a lot of detail to these shared library mechanisms, and here we only outline their purpose and functionality. For full details, please refer to the WebLogic Server documentation at Link 8-3.

Optional packages are part of the Java EE 5 specification. An optional package is a plain `.jar` file containing compiled classes and resources that can be deployed to a server. Applications and other optional packages can refer to the optional packages they depend on in their manifest files — this reference will be resolved at deployment time. Optional packages can also have a version, and different versions of the same optional package can be deployed to the server. The manifest file of the referring application will determine which version of the library it will use.

At runtime, optional packages are loaded in the application classloader, and so behave in a similar fashion to bundled libraries packaged in the application. If two applications deployed to a server use the same optional package, there will be two separate copies of the classes loaded in the server. Optional packages are not a way to reduce the memory footprint of an application.

Shared Java EE libraries are specific to WebLogic Server and are very similar to optional packages. Like optional packages, shared Java EE libraries can be deployed to a server; optionally can have a version; and can be referred to by applications or by other shared Java EE libraries. The main difference from optional packages is that shared Java EE libraries can also be enterprise applications, EJB modules, or web application modules, as well as plain .jar files containing classes and resources. The shared Java EE library name refers to this ability to contain Java EE applications and modules, but it is important to remember that this is a WebLogic Sever–specific feature.

When an application that refers to a shared Java EE library is deployed, it behaves as if the files in the shared library were merged with its own. Like optional packages, shared Java EE libraries provide a way to share code between applications, but each referring application is deployed with its own runtime copies of the classes and resources.

Optional packages and shared Java EE libraries have much the same runtime characteristics as bundled libraries. The benefit of optional packages and shared Java EE libraries is that they allow common libraries to be managed independently from applications, making the application archives smaller and often faster to deploy. On the other hand, an application that relies on optional packages is less self-contained and less independent.

Optional packages and shared Java EE libraries come into their own when used to provide common functionality for one or more applications, where you wish to be able to upgrade that common functionality without having to change the applications. Another less common use case is to ensure that each application is using exactly the same version of a library. If neither of these applies, it is simpler to build independent applications by fixing their dependencies at build time and use bundled libraries.

Best Practice

There are two good use cases for optional packages or shared Java EE libraries. The first is to allow common functionality to be upgraded without having to change dependent applications. The second is to ensure all deployed applications use the same version of a common library. If neither of these applies, using bundled libraries is simpler and results in more independent applications.

Following this best practice, we have used bundled libraries for bigrez.com. Toward the end of this chapter, we show what we would have to do to repackage one of these bundled libraries as a shared Java EE library.

Other Types of Modules

According to the Java EE specification, an enterprise application may contain four types of modules, namely web applications, EJB modules, client applications, and resource adapters.

WebLogic Server applications can also contain three other types of modules — JDBC modules, JMS modules, and WebLogic Diagnostic Framework (WLDF) modules. Each of these module types is defined by a single XML configuration file, and the module does not include other classes or resources, in contrast to the standard Java EE modules. Because they provide declarative configuration that configures how WebLogic Server manages the application, you can think of these JDBC, JMS, and WLDF modules as special types of deployment descriptor.

A JDBC module defines a JDBC data source. A JMS module defines JMS resources, including queues, topics, and connection factories. A WLDF module defines custom instrumentation points for the application. You can choose whether to package JDBC and JMS modules in the application as *application modules*, in the domain configuration as a *system module*, or deploy them on their own as *standalone* modules. In contrast, you can only add instrumentation to an application using a WLDF application module. We cover WLDF instrumentation in more depth in Chapter 12.

The JDBC and JMS configuration files for application modules and standalone modules are the same as those used for system modules. When you create a system module by adding a JDBC data source or JMS module to a domain using the WebLogic Server console, the XML configuration file is placed below the `config/jdbc` or `config/jms` directory of the domain. To convert a system module to an application module, include this file somewhere in the application, and declare the module using the `<module>` element of `weblogic-application.xml`. Conventional practice is to place modules alongside descriptors in `META-INF`. You will need to delete the system module before you can deploy your application, because otherwise the JNDI names and other resource names will clash.

JDBC and JMS modules can also be deployed in a standalone fashion. To do this, you use the module's XML file as the parameter to the `weblogic.Deployer` tool, or deploy it through the console.

The system, standalone, and application deployment types for JDBC and JMS modules are compared in Table 8-4.

Table 8-4: Comparison of Deployment Types for JDBC and JMS Modules

	System Modules	Standalone Modules	Application Modules
Resource Binding Options	Global JNDI.	Global JNDI.	Global JNDI — available for use by other applications. Application-scoped JNDI — inaccessible to other applications. JMS modules can be linked directly with `<resource-link>`.
Administration Options	JMX, WLST, or the console.	JSR-88 API and deployment plans, with console support. No JMX API for configuration. No support for WLST.	JSR-88 API and deployment plans, with console support. No JMX API for configuration. No support for WLST.

Standalone modules are of benefit over system modules if you wish to administer your domain using the standard JSR-88 API rather than the WebLogic Server–specific WLST or JMX management beans. This is a rare requirement. Standalone modules should also be considered if a separate team is responsible for defining the required JDBC or JMS resources. It may be easier to supply a standalone module, rather than a WLST script.

Application modules can make an application more self-contained, but they do not totally remove the burden on an administrator to understand and customize the resource configuration for deployment to a particular environment.

When deploying JDBC application modules, the database URL and passwords will usually need to be changed, and connection pool sizes frequently need to be tuned. If the application is not to be changed, this customization must be done in a deployment plan. Some JDBC features, such as the use of the logging last resource optimization, require the use of system modules.

JMS modules can have resources with specific targeting requirements, and the administrator must provide the appropriate *subdeployment* targets in the domain configuration. See Chapter 10 for more details on targeting JMS resources. JMS queues and topics often contain data that should survive the redeployment of applications. When undeploying an application with a JMS module that contains a queue, any messages in the queue will be discarded. On the positive side, a JMS application module is a good way to package a uniform distributed topic that provides non-persistent messaging within an application deployed to a cluster.

Best Practice

Consider using JDBC and JMS application modules instead of system modules to make applications more self-contained, but assess carefully whether they truly decrease the administration overhead. This will depend on exactly which resources the modules provide, and the degree to which the configuration must be customized for each target environment. When unsure, choose system modules.

Standalone modules can be simpler to use than WLST if a separate team is responsible for defining JDBC or JMS resources.

Administrators will often need to modify supplied application and standalone modules. This can be done using a deployment plan.

Customizing Classloading

The classloader hierarchy used by an application can be completely changed using the `<classloader-structure>` element of `weblogic-application.xml`. This is a development-only feature that can be used to allow more fine-grained redeployment of parts of the application. However, WebLogic Server already provides a wealth of redeployment and class redefinition features, so there is little reason to do this. Unless you have a deep understanding of classloader behavior, using a non-default structure can be the cause of many headaches.

Two other features allow more specific customization of the classloading behavior — individual EJB classloaders and filtering classloaders.

Individual EJB classloaders are only supported for EJB 1.x and EJB 2.x beans. An individual EJB classloader is a development feature that is useful if you are making many changes to an EJB implementation belonging to a larger enterprise application and using an exploded application structure. By default, EJBs are loaded in the application-level classloader. If you enable individual EJB classloaders with the `<enable-bean-class-redeploy>` element of `weblogic-ejb-jar.xml`, each EJB implementation is loaded in a separate classloader in a similar manner to that used for JSPs. Individual EJBs can then be redeployed using the `weblogic.Deployer` tool, without having to reload the entire application. Session EJB interfaces and associated classes are still loaded in the application classloader, because they are required to be visible to other components, and require a full redeploy of the application if changed.

> **Best Practice**
>
> Individual EJB classloaders pre-date FastSwap, are not supported for EJB 3.0 beans, and are deprecated in WebLogic Server 11g. FastSwap has some additional restrictions on changes to EJBs, but is a more general and easier-to-use alternative than the individual EJB classloader feature.

Filtering classloaders are used to resolve clashes between classes that are present in the application and on the system classpath, or in the domain `lib` directory. By default, if a class is present on both the system classpath and in the application, the system classpath copy is used. Filtering classloaders are commonly used to package a different version of a third-party library in the application. This is similar to the `<prefer-web-inf-classes>` web application feature, but applies to enterprise applications and can target specific classes using a simple wildcard syntax.

Filtering classloaders are controlled using the `<prefer-application-packages>` element in `weblogic-application.xml`. Suppose you wanted to use a later version of EclipseLink than the one packaged with WebLogic Server. You could package EclipseLink as a bundled library in the application, and use the following descriptor entry.

```
<prefer-application-packages>
  <package-name>org.eclipse.persistence.*</package-name>
</prefer-application-packages>
```

The `<package-name>` expression can have an optional wildcard * for its last character, which matches any characters.

In addition to classes, Java classloaders are responsible for providing access to resources that are packaged with the classes, such as property files or images. The `getResource()` method searches the classloaders in priority order, and returns the first match. The `getResources()` method returns all matches found, in priority order. The priority of classloaders for loading resources normally follows that for loading classes, with a parent classloader having priority over its children.

If you configure a filtering classloader that filters one or more packages, WebLogic Server will adjust the classloader priority so that the resources in classloaders that are parents of the application classloader are considered after the application classloaders. For an application containing a web application, the resource loading order will be the application classloader, the web application classloader, the system classpath, finally followed by the domain `lib` directory. The configured package filters are irrelevant — the resource loading order is changed if there is at least one filter. In contrast to the loading of classes that match a package filter, the system and domain `lib` classloaders are still consulted, albeit with a lesser priority. This allows you to package a bundled library in an application and place its configuration files on the system classpath.

WebLogic Server 11g allows you more precise control over the resource loading, using a new `<prefer-application-resources>` element in `weblogic-application.xml`. For example:

```
<prefer-application-resources>
  <resource-name>com/bigrez/*</resource-name>
</prefer-application-resources>
```

As for `<package-name>`, the `<resource-name>` expression can have an optional wildcard * for its last character, which matches any characters. Resources with names matching a `<resource-name>` expression will only be loaded from the application classloaders. The system and domain `lib` classloaders will not be consulted at all. For applications that frequently attempt to load resources, this can provide a significant performance benefit. Resources that do not match a `<resource-name>` expression are loaded by the old rules.

Packaging `bigrez.com`

We've reviewed the options for packaging an enterprise application. This section looks at how the `bigrez.com` application is put together.

The bigrez.com Components

The `bigrez.com` application is composed of four modules and several bundled libraries, as listed in Table 8-5. We covered the web application modules and `bigrez-web-common.jar` in Chapter 4, the `bigrez-domain.jar` library and `bigrez-services.jar` EJB module in Chapter 7, and we'll come to the `bigrez-webservices.jar` module in Chapter 9.

Table 8-5: The bigrez.com Components

Component Name	Type	Purpose
`bigrez-domain.jar`	Bundled library	JPA domain model.
`bigrez-services.jar`	EJB module	EJB 3.0 session beans providing services as a session façade.
`bigrez-web-admin.war`	Web application module	Web interface for hotel administrators.
`bigrez-web-user.war`	Web application module	Web interface for end users.
`bigrez-web-common.jar`	Bundled library	Common functionality shared by `web-admin` and `web-user`.
`bigrez-webservices.war`	Web application module	Web services implementation.

The dependencies between the components are shown in Figure 8-5. The web application modules depend on third-party libraries for Spring MVC, JSTL, and Tiles that are packaged as bundled libraries. These have been placed in the application's `APP-INF/lib` directory.

The bigrez.com Projects

The application and each of the components has its own project directory. Each project has an Apache Ant build file. There is also a `unittests` project containing JUnit unit test code that is not packaged in the application.

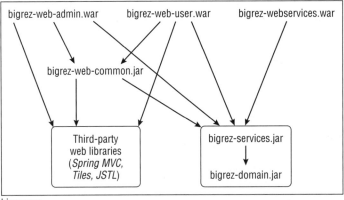

bigrez.ear

Figure 8-5: Dependencies between the `bigrez.com` **components.**

IDEs encourage a separate project per module or library, and one for the enterprise application. Splitting an application into projects allows the same directory structure to be used by an IDE, and allows the application to be built using Ant build scripts. Additionally, dependencies between components correspond directly to dependencies between projects.

Best Practice

Develop each Java EE module as a separate project, with its own build file.

The `bigrez.com` application is small enough for its inter-component dependencies to be understood easily. As applications grow, dependency management becomes a significant concern.

Best Practice

As your applications grow in size, you will need to manage dependencies between various components and third-party libraries. Consider automating dependency management using Apache Maven or Apache Ivy.

Altering bigrez.com to Use a Shared Library

Following the best practice suggested earlier in this chapter, we have used bundled libraries for `bigrez.com`. As an exercise, let's look at what we would do if we wanted to convert one of the bundled libraries to a shared Java EE library. We'll pick on the largest bundled library in `bigrez.com` — the Spring Framework jar file, `spring.jar`. This is 2.9 MB in size, which accounts for more than half of the `bigrez.ear` archive file.

First, we deploy `spring.jar` to the server as a library. We could do this through a variety of means, including using the WebLogic Console or the `weblogic.Deployer` tool. We cover deployment in more depth later. For now, here is a suitable `weblogic.Deployer` command and its output.

```
% java weblogic.Deployer -adminurl t3://localhost:7001 -username weblogic -password
weblogic1 -name springframework -library -libspecver 2.5.4 -deploy ./spring.jar
weblogic.Deployer invoked with options:  -adminurl t3://localhost:7001 -username
weblogic -name spring -library -libspecver 2.5.4 -deploy ./spring.jar
...
Task 11 completed: [Deployer:149117]deploy library springframework
[LibSpecVersion=2.5.4,LibImplVersion=2.5.4] on AdminServer.
```

Here we have deployed the `spring.jar` file as a shared library called `springframework`, and given it the specification version `2.5.4`. We didn't specify the implementation version, but the deployer has found it from the jar file's manifest.

To change the `bigrez.com` application to use the shared library, we remove the bundled library from the archive and add the following element to the `weblogic-application.xml` deployment descriptor.

```
<library-ref>
  <library-name>springframework</library-name>
  <implementation-version>2.5.4</implementation-version>
  <exact-match>true</exact-match>
</library-ref>
```

For web application shared libraries, the `<library-ref>` element allows the referring application to override the context root.

We can now deploy the `bigrez.ear` application.

Optional packages are deployed in exactly the same way. The difference is that they are referred to from the manifest file of the application or one of its modules. To refer to the `springframework` library as an optional package, you could use the following `META-INF/MANIFEST.MF` file for the `bigrez.ear` file.

```
Manifest-Version: 1.0
Extension-List: springfw
springfw-Extension-Name: springframework
```

Both the optional package and the shared Java EE library referring mechanisms have various options that control which versions of the shared library are acceptable; refer to the WebLogic Server documentation for full details (see Link 8-3).

Compiling Production Builds with appc

In Chapter 6, we recommended using the WebLogic Server `appc` compiler to compile production builds of EJB modules and enhance JPA entity classes. This reduces deployment time and provides early warning of any problems. The `appc` compiler precompiles JSP pages, and performs validation checks against deployment descriptors.

The build file for the `bigrez.com` enterprise application includes a target that compiles the `bigrez.ear` file with `appc`. Rather than using the `appc` tool directly, as we did in Chapter 6, the build file uses the WebLogic Server `wlappc` Ant task.

```
<target name="do.package">
  <mkdir dir="${output.dir}" />
```

```
<property name="output.jar" location="${output.dir}/bigrez.ear"/>
<!-- We don't use the standard Ant EAR task as that expects an
     application.xml deployment descriptor, and we don't have one. -->
<jar jarfile="${output.jar}">
  <zipfileset dir="../domain/output" includes="**/*.jar"/>
  <zipfileset dir="../web-common/output" includes="**/*.jar"/>
  <zipfileset dir="../services/output" includes="**/*.jar"/>
  <zipfileset dir="../web-admin/output" includes="**/*.war"/>
  <zipfileset dir="../web-user/output" includes="**/*.war"/>
  <zipfileset dir="../webservices/output" includes="**/*.war"/>
  <zipfileset dir="EarContent"/>
</jar>
<taskdef name="wlappc"
         classpathref="build.classpath"
         classname="weblogic.ant.taskdefs.j2ee.Appc"/>
<wlappc source="${output.jar}" classpathref="build.classpath"/>
</target>
```

As we noted in Chapter 6, for this precompilation to be effective, the appc compilation must use the same version and patch level as the expected production environment. Otherwise WebLogic Server will repeat the compilation when the application is deployed.

The bigrez.ear file is now complete and ready for deployment. We discuss deployment in a development environment in the next section, and Chapter 12 covers the deployment of bigrez.com in a production environment.

Deploying Applications

You can deploy a module or an enterprise application to a WebLogic Server environment in many ways.

❑　Automatic deployment

❑　WebLogic Server deployer utility

❑　WebLogic Console deployment

❑　The wldeploy Ant task

❑　The WebLogic Scripting Tool (WLST), in both online (connected) and offline modes

❑　The Java EE Deployment API standard (JSR-88) and the WebLogic Server deployment API

The first three methods were examined in the context of deploying web applications in Chapter 5. The same rules, best practices, and limitations discussed in that chapter apply to their use with other module types and enterprise applications. In this section, we discuss preparing the environment for deployment and then walk through the deployment process for the bigrez.com enterprise application using these three methods: automatic deployment, the WebLogic Server deployer utility, and WebLogic Console deployment. See Chapter 5 for a further discussion of deployment tools, and Chapter 12 for information about WLST.

JSR-88 and the WebLogic Server deployment API are primarily of interest to Java EE tool vendors, and we do not consider them further. Refer to the WebLogic Server documentation for information (see Link 8-4).

Creating Required Services

Before attempting to deploy a module or enterprise application, you should configure the required shared libraries and services (JDBC data sources, JMS resources, and so on) in the server environment. Although some applications may deploy properly without the required services, others, such as applications with JPA persistence units, will not deploy.

When an MDB component is deployed, for example, the server will attempt to connect the MDB to the JMS destination defined in its descriptor file. If the JMS destination is not available the server will display an error message in the log and attempt to reconnect to the destination periodically until it is available. This will not stop the MDB from deploying, although it will not operate properly until the JMS resource is created.

An application with a JPA persistence unit will fail to deploy if the associated data sources don't exist. Deployment may also fail if the database connections can be made, but the database schema does not match that used to develop the application.

As a general rule, you should configure the required services and resources before attempting to deploy the application.

> **Best Practice**
>
> Create and configure all required shared libraries, services, and resources before attempting to deploy the application.

Table 8-6 lists the resources that `bigrez.com` expects from its environment.

Creating services and resources in a single server development environment is fairly easy. The WebLogic Console provides straightforward screens for creating resources in the current domain. For `bigrez.com`, it is even simpler to use the WLST script `setUpDomain.py` supplied in the distribution that automates all of the necessary tasks. You can find full details of how to run this script in the accompanying `README.txt` file. The `setUpDomain.py` script reads properties that change for each environment from the `local.properties` file. You should edit this file to suit your local environment before running the script. The Ant build scripts also use this file.

> **Best Practice**
>
> Take the time to create WLST scripts that set up the domain for your application. Otherwise all of the developers on your team will have to master the WebLogic Server configuration, and time will be lost due to configuration mistakes in individual environments.

The data sources connect to a particular database account. This database account should be pre-initialized with the appropriate schema. Please refer to the `README.txt` file for full details.

Having created a new domain, started the administration server, and executed the WLST script, the domain is now prepared for the deployment of the `bigrez.com` enterprise application.

Table 8-6: The Resources bigrez.com Requires in the Environment

Resource Name	Type	Purpose
BigRezJTADataSource	JDBC Data Source	Data source connected to the `bigrez.com` schema. Configured to honor global JTA transactions.
BigRezNonJTADataSource	JDBC Data Source	Data source connected to the `bigrez.com` schema. Configured to ignore global JTA transactions.
BigRezJMSServer	JMS Server	A JMS server must be targeted to any server instance that hosts JMS resources. In the development environment, the JMS server will use the default file store; for production you may want to configure a separate persistent store. Refer to Chapter 10 for details.
BigRezJMSModule	JMS Module	A JMS module is a deployable collection of JMS resources. This module contains the JMS resources listed below in this table.
BigRezConnectionFactory	JMS Connection Factory	JMS connection factory. Configured to be XA-aware, so JMS sessions created from its connections will support global JTA transactions.
BigRezEmailQueue	JMS Queue	Queue used for storing outbound email messages. Redelivery options configured to attempt to redeliver a message to a consumer five further times after a delay of a minute before placing the message in the error queue.
BigRezEmailErrorQueue	JMS Queue	Queue configured as an error destination for `BigRezEmailQueue`.
JMSServerSubDeployment	JMS Subdeployment	JMS subdeployment used to target the queues correctly.
BigRezMailSession	JavaMail Session	Mail session configured with details of a STMP server that can send emails.
BigRezAdministrators	Security Group	Hotel administrators must belong to this group to access the administration pages.

Automatic Deployment and weblogic.Deployer

We discussed automatic deployment at some length in Chapter 5. Here, we simply review the technique and present the steps required to deploy the `bigrez.com` application.

First, ensure that the domain is running in development mode so that automatic deployment is enabled. The administration server will now scan the `autodeploy` directory in the domain for new (or modified) application archives and exploded directory structures during each boot process and periodically during server operation.

Next, copy the `bigrez.ear` archive file or the entire exploded application structure to the `autodeploy` directory in the domain. The server can be running, if desired, although with exploded applications it is usually best to copy the structure with the server stopped to avoid the race condition discussed in Chapter 5.

Automatic redeployment of the application occurs whenever the `bigrez.ear` file is overwritten or the `META-INF/REDEPLOY` file is touched so that its timestamp changes. These rules were discussed at length in Chapter 5.

The ability to redeploy the application quickly without rebooting the server or accessing the WebLogic Console is very useful during development. Automatic deployment is a popular way of deploying exploded and archived enterprise applications in a single server development or test environment. However, it does involve additional copying of files, which can take some time for large applications. It is often simpler to use the `weblogic.Deployer` command-line tool to deploy the application from wherever it was built.

```
% java weblogic.Deployer -username weblogic -password weblogic1 -deploy bigrez.ear
weblogic.Deployer invoked with options:  -username weblogic -deploy bigrez.ear
<29-Mar-2009 11:30:37 o'clock BST> <Info> <J2EE Deployment SPI> <BEA-260121>
<Initiating deploy operation for application, bigrez.ear [archive:
/home/philipa/writing/pows/bigrez2/ear/output/bigrez.ear], to configured targets.>
Task 55 initiated: [Deployer:149026]deploy application bigrez.ear on AdminServer.
Task 55 completed: [Deployer:149026]deploy application bigrez.ear on AdminServer.
Target state: deploy completed on Server AdminServer
```

In this use of `weblogic.Deployer`, we've relied on the server running on the default host (`localhost`) and the default port (7001), so we haven't needed to use the tool's `adminurl` option.

It is similarly easy to redeploy and undeploy the application.

```
% java weblogic.Deployer -username weblogic -password weblogic1 -redeploy -name
bigrez.ear
. . .
% java weblogic.Deployer -username weblogic -password weblogic1 -undeploy -name
bigrez.ear
. . .
```

Better still, modern IDEs can easily be configured to use WebLogic Server features such as the partial redeployment, split development directory structure, and FastSwap, and make the minimal required deployment changes through the push of a button. We return to this in Chapter 14 where we show how to set up Eclipse and JDeveloper for bigrez.com development.

WebLogic Console Deployment

Chapter 5 also walked through the process of deploying a simple web application using the WebLogic Console. Deploying an enterprise application to an environment is very similar to deploying a web application.

1. Start the server and open the WebLogic Console.

2. Open the list of current applications, modules, and libraries deployed in the server using the Deployments folder on the left side of the screen.

3. If you have unset the console preference to acquire the edit lock and apply changes automatically, select Lock & Edit.

4. Click the Install link. Use the supplied screens to navigate to the location of your new application, and select the application archive file or root directory to be deployed.

5. Continue the process by selecting that you want to deploy an application rather than a library, targeting the new application to your server, and clicking the Finish button to deploy the application.

6. If you have unset the console preference to acquire the edit lock and apply changes automatically, select Apply Changes.

7. If the domain is running in production mode, an additional step is necessary to start the application. Select the application in the list of deployments, and chose Start / Servicing All Requests.

The application is now deployed and ready for users. To redeploy an application with the WebLogic Console, acquire the edit lock, set the checkbox next to the application on the Deployments page, and select Update. You can optionally change the path to the application, and associate a deployment plan with the application. The application may be undeployed in a similar manner.

Chapter Review

This chapter discussed the steps required to package and deploy an enterprise application to the WebLogic Server environment.

The first section reviewed the structure and contents of an EJB module, and the various WebLogic Server configuration options for EJBs. The second section considered how to package JPA persistent units in applications.

The third section covered enterprise applications. We reviewed the structure and contents of an enterprise application including the settings in application descriptor files, bundled libraries, and other WebLogic Server module types. We also looked at related subjects, including exploded deployments, optional packages, and shared Java EE libraries and classloading.

The final section presented the steps necessary to deploy your enterprise application and discussed the importance of preparing the environment before deployment.

The `bigrez.com` application is now complete and ready for deployment in production, a task we tackle in Chapter 12. The following chapters continue our discussion of development-related techniques by examining best practices and WebLogic Server features in the areas of web services, JMS messaging, and security.

9

Developing and Deploying Web Services

In this chapter, we show you how to develop web services using WebLogic Server and we highlight best practices for running web services on WebLogic Server.

This chapter is not intended as a general primer or introduction to web services standards and technologies. Our primary emphasis is the web services development model, and the WebLogic Server Web Services container and its unique features and capabilities. If you're unfamiliar with the basics of web services, we suggest you read *Developing Java Web Services* by Ramesh Nagappan, Robert Skoczylas, and Rima Patel Sriganesh (Wiley, 2003).

We begin by briefly summarizing the relevant web services terms and key concepts. Next, we show you how to create simple web services using WebLogic Server, followed by a demonstration of the more advanced web services capabilities built into WebLogic Server. Finally, we show you how to implement a web service for integrating with `bigrez.com`.

Throughout the chapter, we refer to standalone examples that are available on the companion web site at `http://www.wrox.com`. We use code fragments in the text to demonstrate key points, but we encourage you to download and look through the complete examples as well.

Summarizing Web Services Standards

Before we dive into building web services on WebLogic Server, let's summarize the key underlying standards that are most frequently used to make web services work.

SOAP   Simple Object Access Protocol (SOAP) is a specification for exchanging structured information between distributed systems, using XML as the message format (see `http://www.w3.org/TR/soap/`). We can use SOAP to implement synchronous remote procedure calls (RPC) between *service consumers* and *service providers* or to implement asynchronous messaging between distributed components. SOAP messages have an XML structure known as a SOAP envelope. This envelope is composed of a header element and a body element. The header contains a set of optional elements that we use to transmit extra information about the context of the message such as security- or addressing-related data. We place the real business data in the SOAP body, using XML elements that typically conform to one or more XML schemas.

WSDL   The Web Services Description Language (WSDL) is the specification that defines the XML-based, interface definition language used to describe web services (see `http://www.w3.org/TR/wsdl`). A WSDL document specifies the details of a web service's operations, input and output XML message formats, transport protocol, and endpoint URL.

WS-Security   WS-Security is a specification that defines how to secure web services at the SOAP message–level rather than just relying on existing transport-level security mechanisms like HTTP basic authentication or Secure Sockets Layer (SSL). It includes mechanisms for service client authentication and for message content encryption and digital signing. Security Assertion Markup Language (SAML) is a related specification that complements WS-Security by providing an XML token-based mechanism for exchanging authentication and authorization data between different web service security domains. We cover SAML in more detail in Chapter 11.

WS-I Basic Profile   The WS-Interoperability (WS-I) Organization is an umbrella organization of software vendors and consumers who are interested in promoting best practices for web services interoperability (see `http://www.ws-i.org`). This group produces a set of profiles, which are specifications for implementing web services to maximize interoperability. The WS-I Basic Profile is the most widely used profile; it defines the rules for using SOAP and WSDL to implement interoperable web services.

JAX-WS   The Java API for XML-based Web Services (JAX-WS) is a specification that defines a standard Java programming model for building web services and web service clients (see `http://jax-ws.dev.java.net/`). JAX-WS 2.0 is part of the Java EE 5 specification. In JAX-WS, the term Service Endpoint Interface (SEI) refers to a strongly-typed JAX-WS implementation of a web service. JAX-WS also provides facilities for more loosely-coupled web services and *handlers*. Handlers provide reusable message processing logic that can be injected into the invocation path of the service providers and consumers.

JAXB   The Java API for XML Binding (JAXB) specification describes how XML schema types are mapped to and from Java types (see `https://jaxb.dev.java.net/`). Strictly speaking, JAXB is not specifically a web services–related standard; it applies to XML and Java in general. However, the JAX-WS standard uses JAXB to define how Java classes are used as parameters and return types for web service operations, and how they are marshalled to and unmarshalled from XML.

EJB 3.0   The EJB 3.0 specification requires EJB containers to support exposing a stateless session bean via a web service interface using WSDL and SOAP or plain XML over HTTP.

WebLogic Server supports a plethora of other web services–related standards, including the Universal Description, Discovery, and Integration API (UDDI) for accessing web service registries, WS-Addressing for including address-related information in SOAP headers (for example, a reply-to address for asynchronous messages), and WS-ReliableMessaging (WS-RM) for reliable delivery of messages between SOAP consumers and producers, just to name a few.

Creating Web Services with WebLogic Server

In this section, we begin by describing WebLogic Server's Web Services container architecture. Next, we show you how to develop web services with WebLogic Server and provide two detailed examples, one starting from Java and the other starting from WSDL. Finally, we show you how to create a client application to invoke these web services.

Web Services Container Architecture

WebLogic Server provides a web services container for hosting Java code that processes SOAP requests and generates SOAP responses. The container implements the JAX-WS 2.1 specification and provides built-in WS-I Basic Profile 1.1 interoperability support. It also is integrated with WebLogic Server's Security Service to provide pluggable authentication and authorization, and support for web services security standards such as WS-Security and SAML for any deployed web services. Figure 9-1 shows the structure of WebLogic Server's Web Services container and its relationship to some of the other WebLogic Server subsystems.

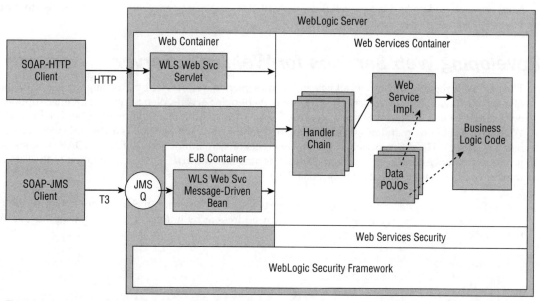

Figure 9-1: WebLogic Server's Web Services Container.

The web services container provides two transport mechanisms for invoking web services: SOAP over HTTP and SOAP over JMS. Both mechanisms also support transport-level security using SSL. SOAP over HTTP requests are initially processed by the web container, which dispatches them to a built-in servlet known as the `WebServiceServlet`. This servlet simply routes the requests to the web services container for processing. SOAP over JMS uses WebLogic JMS queues as intermediaries and the normal WebLogic JMS mechanisms to deliver the message to the JMS queue. Once in the queue, WebLogic Server uses a built-in message-driven bean that dequeues the requests and dispatches them to the web services container.

Once a SOAP request arrives at the web services container, the first step is to identify the target web service implementation class to invoke. The implementation class is a Java class that has been developed using the JAX-WS or JAX-RPC programming model and deployed to WebLogic Server. Later in this chapter we briefly discuss the older JAX-RPC-based web services technology also included in WebLogic Server. Before invoking the class, the container invokes any of the handlers that are registered. Assuming that the handlers do not short-circuit the processing, the container uses JAXB to unmarshal the incoming SOAP message body into the appropriate set of Java objects that are then passed as arguments to the relevant Java method in the implementation class. Once the Java method completes, the container marshals the Java method's return value into the appropriate SOAP message body for the response, invokes the registered handlers, in reverse order, and returns the resulting SOAP response to the client.

From a high level, this is really all there is to WebLogic Server's Web Services container. WebLogic Server's client-side container provides a similar architecture. When a Java client invokes a service, the container intercepts the invocation, marshals the Java arguments, invokes any client-side handlers we have defined, and finally invokes the remote web service. The response unwinds through the same steps, until the Java client's method invocation returns the response as a Java object to the client application.

Now that you understand the overall flow, we will look at the basic mechanisms that you use to write your own web service providers and clients.

Developing Web Services for WebLogic Server

The JAX-WS programming model allows you to implement a web service by exposing the public methods of a regular Java class as web service operations. WebLogic Server's Web Services container supports both SOAP 1.1 and 1.2 and WSDL 1.1. Because SOAP 1.1 is still the most commonly used version and the WS-I Basic Profile 1.1 mandates its use for interoperability, we will develop our example web services using SOAP 1.1. The differences between the two versions are minor and switching SOAP versions does not require changes to the Java code apart from adding a new @BindingType annotation to the service implementation class to specify that SOAP 1.2 is to be used.

Throughout this chapter, we use a BigRez property search web service in our examples. Our property search service supports searching for a property by address or by unique id. The outline of the Java Web Service (JWS) class that we use to define the property search web service is shown here.

```
@WebService
public class PropertySearchService
{
    public PropertyInfo
        getPropertyDetailsByAddress(PropertySearchAddress searchAddress)
    {
        ...
    }

    public PropertyInfo getPropertyDetailsById(PropertySearchId searchId)
    {
        ...
    }
}
```

As you can see, the JWS class is just a normal Java class. There is no need for code associated with SOAP message processing. We simply tell WebLogic Server that this class should be exposed as a web service using JAX-WS's @WebService annotation and the web services container takes care of the plumbing for us. By default, all public methods of the class — except those inherited from java.lang.Object — are exposed as web service operations.

When running in a WebLogic Server environment, each JWS class can receive multiple, concurrent requests — very similar to a Java servlet. As such, your JWS class, and all utility classes and third-party libraries that it might use, must be thread-safe. As with servlets, do not overly synchronize your JWS class or risk performance and scalability problems that may not surface until stress testing or production.

> **When using regular Java classes to implement a web service, you must ensure that your code is thread-safe. This includes any utility classes and third-party libraries you use.**

WebLogic Server also allows you to implement a web service by exposing the methods of a stateless session bean as web service operations. By mixing both JAX-WS and EJB annotations together in the same stateless session bean class, we can provide both a normal EJB client and web service client view to a stateless session bean. One advantage of using a stateless session bean to implement a web service is that the JWS class is an EJB and as such, the EJB container will pool the objects and make sure only one thread at a time accesses the object. Of course, the EJB container does not do this for other classes the EJB accesses, so this isn't a magic solution for thread-safety problems. We don't recommend this approach for building externally exposed web services anyway, because it creates tighter coupling between the business logic in the EJB and the external web service interface.

Do not place your core business logic code directly into the JWS implementation class. Instead, write the core business logic independently of the web service interfaces. The JWS implementation class should focus on logic specific to the web service and delegate the business logic to other components. This provides the opportunity to expose the same business logic via other interfaces like EJB or JMS and to unit-test the business logic code in a standalone environment. Think of the JWS class as a wrapper class that makes your business logic remotable. By following this approach, you have the option of using dependency injection to have a reference to the business class instances injected into your JWS class.

> ### Best Practice
> To expose business logic services as web services, create separate JWS classes that invoke the business logic rather than mixing business logic with the JWS class. Only use the JWS class as a thin wrapper class to make your business logic remotable.

JAX-WS defines Java annotations, such as @WebService, that we use to decorate parts of our Java class. These annotations tell WebLogic Server's JAX-WS tools that our Java class represents a web service and they describe various details about the web service we want to create. WebLogic Server's JAX-WS tools introspect the Java class and its annotations to determine exactly what code it must generate to wire the web service provider or consumer to the container. This generated code transparently handles the communication between the remote client and the web service. On the client side, this generated code is called a web service *stub*. The stub acts like a proxy, turning local Java method calls into SOAP requests to invoke the remote web service.

WebLogic Server's JAX-WS tools also take care of mapping between XML and Java using the rules defined by JAXB. This capability is especially powerful when the inputs and outputs for the web service operations are complex data types. JAXB contains rules for mapping between XML schema types and data-oriented Java objects (data POJOs) in such a way as to maintain equivalence between the two representations when performing round-trip mappings between the two representations. These data POJOs are very similar to JavaBeans in that they each contain a *no-args* constructor, getter and setter methods for each member variable, and no actual business logic.

Once we have written our web service, WebLogic Server's JAX-WS tools help us package the implementation class, the generated code, and other related artifacts, like data POJOs, WSDLs, and XML schemas, into an exploded EAR directory structure containing a deployable WAR file. Use the EAR directory structure to add other application artifacts, package it into an EAR file, and deploy to a WebLogic Server domain just like any other EAR file. The WAR file itself is also deployable without the EAR structure around it, so you might decide to deploy it standalone. Throughout the rest of the chapter, we will refer to the output as a WAR file rather than specifying that it is an exploded EAR directory structure containing a deployable WAR file. WebLogic Server's Web Services container automatically detects the presence of any web service endpoints when deploying the application and makes them available for processing incoming SOAP requests.

When designing and developing a web service, we can follow one of two approaches.

> **Code-First**   This is a bottom-up, implementation-first strategy where we write the Java class and the data POJOs representing the complex data types used by the web service operations. Then, we use WebLogic Server's JAX-WS tools to generate the web service's WSDL interface and associated XML schema types. In JAX-WS terminology, this approach is often referred to as *Java-to-WSDL*.
>
> **WSDL-First**   This is a top-down, interface-first strategy where we manually create the web service's WSDL interface and any associated XML schemas. Then, we use WebLogic Server's JAX-WS tools to generate the Java interface and the data POJOs. Finally, we complete the web service implementation by writing a class that implements the generated Java interface. In JAX-WS terminology, this approach is often referred to as *WSDL-to-Java*.

Is one approach more preferable than the other? Well, this is difficult to answer because each approach has advantages and disadvantages. One might claim that the code-first approach enables more rapid development of web services, especially if we just want to expose existing application functionality. However, the code-first approach forces the developer to create all the data POJO classes manually, whereas the WSDL-first approach generates them for you.

Typically, the WSDL-first approach provides a looser coupling between the web service and its consumers because it has the developer create the external interface first. Theoretically, if you spend enough time designing the interface to match the business purpose and data exchanged, the external interface becomes less likely to change over time — even when the underlying systems that implement the business logic change. While we agree with the theory, our experience tells us that many people simply do not spend enough time designing the interface to achieve these benefits. Even so, we do recommend the WSDL-first approach for external web services in the hope that forcing people to come up with the WSDL and XML schemas first will help them put more thought into the design.

> **Best Practice**
>
> If you need to share the same set of XML message formats across many different web services and even across different systems in your organization, use a WSDL-first approach to enable the externally defined XML schemas to be reused.

Developing Code-First Web Services

When developing code-first web services, you follow these basic steps:

1. Write and compile the data POJO classes.

2. Write and compile the JWS class containing the appropriate JAX-WS annotations.

3. Run WebLogic Server's Java Web Service Compiler (JWSC) using the `jwsc` Ant task to generate a deployable WAR file.

4. Deploy the WAR file to one or more WebLogic Server instances or clusters using any of WebLogic Server's deployment tools, such as the WebLogic Console or `wldeploy` Ant task.

Note that the WSDL for the web service is not generated by JWSC at compile time by default, but JWSC does provide an option to enable generation at compile time. Normally the WebLogic Server Web Services container generates it on demand at runtime.

Listing 9-1 shows the outline of the Java class that implements the BigRez property search web service in Example 1 of the downloadable examples for Chapter 9.

Listing 9-1: Outline of Example 1's PropertySearchService.java.

```java
package com.bigrez.ws.service;

import javax.jws.WebService;
import javax.jws.WebMethod;
import javax.jws.soap.SOAPBinding;

import com.bigrez.ws.property.PropertyInfo;
import com.bigrez.ws.property.PropertyInfoFault;
import com.bigrez.ws.property.PropertyInfoFaultException;
import com.bigrez.ws.property.PropertySearchAddress;
import com.bigrez.ws.property.PropertySearchId;

@WebService(
    serviceName="PropertySearchService",
    targetNamespace= "http://www.wrox.com/professional-
weblogic/PropertySearchService"
)
```

Continued

Listing 9-1: Outline of Example 1's PropertySearchService.java. *(continued)*

```java
@SOAPBinding(
    style=SOAPBinding.Style.DOCUMENT,
    use=SOAPBinding.Use.LITERAL,
    parameterStyle=SOAPBinding.ParameterStyle.WRAPPED
)
public class PropertySearchService
{
    public PropertyInfo
        getPropertyDetailsByAddress(PropertySearchAddress searchAddress)
        throws PropertyInfoFaultException
    {
        PropertyInfo property;
        String address1 = searchAddress.getAddress1();
        String postalCode = searchAddress.getPostalCode();

        if ((address1 == null) ||
            (address1.trim().length() <= 0) ||
            (postalCode == null) ||
            (postalCode.trim().length() <= 0)) {
            throwFaultException();
        }

        // Call business logic to search for property
        //
        ...

        return property;
    }

    public PropertyInfo getPropertyDetailsById(PropertySearchId searchId)
        throws PropertyInfoFaultException
    {
        PropertyInfo property;
        int id = searchId.getId();

        if (id <= 0) {
            throwFaultException();
        }

        // Call business logic to search for property
        //
        ...

        return property;
    }
```

```
      private void throwFaultException()
         throws PropertyInfoFaultException
   {
         String error = "Property search criteria is empty";
         PropertyInfoFault fault = new PropertyInfoFault();
         fault.setCode("BIGREZERR-01234");
         fault.setMessage(error);
         throw new PropertyInfoFaultException(error, fault);
   }
}
```

As we mentioned previously, the `@WebService` annotation tells WebLogic Server that this is a JWS class. If not specified, the default name of the web service is the class name with the word `Service` appended to it (for example, `PropertySearchServiceService`). Likewise, the default namespace for the resulting SOAP body elements is the reverse of the package name of the class (for example, `http://service.ws.bigrez.com/`). Rather than accept these default values, we explicitly specify the web service name and target namespace using the `@WebService` annotation's `name` and `targetNamespace` elements.

We could annotate the public methods of our class with `@WebMethod`. In most cases, this is redundant; by default, all public methods of a JWS class are mapped to web service operations. The `@WebMethod` annotation allows you to specify a different name for the web service operation or exclude a public method from becoming a web service operation. Because the default behavior works for our example, we do not use the `@WebMethod` annotation.

We also use the optional `@SoapBinding` annotation. This annotation gives us influence over the XML structure that surrounds the parameters and return values of a SOAP request and response. In the "Understanding Style and Use" section later in this chapter, we discuss why such settings are important. Actually, we could omit this annotation because DOCUMENT, LITERAL, and WRAPPED are the default values.

The JAX-WS 2.0 classes and annotations are part of both Java EE 5 and Java SE 6 and contain classes from the following packages:

- javax.jws
- javax.jws.soap
- javax.xml.ws
- javax.xml.ws.handler
- javax.xml.ws.handler.soap
- javax.xml.ws.http
- javax.xml.ws.soap

However, WebLogic Server 10.3.1 actually implements version 2.1 of JAX-WS, so the best place to find the Javadocs for the JAX-WS classes is shown in Link 9-1 in the book's online Appendix at `http://www.wrox.com`.

Because our JWS class uses complex arguments and return types, we have to create the data POJOs for these complex types. Listing 9-2 shows the Java code for one of these data POJOs.

Listing 9-2: Example 1 Data POJO PropertySearchAddress.java.

```java
public class PropertySearchAddress
{
    private String address1;
    private String postalCode;

    public String getAddress1() { return address1; }

    public void setAddress1(String value)
    {
        this.address1 = value;
    }

    public String getPostalCode() { return postalCode; }

    public void setPostalCode(String value)
    {
        this.postalCode = value;
    }
}
```

As you can see, a data POJO is just a JavaBean-like class with property getter and setter methods. It purely holds data. To allow more hierarchical information, data POJO member variables can be other data POJO types, arrays of other data POJO or primitive types, or strongly-typed Java collections used to hold other data POJO or primitive types. When using arrays or other collection types, you must provide the appropriate getters and setters to allow access to these collection-based member variables.

We also declared that the JWS methods could throw an exception. JAX-WS gives us a convention for declaring custom exceptions, which can easily be converted into custom SOAP faults. A *wrapper* exception (for example, `PropertyFaultException`) extends `java.lang.Exception` and contains a method called `getFaultInfo()` for accessing a JavaBean-like *fault* object (for example, `PropertyFault`). In our example, the fault object contains getters and setters for two properties that we have called `Code` and `Message`. These will provide more information about the errors. The web service container is able to catch the exception thrown by our JWS class, at runtime, and convert this information into the appropriate XML data as part of the fault's detail element of the SOAP response. The SOAP fault response generated by our service implementation is shown here.

```xml
<soap:Envelope xmlns:soap="http://schemas.xmlsoap.org/soap/envelope/">
  <soap:Body>
    <soap:Fault>
      <faultcode>soap:Server</faultcode>
      <faultstring>Property search criteria is emtpy</faultstring>
      <detail>
        <PropertyInfoFault xmlns="http://www.wrox.com/professional-
weblogic/PropertyInfo">
          <Code>BIGREZERR-01234</Code>
          <Message>Property search criteria is emtpy</Message>
        </PropertyInfoFault>
      </detail>
    </soap:Fault>
  </soap:Body>
</soap:Envelope>
```

Once the data POJO and JWS classes are complete, we create an Ant `build.xml` file to automate compiling the Java code, running the JWSC, and deploying the resulting WAR file to WebLogic Server. We show portions of our example's `build.xml` file that pertain to the use of WebLogic Server's `jwsc` Ant task here.

```
<taskdef name="jwsc" classpathref="${weblogic.classpath}"
         classname="weblogic.wsee.tools.anttasks.JwscTask"/>

<jwsc srcdir="src" destdir="earcontents" classpathref="${app.classpath}">
   <jws file="com/bigrez/ws/service/PropertySearchService.java"
        contextpath="PropertySearchService_CodeFirst"
        type="JAXWS"/>
</jwsc>
```

Best Practice

Write a single Ant `build.xml` file that compiles your Java code, runs WebLogic Server's JWSC, and deploys the resulting WAR file using a single command.

WebLogic Server's JWSC generates the deployable web services artifacts and packages them into a WAR file that is ready for deployment to WebLogic Server. These deployable artifacts include the compiled JWS and any data POJO classes as well as the relevant deployment descriptors. The `web.xml` deployment descriptor contains a servlet mapping to the `WebServiceServlet` that dispatches the SOAP requests to the JWS class via WebLogic Server's Web Services container.

The `jwsc` Ant task supports a multitude of attributes to customize its behavior. Typically, you only need to specify a few of them; the most common attributes are:

❑   `srcdir` — The top-level directory where all JWS files are located.

❑   `destdir` — The directory to contain the generated EAR file's unpacked contents.

❑   `classpathref` — The classpath for the compiled classes that the JWS class relies upon.

Setting the `jws` element's type attribute value to JAXWS tells WebLogic Server to generate a JAX-WS web service. If you forget to set this attribute, the `jwsc` Ant task will generate a JAX-RPC web service. Later in this chapter we briefly discuss the older JAX-RPC-based web services toolkit included in WebLogic Server.

So once we've deployed the web service, how do we determine what the web service's URL is? The answer depends on the JAX-WS annotations and Ant task attributes we used to compile the web service. For our example, the web service's URL is composed of the following elements:

```
http://<host>:<port>/<contextpath>/<webservice-annotation-service-name>
```

In our case, we specified a `contextPath` attribute in our Ant `jws` element. The following list shows how the context path of the URL is determined, in order of precedence:

❑   The `contextPath` attribute of the `jws` element.

- ❏ The `contextPath` attribute of the `WLHttpTransport` or `WLJMSTransport` child element of `jws`. `WLHttpTransport` and `WLJMSTransport` are optional and provide the ability to define additional transport specific settings for the generated web service.

- ❏ The name of the JWS file without any extension.

Assuming the example WAR is deployed to a local, single server WebLogic Server domain listening on the default port, the BigRez property search web service's URL is:

```
http://localhost:7001/PropertySearchService_CodeFirst/PropertySearchService
```

To view the WSDL for a deployed web service, simply append `?wsdl` to the URL, as shown here.

```
http://localhost:7001/PropertySearchService_CodeFirst/PropertySearchService?wsdl
```

Another way to determine the URL of a deployed web service and view its WSDL is to use the WebLogic Console. Simply select the `Deployments` folder, expand the link to the deployed web service WAR (for example, `PropertySearchService_CodeFirst`), and then select the web service sub-element of this WAR (for example, `PropertySearchService`). This page of the WebLogic Console provides configuration, security, and monitoring information about our web service. The `Testing` tab provides links to the WSDL and Test Client, as shown in Figure 9-2.

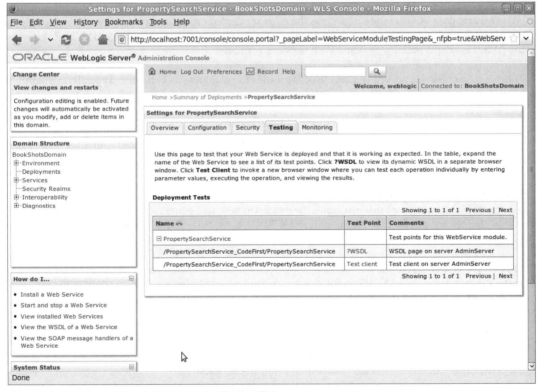

Figure 9-2: WebLogic Console Web Service Testing Tab.

We have many ways to test our deployed web service. Perhaps the easiest way is to use the WebLogic Test Client. To access it, point your browser at your local WebLogic Server instance using the URL `http://localhost:7001/wls_utc/`. This tool allows you to enter the URL of any web service's WSDL to test, even if the web service isn't running on WebLogic Server. For deployed WebLogic Server web services like our property search service, we can simply select the `Test client` link, as shown in Figure 9-2. This automatically launches the WebLogic Test Client ready to test our web service, as shown in Figure 9-3.

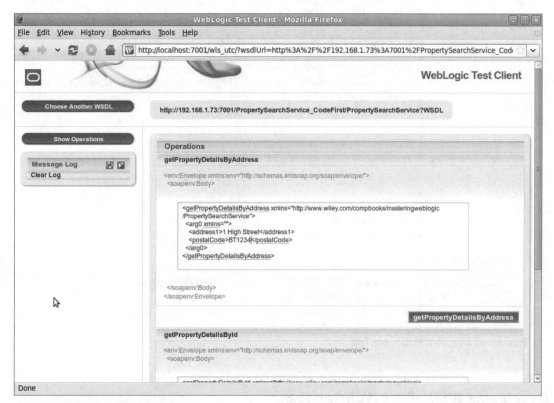

Figure 9-3: WebLogic Test Client.

The WebLogic Test Client makes things easy for us by automatically generating a sample XML payload. Simply change the sample data to reflect real property details and press the operation's submit button to test the service. The WebLogic Test Client result page will show the content of the original SOAP request and the resulting SOAP response.

Another useful tool for testing web services is a free, open-source tool called SoapUI. This is a stand-alone, Java Swing–based application, downloadable from `http://www.soapui.org/`. SoapUI is easy to use and once it has been given a web service WSDL, it provides powerful tools for creating and submitting sample SOAP requests. Figure 9-4 shows SoapUI being used to test our web service.

SoapUI provides some added benefits, including the ability to view the *raw* HTTP request and response. It also provides other tools, such as WSI Analyzer and TCPMon. WSI Analyzer checks the WS-I Basic

Profile compliance of a web service. TCPMon acts as a tunnel between a web service consumer and provider to enable you to see the raw message traffic passed over the wire.

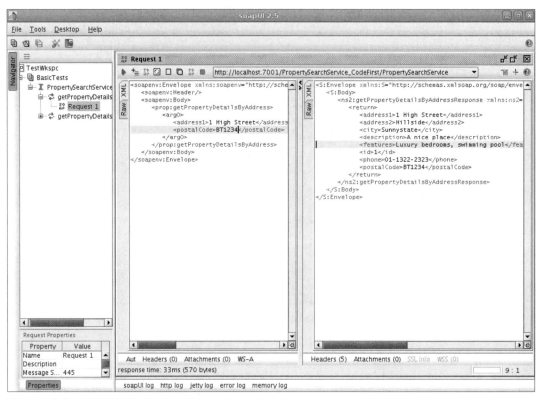

Figure 9-4: SoapUI Web Service Test Tool.

Developing WSDL-First Web Services

When developing WSDL-first web services, you follow these basic steps.

1. Write the WSDL for the web service and the XML schemas for any complex data types that are referenced in the WSDL's input and output message parts.

2. Run WebLogic Server's Web Services Description Language Compiler (WSDLC) using the `wsdlc` Ant task to generate the JWS interface class and any data POJO classes. The output of the `wsdlc` Ant task is a single JAR file containing all the generated artifacts.

3. Write and compile a concrete JWS class that implements the generated JWS interface class and uses the appropriate JAX-WS annotations.

4. Run the `jwsc` Ant task specifying the location of the JWS class and the location of the `wsdlc`-generated JAR file from step 2. As we saw before, this generates the deployable WAR file.

5. Deploy the WAR file to one or more WebLogic Server instances or clusters.

At this point, please locate the `PropertySearchService.wsdl` and `PropertyInfo.xsd` files contained in Example 2 of the downloadable examples before proceeding.

`PropertySearchService.wsdl` contains the WSDL we created to define the interface for the property search web service. WSDL can be a little intimidating at first glance. To understand a WSDL definition, it's usually best to start from the end and work backwards. At the base of our WSDL, we define a web service called `PropertySearchService` containing the URL of the service endpoint. When we wrote this WSDL, we did not know where the service would be hosted, so we included a dummy URL. At runtime, WebLogic Server will generate a version of the WSDL containing the correct URL based on the environment to which the web service is deployed.

The `binding` section of our WSDL identifies the two operations we require, the protocol the service will use (that is, SOAP over HTTP) and the `style` and `use` of SOAP message structure to use (that is, `document` and `literal`). We discuss style and use in the "Understanding Style and Use" section later in this chapter.

In the WSDL's `portType` section, we map input, output, and fault message types to the web service operations. The `messages` section defines the top-level data structures that can be used as inputs or outputs for any of our web service's operations. These message definitions reference XML schema types that the WSDL either explicitly defines in the `types` section or imports from externally-defined XML schema files. In our example, we define types for the top-level XML elements for the SOAP body payloads directly in the WSDL and then reference imported schema types to define the complex XML data structures relating to BigRez properties.

In `PropertyInfo.xsd`, we define several complex XML types to represent business data. `PropertySearchAddress` and `PropertySearchId` provide structures that we use to pass input data to the web service operations. `PropertyInfo` and `PropertyInfoFault` provide structures for returning response data and error details, respectively. You may ask why define some of the XML types in the WSDL and some in an XML schema?

Ideally, all of the XML types would be defined in an XML schema. Nevertheless, to help the SOAP clients and servers map requests to their target operations, a *wrapped* convention is used whereby the top-level element in a SOAP request body element identifies the name of the target operation (for example, `GetPropertyDetailsByAddress`). Inside this wrapper is the real XML business data. From a web service design perspective, we could have chosen not to use this wrapper element. We discuss the guidelines about when and when not to use wrapper elements in the "Understanding Style and Use" section later in this chapter.

Once we finish writing the WSDL and associated XML schemas, we need to run WebLogic Server's WSDL compiler to generate the JAR file containing the JWS interface class and any JAXB data POJOs. The `wsdlc` Ant task–related portions of the example's Ant `build.xml` file are shown here.

```
<taskdef name="wsdlc" classpathref="${weblogic.classpath}"
        classname="weblogic.wsee.tools.anttasks.WsdlcTask"/>

<wsdlc srcWsdl="WebContent/wsdls/PropertySearchService.wsdl"
      destJwsDir="tmp"
      destImplDir="tmp"
      packageName="com.bigrez.ws.property"
      type="JAXWS"/>
```

As for the `wsdlc` attributes, `srcWsdl` specifies the location of the WSDL to compile, `destJwsDir` specifies the output JAR file destination, `destImplDir` specifies the base directory to generate the stubbed-out Java class to, and `packageName` specifies the Java package name to use for the generated Java classes.

If you explore the example `build.xml` file some more, you will see that the `generate` target that runs the WSDL compiler is not part of the default target's dependency chain that builds and deploys the web service. This is intentional. By doing this, you run the `generate` target once to generate the initial set of Java classes. Run the default target whenever you change the JWS class to compile, package, and deploy the web service. You don't need to re-run the `generate` target unless you change the WSDL or XML schema.

Best Practice

Run the `wsdlc` Ant task in a separate target that is not part of the chain of dependencies for the default target in the `build.xml` file. You don't need to re-run `wsdlc` unless you change the WSDL or XML schema. This will help speed up your development process.

It is relatively easy to write the JWS class when using a WSDL-first approach. We just need to implement the generated interface and its declared methods, using the JAXB-generated data POJO classes. The code snippet that follows shows the outline of the `PropertySearchServiceImpl` JWS class that implements the BigRez property search web service.

```
@WebService(serviceName="PropertySearchService",
    targetNamespace="http://www.wrox.com/professional-weblogic/PropertySearchService",
    endpointInterface="com.bigrez.ws.property.PropertySearchService"
)
public class PropertySearchServiceImpl implements PropertySearchService
{
    ...

    public PropertyInfo
        getPropertyDetailsByAddress(PropertySearchAddress searchAddress)
        throws PropertyInfoFaultException
    {
        // SAME AS CODE-FIRST EXAMPLE
    }

    public PropertyInfo getPropertyDetailsById(PropertySearchId searchId)
        throws PropertyInfoFaultException
    {
        // SAME AS CODE-FIRST EXAMPLE
    }

    ...
}
```

This class is practically the same as the class in the code-first example, except that this time the JWS class implements a generated Java interface and the `@WebService` annotation specifies the `endpointInterface` element to help the WebLogic Server tools determine that this is actually a WSDL-first implementation. This time we did not use the `@SOAPBinding` annotation to specify the web service format because we already defined this structure when we wrote the WSDL.

Next, we need to run the JWS compiler on our JWS class to generate the web service WAR, just as we did in the code-first approach. Because we are using a WSDL-first approach, we must specify the `compiledWsdl` attribute, which specifies the location of the `wsdlc` Ant task–generated JAR file. We show the `jwsc` Ant task–related portions of the example `build.xml` file here.

```
<taskdef name="jwsc" classpathref="${weblogic.classpath}"
        classname="weblogic.wsee.tools.anttasks.JwscTask"/>

<jwsc srcdir="src" destdir="earcontents" classpathref="${app.classpath}">
  <jws compiledWsdl="PropertySearchService_wsdl.jar"
       file="com/bigrez/ws/service/PropertySearchServiceImpl.java"
       contextpath="PropertySearchService_WSDLFirst"
       type="JAXWS"/>
</jwsc>
```

Once we have run JWSC, the content of the web service WAR is the same as it was for the code-first approach. When we deploy the web service WAR to our local WebLogic Server instance listening on its default port, the URL for the web service will be:

```
http://localhost:7001/PropertySearchService_WSDLFirst/PropertySearchService
```

The URL for the WSDL will be:

```
http://localhost:7001/PropertySearchService_WSDLFirst/PropertySearchService?wsdl
```

And we can use the same tools to test the web service.

At this point it is probably worth looking at the shape of the XML used for the SOAP request and response. We show the SOAP request structure for the WSDL-first web service we have been discussing here.

```
<soapenv:Envelope xmlns:soapenv="http://schemas.xmlsoap.org/soap/envelope/">
  <soapenv:Body>
    <wrapper:GetPropertyDetailsByAddress
        xmlns:wrapper="http://www.wrox.com/professional-
weblogic/PropertySearchService">
      <PropertySearchAddress
          xmlns="http://www.wrox.com/professional-weblogic/PropertyInfo">
        <Address1>1 High Street</Address1>
        <PostalCode>BT1234</PostalCode>
      </PropertySearchAddress>
    </wrapper:GetPropertyDetailsByAddress>
  </soapenv:Body>
</soapenv:Envelope>
```

The WSDL-first web service's SOAP response looks like the one shown here.

```
<soapenv:Envelope xmlns:soapenv="http://schemas.xmlsoap.org/soap/envelope/">
  <soapenv:Body>
    <wrapper:GetPropertyDetailsByAddressResponse
        xmlns:wrapper="http://www.wrox.com/professional-
weblogic/PropertySearchService">
```

317

```
<PropertyInfo xmlns="http://www.wrox.com/professional-weblogic/PropertyInfo">
  <Id>1</Id>
  <Description>A nice place</Description>
  <Features>2 bedrooms</Features>
  <Address1>1 High Street</Address1>
  <Address2>Hillside</Address2>
  <City>Sunnystate</City>
  <PostalCode>BT1234</PostalCode>
  <Phone>01-1322-2323</Phone>
</PropertyInfo>
    </wrapper:GetPropertyDetailsByAddressResponse >
  </soapenv:Body>
</soapenv:Envelope>
```

If you look closely at the three namespaces the request and response use, it starts to become evident why we declare the wrapper elements in the WSDL and the inner XML content in a separate XML schema. The SOAP message contains three namespaces referenced by different prefixes:

❑   soapenv — This namespace refers to the SOAP envelope schema defined by the SOAP specification.

❑   wrapper — This namespace refers to the wrapper type we defined in the types section of the WSDL.

❑   none — XML elements without prefixes use the default namespace, which refers to the business data types we defined in our XML schema.

Using this approach helps us clearly separate the three concerns: the SOAP protocol, the wrapper type, and the self-contained XML document payload containing the real business data. Because of this, our XML schema is purely defining the structure of our business data; this makes it suitable for use in all parts of our application and potentially across other applications. We define web service–specific types like the wrapper in the WSDL because these types are specific to the web service represented by the WSDL.

Best Practice

Define web service operation wrapper types directly in the WSDL using the WSDL's target namespace. Define the XML types for the web service operation request and response data in a separate XML schema file using a different namespace. This approach decouples the XML schema of the business data types from the web service–specific wrapper types to make it easier to standardize business data type schemas across your application or organization.

Developing Web Service Clients

A web service client application uses a generated Java web service *stub* class, also known as a *proxy*, to invoke the web service. The client uses a set of generated data POJO classes to pass the request data into and receive the response data back from the stub. The generated web service stub's API has methods that mirror the remote web service's operation names, arguments, and return types. Regardless of how the web service was implemented, the process for creating the WebLogic Server Web Services client always uses a WSDL-first approach.

To implement a WebLogic Server Web Services client, we always use the same basic steps.

1. Run WebLogic Server's `clientgen` Ant task against the WSDL for the web service to generate the stub and data POJO classes.

2. Write the client application using the generated stub's exposed API and compile the client application.

3. Run the client.

We show the `clientgen` Ant task–related portions of Example 3's `build.xml` file here.

```
<taskdef name="clientgen" classpathref="${weblogic.classpath}"
        classname="weblogic.wsee.tools.anttasks.ClientGenTask"/>

<clientgen wsdl="http://localhost:7001/PropertySearchService_WSDLFirst/
PropertySearchService?wsdl"
        destDir="stubcode"
        packageName="com.bigrez.ws.property"
        classpathref="${app.classpath}"
        type="JAXWS"/>
```

As for the `clientgen` task attributes, `wsdl` is the complete path or URL to the web service's WSDL, `destDir` is the output directory to which to write the generated class files, and `packageName` is the Java package name of the generated classes.

Once we generate the stub and data POJO classes, we use the stub's API to invoke the web service. The standalone Java client class from Example 3 is shown in Listing 9-3.

Listing 9-3: Example 3's PropertySearchClient.java.

```java
public class PropertySearchClient
{
    public static void main(String[] args)
    {
        try {
            new PropertySearchClient();
        }
        catch (Exception e) {
            e.printStackTrace();
        }
    }

    public PropertySearchClient() throws PropertyInfoFaultException
    {
        // Construct request data
        PropertySearchAddress searchAddress =
            new PropertySearchAddress();
        searchAddress.setAddress1("1 High Street");
        searchAddress.setPostalCode("BT1234");
```

Continued

Listing 9-3: Example 3's PropertySearchClient.java. *(continued)*

```
        // Invoke service operation
        PropertySearchService_Service service =
            new PropertySearchService_Service();
        PropertySearchService port =
            service.getPropertySearchServiceImplPort();
        PropertyInfo property =
            port.getPropertyDetailsByAddress(searchAddress);

        // Process response data
        if (property != null) {
            int id = property.getId();
            String city = property.getCity();
            System.out.println("Found Property: Id=" + id +
                            ", City=" + city);
        }
        else {
            System.out.println("No Property found");
        }
    }
}
```

In our example code, we first populate the JAXB-generated POJO class (`PropertySearchAddress`) with data representing the address information for a property search. Next, we use a set of three steps to locate and invoke the web service operation. In step 1, we obtain a handle to the class that represents the remote web service by instantiating the generated stub via its *no-args* constructor. A web service can have multiple invocation points; these invocation points are known as ports. For example, a web service might have one port for SOAP over HTTP access and another port for SOAP over JMS access. In step 2, we locate the actual service invocation endpoint (port) that we require. At this point, we have a proxy object that represents the remote web service and contains methods with the same names as the remote web service's operations. In step 3, we invoke the appropriate method on the proxy object, passing the property search data and receiving the property search result in a data POJO.

Once we compile the client class, we run the example just like any other ordinary Java standalone application using the command shown here.

```
> java com.bigrez.ws.client.PropertySearchClient
```

Before running this command, we must ensure that the Java classpath contains our client application classes, the generated property search client classes, and WebLogic Server's Web Services client container classes. For the web services client container classes, copy the `$WL_HOME/server/lib/wseeclient.zip` file to the client machine, unzip its contents into a directory, and add the `wseeclient.jar` file to the Java classpath. Note that this works because the `wseeclient.jar` file's Manifest contains references to all the other JARs, so don't be fooled into thinking you don't need the other JAR files.

It is worth noting that when the web service client code runs, the service stub actually downloads the WSDL from the server. By default, the stub uses the URL you specify when you run `clientgen` to generate the stub. Having runtime access to the WSDL significantly reduces the amount of client code and annotations that we need to write, so the JAX-WS specification authors felt this was an acceptable trade-off. As such, web service annotations are really intended to provide additional metadata over and above the data already contained in a web service WSDL.

The JAX-WS APIs allow you to override the default WSDL URL dynamically at runtime, as shown here.

```
URL wsdlURL = new URL("http://localhost:7001/PropertySearchService_WSDLFirst/" +
                      "PropertySearchService?wsdl");
QName serviceQName =
    new QName("http://www.wiley.com/compbooks/professional-" +
              "weblogic/PropertySearchService", "PropertySearchService");
PropertySearchService_Service service =
    new PropertySearchService_Service(wsdlURL, serviceQName);
```

The URL of the WSDL can refer to a local file , by using a URL of the form `file://<path_to_file>`. To construct the qualified name (`QName`), we specify the WSDL's target namespace and the web service's name, as defined by the `service` element of the WSDL.

Sometimes a WSDL may be accessible at the time of web service client generation, but may no longer be accessible when the client is run. For these situations, WebLogic Server provides a handy Ant task called `wsdlget` that downloads a remote WSDL to the local file system plus all its imported XML schemas. This task also changes the WSDL's import references to point to the local copies of the schemas. The following example shows how `wsdlget` can be used to download a copy of a remote WSDL into the current working directory:

```
<wsdlget wsdl="http://remoteserver/ws/PropertySearchService?WSDL" destDir="."/>
```

We then just change the `wsdl` attribute of our `clientgen` Ant task to use the local file URL of the downloaded WSDL.

Alternatively, we can use WebLogic Server's XML Catalog feature to override the locations from which WebLogic Server retrieves the WSDLs and XML schemas. See Link 9-2 for more information on using XML Catalogs.

We can even override the URL of the actual web service endpoint dynamically at runtime. The JAX-WS API provides a special `BindingProvider` interface that supports performing HTTP protocol-specific actions. We use this interface to specify the HTTP endpoint URL in the following example.

```
Map<String, Object> rc = ((BindingProvider) port).getRequestContext();
rc.put(BindingProvider.ENDPOINT_ADDRESS_PROPERTY,
    "http://localhost:7001/PropertySearchService_WSDLFirst/PropertySearchService");
PropertyInfo property = port.getPropertyDetailsByAddress(searchAddress);
```

Regardless of how you do it, you should minimize the number of remote calls to obtain and the number of parses required to process a single WSDL file. A naïve approach of always creating a new service stub each time you want to invoke a web service operation will require a remote call to retrieve the WSDL, parsing the WSDL (which may require retrieving one or more remote XML schemas), and another call to execute the operation. A better approach would be to cache and reuse the service stub. You should also consider making local copies of the WSDL and XML schemas.

> **Best Practice**
>
> Lookup and cache a service stub just once in your client code, rather than looking up the service each time you want to call a web service operation. This improves performance by reducing the need for the client code to repeatedly obtain and parse a WSDL. This also reduces the risk of errors if the WSDL is hosted remotely and is sometimes unavailable for access.

Of course, not all web service clients are standalone Java programs. In many cases, server-side Java EE components need to make web services calls. When writing web service client code that will run inside WebLogic Server, we can include a JAX-WS `@WebServiceRef` annotation to instruct the container to inject the web service client stub directly into a member variable in a Java EE component class, as shown here.

```
@WebServiceRef
PropertySearchService_Service service;
```

This annotation can be used from within servlets, EJBs, and even other web services running in a WebLogic Server.

We can override the web service's WSDL's URL built into the generated client stub by specifying a `wsdlLocation` element for the `@WebServiceRef` annotation, as shown here.

```
@WebServiceRef(wsdlLocation="http://localhost:7001/PropertySearchService_WSDLFirst/
PropertySearchService?wsdl")
PropertySearchService_Service service;
```

When web service client code is running within a WebLogic Server deployed application, we don't have to worry about setting up the classpath to include WebLogic Server's Web Service client JARs. This is because all the required WebLogic Server classes are automatically available to our code, by virtue of the server's default classpath.

Moving Past the Basics

In the previous section, we showed you how to write basic web services using two different approaches and how to write a web service client to call these services. Now, we show you how to use some of the more advanced features of WebLogic Server's Web Services container.

Using JAX-RPC

JAX-RPC 1.1 is an older Java web services standard whose name reflects its emphasis on a remote procedure call–style programming model for web services development. The specification was renamed to JAX-WS during the move from version 1.1 to 2.0, to reflect the fact that the specification now supports both RPC and message-centric programming models. Although JAX-WS is not a radical departure from the previous versions of the specification, JAX-WS is not backward-compatible with JAX-RPC. Consequently, WebLogic Server still provides support for the old JAX-RPC programming model to support users who have existing applications using the older model that want to upgrade to the latest version of WebLogic Server.

For the most part, the WebLogic Server provides feature parity between its JAX-RPC 1.1 implementation and its JAX-WS 2.1 implementation. For example, both implementations support the WS-Security, SAML, and WS-Addressing standards plus features like asynchronous messaging and callbacks. Currently, only WebLogic Server's JAX-RPC implementation supports the following standards and features:

WS-Trust 1.3 (clients-only)   WebLogic Server–based web services clients use WS-Trust to request security tokens from third-party security token services (STS).

WS-ReliableMessaging 1.1   Web services applications use WS-ReliableMessaging to enable a web service consumer to reliably send messages to a web service provider with a specified quality of service.

SOAP over JMS   Web services applications use SOAP over JMS to enable a web service consumer to send SOAP messages asynchronously to a web service provider via a WebLogic JMS Queue.

If we require any of these features, we must use WebLogic Server's JAX-RPC implementation. Otherwise, we should use the JAX-WS programming model because it is part of the Java EE 5 specification.

JAX-RPC development uses the same WebLogic Server Ant tasks as JAX-WS. Simply change the value of the `type` attribute from `JAXWS` to `JAXRPC`. Be aware that the default value for the type attribute is `JAXRPC`. The annotations and XML-Java mapping technologies JAX-RPC provides are, for the most part, different from JAX-WS. See Link 9-3 for more information on using the JAX-RPC programming model with WebLogic Server.

> For the WebLogic Server web services–related Ant tasks, the `type` attribute determines whether your web services will use the JAX-RPC or JAX-WS web services models. If you fail to specify the `type` attribute, it defaults to `JAXRPC`.

Understanding Style and Use

SOAP defines two *styles* of operation. As web service developers, we need to choose one and specify this decision in the binding section of the WSDL or in the `@SOAPBinding` annotation of the JWS class. The two styles are:

❑   `rpc` — Historically, this style has been associated with synchronous, request/response operations. This style implies that the SOAP body structure reflects the operation name, zero or more arguments, and a return value.

❑   `document` — Historically, this style has been associated with asynchronous, one-way message passing. This style implies that the SOAP body is made up of one or more XML documents.

This categorization is somewhat arbitrary because most modern SOAP engines support the use of `document` style for both the RPC and message-passing models. WebLogic Server correctly maps web service operations to the corresponding JWS class's methods regardless of whether we specify the `rpc` or `document` style. The style attribute has no real effect.

Unfortunately, to confuse matters further, SOAP also defines a *use* attribute, which we must specify on each input, output, and fault sub-element of each operation in the WSDL binding section, or in the JWS class's @SOAPBinding annotation. The two uses are:

❑ encoded — The SOAP body content adheres to a set of rules for serializing a graph of typed objects. Although the individual types are based on XML schema types, the SOAP body as a whole does not conform to an XML schema.

❑ literal — The SOAP body content conforms to one or more XML schemas.

So as a web service developer, what style and use should we adopt when building our web services?

The two styles and two uses come together as four possible style/use combinations that could be supported by SOAP implementations. WebLogic Server and the applicable industry standards support only a subset of these combinations, as shown in Table 9-1.

Table 9-1: Support for the SOAP Style/Use Combinations

Style/Use	WebLogic Server	JAX-RPC 1.1	JAX-WS 2.1	WS-Basic Profile 1.1
RPC-encoded	Yes (JAX-RPC impl. Only)	Yes	Optional (deprecated)	No
RPC-literal	Yes	Yes	Yes	Yes
document-encoded	No	Optional	Optional (deprecated)	No
document-literal	Yes	Yes	Yes	Yes

As you can see, using RPC-literal or document-literal web services maximizes interoperability with other SOAP implementations. To maximize reuse of XML schemas, prefer document-literal over RPC-literal.

Best Practice

Use document-literal–based web services to maximize SOAP interoperability and XML schema reuse.

To confuse matters even further, there is an unofficial fifth style/use combination called document-literal-wrapped. In the early days of web services, Microsoft-based technologies preferred to use the document style for remote procedure call–enabling .NET components, rather than the more popular RPC style of the time. The problem with using *bare* document style SOAP requests is that the SOAP body has no top-level element that identifies the target operation name. Even though there are other possible means for addressing the operation (which we discuss in the next section), a wrapped convention became popular for enabling the RPC model of programming when using document-based web services.

As we discussed previously, the wrapped style names the top-level element inside the SOAP body to match the name of the target operation, rather than using that element as the root element of the regular business data. The SOAP standard does not mention or define the wrapped style because it is just a convention. However, the JAX-WS 2.1 specification does refer to this convention and states how such web services should be mapped to and from Java classes.

Should you use the wrapped or bare style?

Our answer is that it depends on the web services programming paradigm you want to use. When using a synchronous RPC model, use the document-literal-wrapped convention. The top-level wrapper allows you to pass multiple arguments without violating the WS-I Basic Profile 1.1 rule that allows only a single top-level element within a SOAP body. When using a message-passing model, use document-literal (bare). With this model, you generally just want to pass a business document between systems, often asynchronously. Most times, the web services using this model have only a single operation so there is no need for the wrapper. If for some reason a message passing–style web service has more than one operation, you must use the wrapped convention to conform to the WS-I Basic Profile 1.1 standard.

Best Practice

There are different recommendations concerning which style of web service to adopt depending on whether you want to use an RPC programming model or a message passing programming model.

❏   Use the document-literal-wrapped convention when using web services for an RPC programming model.

❏   Use the document-literal (also known as, document-literal-bare) convention when using web services for a message passing programming model.

❏   If a message passing-style web service has more than one operation, use the document-literal-wrapped convention to conform to the WS-I Basic Profile 1.1 standard.

Influencing which Operation to Invoke

As we have seen in the previous section, the WS-I Basic Profile requires web services with multiple operations to have unique top-level elements inside the SOAP body. By default, WebLogic Server looks at the top-level element name and tries to match it to an operation name when determining which operation to invoke. However, WebLogic Server is quite versatile; if the top-level element is not unique, WebLogic Server looks at the next level of child elements and so on, until it finds a matching operation signature in the WSDL.

What happens for document-literal-bare web services when more than one operation has the same shape? At build-time, WebLogic Server's WSDL and JWS compilers justifiably produce a warning saying that the web service has non-unique body parts and that message dispatching may fail. For such ambiguous situations there needs to be another way for us to influence the operation addressing decision that WebLogic Server's Web Services container makes.

HTTP-based SOAP services can include an HTTP header as a hint for the operation to invoke. SOAP 1.1 uses the SOAPAction header for this purpose, but this has changed in SOAP 1.2. Unfortunately, this mechanism is transport-specific and can legally be ignored or overruled by the web service implementation, as it is with WebLogic Server. As a consequence, we should never rely upon the values of such transport headers to direct the behavior of the web services container.

WebLogic Server supports another mechanism for a client to specify the name of the operation to invoke. This feature relies on WebLogic Server's support for the WS-Addressing 1.0 standard. The WS-Addressing specification defines various elements that can be used in a SOAP body or a SOAP header. The following example shows a SOAP request that includes WS-Addressing elements in the SOAP header.

```
<Envelope ....>
  <Header xmlns:wsa="http://www.w3.org/2005/08/addressing">
    <wsa:To>....</To>
    <wsa:Action>....</Action>
  </Header>
  <Body>
    .....
  </Body>
</Envelope>
```

Although WS-Addressing specifies other header elements that we can include, only the `Action` element is mandatory when using WS-Addressing. The `To` element identifies the URL of the target web service (for example, its URL) and the `Action` element names the target operation. The `Action` element value needs to match the `soapAction` attribute value specified in the web service's WSDL, as shown in the following WSDL snippet for our property search web service.

```
<definitions>
  ...
  <operation name="GetPropertyDetailsByAddress">
    <soap:operation
        soapAction="http://www.wrox.com/professional-
weblogic/PropertySearchService/GetPropertyDetailsByAddress"
    />
  </operation>
  ...
<definitions>
```

Even though the `soapAction` attribute in the WSDL looks like an endpoint URL, it is really just a unique identifier for our `GetPropertyDetailsByAddress` operation. For code-first–style web services, we specify the WSDL's `soapAction` attribute value using the `@Action` annotation on the corresponding JWS method. To tell WebLogic Server to actively look for and use the WS-Addressing `Action`, the JWS class must use the `@Addressing` annotation, as shown here.

```
@WebService
@Addressing(enabled=true, required=true)
public class PropertySearchServiceImpl implements PropertySearchService
{
    ...
}
```

By including this annotation in our JWS class, the WSDL that WebLogic Server generates for our web service will contain a WS-Addressing element called `UsingAddressing`. This element advertises that the service supports the use of WS-Addressing, as shown in the following example.

```
<definitions>
  ...
  <binding name="PropertySearchServiceImplPortBinding"
          type="tns:PropertySearchService">
```

```
<wsaw:UsingAddressing/>
    ...
  </binding>
  ...
</definitions>
```

We do not need to change any of our code in our web service client to include the addressing headers in the SOAP requests. This is because WebLogic Server–based clients will detect that WS-Addressing is required, from the WSDL, and automatically include an `Action` header matching the `soapAction` for the operation. On the server side, WebLogic Server will now base its operation routing decision for our web service purely on the value of the `Action` addressing header and will ignore any operation-specific signature that may be present in the SOAP body.

If for some reason the WSDL for a web service does not advertise a `UsingAddressing` element, JAX-WS provides a feature the client applications can use to force the client container to always send an `Action` WS-Addressing header regardless of what the WSDL says. To enable this feature in our SOAP client, we use the following code:

```
PropertySearchService_Service service = new PropertySearchService_Service();
WebServiceFeature[] actionAddressingRequired = {new AddressingFeature(true, true)};
PropertySearchService port =
    service.getPropertySearchServiceImplPort(actionAddressingRequired);
```

Best Practice

To enable clients to uniquely specify which operation of a web service to invoke, choose one of the following three options:

1. Use a document-literal-wrapped style to guarantee that each operation has a unique SOAP body shape that WebLogic Server can match with the operation.

2. Use a document-literal-bare style if the web service has only one operation because no routing decision is required.

3. Use a WS-Addressing `Action` header to identify the operation if both the client and service provider support WS-Addressing.

Creating More Dynamic Web Services

So far in this chapter, we have concentrated on implementing web services using the SEI approach where we generate strongly-typed data POJOs and a Java implementation class that has methods matching a web service's operations. This SEI-based approach is essentially an RPC programming model, which is very popular when you want to web service–enable existing applications.

What if we need to support a more dynamic and loosely-coupled approach, such as to support a message-passing model? Imagine you need to build a system that receives complex XML messages from other systems where the XML schemas for the messages vary from one request to another. The message header might even contain metadata specifying the format of the message. For such situations, the use of a fixed, strongly-typed web service interface may be difficult or even impossible.

JAX-WS provides two APIs to address this need: `Provider` and `Dispatch`. In the SEI-based approach, JAX-WS uses a high-level, object-oriented abstraction for implementing services that hides the plumbing of converting between XML and Java. The `Provider` API gives the service implementation direct access to the SOAP messages, and the `Dispatch` API provides the equivalent functionality for the client.

To demonstrate the use of the Provider API, Example 4 contains a simple property change web service. Clients send messages containing the details of the property to change. For example, we may need to update the property's description and features fields in the database if the property has been newly refurbished and extended. Listing 9-4 shows the Java code for the property change web service that implements the `Provider` interface.

Listing 9-4: Example 4's PropertyChangeService.java.

```java
@WebServiceProvider(
    serviceName="PropertyChangeService",
    targetNamespace="http://www.wrox.com/professional-
weblogic/PropertyChangeService",
    portName="PropertyChangeServiceSOAP",
    wsdlLocation="wsdls/PropertyChangeService.wsdl"
)
@ServiceMode(value=Service.Mode.MESSAGE)
public class PropertyChangeService implements Provider<SOAPMessage>
{
    private final static String PREFX = "prpty";
    private final static String NMSPC =
        "http://www.wrox.com/professional-weblogic" +
        "/PropertyChangeData";

    public SOAPMessage invoke(SOAPMessage request)
    {
        try {
            // Process request
            //
            Iterator<SOAPElement> children =
                request.getSOAPBody().getChildElements(
                new QName(NMSPC, "PropertyChangeInfo"));
            SOAPElement propertyChangeInfo = children.next();
            String id = getChildValue(propertyChangeInfo, "Id");
            System.out.println("Changing prop '" + id +
                            "' info with values:");
            System.out.println("Description: " +
                getChildValue(propertyChangeInfo, "Description"));
            System.out.println(" -Features: " +
                getChildValue(propertyChangeInfo, "Features"));

            // Generate response
            //
            SOAPMessage response =
                MessageFactory.newInstance().createMessage();
            SOAPEnvelope envelope =
                response.getSOAPPart().getEnvelope();
```

```
                Name propChangeAckElementName =
                    envelope.createName(
                    "PropertyChangeAcknowledgement" , PREFX, NMSPC);
                SOAPElement propChangeAckNameElement =
                    response.getSOAPBody().addBodyElement(
                    propChangeAckElementName);
                Name ackElementName =
                    envelope.createName("Ack", PREFX, NMSPC);
                propChangeAckNameElement.addChildElement(
                    ackElementName).addTextNode("SUCCESS");
                Name receiptNumberElementName =
                  envelope.createName("ReceiptNumber", PREFX, NMSPC);
                propChangeAckNameElement.addChildElement(
                    receiptNumberElementName).addTextNode(
                    System.currentTimeMillis() + "-" + id);
                Name commentElementName =
                    envelope.createName("Comment", PREFX, NMSPC);
                propChangeAckNameElement.addChildElement(
                    commentElementName).addTextNode("Successfully " +
                    "processed info change for property: " + id);
                return response;
            }
        catch (SOAPException e) {
            throw new WebServiceException("Error occurred in " +
                                         "JAX-WS Provider", e);
        }
    }

    private String getChildValue(SOAPElement parent,
                                 String nodeName)
    {
        // Function to get the child soap element
        // with matching name
        //
        ...
    }
}
```

In the example, the service response is just an acknowledgment XML document containing a SUCCESS flag, a comment, and a receipt number for the consumer's future reference. For brevity, our example code just prints out the property's data rather than updating the property database. We include a receipt number in our reply because our service is intended to be used by business partners who may need to contact us at a later date, to query a problem with the update of a property. Internally our service implementation could generate a unique receipt number for tracking purposes and store this in an audit table along with the date and time that the update occurred and the user id of the business partner that performed the update.

To create this class, we just implement the Provider interface and specify the type as either javax.xml.soap.SOAPMessage or javax.xml.transform.Source. By setting the type to SOAPMessage, we tell WebLogic Server that we want use the loosely-typed XML DOM-based API to process the request and construct the response. This DOM-based API uses the org.w3c.dom package plus some wrapper and helper classes from the javax.xml.soap package, both packaged with the standard JDK. This is the same set of APIs we use for handling SOAP messages with attachments later in this chapter.

Our `Provider` class has a single `invoke()` method that processes all calls to the web service, regardless of the target operation. Unlike an SEI class, we must annotate this class with `@WebServiceProvider` rather than `@WebService`. The other interesting annotation is `@ServiceMode`, which is set to `MESSAGE`. This tells WebLogic Server that our `invoke()` method wants to receive the entire SOAP envelope. A value of `PAYLOAD` says to receive only the SOAP body content.

The process for building and deploying a `Provider`-based web service is very similar to the WSDL-first process detailed earlier. First, we create the XML schemas and WSDL for the web service. Next, we implement the web service using the `Provider` interface. Then, we run WebLogic Server's `jwsc` Ant task to generate the web service WAR. Finally, we deploy the WAR. The only difference is that we have no need to run the WSDL compiler because we don't need the generated interface or data POJO classes. In fact, we can also choose to not use `jwsc` to create the WAR file. When we deploy a custom-built WAR file, WebLogic Server automatically detects the presence of a JWS class and maps it to the built-in `WebServiceServlet` using a servlet mapping where the name of the JWS class is part of the service's URL. If we want better control of the URL, we can simply add a `<servlet>` definition for the `Provider` JWS class and the `<servlet-mapping>` we require to the `web.xml` deployment descriptor.

On the client, we don't need to use any WebLogic Server Ant tasks at all when we use the Dispatch API to call our web service. The class is just a normal Java class using the generic JAX-WS API. Listing 9-5 shows the example code for our service client. Again, we just use the XML W3C DOM API to construct requests and process responses.

Listing 9-5: Example 4's PropertyChangeClient.java.

```
public class PropertyChangeClient
{
    private final static String WSDL_URL_SUFFIX = "?WSDL";
    private final static String WSDL_NMSP =
        "http://www.wrox.com/professional-weblogic" +
        "/PropertyChangeService";
    private final static String WSDL_SRVC_PORT =
        "PropertyChangeServiceSOAP";
    private final static String WSDL_SRVC_NAME =
        "PropertyChangeService";
    private final static String XSD_PRFX = "prpty";
    private final static String XSD_NMSP =
        "http://www.wrox.com/professional-weblogic" +
        "/PropertyChangeData";

    public PropertyChangeClient(String endpointURL)
        throws SOAPException, MalformedURLException
    {
        // Construct request
        //
        SOAPMessage request =
            MessageFactory.newInstance().createMessage();
        SOAPEnvelope envelope =
            request.getSOAPPart().getEnvelope();
        Name messageRootName =
            envelope.createName("PropertyChangeInfo",
                            XSD_PRFX, XSD_NMSP);
```

```
            SOAPElement topElement =
                request.getSOAPBody().addBodyElement(messageRootName);
            topElement.addChildElement(
                envelope.createName("Id", XSD_PRFX,
                XSD_NMSP)).addTextNode("1");
            topElement.addChildElement(envelope.createName(
                "Description", XSD_PRFX, XSD_NMSP)).
                addTextNode("Recently re-furbished");

            // Invoke service operation
            //
            QName portName = new QName(WSDL_NMSP, WSDL_SRVC_PORT);
            Service service =
                Service.create(new URL(endpointURL + WSDL_URL_SUFFIX),
                                new QName(WSDL_NMSP, WSDL_SRVC_NAME));
            Dispatch<SOAPMessage> dispatcher =
                service.createDispatch(portName, SOAPMessage.class,
                                        Service.Mode.MESSAGE);
            SOAPMessage response = dispatcher.invoke(request);

            // Process response
            //
            String ack =
                response.getSOAPBody().getElementsByTagNameNS(XSD_NMSP,
                "Ack").item(0).getFirstChild().getNodeValue();
            String receiptNum =
                response.getSOAPBody().getElementsByTagNameNS(XSD_NMSP,
                "ReceiptNumber").item(0).getFirstChild().
                getNodeValue();
            String comment =
                response.getSOAPBody().getElementsByTagNameNS(XSD_NMSP,
                "Comment").item(0).getFirstChild().getNodeValue();
            System.out.println("Change property result: " + ack +
                                " (Receipt=" + receiptNum +
                                ", Comment=" + comment + ")");
        }
    }
```

To obtain a reference to the web service proxy, the client code specifies the URL of the WSDL and the specific service's qualified name, as defined in the WSDL. We use the proxy to create the `Dispatch` object by specifying the qualified name of the port. Additionally, we specify that we want to use the `SOAPMessage` W3C DOM API and `MESSAGE` mode.

We only need to compile the client using the Java compiler. To run the client, just make sure that the WebLogic Server Web Services client JAR (`wseeclient.jar`) is on the classpath, as discussed previously.

As you can see, this approach allows you to write web service clients and implementations that are much more dynamic. If we use `javax.xml.transform.Source` instead of `javax.xml.soap.SOAPMessage` as the type, we can use alternative mechanisms for processing the XML data of web service requests and responses. Example 5 has an alternate implementation of the service that uses a different XML processing technique, as shown in Listing 9-6.

Listing 9-6: Example 5's PropertyChangeService.java.

```java
@ServiceMode(value=Service.Mode.PAYLOAD)
public class PropertyChangeService implements Provider<Source>
{
    private final static String NMSPC =
        "http://www.wrox.com/professional-weblogic" +
        "/PropertyChangeData";

    public Source invoke(Source request)
    {
        try {
            // Process request using a W3C DOM API
            //
            Transformer transformer =
                TransformerFactory.newInstance().newTransformer();
            DOMResult dom = new DOMResult();
            transformer.transform(request, dom);
            Document doc =
                dom.getNode().getFirstChild().getOwnerDocument();
            Element topElement = doc.getDocumentElement();
            String id = getChildValue(topElement, "Id");
            System.out.println("Changing property '" + id +
                                "' with values:");
            System.out.println(" -Description: " +
                                getChildValue(topElement, "Description"));
            System.out.println(" -Features: " +
                                getChildValue(topElement, "Features"));

            // Generate response using a text stream
            //
            String response =
                "<?xml version=\"1.0\" encoding=\"UTF-8\"?>\n" +
                "<PropertyChangeAcknowledgement " +
                "xmlns=\"http://www.wrox.com/professional-" +
                "weblogic/PropertyChangeData\">\n" +
                "  <Ack>SUCCESS>\Ack>\n" +
                "  <ReceiptNumber>" + System.currentTimeMillis() +
                "-" + id + "</ReceiptNumber>\n" +
                "  <Comment>Successfully processed info change " +
                "for property: " + id + "</Comment>\n" +
                "</PropertyChangeAcknowledgement>";
            return new StreamSource(new StringReader(response));
        }
        catch (Exception e) {
            throw new WebServiceException("Error occurred in " +
                                            "JAX-WS Provider", e);
        }
    }
    ...
}
```

In this example, we chose to use a W3C DOM-based API to process the request and to construct the response we just used a text stream. Obviously, we could retrieve the actual XML text from somewhere else. We set the value of the @ServiceMode annotation to PAYLOAD; this allows us to concentrate on processing just the business data and not worry about the SOAP-specific elements.

Using the javax.xml.transform.Source interface allows us to use any XML API we want for processing SOAP requests and responses, including the following standard Java APIs, which have classes that implement Source and Result:

❑ W3C XML DOM API

❑ SAX XML Parser API

❑ StAX XML Streaming API

❑ Raw XML text stream

❑ JAXB-generated Java types

Using these low-level XML APIs, we can then go on to use richer XML processing tools like XPath and JDOM or even XML processing languages like XSLT and XQuery. On the client side, we are also free to use the javax.xml.transform.Source interface with the Dispatch API, as shown in the Example 5 version of PropertyChangeClient.java in the downloadable examples.

When should you use the SEI approach and when should you use the Provider/Dispatch approach to building web service consumers and providers? Although there are no hard and fast rules, each approach has its advantages. These advantages tend to mirror the fact that SEI is a strongly-typed, compile-time approach whereas Provider/Dispatch is a loosely-typed, runtime-based approach that exposes you directly to the underlying SOAP messages. The following list provides some examples of situations that might lead you to consider using the Provider/Dispatch approach; however, even with these scenarios, you should carefully weigh the different design alternatives to choose the best one for your situation.

Enable a Message-Passing Model   RPC-based models can lead to tight coupling between service implementations and clients that are resistant to change. However, using loosely-typed interfaces that accept any and all XML messages tends to increase the complexity of the application, which may lead to less robust implementations. Do you really need a single service implementation that accepts multiple XML message types? Are there other designs (for example, one operation per message type) that allow you to handle multiple message types without losing the benefit of a strongly-typed interface? Choose a design that meets your known requirements rather than designing a solution to the general problem that you may never need to solve. Focus on defining the appropriate WSDL interface for a service versus one that only reflects your currently planned implementation of it.

Act as an Intermediary   A web service may only be acting as a messaging intermediary, taking some action on a small portion of the message before passing it on. Enforcing strongly-typed interfaces and message validation on the intermediary makes your intermediary less flexible and may force you to change it every time the end-service changes. On the other hand, blindly passing along invalid messages to the backend puts additional burden on your system. Choose a design that provides the right balance for your intermediaries and the services they perform.

Support Other XML Processing Tools   When using an SEI-based approach, there is one and only one way to operate on data. If your service requires access to only part of a message, having the option to use a SAX parser or just an XPath-based Java API may significantly reduce complexity of your XML processing code, especially for large messages. Also, if languages like XQuery or XSLT offer you a better abstraction and a quicker development model, then these can be plugged in to your service implementation for processing XML requests and responses.

Allow Performance Optimization   Marshalling between XML and Java types can have a major negative performance impact, especially for high-volume services that work with large XML payloads. For your critical web services, you want to have the capability to use a leaner and faster mechanism for XML processing, such as XML streaming parsers and SAX parsers where your application encounters real bottlenecks. However, be careful to choose a design that supports adding optimizations without adding extra complexity or requiring significant rework. Only optimize actual bottlenecks that significantly impact your application in real-world stress testing or production environments.

Best Practice

Choose the right application design to meet your known requirements. By default, use the SEI approach to web services application development to simplify the programming model and resulting application code. Using the `Provider/Dispatch` approach gives you more flexibility in choosing your web services programming model to address specific scenarios, but can lead to an overly complex design.

Using Web Service Handlers

Web services, like most types of components, tend to encapsulate and expose business functions or capabilities. However, there are invariably other non-functional concerns that we need to apply to some or all of our web services. These concerns are often pieces of re-usable *system* logic that are orthogonal to the *application* logic contained within individual web services. For example, applications often require support for auditing, reporting, custom security schemes, and alerting. Ideally, we would like to write such system-level logic once and then apply it to multiple services, as needed.

In the Java SE world, Aspect Oriented Programming (AOP), and technologies like AspectJ and Spring that support it, provides the mechanisms to apply such cross-cutting logic to multiple components. AOP allows you to *inject* logic around existing components without requiring changes to the components. In the Java EE world, we use an interceptor model to register code to execute around existing components. Each of the Java EE technologies calls these pieces of code by a different name, but they all work in a similar fashion. The servlet specification calls these pieces of code *filters*, the EJB specification calls them *interceptors*, and the web services specifications call them *handlers*. Unlike servlet filters and EJB interceptors, web service handlers also support client-side registration and use.

JAX-WS handlers allow us to apply reusable logic before and after the invocation of a web service, and even short-circuit the actual invocation, if that is appropriate. The JAX-WS specification defines two categories of handlers:

Logical Handler   A logical handler provides access to only the message context properties and message payload. It is protocol-agnostic and cannot affect the protocol-specific portions of the message. Logical handlers implement the `java.xml.ws.handler.LogicalHandler` interface.

Protocol Handler   A protocol handler provides access to the entire message, including the protocol-specific elements of the message like the SOAP envelope, header, and body for the SOAP protocol. Protocol handlers implement any interface that derives from `javax.xml.ws.Handler` except `javax.xml.ws.handler.LogicalHandler`.

A handler is just a Java class that implements an appropriate handler interface and a small set of life cycle methods. The web services container invokes the `handleMessage()` method before and after a web service invocation. Figure 9-5 shows the relationship between handlers, the web service client, and web service provider.

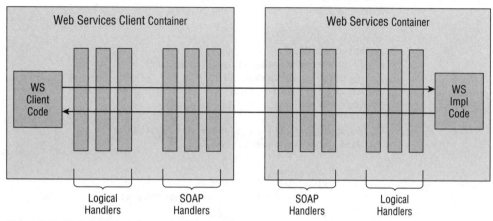

Figure 9-5: Web Services Handlers Framework.

To use handlers in our applications, we define handler chains to collect together a set of related handlers to be run one after the other, before and after a web service invocation. We define a chain of handlers in an XML file, which is then included in the deployable web services WAR. This approach allows each web service implementation class to share the same handler chain XML file using a `@HandlerChain` annotation.

Example 6 demonstrates the use of a protocol handler to enforce a custom security mechanism for clients who wish to access the web service. We apply this handler to the same WSDL-first property search service that we implemented earlier in this chapter. Service clients will need to provide a *secret key* that only trusted clients and we know. Our handler looks for the presence of a custom SOAP header element called `MagicKey` with a secret value of `012345` and allows normal request processing to occur only if the key is present and valid. Otherwise, the handler throws an exception to abort the handler chain and return a fault to the client without ever invoking the actual web service. Listing 9-7 shows our protocol handler code.

Listing 9-7: Example 6's CheckMagicHeaderKeySOAPHandler.java.

```
public class CheckMagicHeaderKeySOAPHandler
    implements SOAPHandler<SOAPMessageContext>
{
    private final static String NMSPC =
        "http://www.wrox.com/professional-weblogic/MagicKey";
    private final static String MAGIC_KEY_HEADER_NAME = "MagicKey";
    private final static String MAGIC_KEY_HEADER_CORRECT_VALUE =
        "012345";

    public boolean handleMessage(SOAPMessageContext context)
    {
        try {
```

Continued

335

Listing 9-7: Example 6's CheckMagicHeaderKeySOAPHandler.java. *(continued)*

```
            boolean isOutboundDirection =
                ((Boolean)context.get(
                MessageContext.MESSAGE_OUTBOUND_PROPERTY)).
                booleanValue();

        if (!isOutboundDirection) {
            NodeList headers =
                context.getMessage().getSOAPHeader().
                getElementsByTagNameNS(NMSPC,
                MAGIC_KEY_HEADER_NAME);
            String value = null;

            if (headers != null && headers.getLength() > 0) {
                Node node = headers.item(0);

                if (node != null) {
                    value =
                        node.getFirstChild().getNodeValue();
                }
            }

            if ((value == null) ||
                (!value.equals(
                MAGIC_KEY_HEADER_CORRECT_VALUE))) {
                throw new ProtocolException("Mandatory SOAP " +
                    "header '" + MAGIC_KEY_HEADER_NAME +
                    "' not specified with correct value");
            }
        }
    }
    catch (SOAPException e) {
        throw new ProtocolException(e);
    }
    return true;
}

// Some other lifecycle methods including handleFault(),
// getHeaders(), and close()
//
...
}
```

Because logical handlers only provide access to the message payload, the `handleMessage()` method always receives the message as a `javax.xml.transform.Source` data type. In our protocol handler example, the `handleMessage()` method receives the messages as a `javax.xml.ws.handler.soap.SOAPMessageContext` data type. This type provides full access to the SOAP message using a W3C DOM-based API.

At runtime, the web services container invokes the same `handleMessage()` method both before invoking the service and after the service invocation returns. On the way in, this allows a handler to inspect and modify the SOAP request before the container invokes the web service, or even abort the invocation altogether. On the way out, this allows a handler to inspect and modify the SOAP response returned by the web service invocation before the container sends it back to the client. In our example, we use the `MessageContext` object to ensure that we only run security header checking code on the inbound request. By returning true, we tell the container to proceed with the normal invocation procedure that executes the rest of the handler chain and the actual web service. If any of the handlers or the web service implementation throw an exception or generate a SOAP fault, the container invokes the `handleFault()` method of each previously invoked handler, giving these handlers the opportunity to perform custom error logging or to transform the SOAP fault into a more user-friendly format.

Example 6 uses a `handler-chain.xml` file to define the handler chain that includes our handler, as shown here.

```xml
<handler-chains xmlns="http://java.sun.com/xml/ns/javaee">
  <handler-chain>
    <handler>
      <handler-class>
        com.bigrez.ws.service.CheckMagicHeaderKeySOAPHandler
      </handler-class>
    </handler>
  </handler-chain>
</handler-chains>
```

Our JWS class refers to the `handler-chain.xml` file that includes our handler using the `@HandlerChain` annotation shown here.

```java
@WebService
@HandlerChain(file="handler-chain.xml")
public class PropertySearchServiceImpl implements PropertySearchService
{
    ...
}
```

The `@HandlerChain` annotation supports both absolute and relative paths to the `handler-chain.xml` file. Relative paths are relative to the location of the JWS class, which is in the same directory in this case. We then generate and package the web service in exactly the same way as we have done before.

Listing 9-8 shows the client-side protocol handler that injects the secret key into the SOAP request header.

Listing 9-8: Example 6's InjectMagicHeaderKeySOAPHandler.java.

```java
public class InjectMagicHeaderKeySOAPHandler
    implements SOAPHandler<SOAPMessageContext>
{
    private final static String NMSPC =
        "http://www.wrox.com/professional-weblogic/MagicKey";
    private final static String MAGIC_KEY_HEADER_NAME = "MagicKey";
    private final static String MAGIC_KEY_HEADER_CORRECT_VALUE =
        "012345";

    public boolean handleMessage(SOAPMessageContext context)
    {
```

Continued

Listing 9-8: Example 6's InjectMagicHeaderKeySOAPHandler.java. *(continued)*

```java
            try {
                boolean isOutboundDirection =
                    ((Boolean)context.get(MessageContext.
                    MESSAGE_OUTBOUND_PROPERTY)).booleanValue();

                if (isOutboundDirection) {
                    SOAPEnvelope envelope =
                        context.getMessage().getSOAPPart().
                        getEnvelope();
                    SOAPHeaderElement newHeader =
                        envelope.addHeader().addHeaderElement(
                        new QName(NMSPC, MAGIC_KEY_HEADER_NAME));
                    newHeader.setValue(MAGIC_KEY_HEADER_CORRECT_VALUE);
                }
            }
            catch (SOAPException e) {
                throw new ProtocolException(e);
            }
            return true;
        }

        // Some other lifecycle methods including handleFault(),
        // getHeaders(), and close()
        //
        ...
    }
```

Once we compile our client-side handler class, the only thing left to do is to alter our code to use the JAX-WS `javax.xml.ws.Binding` API to associate the handler with the service client, as shown here.

```java
Binding binding = ((BindingProvider)port).getBinding();
List<Handler> handlerList = binding.getHandlerChain();
handlerList.add(new InjectMagicHeaderKeySOAPHandler());
binding.setHandlerChain(handlerList);
```

Our example handler is effectively implementing its own custom security mechanism to protect the web service. Later in the chapter we discuss how to use more standards-based security mechanisms to protect web services.

Using SOAP Attachments

SOAP attachments provide a way to attach any type of data to a SOAP message. This is particularly useful when you need to pass a binary file, such as JPEG images or PDF document to a web service. The SOAP Messages with Attachments specification (see http://www.w3.org/TR/SOAP-attachments) defines how to pass attachments with SOAP messages. Attachments are not passed within the SOAP envelope, but are passed in a separate part of the HTTP POST request or response. The HTTP Content-Type header is set to Multipart/Related rather than just text/xml, as is the case with normal SOAP messages. In the HTTP body, a special piece of text called a *MIME boundary* divider separates the actual SOAP envelope from the contents of the attachment(s). If the attachment has a binary format, its content is base 64 encoded before being placed into the HTTP body.

Fortunately, JAX-WS hides and encapsulates the complex details of handling multi-part HTTP messages and base 64 encoding. To create a web service that receives an attachment, we just need to create two protocol handlers, one to add the attachment on the client-side and another to extract it on the server-side. Example 7 uses the same property change WSDL-first web service to receive updated data about a particular property. In this example, we enhance the web service to accept one or more attached documents relating to the property. For example, the caller might include a JPEG picture of the refurbished hotel.

For simplicity, our handler persists the image file to disk. Obviously, more realistic examples might use a different storage mechanism, like a database BLOB field. Listing 9-9 is an excerpt from AttachmentPersisterSOAPHandler.java that shows the server-side protocol handler code we use.

Listing 9-9: Example 7's AttachmentPersisterSOAPHandler.java.

```java
private final static String FILE_LIST_KEY = "AttachedFilePathList";
...


public boolean handleMessage(SOAPMessageContext context)
{
    try {
        boolean isOutboundDirection =
            ((Boolean)context.get(MessageContext.
            MESSAGE_OUTBOUND_PROPERTY)).booleanValue();

        if (!isOutboundDirection) {
            Iterator<AttachmentPart> attachments =
                context.getMessage().getAttachments();
            List<String> filePathList = new ArrayList<String>();

            while (attachments.hasNext()) {
                AttachmentPart attachment = attachments.next();
                File tempFile =
                    File.createTempFile(attachment.getContentId(),
                                        ".tmp");
                OutputStream out =
                    new BufferedOutputStream(new FileOutputStream(tempFile));
                out.write(attachment.getRawContentBytes());
                out.close();
                System.out.println("Saved attached file to: " +
                    tempFile.getAbsolutePath());
                filePathList.add(tempFile.getAbsolutePath());
            }

            context.put(FILE_LIST_KEY, filePathList);
            context.setScope(FILE_LIST_KEY, Scope.APPLICATION);
            context.getMessage().removeAllAttachments();
        }
    }
    catch (Exception e) {
        throw new ProtocolException(e);
    }
    return true;
}
```

The W3C DOM-based API includes a `getAttachments()` method that returns the list of files attached to the request. For the inbound direction, we remove all the attachments from the request and save their binary content to temporary files. The container passes the `handleMessage()` method a `SOAPMessageContext` object that we use to store the list of file names we will look up in the actual web service implementation. This works because we set the context scope to `APPLICATION`.

Listing 9-10 shows an excerpt from `PropertyChangeServiceImpl.java` that highlights the attachment-handling code in our web service implementation. We access the message context property containing the list of temporary file names and, for simplicity, just print the path and size of each file to standard out.

Listing 9-10: Example 7's PropertyChangeServiceImpl.java.

```
@Resource
private WebServiceContext context;
private final static String FILE_LIST_KEY = "AttachedFilePathList";


    ...
    List<String> filePathList =
     (List<String>)context.getMessageContext().get(FILE_LIST_KEY);

    for (String path : filePathList) {
        File file = new File(path);
        System.out.println("Using file attachment saved at '" +
                           file.getAbsolutePath() + "', size=" +
                           file.length());
    }
    ...
```

The handler chain and web service implementation share the message context. We use resource injection to get a reference to the message context by defining a member variable of type `WebServiceContext` and annotating it with `@Resource`. This message context object also provides access to HTTP protocol-specific request headers and the name and roles of the user who invoked the service, if any.

On the client side, we need to write a protocol handler to add the attachment to the outbound message. Listing 9-11 is an excerpt from `AddAttachmentSOAPHandler.java` that shows how the `handleMessage()` method uses the W3C DOM-based API to add the image's binary content to the request as an attachment.

Listing 9-11: Example 7's AddAttachmentSOAPHandler.java.

```
public boolean handleMessage(SOAPMessageContext context)
{
    try {
        boolean isOutboundDirection =
            ((Boolean)context.get(MessageContext.
            MESSAGE_OUTBOUND_PROPERTY)).booleanValue();

        if (isOutboundDirection) {
            AttachmentPart attachment =
                context.getMessage().createAttachmentPart();
            File file = new File("./hotel_picture.png");
```

```
        attachment.setRawContent(new BufferedInputStream(
            new FileInputStream(file)), "image/png");
        attachment.setContentId(file.getName());
        context.getMessage().addAttachmentPart(attachment);
        System.out.println("Handler added attached file '" +
                           file.getCanonicalPath() +
                           "', size=" + file.length());
      }
   }
   catch (Exception e) {
      throw new ProtocolException(e);
   }
   return true;
}
```

The API we use to access the SOAP message's content and its attachments was originally defined in Sun's SOAP with Attachments API for Java (SAAJ) specification. Today, many other parts of the JAX-WS specification use this API and it is part of Java SE 6. As a result, it's now pretty uncommon to refer to the ability to access attachments using the term SAAJ.

Sometimes, as developers we may be tempted to use the SOAP Message with Attachments approach as a workaround when really we would like the binary documents to actually be part of the SOAP body payload and be defined in a WSDL or schema as part of the XML structure. However, we may resort to using attachments to reduce the performance cost of encoding binary documents inside XML and to avoid the performance penalty of transmitting these expanded documents. WebLogic Server's Web Services container provides support for another web services standard called Message Transmission Optimization Mechanism (MTOM), which addresses these types of problems. MTOM defines a method for optimizing the transmission of XML data of type base64Binary and hexBinary in SOAP messages. Unlike attachments, the structure of the XML (also known as the XML infoset) within the SOAP messages stays the same. MTOM just optimizes the transmission of any binary data that we have in our messages. When MTOM is enabled, this binary data gets sent as a binary attachment saving time and space. If the transport protocol is HTTP, MIME attachments are used to carry that data while at the same time allowing both the consumer and the provider direct access to the XML data in the SOAP message without having to be aware that any MIME artifacts have been used. For larger binary data, at runtime WebLogic uses the XML-binary Optimized Packaging (XOP) optimization for transmitting this data. XOP is a mechanism that relies on compression for efficient transmission.

To use MTOM in our web services, annotate any base64Binary types we have defined in our WSDL or schema with a special attribute identifying the MIME type of the element, as shown in the following example.

```
<element name="image" type="base64Binary"
        xmime:expectedContentTypes="image/png"
        xmlns:xmime="http://www.w3.org/2005/05/xmlmime"/>
```

Then annotate our web service implementation class with @javax.xml.ws.soap.MTOM to tell WebLogic Server to use the MTOM/XOP optimization. In the service client code, we must tell the client container to use the MTOM feature, at the point in the consumer where we get a handle on the service stub, as shown in the following code excerpt.

```
import javax.xml.ws.soap.MTOMFeature;
....
PropertySearchService port =
    service.getPropertySearchServiceImplPort(new MTOMFeature());
```

Implementing Stateful Web Services

It is widely acknowledged as a best practice that web services are stateless. Ideally, each new SOAP request contains all required data, including any context information that relates to previous interactions. This helps a distributed system to maintain a loose coupling between service providers and service consumers. It is also easier to scale a system to support a large number of concurrent requests if the system does not need to maintain user state between requests.

WebLogic Server provides a mechanism that allows us to maintain session state between web service requests. For HTTP-based SOAP services, our web service implementation code runs in the context of WebLogic Server's Web Application container. The JAX-WS WebServiceContext object provides access to protocol-specific objects like HttpServletRequest and HttpSession. As a result, we can access and store state in the HttpSession in the same way a servlet does.

Listing 9-12 shows an excerpt of Example 8's PropertySearchServiceImpl.java that uses the HttpSession to maintain a counter that tracks how many times a specific client calls the service.

Listing 9-12: Example 8's PropertySearchServiceImpl.java.

```
@Resource
private WebServiceContext context;

...

HttpServletRequest servletRequest =
    (HttpServletRequest)context.getMessageContext().
    get(MessageContext.SERVLET_REQUEST);
HttpSession session = servletRequest.getSession(true);
Integer count = (Integer)session.getAttribute("CalledCount");

if (count == null) {
  count = 0;
}

session.setAttribute("CalledCount", ++count);
System.out.println(count);
```

WebLogic Server uses an HTTP cookie to track the HTTP session between each of our consumers and our provider. By calling getSession(true), we tell the web container to create a session, if one is not present. WebLogic Server adds a Set-Cookie HTTP header to the HTTP response whenever a request has an associated session. This cookie contains the session ID that uniquely identifies the specific user session, as shown here.

```
Set-Cookie: JSESSIONID=cCdnJKLDn0t2TLS2b1GHhcLr!90514; path=/
```

On the client-side, we need to tell our client that it is participating in a stateful interaction. When the client receives the Set-Cookie header, it must attach this cookie to all subsequent requests to enable the web service to associate it with the same HTTP session. By default, WebLogic Server Web Services clients ignore the Set-Cookie header, which prevents stateful interaction. Using the JAX-WS API to enable a special SESSION_MAINTAIN_PROPERTY property will force the WebLogic Server Web Services client container to accept and pass the Cookie header to the web service. Listing 9-13 contains an excerpt from PropertySearchClient.java that demonstrates how to set this property to support stateful interaction.

Listing 9-13: Example 8's PropertySearchClient.java.

```
PropertySearchService_Service service =
    new PropertySearchService_Service();
PropertySearchService port =
    service.getPropertySearchServiceImplPort();
Map<String, Object> rc =
    ((BindingProvider)port).getRequestContext();
rc.put(BindingProvider.SESSION_MAINTAIN_PROPERTY, Boolean.TRUE);
PropertyInfo property = null;
property = port.getPropertyDetailsByAddress(searchAddress);
property = port.getPropertyDetailsByAddress(searchAddress);
property = port.getPropertyDetailsByAddress(searchAddress);
```

Once the web service client stub receives the server's `Set-Cookie` header in response to the first call to `getPropertyDetailsByAddress()`, the stub transparently adds the session cookie to all subsequent calls to the same web service. We show an example of the `Set-Cookie` HTTP header that the client sets here.

```
Cookie: JSESSIONID=cCdnJKLDn0t2TLS2b1GHhcLr!90514
```

On the server side, the three property searches by the same client causes the HTTP session tracking code to increment the counter three times.

Because these stateful web services use normal HTTP sessions and session tracking, any SOAP clients that support HTTP cookies can use the stateful web service that we have hosted on WebLogic Server. If the SOAP client container does not directly support HTTP cookies, the client may still work provided the client has access to HTTP request and response headers. If this access is available, it should be possible for the client application to retrieve the `Set-Cookie` header from each SOAP response and to then add the `Cookie` header to the next SOAP request. Always get the `Set-Cookie` header from the last response to use with the next request because WebLogic Server supports HTTP session replication and failover. If failover occurs, the session ID for a particular session will change. Using the old session ID after a failover happens will cause you to lose your state.

It is worth noting that the WS-I Basic Profile mentions that SOAP over HTTP implementations can support the use of HTTP cookies, but it is not mandated.

Implementing Asynchronous Web Services

Not all web service requirements map neatly onto the typical synchronous request and response pattern. There are other types of usage patterns that we may require that are much more asynchronous in nature. WebLogic Server supports several of these asynchronous patterns. See Example 9 for working samples of these patterns.

Calling Web Services Asynchronously

Typical web service clients call a web service and block waiting for the response. Sometimes, it is useful to allow the client to do other work while waiting for the response. WebLogic Server–generated client stubs not only provide an `invoke()` method (for example, `getPropertyDetailsById(id)`) but also provide two `invokeAsync()` methods (for example, `getPropertyDetailsById Async(id)` and `getPropertyDetailsById Async(id, handler)`). The first returns an object reference that we poll to determine when the response returns and extract it. The second uses a callback mechanism that invokes our specified callback method when the SOAP response comes back. With both methods, the web service on the server side still acts in a synchronous manner and is unaware that the client is using its operations in an asynchronous fashion.

The stub's `invokeAsync()` methods are not generated by default. To generate these, we add a `binding` element to our `clientgen` Ant task, as shown in this example.

```
<clientgen
     wsdl="http://localhost:7001/PropertySearchService_WSDLFirst/
PropertySearchService?wsdl"
     destDir="stubcode"
     packageName="com.bigrez.ws.property"
     classpathref="${app.classpath}"
     type="JAXWS">
  <binding file="jaxws-binding.xml"/>
</clientgen>
```

The content of the binding XML file tells WebLogic Server's `clientgen` Ant task that our service supports the asynchronous model, as shown here.

```
<bindings wsdlLocation="PropertySearchService.wsdl" .....>
  <bindings node="wsdl:definitions">
    <package name="com.bigrez.ws.property"/>
    <enableAsyncMapping>true</enableAsyncMapping>
  </bindings>
</bindings>
```

When using the dynamic `Dispatch` interface, rather than a generated stub, the two asynchronous invocation methods are provided by default, named `invokeAsync()`.

Creating One-Way Web Services

JAX-WS provides a `@OneWay` annotation to mark a web service method in the JWS class as being a one-way operation. This tells the container that the client does not need to wait for a response and that if the client expects an empty response the container can return an empty response immediately without waiting for the web service to finish processing the request. In practice, WebLogic Server returns an HTTP 202 Accepted status to the client as soon as the request stream has been consumed. This allows the client to fairly quickly continue processing its other work but the caller will block until the response is received. We can further help the client by using one of the client-side `invokeAsync()` methods to invoke the one-way operations to enable the application to fully achieve one-way, asynchronous messaging.

Returning Multiple Asynchronous Responses

When a client calls a web service, the web service may not need to send a response back for some requests. For others, it may need to send back multiple responses at different times, such as when implementing a subscribe-notify usage pattern. To implement such a pattern, we use a one-way web service operation to initiate the interaction. Optionally, the client code can also use one of the `invokeAsync()` methods to call the web service to prevent blocking to wait on the HTTP 202 Accepted response.

If and when our web service needs to send one or more responses back to the client, it needs to know the web service endpoint to call back to the originating client application. To determine the URL of this location, the original SOAP request must supply its specific callback endpoint URL. Typically we use WebLogic Server's WS-Addressing support to pass this callback URL.

The best way for the client to provide its callback URL is to actually pass the callback URL as part of the normal SOAP body payload data. To support this mechanism, WS-Addressing defines a schema type called an Endpoint Reference (EPR) to use in WSDL and schemas for a web service. WebLogic Server understands how to convert between this EPR XML type and a special JAX-WS data type called `W3CEndpointReference`. As a result, our web service operations will receive the correct callback URL in a special Java type parameter passed to the operations.

Listing 9-14 shows the outline of an example SEI implementation for a web service that can be invoked by a client to register for callback events, whenever the details for a given property changes. This service uses the EPR-typed argument as an operation parameter in addition to a normal data parameter. The service can then use the URL it receives, for invoking the callback service. This example code is hard-coded to just send two updates about the property with a short sleep between the two callback notifications.

Listing 9-14: Example 9's PropertyUpdateRegister.java Notifier Service.

```java
@WebService
public class PropertyUpdateRegister
{
    public boolean registerInterest(int propId,
                            W3CEndpointReference callbackReference)
    {
        PropertyUpdateReceiver_Service service =
            new PropertyUpdateReceiver_Service();
        PropertyUpdateReceiver port =
            service.getPort(callbackReference, PropertyUpdateReceiver.class);
        port.receiveUpdate(propId, "Closed for re-furbishment");
        try {
            Thread.sleep(200);
        }
        catch (InterruptedException e) {
        }
        port.receiveUpdate(propId, "Now fully furninshed");
        return true;
    }
}
```

In order for this to work, the two parties (that is, the subscriber client and the notifier service) need to agree on a common shape for the callback web service. This is the service that the subscriber will implement and the notifier will invoke each time a property's details change. This can be achieved by agreeing on an abstract WSDL to define the shape of the callback web service. The abstract WSDL contains a dummy endpoint URL, because the actual URL will be provided dynamically at runtime.

In addition to hosting a callback web service, the client application also needs to construct an EPR to represent the endpoint URL of its callback service. Listing 9-15 shows an example of how our subscribing client application generates an EPR Java type from a URL and then passes this to the notifier service.

Listing 9-15: Example 9's PropertySubscribeClient.java Subcriber Client.

```
// Get ref to local 'callback' web service for receiving replies
QName callbackPortName =
    new Qname("MyCallbackNmspc", "PropertyUpdateReceiverPort");
Service callbackService =
    Service.create(new URL("http://localhost:7001/MyCallBackSrvc"),
                   new QName("MyCallbackNmspc", "MyCallBackSrvc"));
Dispatch<Source> callbackDispatcher =
    callbackService.createDispatch(callbackPortName, Source.class,
                                   Service.Mode.PAYLOAD);
W3CEndpointReference callbackEndpointRef =
    callbackDispatcher.getEndpointReference(
    W3CEndpointReference.class);

// Call notifier service with address of callback service
PropertyUpdateRegister_Service service =
    new PropertyUpdateRegister_Service();
PropertyUpdateRegister port =
    service.getPropertyUpdateRegisterPort();
port.registerInterest(1, callbackEndpointRef);
```

Customizing Mappings between Java and XML

JAX-WS relies on the JAXB specification to map between XML schema types and Java types. Even though JAX-WS supplements JAXB by defining how certain WSDL-specific artifacts map to and from Java, it still uses the JAXB data-binding rules even for these cases.

JAXB provides default XML to Java mapping rules for practically all XML schema types. For mapping Java to XML, JAXB has default mapping rules for a large set of built-in Java types. It also supports many custom types, especially if the custom types follow a JavaBean-style approach by supplying a *no-args* constructor, property getters and setters, and strongly-typed arrays or collection classes for child objects.

In practice, it is very rare to have a problem when converting XML schemas to Java when relying on the default mapping rules. For Java to XML, following the JavaBean-style approach will minimize possible problems in generating the XML schemas.

Best Practice

When using a code-first approach, data POJOs should be seen as lightweight data containers that do not contain behavior or business logic. Following this advice will make it easy to adopt a JavaBeans-style implementation approach to help avoid potential Java-to-XML mapping issues.

If we do have problems or want to override the mapping behavior, we can use JAXB customization declarations in one of the following two ways:

Customizing Java-to-XML Mappings Define JAXB annotations like @XmlElement and @XmlType in the data POJOs and the service implementation class to influence the names and other aspects of the XML elements and complex types in the generated XML schemas and WSDL.

Customizing XML-to-Java Mappings   Embed JAXB *binding declarations* directly inside the WSDL and schema files. The WSDL declarations control features such as the wrapper style and the generated method parameter names for operations. The XML schema declarations control the generated structure and content of the JAXB generated classes for the data POJOs. Alternatively, an external JAXB *binding declarations* file can specify these features and then be associated with the generated web service by adding a <binding> child element to WebLogic Server's wsdlc and clientgen Ant tasks.

We show how we can use the JAXB @XmlElement annotation to customize the name of the description XML element, which will be generated for the PropertyInfo data POJO. The resulting XML element in SOAP responses will now be named FullDescription instead of description.

```
@XmlAccessorType(XmlAccessType.FIELD)
public class PropertyInfo
{
    private int id;
    @XmlElement(name = "FullDescription")
    private String description;
    private String features;

    ...
    // All the other property members variables
    //  plus all the property getters and setters
    ...
}
```

We also needed to add the annotation @XmlAccessorType for this class to ensure that every non-static, non-transient field in the Java class is automatically bound to XML by the JAXB compiler. When no JAXB annotations are defined in the class, this is the default behavior.

The following XML fragment shows how we can add a declaration to the PostalCode element of the XML schema for the web service to change what is generated in the PropertyInfo data POJO class. Here we add a JAXB property annotation to instruct the JAXB compiler to generate a data POJO with a property called zipCode instead of postalCode plus the associated getZipCode() and setZipCode() accessor methods.

```
<element name="PostalCode" type="tns:PostalCode">
  <annotation>
    <appinfo>
      <jaxb:property name="ZipCode"/>
    </appinfo>
  </annotation>
</element>
```

JAXB also provides additional control for marshalling and un-marshalling of awkward Java classes or XML fragments. We create JAXB adapter classes to dictate exactly how to convert a specific section of XML content to a Java class and vice versa. This is useful if, for example, we have a Java class without a *no-args* constructor and we cannot change the source code. Our adapter class must implement javax.xml.bind.annotation.adapters.XmlAdapter and provide a method called marshal() to convert a Java type into an XML representation and a method called unmarshal() to convert from XML back to Java.

Using Web Services Security

WebLogic Server provides a wealth of security-related features and capabilities to help secure web services and their clients. These features include various authentication mechanisms, declarative and programmatic access control, message confidentiality, message integrity, auditing, and identity propagation. WebLogic Server's Web Services container integrates directly with WebLogic Server's Security Service. This means that web services leverage the WebLogic Server domain's security providers. We discuss WebLogic Server's Security Service in detail in Chapter 11.

The two primary mechanisms to secure web services are:

Transport-Level Security Transport-level security refers to securing the connection between a client and a web service, which relies heavily on the underlying transport protocol's standard security mechanisms. For example, SOAP can use HTTPS instead of HTTP to secure the underlying network connection with SSL. SSL provides both confidentiality and integrity. HTTP and HTTPS provide support for HTTP basic authentication that gives you simple username/password-based authentication. By configuring two-way SSL, WebLogic Server also supports client certificate-based authentication.

Message-Level Security Message-level security refers to securing some or all of the message content, which relies on the WS-Security specification. WS-Security provides support for encrypting and/or signing part or all of a message. It also provides authentication using token-based credentials. In addition to WS-Security, WebLogic Server also supports the WS-SecureConversation standard to enable a secure session to be established between two trusted parties to facilitate the exchange of multiple messages in a stateful and secure manner.

The main benefit of transport-level security is that it relies on very mature and widely adopted standards and protocols that virtually every web services container supports. Message-level security standards are maturing but not yet as widely and uniformly adopted by web service technologies; this often leads to interoperability problems.

Message-level security provides many more mix-and-match security options than transport-level security and enables encrypting and signing only parts of a message. This is advantageous in more complex web service environments where there may be one or more web service intermediaries, like an Enterprise Service Bus (ESB), between web service clients and providers. For example, a client might encrypt and sign sensitive personal information within the message using the service provider's public key. Because decrypting the information requires the provider's private key, the client knows that its sensitive data is safe regardless of what intermediaries exist or what they do with the message. Whether or not a client is encrypting part of a message, a client might want to ensure some part of the SOAP message body is not modified along the way to the web service provider. WS-Security provides the client with a means to sign a portion of the message, leaving other parts unsigned so that intermediaries are free to modify them.

When using a transport-level security mechanism like SSL, intermediaries typically must terminate the SSL connection, which forces the decryption of the data at it enters the intermediary. Even if the intermediary forwards the message over SSL to the provider, neither the client sending the message nor the web service provider receiving it knows what happened to the data along the way. An intermediary might modify the data or log the message, potentially exposing credit card numbers or other personal information. As you can see, transport-level security is not sufficient for ensuring end-to-end data security when there are intermediaries in the path of the web service flow.

Finally, message-level security provides potential performance benefits as well. By only encrypting the sensitive information but not the entire SOAP envelope, an intermediary can pass messages through without decrypting and re-encrypting the message. Intermediaries are free to use and modify parts of the message to perform their task, such as routing a message to different providers based on location data in the message or adding a security token in a SOAP header.

WebLogic Server supports combining transport- and message-level security to protect a web service. For example, we may want to use one-way SSL to provide confidentiality and integrity but use a WS-Security password digest authentication token to authenticate.

Defining Security Policies

With the introduction of the WS-Security standards for implementing message-level security, there needs to be a way for us to define what type of security policies we want to apply to our web services. As a result, two related standards were introduced at the same time as WS-Security to enable us to define our WS-Security-related policy rules in an XML format. These standards are WS-Policy and WS-SecurityPolicy.

WS-Policy enables web services to express their constraints and requirements in XML that conforms to the WS-Policy schema. WS-SecurityPolicy is an extension of WS-Policy that defines a set of security policy assertions for describing web service messages security. WebLogic Server takes WS-Policy and WS-SecurityPolicy a step further by not just using it to define message-level security policies, but also to define the security policies when using transport-level security.

To define how we want to secure our web service's operations, we include WS-Policy declarations either within our WSDL or in a separate XML file, which is referenced by our WSDL. These WSDL WS-Policy declarations are used in two ways. First, it tells WebLogic Server's Security Service how to enforce protection of our web service. Second, it tells potential clients exactly how they should invoke our web service with the relevant security elements. Using WS-Policy in our WSDL gives us a declarative security enforcement mechanism rather than a programmatic one. Even with a code-first approach, little extra coding is required. All we need to do is add a security policy annotation to our JWS class's public methods to define how WebLogic Server should secure these operations. An example of this policy annotation is shown here.

```
@Policy(uri="../policies/MyPolicy.xml")
```

The `@Policy` annotation's `uri` attribute specifies the path of the WS-SecurityPolicy file. As with other annotations that reference files, the path is relative to the location of the JWS class. WebLogic Server's Web Services container will automatically include the policy in the generated WSDL.

The WS-Policy specification is extremely flexible; but it is also verbose and therefore hard to get right. Fortunately, there is a common set of use cases for web services security and as a result WebLogic Server provides a large set of predefined, prepackaged policy files. These prepackaged policy files reflect many of the common use cases and therefore, their interoperability with other web service vendors has been tested. For the full list of predefined policy files, see Link 9-4. To reference one of these WebLogic Server–provided policy files, we prefix the `@Policy` annotation's `uri` attribute value with `policy:`, as shown here.

```
@Policy(uri="policy:Wssp1.2-Wss1.1-X509-EncryptRequest-SignResponse.xml")
```

Best Practice

Whenever possible, use the WebLogic Server prepackaged policy files. You can avoid errors and take advantage of WebLogic Server optimizations by using these predefined policies. In addition, these prepackaged policy files tend to reflect common use cases that have been tested with other web service vendors for interoperability.

WebLogic Server also allows us to associate one or more security policy files with a web service after it is deployed. Using the WebLogic Console, navigate to the web service deployment's WS-Policy Configuration tab to associate a WS-Policy file with the web service. Note that this only works for web services that do not already have compile-time WS-Policy file associations.

Transport-level Security

To authenticate a client using HTTP basic authentication, we must base 64 encode the username and password before transmission. The following example SOAP request HTTP header shows an encoded username and password in a header called Authorization.

```
POST /PropertySearchService/PropertySearchService HTTP/1.1
Authorization: Basic d2VibG9naW5hWM6d2VibG9naW5hWM=
SOAPAction:"http://www.wrox.com/professional-weblogic/PropertySearchService
/GetByAddress"
Content-Type: text/xml;charset="utf-8"
Host: 127.0.0.1:7001
Content-Length: 464
```

Example 10 demonstrates how to provide a username and password to a web service client, an excerpt of which is shown here.

```
PropertySearchService_Service service = new PropertySearchService_Service();
PropertySearchService port = service.getPropertySearchServiceImplPort();
Map<String, Object> rc = ((BindingProvider)port).getRequestContext();
rc.put(BindingProvider.USERNAME_PROPERTY, "weblogic");
rc.put(BindingProvider.PASSWORD_PROPERTY, "weblogic1");
PropertyInfo property = port.getPropertyDetailsByAddress(searchAddress);
```

The JAX-WS BindingProvider class contains username and password properties that we set to specify the user's credentials. The underlying web service stub takes care of base 64 encoding these credentials and including them in the HTTP headers of the SOAP request.

On the server-side, we just need to add an access control rule to the web service that limits access to a particular set of users or roles. We don't need to make any server-side code changes.

We can use SSL (SOAP/HTTPS) to provide a secure transport for web services. For one-way SSL, we need to make the following changes to our HTTP basic authentication example:

1. Configure the WebLogic Server domain to support SSL, listening on an appropriate port (for example, 7002).

2. Add a `@weblogic.jws.Policy` annotation to the service implementation class to specify that both one-way SSL and HTTP basic authentication are required. When deployed, WebLogic Server checks that there is an available HTTPS channel. Whenever WebLogic Server receives a request for the WSDL, it will set the protocol, address, and port of the WSDL's endpoint URL to `https` and the listen address and port of the HTTPS channel. The additional policy file annotation that we need to add to the service implementation class is shown here.

```
@Policy(uri="policy:Wssp1.2-2007-Https-BasicAuth.xml")
public class PropertySearchService
{
    ...
}
```

3. When running the Java web service client application, include a system property in the JVM start-up command line to specify the path of a trust keystore. This trust keystore must include a Certificate Authority certificate, which must match the signer of the certificate that the server will present. An example of the JVM system properties to reference WebLogic Server's Demo Trust store is shown here.

```
-Djavax.net.ssl.trustStore=/oracle/middleware/wlserver_10.3/server/lib/DemoTrust.jks
-Djavax.net.ssl.trustStorePassword=DemoTrustKeyStorePassPhrase
```

Chapter 11 describes in greater detail the primary tasks involved in configuring WebLogic Server SSL with the appropriate private keys and X.509 certificates on both the server and the client.

WebLogic Server also provides a pre-built policy file to enforce the use of two-way SSL using a client presented certificate for authentication, rather than using HTTP basic authentication. To enable this, we need to make the following changes to our previous example:

1. Further configure the WebLogic Server domain's SSL settings. Set the `Two Way Client Cert Behavior` field to the value `Client Certs Requested And Enforced`.

2. For the domain's security realm, configure the `DefaultIdentityAsserter` provider to support certificate-based identity assertion, by adding `X.509` as an active type and setting the `Default User Name Mapper Attribute Type` field to the value `CN`. We will use the CN part of a certificate to match to a WebLogic Server username.

3. Change the `@weblogic.jws.Policy` specified in our JWS class to use a different predefined policy file:

```
@Policy(uri="policy:Wssp1.2-2007-Https-ClientCertReq.xml")
```

4. In the `web.xml` deployment descriptor for the web service, set the value of the `<auth-method>` to `CLIENT-CERT` to tell the web container to use certificate-based authentication.

5. Create the service client's identity keystore containing its private key and X.509 certificate. Make sure that the CN for the certificate includes the WebLogic Server username. Chapter 11 describes this process in detail. For this example, we use WebLogic Server's CertGen and ImportPrivateKey utilities; this means that the client's X.509 certificate will be signed by WebLogic Server's Demo Certificate Authority.

6. Add the client certificate's CA certificate to the server's trust store, if needed. Because we use the demo CA and the demo trust keystore on the server, we can skip this step.

7. When running the service client Java application, include the following system properties in the JVM start-up command line to specify the path of the demo trust keystore, the password for the demo trust store, the path for our new identity keystore, and the password for the identity keystore, as shown here.

```
-Djavax.net.ssl.trustStore=/oracle/middleware/wlserver_10.3/server/lib/DemoTrust.jks
-Djavax.net.ssl.trustStorePassword=DemoTrustKeyStorePassPhrase
-Djavax.net.ssl.keyStore=/home/myuser/ClientIdentity.jks
-Djavax.net.ssl.keyStorePassword=mypassword
```

The Java SE SSL package used for client-side SSL support does not provide Java system properties to specify the client identity store's private key passphrase or key pair alias that the client should use as its identity. This lack of Java system properties effectively requires that the passphrase for private key be the same as the password for the keystore that contains the key for Java SE-based 2-way SSL web service clients. It also means that the client keystore can include only one private key and X.509 certificate pair to enable the Java runtime to locate the required key pair.

Message-level Security

WS-Security covers three main security capabilities, which we can use in isolation or in combination:

1. Authentication

2. Confidentiality

3. Integrity

WebLogic Server Web Services container supports three different authentication token types: Username, X.509, and SAML. The username token can be in one of two formats. The first format places both the username and password in clear text in the SOAP header. The second replaces the clear text password with a *password digest*, which is a cryptographic hash generated by combining the password, a *nonce* (a randomly generated *number used once*), and a timestamp. On receiving a password digest, WebLogic Server determines whether the password digest is correct for the given nonce and timestamp. WebLogic Server also remembers the nonces that it receives to prevent a password digest from being used more than once. This helps to prevent replay attacks.

We will now look at a simple example that uses WS-Security to authenticate with a username and password. Example 11 uses our code-first property search web service and adds username token-based WS-Security authentication. This example is similar to the HTTP basic authentication example from Example 10, except in this case we pass the credentials in the SOAP header instead of the HTTP header. Doing this removes the dependencies on the HTTP protocol thus enabling its use with other SOAP transport protocols. The following example SOAP request shows how the client request passes the Username and Password elements in the SOAP header.

```
<Envelope xmlns:S="http://schemas.xmlsoap.org/soap/envelope/">i
  <Header>
    <wsse:Security xmlns:wsse="http://docs.oasis-open.org/wss/2004/01/oasis-200401-
wss-wssecurity-secext-1.0.xsd">
```

```
      <wsse:UsernameToken>
        <wsse:Username>weblogic</wsse:Username>
        <wsse:Password Type="http://docs.oasis-open.org/wss/2004/01/oasis-200401-
wss-username-token-profile-1.0#PasswordText">weblogic1</wsse:Password>
      </wsse:UsernameToken>
    </wsse:Security>
    ...
  </Header>
  <Body>
    ...
  </Body>
</Envelope>
```

In our JWS class that implements the web service we just add a reference to our WS-Security policy file using the @Policy annotation, as shown here.

```
@WebMethod
@Policy(uri="UsernameTokenPolicy.xml", direction=Policy.Direction.inbound)
public PropertyInfo getPropertyDetailsByAddress(PropertySearchAddress searchAddress)
{
    ...
}
```

The annotation also defines the direction to which we want to apply the policy file, in this case for SOAP requests only. WebLogic Server does not provide a predefined policy file that uses a username token. This is because it can introduce a security risk as the password is transmitted in clear-text and is not supported by some other common web services technologies like .NET. Nevertheless, it is a requirement that is sometimes needed and serves as a good example to show how we can create our own custom policy file, as shown in Listing 9-16.

Listing 9-16: Example 11's Custom Username Token WS-Policy file.

```
<wsp:Policy xmlns:wsp="http://www.w3.org/ns/ws-policy"
            xmlns:sp="http://docs.oasis-open.org/ws-sx/ws-
securitypolicy/200702">
  <sp:SupportingTokens>
    <wsp:Policy>
      <sp:UsernameToken
          sp:IncludeToken="http://docs.oasis-open.org/ws-sx/ws-
securitypolicy/200702/IncludeToken/AlwaysToRecipient"/>
    </wsp:Policy>
  </sp:SupportingTokens>
</wsp:Policy>
```

Now, we use the jwsc Ant task to generate the deployable web service WAR. When we access the WSDL for the deployed web service, we see that the generated WSDL contains the policy-related XML elements inline. Our WSDL also contains the policy statement <wsp:UsingPolicy Required="true"/> to indicate to potential service clients that the use of the WS-Security policy is mandatory.

On the client-side, we need to add code to specify the WS-Security-related username and password, as shown here. Note that we have to use the WebLogic Server–specific weblogic.xml.crypto.wss.

provider.CredentialProvider and weblogic.wsee.security.unt.ClientUNTCredentialProvider classes because JAX-WS does not provide a standard way to set these credentials.

```
import weblogic.wsse.security.unt.ClientUNTCredentialProvider;
import weblogic.xml.crypto.wss.provider.CredentialProvider;
...
PropertySearchService port = service.getPropertySearchServicePort();
List<CredentialProvider> credProviders = new ArrayList<CredentialProvider>();
CredentialProvider cp =
    new ClientUNTCredentialProvider("weblogic".getBytes(),
                                    "weblogic".getBytes());
credProviders.add(cp);
Map<String, Object> rc = ((BindingProvider)port).getRequestContext();
rc.put(WSSecurityContext.CREDENTIAL_PROVIDER_LIST, credProviders);
PropertyInfo property = port.getPropertyDetailsByAddress(searchAddress);
```

Next, let's look at a more secure WS-Security example that uses a predefined WebLogic Server security policy to enforce that the SOAP body of our request and response is signed and encrypted and define that the service consumer and provider should provide certificates to each other, for authentication. Example 12 uses the same code-first property search web service. In this example we declare a @Policy annotation on the web service as a whole, as shown here. We reference the WebLogic Server–provided Wssp1.2-2007-Wss1.1-X509-Basic256.xml policy file that requires mutual authentication between the service consumer and provider using X.509 certificates.

```
@WebService
@Policy(uri="policy:Wssp1.2-2007-Wss1.1-X509-Basic256.xml")
public class PropertySearchService
{
    @WebMethod
    @Policies({
        @Policy(uri="policy:Wssp1.2-2007-SignBody.xml",
                direction=Policy.Direction.both),
        @Policy(uri="policy:Wssp1.2-2007-EncryptBody.xml",
                direction=Policy.Direction.both)
    })
    public PropertyInfo getPropertyByAddress(PropertySearchAddress searchAddress)
        throws PropertyInfoFaultException
    {
        ...
    }
}
```

WebLogic Server also provides some pre-built protection assertion policies that identify which part of a message's content to protect. These policies only work in conjunction with an X.509 token policy. We use two @Policy annotations for each operation: Wssp1.2-2007-SignBody.xml and Wssp1.2-2007-EncryptBody.xml. These policies indicate that we want to encrypt and sign the whole SOAP body for both the request and response.

Before we can deploy this web service and create the client, we must do the following things:

1. Configure the WebLogic Server domain to support SSL, listening on an appropriate port (for example, 7002).

2. Configure the security realm's `DefaultIdentityAsserter` provider to support certificate-based identity assertion by adding `X.509` as an active type and setting the `Default User Name Mapper Attribute Type` field to the value `CN`. We will use the CN part of a certificate to match to a WebLogic Server username.

3. Create two identity keystores containing the private key and X.509 certificate, one for the server and one for the client.

4. Create or locate two trust keystores, one for the server and one for the client, containing the other's CA certificate. For our example, we will use the demo trust keystore.

Because Chapter 11 covers obtaining, installing, and using X.509 certificates with WebLogic Server and Java clients, we will not discuss the details here. Please refer to the `README.txt` file with Example 12 for details about the steps you need to perform to generate and configure the public and private keys, associated X.509 certificates, and keystores for this example. To simplify the setup, the common name (cn) for the X.509 certificate we will use is set to `weblogic` so that the X.509 identity asserter can map the certificate to the WebLogic Server user named `weblogic` that already exists in the WebLogic Server domain's embedded LDAP directory.

On the client-side, for our standalone Java application, we must add additional Java code, using WebLogic Server–specific APIs, to declare what keys and certificates to use when invoking the secured web service, as shown in Listing 9-17.

Listing 9-17: Example 12's Web Service Client Certificate Handling Code.

```
private final static String KEYSTORE_TYPE = "JKS";
private final static String CLIENT_KEYSTORE_PATH =
    "./ClientIdentity.jks";
private final static String CLIENT_KEYSTORE_PASSWD =
    "ClientStorePass";
private final static String CLIENT_KEY_ALIAS = "clientcert";
private final static String CLIENT_KEY_PASSWD = "ClientKeyPass";
private final static String SERVERCERT_KEY_ALIAS = "servercert";
private final static String TRUST_KEYSTORE_PATH =
    "/opt/middleware/wlserver_10.3/server/lib/DemoTrust.jks";
private final static String TRUST_KEYSTORE_PASSWD =
    "DemoTrustKeyStorePassPhrase";
private final static String RSA_AUTH_TYPE = "RSA";

...

// Get web service stub handle
//
PropertySearchService_Service service =
    new PropertySearchService_Service();
PropertySearchService port =
    service.getPropertySearchServicePort();
Map<String, Object> rc =
    ((BindingProvider)port).getRequestContext();

// Load the server certificate from local keystore
//
```

Continued

Listing 9-17: Example 12's Web Service Client Certificate Handling Code. *(continued)*

```
KeyStore keyStore = KeyStore.getInstance(KEYSTORE_TYPE);
keyStore.load(new FileInputStream(new File(CLIENT_KEYSTORE_PATH)),
    CLIENT_KEYSTORE_PASSWD.toCharArray());
X509Certificate serverCert = (X509Certificate)
    keyStore.getCertificate(SERVERCERT_KEY_ALIAS);
serverCert.checkValidity();

// Set-up credential provider using client key and server cert
//
List<CredentialProvider> credProviders =
    new ArrayList<CredentialProvider>();
CredentialProvider bstCP = new ClientBSTCredentialProvider(
    CLIENT_KEYSTORE_PATH, CLIENT_KEYSTORE_PASSWD, CLIENT_KEY_ALIAS,
    CLIENT_KEY_PASSWD, KEYSTORE_TYPE, serverCert);
credProviders.add(bstCP);
rc.put(WSSecurityContext.CREDENTIAL_PROVIDER_LIST, credProviders);

// Create Trust Manager to check certs against Trust Keystore
//
KeyStore trustStore = KeyStore.getInstance(KEYSTORE_TYPE);
trustStore.load(new FileInputStream(new File(
    TRUST_KEYSTORE_PATH)), TRUST_KEYSTORE_PASSWD.toCharArray());
TrustManagerFactory tmf = TrustManagerFactory.getInstance(
    TrustManagerFactory.getDefaultAlgorithm());
tmf.init(trustStore);
final X509TrustManager tm =
    (X509TrustManager)tmf.getTrustManagers()[0];
rc.put(WSSecurityContext.TRUST_MANAGER, new TrustManager() {
    public boolean certificateCallback(X509Certificate[] chain,
                                       int validateErr)
    {
        try {
            tm.checkServerTrusted(chain, RSA_AUTH_TYPE);
        }
        catch (CertificateException e) {
            return false;
        }
        return true;
    }
});

// Invoke web service
//
PropertyInfo property =
    port.getPropertyDetailsByAddress(searchAddress);

...
```

Our code loads and validates the server certificate from the local client keystore, which it uses to encrypt the SOAP request's body and validate the server's signed response. We use WebLogic Server's CredentialProvider class to create our Binary Security Token (BST) provider based on the client's private key and certificate from the client's keystore (`ClientIdentity.jks`). The provider uses the client's private key to sign the request and decrypt the response. The client's certificate will also automatically be transmitted in the SOAP request header so that the server can decide if it trusts the client, use it to verify the request's signature, and encrypt the response. Table 9-2 shows which keys are used by the client and server for each action.

Table 9-2: Message Encryption and Signing Public/Private Key Usage

Action	Key Used by Client	Key Used by Server
Client sends encrypted message to the server	Server's public key used to encrypt	Server's private key used to decrypt
Client signs message to send to the server	Client's private key used to sign	Client's public key used to verify signature
Server returns encrypted response to the client	Client's private key used to decrypt	Client's public key used to encrypt
Server signs response message to return to the client	Server's public key used to verify signature	Server's private key used to sign

We create a `TrustManager` class to provide a callback method that allows us to check the client and server certificates that we receive, using our client's demo trust keystore, to assert that we trust the X.509 certificates.

If we run our web service consumer inside of WebLogic Server, instead of using WebLogic Server's client container, we do not need to add any of the security-related code in Listing 9-17. Instead, we simply configure a WebLogic Server PKI Credential Mapper to perform these actions for us. WebLogic Server Credential Mappers are covered in detail in Chapter 11. By configuring the PKI Credential Mapper, when the web service consumer attempts to call the remote web service, WebLogic Server's Web Services container transparently asks the WebLogic Server Security Service for the relevant private key and certificate associated with the endpoint of the web service being invoked. If they exist, the web services container automatically uses these credentials to fulfill the required security policy.

To enable credential mapping for the web service consumer running in WebLogic, we must do the following things:

1. Import the service provider's certificate into the consumer's keystore using the Java `keytool` utility.

2. Create a new PKICredentialMapper and configure the provider settings to reference the consumer's keystore.

3. Add a new PKI Security Credential Mapping referencing the consumer's private key in the keystore.

4. Add a new PKI Security Credential Mapping referencing the service provider's certificate that we just imported into the keystore.

Figure 9-6 shows the WebLogic Console being used to define the PKI credential mappings for our client key pair and server certificate.

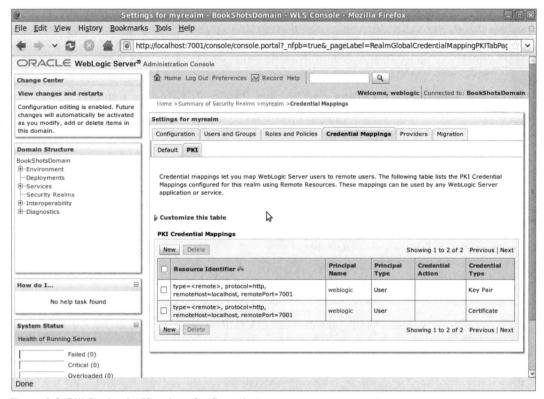

Figure 9-6: PKI Credential Mappings Configuration.

As you can see, you get a lot of benefit from running your web service consumer application inside WebLogic Server. WebLogic Server's Security Service does a lot of the security-related heavy-lifting for you and helps you avoid polluting your code with what really should be configuration settings.

Web Service Security Configuration

As we have seen, we can implement many common web service security use cases using WebLogic Server's default security configuration, private key, and certificate. This is because WebLogic Server has sensible defaults. However, certain security-related use cases require additional information to allow WebLogic Server to determine exactly how it should fulfill the web services' security policies. Some examples of these use cases that require additional information are:

❑ Using a password digest in SOAP messages

❑ Specifying a different key pair used to sign SOAP messages

❑ Specify a different key pair used to encrypt SOAP messages

We specify these optional web service–related security settings at the domain-level by creating a new Web Service Security Configuration. We can create a Web Service Security Configurations using the WebLogic Console, WLST, or JMX. Once we create this new configuration, we associate it with our web services using the `@weblogic.jws.security.WssConfiguration` annotation in our service provider implementation class. Alternatively, if we want the server to use a custom configuration as its default for all deployed web services, we simply create a security configuration with the name `default_wss`.

For our encrypted, signed, and mutual-certificate authenticated web service from Example 12, what if we needed to use a different server private key and certificate rather than using the server's default identity private key and certificate? To achieve this, we would create a new `Web Services Security Configuration` and apply it to our web service, or set it as the default for all web services. Rather than manually configuring this using the WebLogic Console, we can use a WLST script that ships as part of the standard set of WebLogic Server example projects. The WebLogic Server installation provides an *online* WLST script called `configWss.py` that performs the following actions:

❑ Creates the `Web Services Security Configuration` object called `default_wss`, if not already present

❑ Creates a new x.509 credential provider in `default_wss`

❑ In the new x.509 credential provider, defines a custom keystore for XML encryption and for XML digital signatures (in this case, both will use the `ServerIdentity.jks` file that we created)

We can run this WLST script with the following command-line arguments:

```
% java weblogic.WLST
$WL_HOME/samples/server/examples/src/examples/webservices/wss1.1/co
nfigWss.py weblogic weblogic1 localhost 7001
$DOMAIN_HOME/ServerIdentity.jks ServerStorePass servercert
ServerKeyPass
```

After restarting the server to allow the changes to take effect, the next time we run our protected web service it will use the key and certificate from the web service–specific custom identity keystore rather than the one associated with the server's SSL configuration.

Adding Web Services to `bigrez.com`

We finish this chapter by creating a new example BigRez property search web service that integrates with the `bigrez.com` application by using the PropertyServices EJB from Chapter 6. We package the web service in its own web service WAR file and bundle it into the existing BigRez EAR. We use a WSDL-first approach to build the BigRez property search service. The WSDL and XML schema are almost identical to the ones that we have used throughout this chapter with only two minor differences. First, the unique property ID is a string in `bigrez.com`, rather than an integer. Second, the operation to find a property by address returns a list of matched properties rather than just one property.

The process we use for generating the Java SEI interface and the data POJOs is exactly the same as the WSDL-first approach described throughout this chapter. The main difference this time is in the actual code we use to implement the web service. We use the `PropertyServices` stateless session bean, which contains the core business logic. This EJB uses JPA to query the database to find the matching properties. We also use an `@EJB` annotation in our JWS class to have WebLogic Server automatically inject an instance of this EJB for us. Listing 9-18 shows our new JWS class.

Listing 9-18: bigrez.com PropertySearchServiceImpl.java.

```java
@WebService(
    serviceName="PropertySearchService",
    targetNamespace="http://www.wrox.com/professional-weblogic/
PropertySearchService",
    endpointInterface="com.bigrez.ws.property.PropertySearch
Service"
)
public class PropertySearchServiceImpl
    implements PropertySearchService
{
    @EJB
    private PropertyServices propertyServices;

    public PropertiesInfo
        getPropertyDetailsByInfo(PropertySearch Info searchInfo)
    {
        PropertiesInfo propertiesInfo = new PropertiesInfo();
        List<PropertyInfo> propertyInfoList =
            propertiesInfo.getPropertyInfo();

        for (Property property :
             propertyServices.findByCityAndState(
             searchInfo.getCity(), searchInfo.getState())) {
            propertyInfoList.add(
                convertPropertyToPropertyInfo(property));
        }
        return propertiesInfo;
    }

    public PropertiesInfo
        getPropertyDetailsById(PropertySearchId searchId)
    {
        PropertiesInfo propertiesInfo = new PropertiesInfo();
        List<PropertyInfo> propertyInfoList =
            propertiesInfo.getPropertyInfo();

        try {
            Property property =
                propertyServices.findPropertyByExternalIdentity(
                searchId.getId());
            propertyInfoList.add(
                convertPropertyToPropertyInfo(property));
        }
        catch (Exception e) {
            /* OK - no property to add */
        }
        return propertiesInfo;
    }

    private static PropertyInfo
        convertPropertyToPropertyInfo(Property property)
```

```
        {
            PropertyInfo propertyInfo = new PropertyInfo();
            propertyInfo.setId(property.getExternalIdentity());
            propertyInfo.setDescription(property.getDescription());
            propertyInfo.setFeatures(property.getFeatures());
            propertyInfo.setAddress1(
                property.getAddress().getAddress1());
            propertyInfo.setAddress2(
                property.getAddress().getAddress2());
            propertyInfo.setCity(property.getAddress().getCity());
            propertyInfo.setState(
                property.getAddress().getStateCode());
            propertyInfo.setPostalCode(
                property.getAddress().getPostalCode());
            propertyInfo.setPhone(property.getPhone());
            return propertyInfo;
        }
    }
```

As you can see, we intentionally make the web service a very thin façade to promote the reuse of the existing business logic components that we have in our application. The main work we do directly in the web service code is copying data from the EJB's JPA entity objects into our web service–generated data POJOs. You might wonder why we chose to do this. After all, the JPA entities are just POJOs so why not combine the two data models into a single set of objects? The answer is that we do this to reduce coupling between our JPA objects that represent our relational model and our web service's data objects that we expose to other applications. Using the JPA entities in the web service interface would make it more difficult to change the web service interface or the relational model because a change to either would likely affect the other.

Best Practice

When combining a web service with other components that have their own model for representing structured data in Java, be wary of using the same data model to define the web service's external interface. Exposing your internal data model via a web service interface will make your application resistant to change. The web service's interface would be far too tightly coupled to the internal data model and vice versa. Whenever the internal model changes, the impact on the rest of your code would be much greater than it otherwise should be.

By the same token, we could add the @WebService and other JAX-WS annotations directly to the EJB to create the web service directly. Again, doing this will increase the coupling between your business logic components and your web service interface. We recommend making your web services delegate all business logic to the other components in the application.

Chapter Review

We have covered a lot of ground in this chapter. We started by looking at how WebLogic Server supports web services. We looked at examples for building WebLogic Server–based web services and clients. Next, we looked at some of the more advanced features of WebLogic Server's Web Services container. Finally, we showed how we could easily add a web service to integrate with the bigrez.com application.

Using WebLogic JMS

The Java Message Service (JMS) specification defines a standard set of interfaces for accessing messaging systems. WebLogic Server provides an enterprise-class messaging system that completely supports the JMS APIs. In addition, WebLogic Server goes the extra mile to make it easy to use other JMS-accessible messaging systems transparently from your Java EE applications. In this chapter, we begin by giving you a brief review of some key JMS concepts. Next, we jump into a detailed discussion of how the WebLogic JMS provider works. Then, we spend some time talking about WebLogic JMS design considerations. We follow that with a brief discussion of WebLogic JMS programming. Finally, we finish up this chapter with a discussion on integrating external JMS providers with WebLogic Server.

Like the rest of this book, this chapter is not intended as an introduction to either JMS or WebLogic Server's JMS implementation. If you are unfamiliar with the basics of JMS, we suggest that you study the book *Java Message Service, Second Edition* by Mark Richards, Richard Monson-Haefel and David A. Chappell (O'Reilly, 2009) for a complete treatment of JMS. For more information on WebLogic JMS, please refer to the WebLogic Server JMS documentation at Link 10-1, as listed in the book's online Appendix at `http://www.wrox.com`.

JMS Key Concepts

In this section, we give you a brief review of key JMS concepts. We begin by discussing the messaging models that JMS supports. We spend the rest of this section reviewing the JMS API, which will be important for our discussions in the following sections.

Understanding the Messaging Models

JMS supports two distinct messaging models: *point-to-point* and *publish-and-subscribe*. With point-to-point messaging, the message *producer*, also known as the *sender*, creates a message and sends it to a destination known as a *queue*. Messages sent to queues can be *persistent* or *non-persistent*. Persistent messages sent to a queue will survive server shutdowns and failures. When a message arrives at a queue, the JMS provider places the message in the queue in the order in which it was received. Each message is held in the queue until one of the following events occurs:

❑ A message consumer successfully processes the message.

❑ The message time-to-live expires.

❑ If the message is non-persistent, the server on which the queue resides shuts down or fails.

❑ The queue is deleted.

Message *consumers*, also known as *receivers*, process messages placed in a queue. Each message will be processed by a single receiver. By default, JMS delivers messages in first-in-first-out (FIFO) order. If multiple receivers are concurrently processing messages from a single queue, the JMS provider makes sure that each message goes to only one receiver.

With the publish-and-subscribe model, the message producer creates a message and sends it to a destination known as a *topic*. Messages sent to topics can be persistent or non-persistent. Messages sent, or *published*, to a topic are delivered only to the active consumers, also known as *subscribers*, which have registered their interest, or *subscribed*, to messages sent to the topic. Subscriptions can be either *durable* or *nondurable*. When a consumer subscribes to the topic, that subscriber will receive messages sent only during the lifetime of that subscription. A nondurable subscription will never last longer than the subscriber's JMS connection. In contrast, a durable subscriber can disconnect. Once the subscriber reconnects, it will receive all messages published since it disconnected: Note that message persistence may affect the availability of previously published messages in the event of server failures, depending on the JMS provider.

The JMS provider will save a message until one of the following events occurs:

❑ All subscribers successfully process the message. A nondurable subscription ends when the subscriber disconnects. A durable subscription ends when the subscriber calls unsubscribe() or specifies a new selector.

❑ The message time-to-live expires.

❑ If the message is non-persistent, the server on which the topic resides shuts down or fails.

❑ The topic is deleted.

Reviewing the JMS API

In this section, we briefly review the primary objects associated with the JMS 1.1 APIs. We expect that most readers are already familiar with the older, domain-specific JMS APIs so we will focus on the newer, domain-independent versions of the APIs. This review is intended to make it easier for you to differentiate between what the JMS specification provides and what WebLogic JMS provides. As we hope will become clear, JMS is just an interface to messaging systems that defines some of the expected behavior of the underlying messaging provider. The JMS specification stops well short of defining everything you need to build enterprise-class messaging applications using Java EE.

Connection Factories

In JMS, you use a connection factory to create connections. Applications look up connection factories in JNDI. You can think of connection factories as a set of templates used by an administrator to define common attributes about connections. Connection factories implement the `javax.jms.ConnectionFactory` interface and provide methods to create connections. JMS also provides an XA version of the connection factory for use in distributed transactions. To get a connection factory, an application uses code similar to the following:

```
InitialContext ctx = new InitialContext(contextProperties);
ConnectionFactory connectionFactory =
    (ConnectionFactory)ctx.lookup("MyConnectionFactory");
```

Applications can also use annotations to have the connection factory reference injected by the container rather than using JNDI lookups, as shown here.

```
@Resource(mappedName="MyConnectionFactory")
ConnectionFactory connectionFactory;
```

Connections

A JMS connection conceptually represents a physical connection to the underlying messaging system. Each JMS application will require a JMS connection in order to communicate with the JMS provider. For multithreaded applications, the specification guarantees JMS connections to be thread-safe and does not provide any specification-related reason to require more than one JMS connection to a particular JMS provider. Of course, you may find reasons for needing multiple JMS connections when working with a specific provider.

A JMS connection implements the `javax.jms. Connection` interface. Applications may use the connection object to authenticate themselves to the provider, to create sessions, to obtain metadata about the provider, and to register for callbacks when JMS detects there is a problem with the connection. To create a connection, just invoke the appropriate method on the connection factory.

```
Connection connection = connectionFactory.createConnection();
```

Destinations

Destinations represent the intermediate location that producers and consumers use to exchange messages. JMS applications typically look up a destination from JNDI and use it to create a producer or consumer tied to that destination. JMS also provides methods on the session objects for obtaining references to existing destinations using a provider-specific naming syntax. Like JMS connections, destinations are thread-safe. Destinations come in two primary flavors: `javax.jms.Queue` and `javax.jms.Topic`. The JMS 1.1 APIs use the domain-independent `javax.jms.Destination` interface to refer to destinations of either type. To get a destination, an application uses code similar to this:

```
InitialContext ctx = new InitialContext(contextProperties);
Destination destination = (Destination)ctx.lookup("MyQueue");
```

As an alternative to JNDI lookups, applications can use resource injection.

```
@Resource(mappedName="MyQueue")
Destination myQueue;
```

JMS also provides a mechanism for creating temporary destinations that are specific to the JMS connection on which they are created. These temporary destinations are often used to specify a response destination in the JMSReplyTo message header to tell the receiver where to send the response to that particular message.

Sessions

Sessions exist to allow coordination of message delivery between the application and the JMS provider. Sessions represent a single-threaded context for producing and consuming messages and are not thread-safe. If an application wants to share a session across multiple threads, it is the application's responsibility to synchronize access to the session. Applications use sessions as factories for creating different types of objects: message producers and consumers, temporary destinations, references to existing destinations, and messages. In addition, sessions provide a mechanism for defining transaction boundaries, serializing the consumption of messages, and limiting the scope of message acknowledgment. Sessions implement the javax.jms.Session interface. An XA version of the session interface also exists.

When a JMS message consumer finishes processing a message or set of messages, it needs to notify the JMS provider that it may delete the message(s). JMS provides two mutually exclusive ways to do this: *message acknowledgment* and *transacted sessions*. Message acknowledgment simply involves sending the JMS provider a message that tells it the messages are no longer needed. JMS sessions offer three distinct acknowledgment modes that can be used with nontransacted sessions. The message acknowledgment modes are as follows:

AUTO_ACKNOWLEDGE Messages are automatically acknowledged by the underlying provider after the consumption of each message. Although this is the easiest form of message acknowledgment, it is generally the most inefficient because it acknowledges only a single message at a time. With AUTO_ACKNOWLEDGE mode, there is a small window during which it is possible for the last message received, but not yet acknowledged, to be redelivered in the event of a failure.

DUPS_OK_ACKNOWLEDGE This is similar to AUTO_ACKNOWLEDGE mode except that the underlying provider can acknowledge the messages in a lazy fashion, making it more efficient. As the name indicates, this lazy acknowledgment can result in the application receiving sets of duplicate messages. Typically, duplicate messages are the result of a client or server failure where the JMS provider redelivers messages that the application has already processed but not yet acknowledged. This is generally the most efficient form of acknowledgment because it minimizes the work done by the session to eliminate duplicate messages and allows the provider to optimize acknowledgments. This mode exposes the application to the possibility of receiving sets of duplicate messages.

CLIENT_ACKNOWLEDGE Messages are acknowledged only when the client explicitly calls the acknowledge() method on a message. Calling acknowledge() acknowledges all consumed messages on the current session, not just the message on which it is invoked. The efficiency of this mode and the application's exposure to duplicate messages depend on the application's acknowledgment strategy. We talk more about acknowledgment strategies later.

Transacted sessions allow you to define units of work that allow the processing of groups of messages together and apply only to messages sent or received in the scope of the JMS session. In contrast, transacted sessions do not include any other external resources such as EJBs, databases accessed via JDBC, or enterprise information systems accessed through J2EE Connector Architecture adapters. Message acknowledgment is handled automatically when transacted sessions either commit or roll back their units of work.

When creating sessions, applications must specify the transaction and message acknowledgment modes. The transaction mode defines whether you want to use a transacted session; message acknowledgment mode defines which of the acknowledgment modes you want to use for nontransacted sessions. To create a nontransacted session that uses AUTO_ACKNOWLEDGE mode, an application would use code similar to this:

```
Session session = connection.createSession(false, Session.AUTO_ACKNOWLEDGE);
```

JMS also supports the use of XA transactions with providers that implement the XA versions of the JMS objects. Many large enterprise applications that use JMS will also use XA transactions. As is the case with transacted sessions, message acknowledgment is handled automatically at transaction commit or rollback. When using XA transactions, make sure to create the session with the *transacted* argument (the first argument) set to false and any message acknowledgment mode you like because the message acknowledgment mode will be ignored when a transaction context is present. If a transaction context is not present, WebLogic JMS processes the message nontransactionally according to the session's acknowledgment mode. Note that this is a gray area in the JMS specification so other JMS providers may behave differently.

Message Producers and Consumers

Message producers allow an application to send a message to a destination. Like sessions, message producers are not thread-safe. Producers also have characteristics that affect messages sent through them. These characteristics include things such as whether to use persistent delivery, the priority of the message, and the message's time-to-live. Message producers implement the javax.jms.MessageProducer interface. The code to create a message producer looks like this:

```
MessageProducer messageProducer = session.createProducer(destination);
```

Message consumers implement the javax.jms.MessageConsumer interface. Like sessions and producers, consumers are not thread-safe. Message consumers provide the context by which an application can receive messages from a particular destination. By specifying a message selector, consumers can limit the messages they receive to only the subset of messages in which they have an interest. Message consumers can receive messages synchronously by explicitly calling the consumer's receive() method or asynchronously by registering a callback object that implements the javax.jms.MessageListener interface using the consumer's setMessageListener() method:

```
MessageConsumer messageConsumer = session.createConsumer(destination);
messageConsumer.setMessageListener(new MyMessageListener());
connection.start();
```

Notice that we are calling the connection's start() method to tell the connection we are ready to start receiving messages. JMS requires that you explicitly start a connection before any messages can be received.

> ### Tip to Remember
> When creating a consumer, don't forget to call the `start()` method on the JMS connection. Your consumer will not start receiving messages until after your application calls the `start()` method.

Durable Subscribers

A topic's message consumers are usually called *subscribers*. When subscribing to a topic, you can create either a durable or nondurable subscription. Nondurable subscriptions are valid only from the time that you create them until the time you either unsubscribe or otherwise disconnect from the messaging system. This means that any failure that disconnects the application will automatically terminate the subscription. When you resubscribe, any messages sent between the time that you were disconnected and you resubscribed will not be delivered — even if the message's delivery mode is persistent. In many situations, this is the desired behavior; if it is not, you need to use a durable subscription. Note that JMS creates nondurable subscriptions by default unless you explicitly invoke one of the `createDurableSubscriber()` methods on the session object.

With durable subscriptions, the subscriber provides a unique identifier to identify the subscription. Once the subscription is accepted, the messaging system will try to deliver all messages it receives to the durable subscriber. If the subscriber disconnects without unsubscribing, the JMS provider will buffer all of the messages the subscriber has not seen until the subscriber returns. If the delivery mode is non-persistent, the messages are buffered in memory and thus subject to message loss during failures.

Asynchronous Consumers and Transactions

JMS supports asynchronous message consumers. These asynchronous message consumers can use transacted sessions to define JMS-only units of work. They cannot, however, generally support JTA transactions that include the asynchronous delivery of the message. The reasons for this are somewhat complex. When registering an asynchronous `MessageListener`, JMS does not provide a mechanism to tell the JMS provider to start a JTA transaction before delivering the message. Because the JMS provider does not start the transaction before it delivers the message, the only other way that we could include the message delivery in the JTA transaction would be if JMS supported a callback mechanism to tell it that a previously delivered, but unacknowledged message should be considered part of a JTA transaction.

The story gets worse when you consider the EJB specification's requirements for supporting JTA transactional delivery of messages to message-driven beans. Two primary strategies exist for addressing this issue. The first strategy is for the JMS provider to provide a nonstandard API that can be used to associate a previously delivered, but unacknowledged message with a JTA transaction. Although this works fine for applications that use the same vendor for both the EJB and JMS providers, it clearly does not work when mixing vendors unless the vendors can agree on the nonstandard API and semantics. The other strategy is to simulate asynchronous delivery using synchronous delivery under the covers. As you will see later, WebLogic Server supports both of these strategies to make it possible to integrate Java EE applications with any JMS provider that supports XA transactions.

Message Selectors

Sometimes a consumer is interested in only a subset of the messages delivered to a destination. JMS provides a standard filtering facility for message consumers, known as *message selectors*. Message selectors use a syntax similar to an SQL WHERE clause to create expressions that JMS will evaluate against message headers or properties. You can specify a selector when you create a message consumer:

```
MessageConsumer messageConsumer =
    session.createConsumer(destination, "JMSPriority > 5");
messageConsumer.setMessageListener(new MyMessageListener());
connection.start();
```

This selector ensures that messages will be delivered to this consumer only if the value of the JMSPriority header is greater than 5.

Message selectors are static. You cannot change them without first closing the current consumer and creating a new one. Changing a durable subscription's selector ends the subscription; all unconsumed messages for that subscription are deleted and the subscription is recreated, as required by the JMS specification.

As you can imagine, the use of selectors adds overhead to message delivery that will affect the performance and scalability of the application. When designing a JMS application, consider splitting a destination into multiple destinations to eliminate the need for message selectors. We discuss message selector design and performance implications in more detail later.

Messages

Messages form the foundation of any JMS application. Applications use messages to carry data associated with a particular event. As shown in Figure 10-1, JMS divides messages into three logical parts: headers, properties, and the body.

Message headers specify certain characteristics of a message potentially of interest to applications. For most JMS headers, the JMS provider is responsible for setting the values of these characteristics. JMSReplyTo and JMSCorrelationID are two notable exceptions often used by applications to implement a request/reply pattern of message exchange.

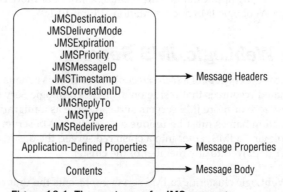

Figure 10-1: The anatomy of a JMS message.

Message properties allow applications to define additional characteristics about a message. The JMS specification reserves all property names that begin with JMSX. Typically, message properties are most useful for applications that need to apply message selectors to application-specific data.

The message body contains the payload of the message. The type of information a message contains depends on the type of message the application chooses to use. JMS defines five different types of message objects, all of which derive from javax.jms.Message:

TextMessage   Applications use this message type to send simple text strings or more complex, text-based data structures like XML messages.

BytesMessage   Applications use this message type to send a raw array of bytes. Typically, you would use this to retain an application's native data format.

ObjectMessage   Applications use this message type to send a serialized Java object.

StreamMessage   Applications use this message type to send an ordered stream of Java primitive types or the object versions of these primitive types, such as java.lang.Integer or java.lang.Double.

MapMessage   Applications use this message type to send an unordered set of name-value pairs. All names must be unique, and the values must be Java primitive types or the object versions of these primitive types.

To create a message and send it to a destination, use code like that shown here:

```
TextMessage message = session.createTextMessage("message body");
messageProducer.send(message);
```

The WebLogic JMS Provider

In this section, we take a detailed look at the WebLogic JMS provider implementation. As you will see, WebLogic JMS not only provides a messaging system that fully implements the JMS specification but also provides other configuration and programming options that go well beyond what JMS defines to provide enterprise-class messaging features. We do not attempt to provide comprehensive coverage of WebLogic JMS, but instead focus our discussions on the details that are most important for designing and building robust messaging applications with WebLogic JMS. For more comprehensive coverage of JMS, we refer you to the WebLogic JMS documentation at Link 10-1.

Understanding WebLogic JMS Servers

WebLogic JMS introduces the concept of a *JMS server*. A JMS server is a management entity and container for JMS destination-related resources that reside on a single WebLogic Server instance. A WebLogic Server instance can host zero or more JMS servers and can serve as a migration target for zero or more JMS servers. All destination names must be unique across every JMS server in a WebLogic Server instance. If you are deploying a JMS server into a clustered server, the destination names must be unique across every JMS server deployed to any member of the cluster.

When you are using WebLogic clustering, a JMS server represents the unit of migration when failing over a set of destinations from one WebLogic Server instance to another. By associating destinations with a JMS server, WebLogic JMS makes it easier to migrate a set of destinations from one WebLogic Server instance to another. We talk more about JMS server migration in the next section.

Clustering WebLogic JMS

WebLogic JMS clustering is built on top of the basic WebLogic Server clustering mechanisms. It provides a JMS application with the features you would expect from a clustered messaging infrastructure. In this section, we take a closer look at WebLogic JMS clustering, which includes discussions on the following features of clustering:

❑   *Location transparency* provides the application with a uniform view of the messaging system by hiding the physical locations of JMS objects.

❑   *Connection routing, load balancing,* and *failover* provide the application with a single, logical connection into the messaging system.

❑   *Distributed destinations* provide a single, logical destination distributed across multiple servers in the cluster to support both load balancing and high availability.

❑   *Automatic migration* for JMS servers provides the ability to restart failed destinations automatically, without human interaction in the event of server failure or maintenance outage.

Location Transparency

WebLogic JMS registers managed objects such as connection factories and destinations in JNDI. Because WebLogic Server provides JNDI replication across a cluster, an application can simply look up the objects by their JNDI name, regardless of which servers in the cluster are hosting the objects. For example, applications can access a JMS destination without knowing which WebLogic Server instance hosts the JMS server that holds the destination. In the same way, you can create a JMS connection and session without having to worry about what servers are in the cluster or where the destinations you are using reside.

Connection Routing, Load Balancing, and Failover

When deployed to a cluster, WebLogic JMS connection factories provide transparent access to all JMS servers in the cluster. This means that any JMS connection you create using one of these factories will have access to every JMS destination across the cluster. How this works depends on where the application is located in relation to the WebLogic Server cluster.

For client applications not running in a WebLogic Server instance, WebLogic JMS defaults to using a simple round-robin algorithm to distribute connection requests across all running servers in the cluster on which the connection factory is deployed. The algorithm's state, however, is tied to each client's copy of the connection factory. The overall load distribution will be relatively uniform because the load-balancing algorithm is initialized by randomly selecting the initial server. Connection factories provide failover by routing requests to create a new connection around failed servers.

Once the client creates a connection, WebLogic JMS routes all JMS operations over that same connection to the appropriate WebLogic Server instance in the cluster. This enables WebLogic JMS clusters to support a large number of concurrent clients but does expose the client to failures if the server to which it is connected fails. Another interesting failure scenario occurs when the JMS connection is still operational but the WebLogic Server instance on which a particular JMS destination resides fails. For example, the client's JMS connection is talking with server1, but it is asynchronously consuming messages from a destination on `server2`. If the client is asynchronously consuming messages using one of the failed destinations, you need some way to notify the client application that the `MessageConsumer` is no longer valid. Though the JMS specification does not indicate how to handle this type of problem, WebLogic Server calls the standard `onException()` message on the connection's exception listener.

WebLogic JMS has the ability to attempt to failover message producers and consumers to another server instance in the cluster when failures occur. This capability is enabled by default for message producers but disabled by default for message consumers. This functionality can be controlled programmatically via the `WLConnection.setReconnectPolicy()` method or administratively via settings on the WebLogic JMS connection factories. See Link 10-2 for more information about automatic JMS client failover.

When using this functionality, the WebLogic JMS code tries to refresh the connection, session, and message producer/consumer objects without intervention by the application code. In a number of situations the implicit refresh may not work or is not completely transparent to the client. Any exception listener registered for the connection will be invoked — even if the reconnection/refresh is successful. There is no real way for the exception listener to determine whether the reconnect/refresh worked. That means you have two choices. First, you might decide that you can live with the limitations of the reconnect/refresh feature and rely on this without an exception listener. Second, you might decide that you need an exception listener to handle the situation more robustly. With an exception listener, you end up recreating the JMS objects anyway so you should disable the implicit reconnect/refresh feature.

In our opinion, the exception listener approach is more robust and generally a better approach because it can handle all situations. As such, we recommend not relying on this implicit reconnect/refresh mechanism and implementing your own exception listeners to re-establish your JMS connectivity.

Best Practice

WebLogic JMS applications should not rely on the automatic failover of message producers and consumers. Though convenient, they do not handle every situation transparently. Use exception listeners to detect the failures and use the ConnectionFactory and Destination objects previously looked up from JNDI to re-establish your JMS connectivity.

To detect JMS failures, clients must use the standard JMS mechanism to register an object that implements that `javax.jms.ExceptionListener` interface with the connection by calling the `setExceptionListener()` method. To recover, you will need to use the connection factory to create a new connection and any other objects that were associated with the failed connection object.

For server-side applications, WebLogic JMS avoids extra network traffic by processing connection requests locally wherever possible. If the connection factory is not deployed locally, the server-side application will connect to one of the servers where the connection factory exists. In most applications, it is very desirable to distribute the load across all servers in a cluster. There are multiple ways to achieve this. In almost all situations, it is best to distribute the load as it enters the cluster and keep all processing of a particular message within the local server to which the message was delivered. Therefore, we recommend deploying your applications and JMS resources homogeneously across the cluster. Because any particular destination must reside on only one server in the cluster, we need to use distributed destinations to accomplish this homogenous distribution.

> **Best Practice**
>
> For JMS server-side applications accessing destinations within the same cluster, deploy your connection factories to all servers in the cluster. Likewise, deploy your connection factories to all servers in the cluster for remotely connected JMS applications accessing a cluster with a distributed destination with members in every cluster member.
>
> For remotely connected JMS applications that use only a subset of the cluster for hosting JMS destinations, deploy the connection factories on the WebLogic Server instances where the JMS servers reside.
>
> Following these rules will help eliminate unnecessary routing of JMS requests through servers with no JMS server deployed.

Distributed Destinations

Distributed destinations give WebLogic JMS the ability to make JMS destinations highly available and load balanced. To create a distributed destination, simply map multiple member JMS destinations to a single, logical, distributed JMS destination. JMS applications use distributed destinations just like any other JMS destination. How WebLogic JMS routes application requests to the underlying member JMS destinations depends on many different factors, such as where the application resides (in a remote client or in a server), what the application is doing (sending messages or receiving messages), what type of destination is used (queue or topic), and how many consumers there are.

WebLogic JMS can load balance message producers to a distributed destination on a request-by-request basis. This means that, all other things being equal, the messages produced by a single client can be evenly distributed across the member destinations of the distributed destination. For message consumers, WebLogic JMS load balances them at creation time, thereby pinning each consumer to a member destination. WebLogic JMS also looks at several other factors when load balancing producers and consumers, such as the number of consumers for a member destination, the location of the member destinations, the availability of a persistent store (if the message delivery mode is persistent), and the current transaction context. Any of these other factors can cause WebLogic JMS to alter its default load balancing policy for a particular message or destination. We spend the rest of this section explaining how WebLogic JMS routes application requests that use distributed destinations.

In general, we highly recommend that you deploy distributed destinations homogeneously across the cluster using similar configurations for each participating JMS server and its associated destinations. WebLogic Server 9.0 introduced *Uniform Distributed Destinations* to simplify the configuration of homogenously deployed distributed destinations. Therefore, we focus on describing the behavior of distributed destinations when deployed in homogenous configurations. For more complete information, please refer to the WebLogic Server documentation at Link 10-3.

> **Best Practice**
>
> When you are deploying distributed destinations, always use uniform distributed destinations and similar settings for every JMS server in the cluster.

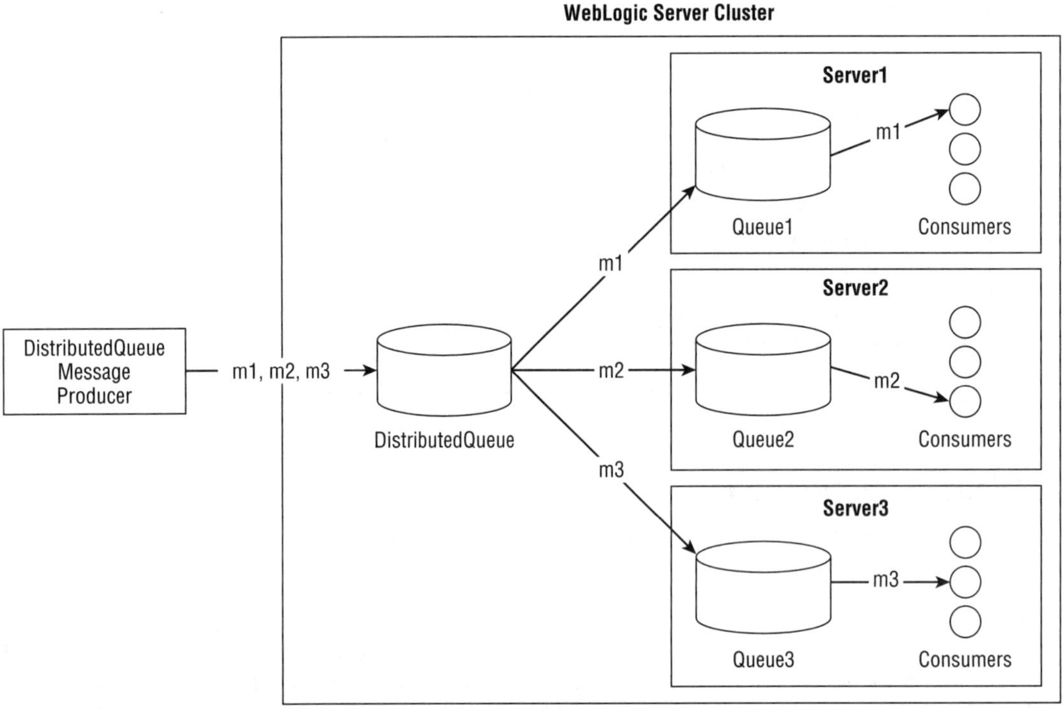

WebLogic Server Cluster

Figure 10-2: Sending messages to a distributed queue.

Producing Messages to a Distributed Queue

Figure 10-2 illustrates the producer's perspective of distributed queue operation using the common load-balancing configuration. There are three WebLogic Server instances running in a cluster, each hosting a member destination (Queue1, Queue2, and Queue3) of the distributed queue, DistributedQueue. Each message sent by the producer is load balanced across the member destinations. Because this is a point-to-point messaging model, only one consumer will receive each message.

When a producer sends messages to a distributed queue, WebLogic JMS first determines how to load balance the send() requests. You can control this with the connection factory's Load Balancing Enabled checkbox, which is enabled by default, and the distributed destination's Load Balancing Policy, which is round-robin by default. If load balancing is enabled, WebLogic JMS load balances each queue producer on every send() call using the algorithm specified by the load balancing policy. If it is disabled, WebLogic JMS load balances only each producer's first call to send(); all subsequent messages from a particular producer will be sent to the same member destination.

WebLogic JMS uses several other heuristics that override the default load balancing behavior; the heuristics are applied in this order:

❑ *Persistent store availability* means that WebLogic JMS will prefer destinations whose underlying JMS server does not explicitly disable its Store Enabled attribute.

❑ *Transaction affinity* means that WebLogic JMS will try to send all messages associated with a particular transaction context to the same JMS server to minimize the number of JMS servers involved in the transaction. Note that at the time of writing the transaction affinity heuristic only applies to transacted session transactions and not to global XA transactions.

❑ *Server affinity* means that WebLogic JMS will try to use a destination in the local process. WebLogic JMS will use member destinations in the WebLogic Server instance in which the producer/consumer is running or to which the producer/consumer's JMS connection is connected. Although this is the default behavior, you can disable this behavior by deselecting the connection factory's `Server Affinity Enabled` checkbox.

❑ *Zero consumer queues* means that WebLogic JMS will do its best to avoid sending messages to member queues with zero consumers, unless all member queues have zero consumers. Because of the transient nature of some message consumers, it is still possible for messages to end up on queues with zero consumers.

Figure 10-2 portrays a conceptual view of how a distributed queue works. In reality, all routing to a member queue occurs inside a WebLogic Server process. Each producer has a JMS connection attached to one WebLogic Server in the cluster. By default, server affinity causes WebLogic JMS to attempt to send the messages from a particular producer to a member destination on the server to which the producer's JMS connection is attached. The message may be routed to a different destination if server affinity is disabled, there is no local member destination, or one of the other heuristics takes precedence.

> **Tip to Remember**
>
> By default, server affinity causes message producers sending messages to a distributed queue always to send to the member queue in the JMS server to which the producer is connected. To enable a producer to load balance messages across member destinations, disable server affinity on the connection factory the producer is using. Of course, this load balancing will still be subject to other heuristics that might skew the distribution of messages.

Another important feature of distributed queues is message forwarding. The zero consumer queues heuristic will try to prevent routing point-to-point messages to a member destination with no consumers if there are other member destinations with consumers. It is still possible, though, for messages to end up on a queue with no consumers if, for example, a consumer exits after the message is sent but before it is received. WebLogic JMS provides a forwarding mechanism by which messages can be forwarded from a member queue with no consumers to a member queue with consumers after a specified amount of time. The distributed queue's `Forward Delay` attribute controls the number of seconds WebLogic JMS will wait before trying to forward the messages. By default, the value is set to −1, which means that forwarding is disabled. Setting a `Forward Delay` is incompatible with strictly ordered message processing, including the Unit-of-Order feature discussed later.

> Setting a `Forward Delay` is incompatible with strictly ordered message processing, including the Unit-of-Order feature.

Consuming Messages from a Distributed Queue

When an application creates a message consumer for a distributed queue, WebLogic JMS associates the consumer with one of the member destinations of the distributed queue. From that point on, the

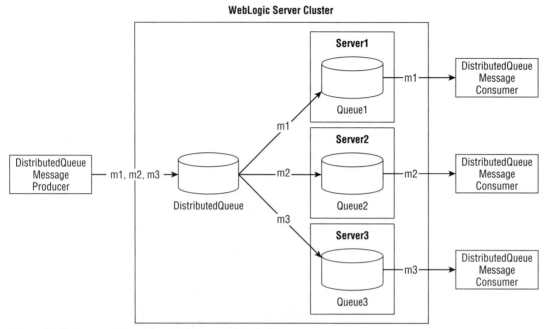

Figure 10-3: Consuming messages from a distributed queue.

consumer is pinned to that member destination. Figure 10-3 illustrates the operation of a distributed queue from the consumer's perspective. In this figure, the three DistributedQueue consumers have each been associated with one of the member destinations. Each consumer will be eligible to receive only messages routed to his or her respective member destinations.

When consumers are created, WebLogic JMS associates the consumer with a member destination by load balancing the consumers across the available member destinations. Although this load balancing is done only once for each consumer, the mechanisms used are very similar to those used for load balancing messages sent to a distributed queue. All other things being equal, WebLogic JMS will use the distributed destination's load balancing policy to distribute the consumers across all member destinations. Just as before, WebLogic JMS uses heuristic optimizations that will override the default load balancing mechanism. If server affinity is enabled, WebLogic JMS will try to associate the consumer with a local member destination, as described previously. WebLogic JMS will also try to associate new consumers with member destinations that currently have zero consumers, unless server affinity prevents this.

When a WebLogic Server hosting a member of a distributed queue fails, all unconsumed persistent messages remain on the failed server's queue. These messages will not be available until either the WebLogic Server instance is restarted or the JMS server containing the member queue is migrated to another WebLogic Server instance. We talk more about JMS server migration later in this section. If the messages are non-persistent, all of the unconsumed messages will be lost.

WebLogic JMS distributed queue consumers are essentially the same as nondistributed queue consumers once the association between the consumer and the member destination has been established. If the WebLogic Server hosting the member queue fails, WebLogic JMS throws a javax.jms.JMSException to all synchronous consumers. For asynchronous consumers, the connection's ExceptionListener is notified and the application will have to recreate the JMS connection and all of its associated objects (sessions, consumers, producers, and so on).

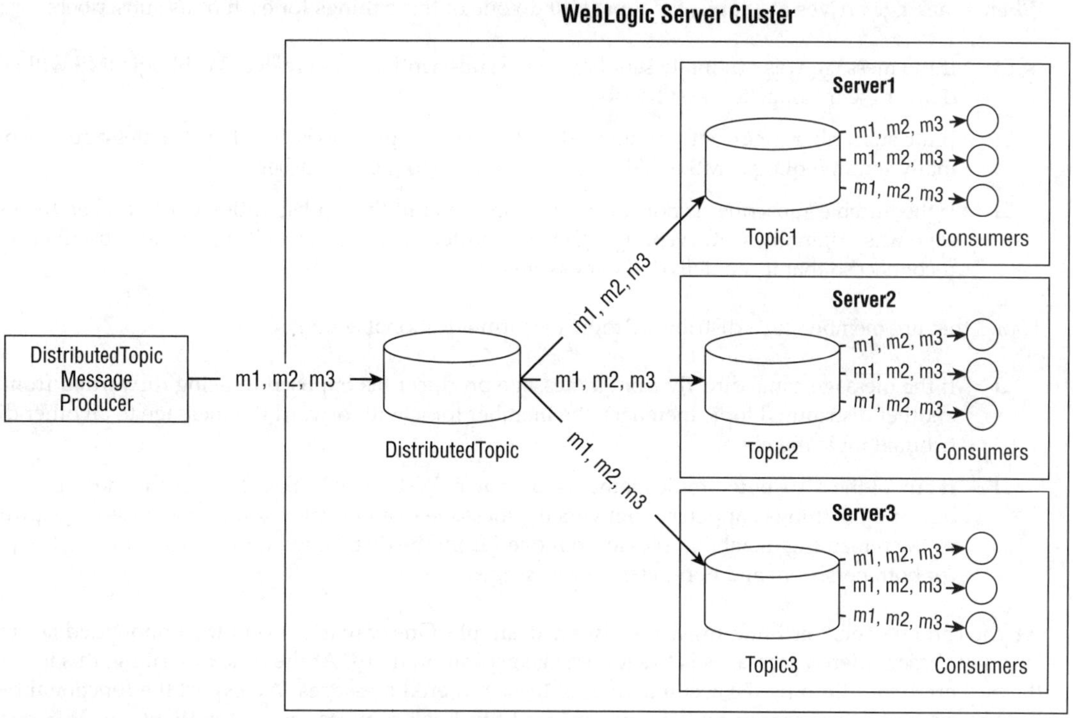

WebLogic Server Cluster

Figure 10-4: Publishing messages to a distributed topic.

Producing Messages to a Distributed Topic

Figure 10-4 illustrates the conceptual operation of a distributed topic from the producer's perspective. As in the previous example, there are three WebLogic Server instances running in a cluster, each hosting a member destination (Topic1, Topic2, and Topic3) of the distributed topic, DistributedTopic. When a producer sends messages to a distributed topic, WebLogic JMS sends a copy of the message to every available member topic that has at least one consumer. Because all member topics in Figure 10-4 have at least one consumer, every message is sent to the three member topics. If the three consumers attached to Topic3 were to unsubscribe from DistributedTopic, any future messages would be sent only to Topic1 and Topic2 until a new consumer was assigned to Topic3.

In reality, a distributed topic producer always sends each message to a single member topic. The member topic then forwards the message to all other member topics. If you publish messages directly to the member topic, WebLogic JMS will still replicate the messages to every member of the distributed topic, just as it would if you had published the messages to the distributed topic itself. This means that any topic associated with a distributed topic will distribute messages just as the distributed topic does. It is important to note that distributed topic producers maintain an affinity to a member topic after they send their first message. This affinity overrides any load balancing settings on the connection factory. They will, however, failover to another member topic in the event of failure. When this happens, the producer pins itself to the new member for future messages.

As we discuss later in the "Persistent Stores" section, persistent messages sent to a nondistributed topic are not actually persisted unless there are one or more durable subscribers. For distributed topic members, the message is always persisted before forwarding on to other member topics.

When a message arrives at a topic, the topic will do one of three things for each of its subscribers:

- If the message was originally sent before the subscription was created, WebLogic JMS will not deliver the message to the subscriber.

- If the subscriber is currently connected and the subscription existed when the message was originally sent, WebLogic JMS will deliver the message to the subscriber.

- If the durable subscriber is not currently connected but their subscription existed when the message was originally sent, WebLogic JMS will buffer the message waiting on the subscriber to reconnect so that it can deliver the message.

Topics that are members of a distributed topic perform additional actions.

- If the message came directly from a message producer (as opposed to being forwarded from another distributed topic member), the member topic will forward the message to all other distributed topic members.

- If any of the distributed topic members are down, WebLogic JMS will buffer the message until one of three things happens: it delivers the message to all member topics, the message expires, or the remaining member topics are removed from the distributed topic. This buffering happens for both persistent and non-persistent messages.

As you can imagine, this buffering is not always desirable. One way to prevent the unbounded accumulation of these buffered messages is to set message expiration times. At the time of writing, this is really the best option for limiting the accumulation of these buffered messages. We expect the functionality of distributed topics may change by the time you read this book so please check the WebLogic JMS documentation for more information. We talk more about durable subscribers and message persistence later.

Consuming Messages from a Distributed Topic

Distributed topic consumers are similar to distributed queue consumers; WebLogic JMS associates them with a member destination at the time they are created. WebLogic JMS uses the same load balancing mechanisms and optimization heuristics for distributed topic consumers that it uses for distributed queue consumers. The same error-handling mechanisms that we discussed for distributed queue consumers also apply to distributed topic consumers. Two important differences exist in how consumers work with distributed topics that we need to mention.

First, any durable subscriptions must be made directly with a distributed topic's member destinations. WebLogic JMS does not currently support creating a durable subscription on a distributed topic directly. This is unfortunate because although it does not prevent you from building an application that leverages distributed topics with durable subscribers, it does make it more difficult. In most cases, the subscriber must look up one of the member topics directly. The WebLogic Server documentation lists two approaches that applications can use to handle this situation:

1. Give each member topic a unique JNDI Name and have the durable subscribers use those JNDI names to look up the member topic explicitly. Note that the JNDI Name attribute binds the member topic into JNDI and WebLogic Server replicates that binding across the cluster.

2. Give each member topic the same Local JNDI Name so that the durable subscribers use the same JNDI name to look up the member topic and will always get the one on the local server to which they are connected. Note that the Local JNDI Name attribute allows you to specify a JNDI name that is not replicated across the cluster.

Both of these approaches have serious drawbacks for remote subscribers. For example, the first approach makes it easy for durable subscribers to reconnect to the appropriate member topic but requires subscribers to understand the current topology of the cluster and invent their own mechanisms to ensure load balancing and server affinity. The second approach tries to hide the cluster topology but at the expense of making it easy for the consumer to reconnect to their existing durable subscription. That is, because the durable subscription is associated with the member topic and each member topic has the same JNDI name, the subscriber has to invent its own mechanisms to reconnect to the same cluster member to find the durable subscription. You might decide to solve this problem by using one JMS connection factory per member topic. However, this causes exactly the same problems and options. At the end of the day, you end up needing to build load balancing and failover machinery into the application. We feel that this makes remote durable subscribers on distributed topics (in their current form) too complex and recommend that you avoid their use.

Fortunately, things are much better if the durable subscribers are server-side components deployed in the same cluster. In fact, WebLogic Server's MDB container actually allows an MDB to specify the JNDI name of a local distributed topic when creating a durable subscription. The container simply determines the correct member topic for the local managed server and creates the durable subscription against it.

The second important difference is that message-driven bean (MDB) deployments are treated as a single consumer per member topic. This means that regardless of how many MDB instances are in the pool on each server, messages will be sent to a single MDB instance for each member topic. If you stop to think about it, this is desirable because the whole idea of deploying an MDB is to create one virtual consumer per deployment. You probably do not want each message sent to the topic to be processed by multiple MDB instances in the same server. Where this becomes less clear is when you think about deploying an MDB to a cluster using a distributed destination. In some cases, you might actually want each message processed in each server; in others, it might be desirable to process each message once across the entire cluster. Currently, WebLogic JMS supports only sending each message to all servers hosting the MDB.

Related to this, it is important to note that WebLogic JMS requires all durable subscribers connected to a cluster to have a unique *client identifier*. This client identifier is what uniquely identifies the durable subscription. To make it easier to deploy MDB durable subscribers, WebLogic Server's MDB container supports a `<generate-unique-jms-clientid>` element in `weblogic-ejb-jar.xml` that tells the server to generate unique durable subscriber client identifiers automatically for each MDB deployment. This capability, when combined with the ability to use the distributed topic as the target destination for the MDB, makes it easy to deploy an MDB that acts as if it were a durable subscriber to a distributed topic.

As you can see, at the time of writing there are a number of significant limitations resulting from the lack of support for durable subscriptions directly on distributed topics in WebLogic Server 10.3.1 and earlier. While this is a limitation that we expect will be addressed in an upcoming release, at the time of writing the only reasonable way to use durable subscriptions in combination with distributed topics is to use MDB durable subscribers where the MDB is deployed to the same cluster as the distributed topic.

> **Best Practice**
>
> At the time of writing, WebLogic Server does not support durable subscriptions directly on distributed topics. You must create the durable subscription directly on the member topic. Until this situation changes the only effective way to emulate a durable subscription on a distributed topic is to use an MDB deployed to the same cluster as the distributed topic.

We expect that the capabilities and options surrounding distributed topics will be changing in an upcoming version of WebLogic Server — possibly by the time you are reading this book. Please consult the WebLogic Server documentation at Link 10-4.

Automatic Failover for JMS Servers

It's important that a JMS server is running so that its queues and topics are always available. WebLogic Server provides two mechanisms to support the automatic failover for a JMS server: whole server migration and service migration. With whole server migration, the WebLogic Server instance is restarted on another machine. Service migration provides the ability to migrate specific services from one WebLogic Server instance to another in the same cluster.

WebLogic JMS supports service migration, which simplifies the migration of a JMS server from one instance of WebLogic Server to another instance of WebLogic Server in the same cluster, if properly configured.

Migrating a JMS server from one WebLogic Server instance to another is simple provided that the target server has access to all of the JMS server's resources used by the source server. If a persistent store is involved, the persistent store will need to be available on the target server. If the source server failed with transactions in flight, you will also need to migrate the JTA service, and its associated transaction log files, so that these in-flight transactions can be recovered. You can find a complete discussion of the configuration and use of the WebLogic Server service migration and whole server migration in Chapter 12.

> **Best Practice**
>
> If you need to be able to move a JMS destination to another server to handle failover, always use automatic whole server migration or automatic service migration rather than trying to do it yourself.

WebLogic JMS Clients

External clients connect to a remote WebLogic Server over TCP/IP network connections which are automatically established using standard JNDI and JMS APIs.

WebLogic JMS supports several options for external clients including three Java clients as well as a C client and a .NET client. All clients support transacted session-style transactions. Only the Java clients support the JTA transaction API; the .NET and C clients do not. The Java clients also support an optional client Store-and-Forward (client SAF) feature that will automatically store messages in a local file before forwarding them on to the remote JMS server. This feature allows clients to send messages even when disconnected and have those messages forwarded to the target destination once a connection is re-established. See the "Understanding the Store-and-Forward Service" section later in this chapter for more information about SAF.

The five different types of clients are briefly described in the following list.

Java Install Client   The Java Install Client is a client that uses the `$WL_HOME/server/lib/weblogic.jar` file located within a full WebLogic Server installation. This distinction is important because `weblogic.jar` was split up into modules as of WebLogic Server 10, and the jar file itself is no longer sufficient to run a remote client application (that is, copying the `weblogic.jar` file from a WebLogic Server 10.x installation to another machine to run the client does not work anymore). This client uses the T3 protocol, which may be secured with SSL or tunneled over HTTP (specified by t3, t3s, http, or https in a URL). It does not support the IIOP protocol when calling into JMS APIs.

Java Full Client   The Java Full Client is the WebLogic Server 10.x replacement for the older *copy the* `weblogic.jar` *file* clients. It is equivalent to the Java Install Client except that it uses a stand-alone `wlfullclient.jar` file that you build using the WebLogic JarBuilder utility (see Link 10-5). Once you generate the `wlfullclient.jar` file, you can copy it around and use it exactly like you used to use `weblogic.jar` in earlier releases.

Java Thin Client   The Java Thin Client uses several small jars that contain different pieces of functionality that you can mix and match depending on what functionality your client application uses. The primary jar file required for all thin clients is `wlclient.jar`. For a JMS client, you also need `wljmsclient.jar`, and optionally `wlsafclient.jar` if using client SAF. This client supports SSL, HTTP tunneling, and the IIOP protocol. If a thin client application URL specifies the T3 protocol, the thin client will automatically convert it to the IIOP protocol. The thin client is considerably less performant and scalable than the full or install clients and, therefore, is generally not recommended in any server-to-server scenarios. We recommend only using the thin client with real clients where the small jar size is an absolute requirement (for example, with a Java applet).

C Client   The WebLogic JMS C client is a C API that works on top of one of three Java clients. The client process must embed a Java client library and JVM in order for the C client to work. As with using the thin client, the C client should not be used with the thin client in a server-to-server scenario.

.NET Client   The WebLogic JMS .NET client is a fully managed .NET runtime library and application programming interface (API) that closely resembles the standard JMS API. It allows programmers to create simple native .NET C# client applications that can directly communicate with WebLogic JMS. The .NET client consists of a standalone dynamic link library (`modules/com.bea.weblogic.jms.dotnetclient_1.1.0.0/WebLogic.Messaging.dll`) that has no dependencies on a JVM or any WebLogic Server Java client library. It currently supports the T3 protocol and has a number of limitations (see Link 10-6 for more information).

Before we move one to discuss WebLogic JMS configuration, we should briefly discuss the JNDI URL formats supported by WebLogic JMS clients, and WebLogic Server clients in general.

WebLogic Server Client URLs

Applications that are not running within a WebLogic Server instance must specify a PROVIDER_URL when creating their JNDI InitialContext objects in order to connect to a server or a cluster. If a URL resolves to multiple addresses, WebLogic Server clients will randomly select an address in the list to start with and then automatically try each address in turn until one succeeds. The URL syntax is as follows:

```
[t3|t3s|http|https|iiop|iiops]://address[,address]...
where:   address = hostlist : portlist
         hostlist = hostname [,hostname]...
         portlist = portrange [+portrange]...
         portrange = port [-port]
```

Use port-port to indicate a port range, and + to separate multiple port ranges. For example, a simple address is typically something like t3://hostA:7001; the address t3://hostA,hostB:7001-7002 is equivalent to the following addresses.

```
t3://hostA,hostB:7001+7002
t3://hostA:7001-7002,hostB:7001-7002
t3://hostA:7001+7002,hostB:7001+7002
t3://hostA:7001,hostA:7002,hostB:7001,hostB:7002
```

> ### Tip to Remember
> If your application is running inside a WebLogic Server instance or cluster, do not specify a URL when creating the JNDI InitialContext. Creating an InitialContext without specifying a URL implicitly returns the JNDI context for the local server or cluster.

While this URL list notation is convenient, you may want to consider other schemes for production environments. You can replace the list of hostnames with a single hostname that resolves to the list of IP addresses for your cluster. This technique is known as DNS round-robin. One potential problem with DNS round-robin is DNS lookup caching, which can occur in the JVM or in a DNS server. If you update your DNS entry to account for a server that is down or a new server that was added, it could take a long time before your WebLogic Server–based application is able to see this change if you don't ensure that DNS lookup caches for your clients are short-lived.

For Java clients, you can control the JVM caching using the Java system property networkaddress. cache.ttl (see Link 10-7 for more information). Remember, DNS lookups are generally expensive so reducing the effectiveness of the JVM's cache can have negative performance implications for applications that do frequent DNS lookups.

For DNS servers, the situation is more complex. If all your clients (for example, your web service plug-ins) use the same DNS server that holds your cluster's DNS entry, changes to the entry will generally be immediate. However, if your clients use other DNS servers, caching will likely be an issue since DNS servers communicate with other DNS servers to resolve addresses. These DNS server to DNS server lookups are almost always cached for extended periods of time to improve performance. Changes to

DNS entries can take days to propagate across a set of DNS servers. Even if you control all of the DNS servers involved, you typically won't be able to tune the caches time-to-live down or risk slowing your DNS servers (and therefore, all your network-based applications that do DNS lookups) to a crawl. In these situations, you'll need to look at more sophisticated solutions involving a hardware load balancer rather than DNS round-robin.

When using a hardware load balancer with RMI-based applications, you must ensure that the load balancer is only used to resolve the initial hostname to an IP address.

Best Practice

For production systems, consider using DNS round robin or a hardware load balancer (for initial hostname resolution only) rather than using the PROVIDER_URL list notation.

Configuring WebLogic JMS

Now that you understand the high-level overview of WebLogic JMS clustering, let's take a more detailed look at the many different configuration options that can affect your JMS applications. We cover only a subset of the functionality, and we recommend that you consult the WebLogic JMS documentation for more information.

JMS Modules

A JMS module is a configuration container for other JMS resources, such as destinations and connection factories. JMS modules come in two flavors: system modules and application modules. Application modules can be packaged or standalone. WebLogic JMS administrators create system modules using the WebLogic Console. These modules are visible and accessible to all applications deployed on the server/cluster. WebLogic JMS developers create application modules and package them together with their application. Application modules are typically visible only to the application in which they are defined, though they can also be made visible to all applications. The idea of an application that packages its JMS artifacts internally so that it is easy to move between environments is appealing. Nevertheless, you should consider the following points before choosing to use application modules.

❏ Application module configuration is not manageable via JMX (for example, the WebLogic Console).

❏ Non-default targeting of application modules significantly complicates deployment.

❏ Undeploying the application destroys the JMS destination, discarding any undelivered messages.

❏ Application modules only support a subset of JMS resources.

In our opinion, these negative points about application modules outweigh their promised benefit of providing self-contained JMS resources to an application. We have not found a need for application modules in a real production system. As such, all of our discussion of JMS modules throughout the rest of the book focuses on system modules.

Best Practice

We recommend avoiding the use of JMS application modules and only using JMS system modules due to the ability to manage system modules through JMX and all the standard WebLogic Server management tools.

JMS modules can contain connection factories, destinations, distributed destinations, quotas, destination sort keys, and some other integration-related artifacts that we discuss later. JMS modules are targeted to zero or more WebLogic Server instances or clusters. If you remember from our earlier discussion, physical destinations can only be deployed to a single JMS server. So how is it that JMS modules can be targeted to WebLogic Server instances or clusters if they contain nondistributed destinations?

JMS modules also contain *subdeployments*. Subdeployments allow a subset of a module's resources to be selectively targeted. Here are some rules of thumb to help you use modules and subdeployments in their recommended way.

❑ Define one JMS module per homogenous deployment target set: a cluster, a set of WebLogic Servers within a single cluster, or a single WebLogic Server instance. Target the module to that target set.

❑ Define one subdeployment per JMS module and target it to the set of JMS servers running on the WebLogic Server instances targeted by the JMS module.

❑ Target all destination resources to the subdeployment. If the subdeployment targets more than one JMS server in a cluster, you will have to use distributed destinations and the `Advanced Targeting` button to assign them to the subdeployment.

❑ Target connection factories to the module (not to the subdeployment) by accepting the default targeting option. The default targeting option implicitly sets the connection factory targets based on the module's target.

By following these guidelines, each module will equate to a single deployment target set. Destinations will end up on exactly the desired JMS servers and the connection factories will be targeted to all of the servers.

Using JMS modules and subdeployments, it is possible to create a single module that contains all WebLogic JMS resources for deployment. However, best practice suggests that every JMS module should correspond to a single deployment target set (for example, a cluster or a WebLogic Server instance). Likewise, we suggest that each subdeployment be targeted to the JMS servers running on the WebLogic Server instances targeted by the module.

Best Practice

We recommend defining one JMS module per homogenous deployment target set and configuring one subdeployment per JMS module. Target the subdeployment to JMS servers that are hosted among the target set's managed servers. Target destinations to the subdeployment but connection factories to the module's default target set.

Connection Factories

A JMS connection factory can be thought of as a template defining common connection attributes. Once you create connection factories using the WebLogic Console, the connection factories are bound into JNDI when WebLogic Server starts up. Each connection factory can be deployed on multiple WebLogic Server instances or clusters through its associated JMS module. An application accesses JMS by looking up a connection factory and using the connection factory to create a connection. Once the connection is established, all predefined connection factory attributes are applied to the connection.

Let's look at a few of the more important connection factory attributes. A complete discussion of individual attributes is outside the scope of this chapter, and you should consult the WebLogic JMS documentation if you're interested. Using the WebLogic Console, navigate to the `Services` ➪ `Messaging` ➪ `JMS Modules` folder in the left-hand navigation bar and create a new JMS module and connection factory. The following list explains some of the more important settings on the connection factory's various configuration tabs.

Default Message Delivery Attributes   These settings include `Priority`, `Time to Live`, `Time to Deliver`, `Delivery Mode`, `Redelivery Delay`, and `Compression Threshold`. Values set here are used for messages for which these attributes are not explicitly set in the application or not overridden by other configuration parameters.

Maximum Messages per Session   This parameter is not a true message quota, as the name might lead you to believe. For a normal JMS session, this value indicates the maximum numbers of outstanding messages (that is, messages that have not yet been processed by the consumer's business logic) that a consumer is willing to buffer locally. This buffer is also known as the message pipeline and exists on both local and remote JMS consumers.

WebLogic JMS tries to keep the consumer's pipeline full. It will deliver batches of messages to speed up processing and amortize the cost of coordinating message delivery across multiple messages. If a consumer falls behind to the point where it has too many outstanding messages, WebLogic JMS will leave the messages in the destination until the client starts to catch up. If the session is a WebLogic JMS multicast session, the server will not buffer the overflowed messages and will instead discard them based on the policy specified by the `Overrun Policy` attribute.

By default, WebLogic JMS sets this value to 10 messages. There are several situations where you might want to change the value:

❑   Applications that pass very large messages should typically reduce the value to 1 to control the number of messages in the client application's memory, keep the server from running into maximum T3 message sizes, and allow better parallelization of message processing (assuming that processing these very large messages takes time).

❑   Applications where the messages are very time sensitive should reduce the value to 1 so that messages don't get stuck in a slow client's buffer.

❑   Applications that need strict ordered processing and aren't using the Unit-of-Order feature must set the value to 1. Setting it to anything else will cause messages to get out of order if message processing fails and the message goes back to the destination for redelivery.

❑   Applications that want to maximize throughput for small messages (for example, a few kilobytes or less) should increase the value to allow the server to push more messages to a single consumer in a single batch.

Client Reconnect Attributes   The `Reconnect Policy` determines whether or not message producers and consumers attempt to automatically reconnect when they are unexpectedly disconnected. `Reconnect Blocking Time` specifies the maximum amount of time in milliseconds that a JMS call will block the calling thread while attempting to reconnect. `Total Reconnect Time` defines the maximum amount of time in milliseconds that asynchronous consumers will try to reconnect. As discussed previously, the default reconnect policy is `Producers` but we recommend handling all reconnect attempts in your JMS client code using exception listeners and disabling client reconnect by setting `Reconnect Policy` to `None`.

XA Connection Factory Enabled   All WebLogic JMS applications that wish to send or receive JMS messages as part of global JTA transactions must enable XA connection factory support. Applications that use WebLogic JMS connection factories that have not explicitly enabled this property will not participate in JTA transactions.

Load Balancing Enabled   This setting indicates whether to load balance the messages sent to a distributed destination on a per-call basis. If checked (the default), associated producers' messages are load balanced across the member destinations on every call to `MessageProducer.send()`. Otherwise, the load balancing occurs only on the first invocation, and all future invocations will go to the same member destination, unless a failure occurs. This attribute has no effect on the consumers and applies only to *pinned* producers created through this connection factory. A pinned producer sets its destination when it is created and cannot change it afterward.

Server Affinity Enabled   This checkbox controls how WebLogic JMS load balances consumers or producers running inside a WebLogic Server instance across a distributed destination. If enabled, WebLogic JMS prefers to associate consumers and producers with member destinations located in the same server process. If disabled, WebLogic JMS load balances them across all member destinations in the distributed destination just as it would if the consumers and producers were running in a remote client process.

Best Practice

Most applications should use the default values for Server Affinity Enabled and Load Balancing Enabled, which are true for both settings.

WebLogic JMS defines two connection factories, `weblogic.jms.ConnectionFactory` and `weblogic.jms.XAConnectionFactory`, which are enabled by default. You can disable them by deselecting the `Enable Default Connection Factories` checkbox in the server's `Services Configuration` tab of the WebLogic Console. Because the default connection factory settings cannot be changed, we recommend that you always define application-specific connection factories. When choosing JNDI names for user-defined connection factories (or, for that matter, anything else), avoid using JNDI names in the `javax.*` and `weblogic.*` namespaces.

Best Practice

Always define application-specific JMS connection factories and disable the default JMS connection factories. Avoid using JNDI names in the `javax.*` or `weblogic.*` namespaces.

Templates

Templates provide an efficient way to define multiple destinations with similar attribute settings. By predefining a template, you can very quickly create a set of destinations with similar characteristics. Changing a value in a template changes the behavior for all destinations using that template. Each destination can override any template-defined attribute by setting the value for the attribute explicitly on the destination itself. Using JMS templates is completely optional for applications that use predefined destinations. Any application wishing to use temporary destinations, though, is required to assign a Temporary Template to the WebLogic JMS server(s) involved.

> **Best Practice**
>
> Use JMS templates to create and maintain multiple destinations with similar characteristics. JMS servers that support temporary destinations must tell the JMS server which template to use when creating temporary destinations.

Destination Keys

By default, WebLogic JMS destinations use first-in-first-out (FIFO) ordering. Simply put, the next message to be processed by a consumer will be the message that has been waiting in the destination the longest. WebLogic JMS also gives you the ability to use message headers or property values to sort messages in either ascending or descending order. To do this, you need to define one or more *destination keys* and associate these keys with a JMS destination, either directly or through the use of a template. Any destination can have zero or more destination keys that control the ordering of messages in the destination. By creating a descending order destination key on the JMSMessageID message header, we can configure a destination to use last-in-first-out (LIFO) ordering. By creating a destination key on the JMSPriority message header, we can configure a destination to use priority ordering where WebLogic JMS will process the highest priority messages first and use FIFO ordering for messages with the same priority.

It is important to note that using sorting orders other than FIFO or LIFO increases the overhead of sending a message. WebLogic JMS will have to scan some portion of the messages in a destination to determine where to place the incoming message. Though this is not a big deal for destinations with a small backlog of messages, it can be a huge performance penalty for destinations containing a large backlog of messages. Therefore, we recommend avoiding sorted destinations unless the price of not sorting the destination (for example, in increased application complexity) is higher than the cost of the potential performance degradation.

In most cases, the default FIFO sort order works best and will always give the best performance. You can change the sorting order to LIFO using the JMSMessageID without any significant performance penalty. Sorting destinations by any other property can cause significant performance degradation on the producer or the consumer. The amount of performance degradation will depend on the number of undelivered messages stored in the destination at any point in time.

> **Best Practice**
>
> FIFO or LIFO sort orders provide the best performance. Any other sorting order can cause significant performance degradation that will be proportional to the number of undelivered messages stored in the destination.

Time-to-Deliver Extension

WebLogic JMS provides a *time-to-deliver* extension, which allows sending messages that will not be delivered until some time in the future. This extension can be a very useful feature for implementing certain types of application functionality. To use it, simply set the producer's time to deliver before sending the message, as shown here. This will cause the producer to set the WebLogic JMS–specific JMSDeliveryTime header when the message is sent. Note that you must cast the standard JMS producer to a WebLogic JMS–specific type in order to use this extension:

```
// Send the message one minute from now...
long timeToDeliver = 60 * 1000;
weblogic.jms.extensions.WLMessageProducer producer =
    (WLMessageProducer)queueSender;
producer.setTimeToDeliver(timeToDeliver);
queueSender.send(message);
```

One important point to note: The JMS provider sets most JMS message header fields. This means that regardless of what values are set using the JMS Message interface, the JMS producer will overwrite them. We mention this here because the weblogic.jms.extensions.WLMessage interface provides a setJMSDeliveryTime() method. Trying to use this mechanism to set the JMSDeliveryTime header will have no effect because the message producer will overwrite this header field value when it sends the message.

WebLogic JMS also allows you to administratively delay all messages for a particular destination. Using the destination's Overrides Configuration tab, the Time-to-Deliver Override attribute supports delaying all messages either by the same number of seconds or to be delivered at the same time each hour or day (for example, at 6:00 PM each day).

> The setJMSDeliveryTime() method in the weblogic.jms.extensions.WLMessage interface is like most of the other setter methods on the javax.jms.Message interface. Setting a value on WLMessage has no effect because the producer overwrites it when a message is sent. Use the setTimeToDeliver() method on the weblogic.jms.extensions.WLMessageProducer interface instead.

Persistent Stores

WebLogic Server provides a high performance persistent storage system for all services that require persistence. The WebLogic Persistent Store supports both file- and database-based persistent stores. Each WebLogic Server instance has a default file-based store it uses to store the server's JTA transaction log. The server can use the default store for other purposes, such as storing JMS persistent messages, though doing so limits your ability to use JMS service migration. See Chapter 12 for a more complete discussion of the automatic failover using whole server migration or service migration.

When WebLogic JMS determines that a message should be persistent, it uses the Persistent Store associated with the destination's JMS server to store the entire message. By default, WebLogic JMS keeps all messages in memory for faster access — even persistent messages that it has already written to secondary storage. If the backlog of messages is small, this can significantly improve performance without consuming significant amounts of memory. Of course, as the backlog of messages gets larger, the memory demands can cause the JVM to run out of memory.

As you will see in the "Delivery Overrides, Destination Quotas, and Flow Control" section, you can use quotas, thresholds, and paging to help control the amount of memory consumed.

Configuring Persistent Stores

WebLogic Server supports two types of persistent stores for saving JMS messages: JDBC and file-based persistent stores. The choice of a particular store type has no effect on the application code. As their name suggests, JDBC persistent stores save messages in database tables, whereas the file stores save messages in files. To use a persistent store, create a persistent store and assign it to a WebLogic Server instance. Each JMS server should have its own backing JDBC or file store, though it is possible for multiple JMS servers on the same server instance to use the same persistent store. If a JMS server does not have a configured persistent store, it will use its host WebLogic Server instance's default store. To use service migration to migrate a JMS server with an associated persistent store, you must create a custom persistent store rather than using the host's default store. In addition, the persistent store must be accessible via the same path on the target WebLogic Server. The path is either the JDBC data source name or the directory where the file resides.

JDBC-based stores may share the same physical database schema, but each must have its own uniquely named table. The JDBC store uses one table whose base name is `WLStore`. By using the `Prefix Name` parameter, you can prepend values to these base names to create unique names per store. By knowing the table naming syntax for your database, you can force the tables to be in different schemas; for example, specifying a `Prefix Name` of `bigrez.JMS_Store1_` will cause the JDBC store to create a table in the `bigrez` schema with the name `JMS_Store1_WLStore`. Failure to specify unique table names for multiple stores sharing the same database can result in message corruption or loss. JDBC-based stores will normally detect and prevent attempts by more than one store to use the same backing table; however, you should not rely on this check.

> Multiple WebLogic Server instances cannot share the same persistent store. For JDBC-based stores, you must specify a unique **Prefix Name** value for every store that uses the same database schema. Failure to do so can result in message corruption or message loss.

In the case of file stores, multiple WebLogic Server instances can share the same directory. WebLogic Server will automatically create unique names of the form `<FileStoreName>######.DAT`, where `######` is a unique number. WebLogic Server will prevent you from creating two file stores with the same name within a single domain, which prevents you from accidentally having two WebLogic Server instances trying to share the same file store. However, there is no enforcement across domains; therefore, you need to make sure that you don't create a situation where two different servers in two different domains are using the same file store directory and file store name. Now, let's compare and contrast the two types of stores.

File stores generally perform better than JDBC stores. By default, writing to a file store is a synchronous operation. WebLogic Server provides three Synchronous Write Policy settings for controlling how messages (and all other persistent data) are written to the store:

❑ Direct-Write is the default policy as of WebLogic Server 9.0. It forces all message create and delete requests to *safe storage* (which might be a disk or a battery backed cache on some high-end storage devices) on each physical write, thereby eliminating the need for a separate flush operation at the end of the transaction. In general, Direct-Write is faster than Cache-Flush and uses a native file I/O library called wlfileio2 (for example, libwlfileio2.so on Linux); however, this policy's reliability and performance depend on operating system and hardware support of on-disk caches.

❑ Cache-Flush was the default setting prior to WebLogic Server version 9.0. It forces all message create and delete requests to be flushed from the operating system cache to disk before the completion of a transaction, or a JMS operation in the nontransactional case. The Cache-Flush policy is reliable and scales well as the number of simultaneous users increases but is almost always slower than Direct-Write.

❑ Disabled allows for maximum performance, but because messages may remain in operating system caches, it exposes the application to possible message loss or duplicate messages in the event of a failure.

Before WebLogic Server version 9.0, the Direct-Write policy's performance and scalability were significantly reduced without the use of an on-disk cache. The use of an on-disk cache can expose the application to message loss or duplication in the event of a power failure unless the on-disk cache is reliable. Many high-end storage devices that offer on-disk caches also provide a battery backup to prevent the loss of data during a power failure.

To add to the complexity of the Direct-Write setting, Windows provides an OS option to enable write caching on the disk; this is enabled by default on most consumer-grade installations (for example, laptops and desktops). The problem is that some versions of Windows do not send the correct synchronization commands to tell the disk to synchronize the cache (for more information, please refer to Link 10-8). You can disable write caching with most disk drives using the Windows Device Manager entry for the disk in question; the Write Cache Enabled checkbox is located on the Disk Properties tab.

> Direct-Write writes through to safe storage, which might be an on-disk cache. Remember, using on-disk caches without battery backup can cause data loss or corruption should a power failure occur.

One final word of caution: Some third-party JMS providers set their default write policy to the equivalent of WebLogic Server's Disabled policy, which allows the operating system to buffer all file writes without flushing them to disk. Though this is great for performance, it can cause data loss and corruption in the event of a power failure. Before you try to compare performance numbers for persistent messages with WebLogic JMS, make sure you understand the write policy configuration for each JMS provider.

> Some third-party JMS providers default to the equivalent of WebLogic Server's `Disabled` policy, so make sure you check before trying to compare performance numbers with those of WebLogic JMS.

Because file stores are often collocated with the JMS server, writing to a file store may generate less network traffic. File store availability, however, is subject to hardware failures so it is often desirable to place file stores on shared disks or storage area networks (SANs). Be particularly wary if you are considering using NFS to host file stores. NFS historically has provided no support for synchronous writes, and also suffered from file locking issues. Some NFS implementations have matured in recent years, you should check that yours guarantees that a write operation will not return until the data is safely stored on disk. Because of these issues, JDBC stores may provide an easier solution for addressing the failover issues because the database typically resides on a separate machine from the application servers.

> ### Best Practice
>
> File store availability is subject to hardware failure. In situations where you need to failover, you must put the file stores on some sort of shared disk. Do not use NFS as a means to share file stores.

WebLogic Server never attempts to reduce the size of a file store. The file store grows as needed to hold all unconsumed messages up to the quota limits configured for the JMS server or its individual destinations. Although the entire file store can be reused to store new messages, the amount of disk space that the store consumes will never shrink even when the file store has no messages in it. Starting in WebLogic Server 9.2, WLST supports the `compactstore` command to compact a file store, but this only works when the WebLogic Server that hosts the store is shut down. For more information on persistent store administration, see the WebLogic Server documentation at Link 10-9.

> WebLogic Server will never shrink the size of a file store, though it will reclaim the space inside the file for future use. Set quotas on the JMS server to limit the maximum size of the store. Use the WLST `compactstore` command should you feel the need to reduce the size of the store.

Finally, a file store can be thought of as a database. For JMS applications that process large numbers of persistent messages, you should configure disk access just as you would when setting up high performance database servers. Isolate file stores on separate disks. When using multiple file stores, you may need to put each store on a separate disk, or even disk controller. Using advanced, on-disk caching technology can provide large performance improvements without sacrificing the integrity of the message store. If the messages are important enough to store to disk, they are probably too important to lose due to hardware failure. Consider using a SAN, a multiported disk, or disk mirroring technology to make the file store highly available to allow for JMS service or whole server migration.

Understanding When Messages Are Persisted

On the surface, message persistence seems straightforward, and for point-to-point messaging it is. Point-to-point message producers can specify a message's delivery mode, which determines whether the message is persistent. For WebLogic JMS, the producer's desired delivery mode can be overridden by several JMS configuration options. In the end, the message will either be persistent or non-persistent based on the application's request and the WebLogic JMS configuration. The section on overrides, quotas, and flow control provides more information on how to control message delivery characteristics such as persistence.

For publish-and-subscribe messaging, the message's delivery mode and WebLogic JMS configuration do affect the decision of whether or not to persist a message, but WebLogic JMS also considers the number and type of subscribers to the topic. If a nondistributed topic has one or more durable subscribers, messages that are sent with a persistent delivery mode will always be stored in the persistent store and will be retained until all of the durable subscribers have received a copy of the message, even in the event of a server failure and restart. If the delivery mode for the message is non-persistent, WebLogic JMS retains the messages by buffering them in memory (or paging them out to the paging directory, if needed). If there are no durable subscribers currently subscribed to a nondistributed topic, WebLogic JMS will not persist a message, regardless of whether the producer set a persistent delivery mode on the message, because there is no need to recover the messages in the event of a server failure. In the event of a server failure and recovery, the JMS specification requires only that durable subscribers that existed before the time that the persistent message was originally produced actually receive the message.

The durable subscription itself is persisted to ensure that it survives server restarts or system crashes, as required by the JMS specification. Because of this, WebLogic JMS requires that a persistent store be configured on any WebLogic JMS server that hosts topics that will have durable subscribers, even if all of the messages are non-persistent. By default, WebLogic Server will use the default persistent store if you do not explicitly associate a persistent store with the JMS server. WebLogic JMS will throw a `javax.jms.JMSException` if an application attempts to create durable subscribers on a topic that is hosted by a WebLogic JMS server with its `Store Enabled` attribute set to `false`.

Delivery Overrides, Quotas, and Flow Control

As we discussed previously, you can override default delivery attributes for messages either programmatically in the application or administratively using the WebLogic Console. In this section we take a look at how to use delivery overrides. We then examine different WebLogic JMS throttling features such as quotas, paging, and flow control.

Overriding Message Delivery Characteristics

Message delivery attributes include `Priority`, `Time to Live`, `Time To Deliver`, `Delivery Mode`, `Redelivery Delay`, and `Compression Threshold`. As you saw earlier, default values for these can be set in the connection factory; however, the application can override these values by setting them explicitly in the code. In addition, the WebLogic JMS destination configuration can override both the connection factory and the application-specified values. You can specify destination configuration overrides either directly in the destination's settings or indirectly in the destination's template settings. Any settings in the destination override the setting in the destination's template.

Let's look at an example to make sure that you understand how this works. In our example, we list the different ways to configure the `Delivery Mode` for a message being sent to a particular destination in ascending order of precedence. Each subsequent method will override all of the previously mentioned methods so that the last one that is applicable will define the actual `Delivery Mode` for the message.

1. The connection factory specifies the `Default Delivery Mode`, which defaults to persistent.

2. The application may override the `Delivery Mode` by explicitly setting it in the application code prior to sending the message. For example,

    ```
    queueSender.setDeliveryMode(deliveryMode);
    queueSender.send(message);
    ```

    where `deliveryMode` can be set to one of the following constants:

    ```
    javax.jms.DeliveryMode.PERSISTENT
    javax.jms.DeliveryMode.NON_PERSISTENT
    ```

3. The destination optionally can have a template that can override the `Delivery Mode` by setting it to `Persistent`, `Non-Persistent`, or `No-Delivery`, where `No-Delivery` is the default and simply means that the template does not override the values specified by the application or the connection factory.

4. The destination can override the `Delivery Mode` by setting it to `Persistent`, `Non-Persistent`, or `No-Delivery`, where `No-Delivery` is the default and simply means that the destination does not override the values specified by the template, the application, or the connection factory.

5. The JMS server can implicitly override a `Delivery Mode` value of `Persistent` by explicitly disabling `Store Enabled` and enabling `Allow Persistent Downgrade`. This combination will force all messages delivered to destinations associated with the JMS server to be non-persistent. If the JMS server has not been configured with this combination of options, this simply implies that the JMS server is not overriding the `Delivery Mode`.

> If an application invokes the `setJMSDeliveryMode(deliveryMode)` or `setJMSPriority(priority)` methods from the `javax.jms.Message` interface, WebLogic JMS will override these values, because the JMS specification designates that these methods are strictly for use by JMS providers. You must set the delivery mode or priority using the appropriate producer method calls for them to take effect.

Understanding Quotas

WebLogic JMS provides mechanisms for establishing quotas on individual JMS destinations, on a set of destinations, or on the entire JMS server. These quotas control the maximum amount of data that can be stored, either in a persistent store or in memory. Without quotas in place, producers can continue to produce messages until their messages consume all available space in the persistent store or all available memory in the JMS server.

WebLogic JMS quotas are JMS module-level artifacts. The `Bytes Maximum` and `Messages Maximum` attributes specify the quota's maximum number of bytes and messages, respectively. By default, quotas are not shared; each destination that uses the quota can hold the maximum number of bytes or messages the quota defines. Quotas are also sharable. This means that all destinations compete for the allowed number of bytes or messages. It is important to note that the scope of a shared quota is a single JMS server — shared quotas are never shared across JMS server boundaries.

WebLogic JMS also supports setting a quota directly on the JMS server itself. As of WebLogic 9.0, this JMS server-level quota applies only to destinations that aren't using a named quota. For example, `JMSServer-1` contains three queues, `Queue1`, `Queue2`, and `Queue3`, and defines a JMS server-level quota of 50 megabytes. `Queue1` is using a named quota whose message maximum attribute is set to 25 megabytes. This effectively sets a private quota of 25 megabytes on `Queue1` and a shared quota of 50 megabytes on `Queue2` and `Queue3` for a maximum possible memory footprint for `JMSServer-1` of 75 megabytes.

> **The scope of a shared quota is a single JMS server. JMS server–level quotas apply only to destinations not using named quotas.**

When the quota is reached, WebLogic Server JMS producers will wait for a limited time until space becomes available up to the user-defined timeout period. If the quota condition does not subside before the timeout period, producers get a `javax.jms.ResourceAllocationException`. It is up to the application how to handle this condition.

The connection factory's `Send Timeout` attribute controls the maximum number of milliseconds a producer will block when waiting for space. By default, it is set to 10 milliseconds. You can disable blocking sends by setting this value to 0. An application may choose to override this setting by changing the value on the producer:

```
weblogic.jms.extensions.WLMessageProducer producer =
    (WLMessageProducer)queueSender;
producer.setSendTimeout(sendTimeoutMillis);
queueSender.send(message);
```

You should be very careful about using blocking sends with message producers running inside a WebLogic Server instance. These will cause the server's execute threads to block during quota conditions and could bring the entire server to a grinding halt and possibly deadlock the server for the amount of blocking time. In most cases, application message producers running inside the server should either disable blocking sends or set their values very small to prevent thread starvation. Also, be careful about retrying sends indefinitely inside the server for similar reasons.

> **Blocking sends are a convenient way to shield applications from temporary quota limits. Care needs to be taken, though, when the producers are running inside a WebLogic Server so as not to completely block execute threads that are needed to consume messages and clear the quota limit condition. To disable blocking sends, set the `Send Timeout` to 0.**

The `Blocking Send Policy` attribute of the JMS server defines the expected behavior when multiple senders are competing for space on the same JMS server. The valid values are as follows:

FIFO   This value indicates that all send requests are to be processed in the order in which they were received. When the quota condition subsides, requests for space are considered in the order in which they were made.

Preemptive   This value indicates that any send operation can preempt other blocking send operations if space is available. That is, if there is sufficient space for the current request, that space is used even if there are other requests waiting for space. This can result in the starvation of larger requests. If sufficient space is not available for the request, the request is queued up behind other existing requests.

Best Practice
Always configure quotas to prevent the server from consuming all available space while storing unconsumed messages. A good rule of thumb is to assume that each message will consume 512 bytes — even if the message has been paged out.

Understanding Message Paging

A WebLogic JMS server will automatically move in-memory messages out of the server's memory to secondary storage to prevent trying to hold too many messages in memory; this is known as *paging*. When a message that has been paged out of memory is needed, the server moves it back into memory. This paging behavior is completely transparent to the JMS application. Of course, reading and writing messages to disk will have a significant performance impact, but this is much better than filling up all of the server's available memory.

WebLogic JMS keeps all messages in memory for faster access — even persistent messages. This can cause problems as the number and size of the persistent messages in the destination grow. Fortunately, WebLogic JMS automatically pages messages out of memory when its message buffer fills up. The JMS server determines the size of its message buffer using the `Message Buffer Size` attribute if it is set to a nonnegative number of bytes. By default, the `Message Buffer Size` is set to -1, which means that the JMS server will automatically determine the size of its message buffer. When automatically determining the message buffer size, the JMS server sets the message buffer size to either one-third of the maximum heap size or 512 megabytes, whichever is smaller.

Tip to Remember
Paging is important for both persistent and non-persistent messages.

A JMS server uses its `Paging Directory` to store paged messages. By default, every JMS server uses `$DOMAIN_HOME/servers/<server-name>/tmp` as the paging directory. Of course, you probably want to configure the paging directory explicitly so that you can control the location of the store, which might be on a RAID disk array to increase performance for high-volume systems.

For persistent messages stored in a file store, WebLogic JMS actually does not use the paging directory to page messages larger than 64 kilobytes because they already exist locally in the persistent store. For smaller messages, it writes the messages to the paging store to improve the performance when it needs to page in the messages. One important thing to note is that even though the paging process writes non-persistent and persistent messages to the paging directory as needed, these messages will not survive server restarts or system crashes. Because of this, there is no need to worry about high availability of a paging directory.

Paging is an important preventive mechanism. Most non-persistent messaging applications, however, choose to use non-persistent messages for speed. Because paging will significantly reduce the performance of your messaging application, you should tune your application configuration to try to prevent paging from ever occurring. Remember, a healthy messaging system requires consumers to keep up with producers over time.

> **Best Practice**
>
> Paging should be a last line of defense because of its impact on performance. Always design and tune your JMS application to avoid paging during normal peaks in message load.

Understanding Flow Control

WebLogic JMS flow control can slow down the rate at which message producers are sending messages in an attempt to allow consumers to catch up before quota limits are reached. Once it starts controlling the flow of messages to a particular JMS server or destination, it will continue to do so until the number of unconsumed bytes or messages drops below the configured lower threshold. At that point, WebLogic JMS will tell the producers to start increasing their flow of messages gradually until message rates are no longer being throttled.

Flow control configuration involves settings on the producer's connection factory and on either the JMS server or a destination. By default, WebLogic JMS enables flow control on all connection factories but effectively disables it from ever occurring through the default thresholds on JMS servers, templates, and destinations.

To configure thresholds, use the `Thresholds & Quotas Configuration` tab of the JMS server, JMS template, or JMS destination. Like quotas, thresholds can be set in terms of the number of bytes or the number of messages. `Bytes Threshold High` and `Messages Threshold High` specify the upper threshold that WebLogic JMS uses to determine when to start flow control. When the number of bytes or messages exceeds the upper threshold, WebLogic JMS will log a warning message and start limiting the producers' message flows for any producers using connection factories with flow control enabled.

`Bytes Threshold Low` and `Message Threshold Low` specify the lower threshold that WebLogic JMS uses to determine when to stop flow control. When the number of bytes or messages drops below the lower threshold, WebLogic JMS logs a message and disarms any flow control that was occurring and instructs all of the flow-controlled producers to begin increasing their message flow rates gradually.

The attributes that control the tuning of the flow control algorithm are set via a producer's connection factory. When you create a connection factory, flow control is enabled by default and the flow control tuning parameters are given some default values, as shown in Figure 10-5. Of course, you can change the default values as necessary. Let's spend some time looking at the flow control algorithm and how these tuning parameters affect its behavior.

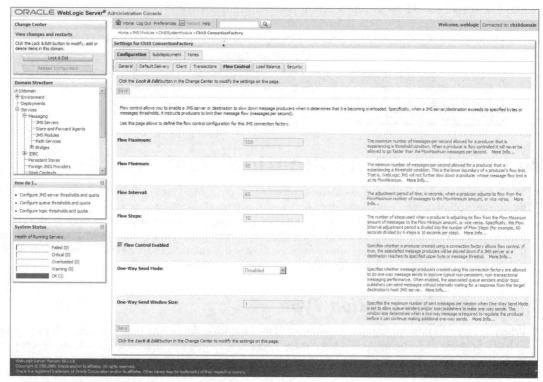

Figure 10-5: Configuring the flow control parameters.

WebLogic JMS engages the flow control algorithm when an upper threshold is reached. At that point, WebLogic JMS will limit the flow rate of all producers by setting their maximum allowable flow rate to that specified by their connection factory's Flow Maximum parameter. Unless the lower threshold is reached first, WebLogic JMS will continue to slow down producers over time until all producers are at their minimum flow rate, as specified by the connection factory's Flow Minimum parameter. The rate at which WebLogic JMS slows down producers is controlled by the Flow Interval and Flow Steps parameters. Flow Interval defines the time interval over which a producer is slowed from its maximum rate to its minimum rate. Flow Steps is the number of incremental steps WebLogic JMS uses in the slow-down process. It reduces the flow rate more rapidly in earlier steps, so the server reacts quickly to a breach of the maximum threshold.

Once the maximum allowable flow rate reaches the Flow Minimum value, WebLogic JMS will maintain the producers' flow rates until the JMS server or destination backlog reaches the lower threshold. At that point, WebLogic JMS will linearly increase the producers' maximum allowable flow rates Flow Steps times over the Flow Interval period, with the final step disengaging flow control completely.

As with paging, flow control should be used as a preventive measure. Flow control is no substitute for proper application design and tuning so that consumers can keep up with producers. Under the covers, flow control causes the producer's sending thread to sleep for a period of time. This has two implications. First, flow control only works for message producers that send multiple messages. Second, you should think carefully before using flow control on producers running inside the WebLogic Server because flow control effectively slows down the sending thread. We discuss this more in the next section, where we go into more detail about how to design JMS applications properly with WebLogic Server.

> **Best Practice**
>
> Use flow control as a preventive measure for producers that run outside the WebLogic Server process. Be careful using flow control inside the server because it will cause server threads to slow down.

WebLogic JMS Application Design

The previous section looked at the different throttling mechanisms WebLogic JMS provides to help offset temporary spikes in message production. In general, you need to design your messaging applications so that the consumers can keep up with the producers over long periods of time. If messaging applications tend to produce more messages than they can consume, eventually the application will fall so far behind that it runs into physical resource constraints such as running out of memory or disk space. In this section, we discuss some design considerations for messaging applications.

Choosing a Destination Type

When designing a JMS application, a commonly asked question is whether to use queues or topics. Trying to think in terms of destination type often leads to confusion. Instead, you should think about what type of messaging your application requires. In general, point-to-point style messaging should use queues, whereas publish-and-subscribe style messaging should use topics. Of course, there is no hard and fast rule, and it is possible to use either type of destination with most applications if you are willing to do enough work. When using queues, some things to remember are:

- ❏ Each message will be processed by one consumer.
- ❏ Messages will remain on the queue until they are consumed or expire.
- ❏ Persistent messages are always persisted.
- ❏ Using message selectors becomes expensive as the number of messages in the queue gets large.

When using topics, some things to remember are:

- ❏ Each message can be processed by every consumer.
- ❏ Unless you are using durable subscriptions, messages will be processed only if at least one consumer is listening at the time the message is sent.
- ❏ Persistent messages are persisted only when durable subscriptions exist.
- ❏ Using message selectors with topics becomes expensive as the number of consumers gets large.
- ❏ Unlike queues, which can divide their messages across multiple parallel consumers, a single topic subscription usually has a single active consumer. An exception is WebLogic Server MDBs

that subscribe to a WebLogic JMS topic but don't use container-managed transactions. In this case, an MDB will multiplex a single topic subscription over multiple instances within a server, and so process the messages in parallel. This is a useful feature; it is not possible to arrange such parallel processing of messages for a single subscription using the standard JMS API.

Best Practice

Choose your destination type based on the type of messaging. Point-to-point messaging implies queues, and publish-and-subscribe messaging implies topics.

Locating Destinations

In WebLogic JMS, a destination physically resides on a single server. JMS provides two ways for an application to obtain a reference to a destination. First, you can explicitly look up the destination using the JNDI API and cast it to the appropriate destination type, `Queue` or `Topic`, or implicitly have the container inject the reference using an annotation.

Second, you can use the `Session.createQueue(destinationName)` or `Session.createTopic(destinationName)` methods to locate an existing queue or topic. Note that these methods are really misnamed since they will not create new destinations, only return a reference to a pre-existing destination. These create methods require an application to pass destination names using a vendor-specific syntax.

For WebLogic JMS, the default syntax is:

```
<jms-server-name>/<jms-module-name>!<jms-destination-name>
```

For example, to obtain a reference to a destination named `queue1` from the module named `module1` that resides in the JMS server named `JMSServer1`, you would use a destination name of `JMSServer1/module1!queue1`. You can replace the `<jms-server-name>` with a "." to restrict the search to the local server — that is, the one with which your JMS connection is associated (for example, `./module1!queue1`).

When referring to a distributed destination, omit the JMS server name and forward slash because a distributed destination spans JMS servers; for example, `module1!MyDistributedQueue`. To refer to an individual member destination of a uniform distributed destination, use the following syntax:

```
<jms-server-name>/<jms-module-name>!<jms-server-name>@<udd-name>
```

If `queue2` is the name of a distributed queue, you could use `JMSServer1/module1!JMSServer1@queue2` or `./module1!JMSServer1@queue2` to get the member queue on `JMSServer1`.

WebLogic Server also allows you to influence the name used to call the `createQueue()` or `createTopic()` method. This feature allows you to remove, or at least reduce, the WebLogic JMS configuration-related information from the name passed to these create methods. Simply use the `Create Destination Identifier` (CDI) under the `Advanced` portion of the destination's `General Configuration` tab to specify a name for the destination. Now, the syntax for a nondistributed destination or a member of a uniform distributed destination will be `<jms-server-name>/<cdi-name>`

or ./<cdi-name>. Even with a CDI specified, the reference to the distributed destination remains the same (<jms-module-name>!<udd-name>).

Given that the default behavior for the createQueue() and createTopic() methods require specifying the WebLogic JMS server, module name, or both, we feel that these methods are of limited value (unless you can use the CDI name with the *dot* notation) because:

❑   We generally want to hide the location of the destination from the application. Any advantages that might be gained by using these methods rather than JNDI are likely to be offset by requiring the application to understand what JMS server or module the destination lives in. Any change in deployment topology would likely require changing the value of the names passed to these methods.

❑   As we mentioned previously, these methods use a vendor-specific naming syntax that is not portable across providers.

As a result, we recommend using JNDI or annotations to obtain references to JMS destinations. JNDI lookups, though, are relatively expensive so applications should attempt to look up JMS destinations once and cache them for reuse throughout the life of the application.

Best Practice

Use JNDI to locate destinations. Caching and sharing JMS destinations or using annotations throughout the application will help to minimize the impact of the JNDI lookup overhead.

Choosing the Appropriate Message Type

Choosing a message type is the second design choice you face when designing JMS applications. TextMessage is one of the more commonly used message types simply because of the type of data typically exchanged. As the popularity of XML increases, TextMessage popularity increases because the JMS specification does not explicitly define a message type for exchanging XML documents. However, serializing a string is more CPU-intensive than serializing other Java primitive types. Using strings as the message payload often implies that the receiver must parse the message in order to extract the data encoded in the string. WebLogic JMS also provides an XMLMessage type. The primary advantage of the XMLMessage type is the built-in support for running XPath-style message selectors on the body of the message.

Let's take a minute to talk more about XML messages. Exchanging XML messages via JMS makes it easy to think about solving many age-old application integration problems. Although JMS uses Java and Java already provides a platform-independent way of exchanging data, not all messaging applications are written in Java. Fortunately, many popular legacy messaging systems, such as IBM's WebSphere MQ, offer a JMS API in addition to their other language bindings. Oracle also provides both a C and .NET API to WebLogic JMS. This solves the message exchange part of the problem.

XML solves the data exchange part of the problem by providing a portable, language-neutral format with which to represent structured data. As a result, it is not surprising to see many JMS applications using XML messages as their payload. Of course, the portability and flexibility of XML do not come without a cost. Not only are XML messages generally sent using TextMessage objects, which makes their serialization more costly, but they also generally require parsing the data in order to convert it into language object representations that the application can manipulate more easily. All of this requires that the receivers do more work just to be able to get the message into a form where it can be processed.

This is not to say that you should avoid XML messages completely. XML is the format of choice for messages that cross application or organizational boundaries. When talking about applications here, we define an application as a program or set of programs that are designed, built, tested, and more importantly, deployed together as a single unit. What we want to caution you on is using XML message formats everywhere — even within the boundaries of a single application — just to be using XML. Use XML where it makes sense, and use other binary representations where XML is not required.

> **Best Practice**
>
> Use XML messages for inter-application messaging and binary messages for intra-application messaging.

When choosing the message type for an application, there are several things you should consider. A well-defined message should have just enough information for the receiver to process it. You should consider how often the application will need to send the message and whether the message needs to be persistent. Message size can have a considerable impact on network bandwidth, memory requirements, and disk I/O. Keep messages as small as possible without removing information needed to be able to process the message efficiently.

Once you decide on the information to pass, use the simplest message type that can do the job. If possible, use a message format that is directly usable by the receiver, such as a `MapMessage` or `ObjectMessage`.

If you have only a few primitive types to send in a message, try using a `MapMessage` instead of an `ObjectMessage` for better performance. As the number of fields gets larger, however, the mapping code itself can add complexity. You might find that the performance benefit is outweighed by the additional maintenance burden. `MapMessage` also provides some extensibility in the sense that you can add new name-value pairs without breaking existing consumers. When you are using an `ObjectMessage`, providing your own custom serialization by implementing `Externalizable` rather than relying on the default Serializable implementation can improve the marshalling performance.

We should caution you about the implications of using an `ObjectMessage` to pass data across application boundaries. `ObjectMessage` uses Java serialization, which relies on the sender and the receiver having serialization-compatible versions of the class available. This can lead to tightly coupled producers and consumers — even though you are using asynchronous messaging for communication. It might be possible to escape some of this coupling by implementing `Externalizable`, but this just means that your externalization code has to deal with object versioning. In contrast, XML provides more loosely-coupled message passing between applications. XML schemas can be written to validate different versions of a message, optional content can be ignored by systems that don't understand it, and an XML message can easily be transformed and adapted.

`BytesMessage` generally will produce the smallest message sizes. However, you need to carefully weigh the benefits of the smaller message sizes against the expense and complexity of marshalling and unmarshalling your data into and out of an array of bytes. Like with using an `ObjectMessage` to cross application boundaries, using a `BytesMessage` to cross application boundaries can produce a similar coupling problem in that the sender and receiver must understand the format of the byte array being passed.

Best Practice

Use the simplest and smallest message type that is directly usable by the receiving application. Favor `MapMessage` when sending small collections of primitive data types, and avoid `ObjectMessage` and `BytesMessage` to reduce coupling between disparate systems.

Compressing Large Messages

XML messages tend to be larger than their binary counterparts. As you can imagine, larger messages will require more network bandwidth, more memory, and more importantly, more storage space and disk I/O to persist. If the messages are infrequent, this may not be an issue, but as the message frequency increases, the overhead will compound and start affecting the overall health of your messaging system. One way to reduce this impact is to compress large messages that carry strings as their payload. Compressed XML messages may actually provide a more compact representation of the data than any other binary format.

WebLogic JMS connection factories provide a `Default Compression Threshold` parameter to compress messages automatically whose serialized message body exceeds the configured value. The performance impact of message compression, however, is not clear cut and needs to be evaluated on a case-by-case basis. When considering the use of compression, there are a number of things to weigh. First, are your messages big enough to warrant compression? Small messages do not generally compress very well so using compression can, in some cases, actually increase the size of your message.

Second, will the extra overhead of compressing and decompressing every message prevent your applications from meeting your performance and scalability requirements? Compressing messages can be thought of as a crude form of throttling because the compression step will slow down your message producers. Of course, this isn't necessarily a good thing because your consumers will also have to decompress the message before processing it.

Finally, will compression significantly reduce your application's network and memory resource requirements? If the producers and consumers are not running inside the same server as the destination, compressing the messages can reduce the network transfer time for messages. It can also reduce the memory requirements for your WebLogic JMS server. If the messages are persistent, it can also reduce the amount of disk I/O for saving and retrieving the messages. When the persistent store type is JDBC, it can reduce the network traffic between the WebLogic Server and the database. If the producers, consumers, and JMS server are all running inside the same WebLogic Server instance, many of these benefits may be outweighed by the additional CPU and memory overhead of compression and decompression.

> **Best Practice**
>
> The decision whether to use compression is something that needs to be carefully considered. It is usually only beneficial when transferring messages to and from remote clients over low speed networks. If the producers, consumers, and destinations are collocated inside a WebLogic Server instance, it is generally better not to use compression.

Selecting a Message Acknowledgment Strategy

WebLogic JMS retains each message until the consumer acknowledges that it has received the message. Only at this point can WebLogic JMS remove the message from the server. Committing a transaction is one way for an application to acknowledge a message has been received. If transactions are not being used, an application uses message acknowledgments to acknowledge that a message, or set of messages, has been received. Message acknowledgments and transactions, whether they are JMS transacted sessions or JTA transactions, are mutually exclusive. If you specify both transactions and acknowledgments, WebLogic JMS will use transactions and ignore the acknowledgment mode.

Your application's message acknowledgment strategy can have a significant impact on performance and scalability. WebLogic JMS defaults to using AUTO_ACKNOWLEDGE mode. This means that WebLogic JMS will automatically acknowledge each message after the receiver processes it successfully. Using AUTO_ACKNOWLEDGE mode can reduce the chance of duplicate messages; however, it comes at a cost because the receiver's runtime must send an acknowledgment message to the JMS server after each message to tell the server to remove the message.

If your application can tolerate duplicate messages, JMS defines the DUPS_OK_ACKNOWLEDGE mode to allow the receiver's runtime to acknowledge the messages lazily. Another technique that gives you a little more control is using CLIENT_ACKNOWLEDGE mode to explicitly acknowledge groups of messages rather than each message individually. Though message duplication is still possible, it typically occurs only because of a failure where your receiver has already processed some messages but had not acknowledged them. You could imagine building a strategy that tries to detect duplicate messages when starting up or recovering from a failure condition.

In addition to the standard JMS message acknowledgment modes, WebLogic JMS provides two additional acknowledgment modes through the weblogic.jms.WLSession interface:

> **NO_ACKNOWLEDGE**   This mode tells WebLogic JMS not to worry about message acknowledgments and simply provide a best-effort delivery of messages. In this mode, WebLogic JMS will immediately delete messages after they have been delivered, which can lead to both lost and duplicate messages in the event of a software or hardware failure. Applications that want to maximize performance and scalability and can tolerate both lost and duplicate messages should use this acknowledgment mode.
>
> **MULTICAST_NO_ACKNOWLEDGE**   This mode can only be used for nondurable topic subscribers, and tells WebLogic JMS to use IP multicast to deliver messages to consumers. This has large performance and scalability benefits, because the network only deals with one message regardless of the

number of subscribers, but it does require a fast, reliable network and the application must be able to tolerate occasional message loss. As the name implies, this mode has similar acknowledgement semantics to the NO_ACKNOWLEDGE mode.

For remote, nondurable subscribers, WebLogic JMS pushes local copies of the message to every client JVM to optimize network overhead. Because this strategy also includes message acknowledgment optimizations, these subscribers really will not benefit from using the aforementioned CLIENT_ ACKNOWLEDGE strategy or from using NO_ACKNOWLEDGE; AUTO_ACKNOWLEDGE should perform equally well.

We talk more about using multicast sessions later in this section.

Best Practice

Applications that explicitly acknowledge sets of messages will generally be faster and more scalable than those that acknowledge each message individually to minimize the possibility of receiving duplicate messages.

Designing Message Selectors

As we discussed earlier in the "JMS Key Concepts" section, message selectors allow consumers to filter the set of messages they want to receive. Consumers specify a logical statement using an SQL WHERE clause–like syntax that the JMS provider evaluates against each message's headers or properties to determine whether the consumer should receive the message. WebLogic JMS adds another type of selector for use with the WebLogic JMS XMLMessage type. With this message type, you can specify XPath expressions that evaluate against the XML body of the message.

In WebLogic JMS, all selector evaluation and filtering takes place on the JMS server, with the exception of multicast subscribers, which we discuss later. For topics, WebLogic JMS evaluates each subscriber's message selector against every message published to the topic to determine whether to deliver the message to the subscriber.

For queues, the evaluation process is more complex. A message is always delivered to a queue, and WebLogic JMS will evaluate the message against each *active* consumer's message selector until it finds a match. An active consumer is either a synchronous receiver that is waiting in a receive() call or an asynchronous listener that has room for more messages in its local buffer, whose size is controlled by the consumer's connection factory's Maximum Messages per Session attribute. If no active consumer's message selector matches the message, the message will remain in the queue. When a new active consumer associates itself with the queue, WebLogic JMS must evaluate the consumer's message selector against each message in the queue, delivering matching messages. This may take some time.

What does this all mean? It means that while a queue consumer stays active, WebLogic JMS maintains state about which messages have been tested against the consumer's selector. As soon as it becomes inactive, that state is lost. The next time it becomes active, it must start from the beginning of the queue, testing each message until it either becomes inactive or reaches the end of the queue. Once it reaches the end of the queue, the consumer's selector will be added to the set that is evaluated when new messages arrive — a much more efficient process. If your queue maintains a large backlog and your consumers are going in and out of the active state frequently, your consumers will likely end up evaluating their selectors against the same messages multiple times.

Be wary of applying selectors where consumers are frequently connecting to queues — which includes those switching in and out of the active state — that contain an existing backlog of messages. In these circumstances, performance of queue selectors may be greatly degraded. In contrast, the performance of topic message selectors is stable, and the cost of adding a new subscriber is small. See our discussion of indexed subscribers later in this section.

It is often better to split a destination into multiple destinations and eliminate the need for message selectors. For example, imagine an application that sends messages to the `trade` queue. If the application's consumers that use message selectors to select only `buy` or `sell` orders, we can split the `trade` queue into `buy` and `sell` queues and eliminate the need for a message selector. When a producer sends a `buy` message, it sends the message directly to the `buy` queue, and only `buy` consumers need to listen to that queue. Partitioning applications in this way has other advantages besides performance. With this architecture, you can monitor each message type individually in each queue, and if performance does become an issue down the road, you can even separate the queues onto separate servers.

> **Best Practice**
>
> Always evaluate the advantages and disadvantages of using multiple destinations before deciding to use message selectors. Favor splitting destinations over the use of message selectors when there is a clear separation of message types.

Of course, there will be situations when using a message selector is appropriate. In these situations, there are several things to keep in mind when designing your message selector strategy. First, what fields does your selector need to reference? Message header and property fields are the fastest to access. Examining an `XMLMessage` message body adds a significant amount of overhead and, therefore, will be much slower.

Suppose that the producer sends a message in XML format like the one shown here:

```
<order type="buy">
    <symbol>beas</symbol>
    <quantity>5000</quantity>
</order>
```

The consumers can use an XPath message selector like this:

```
"JMS_BEA_SELECT('xpath','/Order/attribute::type') = 'buy'"
```

These XPath message selectors are the most expensive expressions to evaluate because they involve parsing at least some portion of the XML document. Of course, XPath selectors are convenient to use, but you should realize that they are expensive and plan your use of them accordingly.

Second, what type of operators do you need to use? In general, you should strive to keep selectors as simple as possible. Avoid complex operators such as `like`, `in`, or `between` in favor of primitive operators such as =, >, or <. The more complex the selector is, the slower its evaluation will be. In general, an XPath expression will be the most expensive because it has to scan the XML body of the message looking for the element or attribute value to compare.

> ### Best Practice
> Keep message selectors as simple as possible. Try to avoid more complex operators such as `like`, `in`, or `between`.

Third, what data type do you need to use for the selector? Where possible, avoid the use of strings in message properties, especially if they are large. Strings are more expensive to serialize and more expensive to compare than other primitive types. In our previous example, if we decided to use message selectors to distinguish between `buy` and `sell` messages, we would be better off performance-wise defining the message property as an integer (for example, 1 = buy, 2 = sell) rather than using the strings `buy` or `sell`.

WebLogic JMS supports the concept of *indexed subscribers* for topic applications that have many subscribers and a need to efficiently use selectors to differentiate messages. With an indexed subscriber, an application uses message property names, rather than the value of a particular message property, to distinguish the messages. To obtain a performance boost, an indexed subscriber's selector must be exactly of the form `<property_name> IS NOT NULL`. For example, the application would set the `buy` message property to any value on all `buy` messages and the `sell` message property to any value on all `sell` messages. Consumers only interested in `sell` messages would use the expression `sell IS NOT NULL` for its message selector. Because the subscribers are indexed based on the message property names in the selector, it is generally faster to use an indexed subscriber than it is to use the strings `buy` and `sell` as the value for the `trade_type` message property.

> ### Tip to Remember
> String data types are typically the slowest, most expensive types to compare. Using other primitive data types will generally improve the efficiency of your application. If your topic-based application needs to use strings to differentiate messages, use indexed subscribers to improve the performance of the message selectors.

Fourth, when using compound selectors, which elements are most efficient to process and which elements are most selective? If a selector involves both message header fields and message property fields, place the message header field to the left of the expression. It is less expensive to use the expression `JMSPriority > 5 AND (trade_type = 'buy')` than it is to use the expression `(trade_type = 'buy') AND JMSPriority > 5`. When a selector involves multiple evaluation criteria where one field is much more selective than the other, it may make sense to put this one first to reduce the number of evaluations necessary to rule out a particular message. For example, if you had a selector that did something like `(trade_type = 'buy') AND (trade_num_shares > 100000)`, it would make more sense to reverse the order because presumably there are many more buy orders than there are orders that involve more than 100,000 shares. Selector evaluation is always left-to-right, except where parentheses explicitly preclude it.

> ### Tip to Remember
> With compound selectors, order matters. WebLogic JMS will short-circuit message selector evaluation once it determines the message does not match. Design your selectors to take advantage of this default left-to-right evaluation order.

Finally, what type of messaging do you need to use? We certainly do not recommend that you choose the messaging model based on whether you need to use message selectors. You should know, though, that message selectors generally tend to be faster and more predicable with topics than with queues. Of course, this is not always the case. When using message selectors with queues, the performance will be very dependent on the consumers keeping up with the producers and with quick matching of a message to a consumer. In cases where the queue is typically empty and it is easy to find a match between a message and a consumer, queues will actually outperform topics. The problem is that when something happens to make the consumers not keep up, the performance of message selectors with queues will degrade much faster than with topics because the performance can degrade proportionally to the number of messages in the queue.

One last thing to mention before moving on to other design considerations is the interaction between message selectors and paging. WebLogic JMS maintains messages in memory whenever possible. Whenever paging is necessary, only the message body is paged out of memory. This means that WebLogic JMS can evaluate most selectors even if the message body itself is paged out. The exception to this would be XPath selectors. Because WebLogic JMS evaluates the selectors on topics at the time the message is published, this is only a big concern for XPath selectors used in conjunction with queues.

Choosing a Message Expiration Strategy

By default, JMS messages never expire. When your application is sending messages to queues or topics with durable subscribers, WebLogic JMS must retain the message until it is consumed. This is fine in most point-to-point messaging applications because consumers are constantly consuming messages. Any message sent to a queue will typically be consumed in a relatively short period of time. If the queue consumers get disconnected, they will usually reconnect as soon as possible and start processing any messages that might have built up in the queue.

For durable subscribers to a topic, this is not necessarily true. The messaging system is forced to retain any message that has not been consumed by a durable subscriber, regardless of whether that durable subscriber will ever return. In this case, WebLogic JMS is at the mercy of the durable subscriber to unsubscribe when it no longer wishes to receive the messages. If the durable subscriber logic is flawed in such a way that the subscribers do not unsubscribe properly, the messaging system will start to fill up with messages that may never be delivered. As you can imagine, this calls for real caution in your use of durable subscribers. Fortunately, there is another way to help deal with this problem.

Conventional wisdom suggests that the time-sensitive messages should be sent only to nondurable subscribers, and that is true for the most part. In some situations a producer may wish to publish time-sensitive messages even when a subscriber is not connected. For example, an employee portal application may wish to publish messages to a topic that represents all employee mailboxes. If each employee uses his or her login ID as the durable subscription's client ID, the employees can receive published messages every time they log in. Imagine that you want to send pension plan enrollment information to all your employees. The problem is that the JMS server must retain the message until every employee reads the message, which may never happen. Because the message is really irrelevant after the enrollment period ends, it is better to set an expiration time on the message so that WebLogic JMS can discard the message when it becomes unimportant — even if some employees never read it.

Message expiration can be set at the connection factory level or via any of the other override mechanisms discussed earlier. Using a connection factory's `Default Time-to-Live` attribute, using a JMS template's or destination's `Time-To-Live Override` attribute, or by explicitly calling the `setTimeToLive()` method on the `MessageProducer`, you can specify the number of milliseconds that WebLogic JMS should retain an undelivered message after it is sent.

Best Practice

For messages that become irrelevant after a certain time, set the connection factory's `Default Time-to-Live` attribute, use the JMS template's or destination's `Time-To-Live Override` attribute, or call `setTimeToLive()` on the producer to avoid message buildup.

Active Expiration

Prior to WebLogic Server 8.1, WebLogic JMS used a lazy message expiration policy. This means that it would remove expired messages from the system only when it happened to discover them in its normal course of processing messages. If a destination was idle, it was possible for expired messages to accumulate and continue to consume system resources. This meant that, under certain conditions, it was possible for a new message to be rejected because of quota restrictions even though the destination or JMS server contained expired messages that, if removed, would have cleared the quota condition and allowed for the delivery of the message.

WebLogic Server 8.1 added support for active message expiration, in addition to the lazy message expiration scheme. Active message expiration works by having each JMS server periodically scan all destinations for expired messages. The JMS server's `Expiration Scan Interval` property controls the frequency of the scans. If a message expires at time t, the maximum length of time that the message will be retained is t + ExpirationScanInterval + s, where s is the time it takes to scan all message expiration times in the JMS server at the next scan interval. Some messages may be removed almost immediately, by lazy message expiration. Other messages may not be removed until the full amount of `ExpirationScanInterval` + s seconds has elapsed. Setting `ExpirationScanInterval` to 0 disables active message expiration. Even with active expiration disabled, messages will still expire and be removed during normal message processing by the lazy message expiration mechanism.

Setting `ExpirationScanInterval` to a very large value effectively disables active scanning for expired messages. Of course, expired messages will still be removed during normal message processing by the lazy expiration mechanism.

Expiration Policies

WebLogic JMS supports the concept of an *Expiration Policy* on a destination. Expiration policies allow you to define the action that WebLogic JMS should take when it finds an expired message. Configure the `Expiration Policy` using the JMS template's or destination's `Delivery Failure Configuration` tab in the WebLogic Console. The valid values are as follows:

Discard WebLogic JMS removes expired messages from the destination. This is the default.

Log WebLogic JMS removes the expired messages from the destination and writes an entry to the server log file indicating that the messages have been removed. The `Expiration Logging Policy` defines the actual information that is logged.

Redirect WebLogic JMS moves the expired messages from their current destination to that destination's configured `Error Destination`, if defined.

> You cannot use the `Redirect` policy when there is no valid error destination defined for the destination. Similarly, you cannot remove the error destination for a destination that is using the `Redirect` policy.

By setting the `Expiration Policy` to `Log`, you are telling WebLogic JMS to write a log entry for every expired message it removes. Using the `Expiration Logging Format` attribute, you can tell WebLogic JMS what information to log. WebLogic JMS will always write the `JMSMessageID` header; by default, this is the only information logged. You can add message headers or properties to the list by explicitly listing their names using a comma to separate the entries. WebLogic JMS also provides two wildcard values, `%header%` and `%properties%`, that will write all message headers or all message properties to the log, respectively.

> **Tip to Remember**
>
> When the `Expiration Policy` is set to `Log`, WebLogic JMS always writes the `JMSMessageID` field to the log. If you forget to set the `Expiration Logging Format`, the log entry will contain only the message's `JMSMessageID` value.

Handling Poison Messages

At some point, most messaging applications encounter situations where they are unable to process a message successfully. This might occur for multiple reasons; for example, the message could contain bad data, or the business logic might require access to a backend system that is temporarily unavailable. In these situations, the message consumer cannot successfully process the message and needs to do something with that message so that it can move on to do other useful work, if possible. For example, a message-driven bean using transactional delivery might call `setRollbackOnly()` on its `MessageDrivenContext` object to prevent the transaction from committing, thus forcing the JMS provider to requeue the message.

The problem with our example is that the JMS provider will simply try to redeliver the message at some point in the future. If the redelivery occurs and the application is still unable to process the message, the application can end up in a deadly cycle of trying to process a *poison* message. When designing your messaging application, you need to understand in what situations your application might encounter poison messages and come up with strategies that make sense to reduce the burden on the underlying messaging system.

If your application accepts messages from another application, you might want to plan for unexpected or invalid message formats or data. Although you could use WebLogic JMS's support for *error destinations* to handle this situation, it doesn't solve the problem. In this case, the problem is not a system-level problem with the actual delivery of the message, but an application-level problem with the expected contents of the message. As a result, asking the messaging system to try to redeliver the message is a waste of resources because the application will never be able to process the message. Furthermore, the offending message producer might continue to try to resend this message or, worse, all messages with this invalid message format or data. In this situation, you almost always want the application to reject the message, possibly by notifying the sending application that the message was rejected because of a bad message format or bad data. This means that you need the receiving application to divert the poison message to an error-handling process that will notify the sender of the problem rather than rejecting the message and forcing the messaging system to try to redeliver it.

> **Best Practice**
>
> Use application-level error handling rather than redelivery and error destinations to handle errors in message content, including invalid formats and bad data.

Another common situation that occurs in the message processing application is that a backend system becomes temporarily unavailable. Because the receiving application may require access to this backend system to be able to process the incoming messages, the application must somehow delay the processing of the messages until the backend system becomes available. Ideally, you could somehow detect that the backend system is unavailable and simply tell the application to stop trying to consume any messages until further notice. Today this means writing your application to support this. Fortunately, WebLogic JMS provides several features that support this.

First, WebLogic JMS supports pausing and resuming JMS destinations either at server startup or at runtime. Destinations can be paused for message production, insertion, and consumption. Pausing a destination for insertion pauses it for production, but also affects in-flight operations such as:

- ❑ Messages that have not yet reached their time-to-deliver.
- ❑ Messages that are part of a transaction that has yet to be committed.
- ❑ Messages that are awaiting available quota.

Pause a destination for insertion if you want to make sure no new messages appear on the destination. With these management capabilities, it is much simpler to pause message consumption to prevent MDBs from continually trying to consume the messages and resume message consumption only once the back-end system becomes available. For cases where you expect, or at least want to plan for, long periods of backend system unavailability, you should carefully consider using a mechanism for automatically pausing and resuming the consumption of messages.

Second, WebLogic Server automatically disconnects an MDB if its source destination becomes unavailable. WebLogic Server will periodically try to re-establish the JMS connection to the source destination until it successfully reconnects.

You can also suspend and resume the MDB's JMS connection manually through the WebLogic Console or WLST. If the destination your MDB is listening on has multiple consumers and not all of them access the unavailable backend application, suspending the MDB may be a better option than pausing consumption from the WebLogic JMS destination.

Third, WebLogic MDBs will heuristically pause themselves after a certain number of consecutive application failures. See the discussion of this in the "Message-Driven Bean Settings" section of Chapter 8 for a detailed discussion of this capability.

Finally, if your backend systems are highly available and you never expect more than transient periods of unavailability, you might want to rely on the JMS provider's ability to redeliver the message at some point in the future. WebLogic JMS supports this through the use of `Redelivery Delay`, `Redelivery Limit`, and `Error Destination`.

Tip to Remember

For receiving applications that require access to external systems that are known to be unavailable occasionally, consider manually pausing message processing when the system becomes unavailable and resuming it after the system comes back online.

Redelivery Delay, Redelivery Limit, and Error Destination

`Redelivery Delay` instructs WebLogic JMS to defer the redelivery of messages for a specified amount of time. Messages with a redelivery delay do not prevent other messages behind the delayed message from being delivered and can alter message ordering for those applications not using WebLogic JMS's Unit-of-Order or Unit-of-Work features. You can set the `Default Redelivery Delay` on your WebLogic JMS connection factory. From there, you can explicitly override the `Redelivery Delay` on the session by using the WebLogic JMS extensions:

```
((WLSession)session).setRedeliveryDelay(redeliveryDelayMilliseconds);
```

You can also administratively override both the connection factory and session settings by setting the `Redelivery Delay Override` on a template or destination.

`Redelivery Limit` controls the number of times that WebLogic JMS will attempt to deliver a message before declaring it undeliverable. When a message is determined to be undeliverable, WebLogic JMS will move the message from its current destination to that destination's associated `Error Destination`. If no `Error Destination` is configured, the messages are silently deleted.

If the `Error Destination` has reached its quota, WebLogic JMS will drop the message and log an error message once every five minutes until the quota problem is resolved. For non-persistent messages, this means that the message is discarded; for persistent messages, the message will remain in the persistent store and will reappear in the original destination the next time the server starts.

Message producers can set the redelivery limit for messages they produce using the WebLogic JMS `WLMessageProducer` extension:

```
((WLMessageProducer)producer).setRedeliveryLimit(3);
```

If you pass –1 as the argument to `setRedeliveryLimit()`, it means that there is no limit unless it is overridden by the destination. Both the `Redelivery Limit` and `Error Destination` are configurable on a JMS template or destination. Setting the `Redelivery Limit` on a template or destination overrides any setting passed in from the producer; a value of –1 specifies that there is no override. An `Error Destination` can be a queue or a topic but must physically reside in the same JMS server as the associated destination.

When using error destinations, it is very important to incorporate the processing of messages from this destination in your application. One of the biggest challenges in doing this can be determining why the message was not successfully processed and what your application needs to do with it. We highly recommend that you do not let the error queue be used to handle application-level message content errors. If you can handle these errors through a separate process, you should be able to treat all messages in the error destination as messages that could not be processed due to transient failures. One way of processing them would simply be to resend them to their original destination once you know that the transient failure has subsided. If you are using an Expiration Policy of Redirect, you may also have to look at message expiration times to segregate the messages to retry from those that expired. This isn't a big deal because it is easy to accomplish. Trying to segregate application-level errors from transient system-level errors placed onto the error queue is much more difficult.

> **Trying to separate messages on an error queue that got there because of both application-level errors and system-level errors can be very difficult, if not impossible. Designing your application to use a separate application-level destination for application errors will make processing messages in an error destination much simpler.**

Redelivered Flag and Redelivery Count

Nontransactional applications may want to perform extra checking when receiving a message to determine if it has been delivered previously. This extra checking often involves checking some persistent history to determine whether or not the message has already been processed. To support this type of checking, the JMS specification requires JMS providers to support the Message.getJMSRedelivered() method, which must return true if the message has already been delivered.

WebLogic JMS also supports the JMSXDeliveryCount property that returns the number of delivery attempts. If a message has potentially already been delivered once, the value of this field will always be at least 2. WebLogic JMS tries to persist the value of JMSXDeliveryCount so that it survives server restarts. In the event of a server crash or forced shutdown, the returned value may be lower than actual number of delivery attempts, but will always be at least 2 if at least one delivery attempt has already been made.

Handling Message Ordering Issues

Many applications require processing of messages in the order in which they were sent. The problem is that the only way to guarantee that messages are processed in order is to have a single consumer processing one message at a time. For example, imagine that you have to send three messages to a queue in the following order: message1, message2, and message3. If you have two consumers, consumer1 and consumer2, processing messages concurrently from that queue, WebLogic JMS will pick up message1 and hand it to consumer1 and then pick up message2 and hand it to consumer2. From a WebLogic JMS perspective, it has delivered the messages in order; from an application perspective, the messages may or may not be processed in order, depending on the thread or process scheduling between the two consumers. It is a race condition at this point. As such, it is entirely possible for consumer2 to get more resources than consumer1 and complete the processing of message2 before consumer1 completes the processing of message1. Furthermore, it is also possible for consumer2 to go back to WebLogic JMS to get message3 and complete the processing of message3 before consumer1 ever finishes with message1. In short, as soon as you start parallel processing, message ordering across the threads or processes can no longer be guaranteed.

Other factors besides having a single JMS consumer can affect message ordering. To summarize, ordered processing of messages requires you to:

1. Have a single JMS consumer processing the messages.

2. Set the JMS Connection Factory's `Maximum Messages per Session` attribute to 1.

3. Ensure that all messages requiring ordering go to the same physical destination.

4. Do not use custom destination sort orders that alter the normal FIFO ordering.

5. Do not set redelivery delays.

Clearly, you need a way to maintain ordering without creating a bottleneck in your application that can process only one message at a time. The typical way to handle message ordering issues is to try to define sets of messages that require ordering only within the set and parallelize the processing by assigning different sets of messages to different threads/processes. WebLogic JMS's *Unit-of-Order* feature allows JMS applications to easily define sets of messages that require ordered processing while allowing different message sets to be processed in parallel.

Unit-of-Order

WebLogic JMS provides a unit-of-order capability to allow JMS applications to group messages into sets that require strict ordered processing. A unit-of-order set is identified by its name and its associated destination. For each destination, all message producers using the same unit-of-order name will produce messages that are part of the unit-of-order.

When unit-of-order messages are processed, they will be processed in strict order. While the current unit-of-order message is being processed by a message consumer, the next message in the unit-of-order will not be delivered unless it is to the same transaction or session. If no message associated with a particular unit-of-order is processing, then a message associated with that unit-of-order may go to any session that's consuming from the message's destination. This guarantees that all messages will be processed one at a time and in order, and any rollback or recover will not prevent ordered processing of the messages. Unit-of-order works with distributed destinations and with the WebLogic Store-and-Forward service, which we discuss later in the "External JMS Providers" section.

As you can see, the choice of the unit-of-order name changes how the messages are processed. If the unit-of-order name is an account number, no two sessions or transactions will process the same account at the same time. This helps the overall application design to know what overlapping processing is prevented. Moreover, this can help speed up processing of shared resources. You may need locks for correctness, but the locks for a resource associated with a unit-of-order should not be contended.

You can set WebLogic JMS units-of-order administratively on connection factories, templates, or destinations, or your application can set it directly by calling a method on its producer.

The connection factory's `Default Unit-of-Order for Producer` attribute allows you to specify one of the following values.

❑ None — Specifies no default unit-of-order for producers created using the connection factory; this is the default value.

❏   System-generated — Specifies that WebLogic JMS should use a system-generated unit-of-order name for producers created using the connection factory.

❏   User-generated — Specifies that WebLogic JMS should use the value of the User-generated Unit-of-Order Name attribute as the unit-of-order name for producers created using the connection factory.

WebLogic JMS templates and destinations can also be configured to assign a default system-generated unit-of-order name to any messages arriving at a destination that is not already part of a unit-of-order. Be careful when using this default unit-of-order option with distributed destinations, as WebLogic JMS scopes the ordering to a particular member destination. If a producer sends messages to two different members, the producer's messages may not be processed in the order in which they were sent. To ensure strict ordering when using a default unit-of-order with a distributed destination, the producer for an ordered set of messages must pin itself to a single member destination so as not to divide the ordered set of messages across more than one member destination.

Finally, JMS applications can programmatically configure a system- or user-generated unit-of-order using one of the setUnitOfOrder() methods from the weblogic.jms.extensions.WLMessageProducer interface, as shown here.

```
Destination queue = (Destination)ctx.lookup("java:comp/env/jms/myqueue");
MessageProducer producer = session.createProducer(queue);
((WLMessageProducer)producer).setUnitOfOrder();   // use system-generated UOO
String uooName = ((WLMessageProducer)producer).getUnitOfOrder();
```

As you can see, you have multiple ways to set up your JMS applications to use the unit-of-order feature. With some applications, administratively configuring unit-of-order may allow your application code to take advantage of this advanced feature without requiring code change. As the logic that determines the unit-of-order to use becomes more complex, the application may need to choose different connection factories or destinations to send messages to the proper unit-of-order or they may need to programmatically change the unit-of-order before each message send. If you find that you need to create large numbers of connection factories or destinations to meet your application's unit-of-order requirements administratively, you may be better off setting the unit-of-order programmatically.

> **Best Practice**
> Administratively configure unit-of-order when your application's ordering requirements are simple. As the complexity of choosing which unit-of-order to use for each message increases, consider specifying the unit-of-order programmatically, because it may be simpler.

A unit-of-order's scope is a destination; that is, all messages associated with a particular unit-of-order must be sent to the same destination. As such, multiple destinations using the same unit-of-order name will each define separate units-of-order. If a unit-of-order is defined on a distributed destination, by default WebLogic JMS routes all messages for that unit-of-order to one member destination since only one physical destination at a time can own a unit-of-order. If the unit-of-order's member destination is unavailable, producers associated with the unit-of-order will receive a weblogic.jms.extensions.JMSOrderException when sending a message because the specified quality of service is not available. When using unit-of-order with distributed destinations, you should always send the messages to the distributed destination rather than to one of its members. If you are not careful, sending messages directly to a member destination may result in messages for the same unit-of-order going to more than one member destination and cause you to lose your message ordering.

> **Messages sent as part of a unit-of-order associated with a distributed destination are always sent to one member destination. If that member destination becomes unavailable, the producer will receive a `JMSOrderException` when sending the message because the specified quality of service is not available.**

You might be wondering how WebLogic JMS knows which member destination to use when multiple producers are sending messages associated with the same unit-of-order to a distributed destination. WebLogic JMS supports two routing mechanisms to accomplish this: Path Service–based routing and hash-based routing. Before we talk about the routing mechanisms, let's discuss another message grouping feature of WebLogic JMS called *Unit-of-Work*. Before we do that, we need to talk about using unit-of-order with topics.

Using Unit-of-Order with Topics

Unit-of-order is most commonly used with queues. While it can be used with topics, care must be taken when the message consumers are MDBs. As mentioned previously, WebLogic MDBs not using container-managed transactions will multiplex the messages from a topic subscription across multiple MDB instances, thus processing the messages in parallel. This feature is useful to speed up message processing but, at the time of writing, it does not take into account any unit-of-order. You must disable this parallel processing to preserve the order by either using container-managed transactions or by setting `<max-beans-in-free-pool>` to 1.

When producing unit-of-order messages to a distributed topic, you must target the distributed topic itself. Unlike other JMS messages, sending unit-of-order messages directly to a member topic is not recommended and may cause messages to be delivered out of order. Sending the messages directly to the distributed topic is the natural approach so this restriction shouldn't cause any problems.

Unit-of-Work

Whereas unit-of-order provides JMS applications with a way to achieve strict ordered processing within a group of messages, some applications need additional guarantees that require the entire group of messages to be processed as a unit by a single consumer. This is exactly what WebLogic JMS's Unit-of-Work feature provides. One or more message producers define messages belonging to a unit-of-work by name. Each message contains JMS message properties that specify the unit-of-work name, the message's position in the unit-of-work sequence, and whether or not the message is the last message in the unit-of-work. Unit-of-work messages can pass through any number of intermediate destinations; consumers at these intermediate destinations can process the messages individually, in any order, and even in parallel — no grouping semantics are enforced at intermediate destinations. When the messages in the unit-of-work reach the terminal destination, they are held until all messages in the group arrive. Once they all arrive, the entire group of messages is passed to a single consumer as a `java.util.List` of messages stored inside a `javax.jms.ObjectMessage`.

To create messages that are part of a unit-of-work, simply use the standard JMS methods to set the JMS message properties listed in Table 10-1 on each message before sending it.

415

Table 10-1: Unit-of-Work Message Properties

Property Name	Property Type	Example Value
JMS_BEA_UnitOfWork	String	"myUnitOfWork"
JMS_BEA_UnitOfWorkSequenceNumber	int	5
JMS_BEA_IsUnitOfWorkEnd	boolean	false

At some point, all messages in a unit-of-work must end up at a *terminal destination*. A terminal destination is any destination whose Unit-of-Work (UOW) Message Handling Policy is set to Single Message Delivery. Terminal destinations also have an Expiration Time for Incomplete UOW Messages property to specify how many milliseconds a destination should wait before expiring messages in an incomplete unit-of-work. By default, messages never expire. If an incomplete unit-of-work is expired, the expired messages are handled using the destination's specified expiration policy.

To consume the messages at a terminal destination, the message consumer code will look similar to that shown here.

```
void onMessage(Message message)
{
    List msgList = (List)((ObjectMessage)message).getObject();
    for (int i = 0; i < msgList.size(); i++) {
        TextMessage msg = (TextMessage)msgList.get(i);
        ...
    }
}
```

Like unit-of-order, unit-of-work can be used with distributed destinations. Terminal destinations that are distributed destinations route all messages for each unit-of-work to the same member destination. This is accomplished via either the Path Service or hash-based routing.

Unlike a unit-of-order where the messages effectively stream through the system one at a time, applications must take care to control the size of a single unit-of-work. All of the messages comprising a particular unit-of-work are ultimately collected into a single ObjectMessage for delivery to the final consumer. As such, both the server that delivers this message and the client that receives it must have enough memory to hold the entire message.

Path Service and Hash-Based Routing

The *Path Service* is a singleton service that runs on one server in the cluster and routes all messages associated with a particular unit-of-order and unit-of-work to the same member destination of the targeted distributed destination. It uses a WebLogic Server persistent store to save the state of which member destination a particular unit-of-order or unit-of-work is currently using. When a Path Service receives the first message for a particular unit-of-order or unit-of-work bound for a distributed destination, it uses the normal JMS load balancing heuristics to select which member destination will handle the unit and writes that information into its persistent store. Note that when a unit-of-order has no unconsumed messages pending, the Path Service entry is removed and future messages may be sent to other member destinations.

By default, the Path Service uses the server's default persistent store. For high availability purposes, the Path Service can be targeted to a migratable target to allow for automatic or manual migration; however, this requires the use of a custom store.

If the Path Service is not configured, WebLogic JMS uses a hash-based routing mechanism. The hash-based routing algorithm uses the unit-of-order name to determine to which member destination the unit-of-order is associated. This means that the routing decision is made in the client based on the number of configured member destinations without any considerations for the normal JMS load balancing heuristics.

Both styles of routing have strengths and weaknesses. Hash-based routing makes the routing decision in the client so it is more efficient and does not require service or whole server migration to make the routing service highly available. However, hash-based routing is static in the sense that it doesn't take into account which members are up and running. If a member is down, producers for that unit-of-order will throw `weblogic.jms.extensions.JMSOrderException` — even if there are no outstanding messages for that unit-of-order. In addition, administratively adding or removing members will cause the hash results to change and will break the ordering guarantee for any executing unit-of-orders when messages start getting routed to new locations.

The Path Service provides a more resilient ordering guarantee. Unlike hash-based routing, the Path Service ensures that a new UOO, or an old UOO that has no messages currently on any destination, can be enqueued anywhere in the cluster. Adding and removing member destinations will not disrupt any existing unit-of-order because the routing decision is made dynamically and those decisions are persistent. Of course, use of the Path Service requires accessing the Path Service and potential disk access to make the routing decision, which can add overhead to your application.

The major drawback of the Path Service is that it is a singleton service. You must provide for high availability of this service either via JMS service or whole server migration. If the Path Service is unavailable, any requests to create new units-of-order will throw the `JMSOrderException` until the Path Service is available. Information about existing units-of-order are cached in the connection factory and destination servers so the Path Service availability typically will not prevent existing unit-of-order messages from being sent or processed.

If you can accept the occasional loss of ordering (perhaps you are just using UOO to avoid locking problems), or you will only change distributed destination configuration when the system is shut down, hash-based routing is fine. If you need strict message ordering that can cope with the reconfiguration of distributed destinations, or you wish to use the producer load balancing heuristics for each new unit-of-order (important if you want server affinity), you should configure the Path Service, and further consider making it highly available.

We hope that some future version of WebLogic Server provides a new and improved routing option that combines the best of these two mechanisms and eliminates most of the drawbacks. Check your WebLogic Server documentation for more information on the current options, capabilities, and limitations.

Using Transactions

Transactions are used when multiple operations need to be treated as single atomic unit. As discussed earlier, the JMS specification introduces the concept of a transacted session to allow multiple JMS operations to be performed within the scope of a transaction. If your transactions involve multiple

JMS operations only within a single session, you should use transacted sessions. For transactions that involve multiple JMS sessions or other resources, you will need to use JTA transactions. You can make your JMS session *JTA-aware* by enabling XA transaction support on your connection factory. Using the WebLogic Console, simply check the XA Connection Factory Enabled checkbox on the Transactions Configuration tab. This will make WebLogic JMS return a connection factory that implements the javax.jms.XAConnectionFactory interface whenever you look up the connection factory from JNDI.

If your transaction involves multiple resources, the WebLogic JTA transaction manager detects this and switches automatically to the two-phase commit (2PC) protocol. WebLogic JMS implements its own XA resource manager and therefore can participate in a 2PC transaction without requiring support from the underlying storage manager (for example, the JDBC driver for JDBC-based message stores). One side effect of this is that transactions that involve JMS and any other database resource — even if JMS is using the same database as its persistent store — will always involve a 2PC transaction. Another side effect of this is that JMS JDBC-based persistent stores do not use XA JDBC drivers. You must use the non-XA version of the driver for accessing the persistent store; WebLogic JMS will update the database to reflect the commit or rollback of JMS transaction branches without enlisting the database itself in the global transaction.

> ### Tip to Remember
> Do not use an XA JDBC driver to create JMS JDBC stores even when the store would participate in global transactions.

For any other database work done by other components as part of the transaction, you need to use a JTA-aware DataSource. A JTA-aware DataSource means one that has the Supports Global Transactions attribute selected. Typically, you will want your JTA DataSource to use an XA-compliant JDBC driver so that it can participate in 2PC transactions using the XA protocol. It is possible for WebLogic JTA to involve one non-XA JDBC resource in a global transaction. For a DataSource that refers to a JDBC connection pool that is not using an XA-compliant driver, you can use either the Emulate Two-Phase Commit option or the Logging Last Resource option. In the "Selecting Transaction Options for a Data Source" section of Chapter 12, we discuss why you should always use the Logging Last Resource option when using a non-XA JDBC driver to perform work as part of a larger JTA transaction involving XA resources.

> ### Best Practice
> When your application uses transactions that contain JMS resources and other resources, using XA JDBC drivers will give you transactional safety and the most flexibility. One of the database resources can be configured to use the Logging Last Resource option without sacrificing the transactional safety of pure XA and with better performance.

If you are going to be using global transactions that involve JMS, the most important thing to keep in mind is that WebLogic JTA will optimize global transaction coordination for collocated resources. Some of the ways that you can collocate resources are as follows:

❑ If your transactions involve JMS and one or more EJBs, deploy all of your EJBs and JMS destinations on the same WebLogic Server instances. If you are using distributed destinations, deploy all of the EJBs to every server that hosts a member destination.

❑ If your transactions involve an MDB and distributed destinations that both run in the same cluster, target the MDB to the cluster. This combination will cause WebLogic Server to automatically deploy an MDB instance on each distributed destination member and to dynamically respond as destination members are migrated, created, or deleted.

❑ If your transactions involve JMS and JDBC resources, deploy your JDBC connection pools, JTA-aware `DataSource` objects, and JMS destinations on the same WebLogic Server instances. Again, for distributed destinations this means deploying them to every server that hosts a member destination.

❑ If your transactions involve multiple JMS destinations, deploy all of the destinations on the same WebLogic Server instance. For applications accessing multiple distributed destinations, make sure to collocate the members of each distributed destination on the same WebLogic Server instances. In both cases, it is even more efficient if you can deploy them in the same JMS servers.

Using Multicast Sessions

Multicast sessions are a WebLogic JMS extension for publish-and-subscribe messaging that can improve performance dramatically, especially when your application needs to send individual messages to a large number of subscribers. When using IP multicast to transmit messages, the underlying network needs to carry only one copy of the message regardless of the number of subscribers. Because of the inherent unreliable nature of the UDP protocol on which IP multicast is based, WebLogic JMS does not guarantee delivery of messages sent using multicast sessions. Network congestion plays a big role in the quality of service. Clearly, applications that cannot tolerate message loss should not consider the use of multicast sessions.

Multicast also requires a tightly controlled network environment. Most routers and firewalls are not configured to allow multicast traffic to pass through them. Though it is possible to configure them to do so, it requires that your subscribers and WebLogic JMS servers are all connected by a network that you can control. Multicast messages use a *time-to-live* (TTL) concept that routers use to control the propagation of multicast messages. Each router that forwards a multicast packet decrements the packet's TTL; once the TTL reaches zero, the packet will no longer be forwarded between network segments. Multicast uses a special class of IP addresses, known as *Class D addresses*, which range from 224.0.0.0 to 239.255.255.255. Typically, addresses in the 224.0.0.x range are reserved for multicast routing.

WebLogic JMS supports only multicast sessions for topics. This makes sense because the benefit of multicast is seen only when the same message is sent to large numbers of consumers. To use multicast sessions, you need to configure the multicast information for your topics. When using multicast, we highly recommend that you select unique multicast address and port combinations for each topic that will be using multicast for message delivery. Doing this will help segregate the traffic for a particular topic and will reduce the chances of message loss.

> **Best Practice**
> Always select unique multicast address and port number combinations for each topic that will use multicast message delivery. Never use the same multicast address and port number used by your WebLogic clusters.

419

Once the topics are properly configured, you need to create a JMS session that uses the WebLogic JMS-specific `MULTICAST_NO_ACKNOWLEDGE` acknowledgment mode, as shown here. Note that multicast sessions cannot use transacted sessions or JTA transactions. Use the following code to create a multicast session:

```
Session session =
    connection.createSession(false, WLSession.MULTICAST_NO_ACKNOWLEDGE);
```

Next, we create the `MessageConsumer` as we normally would, as shown here. This call will fail if the topic is not configured to support multicast. Also note that multicast consumers cannot be durable subscribers.

```
MessageConsumer consumer = session.createConsumer(topic);
```

Finally, we need to register our `MessageListener` and start the connection, if it is not already started. Multicast sessions must use asynchronous delivery via the `MessageListener`:

```
consumer.setMessageListener(new MyMessageListener());
connection.start();
```

For multicast sessions, WebLogic JMS tracks the message sequence. A sequence gap occurs when messages are lost or received out of order. When WebLogic JMS detects a sequence gap, it will deliver a `weblogic.jms.extensions.SequenceGapException` to the multicast session's `ExceptionListener`, if one is registered.

Tip to Remember

If your application cares about sequence gaps when using multicast delivery, you can register an `ExceptionListener` with the WebLogic JMS session to be notified when sequence gaps occur.

At the time of writing, you should avoid using multicast sessions with distributed topics. The semantics of this combination are not well defined and your subscribers may well receive multiple copies of each message (because each member topic that receives the message will rebroadcast it). Please check the WebLogic JMS documentation for any updates that may have happened since this book was published.

At the time of writing, the semantics of using multicast sessions with distributed topics is not well defined. As such, you should avoid this combination. Check the WebLogic JMS documentation for any recent updates that may have occurred since this book was written.

Handling Request/Reply Style Message Exchange

JMS is all about sending and receiving messages. Whenever an application sends a message to another application, it is not uncommon for the sending application to require a response message after its original message is processed. This pattern is so common that JMS explicitly supports the pattern in several ways.

First, JMS supports the concept of a temporary destination, and the JMS message headers include a `JMSReplyTo` field for passing a reference to a *reply-to* destination as part of a message. Though there is nothing that requires the reply-to destination to be a temporary one, this is a common pattern that clients use to prevent having to use message selectors to find their response among responses for other clients. Be very careful about using a distributed queue as the reply-to destination. Because the responding application uses a different JMS connection to reply, it is very possible that the reply message could end up on a different member destination than the one the requestor is using to listen for the reply. As such, only applications where any node in the cluster can handle the response should use this pattern.

> Be very careful about using a distributed queue as the reply-to destination. Doing so will likely cause situations where the reply message is sent to a different member queue that the one the requestor is using to listen for the reply. Only applications where any node in the cluster can handle the response should use this pattern.

An example of how you might use the `JMSReplyTo` field for passing a reference to a temporary reply-to destination is shown here:

```
Queue responseQueue = session.createTemporaryQueue();
MessageConsumer consumer = session.createConsumer(responseQueue);
consumer.setMessageListener(new MyMessageListener());
textMessage.setText("My Request Message");
textMessage.setJMSReplyTo(responseQueue);
producer.send(textMessage);
...
responseQueue.delete();
```

Now, let's look at the consumer of the request message. In the consumer, we simply get the `JMSReplyTo` destination from the request message, generate our response message, and send the response message to the destination:

```
Queue replyQueue = (Queue)requestMessage.getJMSReplyTo();
producer.send(replyQueue, replyMessage);
```

In this example, our request producer is using the `MessageListener` to asynchronously receive the response that will be sent to the temporary destination. This is the recommended way of accomplishing the request/response pattern. Of course, applications sometimes want to block until the response comes back. You could achieve this using the synchronous `receive()` method:

```
Queue responseQueue = session.createTemporaryQueue();
MessageConsumer consumer = session.createConsumer(responseQueue);
textMessage.setText("My Request Message");
textMessage.setJMSReplyTo(responseQueue);
producer.send(textMessage);
Message responseMessage = consumer.receive();
responseQueue.delete();
```

Here, we used the *no-args* `receive()` method that blocks until a message arrives. There is also a version that accepts a timeout value, after which the method will return control to the application even if no message has arrived. Finally, there is a `receiveNoWait()` method that does not block and will return `null` if no message is waiting.

> Use the `receive(long timeout)` or `receiveNoWait()` methods inside server applications that need to receive a response message synchronously from another application. Even in standalone JMS client applications, think twice before using the *no-args* `receive()` method, which can cause the application to block for an uncontrolled length of time.

Notice that, in both cases, we call the `delete()` method on the temporary destination when we are through with it. Applications should try to reuse temporary destinations rather than continually creating and deleting them, wherever possible. WebLogic Server will automatically delete temporary destinations when the JMS connection is closed.

The JMS specification authors thought that this pattern was so common that they created an easier way to accomplish the same thing by using a *Requestor* object. The code shown here demonstrates how to accomplish the same synchronous request/response pattern using a temporary queue.

```
QueueRequestor queueRequestor =
    new QueueRequestor(queueSession, requestQueue);
textMessage.setText("My Request Message");
Message responseMessage = queueRequestor.request(textMessage);
```

The `QueueRequestor` and `TopicRequestor` utility classes automatically create the temporary destination and block waiting for the response. Be forewarned that these classes do not allow you to perform non-blocking or blocking with a timeout request. You must use nontransacted sessions with these classes. As with all temporary destinations, the messages sent to them are non-persistent because temporary destinations, by definition, do not survive application restarts or failures.

> **Best Practice**
>
> When using request/response style messaging inside a WebLogic Server instance, be very careful about calling blocking methods to receive the response. If you must call `receive()`, always use a relatively short timeout to prevent tying up WebLogic Server execute threads for extended periods of time. Wherever possible, use the asynchronous `MessageListener` to wait for the reply. Or better still, use a non-temporary reply queue and process responses in an MDB.

The other major approach for supporting request/reply messaging is through the use of a *correlation ID*. Correlation IDs provide you with the ability to assign a unique identifier to a message and its reply. JMS doesn't do anything with these correlation IDs; it is up to the application to use them to correlate requests with replies. By using correlation IDs, you have much more freedom about where and when you send the reply. Using correlation IDs can be useful even when used in conjunction with temporary destinations to help applications that can have multiple outstanding messages at any point in time.

To use correlation IDs, the first thing you need to decide on is what unique identifier you are going to use to correlate the messages. The JMS provider creates a unique identifier for every JMS message that it stores in the JMSMessageID header. As a result, using the JMSMessageID as the correlation ID is a common practice. JMS messages also contain a JMSCorrelationID header that applications can use to set the correlation ID for a particular message.

When using this scheme, the producer sending the message needs to call only the getJMSMessageID() method on the Message *after* the message is sent. It is important to wait until after the message is sent because WebLogic JMS does not actually set the message's JMSMessageID header until the message is sent. The producer doesn't actually need to set the JMSCorrelationID field in the request message because the consumer is going to associate the JMSMessageID of the request message with the JMSCorrelationID of the reply message:

```
replyMessage.setJMSCorrelationID(requestMessage.getJMSMessageID());
```

Of course, there is nothing preventing you from using your own correlation ID scheme. Simply set the correlation ID in the original request message, and have the consumer read the incoming request message's correlation ID using the getJMSCorrelationID() method and then set it on the outgoing reply message.

The last thing we need to discuss as it relates to correlation IDs is the use of a shared reply queue across all requests. A very common pattern we see occurs where you have a synchronous client, such as a web application responding to a request from a browser, needing to call a backend system that is accessible only via a messaging system. Usually, the synchronous client wants to send a message and wait for the response. The client, however, will typically wait only so long and then give up on the response, possibly even resending the original request. This causes a problem if your backend system is slow but still working, in that the shared reply queue may end up with reply messages that have already been abandoned by the requestor. Fortunately, you can do several things to handle this problem.

First, you can use message expiration on the reply messages to prevent them from accumulating. For that matter, you might want to use expiration times on the request messages to try to prevent the backend from receiving messages that the client has given up on. Finally, you could just use temporary destinations that the client deletes when giving up on the reply. This will also give your backend system some indication that the client has left when it gets an error trying to send the response to the temporary destination that no longer exists. None of these solutions really solves all of the application-level problems associated with this type of scenario, but at least they help keep the messaging system healthy.

WebLogic Server provides an asynchronous servlet programming model that allows the server to release execute threads while waiting for the data needed to generate the HTTP response. While this will help you build a more scalable, resource-friendly application for this type of scenario, it does not solve the fundamental problems with the messaging system since the client request may still timeout. The preferred approach to dealing with this type of scenario is to try to separate the synchronous client request into two separate requests, one to submit the backend request and another to look for the backend response.

Before we move on, we need to discuss another issue you may need to consider when using the JMS request-response pattern. The JMS request-reply mechanisms discussed in this section assume that the responder knows how to send a message to the reply-to destination. If both the requestor and the responder are using the same logical JMS server (for example, WebLogic JMS resources deployed to the same cluster), the responder can simply use a local JMS connection factory to send the reply message. What happens if the reply-to destination is hosted in another logical JMS server (for example, a WebLogic JMS destination deployed to a remote WebLogic Server cluster)?

Your responding application must use a connection factory that knows how to route the message to the reply-to destination. Since the JMS specification does not define a standard way to pass the connection factory along with the JMSReplyTo header, your application must define a mechanism to pass this information to the responder. Typically, you will want to pass the information as part of the JMS message; for example, in custom JMS message properties.

We do not recommend trying to pass the actual connection factory object. Instead, we recommend passing enough information to perform a JNDI lookup of the appropriate connection factory. One approach would be to pass the required JNDI InitialContext properties and the connection factory's JNDI name so that the responder knows how to look up the connection factory from the remote JNDI provider. Another approach is to leverage WebLogic JMS's Foreign Server or WebLogic Server's Foreign JNDI Provider capabilities to create a local JNDI binding to the remote JMS connection factory. This would eliminate the need to pass the JNDI InitialContext properties so that only the JNDI name needs to be passed. One drawback of this approach is that the JNDI name the requesting application needs to pass changes to the JNDI name in the responding application's JNDI tree rather than its own local JNDI tree, which makes for slightly tighter coupling of the requesting and responding application. We discuss the WebLogic JMS's Foreign Server and WebLogic Server's Foreign JNDI Provider capabilities in more detail later in the "Mapping External JMS Objects to WebLogic JNDI" section.

WebLogic JMS Application Programming

In this section, we look at how to use WebLogic JMS in your application. We start out by talking about the WebLogic JMS resource pooling and how to leverage that support with web applications and EJBs. We finish this section with a discussion of how to use WebLogic Server's message-driven bean support to consume JMS messages from server-side applications.

Using WebLogic JMS with Servlets and EJBs

Using WebLogic JMS from within your server-side application can be simpler than using it from within standalone client applications. By making use of the Java EE–defined mechanisms for referencing JMS objects through deployment descriptor resource reference mappings, WebLogic JMS transparently substitutes the real JMS objects for wrappers that pool JMS resources like connections and sessions. This also works with foreign (third-party) JMS providers. To use this, you simply add a resource-ref into your standard Java EE deployment descriptor (that is, web.xml or ejb-jar.xml):

```
<resource-ref>
  <res-ref-name>jms/BigRezEmailConnectionFactory</res-ref-name>
  <res-type>javax.jms.ConnectionFactory</res-type>
  <res-auth>Container</res-auth>
  <res-sharing-scope>Shareable</res-sharing-scope>
</resource-ref>
```

Then, you add a matching resource-description entry in your WebLogic Server–specific deployment descriptor (that is, weblogic.xml or weblogic-ejb-jar.xml):

```
<resource-description>
  <res-ref-name>jms/BigRezEmailConnectionFactory</res-ref-name>
```

```
    <jndi-name>BigRezEmailConnectionFactory</jndi-name>
  </resource-description>
```

Finally, you simply look up the connection factory and write standard JMS code, as shown here:

```
ConnectionFactory factory = (ConnectionFactory)
    jndiCtx.lookup("java:comp/env/jms/BigRezEmailConnectionFactory");
Queue queue = (Queue)
    jndiCtx.lookup("java:comp/env/jms/BigRezEmailQueue");
Connection connection = null;
try {
    connection = factory.createConnection();
    ...
}
catch (JMSException jmse) {
    ...
}
finally {
    if (connection != null) {
        try { connection.close(); } catch (JMSException ignore) { }
    }
}
```

Java EE 5 makes obtaining the JMS connection factory and destination objects even easier through the use of annotations. Using the @Resource annotation, we can eliminate the need for the deployment descriptor entries and simplify the code, as shown in this excerpt from the EmailServicesImpl stateless session bean in our bigrez.com example.

```
@Resource(mappedName=bigrez.jms.connectionfactory)
private ConnectionFactory jmsConnectionFactory;

@Resource(mappedName=bigrez.jms.emailQueue)
private Destination emailQueue;

...
try {
    Connection connection = null;
    try {
        connection = jmsConnectionFactory.createConnection();
        ...
    }
    finally {
        if (connection != null) {
            connection.close();
        }
    }
}
catch (JMSException jmse) {
    ...
}
```

The @Resource annotation's mappedName attribute specifies the global JNDI name where the resources can be located. This value is used only if it has not been provided or overridden in one of the deployment descriptors.

Notice that we are closing our connection at the end of each use inside the `finally` block. This is critical when using pooled resources and is just like what you would do when using JDBC connection pools. In our example, we are using injection to obtain the connection factory and queue references. Do not try to cache any of the intermediate objects like the connection, session, or sender. WebLogic JMS is already pooling these objects so it is important to release them back to the pool when you have finished using them.

Best Practice

From your server-side applications, take advantage of JMS resource pooling by using Java EE resource references to obtain your JMS connection factory. Always close your connection objects at the end of each use to allow WebLogic JMS to release these pooled objects back into the pool.

If you use JMS within XA transactions, you do not need to reference the XA versions of the JMS objects when using the WebLogic JMS pooling mechanism. The wrapper object is smart enough to detect the presence of a JTA transaction and will automatically use the XA capabilities of the JMS provider to enlist it in the XA transaction. If the underlying JMS provider does not support XA (or you haven't enabled XA support), you will need to suspend the JTA transaction either by telling the container that the EJB does not support transactions or by using the JTA APIs. We talk more about integrating with foreign JMS providers in the last section of this chapter.

At this point, it is important to discuss another transaction-related feature of these wrappers that greatly simplifies your application. Although the WebLogic Server MDB container transparently handles all JTA transaction manager registration and transaction enlistment of foreign JMS providers for inbound messages, it is your responsibility to register and enlist any foreign JMS providers you use to send messages to foreign JMS providers from within your applications. This registration and enlistment process can be tricky and error prone; see Link 10-10 for more information on manual registration and enlistment. Note that the WebLogic Messaging Bridge, which we discuss later, also handles this registration and enlistment process for both the inbound and outbound foreign JMS providers.

Fortunately, the wrapper framework we are discussing can take care of registering the foreign JMS providers' XA resource and enlisting it in the transactions. To create a resource reference for a foreign JMS provider, simply use the same process to create the connection factory reference. Since resource references require a local JNDI binding, the only additional step you need to do is to tie that foreign provider's connection factory into WebLogic JNDI using WebLogic JMS's Foreign Server support, which we discuss later in the "Mapping External JMS Objects to WebLogic JNDI" section of this chapter.

One other thing to be aware of is that these wrapper objects enforce some Java EE restrictions on these pooled objects that are not enforced when working directly with the real JMS objects. These restrictions basically prevent you from calling certain JMS methods that require asynchronous delivery and thus require a thread to be created. For example, you are not allowed to associate a `MessageListener` with a consumer. What this means is that the only way to asynchronously consume messages from a Java EE application is to use either a message-driven bean or a server session pool, which we discuss in the next section. Because both of these mechanisms are using pooled objects that are not specific to a particular client or request, the main thing that you lose through this is the ability to create a `MessageListener` that contains state about the specific client or request. This simply means that any state that you require the asynchronous listener to have must be passed through or accessible using the contents of the message.

For more information on the methods that are not allowed, see the "Java EE Compliance" section of Link 10-11.

> WebLogic JMS resource pooling enforces the restrictions laid out for server-side applications in Section 6.6 of the Java EE 5 specification. This means that existing server-side applications that use the asynchronous `MessageListener` pattern will no longer work properly if resource pooling is in use.

Consuming Asynchronous Messages on the Server

When building server-side applications that asynchronously consume JMS messages, you have two primary options for how to do this: message-driven beans (MDBs) and server session pools. WebLogic JMS server session pool support has been deprecated for several years because there were few reasons left for them since message-driven beans arrived. As a result, we will focus our discussion on MDBs. For more information on using WebLogic JMS support for server session pools, please refer to the WebLogic JMS documentation at Link 10-12.

Message-Driven Beans

Our coverage of MDBs is not intended to be exhaustive. If you want to learn more about MDBs, please refer to the WebLogic Server documentation at Link 10-13.

Understanding Concurrency

Like stateless session beans, the WebLogic Server EJB container pools message-driven bean instances in memory. You can control the size of the pool using the `<initial-beans-in-free-pool>` and `<max-beans-in-free-pool>` parameters found in the `weblogic-ejb-jar.xml` deployment descriptor. When messages arrive at the associated destination, the EJB container tries to find a bean in the free pool to handle the message. If no instance is available, the container will create a new instance if the size of the pool is currently less than `<max-beans-in-free-pool>`. If the pool is already at its maximum size, the message will remain in the destination until a bean in the pool becomes available. Of course, the maximum amount of parallelism, and therefore the maximum number of beans the EJB container will ever create, is also controlled by the maximum number of threads available for use by the MDB instances. Unlike stateless session beans, the maximum number of available threads varies depending on how the MDB is deployed.

When you deploy an MDB, the WebLogic EJB container limits the maximum number of threads the MDB can use using the following rules, in order of precedence.

1. If WebLogic Server self-tuning thread pool is disabled and the MDB is using a custom execute queue, the maximum number of threads will be equal to the execute thread count.

2. If the MDB is using a custom work manager with a `<max-threads-constraint>`, the maximum number of threads will be equal to the value of `<max-threads-constraint>`.

3. If self-tuning is disabled and the MDB is using the default execute queue, the maximum number of threads will be equal to (execute thread count/2) + 1.

4. Otherwise, the maximum number of MDB threads equals 16.

The maximum number of threads used will be further restricted by the `<max-beans-in-free-pool>` setting.

You should never need to disable the self-tuning thread pool. If you want to alter the maximum concurrency for an MDB to be greater than 16, configure a custom work manager with a `<max-threads-constraint>` and associate it with your MDB. If you want the maximum concurrency to be less than 16, you can either set `<max-beans-in-free-pool>` or use a custom work manager. We recommend using a custom work manager in both cases. Bear in mind that the maximum number of threads will only be used if there are a sufficient number of queued messages, and the self-tuning thread pool has determined that the additional threads will improve throughput or the work manager also has a `<min-threads-constraint>`.

When you deploy an MDB to listen for messages on a queue, WebLogic Server uses one JMS session and consumer per bean instance in the pool. This allows for parallel processing of queued messages. In contrast, WebLogic Server uses one JMS session and consumer per pool for MDBs listening for messages on topics. Although this means that the EJB container receives one message at a time, it actually dispatches the messages to the bean instances in parallel for non-XA MDBs listening on WebLogic JMS topics.

These algorithms may differ somewhat between different WebLogic Server releases so we recommend that you check the MDB section of the Performance & Tuning Guide for your particular version (see Link 10-14).

Using Transactions

MDBs support both container-managed and bean-managed transactions. You can control the transactional semantics for your MDBs through Java annotations or the `ejb-jar.xml` deployment descriptor, just as you do for any other type of EJB. When using container-managed transactions, WebLogic Server will automatically start a JTA transaction before invoking an MDB's `onMesssage()` method so that the incoming message delivery is part of the JTA transaction. If you want to force the container to roll back the transaction, you should call the `setRollbackOnly()` method on the `MessageDrivenContext` object. In general, you should avoid throwing a `RuntimeException` like `EJBException` from the `onMessage()` method. Although this will cause the container to roll back the transaction, it also forces the container to remove the MDB instance from the pool, as required by the EJB specification. Of course, the container is free to create another instance should it need to do so.

Best Practice

Avoid throwing a `RuntimeException`, such as `EJBException`, from an MDB's `onMessage()` method to roll back transactions. If an MDB does throw a `RuntimeException`, the EJB specification requires the container to remove the instance that threw the exception from memory. Calling `setRollbackOnly()` works just as well and does not force the container to remove the instance from memory.

To deploy an MDB that uses container-managed transactions, the MDB must use an XA connection factory. If the referenced connection factory does not support XA, WebLogic Server will not deploy the MDB.

MDBs provide a declarative mechanism to tell the EJB container to start a transaction before delivering a message to them. As we discussed earlier, JMS does not generically support the concept of transactional delivery of asynchronously received messages. For JMS providers whose session objects implement the weblogic.jms.extensions.MDBTransaction interface, WebLogic Server will support truly asynchronous transactional delivery by receiving the message using the CLIENT_ACKNOWLEDGE mode, start a JTA transaction, and then use this callback interface to associate the message delivery with the JTA transaction. Obviously, this interface is specific to WebLogic Server, but at least one other third-party JMS vendor (Progress Software's SonicMQ) implements this interface. For JMS providers that do not implement this interface, WebLogic Server uses synchronous polling to support transactional delivery of JMS messages to MDBs.

MDBs also support bean-managed transactions. When using bean-managed transactions, the incoming message delivery cannot be included as part of the transaction. In the onMessage() method, the WebLogic EJB container gives you access to the JTA UserTransaction object through the MessageDrivenContext so that your application can begin, commit, and roll back transactions as necessary. In all cases, you must end your transaction before the onMessage() method returns. Once the onMessage() method returns, the EJB container will acknowledge the message. To prevent this message acknowledgment from occurring, you must throw a RuntimeException *after* ending the transaction.

To help applications prevent message acknowledgement and force redelivery more efficiently, WebLogic Server will not destroy the MDB instance if the MDB throws a weblogic.ejb.NonDestructiveRuntimeException. While this exception works for all MDBs, it is most important for MDBs that are not using container-managed transactions since throwing a RuntimeException is the only way to prevent the container from acknowledging the message. MDBs using container-managed transactions should use setRollbackOnly() instead.

You have several choices for controlling the type of message acknowledgment that the container uses. By using the @ActivationConfigProperty annotation to set the acknowledgeMode property or setting the <acknowledge-mode> element in the ejb-jar.xml deployment descriptor, you can control the acknowledgment mode for any MDB that is not using a container-managed transaction. When container-managed transactions are being used, this attribute is ignored. By default, the container uses AUTO_ACKNOWLEDGE mode when container-managed transactions are not in use (or the transaction type is set to NotSupported). You can also choose to use DUPS_OK_ACKNOWLEDGE or one of the WebLogic JMS–specific modes, NO_ACKNOWLEDGE or MULTICAST_NO_ACKNOWLEDGE. An MDB is prohibited from using client acknowledgment by the EJB specification.

Dealing with Durable Subscriptions

MDBs can also use durable subscriptions. Durable subscriptions require a unique client identifier. WebLogic Server lets you set the client identifier for an MDB's durable subscription in two ways: using the <jms-client-id> element in the weblogic-ejb-jar.xml deployment descriptor or using the Client ID for Durable Subscribers attribute on the connection factory's Client Configuration tab in the WebLogic Console.

As we previously discussed in the "Consuming Messages from a Distributed Topic" section, this create a problem when deploying the MDB to a cluster. When you target an MDB to a cluster, WebLogic Server deploys a copy of the MDB in each WebLogic Server instance. Because each copy of the MDB deployed to the individual servers is treated as a separate deployment, this causes a problem because, as far as WebLogic JMS is concerned, you have just deployed multiple durable subscriptions that are using the same client identifier.

To solve this problem, simply set the MDB's `<generate-unique-jms-client-id>` element to `true` in the `weblogic-ejb-jar.xml` deployment descriptor and WebLogic Server will generate a unique subscription ID for each managed server's MDB deployment. This allows each managed server's MDB deployment to create and consume from a unique durable subscription so that each managed server receives one copy of each published message. When a managed server's MDB is unavailable, other cluster members will store the published messages and forward them once the MDB reconnects.

As previously discussed, WebLogic Server did not support creating durable subscriptions directly on distributed topics when we were writing this book. The WebLogic EJB container actually allows you to deploy durable subscriber MDBs that reference the JNDI name of a distributed topic that is running in the same cluster, rather than one of its member topics. This is purely a convenience mechanism that makes it easier to create MDBs that are durable subscribers, and MDBs using this approach must still set `<generate-unique-jms-client-id>` to `true`. Behind the scenes, the EJB container actually creates each server's MDB durable subscription against the member topic.

WebLogic Server MDB's also provide a `<durable-subscription-deletion>` element to tell the server whether to automatically delete the durable subscription when you undeploy or remove the MDB. By default, this value is set to `false`.

Tip to Remember

If you need to use durable subscriptions with message-driven beans in a WebLogic Server cluster, use the `<generate-unique-jms-client-id>` feature to prevent client identifier conflicts. If using durable subscriptions in conjunction with distributed topics that are running in the same cluster as the MDB, use the distributed topic's JNDI name in your MDB — WebLogic Server will create the appropriate durable subscriptions on the member topics automatically.

We expect that the capabilities and options surrounding distributed topics will be changing in an upcoming version of WebLogic Server — possibly by the time you are reading this book. Please consult the WebLogic Server documentation at Link 10-4.

Connecting to Distributed Destinations

As previously discussed, WebLogic JMS consumers are pinned to a distributed destination member at the time you create them. This behavior, in conjunction with server affinity, usually provides you with exactly what you want — an optimized connection where your consumer is listening for messages on a local member destination. By default, WebLogic Server MDBs also exhibit this exact same behavior when deployed into the same cluster as the distributed destination. Again, this is typically what you want.

What happens if your distributed queue and MDB are in two different clusters? It used to be that the behavior was exactly the same as any other remote consumer — each managed server's MDB would connect into the remote cluster and get pinned to a member queue. Assuming load balancing was working, you typically got a reasonable distribution across the distributed destination's members. The problem started when the managed servers hosting the distributed queue's members were shut down and restarted.

When a queue member's managed server was shut down, the MDB container would detect that and attempt to reconnect to the distributed queue. Because one server was down, that connection request would be processed by a server that was still running. When the member queue's managed server comes back up, it will have no consumers until a server shuts down or a consumer is forced to reconnect. Imagine if the WebLogic Server administrator for the cluster hosting the distributed queue shut down the entire cluster and brought each server back up one at a time. Because the EJB container is periodically trying to reconnect to the JMS destination, it is very possible that all MDBs in the cluster might connect to one, or maybe two, member queues. If no failures or server shutdowns occur, the MDBs might all be listening to a single member destination for a very long time. Also, as more distributed queue members are added, the MDBs won't use them until they are forced to reconnect. As you can tell, this was problematic.

In all current versions of WebLogic Server, MDBs use a more appropriate load balancing algorithm when the distributed queue is in a remote cluster. Each MDB pool in the cluster creates consumers on every member queue in the remote distributed queue. Additionally, the MDB pools will respond dynamically to changes in the remote distributed destination — even when members shut down, restart, or migrate.

WebLogic Server MDBs also have advanced capabilities when interacting with distributed queues in the same cluster. When the MDBs are targeted to the same cluster as a distributed queue, WebLogic Server will create a pool of MDB instances for each member of the distributed queue. The MDBs will move automatically if the members migrate from server to server.

WebLogic Server also supplies the `<distributed-destination-connection>` element in the `weblogic-ejb-jar.xml` deployment descriptor that allows you to change the default behavior where each MDB pool only creates consumers on the local member (`LocalOnly`) and force it to create them on every member (`EveryMember`).

Application Design Considerations

When designing your MDB-based application, there are several things to keep in mind. First, it is generally better to use a delegation model to keep the business logic inside the `onMessage()` method to a minimum. By delegating the actual message processing to another component, you can turn the MDB into a controller that does nothing more than dispatch messages to the right business component. This promotes modular design and component reusability.

Remember that an MDB instance can process only one message at a time. This creates a problem if the business logic takes a relatively long time to process a message. As we have mentioned several times throughout this chapter, a well-designed messaging application requires consumers to be able to keep up with producers over long periods of time. If your message processing takes a long time, you need to make sure that you have enough concurrency to handle the incoming message volume. Also remember that WebLogic JMS consumers use a message pipeline to help speed up delivery of messages — this applies to MDBs as well. Therefore, you should typically create your own JMS connection factory and set `Maximum Messages per Session` to 1 for any MDB that will take tens of seconds, or even longer, to process each message. This ensures that messages do not accumulate in an MDB's message pipeline waiting for MDBs to finish processing the current message when there might already be MDBs available to process the message. Please refer to the "Connection Factories" subsection of the "Configuring WebLogic JMS" section earlier in this chapter for a more complete discussion of the message pipeline.

When deploying MDBs, it is best to deploy them to the same WebLogic Server instance that hosts the destination whenever possible. When deploying to a cluster which hosts both the MDBs and their JMS destinations, you should make sure that the MDBs are listening only on destinations in the same server instance. This happens by default when you deploy the MDB to the cluster (that is, its target is a cluster as opposed to the individual managed servers) and you set the MDB to listen to a distributed destination. When you do this, WebLogic Server starts the MDB instances only on servers that contain a member destination.

While using distributed destinations that contain multiple member destinations is not appropriate for every application, you can leverage this capability even with an application that uses a single physical destination by wrapping it in a distributed destination with only one member. Assuming that you do this and target the MDB to the cluster, the MDB will only activate on the managed server currently hosting the single member destination. That means that if you use service migration to migrate the destination to another server in the cluster, WebLogic Server will activate the MDB on the new hosting server as part of the migration process.

Of course, all of the other considerations we discussed previously in the "WebLogic JMS Application Design" section apply to MDBs as well.

External JMS Providers

Sometimes, you may need to use a remote WebLogic JMS system or another vendor's messaging system to be able to access as application. Many of the messaging systems in use today are starting to provide JMS APIs that make this job easier. The Java EE 5 specification does not really define exactly how Java EE applications deployed using one vendor's application server should be able to integrate with JMS providers from another vendor. For example, the EJB 3.0 specification does not define how the MDBs should support interaction with a foreign (third-party) JMS provider. Fortunately, WebLogic Server provides seamless integration with foreign JMS providers.

In general, two strategies exist for integrating your Java EE applications deployed in WebLogic Server with external JMS providers: direct and indirect integration. These external JMS providers might be another vendor's JMS product or just another WebLogic Server instance that hosts the JMS destinations. With direct integration, the application interacts directly with the external JMS destinations from the application code or the MDB's deployment descriptors. This method has the advantage of being the most efficient but exposes the Java EE application to the availability of the external provider.

Indirect integration uses a *store-and-forward* model where the application produces messages to or consumes messages from local JMS destinations. A *message forwarding agent* is responsible for moving messages between the local and external destinations. Because all availability and reconnection issues are handled by the agent, the application itself never has to worry about the external JMS provider. WebLogic Server provides two message forwarding agent technologies for use in different scenarios.

In this section, we start by looking briefly at the capabilities of the two message forwarding agent technologies: WebLogic Messaging Bridge and WebLogic Store-and-Forward (SAF). We follow that with a discussion of MDB support for foreign JMS providers. Next, we discuss WebLogic JMS's new *Foreign Server* support, which allows an administrator to maintain the configuration details required to establish the connections as part of the WebLogic Server domain configuration. We end this section with a brief discussion of the trade-offs of the different approaches.

Understanding the Messaging Bridge

WebLogic Server provides a built-in messaging bridge that you can configure using the WebLogic Console to move messages between any two JMS destinations. The WebLogic Messaging Bridge provides three alternative qualities of service (QoS) that control the message delivery: `Exactly-once`, `Atmost-once`, and `Duplicates-okay`. `Exactly-once` delivery means just that; the message will be delivered from the sending destination to the receiving destination using XA transactions so that the receiver gets exactly one copy of each message. `Atmost-once` delivery makes sure that the receiving destination receives only a single copy of the message or does not receive it at all. With the `Duplicates-okay` delivery mode, the bridge acknowledges receiving the message from the source destination only after writing it to the target destination. Because this is done outside the scope of a transaction, failures after writing the message to the target and before acknowledging the source can result in duplicate messages being delivered but should never result in a message being lost. This type of delivery is better known as *at-least-once* delivery.

The bridge uses J2EE Connector Architecture adapters to connect to the different messaging systems, though the adapters it can use are currently limited to the following built-in set of adapters:

> **eis.jms.WLSConnectionFactoryJNDIXA**   The bridge uses this adapter to communicate with any XA-compliant JMS provider to provide `Exactly-once` delivery.

> **eis.jms.WLSConnectionFactoryJNDINoTx**   The bridge uses this adapter to communicate with any JMS provider to provide either `Atmost-once` or `Duplicates-okay` delivery.

You must create an instance of the Messaging Bridge that maps each source destination with a target destination. Each destination is configured using one of the bridge's adapters. Each bridge instance is targeted to a specific WebLogic Server instance. If the source is a distributed destination, the JMS consumer load balancing rules will associate the bridge with a single destination. In this case, it is best to connect a separate bridge instance to each member of the source destination. This leads to a proliferation of bridge instances that must be reconfigured if the cluster membership changes.

The WebLogic Messaging Bridge provides many different configuration options that we will not spend time on here. For a complete discussion of the bridge, please refer to the WebLogic Server documentation at Link 10-15.

Best Practice

Use the WebLogic Messaging Bridge to store and forward messages between JMS destinations where one or both destinations are either hosted by foreign JMS providers or running on older versions of WebLogic Server that do not support the new Store-and-Forward service.

Understanding the Store-and-Forward Service

WebLogic Server 9.0 introduced the *Store-and-Forward* (SAF) service that allows applications to send messages reliably to destinations hosted by remote WebLogic Server instances without worrying about the availability of the remote environment. The WebLogic Server Web Services container relies on SAF to support Web Services Reliable Messaging (WS-RM)–based applications. SAF also provides JMS clients running in standalone JVMs with the ability to reliably send messages to a WebLogic JMS system, providing a mechanism by which you can build disconnected client applications (see Link 10-16 for more information about the SAF client).

Both WebLogic SAF and the Messaging Bridge provide the JMS applications a message forwarding agent-based technology and the same three qualities of service. However, a few key differences exist:

❑ SAF supports only WebLogic JMS 9.0 and higher endpoints. The Messaging Bridge can supports all versions of WebLogic Server, and any third-party JMS endpoint.

❑ SAF supports clustered deployment with distributed destinations. Though the Messaging Bridge can be used in a cluster and with distributed destinations, you must configure a bridge instance for each member of the source distributed destination.

❑ SAF cannot be used with temporary destinations to support the request-reply pattern using the JMSReplyTo field. However, it supports JMSReplyTo using permanent/preconfigured destinations. JMSReplyTo using temporary destinations is supported by the Messaging Bridge.

❑ WebLogic Server provides a version of the SAF agent that runs in a standalone client. The Messaging Bridge must be deployed to a WebLogic Server instance.

❑ SAF tends to perform better than the Messaging Bridge for the exactly-once quality of service. It uses an internal duplicate elimination algorithm that does not require XA transactions.

❑ SAF provides exactly-once messaging without requiring distributed transactions that span between the source and the target systems.

SAF is the preferred mechanism to store and forward in WebLogic Server 9.0 and higher. You should always choose to use SAF for routing messages between two standalone WebLogic Server instances, between server instances in a cluster, across clusters in a domain, or across domains. Use the Messaging Bridge when forwarding messages to older WebLogic JMS servers, interoperating with foreign JMS providers, and when using the request-response pattern with temporary destinations.

When forwarding messages between remote applications, both sides must coordinate to guarantee delivery with the specified quality of service: the local sending side and the remote receiving endpoint. SAF uses agents to store and forward the messages between the sending and receiving sides. You must configure SAF agents to support sending, receiving, or both; the appropriate settings depend on what technology is used and which side the agent is supporting, as shown in Table 10-2.

SAF agents are similar to JMS servers in that they have persistent stores, paging directories, and destinations, as well as quotas, thresholds, and other similar configuration parameters. The primary difference is that SAF agents only support imported destinations, a local representation of remote destinations to which messages are stored locally and then forwarded. SAF agents also support targeting to migratable targets to enable SAF agent service migration.

Table 10-2: SAF Agent Configuration

Technology	Side	Required Agent
JMS	Sending	Sending agent only
JMS	Receiving	No agent needed
WS-RM	Sending	Sending and receiving agent
WS-RM	Receiving	Receiving agent

Reliability in SAF is time-based in that the `Time-To-Live` attribute determines how long the agent will attempt to forward the message before expiring it. The rules to determine a message's time-to-live on the sending side are:

❑ A connection factory used by a `MessageProducer` can specify the `Default Time-to-Live` for all messages it sends. This value defaults to `0`, which means the messages never expire.

❑ An application can override the connection factory's `Default Time-to-Live` setting using the `MessageProducer.setTimeToLive()` method. By default, messages never expire.

❑ SAF can override all messages' time-to-live that were set by the application calling the `MessageProducer.setTimeToLive()` method before sending the message. Here is how it works:

    ❑ A `Store-and-Forward Agent` can set their `Time-To-Live` attribute to set the expiration time for all messages sent to imported destinations whose `Enable SAF Default Time-to-Live` attribute is set.

    ❑ The `SAF Imported Destinations` artifact that you create in a JMS module and associate with a `Store-and-Forward Agent` acts as a *container* for the imported queues or topics it defines. At this container level, you can set the default values of the `Enable SAF Default Time-to-Live` and `SAF Default Time-to-Live` attributes. These values will apply to all imported queues or topics defined by the container.

    ❑ Each imported queue or topic can set the `Enable SAF Default Time-to-Live` and `SAF Default Time-to-Live` attributes to override those set by the `SAF Imported Destinations` container.

If an imported queue or topic does not enable the `Enable SAF Default Time-to-Live` attribute, SAF will not override the messages' time-to-live for messages sent to that imported queue or topic. When setting a time-to-live on one of these SAF objects, a value of `-1` means that the value is not set, `0` means that the message never expires, and a positive value defines the number of milliseconds after the message was created that the message will expire.

If a message expires, SAF error handling provides four expiration policies from which to choose: `Discard`, `Log`, `Redirect`, and `Always-forward`. The first three have the exact same meaning and semantics as the JMS server expiration policies we discussed previously in the "Choosing a Message Expiration Strategy" section. `Always-forward` ignores the default `Time-To-Live` setting on the imported destinations and any message expiration time and forwards the message even after it has expired. Typically, you would use this option if your application had expiration policies set up on the remote destinations and you want the expired messages to be handled using these policies.

Once the message reaches the target destination on the remote server, the remote destination's `Time-to-Live Override`, if set, will override the time-to-live values on any incoming messages. If a message expires after arriving at the target destination, the destination's normal WebLogic JMS expiration policy settings apply.

When using SAF to forward messages between WebLogic Server domains, setting up cross domain security is not required. It is required if one domain has enabled cross domain security and the SAF agent is importing uniform distributed destinations whose membership may change, either through configuration or at runtime. Please see the "Setting up Cross Domain Security and Single Sign On (SSO)" section of Chapter 11 for more information about setting up cross domain security.

The WebLogic Store-and-Forward service provides a wide variety of configuration options and has numerous design considerations that need to be accounted for when configuring applications to use it. Please see the WebLogic Server documentation at Link 10-17 for more information.

Using Message-Driven Beans

MDBs use JNDI to retrieve connection factories and destinations. You can use MDBs in WebLogic Server to work with any JMS provider that supports and implements the JMS and JNDI specifications. When configuring an MDB to use a remote JMS provider, you must provide the JNDI information needed to look up the remote connection factory and destination using the MDB's deployment descriptors. This information may include the values of the JNDI `Context.INITIAL_CONTEXT_FACTORY` and `Context.PROVIDER_URL` parameters that WebLogic Server should use to create the `InitialContext`, as well as the JNDI names of the connection factory and destination. However, there is no support in the deployment descriptor for providing the authentication information needed if the foreign JNDI provider requires authentication. For this, you need to use WebLogic Server's Foreign JNDI Provider or WebLogic JMS's Foreign Server support discussed in the next section.

WebLogic Server also supports using container-managed transactions with foreign JMS providers to provide transactional delivery of messages to the MDBs. Make sure that the connection factory the MDB deployment descriptors references is an instance of `javax.jms.XAConnectionFactory` so that WebLogic Server will fully support the transactional settings of the MDB and provide for transaction coordination between the external provider and any other resources your business logic might involve in the transaction.

At the time of writing, WebLogic JMS cannot participate in distributed transactions managed by a foreign (third-party) transaction manager. The WebLogic JMS client does not support the `javax.jms.XASession.getXAResource()` method unless it is running inside a WebLogic Server instance. Because of this, it is not possible to enlist WebLogic JMS in an XA transaction managed by a foreign transaction manager. This means that, for example, you cannot deploy an MDB that is using container-managed transactions with a WebLogic JMS destination to another vendor's Java EE application server.

Mapping External JMS Objects to WebLogic JNDI

WebLogic Server provides two facilities that give you the ability to create an administrative link between objects in an external JNDI provider and a binding in your local WebLogic Server's JNDI tree. This makes it easier for your applications, or the messaging bridge configuration, to abstract itself away from the external JNDI provider's configuration details. The two facilities are:

WebLogic Server's Foreign JNDI Provider   WebLogic Server provides a general JNDI mapping capability that allows you to map objects stored in remote JNDI providers' JNDI trees to WebLogic Server's JNDI tree. Though not specific to JMS objects, you can use this facility to map JMS connection factories and destinations from remote or foreign JMS providers' JNDI tress to your server's local JNDI tree.

To use this facility, you start by using the WebLogic Console to create a `Foreign JNDI Provider` entry for each of your external JMS providers. This entry contains the information about how to connect to the external JMS provider's JNDI provider. Once the `Foreign JNDI Provider` entry exists, you can add any number of links between external connection factories and destinations for that server and local JNDI bindings. For more information about using this feature, see Link 10-18.

WebLogic JMS's Foreign Server   WebLogic JMS supports defining a *Foreign Server* as a resource configured in a JMS module. This Foreign Server resource represents a remote or foreign JMS provider and its connection factory and destination objects. Like the WebLogic Server Foreign JNDI Provider, the idea is to bind references to the remote JMS connection factories and destinations into the local WebLogic Server JNDI tree. This Foreign Server feature is specific to JMS and is simpler to use than a Foreign JNDI Provider for mapping remote JMS connection factory and destination objects into the local JNDI tree. In addition, it has some additional capabilities such as providing support for specifying that the username and password that the server should use for creating JMS connections.

To use this facility, first you must create a new `Foreign Server` resource in an existing JMS module by giving it a `Name` and specifying the `Targets`. Typically, you should accept the JMS module's default targeting.

Next, edit the new Foreign Server and use the Foreign Server's `General Configuration` tab to specify the foreign provider's JNDI information. WebLogic Server will use this information to establish a JNDI `InitialContext` and perform lookups of the connection factories and destination, as needed.

Finally, use the `Destinations Configuration` tab to create new destination references and the `Connection Factories Configuration` tab to create new connection factory references. With both types of references, you specify the following attributes:

❑   `Name`: The logical name used in the WebLogic Server configuration.

❑   `Local JNDI Name`: The JNDI name to use to bind the reference into the local JNDI tree

❑   `Remote JNDI Name`: The JNDI name to use to look up the object in the foreign server's JNDI tree.

After creating a connection factory reference, you can also specify a `User Name` and `Password` that WebLogic JMS will use to call the `ConnectionFactory.createConnection(username, password)` method. Not all providers require this — check your JMS provider documentation to determine if you need to supply these credentials to create JMS connections.

Of course, the Foreign Server mechanism is tightly integrated with the WebLogic Server JMS and MDB subsystems so we recommend using this approach for foreign or remote JMS provider integration. For more information on the WebLogic JMS's Foreign Server support, please see the WebLogic JMS documentation at Link 10-19.

Best Practice

Use the WebLogic JMS Foreign Server capabilities to isolate the rest of your application configuration away from the external JMS provider's configuration by making the objects visible from the local JNDI tree. Use the WebLogic Server Foreign JNDI Provider to achieve the same sort of isolation with non-JMS objects.

Integrating Oracle Advanced Queuing

Many Oracle customers have applications that use Oracle Advanced Queuing (AQ), which comes as part of the Oracle Database, as their messaging provider. Oracle AQ provides a JMS interface that allows applications to use the JMS interface to send and receive messages. Though we do not cover AQ or AQ JMS in this book, we do need to discuss the subject of AQ JMS integration because there are some caveats to the normal foreign JMS provider integration approach we have been discussing.

With the release of Oracle WebLogic Server 11g, AQ JMS now integrates directly using the standard JMS foreign server approach described previously. The initial release has some limitations which include only supporting the Oracle 11g Thin driver and the lack of support for any of the options that allow using a non-XA data source within a global transaction (for example, Logging Last Resource). We expect the support for other options to be added over time so please consult the WebLogic Server documentation at Link 10-20 for details.

To configure this integration, start by setting up AQ in the database. For the purpose of this section, we use the following SQL commands to create our `jmsuser` database user.

```
% sqlplus SYS/manager1@ORCL AS SYSDBA
SQL> grant connect,resource,aq_administrator_role to jmsuser identified by jmsuser;
SQL> grant select on sys.DBA_PENDING_TRANSACTIONS to jmsuser;
SQL> grant execute on sys.dbms_aqadm to jmsuser;
SQL> grant execute on sys.dbms_aq to jmsuser;
SQL> grant execute on sys.dbms_aqin to jmsuser;
SQL> grant execute on sys.dbms_aqjms to jmsuser;
SQL> exec dbms_aqadm.grant_system_privilege('ENQUEUE_ANY','jmsuser');
SQL> exec dbms_aqadm.grant_system_privilege('DEQUEUE_ANY','jmsuser');
```

Next, we create our AQ queue tables and queues using the commands shown here.

```
% sqlplus jmsuser/jmsuser AS SYSDBA;
SQL> exec dbms_aqadm.create_queue_table(queue_table=>'jmsdemo_queue_table',
        queue_payload_type=>'sys.aq$_jms_text_message',multiple_consumers=>false);
SQL> exec dbms_aqadm.create_queue_table(queue_table=>'jmsdemo_topic_table',
        queue_payload_type=>'sys.aq$_jms_text_message',multiple_consumers=>true);
SQL> exec dbms_aqadm.create_queue(queue_name=>'JMSDEMO_QUEUE1',
```

```
                         queue_table=>'jmsdemo_queue_table');
SQL> exec dbms_aqadm.create_queue(queue_name=>'JMSDEMO_TOPIC1',
                         queue_table=>'jmsdemo_topic_table');
SQL> exec dbms_aqadm.start_queue(queue_name=>'JMSDEMO_QUEUE1');
SQL> exec dbms_aqadm.start_queue(queue_name=>'JMSDEMO_TOPIC1');
```

Creating a queue with `multiple_consumers` set to `true` will allow us to use the AQ queue as a JMS topic.

Once AQ is properly configured, we need to set up a WebLogic Server data source to connect to our database as our AQ user: `jmsuser`. We will not go through the details here but remember that you must select either the Oracle Thin XA driver or the Oracle Thin driver for AQ integration in WebLogic Server 11g. If you choose the non-XA driver, accept the defaults of `Supports Global Transactions` and `One-Phase Commit` on the `Transaction Options` screen of the WebLogic Console's data source creation wizard.

Next, we need to create the WebLogic JMS resources needed to configure a foreign server for our AQ integration by doing the following:

1. Create a JMS module called `AQSystemModule` using the WebLogic Console and target that module to your server or cluster.

2. In the module, create a `Foreign Server` resource named `AQForeignServer` and accept the default targeting it inherits from the module (that is, do not use the `Advanced Targeting` button).

3. Using the foreign server's `General Configuration` tab, set the `JNDI Initial Context Factory` to `oracle.jms.AQjmsInitialContextFactory` and add the `datasource` property to the `JNDI Properties` field and set its value to the JNDI name of the data source you created for accessing AQ (for example, `datasource=AQJMSDataSource`).

4. Set up the foreign server's connection factories using its `Connection Factories Configuration` tab. Note that AQ JMS does not require predefining the connection factories in the database. AQ JMS provides the six connection factories shown in Table 10-3. Map each AQ JMS connection factory your application requires to an appropriate `Local JNDI Name` using the `Remote JNDI Name` from Table 10-3. We chose to map `ConnectionFactory` to `AQJMS_ConnectionFactory` and `XAConnectionFactory` to `AQJMS_XAConnectionFactory`.

5. Set up the foreign server's destinations using its `Destinations Configuration` tab. For queues, the `Remote JNDI Name` will be of the form `Queues/<AQ queue name>`, where the AQ queue name is the one specified in the database (for example, `Queues/JMSDEMO_QUEUE1`). For topics, it will be of the form `Topics/<AQ queue name>` (for example, `Topics/JMSDEMO_TOPIC1`).

Once you complete these steps and activate your changes, you should be able to see the JNDI bindings you just created for these JMS resources in the server's JNDI tree, which you can view using the server's `General Configuration` tab in the WebLogic Console. MDBs can reference these artifacts using WebLogic JNDI and the local JNDI names you chose so your MDB is completely decoupled from the AQ-specific configuration data. Note that in this first release of native AQ JMS integration with WebLogic Server, this is the only supported integration mechanism. MDBs cannot integrate directly with AQ JMS's JNDI provider and the Messaging Bridge is not supported. Be sure to check the documentation for your release to see if anything has changed.

Table 10-3: AQ JMS Connection Factory Remote JNDI Names

Remote JNDI Name	JMS Object Type
QueueConnectionFactory	javax.jms.QueueConnectionFactory
TopicConnectionFactory	javax.jms.TopicConnectionFactory
ConnectionFactory	javax.jms.ConnectionFactory
XAQueueConnectionFactory	javax.jms.XAQueueConnectionFactory
XATopicConnectionFactory	javax.jms.XATopicConnectionFactory
XAConnectionFactory	javax.jms.XAConnectionFactory

Integrating AQ with Older WebLogic Server Releases

Older releases of the AQ JMS library and WebLogic Server are not able to take advantage of this new support. Prior to the release of WebLogic Server 11g, AQ JMS did not provide its own JNDI provider. Instead, it relied on Oracle Internet Directory's (OID) or the Oracle Containers for Java (OC4J) application server's JNDI providers. AQ JMS also provides proprietary APIs to obtain connection factory and destination object references; however, these references do not implement standard JNDI interfaces so they are incompatible with WebLogic Server JNDI.

At the time of writing, the only solution for pre–WebLogic Server 11g integration with AQ JMS is an open source framework written by one of the book's authors. This package provides a startup class–based mechanism to integrate AQ JMS connection factories and destinations into WebLogic JNDI. Because this is all that it does, it has the same caveats that we previously mentioned concerning automatic XA resource registration and enlistment. That is, WebLogic Server handles XA resource registration and enlistment for inbound messages being consumed by MDBs; it doesn't handle automatic registration and enlistment for outbound messages sent by your applications. We recommend using the JMS wrapper mechanism described in "Using WebLogic JMS with Servlets and EJBs" section to leverage automatic registration and enlistment for outbound connections. Please note that at the time of writing, you can use the wrapper approach only for the connection factory and not the destination. Though this is sufficient to obtain the benefits of wrapper, we hope to address this limitation by the time you are reading this book. Please check the readme file included in the package for further information.

You can download the source code for this framework at Link 10-21. You should use this framework only after you understand its implementation, have tested it with your application, and are willing to accept the risks associated with the lack of commercial support for this package.

Choosing an Integration Strategy

When your application is consuming messages from an external JMS provider, consider using the direct integration approach with MDBs rather than the indirect bridging approach. MDBs deployed in WebLogic Server can support the same qualities of service supported by the message forwarding agents. MDBs support exactly-once delivery through the use of XA transactions. If you are not using transactions, use either AUTO_ACKNOWLEDGE or DUPS_OK_ACKNOWLEDGE modes to get at-least-once delivery. The trade-offs between the two acknowledgment modes are really about reducing the chances for duplicate messages versus improving performance. By using the WebLogic JMS–specific modes of NO_ACKNOWLEDGE or MULTICAST_NO_ACKNOWLEDGE, you can achieve at-most-once delivery of your messages. MDBs also support automatic reconnection to the external provider should the connection fail, such as when the external JMS provider is restarted. You can tune the polling interval with which the MDBs will try to reconnect by using the <jms-polling-interval-seconds> element in the weblogic-ejb-jar.xml deployment descriptor. The default value is to try to reconnect once every 10 seconds. Use of the Foreign Server mechanism allows you to handle situations where the JNDI objects change when the external JMS provider is restarted, as well as remove environment-specific settings from the MDB deployment descriptors.

For applications that are sending messages to a foreign provider, using the indirect integration approach via SAF or the Messaging Bridge is typically a better option unless the application is waiting on a response to be able to continue processing. For example, a web application that is using request/reply style messaging to an external backend system in order to be able to send a web page back to the client's browser would not be a good candidate for the indirect integration approach. In this situation, direct integration is better because the application will receive a system exception and can immediately abort the web request if its message cannot be sent to the remote system. Of course, we could argue that this isn't the best design, as we did earlier in the chapter, but we hope that the example gets our point across. Using the indirect approach allows the application to complete requests by writing the message to a local JMS queue. This means that the application will continue to function properly even when the remote system is down. The SAF agent or Messaging Bridge handles all of the reconnect logic to deal with the external JMS provider being unavailable for a period of time.

Chapter Review

We covered a lot of ground in this chapter. We started off by reviewing some key concepts of JMS. We spent quite a bit of time talking about the WebLogic JMS provider, covering how it works and what features it provides. After that, we discussed things to consider when designing WebLogic JMS applications. Next, we talked briefly about WebLogic JMS programming and how to best use WebLogic JMS from within Java EE applications. This discussion included the server-side JMS resource pooling and a discussion of message-driven beans. We finished up the chapter with a discussion of how to integrate WebLogic Server applications with external JMS providers using either the direct or indirect approach to integration. In the next chapter, we talk in detail about WebLogic Server security.

11

Using WebLogic Security

In this chapter, we discuss the WebLogic Server Security Service. If you are unfamiliar with general security concepts or Java EE security features, you should consult the WebLogic Server documentation at Link 11-1 in the book's online Appendix at http://www.wrox.com/ for more information.

We begin with an overview of WebLogic Server security, from both a runtime and administrative perspective. This is important so that you understand the big picture of how interactions with WebLogic Server are secured. Next, we dive into the details of the WebLogic Security Framework and the security providers that are available to the security service. We follow that with a brief discussion of how to use external security stores with WebLogic Server. Next, we show you how to set up WebLogic Server to use Secure Socket Layer/Transport Layer Security (SSL/TLS). From there, we move into a discussion of client-side programming to the WebLogic Server Security Service. This includes a detailed discussion of how to set up and use two-way SSL between different types of Java clients and WebLogic Server. Then, we briefly discuss how to manage application security using both Java EE security features and WebLogic Server's own application security. We end the chapter with a discussion of how to provide single sign-on (SSO) to WebLogic Server across domains and across the Internet.

In this chapter, the term *server* refers to one instance of a WebLogic Server or multiple instances of WebLogic Server acting as a cluster. We will treat the cluster of servers as one logical entity. Throughout the chapter, we refer to several examples when discussing certain features. As with the other chapters, these examples are available on our companion Web site at http://www.wrox.com/.

WebLogic Security Overview

Let's start our discussion of WebLogic Server security by looking at the different types of clients and how they can access a WebLogic Server application. WebLogic Server supports many different types of clients and protocols for accessing the server, as shown in Figure 11-1. As far as security is concerned, three primary types of clients will be calling into the server.

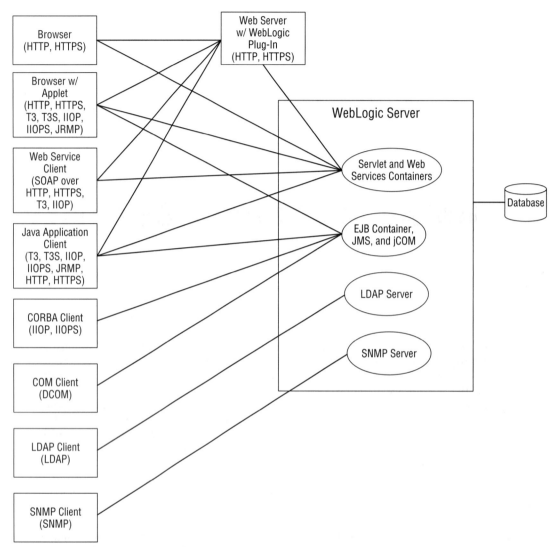

Figure 11-1: Client connectivity options.

The first type is typically a browser that either calls directly into the server or accesses the server via an intermediate web server running one of the WebLogic Server web server plug-ins. Java or non-Java applications that make standard HTTP requests would also fall into this category. These clients generally authenticate themselves to the WebLogic Server using one of the standard HTTP authentication mechanisms: basic authentication or certificate-based authentication using two-way SSL. SSL also provides confidentiality by protecting the contents of the HTTP messages from being seen in clear text by parties other than the sender and the receiver.

The second type is the application client that typically calls directly into the server using a distributed object–based protocol like T3, IIOP, or JRMP. These clients generally authenticate themselves using the security mechanisms associated with the particular protocol or programming model, such as the Java Authentication and Authorization Service (JAAS) or the Common Secure Interoperability Version 2 (CSIv2) in the case of CORBA clients. Although HTTP tunneling of these protocols can allow these clients to communicate through an intermediate web server, authentication still uses the same mechanisms that it would if the protocols were not being tunneled.

The third type is a SOAP web services client. The web services client could be the WebLogic Server web service client or any other Java or non-Java web service client. Normally, these clients access WebLogic Server over HTTP in which case the protocol-level security mentioned previously can be used. In addition, the SOAP messages themselves can have protections applied — identity tokens, encryption, and digital signatures. The binding of security information to SOAP messages is defined by the OASIS WS-Security specification. Message-level security should be used when multiple parties have different access to the same message. For example, a loan application contains the applicant's credit history along with information about the property. A home inspection service needs to have access to the information about the property, but should not be able to see the credit information. In this case, the part of the message containing the credit information can be encrypted. Message-level security should also be used when the message is part of an asynchronous process because the protections provided by the transport protocol are not there once the message is enqueued. In the case of simple synchronous requests, protocol-level security is often sufficient.

With any type of client, the calls could be routed through one or more firewalls. We talk about suggested firewall layouts in Chapter 15. In addition to external firewalls, WebLogic Server has its own software firewall called a connection filter. The connection filter can grant or deny access to different protocols and ports running on WebLogic Server by domain, machine, or network mask. For example, you might use a connection filter to ensure that all traffic coming to WebLogic Server is coming from your web servers running the WebLogic Server web server plug-in.

As these clients make calls into the various business applications on the server, these applications use the WebLogic Server Security Service to authenticate the client's identity, authorize their access to application functionality, audit security decisions, map the caller's identity into a different credential needed to access another system, and perform other security-related tasks. The WebLogic Server Security Service supports the Java EE security features as well as specialized WebLogic Server security features. Depending on the security mode used to deploy the application, WebLogic Server can apply roles and security policies defined in the application's deployment descriptors or manage access to application resources using roles and policies defined by WebLogic Server.

When the WebLogic Server Security Service is called, it makes calls into the security framework for security decisions. The security framework defines a rich set of service provider interfaces (SPIs) that the security service calls when security decisions must be made. Through these provider interfaces, the framework calls into one or more security providers that are configured for the server. Figure 11-2 shows the architecture and where each component fits into the big picture.

WebLogic Server also supports JSR-115: Java Authorization Contract for Containers (JACC). JACC is an alternative to the WebLogic Security Framework for EJBs and web applications. JACC defines a mapping between Java security permissions and Java EE objects such as servlets and EJBs. You can find details on WebLogic Server and JACC at Link 11-2. The capabilities defined in the JSR-115 are not as rich as those found in WebLogic Server. Though fully supported, using JACC with WebLogic Server is not recommended.

Compatibility security is the ability to secure WebLogic Server with a WebLogic Server 6.x–style security realm. The older realm architecture defined all of security services in a single object — for example, LDAP Realm. In this model, all of the security information (users, groups, ACLs) was maintained in LDAP. Compatibility security has been deprecated since WebLogic Server 7.0. You can find details about compatibility security at Link 11-3. This chapter only focuses on the current security architecture.

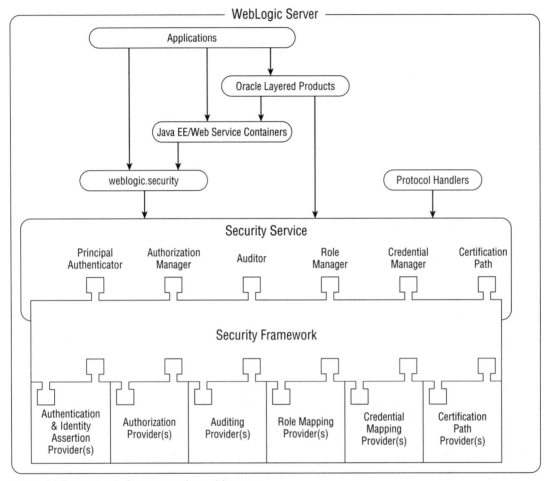

Figure 11-2: WebLogic Server security architecture.

The term *realm* persists in the current version of WebLogic Server, but a realm now is a named configuration of individual security providers. In the current version of WebLogic Server, for example, authentication can occur in LDAP, but the groups can be retrieved from an RDBMS. The roles and policies stored inside of WLS using eXtensible Access Control Markup Language (XACML) go well beyond a simple ACL-based model. XACML is a standard for defining authorization policy, and we discuss it in more detail later in the chapter. Though many applications won't have such elaborate security requirements, the point is that the security provider–based model is much more flexible and powerful than its predecessor.

Administration

The bulk of this chapter is organized around and focuses on the runtime behavior of WebLogic Server security. As each topic is covered there is an explanation of how to configure WebLogic Server to provide the functionality. As a reference, the WebLogic Console tab names for the administrative operations covered in this chapter are listed in Table 11-1, Table 11-2, Table 11-3, and Table 11-4 in this section. The security administration functionality is organized by resource scope — there is no one single security area of the WebLogic Console. Rather in the context of the resource being secured, the appropriate security options are available. This section provides an overview of security administration and the location of the specific tasks in the WebLogic Console as well as in the JMX MBean hierarchy. To represent the location in the MBean hierarchy, this section uses the WebLogic Scripting Tool (WLST) directory structure.

Table 11-1: Domain Level Security Administration

Operation	Domain's Tab Name
Set the Default Realm	General Security
Enable/Disable Cross Domain Trust	General Security
Unlock a User	Unlock User Security
Define a Connection Filter	Filter Security
Manage the Embedded LDAP	Embedded LDAP Security
Configure Admin Policies (Who is authorized to Unlock Users, Upload/Download Files, View Logs, and Assert Identities)	Roles Security Policies Security
Configure Web Services Token Handler	Web Services Security
Configure Credential Provider	Web Services Security

Table 11-2: Server Level Security Administration

Operation	Server's Tab Name
Configure Trust and Identity Keystore	Keystores Configuration
Configure SSL	SSL Configuration
Configure SAML SSO and other SAML-based Services	Federation Services Configuration
Define Server Policies (start and stop server)	Policies Security

Table 11-3: Realm Level Security Administration

Operation	Realm's Tab Name
Configure the Security Model for the Domain	General Configuration
Configure RDBMS as a Security Store	RDBMS Security Store Configuration
Configure the User Lockout Policy	User Lockout Configuration
Manage Users and Groups	Users and Groups
Manage Global Roles	Roles and Policies
Manage Root Level Policies	Roles and Policies
Configure Credential Mappings for Cross Domain Users	Default Credential Mappings
Configure which Keys to use by a user when Signing/Encrypting Web Services	PKI Credential Mappings
Manage Security Providers — Authentication, Authorization, Adjudication, Role Mapping, Auditing Credential Mapping, Certification Path, Keystores	Providers
Import/Export of Security Policy	Migration

Domain Level

Domain is the highest level of security configuration. The following administration operations are performed on the domain in the WebLogic Console. With the exception of the roles and policies, these operations are also performed from WLST from /<domain name>/serverConfig/SecurityConfiguration/<domain name>. Roles and policies are managed using the active realm's XACMLRoleMapper and XACMLAuthorizer MBeans for the active realm.

Server Level

Some security properties are defined at the server level. The following administrative operations are performed on the server in the WebLogic Console. With the exception of the roles and policies, the operations are also performed from WLST /<domain name>/ serverConfig/Servers/<server name>.

Realm Level

A domain has only a single active security realm, so realm-level settings for the active realm are at the same level/scope as the domain security settings, but are managed on the active security realm in the WebLogic Console. The roles and policies for the entire domain are visible and can be administered from the Roles and Policies tab. This is for convenience. The same roles and policies are visible on the Roles Security and Policies Security tabs of the individual objects as well.

With the exception of the management of roles and policies, the operations are also performed from WLST from /<domain name>/serverConfig/SecurityConfiguration/<domain

name>/Realms/<realm name>. Roles and policies are managed from the XACMLRoleMapper and XACMLAuthorizer MBeans for the active realm.

Table 11-4: Provider Management Level Administration

Operation	Realm's Tab Name	Provider-Specific Type
Configure SAML WebSSO Identity Provider Partner	Authentication Providers	SAML2IdentityAsserter
Configure SAML WebService Identity Provider Partner	Authentication Providers	SAML2IdentityAsserter
Configure Trusted Certificates	Certification Path Providers	CertificateRegistry
Configure SAML WebSSO Service Provider Partner	Credential Mapping Providers	SAML2CredentialMapper
Configure SAML WebService Service Provider Partner	Credential Mapping Providers	SAML2CredentialMapper

Provider Management Level

A realm is a collection of individual security providers. A few of the built-in providers have their own management operations that are accessible from the WebLogic Console via the Management tab of the provider. WebLogic Server has extensive Security Assertion Markup Language (SAML) capabilities. SAML is a standard for propagating identity and WebLogic Server can use it in both a web and web services context. The SAML security providers make extensive use of this provider-level management feature. The details of SAML are discussed later in this chapter.

From WLST, access the management operations of the provider from <domain name>/serverConfig/ SecurityConfiguration/<domain name>/Realms/<realm name>/<provider type>/<provider name>.

The roles and policies for the entire domain are accessed via WLST by accessing the XACMLRoleMapper and XACMLAuthorizer, respectively.

WebLogic Security Framework

This section discusses the WebLogic Security Framework in detail, with particular emphasis on the out-of-the-box functionality. As you may have noticed in Figure 11-1, WebLogic Server ships with an embedded LDAP server. This server is used as the default security store — the persistent repository of security policy information for authorization, roles, credential mapping, and certificate registry providers. Our first topic in this section is describing how the embedded LDAP server or an external RDBMS is used as the security store. By default, the embedded LDAP server is also used to store users and groups. These capabilities are discussed here as well. Next, we present an overview of the default security providers. Because these providers are fairly complex, we cover only some of the more important features. For more detailed information, please refer to the WebLogic Server security documentation at Link 11-4.

Embedded LDAP Server

WebLogic Server's default security providers use an embedded LDAP server to persist all security-related data. Each server stores this data locally, including all of the user, group, role, access control policy, and credential information. For each domain, the admin server acts as the master LDAP server and replicates new information to the embedded LDAP running on each of the managed servers.

In addition to the normal replication flow, the embedded LDAP server supports some additional scenarios. Configuration changes made on a managed server are first sent to the admin server's embedded LDAP server and then from there replicated to all other managed servers' embedded LDAP servers. Also, managed servers can be configured to receive an entire replica of the configuration from the admin server at startup. The default behavior is to receive the set of incremental updates. Changing this setting is useful in situations where a managed server has been off-line for an extended period, thus making it inefficient for the admin server to send each individual change to the managed server.

Each LDAP server does automatic backups of the entire LDAP directory tree once a day. You can configure the time that the backup task kicks off with the Backup Hour and Backup Minute parameters found on the domain's Embedded LDAP Security tab in the WebLogic Console. All backup files are compressed and stored with the LDAP server's data files; the maximum number of backup files the server will keep is also configurable through the same Embedded LDAP Security tab in the console.

Whenever a WebLogic Server is started, it places all of its internal files in a server instance–specific directory. By default, the server's directory is located in the directory it was started from and has the same name as the server instance (for example, user_projects/domains/<domain name>/servers/<server name>). Inside this server directory is a data/ldap subdirectory where you will find the LDAP server's files. Table 11-5 shows the full directory structure and description of the embedded LDAP server directory contents. If you ever encounter a problem where a managed server won't start and you suspect that its LDAP data may be corrupt, you can either try to use one of the backup zip files from the backup directory to revert the contents of the ldapfiles directory, or simply remove the entire ldap directory and let it be recreated when the managed server starts up and connects to the admin server.

Table 11-5: Embedded LDAP Server Directory Structure and Usage

Directory	Information Stored
backup	Zipped backup files created once a day from the ldapfiles directory
conf	Configuration files that are generated on the first server start
ldapfiles	LDAP server data files
log	LDAP server log files
replicadata	Managed server replicated data

Within the ldapfiles directory, you will find seven data files. EmbeddedLDAP.tran, EmbeddedLDAP.trpos, and EmbeddedLDAP.twpos are the transaction tracking files. If there is ever an internal problem with the embedded LDAP server these files can be deleted without loss of data. EmbeddedLDAP.data is the main data file where all the users, groups, roles, and policies are stored. EmbeddedLDAP.delete contains information about deleted entries, and EmbeddedLDAP.index is the index of data files. Finally, the `EmbeddedLDAP.lok` file is used to ensure access consistency to the LDAP information. In some cases, a WebLogic Server might shut down without allowing the embedded LDAP server to unlock the data. If this happens, the server will go into a loop, waiting for the file to be removed and printing out a warning message:

```
####< Jun 21, 2009 9:42:54 PM CDT> <Warning> <EmbeddedLDAP> <lhotse>
<AdminServer> <[ACTIVE] ExecuteThread: '0' for queue:
'weblogic.kernel.Default (self-tuning)'> <<WLS Kernel>> <> <> <1245638574219>
<BEA-171520> <Could not obtain an exclusive lock for directory:
.\servers\AdminServer\data\ldap\ldapfiles. Waiting for 10 seconds and then
retrying in case existing WebLogic Server is still shutting down.>
```

Typically, deleting the `EmbeddedLDAP.lok` file will resolve this issue.

WebLogic Server stores the default security providers' default configuration information in a set of files with the `ldift` extension. Most of these files are located in the `$WL_HOME/server/lib` directory, though you will also see a couple of these `ldift` files in your WebLogic Server domain's security directory. WebLogic Server runs these `ldift` files through a preprocessor to convert them into standard LDAP `ldif` files that can then be fed directly into the embedded LDAP server.

The embedded LDAP server listens on the normal WebLogic Server listen port. Because the WebLogic Server installation program automatically generates a random, unique password for the LDAP server, this does not pose any significant security threat. You should avoid changing this password unless you absolutely need to because the generated password is typically harder to crack than those you might normally choose. If you need to access the embedded LDAP server using standard LDAP mechanisms, you will need to change the security credential. You can change the embedded LDAP server's credential through the same `Embedded LDAP Security` tab we previously discussed. Once you have set this credential to a known value, you can use any LDAP tool to access the server's LDAP directory by setting the `Base DN` to the pattern `dc=<your_domain_name>`, the username to `cn=Admin`, and the password to the value used to set the credential through the WebLogic Console.

The embedded LDAP server uses replication between the administration server and any managed servers. This replication uses the server's SSL port, if it is enabled. Therefore, if you are concerned about the security of your LDAP replication data flowing between the admin server and any managed server, you should configure and enable SSL on all servers in the domain. We talk about how to enable and configure SSL a little later.

Best Practice

If the network connecting the WebLogic Server instances in your domain is not trusted, make sure you enable SSL on each server in the domain so that WebLogic Server can use SSL for all LDAP replication between the admin server and all managed servers.

RDBMS Security Store

WebLogic Server 10.3 introduced an option to configure a domain to use an RDBMS security store. This means that instead of storing the security policy information in the embedded LDAP server, the information is stored in a relational database.

Using an RDBMS security store is strongly recommended when using SAML SSO in a domain with more than 1 server. With the embedded LDAP, any updates made at the managed server need to be first sent to the admin server and then replicated to the other managed server. This resulting latency creates problems with some of the SAML 2 capabilities. You can find the scripts for creating and removing the security store database in `$WL_HOME/server/lib`. For example, the create and remove scripts for the Oracle database are `rdbms_security_store_oracle.sql` and `rdbms_security_store_oracle_remove.sql`, respectively. Note that you must create the security store database before starting the domain.

We recommend that you consider the type of security store needed before creating a domain since there is no easy migration path to moving from using embedded LDAP to the RDBMS security store. If you do need to upgrade an existing domain, the process is essentially creating a new domain using the RDBMS security store, exporting the data from the existing domain, importing it into the new domain, and redeploying any existing applications. The WebLogic Server Configuration Wizard allows you to configure an RDBMS security store as part of the domain creation process. We recommend this method since the Configuration Wizard validates the database configuration for you. This helps ensure that your domain will be able to retrieve its security policies and start up correctly.

When using an RDBMS security store, you must configure a shared JMS topic for synchronizing changes. The JMS shared topic ensures that configuration or policy changes made to a security provider are communicated to the other servers in the domain. If a server cannot connect to the shared topic, its caches will become stale, and will have to be restarted to pick up any changes. At restart, the managed server directly communicates with the database to get the latest data. To avoid the complexities of configuring cross-cluster, domain-wide, highly available JMS topic, we recommend that you only use the RDBMS security store in a domain that contains a single cluster.

> When using the RDBMS security store, prefer configurations that limit the domain to a single cluster to avoid the complexities of configuring a cross-cluster, domain-wide, highly available JMS topic.

The security providers that leverage the RDBMS security store are:

❑   XACML Authorization and Role Mapping providers

❑   WebLogic Credential Mapping provider

❑   PKI Credential Mapping provider

❑   Certificate Registry

❑   SAML 1.1 providers: SAML Identity Assertion provider V2, and SAML Credential Mapping provider V2

❑   SAML 2.0 providers: SAML 2.0 Identity Assertion provider, and SAML 2.0 Credential Mapping provider

The next section covers the XACML Authorization and Role Mapping, WebLogic Credential Mapping, PKI Credential Mapping and Certificate Registry in detail. Details of the SAML 1.1 and SAML 2.0 providers are discussed later in the "Single Sign-On" section of this chapter.

Security Realms and Providers

WebLogic Server includes a wide range of security providers that plug into the security framework. In this section, we begin by looking at the providers that are configured in a realm by default — the default providers — in more detail. WebLogic Server includes other providers that we use for situations where more advanced security functionality is required. We discuss those providers in detail later in the "Using External Security Stores" and "Single Sign-On" sections of this chapter. Finally, we end this section with a look at how to manage these default providers using the JMX capabilities of WebLogic Server.

Let's start by looking at the different types of security providers. Table 11-6 shows the different types of providers and explains their functionality. To see the security providers running in your server, use the WebLogic Console to navigate to the `Security Realms` folder. Select the active realm, which in most cases is called `myrealm`, and then click the `Providers` tab.

Table 11-6: Security Provider Types and Features

Provider Type	Features
Authentication	The default security provider allows for username-and-password-based, direct-to-server certificate-based, and HTTPS certificate-based authentication. The authentication provider gives the server a JAAS configuration that points at a specific JAAS `LoginModule`.
Identity Assertion	This security provider maps an outside authentication token to a username. This allows for functions like perimeter authentication. The identity asserter provides an implementation of a JAAS `CallbackHandler`. The default identity asserter supports WebLogic Server security tokens, X.509 certificates, CSIv2, and WS-Security password digest.
Authorization	This security provider decides whether an authenticated `Subject` may access a set of resources given a certain application context.
Adjudication	When using multiple authorization providers, this provider tallies the decisions from each provider and decides on the final verdict of authorization. It is unnecessary if there is only one authorization provider.
Audit	This security provider collects and stores the security logs.
Role Mapper	After a `Subject` is authenticated, as it tries to access resources, the role mapper decides what roles apply to the `Subject` and stores them in the `Subject` object.
Credential Mapper	This security provider supplies the credentials for legacy systems to an authenticated `Subject` when needed.
Certification Provider	This provider, also referred to as Certificate Lookup and Validation (CLV), performs two important functions for working with X.509 certificates. It completes certificate chains and validates certificates.

Figure 11-3 describes the typical call flow to those security providers.

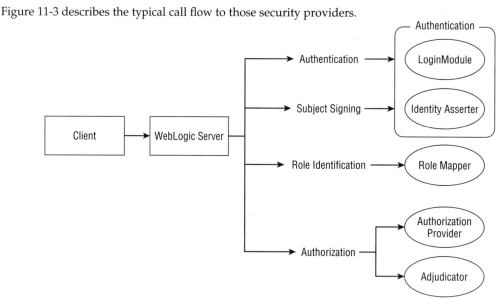

Figure 11-3: Authentication and authorization call flow.

WebLogic Server loads the default security providers from the Java archive files in the `server/lib/mbeantypes` directory. These files contain not only the default security provider implementation classes but also their JMX configuration MBeans. When loading the security providers, WebLogic Server does not load these files from the classpath, but rather dynamically loads them using an internal class loader.

Before we move on to explore the different provider types in detail, we need to point out that the WebLogic Server supports multiple application security models. By default, it supports the standard Java EE deployment descriptor–based model that defines roles and authorization policies in deployment descriptors, or the equivalent Java annotations. For simplicity, we will not distinguish between defining the roles and policies using deployment descriptors or annotations, and will simple refer to them as being defined in deployment descriptors. It also supports more dynamic security models where some or all of this information is managed by WebLogic Server or some external provider. This results in WebLogic Server exposing four high-level application security models from which to choose:

DD only Only use the roles and policies defined in the Java EE application deployment descriptors.

Custom Roles Use the roles and policies defined in the deployment descriptors but, rather than mapping roles to principals in the WebLogic Server–specific deployment descriptors, map them using the WebLogic Console.

Custom Roles and Policies Use only the WebLogic Console to define roles and policies, ignoring any roles and policies defined in the deployment descriptors.

Advanced Use the roles and policies defined in the deployment descriptors to seed the WebLogic Server security roles and policies, and use the WebLogic Console to modify roles and policies from that point onward.

We discuss the details of these various models later in the "Setting Up WebLogic Server Application Security" section.

The realm defines a default security model for the applications being deployed in the domain. As you deploy applications, the WebLogic Console asks you to choose a security model for the application with the default value being the value set by the realm. Each application can accept or override this value but regardless of their choice, the application's security model is recorded in the `config.xml` file. The only way to change the application's security model choice is to redeploy the application.

Some security providers can also affect the application's security model. The `XACMLAuthorizer`, `DefaultAuthorizer`, `XACMLRoleMapper`, `DefaultRoleMapper`, and `DefaultCredentialMapper` security providers each have an option to *enable deployment*. Enabling deployment, which is the default, means that the provider uses the role or policy definitions from Java EE deployment descriptors. We discuss these details in each of the provider-specific sections below.

Authentication

In addition to the preconfigured providers, WebLogic Server comes with several built-in, configurable authentication providers. These providers primarily include support for external LDAP servers; these include support for Active Directory, Sun Java System Directory Server (formerly known as iPlanet and SunOne), OpenLDAP, and Novell eDirectory, Oracle Internet Directory, and Oracle Virtual Directory LDAP servers. WebLogic Server also ships with a generic LDAP provider that serves as a template for any LDAP v3–compliant server. WebLogic Server still ships a Windows NT Domain authentication provider, but it is deprecated. As an alternative, use the Active Directory authentication provider.

If you want to use an external LDAP server as your sole authentication provider, you must map WebLogic Server's `Admin` role to at least one group or user. By default, this `Admin` role maps to the `Administrators` group, so simply defining an `Administrators` group in your external LDAP tree is sufficient.

WebLogic Server's security framework fully supports the Java Authentication and Authorization Service (JAAS) specification. JAAS specifies that all authentication requests are to be routed through a `LoginModule` interface. `LoginModules` can be stacked together to form a pluggable framework. WebLogic Server's security framework supports multiple authentication providers in exactly the same way, thus allowing for multiple, pluggable providers. Each authentication provider supports one `LoginModule`; therefore, using multiple `LoginModules` requires using multiple authentication providers. `LoginModules` do not interact directly with the environment. They interact with a `CallbackHandler` through the `handle(Callback[])` method. A typical `LoginModule` passes a `NameCallback` and a `PasswordCallback`. In WebLogic Server, the identity asserter provides the specific `CallbackHandler` implementation. In the case of perimeter authentication, the security framework uses the identity asserter that matches the *token type* being presented (SAML, X.509 certificate, digest authentication). Identity asserters are discussed in more detail later in this section.

Each authentication provider has a configuration option called a *control flag*. This control flag allows the provider to specify how its authentication results affect the overall authentication process. These control flag options, which are the same as the JAAS `LoginModule` configurations that we discuss in the "Writing Java Clients That Use JAAS" section later in this chapter, can have the following values:

Required The authentication provider is required to succeed. If it succeeds or fails, the authentication process continues to proceed through the list of configured providers.

Requisite The authentication provider is required to succeed. If it succeeds, the authentication process continues through the list of configured providers. If it fails, the authentication process immediately fails and returns control to the application.

455

Sufficient   The authentication provider is not required to succeed. If it does succeed, the authentication process succeeds and control immediately returns to the application. If it fails, the authentication process continues down the list of configured providers.

Optional   The authentication provider is not required to succeed. If it succeeds or fails, the authentication process continues down the list of configured providers.

When you create a new authentication provider, you should use a less strict control flag while in development. The primary reason is that a value of Required or Requisite will cause the authentication to fail if the new provider fails. Because the server must authenticate the administrative user used to start the server, a misconfigured provider using one of these strict control flags will prevent the server from starting. If the control flag is set to either Sufficient or Optional, the server will show you the error information about the incorrectly configured provider but will start, thus allowing you to use the WebLogic Console to modify the configuration. Once you verify that everything is working in the new provider, set the control flag to the desired value.

Best Practice
Set the control flag for all authentication providers to OPTIONAL before applying any changes to prevent a configuration error from causing the server not to boot.

The WebLogic Console now sets the default value for the Control Flag attribute to OPTIONAL. You should be aware, though, that the default value in the underlying MBean is still REQUIRED. This means that if you create the MBean by hand, through hand editing of the config.xml file or writing JMX programs, you need to set the Control Flag attribute explicitly or it will automatically be set to REQUIRED. Because most people use the WebLogic Console, this should not be a problem.

If you find yourself in a situation where your server will not boot because of a security realm configuration issue, you can simply edit the provider's config.xml entry to change the control-flag setting:

```
<sec:authentication-provider xsi:type="wls:custom-dbms-authenticatorType">
  <sec:name>SQLAuthenticator</sec:name>
  <sec:control-flag>OPTIONAL</sec:control-flag>
  ...
</sec:authentication-provider>
```

Of course, you can also restore the config.xml file from one of the backups that WebLogic Server automatically makes.

When using an external LDAP authentication provider, you might want WebLogic Server to continue to serve any unprotected information even when it cannot get authentication information from the external server, such as when the server is unavailable. To accomplish this, you must make certain the server's boot identity is defined in the embedded LDAP server, so it can be used regardless of whether the external LDAP server is operational. You can use the WebLogic Console to set connection and search result timeout values on the external LDAP authentication provider. This will ensure that the server does not hang when attempting to authenticate against the external LDAP server. Following these steps will allow you to boot and serve up unprotected information with the WebLogic Server even when your external server is unavailable.

> **Best Practice**
>
> When using an external authentication provider, it is a good idea to store the server's boot identity in the embedded LDAP server. By doing this and setting timeouts on the external authentication provider, you can continue to boot and serve up unprotected information with WebLogic Server when the external server is unavailable.

Before we move on to talk about identity assertion, we should talk about what to do if you forget your administrative password and cannot boot the server. Please note that the following procedure works only for the default authenticator using the embedded LDAP server and only if you have not modified the global `Admin` role, which by default is granted to the `Administrators` group. For our example, we will assume that your server name is `AdminServer`. To reset the password, follow these steps:

1. Using the command line, change the directory to your WebLogic Server domain's root directory and run your `bin/setDomainEnv` script to set up your `PATH` and `CLASSPATH`.

2. Create a new initialization file for the default authenticator by running the following command that creates a new `DefaultAuthenticatorInit.ldift` file in the `$DOMAIN_HOME/security` subdirectory:

    ```
    java weblogic.security.utils.AdminAccount <tempadmin>
        <temppassword> $DOMAIN_HOME/security
    ```

3. Remove the initialized status file `DefaultAuthenticatormyrealmInit.initialized` from the `$DOMAIN_HOME/servers/AdminServer/data/ldap/` subdirectory.

4. Restart the server, and enter the `<tempadmin>` username and `<temppassword>` password supplied in step 2.

Identity Assertion

Identity asserters take an outside identity token, validate it, and provide information in the form of callbacks to the authentication provider(s) so that WebLogic Server can authenticate the caller. Identity asserters almost always provide the name of the user, but can provide additional information such as the groups to which the user belongs. The default identity assertion provider, known as the `DefaultIdentityAsserter`, can validate WebLogic Server security tokens, X.509 certificates, IIOP CSIv2 tokens, and WS-Security password digests.

By default, the `DefaultIdentityAsserter` is enabled only to support WebLogic Server security tokens; use the WebLogic Console to enable support for the other supported token types. This default identity assertion provider does its work via a `UserNameMapper` interface, which maps either an X.509 certificate array or an X.501 distinguished name to a username. Using the WebLogic Console, you can enable and configure the `Default User Name Mapper` that comes with the server to extract the username automatically from most fields in an X.509 certificate. You can also write your own username mapper implementation class by implementing the `weblogic.security.providers.authentication.UserNameMapper` interface and configuring the `DefaultIdentityAsserter` to use it.

Probably the most common reason to change the default configuration of the `DefaultIdentityAsserter` is to support authentication via client certificates from a two-way SSL connection. To enable identity assertion for X.509 certificates, first you need to add `X.509` to the list of chosen types at the bottom of the `DefaultIdentityAsserter`'s `Common Configuration` tab in the WebLogic Console. Next, you need to enable and configure the `Default User Name Mapper`, using the `Provider Specific Configuration` tab.

The `Default User Name Mapper Attribute Type` allows you to choose which field in the distinguished name (DN) of the `Subject` of the X.509 certificate to use to obtain the username. If the field being used contains more than the username, the `Default User Name Mapper Attribute Delimiter` can be used to truncate the extraneous information. For example, if you select the `E` value for the attribute type, you may need to strip off the domain name information from the email address. If the email address were `someuser@bigrez.com` and the WebLogic Server username were `someuser`, setting the delimiter to @ would allow the username mapper to map the email address field in the certificate to the correct WebLogic Server username properly.

Another reason to modify the configuration of the `DefaultIdentityAsserter` is to change the behavior of WebLogic Server's digest authentication. Digest authentication is more secure than HTTP basic authentication because it adds protection against replay attacks. It does this through the use of timestamps and a *nonce* — a number used only once. Using the `Provider Specific Configuration` tab of the `DefaultIdentityAsserter`, you can change the default `Digest Expiration Time Period` of 300 seconds. WebLogic Server also has the ability to detect digest replays by persisting the digest in a database. To enable this feature on the `DefaultIdentityAsserter`, select the `Digest Replay Detection Enabled` attribute and set the `Digest Data Source Name` attribute to point to a preconfigured WebLogic Server data source. Note that the `DefaultIdentityAsserter` will create the `WLS_NONCE_2` table to store this data so the database user needs permissions to create and drop tables as well as to read from and write to this table. At the time of writing, WebLogic Server only supports digest authentication for web services. Enabling digest authentication for web services requires the creation of a domain-level Web Services Security Configuration, which was discussed in Chapter 9.

Authorization, Role Mapping, and Adjudication

In the current version of WebLogic Server, the default realm's authorization and role mapping providers are the `XACMLAuthorizer` and the `XACMLRoleMapper`, respectively. The eXtensible Access Control Markup Language (XACML) is a standard way of defining authorization policies. Though WebLogic Server essentially hides all of the details of XACML, it stores the role and security policies you define in the WebLogic Console as XACML objects behind the scenes. As the XACML standard continues to mature, the expectation is that third-party tools will emerge to help validate/optimize XACML-based authorization policies against relevant governance and compliance policies. In the meantime, the important thing to note is that the `XACMLAuthorizer` is the default authorizer — not the `DefaultAuthorizer`. The `DefaultAuthorizer` is the previous generation default authorization provider based on a WebLogic Server proprietary entitlements language. One additional difference between the two providers is that the `XACMLAuthorizer` has the ability to work with the RDBMS security store. `DefaultAuthorizer` can only persist its policies to the embedded LDAP server.

The authorization and role mapping providers that WebLogic Server ships with have a setting called `Policy Deployment Enabled` and `Role Deployment Enabled`, respectively. This setting determines if the provider should deploy role or policy information in the application deployment descriptors. WebLogic Server currently requires the active security realm to have at least one authorization provider and one role mapping provider that supports deploying policies and roles from deployment descriptors. The default providers enable deployment by default. Changing these values requires extreme caution, and you should leave these set to the default value in most cases. Read the "Setting Up WebLogic Server Application Security" section for more information before changing these values on the providers themselves.

When an authenticated user attempts to access a resource, the security framework uses three types of providers that together to issue a yes or no answer. First, the role mapping provider determines the list of roles that the user has for that resource. If multiple role mapping providers are specified, the resulting sets of roles returned from the providers are combined to determine the set of applicable roles. Next, the security framework passes the authenticated user and its roles to the realm's configured authorization providers. Each authorization provider issues an access decision of yes, no, or abstain. When using multiple providers, it is possible that some providers may permit access whereas others either abstain or deny access. This is where the adjudication provider comes in. An adjudicator looks at all of the responses from the different authorization providers and decides whether to grant or deny access.

When making authorization calls into the WebLogic Server Security Service, the server passes information about the identity of the caller, the resource being accessed, and other contextual information about the call to the authorization provider. The authorization provider instantiates an `AccessDecision` object that uses this information to make its authorization decision. For example, when a caller tries to access a protected method of an EJB, the EJB container passes the `AccessDecision` object the parameters of the EJB method call along with the method name itself. Having this additional contextual information about the request allows the `AccessDecision` object to make access decisions using arbitrarily complex security policies. Of course, the complexity of the authorization decisions depends on what type of contextual information the server provides for a given type of resource.

The security framework passes this contextual information using objects that implement the `weblogic.security.service.ContextHandler` interface. A `ContextHandler` is essentially a list of name-value pairs. WebLogic Server's default authorization provider uses the information in the `ContextHandler` to decide whether a given subject may have access to a given resource. We hope that you will not need to write your own authorization provider because the default provider supports fairly complex policy statements. If you do, we encourage you to look at the "Developing Security Providers for WebLogic Server" documentation at Link 11-5 and the sample providers on the Oracle Technology Network web site at Link 11-6 for more information.

> **Tip to Remember**
>
> If you need to extend or implement your own security providers, some very good example providers are available on the Oracle Technology Network web site at Link 11-6. These are source code examples of everything it takes to write a set of providers, and we highly recommend them.

Unless you develop your own authorization provider, you may never need to use the adjudication provider. Even if you add a second authorization provider, the default adjudication provider can be configured to resolve almost any conflict.

Auditing

WebLogic Server's default audit provider simply sends security events to the `DefaultAuditRecorder.log` file in the server's logs directory. The directory can be changed by setting the `-Dweblogic.security.audit.auditLogDir` Java system property. The default realm does not include this audit provider by default. To use it, use the WebLogic Console to create an instance of the `DefaultAuditor`. In the auditor's `Provider Specific Configuration` tab, you can select which `ContextHandlers` to audit. This allows you to determine what information is sent to the audit log. By the way, these are the same `ContextHandlers` that are passed to the roles and authorization providers.

WebLogic Server can also audit administrative changes by pushing administrative changes to the security framework's configured audit providers. By default, configuration auditing is disabled. To enable configuration auditing, use the `Advanced` area of the domain's `General Configuration` tab to set the `Configuration Audit Type` to one of the following values:

Change Log   This setting will only write configuration change information to the server's log file. The domain's audit providers are not called.

Change Audit   This setting will only pass the configuration changes to the audit providers. No change information is written to the server log.

Change Log and Audit   This setting will cause changes to be written to the server log and passed to the audit providers.

Since the `DefaultAuditor` writes all events to the server's audit log, setting the `Configuration Audit Type` to `Change Audit` or `Change Log and Audit` will result in the changes appearing in the server's audit log.

You could write your own audit provider to send security logs to a specialized, non-repudiation data store. To do this, your provider must implement the `weblogic.security.spi.AuditChannel` interface, which receives a `weblogic.security.spi.AuditEvent` whenever an audit message occurs.

Credential Mapping

The credential mapping provider supplies credentials for downstream systems. It is essentially the inverse of the identity assertion provider. Identity asserters take credentials and establish a JAAS subject. Credential mappers take a JAAS subject and convert it to a credential of a specified type. WebLogic Server uses the `DefaultCredentialMapper` to store and retrieve username/password credentials when:

❑   Defining cross domain trust in WebLogic Server. We discuss this in more detail later in the "Setting Up Cross Domain Security and Single Sign-On" section of this chapter.

❑   Defining a credential mapping for a JDBC data source.

❑   Managing credentials for connections to external EIS systems in resource adapters.

There is a provider-specific flag on the `DefaultCredentialMapper` called `Credential Mapping Deployment Enabled`. Like the `Policy Deployment Enabled` and `Role Deployment Enabled` properties on the authorization and role mapping providers, this controls whether or not the provider copies relevant information from the application deployment descriptors. In the case of the `DefaultCredentialMapper`, this determines whether the provider stores the credential maps defined in the resource adapter's deployment descriptors.

WebLogic Server provides two other credential mappers that we'll discuss later: the `PKICredentialMapper` and the `SAML2CredentialMapper`. These credential mappers support web services security and SAML single sign-on services. We discuss their use in more detail in the "Setting Up Cross Domain Security and Single Sign-On" section of this chapter.

Certification Path

WebLogic Server provides an X.509 certificate lookup and validation (CLV) framework that consists of two components: the `CertPathBuilder` and the `CertPathValidator`. The `CertPathBuilder` takes an X.509 certificate and builds the entire certificate chain up to the root Certificate Authority certificate, as needed. From there, the `CertPathValidators` takes over and validates the certificate chain. The CLV framework requires exactly one `CertPathBuilder` but allows for zero or more `CertPathValidator` instances. Together, the `CertPathBuilder` and the `CertPathValidator` ensure that the server only accepts registered and valid certificates. For more information, see Link 11-7.

WebLogic Server provides two CLV providers that implement both the `CertPathBuilder` and a `CertPathValidator` interfaces: the `CertPath` and `Certificate Registry` providers. The `CertPath` provider performs rigorous checking of the entire certificate chain to ensure its validity. The `Certificate Registry` stores a list of client certificates that are allowed to access the server. In this context, accessing the server means one of two things:

❑ A client calling a WebLogic Server–based application over two-way SSL or using WS-Security message-level security (that is, where the client must present its certificate to WebLogic Server)

❑ Another server that a WebLogic Server–based application (acting as a client) is calling over SSL or with WS-Security message-level security (that is, where the other server must present its certificate to WebLogic Server)

If you create a `Certificate Registry` then the WebLogic Server will only trust certificates in the registry regardless of whether WebLogic Server trusts the certificate's root CA. For certificates that the server receives, the `Certificate Registry` provider will check to see that the certificate is in the registry and that the root CA is trusted — it performs no other validation of the certificate chain. The `Certificate Registry` provider allows you to manage the list of valid certificates using the WebLogic Console.

By default, WebLogic Server configures the `CertPath` provider; it is sufficient for most use cases. If you need a simple way of managing and revoking a certificate's access to the server then consider using the `Certificate Registry`.

In the "Setting up SSL/TLS" section later in this chapter, there is a lengthy discussion of the WebLogic Server identity and trust models. There is an option to use the certification path provider to validate the inbound or outbound SSL connections. This feature is really only useful if you are using the `Certificate Registry` or some other enhanced custom provider, since the `CertPath` provider uses the exact same trust model as the WebLogic Server SSL stack. The web services security stack also uses the certification path providers. Some WS-Security scenarios like responses signed with an X.509 certificate require configuring the `Certificate Registry`. The reason for this is that the `CertPath` provider doesn't support building a certificate path based on the issuer DN serial number — an advanced capability required for this scenario.

Managing Security Providers

Like the rest of the server's configuration data, WebLogic Server stores the server's security configuration data in the `config.xml` file. In addition to their configuration data, most security providers have their own data that they use to make security decisions (for example, the authentication provider stores user and group information). WebLogic Server also provides import/export facilities for the security data that those providers use. Each security provider, as well as the realm itself, has a JMX-based management interface that is accessible from any JMX-based tool, such as WLST. This section discusses how to perform common administrative tasks and how to use those programmatic interfaces to automate the management of a realm and its underlying providers. If you are unfamiliar with JMX and WLST, see the "Monitoring WebLogic Server Applications" section in Chapter 12 for more information.

When changing a server's security realm configuration, it is a good idea to create a new realm just in case you make a mistake and end up with a configuration that doesn't work. While a WebLogic Server domain can only have one active realm, it can have any number of inactive realms so it is easy to keep a backup copy of the working realm. Doing so will allow you to quickly recover from your mistake.

The WebLogic Console does not provide a mechanism to *clone* a realm, but it is easy enough to do. If you create a new realm using the WebLogic Console, the new realm will be empty so you will have to configure all the providers and other attributes you want. A simpler way to create the new realm is to edit the `config.xml` file by hand while the admin server is shut down. Simply copy everything in the `<realm>` element and then paste it directly below.

```
<realm>
  ...
  <sec:name>myrealm</sec:name>
</realm>
<realm>
  ...
  <sec:name>myrealm2</sec:name>
</realm>
```

Make sure to change the `<sec:name>` element to give the new realm a unique name! After saving the file, restart the admin server. At this point, the providers are the same between the old realm and the new realm, but the data is not. Before we show you how to copy the data, let's talk about the facilities we will use to copy the data.

All WebLogic Server–provided security providers have the ability to import and export their security data. You can perform these operations on the entire realm or on a provider-by-provider basis. What information a provider exports and the format that it uses depends on the provider.

To export a realm's data, use the realm's `Export Migration` tab and specify the directory to which the export files should be written. When WebLogic Server exports a realm, it writes an `exportIndex.dat` file plus one additional file for each of the realm's providers into the directory that you specify. The `exportIndex.dat` contains a list of all of the provider-specific files and which provider each file came from. Note that only providers that store their security data in the security store support exporting their data with this facility. For providers that store their information in a different store, like any of the LDAP authentication providers, WebLogic Server assumes that there is some other export facility available for you to use to accomplish exporting that provider's security data.

Using each provider's `Export Migration` tab, you can control what information it exports and the form that it uses. Likewise, each provider's `Import Migration` tab allows you to control what information it imports. Each provider may support a set of optional constraints that give the administrator more control over the export/import process. You will find the full list of constraints at Link 11-8. There are a few additional subtleties about constraints that are worth noting.

> **Specifying Constraints** While the WebLogic Server documentation lists all constraints each provider supports, it does not currently document the possible values for each constraint and each provider. Some constraints require specifying a `name=value` form; others do not. For example, the `DefaultAuthenticator` constraints `users` and `groups` don't require a value. Simply putting the word `users` or `groups` in the `Export Constraints (name=value)` or `Import Constraints (name=value)` field is sufficient.
>
> When specifying multiple constraints, place each constraint on a separate line in the `Export Constraints (name=value)` or `Import Constraints (name=value)` field.

Exporting Passwords   Some providers support the `passwords` constraint to give you additional control over the exporting of passwords. For example, the SAML identity asserter and credential mapper providers support exporting passwords as clear text by specifying the constraint `passwords=cleartext`. However, not all providers that support the `passwords` constraint support exporting clear text passwords. For example, the `DefaultAuthenticator` stores passwords using a one-way hash by default. As such, there is no way to determine the clear text password so the export process will ignore a constraint of `passwords=cleartext` and will export the passwords in their hashed format.

If you need to support exporting clear text passwords, you will need to check `Enable Password Digests` on the `DefaultAuthenticator`'s `Provider Specific Configuration` tab. Note that enabling this option requires you to reset all user passwords so that the `DefaultAuthenticator` can store them using a reversible encryption scheme.

Controlling SAML Partner Exports   When using SAML, the identity asserter and credential mapper providers store information about the different identity and service provider partners for the domain. Both the `SAMLIdentityAsserterV2` and `SAMLCredentialMapperV2` support the ability to export only a subset of the entries using the `partners` and `certificates` constraints. For the `partners` constraint, list the names of the partners you want to export (for example, `partners=ap_0001,rp_0002`). For the `certificates` constraint, list the aliases of the certificates (for example, `certificates=cert1,cert2`).

These provider-specific settings and constraints are non-persistent, which means that you cannot use them to configure a realm-level export since they are lost as soon as you leave the provider's `Export Migration` tab. This is a shame since it really limits the value of the realm-level export. Fortunately, the realm level export uses a set of defaults that are sufficient to accomplish the primary use case: migrating of security data from one domain to another.

The export process only exports the security data of the providers, not the security configuration itself. You still need to migrate the realm and its providers' configuration information manually, as described earlier in this section. Once you have the new realm configured, use either the realm's or the individual providers' `Import Migration` tabs to import the data.

Now that the new realm is exactly the same as the old realm, make the configuration changes to the new realm. To test the changes, make the new realm the active realm by changing the `Default Realm` attribute on the domain's `General Security` tab. The advantage of this approach is that it preserves the existing security configuration. If there is some issue with the new configuration, you can restore the old configuration by simply setting the old realm as the active one, and restarting.

Rather than trying to describe everything you need to do to back out from a bad realm configuration, we recommend that in addition to testing your realm you make a backup of the entire domain directory tree just before activating the new realm. This way, you can revert by simply restoring the entire domain directory and restarting the server.

These facilities are useful when trying to move between environments (for example, from a development to a test environment). If your applications define all their security policies using Java EE deployment descriptors, simply deploying the applications will automatically populate the new environment's security database with this information. If the security information goes beyond that, or the application is not using the DD-only security model, you will need to migrate the data using either the import/export capabilities or through manually copying the embedded LDAP tree and the `SerializedSystemIni.dat` file to the new domain. If the RDBMS security store is being used then you could use either the import/export facility of the providers or the native capabilities of the database. Regardless of the security data and its storage, you will need to migrate the configuration information in the `config.xml` file manually.

You can gain programmatic access to the security providers through JMX and WLST. You can locate the WebLogic Server Security MBeans in the `weblogic.management.security` package. By looking through the Javadocs of these MBean interfaces, you can see how to manipulate both the default security providers and any third-party security providers that are capable of management. By default, these methods are available only to programs running with the `Admin` role. We talk more about the `Admin` role and the other default roles later in this chapter.

The following example, `PasswordChanger`, shows how to modify a user's password programmatically using WLST. You can find a complete source code version of this program on this book's companion web site (http://www.wrox.com/).

```
connect("weblogic","weblogic1")
cd("SecurityConfiguration")
cd(domainName)
defaultRealm = cmo.getDefaultRealm().getName()
print defaultRealm
cd("Realms")
cd(defaultRealm)
cd("AuthenticationProviders")
providers=ls(returnMap="true")
print providers
for authProvider in providers:
    print authProvider
    cd(authProvider)
    operations=ls("o")
    resetPasswordCount = operations.count("resetUserPassword")
    if resetPasswordCount==1:
        print "RESETING THE PASSWORD"
        cmo.resetUserPassword("temp2","wlstworks")
    cd("..")
disconnect()
```

Debugging

Before we continue, we should tell you that the security framework has its own debug scope. You enable debugging for the security scope using the WebLogic Console. Use the server's `Debug` tab and locate the `weblogic.security` node in the debug scope tree. The nodes under `weblogic.security` are roughly organized by the provider types, with some special debug scopes for tricky things like SSL and SAML. Using the debug scope `weblogic.security` is crucial to solving security issues. ·

Tip to Remember

Using the debug scope `weblogic.security` is crucial to solving security issues.

Using External Security Stores

WebLogic Server can also use external security stores for storing security data. In this section, we look at a few of the most common external stores used with WebLogic Server. We focus on using these external stores for authentication data because that is by far the most common usage. Most applications still use Java EE deployment descriptor security, third-party application security products, or custom application code to do authorization. As you see later in the "Setting Up WebLogic Server Application Security" section, WebLogic Server has its own application security functionality that provides parametric, policy-based authorization that can be configured outside of the application code or deployment descriptors.

Managing External LDAP Authentication

LDAP servers have become the de facto standard for managing corporate user information. Current versions of WebLogic Server support using both its embedded LDAP server as well as several of the more popular commercial and open source LDAP servers on the market today. Supporting different LDAP servers generally means that WebLogic Server has built-in knowledge of the default schemas these servers use, which makes them easier to configure. Just because WebLogic Server does not support a particular LDAP server out of the box, it does not mean you cannot use it. Typically, it is possible to make it work; you just need to customize the authentication provider configuration to match the LDAP schema and server information.

The security framework has a series of built-in LDAP authentication providers. These options include support for Active Directory, Sun Java System Directory Server (formerly known as iPlanet and SunOne), OpenLDAP, Novell eDirectory, Oracle Internet Directory, and Oracle Virtual Directory LDAP servers. WebLogic Server tailors each authentication provider to understand the default or standard schemas used by that LDAP server. WebLogic Server also includes a generic LDAP authentication provider that you can use with any LDAP v3–compliant directory. You create and configure these providers using the WebLogic Console.

All LDAP authentication providers use the following attributes:

> **Principal** Distinguished Name (DN) of the user connecting to the LDAP server
>
> **Credential** Password of that user
>
> **Use Retrieved User Name as Principal** Selected, unless the user is authenticating in a different directory and the LDAP server is only used for groups
>
> **User Base DN** All user search queries are relative to this DN
>
> **Group Base DN** All group search queries are relative to this DN
>
> **User Object Class** Object class for the users in the LDAP directory
>
> **User Name Attribute** Attribute of the User Object Class that contains the username

These attributes are important in describing how WebLogic Server authenticates to an external LDAP server. WebLogic Server uses the `Principal` and the `Credential` to create the connection (bind) to the LDAP server. When a user attempts to authenticate, LDAP provider needs to map the username passed in the login to a DN. It does this by performing a subtree search from the `User Base DN` for objects of the defined object class where the `User Name Attribute` matches the username entered. It then compares the password of the user to the entry in the LDAP server. Assuming that they match and the `Use Retrieved`

User Name as Principal is selected, the LDAP provider adds the username as a WLSUser principal object to the JAAS subject.

The next step is to retrieve the groups that the user is a member of. It does this by performing a subtree search from the Group Base DN for objects of the Group Object Class that have the user as a member (that is, the username matches the Group Membership Attribute of the Group Object). For each of the groups that the user is a member of, WebLogic Server performs another search to see whether that group is a member of any other groups. The implication is that the user is also a member of those groups. To control the hierarchical searching of group memberships, set the Group Membership Searching to limited and the Max Group Membership Search Level to the appropriate number of levels. Finally, WebLogic Server adds all of the groups found as WLSGroup principal objects to the JAAS subject.

Each LDAP provider has a slightly different configuration. The configuration for the Active Directory authentication provider is as follows:

UserNameAttribute   sAMAccountName

Principal   <DN of the Administrator User> (for example, cn=Admininistrator,cn=Users, dc=<domain>)

Credential   <password for the Administrator user>

User From Name Filter   (&(sAMAccountName=%u)(objectclass=user))

User Base DN   CN=Users,DC=<domain>

Group Base DN   CN=Users,DC=<domain>

Use Retrieved User Name as Principal   Selected

Use Token Groups for Group Membership Lookup   Selected

By default, the provider sets the User Name Attribute to cn. This creates issues with users created via the Active Directory Console. Changing the attribute to sAMAccountName in both the User Name Attribute and the User From Name Filter fixes this issue. The Principal and Credential are nothing more than the Administrator DN and password. In many Active Directory deployments you will find user and group objects under the same base DN — CN=Users. If the groups are in a separate subtree, change the configuration accordingly.

The Active Directory provider has a few capabilities that are specific to the Active Directory schema. First, there is an alternate way to retrieve the group memberships for a user. Users in Active Directory have an attribute called TokenGroups. This attribute stores the objectSID of all of the security groups that the user is a member of. This technique is typically faster than recursively searching through the groups. Second, only users that are enabled in Active Directory can authenticate. Active Directory does this by checking that the UF_ACCOUNTDISABLE bit of the userAccountControl attribute of the user is not set. By default, this check is only performed at authentication time. To prevent having disabled users show up in the WebLogic Console, set the All Users Filter to:

    (&(objectclass=user)(!(userAccountControl:1.2.840.113556.1.4.803:=2)))

The details of the Active Directory are different from other LDAP providers, so we cover them here. As we mentioned before, just because your LDAP server vendor is not listed, it does not mean you cannot use it with WebLogic Server. Consult your LDAP administrator to find the best match between the supplied LDAP providers and your schema. This is the best way to create a specialized LDAP authentication provider. Using the WebLogic Console, map the preceding configuration information to the new LDAP providers by simply providing the information in the appropriate fields under the provider's `Provider Specific Configuration` tab.

Working with multiple authentication sources is common. The most typical scenario is for administrators to authenticate against the embedded LDAP server and for users to authenticate against an external directory. In that case, you need to make a decision on how to order the authentication providers. Typically, you would want to list the customer authentication provider first and set its `Control Flag` to SUFFICIENT. You would list the administrator's authentication source — the embedded LDAP server — second and also set its `Control Flag` to SUFFICIENT. The assumption in this approach is that it is better for administrators to pay the marginal performance hit of failing to authenticate to the external LDAP server than it is for users. In cases where there are two distinct user populations authenticating against two separate directories, you need to make a similar, yet slightly more difficult choice. One directory goes first and users in that directory will have a slightly better experience than the second group of users.

For most applications, it will be very important to optimize the performance of your LDAP-based authentication and group membership queries. You should try to tune your WebLogic Server LDAP configuration filters to be as specific as possible. Another critical step in enhancing your performance is to have your LDAP server index all of the attributes that you will use as search keys in your LDAP search filters. Failing to index these attributes will typically cause performance problems as the number of objects in your LDAP server grows because it forces the LDAP server to perform linear searches. Each LDAP provider has caching configuration options. You will find these options on both the `Provider Specific Configuration` and `Performance` tabs of the LDAP-based authentication provider inside of the WebLogic Console.

Best Practice

Always tune your WebLogic Server LDAP configuration filters to be as specific as possible. Indexing LDAP attributes that are used as search keys is critical for achieving good performance with LDAP servers that contain more than a handful of objects.

Managing RDBMS Authentication

There are three different options for using an RDBMS for authentication: `SQLAuthenticator`, `ReadOnlySQLAuthenticator`, and `CustomDBMSAuthenticator`. The `SQLAuthenticator` is the most fully featured provider. It supports authentication and read/write access to the user/group information via the WebLogic Server domain's admin server. The `ReadOnlySQLAuthenticator` supports authentication and read-only access to the user/group information in the WebLogic Console. The `CustomDBMSAuthenticator` supports only authentication but requires the creation of a plug-in class. The plug-in class has to implement the `weblogic.security.providers.authentication.CustomDBMSAuthenticatorPlugin` interface. This interface gets access to a connection for the configured JDBC data source. The code sample below shows how to implement the `lookupPassword` method. The other key methods of the interface, `userExists`, and `lookupGroups` all follow the same pattern.

```java
package rdbmsplugin;

import java.sql.*;
import weblogic.management.security.ProviderMBean;
import weblogic.security.providers.authentication.CustomDBMSAuthenticatorPlugin;
import weblogic.security.providers.authentication.CustomDBMSAuthenticatorMBean;

public class SampleDBMSAuthPlugIn implements CustomDBMSAuthenticatorPlugin
{
    public SampleDBMSAuthPlugIn()
    {
        System.out.println("Instantiating the Sample Auth PlugIn......");
    }

    //You can access the information configured in the console through the MBean.
    //This is useful for things like setting your own plugin properties
    public void initialize(ProviderMBean providerMBean)
    {
        CustomDBMSAuthenticatorMBean customMBean =
            (CustomDBMSAuthenticatorMBean)providerMBean;
        System.out.println("The plugin properties are " +
                            customMBean.getPluginProperties());
    }

    public String lookupPassword(Connection conn, String user)
    {
        try {
            PreparedStatement stmt =
                conn.prepareStatement("select password from users where user=?");
            stmt.setString(1,user);
            ResultSet rs = stmt.executeQuery();
            if (rs.hasNext()) {
                return rs.getString(1);
            }
            else {
                return null;
            }
        }
        catch (SQLException e) {
            e.printStackTrace();
            return null;
        }
        finally {
            try {
                connection.close();
            }
            catch (Exception otherException) {
                otherException.printStackTrace();
            }
        }
    }

    public boolean userExists(Connection connection, String user)
    {
```

```
        ...
    }

    public String[] lookupUserGroups(Connection connection, String user)
    {
        ...
    }

    public void shutdown()
    {
        ...
    }
}
```

The `CustomDBMSAuthenticator` is a simple way to integrate your database with WebLogic Server for username and password authentication and retrieval of groups at authentication time, especially if you have existing stored procedures. If you need the groups in the database to be visible in read-only mode through the WebLogic Console or your database schema is fairly simple, use the `ReadOnlySQLAuthenticator`. Use the `SQLAuthenticator` only if you need to manage users and groups using the WebLogic Console.

Setting Up SSL/TLS

WebLogic Server supports secure communications with clients and other servers using either Secure Sockets Layer (SSL) or Transport Layer Security (TLS) connections. We assume that everyone is familiar with SSL; for those not familiar with TLS, all you really need to know is that TLS is essentially the next generation of SSL and that WebLogic Server currently supports TLS version 1.0. For the remainder of this book, we will not bother to make the distinction between SSL and TLS and will simply refer to both as SSL. Should we need to differentiate between the two, we will do it explicitly.

In this section, we begin by giving you a brief review of SSL technology. Next, we talk about how to obtain X.509 certificates, private keys, and the CA certificates needed to configure SSL. We end this section with a detailed walkthrough of how to configure WebLogic Server to use SSL.

Overview of SSL and X.509 Certificates

SSL supports two different connection modes or types. The two types are commonly called one-way and two-way SSL. *One-way SSL* allows the SSL client to verify that the SSL server is, in fact, who it claims to be. *Two-way SSL* extends one-way SSL by allowing the SSL server to verify that the client is who it claims to be.

These verifications are accomplished through the use of public/private key technology. This technology uses a set of two related keys known as a public key and a private key for encryption and signing purposes. Anything encrypted using the public key can only be decrypted using the private key, and vice versa. As the names suggest, the owner of the private key keeps this key locked away where only the owner has access to it and gives its public key to everyone who might need it. In almost all cases, private key files are additionally encrypted with a passphrase that must be supplied to get the actual private key as an additional safety check against unauthorized use. The standard way of distributing public keys is to use X.509 certificates that contain information about the certificate's owner and the public key.

X.509 certificates are issued by certificate authorities that digitally sign the certificates with their private key to allow verification (through the use of their public key) that they did, in fact, issue the certificate and that it has not been tampered with. In some cases, the signing authority's certificate might have been signed by another authority and so on. This brings about the notion of a certificate chain where the top of the chain is known as the root certificate authority (CA) whose certificate is always self-signed. When you get the CA's certificate, that certificate will generally contain the entire certificate chain back to the root CA. This root CA or certificate chain is used by the receiver of the original certificate to determine whether he or she trusts that the certificate is legitimate.

With one-way SSL, the SSL client uses the server's certificate (actually, the public key contained in the certificate) to encrypt a symmetric session key that is sent to the server. The server decrypts the session key with its private key. Both the client and the server use that key to encrypt and decrypt data for the duration of the session. This is why it is critical for the server to keep its private key safe and its passphrase a secret. With two-way SSL, the server will request a certificate from the client that it then uses to identify and authenticate the client. In order for the client to trust the certificate provided by the server, it must verify the signing chain of the server's certificate. If the client trusts the server's certificate authority, it can verify the server's certificate and prove that it is real and has not been tampered with. This verification requires the client to have the CA's certificate for the server available locally, as a notion of which certificates the client will *trust*.

In the case of two-way SSL, the server must use the exact same mechanisms to verify the client's certificate. The server requires the client's root CA's certificate locally for two-way SSL. See Table 11-7 for this listing of required data on either side. Notice the concepts of *identity* and *trust* for both the SSL server and the SSL client. The identity is the certificate and private key. The trust is the certificate authority.

Table 11-7: Required SSL Configuration Data

SSL Mode	Client	Server
One-way SSL	Copy of server root CA certificate and chain	Server root CA certificate and chain Server certificate Server private key
Two-way SSL	Copy of server root CA certificate and chain Client root CA certificate and chain Client certificate Client private key	Server root CA certificate and chain Server certificate Server private key Copy of client root CA certificate and chain

Obtaining X.509 Certificates

Now that you understand what you need, we can walk through the process of generating a new certificate and private key for the server. WebLogic Server provides two utilities you can use to generate a new certificate and private key, or you can use the `keytool` program that comes with Java SE. If you want to generate certificates and private keys quickly for demonstration or development purposes, you can use the `utils.CertGen` utility. We will use `utils.CertGen` in the "Configuring Two-Way SSL" section, so we won't spend any time on it here.

If you need certificates for a production server, you will probably want to get your certificates signed by a well-known certificate authority (CA) or use a public key infrastructure (PKI) product. This means that in addition to generating the certificate and the private key, you will need to generate a *Certificate Signing Request* (CSR) and submit it to a certificate authority.

Oracle recommends using the `keytool` program that comes with Java SE. The `keytool` program is at times tedious and unforgiving, so we will walk you through the certificate-generation process step by step. First, you need to generate your self-signed certificate and private key.

```
keytool -v -genkey -alias server_cert -keyalg RSA -keysize 1024
        -dname "CN=www.bigrez.com,OU=Operations,
                O=BigRez.com,L=Dallas,S=Texas,C=US"
        -keypass secret_key_passphrase
        -keystore server_keystore.jks
        -storepass secret_store_password
```

This command generates a self-signed certificate and private key, whose passphrase is `secret_key_passphrase`, using a 1024-bit RSA algorithm and stores them in the key store file `server_keystore.jks`, whose password is `secret_store_password`, under the alias `server_cert`. Pay special attention to the key size and CN element of the distinguished name. The hostname you enter for the CN here *must* be the same as the hostname your SSL clients will use to connect to your SSL server.

> **Set the CN field to the hostname that your SSL clients will ultimately use to reach your server. Failure to do this will result in a certificate that your SSL client may reject because the hostname does not match the IP address the client is using to reach the server.**

You should set the key size to the highest value your WebLogic Server license will allow. At the time of writing, WebLogic Server supports 512-, 1024-, and 2048-bit key lengths.

> **Key lengths of less than 1024 bits are generally considered too weak. If SSL is important enough to use in your environment, use a 1024-bit or larger key.**

The next step is to generate a certificate signing request:

```
keytool -certreq -v -alias server_cert
        -file www_bigrez_com-request.pem
        -keypass secret_key_passphrase
        -storepass secret_store_password
        -keystore server_keystore.jks
```

The result of this command will be a text file called `www_bigrez_com-request.pem` containing your certificate signing request.

Once you have the CSR, you can go to your certificate authority and request a signed certificate. Several different, well-known certificate authorities will sell you a signed certificate. Some CAs will allow you to use a CSR to get a temporary trial server certificate in about 15 minutes. These can be very useful for development and testing efforts prior to production. VeriSign will give you a 14-day trial certificate when you submit your CSR at Link 11-9.

Depending on your CA, you might get your signed certificate or the CA's certificate in one of several different formats. Privacy-Enhanced Mail (PEM) format is the most common and is just a text file containing special beginning and ending delimiters with the certificate information Base64-encoded in between. Look at the `www_bigrez_com-request.pem` file in the downloadable example code to see what a PEM-formatted certificate looks like. Distinguished Encoding Rules (DER) is the other common format, which is a binary format.

Some certificate authorities might give you a certificate file with a `.cer` file extension. This is a Microsoft file extension for certificates and can contain either a binary-encoded (DER format) or a Base64-encoded (PEM format) certificate. Some tools may check the file extensions and refuse to recognize the `.cer` file as a valid certificate. If this happens, open up the file in a text editor to see if the file is Base64-encoded or binary. If it is Base64-encoded, rename the file using a `.pem` extension; if the file is binary, use a `.der` extension.

Should you ever need to convert between PEM and DER formats, WebLogic Server provides two utility programs, `utils.der2pem` and `utils.pem2der`, that will convert between PEM and DER formats. See Link 11-10 for more information on these utilities.

Once you have your signed certificate and the CA's certificate chain available in either PEM or DER format, you will need to import your signed certificate into the key store. Because the `keytool` program will not allow you to import a certificate for which it cannot verify the certificate's signing chain, you need to import the CA's certificate chain as a trusted CA certificate before importing the signed certificate.

```
keytool -import -v -noprompt -trustcacerts -alias cacert
        -file getcacert.der -keystore server_keystore.jks
        -storepass secret_store_password
```

Now you are ready to import the signed certificate that will replace the self-signed certificate you created earlier.

```
keytool -import -v -alias server_cert
        -file www_bigrez_com-cert.pem
        -keystore server_keystore.jks
        -keypass secret_key_passphrase
        -storepass secret_store_password
```

At this point, you have a key store that contains the server's signed certificate, the server's private key, and the trusted CA certificate, which should include the entire certificate chain. All you need to do now is to configure the server and provide the client with the trusted CA certificate, if the client doesn't already have it.

Configuring One-Way SSL

You finished all of the hard configuration work in the last section; now we'll help you set up the server to use your key store. All you need to do is to edit the server's configuration to enable one-way SSL and use the key store you created. First, change the key store information by selecting the server's `Keystores Configuration` tab. Because you are going to supply a new certificate but use the Java SE–supplied key store, select the `Custom Identity and Java Standard Trust` option for the `Keystores` attribute.

Now, you simply fill in the file name, key store type, and key store password for the `Custom Identity Keystore` and the password for your `Java Standard Trust Keystore`. The standard Java trust key store is always found at `$JAVA_HOME/jre/lib/security/cacerts` and has a default key store password of `changeit`. You can change the password of this key store using the `keytool -storepasswd` command; however, we recommend that you do not modify this file. If you are not comfortable with having this trust key store with this well-known password, we recommend copying this key store to another location, resetting the password, and switching to use a custom trust key store. This makes it easier to upgrade your WebLogic Server software without running the risk of losing your customized trust key store.

> **Best Practice**
> Never modify the standard Java trust key store directly. If you want to use it as a starting point and customize it, make a copy of it into someplace that is associated with your application configuration and modify the copy.

The downloadable example places the identity key store file in the server-specific directory. You can place the file anywhere you want but remember that this file must be protected, so we recommend keeping it close to the rest of your server's configuration files. Any relative path that you enter for the key store file name is relative to the domain's root directory. The key store type is JKS (short for Java key store), and the value of the Custom Identity Keystore Passphrase attribute is simply the key store's password you used when creating the key store — secret_store_password in our example.

Next, you need to configure SSL to use the private key from the key store. Using the server's SSL Configuration tab, enter the private key's alias in the key store and its passphrase. The private key alias you should use in this example is the alias for the server's certificate: server_cert. Once this is finished, simply restart the server for your changes to take effect. Don't forget to enable the SSL Listen Port on the server's General Configuration tab.

Finally, you need to make the server's CA certificate chain available to the client. If you are using real certificates from well-known authorities, your client will probably already have the certificate chain in its trusted CA certificates store. If not, you will need to make the CA's certificate chain available to the client.

For browser-based clients, the browser will simply prompt the user to ask whether he or she wants to trust this certificate, as well as giving the user an option to install it. You can also proactively install the trusted CA certificate chain on the client. For Internet Explorer, you need to install the trusted CA certificate chain in the operating system. Please talk to your Windows administrator or refer to the MSDN article on how to manage end user certificates at Link 11-11. For Firefox or other browsers, please refer to the browser documentation.

For Java-based clients, you can either add the new certificates to the Java SE's $JAVA_HOME/jre/lib/security/cacerts key store or create a new client trust key store. If you create a new client trust key store, you need to tell your Java client to use it. If you are using JSSE, you do this by setting the Java system properties as follows:

```
-Djavax.net.ssl.trustStore=<trust key store file name>
-Djavax.net.ssl.trustStorePassword=<trust key store passphrase>
```

If you are using WebLogic Server SSL, you do this by setting the Java system properties as follows:

```
-Dweblogic.security.TrustKeyStore=CustomTrust
-Dweblogic.security.CustomTrustKeyStoreFileName=<trust key store file name>
-Dweblogic.security.CustomTrustKeyStorePassPhrase=<trust key store passphrase>
```

We talk more about how to do this in the "Writing Java Clients That Use SSL" section later in this chapter.

Configuring Two-Way SSL

Now that you have seen how to configure the server for one-way SSL, getting to two-way SSL is pretty simple. In this section, you use the `utils.CertGen` utility that comes with WebLogic Server to generate client certificates. Remember that `utils.CertGen` is not intended for use in production environments. You could just as easily use the same keytool-based process used to generate certificates for the server to generate the client certificates. Our primary motivation for using `utils.CertGen` here is to show you how you can use it to generate certificates for demonstrations or development environments without incurring the cost of buying real certificates for every demo/development machine.

First, let's generate the client certificate, private key, and key store. `utils.CertGen` is a simple utility that can generate certificates. The syntax of the command is as follows:

```
java utils.CertGen -certfile <cert_file_name> -keyfile <key_file_name>
    -keyfilepass <key_file_pass> -cn <hostname>
    [-strength <key length (1024 by default)>]
```

In this example, you want to generate a certificate for a machine called `rpatrick.bigrez.com` so that you can run the following command on any machine. The output of this command is four files containing the certificate and the primary key in both PEM and DER formats:

```
java utils.CertGen -certfile client_cert -keyfile client_key
    -keyfilepass client_key_passphrase -cn rpatrick.bizreg.com
```

You can find the CA certificate used to sign all certificates generated by `utils.CertGen` at `$WL_HOME/server/lib/CertGenCA.der`. For more information on the `utils.CertGen` utility, see Link 11-12.

You will need to make the client's CA certificate available to the server. Because your server is currently configured for one-way SSL and using the standard Java trust key store, you either need to add the client CA certificate to the standard Java key store or create a new server trust key store. Recall that we don't recommend modifying the standard Java trust key store. We recommend copying the standard Java trust key store because it already contains most of the root CA certificates you will need. If your application is an internal application, you may want to start with a new key store and add only the CA certificates approved for use within your organization.

Tip to Remember

For sites using two-way SSL with external clients, starting with the standard Java trust key store will ensure that most clients will be able to connect using their existing certificates.

Start by copying the standard Java trust key store to a file called `server_trust_keystore.jks` in the domain's root directory and changing its password.

```
keytool -storepasswd -new secret_trust_password
    -keystore server_trust_keystore.jks -storepass changeit
```

Then, import the client's CA certificate, just as you did before, using the `keytool -import -trustcacerts` command.

```
keytool -import -v -noprompt -trustcacerts -alias cacert3
        -file %WL_HOME%\server\lib\CertGenCA.der
        -keystore server_trust_keystore.jks
        -storepass secret_trust_password
```

Now, you need to reconfigure the server to use this new trust key store. Simply go back to the server's `Keystores Configuration` tab in the WebLogic Console and select the `Custom Identity` and `Custom Trust` option for the `Keystores` attribute. Next, set the trust key store name, type, and passphrase to the appropriate values (`server_trust_keystore.jks`, `JKS`, and `secret_trust_password`, respectively). You can leave everything else unchanged and finish applying the changes. Before restarting the server, make the other SSL changes to enable two-way SSL.

Back on the `SSL Configuration` tab, scroll down to the bottom of the page and select the `Advanced` heading. It has a few settings of interest to our current discussion. First, you need to change the `Two Way Client Cert Behavior` attribute that tells the server how to handle client certificates. Setting it to a value of `Client Certs Requested But Not Enforced` will turn on two-way SSL, but the SSL connection process will continue even if the client does not provide a certificate. If you want to require two-way SSL, set the value to `Client Certs Requested And Enforced`. We will use the last setting because we want to verify that two-way SSL is working properly.

Another attribute of interest is `Hostname Verification`, which controls the behavior that the server uses when validating a certificate sent to it. This applies when the server is acting as a client to another SSL server. By default, this is set to the value `BEA Hostname Verifier`, which tells the server to use the internal implementation for verifying that the hostname in the certificate matches the destination from which the certificate originated. In some cases, you might want to change this setting to `None` to allow the use of certificates that do not match while in development. Never use this setting in a production environment. In extreme circumstances, you might need to provide your own implementation of the hostname verifier. You can do this by setting the value to `Custom Hostname Verifier` and setting the `Custom Hostname Verifier` attribute to the fully qualified class name of a class that implements the `weblogic.security.SSL.HostnameVerifier` interface.

It is also possible to disable all hostname verification completely in any WebLogic SSL client or server by setting the Java system property `weblogic.security.SSL.ignoreHostnameVerification` to true. Of course, another way to do this would be to provide your own hostname verifier class that always returns true. Either way, this is extremely dangerous because it disables verification that the certificate being used is actually from the host specified in the certificate. It can be useful, though, in a development or demonstration environment when you simply want to use the demonstration certificates that come with WebLogic Server. Do not forget to re-enable hostname verification when migrating your configuration to a production environment.

Best Practice

Disabling hostname verification can make things simpler in a development or demonstration environment; always re-enable hostname verification for your production environments.

The last attributes of interest are the inbound and outbound certificate validation. For each of these attributes there are two options: Built in SSL Validation or Built in SSL and Cert Path Validation. The second option additionally uses the certification path providers configured for the domain to validate certificates. WebLogic Server provides a certification path provider called Certificate Registry that is used to manage trusted certificates. This includes the ability to revoke certificates from the WebLogic Console without restarting the server. Also, custom certification path providers could be written to integrate Online Certificate Status Protocol (OCSP) and Certificate Revocation Lists (CRL) checking into WebLogic Server. OCSP and CRL are two different techniques for ensuring that a certificate is still valid.

If you are using browser-based clients, you will need to install the client certificates used by the browsers. Of course, these client-side, browser-based certificates will likely be user-specific certificates, so make sure to install them appropriately. If you intend to use two-way SSL as an application authentication mechanism, make sure that each user's certificate contains his or her WebLogic Server username somewhere in the distinguished name. We talk more about application authentication after we discuss configuring Java clients.

For Java clients, you need to create identity and trust key stores for the client to use. Again, these key stores can be the same or different key stores. In this example, you use two separate key stores to help you understand what needs to go in each key store. The identity key store needs to contain the client's certificate and private key. To create this client key store, you will use another WebLogic Server–provided utility called utils.ImportPrivateKey, whose syntax is as follows.

```
java utils.ImportPrivateKey -keystore <keystore_file>
      -storepass <keystore_password> -alias <certificate_alias_to_use>
      -keyfilepass<private_key_passphrase> -certfile <certificate_file>
      -keyfile <private_key_file> -storetype [<keystore_type>]
```

If the keytool program provided an easy way to import an existing private key from a file, you would not need this utils.ImportPrivateKey utility. Because it doesn't, use the following command to create your identity key store and import your existing certificate and private key.

```
java utils.ImportPrivateKey -keystore  client_keystore.jks
      -storepass client_key_passphrase -alias client_cert
      -keyfilepass client_key_passphrase
      -certfile  rpatrick-cert.pem
      -keyfile rpatrick-key.pem -storetype JKS
```

Notice that by using the utils.ImportPrivateKey utility you did not have to import the CA certificate chain first. For more information on the utils.ImportPrivateKey utility, see Link 11-13.

Next, you need to create your trust key store. Because Java client programs are not typically talking with a large number of servers controlled by different organizations, we have chosen to create a new trust key store rather than starting with the one included with Java SE. You will place both the client's and the server's CA certificate chain in the trust key store. Once again, you can use the keytool program to create the new store and import both certificate chains.

```
keytool -import -v -noprompt -trustcacerts -alias client_cacert
      -file %WL_HOME%\server\lib\CertGenCA.der
      -keystore trust_store_keystore.jks
      -storepass trust_store_password
```

```
keytool -import -v -noprompt -trustcacerts -alias server_cacert
        -file getcacert.der -keystore trust_store_keystore.jks
        -storepass trust_store_password
```

Finally, you just need to get your Java client programs to use these new key stores. You use the same Java system properties we discussed at the end of the "Configuring One-Way SSL" section to tell your client which trust key store to use. As you see later in the "Writing Java Clients That Use SSL" section, you specify the identity key store to use directly from within the client-side Java code.

The last thing we need to discuss is how to use two-way SSL as an application authentication mechanism. To use client certificates to authenticate your client users, you need to configure the server to support this. If you want to require users to have a client certificate, make sure that you set the Two Way Client Cert Behavior attribute to Client Certs Requested And Enforced. Otherwise, WebLogic Server will permit clients that do not present a certificate access. For web applications only, there is an additional step on the server. Make sure that the application is configured in the web.xml to use the <login-method> of CLIENT-CERT and that the resources that you want to protect are included in a <security-constraint>. These settings tell WebLogic Server to look for the identity in the X.509 certificate of the caller when those protected resources are being accessed. Next, you need to create WebLogic Server users for mapping to client certificates. We talk more about user management in the "Setting Up WebLogic Server Application Security" section later in this chapter. Finally, you need to configure the DefaultIdentityAsserter to support X.509 token types and set up the username mapper to extract the mapping information from the certificate and return the username, as previously discussed in the "Identity Assertion" section.

In this example, because the CN of our utils.CertGen-created client certificates contains the fully qualified hostname, you should set the Default User Name Mapper to extract the user information from the CN field and use the "." character as the delimiter to map the hostname rpatrick.bigrez.com properly to the WebLogic Server user rpatrick. Once you have everything configured correctly, you should be able to use normal Java EE or WebLogic Server security mechanisms with your users without requiring them to log in or supply a password.

To test two-way SSL from a browser, you'll need to install the user's private key and certificate. Both Internet Explorer and Firefox can import a PKCS12 key store containing the private key. The Java keytool program is used to export a key store into another format including PKCS12. The only trick is that the password for the newly created PKCS12 key store has to be the same as the password for the user's private key.

```
keytool -importkeystore -v -srckeystore client_keystore.jks
        -destkeystore client.p12 -deststoretype pkcs12
        -deststorepass client_key_passphrase -srcstorepass client_store_password
        -srcalias client_cert -srckeypass client_key_passphrase
```

This will result in the creation of a PKCS12 file called client.p12 that can then be imported into Internet Explorer or Firefox. When prompted in the browser to enter the password for the certificate, enter client_key_passphrase. We cover more of the details of the keytool and two-way SSL in the section "Writing Java Clients That Use SSL."

Debugging SSL Problems

Debugging problems with SSL configurations can be a frustrating task because most of the real work happens during the initial SSL handshake, before the server-side application code is ever invoked.

Fortunately, WebLogic Server has some debugging flags that cause the server to print out very detailed information during the handshake. Without this sort of information, it is almost impossible for you (or Oracle Customer Support) to debug the problem. To turn on this debugging output, use the server's `Debug` tab to enable the `default.DebugSSL` and the `weblogic.security.ssl` debug scopes. On the client side use `-Dssl.debug=true` and `-Dweblogic.StdoutDebugEnabled=true`.

When running WebLogic Server with 1-way SSL, if the server starts up and the server is listening on the SSL port then there are no issues on the server. If the server fails to listen on the SSL port then there is either an issue with the server's certificate or with one of the trusted CAs. Common issues with the server certificate are that it's expired or it's not trusted — not all of the CAs in the certificate's chain are trusted. Issues with individual CAs are unlikely, but on occasion issues with expired CA certificates or invalid certificates could cause the SSL listener to not start properly.

Assuming that the server has started, if the client cannot connect to the server over 1-way SSL then the next place to check is on the client. The most common client issue is that the certificate of the server is not trusted. Adding the server's CA certificates to the client's trust store fixes this problem. Another common issue is that the hostname verification fails. This normally means that the CN in the SubjectDN of the certificate does not match the hostname of the server. As was previously discussed, for non-production environments, simply changing the client to use a less rigorous `HostnameVerifier` will suffice. For production environments make sure that the IP address of the server can be resolved to the hostname that matches the CN in the server's certificate. Alternatively, get the server a certificate for the hostname that does match the IP address of the server it is running.

Debugging a client that is using 2-way SSL is just an extension of the checks done for a 1-way SSL client. In addition, there is the possibility that the client when prompted by the server to pass a certificate is unable to do so. The most common reason for this is that when the server presents the client with the list of CAs that it trusts, the CA for the client's certificate is not present, so the SSL handshake fails. The remedy in this case is to add the client's CA certificates to the server's trust store.

Tip to Remember

When having SSL problems, first check the release notes for any known problems that may apply to your particular configuration. Turning on the SSL debugging flags can make debugging SSL configuration problems much simpler.

Writing Security-Aware Java Clients

In this section, we show you how to write security-aware Java clients that interact with WebLogic Server. The focus is primarily around authentication and the use of SSL. First, we talk about how your Java application client can use JAAS to authenticate to WebLogic Server. Then, we show you how to set up an SSL connection between your application client and WebLogic Server. In Chapter 9, we showed you how to write security-aware web services clients that use SSL for transport security and WS-Security for providing message-level protection.

Writing Java Clients That Use JAAS

Before we jump into the details of how to use JAAS with your WebLogic Server Java client application, let's briefly look at the theory behind it. JAAS provides a standard way to authenticate specific users and authorize those users for specific sets of code and resources.

JAAS authentication is designed to be a pluggable framework that removes authentication methods and decisions from business logic entirely. This framework allows for a new method of authentication to be added to an application to either replace or augment the current authentication modules without requiring the application code to change. We spend the bulk of this section looking at how JAAS authentication works.

JAAS authorization is built using the existing Java security model, which uses a security policy to restrict the rights of executing code. JAAS extends this model by allowing the policy to be defined for specific users and groups. Typically and by default, this policy is defined in a text file that uses a special syntax; this file is `java.policy`. Through this mechanism, JAAS allows the Java runtime to restrict access based on where the code came from, who the code might be digitally signed by, and what authenticated principal the code is running on behalf of. The granularity of restriction is still limited to the same low-level system resources of the Java runtime. For example, you could restrict access to reading or writing specific Java system properties, files, or network ports. JAAS authorization does not address the problems associated with protecting a server's application-level resources such as an EJB method or JMS queue. Java Authorization Contract for Containers (JACC) uses JAAS as a foundation, and provides a standard solution for some of these issues, but in general JAAS authorization is not used to secure Java EE container resources.

You can turn on JAAS authorization by adding the following two Java command-line options to set the required Java system properties:

```
-Djava.security.manager -Djava.security.policy=weblogic.policy
```

The `java.security.debug` system property is helpful in resolving issues with JAAS authorization. Using a combination of the `access` and `policy` values should help get to the root issue with any unexpected behavior.

JAAS authorization might be useful to restrict the Java runtime permissions for untrusted code running on your server. Most production environments, though, typically are not running untrusted code on the server, so using JAAS authorization to control access on your application server is probably not worth pursuing. A typical Java EE environment has at least minimal audits of the business applications and code running on the server. The only real-world situation where the extra performance hit of using JAAS authorization might be useful would be for application service providers (ASPs). JAAS authorization makes sense only if you host applications that you don't directly control or have the ability to audit. In most cases, the benefits do not justify the runtime performance overhead.

> **Best Practice**
>
> JAAS authorization addresses authorization only for low-level system resources or capabilities like reading or writing to a file or creating a new class loader. All application-level resources are left as an exercise for the application server or application security vendors. Most production server environments are not typically running untrusted code, and the performance overhead of JAAS authorization can be substantial. Therefore, we do not recommend JAAS authorization for most application authorization needs.

JAAS authentication occurs in a few basic steps. A JAAS client application begins the authentication process by instantiating a `LoginContext` object with the client type and a new custom `CallbackHandler`, as shown in the following code fragment.

```
CallbackHandler callback =
    new ProfessionalWebLogicCallbackHandler(username, password, url));
LoginContext loginContext =
    new LoginContext("ProfessionalWebLogic", callback);
```

In this case, the client type is `ProfessionalWebLogic` and the custom `CallbackHandler` is the `ProfessionalWeblogicCallbackHandler`.

When this client code executes, the `LoginContext` looks up its configuration to determine the required authentication types, or `LoginModules`, to be used in performing the authentication. Whereas JAAS supports a pluggable configuration model, the Java runtime ships only with the file-based implementation, so the configuration typically comes from a file. The `LoginContext` matches the client type with the `LoginModule` and its associated flags. In our example, the configuration information is stored in the `professionalweblogic.config` file, whose contents are as follows:

```
ProfessionalWebLogic {
    weblogic.security.auth.login.UsernamePasswordLoginModule required debug=false;
};
```

When the `LoginContext` reads this file, it finds the entry for its client type, `ProfessionalWebLogic`, and determines that the correct `LoginModule` to use is `weblogic.security.auth.login.UsernamePasswordLoginModule`, whose control flag is set to `Required` and `debug` flag is set to `false`. This control flag value has the exact same semantics as we previously discussed when covering `LoginModule` settings in the "Authentication" section.

So, the next question that should come to mind is how does the `LoginContext` know where to find its configuration? Java provides two mechanisms for telling the `LoginContext` where to find its configuration information. One way to specify the location of the JAAS login configuration is through the Java system property `java.security.auth.login.config`, which can be set to point to the configuration file the Java program should use. If this system property is not set, the Java runtime will search through the list of entries like the one shown next in the `$JAVA_HOME/jre/lib/security/java.security` file looking for a configuration file that contains an entry that matches our client type:

```
login.config.url.1=file:/c:/powls/ch11/professional-weblogic.policy
```

The next step in the application is to call the `LoginContext`'s `login()` method, which starts the whole authentication process. The `LoginModules` are called with the original `CallbackHandler`. A basic `LoginModule` might simply use the `CallbackHandler` to prompt for a username and password on the command line. More complex methods might require an X.509 certificate, a Kerberos token, or even some biometric information. Each new authentication method requires a new `LoginModule`, and possibly a new `CallbackHandler` to deal with any new `Callback` types the `LoginModule` might need. Each `LoginModule` uses the `CallbackHandler` to decide whether to authenticate this subject.

In our example, we use a `ProfessionalWebLogicCallbackHandler` to hold the username and password. We chose this approach so that you could see the inner workings of the `CallbackHandler`. In this case, it would be just as easy to use the WebLogic Server's built-in `weblogic.security.SimpleCallbackHandler` or `weblogic.security.URLCallbackHandler`. The `SimpleCallbackHandler` supports only prompting for the username and password; the `URLCallbackHandler` supports prompting for the username, password, and server URL.

Upon success, `LoginModules` associate various `Principals` with the newly created `Subject`. If the `LoginContext` is successful, the application can then retrieve the `Subject` from it. This new `Subject` has a list of `Principal` objects that represent the identity of the currently authenticated user. To invoke business logic, you must create a class that implements `PrivilegedAction` and contains the business logic, and you must pass it to the WebLogic Server security subsystem along with the newly created `Subject`.

```
loginContext.login();
Subject subject = loginContext.getSubject();
JAASExampleAction clientAction = new JAASExampleAction(url);
Security.runAs(subject, clientAction);
```

You should notice right away that the business logic is now encapsulated inside a `PrivilegedAction` object, which is just a wrapper of a `Runnable`. We pass the `PrivilegedAction` object to the WebLogic Server security subsystem, along with the authenticated `Subject`, to be run. This is different from standard JAAS, which uses the `Subject` itself to run the `PrivilegedAction`. Although covering the rationale for this is beyond the scope of this book, suffice it to say that there are problems with losing the user identity when combining the JAAS-specified `Subject.doAs()` with `AccessController.doPrivileged()`. Because Java EE requires the use of `AccessController.doPrivileded()` in certain conditions, WebLogic Server provides a `Security.runAs()` method that is similar in spirit to `Subject.doAs()` and works with all of your JAAS code, but does not suffer from the user identity problem.

Another important point is that the `LoginModule` being used by the client is not the same as the one being used by the WebLogic Server Security Service on the server. The client-side `LoginModule` calls to the server to try to authenticate the client. As a result of this request, the server will call into the security framework, which will end up invoking the server-side `LoginModule`(s) to make the actual authentication decision. Your application client should either use the WebLogic Server–provided `LoginModule`, called the `UsernamePasswordLoginModule`, or provide its own custom `LoginModule`. If you use a custom `LoginModule`, always call `weblogic.security.auth.Authenticate.authenticate()` from within its `login()` method, as shown here:

```
Subject subject = new Subject();
weblogic.jndi.Environment env = new weblogic.jndi.Environment();
env.setProviderUrl(url);
env.setSecurityPrincipal(username);
env.setSecurityCredentials(password);
weblogic.security.auth.Authenticate.authenticate(env, subject);
```

The basic idea here is that the client application running the custom `LoginModule` must contact the server to allow the server to do the authentication. As a part of this server-side authentication process, the server will populate and digitally sign the `Subject` before returning. You can place any `Serializable` object in the `Environment` to act as the credential instead of a password as long as the server's configured authentication provider knows how to use it to authenticate the user. This `authenticate()` method is only for authentication to a remote server. To authenticate to the server from code running inside that server, you need to use the `weblogic.security.service.Authenticate.login()` method.

Best Practice

Use only the `weblogic.security.auth.Authenticate.authenticate()` method to authenticate to a remote server process. Always use the `weblogic.security. services.Authenticate.login()` method for code running inside the server to which you want to authenticate.

Writing Java Clients That Use SSL

When writing a Java client that uses SSL, there are three main types of application clients to consider: RMI clients, programmatic HTTP clients, and web services clients. We discuss RMI clients and HTTP clients in this section, since we covered the discussion of web services clients in Chapter 9. We end this section with a discussion of application authentication, hostname verification, and trust managers.

RMI Clients

The first type of client to discuss is an RMI client using SSL. For one-way SSL, it is as simple as specifying an SSL protocol and port in the `PROVIDER_URL` that you use to create the JNDI `InitialContext` object:

```
Hashtable ht = new Hashtable();
ht.put(Context.INITIAL_CONTEXT_FACTORY,
        "weblogic.jndi.WLInitialContextFactory");
ht.put(Context.PROVIDER_URL, "t3s://localhost:7002");
InitialContext ctx = new InitialContext(ht);
```

Of course, this assumes that the server's certificate is trusted by the client — the server's root CA certificate is in the client's standard Java trust store. If not, you either need to add it or use a custom trust key store that contains this root CA certificate. If using the custom trust key store, you will need to use the Java system properties previously described in the "Configuring One-Way SSL" section to tell the JVM where to find the trust store.

Making a two-way SSL connection from a standalone client is a little bit more work. In this case, you simply need to get the certificate chain and private key from the key store and pass it into the `InitialContext` constructor. You also need to establish trust with the certificate being returned by the server. We explore in the next section the use of JSSE `TrustManagers` to accomplish this. Java Secure Socket Extension (JSSE) is the standard set of libraries that the JDK provides for SSL, most of which are located in the `javax.net.ssl` package. The WebLogic Server environment has the ability to specify the MD5 fingerprint of the CAs that this client trusts. You can easily retrieve the MD5 fingerprint of the certificate by using the `keytool -list -keystore <keystore>` command. The MD5 fingerprint in the following example is for the VeriSign Trial CA certificate.

```
KeyStore ks = KeyStore.getInstance("jks");
ks.load(new java.io.FileInputStream("client_keystore.jks"), null);
PrivateKey key =
    (PrivateKey)ks.getKey("client_cert", "client_key_passphrase".toCharArray());
Certificate [] certChain = ks.getCertificateChain("client_cert");
weblogic.jndi.Environment env = new weblogic.jndi.Environment();
env.setProviderUrl(url);
env.loadLocalIdentity(certificateChain, privateKey);
env.setSSLRootCAFingerprints("B69DA4405202500DD59CE1B84B66C4AC");
Context ctx = env.getInitialContext();
```

Another example available for downloading shows how to accomplish the same thing using the thin RMI client that also supports using a key store but does it by using JSSE under the covers. Java Secure Socket Extension (JSSE) is the standard set of libraries that the JDK provides for SSL, most of which are located in the `javax.net.ssl` package. Notice that instead of using the MD5 serial number check, this example uses JSSE `TrustManagers` to establish trust. This example will work only if the client is using the thin client jar file, `wlclient.jar`, and not running inside a WebLogic Server. As mentioned previously, you don't need to worry about outgoing SSL connections from the WebLogic Server as long as you have the server configured with the proper information to find its certificate and private key.

When using JSSE, you can configure the SSL client information either through a set of system properties or programmatically through the instantiation of a `SSLContext` object. Unfortunately, current versions of WebLogic Server no longer provide a way to pass the `SSLContext` into the `InitialContext` programmatically. Therefore, the RMI client example below specifies the information as Java system properties. You specify the trust key store to use by setting the Java system property `javax.net.ssl.trustStore`. To verify the integrity of the data it retrieves from the key store, specify the key store password using the `javax.net.ssl.trustStorePassword` Java system property.

You also need to configure JSSE to use a client identity key store by setting the Java system property `javax.net.ssl.keyStore`. To retrieve the client's certificate and private key from the key store, set the Java system property `java.net.ssl.keyStorePassword` to the key store password and private key passphrase. Also, if you are using a key store type other than JKS, such as PKCS12, set the Java system property `javax.net.ssl.keyStoreType` accordingly. So, the code is the same as the one-way SSL example above, but we must set the `javax.net.ssl.keyStore` and the `java.net.ssl.keyStorePassword` properties to specify the client certificate information.

```
Hashtable props = new Hashtable();
props.put(Context.INITIAL_CONTEXT_FACTORY,
        "weblogic.jndi.WLInitialContextFactory");
props.put(Context.PROVIDER_URL, "iiops://127.0.0.1:7002");
InitialContext ctx = new InitialContext(props);
```

One important thing to point out is the JSSE Java system properties do not provide a property for the identity key store certificate alias or for the private key passphrase. This means:

❑   JSSE only supports a client identity key store that has a single certificate/private key pair.

❑   Through its Java system properties, JSSE requires that the password for the key store and the passphrase for the private key be identical.

> When using a two-way SSL JSSE client, you need an identity key store that has one
> certificate/private key pair. When using the Java system properties, JSSE requires
> that the identity key store's password and the private key's passphrase be identical.

Programmatic HTTP Clients

The next type of client is a Java application client making HTTP requests over SSL using `URLConnection`
objects. You might wonder how common it is to need a Java client that makes HTTP requests. The answer
is that although it may not be very common for a true client application, it is a relatively common thing
to do when writing server-side code that may need to call out to some other site to get information.

When writing these types of clients, you have two main ways of establishing the SSL connection:
WebLogic SSL APIs or JSSE APIs. First, let's look at using the WebLogic SSL APIs. For one-way SSL you
simply create your `HttpsURLConnection` object.

```
URL url = new URL("https", hostname, sslPortNumber, page);
weblogic.net.http.HttpsURLConnection sslConn =
    new weblogic.net.http.HttpsURLConnection(url);
sslConn.connect();
```

As with the RMI client, this assumes that the client trusts the server's certificate. If not, you must take the
appropriate steps to configure the client to trust the server's certificate, as previously described.

The same exact code will work for 2-way SSL from inside WebLogic Server. There is no need to supply
the credentials because the server can be configured to automatically provide them for any outgoing SSL
connection in which the remote SSL server requests them. You can do this by enabling `Use Server Certs`
from the `Advanced` area of the `SSL Configuration` tab of the server. This only applies to clients using the
WebLogic Server SSL stack

If you want to make a two-way SSL connection from outside the server, you need to do a little bit
more work. You need to get the X.509 certificate chain and the private key and use these to store
the client's identity in WebLogic Server's version of the `SSLContext`. Then, you get the WebLogic
Server `SSLSocketFactory` from the `SSLContext` and use it to call `setSSLSocketFactory()` on the
`weblogic.het.http.HttpsURLConnection` object before you call `connect()`. The downloadable
examples contain a complete working example, the highlights of which are shown here.

```
import weblogic.net.http.HttpsURLConnection;
import weblogic.security.SSL.SSLContext;
import weblogic.security.SSL.SSLSocketFactory;

. . .

SSLContext ctx = SSLContext.getInstance("https");
ctx.loadLocalIdentity(certChain, privateKey);
SSLSocketFactory sslSocketFactory = ctx.getSocketFactory();

URL url = new URL("https", hostName, sslPortNumber, page);
HttpsURLConnection sslConn = new HttpsURLConnection(url);
```

```
sslConn.setSSLSocketFactory(sslSocketFactory);
sslConn.connect();
```

For JSSE clients making a one-way SSL connection, it is simply a matter of changing the package of `HttpsURLConnection` object to `javax.net.ssl.HttpsURLConnection`:

```
URL jsseUrl = new URL("https", hostname, sslPortNumber, page);
javax.net.ssl.HttpsURLConnection sslConn =
    (javax.net.ssl.HttpsURLConnection)url.openConnection();
sslConn.connect();
```

Unlike the 2-way SSL RMI example using JSSE, you can instantiate the `SSLContext` object and pass it to initialize your HTTP client connection. You simply use the JSSE `SSLContext` object to get a JSSE `SSLSocketFactory` and use it to call `setSSLSocketFactory()` on the `javax.net.ssl.HttpsURLConnection` object before you call `connect()`, as highlighted here. See the downloadable examples on the companion Web site for a complete working example.

```
import javax.net.ssl.HttpsURLConnection;
import javax.net.ssl.KeyManagerFactory;
import javax.net.ssl.SSLContext;
import javax.net.ssl.SSLSocketFactory;
import javax.net.ssl.TrustManagerFactory;

...

KeyManagerFactory kmf =
    KeyManagerFactory.getInstance("SunX509", "SunJSSE");
kmf.init(identityKeyStore, args[1].toCharArray());
TrustManagerFactory tmf =
    TrustManagerFactory.getInstance("SunX509", "SunJSSE");
tmf.init(trustKeyStore);

SSLContext ctx = SSLContext.getInstance("SSL");
ctx.init(kmf.getKeyManagers(), tmf.getTrustManagers(), null);
SSLSocketFactory sslSocketFactory = ctx.getSocketFactory();

URL url = new URL("https", serverName, sslPortNumber, page);
HttpsURLConnection sslConn =
    (HttpsURLConnection)url.openConnection();
sslConn.setSSLSocketFactory(sslSocketFactory);
sslConn.connect();
```

JSSE uses the `KeyManagerFactory` to handle all interaction with the `KeyStore`. It queries the `KeyStore` to determine which certificate and private key to use when asked to provide credentials. While this programmatic API allows the identity key store password and private key passphrase to be different, there is still no way to specify which certificate/private key pair to use. As such, you still need to use an identity key store with a single certificate/private key pair.

> When using JSSE's `KeyManagerFactory`, there is no way to specify which certificate/private key pair to use. As such, you still need to use an identity key store with a single certificate/private key pair.

Web Services Clients

The use of SSL for web services clients is covered in Chapter 9. This chapter includes both transport- and message-level security. Before we leave the topic of SSL, we need to discuss a few miscellaneous options related to SSL: application authentication, hostname verification, and trust managers.

Application Authentication

You can use two-way SSL to authenticate a client to your WebLogic Server application. To do this, you simply need to map the client certificate presented to the server to a WebLogic Server username. You can do this using the identity assertion capabilities of the WebLogic Security Framework, as discussed earlier in the "Identity Assertion" section. All of the two-way SSL examples we just discussed use this capability to allow the server-side application to determine the username. Once the WebLogic Server identity is established, you can use any standard Java EE or WebLogic Server authorization capabilities to restrict access to protected resources.

Hostname Verification

Both WebLogic Server and JSSE try to verify that the certificate a remote process presents matches its hostname. They do this by invoking a default set of rules to try to match the common name (CN) field of the X.509 certificate's distinguished name (DN) to the host from which it came. If they are unable to do that, they will invoke the registered hostname verifier class to verify that the certificate is, in fact, from the host. In most situations, the hostname verification process will not need the hostname verifier. By default, both WebLogic Server and JSSE are configured to fail all verification calls that need to call the hostname verifier. This means that if your certificates are failing the default verification rules, you will need to get new certificates or provide your own implementation of the `weblogic.security.SSL.HostnameVerifier` or `javax.net.ssl.HostnameVerifier` interface, depending on which SSL implementation you are using.

There are three ways to register your custom hostname verifier class with WebLogic SSL. You can call the `setHostnameVerifier()` method on either the WebLogic `HttpsURLConnection` or `SSLContext` objects. If your code is running in the server, you can use the `Advanced` section of the server's `SSL Configuration` tab in the WebLogic Console. Finally, you can use the Java system property `weblogic.security.SSL.HostnameVerifier` to point to the fully qualified class name of your hostname verifier class.

Trust Managers

Our last topic is the `TrustManager` interface. A `TrustManager` is a secondary means of verifying the certification chain supplied by the other party participating in the SSL handshake. It is a simple interface that is called only if the default certificate chain verification fails. A common example of this occurs when an SSL client connects to an SSL server that has a single expired certificate somewhere in its certificate signing chain and the expired certificate has been replaced with a new certificate, next to it in the chain. Using the new certificate in the server certificate chain and simply ignoring the expired certificate will verify correctly. The problem is that standard SSL certificate verification will not accept a certificate chain like this. It is considered untrusted, and the SSL handshake will fail.

If the SSL client has been set up with a `TrustManager`, the client's `TrustManager` will be called with the unverified server certificate chain. The `TrustManager` can then decide whether to allow the certificate chain verification and thus the SSL handshake to continue. Use of a `TrustManager` is not required if the default SSL certificate chain verification is all that is needed. Both WebLogic SSL and JSSE support registering a custom `TrustManager`. With WebLogic SSL, you need to provide an implementation of the `weblogic.security.SSL.TrustManager` interface and register it with the weblogic.security.SSL.SSLContext object. For JSSE, you need to create and register your own javax.net.ssl.TrustManagerFactory or implement the javax.net.ssl.X509TrustManager interface directly. Both of these are then used in conjunction with the javax.net.ssl.SSLContext object's init() method.

Managing Application Security

In this section, we present a brief overview of the setup, management, and administration of the WebLogic Server application security features. We start with a brief description of the various application security models in WebLogic Server. We continue with a review of the Java EE standard security settings in various deployment descriptors. Next, we show you how to set up roles and access control policies using the built-in WebLogic Server security providers' capabilities. We finish by talking about the different ways to specify the username and password needed to boot the WebLogic Server.

Application Security Models

As we discussed in the "Security Realms and Providers" section, WebLogic Server supports several application security models. An application security model essentially describes how WebLogic Server should define and manage an application's role and authorization policies. The realm defines the default application security model for applications but each application has the choice to accept the default model or choose one of the other models at deployment time. By default, WebLogic Server sets the realm's default application security model to DD Only (DD stands for deployment descriptor); this mode gives you the standard Java EE security model. Both the role and authorization policies are defined inside of the application's deployment descriptors. This chapter covers the Java EE model in great detail.

Another security model is Custom Roles. In this model, administrators can define role policies inside of the WebLogic Console. Custom Roles allow the assignment of users to roles based on more than just group membership (for example, time of day) or to have application- or resource-scoped roles (for example, a Sales role for a specific web service). The DD Only model allows for the mapping of users or groups to roles but those roles are for the entire application.

The Custom Roles and Custom Policy model extends the Custom Roles model with the ability to manage authorization policy through WebLogic Console. Custom policies allow for finer-grained authorization based upon information in the request — that is, contextual authorization. For example, role X can access an EJB if the amount parameter is less than 50. The DD Only model only allows for granting roles access to URL paths or EJB methods inside of the deployment descriptors.

In both the Custom Roles and Custom Roles and Policies models, all activity is delegated to the role mapping and authorization providers configured in the realm. In the "Setting Up WebLogic Server Application Security" section, we describe in detail the capabilities provided by the default XACML providers.

The Advanced model allows you to combine roles and policy definitions from deployment descriptors and the WebLogic Console. We discuss this model in more detail in the "Setting Up WebLogic Server Application Security" section.

Setting Up Java EE Application Security

In this section, you learn how to use Java EE security mechanisms to set up authentication requirements, configure access control policies, and define role mappings for web applications, Enterprise JavaBeans (EJB), resource adapters, and enterprise applications. We cover web services security in Chapter 9.

With most Java EE component types, WebLogic Server uses a two-level process for mapping roles defined in the Java EE standard deployment descriptors or annotations to actual WebLogic Server users or groups in the WebLogic Server–specific deployment descriptor. This mechanism allows you to use standard role names in your application and then map them to physical users or groups at deployment time.

Securing Web Applications

When setting up web application security, the first decision you need to make is the type of HTTP authentication mechanism to use. In the following `web.xml` deployment descriptor, we define the desired HTTP authentication mechanism in the `<auth-method>` element, within the `<login-config>` element.

```
<login-config>
  <auth-method>FORM</auth-method>
  <form-login-config>
    <form-login-page>/login.jsp</form-login-page>
    <form-error-page>/login_error.jsp</form-error-page>
  </form-login-config>
  <realm-name>BigRez Realm</realm-name>
</login-config>
```

This tells the Web container that the web application will be using form-based authentication. Three different types of authentication are supported.

BASIC   Using this method causes the web browser to pop up the HTTP authentication dialog box requesting a username and password. To define basic authentication in your web application, simply replace FORM with BASIC in the `<auth-method>` element and eliminate the entire `<form-login-config>` element. The `<realm-name>` tag is used only with BASIC authentication to specify the authentication realm displayed in the browser's pop-up authentication dialog box. It is completely cosmetic and has no other purpose at this time.

FORM   When using form-based authentication, the browser is redirected to the configured HTML login form, as defined in the `<form-login-page>` element, whenever the user tries to access a protected URL. Once authentication succeeds and authorization is granted, the Web container automatically redirects the browser to the originally requested HTTP resource, complete with its original HTTP headers. If this authentication fails, the browser will be redirected to the HTTP resource defined in the `<form-error-page>` element. When using form-based authentication, your form must use the `j_username` and `j_password` form element names to identify the username and password attributes to the container. The form's action attribute must be set to `j_security_check`, as shown here. These form element and action names are required by the Java Servlet specification.

```
<form method="POST" action="j_security_check">
  <input type="text" name="j_username">
  <input type="password" name="j_password">
  <input type="submit" name="Login">
</form>
```

CLIENT-CERT If you are using two-way SSL between the browser and the server, you can choose client certificate–based authentication. This option requires not only two-way SSL connections but also the use of an appropriate identity asserter to map the certificate to a WebLogic Server username, as we discussed at length in earlier sections of this chapter. To specify client certificate–based authentication, simply replace FORM with CLIENT-CERT in the <auth-method> element. When using this type of authentication, the <form-login-config> and <realm-name> elements may be omitted.

Also, specify the <auth-method> as CLIENT-CERT if users authenticate to the application using SSO of any token type including Microsoft Desktop SSO, SAML Web SSO, or any other custom token type.

It is important to remember that with any of these authentication options, the container will not authenticate the user until the browser tries to access a protected URL. Though this seems intuitive with either basic or form-based authentication, it also applies to client certificate–based authentication. This means that even though the SSL handshake is complete and the client certificate is available to the server, WebLogic Server will not invoke the identity asserter until you try to access a protected resource.

Because the security realm is defined at the domain level, all web applications on the server use the same authentication realm. By default, WebLogic Server uses the same cookie name (JSESSIONID) for all web applications on the server. That way, no matter what type of authentication method is used in a particular web application, an authenticated user will have single sign-on to all other web applications in the WebLogic Server. You can modify this behavior by changing the cookie path or cookie name for specific web applications. The following extract from the weblogic.xml deployment descriptor shows how to modify the cookie name. To modify the cookie path instead, simply change the element from <cookie-name> to <cookie-path>.

```
<session-descriptor>
  <cookie-name>ApplicationSpecificCookie</cookie-name>
<session-descriptor>
```

Now that you have set up the authentication mechanism, you are ready to set up the access control policies and roles for the web application. The policies themselves are specified exclusively in the web.xml deployment descriptor within the <security-constraint> element, as shown here.

```
<security-constraint>
  <web-resource-collection>
    <web-resource-name>SecureArea</web-resource-name>
    <description>Our Secure Area</description>
    <url-pattern>/secure/*</url-pattern>
    <! - - no http-method elements specified -->
  </web-resource-collection>
  <auth-constraint>
    <description>Constraints for secure area</description>
    <role-name>manager</role-name>
    <role-name>security-admin</role-name>
  </auth-constraint>
  <user-data-constraint>
    <description>SSL is not required</description>
    <transport-guarantee>NONE</transport-guarantee>
  </user-data-constraint>
</security-constraint>
```

As the bold highlighting shows, all requests for any URL matching the pattern /secure/* relative to the root context of this web application will be protected. Even though the specification allows the further restriction of the <web-resource-collection> with <http-method> elements, it's best not to define any methods here. If no methods are specified, all are protected. If some methods are specified, those not specified are not protected — a security vulnerability that has been publicly exploited.

Best Practice

Don't specify an <http-method> when restricting resources. This makes all methods protected. If any methods are specified, any other HTTP methods not specified will be unprotected — a security vulnerability that has been publicly exploited.

We have restricted access to these resources so that only users in the role manager or security-admin can access them, but we are not requiring the use of SSL transport for access. Setting the <transport-guarantee> to CONFIDENTIAL or INTEGRAL would further restrict access to only those users in one of the specified roles who are using SSL to access the page. For WebLogic Server to grant access to a resource that has set <transport-guarantee> to CONFIDENTIAL or INTEGRAL, the SSL connection must terminate at WebLogic Server. If there is a proxy such as a web server or hardware load balancer in front of WebLogic Server that terminates the SSL connection, the request does not meet the requirement of <transport-guarantee>, and the request is denied.

Another situation that requires the SSL request to be terminated at WebLogic Server to work properly is *secure cookies*. In order to prevent session stealing, an application can be configured to use one of two protection schemes available in WebLogic Server. The first is to configure the JSESSIONID cookie as a *secure* cookie. Secure cookie in this context means that the cookie is marked as secure before it is returned to the browser. The browser will only send the cookie back to the server in subsequent requests that are made over SSL. This feature can be enabled in the weblogic.xml using the <cookie-secure> element shown here.

```
<session-descriptor>
  <cookie-secure>true</cookie-secure>
</session-descriptor>
```

WebLogic Server has an enhanced secure cookie scheme that uses a secure cookie called the *AuthCookie*. The actual cookie name is _WL_AUTHCOOKIE_JSESSIONID. When the user authenticates over HTTPS, WebLogic Server sends this secure cookie back along with the JSESSIONID cookie. Even if the JSESSIONID is not marked as secure, the AuthCookie is and will only work with the JSESSIONID that was established at authentication time. This means that all resources that are accessed over SSL check that the JSESSIONID value in the AuthCookie is the same as the JSESSIONID cookie passed from the browser. This ensures that the JSESSIONID cookie is valid. WebLogic Server enables this feature by default and stores the configuration setting in the config.xml file.

```
<WebServer Name="AdminServer" AuthCookieEnabled="true">
```

If there is a proxy (such as a web server or hardware load balancer) in front of WebLogic Server that terminates the SSL connection, the request does not satisfy the requirement of coming from an SSL connection. Requests between the proxy and WebLogic Server that come over an HTTP connection will not meet the CONFIDENTIAL or INTEGRAL <transport-guarantee> so WebLogic Server will deny access. If the application uses <cookie-secure>, WebLogic Server will not return the JSESSIONID cookie and the enhanced session stealing prevention provided by the AuthCookie will not work.

If you require these features in conjunction with a proxy-based architecture, you must configure the proxy to connect to WebLogic Server over SSL. Please refer to Link 11-14 for details on how to configure the WebLogic Server web server plug-ins to use SSL.

> **The SSL connection must terminate at the WebLogic Server in order for the server to consider the request to be *over SSL*. If an intermediary such as a web server or hardware load balancer terminates the SSL connection and the request from the intermediary to WebLogic Server is not over SSL, CONFIDENTIAL and INTEGRAL `<transport-guarantees>`, `<cookie-secure>`, and AuthCookie functionality will not work.**

Now that we have the security constraints defined, you need to declare the roles used in the `<auth-constraint>` elements, using the `<security-role>` elements.

```
<security-role>
  <description>the managers role</description>
  <role-name>manager</role-name>
</security-role>
<security-role>
  <description>the security-admin role</description>
  <role-name>security-admin</role-name>
</security-role>
```

If we stopped here, WebLogic Server would try to map these roles to principals, either users or groups, with the same name, as defined in the active security realm's authentication provider. In most cases, you don't actually want this, so you need to define the mapping from these roles to actual principals defined in the WebLogic Server security realm.

To map these roles to principals in the underlying security realm, you use the `<security-role-assignment>` element in the `weblogic.xml` deployment descriptor. As our example here shows, we are mapping the `manager` role to the `Administrators` group and the `security-admin` role to three unique users: `phil`, `robert`, and `paul`.

```
<security-role-assignment>
  <role-name>manager</role-name>
  <principal-name>Administrators</principal-name>
</security-role-assignment>
<security-role-assignment>
  <role-name>security-admin</role-name>
  <principal-name>phil</principal-name>
  <principal-name>robert</principal-name>
  <principal-name>paul</principal-name>
</security-role-assignment>
```

We should point out that changing these role mappings in the `weblogic.xml` deployment descriptor requires that you redeploy the application for the changes to take effect. In most cases, you will want to map roles to groups defined in the underlying realm so that you can dynamically change who has access to your protected resources by simply changing the group membership in the underlying security realm.

491

> ### Best Practice
> Always explicitly specify the mapping of your deployment descriptor roles to principals in the underlying security realm. In most cases, you will want to map these roles to groups, rather than users, to allow you to change dynamically who has access to protected resources without redeploying the application.

Web applications also support the ability to run the application always as a specific principal, regardless of any authentication that may have occurred. This is an alternative to the authentication and protection mechanisms already discussed. To configure your web application to run as a specific principal, you first need to specify the role using the `<run-as>` element in the `web.xml` deployment descriptor, as shown here. This declaration will tell the container to run the web application always as the `AppAdmin` role.

```
<run-as>AppAdmin</run-as>
```

Next, we want to specify the mapping of the role to a specific principal in the underlying security realm. The best way to do this is to use the `<run-as-role-assignment>` element in the `weblogic.xml` deployment descriptor, as shown here.

```
<run-as-role-assignment>
  <role-name>AppAdmin</role-name>
  <run-as-principal-name>lauren</run-as-principal-name>
</run-as-role-assignment>
```

This mapping applies for the entire web application. If you don't define the `<run-as-role-assignment>` for a given role, the container will choose the first principal name defined for that role in the `<security-role-assignment>` stanza.

It is also possible to scope the `<run-as>` configuration to a specific servlet in the web application. This servlet-scoped `<run-as-principal-name>` configuration overrides the more general one specified using the `<run-as-role-assignment>` stanza. In this example, we will always run the `SampleServletName` servlet as the user `hugh` in the underlying realm.

```
<servlet-descriptor>
  <servlet-name>SampleServletName</servlet-name>
  <run-as-principal-name>hugh</run-as-principal-name>
  . . .
</servlet-descriptor>
```

If needed, you can use programmatic security checking in the business logic of your web applications. Though we won't bother to go through all of the servlet security–related APIs, one interesting method to point out is the `isUserInRole()` method.

```
boolean isUserInManagerRole = request.isUserInRole("manager")
```

Using this method, you can test whether the current user should get certain types of options or data. By defining this role and mapping it to one or more principals in the web application deployment descriptors, the application code can do fine-grained security checks without sacrificing the level of indirection that role mapping gives you.

Just to be complete, there is another way to restrict what a web application can do by using JAAS authorization policies. As discussed previously, JAAS authorization typically uses a policy file to store its authorization policies. This policy file specifies a set of Java runtime permissions based on where the code originated. Because that file doesn't know where the deployed web application will exist on the server's filesystem, the `CodeBase` cannot be statically defined. As a result, you cannot define a JAAS authorization policy for web applications in the server-wide `weblogic.policy` file. To get around this limitation, WebLogic Server allows you to define a JAAS authorization policy for a web application in the `weblogic.xml` deployment descriptor. This example shows how to restrict the web application's `java.net.SocketPermission` to allow it to connect only to the Oracle web site.

```
<security-permission>
  <description> Connect permission to Oracle Web site</description>
  <security-permission-spec>
    grant {
        permission java.net.SocketPermission
                   "www.oracle.com:80", "connect"
    };
  </security-permission-spec>
<security-permission>
```

As we alluded to earlier, most applications running on a server are audited by other means to make sure that they are not doing something they shouldn't. The runtime overhead of JAAS authorization is high so we recommend very careful consideration and performance testing before going too far down this path.

> JAAS authorization provides very fine-grained, system-level control of Java runtime resources. This system-level control comes at a high price in runtime overhead. Always prototype and performance test any application making use of JAAS authorization before committing to that approach.

Managing EJB Security

To set up an access control policy in an EJB, you use the `<security-role>` and `<method-permission>` elements of the `ejb-jar.xml` deployment descriptor. In the following example, we restrict access to the `AdvertiseProduct` EJB's `getResults()` method to users in either the `manager` or `ejb-admin` roles.

```
<assembly-descriptor>
  <security-role>
    <role-name>manager</role-name>
    <role-name>ejb-admin</role-name>   </security-role>
  <method-permission>
    <role-name>manager</role-name>
    <role-name>ejb-admin</role-name>
    <method>
      <ejb-name>AdvertiseProduct</ejb-name>
      <method-name>getResults</method-name>
    </method>
  </method-permission>
        . . .
</assembly-descriptor>
```

EJB 3.0 also allows for declaration of EJB security constraints through annotations found in the `javax.annotations.security` package. The same example could be implemented using annotations.

```
import javax.annotations.security.*;
@Stateless(name="AdvertiseProduct")
@DeclaredRoles(value={"manager","ejb-admin"})
public class AdvertiseProduct
{
    @RolesAllowed(value={"manager","ejb-admin"})
    public Results getResults()
    {
        ...
    }
}
```

EJBs also support the concept of role mapping. Similar to web applications, the application server–specific deployment descriptor, `weblogic-ejb-jar.xml`, contains the actual mapping data. The following example maps the `manager` role to both the `Administrators` group and the user `someadminuser`. Additionally, you can use the `<externally-defined>` element to force a role to be defined in the role mapping security provider.

```
<security-role-assignment>
  <role-name>manager</role-name>
  <principal-name>Administrators</principal-name>
  <principal-name>someadminuser</principal-name>
</security-role-assignment>
<security-role-assignment>
  <role-name>ejb-admin</role-name>
  <externally-defined/>
</security-role-assignment>
```

As you might expect, EJBs also support the ability to run as a specific principal. Similar to web applications, we start by specifying the `<run-as>` role in the `ejb-jar.xml`, as shown in the following example where we set the `<run-as>` role to `EJBAppAdmin`.

```
<security-identity>
  <run-as>EJBAppAdmin</run-as>
</security-identity>
```

Now, we map the specified `<run-as>` role to a specific principal using the `<run-as-role-assignment>` tag in the `weblogic-ejb-jar.xml` deployment descriptor. Here, we map the `EJBAppAdmin` role to the user `bob`.

```
<weblogic-ejb-jar>
  ...
  <run-as-role-assignment>
    <role-name>EJBAppAdmin</role-name>
    <run-as-principal-name>bob</run-as-principal-name>
  </run-as-role-assignment>
</weblogic-ejb-jar>
```

We can also scope the `<run-as>` configuration to a specific EJB within the jar file, as shown in the code that follows, where we map the `<run-as>` role to the user `jason` for the `BandEJB`. As before, this

EJB-scoped `<run-as-principal-name>` configuration overrides the more general one. If there is no `<run-as-principal-name>` element specified in either place, the container will match the `<run-as>` role to the first principal listed in the normal role mapping elements.

```
<weblogic-enterprise-bean>
  <ejb-name>BandEJB</ejb-name>
  ...
  <run-as-principal-name>jason</run-as-principal-name>
</weblogic-enterprise-bean>
```

You can use programmatic security checking in the business logic of an EJB. This can allow for business logic with very specific requirements to test whether the current user should get certain types of information. To get the currently authenticated user, use the `getCallerPrincipal()` method:

```
Principal currentUser = ejbContext.getCallerPrincipal();
```

To check whether the currently authenticated user has a specific role, use the `isCallerInRole()` method:

```
boolean isUserInRole = ejbContext.isCallerInRole("manager");
```

WebLogic EJBs also support using JAAS authorization policies in the `weblogic-ejb-jar.xml` deployment descriptor to restrict the system-level resources an EJB can use. To do this, you use the `<security-permission>` element, whose syntax is exactly the same as that of the `<security-permission>` element in the `weblogic.xml` deployment descriptor entry. For the same reasons, we caution you against trying to use JAAS authorization without first proving to yourself that the benefits are worth the costs.

Securing J2EE CA Resource Adapters

J2EE Connector Architecture (J2EE CA) resource adapters access the resources of the container in the context of an identity. This behavior is configured in the `<security>` element of the `weblogic-ra.xml`. WebLogic Server provides the ability to the specify different identities for different aspects of the J2EE CA life cycle:

1. An identity used when making connections (`<run-as-principal>`)
2. An identity for launching work instances (`<run-work-as-principal>`)
3. An identity for management operations such as startup and shutdown (`<manage-as-principal>`)

A resource adapter can also specify a default identity to use (`<default-principal-name>`) if you don't specify the identity for a particular phase.

WebLogic Server also manages credential mappings for outbound resource adapters. A credential mapping allows the resource adapter to define the credentials that specific users and groups in WebLogic Server should use when accessing the target system. You configure these credential maps at the connection factory or global level. Through the WebLogic Console, you can define credential mappings using the `Credential Mappings Security` tab of a deployed resource adapter. WebLogic Server stores the mappings for the resource adapter in the security store.

Securing Enterprise Applications

One problem with defining roles in the web application and EJB components is that you may need to define them in multiple places. Enterprise applications can define roles that apply to all of their containing components in their `application.xml` deployment descriptor. This allows application-scoped role definitions using the same techniques as web applications and EJBs.

For enterprise applications, `weblogic-application.xml` is the WebLogic Server–specific deployment descriptor used to define application-scoped configuration information. This descriptor provides the ability to map roles in the `application.xml` to principals (users or groups). This is done with the `<security-role-assignment>` element inside of the `<security>` element. This eliminates the need to map application-level roles in component-level deployment descriptors.

Setting Up WebLogic Server Application Security

This section begins with a very brief discussion of how to create and manage WebLogic Server users and groups because every application that uses application-level security will need to do this. Next, we talk about roles, both application-scoped and global. From there, we explain setting up access control on specific server resources and then forming a set of policies. We end this section with a brief explanation of how to set up single sign-on across WebLogic Server domains.

Managing Users and Groups

If you are using the default configuration — which uses WebLogic Server's embedded LDAP server as the security store — you can manage users and groups using the WebLogic Console. By selecting the `Security Realms` folder in the left navigation bar and clicking on the `myrealm` provider, you will see the `Users and Groups` tab. Selecting the `Users` or `Groups` subtab displays pages that allow you to add, delete, modify, and view different users or groups in the domain. Each user and group must be uniquely identifiable in a WebLogic Server domain. Because users and groups are identified only by their names and a WebLogic Server principal can refer to either a group or user, every user and group must have a unique name.

Before moving on, we should mention WebLogic Server's User Lockout feature. By default, a user has five attempts to enter the correct password before being locked out of the server. You can adjust the user lockout characteristics using the active security realm's `User Lockout Configuration` tab. Anyone with the `Admin` role can unlock the user prior to the timeout. To unlock a locked out user, use the domain's `Unlock User Security` tab, enter the username in the `Unlock User` field, and click the `Save` button.

WebLogic Server has a special type of group that cannot be managed through the WebLogic Server console called a *runtime group*. There are two of these groups. WebLogic Server adds a caller to the `users` group after they successfully authenticate. All callers, authenticated and not, belong to the `everyone` group. Later on in the section, you see how WebLogic Server uses these groups to define some of the default global roles.

Resources

A resource in WebLogic Server is anything that a subject is attempting to gain access to or perform an action on. The following are some common resource types:

❑ Administrative Resources — file uploading, viewing domain logs, unlocking users

❑ Application Resources — access to a standalone deployment (EAR or standalone deployment of an WAR, RAR or EJB JAR)

- ❏ EIS Resources — connect to the resource adapter

- ❏ EJB Resource — invoke methods on EJBs

- ❏ JDBC Resource — connect to the JDBC data source

- ❏ JMS Resource — produce/consume messages to/from a JMS Destination

- ❏ JNDI Resource — modify, lookup, list elements in the JNDI tree

- ❏ Server Resource — boot, shutdown, suspend, or resume a server

- ❏ URL Resource — access a URL

- ❏ Web Service Resource — access a web service module or operation

Resources are hierarchical. When WebLogic Server evaluates if a user has access to a resource, the user must have access to all of the objects in the hierarchy. For example, when accessing a web service that uses an EJB implementation, the user needs access to the application, the web service module, the web service operation, and the EJB method.

Working with Roles and Policies

WebLogic Server has the concept of global roles and root-level policies. Global roles, like `Admin`, `Anonymous`, `Operator`, and `Monitor`, are available in the entire domain. Root-level policies define the default access for each resource type. Additionally, WebLogic Server defines roles and policies for individual resources. To view the security realm's roles and policies, select the `Roles and Policies` tab. The `Realm Roles` subtab allows you to manage both the global roles and resource-specific roles for any resources in the domain. The `Realm Policies` subtab allows you to manage the root-level policies.

Table 11-8 explains the default roles and group mappings.

Each default administrative role has a mapping to a specific default group. If users are a member of that group, they are in the matching role. As you can see, the default role names are all singular whereas the default group names are plural. This is done solely to make it easier to differentiate which names are roles and which names are groups.

> ### Best Practice
> Keeping role names singular and group names plural will help make security discussions involving roles and groups less confusing.

You can also manage roles and policies for a resource outside of the security realm by selecting the resource's `Security` tab. A role or policy is created based on predicates. Predicates can include information about the user (username, group, role), environment (server is in development mode, time of day, day of the month), or about the context (values in the request, message signatures). The context that is available depends on the resource being accessed. For a URL resource, the context includes HTTP headers. For EJB resources, the context includes the EJB method parameters. You can use these predicates to form very simple roles and policies (people in the `Managers` group are assigned the `Manager` role) or very complex ones (if the server is in development mode then grant `everyone` access, or if it is after 5 pm only people in the `Manager` role can have access unless the context value `priority = "Urgent"`). All of these roles and policies are stored inside of the security store by the `XACMLRoleMapper` and `XACMLAuthorizer` providers.

Table 11-8: Default Roles and Groups

Default Global Roles	Access Policy	Default Groups
Admin	All access to the console. This means deploying applications, startup and shutdown classes, web services, and J2EE connectors. It can also modify server configuration and edit deployment descriptors.	Administrators
AdminChannelUser	Access the administrative channel, `AdminChannel`.	AdminChannelUsers, Administrators, Deployers, Operators, Monitors, and AppTesters
Anonymous		everyone
AppTester	Access applications for testing purposes that are running in `Admin` mode.	AppTesters
CrossDomainConnector	Make inter-domain calls to foreign domains	CrossDomainConnectors
Deployer	May deploy applications, startup and shutdown classes, web services, and J2EE connectors. It may view the server configuration.	Deployers
Operator	Start, stop, and resume servers. It may view the server configuration (except for encrypted attributes).	Operators
Monitor	View the server configuration.	Monitors
No Matching Role	Any authenticated user.	users

The WebLogic Console will not allow you to create scoped roles and policies for URL and EJB resources if the application security model does not allow it. If the security model is anything other than DD Only, WebLogic Server uses resource-scoped roles. The security model must be Custom Roles and Policies or Advanced to use resource-scoped policies.

Table 11-9 explains the default roles and group mappings.

Now that you know how to define both global and scoped roles and access control policies using both the WebLogic Console and Java EE deployment descriptors, you need to understand the persistence of this information. For deployment descriptors, it's easy to see that the persistence mechanism is the deployment descriptor itself. For Custom Roles and Custom Roles and Policies, WebLogic Server stores them in the default security provider's store.

Table 11-9: Default Policy

WebLogic Resource	Default Security Policy
Administrative resources	Roles: Admin, Deployer, Operator, Monitor
Server resources	Roles: Admin, Operator
COM resources	None
EIS resources	Group: everyone
EJB resources	Group: everyone
JMS resources	Group: everyone
JDBC resources	Group: everyone
JNDI resources	Group: everyone
MBean resources	Group: everyone
Web service resources	Group: everyone

In the `Advanced` mode, administrators can control the loading of roles and policies from the deployment descriptor. This is useful when initially installing an application and you want to load the policies from the deployment descriptors into the realm but then manage them from the WebLogic Console. To do this, first configure the realm in `Advanced` mode, with `Check Roles and Policies` set to `All Web applications and EJBs`, and then toggle `Initialize/Ignore roles and policies from DD` to `Initialize`. When the application is deployed, all of the information will be copied to the provider. Next, toggle `Initialize/Ignore roles and policies from DD` to `Ignore`, and then modify the policies via the WebLogic Console.

Another use for `Advanced` mode is to combine policies from the deployment descriptors and the WebLogic Console. To do this, set the `Initialize roles and policies from DD` setting in the `Advanced` mode. Then, configure two authorization providers but only one with `Policy Deployment Enabled`. Once you have this set up, you can control how WebLogic Server combines the results via the `DefaultAdjudicator`. Checking `Require Unanimous Permit` means that the user must be granted access to the resource in the deployment descriptor and in the policies inside of WebLogic Server. Unchecking `Require Unanimous Permit` allows users access if either the deployment descriptor or the WebLogic Server policies apply.

If you are not careful, the complexity of the merging and storing of role and policy definitions can get you into trouble. We recommend that you come up with a simple plan that specifies where the role mapping and policy information will live and stick to it.

> **Best Practice**
> Define a simple set of guidelines for where you will define the roles and policies your application needs and then stick to them to reduce confusion resulting from WebLogic Server's complex merging policies.

To summarize, you have four different ways to restrict access to Web applications and EJBs:

Use only the Java EE Deployment Descriptors (DD Only)   At deployment time, WebLogic Server reads the role and policy information from the deployment descriptor and uses it throughout the life of the application. Using this option, you define users and groups in the authentication provider but define the roles, policies, and the mapping of roles to principals using Java EE deployment descriptors or annotations. If you need to modify the access control information at runtime, you typically do this by modifying the group membership of one or more groups that are mapped to the relevant roles in the deployment descriptors. In WebLogic Server, the default configuration uses roles and enforces policies only for web applications and EJBs that define roles and policies in their deployment descriptors or annotations.

Configure the Policies in the Deployment Descriptors but Configure the Role-to-Principal Mapping in the WebLogic Console (DD Only or Custom Roles)   With this second option, you use the ejb-jar.xml or web.xml to set up the access control policy for specific roles. Then, you have two options for mapping the roles. First, you can the DD Only security model and <externally-defined/> roles in the WebLogic Server–specific deployment descriptors to map the application-defined roles to a global role. Second, you can use the Custom Roles security model to define roles via the WebLogic Console and map them to the application-defined roles.

Use only the WebLogic Console (Custom Roles and Policies)   When using Custom Roles and Policies, you define all of the access control information using the WebLogic Console. To prevent accidentally picking up any deployment descriptor information that might be present, you should change the default setting on the realm. To do this for WebLogic Server, set the active realm's Security Model Default attribute to Custom Roles and Policies.

Seed the Roles and Access Control Policies with Values from the Deployment Descriptors and Then Use the WebLogic Console to Modify them from That Point Forward (Advanced)   Use the Advanced security model to bootstrap the WebLogic Server security providers with roles and policies that the application deployment descriptors define. Use the Advanced area of the active realm's General Configuration tab to set Check Roles and Policies to All Web Applications and EJBs and make sure that When Deploying Web Applications or EJBs is set to Initialize roles and policies from DD. Deploy the application and then set When Deploying Web Applications or EJBs to Ignore roles and policies from the DD. From that point on, you use the WebLogic Console to manage all of the access control information, just like with Custom Roles and Policies.

Booting WebLogic Server

When you start a WebLogic Server, it needs a username and password for a user in the Admin role. Because this username and password will authenticate a user in the Admin role, it is vital to keep this information as secret as possible. There are several different ways to make the username and password available to the server for booting.

The preferred way to provide the username and password is to use the boot.properties file, stored in the server's security subdirectory. This file contains the boot identity in an encrypted form. Both the username and password are encrypted. If you set the weblogic.system.StoreBootIdentity Java system property to true, the server will use the supplied boot information to create the file for you. The easiest way to create the file, however, is simply to create a two-line text file that looks like the one shown here for a server using the weblogic username with a password of weblogic1:

```
username=weblogic
password=weblogic1
```

The WebLogic Configuration Wizard will automatically create this file for you when creating a new domain that uses development mode. For more information about development mode, see Link 11-15.

After creating this file manually, simply start the server once and it will encrypt the values of the username and password. If you want to rename the file to something less obvious, you can use the `weblogic.system.BootIdentityFile` Java system property to specify the name of the `boot.properties` file. Finally, you can tell the server to delete the file after it uses it. You might use this in conjunction with a shell script that copies the file from a secure location to the local directory just prior to starting the server. Setting the `weblogic.system.RemoveBootIdentity` Java system property to `true` will tell the server to delete the file:

```
java -Dweblogic.system.RemoveBootIdentity=true ...
```

> **Best Practice**
> Use the `boot.properties` file mechanism to specify the server's boot identity on startup.

Another simplified technique is to specify nothing on the command line. This will cause the server to prompt for a username and password in the shell. This may be acceptable for development purposes, but it has an obvious drawback for production systems where you do not want to rely on human intervention to start the server. You can also provide the username and password through Java system properties specified either as command-line arguments, as shown here, or programmatically using a Java program that wraps the call to `weblogic.Server.main()`:

```
java -Dweblogic.management.username=someuser
     -Dweblogic.management.password=password ... weblogic.Server
```

Of course, this is not an elegant solution for a production system either because the command-line arguments may be seen by users having access to the operating system — for example, by using the UNIX `ps` command to list the processes running on the machine. We do not recommend specifying the password via command-line arguments.

Single Sign-On

WebLogic Server has rich capabilities when it comes to identity propagation; that is, passing identity from one security domain to another. This type of identity propagation is often referred to as single sign-on (SSO). This section starts by covering WebLogic Server's uses of SAML for both web services and web SSO. It continues by looking at two additional SSO models: the WebLogic Server–specific capabilities around Cross Domain Security and WebLogic Server SSO with Microsoft Windows desktops. We conclude this section with a brief discussion of how you can extend WebLogic Server to achieve SSO using other protocols by creating custom security providers.

Security Assertion Markup Language (SAML)

WebLogic Server makes extensive use of SAML. This section begins with a brief overview of SAML. Next, it describes how the security framework provides the core building blocks for all of the SAML services on WebLogic Server. Finally, it ends by describing how WebLogic Server uses those building blocks to provide Web SSO and support for using SAML to pass the user's identity in a SOAP message.

Overview of SAML

SAML is a standard way of conveying identity on the Internet. The core concept of SAML is that it passes security information between security domains using *assertions*. Parties make assertions; for example, Server 1 asserts that User X authenticated at 10:00 AM using an X.509 certificate. Another party (known as the *relying party*) gets the assertion. The relying party cannot 100% validate the assertion — How do I *really* know that User X authenticated at 10:00 AM? The relying party has to trust the asserting party. SAML defines a set of *profiles*. These profiles are mechanisms for asserting and relying parties to exchange information in different situations in such a way that the relying party can decide whether to trust the asserting party or not.

WebLogic Server uses SAML in two scenarios: web SSO and web services security. SAML is a very useful standard in both of these scenarios because it allows systems to assert and trust users' identities without having the user's credentials. This is especially useful in scenarios where the producer and the consumer of a service are in different security domains (for example, a company portal calling an outsourced benefits provider service). In this model, it is beneficial to both parties not to have to synchronize usernames and passwords. It is simpler if the partner can just grant the user access to their service because they received a SAML assertion from Company A that says this user is employee 12345.

SAML is not a replacement for PKI and X.509 certificates. In fact, much of the true *trust* of SAML relies upon digitally signing SAML assertions and other SAML messages. One benefit of SAML over issuing individual users X.509 certificates is that managing a large PKI can be very challenging. SAML does not require certificates for users; it only requires them for the asserting and relying parties. This is typically a much smaller number than the number of actual users. The other advantage is that SAML assertions support arbitrary *attribute statements*. This means that when issuing an assertion the asserting party can add unlimited additional information about the user. WebLogic Server uses attribute statements to convey the groups to which the user belongs. Certificates are much less flexible when it comes to attributes.

SAML Security Providers

WebLogic Server supports both SAML 1.1 and SAML 2.0. This section focuses on the SAML 2.0. The configuration of SAML 1.1 in WebLogic Server is very similar, and the core concepts we cover in this section are also applicable to the SAML 1.1 providers.

The core of SAML is the production and consumption of SAML assertions. As previously discussed in this chapter, WebLogic Server supports both producing and consuming SAML assertions through the security framework. WebLogic Server uses the SAML credential mapper to generate a SAML assertion for a user, whereas the SAML identity asserter can consume (validate and parse) a SAML assertion. The SAML authentication provider works in concert with the SAML identity asserter to support advanced federated identity use cases.

Like other credential mappers, you create the `SAML2CredentialMapper` using the active security realm's `Credential Mapping Providers` tab. Make sure to create a `SAML2CredentialMapper` and not a `SAMLCredentialMapper` (a SAML 1.1 provider introduced in WebLogic Server 9.0 and since deprecated) or a `SAMLCredentialMapperv2` (a SAML 1.1 provider introduced in WebLogic Server 9.2). Once you create the provider, you should configure some of the provider-specific attributes. The `Issuer URI` is the name of the party creating these assertions for the user — for example, `http://saml.oracle.com`. Use the Name Qualifier attribute to disambiguate users from the same issuer (for example, employees or customers), if needed. SAML assertions are only valid for a certain period of time. Set this value using the Default Time to Live attribute. While the two-minute default setting is reasonable, SAML assertions for long-running asynchronous SOAP requests may require a longer timeout value. This value is only the default. Individual partners may override this value with their own timeout value. If you are using this SAML credential mapper for web services where the SAML assertions will be signed, you will also need to provide the alias and passphrase for the signing key. We cover the specifics of how to configure the signing key for SAML assertions used in web SSO later in this section.

Like other identity asserters, you create the SAML2IdentityAsserter using the active security realm's Authentication Providers tab. Make sure to create a SAML2IdentityAsserter and not SAMLIdentityAsserter (a SAML 1.1 provider introduced in WebLogic Server 9.0 and since deprecated) or a SAMLIdentityAsserterV2 (a SAML 1.1 provider introduced in WebLogic Server 9.2). Once you create the provider, there isn't much else to do. The SAML2IdentityAsserter and the SAML2CredentialMapper support the configuration of a custom name mapper class. The default name mapper uses the JAAS principal name, but it's conceivable that you might want to use other names (for example, the subject's email address). Also, you can configure name mappers on a per-partner basis.

Both the SAML2CredentialMapper and SAML2IdentityAsserter define a set of default values for the realm. You can override these values for individual partners. For a SAML2CredentialMapper, Service Provider Partners are relying parties; the entities that will consume the SAML assertions generated by the credential mapper. For a SAML2IdentityAsserter, Identity Provider Partners are asserting parties; entities that will generate the SAML assertions consumed by the identity asserter. You manage the definitions for Service Provider Partners and Identity Provider Partners on the Management tab of each of the providers. Both Identity Provider Partners and Service Provider Partners are further specialized for web SSO and web services. Later in this section, we cover the details of configuring partners while discussing web SSO and web services security configuration.

In addition to managing partners through the WebLogic Console, partners are manageable through JMX/WLST. One notable difference between partners and security providers is that WebLogic Server picks up partner changes in real time without requiring a server restart. Making changes to security providers almost always requires a restart. Consequently, you manage partners through the ServerRuntime MBean. The following WLST script demonstrates how to enable all the partners for a SAML2CredentialMapper.

```
connect('weblogic', 'weblogic1', 't3://127.0.0.1:7001')
cd('serverRuntime:/ServerServices/RuntimeService/DomainConfiguration')
cd(domainName)
cd('SecurityConfiguration')
cd(domainName)
cd('DefaultRealm/myrealm/CredentialMappers/SAML2CM')
partners_cursor = cmo.listSPPartners('*', 10)
while cmo.haveCurrent(partners_cursor):
    partnerName = cmo.getCurrentName(partners_cursor)
    cmo.advance(partners_cursor)
    partner = cmo.getSPPartner(partnerName)
    print partnerName
    print partner.isEnabled()
    partner.setEnabled(true)
    cmo.updateSPPartner(partner)
cmo.close(partners_cursor)
disconnect()
```

WebLogic Server also provides a SAML authenticator. The SAML authenticator is a special type of authenticator that works in conjunction with the SAML identity asserter to provide some SAML-specific capabilities. Most notably, the SAML authenticator enables support for *virtual users*. Virtual users are users that do not exist in any of the locally configured authentication providers. This is a very common case in federated environments. The SAML authenticator will also create groups using any group attribute statements defined in the SAML assertion.

Configuring Federation Services

Once you create either a SAML2CredentialMapper or SAML2IdentityAsserter, you can specify additional information describing the SAML 2.0 service(s) running on WebLogic Server. You do this using the server's Federation Services Configuration tab and selecting the SAML 2.0 General subtab. Notice that you configure the federation services on a per-server, rather than a per-domain or per-cluster, basis.

> ### Best Practice
> Configure federation services on the managed servers in the cluster — not on the admin server. Configure all of them identically. If the SAML services are running on more than one instance, using the RDBMS security store is highly recommended. Upgrading from an LDAP security store to an RDBMS security store is difficult, so consider upfront if the domain is going to use SAML Federation Services.

This information configured in the SAML 2.0 General subtab is common across all of the SAML 2.0 services running on the server. This information includes contact information so that partners can contact the appropriate people if they are having problems. In the Site Info section, there are two attributes that bear some special mention. The Published Site URL is the base URL for federation services on the server. This should be a public URL for the server or cluster. Typically, a server publishes the service at the relative URL /saml2 so the value of this attribute might be something like http://www.bigrez.com/saml2. The other attribute of note is the Entity Id. It uniquely identifies this server to partners. All SAML credential mappers should use the value of this attribute as their entity id. The rest of the attributes specify additional security measures required for partners' communication: authentication requirements, artifact and document signing restrictions, and associated configuration.

> ### Tip to Remember
> The myriad of security options for SAML 2.0 can provide very detailed security control over access to the service, but with each additional option, there is more work and complexity for partners — which could affect integration and adoption. Keep that in mind when configuring these settings.

Once you configure the SAML 2.0 General settings, you configure the SAML 2.0 Identity Provider or Service Provider services. This section describes how to configure those services. Later on in the section, we will discuss how to manage the definitions of Web Single Sign-On Identity Provider Partners and Web Single Sign-On Service Provider Partners. The partners are the users of the federation services. A Web Single Sign-On Identity Provider Partner represents the metadata of a server accessing WebLogic Server's SAML 2.0 Service Provider. Likewise, a Web Single Sign-On Service Provider Partner defines the SAML 2.0 Identity Provider's behavior when interacting with another server. Table 11-10 explains the relationship among the federation service, security provider, and partner objects.

Table 11-10: Default Policy

Federation Service	Security Provider Used	Partner Definitions Managed
SAML 2.0 Service Provider	SAML2IdentityAsserter	Single Sign-On Identity Provider Partner
SAML 2.0 Identity Provider	SAML2CredentialMapper	Single Sign-On Service Provider Partner

A SAML 2.0 Identity Provider uses the SAML2CredentialMapper to generate the actual SAML assertions. The role of the SAML 2.0 Identity Provider is to gather the user's credentials, generate the SAML assertion, and communicate with the relying party — the service provider — about the assertion over one or more of three possible bindings. The SAML 2.0 specification goes into gory detail to define three different bindings: artifact, redirect, and post. In summary, redirect and post are *front-channel* methods where the identity provider passes the SAML assertion to the service provider via the user's browser. artifact is a *back-channel* binding. When the service provider receives an artifact — a unique identifier for the assertion — it uses SOAP to communicate with the identity provider to retrieve the assertion.

By default, when the identity provider challenges the user for credentials, WebLogic Server uses HTTP basic authentication. Configuring the identity provider to present the user with a custom HTML form is also an option. To use a custom form, you must configure two parameters:

1. URI of the form: Path to the custom form.

2. Return parameter: The name of the query string parameter the identity provider should use to pass the return URL to the form. The custom form must redirect the successfully authenticated user to this URL to complete the SSO process.

Let's look at an example. If the URI of the custom form is /myapp/login and the return parameter is returnURLParam, the request will be something like the one shown here.

```
http://www.bigrez.com/myapp/login?returnURLParam=http://www.bigrez.com/sam
l2/idp/sso/login-return
```

The SAML 2.0 Identity Provider custom form is a separately deployed web application. When developing custom login forms, you may want to provide a customized authentication experience. This might include gathering additional information or registering the user prior to redirecting the user to the service provider. The standard Java EE form-based authentication does not support this functionality. To realize this use case, you will need to programmatically authenticate the user using the WebLogic Server security API. The following code sample is a servlet implementation of an identity provider custom login form using the weblogic.security.servlet.ServletAuthentication.login() method.

```
import weblogic.security.servlet.ServletAuthentication;

...

protected void doPost(HttpServletRequest request, HttpServletResponse response)
    throws ServletException, IOException
{
```

```
String user = request.getParameter("user");
String password = request.getParameter("password");
String returnURL = request.getParameter("returnURL");
try {
    int rc = ServletAuthentication.login(new CallbackHandler() {
        @Override
        public void handle(Callback[] callbacks)
            throws IOException, UnsupportedCallbackException
        {
            for (int i = 0; i < callbacks.length; i++) {
                Callback c = callbacks[i];
                if (c instanceof NameCallback) {
                    NameCallback nc = (NameCallback) c;
                    nc.setName(user);
                }
                else if (c instanceof PasswordCallback) {
                    PasswordCallback pc =(PasswordCallback) c;
                    pc.setPassword(password.toCharArray());
                }
            }
        }
    }, request);
    response.sendRedirect(returnURL);
}
catch (LoginException le) {
    le.printStackTrace();
    response.sendRedirect("login.jsp?returnURL="+returnURL);
}
}
```

The role of the SAML 2.0 Service Provider is to redirect the user to the appropriate identity provider, retrieve the SAML assertion from the identity provider, and validate it. The service provider uses the SAML identity asserter to validate the SAML assertions it receives. The SAML 2.0 Service Provider has some additional security options including signing authentication requests and requiring that assertions be signed. It also has the option to force the identity provider to authenticate the user every time it asks for an assertion. This means that even if the identity provider has the user logged in with a valid session, the service provider wants the user to reauthenticate.

Managing SSO Partners

SAML 2.0 formalizes information about partners in a partner metadata document. This greatly simplifies getting SAML 2.0 identity and service providers communicating. Once you configure WebLogic Server with either a SAML 2.0 service provider or identity provider, WebLogic Server can generate the SAML 2.0 partner metadata. To do this, use the Publish Meta Data button on the SAML 2.0 General subtab under the Federation Services Configuration tab.

This same partner metadata document provides the input for the first step in onboarding a Web SSO partner. By importing this document, WebLogic Server uses it as the foundation for its partner definition. You manage partners from the Management tab of either the SAML2IdentityAsserter or the SAML2CredentialMapper.

When WebLogic Server is acting as a service provider, select the Management tab from the SAML2IdentityAsserter and create a new Web SSO Identity Provider Partner. Import the metadata file that the partner provided. Besides specifying additional security constraints around artifact signatures and identity provider credentials, the General tab of the Web SSO Identity Provider Partner has some important functional attributes as well. The Redirect URIs are a list of URIs which, if hit by an unauthenticated user, will cause a request to be redirected to the identity provider for authentication. This allows you to specify individual identity providers on a per-application basis. However, simply specifying the Redirect URIs is not enough to cause WebLogic Server to redirect requests to the identity provider for authentication. You must protect the resource using WebLogic Server security; for example, by specifying a <security-constraint> in the deployment descriptor. You can configure the service provider to accept virtual users for a specific identity provider partner. For this feature to work, you need to configure the realm to use a SAMLAuthenticator, allowing the service provider to authenticate users not found in any of the authentication providers. You can even instantiate virtual users' group memberships by enabling the Process Attributes attribute. When enabled, the SAMLAuthenticator uses the SAML attribute statements in the SAML assertion to populate the virtual user's JAAS subject with the groups.

When WebLogic Server is acting as an identity provider, select the Management tab from the SAML2CredentialMapper and create a new Web SSO Service Provider Partner. Import the metadata file the partner provided. If the identity provider requires the service provider partner to use two-way SSL then import the service provider partner's client certificate using the Transport Layer Client Certificate tab. You can configure the identity provider to generate a SAML assertion with a different Time to Live than the default or with attributes (attribute statements of the groups in the user's JAAS subject). A Service Provider Partner definition contains additional signing and transport level security controls.

Managing Web Services Partners

In WebLogic Server, a web service partner is a configuration that defines how the container should generate or validate SAML assertions that are included in SOAP messages. The *SAML Token Profile* is the WS-Security specification that defines how to use SAML assertions with SOAP message-level security; see Link 11-16 for more information.

WebLogic Server provides a number of WS-SecurityPolicy 1.2 policies for the SAML Token Profile. There are four policies for SAML 2.0 covering the three confirmation methods defined in the SAML 2.0 specification. A confirmation method defines how the sender of the SOAP message containing the SAML assertion can prove to the recipient (in a trusted fashion) that this SAML assertion is valid. The three confirmation methods are:

Holder-of-Key   In the holder-of-key (HOK) confirmation method, the SAML assertion includes the public key of the user. The issuer signs the assertion to protect the integrity of the public key. The sender signs the message using the user's private key. If the recipient trusts the issuer then the recipient trusts the public key in the assertion and can use the public key to validate the message using the message signature. If the recipient is able to validate message using the public key, this implies that the sender has the private key and therefore is the holder of (the private) key.

Sender-Vouches   In the sender-vouches confirmation method, the message contains the SAML assertion and the message is signed by the sender. If the recipient trusts the sender then the recipient trusts the SAML assertion; the sender vouches for the validity of the assertion.

Bearer   In the bearer confirmation method, there is nothing beyond the presence of the assertion that is used to confirm who the subject is.

You can easily associate the policies for the SAML Token Profile, like other web services security policies, with a JAX-WS web service by using the @Policy annotation. The following values for the uri attribute of the @Policy annotation represent the four SAML Token Profile WS-SecurityPolicy policies in WebLogic Server.

❏   `policy:wssp1.2-2007-Saml2.0-SenderVouches-Wss1.1-Asymmetric.xml`

❏   `policy:wssp1.2-2007-Saml2.0-SenderVouches-Wss1.1.xml`

❏   `policy:wssp1.2-2007-Saml2.0-HolderOfKey-Wss1.1-Asymmetric.xml`

❏   `policy:wssp1.2-2007-Saml2.0-Bearer-Https.xml`

In these policies, the reference to asymmetric in the name refers to asymmetric encryption, which means the sender uses one key to encrypt/sign a message and the recipient uses a different key to decrypt/validate the signature. When WebLogic Server applies these policies, it uses the sender's and recipient's public and private keys. In the case of `policy:wssp1.2-2007-Saml2.0-Sender Vouches-Wss1.1.xml`, WebLogic Server uses the same key to encrypt and decrypt the message. Even though the message is secured with a symmetric key, WebLogic Server still encrypts the key itself with the recipient's public key asymmetrically — ensuring only the recipient can decrypt it. With the bearer assertion, WebLogic Server sends the message over one-way SSL to at least ensure that the sender trusts the recipient of the SOAP message before sending the SAML assertion.

Identity Provider Partners

Understanding what each of the WS-SecurityPolicy types does is important for configuring them in WebLogic Server. First, securing a web service with any of these policies requires the configuration of a `SAML2IdentityAsserter`, as described earlier. The next step is to create a `Web Service Identity Provider Partner` for the requestors using the `Management` tab of the `SAML2IdentityAsserter`. The partner definition defines which services to apply this definition in the `Audience` attribute. The values of the attribute take one of the following forms:

❏   `target:*:<URI>`: a wildcard match

❏   `target:-:<URI>`: an exact match and does not include the target in the audience URI in the SAML assertion

❏   `target:+:<URI>`: an exact match and does include the target in the audience URI in the SAML assertion

❏   `<URI>`: an audience URI for the SAML assertion — always included in assertion, not used for partner matching.

In SAML, the audience URI defines the scope of the assertion. In some cases, the assertion is only intended for the specific target service whereas in others, the SAML assertion can be used more broadly. The flexibility in configuring the `Audience` attribute covers both of these scenarios.

The `Issuer` attribute uniquely identifies this partner. The partner definition needs to be set to the appropriate `Confirmation Method`: `Sender Vouches`, `Bearer`, or `Holder of Key`.

WebLogic Server will not validate the SAML assertion if the identity asserter cannot locate a matching partner definition. The identity asserter attempts to match the `Audience` attribute, the `Confirmation Method`, and the `Issuer` of the SAML assertion it receives against its partner definitions. If it does, the identity asserter attempts to validate the assertion using the specified confirmation method in accordance with the SAML 2.0 specification.

The `Process Attributes` and `Virtual User` attributes determine if the server should use the attributes of the SAML assertion as groups and if the server should allow the user access even if it doesn't exist in any of the authentication providers defined in the realm, respectively. To use these features, you must configure a `SAMLAuthenticator` in the active security realm.

For the `policy:wssp1.2-2007-Saml2.0-Bearer-Https.xml` policy, the caller must send the request over one-way SSL so you must configure WebLogic Server for one-way SSL support (see the section "Configuring One-Way SSL" in this chapter). For the sender-vouches confirmation method, the sender of the request must sign and encrypt the message; therefore, the server needs to trust the sender. To accomplish this, configure the server to trust the sender's certificate authority by adding the CA certificate to the server's trust key store. For the holder-of-key confirmation method, the SAML issuer signs the assertion and the sender signs the message so WebLogic Server needs to trust both the sender and the SAML issuer. You configure the server to trust the SAML issuer's certificate by importing it from the `Assertion Signing Certificate` tab of the `Web Service Identity Partner Provider`, and to trust the sender's signing certificate by adding the CA certificate to the server's trust key store.

Service Provider Partners

The requestor also needs to understand what the web service expects so that it is properly configured. In all cases, you need to configure the `SAML2CredentialMapper`. Next, create a new `Web Service Service Provider Partner` from the `Management` tab of the identity asserter. WebLogic Server uses these partner definitions to determine what type of SAML assertion to generate. WebLogic Server provides the ability to configure specific SAML settings on a per-partner basis. Configuring a service provider partner is very similar to configuring an identity provider partner. The differences are that the audience attribute of the identity provider needs to include the URL for the web service (for example, `http://www.bizreg.com/WebService/HelloWorld`) and that you cannot configure the issuer on a per-partner basis. The issuer is set on the credential mapper itself and applies to all partners.

If the partner is using the confirmation method sender-vouches then the sender is going to sign the SOAP request that will include the SAML assertion. In order to configure a signer's identity, the first step is to create a `PKICredMapper`. The `PKICredMapper` references a key store that contains the certificates that the server uses to sign/encrypt messages. Once you configure the `PKICredMapper`, the next step is to configure the credential mappings for the realm. The credential mappings define which key in the `PKICredMapper`'s key store a user or group should use when making remote requests. This is not part of SAML specifically, rather the SAML sender-vouches and holder-of-key policies provided by WebLogic Server requires that the SOAP messages be signed. This process of configuring the `PKICredMapper` is exactly the same as configuring any message protection scheme that requires digital signatures.

If the partner is using the confirmation method holder-of-key, the issuer of the SAML assertion includes the sender's public key in the signed SAML assertion. Then, the sender uses their private key to sign the SOAP request, which contains the signed SAML assertion and the sender's public key. In this case or any other where the issuer signs the assertions, you must configure the `SAML2CredentialMapper` with an identity to use for this purpose. The `SAML2CredentialMapper` uses the server's configured identity store. If there isn't a separate identity for the SAML issuer, the `SAML2CredentialMapper` can use the server's certificate by simply entering the server certificate's alias and private key passphrase, which were previously defined on the server's `SSL Configuration` tab in the WebLogic Console.

Debugging SAML

WebLogic Server has a `weblogic.security.saml2` debug category that you should enable when trying to diagnose SAML2 issues. Also, it may be helpful to enable the `weblogic.security.credmap`
(when acting as an identity provider), `weblogic.security.atn` (when acting as a service provider),
and `weblogic.security.ssl` categories as well.

Most SAML issues occur when the server can't find a matching partner definition. This will manifest
itself in a message like "Unable to generate credential for Identity" or "Invalid Token." These messages
are deliberately vague; the logs have all of the details. When producing a SAML assertion, WebLogic
Server performs the search based on confirmation method and target. When validating the assertion, the
search is based on confirmation method, target, and issuer. Also, partners are not enabled by default so
make sure that the partner is enabled.

Tip to Remember

Most SAML issues occur when the server can't find a matching partner definition. Also,
partners are not enabled by default, so make sure that the partner is enabled.

Setting Up Cross Domain Security and Single Sign-On

This section covers two additional scenarios for identity propagation or single sign-on. The first is identity
propagation between WebLogic Server domains. WebLogic Server has two models for inter-domain
identity propagation: *Cross Domain Security* and *Global Trust*. The second SSO scenario is from Microsoft
Windows desktops to WebLogic Server web applications. This scenario uses the **S**imple and **P**rotected
GSSAPI **Nego**tiation (SPNEGO) mechanism. Setting this up can be complicated, so this section contains
an overview of the process, and concludes with some best practices and troubleshooting tips.

Trust Between Domains

By default, a principal from one WebLogic Server domain will not be valid in another WebLogic Server
domain. This is because the keys used by one domain to sign the principal are different than the keys
used by the other domain to validate the principal. In previous versions of WebLogic Server, in order to
achieve cross domain trust, you simply needed to change the keys in the two domains to be the same.

This approach is fine except that it has some limitations. The first is that the trust is transitive. For
example, if domains A and B have cross domain trust established and domains B and C have cross
domain trust established, that implies that domains A and C will also have cross domain trust established. The second limitation is that WebLogic Server will trust all users in this cross domain trust model.
For example, if Domains A and B have cross domain trust established and a user is an administrator in
Domain A, the user will also be an administrator in Domain B.

Recognizing these and other limitations, WebLogic Server 9.2 MP2 introduced two types of cross domain
security. The first type, known as *global trust*, is simply a new name for the older cross domain trust
previously described. It still has all the same limitations, which in many cases may not be relevant.
Global trust is far easier to use than the second model and is sufficient for many deployments. Global
trust is currently the only option for RMI/EJB. To enable global trust, simply change the credential under
the `Advanced` section of the domain's `General Security` tab using the WebLogic Console.

The second model is simply called *cross domain security*. This model is available for JMS, JTA, MDB, and WAN replication subsystems. Using this model overcomes the limitations with the global trust model. Trust is established pair-wise between domains, not transitively. In this model, if Domain A trusts Domain B, and Domain B trusts Domain C, Domain A does not trust Domain C. You would need to specifically configure Domain A and Domain C to trust each other. To enable cross domain security, use the WebLogic Console to select the `Cross Domain Security Enabled` option on the domain's `General Security` tab.

You configure the domain-to-domain trust in two parts. In the Domain A, you need to create a user, known as the *cross domain user*, and assign that user to the `CrossDomainConnectors` group. In Domain B, you need to set up a credential mapping for Domain A. To do this, create a new credential mapping entry using the `New` button on the security realm's `Credential Mapping` tab. In the resulting wizard pages, choose the `Use cross-domain protocol` option, enter the other domain's name (for example, Domain A) in the `Remote Domain` field, and then enter the cross domain user's username and password for the other domain in the `Remote User` and `Remote Password` fields. You will need to repeat these two steps on the other domain as well by creating a cross domain user in Domain B and a credential mapping for that user in Domain A. This process gives the domain administrator explicit control over which domains to trust. The domain administrator can also explicitly exclude domains from being trusted by adding their names to the `Excluded Domain Names` attribute on the domain's `General Security` tab in the WebLogic Console.

> **Best Practice**
>
> If you need to establish trust between domains, use global trust. If transitive trust is a concern, you can use cross domain security but only for JMS, JTA, MDB, and WAN replication purposes. The EJB/RMI subsystems require global trust.

SSO from Microsoft Windows Desktops

Using the capabilities of WebLogic Server to achieve SSO from a Microsoft Windows desktop is not a simple task. Conceptually, it is a very desirable feature — users log in to their workstation once and then can access web applications without re-entering their username or password. In practice, getting this to work requires changes to the user's browser, to Active Directory, and to WebLogic Server. Understanding what needs to be done up front is important in planning and executing the deployment of this feature. This section is essentially an outline of how to configure this capability but it is not meant to be a comprehensive manual covering every deployment scenario and every conceivable issue. Please refer to the Oracle Support web site for a more comprehensive troubleshooting guide (Link 11-17).

The first step is to configure WebLogic Server's JVM to talk to the Kerberos Key Distribution Center (KDC) for the Windows domain. You do this by creating a configuration file that the Kerberos libraries inside of WebLogic Server use to exchange information with the Windows domain. On Windows, create a file called `%windir%\kbr5.ini`; on UNIX, create a file called `/etc/kbr5.conf`. Use the following sample as a template.

```
[libdefaults]
default_realm = BOOK.LOCAL
default_tkt_enctypes = rc4-hmac des-cbc-crc
default_tgs_enctypes = rc4-hmac des-cbc-crc
permitted_enctypes = rc4-hmac des-cbc-crc
ticket_lifetime = 600
```

```
[realms]
BOOK.LOCAL = {
kdc = 123.45.67.89
admin_server = dc.book.local
default_domain = BOOK.LOCAL
}
[domain_realm]
.book.local = BOOK.LOCAL
[appdefaults]
autologin = true
forward = true
forwardable = true
encrypt = true
```

You'll need the following three pieces of information to adapt this sample into your environment:

❑ Domain Name: The name of Windows domain (for example, book.local). Make sure to use the same capitalization as the sample above does.

❑ Domain Controller IP address: The IP address of the domain controller for the domain (for example, 123.45.67.89).

❑ Domain Controller Hostname: The hostname of the domain controller for the domain (for example, dc.book.local).

The next step is to create an account in Active Directory and associate this account with one or more service principal names (SPN). The Windows domain controller uses the service principal name to uniquely identify the service (for example, http/www.bizreg.com) that it is communicating with, and to generate a request that only that service can understand. In most environments, create a single user in Active Directory, and then add all of the SPNs for all of the machines in the domain/cluster to that user. This can minimize the number of *pseudo-user* records created in Active Directory. In an environment where there is a web server running a WebLogic Server web server plug-in in front of WebLogic Server, create an SPN for that machine as well. If the SPN is incorrect, has the wrong case, or has multiple user accounts mapped to the same SPN, the SSO will not work.

When working with Kerberos, case is very important. Make sure that realm names are in ALL CAPS, and that the protocol of the services in the SPNs are in lowercase (for example, http). Be sure to create an SPN for any web server machines used to proxy to WebLogic Server as well. Make sure that there is only one account associated with the SPNs. If there are multiple user accounts associated with the SPN, the browser won't send the credentials to WebLogic Server. Remove the SPN from the other accounts.

You must create the Active Directory user account with certain conditions. It should never expire the password and it must not use Kerberos pre-authentication.

As of JDK 1.6, the Java GSS API supports RC4-HMAC encryption, which is the default Kerberos encryption type of Active Directory (see Link 11-18). This means that you no longer need to mark the user account to Use DES Encryption.

Once you add the SPNs to the account, you will export the information into a keytab file that WebLogic Server uses to identify itself to the Windows domain controller. If WebLogic Server is running on Windows, perform the following steps to generate a keytab file for the user account.

1. Use the `setspn` utility from Microsoft to create the following SPN:

    ```
    setspn -a http/<machine name> <created account>
    ```

    For example, if the machine name running WebLogic Server is `wls` and the Active Directory user account is `wlsuser`, the commands would be:

    ```
    setspn -a http/wls.book.local wlsuser
    ```

2. Next, create a keytab file for the user account. WebLogic Server uses the keytab file to identify itself to the domain controller.

    ```
    ktab -k keytab-file-name -a account-name@REALM.NAME
    ```

    Following the example, the command would be:

    ```
    ktab -k wls.keytab -a wlsuser@BOOK.LOCAL
    ```

    When prompted, enter the password for the Active Directory user account.

3. Copy the keytab file to the `$DOMAIN_HOME` directory of the WebLogic Server instance.

If WebLogic Server is running on UNIX, perform the following steps to generate the keytab file.

1. Use the `ktpass` command to both set the SPN and generate the keytab file.

    ```
    ktpass -princ http/<weblogic-server-host-name>@<REALM-NAME>
           -mapuser <account-name> -pass password -out <keytab-file-name>
    ```

    Following the example, the command would be:

    ```
    ktpass -princ http/wls.book.local@BOOK.LOCAL -mapuser wlsuser
           -pass password -out wlsuser.keytab
    ```

2. Copy the keytab file to the `$DOMAIN_HOME` directory of the WebLogic Server instance.

Before we continue, we need to point out that running `ktpass` has a serious side effect — it changes the name of the user in Active Directory from <accountname> to http/<accountname>. This is one reason why Oracle recommends creating a separate account. Also under some circumstances, `ktpass` does not update the user account to http/<accountname>. Make sure that the username change has occurred; if it has not, manually change the username.

> **Running `ktpass` is supposed to change the name of the user in Active Directory from <accountname> to http/<accountname>. Make sure that `ktpass` changed the username and if not, make the change manually.**

Once you copy the keytab file to the WebLogic Server domain, use the JVM's `kinit` utility to test that the configuration to the Windows domain controller is correct and that the keytab file is working properly. Set up the Java environment for the domain and run the following command:

```
kinit -k -t <keytab file name> <accountname>
```

Following the example, the command would be:

```
kinit -k -t wlsuser.keytab wlsuser
```

If the command is successful, `kinit` will return a message like "New ticket is stored in cache file x." If `kinit` returns an error, check the Kerberos configuration. Make sure that the IP address of the KDC is correct, that the Windows realm name is capitalized, that the Windows domain controller is available, and that WebLogic Server can connect to the Windows domain controller. Other possible issues include clock skew (that is, time on the two machines is more than 5 minutes apart) or some problem with the user account (for example, wrong password or mismatched encryption type).

That completes the configuration of the Windows domain. The next step is to configure the client (in most cases, Microsoft Internet Explorer) to trust WebLogic Server and send the user's credentials. This behavior is off by default so it needs to be turned on for each and every end user.

Configure the WebLogic Server and any web server proxy machines as members of the `Local Intranet Zone` by doing the following:

1. Open the `Tools` ➪ `Internet Options` menu item.

2. Select the `Security` tab.

3. Select the `Local Intranet Zone` and click the `Sites` button.

4. Click the `Advanced` button and add the site. From the example, that would be `http://wls.book.local`.

5. Back on the `Security` tab with the `Local Intranet Zone` selected, click the `Custom Level` button and make sure that the `Logon` setting under `User Authentication` is set to `Automatic Logon Only in Intranet`.

6. In Internet Explorer 6 only, back on the `Internet Options` page, select the `Advanced` tab and make sure that `Integrated Windows Authentication` is enabled.

The final step is to configure WebLogic Server to use the keytab file and to challenge a properly config-ured client for their credentials. This process starts with the creation of a file called `krb5Login.conf` in the WebLogic Server `$DOMAIN_HOME` directory.

WebLogic Server uses the standard Kerberos JAAS Login Module to authenticate the WebLogic Server instance to the Windows domain. The JAAS Login Module uses the login entry names to identify the configuration to use for each of the two login phases. The *initiate* phase has a login entry name of `com.sun.security.jgss.initiate` and is called when WebLogic Server authen-ticates the SPN using the keytab file for the account. The *accept* phase has a login entry name of `com.sun.security.jgss.krb5.accept` and is called when a browser sends a valid SPNEGO request and that ticket is validated by WebLogic Server.

Below is a template for the `krb5Login.conf` file containing the login entries for both the initiate and accept phases of the process

```
com.sun.security.jgss.initiate {
    com.sun.security.auth.module.Krb5LoginModule required
    principal="<account>@REALM.NAME" useKeyTab=true
    keyTab=<keytab-file-name> storeKey=true debug=true;
};

com.sun.security.jgss.krb5.accept {
    com.sun.security.auth.module.Krb5LoginModule Required
    principal="<account>@REALM.NAME" useKeyTab=true
    keyTab=<keytab-file-name> storeKey=true debug=true;
};
```

> **Tip to Remember**
>
> If you are using a Java SE 5 JVM, the JAAS login entry name for the *accept* phase should be changed from `com.sun.security.jgss.krb5.accept` to `com.sun.security.jgss.accept`.

The next step is to modify the WebLogic Server domain's `setDomainEnv` script to include the following system properties:

```
-Djava.security.auth.login.config=krb5Login.conf
-Djava.security.krb5.kdc=<IP address of the KDC - Same as in krb5.conf/ini>
-Djava.security.krb5.realm=<Realm - Same as in krb5.conf/ini>
-Djavax.security.auth.useSubjectCredsOnly=false
```

Optionally, set the Java system property `sun.security.krb5.debug` to `true` for detailed debugging of the calls WebLogic Server makes to the Windows domain controller.

```
-Dsun.security.krb5.debug=true
```

Finally, configure the security realm to use the `NegotiateIdentityAsserter`. The `Forms Based Negotiation Enabled` option triggers WebLogic Server to attempt SSO for all applications that are using form-based authentication. WebLogic Server enables this option by default. Once desktop SSO is set up properly, consider turning this option on; but while trying to debug the configuration, set this option to false. If not, then all applications with form-based authentication — including the WebLogic Console application — will be affected. Assuming that this setting is disabled, SSO should now work for any web application that is protected and has its `<login-method>` set to `CLIENT-CERT`. See the "Securing Web Applications" portion of the "Managing Application Security" section of this chapter for the details on how to protect the web application in this way.

Debugging the WebLogic Server environment is crucial to getting Desktop SSO to work. Turn on the `weblogic.security.atn` and `weblogic.servlet.security` debug categories. Also set the `-Dsun.security.krb5.debug=true` Java command-line option. The Kerberos debug logging information is sent to standard out. The `weblogic.security.atn` debug logging is sent to the server's log file. In this situation, configuring the server to write debug information to standard out makes it easier to debug the scenario because all of the information is available in standard out.

One of the most common problems is that the browser does not send the user's credential. Instead it sends a request to use NTLM authentication. A proper response from the browser is an `Authorize: Negotiate <Base64 encoded bytes>`, where the Base64 encoded bytes contain the service ticket authorizing the user for the service. The size of this message is typically over 1,000 bytes. In contrast, an NTML response is much shorter — about 50 bytes. There will also be a message in the server log — "Didn't find any token." In this case, double-check that the browser has the server configured in the Intranet Zone, and that the SPN is correct. Once the browser is sending the credential, the issues are much easier to diagnose.

Custom Authentication Providers

WebLogic Server provides SSO support for the SAML and SPNEGO industry standards. There are a number of other standard and proprietary SSO technologies that you might need to support. You can integrate other SSO technologies into WebLogic Server by creating a custom authentication provider. While all of the provider types support custom providers, custom identity asserters that work in conjunction with WebLogic Server's authentication providers or custom authentication providers is the most common use case. There are several source code examples that you can use to get started. As we mentioned previously, the Oracle Technology Network web site contains an example authentication provider (see Link 11-6).

At this point, we need to warn you about trying to use these examples as your production providers. The code examples are meant to help you understand how to build your own custom providers — they are not designed to be production-ready implementations. At a minimum, you should make certain performance and fault-tolerance enhancements before trying to use them in a production environment.

> The example security providers are intended to be used only as learning tools to help you understand how to interface with the WebLogic Server Security Service. These examples lack performance optimizations and fault-tolerance features required in any production-ready security provider.

Also, the `SimpleSampleIdentityAsserter` uses only a clear text username to identify the user to WebLogic Server. This is a security vulnerability exploitable by knowledgeable users who have direct network access to WebLogic Server. By creating an HTTP request that contains this token (that is, the username), it is simple to assume the identity of any user without their password.

It is strongly discouraged to use the `SimpleSampleIdentityAsserter` in a production environment without modifications. Modifications include adding encryption to the token or using a connection filter to restrict access to WebLogic Server from only the HTTP servers running the WebLogic Server plug-in.

> The **SimpleSampleIdentityAsserter** allows access to WebLogic Server by simply knowing the name of the user. This information can easily be obtained or guessed. It is strongly discouraged to use this in a production environment.

Servlet Authentication Filter

The Servlet Authentication Filter feature of the security framework enables support for authentication methods other than those provided by the Java EE specification: basic, form, and X.509 certificate. The authentication providers that WebLogic Server provides out of the box for single sign-on — negotiate identity asserter and SAML identity asserter — use this feature. A servlet authentication filter is very similar to a servlet filter, except that it is global for the domain and therefore doesn't need to be configured on a per-application basis. The servlet authentication filter gets invoked before the security framework so it can interact with the user to get the appropriate credentials.

Tip to Remember

Consider using a servlet authentication filter instead of application-level servlet filters for the purpose of providing authentication mechanisms other than those provided by Java EE such as integration with SSO.

Chapter Review

In this chapter, we covered a large amount of information related to the WebLogic Server security features. We started with an overview of the WebLogic Server Security Service. From there, we went on to discuss the WebLogic Security Framework and its built-in providers. We touched on how to use external authentication providers with WebLogic Server and followed that with a detailed discussion of how to configure SSL/TLS support. After that, we talked about how to write different types of Java application clients that use SSL. Then we discussed managing application security, starting with the use of Java EE deployment descriptors to define access policies, discussing the use of WebLogic Security access control policies, and finishing with a brief discussion about server boot identity security. We finished off the chapter with how to configure WebLogic Server for single sign-on across domains, using SAML and with Microsoft Windows desktops. In the next chapter, we concentrate on WebLogic Server administration and management.

12

Administering and Deploying Applications in WebLogic Server

In this chapter, we discuss the finer points of WebLogic Server administration. If you are unfamiliar with WebLogic Server administration, you should consult the WebLogic Server documentation at Link 12-1, as listed in the online Appendix on the book's web site at http://www.wrox.com, for more information. We begin by reviewing the key WebLogic Server architectural concepts. The purpose of this discussion is to give you a big picture understanding of how the WebLogic Server product works. Next, we discuss WebLogic Server administration concepts. Finally, we end the chapter by discussing WebLogic Server configuration, management, and monitoring.

WebLogic Architecture Key Concepts

In this section, we review some of the key concepts associated with the WebLogic Server deployment architecture. Before jumping into the details, we need to define a few terms that will be used throughout the rest of this chapter. In this chapter, the terms *server* and *instance* are used to describe a Java Virtual Machine process that is running the WebLogic Server software program. We use the term *machine* to describe a computer with its own CPU, memory, and secondary storage that is running its own copy of the operating system software. Even though it is often possible to partition large computers into several logical, smaller computers, we will not make a distinction between multiple machines that, through logical partitioning, are part of the same chassis and those that are not. Now, we are ready to review the WebLogic Server deployment architecture.

Domain Architecture

A *WebLogic Server instance* is the process responsible for receiving incoming requests from the user, dispatching those requests to the appropriate Java EE application component(s), and returning responses to the user. This server instance provides the Java EE containers necessary to deploy any

Java EE–based application and handles all of the resource management for the application. We talk more about the internal architecture of the server in the next section.

A *WebLogic Server cluster* is a loosely coupled grouping of WebLogic Server instances that provide a cluster-wide naming service, load distribution, and fault tolerance to hosted applications. WebLogic Server dynamically determines the membership of the cluster using heartbeat messages that are periodically sent via the configured clustering protocol. WebLogic Server supports two clustering protocols: TCP/IP-based unicast or UDP-based multicast. Multicast is still the default clustering protocol, though the WebLogic Console defaults to unicast when creating new clusters. For simplicity, we use unicast in our clustering protocol discussions for the rest of this section even though the mechanisms described are the same for multicast-based clusters. Through these unicast messages, each cluster member maintains its own cluster membership list. In a similar fashion, every server in the cluster maintains a complete copy of the cluster-wide JNDI namespace. WebLogic Server uses a reliable unicast-based protocol to propagate all changes to the JNDI namespace on any particular server to the other cluster members. This loosely coupled clustering architecture allows each server to function independently of any other WebLogic Server process.

Using the ability to define a machine in your WebLogic Server domain, you can tell WebLogic Server which servers run on which machines. The in-memory replication feature of WebLogic Server clustering uses this knowledge to locate the secondary copy of a particular object so that the primary and secondary copies of an object reside on different machines, whenever possible. The administration server also relies on this machine configuration information to determine how to contact a particular WebLogic Server instance's node manager. We talk more about clustering, in-memory replication, and the node manager later.

A *WebLogic Server domain* is an administrative grouping of servers and clusters. You configure, manage, and monitor the domain from a central location; this central location is the *administration* (or *admin*, for short) *server*. The admin server is just a WebLogic Server instance that runs some special administrative applications like the WebLogic Console. Through these applications, the admin server maintains a repository of configuration information for the domain, acts as a centralized location for application deployment, and provides a browser-based administrative console application that the administrator uses to configure, manage, and monitor all aspects of the domain. A *managed server* is the term for any server in the domain other than the admin server. On startup, a managed server contacts the admin server to obtain its configuration information and applications to deploy. WebLogic Server optimizes this transfer of information to include only information that has changed since the managed server was shut down. Once the managed server is running, it no longer depends on the admin server to be able to process client requests. As you see later in this chapter, the admin server introduces a centralized location for configuration, management, and monitoring but does not significantly compromise the benefits of the loosely coupled cluster architecture.

The *node manager* is an optional daemon process that runs on each machine where managed servers may be run. WebLogic Server uses the node manager to allow administrators to start servers on remote machines from the WebLogic Console. As we discuss later, the node manager's role also includes server monitoring and automatic restart capabilities. It also plays a role in automatic service and whole server migration, which we discuss in detail later in this chapter.

Figure 12-1 shows how all the pieces fit together. In this example, we have the admin server for the `mydomain` domain running on machine `m1`. This admin server manages the configuration information for two different clusters, `abc` and `mycluster`, and one standalone server, `X`. Each machine has a node manager running on it; the configuration information would also specify which servers are running on each machine.

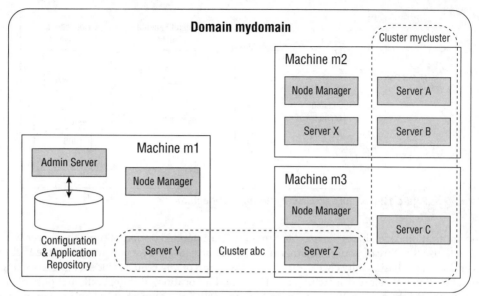

Figure 12-1: WebLogic Server domain architecture.

WebLogic Server Architecture

A high-level understanding of the server's internal architecture is important to understanding how to design, build, deploy, and debug applications that will run on WebLogic Server. Although many things have changed since the early versions of Tengah (the name of the server before the BEA acquisition), the fundamental message processing architecture remains relatively unchanged. As shown in Figure 12-2, the core components of the server are the *listen threads*, the *socket muxer*, and the *execute queue* with its associated *execute threads*. When the server process starts up, it binds to one or more ports and assigns a thread to each port to listen for connection requests. Once the server accepts the connection request and establishes the connection, the server hands off control of the connection to the socket muxer, which waits for incoming requests. At a high level, the socket muxer detects an incoming request, reads the request off of the socket, and places the request along with any associated security or transaction context onto the appropriate execute queue (typically, the self-tuning execute queue). Once a request appears on the execute queue, an idle execute thread takes the request off of the queue, assumes the identity of the user who submitted the request, executes the request, returns the response to the caller, and goes back to wait for the next request.

Execute Queues, Execute Threads, and Work Managers

Once an execute thread invokes the target component of the request, that execute thread will, under most circumstances, process the entire request. Figure 12-2 depicts this fact by showing a single execute thread spanning the servlet, EJB, and JDBC components in the application container. The call to the servlet, its call to a method on an EJB, and the EJB's use of JDBC to query a database will all occur within the same execute thread. During the execution of a request, the execute thread will be unavailable to process any other requests until the request processing code completes successfully or throws an exception. This is an extremely important point to recognize.

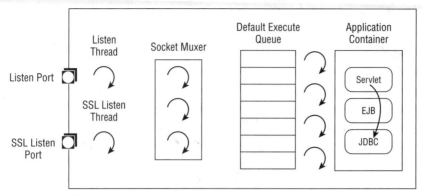

Figure 12-2: WebLogic Server internal architecture.

If the application code blocks the execute thread for an extended period of time, the server will not be able to use that thread to process other requests coming into the execute queue. While WebLogic Server does some basic sanity checks during the execution of any request (for example, checking the transaction timeout before dispatching an EJB method invocation), it is generally not possible for the server to tell the execute thread to abort the processing of a request. If the application gets into a state where every execute thread is blocked for an extended period of time, the server will either become nonresponsive (for requests targeted to that execute queue) or have to spawn additional execute threads to try to cope with the situation. Although the listen threads and the socket muxer are able to accept new requests from clients and place them into the execute queue, no execute threads will be available to process the request and return the response to the client unless the server is able to spawn new execute threads. Of course, spawning new threads that end up blocking on the first application request does not improve the overall situation.

When these long-running requests cause the execute threads to block, the incoming requests will start to back up in the execute queue. Even if the condition causing the execute threads to block goes away, it is very likely that the execute queue will end up with a relatively large number of messages. This not only will cause degradations in response time but also may cause users to cancel their requests (by clicking the stop button on their browsers) and to resubmit them. Typically, this will only make the situation worse because WebLogic Server currently processes every message on the execute queue in first-in-first-out order. In certain conditions (for example, reading HTTP POST data associated with a web application request), WebLogic Server will detect that the client is no longer waiting for the response and will short-circuit the request processing. Other conditions, though, may cause WebLogic Server to process the request even if the client is no longer waiting for the response. Fortunately, WebLogic Server provides a mechanism to limit the number of requests it will accept to prevent this execute queue overload condition, which we discuss shortly.

Current versions of WebLogic Server use a single, priority-based, self-tuning execute queue that increases and decreases the number of execute threads dynamically based on historical performance data. When the server receives a request, it determines the request class to which the request belongs, either implicitly based on the application or explicitly based on an applicable work manager configuration. Using the request class information, the server assigns the request an internal priority and places it on the execute queue, with higher priority requests going closer to the front of the queue. The closer to the front of the queue, the faster the request will be assigned to an execute thread for processing. WebLogic Server determines the internal priority of each request using the *work managers* you create to manage your applications.

Work managers provide a way for administrators to describe how they want the server to partition its resources across applications. To describe resource partitioning, WebLogic Server work managers contain four component types:

1. Request Class
2. Minimum Threads Constraint
3. Maximum Threads Constraint
4. Capacity Constraint

All four components are optional.

Think of a request class as a mechanism to define the runtime behavior of the set of requests to which it is associated. All requests that share a runtime behavior should share a request class. For example, if all of the HTTP requests within your web applications are equally important, you should associate your web applications with the same request class so that they get equal runtime prioritization when being dispatched by the server. By default, each application belongs to its own request class. WebLogic Server supports three request class types:

Fair Share Request Class   A fair share request class specifies the relative thread usage time of an application as compared to other applications running in the same instance. Imagine a managed server with two applications deployed, A and B. Application A uses a work manager with a fair share of 50 and Application B uses a work manager with a fair share of 150. When the server is receiving a steady stream of requests from both applications that exceed the number of execute threads, the server will assign Application A's requests to 25% of the available threads and Application B's requests to 75% of the available threads, assuming that requests for both applications, on average, take the same amount of time to execute. The allowable values of a fair share request class are 1 to 1000. Each application that uses a work manager that does not explicitly reference a request class gets an exclusive fair share value of 50.

Response Time Request Class   A response time request class specifies the target response time in milliseconds. Using our previous example, imagine that Application A uses a work manager with a response time of 3000 milliseconds and Application B uses a work manager with a response time of 5000 milliseconds. When the server is receiving a steady stream of requests from both applications that exceed the number of execute threads, the server will keep the average response times of the two applications in a 3 to 5 ratio, where the actual response times will be some fraction or multiple of the response time goal.

Context Request Class   A context request class is a compound class that maps between the context of a request and a fair share or response time request class. Currently, a context request class supports using the authenticated user and group names to map to different fair share or response time request classes. For example, a stock quote application might assign a higher fair share to logged-in users (which implies that they have accounts) by routing all requests associated with the built-in group name users to which all authenticated users belong to a higher fair share request class, and all requests associated with the built-in user name <anonymous> to a lower fair share request class.

Constraints allow you to set limits on what a work manager can do. By default, a work manager has no constraints. The minimum thread constraint has nothing to do with the minimum size of the execute thread pool. Instead, it allows you to ensure that the server will have a certain number of threads available for processing requests associated with work managers using this constraint. This is really only useful to prevent deadlock in certain server-to-server callback scenarios. We provide an example.

Imagine that Application A runs on Managed Server 1 and Application B runs on Managed Server 2. If Application A makes an EJB call to Application B and Application B calls back to Application A (or any other application running on Managed Server 1) while processing the EJB call, it is possible to deadlock the two managed servers. If all of Managed Server 1's threads are waiting on the EJB call to Application B to respond, Managed Server 1 will not have any threads available to process the callback requests and the two servers will deadlock waiting on each other. To prevent this deadlock situation, you might assign the callback requests from Application B a higher fair share than the calls generating the EJB calls to Application B. You might also add a minimum threads constraint for the callbacks to ensure that some threads will always be available for processing callbacks.

Best Practice

Only use minimum thread constraints when your application contains callbacks that can cause server-to-server deadlock.

Maximum thread constraints are useful in a number of situations. For example, if a particular type of request requires a database connection, you might want to set a maximum thread constraint to a value equal to the maximum number of database connections available to your application so that execute threads won't block waiting for a connection to be available. This example is such a common use case that the maximum thread constraint supports either specifying a numeric value or the name of a WebLogic Server–defined JDBC data source. In the latter case, the maximum thread constraint value changes as the maximum size of the JDBC data source's connection pool changes.

Best Practice

Always specify a maximum thread constraint to prevent contention for JDBC or other backend system connections.

Capacity constraints allow you to specify the maximum number of requests a server will accept. The capacity constraint gives you a mechanism to prevent the execute queue overload condition we discussed earlier in this section. When determining capacity, the server counts all requests currently executing on an execute thread and all requests waiting in the execute queue. When a capacity constraint is reached, the server takes overload protective action; for example, by returning an HTTP 503 response to indicate that the server is too busy or returning a `RemoteException` for RMI calls to allow the request to fail over to another server in the cluster. WebLogic Server also provides a `Shared Capacity for Work Managers` parameter that limits the total capacity of the server.

> **Best Practice**
>
> Do not allow the execute queue to get so long that the response time for new requests would be longer than most clients are willing to wait.

During certain types of failure conditions, execute threads may block for extended periods of time waiting for slow backend systems or TCP/IP timeouts in the case of machine or network failures. These conditions can cause execute threads to block for minutes at a time. If the server's incoming request load is high enough, all available execute threads will be blocked and the server will create more execute threads in an attempt to continue doing useful work. Because the server does not understand the nature of the problem or the applications it is servicing, it cannot make an intelligent decision about whether creating new execute threads will in fact help. The real issue in these situations is that the server is unable to process any requests because of this failure condition. Your first thought might be to create a maximum thread constraint to prevent the server from creating too many threads; however, this would be treating the symptom and not the root cause. The real problem is that the requests keep piling up in its execute queue. As discussed previously, there is no point in the server accepting work if the time it will take to process that work exceeds the time for which the clients are willing to wait on the response. A better way to protect the server in these situations is to define a capacity constraint so that the server starts rejecting work when it is unable to keep up. By combining a capacity constraint with proper tuning of the stuck thread detection capability (that we discuss later), you can protect the server from overloading itself during these types of failures.

> **Best Practice**
>
> Combining capacity constraints and stuck thread detection will help protect the server in certain types of failure conditions.

WebLogic Server allows you to define work managers, request classes, and constraints at the global, application, and component levels. Request classes and constraints can either be shared across work managers or be exclusive to a single work manager. All applications share any request classes and constraints associated with their work manager. The only exception to this rule, which we will discuss later, is for work managers that do not specify a request class and, therefore, use the default fair share request class.

Use the `Environment ⇨ Work Managers` page in the WebLogic Console to define global work managers, request classes, and constraints. All globally-defined request classes and constraints are inherently sharable — whether they are defined within or outside the context of a specific global work manager. For example, if multiple work managers share the same capacity constraint, this means that the sum total of all requests across all work managers sharing the capacity constraint will never exceed the capacity value in each server instance. If multiple applications use the same global work manager that defines an exclusive capacity constraint, this means that the sum total of all requests across all applications sharing the work manager will never exceed the capacity value in each server instance.

WebLogic Server also supports defining work managers, request classes, and constraints at the application and application component level by adding definitions to `weblogic-application.xml`, `weblogic.xml`, or `weblogic-ejb-jar.xml`. When using deployment descriptors to define request classes and constraints, you have the option to define them inside a specific work manager, as shown in the following code.

```
<work-manager>
  <name>mylowpriority_workmanager</name>
  <fair-share-request-class>
    <name>mylowpriority_requestclass</name>
    <fair-share>20</fair-share>
  </fair-share-request-class>
  <max-threads-constraint>
    <name>mylowpriority_maxthreadsconstraint</name>
    <count>15</count>
  </max-threads-constraint>
</work-manager>
```

Doing this implies that the request class or constraint is exclusive to the work manager in which it was defined.

You can also define the request classes and constraints outside the context of a work manager and then reference them by name from a work manager definition, as shown here:

```
<work-manager>
  <name>mylowpriority_workmanager</name>
  <request-class-name>
    mylowpriority_requestclass
  </request-class-name>
  <max-threads-constraint-name>
    mylowpriority_maxthreadsconstraint
  </max-threads-constraint-name>
</work-manager>
```

WebLogic Server supports defining request classes and constraints outside the context of a work manager at the global and application levels only. Work managers refer to these shared request classes and constraints by name. The scope of these shared definitions is as you would expect. Shared application-defined request classes and constraints are visible only to work managers defined in the same application or application components within the application. Globally-defined request classes, which are always sharable, are visible to any work manager on the targeted servers.

If a work manager does not specify a request class, it gets a copy of the default fair share request class whose fair share value is 50. Unlike with explicitly-defined request classes, all applications using a work manager associated with the default fair share request class get their own fair share of 50, rather than sharing the fair share. WebLogic Server defines a global work manager called `default` that does not define a request class or any constraints. As such, each application that uses the `default` work manager will have its own fair share of 50. You can modify the default work manager by creating a global work manager definition with the name `default`.

To configure a servlet or JSP to use a work manager, use the `<wl-dispatch-policy>` initialization parameter to specify the name of the work manager in the web application's `web.xml` deployment descriptor:

```
<servlet>
  <servlet-name>HighPriorityServlet</servlet-name>
  <jsp-file>high_priority.jsp</jsp-file>
  <init-param>
    <param-name>wl-dispatch-policy</param-name>
    <param-value>MyHighPriorityWorkManager</param-value>
  </init-param>
</servlet>
```

To map the entire web application to a work manager, use the `<wl-dispatch-policy>` element in the `weblogic.xml` deployment descriptor:

```
<weblogic-web-app>
  ...
  <wl-dispatch-policy>MyHighPriorityWorkManager</wl-dispatch-policy>
  ...
</weblogic-web-app>
```

To map an EJB to a work manager, use the `<dispatch-policy>` element in the `weblogic-ejb-jar.xml` file:

```
<weblogic-enterprise-bean>
  <ejb-name>HighPrioritySessionEJB<ejb-name>
  ...
  <dispatch-policy>MyPriorityQueue</dispatch-policy>
</weblogic-enterprise-bean>
```

WebLogic Server checks for stuck threads. Stuck threads are threads that have been processing a particular request for more than the configured amount of time. If the server determines that execute threads are stuck, it will take the configured action on the component specifying the stuck thread detection behavior. WebLogic Server supports configuring stuck thread detection behavior at the server, work manager, and application levels. We discuss stuck thread detection behavior in detail in the "Server Self-Health Monitoring" section later in this chapter.

Socket Muxer

The socket muxer manages the server's existing socket connections. The first thing it does is determine which sockets have incoming requests waiting to be processed. Then, it reads just enough of the data to determine the protocol, packages the socket up into a protocol-specific data structure, and dispatches the socket to the appropriate runtime layer. In this runtime layer, the socket muxer thread reads the request off the socket, sets up any required context information, determines which work manager to use, and places the request onto the execute queue.

WebLogic Server has two versions of the socket muxer: an all-Java version that currently has to poll each socket to determine whether a request is waiting and a version that uses a small native library leveraging the more efficient operating system call to make that determination. The `Enable Native IO` checkbox on the server's `Tuning Configuration` tab tells the server which version to use; this is on by default on most platforms. It is important to remember that in order to use native I/O, you must make sure that the native library is in the server's shared library path. The default scripts that come with the server set this up for you. If the server fails to load the native library, it will throw a `java.lang.UnsatisfiedLinkException` and then load the all-Java version, so you need to pay close attention to the server output and log file to make sure that you are, in fact, using the native version.

With a small number of concurrent connections, the all-Java version tends to be faster; this is probably due to the huge overhead associated with making JNI method calls compared to making Java method calls. As the number of concurrent socket connections grows, however, the native I/O muxer quickly becomes more efficient. We recommend using the native I/O muxer in most production environments if it is available on the target platform.

Best Practice

Always enable native I/O, if available, and check for errors at startup to make sure it is being initialized properly.

WebLogic Server 8.1 added has a new socket muxer based on the non-blocking I/O (NIO) capabilities introduced in JDK 1.4. Presumably this new muxer will eventually replace the native muxer because the operating system calls used by the native muxer are now being surfaced in Java. At the time of writing, the NIO muxer is still not officially supported by Oracle and still does not support SSL. We expect both of these to change, so check the WebLogic Server documentation for more information. To enable the NIO muxer, set the Java system property `weblogic.MuxerClass` to `weblogic.socket.NIOSocketMuxer` on the Java command line. One advantage of the NIO muxer is that it also works on the WebLogic Server client run time, unlike the native I/O muxer. Remember, however, never to use an unsupported feature in a production environment.

The Java socket muxer steals threads from the default execute queue's thread pool (on the server side, this is the self-tuning thread pool). The `Socket Readers` parameter controls the maximum number of threads the Java socket muxer can steal as a percentage of the *maximum* number in the pool. When using the self-tuning thread pool there is no maximum number of threads in the pool so the server uses the value returned by the `weblogic.management.configuration.KernelMBean.getThreadPoolSize()` method, which has a default value of 15. At this point in time, there is really no good reason to use the Java socket muxer on the server. WebLogic RMI clients always use the Java socket muxer (or the NIO muxer).

By default, the `Socket Readers` parameter is set to 33, meaning that the socket muxer can take up to 33 percent of the maximum number of execute threads from the default execute queue. For example, if the default execute queue has 15 threads, we may have only 10 threads processing requests and 5 threads reading incoming requests off the sockets. The `Socket Readers` parameter is also configurable using the server's `Tuning Configuration` tab.

The native I/O muxer uses its own execute thread pool (associated with the `weblogic.socket.Muxer` queue) and uses $n + 1$ threads by default, where n is the number of CPUs. Note that multi-core CPUs and hyper-threading also impact the CPU count for determining the number of threads.

It is possible to change the number of socket muxer threads. WebLogic Server uses Java system properties to control the number of threads used by the native I/O muxer. WebLogic Server uses the `weblogic.SocketReaders` Java system property to control the number of socket reader threads for the native I/O muxer. In our experience, the only reason we have ever increased the number of socket reader threads was to allow Java application clients to be more responsive when talking to a large cluster of servers, and even then, the change was made only on the Java application client and not on the server. Changes in the client runtime have made even this unnecessary. On machines with multi-core CPUs with hyper-threading enabled, you may end up with an artificially large number of muxer threads. For example, 2 quad core CPUs with hyper-threading will cause WebLogic Server to create 17 muxer threads. In most cases, it makes sense to reduce this number to eliminate the double counting of CPUs caused by hyper-threading. We have observed cases where too many native muxer threads had an impact on performance. In those cases, reducing the number of muxer threads — even as low as 1 — may improve your application's performance.

Listen Ports and Listen Threads

By default, WebLogic Server starts up listening on two ports. The plain text listen port accepts connections for HTTP, T3, IIOP, COM, LDAP, SNMP, and WebLogic Server's `cluster-broadcast` protocols. The SSL listen port accepts connections for HTTPS, T3S, IIOPS, LDAPS, and WebLogic Server's `cluster-broadcast-secure` protocols. Each port has a listen thread associated with it. This thread simply waits for connection requests, accepts the connection, hands the connection off to the socket muxer, and goes back to listen for the next connection request.

WebLogic Server also has the concept of an *administration* (*admin*, for short) *port*, allowing administration requests to the server to be directed to a separate port and associated listen thread. When using the admin port, WebLogic Server will reject all administrative requests that arrive at any listen port other than the admin port. Use of the admin port also requires all administrative requests to use SSL.

In addition to the default network configuration (also known as the default *channel*) described already, WebLogic Server gives the administrator more flexibility and control over the server's network configuration. While the server still requires at least one enabled port on this default channel, it gives us the ability to turn off the default channel's plain text listen port. We talk more about these more advanced network configuration capabilities in the "Network Channels" section.

Application Container

The *application container* is simply the mechanism in which the server deploys applications. WebLogic Server requires that all application components be packaged as some type of Java EE application component. This packaging has multiple benefits that we discuss in other portions of this book, but the main implication that affects administration is the ability to perform what is known as *hot deployment*. Using hot deployment, we can deploy, redeploy, or undeploy an application while the server is running without affecting other applications or requiring a server restart.

To support unloading an application and achieving hot deployment, WebLogic Server relies on Java's ability to define custom classloaders. The reason for using custom classloaders is simple: Java does not provide any mechanism to unload or reload classes loaded by its default classloader, known in the WebLogic Server documentation as the *system classloader* (the one that uses the `CLASSPATH` environment variable for its search path). The system classloader simply loads the class from disk the first time it encounters a need for that class and then never looks at the class file on disk again. This means that once the system classloader loads a class, it will never pick up any changes to that class. Restarting the JVM is the only way to reload a class with the system classloader. Fortunately, Java does provide the ability to define and use custom classloaders. WebLogic Server deploys Java EE applications using custom classloaders so that you can unload or reload an application without restarting the server. See the discussion in Chapter 8 or the WebLogic Server documentation at Link 12-2 for more information.

WebLogic Server supports three models for redeploying applications in a running server: production redeployment, in-place redeployment, and partial redeployment. Production redeployment supports a side-by-side application versioning model through which you can deploy a new version of an application, verify that it is working, and activate the new version — all without disrupting existing client requests using the old version of the application. We discuss the redeployment models in more detail in the "Versioning Applications" section later in this chapter.

In this section, we have discussed the primary architectural features of WebLogic Server. A thorough understanding of these features will go a long way toward helping application architects, developers, and administrators make good decisions about application design, development, debugging, configuration, management, and monitoring. Many problems with WebLogic Server applications can be explained in terms of the concepts discussed in this section, so always keep these concepts in mind when looking for the root cause of a problem. Next we take an in-depth look at the WebLogic Server clustering architecture.

WebLogic Server Clustering Architecture

WebLogic Server clustering provides load balancing and failover capabilities to Java EE–based applications. Through its clustering mechanisms, WebLogic Server loosely couples together a set of server processes, distributed across one or more machines, so that they can share the responsibilities of processing requests for the applications deployed to the cluster. Exactly what facilities WebLogic Server clustering provides to an application depends on whether the application is web-based or RMI-based. Before we get into the details of the application-level facilities provided, let's look under the hood to see how WebLogic Server clustering works.

As previously mentioned, WebLogic Server clustering provides a loose coupling of the servers in the cluster. Each server in the cluster is independent and does not rely on any other server for any fundamental operations. Even if contact with every other server is lost, each server will continue to run and be able to process the requests it receives. Each server in the cluster maintains its own list of other servers in the cluster through periodic heartbeat messages. Every 10 seconds, each server sends a heartbeat message to the other servers in the cluster to let them know it is still alive. Heartbeat messages are sent using TCP/IP unicast or UDP multicast technology built into the JVM. Each server receives these heartbeat messages from other servers and uses them to maintain its current cluster membership list. If a server misses receiving three heartbeat messages in a row from any other server, it takes that server out of its membership list until it receives another heartbeat message from that server. This heartbeat technology allows servers to be dynamically added and dropped from the cluster with no impact on the existing servers' configurations.

It is possible to change the number of missed heartbeats necessary to remove a server from the cluster by changing the value of the Idle Periods Until Timeout parameter located in the Advanced area of the cluster's Messaging Configuration tab. Typically, you should leave this setting alone. In cases where you can guarantee your network is reliable and the servers are able to process these heartbeat messages in a timely fashion, you might want to experiment with a lower setting to speed up the time it takes to detect server death so as to speed up failover. However, we caution you from changing this setting without careful consideration and thorough testing as it may cause servers to leave and re-enter the cluster unnecessarily.

WebLogic Server also provides a cluster-wide JNDI namespace. Again, each server maintains its own view of the cluster-wide JNDI namespace, and any changes to the cluster-wide JNDI namespace on one server are propagated to the other servers via a reliable TCP/IP unicast– or UDP multicast–based protocol. This allows applications to have a global view of the cluster-wide JNDI namespace from any server in the cluster. Recognize that this JNDI replication is designed for service advertisement across the cluster, and not for replicating or sharing non-RMI-based objects across the cluster. Any object bound into the cluster-wide JNDI tree is always associated with the server that did the binding. If that server goes down, all JNDI references to the object will be removed from every server in the cluster. Of course, this is what you want for RMI-based references, but probably not what you would expect or want for cluster-wide sharing of non-RMI-based objects.

> At the time of writing, unicast-based clustering requires an explicit `ListenAddress` to cluster across machines. There are two ways to accomplish this. You can simply set each servers' `ListenAddress` explicitly rather than leaving it blank. As an alternative, you can define a custom network channel for unicast traffic and explicitly set the `ListenAddress` for that network channel.

Clustering for Web Applications

For web applications, WebLogic Server clustering provides persistence mechanisms for `HttpSession` objects. Through these persistence mechanisms, web applications that make use of `HttpSession` objects to store temporary state information can transparently fail over when a server in the cluster fails. Configuring the persistence mechanisms involves making changes to the web application's `weblogic.xml` deployment descriptor.

The most popular form of session persistence is in-memory replication. WebLogic Server uses a primary-secondary replication scheme in this form of persistence. The primary copy of the `HttpSession` object will be created by whichever server happens to be processing the user's first request requiring access to the `HttpSession`. At the end of that request, and before the response is returned to the user, the server will create a secondary copy of the `HttpSession` on another server in the cluster, encode the location of the primary and secondary copies of the `HttpSession` in the session ID, and add a cookie that contains the session ID to the response (the server can use URL rewriting if cookies are disabled). Typically, the primary server for a particular session will receive all future requests for that session. If the primary server fails, the first request following the failure will be routed to another server in the cluster. When the server receives a request for which it is not the primary, it will become the new primary server and make sure that another server in the cluster is holding the secondary.

Three burning questions may occur to you at this point:

- ❑   How is the routing accomplished?
- ❑   How does WebLogic Server determine where to place the secondary copy of a session?
- ❑   How does WebLogic Server detect changes to the primary copy and transmit them to the secondary?

Session-Based Routing

WebLogic Server supports two different mechanisms for accomplishing the routing of HTTP requests. The first routing mechanism uses a web server plug-in to proxy requests from a web server to the WebLogic Server cluster. Though Chapter 15 discusses deployment models in more detail, Figure 12-3 shows a common deployment model for this architecture. Web server plug-ins are available for Sun Java System Web Server, Microsoft IIS, and Apache-based web servers and for WebLogic Server itself. It is important to note that the web server plug-in routing behavior was changed in 2005 so that it now behaves like a hardware load balancer — that is, it ignores the secondary session location information when routing a request for a session whose primary server is down. This change was made to allow better distribution of a failed server's load across the remaining cluster members.

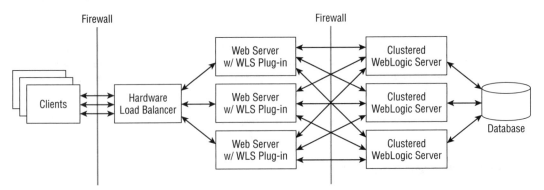

Figure 12-3: Web server proxy-based deployment model.

When the plug-in receives a request from the web server, the plug-in looks for a session ID associated with the request. If a request does not contain a session ID, the plug-in uses a round-robin load balancing algorithm to determine the server to which the request should be sent. When a request does contain a session ID, the plug-in uses information encoded in the session ID to determine the location of the primary copy of the particular session. Whenever possible, the plug-in will route the request to the server that contains the primary copy of the session. If the server holding the primary copy is down, the plug-in tries to send the request to another server in the cluster. When a server receives a request with a session ID for which it does not hold the primary copy of the session, it will look at the location information in the session ID to determine the location of the session copies.

If both the primary and secondary servers still exist, the server will call out to the primary server to tell it to send back a copy of the session and to give up its rights as the primary for this session. Once it has the session data, the server processes the request. At the end of the request processing, the server creates a new secondary copy of the session based on the new location of the primary, rewrites the session ID to encode the new primary and secondary location information, and returns the response to the caller. Choosing a new secondary location is necessary to try to keep the secondary on a different machine from the primary.

If only the secondary exists, the server will call out to the secondary server to tell it to send back a copy of the session and invalidate itself as the secondary. At that point, the processing is exactly the same as previously described; the server processes the request, creates a new secondary copy, creates a new session ID, and returns the new session ID along with the response.

If both the primary and secondary servers are down (or have been restarted), the server will treat the request as if it did not contain a session ID and process the request, creating a new session, secondary copy, and session ID. This is an inherent feature of the in-memory replication model and is not a shortcoming of in-memory replication. WebLogic Server replicates only session data as the result of a request for that session. Given that WebLogic Server does not attempt to keep cluster-wide session-to-server mapping information (presumably for performance and scalability reasons), the only way to locate a session is by the information contained in the session ID that is passed back to the browser.

The plug-in also supports transparent retry logic so that if it fails to deliver a request successfully to a WebLogic Server instance, it can resend the request to a different server in the cluster. If the plug-in determines that the server never received the request, it will always try to resend the request to another server in the cluster. In cases where the plug-in successfully sent the request to the server, but never received a response, you can configure the plug-in either to retry the request (the default) or to return an error to the caller. The two plug-in configuration parameters that control this behavior are `Idempotent` and `HungServerRecoverSecs`.

If the `Idempotent` parameter is set to `true` (which is the default value), the plug-in will retry any request for which it does not receive a response within the `HungServerRecoverSecs` timeout interval. The default timeout value is 300 seconds; the accepted range of values is 10 to 600 seconds. When using the `Idempotent` feature, applications must be able to handle duplicate requests properly because the server may have already processed the message (or may process the message later if the server's execute queue is backed up). For applications that are unable to handle duplicate requests, set the `Idempotent` parameter to `false`. For the Sun Java System Web Server and Apache web servers, these parameters can be set differently for different URLs and MIME types.

The second routing mechanism uses a hardware load balancer that routes directly to the cluster. Figure 12-4 shows a common deployment model for this architecture. Because the hardware load balancers generally do not understand the contents of the WebLogic Server session ID, WebLogic Server has to be able to handle situations where requests not directed to the server holding the primary copy of the session can be promoted to the primary. To accomplish this, it uses the same mechanism described in the web server plug-in replication discussion. Though this mechanism is general enough to work with all hardware load balancing schemes, the overhead of copying the session between servers will dramatically compromise both the performance and the scalability of the cluster. Fortunately, most hardware load balancers on the market today support one or more sticky load balancing algorithms.

Using a sticky load balancing algorithm, the load balancer remembers where it sent the last request for the particular user's session and always tries to route all subsequent requests from that session to the same server. The only time the load balancer will route the request to a different server is in the event of a failure of the primary server. When this happens, the load balancer will remember the new location and route all subsequent requests there until another failure happens. Clearly this mechanism is highly desirable because it will prevent moving the session between servers except when the primary server fails. We discuss this deployment model and its advantages and disadvantages in more detail in Chapter 15.

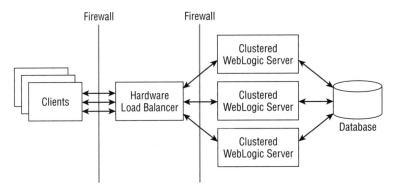

Figure 12-4: Proxy-less deployment model.

Secondary Selection

WebLogic Server uses two mechanisms to help select the secondary server for in-memory replication: machine definition and replication group definition. If we choose not to use either of these mechanisms, WebLogic Server uses a simple ring algorithm to select the secondary server (for example, server 1 has primaries that are replicated to server 2, server 2 has primaries that are replicated to server 3, and server 3 has primaries that are replicated to server 1). While constructing this ring, WebLogic Server tries to determine which servers are running on the same machines and construct the ring to keep primary and secondary session copies on different machines, where possible. Provided WebLogic Server correctly determines the topology, this works fine as long as there are no special circumstances that require more deterministic selection.

By defining machines and assigning server instances to machines, you can tell WebLogic Server which server instances live on which machines so it no longer needs to guess. In addition, you can use replication groups to gain even more control over the secondary selection process. By grouping servers into replication groups, you can tell WebLogic Server that a particular replication group should use another replication group as its preferred secondary replication group. If replication groups are in use, the secondary selection algorithm changes to the following sequence:

1. Is there a server in the preferred secondary replication group?
2. Is there a server in any other replication group that is located on another machine?
3. Is there a server in any other replication group that is located on the same machine?

Although specifying machines and replication groups is completely optional, we recommend specifying the machine information in all environments given the fact that some of the node manager configuration information is set at the machine level. Replication groups, on the other hand, are something that you should use only if you have a specific purpose in mind because, by default, WebLogic Server will make every effort to replicate objects across machines even without the use of replication groups.

> **Best Practice**
>
> Always specify the machine information for servers in a cluster when using in-memory replication. Define replication groups only if you need more control over the secondary selection process.

WebLogic Server also supports two cross-cluster session replication models: metropolitan-area network (MAN) and wide-area network (WAN) replication. MAN replication uses in-memory replication to keep the primary and secondary copies of the session on different clusters. WAN replication uses in-memory replication within the primary cluster and asynchronous replication via a database to keep a third copy of the session at the remote data center. See the "Cross-Cluster Replication" section later in this chapter for a detailed discussion of these capabilities.

Change Detection and Propagation

The server detects changes to the `HttpSession` objects by trapping all calls to the methods used to modify the objects bound into the session. WebLogic Server simply sets hooks in the `setAttribute()` and `removeAttribute()` methods to detect attribute modification during the course of processing a request. At the end of the request processing, but before returning the response to the user, the server will synchronously update the secondary copy of the session (or the persistence store) by propagating only the changes. This implementation has a couple of implications.

First, objects that already exist in the session from a previous request will need to be rebound into the session if we make changes to them during the current request processing. This is somewhat unnatural to most Java programmers. When writing a servlet or JSP to access a previously created object stored in the session, the `HttpSession.getAttribute()` method returns a reference to the existing object. Because the session obviously already has a reference to the object, it seems like an unnecessary step to reset the attribute with the same object's reference, but it is critical because this is how WebLogic Server identifies the modified attributes. We feel that the trade-off of having to invoke `setAttribute()` explicitly every time you modify an existing object is better than the alternative. Without the signal provided by `setAttribute()`, the server would incur more overhead during session persistence, perhaps by copying the entire object every time or using before and after images to determine what, if anything, has changed in the session.

> WebLogic Server will persist the changes to the `HttpSession` object only when using session persistence. The server detects changes to the `HttpSession` objects by trapping calls to the `setAttribute()` and `removeAttribute()` methods. This means that any objects previously bound into the session before the beginning of the current request must be rebound into the session by calling `setAttribute()` if they are modified. Failure to do so will result in changes not being persisted.

Second, the server propagates changes to objects bound into `HttpSession` at the `HttpSession` attribute level. This means that the server propagates any change to an attribute by serializing the entire object associated with the attribute and sending it to the secondary server (or the persistent store), regardless of the magnitude of the change to the object (or even if there is no change at all) whenever you call the setAttribute() method for that object. This means that the size and granularity of the objects bound into the HttpSession will directly affect performance and scalability. We revisit this discussion in Chapter 13.

Clustering for RMI-Based Applications

In RMI-based applications (which include EJB applications), the client uses a stub to invoke a method on the remote, server-side object. In standard, non-clustered RMI, this stub contains a single reference to the server process where the server-side object resides. WebLogic Server clustering introduces the concept of a *replica-aware stub* (also referred to as a *cluster-aware stub*) — a stub that contains references to all servers in the cluster that have a replica of the particular object. The stub load balances method invocations on the stub by distributing the requests across servers in the cluster based on the load balancing algorithm in use. By default, WebLogic Server uses a round-robin algorithm, but it also supports a couple of other load balancing algorithms as well as an extensible mechanism, known as *call router* objects, whereby programmers can supply their own load balancing logic. The current interface for this extensible load balancing mechanism does not provide access to the dynamic cluster list contained in the stub. This makes the mechanism of limited value because without this, there is no dynamic way for the call router object to know which servers are in the cluster and supporting replicas of the target object — at least, not without having the call router make calls to the Java Management Extensions (JMX) APIs in the server to determine this information.

> ### Best Practice
> Use one of the built-in load balancing algorithms rather than trying to use call routers due to their limitation of not having access to the dynamic cluster list maintained by the stubs.

By default, WebLogic Server uses a round-robin load balancing algorithm. It is important to note that the load balancing state is per-stub instance. What this means is that each time the caller gets a new stub (for example, via a JNDI lookup, calling a Remote interface method on an EJB remote object, and so on), the first invocation on the stub will randomly pick a server in the list to use to process the first request. All subsequent requests on that same stub will apply the chosen load balancing algorithm. For example, if the stub's replica list has servers s1, s2, and s3 in it and you are using the default load balancing algorithm, if the first request is sent to s2, the next requests will go to s3, s1, s2, and so on. If, however, the client gets a new stub for every request, the load distribution will be somewhat random based on the fact that each stub instance selects a random starting point in the list to begin applying its algorithm. Keep this point in mind when trying any tests of WebLogic Server clustering to observe the load balancing behavior.

One side effect of this load balancing behavior is that remote RMI-based clients may end up with socket connections to every server in the cluster. While this might be okay for small applications, this limits the scalability of RMI-based applications. For example, 1000 RMI-based clients connecting to a 10-node cluster would end up creating 10,000 socket connections. Many times it is sufficient to distribute the load by simply distributing the client connections across the cluster and having each client communicate with a single server until a time when that server fails. As such, WebLogic Server provides server affinity–based versions of its load balancing algorithms that balance the load on the initial connection and then stick to the first server to which the client connects. A client will not connect to another server unless the first server fails. These server affinity–based algorithms scale linearly with the number of clients since each client typically only requires a single socket connection into the cluster

---

Best Practice

Use one of the server affinity–based load balancing algorithms when you expect to have many more remote RMI-based clients than you have servers in your cluster.

If a server fails, the stub provides retry logic under certain conditions. Much like the previous discussion concerning the proxy plug-in, the stub will always retry requests that it knows never reached the server. The stub, though, will not try to resend failed requests that may have reached the server unless specifically told to do so. One important thing to remember is that if the stub and the target are collocated, no load balancing will be done because it is almost always more efficient to invoke the local replica of the object than it is to call out to another replica on another server.

RMI programmers have a great deal of control and flexibility when configuring the replica-aware stub behavior. For example, the -methodsAreIdempotent switch to WebLogic's RMI compiler (weblogic.rmic) allows the programmer to tell the stub that the object's methods have been written in such a way that it is safe to retry failed requests whose state is unknown. Though this particular option is also surfaced in the deployment descriptor for stateless session beans, the RMI compiler has other options available. Fortunately, most of the important options are available to EJB programmers, and in many cases, the WebLogic Server default settings are often good enough for configuring EJB clustering. Because most Java EE developers are using the EJB programming model instead of the lower-level RMI programming model, we will spend the rest of our time talking specifically about EJB clustering.

WebLogic Server provides a very robust clustering model for EJBs. By default, all EJB home objects, stateless session beans, and entity beans use cluster-aware stubs when they are running in a clustered environment. This means that even if your programmers are not developing in a clustered environment, their deployed beans will generally become cluster-aware once they are put into a cluster. Stateful session beans can also use in-memory replication, much like that previously described for HttpSession objects. The load balancing and failover behavior of the stubs varies depending on the types of objects in question.

All EJB home objects and stateless session beans use load balancing stubs by default. Whether the stubs should be cluster-aware and what load balancing algorithm they should use is configurable on a per-bean basis in the weblogic-ejb-jar.xml deployment descriptor. EJB home stubs for stateless session beans are always set to use idempotent behavior; all other types of EJB home stubs are not. By default, stateless session beans are not set to be idempotent, but they can be configured to use idempotent behavior by setting a flag in the deployment descriptor. All EJB methods (home and remote interface methods) can be configured to be idempotent using the <idempotent-methods> element in the weblogic-ejb-jar.xml deployment descriptor:

```
<weblogic-ejb-jar>
  ...
  <idempotent-methods>
    <method>
```

```
            <ejb-name>TellerEJB</ejb-name>
            <method-intf>Remote</method-intf>
            <method-name>checkBalance</method-name>
            <method-params>
              <method-param>java.lang.String</method-param>
            </method-params>
          </method>
        </idempotent-methods>
      ...
    </weblogic-ejb-jar>
```

By default, stateful session bean instances exist only on the server on which they were created. They can be configured to use in-memory replication, just like the HttpSession object, using the weblogic-ejb-jar.xml deployment descriptor, a topic discussed in Chapter 6. If a stateful session bean is using replication, the stub will be aware of both the primary and secondary copy of the bean but will always route the calls to the primary copy of the bean except in the case of failure. Unlike HttpSession replication, stateful session beans do not require (or support) a routing layer because the stub handles all the routing. Therefore, stateful session bean replication does not use the machinery that redirects a misdirected request in the case of the HttpSession object requests. The change detection mechanism for stateful session beans uses a serialized before and after image to determine the changes that need to be sent to the secondary at the end of the transaction (or method call for nontransactional invocations) because there are no methods by which the server can detect changes to the bean's internal state.

By default, EJB 2.x entity beans use stubs that are cluster-aware; however, entity bean stubs use a sticky routing algorithm to route requests to the cluster. The primary reasons for doing this are to improve the caching capabilities of the server and to reduce transaction propagation across servers in the cluster to improve performance.

In this section, we discussed the details of the WebLogic Server clustering architecture and the application facilities it provides. A thorough understanding of the architecture will help application programmers make good decisions on application design to maximize the benefits of clustering. Administrators should also understand the architecture and its implications when determining production deployment configurations. The next section talks about the admin server and its critical role for the application administrator.

Admin Server

WebLogic Server uses the admin server to configure, manage, and monitor the servers in a domain. The admin server is simply a WebLogic Server with some internally deployed applications that provide administrative capabilities for the entire domain. All servers internally deploy some administrative applications that allow the admin server to send administrative information to them.

The admin server maintains an XML repository of configuration information in the config directory. This directory contains the config.xml file and several subdirectories that can contain other XML files with information about every server, every cluster, every application, and every service deployed in the domain. Although you can edit the config.xml and related files by hand, we strongly recommend that you use the WebLogic Console or other JMX-based tools like the WebLogic Scripting Tool (WLST) to change configuration information.

The typical application deployment model also uses the admin server as the application repository. Under this model, you only need to place the Java EE application package(s) physically on the admin server. You can use the WebLogic Server administration tools to deploy the applications to any server or cluster in the domain. At startup, the managed servers contact the admin server to determine their configuration and download any changes that may exist. In addition, you can deploy applications to a managed server that is already running because the admin server will push the applications out to the managed server and deploy it into the server.

One word of caution: the admin server has a feature known as *auto-deployment* that is enabled when you create a domain using development mode. With this feature, the server watches the autodeploy directory for changes and automatically deploys new or changed applications that it finds there. As discussed in Chapter 5, this feature is useful during development, when the developers are using a single server as both the admin server and the application deployment server. There are several issues with this feature that make it undesirable for any environment other than a single server development environment, however. Before discussing the issues with auto-deployment mode, recognize that disabling auto-deployment mode does not disable hot deployment or redeployment of applications. It only forces the administrator to tell the server when to hot deploy the application via one of the WebLogic Server administration tools (for example, the WebLogic Console).

The first issue with auto-deployment mode is that the admin server will try to deploy a new application only to the admin server. Although this is okay for development on a single server, it is almost never the desired behavior in multi-server environments. The second issue is that there are several limitations to auto-deployment mode, as described at Link 12-3. As such, Oracle recommends that you use the other means to automate deployment, such as the split directory structure and the wldeploy Ant task. We talk more about the split directory structure in Chapter 14.

Fortunately, it is very easy to disable auto-deployment by changing the domain to use production mode. Note that the setDomainEnv scripts created by the WebLogic Configuration Wizard (to be discussed later in this chapter) have an environment variable called PRODUCTION_MODE that controls this feature; set it to true to disable auto-deployment mode.

The WebLogic Console also supports enabling production mode. Simply go to the domain's General Configuration tab, check the Production Mode checkbox, and restart the domain. However, be aware that once you use the WebLogic Console to activate production mode, it adds an entry to config.xml turning on production mode. Once this entry exists, the PRODUCTION_MODE environment variable in the startup script has no effect. To change your domain back to development mode, you must either use the JMX API (for example, by using WLST) or manually edit the config.xml file to either change the value of the entry to false, as shown in the following code, or remove it entirely.

```
<production-mode-enabled>false</production-mode-enabled>
```

We recommend removing it entirely for development mode because that will re-enable the PRODUCTION_MODE environment variable in the setDomainEnv script.

Best Practice

Disable auto-deployment mode for any multiserver environment. Applications
can still be hot deployed using the WebLogic Server administration tools such as
the WebLogic Console even with auto-deployment mode disabled. Even in single
server environments, prefer other mechanisms to automate deployment such as
the split directory structure and the `wldeploy` Ant task.

WebLogic Server uses a two-phase deployment model. In phase 1, the admin server stages the
application by distributing the new application code to each of the target servers and having each
server prepare the application for deployment. Once all target servers complete phase 1, the
admin server tells each target server to activate the application in phase 2. If any failures occur,
the admin server rolls back the activation of the application, giving you the chance to fix the problem
without leaving the application running on some servers but not on others.

As described previously, managed servers typically contact the admin server when they boot to
gather their configuration and application information. In case of an admin server crash, the managed servers will periodically try to contact the admin server until the connection is re-established.

If the admin server is unavailable when a managed server is starting, the managed servers will
start in *managed server independence* (MSI) mode. MSI mode allows a managed server to start up
using its cached copy of the configuration information and applications when the admin server
is not available. When the admin server restarts, the managed server will reconnect to the admin
server, as previously discussed. When this happens, the managed server running in managed server
independence mode will leave this mode and register itself with the admin server for future updates
to its configuration.

Best Practice

Production environments should always use managed server independence,
which is the default.

WebLogic Server supports a flexible deployment model that is configurable via the server's
`Deployment Configuration` tab in the WebLogic Console. The `Staging Mode` parameter controls the
deployment model. The three possible values are:

❑   `stage` — With `stage`, you place the applications on the admin server, and it pushes the
    applications out to the managed servers' staging directories as part of phase 1 of the two-
    phase deployment process.

❑   `nostage` — With `nostage`, the admin server assumes that the files are already available
    to all managed servers via a shared directory. So the admin server does not push the files
    out to the managed servers; rather, it simply tells them to deploy the application from this
    shared directory without copying the files to their staging directory.

❑   `external_stage` — With `external_stage`, the admin server assumes that the files are
    already available in each of the managed servers' staging directories. You are responsible

for making sure that the files in each managed servers' staging directory are up-to-date. At deployment time, the admin server tells each of the managed servers to prepare and deploy the applications from their staging directories.

The default staging mode for managed servers is `stage`; for applications you deploy to the admin server, it uses `nostage`.

Node Manager

The node manager provides a mechanism allowing you to start and force the shutdown of WebLogic Server instances from the WebLogic Console. The admin server depends on the machine definitions for each managed server to know which node manager to contact for a specific server.

WebLogic Server supports two versions of the node manager: a Java node manager and an SSH-based node manager. The SSH node manager started out as a simplified version of the node manager to address the challenges of the Java node manager's requirement for using two-way SSL to communicate with the admin server. In WebLogic Server 9.x and 10.0, the SSH version was the only one that supported some more advanced features (for example, Automatic Whole Server Migration); however, this changed in WebLogic Server 10.3. The SSH version is only supported on Unix-based operating systems. Given that the Java node manager no longer uses two-way SSL, is feature comparable, and provides additional security, we will not discuss the SSH-based node manager in this book. For more information on the SSH-based node manager, please see Link 12-4.

By running the node manager as a daemon process started at machine boot time, the admin server is able to tell the node manager on a remote machine to start or kill a particular WebLogic Server instance. In addition, the node manager monitors the health of the servers for which it is responsible and can restart failed servers — including the admin server itself. This makes the node manager a critical part of any production deployment. By default, WebLogic Server instances allow the node manager to restart them should the JVM process terminate (either because the process dies or because the machine reboots). The node manager can monitor and restart only those servers that it starts. Currently to disable the restart capability of a particular server, you must use the JMX API (or hand edit `config.xml`). The following WLST script shows how you do this.

```
connect('weblogic', 'weblogic1', 't3://127.0.0.1:7001')
edit()
startEdit()
cd ('Servers/AdminServer')
cmo.setAutoRestart(false)
activate()
```

Several additional parameters affect the behavior of this restart capability.

The `Max Restarts Within Interval` parameter tells the node manager the maximum number of times it can automatically restart the server within a specified time interval. Currently, the time interval parameter, formerly known as the `Restart Interval`, is not surfaced in the WebLogic Console so you must use WLST to modify the `RestartIntervalSeconds` attribute on the `ServerMBean` if you want to use an interval other than the default of 3600 seconds. `Restart Delay Seconds` tells the node manager to wait for a period of time before attempting to restart the server. This parameter comes in handy in cases where the underlying operating system does not immediately release

TCP listen ports for reuse — a condition that prevents the server from re-establishing its listen ports upon restart.

WebLogic Server instances monitor their health status by monitoring the status of their critical subsystems. We discuss this in more detail in the "WebLogic Administration Key Concepts" section. The node manager periodically checks the health status of its servers. If any server is in the failed state, the node manager can kill and restart it. To enable the restart of servers in the failed state, use the Auto Kill If Failed checkbox. The Health Check Interval controls the frequency with which the server checks its own health as well as the frequency with which the node manager queries the server for its health status. Remember that the node manager monitors the health of only those servers that it starts.

In this section, we have discussed the important architectural features of the WebLogic Server architecture. This should give you a good fundamental understanding of how the product works and how the pieces fit together. Next, we examine in more detail some important administrative concepts that you will need to understand, before jumping into our discussion of how to administer a WebLogic Server domain.

WebLogic Administration Key Concepts

In the previous section, we discussed the core components of the WebLogic Server architecture. Now, we are ready to talk in more detail about some administrative concepts before jumping into the details of WebLogic Server administration. We begin the discussion by talking about the server life cycle. From there, we proceed to talk in more detail about server self-health monitoring, and we finish up with a discussion of network channels.

Server States

WebLogic Server formally defines the server life cycle. In early versions of WebLogic Server, the server was basically either running or not. This caused two problems for WebLogic Server administrators. First, starting the server involved one long-running step. Depending on the number of applications in use and the required preparation work the server would perform to prepare the applications and services for use, the server could take a very long time to start up to a point where it could start accepting client requests. Second, there was no way to guarantee that the server would process all in-flight requests before shutting down. Other, less obvious problems also existed because the server did not rigorously define the boot order of its subsystems.

Figure 12-5 shows the full server life cycle state transition diagram. The five primary states are *shutdown*, *standby*, *admin*, *running*, and *failed*. A server is in the shutdown state when the JVM process for that server does not exist. When a server first starts up, it initializes itself to a point where it deploys the applications and listens on the administration port, but not on its external listen ports. In standby mode, the server tries to keep its claim on shared resources to a minimum. This allows the server to act as a hot standby in conjunction with a high availability (HA) framework.

For a server to exist in standby mode (rather than just passing through this state on the way to the shutdown or running states), you must enable the domain-wide administration port. The reason for this is simple: if the standby state does not claim the listen port resources, the only way to tell the server to change from the standby state is if it is listening for administrative commands on its administration port.

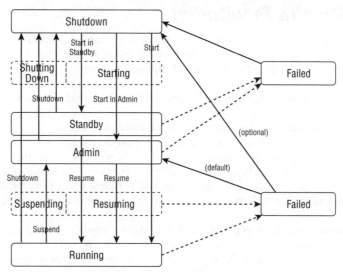

Figure 12-5: Server life cycle state transition diagram.

When a server is in the admin state, it only accepts requests from users in the Admin role. While the WebLogic Console is accessible, all other applications are activated in ADMIN mode which means that only users with the Admin or AppTester roles can submit requests to these applications. This is very valuable in that it allows you to verify that your application is functioning properly before making it available to process end user requests.

Use the resume command to change the state of a server from either the standby or admin state to a running state. The graceful or forceful suspend commands allow you to transition from a running state to the admin state and the graceful or forceful shutdown commands allow you to transition from any of the other states to a shutdown state.

When gracefully shutting down a server, the server passes through standby mode but continues to shut down. There is currently no way to go from running to standby without stopping and restarting the server. When a server is told to shut down gracefully, the server will stop accepting new requests and will continue processing in-flight requests until all requests in its execute queues are complete. Once the server has reached a quiescent state, it will transition itself into the standby mode briefly before continuing to shut itself down. Forcing a server to shut down will not allow any in-flight requests to complete and will cause any in-flight requests to fail.

Once an initializing server reaches the standby state on its way to starting up, it is possible for the server subsystems to fail. If enough of the critical subsystems fail, the server will transition itself into the failed state. At this point, the server process is running, but it is not capable of doing any useful work. A server in the failed state will try to change itself into a non-failed state. If the server fails before reaching the admin state, it will shut itself down. If it fails after reaching the admin state, by default it will simply change back to the admin state; you have the option of having the server shut itself down instead. Fortunately, the node manager can restart servers whose state is failed. For more detailed information on each of the states, please see the WebLogic Server documentation at Link 12-5.

Server Self-Health Monitoring

WebLogic Server subsystems are responsible for monitoring their own status. The criteria each subsystem uses to determine its health status is specific to the particular subsystem. For example, the core server subsystem monitors the health of the default and user-defined work managers. At startup, each subsystem registers itself with the server and specifies whether it is critical to the overall server's operation. Currently, the list of critical subsystems is not configurable and includes systems like RMI, JTA, and core.

The server monitors the health state of each registered subsystem and uses this information to determine the overall health of the server. Currently, the server periodically polls each subsystem to ask for its current health state. The frequency with which the server polls is controlled by the Health Check Interval parameter on the server's Health Monitoring Configuration tab. The health of the server's subsystems is displayed in the server's Health Monitoring tab and available programmatically through the JMX MBean APIs. If any of the server's critical subsystems fail, the server changes its state to failed.

As discussed earlier, WebLogic Server has a notion of stuck threads — threads that have been processing a particular request for longer than a configured amount of time. By default, the server considers a thread stuck if it takes more than 600 seconds to process a single request. What a server does when it determines one or more threads are stuck depends on the server's, its work managers', and its applications' configuration.

Prior to WebLogic Server 9.0, an administrator really had little control over stuck thread behavior. If the server detected a stuck thread, it would log a warning message to its log file and if all execute threads were stuck the server would change its state to failed. A server in the failed state would continue to run until such a time that it was killed and restarted, either automatically by the node manager or manually by an administrator. The Stuck Thread Max Time and Stuck Thread Timer Interval parameters on the server's Tuning Configuration tab are the only controls over this pre-9.0 behavior. Though this behavior is still available, its use is discouraged in favor of the newer mechanisms we discuss next.

WebLogic Server 9.0 introduced more control over stuck thread behavior. Applications, work managers, and servers all have the ability to specify their own stuck thread behavior. At the server level, the server's Overload Configuration tab controls its stuck thread behavior. Max Stuck Thread Time specifies the length of time after which the server considers a thread stuck. If Stuck Thread Count threads become stuck, the server transitions itself to a failed state. Once the server transitions to a failed state, the Failure Action parameter controls what action to take to correct the situation.

Work managers can define how they want to handle stuck threads. At the highest level, a work manager might choose to completely ignore stuck threads. Though this is not something we recommend, it can be useful as a temporary means when porting applications to WebLogic Server that grab hold of execute threads and never release them (for example, for polling purposes). By configuring the offending application component to use its own work manager that ignores stuck threads, you prevent the server from logging these stuck thread warning messages for situations where the application is functioning as expected. Of course, we recommend that you look for ways to restructure your application so it does not grab and hold execute threads for extended periods of time (for example, by using the CommonJ Timer API to schedule periodic work).

Work managers support defining stuck thread behavior using a shutdown trigger. A shutdown trigger tells the work manager that it should shut itself down if there are <stuck-thread-count> threads executing requests on its behalf that are stuck for longer than <max-stuck-thread-time> seconds. At the time of writing, WebLogic Server does not surface work manager shutdown trigger configuration through the WebLogic Console so you must either use other JMX-based tools or hand edit the appropriate work manager definitions. The work manager definition shown here tells the work manager to shutdown if 5 threads are stuck for more than 300 seconds.

```
<work-manager>
  <name>MyStuckThreadWorkManager</name>
  <work-manager-shutdown-trigger>
    <max-stuck-thread-time>300</max-stuck-thread-time>
    <stuck-thread-count>5</stuck-thread-count>
  </work-manager-shutdown-trigger>
</work-manager>
```

In an analogous fashion, enterprise applications support defining stuck thread behavior using an admin trigger. An admin trigger tells the server that it should transition the application into admin mode if there are `<stuck-thread-count>` threads executing requests on its behalf that are stuck for longer than `<max-stuck-thread-time>` seconds. One important difference about the application admin trigger is that it will automatically switch the application back from admin to running mode if the stuck thread condition clears.

You define the admin trigger using the `<application-admin-mode-trigger>` element of the enterprise application's `weblogic-application.xml` deployment descriptor. The admin trigger definition shown here tells the server to put the application into admin mode if 5 threads are stuck for more than 300 seconds.

```
<application-admin-mode-trigger>
  <max-stuck-thread-time>300</max-stuck-thread-time>
  <stuck-thread-count>5</stuck-thread-count>
</application-admin-mode-trigger>
```

Best Practice

Do not set the Max Stuck Thread Time so low that normal requests during peak processing times will be mistaken for stuck threads. Be sure, though, to set them low enough to allow the server to take corrective action before it becomes overwhelmed. For many applications, values on the order of 60 to 120 seconds will be sufficient.

Network Channels

Older versions of WebLogic Server did not support many network configuration options. Server instances could listen on one plain text port and one SSL port. The IP address or DNS name had to be the same across both ports. As a result, the network configuration options available were limited by what the operating system provided naturally for a single TCP port environment. For example, by not specifying a listen address, the server could receive requests sent to the specified port on that machine, regardless of the IP address used to get there. This worked well for supporting machines with a single network interface card (NIC) and one or more IP addresses but it broke down if you tried to use machines with multiple NICs operating on different networks. The server was still able to receive the requests, but it could not always determine the correct IP address to embed in the response data to facilitate the next request reaching the right destination. More recent versions of WebLogic Server support defining additional listen ports (and an associated listen thread) through something called a *network channel*. WebLogic Server allows you to define as many network channels as you want. Use the server's Channels Protocols tab in the WebLogic Console to manage a server's network channels.

A network channel is a conceptual combination of a `Listen Address`, `Listen Port`, and `Protocol` that must be unique within a server. Network channels can share the same address and port number provided that their protocols are different. When this happens, WebLogic Server combines these channels and creates a single listen thread and port that accepts all of the protocols with that address and port number combination. The choice of protocols includes t3, IIOP, HTTP, COM, LDAP, SNMP, t3s, IIOPS, HTTPS, LDAPS, `cluster-broadcast`, `cluster-broadcast-secure`, or admin. WebLogic Server's `cluster-broadcast` protocol supports routing unicast-based cluster messages between servers; `cluster-broadcast-secure` does the same over SSL. The admin protocol is simply a network channel that accepts only administrative requests and requires the use of SSL.

Network channels also support network address translation (NAT) firewalls directly by providing the ability to specify the `External Listen Address` and `External Listen Port` attributes that WebLogic Server should use when communicating with clients through this channel. In addition, each network channel has its own TCP-related configuration parameters that you will find under the `Advanced` area of the channel's `General Configuration` tab in the WebLogic Console.

By providing the ability to define new network channels, WebLogic Server goes a long way toward helping you support the more complex networking requirements often found in production environments. Using network channels is completely optional, however. By default, the server still supports the old model of a single plain text listen port, a single SSL listen port, and an optional domain-wide administration port. This default model is sometimes called the *default channel*; the domain-wide administration port is known as the *administrative channel*. WebLogic Server does not currently allow the default channel to be completely disabled. The good news, though, is that it is possible to disable the plain text listen port on this default channel if the SSL listen port is enabled. If you enable the domain-wide administration port, you must use it or another admin channel instead of the default channel ports for all administrative tasks; however, its use is completely optional.

In the past, WebLogic Server instances in a cluster communicated with each other using the default channel. This made it tedious to separate server-to-server traffic such as replication in its own network because you either had to trick the server into doing this at the individual machines' network configuration level or you had to define network channels explicitly for all your external communications so that the only thing using the default channel was server-to-server traffic. Fortunately, WebLogic Server now supports creating internal channels for communication within a cluster.

To isolate unicast-based cluster heartbeats and JNDI replication traffic to its own network channel, simply create a network channel on each server in the cluster that uses the `cluster-broadcast` protocol; each network channel must have the same name. Then, use the name of the network channel to set the `Unicast Broadcast Channel` property in the cluster's `Messaging Configuration` tab. If you want to secure the cluster's network channel, select the `cluster-broadcast-secure` protocol instead to force the unicast traffic to be sent over SSL.

> **Tip to Remember**
>
> Don't forget that unicast clustering currently requires that you explicitly set the `ListenAddress` on the network channel being used to broadcast cluster messages.

To isolate replication traffic to its own network channel, simply create a network channel on each server in the cluster that uses the t3 or t3s protocol; each network channel must have the same name. Then, use the name of the network channel to set the `Replication Channel` property in the cluster's `Replication Configuration` tab.

We have barely scratched the surface of network administration using network channels. Further reading is available on the Oracle web site at Link 12-6. In the next section, we show an example of using network channels in a WebLogic Server cluster configuration.

In the next three sections, we show the highlights of how to configure, administer, and monitor a WebLogic Server domain and discuss some of the important things to consider. This coverage is intended to provide insights into best practices in WebLogic Server domain configuration, administration, and monitoring, rather than a comprehensive, step-by-step coverage of all of the possible options. For more comprehensive coverage of WebLogic Server administration, please refer to one of the WebLogic Server Administration books available or the WebLogic Server documentation at Link 12-7.

Configuring a WebLogic Server Domain

Determining the best configuration for a particular set of applications requires careful analysis of the applications' resource requirements, service-level agreements, corporate policies, network policies, security policies, and so on. Some of the best practices for choosing production system deployment architectures are covered in Chapter 15 and therefore are not covered here. This section focuses on configuring a typical deployment architecture for a web-based application that also has some Java application and web services clients. Where appropriate, we discuss the available deployment architectures and the things to consider when choosing among the alternatives. The primary purpose of this section, though, is to discuss WebLogic Server domain configuration.

The first thing to do when preparing to configure a WebLogic Server domain is to determine what applications we will need to deploy in the domain. Although there are many things to consider when making this decision, probably one of the most important criteria is whether the same person or group within the organization will be administering all of the applications. The reality is that a WebLogic Server domain is just a logical grouping of WebLogic Server instances, clusters, or both that are controlled through a single administration server. Though it is certainly possible to share a WebLogic Server domain among different sets of administrators, it is typically better for corporate harmony not to do so. Other questions to consider are these:

❏ Do the applications need to interact with one another?

❏ Do the applications share a common security model?

❏ Do the applications need to share critical, but limited resources (for example, connections to legacy system)?

In this section, the example focuses on deploying a single application that has multiple client interfaces. Because there are no other applications to consider, we will create a new domain. The example uses our `bigrez.com` hotel reservation system as the basis for our discussion. Because the `bigrez.com` application doesn't include all features we need for this discussion, we have taken the liberty of assuming that you have extended it to include these other features. In our reservation system, we must support Internet bookings via a web browser–based interface, customer service agent bookings using a Java client application, and web services–based bookings from global reservation systems bookings via a virtual private network (VPN). Although this example certainly won't cover every possible configuration issue, it does attempt to provide a broad overview of common issues you might encounter while configuring a WebLogic Server domain.

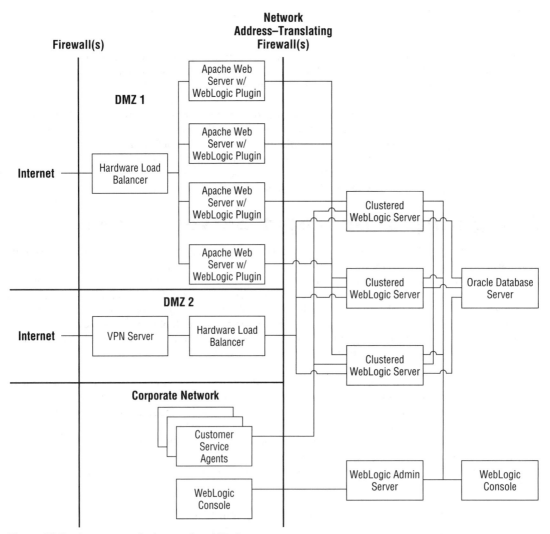

Figure 12-6: `bigrez.com` **deployment architecture.**

Figure 12-6 shows the deployment architecture we chose for this example. The web browser–based Internet requests come in through a firewall to a hardware load balancing device that distributes the requests across the Apache web servers. Using the WebLogic Server Apache plug-in, the Apache web servers proxy requests through a network address–translating firewall to the cluster of WebLogic Server instances. Global reservation systems come into the network through a VPN server. From there, we route the requests through a hardware load balancer and a network address–translating firewall before they finally arrive at our cluster. Because customer service agents use computers connected to the company's internal network, their EJB-based application accesses the servers directly through a network address–translating firewall. The WebLogic Server administrator can also use the WebLogic Console from inside the data center or from any computer connected to the company's internal network through that same network address–translating firewall.

Our configuration assumes that all of the Apache web server and WebLogic Server instances are running on separate machines. The machines running WebLogic Server managed servers have (at least) four separate NICs, one for customers coming in through Apache, one for the global reservation systems coming in through the VPN server, one for corporate users, and one for intra-cluster unicast, replication, and admin traffic. For the purposes of our example, we really do not care which network the database server is on as long as there is connectivity to that network from the application servers.

In Figure 12-6, the admin server is communicating with the managed servers on the same network as the managed servers use for unicast clustering and replication. We could just as easily have separated the admin traffic, the unicast cluster traffic, and the replication traffic each onto different networks. We will use the administrative channel for server administration. We will configure an additional admin network channel that our WebLogic Server administrators can use to access the admin server from the corporate network. Having an administration port accessible from the corporate network may or may not be acceptable in your environment. We believe that this is an acceptable risk given that the administrators may need access to the system at all hours of the night and they already have secure remote access to the corporate network but not to the data center. Now, let's start walking through the process of setting up this configuration and deploying our application.

Setting Up a New Domain

The first step in creating a new domain is to set up and configure the admin server. After installing the WebLogic Server software on the machine where the admin server will reside, you need to create the files that define the admin server. WebLogic Server provides a Configuration Wizard to help create the initial directory structure and configuration files.

On Windows platforms, the WebLogic Configuration Wizard is available through the Windows Start Menu; the `$WL_HOME/common/bin` directory contains the `config` scripts for Windows and Unix. Rather than walking you through creating the domain via the WebLogic Configuration Wizard, we supply a WebLogic Scripting Tool (WLST) script that automates the creation of our domain in the examples that you can download from the book's web site (`http://www.wrox.com`). We discuss WLST in detail in the "Using the WebLogic Scripting Tool" section later in this chapter. This script creates our `bigrezdomain` with an admin server (running on the `AdminMachine`) and a cluster of three managed servers (`Server1`, `Server2`, and `Server3`) running on three machines (`Machine1`, `Machine2`, and `Machine3`) in production mode. In our example, the admin server runs on Windows and the managed servers run on Linux. Though we easily could have included all of the necessary configuration changes we need in this domain creation script, we think that there is value in walking through some of the more important configuration changes. As such, the rest of this section discusses the configuration changes to our domain in detail.

Once the admin server setup is complete, it is time to install the WebLogic Server software and create the configuration files for the managed servers. WebLogic Server provides two command-line utilities, `pack` and `unpack`, that help you create a new managed server directory on a remote machine. These utilities use the same domain templates that the Configuration Wizard uses so they can tailor the managed server's directory contents to different machines with different directory structures, if needed. For more information on these utilities, see Link 12-8.

Most of the time, it is easier just to copy the files needed from the `bigrezdomain` directory from the admin server to the managed servers and edit them as needed. The primary directory of importance for the managed servers is the `bin` directory containing the `setDomainEnv`, `startManagedWebLogic`, and `startWebLogic` scripts — the managed server will create everything else it needs the first time it boots.

Even if you never plan to start or stop the managed server manually using the scripts, you still need to use them to initialize the managed server's directory structure. If you are using a different platform for the managed servers and the admin server, you may need to edit the scripts more extensively. For example, we chose to use the JRockit JVM for the admin server so if the managed servers ran on a platform that does not support JRockit, you would need to edit the scripts to refer to the correct JVM for that platform. Once this process is complete, the next step involves starting the admin server and configuring the domain to match our desired deployment environment.

To make it easy to start the admin server, the Configuration Wizard creates `startWebLogic` shell script files in the admin servers' root directory. Because our admin server will run on a machine using a version of the Microsoft Windows operating system, the relevant shell script file is `startWebLogic.cmd`. Before starting the admin server, we want to configure the server so that you don't have to type in the username and password of the administrative users every time the script is run. The best way to accomplish this is to create the boot identity file; use a text editor to create a two-line `$DOMAIN_HOME/servers/AdminServer/security/boot.properties` file, like the one shown here:

```
# Initial contents of the boot.properties file
username=weblogic
password=weblogic1
```

The next time you start the server it will find the `boot.properties` file and encrypt the username and password property values.

If you are planning to start managed servers using the command-line scripts, you can also create a `boot.properties` file for the managed servers. From the managed server's root directory, simply create the unencrypted `boot.properties` file in the `$DOMAIN_HOME/servers/<server-name>/security` directory. Note that if your managed server's directory does not yet contain the `$DOMAIN_HOME/security/SerializedSystemIni.dat` file, you will need to start the managed server once to initialize its directory structure before it will use the `boot.properties` file. As such, you should start the managed server twice, once to initialize the directory structure and once to encrypt the `boot.properties` file.

Now, start the admin server and bring up the WebLogic Console using your favorite browser. At this stage, we are not ready to go through the network address–translating firewall to our admin server's administration channel or to its admin port (because they have not yet been configured). Therefore, we need to run the console from a machine inside the data center firewalls that can point directly at the admin server's plain text listen port (for example, `http://192.168.1.40:7001/console`). The first thing to do is to obtain your X.509 certificate and configure SSL for the admin server. Because later we enable the domain-wide administration port, the admin server's SSL settings need to be configured properly (actually, all of the managed servers' SSL settings can be configured at this point as well). Don't forget that we need SSL certificates to use with the node managers so plan accordingly. Rather than our covering SSL configuration again here, refer to Chapter 11 for more information on how to do this.

Before moving on to configuring the individual servers, you should configure the domain logging characteristics. Use the domain's `Logging Configuration` tab to verify the `File Name` attribute is set to `logs/bigrezdomain.log` (this should be the default), the `Rotation Type` attribute to `By Time`, and the `Limit Number of Retained Log Files` checkbox to checked. If desired, you can even tell the server to move the old logs to a different location by setting the `Log file rotation directory` property. These changes cause the admin server to place the domain log file in its `logs` subdirectory, rotate the domain log file every day at midnight, and retain only one week's worth of log files. Though in practice the domain log file does not typically grow very quickly unless you configure server log message propagation, it is still a good idea to use log rotation to prevent having to stop the server to remove a large log file that is filling up the file system. In the next section, we enable log rotation for other log files that are more likely to grow very large in a short period of time.

> **Best Practice**
> Always enable log rotation for the domain log file to prevent having to restart the admin server should the log file grow too large.

Configuring Servers

Configuring a WebLogic Server instance is an important part of any WebLogic Server administrator's job. Out of the box, the server comes with a default configuration that will allow you to start it without any additional configuration. Though this default configuration is convenient and contributes much to the ease of use of the product, WebLogic Server has a large number of configuration parameters available to tune the server's behavior for almost any environment. Rather than attempting to cover all of the options, we focus on those parameters that typically require changes from the default values to satisfy production environment requirements. Fortunately, the reservation system example provides us with enough complexity to be able to present these configuration changes in the context of a real-world example.

The first task is to make sure that we properly configure the default network channel. Because the admin server and the managed servers will not be using their default channel SSL listen port, we did not enable the SSL ports of any of the servers when creating the configuration. Check to make sure that the default SSL ports are disabled on the server's General Configuration tab. The Advanced area of the General Configuration tab provides the Local Administration Port Override attribute that allows you to override the domain-wide administration port number for a server. We will not need to do this for our example.

The next item on our list is to configure some of the denial-of-service-related parameters that we discuss more in Chapter 15. Because our example does not use the default channel, we simply set some reasonable defaults for all channels to use. Later, we show you how to configure a channel to use these defaults and how to override these server-level settings for a particular network channel. After talking to our bigrez.com application architects, we know that our customer-facing web application never posts more than a few kilobytes of data and our web service clients never send more than 750 kilobyte messages. As such, we want to limit both the maximum amount of time to receive an entire request's data and the maximum allowable size of a request. Using the HTTP Protocols tab for each managed server, leave the Post Timeout set to the default of 30 seconds and set the Max Post Size to 1,000,000 bytes for all three managed servers. Because the application's Max Post Size is limited to 1,000,000 bytes, limiting the total HTTP message size to 1,200,000 bytes should provide more than enough space to allow all valid HTTP requests to reach the application. Set the HTTP Max Message Size for each managed server to 1,200,000 bytes. Back on the General Protocols tab, you should leave the Complete Message Timeout set to the default of 60 seconds for each of the managed servers. Also, set the Maximum Message Size to 1,200,000.

Several parameters on the server's Tuning Connections tab are important. Accept Backlog controls the length of the underlying TCP/IP listen queue. See Chapter 13 for more information on tuning the length of the listen queue. For now, it is sufficient to understand that this parameter will limit the number of concurrent connection requests to the server. Though the default value of 300 is sufficient for most purposes, you may need to increase this value for servers processing many concurrent HTTP requests to prevent clients from getting "connection refused" errors.

`Login Timeout` is the amount of time the server allows for a newly established connection to start sending request data. In high volume web sites, it may be necessary to increase this parameter to 10 seconds or so to prevent clients from receiving login timed-out errors. Do not set this parameter too high, though, because this could make the server more vulnerable to a denial-of-service attack. For our example, the `SSL Login Timeout` is not important (because we are not using SSL on the default channel), but this parameter serves a similar purpose for SSL connections.

The `Maximum Open Sockets` parameter controls the number of sockets the server can have open at any time. As with the `Accept Backlog` parameter, this parameter provides a mechanism to set a limit that the operating system also controls. A typical use for this parameter would be to limit the number of connections to a server to a number lower than the limit imposed by the operating system. This is one way of throttling requests into the server to prevent overloading the server with so many concurrent requests that the response time for processing a request cannot meet service-level agreements. As previously discussed, setting a capacity constraint on the work manager is probably a better way because doing this will cause the server to return a more meaningful error to the client (for example, an HTTP 503 error indicating that the server is too busy). For this example, we will increase the `Login Timeout` to 10,000 milliseconds (10 seconds). Later, we will create a capacity constraint to prevent server overload.

Because our customer-facing web site is using Apache web servers to proxy requests to our cluster through a NAT firewall, you should set the `WebLogic Plug-in Enabled` attribute for each managed server in the `Advanced` area of the server's `General Configuration` tab. This causes WebLogic Server to return the value of the `WL-Proxy-Client-IP` HTTP header when the application calls the `getRemoteAddr()` method on an `HttpServletRequest` object. By doing this, the application is able to obtain the client information reliably for requests being routed through one of WebLogic Server's web server plug-ins.

Our next task is to configure server logging. Using the servers' `General Logging` tabs, specify the location and name of each server's log file. The `Advanced` area of this tab also controls how verbose the server output to the console window (that is, `stdout`) should be. For the example, the default log file names and `stdout` settings will suffice. We will use the servers' `General Logging` tabs to configure server log rotation. As with the domain log, we will set up server log rotation for all four servers to rotate once a day at midnight and to limit the number of old log files to keep only the log files for the past week. To do this, set the `Rotation Type` to `By Time` and check the `Limit Number of Retained Log Files` checkbox.

Best Practice

Always configure the server and HTTP access logs to use rotation. This will prevent the need to stop the server to remove large log files.

Now, we need to configure HTTP logging for all four of the servers. Using the `HTTP Logging` tab, you can control the format, location, buffering, and rotation of the HTTP access log. The first decision you need to make is whether to use common or extended logging format. Because we want to gather statistical information about site usage, we are going to choose extended logging for the managed servers. The HTTP access log files grow proportionally to the number of requests. This means that the log file sizes can vary greatly depending on the amount of traffic to our web site. Because we hope that our web site will be very popular, we will choose rotation by log file size rather than by time. Though this decision will make it harder to pinpoint a particular day's entries, it will guarantee that you don't end up with a very large log file that could fill up the available disk space, leaving you with no other recourse than to stop and restart the server. Set the Format to extended (under the Advanced area) and the Maximum Log File Size to 10,000 kilobytes.

> HTTP access log files grow proportionally to the number of requests. If you do not configure log rotation properly, the access log file can grow to a very large size and potentially fill up the disk, causing the application and the operating system to stop working. Once this condition is reached, the only way to remove the log file is to stop and restart the application server.

By default, WebLogic Server enables HTTP access logging. Some architectures route all HTTP requests to the cluster through a third-party web server like Apache. Because the web server already creates an HTTP access log, you might want to consider turning off HTTP access logging in WebLogic Server. We will leave it on for our example because we will also receive web service requests that do not pass through our Apache web server.

> **Tip to Remember**
>
> If your WebLogic Server web applications only receive requests from a third-party web server, consider disabling HTTP access logging in WebLogic Server and use the web server's access log instead.

At this point, we are ready to move on to configuring our system for clustering. We have not attempted to cover every possible server option. Some additional parameters are covered in the upcoming sections, and others are covered elsewhere in the book. For a complete discussion of all possible configuration options, refer to the online documentation at Link 12-9.

Configuring the Cluster

The first thing you need to do when setting up a cluster is choose a clustering strategy. As we discussed earlier, WebLogic Server supports both UDP multicast–based and TCP unicast–based clustering with unicast being the WebLogic Console's default for new clusters starting in WebLogic Server 10.0. Multicast clustering is extremely efficient because it leverages low-level network technology to broadcast a message to the entire cluster with a single message send by a WebLogic Server instance. The downside is that multicast requires the operating system and network devices to be properly configured and tuned. If a cluster spans subnets, the routers between the cluster nodes must support UDP message forwarding and the WebLogic Servers must specify a time-to-live (TTL) greater than the number of routers each message must cross using the Multicast TTL attribute under the Advanced area of the cluster's Messaging Configuration tab. Debugging multicast clustering issues can be challenging because many system and network administrators are not familiar with the configuration and tuning parameters for UDP multicast.

When choosing a multicast address and port, it is important to make sure that no other programs on your network are using the same multicast address and multicast port number combination. Although WebLogic Server allows different clusters to share the same multicast address and port number, it is much more efficient, from a server processing standpoint, if they do not. Every server in a cluster must use the same multicast address and multicast port number. Multicast addresses can range from 224.0.0.1 to 244.255.255.255. The general recommendation is to avoid the 224.0.0.x and x.0.0.1 ranges of addresses because these are typically reserved for multicast routing.

Unicast clustering uses TCP/IP sockets to pass cluster messages between members. The benefit of using unicast-based clustering is that it uses TCP/IP sockets; something that system and network administrators should already be very familiar with the details of configuration, tuning, and troubleshooting. To avoid requiring each cluster member to have connectivity to every other cluster member, WebLogic Server uses a group leader strategy whereby the oldest member of the group (in other words, the server that was started first) is designated the group leader. All members of the cluster connect to the group leader so that the group leader acts as the relay point for cluster messages between members. If the group leader goes down, the next oldest member becomes the new group leader.

As you can imagine, the group leader strategy works well for small groups but becomes less efficient as the number of members of the group grows large. As such, WebLogic Server uses a multiple group leader strategy where it limits the number of members in a group to 10. If the cluster is larger than 10 members, WebLogic Server splits into two or more groups, each with their own group leader. The group leaders themselves are all interconnected to minimize the number of hops that a cluster message must traverse to reach all cluster members. Figure 12-7 illustrates this concept, though it is not necessarily representative of the actual group partitioning for a 20 node unicast-based cluster.

Do not try to add the admin server to the cluster. The admin server is not clusterable. We discuss admin server failover later in this chapter.

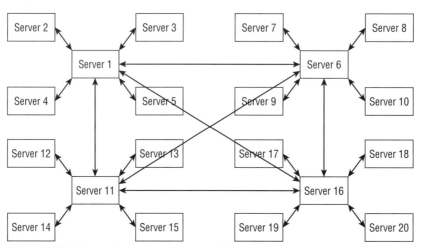

Figure 12-7: Unicast cluster conceptual architecture.

The downside to unicast-based clustering is that as the size of the cluster gets very large, the number of sockets grows large and the burden on the group leaders becomes much higher. If the group leaders become overloaded, this can lead to cluster members dropping out and rejoining the cluster frequently.

As such, we recommend that you consider using multicast-based clustering for very large clusters. As always, you should test whatever clustering mechanism you choose in your environment with your applications under realistic loads to ensure that you system behaves as expected. This is especially important for large, high volume systems!

> **Best Practice**
>
> For very large clusters, prefer multicast-based clustering.

Next, we need to create definitions for the machines on which the managed servers are running. Telling WebLogic Server which servers run on which machines serves two important purposes. First, it lets WebLogic Server be smart about the location of in-memory replicated objects so that it tries to keep copies of the same object on different machines. Because our configuration is currently running only one WebLogic Server instance per machine, this particular aspect is not important in our example. Second, it lets the admin server know which node manager to talk to when starting or stopping a particular managed server. Because our domain configuration WSLT script already created the machines and associated the servers with the machines, you don't need to do anything else.

If we were configuring our system for disaster recovery, we might decide to spread our cluster across two data centers, provided that both data centers were relatively close together and connected by one or more high-speed network links. This type of configuration can support both data centers actively processing requests and allow for failover between data centers. Of course, WebLogic Server clustering does not handle all of the issues involved with setting up this type of environment, such as data replication of backend systems; however, it can support replicating objects between data centers. To accomplish transparent failover of in-memory replicated objects, you need some way to tell WebLogic Server to store the replicated objects' primary and secondary copies in different data centers. Replication groups give you this type of control over how WebLogic Server selects the location of the secondary server.

In our example, we are not considering disaster recovery and do not have any need to control the secondary server selection process. Therefore, we will not set up any replication groups. Before we move on though, let's discuss alternative disaster recovery configurations that use two different clusters instead of one.

Cross-Cluster Replication

In most disaster recovery situations, it is better to create two separate clusters — one in each data center — to provide independent operation of each data center. Cross-cluster replication requires that each cluster be in its own domain; this requirement is no burden. Such a configuration is very desirable because it allows each data center to manage itself independently of the other. This greatly simplifies the application server configuration and administration requirements so that you can adapt your architecture to various levels of cross–data center connectivity. Of course, even this flexibility does not remove all the backend system data replication challenges. As such, it is critical to design the cross–data center application server and backend system architectures together.

As we mentioned earlier in the chapter, WebLogic Server supports two cross-cluster replication models that can be used to replicate HTTP session data between data centers: MAN and WAN replication. Oracle recommends that both domains be identical and have the same cluster and server configurations — including the number of servers per cluster. MAN replication uses the normal in-memory replication except that it always attempts to locate the secondary session on the remote cluster. If connectivity between the data centers is lost, the local cluster will replicate the session within the cluster. On the first request for the session once inter–data center connectivity is restored, WebLogic Server will relocate the session's secondary to the remote cluster.

To configure MAN replication, you first need to set up and configure your local and global load balancers with session affinity, as described in the "Using MAN Replication" section in Chapter 15. Next, you need to enable cross-domain trust between the two WebLogic Server domains, as described in the "Trust Between Domains" section of Chapter 11. Finally, you must configure the `Cross-cluster Replication Type` attribute to `MAN (Synchronous) HTTP Session State Replication` and the `Remote Cluster Address` to point directly to the remote cluster without going through a load balancer. A remote cluster address will be either a DNS name that maps to multiple IP addresses or a comma-separated list of hostnames or IP addresses, such as those shown here. See the "WebLogic Server Client URLs" section of Chapter 10 for a more complete discussion of the URL syntax.

```
t3://remotehost1:7001,remotehost1:8001,remotehost2:7001,remotehost2:8001
t3://remotecluster:7001
```

These attributes are set using the cluster's `Replication Configuration` tab in the WebLogic Console. Optionally, you can define the `Replication Channel` to use for all replication traffic. We talk more about the setting up a replication channel in the "Configuring Network Channels" section.

WAN replication uses the normal intra-cluster, in-memory replication but adds an asynchronous, database-backed replication mechanism to make the session data available to the other data center's cluster should data center–level failover occur. The local server buffers its primary session updates in an in-memory buffer that is periodically flushed. The database-backed replication has two modes of operation:

1. Local cluster periodically flushed the in-memory buffer to its local database. Cross–data center replication is handled externally using some sort of database-level replication technology of your choosing.

2. Local cluster uses RMI to push updates periodically from the in-memory buffer to the remote cluster. The remote cluster writes these updates to its local database.

To configure WAN replication, you first need to set up and configure your local and global load balancers with session affinity just as with MAN replication. If you are planning to use RMI-based data replication (mode 2 in the preceding list), you need to enable cross-domain trust between the two WebLogic Server domains. Next, you need to create the `WLS_WAN_PERSISTENCE_TABLE` in your database and ensure you have a WebLogic Server–managed data source set up for this database.

```
CREATE TABLE WLS_WAN_PERSISTENCE_TABLE (
  WL_ID VARCHAR2(100) NOT NULL,
  WL_CONTEXT_PATH VARCHAR2(50) NOT NULL,
  WL_CREATE_TIME NUMBER(20),
  WL_ACCESS_TIME NUMBER(20),
  WL_MAX_INACTIVE_INTERVAL NUMBER(38),
  WL_VERSION NUMBER(20) NOT NULL,
  WL_INTERNAL_ATTRIBUTE NUMBER(38),
  WL_SESSION_ATTRIBUTE_KEY VARCHAR2(100),
  WL_SESSION_ATTRIBUTE_VALUE LONG RAW,
  PRIMARY KEY(WL_ID, WL_CONTEXT_PATH, WL_VERSION, WL_SESSION_ATTRIBUTE_KEY));
```

Finally, you must configure the `Cross-cluster Replication Type` attribute to `WAN` (Asynchronous) `HTTP Session State Replication` and the `Data Source for Session Persistence` attribute to point the data source previously configured using the cluster's `Replication Configuration` tab. At this point, WebLogic Server will use WAN replication mode 1 and simply flush the session updates to its local database, assuming that you are taking care of making sure that data is available in the remote cluster's database.

To use mode 2, you simply set the `Remote Cluster Address` just as you would if you were using MAN replication. Optionally, you can define the `Replication Channel` to use for all replication traffic.

In the `Advanced` area of the cluster's `Replication Configuration` tab, you control the flushing behavior for the in-memory buffer. The `Session Flush Interval` controls the interval at which session updates are flushed; the default is set to 180 seconds. To protect the server from memory overload, the server flush updates sooner if the number of buffered session updates reaches the `Session Flush Threshold` value.

For more information on cross-cluster replication, see the WebLogic Server documentation at Link 12-10. We discuss disaster recovery considerations and options in more detail in Chapter 15. At this point, we are ready to move on and discuss configuring network channels.

Configuring Network Channels

Our application uses three distinct networks to segment different types of user traffic and one for internal traffic. Using network channels, you can control the network resources, protocols, and tuning parameters of each network independently. Our example is not using the default channel. So, we need to configure three additional channels for user traffic: the `bigrez.com` web site (BigRez) channel, the global reservation systems (GRS) channel, and the internal customer service agents (CSA) channel. To create a network channel, you need to specify the name, listen address and port, cluster address, and protocol that the channel will support.

In this example, the BigRez channel will support only the HTTP protocol because all requests on this channel will be proxied requests from our Apache web servers using HTTP. Because we are using a NAT firewall, we need to set the `External Listen Address` attributes on each managed server. We will use an `External Listen Port` value of 80. The BigRez network channel listen addresses used by each server are shown in Table 12-1.

Next, you will want to tune the settings of the BigRez channel using the `Advanced` area of the channel's `General Configuration` tab. You should make sure that the `Accept Backlog`, `Login Timeout`, `Complete Message Timeout`, and `Idle Connection Timeout` attributes are set to reasonable values. For our example, we will set all four attributes to −1, which tells the network channel to use the server's (in other words, the default channel's) settings. Because server-to-server communication may use network channels and multiple channels may be available, WebLogic Server uses the `Channel Weight` setting to define the preferred channel(s) between two servers. The `Outgoing Enabled` checkbox allows us to enable the initiation of server-to-server communication over a particular channel. `bigrez.com` will not use the BigRez channel for server-to-server communication (all server-to-server communication will use our internal channels) so you should leave the `Outgoing Enabled` checkbox unchecked. Because the BigRez channel is not used for EJB communication, the `Cluster Address` setting is not important. You should, however, adjust the `Maximum Message Size` to a reasonable value based on the application's needs. Because our BigRez channel is transmitting HTTP requests from our public web site that we know to be very small, we will override the server's default channel setting to limit HTTP message sizes to no more than the maximum size expected from our customer web site. After consulting with our application architects, we know that no request from customer web site will ever be larger than 5 KB, so you should set the maximum message size to 10,000 bytes.

Table 12-1: Managed Servers' BigRez Channel Listen Addresses

Server Name	Internal Listen Address	External Listen Address
Server1	192.168.155.41	10.10.1.41
Server2	192.168.155.42	10.10.1.42
Server3	192.168.155.43	10.10.1.43

Table 12-2: Managed Servers' GRS Channel Listen Addresses

Server Name	Internal Listen Address	External Listen Address
Server1	206.168.1.41	10.12.1.41
Server2	206.168.1.42	10.12.1.42
Server3	206.168.1.43	10.12.1.43

Now, we need to create the GRS channel. Create the GRS channel using the internal and external listen addresses from Table 12-2. We will use the same tuning recommendations we applied to the BigRez channel except for Maximum Message Size. Because the GRS channel will carry web service requests from our global reservation system partners whose size we already accounted for when setting the Maximum Message Size for the default channel, set the GRS channel value to –1 to use the default channel setting.

At this point, we are ready to set up the CSA channel that our internal customer service agents will use. Because the Java client application uses RMI to talk with the cluster, the CSA channel will need to support only the t3 protocol.

Now that we understand what needs to be done to support our CSA channel, go ahead and set up the network channel to support only the t3 protocol and deploy it to the cluster. Use the information in Table 12-3 to configure the CSA channel for each managed server. Use the default value for all other parameters.

Next, we want to set up our internal channels for unicast cluster messages and replication. To create a channel for unicast messaging, simply create a channel with its protocol set to cluster-broadcast. If you want to secure these unicast messages between cluster members, you can use the cluster-broadcast-secure protocol. Be forewarned that using SSL to encrypt cluster messages comes with a significant overhead and should be used only when security is more important than performance and scalability. If you choose to use secure cluster messaging, you need to load test your environment using your actual applications with realistic peak loads to ensure that the cluster will hold together under stress with your existing hardware. Use the settings in Table 12-4 to create the Clustering channel.

Table 12-3: CSA Network Channel Configuration Parameter Values

Name	Value
Name	CSA Channel
Protocol	t3
Listen Address	206.11.1.41 for Server1
	206.11.1.42 for Server2
	206.11.1.43 for Server3
Listen Port	7001
External Listen Address	10.11.1.41 for Server1
	10.11.1.42 for Server2
	10.11.1.43 for Server3
External Listen Port	7001
Cluster Address	10.11.1.41:7001,10.11.1.42:7001,10.11.1.43:7001
HTTP Enabled for This Protocol	No (unchecked)
Maximum Message Size	100,000

To make WebLogic Server use a separate channel for replication, you must create a channel on each managed server in the cluster with the same name and then configure the cluster to use that channel for replication. Create the Replication channel using the settings in Table 12-5. Note that you can specify a secure protocol for replication as well. Be forewarned that this will have a direct impact on user response times because in-memory replication is done during the normal request processing. The expense of encrypting replication is directly proportional to the size of your session updates that the server must serialize to the other cluster member and the number of requests (since the server must update the last access time on the other server even for read-only session access). Once the replication channel config-uration is complete, use the cluster's `Replication Configuration` tab to set the `Replication Channel` attribute to the name of your replication channel.

The last step is to set up an additional network channel for the admin server that only supports the admin protocol. Once we do this, all admin traffic must use SSL and we are not ready for this just yet. We define this network channel in the "Administration Port and Channel Configuration" section.

At this point, our network channel configuration is complete and we are ready to move on to the node manager. The configuration of the node manager is relatively simple but debugging problems with the node manager can be tricky. In the next section, we try to point out all of the things to be aware of in order to avoid such problems as well as try to describe the debugging process.

Table 12-4: Clustering Network Channel Configuration Parameter Values

Name	Value
Name	Clustering Channel
Protocol	cluster-broadcast
Listen Address	192.168.1.41 for Server1
	192.168.1.42 for Server2
	192.168.1.43 for Server3
Listen Port	7777
External Listen Address	None
External Listen Port	None
HTTP Enabled for This Protocol	No (unchecked)

Table 12-5: Replication Network Channel Configuration Parameter Values

Name	Value
Name	Replication Channel
Protocol	T3
Listen Address	192.168.1.41 for Server1
	192.168.1.42 for Server2
	192.168.1.43 for Server3
Listen Port	7778
External Listen Address	None
External Listen Port	None
HTTP Enabled for This Protocol	No (unchecked)

Setting Up the Node Manager

The node manager is a daemon process that provides remote server start and stop capabilities, monitors the health of its servers, and allows for automatic restart of failed servers. As such, we recommend installing and configuring the node manager on all machines where WebLogic Server instances will run. WebLogic Server provides two versions of the node manager: one is Java-based and the other is shell script–based. The primary benefit of the script-based node manager is that it relies on SSH for security rather than requiring SSL configuration like the Java-based node manager. However, the script-based node manager does not work on Windows and has several other limitations. As such, we focus our attention on the Java-based node manager. For more information about configuring the script-based node manager, see the WebLogic Server documentation at Link 12-11.

Typically, we recommend installing the node manager so that it starts up when the machine boots. On Windows, this means installing it as a Windows service. On Unix, it generally means writing a boot script to run the node manager start script as the correct user with the correct environment. The Java-based node manager can work in conjunction with `inetd` on Unix-based platforms automatically to restart the node manager upon first access.

Because the managed servers in our example all run in a Unix environment, we will focus primarily on installing and configuring the node manager on a Unix-based operating system. We try to point out places where the process is significantly different under Windows. Our downloadable example also has a node manager set up for our admin server running on Windows. For more complete information, please refer to the WebLogic Server online documentation at Link 12-12.

The first thing you need to do is determine the location from which the node manager will run. Because the default location for the node manager is under the `$WL_HOME/common/nodemanager` directory, we recommend creating a separate directory outside the WebLogic Server software install directory to run the node manager. We will choose to create a directory called `/powls/ch12/Machine#/NodeManager`, where # is either 1, 2, or 3, on each of the three machines where managed servers will run. Now, copy the `$WL_HOME/server/bin/startNodeManager.sh` file (`startNodeManager.cmd` on Windows machines) to the newly created `NodeManager` directory. Edit your copy of the `startNodeManager` script to set the `NODEMGR_HOME` environment variable to the script's current directory.

The `startNodeManager` script takes two arguments: the listen address and the listen port. We could create completely customized scripts to invoke the `startNodeManager` script with proper arguments for each machine. The node manager also looks for a property file called `nodemanager.properties` in the `NODEMGR_HOME` directory for configuration information. If this file doesn't exist, the node manager creates it the first time it is started. By adding the following lines to each node manager's property file, you do not need to create three separate scripts. The `nodemanager.properties` file for `Machine1` looks like this:

```
PropertiesVersion=10.3
ListenPort=5556
ListenAddress=192.168.1.41
```

Rather than do this for our example, we will start node manager using the command-line arguments. Before you do that, let's create another file that the node manager uses for other configuration information.

The node manager optionally uses a `nodemanager.domains` file to specify the list of domains that it controls and a mapping between the domain name and its root directory on the machine. As you see later, this makes it easier for standalone clients (for example, WLST scripts starting the admin server) because they no longer need to specify the domain directory. For our example, create a `nodemanager.domains` file in the `/powls/ch12/Machine1/NodeManager` directory with the following contents.

```
bigrezdomain=/powls/ch12/Machine1/bigrezdomain
```

Now, start the node manager on `Machine1` by running the following command.

```
./startNodeManager.sh 192.168.1.41 5556
```

This should create a `nodemanager.properties` with all the proper settings for `Machine1`. Repeat the process for `Machine2` and `Machine3`. Once the node manager starts successfully, shut it down because we have more work to do before we finish with the node manager!

The admin server can use either one-way SSL or plain text sockets to communicate with the node manager. In a real production environment, you should always configure SSL and use real certificates tied to each machine and configure the node manager to use its machine's certificates and private keys. Rather than our repeating the discussion of SSL configuration here, please refer to Chapter 11. Once you have SSL configured, you can use the `nodemanager.properties` file to tell the node manager to use SSL and point it to the identity keystore. For our example, you simply add the following lines to specify the node manager's SSL configuration for `Machine1`:

```
KeyStores=CustomIdentityAndCustomTrust
CustomIdentityKeyStoreFileName=Machine1_KeyStore.jks
CustomIdentityKeyStorePassPhrase=server_store_password
CustomIdentityKeyStoreType=JKS
CustomIdentityAlias=server_key
CustomIdentityPrivateKeyPassPhrase=server_key_password
```

The next time you start the node manager it will replace the clear text passwords in the property file with encrypted versions.

Best Practice

Always obtain, install, and configure server-specific SSL certificates and enable SSL hostname verification for node managers running in a production environment. Failing to do so can compromise the security of your applications.

By default, the node manager requires authentication to start, stop, and restart servers. The first time you start the node manager, it communicates with the admin server to download the username and password that will be used by the admin server to authenticate to the node manager. You can do this explicitly using WLST's `nmEnroll()` command. This username and password are randomly generated by the admin server. All node managers associated with the domain will use the same username and password. The node manager stores a hashed value of this data in the domain directory's `config/nodemanager/nm_password.properties` file. To change the username and password, use the `Advanced` area of the domain's `General Security` tab to set the `NodeManager Username`, `NodeManager Password`, and `Confirm NodeManager Password` fields for the entire domain. Setting these through the console will synchronize the change across all of the node managers' `nm_password.properties` files.

Next, you need to configure the node manager settings in the WebLogic Console. These settings are split between settings that apply to the node manager on a specific machine and those that contain information the node manager needs to start each individual server on the machine. Using the WebLogic Console, navigate to the machine settings for `Machine1` and select the `Node Manager Configuration` tab. You should see that the `Listen Address` is set to 192.168.1.41 and the `Listen Port` is set to 5556. If not, set these values appropriately for each of the three machines.

The next step is to set the server-specific settings. There are two approaches to providing this information: via the node manager environment or via the server's configuration in the domain. For situations where your node managers are managing one or more servers with identical configurations, customizing the node manager's environment to provide all of the configuration information might be a reasonable approach. For any more complex environments, this quickly becomes unmanageable. Typically, different servers require different JVM tuning parameters, classpath settings, and patch levels because of different applications' requirements.

Using the `Server Start Configuration` tab of each of the managed servers, you can tell the node manager everything it needs to know to start the server with the proper configuration. Though most of the remote start attributes are self-explanatory, we will take a minute to review them because debugging problems with starting servers via the node manager can be frustrating. The server's remote start attributes are as follows:

Java Home The full path to the JDK installation directory on the node manager's machine that will be used to start the server. This parameter must be set such that appending `/bin` to the value of this parameter will give the server the fully qualified directory path to the Java Virtual Machine executable. Typically, this would be set to something like `c:\Oracle\Middleware\jdk160_11` or `/oracle/middleware/jrockit_160_11_R27.6.3-40`, depending on the operating system and where you installed the WebLogic Server software.

Java Vendor The name of the company that makes the JVM. At the time of writing, the valid settings are `Oracle` (or `BEA` for previous WLS versions) for JRockit and `Sun`, `HP`, `IBM`, and `Apple` for their respective JVMs. To determine the current list of applicable values, please refer to the `setDomainEnv` script in the `bin` subdirectory of domain's root directory.

BEA Home The full path to the Oracle software installation directory on the node manager's machine. This directory is also known as the *Oracle Middleware Home* starting in WLS 11g. Typically, this would be set to something like `c:\oracle\middleware` or `/oracle/middleware` depending on the operating system and where you installed the WebLogic Server software.

Root Directory The full path to the domain's root directory on the node manager's machine. The value of this parameter will affect the location of all relative directory and file names. For example, if the root directory is set to `/powls/ch12/Machine1/bigrezdomain` and the server's log file is set to `logs/Server1.log`, the server's log file will be `/powls/ch12/Machine1/bigrezdomain/servers/Server1/logs/Server1.log`. Typically, this would be set to something that includes the WebLogic Server domain name, such as `/powls/ch12/Machine1/bigrezdomain`.

Classpath The complete Java classpath that WebLogic Server requires to start your applications. In most cases, the only things that need to be in the classpath are the JRE's `tools.jar`, the WebLogic Server's `weblogic.jar`, and any JDBC driver's classes or `.jar` files. You should always question developers who require application classes in the server's classpath because this will prevent hot redeployment of these classes with the application.

Arguments The JVM arguments to use to start the managed server on the node manager machine. Typical things to set here are the Java HotSpot Compiler options (for example, `-server`), the JVM heap size (for example, `-Xms32m -Xmx200m`), garbage collection tuning parameters, and any Java system properties required by WebLogic Server or your applications.

Security Policy File The fully qualified name to the Java security policy file to use to start the managed server on the node manager's machine. Typically, it is sufficient to use WebLogic Server's default policy file (for example, `/oracle/middleware/wlserver_10.3/server/lib/weblogic.policy`).

Username   The administrative username to use to start and stop the server and perform other administrative operations. In our examples, we use the username `weblogic` as the administrative user because this has become the de facto standard for development environments. You should always choose a different administrator name for your production environments.

Password   The password of the administrative user that corresponds to the supplied `Username` parameter's value. In our examples, we use the password `weblogic1`. Always choose strong passwords for your production systems' administrative users.

In general, explicitly configuring each server's start parameters is preferred over the node manager environment approach; however, there is one use case that requires some additional consideration.

WebLogic Server provides a feature called *whole server migration*. We discuss whole server migration in detail later in the "WebLogic Server Failures" section, but this feature supports migrating a WebLogic Server instance from one machine to another in case of machine failure. For servers configured to use whole server migration, that means that their server start parameters have to work on more than one machine. If all the machines involved are running the same operating system with the same directory structures, this normally isn't a problem. If the directory structures aren't the same or the operating systems are different, it may not be possible to provide a single set of start parameters that work across the set of machines in question.

If you find yourself in this situation, there are a couple of approaches to address the issue. First, you can combine two approaches such that you specify the machine-dependent configuration options in the node manager's environment. For example, if the JVM location is different for each machine, do not set the `Java Home` parameter in the `Server Start Configuration` tab and rely on the `JavaHome` parameter value in the `nodemanager.properties` file to get the right JVM location. Though this approach may work for simple situations, anything more complex requires a different solution. Fortunately, the Java-based node manager also supports starting and stopping the servers using scripts. Simply modify the `nodemanager.properties` file to set the `StartScriptEnabled` or `StopScriptEnabled` property to `true` and the `StartScriptName` or `StopScriptName` property to point to your script file. This allows you to completely customize your start and stop configuration logic to fit the needs of your environment.

> **Best Practice**
>
> Explicitly configure all remote start attributes for a managed server rather than relying on the node manager's environment for a managed server's configuration. If your deployment environment is heterogeneous and uses whole server migration, have the node manager use custom start and stop scripts tailored to your environment.

After doing the configuration work just described for each of the three machine's node managers, you are ready to start the node managers on the three machines by running the `startNodeManager` scripts on each machine. When you first start the node manager on a particular machine, it will create a `nodemanager.log` file in the node manager's configured home directory. You should look through this file to make sure that the node manager started up properly and that there were no warnings or errors. This file becomes extremely important when running the node manager as a daemon process (for example, a Windows service) where the `stdout` and `stderr` output streams are not visible.

Once the node managers start, you can use each server's `Start/Stop Control` tab to start the managed servers. Because the server runs in the background, you must use log files to troubleshoot any problems with the server configuration. Fortunately, when using the node manager, WebLogic Server captures the `stdout` and `stderr` output streams of the server and writes them to disk. WebLogic Server creates this file in the server's logs directory with a name of `<server-name>.out`. This file allows you to determine why the server failed to start if the server fails before it begins writing to its own log file. Note that there is no way to limit the size of this file or automatically rotate it. To reduce the size of the file, you must stop the server, remove the file, and restart. As such, it is important that your applications do not print information to `stdout` or `stderr`. Also, you should set the `Standard out` logging destination's `Severity Level` to `Critical` (or higher) using the `Advanced` area of the server's `General Logging` tab to limit the amount of output to this file to only that which is required.

> **WebLogic Server instances started with the node manager redirect `stdout` and `stderr` to `$DOMAIN_HOME/servers/<server-name>/logs/<server-name>.out`. It is important for production applications to limit the amount of output to this file since there is no way to reduce the size of this file without stopping the server.**

WebLogic Server currently requires that the node manager start all servers that it monitors. Both the admin server and WLST can tell the node manager to start or stop a server. Allowing WLST to talk directly to the node manager to start a server has two primary benefits. First, it allows the node manager to start, monitor, and, when necessary, restart the admin server itself. Second, it allows WLST to start managed servers when the admin server is down; the managed servers will start in managed server independence (MSI) mode. As discussed previously, MSI mode allows you to start a managed server with a cached copy of its configuration when the admin server is unavailable. This is the preferred way of starting managed servers in MSI mode because it allows the node manager to monitor them in MSI mode and after the admin server comes back up and they switch to back to their normal mode of operation — all without requiring you to restart the managed server.

To start the admin server using the node manager, we need to do two additional tasks above and beyond what we have already done to set up the managed servers' node managers. First, we need to change the domain's node manager username and password to something that we know. By default, WebLogic Server generates a random username and password for the node managers; this works fine as long as only the admin server needs to communicate with the node manager. To allow WLST to connect to the node manager directly, we must supply the correct username and password. Using the domain's `General Security` tab, open the `Advanced` area of the page and change the `NodeManager Username` and the `NodeManager Password`. Don't forget to supply the same password in the `Confirm NodeManager Password` attribute. For our example, we chose to use `weblogic` and `weblogic1` as the node manager username and password for simplicity; however, there is no requirement that the username and password match any user defined within the WebLogic Server security domain.

Next, we need to tell WLST to trust the node manager's X.509 certificate that it presents during the SSL handshake. The easiest way to do this is to edit the WLST start script. Copy the `$WL_HOME/common/bin/wlst.cmd` file to a convenient location (we chose `c:\powls\ch12\AdminMachine\NodeManager\wlst.cmd`) and add the following arguments to end of the line that sets the `JVM_ARGS` environment variable.

```
-Dweblogic.security.TrustKeyStore=CustomTrust
-Dweblogic.security.CustomTrustKeyStoreFileName=C:\\powls\\ch12\cacerts
-Dweblogic.security.CustomTrustKeyStorePassPhrase=changeit
```

Now, we are ready to start WLST by running our edited `wlst.cmd` script file. To connect to the node manager, we run the `nmConnect()` command shown here.

```
nmConnect('weblogic', 'weblogic1', '192.168.1.40', '5556', 'bigrezdomain')
```

The `nmConnect()` command above includes the administrative user's username and password in clear text. To eliminate this, WLST supports storing the user credentials in an encrypted file, known as the *user configuration file*, and passing in its file name rather than the username and password.

After connecting to the node manager, tell it to start the admin server using the `nmStart()` command shown here.

```
nmStart('AdminServer')
```

For more details on WLST and how to create and use the user configuration file, see the "Using the WebLogic Scripting Tool" section later in the chapter.

Before we move on, create your customized WLST start scripts on each of the managed server machines. Note that you don't need to reset the node manager username and password again because all node managers in the domain use the same credentials. Having these customized scripts available for each machine prepares your environment should you need to start the managed servers in MSI mode.

Now that our node managers are configured and working, we move on to discuss configuring the final pieces of our architecture. Namely, the operating system, JVM, and web server plug-in.

Operating System Configuration

Configuring the operating system is an important part of setting up any WebLogic Server deployment. RMI-based applications feature long-lived connections between the clients and the servers, whereas HTTP-based applications feature short-lived connections. Because operating systems represent each connection as a file descriptor, the number of available file descriptors effectively controls the number of client connections. To conserve resources, many operating systems have a default configuration that supports only a relatively small number of file descriptors per process. Though this is fine for many types of applications, it can prove to be a limiting factor with large, server-based applications. Fortunately, most operating systems allow the system administrator to tune the maximum number of file descriptors per process.

In addition to the actual number of file descriptors a process can allocate, processes that open and close a lot of short-lived connections are vulnerable to another related operating system implementation detail. Without going into the details of the TCP/IP protocol, the problem is that the operating system must keep information about a closed TCP socket connection for some period of time. During this period of time, the operating system still considers the file descriptor for this connection to be active and therefore counts it in the process's total number of file descriptors. As you might imagine, applications that open and close a lot of connections in a relatively short period of time (for example, HTTP-based applications) can quickly consume many more file descriptors than you would normally expect given the number of concurrent connections. Fortunately, the period of time that the operating system holds on to these closed connection file descriptors is tunable in most operating systems. Although the name of this parameter varies across operating systems, it is generically known as the *TCP time wait interval*.

From this short discussion of some fundamental operating system concepts and how they affect server-based applications, we hope that it is clear why it is critical to verify the operating system configuration before deploying a production application. Though the details of all possible tuning parameters and operating systems are well beyond the scope of this book, we talk more about operating system tuning in Chapter 13. We highly recommend consulting the WebLogic Server Performance Tuning Guide at Link 12-13 for more detailed recommendations on tuning any particular operating system.

Java Virtual Machine Configuration

Java Virtual Machine (JVM) tuning is another important configuration task for a WebLogic Server administrator. Choosing the right JVM, selecting the right JIT or HotSpot compiler options, selecting the appropriate heap size settings, and tuning the garbage collector are critical to the performance, scalability, and reliability of WebLogic Server–based applications. Although an in-depth discussion of the options is beyond the scope of this chapter, we recommend reading through the "Java Virtual Machine Tuning" section of Chapter 13, reviewing the recommendations on the Oracle and JVM vendors' web sites, and talking with other experienced developers and administrators on the Oracle public newsgroups (see Link 12-14).

Web Server Plug-in Configuration

The final topic in this section is configuring the WebLogic Server web server plug-ins to proxy requests to a WebLogic Server instance or cluster (see Figure 12-3). WebLogic Server supports web server proxy configurations with several different third-party web servers (that is, Oracle HTTP Server, Sun Java System Web Server, Microsoft Internet Information Server, and the Apache Web Server) as well as from another instance of WebLogic Server itself. For the third-party web servers, the proxy support uses a web server plug-in, written to the native extension API of the web server (for example, ISAPI for Microsoft's Internet Information Server), to proxy requests to WebLogic Server. A built-in servlet class, `weblogic.servlet.proxy.HttpClusterServlet`, provides the functionality when using WebLogic Server as the proxy. Though a full discussion of all of the configuration options across all of the different supported web servers is beyond the scope of this book, we cover some of the important points in the context of the Apache web server plug-in configuration. Although the configuration details for each plug-in vary, the general concepts are similar across all web server plug-ins. We believe that the discussion will still be useful even when not using Apache. For more complete and detailed coverage of web server plug-in configurations, please see the WebLogic Server documentation on the Oracle web site at Link 12-15.

In this example, we use the Apache web server, so we will focus on the details of configuring the Apache plug-in. Some knowledge of Apache is useful when configuring the plug-in, but we will try our best to cover the trickier aspects of plug-in configuration without assuming too much prerequisite knowledge. For more complete information about the Apache web server, or to download a copy of the software, please see the Apache web server web site at `http://httpd.apache.org`.

The first step in configuring any plug-in is to install the WebLogic Server plug-in's native libraries and tell the web server to load them. For Apache, this means copying the appropriate shared library to a directory that Apache can find and adding the `LoadModule` directive to the Apache configuration file. Before you do anything, you need to verify WebLogic Server plug-in support for your version of Apache and verify that your version of Apache includes support for Dynamic Shared Objects. Please refer to the WebLogic Server documentation at Link 12-16 for more information on the versions of Apache that WebLogic Server currently supports. To determine whether your version of Apache supports Dynamic Shared Objects, you need to run the server with the -1 option. Change directories to the $APACHE_HOME/bin directory and run the apache2ctl -1 command; the output should look similar to the following snippet and must include mod_so.c. If it does not, please refer to the WebLogic Server Apache plug-in documentation (Link 12-17) or the Apache web server documentation (http://httpd.apache.org/docs/) for procedures for enabling this support.

```
> apache2ctl -l
Compiled in modules:
  core.c
  mod_authn_file.c
  mod_authn_default.c
  mod_authz_host.c
  mod_authz_groupfile.c
  mod_authz_user.c
  mod_authz_default.c
  mod_auth_basic.c
  mod_include.c
  mod_filter.c
  mod_log_config.c
  mod_env.c
  mod_setenvif.c
  prefork.c
  http_core.c
  mod_mime.c
  mod_status.c
  mod_autoindex.c
  mod_asis.c
  mod_cgi.c
  mod_negotiation.c
  mod_dir.c
  mod_actions.c
  mod_userdir.c
  mod_alias.c
  mod_so.c
```

Next, you need to locate the plug-in shared library for the operating system on which Apache is running. The operating system–specific subdirectories under the $WL_HOME/server/plugin directory contain the different plug-in shared libraries. The name of the plug-in varies depending on the version of Apache it supports and the operating system, but it always begins with mod_wl and ends with a shared library extension (for example, so or sl). Please consult the WebLogic Server Apache plug-in documentation for the correct shared library name for a particular platform and version of Apache.

Our example will use Apache 2.2.11 running on 64-bit Linux. Copy the mod_wl_22.so file from the $WL_HOME/server/plugin/linux/x86_64 directory to the $APACHE_HOME/modules directory, which, in our case, is /usr/local/apache2/modules. Locate the httpd.conf file (in the $APACHE_HOME/conf directory) and add the following line at the end of the file:

```
LoadModule weblogic_module modules/mod_wl_22.so
```

At this point, it is a good idea to save these changes and try to restart the server. Run the following command to restart the server (replace `restart` with `start` if the server is not already running):

```
> Apache -k restart
```

To proceed further, you need more information about the application. The example reservation system application will use the Apache web server only for customer self-service bookings. Although we won't be exploring the details of the application until the next section, we will assume that you know from your development staff that you want to redirect all requests to your web site to your WebLogic Server cluster. To do this, you use the `Location` directive in conjunction with the `SetHandler` directive to tell Apache that all requests whose URLs match a particular pattern should be handled by the WebLogic Server plug-in. Add the following lines to the end of the `httpd.conf` to accomplish this:

```
<Location /*>
    SetHandler weblogic-handler
</Location>
```

Of course, this means that Apache will delegate every request to the WebLogic Server plug-in. In many cases, you may not actually want this. For our example application, we simply want to proxy `/user` and `/admin` to our cluster. To do this, we simply add the Location directives shown here:

```
<Location /user>
    SetHandler weblogic-handler
</Location>

<Location /admin>
    SetHandler weblogic-handler
</Location>
```

The plug-in also supports proxying requests by MIME type through the use of the `IfModule` directive in conjunction with the `MatchExpression` directive. Because our use of Apache is simple, you won't need to do this, so we suggest reviewing the WebLogic Server Apache plug-in documentation for more information on how to set this up.

At this point, you have configured Apache to send all requests that begin with `/user` and `/admin` to the plug-in, but how does the plug-in know what to do with the requests once they arrive? You need to tell the plug-in where to send the requests that it receives. To do this, use either the `WebLogicHost` and `WebLogicPort` directives or the `WebLogicCluster` directive, depending on whether you are forwarding to a single server instance or a cluster. We are forwarding requests to the cluster, so you must use the `WebLogicCluster` directive. Before you do this, however, you need to remember that we are using a NAT firewall between Apache and the WebLogic cluster. Therefore, we need to use the external IP addresses of the firewall instead of the actual (internal) IP addresses so that the plug-in can reach the servers. Let's modify the Location directive to add the `WebLogicCluster` directive with the external IP addresses and port number of our cluster.

```
<Location /user>
    SetHandler weblogic-handler
    WebLogicCluster 10.10.1.41:80,10.10.1.42:80,10.10.1.43:80
</Location>
<Location /admin>
```

```
        SetHandler weblogic-handler
        WebLogicCluster 10.10.1.41:80,10.10.1.42:80,10.10.1.43:80
</Location>
```

This completes the basic setup of the Apache plug-in for our simple application. The WebLogic Server plug-ins offer a wide variety of possible configurations and parameters to modify a plug-in's behavior. Though the WebLogic Server documentation covers these in great detail, we cover a few of the most commonly used parameters. The first set of parameters is as follows:

PathTrim   This parameter tells the plug-in to strip off a leading portion of the requested URL before forwarding the request to WebLogic Server.

PathPrepend   This parameter tells the plug-in to add to the leading portion of the requested URL before forwarding the request to WebLogic Server.

DefaultFileName   This parameter tells the plug-in what the default file name should be for URLs that end with /.

The parameters should be self-explanatory, but let's look at an example. Imagine that the request coming from the browser is for `http://www.oracle.com/wls/`. If our `PathTrim` is set to `/wls`, our `DefaultFileName` is set to `index.html`, and our `PathPrepend` is set to `/weblogic`, the plug-in will apply the following steps, in order, to transform the URL before sending it on to WebLogic Server.

1. The plug-in applies the `PathTrim` value to convert the relative URL from `/wls/` to `/`.

2. The plug-in applies the `DefaultFileName` value to convert the relative URL from `/` to `/index.html`.

3. The plug-in applies the `PathPrepend` value to convert the relative URL from `/index.html` to `/weblogic/index.html`.

Therefore, the plug-in transforms the original URL request of `/wls/` to `/weblogic/index.html` before sending the request to WebLogic Server. Though these parameters can be useful, they also can cause unexpected problems you need to watch out for.

The plug-in's `PathTrim` and `PathPrepend` operations are unidirectional. This means that although the plug-in will intercept all requests and remove or add the specified values, it will not parse the HTML responses created by WebLogic Server to fix up any of the embedded URLs by reversing the trimming or prepending process. The browser will therefore see URLs representing the values returned by WebLogic Server rather than the values expected by the plug-in. Though these parameters are useful for making a set of pages appear available at a different URL, the application must modify any navigational links within the pages to fit the new URL scheme. This behavior catches many administrators (and programmers) by surprise because you might expect any URL changes at the plug-in level to be completely transparent to the application — they are not.

The `DefaultFileName` value must match the web application deployment descriptors' welcome file values. The plug-in uses this parameter to append to any URLs that end with /. Therefore, the administrator needs to make sure that the value set for `DefaultFileName` is the same as the welcome file setting the `web.xml` deployment descriptor(s) to which the `Location` parameter is forwarding (because the `Location` directive value might imply forwarding to multiple web applications).

> **PathTrim** and **PathPrepend** do not modify navigational URLs embedded in the
> HTML returned to the browser. As a result, the application must be able to modify
> these navigational URLs to match the values created by these two parameters.
> **DefaultFileName** must match the value of the welcome file for all web applications
> to which it applies.

The plug-in uses the next set of parameters to determine its behavior in the case of response time degradations or failures:

ConnectTimeoutSecs   The total amount of time the plug-in waits for a connection to be established with a server. If the plug-in is unsuccessful, it returns an HTTP 503 (Service Unavailable) response code to the browser. The default value is 10 seconds.

ConnectRetrySecs   The amount of time the plug-in sleeps between connection requests to a server (or other servers in a cluster). Although the plug-in will always try to connect at least twice, the result of dividing the ConnectTimeoutSecs by the ConnectRetrySecs will determine the total number of connection requests before the plug-in gives up. The default value is 2 seconds.

WLIOTimeoutSecs   The amount of time the plug-in will wait for a response from WebLogic Server. If the plug-in submits a request and the server does not respond within a certain time period, the plug-in will declare the server as dead and fail over to another server, if appropriate (see the following Idempotent parameter). The default value is 300 seconds.

Idempotent   Whether the plug-in should try to resend a request for which it did not receive a response within WLIOTimeoutSecs. The default value is ON (which means the plug-in will retry).

ErrorPage   The absolute or relative URL to the page to display when the plug-in is unable to forward a request to WebLogic Server.

The plug-in's default values for ConnectTimeoutSecs and ConnectRetrySecs are usually sufficient for most situations. The appropriate value of Idempotent depends on the semantics of the application. When a request fails in such a way that the plug-in is unsure whether the server received the request, it is only safe for the plug-in to resend the request if the application is idempotent. Essentially, this means that the application state should be the same no matter if the server processes the request in question only once or multiple times. WLIOTimeoutSecs controls the maximum amount of time for a server to process a request. If the time exceeds this, the plug-in will retry the request (if Idempotent is ON) or return an error to the user (if Idempotent is OFF or there are no more servers to accept the request). The ErrorPage simply tells the plug-in what to send back to the browser if it is unable to forward a request to WebLogic Server.

The last set of parameters controls the debugging features of the plug-in.

Debug   The value of this parameter controls how much logging information about requests and response the plug-in writes to the log file. By default, Debug is set to OFF so that no logging occurs.

WLLogFile   This parameter specifies the name and location of the log file (see the Debug parameter). If logging is on, the default log file location is either c:\temp\wlproxy.log or /tmp/wlproxy.log, depending on the platform.

DebugConfigInfo   This parameter controls access to the plug-in's configuration information by supplying the ___WebLogicBridgeConfig query parameter on any URL the plug-in receives. By default, this feature is set to OFF.

The WebLogic Server plug-ins support many levels of logging to help debug problems with proxied requests. The valid values for the Debug parameter are

OFF   The plug-in doesn't log any information.

ON   The plug-in logs only informational and error messages.

HFC   The plug-in logs HTTP headers sent from the client to the plug-in.

HTW   The plug-in logs HTTP headers sent from the plug-in to WebLogic Server.

HFW   The plug-in logs HTTP headers sent from WebLogic Server back to the plug-in.

HTC   The plug-in logs HTTP headers sent from the plug-in back to the client.

ERR   The plug-in logs only error messages.

ALL   The plug-in logs all of the information listed in the other settings.

The Debug parameter also supports combining any of the four individual HTTP header logging values by using a comma-separated list. Of course, turning logging on in a production situation may result in huge log files, so you need to keep this in mind. The WLLogFile parameter simply controls the name and location of the plug-in's log file if logging is enabled.

The DebugConfigInfo parameter offers a quick way of determining the configuration of the plug-in via a browser. By setting the parameter to ON and sending a URL to the plug-in containing the ___WebLogicBridgeConfig query parameter, the plug-in will send back its current configuration information. For example, turn DebugConfigInfo on for your configuration by modifying the Location directive entry to look like this one:

```
<Location /user>
    SetHandler weblogic-handler
    WebLogicCluster 10.10.1.41:80,10.10.1.42:80,10.10.1.43:80
    DebugConfigInfo ON
</Location>
```

Now, restart the Apache server. Enter http://www.bigrez.com/user?___WebLogicBridgeConfig in the browser to ask the plug-in for the configuration information. The return page should look something like the screen shown in Figure 12-8.

Now that we have the Apache plug-in working, all there is left to do is to enable the domain-wide admin port and set up the admin channel to allow our WebLogic Server administrators to get through the corporate firewall to the WebLogic Console.

Administration Port and Channel Configuration

Now that our domain, servers, clusters, network channels, SSL and X.509 certificate keystores, node manager, and web server plug-ins are working, the only task left is to use the domain's General Configuration tab to turn on the Enable Administration Port setting. This change requires that all managed servers be shut down, but once you save and activate the change, the admin server opens up port 9002 and the WebLogic Console is automatically redirected to the administration port — all without restarting the admin server. That was simple, time to move on and start up the managed servers, right? Not just yet!

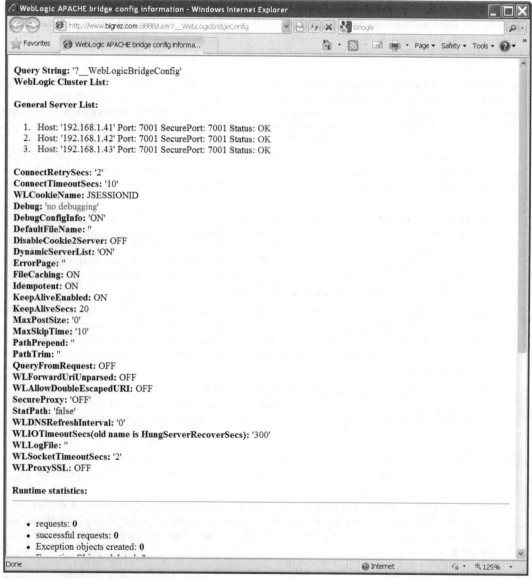

Figure 12-8: Viewing plug-in configuration data.

Once you activate the domain's administration port, all management traffic must use the administration port, which means it must use SSL. That means when a managed server starts up and contacts the admin server for its current configuration it must open an SSL connection to the admin server. No problem right? We already configured the identity and trust keystores for our admin and managed servers. Before we declare victory, there is a bootstrapping problem we need to handle.

Remember when a managed server starts up, it does not yet have its configuration information from the admin server. That means it doesn't know what identity and trust keystores are configured. In this case, it is the trust keystore that can be a problem because during the SSL handshake, the admin server presents its X.509 certificate to the managed server. If the managed server doesn't trust the admin server's certificate, it won't establish the SSL connection and therefore, won't be able to load its configuration to know what trust keystore it should use. As you can see, we have a *chicken and egg* problem.

What the managed server does by default when it boots and needs to use an SSL connection to the admin server is to load its standard trust keystores found in `$WL_HOME/server/lib/DemoTrust.jks` and `$JAVA_HOME/jre/lib/security/cacerts`. If the admin server is using the WebLogic Server demo certificate or a certificate signed by one of the well-known CAs whose root certificates are distributed in the JVM's `cacerts` trust keystore, the managed server will trust the admin server's certificate and everything works perfectly. However, if your admin server's certificate is signed by a different CA or self-signed, you have to do extra work to get the managed server to trust the admin server's certificate. There are a number of possible solutions to this problem should you encounter it.

Update the Standard Trust Keystore With this approach, you add your CA certificate to either the WebLogic Server `DemoTrust.jks` keystore (the store passphrase is `DemoTrustKeyStorePassPhrase`) or the JVM's `cacerts` keystore (the store passphrase is `changeit`). This approach is simple and works well if you don't mind the managed server trusting the other CAs in these keystores. Of course, you could also remove the other CA certificates from the keystore if only your application is using them.

Replace the Standard Trust Keystore A slight variation of the previous solution is to replace one or both of the standard trust keystores. You could accomplish this by either replacing the keystore altogether or simply adding your CA certificate and removing all the other CA certificates. If you decide to replace the keystore, you must make sure that the keystore passphrase is unchanged from the default.

Use Command-Line Arguments to Specify the Trust Keystore With this approach, you modify the startup arguments so that you specify the trust keystore to use. To do this, you must specify the trust store information using these Java command-line arguments to start the managed server:

```
-Dweblogic.security.TrustKeyStore=CustomTrust
-Dweblogic.security.CustomTrustKeyStoreFileName=<keystore_file_name>
-Dweblogic.security.CustomTrustKeyStorePassPhrase=<keystore_passphrase>
```

You specify this information either in the shell scripts used to start the managed servers (for example, the `setDomainEnv` script) or in the servers' `Server Start Configuration` tab's `Arguments` attribute. Though this approach is the preferred solution, there is a potential disconnect that we must point out.

While configuring SSL for the managed servers, most likely we have already configured the managed servers' `Keystores` attribute to `Custom Identity` and `Custom Trust` and specified these same trust store details in the domain configuration. Though there is no specific problem with doing that, you end up needing to maintain the information in two places. It probably isn't a big deal because it is likely that this information won't change, but it is something you must remember if you ever need to change it. A better way to approach this might be to change the managed servers' `Keystores` attribute to `Custom Identity and Command Line Trust`. That way, you no longer specify the trust keystore information in the server's keystore configuration and only maintain it in the server's startup parameters.

For our example, we chose to use command-line trust for our managed servers and modified the managed servers' `Arguments` attribute in the `Server Start Configuration` tab to pass the trust store information to the node manager. Now, we are ready to restart the managed servers.

Our final task is to set up an admin channel to get through the corporate firewall to the WebLogic Console. This allows our administrators to access the WebLogic Console from anywhere inside the corporate network. To do this, simply create a network channel for the admin server by setting the `Name` to `Internal Admin Channel`, the `Protocol` to `admin`, the `Listen Address` to `192.168.1.40`, the `Listen Port` to `443`, the `External Listen Address` to `10.11.1.40`, and the `External Listen Port` to `443`.

At this point, we have finished with the general configuration of the `bigrez.com` production environment. Even though the complexity of the example may seem a little overwhelming, rest assured that most production environments do not require this much configuration complexity. In fact, the simpler you can make the production environment, the better. The whole purpose of choosing such a complex environment was to demonstrate the flexibility of WebLogic Server for supporting almost any imaginable configuration requirement. Now, we are ready to move on to demonstrate how to take an application from your developers and deploy and manage it in a WebLogic Server environment.

Configuring Applications for WebLogic Server

Application developers typically set up their development environment to make it easy to go through the frequent compile, deploy, and test cycles of iterative development rapidly. This often means that when you are ready to promote an application into a more controlled environment, you may want to do some reorganizing and repackaging to make the production deployment environment simpler.

In Chapter 8, we discussed how to package the `bigrez.com` enterprise application into a self-contained enterprise application archive (EAR) file. Though many administrators may not be responsible for application packaging, an understanding of Java EE application packaging will help you identify certain types of problems that may occur. Rather than covering application packaging again here, we suggest that you review the discussion in Chapter 8.

Configuring Database Resources

Most applications depend on databases to read and write pertinent application data. As a result, configuring database resources will be a common task of most WebLogic Server administrators. WebLogic Server provides a database connection pooling framework that provides applications with an efficient, standards-based mechanism for accessing databases without requiring them to optimize connection usage to improve performance. This framework also provides some critical, behind-the-scenes functionality to make sure that Java Transaction API (JTA) transactions have proper database transaction semantics. If your application uses JTA (as most EJB applications do), you must use this framework. Failure to do so can cause data consistency problems in event of rollbacks or failures. In this section, we attempt to cover the important points of setting up a JDBC data source that provides the application with standards-based access to the underlying JDBC connection pooling facilities.

> ### Best Practice
>
> Always use WebLogic Server's JDBC data source and underlying JDBC connection pooling mechanisms rather than some other pooling mechanism. In addition to providing a robust pooling framework, JDBC connection pooling provides some critical, yet hidden transactional semantics to ensure that JTA transactions have the correct transactional semantics without any additional work on the part of the developer. Failure to use this may cause data integrity issues for applications that depend on JTA transactions involving database access.

Selecting and Configuring a JDBC Driver

WebLogic Server supports making connections to any database management system for which a JDBC 2.0-compliant driver is available. WebLogic Server supports JDBC 4.0 so it will expose any JDBC 3.0 or 4.0 APIs that the driver supports. JDBC drivers are available from a number of sources, including the database vendors, application server vendors, and other third-party companies. The quality, features, and performance characteristics of JDBC drivers vary from driver to driver, and sometimes from release to release of the same driver. All other things being equal (which, in our experience, is usually not the case), we recommend using Type 4 drivers over Type 2 JDBC drivers because they do not depend on loading native libraries into the application server (bugs or improper use of native libraries can cause the JVM to crash). Typically, you will want to work with your development team to determine which JDBC driver works best for your application. Remember that although WebLogic Server will support any JDBC 2.0-compliant driver for general application usage, certain subsystems that depend on a database (for example, the JPA provider) may support a more limited set of drivers. Be sure to choose a supported driver for applications that use these database-dependent subsystems.

Once you know which JDBC driver to use, you will need to know a few things about the driver and a few things about the database to which you are connecting. Because the purpose of this discussion is to demonstrate how to configure a WebLogic Server JDBC data source, we are going to choose a database and a JDBC driver and show the details of how to create a data source and its underlying connection pool. For more specific information on a particular JDBC driver configuration, please refer to the JDBC driver documentation and the WebLogic Server documentation.

For our example, we will use an Oracle database and the Oracle Thin JDBC Driver, a Type 4 driver available directly from Oracle. WebLogic Server includes a copy of the driver in the `$WL_HOME/server/lib` directory that it automatically loads with the server. If you were to choose the Oracle OCI (Type 2) Driver, you would have to install and configure the Oracle Client libraries and include them in the shared library path of the WebLogic Server.

The first thing we want to do is to get the right version of the driver available to the server. As mentioned earlier, WebLogic Server ships with a version of the Oracle Thin Driver `ojdbc6.jar` jar file. Although WebLogic Server tries to include the newest version of the driver, bug fixes and enhancements for this driver may mean that you may want to download a newer version from Oracle. Access to the drivers is currently available from Link 12-18, though access to the drivers requires that you register with the Oracle Technology Network.

Once the required files exist on each machine where WebLogic Server instances will connect to the database, you need to make sure that each server's classpath is set to include references to these files before the reference to the WebLogic Server classes (for example, `weblogic.jar`). Because WebLogic Server 10.3.1 includes the latest Oracle 11g Thin Driver, we will use the included driver. If you want to use a different driver, you must modify the servers' `Classpath` attributes in their `Server Start Configuration` tab (and restart the server if it is already running).

If you use a Type 2 driver, you either have to modify the node manager start scripts to put the shared libraries in its shared library search path or add an argument to the `Arguments` entry in the server's Remote `Start Configuration` tab to define the `java.library.path` system property with the correct shared library search path. Both of these mechanisms are somewhat problematic. The node manager start script modification works fine, but it assumes that all servers started by the node manager on a particular machine have the same shared library search path. In many situations, this might be okay, but it can be problematic if different servers are using different software versions of these native libraries (for example, different versions of the Oracle Client). We prefer to use the `java.library.path` system property instead because it is server-specific rather than machine-specific. The only real issue with this mechanism is that you must remember to list all of the directories that need to be in the search path, including the ones that WebLogic Server scripts or your operating system profiles tend to set for you behind the scenes (for example, the platform-specific directories under the `$WL_HOME/server/native` subdirectory).

Now that the server has the necessary class files in the correct place in the classpath, we are ready to move on to setting up the data source and its underlying connection pool.

Configuring JDBC DataSources

WebLogic Server's JDBC connection pools rely on several attributes to determine how to connect to the database:

Driver Class Name   The fully qualified name of the class that implements the `java.sql.Driver` interface. Your JDBC driver documentation should provide this information.

URL   The URL that tells the driver how to locate the correct database. Your JDBC driver documentation should provide information on the expected format. Depending on the information required, you may need some additional information from your database administrator (DBA).

Properties   Properties that allow you to pass in driver-specific information. Every driver has a core set of information that it needs to connect to the database. Some of this information may be contained in the URL, whereas other information may have to be passed via properties. Please refer to the JDBC driver documentation for more specific information on what is required.

Database User Name and Password   Required for connection pools. Connection pools are a set of connections that are functionally equivalent and shared by the application to process requests from all users. Therefore, you will need a database username and password with sufficient permissions to execute all the database work an application requires.

To simplify the process of creating the underlying connection pool, WebLogic Server provides a JDBC Data Source Configuration Wizard in the WebLogic Console that has an underlying knowledge of numerous JDBC drivers so that you don't need to know the driver's class name or the correct syntax for its URL. By selecting from a list of known drivers and filling in the appropriate information, the wizard will populate the `Driver Class Name` and `URL` fields appropriately. If your driver is not in the list of known drivers, simply select Other from the Database Type or Database Driver drop-down menu and the wizard will prompt you for the `Driver Class Name` and `URL` fields on a subsequent screen. To create a data source, we need to specify the following information:

- ❑ `Name` — The logical name of the data source used internally by WebLogic Server.

- ❑ `JNDI Name` — The JNDI name that applications use to locate the `javax.sql.DataSource` object for this connection pool.

- ❑ `Database Type` — The database provider for the database.

- ❑ `Database Driver` — The specific JDBC driver to use for the database type selected.

- ❑ `Transaction Option` — This tells the server what type of transactional behavior you want for this data source.

- ❑ `Database Name` — The name of the database (for example, the Oracle service name or SID).

- ❑ `Host Name` — The hostname or IP address of the server where the database is running.

- ❑ `Port` — The port where the database server is listening.

- ❑ `Database User Name` — The database user to connect as.

- ❑ `Password` — The database user's password.

- ❑ `Properties` — Any extra database-specific properties you need to set.

- ❑ `Test Table Name` — The name of the table or SQL that WebLogic Server should use to test the validity of a database connection.

- ❑ `Targets` — The set of servers or clusters on which to deploy the data source and its underlying connection pool.

Using this information, the WebLogic Console will guide you through the process of creating, testing, and deploying the JDBC connection pool to the cluster. We discuss the `JNDI Name` and `Transaction Option` settings in more detail in the next two sections. Once the pool is deployed, use the data source's `Connection Pool Configuration` tab to set information about the connections in the pool. On this tab, three main parameters control the number of database connections in the pool: `Initial Capacity`, `Maximum Capacity`, and `Capacity Increment`. As you might expect, `Initial Capacity` defines the initial number of connections, `Maximum Capacity` defines the maximum number of connections, and `Capacity Increment` defines the number of connections by which to grow the pool when WebLogic Server determines it needs to increase the size of the pool.

> ### Best Practice
>
> Whenever possible, try to size database connection pools properly so that they never need to grow the number of connections. Trying to grow the number of connections during a peak load situation can aggravate the situation because database connection creation is expensive.

If the application makes use of JDBC `PreparedStatement` objects, WebLogic Server can transparently cache these objects and dramatically improve the performance of the queries whose `PreparedStatement` object is in the cache. The `Statement Cache Size` parameter controls the size of the cache for each connection in the pool (because JDBC prepared statements are scoped to an individual connection). A cache size of zero disables prepared statement caching. By default, WebLogic Server uses a least-recently-used

(LRU) caching algorithm to make room for new statements. It also supports a `FIXED` cache type that simply fills each connection's cache with the first *n* prepared statements it encounters while using that connection, where *n* is the size of the cache. There may be memory, database resource, or other issues associated with the use of this feature. See the "Usage Restrictions for the Statement Cache" section of Link 12-19 in the WebLogic Server documentation for more details on the potential issues with this feature.

Best Practice

Make use of prepared statement caching if the application can tolerate the restrictions.

Under the `Advanced` area of the `Connection Pool Configuration` tab, there are quite a few options that allow you to tailor the way the pool behaves. Though we do not attempt to cover every option, we do discuss several of the more important options. For more complete information, see the WebLogic Server documentation at Link 12-20.

WebLogic Server's `Test Connections On Reserve` feature validates connections as they are requested from the pool by the application. To determine the validity of a connection, WebLogic Server issues a query on the connection. The `Test Table Name` parameter allows the administrator to control the validation query. By default, the query is `SELECT count(*) FROM <Test Table Name>`. Most database systems can optimize this query to avoid a table scan, but it is still a good idea to use a table with no rows just in case. For Oracle, we recommend using the `DUAL` table for maximum performance. WebLogic Server also allows you to use the `Test Table Name` attribute to specify a different validation query. If `Test Table Name` begins with the characters `SQL`, WebLogic Server interprets everything that follows these characters as the literal query to execute.

Because the test is done synchronously as part of the application's request to get a connection, using this option will add some overhead to the application. However, using `Test Connections on Reserve` makes your application more resilient to network glitches that may close existing database connections. For busy applications, the `Seconds to Trust an Idle Pool Connection` attribute allows you to tell the server to skip testing a connection that was recently used. As you might imagine, this can significantly reduce the overhead when the server is busy.

WebLogic Server also provides a mechanism to have the server periodically test unused connections from the pool to make sure that they are still valid. The `Test Frequency` attribute defines the frequency (in seconds) with which the server tests the unused connections.

Best Practice

If you can afford the overhead of testing connections as part of normal request processing, always use `Test Connection On Reserve` to make the application more resilient. Make sure to use an empty table (or `DUAL` if using Oracle) as the `Test Table Name`. Tune the `Seconds to Trust an Idle Pool Connection` parameter so that the server will skip testing frequently used connections.

`Connection Reserve Timeout` specifies the maximum amount of time an application request to get a connection from the pool is allowed to block. By default, WebLogic Server sets this to 10 seconds. The

Maximum Waiting for Connection attribute limits the number of threads that can block waiting for a connection from the pool; by default, this is set to java.lang.Integer.MAX_VALUE. Though this functionality helps applications deal with unexpected loads, never use this as a substitute for properly sizing connection pools. Any threads that have to block to get a connection are slowing down your application request processing.

The last connection pool attribute we need to mention is Connection Creation Retry Frequency. If this attribute is set to zero, it means that WebLogic Server data source creation will fail if the database is unavailable. Although this doesn't sound so important, what you must realize is that WebLogic Server creates the data source every time it boots — not just when you create the definition using the WebLogic Console. What that means is that if any data source for any application deployed on the server has a zero value for this parameter, the server will fail to boot if the database is unavailable. If you do not want the server to fail to boot, set this attribute to a non-zero value and the server will periodically retry to establish the data source's connection pool until it succeeds.

> If a data source's **Connection Creation Retry Frequency** is set to zero, WebLogic
> Server will fail to boot if the database is unavailable.

Before we set up the two data sources for bigrez.com, we need to discuss the Transaction Options and the JNDI Name settings.

Selecting Transaction Options for a Data Source

When creating a data source, WebLogic Server prompts you to specify the transactional behavior for the data source if you select a non-XA JDBC driver. If you select an XA JDBC driver, WebLogic Server automatically configures the data source to use XA (we talk more about what this means later).

The first choice is whether or not the data source supports global transactions. In earlier versions of WebLogic Server, a data source that honors global transactions was known as a TxDataSource and one that doesn't was known as a DataSource. Many people do not understand the differences between the two.

The primary difference is that data sources that support global transactions are JTA transaction-aware. Realize that JTA transactions do not necessarily mean XA transactions and two-phase commits (2PC). JTA transactions also allow two independently written components that modify the same database to participate in a transaction without having to know about each other. Non-XA database transactions require the use of a single database connection to provide the proper transactional semantics. If you choose not to use the Supports Global Transactions option, you need to write your application components in such a way that they get a database connection from the pool at the start of every transaction and pass that connection around to every component that participates in the transaction. This is clearly not desirable and not even possible with certain types of components (for example, JPA managed entities).

A data source that supports global transactions will make sure that your components participating in a JTA transaction get the proper transactional semantics whether or not they are using XA transactions. When not using XA transactions, the data source accomplishes this by associating a database connection with a JTA transaction context. Every time a component asks for a database connection using the data source that supports global transactions, WebLogic Server will check to see if the current transaction already has a database connection, and if so, it will always hand back the same underlying database connection. This allows non-XA transactions to maintain the proper database semantic guarantees without having to worry about what database connection to use and what the transactional boundaries are for the application.

What this means is that every application that uses JTA transactions, which includes most EJB applications and many JMS applications, must use data sources that support global transactions to access their respective database connection pools. Failure to do so will expose the application to database consistency problems during JTA transaction rollback or failures. Data sources that do not honor global transactions will ignore any JTA transaction context. Therefore, unless your application is intentionally trying to do database work outside the scope of a transaction, you must use the `Supports Global Transactions` option. When in doubt, always use the `Supports Global Transactions` option.

Best Practice

When defining data sources you almost always want to use the `Supports Global Transactions` option — even if you are not using XA transactions. By supporting global transactions, WebLogic Server keeps any JTA transactional semantics in sync with the underlying database transaction semantics. When in doubt, always use the `Supports Global Transactions` option.

If the data source supports global transactions and you specify that the data source will use a non-XA JDBC driver, you need to select the transaction commit protocol. The choices are:

One-Phase Commit   This option tells WebLogic Server that your JTA transactions involving this data source will never include more than one transactional resource so the normal single-phase database commit protocol is sufficient. WebLogic Server will prevent any attempt by the application to enlist more than one transactional resource into the same transaction. This is the right setting for applications that only use a single database resource and do not use JMS.

Emulate Two-Phase Commit   This option tells WebLogic Server that you want your non-XA JDBC connections to participate in global transactions. With this option, WebLogic Server will allow at most one non-XA resource to participate in the global transaction and will emulate the XA two-phase commit protocol with this non-XA JDBC connection. Although WebLogic Server orders the XA and non-XA resources during the transaction commit phase to minimize the chance of inconsistency, this option does expose your application to a small window of failure. Because committing the non-XA resource must be performed in a single step, a failure after the commit of the non-XA resource and before writing the XA transaction recovery log will cause the server to forget the global transaction so all XA resources will be rolled back by their respective resource manager (while the non-XA resource has already been committed). The really bad part about this particular failure scenario is that WebLogic Server doesn't realize that the transaction was partially committed because it doesn't remember the transaction.

Last Logging Resource   `Last Logging Resource` is a twist on the `Emulate Two-Phase Commit` option that eliminates the window of failure just discussed by writing the XA transaction recovery log into the database using the non-XA JDBC driver. This ensures that once the non-XA resource commits, the XA transaction recovery log entry is also committed. Even if the server fails immediately after this non-XA resource commit, WebLogic Server will have a permanent record of the transaction so that it can attempt XA recovery on the transaction and warn you if it fails to return the system to a consistent state.

Two-Phase Commit   This isn't an explicit option you choose. WebLogic Server selects this option automatically if you choose to set up a data source with an XA JDBC driver.

As we alluded to at the beginning of this section, selecting an XA JDBC driver for a data source will cause WebLogic Server to select the Supports Global Transaction option automatically and set the transaction protocol to Two-Phase Commit. Before we go on to define our data sources for bigrez.com, let's talk briefly about the data source's JNDI name.

Locating Data Sources in Java EE Applications

Java EE applications use javax.sql.DataSource objects to get access to database connections. As we have been discussing, WebLogic Server allows you to define the data source objects administratively to use application server managed database connection pools. Applications get a reference to the javax.sql.DataSource object you create by looking them up in JNDI by the name you specify in the data source's JNDI Name attribute. There are several ways that an application might use JNDI to find the data source.

First, the application might look up the data source using the *global* JNDI name you set for the data source. Although this works, it tightly couples your application to a global JNDI name. If multiple applications were to expect the same global JNDI name for different resources, this would prevent you from deploying the applications in the same application server instance or cluster. The same is true for applications that use resource injection against the global JNDI name using the mappedName attribute, as shown here:

```
@Resource(mappedName="bigrez.datasource.jta")
DataSource myDataSource;
```

A better way is for the application code to use a logical name specific to the Java EE component (for example, a session EJB might use the logical name java:comp/env/jdbc/BigRezJTADataSource), and the component's deployment descriptor will map this logical name to the actual name that you should specify in the WebLogic Console. For example, the ejb-jar.xml deployment descriptor for one of our session EJBs declares the logical name the code is using by the following entry:

```
<resource-ref>
  <res-ref-name>jdbc/BigRezJTADataSource</res-ref-name>
  <res-type>javax.sql.DataSource</res-type>
  <res-auth>Container</res-auth>
</resource-ref>
```

Notice that the java:comp/env/ prefix in the code tells WebLogic Server that the name is logical, so you don't see it here. Applications using dependency injection will use the name attribute of the @Resource annotation to map to the value of the <res-ref-name> element in the deployment descriptor, as shown here.

```
@Resource(name="jdbc/BigRezJTADataSource")
DataSource myDataSource;
```

Then, this logical name is mapped to the actual global JNDI name with the following entry in the session EJB's `weblogic-ejb-jar.xml` deployment descriptor:

```
<resource-description>
  <res-ref-name>jdbc/BigRezJTADataSource</res-ref-name>
  <jndi-name>bigrez.datasource.jta</jndi-name>
</resource-description>
```

This means that our application is expecting to find the `DataSource` it needs by using the JNDI name of `bigrez.datasource.jta`. The nice part about this is that you can easily change the JNDI name of the `DataSource` objects without having to change the actual application code. Unfortunately, not all Java EE application developers take advantage of this feature, so your application may be using the actual JNDI names in the code.

Best Practice

Encourage developers to use logical JNDI names in their code and leverage the EJB or web application deployment descriptors to map these logical names to the actual names configured in WebLogic Server.

Configuring `bigrez.com` Data Sources

Let's create our two data sources for `bigrez.com`. From Chapter 8, we know that our JPA provider needs both a JTA and a non-JTA data source. Although we haven't talked about configuring JMS yet, our developers have informed us that they are using a persistent JMS queue and need to use XA transactions for operations that involve both the JMS queue and our Oracle database. This means that we want to make sure that our JTA data source uses an XA JDBC driver. Table 12-6 shows the configuration values for our JTA data source. All values not shown should be left at their default values.

For our non-JTA data source, most of the values are the same as for our JTA data source. Table 12-7 lists the values that are different for the non-JTA data source.

Configuring JMS Resources

Many applications use some sort of messaging. Common uses for messaging involve asynchronous communication with other applications, store-and-forward situations where the external system may not always be available, and even situations where you want to avoid the overhead of performing a particular operation synchronously as part of processing a user request (for example, sending an email confirmation). The Java Message Service (JMS) is the Java EE standard API for interacting with messaging systems. WebLogic Server provides a robust, high performance messaging system that fully supports the JMS specification. In addition, WebLogic JMS also supports plugging in external, third-party messaging systems via their JMS APIs to support things like message-driven beans (MDBs) listening directly to externally provided destinations for messages. For more information about WebLogic JMS, please see Chapter 10 and the WebLogic Server documentation at Link 12-21.

Table 12-6: BigRezJTADataSource Configuration Parameters

Name	Value
Name	BigRezJTADataSource
JNDI Name	bigrez.datasource.jta
Database Type	Oracle
Database Driver	Oracle's Driver (Thin XA) for Service Connections; Versions: 9.0.1, 9.2.0, 10, 11
Database Name	ORCL
Host Name	192.168.1.44
Port	1521
Database User Name	Bigrez
Password	Password
Targets	BigRezCluster (All servers in the cluster)
Initial Capacity	60
Maximum Capacity	60
Capacity Increment	0
Statement Cache Type	LRU
Statement Cache Size	100
Test Connections on Reserve	Yes (checked)
Connection Creation Retry Seconds	30

Our example application uses two JMS queues. Internet customer bookings use a queue to buffer email confirmations of interactions with the `bigrez.com` site. We also set up an error queue for email messages that prove to be undeliverable. In this section, we walk through the steps for configuring the JMS services needed for a production deployment of the `bigrez.com` application. We assume that you have read Chapter 10, and therefore we do not spend much time describing particular JMS objects or features here.

Creating JMS Servers and WebLogic Persistent Stores

The first thing we need to do is set up the JMS servers. A JMS server is an administrative grouping of JMS destinations that run on the same WebLogic Server instance and share a set of common characteristics. One WebLogic Server instance can support multiple JMS servers. In the event of failure or maintenance, we can migrate JMS servers from one WebLogic Server instance to another; this is known as *service migration* in the WebLogic Server documentation. As part of JMS service migration, we may need to migrate the JTA service to recover any incomplete transactions involving the JMS server's persistent store, depending on whether we are using JTA transactions with persistent messages for any of the JMS server's underlying destinations.

Table 12-7: Non-JTA Data Source Configuration Parameter Changes

Name	Value
Name	BigRezNonJTADataSource
JNDI Name	bigrez.datasource.nonjta
Database Driver	Oracle's Driver (Thin) for Service Connections; Versions: 9.0.1, 9.2.0, 10, 11
Transaction Options	Supports Global Transactions = No (unchecked)

WebLogic Server also supports relocating the entire server instance, including any JMS servers it might contain, to another machine; this is known as *whole server migration*. We discuss both whole server migration and service migration in the "Managing Failure Conditions" section later in this chapter.

Before we create our JMS servers, we need to determine if we need a JMS persistent store and, if so, what type of store to use. WebLogic JMS supports two types of persistent stores: file-based and JDBC-based. For the file-based store, JMS messages are persisted to disk. The JDBC-based store writes the messages to a database using a WebLogic Server connection pool. In general, the file-based store is much faster than JDBC-based stores. WebLogic JMS provides an XAResource interface to allow the file store to participate in XA transactions. Because the file store is disk-based, migration support for a JMS server using a file store depends on the file store being accessible from another machine.

Applications that choose to use persistent messages generally do so because they cannot afford to lose any messages. Both the file- and JDBC-based stores give the application the persistence that they need. If a WebLogic Server (or the machine on which it is running) goes down, the messages will remain in the JMS store until either the server is restarted or the JMS server is migrated to another machine. The need for migration varies with the application. For some applications, it may be sufficient to wait until the failed server restarts to process the messages in the failed server's JMS store; other applications may be time-sensitive and require the ability to process the messages in the failed server's store.

> ### Best Practice
> Don't automatically assume that your JMS-based applications require support for JMS service migration. Migration is typically important for persistent messages sent to a queue where the processing of those messages is time-critical.

If you need to migrate JMS servers that are using file-based message stores, you need to invest in multi-ported disks, a SAN, or other highly available disk-sharing technology. See the "Configuring Persistent Stores" section of Chapter 10 for more information on what you should consider before using other distributed file sharing mechanisms like NFS for persistent stores. For simplicity, we will use a JDBC-based store to demonstrate JMS migration capabilities without requiring costly disk-sharing technology.

Realize that we are making a trade-off here because a JDBC-based store is generally slower than a file store.

Best Practice

High volume, performance-critical applications should use the file store rather than the JDBC-based store. If migration is required, use a multi-ported disk array, SAN-, or NAS-based solution for making the file store available across servers. Be wary of using NFS to share a file store in a production system.

Before creating the JDBC-based store, you need to set up a JDBC data source for the store. Because WebLogic JMS implements the XAResource interface to allow the file store to participate in XA transactions, the JDBC-based store must use a non-XA connection to the underlying database. Because we already created a non-XA data source, we will use the BigRezNonJTADataSource rather than creating another data source for the JDBC store.

Use the WebLogic Console to create the JDBC-based persistent stores. You need a separate store for each server in the cluster. Table 12-8 shows the values to use for creating the store for Server1. Create similar stores for Server2 and Server3.

Table 12-8: Server1's JDBC-Based JMS Store Configuration Parameters

Name	Value
Name	JDBCStore1
Target	Server1 (migratable)
Data Source	BigRezNonJTADataSource
Prefix Name	Store1_

Finally, you are ready to create the JMS servers. Create three JMS servers with the names JMSServer1, JMSServer2, and JMSServer3 using the persistent stores JDBCStore1, JDBCStore2, and JDBCStore3, and target them to Server1 (migratable), Server2 (migratable), and Server3 (migratable), respectively. Notice that each JMS server can be targeted only to one server instance. We select the migratable options so that we can support JMS server migration, should a need arise.

Creating Distributed JMS Destinations

Each JMS server will contain one or more JMS destinations and will live on a particular server instance. Because our application uses two uniform distributed JMS destinations, you can move directly to creating the distributed destinations. WebLogic Server can create the individual member destinations for you automatically. Because all JMS Servers will have the same configuration, create a single JMS module called BigRezJMSModule and target it to the BigRezCluster.

Within `BigRezJMSModule`, create the `BigRezEmailQueue` distributed queue with a JNDI name of `bigrez.jms.emailQueue`. Like the JDBC data sources earlier, we want to decouple the JNDI names that our application uses to look up the JMS queue from its actual JNDI name. This is just as easy to accomplish using similar deployment descriptor mechanisms. For example, our `ejb-jar.xml` deployment descriptor should have a reference like the one shown here to declare that the application is using the logical JNDI name `java:comp/env/jms/BigRezEmailQueue` to look up the queue or an `@Resource(name="jms/BigRezEmailQueue")` annotation to have the container inject the reference automatically.

```
<resource-ref>
  <res-ref-name>jms/BigRezEmailQueue</res-ref-name>
  <res-type>javax.jms.Queue</res-type>
  <res-auth>Container</res-auth>
</resource-ref>
```

A corresponding entry in the `weblogic-ejb-jar.xml` deployment descriptor will map this logical JNDI name to the actual JNDI name.

```
<resource-description>
  <res-ref-name>jms/BigRezEmailQueue</res-ref-name>
  <jndi-name>bigrez.jms.emailQueue</jndi-name>
</resource-description>
```

This means that the application is expecting us to use the JNDI name `bigrez.jms.emailQueue` when registering this queue.

Distributed queues must also specify a `Load Balancing Policy` that describes the way in which WebLogic JMS distributes incoming messages across the distributed queue's member queues, all other things being equal. Remember that WebLogic JMS uses sophisticated algorithms to optimize processing of messages so that the load balancing policy applies only when every queue has similar runtime characteristics. For our example, we accept the default policy of `Round-Robin`.

Before we look at some of the settings for the `BigRezEmailQueue`, create another distributed queue called `BigRezEmailErrorQueue` with a JNDI name of `bigrez.jms.emailErrorQueue`. Once this distributed queue exists, let's examine some of the settings on the `BigRezEmailQueue`.

Uniform distributed queues have a `Forward Delay` that specifies the number of seconds WebLogic JMS will wait before attempting to forward messages from one member queue to another if the queue in question has no active consumers. For our example, we accept the default of −1, which disables forwarding of messages. Because all of our queues are using MDBs as consumers, we do not expect to ever have a member queue available without any consumers for any extended period of time.

Using the `Delivery Failure Configuration` tab, you can control what happens when message delivery fails. The `Redelivery Delay Override` attribute allows you to specify how many milliseconds the server will wait before attempting to redeliver the message regardless of the `Redelivery Delay` setting on the connection factory or the consumer. By default, the destination does not override the settings of the consumer or connection factory. `Redelivery Limit` controls the maximum number of times WebLogic JMS will attempt to deliver each message before moving it to the `Error Destination`. If the `Error Destination` is not configured, every undelivered message that reaches the `Redelivery Limit` gets discarded.

For our example, we know that our application uses a local MDB to consume messages from this queue and that MDB uses each message's contents to generate and send an email message. The only time WebLogic JMS should ever fail to deliver the message is when the email server is down. As such, we set the Redelivery Delay Override to 60,000 milliseconds, the Redelivery Limit to 5, and the Error Destination to BigRezEmailErrorQueue.

Creating JMS Connection Factories

At this point, we are ready to set up the JMS connection factory. A JMS connection factory is the object through which JMS applications obtain a JMS connection. Configuring a JMS connection factory allows the administrator to customize the behavior of all JMS clients that use the connection factory without requiring code changes. We will add a single JMS connection factory to the BigRezJMSModule for our application.

Creating a JMS connection factory is simple: specify the Name and JNDI Name attributes and accept the default targeting. As with JMS destinations, the JNDI name required during configuration should be entirely dependent on the EJB or web application deployment descriptors. For bigrez.com, create the BigRezConnectionFactory with a JNDI Name of bigrez.jms.connectionfactory.

Connection factories have a large number of configuration parameters you can use to control the JMS application's behavior. For many of these parameters, we will simply use the default values and skip over detailed explanations of what they do. Refer to Chapter 10 or the WebLogic JMS documentation at Link 12-22 for more information. The only thing we need to configure is the transactional semantics of the JMS connection factory. Using the Transactions Configuration tab, you should set the Transaction Timeout to 60 seconds for the connection factory. This tab also lets you enable the use of XA connection factories. Because we are using XA transactions with our queues, you must check the XA Connection Factory Enabled checkbox for the connection factory.

At this point, the configuration of our application's JMS resources is complete. We only have to configure our JavaMail session for our email confirmation service, set up and tune our application-specific work managers, and deploy our application.

Configuring JavaMail Sessions

The bigrez.com application uses the JavaMail API to send email confirmations to our customers via a mail server. To make that process more transparent to the application, WebLogic Server provides the ability to define JavaMail sessions that applications can look up from JNDI and use without having to understand where the mail server lives, how to authenticate, what protocols to use, and so on. For our example, we will use a mail server on our network, mail.bigrez.com. Go to the Services ⇨ Mail Sessions folder in the WebLogic Console's left-hand navigation bar and create a new mail session with the name BigRezMailSession. As with our other resources, the JNDI name that applications use to locate this session will be a logical name. The EJB or web application deployment descriptor will map the logical name to the actual name that the session will use. Use the JNDI name bigrez.email.session to create the mail session. The Properties attribute is simply the JavaMail properties to use when creating the session:

```
mail.transport.protocol=smtp
mail.smtp.host=mail.bigrez.com
```

```
mail.smtp.user=bigrez
mail.smtp.password=password
```

After creating the mail session, don't forget to target it to all servers in the `BigRezCluster`.

Configuring Work Managers, Request Classes, and Constraints

For our application, we are going to define one additional work manager to guarantee that our internal customer service agents' requests get higher priority than our web site and partner web service requests. In reality, what this means is that when the system is busy, requests from our agents on the phone with customers will get a higher fair share of their requests scheduled for execution on an execute threads. To accomplish this, we need to define the work manager and the request class and deploy them to all servers in the cluster. Let's walk through this process.

Using the `Environment` ➪ `Work Managers` folder in the WebLogic Console's left-hand navigation bar, create a new `Fair Share Request Class` whose `Name` is `CSAFairShareReqClass` and `Fair Share` is 100 and target it to the `BigRezCluster`. Now, create a new `Work Manager` whose `Name` is `CSAWorkManager` and target it to the cluster. Next, edit the `CSAWorkManager` and set its `Request Class` to the `CSAFairShareReqClass`.

Because the `default` work manager's `Fair Share` is 50, this means that when the server is busy with a sufficient number of requests for each work manager, assuming that the average request execution time is the same for both request classes, the server will schedule two CSA requests for every one request using the default work manager from within the application. This last part is important! The `default` work manager uses the default fair share request class so each application gets its own fair share of 50 rather than sharing it with other applications. The `CSAFairShareReqClass` is not exclusive. If we deployed another application that used the `CSAWorkManager`, the two applications would share the fair share of 100, rather than each getting its own fair share of 100. In our example, we only have a single application so this configuration will have the desired effect.

We could stop there and have a reasonable configuration that would work well in most situations. However, we want to protect our site from being overwhelmed to the point where response time becomes unacceptable. To do this, we need to create two constraints to protect the server from overload. First, we know that every request coming into the server uses the database and this database access makes up the majority of the request processing time. Therefore, we want to limit the number of threads the work managers create such that we never have more threads processing requests than we have database connections in the connection pool associated with our `BigRezJTADataSource`.

Because both work managers use the connection pool, we want to create a shared constraint to limit the maximum number of threads across both work managers to be no larger than the maximum size of the `BigRezJTADataSource` connection pool. To do this, create a `Maximum Threads Constraint` with a `Name` of `BigRezMaxThreadsConstraint` and a `Data Source` of `BigRezJTADataSource`. Next, go back and assign this constraint to our `CSAWorkManager`. To modify the behavior of the `default` work manager, we need to create a new work manager with the `Name` set to `default` and target it to our cluster. Because the `default` work manager already exists, this will simply give us the ability to modify the behavior of the existing work manager rather than creating a new one. As the final step, assign the max threads constraint to the `default` work manager.

The second constraint we want to create is a capacity constraint to limit the total number of requests being processed and waiting in the execute queue. After load testing of our application, we know that our application response time starts to degrade to unacceptable levels when the total number of in-flight requests per server exceeds 300. As such, we will create a shared capacity constraint to reject additional work when the number of in-flight requests on a server exceeds 300. The process is identical to what we just did for the maximum threads constraint. Create a `Capacity Constraint` named `BigRezCapacityConstraint` with a `Count` of 300, deploy it to the cluster, and assign it to both work managers.

Now, let's deploy the application.

Deploying Applications

Deploying the application is easy. As long as the EAR file is accessible from either the admin server machine or the machine from which you are running the WebLogic Console, you can do everything from the browser. Using the WebLogic Console, open the `Deployments` folder in the left-hand navigation bar and click the `Install` button. If your application files are already on the admin server's file system, simply navigate the file system and locate your application. If not, select the `upload your file(s)` link embedded in the help text, upload the files, and deploy them to the servers or clusters. Don't forget to start the managed servers before trying to deploy the application. If your managed servers are running in production mode, don't forget to start the application because this does not happen automatically upon deployment unless the server is in development mode.

In addition to the WebLogic Console, WebLogic Server provides a rich set of command-line accessible administrative functionality. The first tool we look at is the command-line deployment tool, `weblogic.Deployer`. The `weblogic.Deployer` program allows an administrator to upload, deploy, start, stop, undeploy, and get the status of deployed applications. We will not attempt to cover all of the possible options with `weblogic.Deployer`, but we cover some basic features. For more information, please see the WebLogic Server documentation at Link 12-23.

The first task we want to accomplish is making the deployment tool talk to the administration port of the admin server. Remember that by enabling this administration port, the plain text port can no longer be used to perform administrative functions, and all communication with the admin server requires SSL communication. To accomplish this, you must define a few Java system properties to tell the deployer tool where to find and how to use your trusted CA keystore (see Chapter 11 or Link 12-24 for more information), as shown here.

```
-Dweblogic.security.TrustKeyStore=CustomTrust
-Dweblogic.security.CustomTrustKeyStoreFileName=<keystore file name>
-Dweblogic.security.CustomTrustKeyStorePassPhrase=<keystore passphrase>
```

Note that these are the same command-line Java system properties we described for bootstrapping the managed servers to talk to the admin port in the "Administration Port and Channel Configuration" section earlier in this chapter.

If you are using the demo certificates that came with WebLogic Server, you simply set `weblogic.security.TrustKeyStore` to `DemoTrust` — the other two arguments are not needed because WebLogic Server knows that information implicitly. You may also need to set `weblogic.security.SSL.ignoreHostnameVerification` to `true` to tell the deployer tool to ignore the hostname in the server's certificate. In our example, the first portion of every command you invoke using the deployer tool will look like the following line:

```
java -Dweblogic.security.TrustKeyStore=CustomTrust
    -Dweblogic.security.CustomTrustKeyStoreFileName=C:/powls/ch12/cacerts
    -Dweblogic.security.CustomTrustKeyStorePassPhrase=changeit weblogic.Deployer
```

When using the deployer tool, we also need to specify the URL to use to contact the admin server, a username with sufficient privileges to invoke the command, and the user's password. If you use the `weblogic` account, that means that every time you invoke the deployer tool, the command line will always begin with the following contents:

```
java -Dweblogic.security.TrustKeyStore=CustomTrust
    -Dweblogic.security.CustomTrustKeyStoreFileName=C:/powls/ch12/cacerts
    -Dweblogic.security.CustomTrustKeyStorePassPhrase=changeit
    weblogic.Deployer -adminurl t3s://192.168.1.40:9002
                    -username weblogic -password weblogic1
```

Of course, you also need to make sure that the PATH and CLASSPATH environment variables are set properly so that you find the JVM and the `weblogic.Deployer` class. To make this simpler, let's create the following script file called `weblogicDeployer.cmd` in the Chapter 12 example directory (for example, `c:\powls\ch12\`):

```
@SETLOCAL
@set WL_HOME=c:\Oracle\Middleware\wlserver_10.3
@call %WL_HOME%\server\bin\setWLSEnv.cmd
java -Dweblogic.security.TrustKeyStore=CustomTrust
-Dweblogic.security.CustomTrustKeyStoreFileName=C:\powls\ch12\cacerts
-Dweblogic.security.CustomTrustKeyStorePassPhrase=changeit
weblogic.Deployer -adminurl t3s://192.168.1.40:9002 -username weblogic
-password weblogic1 %*
@ENDLOCAL
```

Note that `weblogic.Deployer` also provides a more secure way of supplying the username and password. See Link 12-25 for more information about how you might modify this script to be more secure.

This script will allow us to run the deployer tool with a command of the form `weblogicDeployer` `<args>*`. For example, let's run the new script using the deployer's `listapp` command to see what applications are deployed:

```
> weblogicDeployer -listapp

bigrez
Number of Applications Found : 1
```

Using the deployer, you can also deploy new applications and undeploy or redeploy running applications. For example, let's say that you just received a new copy of the `bigrez.ear` file from your developers and want to deploy the new version into the `BigRezCluster` that is already running an older version. You need to run the following commands to redeploy the application using the new EAR file.

```
> weblogicDeployer -redeploy -name bigrez
                        -source C:\powls\bigrez\ear\output\bigrez.ear
                        -targets BigRezCluster

<Jun 3, 2009 9:36:16 AM CDT> <Info> <J2EE Deployment SPI> <BEA-260121> <Initiating
redeploy operation for application, bigrez [archive:
c:\powls\bigrez\ear\output\bigrez.ear], to BigRezCluster .>
Task 0 initiated: [Deployer:149026]deploy application bigrez on BigRezCluster.
Task 0 completed: [Deployer:149026]deploy application bigrez on BigRezCluster.
Target state: redeploy completed on Cluster BigRezCluster
```

Note that this command deploys the new version of the application by undeploying the old version and deploying the new version, thus interrupting existing user sessions. We discuss how we can deploy new versions of an application without disrupting existing user sessions later in the "Versioning Applications" section.

Deploying a new application is very similar to redeploying an existing one.

```
> weblogicDeployer -deploy -name bigrez
                        -source c:\ powls\bigrez\ear\output\bigrez.ear
                        -targets BigRezCluster

<Jun 3, 2009 9:38:39 AM CDT> <Info> <J2EE Deployment SPI> <BEA-260121> <Initiating
deploy operation for application, bigrez [archive:
c:\powls\bigrez\ear\output\bigrez.ear], to BigRezCluster .>
Task 2 initiated: [Deployer:149026]deploy application bigrez on BigRezCluster.
Task 2 completed: [Deployer:149026]deploy application bigrez on BigRezCluster.
Target state: deploy completed on Cluster BigRezCluster
```

You now have at least two ways to deploy an application: the WebLogic Console and the `weblogic.Deployer` program. WebLogic Server provides the `wldeploy` Ant task that surfaces the functionality of `weblogic.Deployer` for use from within your Ant scripts; see Link 12-26 for more information. You can also deploy applications from WLST scripts. We favor the `weblogic.Deployer` program, WLST, or their Ant-based equivalents because they lend themselves to scripting common actions and provide a rich set of deployment options.

As we said at the beginning of this section, deploying an application is easy — provided that the application is properly configured for the environment. As we discussed in Chapters 5 and 8, Java EE applications potentially contain some environment-specific configuration information in metadata packaged inside the application itself, either in annotations, deployment descriptors, or both. Fortunately, Java EE provides us a mechanism to reconfigure these metadata settings through the use of *deployment plans*.

Modifying Application Configuration Using Deployment Plans

Information in deployment descriptors often needs to be changed when an application or module is deployed to a new environment. For example, a WebLogic Server administrator may wish to tune an application's work manager settings to make better use of the available hardware. Deployment plans allow you to customize these details without the need to create a different version of an application for each environment. Instead, the application archive is left unchanged and a deployment plan is created for each target environment.

Deployment properties that can be changed fall into two classes. First, there are references to external dependencies; for example, the JNDI name of a JMS topic. These properties are usually declared in a Java EE descriptor. If declarations are not mapped to a resource in a WebLogic Server descriptor, or the supplied value is inappropriate, a deployment plan must be used. Second, there are configurable values that control the application's behavior or tune its performance; for example, a web application's HTTP session timeout. These can optionally be overridden with a deployment plan.

Not every item in a deployment descriptor can be changed with a deployment plan. For example, you can't override the name of an EJB.

Typically, only a few deployment properties need be customized. It is often possible and better to include only logical references in deployment descriptors, and set the environment-specific values in the WebLogic Server configuration. For example, the Foreign JMS feature can be used to provide the host information of a JMS queue in the domain configuration, rather than in a deployment descriptor.

Why is modifying the configuration better than using a deployment plan? Simply put, the various tools to change the configuration (WLST, JMX configuration MBeans, and the WebLogic Console) are easier to use than deployment plans. Some changes to configuration properties in the WebLogic Console cause a deployment plan to be created. However, the WebLogic Console only allows a few settings to be changed. Deployment plans are mostly maintained by hand editing their files, and the development team or WebLogic Server administrators must maintain an appropriate plan for each application and each environment. Oracle Enterprise Pack for Eclipse (OEPE) provides a deployment plan editor that makes creating and editing deployment plans a little easier but avoid this complexity if you can.

Best Practice

Use deployment plans only if you need to override deployment descriptor properties on a per-environment basis.

Minimize the number of deployment descriptor settings that are overridden for each environment by using features such as Foreign JMS and Foreign JNDI. Often deployment plans are unnecessary.

If the application development team can predict in advance that a property is likely to need to be overridden, a template deployment plan should be provided with the application archive.

As you might expect, a deployment plan is an XML file. Currently, the easiest way to create a plan is to use the WebLogic Console. To do this, navigate to the deployed application's `Application Configuration` tab, change one of the values (for example, the session timeout), and save your change. If the application doesn't already have a deployment plan, you will be prompted for a location to save a new one. The WebLogic Server documentation recommends that you store your deployment plans in a `plan` directory alongside the directory containing the application (or archive file). If you follow this guideline, the WebLogic Server deployment tools will automatically look in that location for a deployment plan file called `plan.xml`. However, you can save your deployment plan wherever you like; WebLogic Server will record the location and associate the plan with the application in its configuration.

Using the WebLogic Console to change the session timeout for `bigrez.com` results in a deployment plan similar to the one shown here:

```xml
<?xml version='1.0' encoding='UTF-8'?>
<deployment-plan
    xmlns="http://xmlns.oracle.com/weblogic/deployment-plan"
    xmlns:xsi="http://www.w3.org/2001/XMLSchema-instance"
    xsi:schemaLocation="http://xmlns.oracle.com/weblogic/deployment-plan
        http://xmlns.oracle.com/weblogic/deployment-plan/1.0/deployment-plan.xsd">
  <application-name>output</application-name>
  <variable-definition>
    <variable>
      <name>SessionDescriptor_timeoutSecs_12440079653010</name>
      <value>600</value>
    </variable>
  </variable-definition>
  <module-override>
    <module-name>bigrez</module-name>
    <module-type>ear</module-type>
    <module-descriptor external="false">
      <root-element>weblogic-application</root-element>
      <uri>META-INF/weblogic-application.xml</uri>
      <variable-assignment>
        <name>SessionDescriptor_timeoutSecs_12440079653010</name>
        <xpath>/weblogic-application/session-descriptor/timeout-secs</xpath>
      </variable-assignment>
    </module-descriptor>
    <module-descriptor external="false">
      <root-element>application</root-element>
      <uri>META-INF/application.xml</uri>
    </module-descriptor>
  ...
  </module-override>
  <module-override>
    <module-name>bigrez-services.jar</module-name>
    <module-type>ejb</module-type>
  ...
  </module-override>
  <module-override>
    <module-name>bigrez-web-admin.war</module-name>
  ...
  </module-override>
  <module-override>
    <module-name>bigrez-web-user.war</module-name>
  ...
  </module-override>
  <module-override>
    <module-name>bigrez-webservices.war</module-name>
  ...
</deployment-plan>
```

A deployment plan is split into two parts. First, a `<variable-definition>` element that contains one or more variable names together with the new value supplied by the plan. Variable names are only used within the plan. As you can see from example plan, the console generates a unique name `SessionDescriptor_timeoutSecs_12440079653010`. The second part of the plan is a set of

<module-override> elements. We've removed much of this information in the interest of space. There is a <module-override> element for each deployment descriptor in the application. In the sample, the <module-override> element for the weblogic-application.xml descriptor has a <variable-assignment> element that binds our variable to a specific element in the descriptor using an XPath expression. As you can see from our simple example, deployment plans are very verbose and somewhat cryptic. Writing one by hand is something you should try to avoid if at all possible.

The WebLogic Console allows you to change the deployment plan associated with an application. Both weblogic.Deployer and WLST allow you to supply deployment plans when deploying or redeploying an application, as well as providing a mechanism to update the existing deployment plan for a deployed application. Use the following command to update the deployment plan we use to modify the session timeout for bigrez.com.

```
> weblogicDeployer -update -name bigrez
                          -plan c:\ powls\ch12\plan.xml
                          -targets BigRezCluster

<Jun 3, 2009 11:16:35 AM CDT> <Warning> <WebLogicDescriptorWL> <BEA-2156000>
<"config-root" c:\powls\bigrez\ear\output\plan was not found>
<Jun 3, 2009 11:16:36 AM CDT> <Info> <J2EE Deployment SPI> <BEA-260121> <Initiating
update operation for application, bigrez [archive: null], to BigRezCluster .>
Task 4 initiated: [Deployer:149026]update application bigrez on BigRezCluster.
Task 4 completed: [Deployer:149026]update application bigrez on BigRezCluster.
Target state: update completed on Cluster BigRezCluster
```

Though we have only scratched the surface of all the possible deployment scenarios, it is time to move on. For more information on the details of WebLogic Server deployment, see Link 12-27. During our discussions of WebLogic Server configuration issues and options, we have covered a lot of ground. We hit many of the high points that we feel are likely to be relevant to the largest percentage of applications. However, we haven't covered everything. Our hope is that we provided enough information to give you a good head start on what you need to become an effective WebLogic Server administrator. From this point on, we turn our focus to discussing how to monitor and manage WebLogic Server applications to keep them running optimally and how to handle different types of failure conditions.

Monitoring WebLogic Server Applications

Before we discuss how to manage applications, we are going to cover some techniques for monitoring WebLogic Server applications. Fortunately, WebLogic Server provides numerous tools and techniques for monitoring different aspects of a distributed application. This section starts off by introducing another administration tool, the WebLogic Scripting Tool (WLST). Next, we look into areas of the WebLogic Console that allow you to monitor the runtime behavior of the server and your applications. We spend a little time discussing the Java Management Extensions (JMX) APIs, which provide programmatic access to most of the configuration and runtime monitoring capabilities; these are the same APIs that all of the WebLogic Server administration tools use. We finish off the section by briefly touching on the SNMP capabilities of WebLogic Server.

Using the WebLogic Scripting Tool

WebLogic Server offers access to most administrative functionality through an administration tool called WLST. Through this tool, you can do almost everything from creating new domains and modifying

WebLogic Server configuration, through deploying applications and telling the node manager to start or stop servers, to collecting runtime statistics that allow you to monitor the health of your servers and applications. Although we discuss this tool in multiple places throughout the rest of this chapter, we do not attempt to cover every possible option exhaustively. For more information, see the WebLogic Server documentation at Link 12-28.

WLST uses Jython as its scripting language. Jython is a Java-based implementation of the Python scripting language. See `http://www.jython.org` and `http://www.python.org` for more information on Jython and Python, respectively.

WLST offers three modes of execution:

❏ Interactive Mode — This mode provides a command interpreter where you can enter commands in an interactive shell and receive immediate feedback on their effect.

❏ Script Mode — This mode allows you to execute a Jython script from the command line.

❏ Embedded Mode — This mode allows you to create a WLST interpreter and execute WLST commands from within a Java application.

In addition, WebLogic Server also provides the `wlst` Ant task that allows you to execute either an inline script defined inside your Ant task definition or an external script stored in a file.

As with the deployer tool, WLST requires that the same Java system parameters be defined to support using the SSL protocol to communicate with the administration port on the admin server or a node manager. Because WebLogic Server provides shell scripts to start WLST already, we create a simple script to automate the setting of the SSL-related properties and invoke the provided shell script. Once again, we will place this script in the Chapter 12 examples directory (for example, `c:\powls\ch12\weblogicWlst.cmd`):

```
@SETLOCAL
@set WL_HOME=C:\oracle\middleware\wlserver_10.3
@set WLST_PROPERTIES=-Dweblogic.security.TrustKeyStore=CustomTrust
-Dweblogic.security.CustomTrustKeyStoreFileName=C:\powls\ch12\cacerts
-Dweblogic.security.CustomTrustKeyStorePassPhrase=changeit
@call %WL_HOME%\common\bin\wlst.cmd %*
@ENDLOCAL
```

You'll notice that our script does not provide connection or authentication information. That's because WLST has two operational states: online and offline. When you first start WLST, you enter the WLST offline state. In this state, you can create new domains based on a template or extend existing, inactive domains, much like you can with the WebLogic Configuration Wizard. The other thing that you do in this mode is connect to a WebLogic Server instance or a node manager.

As discussed earlier, the `nmConnect()` command allows you to connect to a node manager so that you can start and stop servers (most importantly, the admin server). However, the most common command to run in offline mode is the `connect()` command to connect to a WebLogic Server instance, typically to the admin server. Once connected, WLST is in online mode until you disconnect. To start up our admin server and connect to it, we run the following WLST commands:

```
wls:/offline> nmConnect(username='weblogic', password='weblogic1',
host='diablo.us.oracle.com', port='5556', domainName='bigrezdmain',
```

```
domainDir='C:\powls\ch12\AdminMachine\bigrezdomain', nmType='ssl')

Connecting to Node Manager ...
Successfully Connected to Node Manager.

wls:/nm/bigrezdomain> nmStart('AdminServer')

Starting server AdminServer ...
Successfully started server AdminServer ...

wls:/nm/bigrezdomain> nmDisconnect()

Successfully disconnected from Node Manager.

wls:/offline> connect(username='weblogic', password='weblogic1',
url='t3s://192.168.1.40:9002')

Connecting to t3s://192.168.1.40:9002 with userid weblogic ...
Successfully connected to Admin Server 'AdminServer' that belongs to domain 'big
rezdomain'.

wls:/bigrezdomain/serverConfig>
```

Before we move on to show you the basics of WLST commands to get or modify data, we should discuss WLST security. Your admin server's configuration directory contains sensitive configuration files for your WebLogic Server domain. Anyone with write access to these files can modify your domain, either via a text editor or using WLST offline mode — regardless of whether or not they know the username and password of an administrative user in your domain. As such, it is important to safeguard these files and not allow everyone write access to them.

Many WLST commands require administrative privileges to run. As such, it is often necessary to supply administrative credentials in your WLST scripts. To prevent needing to store the unencrypted username and password in your WLST scripts, WLST provides a storeUserConfig() command that uses the currently connected user's username and password to create an encrypted credential store and key file. To create the user configuration file for a server, use the following command:

```
wls:/bigrezdomain/serverConfig>
storeUserConfig(userConfigFile='c:\powls\ch12\server-WebLogicConfig.properties',
userKeyFile='c:\powls\ch12\server-WebLogicKey.properties')

Creating the key file can reduce the security of your system if it is not kept in a
secured location after it is created. Do you want to create the key file? y or n y
The username and password that were used for this WebLogic Server connection
are stored in c:\powls\ch12\server-WebLogicConfig.properties and
c:\powls\ch12\server-WebLogicKey.properties.
```

In the same way, you can create the configuration file and the key file for the node manager (when connected to the node manager) by adding the nm='true' argument to the storeUserConfig() command.

Both WLST and weblogic.Deployer provide options for using these files in place of the unencrypted username and password. Even so, the key files are extremely sensitive in that they allow any user to use the configuration file to authenticate as the user stored in the configuration file. You should store the key files in a secure location so that only the authorized users have access to them. To connect to the admin server using the configuration file, use the following `connect()` command:

```
wls:/offline> connect(userConfigFile='c:\powls\ch12\server-
WebLogicConfig.properties', userKeyFile='c:\powls\ch12\server-
WebLogicKey.properties', url='t3s://192.168.1.40:9002')

Connecting to t3s://192.168.1.40:9002 with userid weblogic ...
Successfully connected to Admin Server 'AdminServer' that belongs to domain
'bigrezdomain'.
```

Now that we know how to connect securely, we show how we can use WLST to get information from the server. Once connected to the admin server, WLST provides a file system–like hierarchy of MBeans that we can navigate by using the `cd()` command and list using the `ls()` command. To enable performing operations on the current MBean, WLST automatically assigns the current management object to the `cmo` variable. If we want to determine whether the admin server's SSL listen port is enabled, we need to navigate to its SSL MBean directory and execute `cmo.isEnabled()`, as shown here.

```
wls:/bigrezdomain/serverConfig> cd('Servers/AdminServer/SSL/AdminServer')
wls:/bigrezdomain/serverConfig/Servers/AdminServer/SSL/AdminServer> cmo.isEnabled()

0
```

Although interesting, this isn't very useful by itself. However, because we have the power of the Python scripting language at our disposal, we can define variables to hold the values, perform tests on those values, implement condition logic, iterate over lists, and just about everything else you might expect out of a full-fledged scripting language. Here is a simple example where we iterate over all the servers in our cluster and print out the value of their `ListenAddress` attribute.

```
wls:/bigrezdomain/serverConfig> cd('Clusters/BigRezCluster')

wls:/bigrezdomain/serverConfig/Clusters/BigRezCluster> myServerList =
cmo.getServers()

wls:/bigrezdomain/serverConfig/Clusters/BigRezCluster> for server in myServerList:
...     print server.getName(), ' has a Listen Address = ', server.getListenAddress()
...

Server1  has a Listen Address =  everest.us.oracle.com
Server2  has a Listen Address =  k2.us.oracle.com
Server3  has a Listen Address =  lhotse.us.oracle.com
```

Note that unlike Java, Python uses indentation to demarcate blocks of code. Our `for` loop contains a single line of code and starts with a *tab* character. We close the `for` loop in the interpreter with a blank line.

In addition to looking at the *Config MBeans*, WLST also gives us the ability to view the *Runtime MBeans* to get actual runtime statistics and current state of the running server to which WLST is connected. On the admin server, WLST also has access to the domain runtime MBeans, which allow you to get the actual runtime statistics and current state of every managed server in the domain. The `serverConfig()`, serverRuntime(), and domainRuntime() commands allow you to switch back and forth between views into these three sets of MBeans.

Now that we understand the basics of how to navigate the MBean hierarchy, we need to know how to make changes. The edit() command switches put you into the *Edit MBean* hierarchy. startEdit() locks the configuration so you can safely make changes. Once we have the lock, we make whatever changes we want. At any time during this process, the validate() command will validate our changes. We can save our changes with the save() command or abandon any unsaved changes with the stopEdit() command, which also releases the configuration lock. Once we save any changes, the isRestartRequired() command will tell us whether or not a restart will be required for all of our changes to take effect. We use the activate() command to activate our saved changes, which also releases the configuration lock. Here is an example of changing the BigRezCluster's ClusterAddress property using WLST.

```
wls:/bigrezdomain/serverConfig/Clusters/BigRezCluster> edit()

Location changed to edit tree. This is a writable tree with DomainMBean as the root.
To make changes you will need to start an edit session via startEdit().

For more help, use help(edit)

wls:/bigrezdomain/edit> cd('Clusters/BigRezCluster')

wls:/bigrezdomain/edit/Clusters/BigRezCluster> startEdit()

Starting an edit session ...
Started edit session, please be sure to save and activate your changes once you are
done.

wls:/bigrezdomain/edit/Clusters/BigRezCluster !>
cmo.setClusterAddress('192.168.1.41:7001,192.168.1.42:7001,192.168.1.43:7001')

wls:/bigrezdomain/edit/Clusters/BigRezCluster !> save()

Saving all your changes ...
Saved all your changes successfully.

wls:/bigrezdomain/edit/Clusters/BigRezCluster !> activate()

Activating all your changes, this may take a while ...
The edit lock associated with this edit session is released
once the activation is completed.

The following non-dynamic attribute(s) have been changed on MBeans
that require server re-start:
MBean Changed : com.bea:Name=BigRezCluster,Type=Cluster
Attributes changed : ClusterAddress

Activation completed
```

Though we have barely scratched the surface of what you can do with WLST, it is time to move on. You should explore the WebLogic Server MBean Reference at Link 12-29 to familiarize yourself with the WebLogic Server JMX MBean structure, their attributes, and operations. WLST gives you access to all of these settings — even ones that are not currently surfaced in the WebLogic Console. Before we move on to discuss the WebLogic Console, we need to briefly discuss a deprecated tool that is still an important part of your arsenal.

Using the Deprecated Command-Line Administration Tool

WebLogic Server offers access to some administrative functionality through a deprecated command-line administration tool called weblogic.Admin. Though WLST and other tools offer better access to the functionality exposed by this tool, weblogic.Admin still offers one simple, yet valuable diagnostic feature that we cannot find elsewhere — the PING command.

As with the other command-line tools, the admin tool requires that the same Java system parameters be defined to support using the SSL protocol to communicate with the administration port on the server. In addition, the admin tool requires certain command-line options for every command. Therefore, we will create another script called weblogicAdmin.cmd to automate the process of invoking this program. Once again, we will place this script in the Chapter 12 examples directory (c:\powls\ch12):

```
@SETLOCAL
@set WL_HOME=c:\Oracle\Middleware\wlserver_10.3
@call %WL_HOME%\server\bin\setWLSEnv.cmd
java -Dweblogic.security.TrustKeyStore=CustomTrust
-Dweblogic.security.CustomTrustKeyStoreFileName=C:\powls\ch12\cacerts
-Dweblogic.security.CustomTrustKeyStorePassPhrase=changeit
weblogic.Admin -url %URL% -username weblogic -password weblogic1 %*
@ENDLOCAL
```

The PING command allows us to verify that a server is accepting connections and processing requests. This command connects to the targeted server, sends one or more requests to the server, waits for the server to respond to each request, and measures the round-trip time. These ping requests go through the same mechanism as other requests in that they get placed onto the self-tuning execute queue and an execute thread picks up the request and returns the response to the caller. Using the optional arguments of the PING command that specify the number of requests and the size of each request (in bytes), you can use this tool to measure server response time to these empty ping requests, as shown here:

```
> set URL= t3s://192.168.1.41:9002
> weblogicAdmin PING 1000 10000
Sending 1,000 pings of 10,000 bytes.

    RTT = ~1625 milliseconds, or ~1 milliseconds/packet
```

The results indicate that the total round-trip time (RTT) was about 1.6 seconds, so, on average, the server is processing these empty ping requests in about 1 millisecond. By looking at the latency of processing these empty requests, you can determine whether the server itself is being overloaded during periods of slower-than-normal system response time. This tool is an extremely important diagnostic tool because it enables you to easily see if, and how quickly, the server is processing requests going to the self-tuning execute queue.

Though this tool offers quick and easy access to other administrative functions, Oracle has deprecated it so we recommend that you consider alternative tools such as WLST and weblogic.Deployer wherever possible. For more information about `weblogic.Admin`, please see the WebLogic Server 10.0 documentation at Link 12-30.

For now, let's move on to the WebLogic Console to look at some of its monitoring capabilities.

Monitoring with the WebLogic Console

Most of our use of the WebLogic Console so far has focused on configuration. The WebLogic Console also offers a rich set of monitoring capabilities. In this section, we highlight some of these capabilities that provide insight into the behavior of the application, as well as WebLogic Server. Covering all of the monitoring capabilities of the WebLogic Console in detail is beyond the scope of this book. Please refer to the WebLogic Server documentation at Link 12-31 for more information.

Let's start by discussing the most basic, yet one of the most important, monitoring features of the WebLogic Console. When running a WebLogic Server application, you often need a glimpse inside the server to get a feel for how well it is running. Use the server's `Threads Monitoring` tab to get a look at the request throughput, execute queue backlog, and other execute thread–related statistics. Looking at Figure 12-9, you see that the average request throughput is currently 3 requests per second in this example display.

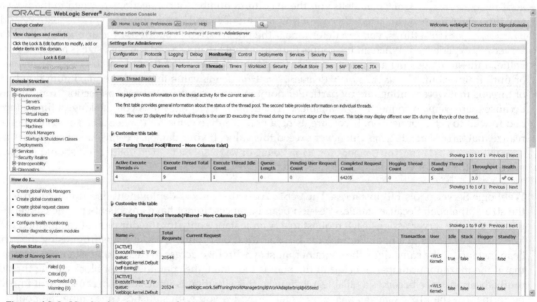

Figure 12-9: Monitoring server performance.

The execute queue length is zero, which means that we don't have more concurrent requests waiting than we have available execute threads to process them. Although this is the optimal situation, it will not always be achievable for actual production systems. The `Performance Monitoring` tab gives you a view into the state of the JVM. Because we are using JRockit, we have the power of JRockit Mission Control at our fingertips should we need to analyze our application or JVM performance in more detail.

Much more runtime information about a server is available through the WebLogic Console. The cluster's Summary Monitoring gives information about the membership of the cluster, and the Failover Monitoring tab gives information about replicated primary and secondary objects on each server. Using the server's Security Monitoring tab, you can view the statistics for failed logins, users that are locked out due to too many authentication failures, and other related information. The JTA Monitoring tab gives you access to transaction statistics and allows you to monitor the particular transactions and view in-flight transactions. On the server's General Configuration tab is a link to view the server's JNDI tree. In the Diagnostics ⇨ Log Files folder, you can access all of the log files for all servers in the domain. Note that by default, only entries from the last five minutes are shown. You will need to choose the Customize this table link to change the information available.

Next, let's look at monitoring JDBC data sources. Under a data source's Monitoring tab, the WebLogic Console provides a configurable view of each database connection pool's runtime statistics. Three particular parameters are especially important in diagnosing the health of your WebLogic Server application: Active Connections High Count, Wait Seconds High Count, and Waiting for Connection High Count. These parameters are not shown by default, but you can add them by using the Customize this view link.

Active Connections High Count tells you the maximum number of connections reached in the pool at any time since the server started. By comparing this number with your pool's Initial Capacity and Maximum Capacity settings, you can determine if the pool is sized properly for the application load the server has experienced. When all the connections in a pool are in use and the pool size is at its maximum value, a thread requesting a connection from the pool will have to wait until one becomes available or until it times out. The Waiting for Connection High Count value tells you the maximum number of threads that were waiting (at any particular point in time) to get a database connection from the pool because there were no connections available. Wait Seconds High Count tells you the longest time a thread had to wait to get a connection. If you are using a non-negative value for Connection Reserve Timeout, realize that Wait Seconds High will never exceed this value. If your database connection pool shows non-zero values for Waiting for Connection High Count or Wait Seconds High Count, you should consider increasing the size of your database connection pool.

WebLogic Server pools EJB instances. The weblogic-ejb-jar.xml deployment descriptor controls the size of the pool. Because stateless session bean instances do not have any client-specific conversational state, the server assigns each request to a bean instance only for the duration of the method call. Idle instances reside in a pool. Because the EJB specification prohibits two threads from using the same bean instance at the same time, the container must synchronize access to each bean instance. This means that if the maximum number of beans in the pool is too small, the container must block calling threads until a bean instance becomes available. Obviously, this situation is undesirable because it will impact performance. The EJB's Running Monitoring tab provides you with statistics concerning the pool. Timeout Total Count tells you the number of threads that have timed out waiting for a bean instance. The Waiter Total Count tells you the cumulative number of times a thread had to wait for a bean instance because none was available. At the time of writing Waiter Total Count is not accessible in the WebLogic Console (it is still available via the EJBPoolRuntimeMBean). Fortunately for stateless session beans, the default value of the <max-beans-in-free-pool> deployment descriptor element that controls the pool size is 1,000, so in practice this problem will occur only if the value is explicitly set too small.

For stateful session beans, the server does not pool idle instances, but it does maintain a cache of recently used bean instances. As this cache starts to fill up, WebLogic Server will passivate bean instances to make room for other instances by writing the bean's state to disk, as discussed in Chapter 6. The next time a request comes in for a passivated bean, the container must read the bean's state in from disk before dispatching the request to the bean. As you might imagine, this can have a significant impact on performance. By default, the `<max-beans-in-cache>` deployment descriptor element that controls the cache size is set to 1,000 instances. Whenever the container must activate or passivate a bean instance, it updates internal statistics that can be seen using the EJB application's `Stateful EJBs Monitoring` tab. For stateful session beans, you should keep an eye on the `Activation Count`. The container passivates bean instances when appropriate, but the cost of reactivating these beans can slow down your application tremendously. If the `Activation Count` for a particular bean is high, you should consider increasing the size of the cache.

WebLogic JMS also supports monitoring through the WebLogic Console. The JMS server's monitoring tab links to monitor JMS servers, destinations, and session pools. Two of the most important statistics to look at for JMS servers and destinations are the `Bytes Threshold Time` and `Messages Threshold Time`. These values will tell you how much time the JMS server or destination has spent controlling flow because the upper threshold was crossed. For more information about JMS monitoring, see Chapter 10 and the WebLogic Server documentation at Link 12-32.

At this point, we have touched on the most important monitoring features of the WebLogic Console. These features provide a quick insight into the operation of your application so that you can determine if configuration changes may help to improve performance or reduce resource consumption. Now, we are ready to move on to talk about WebLogic Server's JMX support.

Programmatic Monitoring with JMX

WebLogic Server implements the Java Management Extensions (JMX) specification and provides JMX-based services to manage server and application resources. While the WebLogic Console can be thought of as a user interface to JMX, the real power of JMX is the ability to programmatically manage resources through either a Java program or from a script using one of the available administrative tools that support JMX (for example, WLST and JConsole). A complete discussion of JMX and JMX programming is beyond the scope of this book; please refer to the WebLogic Server documentation at Link 12-33 and the JMX documentation at Link 12-34 for more information.

In this section, we show how to get the number of execute threads in the pool, the execute queue length, the execute queue throughput, and total number of requests processed using WebLogic Server's JMX MBeans. In the interest of space, we do not list the entire `WebLogicPerformanceMonitor` class, but it is available on the companion web site at `http://www.wrox.com/`. Let's walk through the important parts of this program that are related to JMX.

To execute JMX commands, you will need to obtain an `MBeanServerConnection` object. Remote JMX client applications typically do through the `JMXConnectorFactory.connect()` and `JMXConnector.getMBeanServerConnection()` calls. When connecting to WebLogic Server, you have three different MBean servers to which you might want to connect:

❑   Edit MBean Server — This server provides access to modify the Configuration MBeans that control WebLogic Server configuration.

❑   Runtime MBean Server — This MBean server provides access to the configuration and runtime MBeans of the local server (that is, the server to which you connect). If you only want to monitor configuration changes, connect to the admin server and use this MBean server.

❑   Domain Runtime MBean Server — This MBean server is only hosted on the admin server and provides views of the runtime MBeans for all running servers in the domain.

Our example uses the Domain Runtime MBean Server because we are simply monitoring the statistics in the servers.

```
import java.util.HashMap;

import javax.management.MBeanServerConnection;
import javax.management.remote.JMXConnector;
import javax.management.remote.JMXConnectorFactory;
import javax.management.remote.JMXServiceURL;
import javax.naming.Context;

...

JMXServiceURL serviceUrl =
    new JMXServiceURL(protocol, hostname, port, "/jndi/" +
                        "weblogic.management.mbeanservers.domainruntime");
HashMap<String, String> props = new HashMap<String, String>();
props.put(Context.SECURITY_PRINCIPAL, username);
props.put(Context.SECURITY_CREDENTIALS, password);
props.put(JMXConnectorFactory.PROTOCOL_PROVIDER_PACKAGES,
            "weblogic.management.remote");
connector = JMXConnectorFactory.connect(serviceUrl, props);
connection = connector.getMBeanServerConnection();
```

Once you connect to the proper MBean server, you use the MBeanServerConnection object to get or set attributes, invoke operations, and add or remove JMX notification listeners. When accessing MBeans via JMX, the biggest challenge is determining the correct ObjectName for the MBean you want. Two approaches to locating the MBean exist. First, you can determine the ObjectName for the specific MBean of interest and use it to issue calls directly on it. This works well if you can determine the ObjectName format at the time you are writing your code. The second approach is to navigate the MBean hierarchy at runtime to locate the MBean you want. Doing this is typically much easier because you only need to know the attribute names containing the references since the getAttribute() call will return the ObjectName (or an ObjectName array) for the referenced MBeans. We use the navigation method to locate the ThreadPoolRuntimeMBean for each server in the domain, as shown here.

```
import javax.management.MalformedObjectNameException;
import javax.management.ObjectName;

try {
    service = new ObjectName("com.bea:Name=DomainRuntimeService," +
                        "Type=weblogic.management.mbeanservers." +
                        "domainruntime.DomainRuntimeServiceMBean");
}
catch (MalformedObjectNameException e) {
    throw new AssertionError(e.getMessage());
}
```

```
...

ObjectName[] serverRuntimes =
    (ObjectName[])connection.getAttribute(service, "ServerRuntimes");

int length = serverRuntimes.length;
for (int i = 0; i < length; i++) {
    String serverName = (String)connection.getAttribute(serverRuntimes[i], "Name");

    // Get the nested ThreadPoolRuntime that has the stats we want.
    ObjectName threadPoolRuntime =
        (ObjectName)connection.getAttribute(serverRuntimes[i], "ThreadPoolRuntime");

    ...
```

Once we locate the MBean, we use the same getAttribute() call to get the attribute values.

```
long completedReqCount =
    (Long)connection.getAttribute(threadPoolRuntime, "CompletedRequestCount");
int executeThreadCount =
    (Integer)connection.getAttribute(threadPoolRuntime,
                                     "ExecuteThreadTotalCount");
int pendingUserReqCount =
    (Integer)connection.getAttribute(threadPoolRuntime,
                                     "PendingUserRequestCount");
int queueLength =
    (Integer)connection.getAttribute(threadPoolRuntime, "QueueLength");
double throughput =
    Double)connection.getAttribute(threadPoolRuntime, "Throughput");
```

That is really all there is to using JMX to read information. As you see later, the JMX code to modify configuration information is a little more involved, though it is still relatively simple. You should download the WebLogicPerformanceMonitor example before proceeding.

The WebLogicPerformanceMonitor program takes one argument, the name of the property file where we pass in the relevant information. Once the program reads the information from the property file, it instantiates a WebLogicPerformanceMonitor object, which uses JMXConnectorFactory.connect() and JMXConnector.getMBeanServerConnection() methods to create an authenticated connection to the MBean server. Finally, it goes into an infinite loop periodically calling the getPerfStats() method. getPerfStats() gets the array of ServerRuntimeMBean objects and iterates over each one printing out information from each server's ThreadPoolRuntimeMBean. It is also caching the current values so that the next time through the loop, it can print out information about what has changed since the last iteration.

To run this program, we need to create a property file that looks like the one shown here and pass the name of the property file to the WebLogicPerformanceMonitor class as an argument:

```
interval_seconds=5
protocol=t3s
hostane=192.168.1.40
port=9002
username=weblogic
password=weblogic1
```

As always, when using a Java client to talk to WebLogic Server using SSL, you need to add the appropriate Java system property definitions to the command line. In our example, we use the property file name `perfmon.properties` and create a script called `perfmon.cmd`, as shown here:

```
@SETLOCAL
@set POWLS_HOME=c:\powls
@set WL_HOME=C:\oracle\middleware\wlserver_10.3
@call %WL_HOME%\server\bin\setWLSEnv.cmd
@set CLASSPATH=%POWLS_HOME%\ch12\classes;%CLASSPATH%
java -Dweblogic.security.TrustKeyStore=CustomTrust
-Dweblogic.security.CustomTrustKeyStoreFileName=%POWLS_HOME%\ch12\cacerts
-Dweblogic.security.CustomTrustKeyStorePassPhrase=changeit
professional.weblogic.ch12.example1.WebLogicPerformanceMonitor
%POWLS_HOME%\ch12\perfmon.properties
@ENDLOCAL
```

If you run the `perfmon` script while Server1 is under load, you will get results that look something like the ones shown here:

```
> perfmon
AdminServer Stats at Time: Fri Jun 05 20:09:44 CDT 2009
        528216 Total Completed Requests
        9 Execute Threads
        0 Pending Requests (0 User, 0 System)
        7.000000 Total Throughput
AdminServer Stats at Time: Fri Jun 05 20:09:50 CDT 2009
        528259 Total Completed Requests
        9 Execute Threads
        0 Pending Requests (0 User, 0 System)
        2.500000 Total Throughput

        In the last 6047 milliseconds:
                43 requests were processed
                0 Execute Threads created
                Pending Requests increased by 0 requests
```

You can also use WLST to collect the same information from the server. See `WebLogicPerformance Monitor.py` in the downloadable examples for a WLST script that provides similar statistics for the servers. To invoke this script, run the `perfmonWLST.cmd` script file.

At this point, you have all the information you need to query WebLogic Server to get information via the JMX interface. Of course, the JMX interface also gives us the ability to create new configuration artifacts, to modify existing ones, and to monitor MBean attributes and receive notification when certain types of changes occur. WebLogic Server also supports registering custom MBeans that your application might create. A complete coverage of JMX is beyond the scope of this book. Please see the WebLogic Server documentation and our downloadable examples for some additional JMX examples that demonstrate some of these other use cases.

Before we move on to management, let's have a quick look at WebLogic Server's SNMP support.

Monitoring via SNMP

WebLogic Server supports Simple Network Management Protocol (SNMP) versions 1.0, 2.0, and 3.0. Starting in WebLogic Server 10, WebLogic Server supports two models for SNMP monitoring:

❑ Decentralized Model — As the name implies, this model allows the SNMP manager to communicate directly with SNMP agents within each server in the domain.

❑ Centralized Model — In this model, the SNMP manager communicates with an SNMP agent in the admin server, whose domain MBeans provide the SNMP agent access to runtime information about the entire domain.

Although the centralized model is convenient (and the only one available in earlier versions of WebLogic Server), it has limitations. First and most obvious, when the admin server is down, the SNMP manager loses visibility to the entire domain. Second, for larger domains you will have to filter a large amount of data to find information on a specific resource. Finally, this model adds performance overhead because the admin server's domain MBeans must collect and store runtime information about every server in the domain, thus increasing the load and memory footprint in the admin server. Therefore, we recommend that you use the decentralized model.

> ### Best Practice
> Always prefer the decentralized SNMP model when configuring your domain for SNMP monitoring.

With proper configuration, the WebLogic SNMP agent can act as a proxy for other SNMP agents on the same machine (for example, an Oracle database agent). Though complete coverage of WebLogic SNMP is beyond the scope of this book, we try to cover the basic information needed to communicate with WebLogic Server using SNMP. For more information, please refer to the WebLogic SNMP Management Guide at Link 12-35.

To use SNMP with WebLogic Server, you need to create each server's SNMP agent. To do this using the WebLogic Console, select the Diagnostics ➪ SNMP folder, create a new entry in the Server SNMP Agents table of the Agents tab, and specify the agent's Name. This creates a new agent that uses UDP port 161 and the server's default Listen Port to receive SNMP requests over TCP. At this point, the agent is not enabled or targeted to a server in the domain so we need to do some additional configuration.

On the SNMP agent's General Configuration tab, the Enabled checkbox enables the agent and the SNMP UDP Port allows you to specify what port you want to use for SNMP UDP traffic. The Master AgentX Port attribute specifies which UDP port subagents use to communicate with the SNMP agent. Do not confuse this with the proxy functionality we described earlier. If your server is running on a Unix-based platform, don't forget that you must start the server as root to use port numbers below 1024. Should you want to change the TCP port that the SNMP agent uses, you must create a new network channel and set the Protocol to snmp.

> For the SNMP agent to use its default UDP port of 161, WebLogic Server instances on Unix-based platforms must be started as root.
>
> By default, the SNMP agent uses the server's default `Listen Port`. To change this, you must create a network channel that supports the SNMP protocol.

At the time this book was written, the WebLogic SNMP agent only allows you to configure the UDP port numbers used by the agent — there is no way to specify the IP Address or hostname. As a result, the SNMP agent will bind to the UDP ports without specifying a listen address. This means that if you have multiple agents running on the same machine (for example, one running inside of each managed server on the machine), you should explicitly configure agents to use different port numbers — which means creating individual agents for each server. If you don't, the agent will silently look for the next available port numbers and bind to them. We expect this to change in the near future so please check the WebLogic Server documentation for more information.

This can lead to very insidious behavior. For example, when the SNMP manager sends a request to managed servers on the machine using the configured port, all requests using that port will go to the first server that was started (and found the configured port available). This means that while your SNMP manager is sending a correctly targeted request to each managed server individually, all the requests will actually be processed by the same managed server, thus leading to an incorrect view of your system. Even if you take into account the behavior of the SNMP agents of selecting the next available port, this doesn't help you much because which agents get assigned to which ports really depends on the order the managed servers are started. Always set the `SNMP UDP Port` and `Master AgentX Port` explicitly to different values across SNMP agents hosted on the same machine. Remember to account for possible server migration during failover when choosing these values!

> The WebLogic SNMP agent does not specify a bind address when binding to its UDP ports. By default, the SNMP agent will silently detect a port in use and select the next available port. Even this is problematic because which managed server's agent gets assigned which port is determined purely by the order that the managed servers are started.
>
> When running multiple managed servers on a single machine, always create separate SNMP agents for each managed server and always explicitly specify different `SNMP UDP Port` and `Master AgentX Port` values for each agent.

Before restarting the server, let's talk about some of the other parameters on this tab. SNMP v1.0 and v2.0 uses passwords known as *community names* to authenticate SNMP requests. SNMP v3.0 does not rely on the community name and provides its own mechanisms to support a stronger authentication model. As such, WebLogic Server uses the `Community Based Access Enabled` checkbox on the SNMP agent's `General Configuration` tab to enable WebLogic SNMP support for SNMP v1.0 and v2.0.

Because the admin server has much of the WebLogic SNMP MIB data available for every server in a domain, you need some way for the SNMP manager to tell the admin server's WebLogic SNMP agent what data it wants. The way that WebLogic SNMP accounts for this is by piggybacking the server information with the community name. WebLogic Server's SNMP manager needs to send the community name in the form `<community_name>@<server_name>`. You tell WebLogic SNMP what community name to expect from the SNMP manager via the `Community Prefix` parameter. To get information from the entire domain, connect to the admin server and either replace the server name with the domain name or omit the `@<server_name>` portion of the community name altogether. Note that only the admin server supports this `@<server_name>` syntax because the managed servers only have their own information anyway.

WebLogic Server does not provide an SNMP manager. For this purpose, we will use the WebNMS MIB Browser and Trap Viewer that come with the WebNMS SNMP API 4 product (available from Link 12-36). The MIB Browser allows us to interact with the WebLogic SNMP agent by sending SNMP GET requests to retrieve WebLogic Server configuration and runtime information. This is the same information available through the JMX APIs. WebLogic SNMP does not currently support the SNMP SET operation to make changes to the WebLogic Server configuration.

To communicate with the WebLogic SNMP agent, you need to load the WebLogic Server management information base (MIB) data into the MIB Browser. Using the MIB Browser application's `File` menu, select the `Load MIB` menu item, browse to the `$WL_HOME/server/lib` directory, and select the `BEA-WEBLOGIC-MIB.asn1` file. After expanding the `BEA-WEBLOGIC-MIB` folder on the left, you should see a list of WebLogic SNMP MIB tables and attributes similar to those shown in Figure 12-10. Replace the `Community` entry with the string `public@Server1` and perform an SNMP GET operation targeted to the admin server to get the names of the application deployed to Server1, as shown in Figure 12-10.

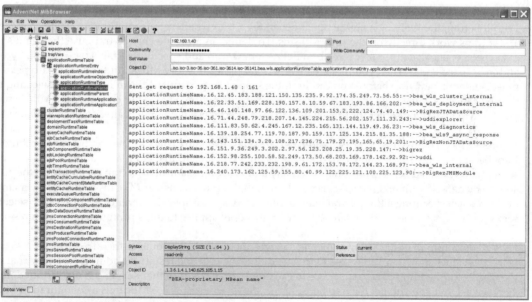

Figure 12-10: Viewing the WebLogic Server MIB.

All of this is interesting, but the main reason to use SNMP is to send unsolicited messages to the SNMP manager whenever something happens. These unsolicited messages are called SNMP *traps*. WebLogic SNMP can generate traps to notify the SNMP manager of certain types of events. WebLogic Server comes with a set of predefined traps for server startup, server shutdown, cold start (admin server startup), and authentication failure. You can also set up three other types of traps: attribute change traps, log message traps, and monitor traps. Before we talk about defining new traps, let's configure the WebLogic SNMP agent and the WebNMS Trap Viewer and verify that we are seeing traps propagate from WebLogic Server to the Trap Viewer.

The first step is to configure the Trap Viewer to listen for traps. Using the MIB Browser's View menu, select the Trap Viewer menu item. Use the Trap Viewer's Start button to tell it to start listening for traps on its default port, port 162, with a Community of public. Now, you need to configure the WebLogic Server side of things. For each SNMP agent, use the agent's Trap Destinations Configuration tab to create a new trap destination. Set the Name to WebNMSTrapViewer, the Community to public, the Host to the IP address or hostname of the machine where Trap Viewer is running (for example, 192.168.1.40), and the Port to 162. Because we are using SNMP v1.0–style traps, we don't need to specify the Security Name or Security Level attributes, which only apply to SNMP v3–style traps. Don't forget to include the SNMP agent on the admin server. Activate your changes once you have finished defining the trap destinations — no server restart is needed.

Now, let's test the trap mechanism by shutting down and restarting Server1. Trap Viewer eventually receives two traps, one for server shutdown and one for server startup. The server shutdown trap has a Generic Type of 6 (that is, an enterprise-specific type) and Specific Type of 70 (that is, server shutdown). Note that if you are running a cluster of managed servers, you may receive multiple copies of each trap. For example, the admin server and other managed servers may all generate a trap saying that Server1 was shut down. We are now ready to explore the other trap types that WebLogic SNMP supports.

WebLogic SNMP supports defining three types of traps. The first type of trap is an attribute change trap. With this trap, the WebLogic SNMP agent generates a trap whenever a configuration value changes. These traps work directly on the JMX MBeans. To define an attribute change trap, use the agent's Attribute Changes Configuration tab to define a new trap and specify the trap's Name, MBean Type, and Attribute Name. When you first create a trap, it applies to every MBean of the specified type. You must create the new trap before you can limit the scope to a particular MBean instance by selecting the desired MBean's name from the Monitored MBean Name drop-down list. After changing the MBean name, you have to restart the server for that change to take effect since the trap has already been initialized.

Before we move on, we need to discuss the Servers tab, also known as the Enabled Servers attribute of a trap. Because a trap is now defined in the scope of an SNMP agent (that is already targeted at one or more servers), the Enabled Servers attribute is actually a filtering mechanism for a trap executing on the admin server. By default with no Enabled Server selected, the trap will consider MBeans from all servers in the domain when executing a trap. If you want to limit the trap to a specific server or set of servers, select the server or servers on the Servers tab. Remember, this only applies to traps running on the admin server!

Let's create a trap to notify you if someone changes the Targets attribute of the BigRezJTADataSource using the values shown in Table 12-9. Once you define the trap and restart the admin server, try changing the targets for the BigRezJTADataSource to exclude Server3. Notice that Server3 is not included in the Servers list, but you still get the trap because the JDBCSystemResource MBean is a configuration MBean and all configuration is controlled by the admin server.

Note that WebLogic Server only supports attribute change traps on configuration MBeans. To monitor attribute changes to runtime MBeans, you must use a monitor trap. Before we discuss monitor traps, we will look at log filter traps.

Table 12-9: BigRezJTADataSource Targets Attribute Change Trap Configuration Parameters

Name	Value
Name	BigRezJTADataSource Targets Attribute Trap
Monitored MBean Type	JDBCSystemResource
Monitored Attribute Name	Targets
Monitored MBean Name	BigRezJTADataSource
Enabled Servers	*<none>*

A log filter trap generates a trap whenever an entry appears in the WebLogic Server log file matching the filter. Log filters can specify several different parameters by which to filter log messages that should generate a trap. Let's examine a WebLogic Server log file entry.

```
####<Jun 9, 2009 12:14:29 AM CDT> <Info> <JDBC> <www1.bigrez.com> <AdminServer>
<[ACTIVE] ExecuteThread: '0' for queue: 'weblogic.kernel.Default (self-tuning)'>
<<WLS Kernel>> <> <> <1244524469593> <BEA-001156> <Stack trace associated
with message 001129 follows:

java.sql.SQLException: The Network Adapter could not establish the connection
        at oracle.jdbc.driver.SQLStateMapping.newSQLException(SQLStateMapping.java:70)
        at oracle.jdbc.driver.DatabaseError.newSQLException(DatabaseError.java:133)
        at oracle.jdbc.driver.DatabaseError.throwSqlException(DatabaseError.java:199)
        at oracle.jdbc.driver.DatabaseError.throwSqlException(DatabaseError.java:480)
        at oracle.jdbc.driver.T4CConnection.logon(T4CConnection.java:413)
        at oracle.jdbc.driver.PhysicalConnection.<init>(PhysicalConnection.java:508)
        at oracle.jdbc.driver.T4CConnection.<init>(T4CConnection.java:203)
        ...
```

Each log file entry has the following format.

```
<Date/Time> <Severity Level> <Subsystem> <Machine> <Server> <Thread> <User Identity>
<Transaction ID> <Diagnostic Context ID> <Raw Time> <Message ID> <Message Text>
```

Imagine that you want to set up a trap every time this message appears (because this message alerts you that the database is no longer reachable). You do this by defining a log filter trap using the settings listed in Table 12-10.

The last type of trap to discuss is the monitor trap. Monitor traps are used to monitor an attribute value of an MBean; they come in three types: counter, string, and gauge. A counter trap simply generates a trap when a particular attribute value meets or exceeds the threshold value. For example, you might want to define a counter monitor trap to let you know when a server is using all of the connections in the `BigRezJTADataSource` JDBC connection pool. To do this, you need to use the

ActiveConnectionsHighCount attribute of the JDBCConnectionPoolRuntime MBean with the Name of BigRezJTADataSource on Server1, Server2, and Server3.

Table 12-10: Database Down Log Filter Trap Configuration Parameters

Name	Value
Name	Database Down Log Filter Trap
Severity Level	Info
Subsystem Names	JDBC
User IDs	
Message IDs	001156
Message Substring	
Servers	Server1, Server2, Server3

A string monitor trap compares the attribute value against a string and can raise a trap when the string matches or when it differs. A gauge monitor trap will alert you whenever the attribute value meets or exceeds the Threshold High value and when it reaches or falls below the Threshold Low. If you had a JDBC connection pool where the Initial Capacity and Maximum Capacity attributes were different, you might want to create a gauge monitor to monitor the maximum and minimum number of connections. By setting the Threshold Low value to be one less than the Initial Capacity, your gauge monitor trap could monitor the ActiveConnectionsCurrentCount attribute of the JDBCDataSourceRuntime MBean and alert you whenever the number of active connections are less than the Initial Capacity (which might indicate database connectivity problems).

Before we move on, we should mention that although WebLogic Server does not provide an SNMP manager, it does provide a Java command-line utility class that you can use to issue SNMP manager commands like GET or GETNEXT. This can allow you to do simple sanity tests of your SNMP agent configuration to make sure that it is working without needing to revert to your SNMP manager console. To get the current number of threads in Server1's thread pool, use the GETNEXT command to get the value of the ExecuteThreadTotalCount attribute on the ThreadPoolRuntime table. Because GETNEXT accepts relative object IDs (OIDs), we simply take the relative OID value for this attribute from the WebNMS MIB Browser and execute the following command on the admin server machine.

```
java weblogic.diagnostics.snmp.cmdline.Manager SnmpGetNext -c public@Server1 -p 161
.1.3.6.1.4.1.140.625.367.1.25

enterprises.140.625.367.1.25.16.200.144.104.202.36.239.133.252.37.194.1.4.239.88
.180.207=6
```

Notice that we set the community name to `public@Server1` so that we get the value for `Server1`. Our GETNEXT command also returned the absolute Object ID for this attribute. Given this attribute, we could use the following GET command to periodically poll the value of this attribute.

```
java weblogic.diagnostics.snmp.cmdline.Manager SnmpGet -p 161
enterprises.140.625.367.1.25.16.200.144.104.202.36.239.133.252.37.194.1.4.239.88.180
.207

enterprises.140.625.367.1.25.16.200.144.104.202.36.239.133.252.37.194.1.4.239.88
.180.207=6
```

For more information in the WebLogic SNMP command-line tool, please see the WebLogic Server documentation at Link 12-37. At the time of writing, the documentation was pretty terse; however, the help output of each command seems to be pretty good, as shown here.

```
java weblogic.diagnostics.snmp.cmdline.Manager SnmpGetNext -?

    USAGE

        java SnmpGetNext [-?|options] <objectID>+

    DESCRIPTION

        Performs a standard SnmpGetNext operation with the given
        objectIDs.

    OPTIONS

        -v1|v2[c]|v3                : snmp version                      [v1]
        -c[ommunity] <community>:   snmp community to use               [public]

        -h[ost]      <host>         : snmp agent host                   [localhost]
        -p[ort]      <port>         : snmp agent port                   [161]
        -r[etries]   <retries>      : # of retries                      [3]
        -t[imeout]   <millis>       : message timeout in millis         [3000]
        -maxvbs      <max_vbs>      : max # of varbinds in a single req.[no-max]

        -metadata    <filename>     : metadata file to load             [mib-2]
        -m[ibs]      <mib-list>     : list of MIBs to load from mibdirs [mib-2]
                                      (def: SNMPv2-MIB:IF-MIB:TCP-MIB)
        -M|mibdirs   <dir-path>     : directories of precompiled MIBs   [default]
        -list                       : list available MIBs               [false]

        -log         <logfile>      : logfile to store debug output     [none]
        -d[ump]                     : dump debug info to stdout         [off]
                                      (note: will not work with -log)

        -pkts                       : display data packets              [off]
        -O outopts                  : display output options            [i]
```

```
                              n: print OIDs in numeric format
                              l: print OIDs with resolved labels
                              i: print OIDs with formatted indexes

        -tcp                  : use TCP rather than UDP              [false]

    NOTE: You may include a 'dsnmp.conf' file in your classpath  or
          filesystem containing default values for the following:

                  mibs=<mib-list>
                  mibdirs=<dir-path>
                  retries=<retries>
                  timeout=<timeout-millis>
                  host=<default-host>
                  port=<default-port>
                  community=<default-community>

          This 'dsnmp.conf' file may be located in any of the following
          directories or JAR file packages:

                  .
                  /
                  /monfox/toolkit/snmp/conf
                  /monfox/toolkit/snmp/appl
                  /etc/dsnmp/conf
                  /etc/dsnmp


    SNMPv3 OPTIONS

        -u[ser] <security-user> : USM username                      [none]
        -A      <auth-passwd>    : Authentication password          [none]
        -a      <auth-protocol>  : Authentication protocol (MD5|SHA) [MD5]
        -X      <priv-passwd>    : Privacy password                 [none]
        -x      <priv-protocol>  : DES | AES128 | AES192 | AES256    [DES]
        -l      <security-level> : noAuthNoPriv|authNoPriv|authPriv [authNoPriv]
        -e      <sec-engine-id>  : security engine id               [none]
        -n      <context-name>   : context name to use              [""]
        -E      <context-eng-id> : context engine id                [none]
        -Z      <boots>,<time>   : engine boots, engine time        [none]
        -crypto <provider>       : security provider class name     [...SunJCE]
```

Hopefully, the documentation issues will improve by the time you read this book.

This ends our discussion of WebLogic SNMP. Although there are very few built-in traps, the ability to define custom traps makes it possible to define most of the types of traps that you might want. Of course, the real difficulty here is that you must know the JMX APIs, what the possible values of each attribute are, what the expected and abnormal ranges of values are, and so on. We hope that future versions of WebLogic Server will simplify this task so that it does not require so much system-level knowledge of the JMX APIs to be able to define custom traps.

Managing WebLogic Server Applications

We are finally ready to talk about the toughest part of a WebLogic Server administrator's job — how to manage WebLogic Server–based applications. This coverage is by no means comprehensive, but we hope to cover the most common problems encountered while managing WebLogic Server applications. We start off this section by discussing how to manage applications by touching on such topics as application troubleshooting and versioning, and we finish with a discussion of handling failure conditions.

Troubleshooting Application Issues

Application troubleshooting can take many forms. Sometimes, you need to figure out why your application is not performing as fast or scaling as well as someone thinks it should. At other times, the application is not functioning properly and you need to determine the root cause of the problem. In a distributed system, this means that you must consider the entire application environment from the client application and hardware, the network and network devices, the server hardware and operating system, the web and application servers, the JVMs, the database, and other backend server hardware and software to the application itself. This can be a daunting task, and the possibilities are endless. Though we cannot expect to cover all the possible problems or diagnostic approaches, we do hope to describe the use of some of the tools that you have at your disposal to make it easier to narrow down the possible causes of the problem.

When problems arise with a distributed system, people naturally suspect the component(s) of the system for which they have the least knowledge or trust. In many cases, this means that WebLogic Server gets the blame, and it is your job as WebLogic Server administrator to prove the problem lies elsewhere (if, in fact, it does). When you encounter a problem, it is important to get as much information about the symptoms of the problem as possible while trying to recognize that people's biases for what they believe to be the problem may cause them to lead you in the wrong direction. Although it is important to listen to all the evidence, it is also important not to jump to conclusions that are not backed up by the facts.

In almost every situation where you suspect a problem might be related to WebLogic Server, you should use either the WebLogic Console or some custom WLST scripts to determine the health of the server. The previous section discussed many of the WebLogic Console's most important monitoring capabilities. Before doing anything, you should look at the relevant WebLogic Server log files to see if they contain any errors that might indicate the cause of the problem. If the problem at hand is performance-related, looking at the relevant server's execute queue length and throughput as well as the JVM's heap usage profile should be one of the first pieces of evidence to examine. To view the server's execute queue length and throughput, use the server's Threads Monitoring tab in the WebLogic Console. If the execute queue is empty or no longer than normal (and garbage collection does not appear to be unusually frequent) even though the clients are experiencing a significant degradation in response time, you need to determine whether the problem is with the server or the components in front of or behind the server.

To narrow down the possible causes of a performance problem, the best solution is to invest in an end-to-end application performance monitoring tool, such as CA Wily Introscope (see Link 12-38) or Oracle Enterprise Manager Application Performance Management extensions (see Link 12-39). Oracle JRockit Mission Control offers a lightweight solution that provides detailed information about what is happening inside the WebLogic Server and the JRockit JVM. You may also want to consider instrumenting your production applications ahead of time using the WebLogic Diagnostic Framework, which we discuss later.

Assuming you don't have such tools in place, you may need to revert to some old-fashioned, though still useful techniques. It is useful to be able to run your client application and the `weblogic.Admin` tool's PING command from various points in your application environment. For example, let's say that your Internet users are complaining of very slow response time. By being able to run a browser on one of the web server machines, you can determine if the cause of the slowdown is between the users and the web server or somewhere starting at the web server and going back into your application and database environment. By again moving the browser to an application server machine, you can isolate or eliminate the web server and the network environment between as potential causes. If the application is not available, the admin tool's PING command can serve a similar purpose.

If you determine through testing that the problem appears to be that WebLogic Server is taking too long to process the requests (even though it is processing PING requests very quickly), the next step is to try to determine what is causing the application request processing to be so slow. Create a series of thread dumps over the span of a minute or so and look at the call stacks for the threads over time. There are a number of ways to generate thread dumps, including sending a `kill -3` signal to the process and using the WebLogic Console or WLST to tell WebLogic Server to do a thread dump. This information will help you understand what the execute threads are doing and may tell you where they are spending most of their time. The optimum frequency and duration of the series of thread dumps depends on how long it takes to process an application request. For example, if a request is taking 15 seconds to process once it is picked up by an execute thread, taking thread dumps 60 seconds apart probably won't help you as much as taking them 5 seconds apart so that you can see if the same thread is in the same place in consecutive thread dumps.

Resource contention is a common cause of performance problems and can occur at many levels. Use the WebLogic Console monitoring tools to detect resource contention for things like JDBC connections and EJB instances. For other types of application-specific resource contention, thread dumps may be your only detection mechanism (outside of either a thorough understanding of how the application works or the use of profiling tools). Data access contention inside the database is best detected by database monitoring tools but may sometimes be seen in application thread dumps.

Best Practice

Configure your production environment with an end-to-end application performance management tool to help troubleshoot performance problems and identify the root cause quickly.

Oracle JRockit Mission Control offers a lightweight solution for gaining detailed insight into what is happening inside the WebLogic Server and the JRockit JVM if you are using the JRockit JVM to run WebLogic Server.

In lieu of proper tools, you can use a series of properly spaced thread dumps to gain insight into the possible causes of long-running requests.

Garbage collection is another common problem. Though modern JVMs have much better garbage collection algorithms than their predecessors, these new garbage collectors can require much more tuning to get optimum, or even reasonable, performance. Most JVMs now have multiple garbage collection algorithms that allow a properly tuned JVM to minimize the number of full garbage collection cycles it runs. Typically, these full garbage collection runs must stop all other activity while the garbage collector scans the heap for unreachable objects, removes unreachable objects, and relocates reachable objects to compact the heap (which packs the reachable objects together so as to maximize the contiguous free memory space within the heap). By looking at the JVM heap usage profile (for example, by turning on the -verbosegc switch to the JVM or better yet by using JRockit Mission Control), you can detect how often these full garbage collection scans are occurring.

Whenever the heap usage reaches a certain percentage of capacity, the garbage collector will perform a full GC to reclaim as much free memory as possible. The result is that users will see that requests that are in-flight during a full GC take longer to process. In extreme situations, full GC sweeps can occur multiple times in the life of a single request. Because most server-side Java applications tend to create a lot of transient objects (ones that are used for a very short time and thrown away), it is often possible to reduce the number of full GC sweeps significantly by tuning the garbage collector. For more information about garbage collector tuning, and performance tuning in general, see Chapter 13, the WebLogic Server documentation at Link 12-40, and your JVM documentation (for example, the Oracle JRockit JVM documentation at Link 12-41).

> **Best Practice**
> Frequent spikes that indicate high JVM heap usage can have a significant effect on the user's experience. Adjusting the heap size and garbage collection tuning parameters can significantly reduce the frequency of full GC sweeps and improve the user experience.

To diagnose application errors, you often need the ability to turn on more verbose logging in targeted areas of WebLogic Server. WebLogic Server has an extensive debug logging framework that allows you to enable entire subsystem-level debugging or drill down to a very specific component to enable debugging output. To modify the default settings, use the server's Debug tab to change the debug scope settings. What makes this so convenient is that you can turn on and off these debug settings at will without interrupting your applications or restarting the server. For example, enabling debugging at the weblogic.security.ssl scope level will make troubleshooting SSL handshake issues immensely easier.

Earlier, we demonstrated how you can define custom SNMP log filter traps to monitor WebLogic Server log files for specific errors. Wouldn't it be nice if you could use this facility for your own application logs? Guess what, you can!

Using WebLogic Server's Logging Services

WebLogic Server provides logging services that allow your developers to write application log messages to the WebLogic Server log files. By having your applications use this service, your applications automatically get access to log-related features like automated log rotation and archiving, support for internationalization and localization, distributed log viewing via the WebLogic Console, severity-based log filtering, and custom JMX- or SNMP-based log filter notifications.

By default, the logging service uses standard Java logging so that developers can get access to the java.util.logging.Logger object that the server uses for logging. With access to the server's Logger object, developers can take full advantage of the Java Logging APIs to add their own custom handlers, filters, and formatters. See the Java Logging API documentation at Link 12-42. WebLogic Server also supports using the Apache Log4J logging service to replace the default Java logging implementation.

Doing this allows the developer to use the Log4J APIs to define their own Log4J loggers, appenders, and layouts.

To produce messages to the log, WebLogic Server provides three mechanisms in which applications can integrate application logging with the WebLogic Server Logging Service: message catalog logging, non-catalog logging, and Apache Commons logging. Let's look at each option now.

Message Catalog Logging

WebLogic Server provides a catalog framework by which you can create a catalog of log messages, internationalize them, and generate Java classes that your application can use to generate these messages to the server log. The process of creating a message catalog logger is simple.

First, you need to create your message catalog. Though the message catalog is just an XML file that could be hand crafted, WebLogic Server provides a simple standalone Java program called `weblogic.MsgEditor` for creating and editing a message catalog. To create a new message catalog, use the `File` menu's `New Catalog` option and provide the values listed in Table 12-11.

Table 12-11: BigRezCatalog.xml Creation Data

Parameter	Value
Message catalog	C:\powls\ch12\MessageCatalog\BigRezCatalog.xml
Catalog Type	Log Messages
i18n Package	com.bigrez.logging.i18n
l10n Package	com.bigrez.logging.l10n
Subsystem	bigrez.com
Prefix	BigRez
Base id	500001
End id	501000
Loggables	unchecked

After creating the new catalog, you need to enter some messages. When creating a new message, the first attribute you must specify is the `Message ID`. This is the numeric value that identifies the log message; its value must be unique and fall within the range specified by `Base id` and `End id` (inclusively) when the catalog was created. The actual log message ID printed in the server log will be a combination of the `Prefix` and `Message ID` fields separated by a hyphen.

The `Method` field lets you define the method name and arguments that your application uses to create the log message. The arguments to your method can be referenced in the `Message Body` field. You refer to arguments positionally using a {#} syntax, where the number is a zero-based index of which argument value you want to insert. Note that the Message Details, Probable cause, and Action fields are only used internally by the WebLogic Server Development team to generate the "Error Message Catalog" section of the WebLogic Server documentation.

If you simply want to collect the log information and write it out later, you can enable the Loggables option. This will cause each logging method to return a weblogic.i18n.logging.Loggable object containing the log message data. Whenever you are ready to write the log message, you simply invoke the log() method on the Loggable object.

Once you complete the base catalog, you may want to add localized versions of the catalog messages for other locales. Again, WebLogic Server provides a standalone Java program called weblogic.MsgLocalizer for creating the localized versions of the message catalog. When you start this tool, locate your Master catalog file, choose the Locale you want, and create the new localized catalog. One thing we found a little confusing is that you need to select the All messages option from the View menu to get a list of the messages in the master catalog. Selecting a message from the master catalog will populate the localized message editor that will allow you to localize the specific message. Use this tool to create as many localized versions of the catalog as required.

Once you finish creating the message catalogs, you need to run compilation tools over them to generate the Java classes and property files required to make the catalog logger work. First, you generate compile the master catalogs using the following command:

```
java weblogic.i18ngen –build –d classes MessageCatalog\BigRezCatalog.xml
```

In the output directory, the i18ngen tool will generate and compile the Java class containing the catalog logger and the property file containing the English text for the master catalog. If you examine the generated Java source file, you will see each catalog entry's method has been mapped to a static method on the logging class. For example:

```
BigRezCatalogLogger.logComplete("this is my test message");
```

If you created any localized catalogs, you can run the l10ngen tool to create the property files for localized catalogs, as shown here. Don't forget to add the output directory of the i18ngen tool to your CLASSPATH first!

```
C:\powls\ch12>set CLASSPATH=c:\powls\ch12\classes;%CLASSPATH%
```

```
C:\powls\ch12>java weblogic.l10ngen -d classes MessageCatalog\BigRezCatalog.xml
```

All that is left to do now is write your application code using the catalog logger and make the generated logging class and property files available to your application at runtime. You can use the catalog logger from a standalone Java client. By default, it will log the messages to stdout instead of to a file. If you want the messages written to a file, set the Java system property weblogic.log.FileName to the name of the log file to use. If you want some subset of log messages to go to stdout, set the Java system property weblogic.log.StdoutSeverityLevel to one of these values: Debug, Info, Notice, Warning, Error, Critical, Alert, Emergency, or Off.

For more information on the catalog logger, see Link 12-43. For more information on the message editor, see Link 12-44. For more information on the i18ngen and l10ngen utilities, see Link 12-45.

Non-Catalog Logging

If you don't need internationalization support and don't want to take the extra steps to create message catalogs, WebLogic Server provides the `weblogic.logging.NonCatalogLogger` class that your applications can use to write application messages to the server log. Note that all messages logged via the non-catalog logger will have the message ID set to `000000`.

```
NonCatalogLogger logger = new NonCatalogLogger("bigrez.com");
logger.info("We are using the WLS NonCatalogLogger");
...
logger.error("Error loading property file", exception);
```

The `NonCatalogLogger` interface supports methods whose names map directly to the different severity levels supported by the logging service. Each severity level maps to two methods of the form:

```
void severity(String message)
void severity(String message, Throwable error)
```

Like the catalog logger, the non-catalog logger can also be used by client applications running outside the server to write to client-side log files. The same client-side Java system property settings apply to both the catalog and non-catalog loggers.

Commons Logging

If desired, your application can use the Apache Commons Logging API instead of either the catalog or non-catalog logging interface provided by WebLogic Server. WebLogic Server does not distribute a version of the Commons Logging classes for use by applications so you will need to download the `commons-logging.jar` from the Apache web site. Once downloaded, you will need to make both `commons-logging.jar` and the WebLogic Server–specific Commons classes (located in `$MIDDLEWARE_HOME/modules/com.bea.core.weblogic.commons.logging_1.3.0.0.jar`) available to your application in any of the standard ways that you would make any other utility classes available to an application (for example, placing them in the enterprise application's library directory).

To use this interface, set the `org.apache.common.logging.LogFactory` Java system property to `weblogic.logging.commons.LogFactoryImpl` and use the `LogFactory` interface to get a `Log` object by name. This name appears as the subsystem name in the server log file.

```
import org.apache.commons.logging.Log;
import org.apache.commons.logging.LogFactory;
...
System.setProperty(LogFactory.FACTORY_PROPERTY,
                   "weblogic.logging.commons.LogFactoryImpl");
...
Log bigRezLogger = LogFactory.getFactory.getInstance("bigrez.com");
...
bigRezLogger.error("BigRezJTADataSource.getConnection() failed", sqlException);
```

Note that Commons Logging defines six severity levels that map directly to method names on the Log interface: `trace`, `debug`, `info`, `warn`, `error`, and `fatal`. Each severity level maps to two methods of the following form:

```
void severity(Object message);
void severity(Object message, Throwable t);
```

Now that we know the options for producing messages to the server log file, we talk briefly about how to configure the logging service and tailor what messages get written to the server log. All of the log configuration we discuss here references settings found under the `Advanced` area of the server's `General Logging` tab in the WebLogic Console. By default, a server logs all messages with a severity level of INFO or higher and sends them to all log destinations, as specified by the `Minimum severity to log` attribute. You can use the `Logger severity properties` field to customize the logging level by subsystem using a semicolon-separated name-value pair syntax.

```
Security=Notice;EJB=Warning
```

You switch a server from using standard Java logging to Log4J using the `Logging implementation` attribute. You can also redirect `stdout` to the logging subsystem by enabling the `Redirect stdout logging enabled` checkbox. Other settings on this page tune the different log listeners' filters that write log messages to the server log file, `stdout`, the domain log file, and the memory buffer used for tailing logs in the WebLogic Console

We have just scratched the surface with what is possible using the WebLogic Server Logging Service. However, it is time to move on to talk about another powerful diagnostic tool WebLogic Server provides — the WebLogic Diagnostic Framework. For more information on the logging service, please refer to the WebLogic Server documentation at Link 12-46.

Using the WebLogic Diagnostic Framework

The WebLogic Diagnostic Framework (WLDF) is a powerful collection of services for monitoring the runtime behavior of your application. Though you can use WLDF for production monitoring, it is particularly useful in pre-production performance testing and troubleshooting situations.

The component services of the WLDF are:

Logging   The WebLogic Server Logging Services belong to the WLDF. These logging services were just covered in the "Using WebLogic Server's Logging Services" section.

Instrumentation   WLDF allows instrumentation monitors to be applied at arbitrary points in application code. Each monitor generates an event whenever the instrumented code is called. The monitored points are specified using declarative rules, and implemented using byte code modification. The events that are captured include a diagnostic context identifier, which allows a stream of related events to be correlated whether they occur within a server, or across JMS messages, remote RMI, or SOAP calls.

Harvester   The harvester regularly schedules a task that records metric data from a configurable set of JMX MBeans.

Data produced from the log sources and instrumentation is in the form of asynchronous events that are *pushed* to the rest of the diagnostic framework. The harvester *pulls* data from the JMX MBeans and translates it into events.

Diagnostic Archive   Each server has a persistent diagnostic archive that is used to store captured historical data from log sources, instrumentation monitors, and the harvester.

The diagnostic archive can be persisted using either a file-based or JDBC-based WebLogic Server persistent store. The archive can be queried through a JMX *accessor* interface using the WLDF query language. The data can also be exported to an XML file using WLST commands.

Watches and Notifications   WLDF watch rules can be used to monitor log messages, instrumentation events, or harvested metric data. By default when a watch rule fires, a message is written to the server log. In addition, external systems can be notified using JMX, SNMP, JMS, or email.

Console Extension   The WLDF console extension provides a Java applet that can display metric data from JMX MBeans as graphs and charts. It can also be used to browse historical metric data that has been stored in the diagnostic archive using the harvester.

Diagnostic Image Capture   A diagnostic image is an archive of information captured at a point in time from many different WebLogic Server subsystems, such as the transaction engine, JDBC, JMS, deployment, JNDI, and so on. The content of a diagnostic image is primarily of interest to Oracle support engineers, but you may occasionally find it useful.

The creation of a diagnostic image can be triggered manually, using the console or WLST, or as the result of notification.

These various WLDF services have been designed to complement each other. They provide primitive capabilities that can be combined in powerful ways. The breadth of the WLDF can be a little daunting at first. Rather than dryly walking through each service in isolation, we show how you might use the WLDF to gain insight into the performance of `bigrez.com`, touching on instrumentation, the harvester, the diagnostic archive, and watches and notifications along the way.

For an advanced example of using WLDF, including diagnostic context propagation between servers, refer to the Oracle Technology Network article *Mining WebLogic Diagnostic Data with WLST* (see Link 12-47) which was written by one of this book's authors.

Instrumenting `bigrez.com`

Let's assume you are interested in the performance cost of searching `bigrez.com` for suitable properties to offer to the user. In particular, you want to know how long it takes the session façade to perform a JPA query against the database, and what further overhead is added by the EJB dispatch (including transaction management and the application interceptor).

To add instrumentation, you need to create an application-specific diagnostic module and a diagnostic system module. Listing 12-1 shows a suitable application diagnostic module. This should be named `weblogic-diagnostics.xml`, and packaged in the application archive below the `META-INF` directory.

Listing 12-1: Sample `weblogic-diagnostics.xml` application module.

```
<?xml version="1.0" encoding="UTF-8"?>
<wldf-resource
  xmlns="http://xmlns.oracle.com/weblogic/weblogic-diagnostics"
  xmlns:xsi="http://www.w3.org/2001/XMLSchema-instance"
  xsi:schemaLocation="http://xmlns.oracle.com/weblogic/weblogic-
diagnostics http://xmlns.oracle.com/weblogic/weblogic-
diagnostics/1.0/weblogic-diagnostics.xsd">
  <instrumentation>
    <enabled>true</enabled>
    <wldf-instrumentation-monitor>
      <name>Trace_facade_getOffersForDisplay</name>
      <action>MethodInvocationStatisticsAction</action>
      <location-type>around</location-type>
      <pointcut>execution(*
com.bigrez.service.impl.PropertyServicesImpl findByCityAndState(...))</pointcut>
    </wldf-instrumentation-monitor>
    <wldf-instrumentation-monitor>
```

```
      <name>Trace_propertySearchController_onSubmit</name>
      <action>MethodInvocationStatisticsAction</action>
      <location-type>around</location-type>
      <pointcut>execution(* com.bigrez.web.PropertySearchController
  onSubmit(...))</pointcut>
      </wldf-instrumentation-monitor>
    </instrumentation>
  </wldf-resource>
```

The example application module defines two custom monitors. One monitor instruments the session façade findByCityAndState() method and the other instruments the appropriate web controller's onSubmit() method. The code instrumented by each monitor is determined by a *pointcut expression*, similar to that used by Aspect Oriented Programming (AOP) frameworks such as AspectJ. The pointcut expression language is powerful: expressions can be based on Java inheritance, visibility modifiers (for example, public or protected), annotations, use wild cards, and can be combined to form composite expressions. We're using the pointcut language in a straightforward manner — the first pointcut in the example instruments any method called findByCityAndState() in the PropertyServicesImpl class, whatever the parameters or return type.

In addition to the instrumentation point, each monitor in the application module configures a number of actions. There are several types of actions that do things such as record the elapsed time, take a stack dump or a thread dump, or simply record that the monitored code has been called. There are three types of monitors:

❑ *Before* monitors fire before the application code is called.

❑ *After* monitors fire after the application code is called.

❑ *Around* monitors fire both before and after the application code is called.

Each action type is compatible with either before and after monitors or around monitors.

Most of the action types cause event information to be stored in the diagnostics archive. Storing data in the archive is useful when you want to record and analyze information about specific events. However, it requires you either to use the accessor API or export the data using WLST, so it is less interactive. Because we're not yet interested in individual events, we've used the MethodInvocationStatisticsAction, which aggregates information for each monitor and stores it in an in-memory JMX MBean that can be easily queried.

A diagnostic system module is also required. Diagnostic application modules only contain application-scoped monitors. System modules contain system-scoped monitors and other WLDF configuration data, such as that for the harvester, watches, and notifications. Note that instrumentation must be enabled in a system module that is targeted to each server you wish to monitor. This allows it to be easily switched on or off. Each server can have at most one targeted diagnostic system module.

Instrumentation for custom monitors is applied using byte code modification, so you must usually redeploy the application whenever you modify the instrumentation. This recreates the application classloader and reloads its classes, instrumenting them as necessary. Alternatively, you can add the *hot-swap* Java agent to the command line used to start the server, which allows the instrumentation to be changed dynamically without requiring redeployment.

```
java ... -javaagent:$WL_HOME/server/lib/diagnostics-agent.jar ... weblogic.Server
```

623

WebLogic Server does not support applying custom monitors to its own classes. Instead, a set of built-in diagnostic monitors is supplied that provide standard instrumentation points throughout the WebLogic Server subsystems. These monitors can be configured in a diagnostic system module. In contrast to custom application-scoped monitors, these standard monitors are rarely useful to application developers.

You can create diagnostic system modules using the WebLogic Console. For our example, we simply need to target the module to the appropriate server and enable instrumentation using the `Enabled` checkbox on the `Instrumentation Configuration` tab.

The information recorded by the `MethodInvocationStatisticsAction` is available through the application's `WLDFInstrumentationRuntime` MBean. This MBean has a `MethodInvocationStatistics` attribute that returns a nested set of maps containing of all the recorded statistics for the application. It also has an `getMethodInvocationStatisticsData()` operation that allows you to query for a subset of the data.

Listing 12.2 is an example WLST script that queries the `bigrez.com WLDFInstrumentationRuntime` MBean and displays all of the results.

Listing 12-2: WLST script to display the WLDF method invocation statistics.

```
connect()
cd("serverRuntime:/WLDFRuntime/WLDFRuntime/WLDFInstrumentationRuntimes/bigrez-ear")
def formatTime(t):
    """Convert nanoseconds double to milliseconds string."""
    return "%.2f" % (t/1e6)

for classStats in cmo.methodInvocationStatistics.entrySet():
    for methodStats in classStats.value.entrySet():
        for signatureStats in methodStats.value.entrySet():
            print "%s.%s(): %d %s %s %s %s" % (
                classStats.key,
                methodStats.key,
                signatureStats.value["count"],
                formatTime(signatureStats.value["min"]),
                formatTime(signatureStats.value["avg"]),
                formatTime(signatureStats.value["max"]),
                formatTime(signatureStats.value["std_deviation"]),)
```

Here are the results produced by the script after a few product searches have been performed.

```
...PropertyServicesImpl.findByCityAndState(): 3 13.62 95.36 193.37 74.28
...PropertySearchController.onSubmit(): 3 15.85 103.24 212.52 81.77
```

The values are the number of the times the method has been called, followed by the minimum, average, and maximum times, and the standard deviation. All the times are in milliseconds. These numbers were obtained by making a few requests to the application using a browser. If we applied a more realistic work load using a performance testing tool such as The Grinder (see Link 12-48), we could get a very good feel for the cost of the JPA query and the overhead of the EJB dispatch.

Harvesting Metric Information

Querying the JMX information using a WLST script can be inefficient. Each time a WLST script is started, it must create a Java virtual machine and a Jython interpreter. Each access to JMX MBeans requires an RMI call to the server. This overhead can be prohibitive when you need to capture lots of data during a performance test run.

This is where the WLDF harvester is useful. The harvester is configured in a diagnostics system module. If you use the WebLogic Console to access the diagnostic system module's `Collected Metrics Configuration` tab, you'll see that you can specify the metric data sampling period, which defaults to 5 minutes. This page also lets you add harvesting rules to collect data from built-in and custom MBeans. For example, you might want to record the number of JDBC connections in use. Simply use the WebLogic Console to define a new harvesting metric that collects the value of the `ActiveConnectionsCurrentCount` attribute of the `JDBCDataSourceRuntime` MBean by selecting the MBean and the attribute from the provided lists.

Continuing our `bigrez.com` example, you might also want to capture the statistics regularly from the application `WLDFInstrumentationRuntime` MBean. The data provided by this attribute is more complex, so you can't simply select it from the list. Instead, you have to provide an *attribute expression* in a particular form. The syntax is straightforward; refer to the WebLogic Server documentation at Link 12-49 for full details. Here's an expression that harvests the count, average, minimum, and maximum statistics from any monitor that uses the `MethodInvocationStatisticsAction`.

```
MethodInvocationStatistics(*)(*)(*)(count|avg|min|max)
```

Listing 12-3 shows the configuration file for the diagnostic system module having configured it to harvest from the `JDBCDataSourceRuntime` and `WLDFInstrumentationRuntime` MBeans.

Listing 12-3: Diagnostic system module with harvester configured.

```xml
<?xml version='1.0' encoding='UTF-8'?>
<wldf-resource ...>
  <name>MySystemModule</name>
  <instrumentation>
    <enabled>true</enabled>
  </instrumentation>
  <harvester>
    <harvested-type>
      <name>
        weblogic.management.runtime.JDBCDataSourceRuntimeMBean
      </name>
      <harvested-attribute>
        ActiveConnectionsCurrentCount
      </harvested-attribute>
      <harvested-instance>
```

Continued

Listing 12-3: Diagnostic system module with harvester configured. *(continued)*

```
           com.bea:Name=BigRezJTADataSource,ServerRuntime=AdminServer,
     Type=JDBCDataSourceRuntime
        </harvested-instance>
        <harvested-instance>
          com.bea:Name=BigRezNonJTADataSource,ServerRuntime=AdminServe
     r,Type=JDBCDataSourceRuntime
        </harvested-instance>
        <namespace>ServerRuntime</namespace>
      </harvested-type>
      <harvested-type>
        <name>
          weblogic.management.runtime.WLDFInstrumentationRuntimeMBean
        </name>
        <harvested-attribute>
          MethodInvocationStatistics(*)(*)(*)(avg,count,min,max)
        </harvested-attribute>
      </harvested-type>
    </harvester>
  </wldf-resource>
```

With the harvester enabled, the server is now recording information in its diagnostic archive. How can you get at it?

If you enable the WLDF console extension, you can see the historic information captured from the JDBCDataSourceRuntime MBean. The console extension is the quickest way to visualize data in the archive, and if you harvest a few key metrics such as heap size, thread usage, and JDBC connection pool usage, it can help you spot trends over time. This is particularly useful during performance testing, or when troubleshooting problems that occur out of office hours.

Due to its complex format, the WLDF console extension cannot display the data from the WLDFInstrumentationRuntime MBean. To get at the historical data, we'll have to export it from the archive.

Exporting Diagnostic Data

Data can be exported from the archive using WLST. There are two ways to accomplish this. First, you can use the exportDiagnosticDataFromServer command while connected to a running server. Second, you can use the exportDiagnosticData command in offline mode while the server is stopped.

> The **exportDiagnosticDataFromServer** command makes a new HTTP connection to the server to perform the bulk download of data. You must run WLST from a location that can make such an HTTP connection.

The archive can contain harvested metric data and event data (from the other types of instrumentation actions that store their results in the archive). Both of the export commands take a `logicalName` parameter that determines which class of data should be read. This can also be set to export from the various log files, but only where the persistent data is stored in the log file itself, not in the diagnostic archive.

The export commands also allow a date range to be specified, or a WLDF query that can precisely specify the information to export.

Here's an example WLST command that exports all of the available harvested data from the connected server.

```
exportDiagnosticDataFromServer(logicalName="HarvestedDataArchive",
exportFileName="myexport.xml")
```

The data is exported in an XML format that represents a set of tabular rows. WebLogic Server does not supply any tools to post-process this exported data. The Oracle Technology Network article referred to at the beginning of this section shows how to process the data using XSLT scripts.

Managing the Diagnostic Archive

Be wary of instrumenting too many methods, harvesting too many metrics, or using very short sampling period. You will quickly fill up the archive, and the overhead of the instrumentation may become measurable.

The data in the archive obviously cannot be allowed to grow indefinitely. WebLogic Server allows data retirement policies to be set for a each class of data in the diagnostic archive that regularly deletes data of a certain age. Data retirement policies can be used for both file- and database-based stores. For file stores, a preferred maximum size can also be configured — WebLogic Server will regularly remove old records to keep the file below the configured size.

Watches and Notifications

A *watch* is a rule that is used to monitor log records, WLDF events, and harvest metric data for some situations. When a watch fires, it triggers one or more *notifications*. A notification allows users and other systems to be informed of the situation using JMX, SNMP, JMS, or email, or for a diagnostic image to be created. Both watches and notifications are configured in a diagnostic system module using the WebLogic Console.

We could, for example, configure a watch rule that fires whenever the harvester discovers there are more than 10 active database connections in use.

Watches can have an associated *alarm* setting. This prevents the same watch from firing within either a configured period (an *automatic reset* alarm), or until an administrator resets the alarm (a *manual reset* alarm).

This concludes our whirlwind tour of the WebLogic Diagnostic Framework. For more information, please see Link 12-50. Now that you understand some of the tools WebLogic Server provides to help troubleshoot applications, we will talk about how we roll new versions of applications into our production system.

Versioning Applications

Applications change. Deployment strategies for putting in new versions of already running applications vary. Certain application characteristics can make rolling out new versions of an application messy. The purpose of this section is to point out the issues around application versioning and to discuss the features that WebLogic Server offers that may help you address these issues with your applications. Note that even these advanced features of WebLogic Server do not address every possible situation. Choosing the right strategy for an application involves analyzing the application requirements and the sorts of application changes occurring, then trading those off against the pros and cons of the available approaches.

WebLogic Server supports the notion of hot deployment of an application. This means that you can take a new version of an application and push it into a set of running servers without restarting the servers. Two primary strategies for hot redeployment:

In-Place Redeployment   In-place redeployment is the default redeployment model used in WebLogic Server today, and the only one available in older releases of the product. With this model, the new version of the application immediately replaces the old version of the application in running server processes. Although WebLogic Server tries to do this in a way to minimize potential disruption of service, the process essentially drops the older version's application classloader and creates a new application classloader to load the new version of the application. This means that there will be some period of time where the application is unavailable and users may lose their non-persisted state. For example, users may lose their HttpSession state if the application has not enabled the <save-session-enabled> element in the weblogic.xml deployment descriptor, or if the new version of the application has made incompatible changes to one or more classes stored in the HttpSession. Therefore, this type of redeployment should ideally be done during scheduled downtime.

WebLogic Server offers some partial redeployment capabilities that allow in-place redeployment of static files like HTML and JSP pages as well as partial redeployment of modules within a larger enterprise application. We do not spend time here discussing these variations because we covered them briefly in Chapter 8. For more information, please see Links 12-51 and 12-52.

Production Redeployment   Production redeployment provides a side-by-side deployment model that does not disrupt service during the redeployment process. Production redeployment support has certain restrictions and limitations (see Link 12-53 for details) and generally works best with applications where client access is via one or more web applications, potentially contained within a larger enterprise application. When you use production redeployment to deploy a new version of the application, existing clients continue to use the old version until their session completes. New clients are directed to the new version of the application. Over time, the old application's client sessions will end and new sessions will be redirected to the new version of the application. Once the old application is no longer needed, it can be safely *retired* without disrupting clients because it is no longer being used. We spend the rest of this section talking about how to use production redeployment.

Production redeployment is probably the right choice for most production applications, assuming they meet the criteria discussed at Link 12-54. For versioning to work well, the application needs to be self-contained. This means that any place your application references global resources is a potential problem unless you are sure that the external resource access will not cause problems when used from the different versions of the application. Things like JMS and JDBC resource have potential to be problematic because many times, what is on the other side of the resource may be application version dependent (for example, your database schema may have changed between application versions). As such, it is typically best to use application-scoped resources wherever possible.

To support this notion and warn application developers and administrators, versioned applications that use global JNDI lookups will result in warnings. To disable these warnings, set the following JNDI properties (expressed as constants on the `weblogic.jndi.WLContext` class) to `true` when creating the JNDI `InitialContext` to perform the lookup:

WLContext.ALLOW_GLOBAL_RESOURCE_LOOKUP This property will disable warnings about JNDI lookups of global resources like JDBC Data Sources and JMS resources from within a versioned application.

WLContext.ALLOW_EXTERNAL_APP_LOOKUP This property will disable warnings about JNDI lookups of external application components like EJBs from within a versioned application.

Versioned applications may also have modules that are bound into the global JNDI tree. These modules should be used only by other modules in the same version of the application. WebLogic Server performs version-aware JNDI bindings and lookups for global resources deployed in a versioned application. By default, a JNDI lookup of a global resource returns a binding for the same version of the application. Setting the `WLContext.RELAX_VERSION_LOOKUP` JNDI property to `true` allows you to get other versions if the same version cannot be found. Only use this property if you are certain that the current version is compatible with the expected version!

To use production redeployment, applications need an explicit version number. Version numbers are strings made up of one or more valid characters. Valid characters are: any lowercase letter (a–z), any uppercase letter (A–Z), any numeric character (0–9), a period (.), an underscore (_), and a hyphen (-). The best way to assign a version number to an application is to explicitly put the application version number in the EAR file's Manifest using a line like the one shown here.

```
Weblogic-Application-Version: v11gR1
```

Any application with a version number assigned in this way will automatically be deployed using production redeployment, assuming that the version number of the application being deployed is different than the one already deployed.

WebLogic Server deployment tools also allow you to provide a version number for applications at deployment time. For example, `weblogic.Deployer` has an `-appversion` argument that allows you to assign a version number to an application that doesn't have a version number in its Manifest file.

WebLogic Server will not support more than two versions of an application at a time. That means that to use production redeployment to deploy a new version of the application, you must ensure that only a single version is deployed before you start your redeployment process. Once you redeploy the new version of the application, the new version becomes the current version of the application and the old version begins the retirement process. Once the retirement process starts, the old version only accepts requests that are part of a pre-existing session (for example, a web application request with an HttpSession associated with the old version) — all new requests go to the current version of the application. Typically, the retirement process completes once every pre-existing session ends. However, it is possible to specify a retirement timeout after which the old version of the application is retired, regardless of whether users have completed their sessions or not.

Once the application is retired, it is safe to undeploy it and remove the files associated with that version of the application. Note that if you are using either nostage or external_stage deployment modes, do not overwrite the old application version's files with the new ones. You must allow both versions' files to exist until you have undeployed the old version of the application.

What happens if you redeploy a new version of the application only to find that there is a problem with it? If you want to roll back the redeployment process, simply redeploy again pointing to the older version's source files. This will reverse the active and retiring processes roles, assuming the retirement process hadn't already completed. If the old application is already retired and undeployed, the redeployment will be the same as deployment any new version of an application — in this case, the new version happens to be the older one but then, WebLogic Server doesn't really know that anyway.

That is really about all there is to production redeployment for applications with web clients. For applications with remote RMI-based clients, WebLogic Server's production redeployment feature currently defines the *pre-existing session* as a JTA transaction (or single request in case of no transaction context). Though from a technical point of view, this might seem reasonable, practically speaking, we are not convinced that this is sufficient to handle the real-world situations that might arise in fat client–based production redeployment use cases. As such, we do not cover the nuances of using this feature with applications using RMI-based clients here. For more information, please consult the WebLogic Server documentation at Link 12-55.

At this point, it is time to move on to our next topic: failure recovery.

Managing Failure Conditions

Failures happen. As an administrator, you want to make your system as resilient as possible. Sometimes it is possible to automate processes so that when a particular type of failure occurs, the system can take steps to recover; other times, it is not. WebLogic Server provides some built-in mechanisms to help make applications fault tolerant and transparently recoverable (for example, clustering, in-memory replication, database connection testing). Newer versions of the product also provide mechanisms to fully automate certain types of failover scenarios. However, when recovering from failures in complex, distributed systems, it is not always possible to provide or use a general purpose failover mechanism. For example, when a WebLogic Server instance fails, how do you decide whether to use whole server migration to migrate the WebLogic Server instance to another machine? In many cases, the machine may restart faster than the WebLogic Server process could be migrated. In this section, we talk about several common failure scenarios and the mechanisms that WebLogic Server provides for recovering from these situations.

Database Failures

A very common scenario is that a database goes down (or is taken down) and restarted, either automatically by a high-availability (HA) framework or by the database administrator. When this happens, the connections in WebLogic Server database connection pools become invalid and the applications trying to use them will begin to fail. As we discussed earlier, WebLogic Server does provide mechanisms to allow the server to eventually recover from the situation without any intervention, although these mechanisms come at the cost of some extra overhead. Depending on the mechanism(s) chosen and the configuration, the application may continue to fail for an extended period of time after the database recovers. Fortunately, WebLogic Server also provides a manual mechanism to tell a server to reset a connection pool.

To reset a database connection pool, you can use the `JDBCDataSourceRuntime` MBean's `reset()` operation. Using this operation, it is possible to provide a script that can reset all of the connection pools associated with a particular database server. Once you have such a script, you need only to have the database administrator or the HA framework run the script whenever the database startup completes (to the point where it is accepting connections). The following WLST script demonstrates resetting the `BigRezJTADataSource` on all running servers in the domain:

```
connect(userConfigFile='C:\powls\ch12\server-WebLogicConfig.properties',
        userKeyFile='C:\powls\ch12\server-WebLogicKey.properties',
        url='t3s://192.168.1.40:9002')
servers=domainRuntimeService.getServerRuntimes()
if (len(servers) > 0):
    for server in servers:
        jdbcServiceRT = server.getJDBCServiceRuntime()
        dataSources = jdbcServiceRT.getJDBCDataSourceRuntimeMBeans()
        if (len(dataSources) > 0):
            for dataSource in dataSources:
                if(dataSource.getName() == 'BigRezJTADataSource'):
                    dataSource.reset()
```

The `JDBCDataSourceRuntime` MBean also provides other operations related to connection pools. Rather than covering them all here, we refer you to the WebLogic Server documentation at Link 12-56. The `forceSuspend()`, `resume()`, and `clearStatementCache()` operations are ones that might prove useful in certain situations. `forceSuspend()` allows you not only to disable all access to the pooled connections but also to destroy all of the existing connections if you choose to do so. For planned database restarts, you might want to suspend the pool and destroy the connections before shutting down the database. This might allow your application to trap the exception raised and display an error page indicating that the system is down. Once the database is back up, you can use the `resume()` operation to re-enable the connection pool, causing the destroyed connections to be recreated. Certain types of database changes may make the prepared statements WebLogic Server is caching invalid. Use `clearStatementCache()` to remove all cached statements after such a database update. This will allow your application to function properly without having to cycle the data source or restart the server.

WebLogic Server also supports *Multi Data Sources*. A multi data source is a data source encapsulates one or more *member* data sources that point to different database instances — a pool of data sources. To an application, a multi data source looks and feels like any other data source. Multi data sources support two different use cases:

Load balancing A multi data source configured to support load balancing will pick a data source from its members to use to honor each `DataSource.getConnection()` request. WebLogic Server uses a round robin algorithm to balance connection requests across the contained data sources. Note that multi data sources configured to support load balancing also support failover, which relies on the Test Connections on Reserve feature we discussed earlier in the "Configuring Database Resources" section.

Failover   Multi data sources configured to support failover will always use the same data source to honor the `DataSource.getConnection()` requests. When processing a `getConnection()` request, the multi data source tests the connection to determine if it is valid before returning it to the caller. If the connection is not valid, the data source will try to replace it first. If that doesn't work, it will go to the next member data source in the pool, get a connection, and test it. It will repeat this cycle until it finds a valid connection or runs out of member data sources.

An important point to note is that multi data sources do not attempt to failover connections that are in use. The application needs to catch any exceptions, close the existing connection, and call `getConnection()` again to try to obtain a valid connection with which the application can restart its database work.

At the time of writing, WebLogic Server relies on multi data sources for high availability scenarios involving Oracle RAC databases and XA transactions. Each member data source is configured to point to a single RAC node. When using XA transactions, each transaction will be pinned to a single RAC node but different transactions will be load balanced across the member data sources, assuming the multi data source specifies its `Algorithm Type` as `Load-Balancing`. This is really required for pre-11g Oracle RAC databases due to lazy propagation of XA transactions IDs across nodes that may lead to XA transaction requests going to a RAC node that has no knowledge of the transaction. Although this limitation is addressed in the 11g RAC database, Oracle still recommends that you do everything possible to keep all branches of an XA transaction on the same RAC node so this transaction affinity will likely not be relaxed.

For non-XA use cases, you have the choice of using multi data sources or using a single data source and the failover capabilities built into the Oracle Thin driver. See Link 12-57 for more information on configuring WebLogic Server to use the Oracle Thin driver's RAC failover capabilities.

> When using WebLogic Server with XA transactions against an Oracle RAC database, you must use multi data sources and each member data source must point to a single RAC node. While WebLogic Server will pin each transaction to a single RAC node, it will load balance transactions across nodes if the multi data source specifies `Load-Balancing` as its `Algorithm Type`.

WebLogic Server Failures

When designing a highly available production system, you must eliminate single points of failure and you must provide mechanisms to ensure your system continues to operate without breaking your service-level agreements. As you know, WebLogic Server clustering provides an excellent first line of defense against single points of failure and provides automatic failover when a server instance or machine fails. However, several situations may require some sort of migration. If you have singleton services running in your cluster, a server process or machine failure may require you to migrate that service to another running instance in the cluster. If you lose a machine, you may need to migrate one or more WebLogic Server instances to another machine to allow the system to continue to service requests without prolonged periods of degraded performance. In this section, we talk about three types of migration: service migration, whole server migration, and admin server migration.

Service Level Migration

WebLogic Server supports running singleton services in a cluster such that the service will always run in one server at a time. The most popular singleton service is a JMS server, which typically includes one or more destinations. WebLogic Server also provides application developers the ability to build their own custom singleton services. We discuss both topics in this section.

As discussed in Chapter 10, WebLogic JMS provides clustering facilities to allow you to build JMS applications that are resilient to server failure. However, the fact remains that when a server hosting one or more JMS destinations fails, it is very likely that the destinations may contain undelivered messages. If the JMS messages represent time-sensitive tasks that need to be processed, your job as a WebLogic Server administrator is to provide a failover mechanism that allows those trapped messages to be delivered in a timely fashion. JMS service migration is one way to achieve this. The other is to use *Whole Server Migration*, a topic we discuss a little later.

Migrating JMS Services

WebLogic Server supports both manual and automatic JMS service migration. If you are using JTA transactions with your JMS application, you will also need to migrate the JTA service. To set up manual JMS service migration, you will need to perform a number of steps. There are many options and variations on the configuration; we list the primary steps to get JMS service migration working.

1.   Create your machines and assign the managed servers to the appropriate machines.

2.   WebLogic Server automatically creates migratable targets for your clustered managed servers. However, you still need to configure them to make sure that the correct `User-Preferred Server` is selected and that the `Service Migration Policy` is set to `Manual Service Migration Only`.

3.   Create and target custom persistent stores for each migratable target. These will be used to store any persistent JMS messages.

4.   Create your JMS servers and target them to the migratable targets.

5.   If any migration policies were modified, you need to restart the admin server and any managed servers affected.

6.   To manually migrate a JMS service, use the migratable targets' Control tab. You can also use WLST (or a custom JMX program) to perform manual server migration.

While manual service migration is good for situations where you have an external HA framework that can invoke a migration script, many WebLogic Server installations simply do not need an external HA framework so that fact that WebLogic Server provides a framework for automatic migration is a real benefit to administrators.

Setting up automatic JMS service migration requires the same steps as setting up manual migration plus a couple more. Before we cover the steps required to perform automatic migration, we need to talk about *leasing* and automatic service migration policies.

When performing automatic migration, WebLogic Server needs a leasing mechanism to ensure that the service only runs on one server at a time. WebLogic Server supports two leasing mechanisms:

Database-Based Leasing This style of leasing relies on a highly available database to coordinate the actions of the servers in the cluster. It is important that you ensure that the database is always available and reachable by each migratable server. A migratable server is only as reliable as the database. If a migratable server is unable to reach the database, it will shut itself down.

Leasing information is maintained in a database table. The schema definition for the table is located in a database vendor–specific directory underneath the `$WL_HOME/server/db` directory in a file called `leasing.ddl`. You must configure a nontransactional data source to access the leasing information. To tell WebLogic Server about the database configuration, use the cluster's `Migration Configuration` tab to set the `Migration Basis` to `Database` and set the `Data Source for Automatic Migration` attribute to point to the nontransactional data source for the database where you created the leasing table. Change the `Auto Migration Table Name` attribute if you named the leasing table something other than the default value of `ACTIVE`.

Consensus-Based Leasing This style of leasing keeps the leasing table in-memory. One server in the cluster is designated as the cluster leader. The cluster leader controls leasing in that it holds a copy of the leasing table in-memory and other servers in the cluster communicate with the cluster leader to determine lease information. The leasing table is replicated across the cluster to ensure high availability should the cluster leader go down.

To tell WebLogic Server you want to use consensus-based leasing, use the cluster's `Migration Configuration` tab to set the `Migration Basis` to `Consensus`. Note that consensus-based leasing requires the use of node manager on every machine hosting managed servers within the cluster.

> Database leasing requires a highly available database. Your migratable targets are only as reliable as the database. If the database becomes unavailable, the migratable servers will shut themselves down.
>
> Consensus leasing requires the use of the node manager on every machine hosting managed servers in your cluster.

WebLogic Server has two automatic service migration policies from which to choose.

- ❏ `Auto-Migrate Exactly-Once Services` — With this policy, WebLogic Server will try to keep the service running if at least one candidate server is available in the cluster — even when an administrator shuts down a server on which the service is running. Note that this can lead to all migratable targets running on a single server.

- ❏ `Auto-Migrate Failure Recovery Services` — With this option, WebLogic Server will not try to migrate services where the `User-Preferred Server` (UPS) is shutdown by the administrator. If the UPS goes down for any other reason, WebLogic Server will try to migrate the service to another candidate server. If the candidate server also goes down, WebLogic Server will first try to reactivate the service on the UPS before searching for another candidate server.

For our purposes with migrating JMS servers that only contain uniform distributed destination members, we will select the `Auto-Migrate Failure Recovery Services` option. This means that if we plan to shut a server down for an extended period of time, we will need to manually migrate the service before shutting the server down; otherwise, the service will be unavailable. This is fine because the only reason we want to migrate the service is to process any message stuck in the queue. Our application will continue to function without the service because the other distributed destination members are still available.

If the JMS destinations had not been part of a distributed destination and our application depended on access to the destinations, we would have selected the `Auto-Migrate Exactly-Once Services` option to ensure that the destinations were made available as quickly as possible to prevent our application from failing for an extended period of time.

So, now that you understand the leasing an automatic service migration policies, you are ready to configure automatic JMS service migration. As with manual migration there are many options and variations on the configuration; we list the primary steps to get automatic JMS service migration working.

1. Create your machines and assign the managed servers to the appropriate machines.

2. Use the cluster's `Migration Configuration` tab to set the `Migration Basis` to either `Database` or `Consensus`. If you choose `Database`:

   a. Create the leasing table, as described previously.

   b. Create a nontransactional JDBC data source for the servers to use to access the leasing table.

   c. On the cluster's `Migration Configuration` tab, set the `Data Source for Auto Migration` attribute to point to your nontransactional data source and verify that the `Auto Migration Table Name` attribute is set to the name of your leasing table.

   If you choose `Consensus`:

   a. Make sure that you configure the node manager on each machine that hosts the cluster's managed servers.

3. WebLogic Server automatically creates migratable targets for your clustered managed servers. However, you still need to use the migratable targets' `Migration Configuration` tab to make sure that the correct `User-Preferred Server` is selected and that the `Service Migration Policy` is set to either `Auto-Migrate Exactly-Once Services` or `Auto-Migrate Failure Recovery Services`.

4. Create and target custom persistent stores for each migratable target. These will be used to store any persistent JMS messages.

5. Create your JMS servers and target them to the migratable targets.

6. Restart the admin server and any managed servers to pick up the new migration policy settings.

7. Even with automatic migration configured, you can still manually migrate a JMS server using the migratable targets' `Control` tab (or WLST), if desired.

One important thing to note is that, as of the time of writing, WebLogic Server does not support automatic failback of migrated JMS services. You will need to perform this task manually, either via the WebLogic Console or a WLST script.

> ### Tip to Remember
>
> At the time of writing, WebLogic Server does not support automatic failback of JMS
> services. After a service has been migrated to another server, you will need to manually
> migrate it back to the original server one that server is ready.

Though we have only covered the basics of WebLogic Server's JMS service migration framework, it is
time to move on. See our discussion of MDB migration in the "Connecting to Distributed Destinations"
section of Chapter 10 to understand how to get your MDBs to migrate with the JMS service. Because JMS
applications often use XA transactions, let's discuss JTA service migration.

Migrating the JTA Service

When machines fail, you need to be able to bring up services on other machines. Migrating the JTA
service can play a critical role in recovery from a failure scenario. In-flight transactions can hold locks
on the underlying resources. If the transaction manager is not available to recover these transactions,
resources may hold on to these locks for long periods of time, making it difficult for the application to
function properly. JTA service migration is possible only if the server's default persistent store (where the
JTA logs are kept) is accessible to the server to which the service will migrate. Once you guarantee this,
migration is simple, although you must be careful how you share these files. Distributed file systems
such as NFS typically do not provide the necessary semantics to guarantee the integrity and content
of transaction logs. Typically, this means using some higher-end means of sharing the files, such as a
multi-ported disk or storage area network (SAN).

Like JMS service migration, you can configure either manual or automatic JTA service migration. Because
one of the most common use cases for JTA service migration is using it in conjunction with JMS service
migration, we only point out the additional steps needed to allow JTA service migration.

To add manual JTA service migration to your cluster already configured to support manual JMS service
migration, you must ensure that the managed servers' default persistent stores are accessible from the
other managed servers to which you want to be able to migrate the JTA service.

By default, WebLogic Server expects to locate a server's default persistent store in the
`$DOMAIN_HOME/servers/<server-name>/data/store/default` directory. For example, say that you
want to be able to migrate `Server2`'s JTA service to `Server1` in the event of failure. That means that
on `Server1`'s machine, the directory `$DOMAIN_HOME/servers/Server2/data/store/default` must contain `Server2`'s default persistent store. The `Server2` directory structure would typically not exist on
`Server1` so you would need to do something to realize this structure. One thing to consider though is
that the addition of the `Server2` directory structure on `Server1` might be confusing for another WebLogic
Server administrator so you might want to think twice before adopting this strategy.

A better approach might be to store the default persistent store directories for all managed servers
using a common mount point outside the domain directories on each machine (for example,
`/mount/BigRezCluster/<server-name>/defaultstore`). Once you do this, you need to reconfigure
your managed server to use this directory by using the server's `Service Configuration` tab and setting
the `Directory` attribute to the absolute path to the directory on the shared file system.

Once the domain is properly configured, use the Advanced area of the managed server's Migration Control tab to migrate the JTA service to another server. Note that JTA service migration is only supported when the server from which you are migrating is not running.

To add automatic JTA service migration to your cluster already configured to support automatic JMS service migration, you must do the following things:

1. Ensure that each managed server's default persistent store is accessible via shared disk, as we just described in our discussion of manual JTA service migration.

2. On each server's Migration Configuration tab, enable the Automatic JTA Migration Enabled checkbox.

3. Restart the managed servers to pick up this change.

4. Even with automatic migration configured, you can manually migrate the service, if desired.

Before we move on to discuss whole server migration, we need to discuss migrating custom singleton services that your application may contain.

Migrating Custom Singleton Services

WebLogic Server provides a mechanism for applications to use the service migration framework to implement singleton services that run on only one server at a time and provide automatic failover to other cluster members when a server fails. To implement a singleton class, you simply write a Java class that implements the weblogic.cluster.singleton.SingletonService interface shown here.

```
package weblogic.cluster.singleton;

public interface SingletonService
{
    public void activate();
    public void deactivate();
}
```

Next, you have to make the class available to the server and tell the server that you want this class to be treated as a singleton service. You have two ways to accomplish this. First, you can package up the class in your enterprise application and add a stanza to the weblogic-application.xml deployment descriptor declaring the singleton, as shown here.

```
<singleton-service>
  <class-name>professional.weblogic.ch12.example3.MySingletonService</class-name>
  <name>My_App_Scoped_Singleton_Service</name>
</singleton-service>
```

When you use this method, the eligible set of candidate servers for migration is defined by the servers to which the application is deployed.

Second, you can simply make the class available to the server (for example, by placing the jar file containing the class in the $DOMAIN_HOME/lib directory) and then use the WebLogic Console to tell WebLogic Server about the singleton service. To create a new singleton service using the WebLogic Console, use the cluster's `Singleton Services Configuration` tab to create a new singleton service by specifying the `Singleton Service Name`, the `Class Name`, and the `User Preferred Server`. By default, the singleton service will use all servers in the cluster as candidate servers. To restrict the candidate servers, simply specify the list of candidate servers in the singleton service's `Migration Configuration` tab using the `Constrained Candidate Servers` attribute.

Of course, the automatic singleton service migration relies on the same sort of configuration needed for automatic JMS and JTA service migration. You must perform the following steps to enable automatic migration of your singleton service:

1. Create your machines and assign the managed servers to the appropriate machines.

2. Use the cluster's `Migration Configuration` tab to set the `Migration Basis` to either `Database` or `Consensus`. If you choose `Database`:

   a. Create the leasing table, as described previously.

   b. Create a nontransactional JDBC data source for the servers to use to access the leasing table.

   c. On the cluster's `Migration Configuration` tab, set the `Data Source for Auto Migration` attribute to point to your nontransactional data source and verify that the `Auto Migration Table Name` attribute is set to the name of your leasing table.

   If you choose `Consensus`:

   a. Make sure that you configure the node manager on each machine that hosts the cluster's managed servers.

3. Restart the admin server and any managed servers to pick up the new migration policy settings.

4. Even with automatic migration configured, you can manually migrate a singleton service using the singleton service's `Control` tab (or WLST), if desired.

At this point, we have covered the basics of WebLogic Server service migration. For more detailed information, please see the WebLogic Server documentation at Link 12-58. An alternative to service migration is to simply migrate the entire server instance to another machine, something WebLogic Server calls whole server migration.

Whole Server Migration

Although service migration provides a great framework for ensuring availability of critical services during failure conditions, it does not change the fact that one or more servers in your cluster have failed and are not available to process incoming requests. If you haven't oversized your cluster to handle such failures gracefully, your applications could experience service level degradation until the failed managed servers are restarted. For extended periods of server downtime (for example, hardware failure), it is often desirable to restart managed servers on another machine to limit your exposure to service level degradation.

Though the ability to restart managed servers on another physical machine is nothing new, automating it used to require the use of an external HA framework like Veritas Cluster Server to detect and trigger the sequence of events necessary to restart the managed server on another machine. For many complex environments, using a full-fledged HA framework still makes sense and WebLogic Server still supports integration into these sorts of environments. However, sometimes all you really need is to restart the managed servers on another machine, and do not require other complex interactions with other hardware or software systems. For those situations, WebLogic Server provides a whole server migration (WSM) framework that supports restarting managed servers on different machines.

Before we dive into the details of configuring WSM, let's talk about some of the requirements for using WSM.

❏   WSM uses a floating IP address, also known as a virtual IP address, for each migratable server. This means that the migratable server candidate machines have to be in the same subnet (because the virtual IP address must be valid on all candidate machines).

❏   WSM requires the use of the node manager. You must make sure the node manager on each candidate machine is properly initialized with the security-related files it need to authenticate and accept commands from the admin server.

❏   WSM uses the node manager to migrate the virtual IP address and assign it to the target machine. As such, the default configuration assumes that the machines are similar; specifically, it assumes the following:

   ❏   The netmask associated with the virtual IP is the same on all machines.

   ❏   The network device name (for example, eth0 on Linux) is the same on all machines.

   ❏   The functional behavior of the platform-specific OS command used to add and remove the virtual IP (for example, ifconfig on Linux) is the same.

❏   WSM only supports migration of a single virtual IP address for each migratable server. Therefore, a migratable server cannot define any network channels that use a Listen Address different from the virtual IP address associated with the server. If you need your servers to use multiple network channels associated with multiple IP addresses, you cannot use the WSM framework.

❏   WSM assumes that any server-specific *state* is already shared through some highly available sharing mechanism. For example, the server's default persistent store where it keeps its XA transaction logs must be accessible on all candidate machines using the exact same path.

Now that you understand the requirements, let's discuss the steps required to set up automatic whole server migration.

1.   Create your domain. Make sure that you set up each managed server's to Listen Address to its virtual IP address and assign it to a machine.

2.   Set up the node manager for each candidate machine. For each machine, edit the nodemanager.properties file to set the NetMask property to the netmask associated with the virtual IP addresses being used and Interface to the network device name with which to associate the virtual IP address. Typically, the nodemanager.properties file is created the first time the node manager is started in the $NODEMGR_HOME directory (by default, $WL_HOME/common/nodemanager).

3. Verify the domain and node manager configuration. Before we proceed, start up the domain and each clustered managed server via its node manager. This not only ensures that the node managers and servers are properly configured but also initializes the node managers with the password files they need to accept commands from the admin server. Don't forget to start managed servers on all candidate machines to ensure that the node manager and domain directory are properly initialized.

4. Choose and configure your leasing mechanism. Like automatic service migration, automatic whole server migration relies on leasing. Use the cluster's `Migration Configuration` tab to select the appropriate `Migration Basis`.

5. If you choose database leasing, be sure to create and configure your nontransactional data source, create the leasing table, and use the cluster's `Migration Configuration` tab to set the `Data Source for Automatic Migration` and `Auto Migration Table Name` appropriately.

6. Grant superuser privileges to the `wlsifconfig` script. Node managers use the `$WL_HOME/common/bin/wlsifconfig.sh` (on Windows, `wlsifconfig.cmd`) script to add and remove virtual IP addresses from the machines. By default, the file is set up to use `sudo`; `sudo` typically prompts you for your password the first time you run it and periodically after that. To do this without needing to input your password, you need to add the `NOPASSWD` option to the relevant entry in your `/etc/sudoers` file. Don't forget to add the `wlsifconfig` script to your `PATH` so that the node managers can locate it.

```
weblogic machine1 = NOPASSWD: /oracle/middleware/wlserver_10.3/common/bin/wlsifconfig.sh
```

7. Enable automatic server migration. The last step is to use each managed server's `Migration Configuration` tab to select the `Automatic Server Migration Enabled` checkbox and restart the servers.

At this point, automatic whole server migration configuration is complete and needs to be tested. Debugging problems with whole server migration can be tricky so you will probably want to add `-Dweblogic.debug.DebugServerMigration=true` to the Java command line used to start your servers. Now, it is time to move onto discuss admin server migration. For more information on whole server migration, please see the WebLogic Server documentation at Link 12-59.

Migrating the Admin Server

The last thing we want to discuss is how to handle admin server availability because the admin server is not currently clusterable. This means that if the admin server goes down, you cannot administer your WebLogic Server domain until you bring it back up. In most cases, you may not be too concerned if the admin server goes down because all you need to do is restart it. If you use the node manager to start the admin server, the node manager can automatically restart a failed admin server just like it can any other server. What happens if the machine where the admin server runs fails in such a way that you cannot restart the admin server? The answer is simple if you prepare for this unlikely event.

Proper operation of the admin server relies on several configuration files and any application files it controls. Typically, the best thing to do is to store the admin server's directory tree on a shared disk. As long as the configuration and application files are accessible, you can restart the admin server on another machine. It is up to you to make sure that you don't have more than one admin server running at a time. If the new machine can assume the original admin server's `Listen Address` (or if it was not set), you can simply start the admin server on the new machine without any configuration changes. Otherwise, you will need to change the admin server's Listen Address. Since the managed servers ping the admin server URL every 10 seconds until it comes back up, you need to devise a way for the admin server URL to allow the managed server to find the restarted admin server on the new IP address. The easiest way to achieve that is using a DNS name that maps to both IP addresses, or better yet that is dynamically updated to point to the correct location of the admin server. If this is a graceful shutdown and migration, use the WebLogic Console to change the Listen Address just before shutting down the admin server. If not, you will need to edit the config.xml file by hand to replace the old Listen Address with the new one. Typically, we recommend planning ahead so that everything you need is already in place to make admin server failover as painless as possible.

Chapter Review

We covered a lot of ground in this chapter. We began with a thorough discussion of the WebLogic Server product architecture to give us a good understanding of how the product works. We followed that with a discussion of other administrative concepts, such as server health states and network channels. The rest of the chapter was dedicated to covering WebLogic Server administration including configuration, monitoring, and management of WebLogic Server and WebLogic Server–based applications. We hope that this gives you the basic fundamentals of WebLogic Server administration. These basics should go a long way toward demystifying the complex task of administering Java EE applications running on WebLogic Server. In the next chapter, we will explore WebLogic Server performance optimization.

13

Optimizing WebLogic Server Performance

This chapter presents best practices for delivering and troubleshooting scalable high-performance systems. It is organized into three major sections:

❑ *System Performance*, a discussion of core principles and strategies for scalable Java EE systems

❑ *Performance Best Practices*, a collection of important design patterns and best practices that affect performance and scalability

❑ *Troubleshooting Performance Problems*, a set of steps and techniques you can use to improve performance and solve scalability issues for your system

This chapter discusses design considerations and best practices we use while delivering scalable systems for numerous BEA and Oracle customers. Information presented in this chapter represents the experience gathered while designing, prototyping, building, and benchmarking distributed systems over the past twelve years. We have had the opportunity to work with very bright architects on many of the largest and most demanding systems deployed using BEA and Oracle software.

This chapter cannot cover all aspects of Java EE performance, which could be the topic of its own book. We instead provide a number of key best practices and troubleshooting tips to help you achieve your performance goals. If you want more information about performance tuning, we suggest looking at some of the existing books and web sites on performance tuning and testing. In our experience, there is no one book that will tell you everything you need to know. For a better understanding of operating system performance tuning, books like *Sun Performance and Tuning: Java and the Internet* by Adrian Cockroft and Richard Pettit (Prentice Hall, 1998) are invaluable. To understand better how to build applications that run in multithreaded Java environments, we recommend *Concurrent Programming in Java: Design Principles and Patterns* by Doug Lea (Addison-Wesley, 1999). To understand web application performance testing models better, we recommend books like *Capacity Planning for Web Performance: Metrics, Models, and Methods* by Daniel A. Menascé and Virgilio A.F. Almeida (Prentice Hall, 1998). Several books are also available on both Java EE and WebLogic Server performance that may provide some additional insight. We also recommend looking at the

WebLogic Server documentation at Link 13-1 in the online Appendix on the book's web site at
`http://www.wrox.com`.

Overview of System Performance

In this section, we discuss the core principles and tuning techniques that underlie many of the performance best practices and troubleshooting tips that we cover later in the chapter. Having a good understanding of the basic operating system, network, JVM, and server resources and tuning options will help you apply these best practices and tips. It is not enough to know what to do; you need to understand why it helps.

Reviewing the Core Principles

Before we get started talking about techniques for achieving *scalability*, we should define the term itself. Scalability generally refers to the ability of an application to meet additional capacity demands without significantly affecting the request processing time. The term is also used to describe the ability to increase the capacity of an application proportional to the hardware resources added. For example, if the maximum capacity of an application running on four CPUs is 200 requests per second with an average of 1-second response time, you might expect that the capacity for the application running on eight CPUs to be 400 requests per second with the same 1-second response time. This type of linear scalability is typically very difficult to achieve, but scalable applications should be able to approach linear scalability if the application's environment is properly designed. Good scalability in multi-tier architectures requires good end-to-end performance and scalability of each component in each tier of the application.

When designing enterprise-scale applications, you must first understand the application itself and how your users interact with it. You must identify all of the system components and understand their interactions. The application itself is a critical component that affects the scalability of the system. Understanding the distribution of the workload across the various tiers will help you understand the components affected most severely by user activity. Some systems will be database-intensive; others will spend a majority of their processing time in the application server. Once you identify these heavily used components, commonly referred to as *application hotspots*, you can use proper scaling techniques to prevent bottlenecks.

This strong understanding of the system itself will also allow you to choose the correct system architecture to meet the demands of the application. Once you choose the system architecture, you can begin to concentrate on the application and apply good performance design practices. There are no silver bullets for choosing the correct system architecture. In our experience, it is best to take an overall system approach to ensure that you cover all facets of the environment in which the application runs. The overall system approach begins with the external environment and continues drilling down into all parts of the system and application. Taking a broad approach and tuning the overall environment ensures that the application will perform well and that system performance can meet all of your requirements.

> **Best Practice**
>
> WebLogic Server–based application performance depends on many different factors that include the network, operating system, application server, database, and application design and configuration. Many of these factors vary from installation to installation, so you should review all recommendations made in this chapter to determine whether they are applicable to your environment.

Before we dive into the lower-level tuning techniques, we will review some system-level approaches for increasing the performance and throughput of your Java EE application.

Use More Powerful Machines   This technique applies equally well across the web, application, and database tiers. If a particular tier's processing is CPU-intensive, using more powerful machines can allow this layer to do the same amount of work in less time or to do more work, thereby increasing throughput. Keep in mind that this technique is effective only on CPU-intensive applications. If your system performance is limited by I/O operations, adding processing power will do very little to improve performance or eliminate bottlenecks. Increasing an application's capacity by adding more CPUs to a machine is often referred to as *vertical scaling*.

Use Clustering   By distributing the load across multiple web or application servers, you can increase the capacity of your application. Increasing an application's capacity by adding more machines is often referred to as *horizontal scaling*. Horizontal scaling also provides a secondary benefit: increased redundancy at the hardware level to improve the overall system reliability.

Take Advantage of Network Appliances   Today, a wide variety of specialized hardware devices are optimized to perform specific tasks, such as fast and reliable data storage, content caching, load balancing, and SSL termination. These devices operate at various layers within the system architecture and can either offload or significantly reduce the processing work that the software needs to do, and do it in a much more scalable way than can be accomplished with software only. As such, they can dramatically increase the performance and scalability of your applications.

Cache Whenever Possible   Caching can significantly improve response time and increase the scalability of web, application, and database servers. Network appliances that cache static content and prevent those requests from ever hitting the web servers can dramatically improve performance. Most web servers also offer page caching, which you should use whenever possible. WebLogic Server also offers dynamic content caching through its JSP caching features, a technique discussed in Chapter 1. WebLogic Server provides various options for both data and object caching; you can use these to cache application data to reduce trips to the database or other backend systems. Of course, caching application data that changes frequently can often create more problems than it solves. In most cases, we recommend using the database to cache this frequently changing data. Most database management systems offer a variety of tuning options for optimizing their caching strategies to better suit a particular application; this can significantly reduce the amount of I/O that the database has to do to answer application queries. For larger-scale systems where caching is mandatory to achieve the performance and scalability goals, Oracle Coherence provides a robust, highly available, distributed object caching solution that integrates seamlessly with WebLogic Server. You should evaluate each of these techniques to determine how best to use caching to improve your application's performance and scalability.

Tuning a WebLogic Server–Based Application

Achieving maximum performance and scalability for your WebLogic Server–based application requires tuning at many different layers within the overall environment. We'll structure our discussion of tuning from the bottom up, starting with the operating system itself and ending with application server tuning.

Operating System Tuning

Many Java EE applications have some sort of web interface through which the users interact. HTTP is a stateless protocol used by browsers to talk to web and application servers. When initiating a request, the browser opens a connection to the server, sends a request, waits for the response, and then closes the connection. Although HTTP keep-alive allows the browser to reuse an existing connection to the server for multiple requests, both the browser and the server will typically close the connection after a fairly short period of inactivity. A typical timeout for one of these connections might be 30 seconds or less. As a result, busy web applications with hundreds, or even thousands, of concurrent users will open and close a large number of connections between the browser and the web or application server.

These HTTP connections to the web or application server are nothing more than operating system–level TCP sockets. All modern operating systems treat sockets as a specialized form of file access and use data structures called file descriptors to track open sockets and files for an operating system process. To control resource usage for processes on the machine, the operating system restricts the number of open file descriptors per process. The default number of file descriptors available for a process depends on the operating system type and its configuration. Without going too far into the gory details of TCP/IP, you should be aware that all TCP connections that have been gracefully closed by an application will go into what is known as the TIME_WAIT state before being discarded by the operating system. The length of time that the socket stays in the TIME_WAIT state is commonly known as the *time wait interval*. While in this TIME_WAIT state, the operating system will maintain the resources allocated for the socket, including its file descriptor and TCP/IP port. To learn more about the details of this, see *Internetworking with TCP/IP Volume II: Design, Implementation, and Internals* by Douglas A. Comer and David L. Stevens (Prentice Hall, 1998).

As a result of this phenomenon, combined with the fact that HTTP servers end up opening and closing a lot of TCP sockets, busy server processes can fill up the server process's file descriptor table, or use up all available TCP/IP ports. To deal with this problem, you often need to tune the operating system to allow your application to scale without running into these operating system limits. When tuning the operating system, you should follow your hardware vendor's tuning recommendations, if these exist. Remember to tune the operating system on all machines that exist in the system, especially any web or application server machines that use the HTTP protocol. On Unix servers, this typically means tuning the number of file descriptors or some of the TCP/IP device driver's tuning parameters. On platforms such as HP-UX, it may be necessary to change some of the kernel parameters. When tuning TCP parameters, you should work with your system administrator to determine what modifications your machines require.

Each operating system sets important tuning parameters differently. Fortunately, most modern server operating systems come configured to minimize the potential impact of the TIME_WAIT problem. We start with detailed coverage of the Solaris operating system and then briefly discuss the differences on other common Unix operating systems and Windows.

Tuning Solaris

On Solaris 8.0 and older, one common problem is that the default value for the time wait interval is too high for high volume HTTP servers. On most Unix operating systems, you can determine the number of sockets in the TIME_WAIT state using the netstat command.

```
netstat -a | grep TIME_WAIT | wc -l
```

This command will count all of the TCP connections that are in the TIME_WAIT state. As this number approaches the maximum number of file descriptors per process, your application's throughput will suffer dramatic degradations because new connection requests may have to wait for a free space in the application's file descriptor table. To determine the current setting for the time wait interval, use the ndd command shown here.

```
/usr/sbin/ndd /dev/tcp tcp_time_wait_interval
```

By default, Solaris 8.0 and earlier sets this parameter to 240,000 milliseconds, or 4 minutes. Our recommendation, which follows the recommendations of both Oracle and SUN, is to reduce this setting to 60,000 milliseconds, or 1 minute; this is the default value starting in Solaris 9. You should use the following `ndd` command to change the `tcp_time_wait_interval` setting dynamically:

```
/usr/sbin/ndd -set /dev/tcp tcp_time_wait_interval 60000
```

This command will change the setting of the TCP device driver for the entire machine and therefore requires superuser privileges. Be forewarned that this value, and any other values you change with `ndd`, will reset to the default value when you reboot the machine. To make the changes permanent, you will need to create a boot script.

According to Solaris 8 tuning recommendations on Sun's web site at Link 13-2, you want the `ndd` boot script to run between the `S69inet` and `S72inetsvc` scripts. This means that you should create the script file in the `/etc/init.d` directory and create symbolic links to your script from the `/etc/rc2.d`, `/etc/rc1.d`, and `/etc/rcS.d` directories. The link names should begin with either `S70` or `S71` because the `S` tells Solaris that this script should run at startup and the numeric value determines the order in which the scripts run.

A number of other TCP-related parameters are available on Solaris that may yield performance improvements in certain situations. To get a list of all of the names of the TCP device driver parameters, use the following `ndd` command.

```
ndd /dev/tcp \?
```

The output from this command will also show you which parameters are *read-write* and which ones are *read-only*. Read-only parameters cannot be changed with `ndd` and must be changed in `/etc/system`. In addition to the `tcp_time_wait_interval` parameter, you may also want to consider changing some of the other parameters like `tcp_conn_hash_size`, `tcp_conn_req_max_q`, `tcp_xmit_hiwat`, and `tcp_recv_hiwat`.

The `tcp_conn_hash_size` parameter controls the size of a hash table that helps quickly locate the TCP socket's data structure in the kernel. If the size is too small, it will result in long hash chains in each bucket that force the operating system into a linear search for the socket entry of interest, and performance will suffer accordingly. By default, Solaris 8 and 9 set this parameter to 512; we recommend raising the value to 8192 for machines hosting HTTP servers. To set `tcp_conn_hash_size`, change the `/etc/system` file, as shown here:

```
set tcp:tcp_conn_hash_size=8192
```

In Solaris 10, the `tcp_conn_hash_size` parameter name changed to `ipcl_conn_hash_size` and its default value changed to 0, which means that Solaris will automatically select the appropriate value at boot time based on available memory. To raise this to the recommended value, change the `/etc/system` file, as shown here:

```
set ip:ipcl_conn_hash_size=8192
```

The `tcp_conn_req_max_q` parameter controls the maximum allowable number of completed connections waiting to return from an accept call (that have completed the three-way TCP connection handshake).

You should increase this parameter only if you notice that your system is dropping connections. You can determine the number of drops using the `netstat` command:

```
netstat -s | grep tcpListenDrop
```

By default, this value is set to 128. If the system is dropping connections, try increasing the value of `tcp_conn_req_max_q` to 1024.

The `tcp_xmit_hiwat` and `tcp_recv_hiwat` parameters control the default size of the *send window* and *receive window* for each TCP connection, respectively. On very fast networks, you should make sure that the values are set to at least 32K. By default, Solaris 8 sets these parameters to 16K and 24K, respectively. Solaris 9 changes the default settings for both parameters to 48K.

Best Practice

Increase the size of key TCP-related parameters to improve system performance and reduce dropped connections.

As we mentioned previously, most operating systems limit the number of open file descriptors a process can have. On Solaris (and most other Unix operating systems), there are actually two file descriptor limits. The first limit is the default limit imposed on each process; this is sometimes called the *soft* limit. The second limit is the maximum number of file descriptors per process that the operating system can support in its current configuration; this is sometimes called the *hard* limit. Use the `ulimit` command to change the soft limit to increase the maximum number of file descriptors for a particular process. You can increase this number only up to the hard limit unless you are the *superuser*, whose username is typically `root` — regardless of any feedback that the `ulimit` command may give you to the contrary. To change the hard limit for processes not running as the `root` user, you need to reconfigure the operating system. On Solaris, this means modifying the `/etc/system` file. The two parameters of interest in the `/etc/system` file are `rlim_fd_cur` and `rlim_fd_max`, which control the soft and hard limits, respectively. You will need to reboot the machine in order for changes to the `/etc/system` file to take effect.

For any machine that will host an HTTP server, we strongly recommend that you increase both the soft and hard limits to 4096 or even 8192. Please make sure to check your operating system documentation and release notes; there are some negative performance implications on some older versions of Solaris if you set these numbers too high. The syntax for adjusting these parameters in the `/etc/system` file is shown here:

```
set rlim_fd_cur=4096
set rlim_fd_max=4096
```

Best Practice

On any machine that hosts an HTTP server, increase the maximum number of file descriptors per process to either 4096 or 8192. On Solaris, this means setting the `rlim_fd_cur` and `rlim_fd_max` parameters in the `/etc/system` file and rebooting the machine.

For more information on tuning the Solaris operating system, please refer to the *Solaris Tunable Parameters Reference Manual*, available on Sun's web site at Link 13-3 (Solaris 8), Link 13-4 (Solaris 9), or Link 13-5 (Solaris 10).

Tuning AIX

On AIX, the `no` command is equivalent to the `ndd` command on Solaris. Running the `no -a` command will display the current values of all network attributes. Issuing the following command will change the time wait interval:

```
no -o tcp_timewait=4
```

This example command sets the `tcp_timewait` parameter to 4 15-second intervals, or 1 minute. For more information on the `no` command, see Link 13-6.

When a server listens on a port for connections, TCP creates a queue that it uses to buffer connection requests while waiting for the server to accept the connection. This *listen queue* is a fixed size, and if it fills up, the operating system will reject any new connection requests until there is space available in the queue. AIX controls the maximum length of this listen queue with the `somaxconn` parameter. By default, AIX sets this to 1024, but on machines with busy HTTP servers, you might want to increase this to 8192. Note that this increases only the maximum allowable length of the listen queue. You will still need to adjust the WebLogic Server instance's `Accept Backlog` parameter so that WebLogic Server will ask for a longer listen queue, using the server's `Tuning Configuration` tab in the WebLogic Console. Of course, this particular configuration is also important for other operating systems, including Solaris. Also, setting this value to allow more pending connection requests has its risks; you should consider how many concurrent connections and requests the WebLogic Server instance can handle without significant degradations in performance and adjust this parameter accordingly.

Some other TCP parameters you may need to tune on AIX include `tcp_sendspace` and `tcp_recvspace`, which control the socket's sending and receiving buffer sizes, respectively. For more information about tuning AIX, please refer to the AIX Performance Management Guide at Link 13-7.

Tuning HP-UX

HP-UX provides the `ndd` command to use for setting the TCP parameters, just like Solaris (although parameter names are slightly different). To adjust the maximum allowable length of the listen queue to 1024, execute the `ndd` command shown here:

```
ndd -set /dev/tcp tcp_conn_req_max 1024
```

By default, HP-UX sets the `tcp_time_wait_interval` to 60000 milliseconds, so you do not typically need to adjust this. HP-UX reads a file in `/etc/rc.config.d/nddconf` to get customized settings for the TCP parameters at boot time. See this file for further information about how to use it to customize the TCP settings for your machine.

On HP-UX, you may also need to modify some kernel parameters to ensure that WebLogic Server performs optimally. Use the `/usr/sbin/sam` program to modify kernel parameters. HP-UX limits the maximum number of threads per process. On older versions of HP-UX, this value defaults to 64, a value that large applications can easily exceed. Newer versions of HP-UX set the default value to 256, but you can change this using the `max_thread_proc` kernel parameter. The maximum number of threads allowed on the system at any point in time is set using the nkthread kernel parameter. Older versions of HP-UX come with a default value of 499 that can be too low on larger multi-CPU machines; newer versions have a default value of 8416. Also remember to adjust the maxfile and maxfile_lim parameters that control the soft and hard limits on the maximum number of file descriptors, if needed. For more information on kernel tuning parameters, see Link 13-8.

Tuning Linux

When tuning Linux operating systems, use either the sysctl command or the /proc file system. Because the sysctl command provides the ability to read from the /etc/sysctl.conf file, we generally prefer to use sysctl over the /proc method. On newer versions of Linux, the default time wait interval is 60 seconds so you really shouldn't need to change this value, which now requires modifying the kernel source (include/net/tcp.h) and rebuilding your kernel.

Linux also limits the maximum number of open files for all users. If this is set too low, your HTTP server process might run out of file descriptors. To change this setting, you can add an entry into the /etc/sysctl.conf file and then run sysctl -p. The required entry is

```
fs.file-max = 20000
```

Then, if you want to allow your HTTP server process to be able to have 8,192 open file descriptors, you need to edit the /etc/security/limits.conf file to add the following entry for your weblogic user (assuming that the server is running as user weblogic). Remember that this number applies across all processes running as the weblogic user. The entry is

```
weblogic hard nofile 8192
```

Finally, you need to use the ulimit command to actually make the setting active for the current login session, as shown here:

```
ulimit -n 8192
```

For more information on Linux tuning, please consult your Linux vendor's documentation or check out some of the Linux resources on the web, such as Link 13-9, which provides a detailed, yet slightly dated description of the TCP/IP tuning parameters available on Linux.

Tuning Windows

The concepts behind tuning the pre-Vista versions of the Windows operating system are similar to those for tuning other operating systems. Most of the TCP/IP parameter settings are located in the registry under the HKEY_LOCAL_MACHINE\SYSTEM\CurrentControlSet\Services folder. To change the maximum length of the TCP listen queue, whose default value is 15, you create a DWORD entry called ListenBackLog in the Inetinfo\Parameters subfolder in your Windows registry. Windows sets the default for the time wait interval to four minutes; the TcpTimedWaitDelay parameter in the Tcpip\Parameters subfolder allows you to change its value. Windows Vista changes the available tuning parameters and their locations significantly. For more information on tuning Windows, please consult the Microsoft Windows documentation. One excellent paper that discusses Windows Server 2008 performance tuning is located at Link 13-10.

Network Tuning

Most networks today are very fast and are rarely the direct cause of performance problems in well-designed applications. In our experience, the most frequent network problems come from misconfigured network devices. Whether it is a network interface card in your server, a firewall, a router, or another, more specialized network device such as a load balancer, improper configuration can lead to insidious problems that are very difficult to figure out. This is why it is important to monitor your network when troubleshooting performance problems. Some very simple tests can indicate problems with the network.

First, you can use the `ping` command to generate network traffic between two nodes in your network and look for packet loss. On a high-speed local area network, you should almost never see any packet loss. If you are only seeing performance problems during peak load, make sure to run your ping tests during these times to make sure that the network is still working properly under load. Second, look for send or receive errors on your machine's network interface. You can use the `netstat` command shown here to do this on Solaris:

```
netstat -I /dev/hme0 5
```

This command will generate output every five seconds that shows the statistics for the `hme0` network interface card. Always remember that the first line of output is the cumulative output since the last reboot, so you should generally ignore it. The output of this command will look similar to that shown here. Pay particular attention to the `errs` columns.

input		/dev/h	output		input	(Total)	output		
packets	errs	packets	errs	colls	packets	errs	packets	errs	colls
0	0	0	0	0	142034	0	40794	242	0
0	0	0	0	0	48	0	6	0	0
0	0	0	0	0	50	0	7	0	0
0	0	0	0	0	48	0	7	0	0

Even when the network is properly configured, it is still important to monitor your network performance in both your testing and production environments, concentrating on three areas: packet retransmissions, duplicate packets, and listen drops of packets.

Packet retransmissions occur when the TCP layer is not receiving acknowledgments (ACKs) from the receiver quickly enough, causing TCP to retransmit the packet. If your retransmission rate is 15 percent or higher, this generally indicates a problem with the network. Bad network hardware or a slow or congested route can cause excessive packet retransmission. You should monitor retransmissions using the `netstat -s -P tcp` command to get the `tcpRetransBytes` and `tcpOutDataBytes` statistics. From these numbers, calculate the retransmission percentage using the following formula:

$$PercentRetransmits = \left(\frac{tcpRetransBytes}{tcpOutDataBytes} \right) \times 100$$

If the remote system is retransmitting too quickly, this will cause duplicate packets. Like packet retransmissions, duplicate packets can also indicate a bad network device or a slow or congested route. Using the same `netstat` command we just showed you, get the `tcpInDupBytes` and `tcpInDataBytes` statistics and calculate the duplication percentage using the following formula:

$$PercentDuplicates = \left(\frac{tcpInDupBytes}{tcpInDataBytes} \right) \times 100$$

Listen drops occur when your system has a full listen queue and cannot accept any new connections. To eliminate listen drops, increase the size of the Solaris TCP parameter `tcp_conn_req_max_q` (or its equivalent on your operating system) or add more servers to handle the network load. Use the `netstat -s -P tcp | grep tcpListenDrop` command to measure the frequency of listen drops.

Best Practice

Modern networks are fast enough to avoid performance problems in well-designed systems, but you should monitor key network statistics such as packet retransmissions, duplicate packets, and listen drops to ensure good performance. When troubleshooting performance problems, don't forget to check your network for packet loss or errors.

Java Virtual Machine Tuning

The Java Virtual Machine (JVM) you use to run your WebLogic Server–based application is a key factor in the final server performance. Not all JVMs are created equal — we have seen certain applications perform up to 20 percent better simply by using a different JVM. Performance is nothing without stability, and fast applications do not do your users any good if they are not running. We recommend that you look for stability first and then performance when selecting the JVM on which to run your application server. If more than one JVM is available and supported on your target deployment environment, you should test them head-to-head to determine which JVM best meets your reliability, performance, and scalability requirements.

Garbage collection is the single most important factor when tuning a JVM for long-running, server-side applications. Improperly tuned garbage collectors or applications that create unnecessarily large numbers of objects can significantly affect the efficiency of your application. It is not uncommon to find that garbage collection consumes a significant amount of the overall processing time in a server-side Java application. Proper tuning of the garbage collector can significantly reduce the garbage collector's processing time and, therefore, can significantly improve your application's throughput.

Though we spend most of our time in the next sections specifically talking about the Sun JVM, a lot of these concepts are similar in other JVMs, such as Oracle's JRockit JVM. Our discussion of JVM tuning starts by reviewing garbage collection. Next, we walk through key JVM tuning parameters and options for the Sun JVM. We also discuss JRockit toward the end of this section.

Understanding Garbage Collection

Garbage collection (GC) is the technique a JVM uses to free memory occupied by objects that are no longer being used by the application. The Java Language Specification does not require a JVM to have a garbage collector, nor does it specify how a garbage collector should work. Nevertheless, all of the commonly used JVMs have garbage collectors, and most garbage collectors use similar algorithms to manage their memory and perform collection operations.

Just as it is important to understand the workload of your application to tune your overall system properly, it is also important to understand how your JVM performs garbage collection so that you can tune it. Once you have a solid understanding of garbage collection algorithms and implementations, it is possible to tune application and garbage collection behavior to maximize performance. Some garbage collection schemes are more appropriate for applications with specific requirements. For example, near-real-time applications care more about avoiding garbage collection pauses whereas most OLTP applications care more about overall throughput. Once you have an understanding of the workload of the application and the different garbage collection algorithms your JVM supports, you can optimize the garbage collector configuration.

In this section, we give you a brief overview of different approaches that JVMs use for garbage collection. For more information on garbage collection algorithms and how they affect JVM performance, we recommend looking at the two very good articles on Sun's web site: "Improving Java Application Performance and Scalability by Reducing Garbage Collection Times and Sizing Memory" by Nagendra Nagarajayya and Steve Mayer (see Link 13-11) and "Improving Java Application Performance and Scalability by Reducing Garbage Collection Times and Sizing Memory Using JDK 1.4.1 — New Parallel and Concurrent Collectors for Low Pause and Throughput Applications" by Nagendra Nagarajayya and Steve Mayer (see Link 13-12).

As we discussed previously, the purpose of the garbage collection in a JVM is to clean up objects that are no longer being used. Garbage collectors determine whether an object is eligible for collection by determining whether objects are being referenced by any active objects in the system. The garbage collector must first identify the objects eligible for collection. The two general approaches for this are reference counting and object reference traversal. Reference counting involves storing a count of all of the references to a particular object. This means that the JVM must properly increment and decrement the reference count as the application creates references and as the references go out of scope. When an object's reference count goes to zero, it is eligible for garbage collection.

Although early JVMs used reference counting, most modern JVMs use object reference traversal. Object reference traversal simply starts with a set of root objects and follows every link recursively through the entire object graph to determine the set of *reachable* objects. Any object that is not reachable from at least one of these root objects is garbage collected. During this object traversal stage, the garbage collector must remember which objects are reachable so that it can remove those that are not; this is known as *marking* the object.

The next thing that the garbage collector must do is remove the unreachable objects. When doing this, some garbage collectors simply scan through the heap, removing the unmarked objects and adding their memory location and size to a list of available memory for the JVM to use in creating new objects; this is commonly referred to as *sweeping*. The problem with this approach is that memory can fragment over time to the point where there are a lot of small segments of memory that are not big enough to use for new objects but yet, when added all together, can make up a significant amount of memory. Therefore, many garbage collectors actually rearrange live objects in memory to *compact* the live objects, making the available heap space contiguous.

In order to do their jobs, garbage collectors usually have to stop all other activity for some portion of the garbage collection process. This *stop-the-world* approach means all application-related work stops while the garbage collector runs. As a result, any in-flight requests will experience an increase in their response time by the amount of time taken by the garbage collector. Other, more sophisticated collectors run either incrementally or truly concurrently to reduce or eliminate the application pauses. Some garbage collectors use a single thread to do their work; others employ multiple threads to increase their efficiency on multi-CPU machines. Look at a few of the garbage collectors used by modern JVMs.

Mark-and-sweep Collector This type of collector first traverses the object graph and marks reachable objects. It then scans the heap for unmarked objects and adds their memory to a list of available memory segments. This collector typically uses a single thread to do its work and is a stop-the-world collector.

Mark-and-compact Collector   A mark-and-compact collector, sometimes known as a mark-sweep-compact collector, uses the same marking phase as a mark-and-sweep collector. During the second phase, it compacts the heap by copying marked objects to a new area of the heap. These collectors are also stop-the-world collectors.

Copying Collector   This type of collector divides the heap into two areas, commonly known as *semi-spaces*. It uses only one semi-space at a time; the JVM creates all new objects in one semi-space. When the garbage collector runs, it copies any reachable objects it finds to the other semi-space as it finds them, thus compacting the heap as it copies live objects. All dead objects are left behind. This algorithm works well for short-lived objects, but the expense of continually copying long-lived objects makes it less efficient. Again, this is a stop-the-world collector.

Incremental Collector   Incremental collectors basically divide the heap into multiple areas and collect garbage from only one area at a time. This can create much smaller, though more frequent, pauses in your application. Numerous approaches exist for defining how the actual collection is handled from traditional mark-and-sweep to algorithms designed explicitly for use with multiple smaller areas like the *train* algorithm. See "Incremental Mature Garbage Collection Using the Train Algorithm" by Jacob Seligmann and Steffen Grarup (see Link 13-13) for more information.

Generational Collector   This type of collector divides the heap into two or more areas that it uses to store objects with different lifetimes. The JVM generally creates all new objects in one of these areas. Over time, the objects that continue to exist get tenure and move into another area for longer-lived objects. Generational collectors often use different algorithms for the different areas to optimize performance.

Concurrent Collectors   Concurrent collectors run concurrently with the application, typically as one or more background threads. These collectors typically have to stop-the-world at some point to complete certain tasks, but the amount of time they halt all processing is significantly reduced because of their other background work.

Parallel Collectors   Parallel collectors typically use one of the traditional algorithms but use multiple threads to parallelize their work on multiprocessor machines. Using multiple threads on multi-CPU machines can dramatically improve the scalability of a Java application on multiprocessor machines.

Tuning the Sun HotSpot JVM Heap Size

Sun Microsystem's HotSpot JVM uses a generational collector that partitions the heap into three main areas: the new generation area, the old generation area, and the permanent generation area. The JVM creates all new objects in the new generation area. Once an object survives a certain number of garbage collection cycles in the new generation area, it gets promoted, or *tenured*, to the old generation area. The JVM stores `Class` and `Method` objects for the classes it loads in a section of the heap known as the permanent generation area. From a configuration perspective, the permanent generation area in the Sun HotSpot JVM is a separate area that is not considered part of the heap. Before we go any further, let's look at how to control the size of these areas.

You can use the -Xms and -Xmx flags to control the initial and maximum size of the entire heap, respectively. For example, the following command sets the initial size of the entire heap to 128 megabytes (MBs) and the maximum size to 256 MBs:

```
java -Xms128m -Xmx256m ...
```

To control the size of the new generation area, you can use the `-XX:NewRatio` flag to set the proportion of the overall heap that is set aside for the new generation area. For example, the following command sets the overall heap size to 128 MBs and sets the new ratio to 3. This means that the ratio of the new area to the old area is 1:3; the new area is one-fourth of the overall heap space, or 32 MBs, and the old area is three-fourths of the overall heap space, or 96 MBs.

```
java -Xms128m -Xmx128m -XX:NewRatio=3 ...
```

The initial and maximum sizes for the new area can be set explicitly using the `-XX:NewSize` and `-XX:MaxNewSize` flags or the `-Xmn` flag. For example, the command shown here sets the initial and maximum size to 64 MBs:

```
java -Xms256m -Xmx256m -Xmn64m ...
```

Configuration-wise, the permanent area is not considered part of the heap. By default, the initial size of the permanent area is 4 MBs. As your application loads and runs, the JVM will resize the permanent area as needed up to the maximum size for this area. Every time it resizes the permanent area, the JVM does a full garbage collection of the entire heap (and the permanent area). By default, the maximum size is 32 MBs. Use the `-XX:MaxPermSize` flag to increase the maximum size of the permanent area. When loading large numbers of classes in your WebLogic Server application, it is not uncommon to need to increase the maximum size of this area. The number of objects stored in the permanent area will grow quickly while the JVM loads classes, and it may force the JVM to resize the permanent area frequently. To prevent this resizing, set the initial size of the permanent area using the `-XX:PermSize` flag. For example, here we have set the initial size to 64 MBs and the maximum size to 128 MBs:

```
java -Xms512m -Xmx512m -Xmn128m -XX:PermSize=64m -XX:MaxPermSize=128m ...
```

> When the permanent area of the heap is too small, the JVM will do a full garbage collection of the entire heap before resizing the permanent area. If you allow the JVM to control the size, these full garbage collections will happen relatively frequently because the JVM is ultra-conservative about grabbing too much space for the permanent area. Always set the `PermSize` big enough for your application to run comfortably.

By default, HotSpot uses a copying collector for the new generation area. This area is actually subdivided into three partitions. The first partition, known as *Eden*, is where all new objects are created. The other two semi-spaces are also called *survivor* spaces. When Eden fills up, the collector stops the application and copies all reachable objects into the current `from` survivor space. As the current `from` survivor space fills up, the collector will copy the reachable objects to the current `to` survivor space. At that point, the `from` and `to` survivor spaces switch roles so that the current `to` space becomes the new `from` space and vice versa. Objects that continue to live are copied between survivor spaces until they achieve tenure, at which point they are moved into the old generation area.

Use the `-XX:SurvivorRatio` flag to control the size of these subpartitions. Like the `NewRatio`, the `SurvivorRatio` specifies the ratio of the size of one of the survivor spaces to the Eden space. For example, the following command sets the new area size to 64 MBs, Eden to 32 MBs, and each of the two survivor spaces to 16 MBs:

```
java -Xms256m -Xmx256m -Xmn64m -XX:SurvivorRatio=2 ...
```

Figure 13-1 shows an overview of the HotSpot JVM heap layout and some of the parameters that we have been discussing.

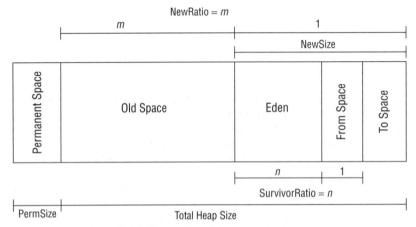

Figure 13-1: Understanding the HotSpot heap partitioning.

As we discussed previously, HotSpot defaults to using a copying collector for the new area and a mark-sweep-compact collector for the old area. Using a copying collector for the new area makes sense because the majority of objects created by an application are short-lived. In an ideal situation, all transient objects would be collected before making it out of the Eden space. If we were able to achieve this, and all objects that made it out of the Eden space were long-lived objects, then ideally we would immediately tenure them into the old space to avoid copying them back and forth in the survivor spaces.

Unfortunately, applications do not necessarily fit cleanly into this ideal model because they tend also to have a small number of intermediate-lived objects. It is typically better to keep these intermediate-lived objects in the new area because copying a small number of objects is generally less expensive than compacting the old heap when they have to be garbage collected in the old heap.

To control the copying of objects in the new area, use the -XX:TargetSurvivorRatio flag to control the desired survivor space occupancy after a collection. Don't be misled by the name; this value is a percentage. By default, the value is set to 50. When using large heaps in conjunction with a low SurvivorRatio, you should probably increase this value to somewhere in the neighborhood of 80 to 90 to better utilize the survivor space.

Use the -XX:MaxTenuringThreshold flag to control the upper threshold the copying collector uses before promoting an object. If you want to prevent all copying and automatically promote objects directly from Eden to the old area, set the value of MaxTenuringThreshold to 0. If you do this, you will in effect be skipping the use of the survivor spaces, so you will want to set the SurvivorRatio to a large number to maximize the size of the Eden area, as shown here:

```
java ... -XX:MaxTenuringThreshold=0 -XX:SurvivorRatio=50000 ...
```

Now that you understand the goals and controls you have for tuning the heap sizes, let's look at some of the information you can get from the JVM to help you make the right tuning decisions.

The -verbose:gc switch gives you basic information about what the garbage collector is doing. By turning this switch on, you will get information about when major and minor collections occur, what the memory size before and after the collection was, and how much time the collection took. Look at some sample output from this switch.

```
[Full GC 21924K->13258K(63936K), 0.3854772 secs]
[GC 26432K->13984K(63936K), 0.0168988 secs]
[GC 27168K->13763K(63936K), 0.0068799 secs]
[GC 26937K->14196K(63936K), 0.0139437 secs]
```

The first line that starts with Full GC is a major collection of the entire heap. The other three lines are minor collections, either of the new or the old area. The numbers before the arrow indicate the size of the heap before the collection, and the number after the arrow shows the size after the collection. The number in parentheses is the total size of the heap, and the time values indicate the amount of time the collection took.

By turning on the -XX:+PrintGCDetails switch, you can get a little more information about what is happening in the garbage collector. Output from this switch looks like this.

```
[Full GC [Tenured: 11904K->13228K(49152K), 0.4044939 secs]
        21931K->13228K(63936K), 0.4047285 secs]
[GC [DefNew: 13184K->473K(14784K), 0.0213737 secs]
        36349K->23638K(63936K), 0.0215022 secs]
```

As with the standard garbage collection output, the Full GC label indicates a full collection. Tenured indicates that the mark-sweep-compact collector has run on the old generation; the old heap size went from 11904K to 13228K; and the total old area size is 49152K. The reason for this increase is that the new area is automatically purged of all objects during a full collection. The second set of numbers associated with the first entry represents the before, after, and total size of the entire heap. This full collection took 0.4047285 seconds. In the second entry, the GC label indicates a partial collection, and DefNew means that the collection took place in the new area; all of the statistics have similar meanings to the first except that they pertain to the new area rather than the old area.

By adding the -XX:+PrintGCTimeStamps switch, the JVM adds information about when these garbage collection cycles occur. The time is measured in seconds since the JVM started, shown in bold here.

```
21.8441: [GC 21.8443: [DefNew: 13183K->871K(14784K), 0.0203224 secs]
        20535K->8222K(63936K), 0.0205780 secs]
```

Finally, you can add the -XX:+PrintHeapAtGC switch to get even more detailed information. This information will dump a snapshot of the heap as a whole.

To get more information on what is going on in the new area, you can print the object tenuring statistics by adding the -XX:+PrintTenuringDistribution switch, in addition to the -verbose:gc switch, to the JVM command line. The output that follows shows objects being promoted through the ages on their way to being tenured to the old generation.

```
java -Xms64m -Xmx64m -XX:NewRatio=3 -verbose:gc
    -XX:+PrintTenuringDistribution ...
```

```
[GC
Desired survivor size 819200 bytes, new threshold 31 (max 31)
- age   1:    285824 bytes,    285824 total
 34956K->22048K(63936K), 0.2182682 secs]
[GC
Desired survivor size 819200 bytes, new threshold 31 (max 31)
- age   1:    371520 bytes,    371520 total
- age   2:    263472 bytes,    634992 total
 35231K->22389K(63936K), 0.0413801 secs]
[GC
Desired survivor size 819200 bytes, new threshold 3 (max 31)
- age   1:    436480 bytes,    436480 total
- age   2:    203952 bytes,    640432 total
- age   3:    263232 bytes,    903664 total
 35573K->22652K(63936K), 0.0432329 secs]
```

Notice the desired survivor size of 819200 bytes. Why is that? Well, let's do the math. If the overall heap is 64 MBs and the NewRatio is 3, this means that the new area is one-fourth of the total heap, or 16 MBs. Because we are using the client JVM, the default value of the SurvivorRatio is 8. This means that each survivor space is one-eighth the size of the Eden space. Because there are two survivor spaces, that means that each survivor space is one-tenth of the overall new area size, or 1.6 MBs. Because the default TargetSurivorRatio is 50 percent, this causes the desired survivor size to be about 800 KBs.

You will also notice that the maximum *threshold* is always 31. The threshold is the number of times the JVM will copy the object between the to and from spaces before promoting it to the old space. Because of the TargetSurvivorRatio discussion previously, the garbage collector will always try to keep the survivor space at or below the target size. The garbage collector will try to age (copy) the objects up to the threshold of 31 times before promoting them into the old area. The garbage collector, however, will recalculate the actual threshold for promotion after each garbage collection. Remember, any full garbage collection cycle will immediately tenure all reachable objects, so always try to tune the garbage collector — especially the PermSize — to prevent full garbage collection cycles from occurring.

In the last entry, you will notice that the garbage collector changed the threshold from the default of 31 to 3. This happened because the garbage collector is attempting to keep the occupancy of the survivor space at its desired survivor size. By adding the size of the objects in all three age categories you will get 903664 bytes, which exceeds the desired survivor size; therefore, the garbage collector reset the threshold for the next garbage collection cycle.

Sun's JVM comes with several garbage collectors that allow you to optimize the garbage collector based on your application requirements. Rather than discuss these alternate garbage collectors here, Sun provides a very good description of these alternate garbage collectors and when to use them in the "Memory Management in the Java HotSpot Virtual Machine" on its web site (see Link 13-14).

Using Oracle JRockit JVM

The Oracle JRockit JVM was designed from the ground up to be a server-side JVM. Instead of lazily compiling the Java byte code into native code as HotSpot does, it precompiles every class as it loads. JRockit also provides more in-depth instrumentation to give you more insight into what is going on inside the JVM at runtime. It does this through Oracle JRockit Mission Control, which provides a stand-alone GUI console but can also be integrated within your Eclipse IDE.

JRockit supports both dynamic and static garbage collection modes. By default, JRockit dynamically selects a garbage collection strategy to optimize application throughput. Dynamic garbage collection supports three modes:

> `throughput`: Optimizes for maximum throughput
>
> `pausetime`: Optimizes for short and even pause times
>
> `deterministic`: Optimizes for very short and deterministic pause times (requires Oracle JRockit Real Time)

JRockit also supports four static garbage collection models:

> **Single-spaced Parallel Collector**   This collector stops the world but uses multiple threads to speed the collection process. It does not segment the heap into multiple areas. Though it will cause longer pauses than the rest, it generally provides better memory utilization and better throughput for applications that don't allocate large numbers of short-lived objects.
>
> **Generational Parallel Collector**   This collector stops the world but uses multiple threads to speed the collection process. It segments the heap into a nursery and an old area. New objects are allocated in the nursery and only promoted to the old area after two collection cycles in the nursery area. Though it will cause longer pauses than the rest, it generally provides better memory utilization and better throughput for applications that allocate large numbers of short-lived objects.
>
> **Single-spaced Mostly Concurrent Collector**   This collector uses the entire heap and does its work concurrently using a background thread. Though this collector can virtually eliminate pauses, you are trading memory and throughput for pause-less collection because it will generally take the collector longer to find dead objects and the collector is constantly running during application processing. If this collector cannot keep up with the amount of garbage the application creates, it will stop the application threads while it finishes its collection cycle.
>
> **Generational Mostly Concurrent Collector**   This collector uses a stop-the-world parallel collector on the nursery area and a concurrent collector on the old area. Because this collector has more frequent pauses than the single-spaced concurrent collector, it should require less memory and provide more throughput for applications that can tolerate short pauses. Remember that an undersized nursery area can cause large numbers of temporary objects to be promoted to the old area. This will cause the concurrent collector to work harder and may cause it to fall behind to the point where it has to stop the world to complete its cycle.

By default, JRockit uses the dynamic garbage collection strategy to optimize for throughput. To change to one of the other dynamic strategies, use the `-XgcPrio:<mode>` flag, where valid mode values are `throughput` and `pausetime`. JRockit Real Time adds a third value to this list: `deterministic`. To specify the collector statically, use the `-Xgc:<gc_name>` flag, where the valid values for the four collectors are `singlepar`, `genpar`, `singlecon`, and `gencon`, respectively. You can set the initial and maximum heap sizes using the same `-Xms` and `-Xmx` flags as you do for the HotSpot JVM. To set the nursery size, use the `-Xns` flag.

```
java -jrockit -Xms512m -Xmx512m -Xgc:gencon -Xns128m ...
```

Although JRockit recognizes the `-verbose:gc` switch, the information it prints will vary depending on which garbage collector you are using. JRockit also supports verbose output options of `memory` (same as `gc`), `load`, and `codegen`. Using the default dynamic throughput collector, the `-verbose:memory` output provides information on both nursery area (*nursery GC*) and old area (*GC*) collections, as shown here.

```
[INFO ][memory ] Running with 32 bit heap and compressed references.
[INFO ][memory ] GC mode: Garbage collection optimized for throughput, initial
strategy: Generational Parallel Mark & Sweep
[INFO ][memory ] heap size: 262144K, maximal heap size: 524288K, nursery size:
131072K
[INFO ][memory ] <s>-<end>: GC <before>K-><after>K (<heap>K), <pause> ms
[INFO ][memory ] <s/start> - start time of collection (seconds since jvm start)
[INFO ][memory ] <end>     - end time of collection (seconds since jvm start)
[INFO ][memory ] <before>  - memory used by objects before collection (KB)
[INFO ][memory ] <after>   - memory used by objects after collection (KB)
[INFO ][memory ] <heap>    - size of heap after collection (KB)
...
[INFO ][memory ] 6.924: parallel nursery GC 159174K->64518K (262144K), 34.992 ms
...
[INFO ][memory ] 48.953-49.041: GC 262144K->81910K (262144K), 88.137 ms
```

Using the -XgcPause switch will cause JRockit to print output each time the JVM has to pause other threads to complete garbage collection. The output looks like this.

```
[INFO ][memory ] 28.787: parallel nursery GC 201290K->105482K (262144K), 30.931 ms
[INFO ][gcpause] nursery collection pause time: 30.930677 ms
[INFO ][memory ] 29.726: parallel nursery GC 223427K->130499K (262144K), 38.595 ms
[INFO ][gcpause] nursery collection pause time: 38.594919 ms
[INFO ][memory ] 30.297: parallel nursery GC 244085K->145013K (262144K), 22.180 ms
[INFO ][gcpause] nursery collection pause time: 22.180263 ms
[INFO ][memory ] 30.822: parallel nursery GC 258605K->159341K (262144K), 21.630 ms
[INFO ][gcpause] nursery collection pause time: 21.629774 ms
[INFO ][gcpause] Threads waited for memory 61.151 ms starting at 31.922 s
[INFO ][gcpause] old collection phase 1-0 pause time: 69.134904 ms, (start time:
31.922 s)
[INFO ][gcpause] (pause includes compaction: 3.539 ms (external), update ref: 9.769
ms)
[INFO ][memory ] 31.922-31.991: GC 262144K->76156K (262144K), 69.135 ms
```

As we discussed, even the concurrent collector occasionally has to stop the application to do certain phases of its work. If you use the -XgcReport switch, JRockit will print out a summary of the garbage collection activity before it exits.

```
[INFO ][memory ]
[INFO ][memory ] Memory usage report
[INFO ][memory ]
[INFO ][memory ] young collections
[INFO ][memory ]     number of collections = 10
[INFO ][memory ]     total promoted =       2473233 (size 129116408)
[INFO ][memory ]     max promoted =         551062 (size 31540352)
[INFO ][memory ]     total GC time =        0.415 s
[INFO ][memory ]     mean GC time =         41.500 ms
[INFO ][memory ]     maximum GC Pauses =    54.765 , 58.583, 64.630 ms
[INFO ][memory ]
[INFO ][memory ] old collections
[INFO ][memory ]     number of collections = 2
[INFO ][memory ]     total promoted =       0 (size 0)
[INFO ][memory ]     max promoted =         0 (size 0)
[INFO ][memory ]     total GC time =        0.142 s (pause 0.142 s)
```

```
[INFO ][memory ]     mean GC time =            71.009 ms (pause 71.007 ms)
[INFO ][memory ]     maximum GC Pauses =        0.000 , 69.135, 72.878 ms
[INFO ][memory ]
[INFO ][memory ]     number of parallel mark phases  = 2
[INFO ][memory ]     number of parallel sweep phases  = 2
```

What really makes the JRockit JVM so compelling is JRockit Mission Control. JRockit Mission Control is a management console for the JRockit JVM that contains the following tools.

JRockit Management Console   This provides a real-time view into the JVM's operation by capturing and displaying live data on the CPU and memory usage, as well as garbage collection pauses. This console also gives you control over CPU affinity, garbage collection strategy, and memory pool sizes so that you can adjust settings without restarting the JVM.

JRockit Runtime Analyzer (JRA)   The runtime analyzer allows you to make low overhead recordings of detailed information about what is happening inside the JVM. Those recordings can then be analyzed offline to get detailed information on garbage collection, object usage, method and lock profiling, and latency statistics.

JRockit Latency Analyzer   Using a JRA recording, the latency analyzer graphically shows you all the latency events occurring in your application. Through this tool, you can easily identify areas of contention where your application threads are blocked waiting on locks, database I/O, and any other type of event that may cause latency.

JRockit Memory Leak Detector   This tool allows you to find memory leaks in production applications with very low overhead without needing to restart the JVM. It can track down even the smallest memory leaks and presents the information in a style that simplifies the task of determining the exact cause of the leak.

We have touched on only the highlights of the JRockit JVM and JRockit Mission Control. For more information on the JRockit JVM, please see the JRockit documentation at Link 13-15. You can find more information on JRockit Mission Control at Link 13-16.

JVM tuning is a complex and challenging topic, and we have barely scratched the surface. Nevertheless, it is time to continue moving up the layers in the architecture to the application server platform.

Application Server Tuning

In this section, we discuss techniques and best practices for tuning the core aspects of your WebLogic Server environment. This discussion includes setting some important connection-related parameters, using the native I/O *muxer*, optimizing thread management, and tuning pool sizes.

Configuring Connection-Related Parameters

During performance tests or on heavily loaded production systems, you may want to increase the length of the TCP listen queue, as we discussed in the "Operating System Tuning" section. Whereas the operating system parameter we discussed controls the maximum length of the listen queue, WebLogic Server uses the Accept Backlog parameter to specify the queue size that the server should request from the operating system. Prior to WebLogic Server 10, the default value of 50 could be too small on heavily loaded systems. Starting in WebLogic Server 10, the new default of 300 should be sufficient for most purposes. However, if valid client connection requests are being rejected, the listen queue may be too small.

WebLogic Server uses the `Login Timeout` parameter to help prevent certain types of denial-of-service attacks. This parameter sets a maximum amount of time for a non-SSL client to complete the process of establishing the connection and sending the first request. By default, WebLogic Server sets the default values to 5,000 milliseconds, which may be too low for heavily loaded systems. If your clients are seeing their connections timed out by the server, then increasing the `Login Timeout` may help. WebLogic Server has a corresponding parameter for SSL connections called the `SSL Login Timeout` that defaults to 25,000 milliseconds. In certain high volume SSL conditions, you may need to raise this limit as well.

Using the Native I/O Muxer

As we discussed in Chapter 12, WebLogic Server has several different socket multiplexing (muxer, for short) implementations: an all-Java muxer and a native I/O muxer. By default, WebLogic Server uses the native I/O muxer whenever it can but will revert automatically to the Java muxer if the native I/O muxer fails to initialize properly — for example, if it cannot locate its shared library. In general, you should always use the native I/O muxer because it is far more scalable than the all-Java muxer.

Optimizing Thread Management

In earlier versions of WebLogic Server, choosing the right number of execute threads for your application was arguably the single most important and difficult parameter to size properly to maximize application performance. As we discussed in Chapter 12, WebLogic Server 9.0 changes the execution model to use a single, priority-based, self-tuning execute queue with a common, self-tuning pool of execute threads. By collecting actual performance information over time, WebLogic Server can dynamically adjust the number of execute threads available for processing work to manage the changing workload demands that are inherent in most applications.

By default, each application uses an instance of the default work manager, which gives each application a fair share of 50 and sets no constraints. This setting gives each application equal priority and prevents applications from using more than their fair share of the server's resources when more work exists for each application than the number of available threads. For many situations, this default work manager is sufficient, so this new model greatly simplifies WebLogic Server tuning. Nevertheless, there are a few things to consider before moving on.

Database Connection Pool Contention If your application depends on database connections for processing requests, allowing the server to schedule more application requests concurrently than the size of the connection pool will cause threads to block waiting on access to a database connection. Administrators limit the number of concurrent requests by setting the maximum thread constraint on the application's work manager.

If two or more applications share the same database connection pool, you should define the maximum thread constraint outside the context of a specific work manager and refer to this shared constraint from each application's work manager (or the default work manager). By doing this, you force all application work managers to share the constraint so that the sum of all threads processing requests for all applications will not exceed the maximum number of database connections configured for the pool. WebLogic Server makes this easy by allowing you to refer to your WebLogic Server data source by name from the constraint. The following `config.xml` excerpt shows you the result of overriding the default work manager in the WebLogic Server instance `MyServer` and setting the maximum thread constraint based on the size of the data source `MyDataSource` such that all applications using the default work manager will share this constraint.

```
<self-tuning>
  <max-threads-constraint>
    <name>MyDataSource_MaxThreads</name>
    <target>MyServer</target>
    <connection-pool-name>MyDataSource</connection-pool-name>
  </max-threads-constraint>
  <work-manager>
    <name>default</name>
    <target>MyServer</target>
    <max-threads-constraint>MyDataSource_MaxThreads</max-threads-constraint>
  </work-manager>
</self-tuning>
```

Server Deadlock   Some applications deploy different components in different server instances or call other applications in other servers. When this happens, care must be given if the remote application calls back into the calling application's server (or cluster) as part of processing the request to prevent a server deadlock. The deadlock occurs if all of the calling server's threads are waiting on remote application requests and none are available to process the callbacks, Though the self-tuning behavior will normally prevent this type of deadlock, we strongly recommend explicitly configuring the work manager associated with the callbacks to tell the server to reserve sufficient resources to process the callback. You have two options to consider.

The first option you might consider is assigning a higher fair share to the work manager associated with the callbacks. This tells WebLogic Server to give higher priority to processing the callbacks than to the requests the create them. Although this approach generally works, it introduces a theoretical race condition that could prevent the callbacks from getting scheduled if the server received a large number of originating requests at nearly the same time while no callback requests were waiting.

A better option is to assign a minimum thread constraint to the work manager associated with the callbacks. Doing this guarantees that the server will always reserve the specified number of threads for processing the callbacks — even if it has to create those threads dynamically.

Best Practice

When dealing with applications that involve request processing that spans multiple servers and uses callbacks, always assign a separate work manager for the callbacks. Do not rely solely on setting a higher fair share for the callbacks' work manager. Always set the minimum thread constraint on the callbacks' work manager to prevent server deadlock.

Server Overload   When tuning WebLogic Server to meet your throughput and response time goals, you must consider the point at which it no longer makes sense to accept new work into the server. If user requests sit in the internal WebLogic Server queue waiting for scheduling on a thread longer than the users are willing to wait, it makes no sense for the server to accepting requests until this condition is cleared. We will provide an example.

From monitoring your system, you know that the server typically self-tunes to run with 25 threads, that your application requests take an average 500 milliseconds to process, and that your users will resubmit requests that take longer than 30 seconds. From this data, you can roughly estimate that as soon as the server exceeds 1500 in-flight requests that the server will be doing work for which no user will ever see the response. Clearly, you want the server doing useful work. To prevent this condition from happening, set a capacity constraint of 1500 on your application's work manager. This will tell WebLogic Server to reject new requests for work associated with this work manager when the capacity is exceeded. When the capacity is exceeded, WebLogic Server responds either by sending the well-known HTTP 503 response code or throwing a `RemoteException` in the case of RMI calls, which permits cluster failover.

Prioritization of Important Requests   Most business applications have a variety of request types and users. For example, a stock trading system might collocate the quotes and trading components in the same servers. By assigning the trading component to its own work manager, you can give higher priority to the trading component so that these trading requests get scheduled with higher priority than do the quote requests. To do this, simply give the trading component's work manager a larger fair share than the quote component's work manager.

In a similar vein, you might want to give your top-tier customers' requests higher priority than anonymous user requests. Using the work manager context request class, you can associate different work managers with the same requests based on the user or group name associated with the request. This allows you to assign a higher fair share or lower response time work manager with your top-tier customers.

JMS Producer and Consumer Balancing   Some applications use JMS messaging as a mechanism to decouple intensive backend processing from user requests. For example, a web application might accept a request to search for available flights from a user, drop that request into a JMS queue, return a page to the user to show that the request is being processed, and periodically poll for the result. The challenge in all messaging applications is having the consumers of the messages keep up with the producers over long periods of time because message production is almost always much cheaper than message consumption. As a result, you will likely need to define a custom work manager to assign a higher fair share to the message consumer component if both the producer and consumer are deployed in the same server.

Tuning Resource Pool and Cache Sizes

WebLogic Server uses resource pooling to optimize server efficiency and performance. Though database connection pools are the most obvious use of pooling, the server also pools stateless session bean instances, message-driven bean instances, and other types of objects. If all the pooled resources are in use, the server will increase the size of the pool dynamically to honor application requests for access to a pooled resource. Increasing the size of the pool dynamically adds overhead to application request processing; the amount of overhead depends on how expensive it is to create the pooled resource. Once the pool reaches its maximum size, the server can no longer grow the size of the pool. When this occurs applications requesting access to a pooled resource when all the resources are in use are forced to wait for a resource to become available. If the maximum size of the pool is dramatically undersized, application requests may be blocked for minutes waiting on an available resource. This can literally kill the performance of an otherwise well-written application.

The rule of thumb for pool sizing is simply to make sure that the pool is large enough for all server threads to get access to the pooled resources they need concurrently. In previous versions of WebLogic Server, this was usually simple. For example, each execute thread needs access to one database connection from each pool, so you always make sure that the maximum capacity of the database connection pool was greater than or equal to the number of execute threads. With the introduction of server self-tuning, the number of execute threads isn't necessarily well defined; however, as we discussed in the previous section, setting a shared maximum threads constraint on the relevant work manager(s) that refer to the data source used to access the connection pool prevents the server from dispatching more requests than the maximum size of the pool.

With stateless session and message-driven bean pooling, the overhead associated with creating additional instances is typically very small. As a result, we recommend not setting the `<max-beans-in-free-pool>` and simply use the default value of 1000. Because the server will not create more instances than it needs unless you set the `<initial-beans-in-free-pool>` setting too high, we find that the default value works well in almost all situations. For more information on how to configure EJB pool sizes, please refer to Chapter 8.

WebLogic Server does not pool stateful session beans; however, it does cache them in memory. Because stateful session bean instances contain client state, the server must retain them for the duration of the session. The size of the stateful session bean cache determines how many instances are kept in memory. If the number of sessions exceeds the size of the cache, WebLogic Server will passivate the session bean instance to disk to make room in the cache for other instances. As you can imagine, this paging of instances in and out of memory can dramatically affect the time it takes to process a request to an instance that is not resident in memory. An order of magnitude increase in response times is not uncommon. Therefore, you must choose the size of your stateful session bean cache carefully to try to balance the need to keep all active sessions in cache with the memory requirements of doing so. Setting the proper `<idle-timeout-seconds>` value and `<cache-type>` parameters in conjunction with `<max-beans-in-cache>` allows you to keep orphaned instances from polluting your cache. For more information on EJB pooling and caching, see Link 13-17.

Verifying Application Server Tuning

Once you have found the optimum settings, you should go back and look at garbage collection to see if there is room for improvement in the garbage collector settings to improve the efficiency of the application. Before moving an application into production, we always recommend that you run a longer test to make sure that the application is stable under heavy load for 24, 48, or 72 hours. These tests can often reveal issues that might not show up in production for weeks or months, such as memory leaks. Skipping these saturation tests may save you time up front but can lead to production downtime later. Do not assume that application server tuning will not impact the long-term stability of your application.

Performance Best Practices

In this section, we turn our attention to application design and configuration best practices that directly affect the performance of your WebLogic Server system. We start by reviewing a few design patterns that can improve performance, then present a series of web container and EJB container best practices, and finish up with some best practices related to database access.

Designing for Performance

Good application performance starts with good application design. Overly complex or poorly designed applications will perform poorly regardless of the system-level tuning and best practices you employ to improve performance. Entire books have been dedicated to good application design, and we have only part of one chapter in this book, so we must limit our discussion to a few key principles and best practices. Many books on Java EE design patterns and anti-patterns are available; two of our favorites are *Bitter Java* by Bruce A. Tate (Manning Publications, 2002) and *EJB Design Patterns: Advanced Patterns, Processes, and Idioms* by Floyd Marinescu (Wiley, 2002).

Design patterns are an important topic in the Java EE development community. Proper use of design patterns can provide significant benefits in the maintainability of application code through standardizing the approach to common design problems. Certain design patterns are also beneficial to performance because they reduce the overhead associated with transactions and inter-component messaging. We discuss three of the more important patterns for Java EE applications. For a more extensive overview of well-known Java EE design patterns, take a look at *Core J2EE Patterns: Best Practices and Design Strategies* by Deepak Alur et al. (Prentice Hall, 2001).

Before we continue, we should point out that the Java EE 5 specification has introduced significant changes that arguably affect the importance of certain patterns in Java EE applications. For example, the introduction of resource injection in Java EE 5 seemingly reduces the value of using the service locator pattern to find other Java EE resources within your application. At the time of writing, there was no definitive design patterns book that accounts for the changes in Java EE 5, though a number of web sites and blogs discuss the implications of Java EE 5, such as Link 13-18.

Session Façade

The session façade pattern is a high-level wrapper for server-side components and was discussed at some length in Chapter 7. Java EE applications commonly implement this pattern by creating a stateless session bean that wraps business process logic and the JPA entities, database interactions, and Java objects required to perform the business process. The `bigrez.com` application makes use of this pattern for key business services such as reservation creation and the rate and availability search processes.

Session façades improve application performance by exposing only high-level business operations and reducing the individual client invocations to the lower-level business components and domain objects. This is especially important when accessing EJB components by remote interfaces, because the network and marshalling overhead for each remote call is substantial. Even with local interfaces, there is some overhead because the EJB container provides security, lifecycle management, and transaction control for each invocation. The guiding principle remains the same: reduce the number of invocations that require network, data marshalling, lifecycle, or transactional services to improve application performance. Session façades are one good way to follow this principle.

> **Best Practice**
> Reduce the number of remote calls or other high overhead invocations in your system to improve performance. Stateless session beans implementing the session façade pattern are one good way to reduce the number of these types of invocations.

Value Object

Another common and important mechanism available to reduce the need for remote invocations is the value object pattern. The EJB 3.0 specification transforms entity beans into plain old Java objects (POJOs). There is no longer any need to create separate value objects representing the entity bean data to return to the client. Clients can simply create these value objects, populate them with information, and either pass them into the server or persist them directly using the JPA persistence manager. This works because the value objects are simply serializable Java objects. Passing the entire object from a client to the server eliminates the need to invoke multiple *setter* methods from the client.

Command Pattern

The command pattern uses a single command object to encapsulate multiple steps or requests that are passed to the server for processing with a single invocation. Use this pattern by itself or in conjunction with the session façade pattern to further reduce individual component remote invocations. Systems that contain many business interfaces implemented as façades often use this pattern to create additional higher-level interfaces without creating additional session beans.

The command pattern resembles the business delegate pattern in that both patterns create a higher-level interface for multiple business services. The command pattern processes the logic within the command class on the server, whereas the business delegate pattern uses the client tier. In other words, though business delegates can simplify the interfaces to backend systems by providing a higher-level interface, they generally execute on the client side of the application and create multiple invocations to backend services. The command pattern may therefore be a better choice if performance is a key requirement for the design.

> ### Best Practice
> Create objects that implement the command pattern to further reduce the number of remote calls or other high overhead invocations in your system. When using remote clients, favor command objects over business delegates for better performance.

Understanding Web Container Best Practices

Many high volume Java EE applications service hundreds, if not thousands, of page requests per second. Small improvements in performance within the web container can therefore lead to big improvements in overall system throughput and scalability. This section touches on a few important best practices related to servlets and JavaServer Pages (JSPs), the core components in most web applications.

Session Management

As discussed in Chapter 1, many applications supplement the stateless HTTP protocol by storing session-specific data in the `HttpSession`. This session data will then be available during subsequent requests from the same browser session. In a reliable application, this session data must be available even if the server originally used to service the HTTP request fails or is shut down. WebLogic Server provides two fundamental options for session persistence within a cluster.

In-memory Replication   Session data is kept in memory on the primary server assigned to this session and replicated to a backup server in the cluster for failover.

JDBC-based Persistence   Session data is stored in a special database table and read in to memory by the server processing an HTTP request.

In-memory replication is much faster than JDBC-based persistence and should be used when it meets your requirements. Recognize, however, that there is a cost associated with session persistence regardless of the persistence option chosen. When a web application updates the `HttpSession` object, WebLogic Server must save these changes at the end of the HTTP request. The quantity of data the server needs to save depends on the structure of the data in the `HttpSession`. WebLogic Server uses the `HttpSession.setAttribute()` method to detect when changes to the session occur. At the end of each request, WebLogic Server saves each new or changed attribute value. This means that WebLogic Server will save the entire object graph bound into the attribute that changed. If your web application updates only one or a few fields in a large object structure, you should consider breaking up this large object structure into smaller objects that are bound into different attributes in the session to reduce the amount of data the server has to save at the end of any particular request.

Best Practice

Avoid placing all session data in a single large object in the `HttpSession`. Use in-memory replication for session persistence unless you need JDBC-based persistence to meet your requirements.

`HttpSession` objects also use system resources, so it is important to clean them up when you finish using them. WebLogic Server releases `HttpSession` objects in two ways:

Session Timeouts WebLogic Server will remove an `HttpSession` object after a period of inactivity, known as a *session timeout*. Session timeouts can be set using either the `<session-descriptor>` element's `<timeout-secs>` attribute in the `weblogic.xml` deployment descriptor or the `<session-timeout>` element in the `web.xml` descriptor. See the WebLogic Server documentation at Link 13-19 for more information.

Explicit Invalidation You can programmatically remove a session by calling the `invalidate()` method on the `HttpSession` object.

Too often, web application programmers abuse the session object. You should carefully consider what you store in session objects. Make sure that you understand all of the other available options and the performance trade-offs associated with using sessions. The following list represents a set of best practices related to sessions.

❑   Avoid using the session to pass data between web application components such as servlet controllers and JSP pages during the processing of a single HTTP request. You should use the `HttpServletRequest` object for passing data needed when forwarding or including other web application components.

❑   Consider other alternatives when state can easily be maintained or derived. You can often store the state in local variables, the database, or client-side cookies.

❑   Keep your session objects as small as possible by always removing objects from the session that you no longer need with the session's `removeAttribute()` method.

❑   Never, ever use the session to store data you cannot afford to lose — even in conjunction with JDBC-based persistence. If the data is too important to lose, store it in the database directly rather than relying on session persistence to avoid losing data when the session times out.

❑   Understand your business requirements for session timeouts. Always make sure that you tune the session timeout interval to the smallest value consistent with your business requirements. This will prevent users from tying up valuable resources when they fail to exit the system when finished. WebLogic Server uses a default value of 3,600 seconds, or 1 hour. A value of 10 or 15 minutes is usually sufficient for most web applications.

JavaServer Pages

Chapter 1 presented a number of the best practices related to JavaServer Pages. Here, we highlight two areas of particular importance to performance.

Using Sessions Efficiently

JavaServer Pages (JSPs) create `HttpSession` objects by default, as required by the JSP specification. If your pages are not using sessions, turning the default behavior off can enhance performance. Include the following JSP page directive to avoid creating unnecessary `HttpSession` objects.

```
<%@ page session="false"%>
```

Using Dynamic Content Caching

Chapter 1 presented the `wl:cache` custom tag and the `CacheFilter` servlet filter, two powerful techniques available for dynamic content caching in WebLogic Server. When determining what content to cache you should consider the following questions.

- ❑ How often is the content requested?
- ❑ How often does the content change?
- ❑ How expensive is it to create or calculate the content with each request?

Content items that change infrequently, such as headers or footers on a portal page, are excellent candidates. Additionally, repetitive database queries that are returning data that changes infrequently also offer the opportunity for performance gains from caching.

Be careful not to go overboard with caching, however, because it consumes memory on the server and there is currently no mechanism to limit the size of the response cache unless you are using *keys*. The `key` parameter in the `wl:cache` tag makes it very easy to cache response data for different key values. Be sure to set the `size` attribute to control the size of the cache when the number of possible key values is large enough to create a very large cache of responses.

> **Best Practice**
> Use dynamic content caching when content is frequently displayed, is infrequently changed, and represents a fair amount of work to create with each request. Limit the size of the cache to avoid competing for heap space with other components.

Servlets

Avoid using the deprecated `SingleThreadModel` for servlets. While the servlet specification recommends using Java synchronization to eliminate the need for the SingleThreadModel, overly synchronizing your servlet class can be even worse from a performance perspective. Try to minimize the need for synchronization in your servlets. Where absolutely required, minimize the scope of synchronization to the smallest possible block of code. Make sure that your synchronized blocks do not involve long, blocking calls that could bring your system to a grinding halt when slowdowns or failure occur.

Use the servlet's `init()` method to perform expensive operations that need to take place only once. Because the web container calls the `HttpServlet.init()` method right after loading the servlet, it is an excellent place to invoke heavyweight operations that you want to perform only once.

In many cases, it is possible to speed up the writing of the output stream by using a `ServletOutputStream` object instead of a `PrintWriter`. `PrintWriter` performs character set conversion; therefore, you should use it only when your requirements demand it. For cases where your servlet returns only ASCII or binary data, use a `ServletOutputStream` to get better performance.

Understanding EJB Container Best Practices

High volume Java EE applications often use Enterprise JavaBean (EJB) components to provide transaction, security, and object lifecycle services for key business processes and objects. The performance of EJB components can have a dramatic effect on overall system performance because they tend to perform much more processing per request than a web component. This section highlights a number of best practices for improving the performance of your EJB components in a WebLogic Server environment.

JNDI Lookup Strategies

Java EE applications use the Java Naming and Directory Interface (JNDI) to locate many different types of resources. Excessive calls to JNDI to look up EJB references, `DataSource` references, and JMS connection factories and destinations can reduce system performance significantly, especially if you are using WebLogic Server's global JNDI namespace. To minimize the overhead of these lookup operations, you should cache and reuse the objects; also, use Java EE resource references to bind the objects in WebLogic Server's global JNDI tree into your application's Environment Naming Context (ENC) namespace. Several techniques are available for caching these objects; we discuss two of them.

For many simple web applications, you can simply look up the objects in the servlet's `init()` method and cache them in instance variables in the servlet. As long as the objects themselves are thread-safe, using instance variables in this way is also thread-safe because your servlet probably uses these objects to create other objects. For example, you use a `DataSource` to get a database connection from the JDBC connection pool.

Java EE 5 supports injecting common resource types directly into your application. An example of resource injection you might use on your servlet's instance variable is shown here. Though this resource injection doesn't eliminate the underlying JNDI lookup, it does simplify the code.

```
@Resource(name=jdbc/MyOracleDataSource)
DataSource myDataSource;
```

Another common approach requires a helper or factory class that you can use throughout your application to locate and cache these types of objects. You can create a separate locator class for each type of object, or create one general purpose locator capable of finding and caching all types of objects. With the introduction of resource injection into the Java EE specification, the desirability and benefits of the service locator pattern are significantly reduced.

> **Best Practice**
>
> Use caching to reduce the number of JNDI lookup operations for EJB references, `DataSource` objects, and JMS connection factories and destinations. Use Java EE resource references to further reduce the cost of your application's JNDI lookups.

One caveat on caching worth noting is that the use of JNDI lookup caching can result in the client having a stale reference if the server on which the object resides shuts down. This is typically an issue only if the client using the object and the object are in separate processes. For example, standalone clients can avoid the problem of EJB reference caching by deploying the EJBs to a WebLogic Server cluster. In a WebLogic Server cluster, each server in the cluster has a copy of the object and the reference bound into JNDI is cluster-aware; that is, it knows about all of the copies of the objects in all of the servers. Should one server fail, the client-side stub can route calls around the failed server to another server with an equivalent component.

Optimizing EJB 3.0 Entities

The EJB 3.0 specification transformed the older specifications' persistence mechanism from one that uses full-blown entity beans to represent your domain objects to one that uses POJOs. This transformation makes it much easier to design and build high performance EJB-based applications. Nevertheless, it does not eliminate the need to optimize your application design to make efficient use of the underlying database interactions. Chapter 6 discusses the tuning considerations for WebLogic Server's default JPA provider, Kodo. If using the EclipseLink provider contained within Oracle TopLink, please refer to Link 13-20.

Taking Advantage of Pass-by-Reference

Enterprise JavaBeans are designed to provide *location transparency*: The caller may call the bean as if it coexists in the same JVM when it may actually be located on a completely different server. EJB components use Remote Method Invocation (RMI) to enable location transparency, but it comes with a cost. RMI uses serialization to pass method parameters and return values using a *pass-by-value* semantic — even if the caller and the bean are in the same JVM.

This marshalling and unmarshalling of data is expensive but necessary when the caller and EJB are in two different processes. It is also necessary if the caller and the EJB are in the same process but loaded using different classloaders. If both the caller and the EJB are in the same JVM and loaded with the same classloader hierarchy, it is possible to skip the marshalling and unmarshalling and pass the arguments and return values using *pass-by-reference* semantics. In many applications, the functional behavior of the application won't change by switching to pass-by-reference semantics; however, certain coding styles and practices can cause functional change. This is why the EJB specification requires the use of pass-by-value semantics for all EJB calls using the EJB's home and remote interfaces, if they exist. EJB 2.0 added support for local interfaces that support pass-by-reference semantics.

This pass-by-reference optimization is available only between components within an enterprise application. Separate applications running in the same JVM use separate classloaders, so attempts to pass data by reference would invariably result in a `ClassCastException`. WebLogic Server uses serialization in these cases. Don't forget that passing data by reference allows the called method to modify the contents of the passed object, in most cases, providing either a powerful feature or a debugging nightmare depending on how you use it.

Best Practice

Deploy related components together in the same enterprise application to allow pass-by-reference semantics and maximize performance.

Historically, WebLogic Server has optimized calls made to EJB components within the same application by passing parameters and return values by *reference*, rather than by *value*, to improve performance. Because of Java EE licensing requirements imposed by Sun, WebLogic Server changed its default behavior to always use pass-by-value semantics. Therefore, we want to emphasize that in order to take advantage of this performance optimization, you now need to enable the optimization explicitly in the `weblogic-ejb-jar.xml` deployment descriptor for every EJB for which you want callers to be able to use pass-by-reference semantics with the EJB's remote interface. This example shows how to enable it:

```
<weblogic-enterprise-bean>
    <ejb-name>CustomerBean</ejb-name>
    <enable-call-by-reference>true</enable-call-by-reference>
</weblogic-enterprise-bean>
```

WebLogic Server 8.1 changed the default behavior for its `<enable-call-by-reference>` optimization. The new default value is false to make WebLogic Server Java EE–compatible out of the box. To take advantage of this performance optimization, you must explicitly enable the optimization in your EJB deployment descriptors.

Applying Database Access Best Practices

Efficient database access is critical to achieving high throughput and good scalability for your system. All of the other tuning and optimizations you perform, whether in the JVM, web container, EJB container, or elsewhere, will be for naught if the database access in the application is slow. Worse yet, the techniques available for increasing database processing capability through hardware upgrades are generally more expensive than the simple clustering techniques available for increasing the processors available for the web or EJB tiers of the application. You simply must start with efficient database access to achieve good overall performance.

This section provides a number of best practices related to database access from within Java EE applications. This section is not intended to provide a complete treatment of database design or performance tuning. For more information about database performance tuning for Oracle, we recommend *Oracle Database 10g Performance Tuning: Tips and Tricks* by Richard Niemiec (Oracle Press, 2007). Numerous books on database design, such as the classic *An Introduction to Database Systems, 7th Edition* by C. J. Date (Addison-Wesley, 2000) and *Case*Method: Entity-Relationship Modelling* by Richard Barker (Addison-Wesley, 1990) are also available.

Basic Database Principles

First, you need an efficient logical database design. Database designers tend to favor highly normalized designs requiring multi-way joins to fetch a typical business object and related data. A design that looks good in the data modeling tool may become a real bottleneck in production. If performance is a key criterion for your system, it is important to push back in this area and work with your database designer to flatten or denormalize some critical tables.

Next, the physical database design must reflect the performance requirements of your application. Your DBA should be employing all of the optimization features available in the chosen database technology to achieve the best possible performance. Make sure to provide your DBA with a complete list of the queries your application uses, including all columns appearing in the WHERE and ORDER BY clauses, so that he or she can create the proper indexes on each table.

After creating and tuning your database, you still need to use efficient database access coding techniques to ensure a high performance application. Some basic rules of thumb include these:

- ❑ Always perform table access using a good, selective index. Work with your database administrator to view statistics on your queries and correct any inefficient database access.

- ❑ Avoid joining multiple tables unless your application logic requires it. This often means creating multiple versions of a query, one that avoids a join and fetches only limited data for each matching object and one that joins with related tables and fetches a fully populated object.

- ❑ Avoid using queries that return extremely large result sets. This becomes even more important when using an ORDER BY clause that does not use the same index that the query's WHERE clause uses. When this happens, the database must order the rows manually — a very time-consuming process.

- ❑ Cache data when the access pattern is mostly read and the hit frequency is high.

Retrieve Columns Explicitly

Use explicit column lists in queries rather than selecting all columns from a table using the SELECT * syntax. Explicitly retrieving only the needed columns avoids internal JDBC operations and reduces the amount of data transferred back to the application, improving query performance. Of course, the other benefit is that your code doesn't break if the table is altered to add new columns.

Cache Prepared Statements

Use prepared statements for database access if your application executes the same SQL statement repeatedly. The first time you execute a prepared statement the database must spend extra time parsing and compiling the statement before it can be executed. Most relational databases will then cache the statement and match new statements against the cached ones to avoid this performance penalty. Keep in mind that for the database to reuse a cached statement, the new statement must match the old statement exactly in all aspects except the values of bind variables.

WebLogic Server supplements this database-level caching with its own JDBC PreparedStatement cache built into its data source support. Whenever your application calls prepareStatement() for a new statement, WebLogic Server will cache the PreparedStatement object returned by the JDBC connection for use during subsequent prepareStatement() requests made using this same JDBC connection. The JDBC model restricts cached statements to a specific connection; therefore, frequently used queries will likely have a cached statement per connection. Reusing JDBC PreparedStatement objects eliminates the need for parsing statements in the database, which reduces CPU usage on the database machine, improving performance for the current statement and leaving CPU cycles for other tasks. You configure a data source's prepared statement cache using the WebLogic Console.

Like most tuning operations, determining the proper size of the prepared statement cache is an iterative process. In general, the more prepared statements your application employs, the larger the cache should be. For example, if the application has 20 SQL statements, setting the pool's prepared statement cache size to 20 will allow WebLogic Server to cache all of the prepared statements because each pool connection has its own cache. One empirical, iterative approach for sizing the cache involves monitoring the SQL parse operations per second occurring in the database during a realistic load test. Continue increasing the size of the prepared statement cache until the number of parse operations per second stops decreasing, representing a point of diminishing returns.

Transaction Model

WebLogic Server supports both the local and distributed JTA transactions. Distributed transactions are transactions that span either multiple database connections or multiple resources. Distributed transactions require additional logging and extra network I/O, making them many times slower than local transactions. Whenever possible, use local transactions involving a single `Connection` object for the best performance.

As we discussed in Chapter 12, there is a three-way relationship between transaction models, JDBC `DataSource` settings, and the underlying JDBC driver. In most circumstances, you want to use a transactional `DataSource`. To create a transactional `DataSource`, you just need to make sure that the `Supports Global Transactions` checkbox is checked when you create the `DataSource` using the WebLogic Console. Note that if you choose an XA JDBC driver, WebLogic Server always uses a `DataSource` that supports global transactions.

It is very common to have multiple EJB components involved in the same unit of work. The only way to accomplish this without using an XA-compliant driver is to have all participants share the same database connection. WebLogic Server will automatically and transparently make sure that all operations use the same connection when your application is using a transactional `DataSource` with a non-XA JDBC driver. You will need to use an XA-compliant JDBC driver if your applications use transactions that span multiple resources, such as a database and JMS or two databases. If a particular transaction involves only a single resource, WebLogic Server's JTA transaction manager will optimize the transaction to use a single-phase commit instead of the more expensive two-phase commit.

WebLogic Server supports an optimization called `Last Logging Resource`, which we discussed in Chapter 12. If you have a situation where you need to involve one or more XA resources and a database in a global transaction, it is possible to use a non-XA JDBC driver with a `DataSource` configured to support global transactions with the `Last Logging Resource` option. Not only is this option transactionally safe, it is generally significantly faster than using XA because the database isn't required to use the XA two-phase commit protocol and the XA transaction log is written into the database as part of the non-XA transaction.

Best Practice

Use a transactional `DataSource` to ensure proper transaction coordination when using EJB components or involving multiple resources in a transaction. When doing distributed transactions, you will generally need to use an XA-compliant JDBC driver.

In certain cases, you may be able to use a non-XA JDBC driver with a transactional `DataSource` configured to use `Last Logging Resource` to improve performance without sacrificing transactional safety.

Commitment Control Level

JDBC connections use a commit control level of `TRANSACTION_NONE` with the `autoCommit` attribute set to `true` by default. These are the correct settings when an application does not need to use transactions, such as when an application invokes a stored procedure or trigger that runs under transaction commitment control. These are unusual circumstances, though; in most cases, you should set `autoCommit` to `false` to increase performance by reducing the number of commit operations. When using nontransactional `DataSource` objects, you should explicitly call `Connection.setAutoCommit(false)` before executing your queries and then call `Connection.commit()` at the end of the transaction, as shown here.

```
DataSource ds = (DataSource)ctx.lookup("java:comp/env/jdbc/TestDB");
conn = ds.getConnection();
conn.setAutoCommit(false);
...
conn.commit();
```

If you are using a transactional `DataSource`, all connections will already have `autoCommit` set to `false`. Any attempt to invoke `setAutoCommit(true)` on the connection will throw a `SQLException`.

Best Practice

Configure commit control properly on JDBC connections obtained from a nontransactional `DataSource` by calling `setAutoCommit(false)` before executing any queries and `commit()` at the end of each transaction to improve performance and avoid committing after every statement.

Batch Updates

A *batch update* refers to a set of SQL statements submitted as a unit for processing. Sending multiple statements together can be much more efficient than sending each update separately. Always set `autoCommit` to `false` or obtain the connection from a JTA-aware `DataSource` when doing batch updates to avoid committing automatically when calling `executeBatch()`. The database will execute the SQL statements in the order they were added to the batch. The following code block illustrates this technique.

```
DataSource ds = (DataSource)ctx.lookup("java:comp/env/jdbc/TestDB");
Connection conn = ds.getConnection();
Statement stmt = conn.createStatement();
stmt.addBatch("INSERT INTO EMPLOYEE " +
            "VALUES (500, 'Jeff', 'Architect', 'Smith', 250000)");
stmt.addBatch("INSERT INTO EMPLOYEE " +
            "VALUES (501, 'John', 'Controller', 'Park', 300000)");
int[] updateNum = stmt.executeBatch();
```

Connection Pools

Establishing a JDBC connection with a database can be very slow and resource intensive. If your application requires database connections that are repeatedly opened and closed, this can become a significant performance issue. WebLogic Server provides a connection pooling mechanism that allows users to access and share persistent database connections to avoid the overhead of constantly opening and closing new connections. When WebLogic Server starts, it creates each connection pool with an initial number of connections. These connections will be available to any application that uses the configured DataSource object. When an application closes the connection it got from the DataSource, the connection will return to the pool and be available for the next time the application needs a connection. Because the call to DataSource.getConnection() only checks a connection out from the pool and its call to Connection.close() does not actually close the connection, using the database connection pool adds very little overhead to the application.

You define and configure the DataSource using the WebLogic Console, as described in Chapter 12. During performance tuning you are interested in two configuration parameters in particular: Initial Capacity and Maximum Capacity. Initial Capacity specifies the initial number of physical database connections to create, as well as the minimum number the pool should try to maintain at all times. Maximum Capacity specifies the maximum number of physical database connections the pool is allowed to create. In production systems, consider setting Initial Capacity equal to the Maximum Capacity so that you don't incur the hit for creating new connections on the fly when the server is busy.

To ensure optimal performance, your connection pool should have enough connections to eliminate *waiters*. Waiters are nothing more than application threads that are forced to wait for a connection because all available connections are in use. You can use two approaches to eliminate waiters.

❑ By using the WebLogic Console to monitor the active JDBC connections during stress testing, you can properly size your connection pool to eliminate waiters.

❑ As discussed earlier, you can set the maximum threads constraint on the work manager(s) to prevent WebLogic Server from dispatching more concurrent application requests than the size of the connection pool.

> ### Best Practice
> Set Initial Capacity and Maximum Capacity to the same value in production systems to avoid creating new connections on the fly during load spikes. Find the proper size during stress testing by monitoring the pool for waiters and then use this value to determine an appropriate value for the maximum threads constraint on the work manager(s) to prevent latency.

Release JDBC Resources

Always release JDBC resources when your application finishes using them. If the application does not release resources in a timely manner, application performance can degrade because other threads may need the resources but have to wait for them if all resources are currently held. JDBC Connection, PreparedStatement, Statement, and ResultSet objects should be explicitly closed when your application component finishes using them. Simply counting on the garbage collector to clean up after the objects is dangerous because there may be situations where these objects hold on to database resources outside the control of the JVM. WebLogic Server will try to clean up after sloppy application coding. Closing a connection should release its underlying resources; however, we advise you not to depend on these mechanisms. We have seen numerous applications with memory leaks that turned out to be the result of not closing JDBC resources properly. The most common errors are not using a finally block to close them and not trying to close every resource in the finally block, even if you get an exception. Always write your JDBC code defensively! It should always be structured similarly to that shown here.

```
Connection conn = null;
PreparedStatement ps = null;
ResultSet rs = null;
try {
... // Do JDBC work here
}
catch (SQLException sqle) {
... // Do error recovery here
}
finally {
    if (rs != null) {
        try { rs.close(); } catch (SQLException ignore) { }
    }
    if (ps != null) {
        try { ps.close(); } catch (SQLException ignore) { }
    }
    if (conn != null) {
        try { conn.close(); } catch (SQLException ignore) { }
    }
}
```

Best Practice

Always close JDBC resources as soon as you are done with them to reduce contention for connections and improve performance. Always write your JDBC code defensively and close JDBC resources inside the finally block — never inside the try block.

Troubleshooting Performance Problems

Your application and environment are now tuned to perfection, users are happy, and the system is taking hundreds of hits per second without batting an eye, right? If not, then read on as we present a tried and true methodology for troubleshooting performance problems.

Successful troubleshooting requires a strong understanding of the system and its components, a good problem resolution process, and knowledge of common performance problems and their solutions. Every system is different, and every performance problem is likely to be different, but a number of best practices are worth outlining to help you through your own troubleshooting efforts. Good tooling and instrumentation can significantly accelerate the root cause analysis process.

Preparing for Troubleshooting

Troubleshooting performance problems can be a difficult and time-consuming process unless you prepare ahead of time. When the users are unhappy and the pressure is on, you must have the proper infrastructure, processes, and people in place to address the problem.

First, the application should have been thoroughly tested and profiled during performance testing. You need to know how the application performed in the test environment to know if the performance problem you are tackling is real or simply a normal slowdown under peak loads. Your test results also indicate the normal resource usage of the individual transaction under investigation for comparison with observed resource usage in production. Good testing is critical to efficient production troubleshooting.

Next, you must have all necessary performance monitoring mechanisms in place to provide information concerning system performance and activity. Recognize that many performance problems do not happen on demand, so you will need some form of logging to reconstruct system resource usage and activity during a period in question. Simple shell scripts that log selected output from system monitoring tools are often sufficient for this purpose. Of course, tools like JRockit Mission Control and other application performance monitoring tools can accelerate the identification and isolation of the problem if they are able to capture data while the problem is occurring.

Finally, you need a team and a process in place before the problem occurs. It is a good idea to form a multi-disciplinary *swat team* and make that team responsible for troubleshooting performance problems. Typically, we recommend using many of the same people who did the original performance testing because they already understand the behavior of the system under various loads. Create a well-documented process for responding to performance problems, including a database or other knowledge repository for storing information on previous incidents and remedies.

Once you've done everything you can to prepare for performance problems, all you can do is wait and see how the system performs. Should a problem arise, the team's first order of business is to identify the root cause of the performance problem, also known as the *bottleneck*.

Bottleneck Identification and Correction

A bottleneck is a resource within a system that limits overall throughput or adds substantially to response time. Finding and fixing bottlenecks in distributed systems can be very difficult and requires experienced multi-disciplinary teams, though modern application performance monitoring tools can make this much easier. Bottlenecks can occur in the web server, application code, application server, database, network, hardware, network devices, or operating system. Experience has shown that bottlenecks are more likely to occur in some areas than in others, the most common areas being these:

❑ Database connections and queries

❑ Application server code

❑ Application server and web server hardware

❑ Network and TCP configuration

Remember that there is rarely a single bottleneck in a system. Fixing one bottleneck will improve performance but often highlights a different bottleneck. Bottlenecks should be identified one at a time, corrected, and the system tested again to ensure that another bottleneck does not appear before reaching the required performance levels.

To identify bottlenecks quickly and correctly you must understand your system. The team responsible for problem resolution must know all of the physical components of the system. For each physical component (server, network device, and so on), the team needs detailed knowledge of all the logical components (software) deployed there. Ideally, all of this information will be documented and available to the swat team members who are responsible for troubleshooting. The team can prepare for problems by identifying all the potential bottlenecks for each component and determining the proper way to monitor and troubleshoot these areas.

The following lists document some of the typical components and areas of concern related to each of them. The team must be aware of these potential bottlenecks and be prepared to monitor the related resource usage to identify the specific bottleneck responsible for a given performance problem quickly.

Common areas of concern for firewall devices include the following:

❑   Total connections.

❑   SSL connections — If you exceed more than 20 SSL handshakes per second per web server you may need an SSL accelerator.

❑   CPU utilization — Make sure CPU utilization does not average above 80 percent.

❑   I/O — If the firewall is logging make sure it is not I/O bound.

❑   Throughput.

Common areas of concern for load balancers include these:

❑   Total connections.

❑   Connection balance.

❑   CPU utilization — Make sure average CPU utilization does not exceed 80 percent.

❑   Throughput.

Common areas of concern for web servers include the following:

❑   CPU utilization — Make sure average CPU utilization does not exceed 80 percent.

❑   Memory — Make sure excessive paging is not taking place.

❑   Throughput — Monitor network throughput to make sure you do not have an over-utilized network interface card.

❑   Connections — Make sure connections are balanced among the servers.

❑   SSL connections — Make sure that the number of SSL handshakes per second is not too much for the hardware and web server software. Consider using SSL accelerators if it is too high.

❑   Disk I/O — Make sure the web servers are not I/O bound, especially if they are serving a lot of static content.

Common areas of concern for application servers include the following:

❑   Memory — Make sure there is enough memory to prevent the JVM from paging.

❑   CPU — Make sure average CPU utilization does not exceed 80 percent.

❑ Database connection pools — Make sure application threads are not waiting for database con-nections excessively. Also, check to make sure the application is not leaking connections.

❑ Execute queue — Watch the queue depth to make sure it does not consistently exceed a prede-termined depth.

❑ Execute queue wait — Make sure messages are not starved in the queue.

Common areas of concern for database servers include these:

❑ Memory — Make sure excessive paging and high I/O wait time are not occurring.

❑ CPU — Make sure average CPU utilization does not exceed 80 percent.

❑ Cache hit ratio — Make sure the cache is set high enough to prevent excessive disk I/O.

❑ Parse time — Make sure excessive parsing is not taking place.

For each area of concern, you may want to put system monitoring tools in place that will take measure-ments of these variables and trigger an alert if they exceed normal levels. If system monitoring tools are not available for a component, you will need to have scripts or other mechanisms in place that you can use to gather the required information.

Best Practice

Identifying bottlenecks quickly in production systems requires a thorough knowledge of the hardware and software components of your system and the types of potential bottlenecks common in each of these areas. Ensure that system monitoring tools cap-ture appropriate information in all areas of concern to support troubleshooting efforts. Consider creating scripts or processes that monitor system resources and notify team members proactively if values exceed thresholds.

Problem Resolution

Troubleshooting performance problems should be accomplished using a documented, predefined prob-lem resolution process similar to the high-level flowchart depicted in Figure 13-2. We will touch briefly on each step in the flow chart to give you a better feel for the process.

The first step in the process is to define the problem. Two primary sources of problems require resolu-tion: user reports and system monitoring alerts. Translating information from these sources into a clear definition of the problem is not as easy as you might think. Reports such as "the system seemed slow yesterday" don't really help you define or isolate the problem. Provide users with a well-designed paper form or online application for reporting problems to ensure that all important information about the problem is captured while it is still fresh in their minds. Understanding how the user was interacting with the system may lead you directly to the root of the problem. If not, move on to the next step in the process.

The next step involves checking all potential bottlenecks, paying special attention to areas that have been problems in the past. Consult your system monitoring tools and logs to check for any suspicious resource usage or changes in normal processing levels. If you are lucky enough to catch the problem while it is occurring, your monitoring tools might help you determine in real time the exact location of the bottleneck.

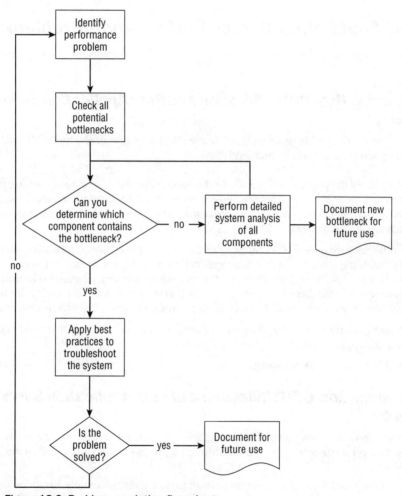

Figure 13-2: Problem resolution flow chart.

If you are unable to identify the location of the bottleneck or root cause of the performance problem you will need to perform a more rigorous analysis of all components in the system, looking for more subtle evidence of the problem. Start by identifying the layer in the application most likely to be responsible for the problem and then drilling in to components in that layer looking for the culprit. If you discover a new bottleneck or area of concern, make sure to document the new bottleneck, adding it to the list of usual suspects for the next time.

Once you've identified the location of the bottleneck you can apply appropriate tuning options and best practices to solve the problem. Document the specific changes made to solve the problem for future use. If nothing seems to work, you may need to step back, revisit everything you've observed and concluded, and try the process again from the top. Consider the possibility that two or more bottlenecks are combining to cause the problem or that your analysis has led you to an incorrect conclusion about the location of the bottleneck. Persevere, and you will find it eventually.

Common Application Server Performance Problems

This section documents a variety of common problems and how you can identify and solve them in your environment.

Troubleshooting High CPU Utilization and Poor Application Server Throughput

The first step in resolving this problem is to identify the root cause of the high CPU utilization. Consider the following observations and recommendations:

❑ Most likely the problem will reside in the application itself, so a good starting point is to profile the application code to determine which areas of the application are using excessive processor resources. These heavyweight operations or subsystems are then optimized or removed to reduce CPU utilization.

❑ Profile the garbage collection activity of the application. This can be accomplished using application profiling tools or starting your application with the -verbose:gc option set. If the application is spending more than 25 percent of its time performing garbage collection, there may be an issue with the number of temporary objects that the application is creating. Reducing the number of temporary objects should reduce garbage collection and CPU utilization substantially.

❑ Refer to information in this chapter and other tuning resources available from Oracle to make sure the application server is tuned properly.

❑ Add hardware to meet requirements.

Troubleshooting Low CPU Utilization and Poor Application Server Throughput

This problem can result from bottlenecks or inefficiencies upstream, downstream, or within the application server. Correct the problem by walking through a process similar to the following:

1. Verify that the application server itself is functioning normally using the weblogic.Admin command-line administration tool to request a GETSTATE and a series of PING operations. Chapter 12 walked through the use of this tool and the various command-line options and parameters available. Because the GETSTATE and PING operations flow through the normal execute queue in the application server, good response times are an indication that all is well within the server. Poor response times indicate potential problems requiring additional analysis.

2. If the GETSTATE operation reports a healthy state but the PING operations are slow, check to see whether the execute queue is backed up by viewing the queue depth in the WebLogic Console.

3. A backed-up execute queue may indicate that the system is starved for execute threads. If all execute threads are active and CPU utilization is low, adding execute threads should improve throughput, so check work managers for any maximum threads constraints and raise them, as appropriate.

4. If the queue appears starved but adding execute threads does not improve performance, there may be resource contention. Because CPU utilization is low, the threads are probably spending much of their time waiting for some resource, quite often a database connection. Use the JDBC monitoring facilities in the console to check for high levels of waiters or long wait times. Adding connections to the JDBC connection pool may be all that is required to fix the problem.

5. If database connections are not the problem you should take periodic thread dumps of the JVM to determine if the threads are routinely waiting for a particular resource. Take a series of four thread dumps about 5 to 10 seconds apart, and compare them with one another to determine if individual threads are stuck or waiting on the same resource long enough to appear in multiple thread dumps. The problem threads may be waiting on a resource held by another thread or may be waiting to update the same table in the database. The JRockit Latency Analyzer can easily identify any resource contention issues without resorting to thread dumps and other types of monitoring. Once the resource contention is identified you can apply the proper remedies to fix the problem.

6. If the application server is not the bottleneck, the cause is most likely upstream of the server, perhaps in the network or web server. Use the system monitoring tools you have in place to check all of the potential bottlenecks upstream of the application server and troubleshoot these components.

Troubleshooting Low Activity and CPU Utilization on All Physical Components with Slow Throughput

If CPU utilization stays low even when user load on the system is increasing, you should look at the following:

1. Is there any asynchronous messaging in the system? If the system employs asynchronous messaging, check the message queues to make sure they are not backing up. If the queues are backing up and there are no message ordering requirements, try adding more dispatcher threads to increase throughput of the queue.

2. Check to see if the web servers or application servers are thread starved. If they are, increase the number of server processes or server threads to increase parallelism.

Troubleshooting Slow Response Time from the Client and Low Database Usage

These symptoms are usually caused by a bottleneck upstream of the database, perhaps in the JDBC connection pooling. Monitor the active JDBC connections in the WebLogic Console and watch for excessive waiters and wait times; increase the pool size, if necessary. If the pool is not the problem, there must be some other resource used by the application that is introducing latency or causing threads to wait. Often, periodic thread dumps can reveal what the resource might be.

Troubleshooting Erratic Response Times and CPU Utilization on the Application Server

Throughput and CPU will always vary to some extent during normal operation, but large, visible swings indicate a problem. First look at the CPU utilization, and determine whether there are any patterns in the CPU variations. Two patterns are common:

❑ CPU utilization peaks or patterns coincide with garbage collection. If your application is running on a multiple CPU machine with only one application server, you are most likely experiencing the effects of non-parallelized garbage collection in the application server. Depending on your JVM settings, garbage collection may be causing all other threads inside the JVM to block, preventing all other processing. In addition, many garbage collectors use a single thread to do their work so that all of the work is done by a single CPU, leaving the other processors idle until the collection is complete. Try using one of the parallel collectors or deploying multiple application servers on each machine to alleviate this problem and use server resources more efficiently. The threads in an application server not performing the garbage collection will be scheduled on processors left idle by the server performing collection, yielding a more constant throughput and more efficient CPU utilization. Also consider tuning the JVM options to optimize heap usage and improve garbage collection using techniques described earlier in this chapter.

❑ CPU peaks on one component coincide with valleys on an adjacent component. You should also observe a similar oscillating pattern in the application server throughput. This behavior results from a bottleneck that is either upstream or downstream from the application server. By analyzing the potential bottlenecks being monitored on the various upstream and downstream components you should be able to pinpoint the problem. Experience has shown that firewalls, database servers, and web servers are most likely to cause this kind of oscillation in CPU and throughput. Also, make sure the file descriptor table is large enough on all Unix servers in the environment.

Troubleshooting Performance Degrading with High Disk I/O

If a high disk I/O rate is observed on the application server machine, the most likely culprit will be excessive logging. Make sure that WebLogic Server is set to the proper logging level, and check to see that the application is not making excessive System.out.println() or other logging method calls. System.out.println() statements make use of synchronized processing for the duration of the disk I/O and should not be used for logging purposes. Unexpected disk I/O on the server may also be a sign that your application is logging error messages. The application server logs should be viewed to determine if there is a problem with the application.

Java Stack Traces

This section discusses the reading and interpretation of Java stack traces in WebLogic Server. A *Java stack trace* displays a snapshot of the current state of all threads in a JVM (Java Virtual Machine) process. This trace represents a quick and precise way to determine bottlenecks, hung threads, and resource contention in your application.

Understanding Thread States

The snapshot produced by a Java stack trace will display threads in various states. Not all Java stack traces will use the same naming convention, but typically each thread will be in one of the following states: runnable, waiting on a condition variable, and waiting on a monitor lock.

Threads in the *runnable* state represent threads that are either currently running on a processor or are ready to run when a processor is available. At any given time, there can be only one thread actually executing on each processor in the machine; the rest of the runnable threads will be ready to run but waiting on a processor. You can identify threads in a runnable state by the runnable keyword in the stack trace, as shown here:

```
"DynamicListenThread[Default[2]]" daemon prio=10 tid=0x2dcb0800 nid=0x4ac
runnable [0x3116f000..0x3116fc94]
    java.lang.Thread.State: RUNNABLE
        at java.net.PlainSocketImpl.socketAccept(Native Method)
...
```

Threads waiting on a condition variable are sleeping, waiting to be notified by their manager that work is ready for processing. The stack trace indicates this with the in Object.wait() message:

```
"[ACTIVE] ExecuteThread: '0' for queue: 'weblogic.kernel.Default (self-
tuning)'" daemon prio=6 tid=0x2ce82000 nid=0x1748 in Object.wait()
[0x2e0cf000..0x2e0cfd14]
    java.lang.Thread.State: WAITING (on object monitor)
        at java.lang.Object.wait(Native Method)
        - waiting on <0x0c89aaa8> (a weblogic.work.ExecuteThread)
        at java.lang.Object.wait(Object.java:485)
        at weblogic.work.ExecuteThread.waitForRequest(ExecuteThread.java:157)
        - locked <0x0c89aaa8> (a weblogic.work.ExecuteThread)
        at weblogic.work.ExecuteThread.run(ExecuteThread.java:178)
```

Applications use monitor locks, or *mutexes*, to synchronize access to critical sections of code that require single-threaded access. When you see a thread that has waiting for monitor entry in its stack trace, the thread is waiting to access synchronized code, such as the thread shown here:

```
"[ACTIVE] ExecuteThread: '1' for queue: 'weblogic.kernel.Default (self-
tuning)'" daemon prio=6 tid=0x2cff8400 nid=0x1630 waiting for monitor entry
[0x2e44f000..0x2e44fd14]
    java.lang.Thread.State: BLOCKED (on object monitor)
        at professional.weblogic.test.MutexServlet.doGet(MutexServlet.java:20)
        - waiting to lock <0x289aefb0> (a professional.weblogic.test.MutexServlet)
        at javax.servlet.http.HttpServlet.service(HttpServlet.java:707)
...
```

Two different types of thread dumps can be produced in a typical environment: system-level process dumps, otherwise known as *core dumps*, and Java thread dumps.

Generating System-Level Process Dumps

System-level process dumps are generated by the JVM itself in response to a system error condition; typically, this happens because some native code is trying to access an illegal memory address. The content of this dump depends on whether the JVM can call the signal handler before the process itself core dumps. If the JVM can call the signal handler, it will typically produce a text file in the current directory containing information about the process and the thread in which the low-level error occurred. If the JVM is unable to call the signal handler, a core dump file will be produced containing information about the JVM's native operating system process rather than the Java classes themselves. This type of dump is much less valuable and should be used only if no Java stack trace is available.

Generating Java Thread Dumps

Sending a special signal to the JVM generates a Java stack trace. On Unix platforms you send the SIGQUIT signal using the kill command. On most Unix platforms, the command kill -QUIT <PID>, where <PID> is the process identifier for the JVM process, will produce a Java thread dump that shows the call stack of every user-level thread in the JVM. On a Windows platform, you generate a thread dump by pressing the Ctrl-Break key sequence in the console window in which the Java program is executing. In addition, you can generate a stack trace either by invoking the static method Thread.dumpStack() or by invoking the printStackTrace() method on an instance of the Throwable class.

WebLogic Server also provides several tools that allow you to generate a thread dump. First, the WebLogic Console provides a Dump Thread Stacks button on the server's Threads Monitoring tab. Second, the deprecated weblogic.Admin tool we briefly discussed in Chapter 12 supports a THREAD_DUMP command. Finally, you can use WLST to get the ThreadStackDump attribute on the JVMRuntime MBean, as shown here.

```
connect('weblogic', 'weblogic1', 't3://127.0.0.1:7001')
cd('serverRuntime:/JVMRuntime/AdminServer')
cmo.getThreadStackDump()
```

When analyzing or troubleshooting an application it is important to generate multiple thread dumps over a period of time to identify hung threads properly and better understand the application state. Start by generating three to five separate thread dumps approximately 15 to 30 seconds apart. If your servers communicate with each other using RMI it may be necessary to perform this operation on all servers in the cluster simultaneously to get a full picture. Depending on the number of servers in the cluster and the number of threads in the execute queue, this process may generate a large amount of output, but the output is invaluable in diagnosing thread-related problems. Later in this section we discuss how to read and interpret these thread dumps.

Reading Core Dumps

Sometimes it will be necessary to examine the core file to determine what has caused the JVM to core dump. When you are examining this core file, remember that Java itself uses a safe memory model and that any segmentation fault must have occurred in either the native code of the application or the native code of the JVM itself. On Unix systems a core file will be produced when a JVM fails. On Windows systems, a drwtsn32.log file will be produced when a segmentation fault occurs in a JVM.

You have several ways to examine these core files, usually through debuggers like gdb or dbx. On Solaris you can also use the pstack command, as shown here:

```
/usr/proc/bin/pstack ./core
```

When using dbx to examine the JVM core file, first move to the directory where the core file resides, then execute the dbx command with the binary executable as a parameter. Remember that the java command is usually a shell script and that you must specify the actual java binary in the command. Once you have started the debugger you can use the dbx where command to show the function call stack at the time of the failure, indicating the location of the segmentation fault.

```
dbx /usr/java/native/java ./core
(dbx) where
Segmentation fault in glink.JNU_ReleaseStringPlatformChars at 0xd074e66c
```

```
0xd074e66c (JNU_ReleaseStringPlatformChars+0x5b564) 80830004
lwz  r4,0x4(r3)
```

From this information you can often determine the location of the error and take the appropriate action. For example, if the segmentation fault is the result of a just-in-time (JIT) compiler problem and you are using the HotSpot compiler you can modify the behavior of the JIT to eliminate the problem. Create a file called .hotspot_compiler in the directory used to start the application, and indicate in this file the methods to exclude from JIT processing using entries similar to the following.

```
exclude java/lang/String indexOf
```

The specified methods will be excluded from the JIT compilation process, eliminating the core dump.

Reading Java Stack Traces

Java stack traces can be very useful during the problem resolution process to identify the root cause for an application that seems to be hanging, deadlocked, frozen, extremely busy, or corrupting data. If your data is being corrupted, you are probably experiencing a race condition. Race conditions occur when more than one thread reads and writes to the same memory without proper synchronization. Race conditions are very hard to find by looking at stack traces because you will have to get your snapshot at the proper instant to see multiple threads accessing the same non-synchronized code.

Thread starvation or thread exhaustion can occur when threads are not making progress because they are waiting for an external resource that is either responding slowly or not at all. One particular case of this happens when WebLogic Server A makes an RMI call to WebLogic Server B and blocks waiting for a response. WebLogic Server B then calls via RMI back into WebLogic Server A before the original call returns from WebLogic Server B. If enough threads on both servers are awaiting responses from the other server, it is possible for all threads in both servers' execute queues to be exhausted. This exhaustion behavior will show itself initially as no idle threads available in the WebLogic Server execute queue when viewed in the WebLogic Console. You can confirm this problem by generating a stack trace and looking for threads blocked waiting for data in the weblogic.rjvm.ResponseImpl.waitForData() method. Look for entries like this:

```
"[ACTIVE] ExecuteThread: '1' for queue: 'weblogic.kernel.Default (self-
tuning)'" daemon prio=6 tid=0x2cff7c00 nid=0x1388 waiting for monitor entry
[0x2e44f000..0x2e44fd14]
    java.lang.Thread.State: WAITING (on object monitor)
        at java.lang.Object.wait(Native Method)
        - waiting on <0x02a03f38> (a weblogic.rjvm.ResponseImpl)
        at weblogic.rjvm.ResponseImpl.waitForData(ResponseImpl.java:87)
    ...
```

If a large number of threads are in this state you need to make appropriate design changes to eliminate RMI traffic between the servers or better throttle the number of threads allowed to call out and block in this way.

Deadlock occurs when individual threads are blocked waiting for the action of other threads. A *deadly embrace* deadlock occurs when one thread locks resource A and then tries to lock resource B, while a different thread locks resource B and then tries to lock resource A. This concept was discussed briefly in Chapter 6 in the context of database locking for entities. Stack traces will show blocked threads within synchronized application code or within code that accesses objects using exclusive locking in one form or another. Remember that it is also possible for the application to be deadlocked across multiple JVMs with one server's threads in a deadly embrace with another server's threads.

A system that is inactive and has poor application performance may, in fact, be performing normally. The problem may instead be indicative of an upstream bottleneck, as described earlier in this chapter. A Java stack trace for a system in this state will display a high percentage of threads in the *default* execute queue blocking until they receive some work, having a stack trace similar to the following.

```
"[ACTIVE] ExecuteThread: '0' for queue: 'weblogic.kernel.Default (self-
tuning)'" daemon prio=6 tid=0x2cf9f000 nid=0x7f0 in Object.wait()
[0x2e0cf000..0x2e0cfb14]
   java.lang.Thread.State: WAITING (on object monitor)
        at java.lang.Object.wait(Native Method)
        - waiting on <0x0c433020> (a weblogic.work.ExecuteThread)
        at java.lang.Object.wait(Object.java:485)
        at weblogic.work.ExecuteThread.waitForRequest(ExecuteThread.java:157)
        - locked <0x0c433020> (a weblogic.work.ExecuteThread)
        at weblogic.work.ExecuteThread.run(ExecuteThread.java:178)
```

The stack trace indicates that this thread is idle, or waiting for a request, rather than busy in application code or waiting on an external resource.

Understanding WebLogic Server Stack Traces

Stack traces of a WebLogic Server instance will also show a number of common elements based on the internal design of the WebLogic Server product. As you know from previous chapters, all client requests enter WebLogic Server through a special thread called the *listen thread*. There will usually be two listen threads visible in a stack trace, one for SSL and the other for nonsecure transport. Here is an example of the WebLogic Server listen thread waiting for a connection to arrive:

```
"DynamicListenThread[Default]" daemon prio=10 tid=0x2d384c00 nid=0x1254
runnable [0x310cf000..0x310cfb94]
   java.lang.Thread.State: RUNNABLE
        at java.net.PlainSocketImpl.socketAccept(Native Method)
        at java.net.PlainSocketImpl.accept(PlainSocketImpl.java:384)
        - locked <0x0cb9ee20> (a java.net.SocksSocketImpl)
        at java.net.ServerSocket.implAccept(ServerSocket.java:453)
        at java.net.ServerSocket.accept(ServerSocket.java:421)
   . . .
```

Socket connections received by WebLogic Server are registered and maintained by the socket muxer. The socket muxer reads data from the socket and dispatches the request to the appropriate subsystem. The socket muxer has its own execute thread pool that it uses to read the requests off the socket by calling the `processSockets()` method, as shown here for the Windows version of the native socket muxer.

```
"ExecuteThread: '1' for queue: 'weblogic.socket.Muxer'" daemon prio=6
tid=0x2d03f400 nid=0x180 runnable [0x2ebff000..0x2ebffc14]
   java.lang.Thread.State: RUNNABLE
        at weblogic.socket.NTSocketMuxer.getIoCompletionResult(Native Method)
        at weblogic.socket.NTSocketMuxer.processSockets(NTSocketMuxer.java:81)
        at weblogic.socket.SocketReaderRequest.run(SocketReaderRequest.java:29)
```

```
    at weblogic.socket.SocketReaderRequest.execute(SocketReaderRequest.java:42)
    at weblogic.kernel.ExecuteThread.execute(ExecuteThread.java:145)
    at weblogic.kernel.ExecuteThread.run(ExecuteThread.java:117)
```

As you become more familiar with your application and better understand the internal implementation of WebLogic Server itself, your ability to interpret stack traces and troubleshoot problems will increase.

Chapter Review

This chapter covered many different areas related to WebLogic Server application performance, including basic principles and tuning options, design patterns and best practices, and specific performance best practices and troubleshooting tips. As you can tell from this wide-ranging discussion, there is a lot to know and consider when tuning or troubleshooting a complex Java EE system. Nothing beats experience when it comes to successful performance tuning, and experience is gained only by doing, so go do some performance tuning!

14

Development Environment Best Practices

Congratulations! Your boss just gave you the go-ahead to build a new Java EE application using WebLogic Server. Months of meetings and proposals are behind you, and it's time to get started on the actual development. It's going to be a fairly large application, requiring a development team of 10 to 15 people. You have a reasonable budget for development hardware and software and the full confidence of management and the other team members. Now what?

It's not enough to know the technology inside and out. You must structure your development effort in a way that optimizes productivity and reduces the risk of failure. This chapter continues the discussion of development best practices with recommendations in the following areas.

- ❑ Defining the required development environment hardware and software.

- ❑ Installing WebLogic Server in the development environment.

- ❑ Configuring the project directory structure.

- ❑ Establishing a build process.

- ❑ Choosing development tools.

- ❑ Creating a unit testing infrastructure.

There can be a lot more to Java EE development than these six items. You need to choose a development methodology and team structure, create realistic plans with measurable deliverables, create useful design artifacts and specifications, and embrace the other development best practices known in the industry. This book does not cover best practices in these general areas. Classic references for information on these topics include *Rapid Development: Taming Wild Software Schedules* by Steve McConnell (Microsoft Press, 1996) and *Extreme Programming Explained: Embrace Change* by Kent Beck (Addison-Wesley, 1999).

Defining Required Hardware and Software

The hardware and software required for your development effort will depend on many details of your application and the chosen platform. The primary goals of the development environment should include the following.

❑ Enable isolated development, execution, unit testing, and debugging of the application on each developer's workstation.

❑ Provide a centralized location for running, unit testing, and debugging a coordinated daily or weekly development build of the application.

❑ Provide a centralized source code management (SCM) repository and database for use by developers and the common build of the application.

❑ Simulate the production hardware and software platform at a level sufficient to support development and debugging.

Most Java EE applications will require at least two servers in the development environment to host the source code management (SCM) server software, the development database, and the development build of the Java EE application. It is common to combine the SCM software and development build on the same server, yielding the following set of hardware and software requirements in the development environment.

❑ *Developer workstations* with WebLogic Server, development tools, database client software, a source code management client, and build scripts and tools.

❑ A *development server* with WebLogic Server, web server software, database client software, source-code management server and repository, and build scripts and tools.

❑ A *database server* with RDBMS software installation and any required legacy system integration software.

Each server and workstation in this environment has a specific role in the development process.

Developers use the workstations to construct the individual components of the application and create local (workstation-based) builds for unit testing and debugging. In addition to all development tools and SCM client applications, the workstations also require a copy of WebLogic Server configured with the appropriate JDBC `DataSource` resources, JMS destinations, and other supporting infrastructure required to run the application. Unless the development team is very small and can share a single development server for builds, you should provide local execution capability for developers on their own workstations.

> **Best Practice**
>
> Provide local execution capability on developer workstations to avoid resource conflicts on shared development servers.

If it is not possible to provide local execution capability for some reason, you may be able to segregate the shared development server and provide an isolated environment to support each developer's execution and testing needs. The easiest way to segregate the server is to create separate domains for each developer with the servers defined in each domain configured to listen on a different port. The developers will still compete for server resources (CPU, memory) but will be able to run multiple copies of the application simultaneously. Again, this is not ideal. It is better to provide local execution capability on each workstation if at all possible.

The development team uses the development server to host the shared source code management (SCM) repository and as a central location for making and testing periodic builds of the application. We discuss the importance of periodic builds and regression testing in a later section. This server also provides an environment more similar to the production environment. A web server can be installed on the machine and configured to proxy appropriate JSP and servlet requests back to WebLogic Server. The development server usually matches the vendor and operating system present in production. Often developer workstations are Windows-based machines and the development, test, and production servers are Unix-based systems.

Best Practice

The development server should match the vendor and operating system of the test and production machines. Developer workstations may use a different platform, if desired.

Sharing a Database Server

The database server is used to host the common development database supporting both developer workstation builds and the central development build of the application. Gateway products and other legacy system integration products can also be hosted on this server. There is no strong reason to separate the database server and the development server apart from the desire to mimic production as early in the process as possible. Production undoubtedly will use separate servers for the WebLogic Server cluster and the database so, if the budget allows, it makes sense to provide this separation in development as well. Often the development database server will be managed by a professional DBA, and will host databases for several project teams.

Sharing a common development database between multiple developers and the common development build may look good on paper, but there is at least one significant problem with this simplistic approach that we need to solve: changes to the database schema and contents can break builds. For example, one developer may need to modify the structure or contents of a database table to support the components he or she is changing and testing on a workstation. Structural modifications are very likely to break the build for all other developers and for the common development build, especially in a JPA application. Remember that the JPA container checks the database schema for every JPA entity when it is used, and will throw exceptions if the schema has been changed to be incompatible with the code.

One approach is to serialize the development process during database schema changes. Essentially, you make the database change, and the entire team waits for the developer to finish the changes, test them, and make the new versions of the components available in the current branch of the application. Everyone retrieves the new copy of the component from the SCM system and is able to build and run the application again. Although this approach might be appropriate for small teams or in circumstances where it can be done very quickly, it simply becomes an untenable solution on a large project.

Fortunately, there is a reasonable solution that provides support for existing builds and for developers requiring database changes: create multiple copies of the development database on the development server, usually as separate schema in a single database instance. In its simplest form, this technique requires two complete copies of the database, called for our purposes DEVDB1 and DEVDB2. As shown in Figure 14-1, the common development build and the builds used by different developers connect to whichever copy of the database matches the components in that build.

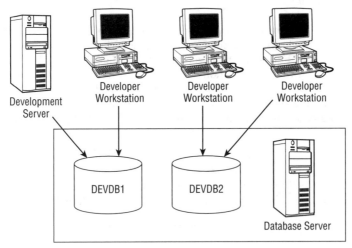

Figure 14-1: Multiple databases support different builds.

In a two-database approach such as this, often a primary database is used for the periodic builds and an alternate database is used for development of components requiring database changes. The database administrator usually toggles back and forth as each new set of changes is made, meaning that DEVDB1 is primary until the changes in DEVDB2 are made part of the common build, at which point DEVDB2 becomes primary and DEVDB1 is used for subsequent database changes. Clearly this technique can be extended to three or more databases, but two are usually sufficient. You can switch between databases without having to modify the application. Ensure that all application components acquire database connections from the JDBC data source using a well-known JNDI name. Create multiple JDBC data sources in the WebLogic Server configuration, and set the data source for appropriate database to use the well-known JNDI name. To switch to another database, simple remove the JNDI name from one data source, assign it to the data source for the new database, and restart the application.

Most development teams go further, and give each developer their own accounts in the database and their own copy of the schema. Each developer configures the data source for their WebLogic Server instance to use their database account. This allows developers to work in isolation from each other, and also have their own copy of the application data. This last point can be important when running unit tests that need to set the database to a known state, execute the code under test, then verify that the new state is as expected. If this approach is taken, a database administrator will usually wish to use synonyms or database views to provide each schema with access to a single copy of tables containing static reference data, and also write database scripts that automate the roll out of schema changes to each developer account.

Best Practice

Use multiple copies of the development database to support builds requiring different database definitions, and to allow each environment to have its own set of data. Switch between databases by changing data source parameters in the WebLogic Server configuration.

Installing WebLogic Server Software

The installation program packaged with WebLogic Server provides a straightforward way to install WebLogic Server on all required machines in the development environment. Follow the instructions in the program, and choose a `Typical Installation` unless you wish to install the WebLogic Server sample code and sample domains, or wish to de-select optional components such as the web server plug-ins to save disk space, in which case choose `Custom Installation`. During the installation, you will be prompted for an Oracle Middleware Home directory. In some limited cases multiple products may share a Middleware Home, but we find it easier to manage multiple installations if we give each its own Middleware Home. You will also be prompted for a `Product Installation` directory; there is no reason to alter the default, which is located below the Middleware Home.

If you are installing WebLogic Server on many machines, you can run the installer as a command-line program in *silent mode,* where it reads installation options from a pre-prepared file. Refer to the WebLogic Server documentation for details, using Link 14-1 from this book's online Appendix at http://www.wrox.com/.

One final comment on installation before we move on: Because you want the development server to mirror a production set up, be sure to install WebLogic Server on the development servers in a manner consistent with your security and network rules. For example, never use the `root` account to install WebLogic Server on a Unix machine. Create a `weblogic` or `oracle` user account for this purpose and limit access to this account to certain developers on the project. Create a `weblogic` group and make the `weblogic` user account a member of that group. Create additional developer accounts in the `weblogic` group and control their level of access to WebLogic Server files and directory structures using the standard operating system permissions facilities.

There are few reasons to need to modify a WebLogic Server installation, and there is often an alternative that does not require the installation to be changed. See Table 14-1 for details. Consequently, we recommend further that you only grant developers read access to the installation, so you can be sure that it is completely standard.

Table 14-1: Reasons for Altering the WebLogic Server Installation, and Alternatives

Reason	Alternative
Install a custom or third-party security provider. Requires placing the file in `$WL_HOME/server/lib/mbeantypes`.	Install the security provider in the `lib/mbeantypes` domain subdirectory for each domain that requires it.
Register a domain with the node manager. Requires that the `nodemanager.domains` file is modified.	Run the node manager from a separate copy of the `$WL_HOME/common/nodemanager` directory.
Apply temporary product patches.	No alternative. Write access to the installation is required because patches may make arbitrary changes to an installation. Patches should be applied under the installation user account.

Best Practice

Install WebLogic Server using a `weblogic` user account, not `root`. Create separate developer accounts in the `weblogic` group to provide limited developer access to WebLogic services and files.

Creating and Configuring a WebLogic Server Domain

When the installation process is complete, each machine will have a copy of WebLogic Server, but it will not yet have a domain to use for your application. You can create a domain for each development environment using the WebLogic Server Configuration Wizard. This program is available from the Start menu in Windows or may be started using the `config` script in the `$WL_HOME/common/bin` directory. The wizard program allows you to set up an empty domain containing a single server quickly, by selecting the defaults, and also provides options to customize the created domain by adding servers, and clusters. The Configuration Wizard's online documentation has detailed instructions; see Link 14-2. The WebLogic Server domain will need to be configured to support your application by adding appropriate JDBC data sources, and JMS queues or topics, integrating the domain with other security systems, tuning network settings, and so on. This configuration often varies between different development environments (we've already noted that each developer may require data sources to connect to different database accounts), and between development and pre-production environments.

The required configuration changes can be made in many ways, including using the WebLogic Console, the `<wlconfig>` Ant task, pre-created domain templates, or the WebLogic Scripting Tool (WLST).

Although it is possible to manage configuration information by hand editing or scripting changes to the XML files in the `config` directory, and Oracle publishes the schema for these files, this is strongly discouraged. The file formats can, and do, change between releases.

The `<wlconfig>` Ant task provides a simplified technique for accessing and manipulating JMX MBeans in the domain, and includes `get`, `set`, `create`, `delete`, and `query` functions. Unfortunately, test and production environments are not typically managed using Ant so the `wlconfig` approach is unlikely to be suitable for migrating and promoting configuration information to those environments.

The WebLogic Server Domain Template Builder and WebLogic Server Configuration Wizard are easy-to-use GUI applications providing a step-by-step process for creating and replaying templates. The Domain Template Builder allows you to create preconfigured domains for your application's environment and use the Configuration Wizard to replay them. This replay capability provides an easy way to bootstrap new domains that already contain the configuration information needed by your application. A silent replay mode is available from the command line to support the build and promotion process. Making changes to domain templates can be tedious, and they do not support incremental change as well as a WLST script. Domain templates are most useful when you want to provide users with a simple installation experience, which fits their primary purpose to support the creation of domains for products that build upon WebLogic Server, such as Oracle Service Bus.

For development environments, the standout winner out of these techniques is WLST, which we covered in depth in Chapter 12. We strongly recommend that you invest the time to master this tool.

You should use the same WLST script to create domains for all of your environments: development, functional and performance test, pre-production, and production. The script should use a small environment properties file that describes the differences between the environments. This makes it easy to recreate an environment at will, and significantly reduces the likelihood of configuration errors.

You can use WLST in either its online or its offline mode. The `bigrez.com` configuration is relatively simple, and we used the online mode for the `setUpDomain.py` script. However, we generally prefer the offline mode for projects that require many domain configuration changes. The offline mode doesn't require a pre-created empty domain and a running server, so is easier to integrate into a build process. You can treat the WebLogic Server configuration like another development project — check changes to the scripts or parameters for a domain into the source code control system, and let the build server create new domains. Additionally, you have to write robust online mode scripts that work correctly if they are reapplied to an existing domain. They need to undo any previous changes before applying new changes, which makes them more complicated. In contrast, an offline script starts from scratch every time.

There are one or two types of changes that require using the online mode; in particular, changes to security policies require a server to be running. Even if you use an offline WLST script as your primary domain creation tool, it is common to need to run a small WLST online script as a post-installation script for production domains.

> **Best Practice**
>
> Use WLST in its offline mode to create and customize WebLogic Server domains for your development, pre-production, and production environments.

Development Project Structure

Once you have hardware and software in place, it is time to configure the working directories used to organize application components.

We outlined the structure we used for `bigrez.com` in Chapter 8. We prefer to have a separate development project and an Ant build file for each Java EE component or library, and called this out as a best practice. We also have an application project that takes the various modules and libraries as input and creates the EAR, and a project containing unit test code. This modular approach is used by IDEs, and is well supported by higher-level build systems such as Apache Maven. Modular projects have many advantages over the alternative of placing the entire source code in one project.

- ❏ Each project is responsible for building a single component. You can easily rebuild single components, and develop and deliver them separately from other components.

- ❏ The structure forces you to address the important issue of the inter-component dependencies, and encourages you to define and use public interfaces and establish a component versioning strategy. In contrast, placing all of the code in a single project allows poor practices to creep in, such as cyclic dependencies between components and direct Java calls to implementation artifacts, leading to a tangled source tree that is increasingly costly to change.

❑   The build files for individual projects are simple, and can be maintained easily. Common build functions can be extracted and reused using the Ant `<import>` task.

Starting with version 10.0, WebLogic Server itself was restructured into modules for these same reasons. You can see the component modules in the `modules` subdirectory below the Middleware Home directory.

Whatever the type of project, it will have source files, artifacts created during build process such as compiled `.class` files, and will produce a component file as output. For `bigrez.com`, these are located below the `src`, `build`, and `output` project subdirectories, respectively. The web application and web services projects have an additional source directory, `WebContent`, which contains the JSPs, TLDs, HTML, images, and deployment descriptors to be packaged in the web application. Similarly, the application project contains an `EarContent` source directory that contains deployment descriptors and the `APP-INF/lib` directory, but has no `src` directory because the application doesn't have any Java source files. The `EarContent` and `WebContent` names happen to be the defaults used by Eclipse Web Tools Project; we use those names because we used Eclipse to create `bigrez.com`.

All of the source files, the build scripts, and ancillary items such as WLST scripts should be stored in a source code management (SCM) repository such as CVS, Subversion, ClearCase, or Perforce. The goal is to have every component and file required to build and deploy the application in the repository to ensure proper control and promotion of the application during the development process.

Streamlining the Development Cycle

Historically, Java EE development has had a bad name for the length of time required to make a change and deploy it the server. In this section, we cover two WebLogic Server features that you should use on developer workstations to avoid lengthy development cycles.

Split Directory Development

The time taken to copy and package compiled classes into libraries and modules, and then to package up the modules into an `.ear` archive, is a significant contributor to lengthy deployment cycles. WebLogic Server has supported *exploded deployments* for many releases, which partly addresses this problem. We considered the many benefits of exploded deployments in Chapter 8, and noted that it removes the need for a packaging step. WebLogic Server's *split directory development* feature builds upon this capability, and lets you deploy an application that is built from separately organized source trees and build directories without first having to merge the application files into a single location.

The Oracle Enterprise Pack for Eclipse (OEPE) uses the split directory development structure to implement its *Virtual EAR* feature, which we cover later. If you use OEPE to create Java EE applications, you'll be using the split directory development structure whether you realize it or not. However, you can make use of this feature even if you're editing your source files with `Notepad` or `vi` and compiling them with build scripts.

The key mechanism that underlies split directory development is a modified deployment process. All of the WebLogic Server deployment tools, including the WebLogic Console, `weblogic.Deployer`, and the `<wldeploy>` Ant task, understand split directory deployment. In a normal exploded deployment of an application, the exploded directory contains a complete enterprise application. The top-level application directory contains subdirectories for each of its components, and all of the compiled classes, descriptors, JSPs, HTML pages, and other resources are present somewhere below the directory structure. An example application is shown in Figure 14-2. This application has an EJB module and a web application module, and contains a mixture of compiled classes, deployment descriptors, third-party .jar files, and JSP files. In a development environment, many of these items would be stored in a source file tree checked out of the SCM repository. Every time we change a source file, we have to copy either it or a derived file (such as a compiled .class file) to the exploded directory. We might be able to configure an IDE or create an Ant build script to automate this step, but this is still an additional interruption to the development cycle.

```
bigapp/
    META-INF/application.xml
    lib/thirdparty.jar
    myejb.jar/
        META-INF/weblogic-ejb-jar.xml
        com/bigapp/
            MyEJB.class
            MyEJBImpl.class
    mywebapp.war/
        WEB-INF/
            web.xml
            index.jsp
            classes/com/bigapp/MyServlet.class
        picture.png
```

Figure 14-2: Example exploded application.

Split directory development allows us to avoid the need to copy files between different locations. Figure 14-3 shows the application restructured for split directory development. Now we have two separate directory structures. The build directory contains various output files that are created as part of the build, such as compiled .class files and third-party libraries that may have been downloaded from a central repository using a dependency management tool. It is straightforward to configure an IDE or build scripts to output files directly into this structure. The source directory contains the application files that you create and edit, and this directory structure can be checked directly into your SCM system.

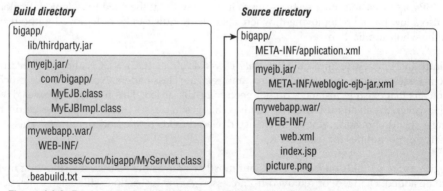

Figure 14-3: Restructured application for split directory development.

The .beabuild.txt file in the build directory contains the magic behind split directory development. When we deploy this application, we pass the build directory as the argument to one of the WebLogic Server deployment tools. The deployment tool then uses the .beabuild.txt file to link the build directory to the source directory. Listing 14-1 shows the contents of a .beabuild.txt file for our application.

Listing 14-1: A .beabuild.txt file for split directory development.

```
bea.srcdir=/opt/development/bigapp/bigappEAR
```

The format of the .beabuild.txt file is very simple: a properties file with a single bea.srcdir property pointing to the source directory. The source directory in the example is /opt/development/bigapp/bigappEAR. If you move the source directory, you will need to edit the .beabuild.txt file to refer to its new location.

WebLogic Server provides the weblogic.BuildXMLGen tool, which takes a source directory and creates an Ant project that uses split directory development. However, this tool generates a build file and imposes a particular Ant build structure upon you. This may be acceptable for simple projects, but we often find it better to create the .beabuild.txt file manually. The caveat is that Oracle does not publicly document the format of the .beabuild.txt file, but it is a simple format that is unlikely to change.

Better still, use a WebLogic Server–aware IDE, such as OEPE, that uses the split directory development feature under the covers.

> **Best Practice**
> Take the time to set up split directory development for your development workstation environments.

FastSwap

Another time-consuming process is the redeployment of a whole application. This can take a particularly long time if an application uses lifecycle listeners to perform initialization tasks, or initializes EJBs and servlets at deployment time. Exploded deployment can also help here. As noted in Chapter 8, WebLogic Server uses change-aware classloaders with exploded deployments that support the refresh of changed HTML, JSPs, servlets, and other web resources in-place without the need to redeploy. Exploded deployments also allow partial redeployment, where a single module can be redeployed without the need to refresh the whole application.

Java 5 introduced a new feature called *dynamic class redefinition* (DCR). DCR allows a container to reload modified classes without the need to destroy and recreate classloaders. Not only is this much faster, but it also means that existing instances do not need to be discarded. This further improves development times. However, the standard DCR only handles changes to classes that leave their *shape* unchanged; that is, changes that do not add, remove, or change declared fields or method signatures. This significantly reduces the opportunities for using DCR.

WebLogic *FastSwap* builds on Java 5 DCR, but mostly removes the restrictions, allowing methods and fields to be added, changed, or removed from classes. A few restrictions still exist; in particular, Java reflection will not be aware of changes to classes, you cannot change the interfaces a class implements, you cannot add or remove methods from an EJB, and you cannot change annotations; refer to the WebLogic Server documentation for details (see Link 14-3). If you make a restricted change to a class, a ClassRedefinitionException will usually be thrown the next time you access the application, indicating that you should either back out the change or redeploy the application.

FastSwap is very easy to use. When enabled, the server loads the application using a special class-loader that handles the class redefinition. FastSwap must detect that classes have changed so they can be reloaded. For web applications, a special servlet filter is automatically deployed that checks for changes when a new request is received. If you are developing a non-web application, you can trigger detection by using the <fast-swap> Ant task.

FastSwap works only with exploded applications; any modifications to archived libraries and modules will require a redeployment of the application.

To enable FastSwap, add the following element to your application's weblogic-application.xml descriptor. You can also use this element in a standalone web application's weblogic.xml descriptor.

```
<fast-swap>
  <enabled>true</enabled>
</fast-swap>
```

FastSwap is a development-time feature, and is disabled if the server is started in production mode. Consequently, you can safely enable FastSwap in the deployment descriptor for all of your applications.

> **Tip to Remember**
>
> You can safely enable FastSwap for all of your applications, because the setting is ignored unless a server is running in development mode.

Establishing a Build Process

The project directories contain everything required to build and package the application. The build process for a project refers to the use of scripts and tools to perform compilation and deployment steps in support of the overall development process. We recommend the use of the Apache Ant build utility to script the build process for your WebLogic Server projects. A wealth of information is available on Ant, including books, white papers, example build scripts, and the Ant project home page at http://ant.apache.org/. Consistent with the intermediate to advanced nature of this book, we assume you have a basic knowledge of Ant and will concentrate on best practices related to its use in WebLogic Server development.

You should organize your Ant build.xml build script based on the major steps required to build, package, test, and deploy the application. These steps or tasks generally fall into five categories: compilation and related activities; creating web application, EJB, and application archives; deploying locally; creating official deployment packages for promotion to test or production; and miscellaneous tasks used during development.

In each category you are likely to have multiple Ant targets, or high-level tasks, that perform a series of steps. The main Ant targets in the build.xml file for bigrez.com projects are listed in Table 14-2.

There is no single correct way to name the targets in your build script, and to set up the dependencies between each target. The Ant utility doesn't mandate a particular scheme, and you'll find many different configurations in different development environments. Pick a scheme that makes sense for your application, but be sure the target names are an accurate reflection of the tasks performed by the target.

Table 14-2: Build Targets for bigrez.com Projects

Task	Purpose
compile	Compile the Java sources. This may involve additional processing steps; for example, JPA weaving.
package	Package the compiled output into the appropriate archive. For example, for a web application project, this creates a .war file.
test	Run any defined unit tests. For bigrez.com, only the unit-tests project defines tests.
clean	Remove the output and intermediate build artifacts such as .class files.
deploy, undeploy, redeploy	The ear project and the top-level build file define these targets that deploy the application to a running server.
report	Produce reports. For most projects, this generates Javadoc output. For the unit test project, it also creates an HTML report of the unit test results.
all	Run the clean, compile, test, package, and report targets to do a full build and test of the project.
initialize-database	The top-level build file defines this utility target that recreates the database schema.

> **Best Practice**
>
> Use the Apache Ant build utility to manage the build process for developer workstations and to create deployment archive files destined for test and production. Choose a consistent naming convention for your build targets, and keep each target focused on a single activity.

Continuous Integration

As you will see shortly, IDEs such as Eclipse and JDeveloper provide rich features for compilation, packaging, and deployment of Java EE projects. Although IDEs can greatly increase developer productivity, you should maintain a set of Ant build files and treat these as the authoritative way of building the application. Throughout this book we've advocated the use of Ant to create a cross-platform, generic build process that is not dependent on a particular IDE's build facilities. There are several important reasons for this. First, different developers prefer to use different IDEs. If you standardize on one particular IDE, you will undoubtedly please some developers and upset others, and there is nothing so unproductive as an unhappy developer. Second, the configuration of an IDE for a particular set of projects can be hard to automate, and the alternative of having every developer be responsible for setting up his or her environment by hand is time-consuming and error-prone. Third, it is usually not possible to automate the IDE build process through a script, so you cannot easily perform regular builds on a central build server.

By having a standard Ant build, you can support multiple IDE products in the same development team. If IDE-specific features are used for building applications it may be difficult to keep all dependencies, steps, and outputs consistent across multiple IDE products. Modern IDEs provide good integration with Ant, so can be used to trigger the standard build scripts as well as supporting interactive development with their own compilation tools.

Best Practice

Use Ant to implement the compile and build process for your application.

It is conventional practice to use a separate build server to run regular builds, unit tests, and report generation, typically overnight. When a build is triggered, an Ant script on the server checks out the latest version of the code from the SCM repository, does a full build, and runs all the unit tests. The build server usually hosts a web server from which the output of the last few builds can be downloaded, and the unit test reports can be browsed.

Teams following a continuous integration approach go one step further, and configure the build server using tools such as Cruise Control (http://cruisecontrol.sourceforge.net/) or Hudson (https://hudson.dev.java.net/) to trigger builds and run unit tests automatically when changes are checked into the SCM repository. Both Cruise Control and Hudson integrate well with Ant. Continuous integration provides quick feedback about problems that break the build, and enables an agile development approach where the team strives continually to evolve a working system, rather than commit major changes at once.

As your portfolio of application projects grows, you will find the management of dependencies between the projects quickly becomes more complex and time-consuming. You may have the need to use different versions of libraries, modules, and third-party components when building different applications. The traditional answer to these problems has been to use SCM features to provide different views or branches on the source code repository; this works, but the overhead of maintaining the SCM configuration can be considerable. More recently, alternative approaches using tools such as Apache Maven (http://maven.apache.org/) and Apache Ivy (http://ant.apache.org/ivy/) have become popular. Using such a dependency management tool in conjunction with a continuous integration server can result in a powerful build system that not only rebuilds an application project when one of its files has changed, but also triggers builds of all the downstream projects that depend on the changed project, deploys the resulting components to a server, and runs the appropriate unit tests.

Best Practice

Use a tool such as Cruise Control or Hudson to create a continuous integration build server that provides a central service for creating authoritative builds.

Code Inspection and Reporting Tools

We recommend you run code quality reports as part of your standard build. Many high-quality reporting tools are freely available.

Checkstyle (`http://checkstyle.sourceforge.net/`) can be used to enforce a coding standard. Developers' passions can run high about the best formatting style, but it is indisputable that a team working on a common code base is more productive if each member uses the same code format conventions. Enforcing conventions with an automated tool such as Checkstyle works much better than using a manual code review process, and allows code reviews to focus on higher-level problems. As well as enforcing a standard source code formatting approach, Checkstyle can perform static code inspection and alert about questionable Java coding practices that may indicate bugs; for example, classes that implement `equals()` but not `hashCode()`. You may even consider applying Checkstyle as part of your SCM check-in rules so that developers can't commit incorrectly formatted code.

FindBugs (`http://findbugs.sourceforge.net/`) is another code inspection tool that analyzes your code for a large number of common problems.

JDepend (see Link 14-4) is a more specialized analysis tool that focuses principally on the identifying coupling and cyclic dependencies between the various components in your code. It is useful to encourage the development of well-defined, loosely-coupled components that are easy to reuse.

Finally, don't forget to generate JavaDoc API documentation. The `javadoc` tool will produce warnings about incorrectly formatted or annotated documentation. Regularly generating and publishing the documentation encourages developers to keep it up to date.

Each of these tools is best applied as an integral part of your development process. They are easy to integrate with Ant. By addressing the problems they identify as early as possible, you will build quality into your code as it grows. In contrast, trying to address a long list of warnings after the code has been written is highly tedious. You should also obtain and install the appropriate IDE plug-ins so developers have access to these tools at their fingertips.

> **Best Practice**
>
> Integrate code inspection and reporting tools such as Checkstyle, FindBugs, JDepend, and JavaDoc into your build process. Fix problems as soon as these tools identify them.

Integrated Development Environments

At this point you have development hardware, software, WebLogic Server domains, a working directory structure, and a basic build process. Next comes the interesting and often difficult choice of development tool or integrated development environment (IDE) appropriate for your project. Let's face it: every developer has his or her favorite tool, whether it's a full-blown IDE, or a minimalist approach using Emacs, TextPad, or some similar editor. Each has its pros and cons, and there is no right answer for all projects or all developers.

Common IDEs used to develop WebLogic Server applications include Eclipse, Oracle JDeveloper, IntelliJ IDEA, and Sun's NetBeans. All four provide powerful, Java-aware editing, support remote debugging, and have features for working with Java EE, such as JSP editing and JPA object relational mapping tools.

In this section, we'll look at how to configure two of these IDEs: Eclipse and JDeveloper. We don't attempt to provide an exhaustive tutorial on each IDE, or to play one off the other. Rather, we show the steps to configure each tool to work well in a WebLogic Server development environment. As a developer, you'll find that the time taken to set up your IDE to support fast, interactive development will quickly be repaid.

Prerequisites

In the discussion that follows, we assume you have obtained the `bigrez.com` source code, installed WebLogic Server 11g, suitably configured a database, and also set up a WebLogic Server domain.

The `bigrez.com` source code is distributed in a `.zip` file, which you should expand into a directory. The directory will contain subdirectories for each of the six components of `bigrez.com` (refer back to Table 8-5 for details), a directory containing the libraries and descriptors to be packaged in the `.ear` file, a directory containing unit tests, and an `etc` directory that contains common build and setup scripts.

The source code contains a `README` file that describes how to build `bigrez.com` using Ant, and how to configure the database and a suitable WebLogic Server domain. You should work through the instructions in the `README` file and check that you can build and run `bigrez.com` before proceeding.

Configuring Eclipse for bigrez.com

The next few pages describe how to set up Eclipse and the Oracle Enterprise Pack for Eclipse for `bigrez.com` development.

The Oracle Enterprise Pack for Eclipse

The standard version of Eclipse has only basic support for WebLogic Server, and for that you must download a separate *server adapter*.

The Oracle Enterprise Pack for Eclipse (OEPE) extends Eclipse to be fully WebLogic Server–aware. If you are an Eclipse user, but don't use OEPE to develop WebLogic Server applications, you are missing out. A full version of Eclipse together with OEPE can be installed using the WebLogic Server 11g installer. Updates to OEPE may be available for download from the Oracle Technology Network (Link 14-5).

OEPE is the successor to the BEA WebLogic Server Tools project, replaces the former BEA WebLogic Workshop IDE, and rolls up several other major contributions to Eclipse by Oracle such as object-relational mapping support. The current version is the Oracle Enterprise Pack For Eclipse 11g, which fully supports WebLogic Server 9.2 and newer, and has limited support for WebLogic Server 8.1, 9.0, and 9.1. Its primary features include:

❑ Support for an enhanced form of WebLogic Server split directory development — a feature it refers to as *Virtual EARs*. We cover this feature later.

❑ Deployment to servers running on local and remote machines, and remote debugging of applications running within a server.

❑ Support for WebLogic Server shared libraries. You can register shared libraries in OEPE, and use them in web application, EJB, and library projects. OEPE will then provide the classes in the libraries to the other Eclipse tools, and maintain the appropriate deployment descriptor entries.

❑   Editing support for WebLogic Server deployment descriptors.

❑   Enhanced wizards for creating and working with web services.

❑   The Oracle Database plug-in for Eclipse, which provides interactive browsing and editing of database schemas.

❑   OEPE has inherited support for Apache XMLBeans (http://xmlbeans.apache.org/) and EJBGen (an annotation-based programming tool for EJB 2.x — see Link 14-6) from WebLogic Workshop. Over time, Oracle plans to move additional WebLogic Workshop features into OEPE.

❑   OEPE also bundles the Spring IDE project, which provides editing support for Spring configuration files.

Installation

Eclipse is available as several different distributions. We started with Eclipse Ganymede Service Release 2, which is Eclipse 3.4 with the Java EE support. This is available online at http://www.eclipse.org/ganymede/. We then installed the Oracle Enterprise Pack for Eclipse 11g from the OEPE site. Experienced Eclipse users will most likely want to take this approach of installing OEPE as a set of plug-ins to their existing Eclipse installation.

If you don't have an Eclipse 3.4 installation, or simply want to try out OEPE without modifying an existing installation, the WebLogic Server 11g installer contains all you need, including the base Eclipse IDE.

Configuring a Target Runtime

We start by configuring our WebLogic Server installation and the domain directory as a *target runtime* for Eclipse. This allows Eclipse to provide the right classes to projects that use the target runtime, to start and stop the server, and to deploy code to the server.

First, configure a runtime environment — this corresponds to a WebLogic Server installation. Open the workspace preferences dialog, and choose Server ➪ Runtime Environments. Click Add, and then select Oracle WebLogic Server 11gR1. Work your way through the rest of the dialog. You'll need to enter the WebLogic Home directory. This is the directory below the Oracle Middleware Home directory that contains the WebLogic Server installation, and is usually called wlserver_10.3.

Now, choose File ➪ New ➪ Other and select Server. This allows you to create a target server that corresponds to a particular domain. The dialog is fairly self-explanatory — apart from specifying the domain directory, you should accept the default settings for now.

Importing the bigrez.com Projects

We'll create a project in Eclipse for each of the six bigrez.com components, and one for the enterprise application. We'll set up dependencies between the projects so that Eclipse understands that they are a single application.

First create the enterprise application project. Select File ➪ New ➪ Enterprise Application Project. Enter bigrez-ear for the project name. For the Contents, deselect Use default and navigate to the ear subdirectory in your expanded bigrez.com distribution. The project will be populated automatically with the existing files. Ensure the Target Runtime is the set to the one you configured for WebLogic Server 11g, and leave all other settings at their default values.

> **Tip to Remember**
>
> Don't use spaces in project names. We've seen several bugs in Eclipse that arise from doing this.

Now create a project for the JPA domain model bundled library. Select File ⇨ New ⇨ Other, and select Utility Project. Name your project bigrez-domain, and ensure the Contents points to the domain subdirectory in your expanded bigrez.com distribution directory. Finally, check Add project to an EAR and select bigrez-ear. Before you move on, note how the project classpath has automatically been set up for WebLogic Server. It includes WebLogic System Libraries — that is, the various modules and APIs that make up WebLogic Server itself, as well as all of the libraries that the EAR has contributed through its APP-INF/lib directory.

> **Tip to Remember**
>
> To set up JPA tooling for the domain project, add the JPA facet in the project properties, and then configure the JPA properties to use a connection to your database. Be sure also to set Discover annotated classes automatically, because we haven't listed the entities in persistence.xml.

Configure the remaining projects in a similar manner, according to Table 14-3. In each case, change the contents directory to be the corresponding one in the bigrez.com expanded directory, and be sure to add the projects to the bigrez-ear EAR.

The Ant build for webservices project follows a two stage process. In the first stage, the web service stubs are generated using the wsdlc and jwsc Ant tools. This creates various Java classes used by the application code, and only needs to be repeated should the WSDL change. The second stage is to compile the application code and package the output as a web application.

The Eclipse webservices project relies on the Ant build to perform the first stage and to generate the classes below WEB-INF/classes. The classes will be included automatically in the Eclipse project build path. It is possible to generate web service stubs in Eclipse, but this task is best automated using Ant. Otherwise whenever the WSDL changes, each developer needs to regenerate the stubs, taking care to use the same IDE options.

> **Best Practice**
>
> IDEs like Eclipse provide integrated tooling to generate web services from WSDL. These features are useful for rapid prototyping, but have many options that must be correctly set by the user, and cannot easily be automated. Formal projects should use the Ant wsdlc and jwsc tasks instead.

Running bigrez.com from Eclipse

Right-click the bigrez-web-user project and select Run As ⇨ Run On Server, check your server is selected, and click Finish.

Table 14-3: Setting Up the bigrez.com Projects in Eclipse

Project Name	Project Type	Notes
bigrez-ear	Enterprise Application	
bigrez-domain	Utility	
bigrez-services	EJB	On the second page, change the Source Folder to src and deselect Create an EJB client jar module. After creating the project, open the project properties and change to the Java EE Module Dependencies Properties tab. Ensure that bigrez-domain.jar is checked.
bigrez-web-common	Utility	
bigrez-web-user	Dynamic Web	On the second page, deselect Generate deployment descriptor, and change the Context Root to user. Ensure that bigrez-domain.jar, bigrez-services.jar, and bigrez-web-common are checked in the Java EE Module Dependencies properties.
bigrez-web-admin	Dynamic Web	On the second page, deselect Generate deployment descriptor, and change the Context Root to admin. Ensure that bigrez-domain.jar, bigrez-services.jar, and bigrez-web-common are checked in the Java EE Module Dependencies properties.
bigrez-webservices	Dynamic Web	On the second page, deselect Generate deployment descriptor, and change the Context Root to webservices. Ensure that bigrez-domain.jar and bigrez-services.jar are checked in the Java EE Module Dependencies properties.

If you have followed the preceding steps carefully, Eclipse will start the WebLogic Server instance, deploy the application, and load the welcome page for bigrez.com. See Figure 14-4.

Once you've played with bigrez.com a little, and browsed around the source code, you may want to experiment with restarting the server in debug mode (right-click the server in the Servers view and select Restart in Debug), and setting breakpoints within the code.

Partial Redeployment

In Eclipse terminology, deployment to a server is known as *publishing*. OEPE tracks the modules in an application that have been modified since the last publish. For the next publish, it will perform a partial redeployment — only deploying the modules that have changed.

As for any deployment, OEPE must acquire the edit lock for the domain when publishing. If you have the WebLogic Console open at the same time, and it is set to automatically acquire the lock and activate changes, you will be prevented from publishing from Eclipse.

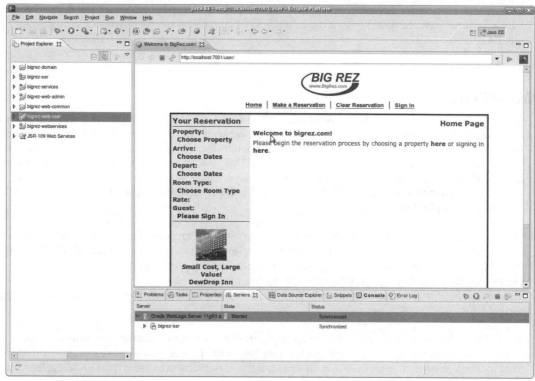

Figure 14-4: `bigrez.com` **running within the Eclipse IDE.**

Tip to Remember

When using the WebLogic Console with OEPE, make sure the `Automatically Acquire Lock and Activate Changes` option is unchecked in the WebLogic Console preferences.

One warning: A partial redeployment of a module that uses a JPA persistence context packaged in a different, unchanged module may sometimes fail. You may find you need to also modify a file in the module containing the persistence context to force the module to be redeployed, or alternatively right-click the server in the `Servers` view and select `Clean` to republish the entire application.

If you edit a file in a module that uses a JPA persistence context packaged in another module, you will occasionally need to touch a file in the JPA module, or republish the entire application.

Partial deployment is a useful time saver, but you'll find you don't need to publish after each change. A publish is required after changes to deployment descriptors and annotations. In most other cases you can simply save your changes in Eclipse, and the application running in a WebLogic Server instance will be updated. Three features enable this — WebLogic Server's change-aware servlet and JSP classloaders, FastSwap, and Virtual EARs. We've already considered change-aware classloaders and FastSwap, but what's a Virtual EAR?

Virtual EARs

Earlier in this chapter, we discussed WebLogic Server's split directory development feature. This feature speeds up development cycles by removing the need to merge source directories and generated output directories into a single exploded application. Even better, the benefits of deploying in an exploded format are inherited, including the ability to change HTML, JSP, other resources, and classes (if FastSwap is enabled) without the need for a partial or full redeployment. However, the split directory development feature relies on the source and build directories both being structured as a set of modules nested within an enterprise application.

When we set up `bigrez.com` for Eclipse, we created an application consisting of a number of modules, organized into seemingly independent project directories within the Eclipse workspace. OEPE deploys the EAR without unnecessary copying of the source files to an exploded application directory, but without nesting the module projects within the application project. How does it do this? It turns out that the `.beabuild.txt` file has more secrets that allow OEPE to link together directories and files into a single virtual EAR.

If you follow the previous steps to deploy an application from Eclipse, and then examine the source path of the application, you'll find it refers to a location below the Eclipse workspace `.metadata` directory. That location contains a `.beabuild.txt` file that ties the various parts of the virtual EAR together. Part of a typical file is shown in Listing 14-2.

Listing 14-2: The .beabuild.txt file generated by OEPE for a Virtual EAR.

```
/work/bigrez/ear/EarContent/APP-INF/classes = APP-INF/classes
/work/bigrez/domain/build/classes = APP-INF/lib/bigrez-domain.jar
/work/bigrez/services/build/classes = bigrez-services.jar
/work/bigrez/web-common/build/classes = APP-INF/lib/bigrez-web-common.jar
/work/bigrez/web-user/WebContent = bigrez-web-user.war
/work/bigrez/web-user/build/weboutput = bigrez-web-user.war
/work/bigrez/web-user/build/classes = bigrez-web-user.war/WEB-INF/classes
/work/bigrez/web-admin/WebContent = bigrez-web-admin.war
...
/work/bigrez/ear/EarContent/APP-INF/lib/commons-beanutils.jar = APP-
INF/lib/commons-beanutils.jar
/work/bigrez/ear/EarContent/APP-INF/lib/commons-codec.jar = APP-
INF/lib/commons-codec.jar
...
```

This is a properties file, like the simple `.beabuild.txt` file in Listing 14-1 for split directory development. However, there are several differences.

❑ The file contains many properties, instead of a single `beasrc.dir` property, allowing many directories and files to be merged into the virtual EAR.

❑ The properties link sources, derived resources, and `.jar` files into the virtual EAR.

❏ The property keys are the absolute paths of the directories to merge into the virtual EAR, and property values are the relative locations in the application. (For the `beasrc.dir` property, the path to the source directory is the property value, not the key.)

We noted previously that the format of the `.beabuild.txt` file is not publicly documented by Oracle, and so it might change in the future. The good news is that you don't need to create or edit this file. OEPE generates the file and keeps it up to date without you having to worry about it. You benefit from faster development cycles with OEPE simply by using the standard Eclipse deployment commands. Virtual EARs are the ideal complement to FastSwap. In most cases, you simply modify and save a file, Eclipse will compile it if necessary, and a running server will automatically pick up the changes.

Configuring JDeveloper for bigrez.com

We'll now look at how to set up JDeveloper for `bigrez.com` development. The high level steps are similar to those for Eclipse, but JDeveloper has a different model of applications and projects.

Oracle JDeveloper

Oracle JDeveloper is Oracle's principal development platform. It is free to download and use, and runs on many platforms including Microsoft Windows, Linux, and Apple Mac OS X. In addition to supporting Java and Java EE development, JDeveloper is the IDE for Oracle's SOA Suite and WebCenter Suite families of products, and provides additional tools for web service, XML, and database development. Most notably, JDeveloper is the tool set for the Oracle Application Development Framework (Oracle ADF). ADF is a commercial framework which extends Java EE and provides a visual and declarative rapid application development approach for enterprise applications.

Installation

Download the latest version of JDeveloper from the Oracle Technology Network site (see Link 14-7). Select the installer appropriate for your operating system.

The installation process is straightforward and similar to that for WebLogic Server described earlier in this chapter.

The JDeveloper 11g installer includes WebLogic Server 11g. This embedded version of WebLogic Server is preconfigured for easy testing and debugging of applications from JDeveloper. To save disk space on developer workstations, you can install JDeveloper into the Oracle Middleware Home directory of an existing WebLogic Server 11g installation. Alternatively, you might chose to rely on the version of WebLogic Server installed by JDeveloper. If you are considering doing so, be aware that the JDeveloper installer is missing several optional components available in the full WebLogic Server installation, including the HTTP Pub-Sub server, third-party JDBC drivers, web server plug-ins, and the WebLogic Server examples.

We prefer to install JDeveloper and WebLogic Server into separate Oracle Middleware Homes. Although this requires more disk space, we benefit from having a full WebLogic Server installation that can be patched and upgraded separately from JDeveloper.

You can now start JDeveloper. If you are using Windows, a suitable menu item will be added to the Start menu. On Linux, run the command `jdeveloper/jdev/bin/jdev`. JDeveloper will start and prompt you to select a role to enable a subset of the JDeveloper features and so simplify the menu options. For now, you should select Default Role to enable all features.

Creating an Application and the First Project

Eclipse uses a separate project to represent the enterprise application. In contrast, in JDeveloper an application configuration is defined to which projects representing the application's modules and libraries are added.

To create the application, choose File ➪ New from the main menu and create a new Generic Application. Name the application BigRez, and set the directory to the top-level directory of your expanded bigrez.com distribution (where the README.txt file is).

If you like, you can set the application package prefix to com.bigrez. This is a convenience that saves typing when creating new Java classes for the application.

The new application dialog creates an initial project. We'll configure this to contain the domain model project, and configure the other projects later. On the second page of the dialog, call the initial project domain, which will set the directory to the bigrez.com domain subdirectory. Also, select the EJB project technology. The default settings on the remaining dialog pages are acceptable, so choose Finish.

JDeveloper uses *deployment profiles* to control the packaging of project output. Create a deployment profile to complete the configuration of the domain project. Open up the project properties by selecting the domain project and choosing Application ➪ Project Properties. Select Deployment, then New, and change the archive name to bigrez-domain. The remaining defaults are acceptable, but to be tidy you may wish to modify the file filters to exclude the Ant build.xml file.

You can now compile the domain project by selecting the Build ➪ Make All menu option, and create the bigrez-domain.jar file by selecting Build ➪ Deploy, then choosing the deployment profile.

Configuring a Server Instance

Select Tools ➪ Preferences from the main menu, then chose Run in the preferences dialog, and select Edit Server Instances. You'll see that an existing Default Server is preconfigured. Rather than make use of this default server, we want to use the WebLogic Server domain that we set up following the instructions earlier in this chapter.

Select New to create a server instance, and change the name to BigRezServer. Check the box to let JDeveloper manage the life cycle of this instance (to start and stop it), and point the Domain Directory to the directory containing your bigrez.com WebLogic Server domain. Replace the Server Instance text with AdminServer. Select Startup and change the listen port to 7001.

Select the Application ➪ Application Properties menu item and choose the Run node in the tree. In the Bind Application to Server Instance list, select the BigRezServer you have just created. When we run the application using integrated WebLogic Server support, it will now use the external bigrez.com domain.

One final bit of configuration is necessary to complete the integration with the external domain. Choose View ➪ Application Server Navigator, right click on IntegratedWLSConnection, and select Properties. Update the Authentication and Configuration settings to correct the administrator user name and password (`weblogic` and `weblogic1`, unless you have changed them), port, and the domain name.

You can now test that the server instance is correctly configured by selecting `Run` ⇨ `Start Server Instance` from the menu.

Creating the Remaining Projects

Next, create the `services` project. Open up the `New Gallery` using the `File` ⇨ `New` menu option. Create a new generic project, and select the `Java` project technology. Change the project name to `services`. This will set the directory to correct subdirectory of the `bigrez.com` distribution. Change the default package on the next page if you wish. The remaining project defaults are suitable, so select `Finish`.

The EJBs in the `services` project depend upon the domain `project`. Open up the project properties and select `Dependencies`. Add a new dependency by clicking the edit icon, expanding the `domain.jpr` project, and selecting the `bigrez-domain` deployment profile. The project also depends upon Java EE and WebLogic Server classes. From the project properties dialog, select `Libraries and Classpath` in the tree, and add the `WebLogic 10.3 Remote-Client` library.

While you have the project properties dialog open, change the Java compiler from the `ojc` compiler to `javac`. This setting can be found under `Compiler`. We found runtime problems with the code produced by `ojc` for the generic types used by the `services` project. Switching to `javac` avoids these problems.

The final step in the `services` project configuration is to create a deployment profile. Call the profile `bigrez-services`, and change the archive type to `EJB JAR File`.

The `bigrez.com` web projects have dependencies on Spring MVC and Tiles. We begin by creating a user library definition which includes all of the required libraries. Choose `Tools` ⇨ `Manage Libraries`, select `User`, then `New`. Name your library `BigRez Dependencies`. Add classpath entries for each of the `.jar` files in the `ear/EarContent/APP-INF/lib` directory (you can select multiple files at once by holding down the shift key). Finally, check `Deployed By Default` so that JDeveloper knows to deploy the library as part of the application.

Now let's create the `web-common` project. Create a new generic project called `web-common`, selecting the `Java` project technology. The remaining project defaults are suitable, so select `Finish`. Open the properties dialog for the new project, choose `Libraries and Classpath` ⇨ `Add Library`, and select the `BigRez Dependencies` library. Also add the `WebLogic 10.3 Remote-Client` library. Create a deployment profile for the project, using the `JAR File` artifact type.

Following the steps in the preceding paragraph, create the three remaining web projects: `web-user`, `web-admin`, and `webservices`. Use the `WAR File` artifact type when creating the deployment profiles. For each project, open the project properties dialog and set up the web content directories, the context root, and the dependencies on other projects as follows:

❑ Locate the `Web Application` node under `Project Source Paths`. Browse and set the `HTML Root` directory to the project's `WebContent` directory.

❑ Go to the `Java EE Application` node and change the `Java EE Web Context Root` to user, admin, or `webservices`, depending on the particular project.

❑ Under the `Dependencies` node, add dependencies to the deployment profiles of the `domain` and `services` projects. For the `web-admin` and `web-user` projects, also add a dependency on the `web-common` deployment profile.

713

If you now try to build the application, you should find that only the webservices project fails to build.

Generating the Web Service

When we set up Eclipse, we relied on our Ant build to perform the generate Web Service stubs below WEB-INF/classes. We pointed out earlier that web service stubs can be generated in Eclipse, but that web service generation is best automated using Ant. As you might expect, JDeveloper also provides IDE options to generate web service stubs if you configure the project with the Web Services project technology. However, it is still better to use Ant to generate the stubs, and we'll do just that.

Unlike Eclipse, JDeveloper can't use the generated classes directly, and requires the generated web service source files to be part of the project. Our Ant build creates the source files in a generated-src directory. If this directory doesn't exist, please first build bigrez.com using Ant as we described in the "Prerequisites" section. If you add the generated-src directory as a project source path for the webservices project, you'll find you can successfully build all of the projects.

There's one final task to do before the webservices project will deploy correctly. Although not required by Java EE 5, JDeveloper expects every web application to have a web.xml descriptor file and the webservices project doesn't have one. Fortunately, a trivial descriptor file will do — it doesn't even need any servlet declarations or mappings. You can generate a suitable descriptor by right clicking on the webservices project and selecting New ⇨ Deployment Descriptors ⇨ Java EE Deployment Descriptor, and then web.xml.

Running and Deploying from JDeveloper

You can now run bigrez.com web projects from JDeveloper by right clicking on the web.xml, and selecting Run. JDeveloper will build the application, start WebLogic Server if necessary, deploy the code, and open the first page of the application in a browser.

To create the bigrez.ear file, set up a deployment profile for the application. Add the modules to the application in the Application Assembly part of the deployment profile dialog. You should also add the ear/EarContent directory as a *contributor* so the application libraries are packaged in the EAR.

Debugging with an IDE

All modern IDEs support debugging of applications running in a remote WebLogic Server instance, and make a debugging session easy to set up. Using Eclipse, for example, it is as simple as right-clicking an application and selecting Debug On Server.

Under the covers, IDEs perform three steps when debugging a WebLogic Server application.

1. Compile the Java components with debugging information included in the .class files.
2. Start WebLogic Server with debug options set in the Java command line used to start the server instance.
3. Attach to the WebLogic Server instance for remote debugging, and set up the breakpoints.

You can perform each of these tasks manually without an IDE. For example, if you compile with javac you can use the -g switch to include debug information, and you can use the command-line jdb debugger to attach to a process. However, this is a somewhat Spartan approach, and using an IDE's debugging capabilities is much easier.

In summary, remote debugging is easy to configure and use with modern IDE products and will save you time when you need to debug your application.

Starting WebLogic Server in Debug Mode

WebLogic Server must be started with the Java Platform Debugging Architecture (JPDA) remote debugging capability enabled. This capability is defined by the Java platform itself, and a JPDA-compliant debugger can debug any Java application running in this mode.

The standard WebLogic Server scripts will start WebLogic Server in debug mode if the `debugFlag` environment variable is set. If this flag is set, the following switches are added to the Java command line.

```
-Xdebug -Xnoagent -Xrunjdwp:transport=dt_socket,address=
${DEBUG_PORT},server=y,suspend=n -Djava.compiler=NONE
```

If you are running multiple WebLogic Server debug sessions on a shared development machine, you should edit the `setDomainEnv` file to set a unique `DEBUG_PORT` for each server.

The WebLogic Server instance will boot up and wait for a debugger to connect to the running application at the port specified or via shared memory. You may notice an increase in server boot time when running in debug mode and a significant slowing of the application when a debugger is attached to the server instance.

Debugging and Transaction Timeouts

One problem to watch out for: If you set a breakpoint inside transactional code such as an EJB component or presentation-tier component with a user-defined transaction, the WebLogic Server transaction manager will time out the transaction after a fairly short period of time. The default transaction timeout is 30 seconds. You should increase the timeout value to at least 600 seconds for development domains to give yourself enough time to examine variables, step through EJB code, and perform other debugging tasks without having the operation time out and roll back.

Best Practice

Increase the Java Transaction API (JTA) timeout value in the domain to at least 600 seconds to provide enough time to step through transactional code and examine variables in the debugger without causing transaction timeouts.

Creating a Unit Testing Infrastructure

Before discussing techniques for unit testing a Java EE application, we provide a brief review of unit testing.

Unit testing is the process of testing an individual software component or program to identify, isolate, and remove software deficiencies as early as possible in the development process. The developer responsible for programming the component is also responsible for unit testing. The component under test is exercised in partial isolation from other parts of the application, and the services it depends upon may be simulated with other test components. This yields a *white box* approach to testing that leverages the developer's knowledge of the component's inner workings to create tests that exercise all critical paths through the code.

The Importance of Unit Testing

A primary goal of unit testing is to detect errors early, at the point where they are easy to fix. Bugs found early in the development process are much cheaper to fix, in terms of time and money, than bugs discovered later in system or user testing. Unit testing has many other benefits as well.

The process of writing unit tests forces a developer to think about how the code should be used, and leads to better interfaces. By exercising the code earlier, a developer can identify and correct inconsistencies in the design before investing in writing a large amount of code.

Unit tests should have repeatable results, and be self-contained to the extent possible. Although the developer creates and initially executes the unit tests as part of the component-development process, the same tests can and should be used as a suite of regression tests that is regularly executed. A strong regression test suite makes design changes and other refactoring efforts less risky. You have the ability to regression test everything after a code change is made. If all the unit tests pass, you have a strong degree of assurance that the changes have not broken previously working code. This is very important if a developer is refactoring code that he or she did not write. Good unit tests also allow you to switch between different third-party implementations of libraries and frameworks with confidence; for example, to change your JPA implementation from Kodo to TopLink.

Unit tests are an effective communication mechanism. They improve the maintainability of code, by providing future developers with solid definitions of expected behaviors and the ability to regression test the application after making changes. They also act as examples that complement the JavaDoc of an API.

Finally, unit tests provide quality assurance before releasing code to other teams. You'll sleep much better going into system and user-acceptance testing knowing that the candidate build has passed the entire suite of unit tests.

Best Practice

Fix unit test failures as soon as possible. If you delay, the cost to fix will increase, trust in the unit test suite will be reduced, and the overall value of your unit tests will be diminished.

Write Unit Tests with the Code

It is easy for developers to delay or eliminate the creation of unit tests when the schedule gets tight. Don't allow this to happen! The result will be lower-quality code that is less maintainable and can't be regression tested, and this will cost you more in the long run.

The Extreme Programming (XP) methodology advocates writing unit tests before writing the component itself, as a means to clarify the expected behavior of the component and facilitate good design before coding begins. Although unit tests are valuable for XP and non-XP development efforts, by requiring unit tests before coding you are more likely to have complete unit tests at the end of the process. Whether or not you start with the test code, we recommend co-developing tests alongside the code. Write a little code, write and execute unit tests to check that it does what you expect, and then repeat. Insist that unit tests be available and that the code successfully passes all unit tests before considering the work complete. A formal code review is a good time to review and sign off on these tests.

A good way to encourage co-development of unit tests with code is to provide developers access to a code coverage tool. We are fans of Atlassian's Clover commercial product (see Link 14-8), but several free, open source coverage tools are also available, including EMMA (http://emma.sourceforge.net/) and Cobertura (http://cobertura.sourceforge.net/). You should set an acceptable unit test coverage goal for all new code — 80% is a typical figure. Developers then have a *score* to aim for, and unit testing becomes more of a game and less of a chore.

Best Practice

Create unit tests for all business components in the system, and require all code to pass the tests before considering it complete. Use the code review process and a code coverage tool to ensure compliance.

Often the problem isn't that developers disagree with the value of unit testing — they just find it burdensome and time-consuming to write and organize the tests. In other words, the cost of writing a detailed unit test often seems to outweigh the apparent benefits. That's where a unit testing framework comes into play by reducing the tedious work of creating, managing, and running unit tests. With a good framework the value of unit testing will always outweigh the cost.

The JUnit Testing Framework

JUnit is by far the most popular Java unit testing framework. It is widely supported, and has strong integration with IDEs, Ant, and other development tools.

JUnit has a small API, and is very simple to use. Unit tests are written as Java methods. From JUnit 4, each unit test method is identified using the `@org.unit.Test` annotation. Here's an abbreviated example from the `bigrez.com` unit tests.

```java
import static org.junit.Assert.assertEquals;
import static org.junit.Assert.fail;
import org.junit.Before;
import org.junit.Test;

import com.bigrez.domain.GuestProfile;
import com.bigrez.service.NotFoundException;
import com.bigrez.testutilties.AbstractEntityManagerTests;

public class TestProfileServices extends AbstractEntityManagerTests
{
    private ProfileServicesImpl profileServices;

    @Before
```

```
    public void setUp() throws Exception
    {
        profileServices = new ProfileServicesImpl();
        profileServices.setEntityManager(getEntityManager());
    }

    @Test
    public void testFindByLogonAndPassword() throws Exception
    {
        GuestProfile guestProfile1 = new GuestProfile();
        guestProfile1.setLogon("logon");
        guestProfile1.setPassword("password");
        GuestProfile createdGP =
            profileServices.createOrUpdate(guestProfile1);
        GuestProfile guestProfile2 =
            profileServices.findByLogonAndPassword("logon", "password");
        assertEquals(createdGP, guestProfile2);
        try {
            profileServices.findByLogonAndPassword("logon", "blah");
            fail("Expected NotFoundException");
        }
        catch (NotFoundException e) {}
    }
}
```

Unlike previous versions of JUnit, there is no requirement for a JUnit 4 test class to extend a standard JUnit superclass. Instead, the integration with the JUnit framework is specified using Java annotations. The preceding example actually does extend a common superclass that is used by several of the bigrez.com unit tests. The AbstractEntityManagerTests class contains convenience functions that set up a JPA EntityManager before each unit test is run, and close it after a test, as well as utility functions for creating instances of various bigrez.com JPA entities.

In our abbreviated example, the unit test class has a single test method testFindByLogonPassword(), indicated by the @Test annotation. Typical unit test classes have tens of such test methods. There is also a setUp() method indicated with the @Before annotation that will be called before each of the test methods. When the test class is run with JUnit, the following will happen for each @Test method.

1. An instance of the class will be created.

2. Any @Before methods will be executed.

3. The @Test method will be called.

4. Any @After methods will be called.

There are also @BeforeClass and @AfterClass annotations that can be used to mark methods that should be called once before or after any test methods defined in a test class.

The other items of interest in our test class are the assertEquals() method, which checks that its arguments are equal, and the fail() method, which will mark a test as failed if it is called. The org.junit.Assert class provides a rich set of other assertion methods.

This short example has demonstrated the principal features of the JUnit API. Complete documentation and examples are available from the JUnit home page at http://www.junit.org/.

Out-of-Container Testing

Before EJB 3.0, EJB applications could only be tested *in-container*; that is, the code to test had to be deployed within a running WebLogic Server instance. To achieve this, one of two techniques was used.

The first technique involves calling EJBs over RMI from JUnit test code running in a remote JVM. This approach clearly can only be used to test EJB methods exposed through a remote interface. It prevents a test case from setting up additional test conditions by making direct Java calls, and from fully asserting the effects of the tests on the internal state of the application. This is *black box* testing, rather than the *white box* testing required for effective unit tests.

The second technique involves running JUnit test code within the server. This can be achieved by calling JUnit directly from a servlet, or using tools such as Jakarta Cactus (http://jakarta.apache.org/cactus/), which automate the process for you. Objections to this approach include that it is complicated to set up, and that the test cycle takes a significant amount of time to run.

Nowadays it is common for all unit tests to be completely run out-of-container. This is possible thanks to the changes toward a POJO-based coding style, embodied in technologies such as EJB 3.0, JPA, and the Spring Framework. The discipline of writing application components to be tested outside of a container promotes good coding practices and results in loosely-coupled, reusable code.

We strongly encourage you to write unit tests that run out-of-container whenever possible. This leads to better code, and test suites that are faster and easy to execute, and so improve productivity.

> ### Best Practice
> Unit tests should run out-of-container wherever possible.

Mocking Frameworks

Of course, components do have dependencies on other components and runtime services provided by a container. To test a component outside of a container, stubs may need to be provided that simulate the behavior of the component or service. Often, it is better to use a mock object rather than a stub. Like a stub, a mock object simulates a component but also provide facilities to check that the component's methods have been called in the expected manner.

Several good mocking frameworks are available, including JMock (http://www.jmock.org/), EasyMock (http://easymock.org/), and Mockito (http://mockito.org/). Mockito is a relatively new framework, and is our favorite of the three. We used Mockito 1.6 in many of the bigrez.com unit tests.

To give you an understanding of how easy it is to use a mocking framework, let's look at an example using Mockito. When using Mockito, you create mock objects, wire them into the classes you want to test, execute the tests, and then verify that the mocks were called in the expected manner. We'll consider the unit tests for the LoggingInterceptor, a class we first encountered in Chapter 6. Recall that LoggingInterceptor is an EJB interceptor that has a single audit() method that logs the entry and exit points of method calls to any EJB to which it is applied. Our test case will simply set up an instance of the interceptor class, call it with an appropriate javax.ejb.InvocationContext, and then check that these two logging messages are written out.

Here's the setup. We first create `java.util.Logger` and `InvocationContext` instances using the Mockito `mock()` method. The `mock()` method takes a class or interface as a parameter and creates a special type of object, a *mock*, that can be substituted for an instance of the class or interface.

```
import static org.mockito.Matchers.eq;
import static org.mockito.Matchers.startsWith;
import static org.mockito.Mockito.mock;
import static org.mockito.Mockito.verify;
import static org.mockito.Mockito.verifyNoMoreInteractions;
import static org.mockito.Mockito.when;
//...   public class TestLoggingInterceptor
{
    private Logger logger = mock(Logger.class);
    private InvocationContext ic = mock(InvocationContext.class);
```

We then complete the setup in a `@Before` method that modifies the behavior of the `InvocationContext` mock's implementation of `getMethod()` to return a particular method. If we didn't do this, the default behavior of the mock would be to return `null` when `getMethod()` was called. In this test we're making fairly minimal use of the `InvocationContext` mock. The interceptor class does call `getMethod()`, but only uses the result in log message output, so the method we return is not particularly important.

```
@Before
public void setup() throws Exception
{
    Method method = TestLoggingInterceptor.class.getMethod("setup");
    when(ic.getMethod()).thenReturn(method);
}
```

Note how clean the Mockito interface is. Some other mocking frameworks would require method names to be passed as strings. Mockito's design uses method names directly, and this means that IDE code completion and refactoring support work naturally.

Now look at a test method. First we create an instance of our interceptor, and stub it with our mock.

```
@Test
public void testLoggingInterceptorGood() throws Exception
{
    LoggingInterceptor loggingInterceptor = new LoggingInterceptor();
    loggingInterceptor.setLogger(logger);
```

Then, we execute the method we want to test. Here we're passing the `InvocationContext` mock as a parameter. We haven't changed the behavior of the mock's `proceedMethod()`, so when our interceptor class calls that method, it will do nothing.

```
    loggingInterceptor.audit(ic);
```

Finally, we verify that the test method called `log()` on the `Logger` stub wrote out exactly twice, passing a suitable message each time.

```
    verify(logger).log(eq(Level.INFO), startsWith("entering"));
    verify(logger).log(eq(Level.INFO), startsWith("exiting"));
    verifyNoMoreInteractions(logger);
}
```

> **Best Practice**
>
> Use a mocking framework, such as Mockito. It's a lot easier than writing stubs by hand.

Dependency Injection and Unit Tests

It is common to have to add unit test accessor methods so that unit tests can set up the test. In the preceding example, you may have noticed that we called the `setLogger()` method to inject the `Logger` mock into the class under test. The `setLogger()` method exists simply to support the unit test.

```
// Obtain default logger using WebLogic Server API
private Logger logger = LoggingHelper.getServerLogger();

// Allow unit tests to override logger.
void setLogger(Logger logger)
{
    this.logger = logger;
}
```

> **Tip to Remember**
>
> Unit test accessor methods need not infect the public interface of your classes. Make the unit test accessor methods package scope, and place the unit test in the same package as the class under test.

Accessor methods are also needed to set up any fields that normally would be populated by a Java EE container; for example, an `EntityManager` field annotated with `@PersistenceContext`. If you are using the Spring Framework, or another dependency injection framework, you might consider using the framework to inject the appropriate dependencies. For unit tests, we find it is usually both clearer and simpler not to do this, and instead wire together the appropriate test context using plain Java.

Database Services as Part of the Unit Test Context

Some things are impractical to stub or mock for unit tests. A relational database is a good example. An application's interaction with a database is usually complicated, and you are as interested in testing that the database does what you expect as you are in the behavior of the application code. In some sense, the database is intrinsically coupled to the class that you are testing.

We've not attempted to mock the database in the `bigrez.com` unit tests. Consequently, some of the unit tests require access to a running database with the correct schema. Further, the tests should have exclusive access to a unique part of the database so they can execute independently of any other use of the database. This is typically straightforward to arrange, following the advice given at the beginning of this chapter.

For `bigrez.com`, we've assumed that the database is pre-populated with a small, standard set of data. Some applications require very large sets of reference data, which are not possible to reload before every unit test run. Unit tests that use a database must take care to restore it to its initial state. For example, the `testFindByLogonAndPassword()` unit test in the `TestProfileServices` test class that we examined creates a `GuestProfile` with a given name. We want to be able to run the test repeatedly, without encountering a database constraint violation. `TestProfileServices`, and most of the `bigrez.com` database tests, achieve this by running each unit test in a transaction, then rolling back the transaction at the end of the test. The `AbstractEntityManagerTests` base class provides support for this transaction management.

> **Best Practice**
>
> Unit tests that use a database should leave its state as they found it, so they can be executed repeatedly.

Time and Other Variable Factors

If unit tests depend on variable factors, such as the current time, or values produced by a random number generator, they may produce different results every time they are called. This makes assertions harder to write, and leads to weaker unit tests.

Where possible, your application code should wrap access to this variable information so that the unit tests can fix the behavior. For example, a class that relies on current time might depend on a `TimeServices` component. Unit tests can then supply an implementation of `TimeServices` that supplies a known fixed time.

This is not a hard and fast rule. Sometimes it is useful for a unit test to generate random input data, because it cannot possibly test the full range of inputs. However, in general, you should aim to write repeatable, well-behaved unit tests. Your goal is to test the application code, not spend forever debugging complicated unit test code.

> **Best Practice**
>
> Allow unit tests to override variable, external factors, such as the current time and random number generators, so they are repeatable.

Testing Web Interfaces

The correct behavior of web interfaces is hard to unit test out-of-container. Of course, there should be no complex business logic in the web components themselves; it should be located in EJBs or in Java helper objects. Still, there remains the need to unit test the user interface of a web application. This is usually achieved by deploying the application to a running server and running some automated external tests that simulate the actions of a web browser.

Two mature, free, open source libraries are available that can make this process easier — HttpUnit (http://httpunit.sourceforge.net/) and HTMLUnit (http://htmlunit.sourceforge.net/). HttpUnit is the older of the two, but HTMLUnit has better support for JavaScript. Many higher-level frameworks are also available, such as JWebUnit (http://jwebunit.sourceforge.net/) and Canoo WebTest (http://webtest.canoo.com/). Both JWebUnit and Canoo WebTest use the HTMLUnit library under the covers.

A full review of these various tools is beyond the scope of this chapter; so let's satisfy ourselves with looking at a simple JWebUnit test case for `bigrez.com`. This is shown in Listing 14-3, and is included in the `bigrez.com` test suite.

Listing 14-3: : An example JWebUnit test case.

```
public class ExampleJWebUnitTestCase extends WebTester
{
    @Before
    public void setUp() throws Exception
    {
        setBaseUrl("http://localhost:7001/");
    }

    @Test
    public void testFrontPage()
    {
        beginAt("/user");
        assertTitleEquals("Welcome to BigRez.com!");
        assertLinkPresentWithText("Choose Property");
    }

    @Test
    public void testSearchProperties()
    {
        beginAt("/user");
        clickLinkWithText("Choose Property");

        assertTextNotPresent("45 Main Street");

        selectOption("stateCode", "MN");
        selectOption("city", "Duluth");
        submit();

        assertTextPresent("45 Main Street");
    }
}
```

JWebUnit is designed for use with JUnit, and our unit test is a JUnit test class. The JWebUnit support is provided through the `WebTester` class, which we've chosen to extend to so that we can call its methods directly from our test methods.

If you look at the `testSearchProperties()` method in Listing 14-3, you can see that the `WebTester` methods almost form a domain-specific language, allowing us to express concisely the browser actions we are simulating. This test starts at the `/user` home page, then navigates through the `chooseProperty.do` link. It then sets up the form options and submits the query, and finally asserts that the resulting page now contains the address of the expected property. JWebUnit deals with the details of translating the `WebTester` method calls into remote HTTP requests, capturing the resulting HTML page, and receiving and resending cookies so each unit test can have its own HTTP session on the server.

How useful is this type of testing in your overall development and unit testing process? We believe all unit testing is valuable, but the benefits must be weighed against the cost. In the case of standard unit tests, the benefits easily outweigh the costs of creating and managing the test cases. The answer is not as clear with web component unit tests. Writing JWebUnit test classes and methods to test every link, form submission, and behavior in the web site can be extremely tedious. Creating form data for submission requires a substantial number of method calls, and many pages respond properly only after many preliminary steps and pages required by the application. For example, the `ReservationThankYou` page in `bigrez.com` cannot be tested without walking through the entire reservation process.

When writing web unit tests, focus on the correctness of the application logic, rather than the aesthetics of the pages, and be sparing with assertions. If you make too many assertions about the page layout, your unit tests will be brittle and will break whenever your page designer decides to reformat the look and feel of your application.

We recommended that web component unit testing be limited to a small number of tests, preferably one test for each page in the application. The resulting test suite can be used as a simple regression test when major changes are made to the application to ensure that all pages build properly (catching runtime JSP compile errors) and generate valid content. Testing critical navigation logic and presentation-layer functionality may also be worthwhile. Leave the complete testing of the web site to the Quality Assurance team during formal system and user acceptance testing.

> **Best Practice**
>
> Create a limited number of unit tests to verify the basic operation of web components in the application. Use the resulting test suites for regression testing.

Web Services

A web service has a well-defined, coarse-grained interface with its own contract, and is quite amenable to unit testing. However, web services need to be tested in-container, just like web applications. Just as for web applications, complex business logic should be located outside of the web services components themselves, but you must still test the translation of Java objects to and from their XML representation.

Because a web services interface usually exists to provide a vendor-neutral interface to your application, interoperability testing is also a concern. We recommend that you test using a variety of client web service stacks and tools, rather than just coding tests that use the WebLogic Server libraries.

> **Best Practice**
>
> Test your web services using a variety of client web service stacks.

soapUI from eviware (`http://www.soapui.org/`) is a popular tool for functional testing of web services. It is available in both a free version and a more fully featured commercial version. soapUI provides a user interface that allows simple web services test cases to be created. You can supply the service's WSDL to the tool, and it will create prototypical messages and requests, and allows these to be composed into test cases, which you can then replay against a deployed service. Different types of assertions can be added to each request to check whether the response complies with the schema, or contains expected content, for example. The resulting test cases can be executed using a command-line tool that is easy to integrate with Ant.

Performance and Concurrency Testing

So far in this section we have considered functional testing; that is, testing that aims to simulate the actions of a single user or system actor. Although not strictly unit testing, it is useful also to provide a load testing facility in the development environment. This allows developers quickly to prove whether a new architectural approach will scale, and to investigate problems that only occur when multiple users access the system. For example, scalability bottlenecks due to a poorly designed synchronization strategy, or database deadlocks that occur because separate parts of the application acquire locks in a different order.

Sometimes it is appropriate to write JUnit tests that spawn threads, or use multiple session objects, to simulate the effect of multiple users. For example, bigrez.com has a TestOptimisticLocking unit test that uses several JPA EntityManagers. This technique can work where you suspect there may be a concurrency issue, but does not find problems that you were not already expecting.

Commercial load testing products can be expensive, and organizations often only license them for use by the test team that runs the formal pre-production performance tests. An application will not reach that team until it is mostly complete, and by that time a concurrency issue may be costly to address. To protect against this risk, we recommend the development team regularly use a lightweight load testing framework, such as The Grinder (http://grinder.sourceforge.net/) or Apache JMeter (http://jakarta.apache.org/jmeter/) to test for concurrency problems. Both products are free and open source, and are written in Java. They are more suited to an application developer than to a professional tester. For example, they both require some coding or scripting skills to get the best out of them. However, unlike many commercial tools, they support testing of many types of application interfaces, including HTTP, remote EJB, web services, and JMS. One of the authors of this book is the primary developer of The Grinder.

Such a setup also allows the development team to do performance testing. Often you are not interested in the absolute numbers (for example, the maximum number of transactions per second you can achieve), because the development environment probably does not provide the same capacity as the target production environment, but regularly measuring relative numbers will allow you to identify performance regressions. Mature development projects often schedule a series of key tests to run every night, when the development server is not needed for other tasks, providing the development team with a regular report on the changing performance of their application.

> ### Best Practice
> Provide the development team with a lightweight load test framework, such as The Grinder or JMeter, to allow informal load tests. Get into the habit of regularly using these tools to check that the application performs well and has no concurrency-related bugs. Consider automating these tests, and running them every night.

Chapter Review

This chapter presented a number of best practices to help you create and organize your development environment. The first section covered the necessary hardware and software in a typical development environment and discussed mechanisms for supporting multiple builds and databases in the same environment. Subsequent sections described the proper way to install WebLogic Server in the development environment, configure your working directory structure, establish an Ant-based build process, and choose the proper development tools for your project. The final section discussed unit testing techniques and frameworks to help increase the quality and maintainability of your application code.

These recommendations should provide a strong starting point in the definition of your development environment and development process. Now all you have to do is build the system. Get to it!

15

Production Environment Best Practices

In this chapter, we discuss strategies and best practices for deploying WebLogic Server applications in a production environment. Our discussion focuses on three strategies:

Deployment   Determining the clustering approach, planning the production site configuration, and choosing the number and types of server machines.

Global Traffic Management   Utilizing local and global load balancers.

Production Security   Securing your production environment and production WebLogic Server applications.

Designing, configuring, and running production systems represent complex topics, those far too broad for us to cover in a single chapter. Unfortunately, it is difficult to refer you to other sources because there just aren't that many books written on the topic. Given the limited space available here, we have chosen these three areas of focus because these are the topics that customers frequently ask us about. We hope that this information proves useful to you in making these types of decisions.

Deployment Strategies

In Chapter 13, we discussed performance tuning and testing strategies. In this section, we examine a number of deployment strategies you can use to meet your requirement for a secure, around-the-clock accessible, high-performance, reliable system in the presence of unpredictable usage and changing market conditions. We focus primarily on two areas: selecting the number and size of machines for running the application server and designing your WebLogic Server clusters to meet your availability requirements.

When deploying highly available, high performance systems, we recommend that you follow the guidelines shown here to allow your system to adapt to the ever-changing needs and complexities of enterprise computing:

❑ Choose solutions that are highly available and manageable.

❑ Choose systems that offer performance regardless of load and can scale to meet new requirements.

❑ Make sure that data is available and protected from corruption.

❑ Look at availability from the user's perspective. Understand that data is only one component of availability and all layers of your system must be available and resilient to failures. In most enterprise systems, achieving high availability will mandate providing redundancy at all layers of the system to avoid single points of failure.

By combining these guidelines with the system's business and technical requirements, you can deploy a system that meets your current and future requirements. In the sections that follow we discuss best practices for selecting and designing a robust deployment environment using these guidelines. Before we jump into the strategies, let's think about how to evaluate the different strategies to come to some conclusion about what works best for your particular situation.

Evaluating Deployment Strategies

As with most architectural decisions, the selection of an appropriate production deployment environment involves trade-offs. Business and technical requirements must be understood in order to select the appropriate deployment environment. When trying to determine the appropriate deployment strategy, we recommend the following steps:

1. Map the business requirements into a technical architecture that allows the system to meet these requirements.

2. Using this technical architecture and the application's additional technical requirements, develop the criteria that your deployment architecture must meet.

3. Assemble a cross-functional team to explore the wide range of possible deployment architectures and narrow them down to a few that best meet the deployment architecture criteria.

4. Wherever possible, reuse existing deployment architectures, or pieces of them, to jump-start your selection criteria.

5. Use proof of concept evaluations to verify that the deployment architecture you've selected can meet the most difficult business and technical requirements.

First and foremost, the deployment architecture must meet the requirements of the business now and in the future. Once you understand the business requirements, you can map them to the technical architecture required to support the business. For example, you may have a business requirement to provide 99.9 percent availability where failing to live up to this will result in non-compliance of service-level agreements (SLAs) imposed on the system. This business requirement maps directly to a technical requirement for high availability that requires software, hardware, and network redundancy, as well as failover capabilities.

728

The application itself will have additional technical requirements defined by application user groups, operations, security, and any other group that interacts with or supports the system. By combining all of these requirements, you can develop criteria for the deployment architecture and apply weights to these criteria depending on the importance to your business. Common criteria include performance, manageability, scalability, flexibility, cost, security, administrative complexity, and maintenance. You can evaluate candidate deployment strategies developed in the next step against this weighted matrix of criteria to determine their appropriateness for your business and application.

Next, work with a group of interdisciplinary architects or technical personnel to select a few candidate deployment architectures that are likely to meet the business and technical requirements. Depending on the complexity of the requirements, scope of the deployment, and the group's experience with similar systems, you can evaluate each candidate either on paper or by doing a proof of concept (POC). One common practice is to select the best paper option and then use a POC to prove that the chosen architecture meets your requirements. It may sometimes be possible to combine this effort with pre-production functionality and performance testing of the application.

Your job is easier if an enterprise deployment environment is already in place and available for testing, requiring only a validation that the existing environment can meet the demands of the new system. Often this approach will not be appropriate because hardware, monitoring, and failover solutions are either not in place or have not yet been chosen. In this case, you should identify and develop an end-to-end slice (or portion) of the application that touches every layer of the system to use in testing the various candidate deployment architectures. This slice of the application should include the most challenging parts of the application and test the most challenging or strictest operational requirements. You can then compare these results with the requirements selection matrix.

By performing POC tests and mapping the results against the requirements matrix, you can choose the best deployment architecture with a high level of certainty that it will meet all requirements. Unfortunately, it is not always possible to run your system in the *best* deployment environment. In many cases, you will have to make trade-offs. For example, you may have to deploy a more tightly coupled system than you would like in order to meet your users' performance requirements. Or you may not be able to use the best availability strategy due to cost considerations. These decisions and trade-offs are best made once you clearly understand the requirements of your business and you are able to differentiate these from other selection criteria.

> **Best Practice**
>
> Evaluate deployment strategies by identifying and prioritizing business and technical requirements for the system, then mapping these requirements against candidate deployment strategies. Use proof of concept tests to validate new or unproven designs.

Now, let's look at a number of key strategies that you should consider when designing and selecting the best, or at least the *appropriate*, deployment architecture for your application.

Server Deployment Strategies

The first deployment strategies to consider are the size and type of server hardware to use in your environment, as well as the way to deploy your WebLogic Server applications on this hardware.

Determining the JVM-to-Processor Ratio

One of the most frequently asked questions is how many instances of WebLogic Server to run on a particular piece of hardware; the next is whether it is better to use a few larger SMP machines or more smaller machines. In an ideal world, applications would scale linearly as you add CPUs to the machine so that a single JVM would use all available CPUs and provide maximum performance. In the real world, many factors can contribute to the nonlinear scalability of a Java application, including things such as I/O bottlenecks, garbage collection, cache memory latency, and thread synchronization.

Garbage collection is of particular interest because it can have a dramatic effect on the application. Many older JVM implementations do not support parallel or concurrent garbage collection so the negative effect of garbage collection on performance grows considerably as we add CPUs on multiprocessor servers. For example, an application that spends 10 percent of its time performing single-threaded, stop-the-world garbage collection will lose 75 percent of its throughput on a 32-processor machine, according to testing performed by Sun Microsystems (see Link 15-1 in the online Appendix on the book's web site at `http://www.wrox.com`). Even on a smaller machine having only five CPUs this same application will lose approximately 20 percent of its throughput.

Most newer JVMs have options to enable either parallel or concurrent garbage collection, though these are not typically the default settings. These can make significant improvements in the effects of garbage collection on JVM scalability across processors. Other factors, though, may still prevent you from achieving the level of scalability you need across a large number of processors.

Determining the ideal JVM-to-CPU ratio for a given application is an iterative process that is ideally done when stress testing the application for acceptance testing or capacity planning. On a multi-processor machine, you should start by taking all CPUs offline except one and then tune the system until you achieve maximum throughput for that application on one CPU. This testing will provide the throughput information for one CPU to use as a baseline for determining linear scalability. From there, bring another CPU online and repeat the process. Continue this process until you cannot fully utilize the CPUs on the node or the linear scalability falls below an acceptable point. Remember, you will need to make sure that you have sufficient load to drive the number of CPUs available and that you watch for bottlenecks in other parts of the system. The goal is to determine the optimal number of CPUs for a single WebLogic Server instance. If you fail to achieve acceptable scalability during this testing, explore the possibility of running multiple instances of WebLogic Server on a machine.

Vertical Scaling

Scaling an application by simply adding more CPUs to a machine is often referred to as *vertical scaling*. Application server vendors have borrowed this term and have expanded it to include scaling an application by adding both processors and application server instances to a machine. A WebLogic Server instance consists of an application server running in its own Java Virtual Machine (JVM), so vertical scaling also implies multiple JVMs on the same machine. Vertical scaling can lead to better utilization of the server hardware and increased application throughput. You should balance this increase in utilization and throughput against the added configuration, maintenance, and monitoring overhead associated with running multiple server instances.

Running multiple instances of WebLogic Server on the same machine can also help minimize the effect of nonparallelized, stop-the-world garbage collection. Because multiple JVM instances will typically not all run garbage collection at exactly the same time, this means that you will almost always have at least one JVM available to schedule application-related work on other processors while another JVM does its stop-the-world garbage collection with a single thread. We recommend using the parallel or concurrent garbage collectors available with the Sun HotSpot JVM, or better yet use the Oracle JRockit JVM that selects the most appropriate garbage collection strategy dynamically, at runtime.

Best Practice

Use parallel or generational garbage collectors to limit the scalability effect that garbage collection has on the application. Even then, you may want to explore the performance benefits of running multiple WebLogic Server instances on larger SMP machines. Before formalizing multiple instances per machine as your deployment strategy, make sure that you understand the effect this will have on configuration, maintenance, and monitoring so that you can make an informed decision.

Horizontal Scaling

Scaling an application by simply adding more machines to your environment is often referred to as *horizontal scaling*. Typically, horizontal scaling is more specifically associated with the practice of employing multiple, relatively small server machines (generally four CPUs or fewer) in a production environment. In this scenario, each machine usually hosts a single instance of WebLogic Server and the application itself. Through the use of WebLogic Server clustering or external load balancers, this approach allows WebLogic Server–based applications to span several machines yet still present a single system view to the end users. You can use this strategy not only to increase scalability but also to improve the failover characteristics of your application. It also provides you with the flexibility of adding more machines on demand to handle increasing throughput requirements.

In many cases, you may want to combine horizontal and vertical scaling techniques to use multiple machines, each running multiple instances of WebLogic Server. This can make it easier to achieve both high CPU utilization and good failover and flexibility characteristics.

Best Practice

Horizontal scaling gives you some failover and flexibility that you normally cannot get with only vertical scaling. Depending on your hardware, you might also want to consider combining the two techniques to increase CPU utilization. Whether this makes sense will depend on your hardware, application, and JVM.

Now, we move on to look at single-site deployment strategies.

Single-Site Deployment Strategies

The next set of strategies relates to the deployment of scalable and highly available systems in a single site or data center. We concentrate on clusters that reside in the application server layer of our system, but we consider other layers where appropriate.

Two different scenarios are discussed in the sections that follow. These scenarios reflect different sets of availability requirements:

❑ A simple WebLogic cluster representing basic availability requirements

❑ A complex WebLogic cluster representing more demanding availability requirements

Many other deployment strategies are possible, of course, each offering varying degrees of availability. It is important that you have a firm understanding of your requirements before choosing a strategy from among the many options available. You must also consider your cost structure and current enterprise standards.

For the purpose of this discussion we make the following assumptions:

1. Local clusters are defined as a grouping of two or more servers residing in the same site or data center with WebLogic Server acting as the middleware.

2. Software, hardware, or a combination of software and hardware are utilized to achieve a high level of availability.

3. The minimum configuration involves at least two instances of WebLogic Server running in a cluster with each instance residing on a different server. This configuration allows protection against failure at the both the node level and the WebLogic Server instance level and is a good, basic configuration for discussing local clusters.

4. Load balancers are used to provide message distribution and failover of requests to the cluster of WebLogic Server instances. In all cases, you could configure web servers as proxy servers to perform the same functionality.

5. Components resident in other layers of the system are redundant and provide high availability.

6. We discuss only symmetric hardware configurations, which are also called *active-active* configurations. Asymmetric, or *active-passive*, configurations are also a viable solution. This type of deployment, though, is not typical at the application server level due to its higher cost caused by the use of passive servers.

Simple WebLogic Server Clusters

First, we will consider a simple WebLogic Server cluster, which provides a basic level of high availability. Figure 15-1 shows a simple cluster that provides a simple, cost-effective, and highly available deployment architecture.

This type of configuration is commonly used under the following situations:

❑ A flexible and cost-effective solution is desirable.

❑ There are no disk-sharing requirements across the WebLogic Server cluster.

❑ Local data storage does not require high availability.

❑ The applications do not use, or participate in, XA transactions because the transaction logs will typically require high availability and failover. In certain situations, WebLogic Server's

Last Logging Resource optimization may be an appropriate way to relax this constraint without requiring shared disk because it uses a database table to store all transaction logs.

❑ The applications do not use file-based JMS persistent messages because the JMS message stores will typically require high availability and failover.

Figure 15-1 depicts an active-active cluster running under normal conditions. Both instances of WebLogic Server are used during normal operation, with load balancing at the connection level provided by load-balancer hardware located between the clients and the WebLogic Server cluster.

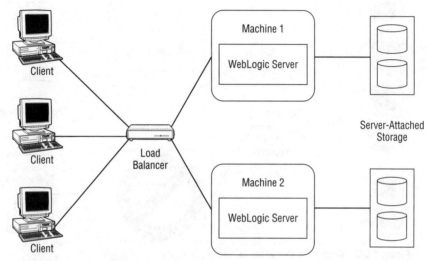

Figure 15-1: Simple cluster before failure.

Figure 15-2 shows the same cluster after a failure of either the WebLogic Server instance or the machine on which it is running.

The load balancer is now providing failover at the connection level, while WebLogic Server clustering software provides a single homogenous system view across both WebLogic Server instances. The key features that WebLogic Server clustering provides are these:

❑ Failover and load balancing of JNDI, RMI, EJB (stateless session beans, stateful session beans with in-memory state replication, and entity beans), and JMS

❑ In-memory `HttpSession` replication

❑ Cluster-wide replication of the JNDI naming service

❑ Cluster membership discovery and cluster health monitoring

❑ Automatic migration of services and servers due to software or hardware failures.

When a failure takes place on either the WebLogic Server instance or the hosting node itself, the load balancer quickly notices that the WebLogic Server listen port is no longer responding to requests. The load balancer then removes that failed server from its list of healthy servers and begins routing all requests to a different, healthy WebLogic Server instance. This failure detection can be achieved in a more intelligent manner by having the load balancer periodically check the health of the WebLogic Server instance using the `weblogic.Admin PING` command, or by making standard HTTP requests for a small static HTML page that just returns OK. If you choose this latter approach, you might even use a JSP to create this HTML page so that it is loaded into memory once, thus minimizing the overhead on the server. Once the WebLogic Server instance is back up and listening on the appropriate port, the load balancer will discover this fact and will once again start distributing requests to that WebLogic Server instance. Refer to Chapter 12 for more detailed information on WebLogic Server clustering.

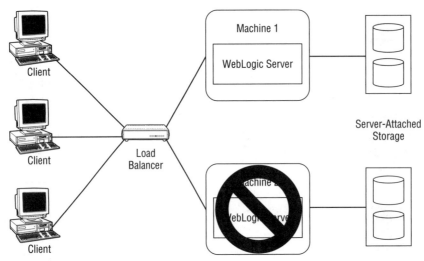

Figure 15-2: Simple cluster after failure.

This simple clustering configuration is a form of horizontal scaling, discussed earlier, in which additional nodes are added to the environment to increase processing capability. When horizontal scaling is used in conjunction with WebLogic Server clustering, it offers a cost-effective method to achieve both flexibility and availability. Servers can be added to the cluster dynamically; once the new WebLogic Server is added to the distribution list of the load balancer, traffic will begin routing to the new instance. If a server fails, the remaining servers will take over the load for the failed server until it can be restarted, thus allowing better utilization of hardware than an active-passive configuration.

> **Tip to Remember**
>
> A simple WebLogic Server cluster is an appropriate strategy for a single-site installation, providing good scalability and failover characteristics.

Complex WebLogic Server Clusters

The second scenario we consider has more demanding availability requirements, such as the following:

❑ The system must support global transactions between local and distributed resources such as JMS destinations and databases.

❑   JMS messages are persisted to the file system and must support failover and be highly available.

❑   Failover of both the node and any WebLogic Server instance-specific functionality, such as JMS destinations and JTA transaction recovery, must take place transparently.

❑   Distributed transactions must be recoverable and restarted in case of node or WebLogic Server failure.

Figure 15-3 presents one possible solution to these more demanding requirements. This solution would utilize the following components:

❑   WebLogic Server instances running in a standard WebLogic Server cluster.

❑   Redundant load balancers (not shown in the figure), which provide load balancing and failover of requests at the connection level.

❑   WebLogic JMS using multiple distributed destinations, providing high availability to both JMS producers and consumers.

❑   Veritas Cluster Server (VCS) or an equivalent product to provide transparent failover across nodes in the hardware cluster. VCS will manage and control both hardware and software resources, bringing resources online and taking them back offline when necessary.

❑   Some type of network- or server-attached storage solution to provide highly available shared disks for JMS queue storage.

❑   Veritas or another highly available file system for high performance and flexible volume management.

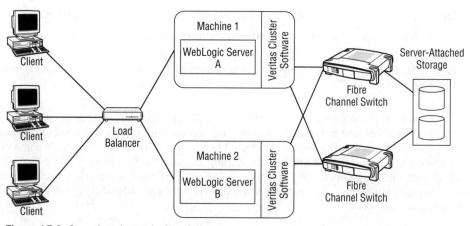

Figure 15-3: Complex cluster before failure.

Should one of the WebLogic Server instances fail, the VCS system will automatically migrate the instance to the other hardware, as depicted in Figure 15-4.

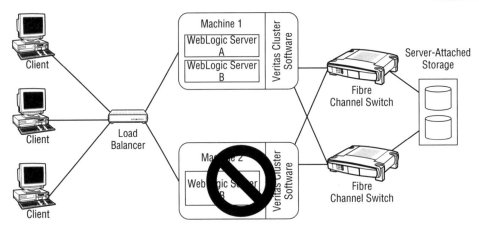

Figure 15-4: Complex cluster after failure.

As noted previously, Veritas Cluster Servers are being used to monitor and control applications running in the configuration, and these clusters respond to a variety of hardware and software faults. Because VCS will be managing and controlling the WebLogic Server cluster, you will need to produce various scripts and determine what type of health monitoring is required. This discussion concentrates on scripts and monitoring of WebLogic Server only, although VCS is actually monitoring and controlling other resources such as IP addresses, disks, and network-interface cards. See the Veritas Cluster Server documentation for a complete description of these activities. Minimally, you will need to develop the following scripts:

Start Scripts   Scripts that start the administrative server as well as all managed servers running in the WebLogic Server cluster.

Stop Scripts   Scripts used to shut down WebLogic Server administrative and managed servers.

Forced Stop Scripts   Scripts that shut down WebLogic Server instances that are not responding to administrative shutdown commands.

Health Monitoring Scripts   Scripts used to determine the health of various subsystems in WebLogic Server.

VCS will use an *agent* to monitor and control the WebLogic Server resources. This agent will start the servers, stop the servers, and fail over the servers after a node failure. You will need to determine the appropriate response when a failure is detected in any monitored resources. We recommend a tiered availability approach concentrated on keeping the active server as available as possible and failing over the cluster only when it cannot be restarted. This approach relies primarily on WebLogic Server's clustering infrastructure and fails over only after a hard failure of a disk, node, or non-redundant device.

You will also need to determine which failures should be handled automatically and which should only be reported so that manual action can be taken. In this scenario, the VCS agent will either perform the appropriate action itself or will propagate the information to a person through a page or send the alert itself to an enterprise monitoring console that will either take action itself or pass the alert to the appropriate personnel.

With our example scenario, no JTA or JMS migration is required during failover. The instances running on a failed VCS node will be migrated by VCS and then brought back online on the targeted node. The instance will come up and start processing just as it would when restarted locally. We should note that this is only one possible approach. We could just as easily have VCS migrate the JMS servers and JTA recovery service from the failed WebLogic Server instance to the other instance running on the other node.

> **Best Practice**
>
> A complex WebLogic Server cluster will cost more than a simple cluster and require additional configuration and testing, but it is appropriate if your installation requires higher levels of availability.

In our solution, we use Veritas Cluster Server because it provides a framework to integrate monitoring and failover of any number of hardware and software resources. However, WebLogic Server also provides two lower-cost options that will typically meet our needs when only failing over WebLogic Server–based resources: service migration and whole server migration.

Manual service migration has been around in WebLogic for a number of releases. It allows you to invoke administrative commands that tell WebLogic Server to migrate JMS servers and JTA transaction managers from one WebLogic Server instance to another. Today, WebLogic Server also supports automatic migration of JMS and JTA services, as well as application-defined singleton services.

Whole server migration provides a framework by which a WebLogic Server cluster will detect the death of a machine and restart the failed WebLogic Server instance on another machine. The framework migrates the virtual IP address of the failed machine to the new machine as part of migrating the WebLogic Server instance.

Although these frameworks only focus on WebLogic Server migration, the gaining popularity of technologies like network-attached storage and Oracle RAC databases significantly reduces the need for larger HA frameworks in many HA architectures. Please see the "WebLogic Server Failures" section of Chapter 12 for a more complete discussion of these capabilities.

Multiple Site Deployment Strategies

Multiple site deployment strategies are often discussed in the context of a continuous business paradigm, combining high-availability solutions with advanced disaster recovery techniques. The ultimate goal is to be able to manage both planned and unplanned outages with minimal disruption. These strategies allow continuous availability during failures as well as software and hardware migration without affecting availability. A complete discussion of this topic is beyond the scope of this chapter, so we limit our discussion to key concepts and examine some configuration options.

Even though local clusters, in which all of the nodes and storage subsystems are in a single data center, offer good protection against smaller disasters such as single node failures or disk crashes, they do not protect against major disasters that could destroy or damage the entire facility. To protect against these kinds of failures you need to make sure that the cluster components are geographically dispersed. Whereas most local clusters are designed around a shared disk-storage architecture where storage resources are either physically connected to all nodes via SCSI or Fibre Channel or connected directly to the network, multi-site clusters usually rely on some type of replicated data architecture.

Designing Multiple-Site WebLogic Clusters

Including WebLogic Server applications in the design of a multi-site cluster is fairly straightforward as long as you ensure that the associated data is properly replicated to all data centers. It becomes more complicated when file-based JMS is used in a distributed transaction environment with multiple resources involved in a two-phase commit transaction (2PC) due to the exactly once nature of these services.

Additional design considerations covered in this section include the following:

❑ Active-passive or active-active cluster design

❑ HttpSession state management and replication

❑ Transaction collocation requirements

❑ Data replication

Cluster Design Options

It is possible to use both active-active and active-passive clusters with WebLogic Server applications. We recommend that you follow the same design that you used for your data-replication solution. For example, if the data replication between the two data centers is bidirectional, then an active-active design of your WebLogic Server applications may be desirable. If data replication is unidirectional, however, it may force you to stick with an active-passive design.

Session Replication

Managing and replicating HttpSession state is a major consideration for most WebLogic Server applications and has been discussed at length in earlier chapters. It tends to be less important in the design of the overall multiple site cluster, however, because the loss of HttpSession data in the event of a data-center loss is often acceptable to the business. If the loss of HttpSession data is not acceptable, several options exist, depending on your situation.

As with all disaster recovery and high availability planning, we recommend that you begin by first examining business requirements and then applying the proper deployment strategy that will meet the requirements. All data is not created equal, and it is likely that only a portion of application data is critical to the basic operation of the application.

Now, let's look at the options for handling HttpSession data replication across data centers. As discussed in Chapter 13, you should never use the HttpSession to store data that you cannot afford to lose. Even so, business requirements may still make losing all user session data during a data center failure undesirable. WebLogic Server provides four possible options for replicating HttpSession data across data centers.

JDBC-Based Session Persistence   WebLogic Server supports a JDBC-based session persistence mechanism that stores the HttpSession data in a database. Storing the session data in the database allows it to be replicated between data centers using your existing database replication technology.

Single Cluster In-Memory Replication   As described in previous chapters, the most popular form of session persistence is in-memory replication. In certain situations, it is possible to create a single cluster that spans two data centers. WebLogic Server uses a primary-secondary replication scheme. To ensure that the primary and secondary are in different data centers, you will typically need to define replication groups. However, some limitations are imposed by this approach; see the "Implementing Clusters That Span Multiple Sites" section later in this chapter for more details.

Cross-Cluster In-Memory Replication   Starting in WebLogic Server 9.0, WebLogic Server supports in-memory replication between clusters; this feature is known as MAN replication in the WebLogic Server documentation. Essentially, it gives applications deployed in two different data centers the ability to keep the primary and secondary copies of the `HttpSession` objects in two different data centers, each running in a different cluster. This eliminates many of the limitations of implementing a single cluster across sites. However, you still need low network latency between data centers to prevent performance and scalability limitations due to the synchronous nature of the replication that happens as part of processing each request.

Cross-Cluster Database-Backed Replication   WebLogic Server 9.0 also introduced support for a feature known as WAN replication in the WebLogic Server documentation. In addition to providing in-memory replication within the local cluster, it provides an asynchronous replication of session data between data centers. Rather than the replication happening during normal request processing, WebLogic Server sends the session data to the remote cluster asynchronously, either by writing to a local database that uses third-party database replication to push the data to the remote data center or by batching RMI calls to the remote cluster, which writes the data to its local database.

It is possible to use a single cluster with in-memory replication across sites. The primary issue is network bandwidth and latency, not only for the replication itself but also for the UDP traffic needed for JNDI replications and cluster membership and monitoring. If using multicast-based clusters, this means that you really need complete control over the link between the sites because most Internet and ISP routers are not configured to forward multicast packets. With unicast-based clustering, this generally isn't an issue. Nevertheless, we have found that if your connection between the data centers has a tendency to lose packets or the latency is over a few hundred milliseconds, this can cause problems with WebLogic Server's clustering mechanisms. With in-memory replication, even a latency of a few hundred milliseconds can have a significant impact on application response times and scalability.

We recommend not clustering between data centers if you can avoid it. When data centers are within the same metropolitan area, WebLogic Server can use synchronous in-memory session replication between two clusters running in different data centers. Though this requires some additional configuration, the mechanism is essentially the same as intra-cluster in-memory replication. Just make sure you have sufficient network bandwidth and low latency to prevent this cross-site replication from becoming a performance bottleneck in your applications.

With geographically distributed data centers where the network bandwidth between the data centers is generally lower and latency generally higher, WebLogic Server supports database-back, asynchronous session replication between data centers. We urge you to carefully weigh the benefits of this option before selecting it as your session replication strategy.

One big advantage of the normal synchronous in-memory replication technique is that it completes the replication before returning the response to the browser. This means that if the primary server were to fail immediately afterwards, the browser would failover to the other server transparently because the other server would have the expected session state. The same is not necessarily true for WAN replication because it is asynchronous. Because the remote updates are performed asynchronously, a data center failure will cause some of your clients to failover only to find stale session state because their latest changes did not get replicated before the data center failure occurred.

As web application programmers, we have no way of knowing when the session data is stale without creating a mechanism to detect this in the application itself. In the worst case, this stale data might cause your web application to fail if the target URL expects to find some session data that is not there. It is possible to come up with web application designs that are more resilient to this sort of anomaly. For example, if you have a multiple forms flow, you might store some identifier in the session to indicate the last form's data that the session contains and transparently redirect the user to the point in the flow reflected by the session. Though a user would likely find it annoying to fill out the same form again, this is certainly better than starting over because of an error that invalidates the session. Frankly, it isn't clear to us that the potential performance gain of WAN replication is worth the added complexity for all applications. Carefully consider your application requirements and choose the appropriate model that best fits your requirements while minimizing complexity.

> ### Best Practice
> Prefer architectures that do not require using WebLogic Server clusters that span data centers. If you do need to support HttpSession failover between data centers, consider using WebLogic Server MAN clustering, where practical. Where MAN replication is not practical, weigh the benefits of WAN replication versus straight JDBC-based persistence in conjunction with your existing data replication technology.

Transaction Collocation Requirements

Your multiple site design should also consider that the application may use certain WebLogic Server services, such as JMS servers and JTA transaction recovery services, which are designed with the assumption that there is only one active instance of the service running in a cluster at any given time. You need to be able migrate the data associated with these services, data that is usually critical for the normal operation of the applications. Additionally, to take advantage of WebLogic Server transaction collocation optimization, it is also desired that all such operations from a specific user be directed to the same data center.

Data Replication

Finally, to provide data center failover capabilities, your design needs to ensure that all *critical* data is replicated to the secondary data center where the services will be restored in the event of primary data center failure. To determine the data-replication requirements, start with the following items:

❏ Domain configuration data stored in the $DOMAIN_HOME/config directory

❏ JTA transaction logs, usually located in the server's default persistent store directory — for example, for a server named Server1, the default persistent store resides in the servers/Server1/data/store/default directory underneath the domain's root directory

❏ JMS persistent messages, which can be stored in an RDBMS or the file system, if applicable — for example, for a server named Server1, the default location for a custom persistent file store is the `servers/Server1/data/store/<file_store_name>` directory underneath the domain's root directory

❑ Data associated with the application business logic, usually stored in an RDBMS

You need to identify the items that must be available at the secondary data center to restart your application and recover all critical data, messages, and transactions.

Implementing Clusters That Span Multiple Sites

Implementing a multiple site WebLogic Server cluster requires reliable, high-speed networking technologies to support the cluster-wide communication used to monitor cluster members and replicate `HttpSession` contents, JNDI naming service information, and other application-level data. This is usually done in a campus cluster where great distances do not separate the cluster nodes.

In the past, one of the primary reasons for considering a single cluster that spans data centers is to achieve cross-data center `HttpSession` in-memory replication. The addition of MAN replication provides a more desirable alternative if the only requirement is session replication across data centers. Even so, there might be other reasons for considering a single cluster across multiple sites. Before settling on this architecture, you should consider the drawbacks to this approach, which include the following:

Network Latency, Bandwidth, and Reliability   As discussed previously, WebLogic Server clustering relies heavily on good, fast, and reliable intra-cluster communication. In addition to in-memory `HttpSession` replication traffic, all JNDI and cluster heartbeat messages will need to traverse the inter-data center network link. Low latency and sufficient bandwidth is critical to proper cluster functionality and good performance. To minimize potential problems, you must ensure reliable connectivity between data centers — this implies redundant network links that are unlikely to go down at the same time.

Inter-Data Center Network Configuration   WebLogic Server clusters use two styles of communication between servers in the cluster. JNDI replication and cluster heartbeat messages use either TCP unicast or UDP multicast messages. Except for a few optional multicast-based features like JMS message multicast delivery, all other server-to-server communication uses normal TCP/IP socket-based protocols like T3. As such, the network links between the data centers must support sending WebLogic Server cluster-related messages between data centers; typically this is only an issue for multicast messages because most network administrators do not allow multicast message forwarding across subnets. Additionally, any firewalls between the data centers will need to allow server-to-server T3 communication.

Highly Available Shared Storage Requirements   As we discussed earlier, certain types of applications may require shared disk access to provide failover when a WebLogic Server node fails. Providing shared disks across data centers typically implies either low-level disk replication (for example, EMC's SRDF) or storage-area network technology.

WebLogic Server Web Server Plug-in Considerations   When using a multi-site cluster, you typically want to process requests that enter one data center inside that data center and not have request processing traversing the inter-data center network link. Because your network administrator must configure each data center's local hardware load balancers, the local load balancer can easily route to only cluster nodes in the local data center. With the web server plug-ins, the plug-in is preconfigured, but they normally update their cluster membership list with data returned by the

WebLogic Server cluster. This causes a problem because now the plug-in will try to load balance requests across both data centers instead of just the local one, putting more load and stress on the network channel between the data centers. You can turn off the plug-in's dynamic configuration update feature by setting `DynamicServerList` to `OFF` in the plug-in configuration; however, this means that the plug-in cannot react to server failures as quickly or elegantly.

Single Admin Server Dependency   A WebLogic Server cluster is, by definition, part of a single domain; therefore, the domain's admin server manages the entire cluster. Because each domain supports only a single admin server, the admin server will always need to manage nodes in the remote data center. You will also need to enable failing over the admin server to the other data center, in the case where a data center goes off-line because the nodes in the remaining data center will have limited manageability until the admin server comes back up.

Figure 15-5 illustrates a possible configuration for a single WebLogic Server cluster that spans both sites.

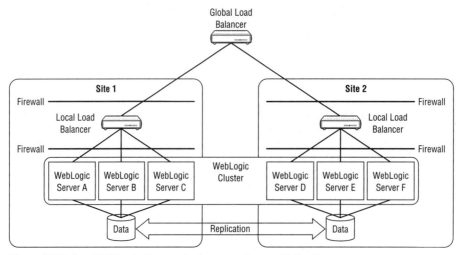

Figure 15-5: One WebLogic Server cluster spanning multiple sites.

To support cross-site `HttpSession` failover properly, you will need to use replication groups to ensure that the `HttpSession` object's primary and secondary copies are in different data centers. Clearly, cross-site session replication adds some latency, but it does provide seamless failure of user sessions in the event of a site failure. All you then need to worry about is the proper replication of application data in the database, JTA transaction logs, and so on. For simplicity, we did not include JMS servers in this design because the exactly once nature makes it more difficult and the appropriate architecture is very dependent on your application's use of JMS and your requirements.

Again, we need to reemphasize the importance of high-speed, reliable, low-latency network connectivity between the sites for this architecture to work successfully. As the distance between the data centers grows, it becomes more difficult and more costly to achieve this type of connectivity. Wherever possible, we strongly recommend that you consider using separate clusters in each data center, the topic of the next section.

> **Best Practice**
>
> Always prefer architectures that do not use a cluster that spans multiple sites. MAN/WAN replication provides cross-site `HttpSession` replication without the challenges imposed by the single cluster approach.

Implementing One Cluster per Site

The previous section described a multiple-site WebLogic Server cluster that used high-speed networking to achieve a single cluster across multiple sites. A single cluster is typically not desirable, however, and this section explores one alternative.

In this alternative design, each site is configured with an independent WebLogic Server cluster. By defining an individual cluster for each site, you immediately eliminate all of the WebLogic Server–specific inter-site communication requirements. Of course, the application may have its own inter-site communication requirements, which will almost certainly include data replication. If it meets your requirements, we believe this multiple cluster design provides a simpler, more flexible architecture while still taking advantage of WebLogic Server clustering features locally in each site. Figure 15-6 illustrates this alternative multiple-site, multiple-cluster design.

When a client first requests the URL for a web application, the global load balancer will route the request to one of the data centers. The local load balancer will then route the request to one of the available servers in the WebLogic Server cluster at that location, and a user session will be created in a primary and secondary server in that cluster. The global and local load balancers remember where they sent the last request for a particular user session and will always attempt to route all subsequent requests from that user to the same data center and server. To accomplish this behavior, you will need to configure the global load balancer using a *static persist* policy and the local load balancer using a *sticky* load balancing algorithm, topics discussed in detail later in this chapter.

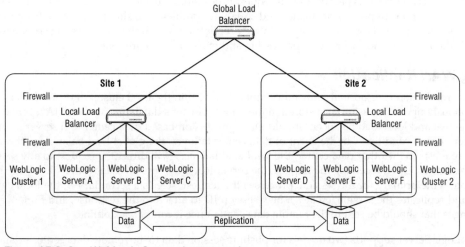

Figure 15-6: One WebLogic Server cluster per site.

When using `HttpSession` replication in a multiple cluster design, you might choose to use normal in-memory replication within the clusters, knowing that data center failover will cause the users to lose their session data. JDBC-based `HttpSession` persistence is another option that enables you to store a user's session in the database and use your normal cross-data center database replication strategy to allow cross-data center failover of user's session data. However, the most interesting options are WebLogic Server's MAN and WAN replication features for replicating session data across clusters.

Using MAN Replication

MAN replication is very similar to normal intra-cluster in-memory replication. WebLogic Server creates the primary session on the server where the user first accesses a page that needs access to the `HttpSession` object. At the end of the request but before the response is returned to the user, the server selects a secondary location on the other cluster, replicates the session data, and encodes location information in the session ID returned with the response. The global load balancer should always redirect requests for that session to the primary data center — the one where the primary copy of the session exists. As usual, the local load balancer uses sticky routing to route the subsequent session requests back to the primary server. When that server fails, the local load balancer redirects the request to another server in its local cluster. That new server reaches out to the secondary server in the other cluster to get a copy of the session data, becomes the new primary server, and generates a new session ID.

If the primary data center fails, the global load balancer directs the request for the session to the other data center and the local load balancer in that data center directs the request to any server in the cluster. When the server receives the request, it reaches out to the secondary server for a copy of the session data, establishes itself as the new primary, picks a new local secondary (assuming that the other data center is still down), and generates a new session ID to return with the response. Once the other data center comes back up, the next request for the session will trigger WebLogic Server to relocate the secondary copy of the session to the other cluster as part of processing the request.

MAN replication gives you all the benefits of in-memory replication within a cluster without the drawbacks of trying to create a single cluster that spans multiple sites. Because the replication is synchronous and done as part of normal request processing, the network bandwidth and latency is important to prevent poor performance and scalability problems. In situations where the network is not sufficient, WebLogic Server offers a WAN replication option that removes the cross-cluster replication from the normal request processing and makes it asynchronous.

Using WAN Replication

WAN replication uses normal in-memory replication within the local cluster and provides asynchronously updated session data stored in the remote cluster's database. As with MAN replication, the global and local load balancers should maintain session-based data center and server affinity under normal conditions. In the event of data center failover, the global load balancer will redirect requests to the other data center; the local load balancer will direct the request to any server in the cluster. Upon receiving the request, the server loads the session data from its local database, becomes the primary for the session, processes the request, selects a secondary in the local cluster and replicates the session, creates a new session ID to attach to the response, and buffers any changes that should be sent to the remote data center once it comes back online.

WebLogic Server supports two models for pushing session data to the remote data center's database. The first model writes the session data to a local database and relies on you to set up database replication between the two data centers using whatever replication technology you desire. Alternatively, WebLogic Server can periodically call out to the remote cluster and push the session data updates via RMI, in which case the remote cluster member receiving the updates writes them to its local database. Regardless of what model you choose, there is a larger window of failure in which updates to session data may be lost if data center failure occurs. When WebLogic Server is pushing the cross-data center updates, the `Session Flush Interval` and `Session Flush Threshold` parameters define the size of the window. When relying on external database replication, the replication technology may increase the size of the window from that defined by your WebLogic Server configuration. See the "Cross-Cluster Replication" section of Chapter 12 for more details.

> ### Best Practice
>
> The multiple-site, multiple-cluster architecture is a very good candidate architecture for applications requiring high availability and good disaster-recovery characteristics.

As we mentioned earlier, applications that use persistent JMS messages or JTA distributed transactions complicate this model. For example, you may need to bring up the JMS server from a failed WebLogic Server instance on another instance, or even another site. Though there are many different ways to use JMS and JTA distributed transactions, the common theme that is usually present is that you need to bring up the JMS server or JTA recovery service from the failed node to process messages or do recovery of the in-flight transactions.

For intra-site failures, typical strategies include either migrating the service to another WebLogic Server instance in the cluster or having another machine bring up the failed instance. For complete site failures, you typically need to have the ability to bring up the entire WebLogic Server cluster at the other site so that it can drain any messages in the JMS persistent stores and recover any in-flight transactions. This is relatively easy to set up provided that you do not need the failed cluster to interact with your users; configuring it to interact with your users is possible, just more difficult.

Unfortunately, space prevents us from going into detailed discussions of the different scenarios. It's time to move on to talk about load balancers and how they work with WebLogic Server.

Global and Local Traffic Management

Global and local load balancers figure prominently in many production environments. Their proper use is the subject of this section. We start with a quick look at some basic configurations that show how load balancers are used in production environments. Next, we discuss using local load balancers with WebLogic Server. We end by discussing the use of global load balancers to load balance and fail over between sites.

Using Load Balancers

As global enterprises have continued to open their systems to new customer channels, system designers have been forced to deal with unpredictable user demands while retaining high performance and high availability. These requirements have driven designers to the use of global and local traffic management devices, or load balancers, to better manage wide area network (WAN) and local area network (LAN) traffic.

Figure 15-7 illustrates a simple example of local traffic management using a set of redundant local load balancers to manage traffic to a cluster of servers.

Figure 15-8 extends this example to global traffic management by adding a global load balancer in front of two identical configurations of servers and local load balancers. Similar configurations were utilized in many of the design strategies discussed in the previous section.

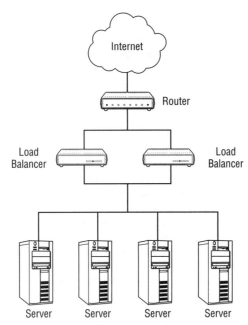

Figure 15-7: Local traffic management using local load balancers.

Many vendors offer these local and global traffic-management devices, including F5, Cisco, and Radware. Although they are commonly called load balancers, most of these devices offer features such as content switching, traffic management, and SSL acceleration in addition to load balancing. You should choose a product that provides at least the following features:

Intercept   The device must be able to intercept the incoming traffic.

Inspect   Once traffic is intercepted it must be inspected to determine its type and how it should be handled. Inspection is performed at different network layers depending on the requirements of the system. Simple inspection is performed at *Layer 4*, one of the seven layers in the ISO Open Systems Interconnection (OSI) Reference Model, and involves IP and port information. For many applications this type of inspection is sufficient to route or transform the message properly. More demanding systems may require inspection of HTTP headers or even the payloads in the packets to handle the traffic properly.

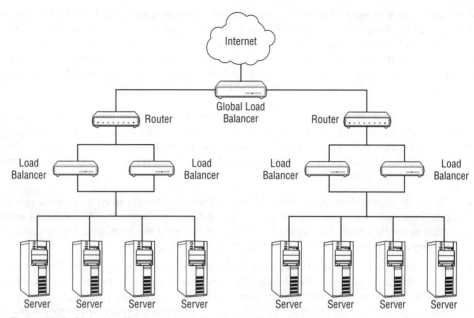

Figure 15-8: Global traffic management using global load balancers.

Transform   The load balancer may be required to transform the traffic in some manner, the simplest example being a change to the destination IP address and port. Advanced transformations can involve re-encryption of traffic, rewriting URL values, or even inserting cookies into HTTP headers.

Direct   The final step involves the actual directing of the traffic to the appropriate resources.

While performing all of these tasks, load balancers must also support multiple IP-based protocols, handle high levels of traffic, and perform very quickly with little overhead. Most load balancers support multiple distribution algorithms, such as round-robin, geography, round-trip time, random, ratio, least connections, application availability, and user-defined quality-of-service (QoS). The simpler algorithms often produce better results. Most commonly used algorithms include round-robin or least connections for local area networks, and user-defined QoS, geography, and application availability for wide area networks and disaster recovery.

Using Local Load Balancers with WebLogic Server

Load balancers can be used to manage traffic to both clustered and non-clustered WebLogic Server instances. Any load balancing algorithms can be used with these configurations, although limitations are associated with certain protocols, SSL support, and stateful HttpSession data.

When using a hardware load balancer with HTTP requests, the load balancer sits in front of the web application and is used to distribute the load across the members of the cluster and provide failover capability. Load balancers present one IP address for all clients and then distribute load to available WebLogic Servers in the cluster.

Load balancers are also used to provide session affinity, routing user requests to the WebLogic Server instance containing the primary copy of that user's session data, a technique known as *sticky* sessions. Once a user establishes a session on a primary server, that user will be pinned to the same WebLogic Server instance for the entire session. As described earlier in the chapter, a failure of the server hosting the primary copy of the user session data will be handled transparently by WebLogic Server using the secondary copy of the session data replicated to another server in the cluster.

If you are using `HttpSession` data with a WebLogic Server cluster, you must use a load balancer that supports a compatible passive or active persistence mechanism, unless you happen to be using JDBC-based session persistence. Even with JDBC-based session persistence, maintaining session affinity has potential performance benefits. The proper configuration for this hardware load balancer depends on the type of persistence you choose:

❑ *Passive cookie persistence* refers to the ability of WebLogic Server to write a cookie containing session information and pass it through the load balancer to the client. The hardware load balancer must be configured to inspect the HTTP header and read the WebLogic Server cookie to route the request to the correct server instance properly.

❑ *Active cookie persistence* exists when the load balancer either creates its own session cookie or overwrites the existing session cookie. The load balancer then examines this cookie to route the request to the proper server instance during subsequent requests. Although active cookie persistence is generally compatible with WebLogic Server, a cluster will work properly only with load balancers that do not modify the WebLogic Server session cookie.

Hardware load balancers can also be used in front of a group of managed servers that are not clustered and do not replicate `HttpSession` data. Traffic will be distributed to the WebLogic Servers according to the load balancing algorithm, and the load balancer will again provide the *sticky* session capability. Should a server instance fail, subsequent requests will be routed to another available managed server. Unless your applications are using JDBC-based session persistence, any session data will be lost. If the session is lost, the user will have to authenticate again and he or she will lose any in-memory state the server was maintaining.

Using Global Load Balancers with WebLogic Server

Unlike local load balancers used for distributing traffic among multiple servers, global load balancers are used to distribute traffic among different sites. Global load balancers can be used with or without clustering software and are often used in conjunction with local load balancers to eliminate single points of failure and route traffic away from poorly performing sites. Global load balancers are also vital for disaster recovery; most products provide policies to ensure that all traffic will be sent to a primary site unless that site is suffering an outage. During an outage, traffic can be manually or automatically routed to a secondary site.

Most global load balancers work by becoming the authoritative DNS server, which means that when a client requests a URL, the query returns the IP address of the global load balancer itself rather than the address of a local load balancer or server. When a client contacts that IP address, the global load balancer then provides the client with the IP address of the data center best suited to serve the request. Global load balancers usually sit outside the LAN and intercept requests before they hit the firewalls at the sites themselves, although configuration options exist for balancing in firewalls as well.

Most global load balancers provide numerous configuration options. For example, the 3-DNS Controller from F5 Networks provides both static and global load balancing policies with various options. In the static mode, connections are distributed according to predefined rules, such as *global availability*, which chooses the server based on the order defined by the administrator, and *static persist*, which ensures that transactions requiring persistence are always routed to same server or data center. *Round-robin* and *return DNS* policies behave like a normal DNS server, whereas *random* and *ratio* modes can be used to do weight-based load balancing. The load balancer also collects various performance metrics that can be used to define dynamic load balancing policies.

Production Security Strategies

In this section, we review some of the key concepts and practices associated with locking down and securing your WebLogic Server installation above and beyond the WebLogic Server and Java EE security topics covered in Chapter 11. First, we review the importance of understanding your application architecture and the potential security threats. We then proceed to discuss firewall and DMZ design, connection filtering, locking down web applications, some miscellaneous security practices, and SSL acceleration approaches.

Understanding Application Data Flow

It's important to first understand the underlying data flow of your application architecture to better define the overall network layout and potential security threats. Once this review is complete you can begin defining and mapping application security requirements to the WebLogic Server Security Service and Java EE security features. As discussed in Chapter 11 and depicted in Figure 11-1, two general types of clients will be calling into the server: Web, or *thin*, clients and application, or *fat*, clients.

The first client type is the thin client, typically a browser or other web services client. Thin clients may call in to the application via the HTTP protocol using direct connections with the WebLogic Server or through a web server running a WebLogic Server proxy plug-in component. Thin clients normally call web application components and web services in the server's servlet engine.

The second client type is the fat client, or application client. Fat clients may use the HTTP, T3, IIOP, or COM protocols to call directly into the server, invoking web application components, web services, EJB components, or JMS services in the server. Both thin- and fat-client calls can be routed through a single firewall or a set of firewalls for security. We talk about suggested firewall layouts later in this section.

To define the specific security threats, also known as the *threat model*, you need to define both *what* you are protecting and *who* you are protecting it from. Once you have identified all of the client types and request paths for your application, you should then identify the data and operations on the server that they will be accessing and the required security for those resources. The security requirement could be as simple as requiring only SSL connections for all authentication or as complex as requiring an X.509 client certificate signed by a specific certificate authority for access. Consider each type of operation or data that will be used by clients and the ramifications if that resource were compromised in some way. Once you understand the security requirements for the server-side data and operations, the various clients, and the network types they will use, you have defined your threat model.

Tip to Remember

One assumption we make in this discussion is the security of the underlying machine on which WebLogic Server runs. The physical security of the machine, the operating system, the user accounts on the machine, and other programs running on the machine, are critical to good security and should be thought through meticulously.

Understanding Firewall Layouts

Firewalls provide a high level of security from untrusted traffic if used and configured properly. In this section, we discuss the positives and negatives of some of the common firewall layouts used to separate corporate resources from the Internet and provide a layered security approach. The specific firewall used in this discussion could be any of the major firewall types. The most basic firewall is a stateless, packet-filtering firewall that performs network address translation (NAT). You can also use the more complex, stateful, packet-inspection firewalls if circumstances warrant their use. Regardless of type, by grouping our network layout in firewalls, we define specific, contiguous regions of a network that operate under a single, uniform security policy.

Another important point about using NAT firewalls is that you need to configure your WebLogic Server instances to be aware of the external addresses that the clients use to contact WebLogic Server. See Chapter 12 for a thorough discussion of this topic.

The simplest and most common firewall layout is a single perimeter firewall protecting the entire application from the untrusted zone, a configuration depicted in Figure 15-9. This untrusted zone might be the Internet, your company's extranet, or even anything outside your data center. This layout is typical of a small enterprise or division. The disadvantage of a single firewall is the lack of a layered approach to security — a single implementation flaw or configuration error in the firewall can lead to a complete loss of security.

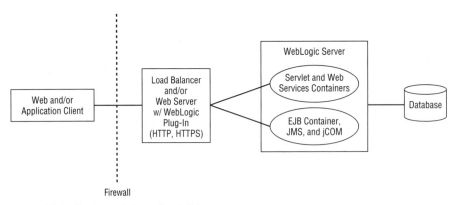

Figure 15-9: Single perimeter firewall layout.

Some corporate security policies can be very strict and may require several well-defined network regions, commonly referred to as *demilitarized zones* (DMZs), having their own security policies. The concept is simple: Putting servers or network appliances, with or without application code, in the DMZ limits your overall security exposure if the machines in that area were somehow compromised. A DMZ could include anything from only a router or hardware load balancer to the entire application; in the latter case, the application has a lower level of protection than other corporate resources not in the DMZ. Typically, the DMZ contains only a hardware load balancer or web servers configured with a WebLogic Server web server plug-in. Figure 15-10 shows a conceptual overview one of the most common configurations.

Of course, we have barely scratched the surface of what is possible with firewall configuration. Most companies have their own policies about how the network should be laid out. Therefore, we will move on to talk about connection filters.

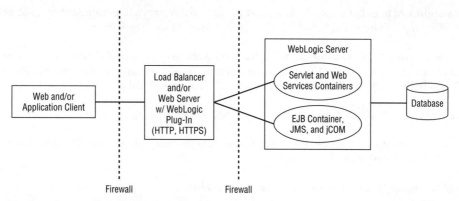

Figure 15-10: Typical DMZ firewall layout.

Using a Connection Filter

One of the first rules of security is to refuse connections from unknown or untrusted sources, denying these sources any foothold in the environment. *Connection filters* are a powerful way to control the types of connections that can access your WebLogic Server instances. Both software- and hardware-based firewalls offer the ability to restrict access to IP/port combinations based on the requestor's IP address, the protocol being used, and so on. For example, many Linux distributions include the iptables software-based firewall that allows you to define connection filters.

WebLogic Server also provides a connection filtering facility that allows you to specify what types of connections your WebLogic Server instances will accept, providing a programmatic control over every new connection with the server. You can configure a WebLogic Server connection filter in two primary ways: use the built-in connection filter in WebLogic Server or write a custom implementation of the ConnectionFilter interface.

WebLogic Server's Built-In Connection Filter

The first and easiest way to filter connections uses WebLogic Server's built-in connection filter facility. You can enable and configure this facility using the domain's Security Filter tab in the WebLogic Console by defining rules that govern the types and sources of network connections to be accepted or denied. By default, no rules are defined in the built-in connection filter, so all connections are accepted. Rules are very specific in format, and ordering is also very important. The first matching rule wins, even if another rule further down contradicts it. Because performance can also be a concern, place more general rules at the top of the list to allow most new connections to be identified quickly and allowed or denied.

To use the default connection filtering, simply set the Connection Filter field's value to weblogic.security.net.ConnectionFilterImpl and define the appropriate rules. Each rule is defined using the following syntax:

```
target localAddress localPort action [protocols]+
```

The target parameter defines the source IP address, including any subnet mask, to be filtered; the localAddress and localPort parameters define the WebLogic Server IP address and port for this rule, making it possible to filter connections on some network channels and not on others. You must set the

751

`action` argument to either `allow` or `deny`, and the optional `protocols` parameters must be one or more of the following values: `http`, `https`, `t3`, `t3s`, `ldap`, `ldaps`, `iiop`, `iiops`, or `com`.

Let's look at a couple of examples. Imagine that you want to deny access to any port on your WebLogic Server listening on 216.148.48.51 from anyone using an IP address that starts with 192.168 for both the HTTP and IIOP protocols. The following entry would accomplish this:

```
192.168.0.0/255.255.0.0 216.148.48.51 * deny http iiop
```

While our entry using the subnet mask is fine, the best practice is to use the Classless Inter-Domain Routing (CIDR) notation, as shown here.

```
192.168.0.0/16 216.148.48.51 * deny http iiop
```

You can also block access specifically to port 7001 on your site to anyone trying to access the site from any host in the baddomain.com domain. The following entry accomplishes this by denying access regardless of the protocol:

```
*.baddomain.com * 7001 deny
```

Note that this rule requires a runtime DNS lookup to evaluate the rule properly for each network connection attempt, potentially creating a performance problem. Try to use IP addresses rather than domain names whenever possible.

This rule-based technique for configuring the connection filter provides significant flexibility. By combining `allow` and `deny` rules, you can configure the connection filter to refuse connections of certain types, perhaps `http` or `t3`, from all external IP addresses while allowing these connections from other servers in the cluster, web servers, or hosts in the corporate LAN subnet.

Custom Connection Filters

The second way to filter connections involves writing a custom implementation of the `weblogic.security.net.ConnectionFilter` interface and configuring WebLogic Server to use this filter rather than the built-in connection filter. Your custom implementation class will receive a `ConnectionEvent` object via the `accept()` callback method whenever a new connection attempt takes place. This `ConnectionEvent` object contains information regarding the inbound connection, including the remote address and port, the local address and port, and the protocol. Your implementation of the `accept()` method should interrogate this object and determine whether to accept the connection, returning from the method without an exception if the connection should be accepted and raising a `FilterException` if the connection should be refused.

What follows is an example implementation of the `ConnectionFilter` interface that accepts all connections from the IP address 127.0.0.1 but refuses all other connection attempts:

```
class SimpleConnectionFilter implements ConnectionFilter
{
    public void accept(ConnectionEvent event)
        throws FilterException
    {
        String target =
            event.getRemoteAddress().getHostAddress();
```

```
            if (! "127.0.0.1".equals(target))
                throw FilterException("Connection refused!");
        }
    }
```

Locking Down Web Applications

Several security considerations related to web applications are not obvious and can lead to confusion if not understood. This section supplements the general security information in Chapter 11 with some additional topics related to web applications.

Access Control Checks during Server-Side Forwards

A web application deployed on WebLogic Server will restrict access to specific pages and resources based on the various `<security-constraint>` elements defined in its `web.xml` deployment descriptor. If the web application sends an HTTP *redirect* to the client with a new resource URL, the client will send a new request to the server for the new URL. This second request will be required to pass any access control checks using the same `<security-constraint>` elements in the deployment descriptor.

If the web application does a server-side *forward* to a new resource URL, however, the client is never involved and no second request is made and checked against the security constraints. The same HTTP request is simply moved on to the next resource on the server side, evading a full access control check. In many web applications, this is fine because the web application development teams understand the access restrictions in place for, and forwarding mechanisms used by, various parts of their application. However, you should be aware that server-side forwarding will not, by default, check authorization to access the target resource. This means that applications that use server-side forwarding can unknowingly create backdoors to allow unauthorized users to access protected resources.

You can configure the web application to perform a full access control check for all server-side forwarding using the `<check-auth-on-forward>` element in the WebLogic Server–specific `weblogic.xml` deployment descriptor:

```
<weblogic-web-app>
  <container-descriptor>
    <check-auth-on-forward/>
  </container-descriptor>
  ...
</weblogic-web-app>
```

Oracle recommends that you not use this mechanism and instead rely on proper application design and security auditing. Though we agree with this recommendation, we felt compelled to point out this potential security hole and a mechanism to prevent it.

Session ID Cookies Safety

Web applications that run over both secure (HTTPS) and insecure (HTTP) sockets must be designed very carefully to avoid compromising the session ID stored in the cookie. Recalling previous discussions in Chapter 1 and elsewhere, the cookie is a token that is generated on the server and sent to the browser client for the purposes of identifying that browser session during subsequent HTTP requests. The browser will resend the cookie with every subsequent request it makes to that domain, and the server will identify the client by the uniquely generated session ID contained in the cookie. In other words, if the browser has authenticated itself, either via FORM or BASIC HTTP authentication, the session ID in the cookie serves as the only information the server needs for proof of the client's identity.

The problem is that if a user begins accessing a web application over a plain text, or insecure, socket, the cookie and the session ID in it are sent in plain text in the HTTP headers. This scenario is very common, and it could represent something like a catalog and shopping cart area in an e-commerce site where it is perfectly acceptable to begin the session over plain text because no private information is being sent over the wire.

The real security problem occurs if the web application later switches to a secure socket and allows the same cookie and session ID to be used during secure operation, the default behavior of a web application. Continuing the e-commerce example, the site might switch to secure mode once a shopping cart is full and the user must log in or provide credit card information to complete the transaction. This new user information and authentication context is still associated with the original session ID and cookie transmitted over plain text even though the secure protocol was used to perform the subsequent authentication or data gathering steps. This is obviously a major concern because anyone who *sniffed*, or intercepted, the original session ID from the plain text socket cookie can now impersonate the newly authenticated user with it, perhaps gaining access to user information or the data gathered during the secure communication. Note that the problem described here is nothing specific to WebLogic Server, but rather a problem in the way secure and insecure HTTP communication is used in typical web applications.

Fortunately, WebLogic Server by default uses a separate secure cookie for HTTPS access. All HTTP requests continue to use the standard JSESSIONID cookie. Any HTTPS requests use a new _WL_AUTHCOOKIE_JSESSIONID cookie that is never transmitted over HTTP. A user that starts by accessing the web application via HTTP will obtain and continue to use the JSESSIONID as normal, with all subsequent requests being treated as authenticated by the session ID. Upon first access to an HTTPS resource, the user must re-authenticate to obtain the _WL_AUTHCOOKIE_JSESSIONID cookie. This is the default behavior starting in WebLogic Server 8.1 SP1. See Link 15-2 for more information.

Examining Other Security Considerations

This section offers additional recommendations and best practices for locking down various parts of a WebLogic Server installation. These include the following:

Use Separate Development and Production Systems   This eliminates any inconveniences associated with production environment security during application development and early stage testing. Areas such as the physical security of the machine, the operating system, the user accounts on the machine, and other programs running on the machine should all be as secure as you can make them. Having separate environments and a specific transfer audit will significantly reduce the risks of improper installation often associated with vulnerabilities.

Precompile All Java Server Pages (JSPs) on the Production System   Some corporate security policies do not allow any source code on live systems. By using the weblogic.jspc or weblogic.appc utilities to precompile all JSPs into the web application's WEB-INF/classes directory, you not only improve the initial response time of the web application but also have a cleaner security audit. To totally eliminate the need for JSP source files on your production system, precompile all of your JSPs and use the WebLogic Server–supplied JspClassServlet instead of the default `JspServlet`. By using the `JspClassServlet`, WebLogic Server will no longer look for the JSP source files.

Use JSP Comments Rather Than HTML Comments   Also consider using only JSP comments in your JSP code, because the JSP comments are removed from the final class at compile time whereas HTML comments are sent to the client and may provide internal implementation details.

Use SSL/TLS Whenever Possible   Though it is certainly true that the performance of SSL is not as good as a plain text socket, the security benefit cannot be overlooked. SSL is a top-heavy protocol. The initial handshake, which uses asymmetric cryptography, is the real performance bottleneck. After the handshake is complete a shared secret exists, and better performing symmetric cryptography is used. This is why it is important to understand SSL session resumption, a technique that allows an SSL client to remember specific SSL session information for reuse when connecting back to an SSL server. The client will then be able to present its SSL session information to the server and skip the expensive SSL handshake.

Using Two-Way SSL Can Prevent Man-in-the-Middle Attacks   If possible, distribute client certificates and set up the server to verify them. By telling the server which certificate authority to use, you know precisely what SSL clients are connecting to the server. This is commonly called a public key infrastructure (PKI). Though some significant management concerns are associated with PKI, the authentication is very secure and could be worth the management and configuration investment.

Modify the Timeout and Maximum Size Values for the Incoming Protocol Ports on the Server to Prevent Denial-of-Service Attacks   The values for some of the main server protocols of T3, HTTP, COM, and IIOP can be adjusted via the server's `Protocols` tab in the WebLogic Console. The settings are located in the `General` and `HTTP` subtabs. The default timeouts are typically acceptable, but the default maximum message size should likely be lowered, subject to the needs of your business applications.

Understand the User Password Lockouts   The default user password lockout values are probably fine, but looking them over is always a good idea. This configuration resides in the security realm's `User Lockout Configuration` tab in the WebLogic Console. If a user does become locked out, you can manually unlock the account before the lockout time is up using the domain's `Unlock User Security` tab.

Use the Underlying Operating System File System Security to Protect the Various Applications and Libraries of the WebLogic Server   Though we have already recommended running with a secure and audited operating system on your production environment, you can also gain superior protection for the applications by using the file system security. Adjusting the ownership of the applications directory for access only by the user account that runs the server can be very helpful, and never install or run your WebLogic Server software as *root*. If you need to bind to a privileged port, make sure to configure the server to switch to a non-privileged user using the machine's `General Configuration` tab in the WebLogic Console.

Use External System Security Facilities When Possible   When connecting to a database from the WebLogic Server, you should specify a username and credential to use. By locking down the database to that specific user, you have reduced the threat against the database significantly. Using a firewall around the database will also limit the threat. The same recommendations hold true for any type of external system we might use from the WebLogic Server. Many backend EIS systems have credentials applied via the Credential Mapper in the WebLogic Server security framework.

Audit the WebLogic Server Log File Often   By routinely monitoring the WebLogic Server system log and the security audit log, you will become familiar with normal operation and be able to identify abnormal use more readily. Without a baseline to compare against, the usefulness of the log files and audit trails is greatly reduced. You might also consider using the audit provider in the security framework as a non-repudiation framework, useful in case an attack succeeds and legal proof of identity is required.

Have a Security Audit Performed by an Internal or External Auditing Group   This can help catch security flaws overlooked in the design, implementation, or deployment of an application. An audit can also qualify the current application deployment and help develop a longer-term security policy for your group or company.

Oracle has an email notification list for vulnerabilities found on the WebLogic Server platform. Email notifications contain information on the vulnerability as well as patching information. This is extremely valuable information for any WebLogic Server production system. You can find more information online at Link 15-3 .

Using SSL Hardware Acceleration

There are at least two good ways to increase your server's SSL performance:

❑   Use a load balancer with built-in SSL support.

❑   Run WebLogic Server on a machine having SSL hardware via the Java Cryptography Extension (JCE).

The first technique uses an external load balancer to handle the SSL. In this solution, the SSL socket is between the client and the load balancer, and all encryption and decryption take place on the load balancer's specialized hardware. The load balancer then uses the plain text HTTP cookie in the decrypted socket to associate the session with a specific standalone server or a server in a cluster. This feature of load balancers is called *SSL persistence*, and many load balancers, such as Nortel and F5, incorporate it in their product offerings.

The second way to accelerate SSL with hardware is via the Java Cryptography Extension (JCE). The Java Cryptography Extension is part of Java SE. WebLogic Server SSL packages use JCE for all cryptographic functions in the server. JCE is a pluggable framework for various cryptographic implementations. New providers for specific features can be added seamlessly and used without requiring modifications to application code. By configuring JCE with a hardware provider, WebLogic Server will be able to use accelerated cryptographic functions available on that platform. This pluggable JCE feature has been supported in WebLogic Server only since version 7.0 Service Pack 2. Prior to that, JCE providers were not configurable in any way.

One thing to remember is that to use specialized JCE hardware, the hardware, the device drivers, and the JCE classes all need to be installed and working correctly. See the WebLogic Server documentation at Link 15-4 for more information about setting up JCE providers.

Chapter Review

This chapter focused on topics and techniques you need to consider when designing a production environment that must be scalable, secure, and highly available. We discussed a number of clustering and multiple-site design strategies, the use of hardware load balancers for global and local traffic management, techniques for employing full-featured clustering solutions with WebLogic, and best practices for securing your production environment and applications.

WebLogic Server provides a wealth of configuration options to support the most demanding requirements. The right combination of hardware, software, and networking strategies is certain to yield a production system that meets all business and technical requirements. It is up to you to identify and document these requirements and choose the proper strategy for achieving your goals.

Index

wsdlc **task, Ant build tool,** 314–316
WS-I (WS-Interoperability)
  overview of, 302
  support for SOAP style/use combinations, 324–325
  supporting HTTP cookies, 343
  web services container architecture, 303
  WSI Analyzer checking, 313–314
WSI Analyzer, SOAP UI utility, 313–314
WS-Interoperability. *See* **WS-I (WS-Interoperability)**
WSM (whole server migration)
  migrating JMS servers and, 585
  overview of, 638–639
  requirements for using, 639
  setting up, 639–640
  WebLogic Server, 564
**WS-Policy, defining web service security
    policies,** 349
WS-RM (WS Reliable Messaging)
  JAX-RPC support for, 323
  SAF support for, 434
  WebLogic Server support, 302
WS-SecureConversation 1.3, 323
WS-Security
  defining web service security policies, 349
  message-level security, 348, 352–358
  overview of, 302
  SAML Token Profile, 507
  Web Service Identity Providers, 508
  web services container architecture, 303
WS-Trust 1.3 (clients only), 323

X

X.509 certificates, 351, 355, 565
  certification path, 460–461
  certification path for, 460–461
  identity assertion and, 457
  obtaining, 470–472
  overview of, 469–470
  SAML and, 502
XA Connection Factory Enabled, JMS, 386
XML
  APIs for dynamic web services, 333
  customizing mappings between Java and XML, 346–347
  embedding XML tags within JSP pages, 12, 16
  mapping to Java, 306
  Provider//Dispatch approach supporting XML processing
      tools, 333
  SOAP using, 301–302
XML Catalog, WebLogic Server, 321
XML **library, JSLT,** 19
XMLMessage, **JMS,** 400–401
XP (Extreme Programming), 716
XPath, 333
XQuery, 333
XSLT, 333

Z

zero consumer queues, JMS, 375